A HISTORY OF ROME

A HISTORY OF
ROME

DOWN TO THE REIGN OF CONSTANTINE

M. CARY, D.Litt.
*Late Emeritus Professor of Ancient History
in the University of London*

and

H. H. SCULLARD, F.B.A.
*Emeritus Professor of Ancient History
in the University of London*

THIRD EDITION

St. Martin's Press   New York

First Edition 1935
Reprinted 1938, 1945, 1947, 1949, 1951

Second Edition 1954
Reprinted 1957, 1960, 1962, 1965, 1967, 1970, 1974

Third Edition 1975
Reprinted 1977, 1978

Preface to the Third Edition

Professor Cary's *History of Rome* has now been widely used both in this country and the United States for nearly forty years in virtually its original form, since the revision in the second edition of 1954 was for practical reasons very limited in scope. The time has therefore come for more radical change and I greatly welcomed the suggestion made by Messrs Macmillan and Mrs Cary that I should undertake this work. That I should attempt this would, I like to think, have been in line with his wishes, since he left a few jottings for revision in an envelope addressed to me; I can only hope that the result has not fallen too far short of what he would have wished.

As the opportunity has arisen for a complete recasting of the format of the book, together with new illustrations and maps, I have taken the chance to rewrite freely where advances in knowledge seem to require fresher treatment: apart from constant minor changes throughout I have rewritten perhaps something like one-third of the book. It has not seemed necessary to attempt to differentiate the contribution of the two authors: since, if anyone were so improbably curious as to wish to try, he could easily pursue this rather fruitless exercise merely by comparing this version with the original work. In general I have written more extensively in the early parts, where archaeological evidence has been accumulating over the years; I have also expanded somewhat near the end in the period of Diocletian and Constantine. Besides making a few changes in the arrangement of some chapters, in places I have added a certain amount of resumptive material: this necessarily involves a little repetition, which may not be bad in itself in a textbook and indeed is perhaps almost inevitable in face of perennial problems such as how far the history of the Empire is to be described under reigns or by topics.

I should like to record my personal gratitude to Professor Cary for friendship, constant help and encouragement to me for over thirty years, first as his postgraduate student and then as colleague and co-editor. My great debt to other fellow historians will I hope be made clear in the bibliographical references in the revised Notes of this book and can scarcely be spelled out in detail here. Among these references I have occasionally included a recent article which, though not necessarily of outstanding importance, provides a useful discussion of the evidence and an up-to-date bibliography of the topic involved. I have also added chronological tables, a general bibliography, some stemmata and the like.

The illustrations of coins have been reproduced at approximately the same size, irrespective of the size of the original coin: it has not been considered necessary in a non-numismatic book to record the degree of enlargement in each case.

All the maps and plans have been redrawn, and many new ones added; for the care with which this has been done my thanks are due to Messrs Lovell Johns. To Mr Rex Allen of Macmillan I owe a very great debt for sharing in the toil of proof-reading and indexing, as well as for his general oversight and care in this complicated task of revision and resetting. Other members of the staff also have been most helpful.

December 1974   H. H. S.

v

Preface to the Second Edition

The object of this book is to provide a comprehensive survey of Roman History down to the dawn of the Middle Ages within the compass of one volume. Its subject is a political system and a civilisation which lasted a thousand years and eventually comprised the whole Mediterranean area and western Europe. Research in this vast field of study is now being conducted more intensively than ever, and our knowledge of it is still being amplified or modified at innumerable points. To write a general history of Rome is therefore to invite criticism on multitudinous matters of detail. But the chief requirement in a work of this kind is not that it should be meticulously exact and up to date in all its facts, but that it should arrange and evaluate the facts in due order and proportion. Its purpose cannot be better stated than in the words of Polybius, the foremost Greek writer on Rome, who declared that his task was to present Roman History 'as an organic whole', so that its meaning and function in world history should stand out clearly.

In a work of this scope it is manifestly out of place to supply full references or to append exhaustive bibliographies. (Readers who wish to pursue their studies in Roman History will find comprehensive and well-arranged bibliographies in the *Cambridge Ancient History*.)

Books and articles which I have found particularly helpful have been cited from time to time in the notes. In addition, I desire to express a more general obligation to various authors in the *Cambridge Ancient History*, notably to Professor Adcock and to Mr Last (who has also given me valuable advice on method and procedure); and to Professors Carcopino, De Sanctis, Tenney Frank, Holleaux and Rostovtseff. I am also indebted to Dr H. H. Scullard for permission to incorporate some details from his forthcoming book on Roman History to 146 B.C.

My acknowledgments are also due to the Roman Society and to Messrs H. Chalton Bradshaw and Geoffrey E. Peachey for leave to reproduce illustrations.

Lastly, I desire to express my thanks to Messrs Macmillan; to the staff of Emery Walker Ltd; and to Mr W. T. Purdom, Assistant Librarian to the Hellenic and Roman Societies, for the every-ready help which I have received from them in preparing the text and the illustrations.

I wish to express my gratitude to Dr H. H. Scullard for his valuable assistance in the preparation of the second edition of this book.

M. CARY

Contents

PART I PRE-ROMAN ITALY

CHAPTER 1

THE GEOGRAPHICAL ENVIRONMENT OF ROMAN HISTORY

CHAPTER 2

THE EARLY INHABITANTS OF ITALY

CHAPTER 3

GREEKS AND ETRUSCANS IN EARLY ITALY

PART II THE ROMAN CONQUEST OF ITALY

CHAPTER 4

LATIUM AND ROME

CHAPTER 5

ROME IN THE PERIOD OF THE KINGS

CHAPTER 6

THE SOURCES FOR EARLY ROMAN HISTORY

CHAPTER 7

THE CONFLICT OF THE ORDERS. THE FIRST STAGE

CHAPTER 8

THE EARLY WARS OF THE REPUBLIC

CHAPTER 9

THE CONFLICT OF THE ORDERS. THE SECOND STAGE

CHAPTER 10

THE LATIN, SAMNITE AND PYRRHIC WARS

CHAPTER 11

THE ROMAN STATE IN THE THIRD CENTURY B.C.

PART III
THE CONQUEST OF THE MEDITERRANEAN

CHAPTER 12

THE FIRST PUNIC WAR AND THE CONQUEST OF NORTH ITALY

CHAPTER 13

THE SECOND PUNIC WAR

CHAPTER 14

THE CONQUEST OF THE WESTERN MEDITERRANEAN

CHAPTER 15

THE MACEDONIAN WARS

CHAPTER 16

THE ROMAN WARS IN ASIA IN THE SECOND CENTURY

CHAPTER 17

THE GOVERNMENT OF THE ROMAN PROVINCES

CHAPTER 18

DOMESTIC POLITICS IN THE SECOND CENTURY

CHAPTER 19

ROMAN SOCIETY IN THE SECOND CENTURY

PART IV   THE FALL OF THE REPUBLIC

CHAPTER 20

TIBERIUS AND GAIUS GRACCHUS

CHAPTER 21

MARIUS AND THE NEW ROMAN ARMY

CHAPTER 22

THE ITALIAN WARS, 91–83 B.C.

CHAPTER 23

THE TEMPORARY MONARCHY OF CORNELIUS SULLA

CHAPTER 24

THE FALL OF THE RESTORATION GOVERNMENT

CHAPTER 25

THE WARS OF LUCULLUS, POMPEY AND CRASSUS

CHAPTER 26

CAESAR'S CONQUEST OF GAUL, AND THE BREAKDOWN OF THE FIRST TRIUMVIRATE

CHAPTER 27

THE RISE OF CAESAR TO SUPREME POWER

CHAPTER 28

THE SECOND TRIUMVIRATE

CHAPTER 29

ROMAN SOCIETY IN THE FIRST CENTURY

PART V

CONSOLIDATION OF THE ROMAN EMPIRE

CHAPTER 30

THE SETTLEMENT OF AUGUSTUS. ROME AND ITALY

CHAPTER 31

THE ROMAN EMPIRE UNDER AUGUSTUS

CHAPTER 32

THE JULIO-CLAUDIAN EMPERORS. INTERNAL AFFAIRS

CHAPTER 33

THE ROMAN EMPIRE UNDER THE JULIO-CLAUDIAN DYNASTY

CHAPTER 34

ROMAN SOCIETY UNDER THE EARLY ROMAN EMPIRE

CONTENTS

CHAPTER 35

THE 'YEAR OF THE FOUR EMPERORS'

CHAPTER 36

THE FLAVIAN EMPERORS

CHAPTER 37

THE 'FIVE GOOD EMPERORS'. GENERAL ADMINISTRATION

CHAPTER 38

THE 'FIVE GOOD EMPERORS'. EXTERNAL AFFAIRS

CHAPTER 39

ROMAN SOCIETY FROM A.D. 70 TO 180

CHAPTER 40

COMMODUS AND THE SEVERI

PART VI   THE DECLINE OF THE ROMAN EMPIRE

CHAPTER 41

THE CRISIS OF THE EMPIRE IN THE THIRD CENTURY

CHAPTER 42

DIOCLETIAN AND CONSTANTINE

CHAPTER 43

ECONOMIC, CULTURAL AND RELIGIOUS DEVELOPMENTS

CHAPTER 44

THE ROMAN EMPIRE. RETROSPECT AND PROSPECT

List of Illustrations

All coins and the Arras Medallion are reproduced by kind permission of the Trustees of the British Museum.

The publishers are indebted to Fototeca Unione of Rome for the use of the following illustrations: 3.1, 3.2, 3.11, 4.1, 4.2, 5.9, 6.1, 11.2, 11.3, 12.2, 12.3, 29.1, 29.2, 29.3, 29.5, 30.1, 30.4, 30.5, 30.6, 30.7, 32.7, 32.8, 34.3, 34.4, 34.5, 34.6, 34.7, 34.9, 34.10, 34.11, 34.12, 34.13, 34.14, 34.15, 34.17, 34.18, 34.19, 34.20, 34.21, 36.4, 36.5, 36.6, 36.7, 36.8, 36.9, 36.11, 37.7, 38.3, 39.2, 39.8, 39.11, 39.12, 39.13, 39.14, 39.15, 39.17, 39.19, 39.21, 39.22, 39.25, 39.31, 39.32, 39.33, 40.10, 41.11, 42.10, 42.14, 42.15, 43.1, 43.2, 43.3, 43.4, 43.5, 43.6, 43.7, 43.8.

List of Maps

PART I

Pre-Roman Italy

1. ITALY

CHAPTER 1

The Geographical Environment of Roman History

1. The Mediterranean Area [1]

Roman history is the record of a state that extended its boundaries from a narrow territory in the Tiber valley to include all the lands of the Mediterranean seaboard. Its scene was laid in every part of Italy and in every district of the Mediterranean area. This geographical background of Roman history will require a brief introductory description.

The Mediterranean basin forms a natural geographical unit. Its constituent lands are on the whole alike in climate and vegetation; they have relatively easy access to each other, but are cut off in a greater or lesser degree from their hinterlands. Intercourse between the Mediterranean area and the three adjacent continents of Europe, Asia and Africa is impeded by an almost continuous barrier of mountains and deserts: only at rare intervals does a river valley or a low pass provide a convenient avenue to the interior. On the other hand, the Mediterranean Sea itself connects rather than separates the surrounding lands. Its winter storms are more than compensated by the regular incidence of its summer trade winds, by the absence of strong currents and tides, and by the abundance of clearly visible islands and headlands which serve as natural signposts to the seafarer. In ancient times its waters were almost deserted from October to April, but in the summer months they were a safe and frequented highway. To the Romans the Mediterranean Sea, or 'Our Sea' (*Mare Nostrum*), as it was appropriately called by them, became an indispensable link of empire. In short, the natural features of the Mediterranean area favour more than they hinder the grouping of its component countries into a unified state-system. The Roman Empire followed rather than cut across the natural lines of its development.

The Mediterranean climate (which in the days of ancient Roman history was substantially the same as the present time)[2] falls into two main seasons with sharply contrasted characteristics. Its winter months are dominated by strong and boisterous winds, mostly from a westerly point, bringing rain-storms of almost tropical violence. Now and again, when the wind veers to the north, a 'cold snap' sets in, and reduces the temperature to that of an English winter. But the rain-squalls pass away as suddenly as they come, and scarcely a day goes by, but the sun breaks through the cloud-banks. The prolonged chilliness, the fog and gloom that mar the northern winter are almost foreign to Mediterranean lands. If the Mediterranean winter is wet and wild, it is also genial and bright.

In the summer months the prevailing wind is a persistent northerly breeze which sweeps the skies clear of clouds and makes an open path for the sun. Under the influence of a dazzling solar radiation the summer temperature of the Mediterranean lands rises to tropical heights. The dryness of the heat renders it wholesome to human life; but the scarcity of summer rain — the drought lasts from one month in northern Italy to six or ten months in Tripoli and Egypt — is destructive to vegetation. Yet the abundance of sunshine which distinguishes the Mediterranean regions – their yearly ration seldom falls below 2000 hours – is on the whole a great boon. Their brisk and bracing winds, and their clear bright skies, under which the forms of objects stand out in sharp outline and their colours show true, tend to foster an active mind in a vigorous body. In a word, the Mediterranean lands were a natural birthplace of a high civilisation.

Their mountain ranges

The structure of the Mediterranean lands is largely the product of an extensive upheaval in the tertiary age, in the course of which the Apennines, the Dalmatian coastal range, the Alps and Pyrenees, the Sierra Nevada and the mountains of North Africa were folded up to their present altitudes. The main ranges of the Mediterranean area, being of relatively recent formation, have not yet weathered into rounded contours, their steeply scarped slopes resemble cliffs rather than downs. The sharp and varied relief of the clear-cut crests seen under a luminous sky gives a peculiar charm to the Mediterranean landscape. But the Mediterranean mountains bring more pleasure to the artist and sightseer than profit to the husbandman. They restrict the area of tillage to the comparatively narrow basins of the level land, and they perform but indifferently the natural functions of mountains as reservoirs of water. Seldom exceeding 10,000 feet in height, they lose their snowcaps before midsummer, and their predominant limestone formations do not store the rain by filtering it into the subsoil, but waste it by pouring it off their impervious flanks. Here and there the water drains off through wide cracks on the limestone face into subterranean caverns, from which copious perennial springs well up at favoured spots in the lowlands. But in general the winter rain and snow do not adequately compensate for the summer drought.

Their vegetation

The peculiar climate and relief of the Mediterranean lands combine to clothe them with a distinctive vegetation. In the lowlands evergreen trees and shrubs replace the deciduous plants of more northerly latitudes, which cannot resist the Mediterranean summer drought. In the mountains forests of oak, beech and chestnut are still to be found at the present day; and in antiquity, when the woodman and the crofter's goat were as yet only beginning their work of destruction, the hill-sides were better clad than their present bald appearance would suggest. But on the lower levels the tree-growth of the Mediterranean lands tends to dwindle into sparse bush.

Among the cultivated plants cereals yield a good return under careful cultivation. Crops sown in autumn mature by June or July, before the season's drought can bring them harm.[3] On the other hand, the lack of summer rain restricts the variety of orchard plants. The common fruits of central and northern Europe thrive only in the neighbourhood of springs, of rivers or of irrigation-canals. But three typical products of the Mediterranean area, the olive, fig and vine, are particularly well adapted to its climate. The olive is favoured by its relatively mild winters; the fig and the grape are matured to perfection by its abundant summer sunshine; and all these three plants have roots sufficiently long to reach down to water-level, however severe the drought.

In the lowlands winter grazing is abundant, but summer pasture is only to be found in river valleys. On the other hand, a summer supply of green fodder sprouts on the mountain-sides after the melting of the snows. In Mediterranean lands accordingly any extensive pastoral industry must depend on the provision of alternate summer and winter grazings, between which the flocks can be driven to and fro, and it must be restricted chiefly to sheep and goats, as being better adapted than horses and cattle to this semi-nomadic existence.

The mineral resources of the Mediterranean region are in general less abundant than those of central and northern Europe. But Spain and Asia Minor contain a rich and varied supply, which was extensively exploited by its ancient inhabitants.

Comparative poverty of the Mediterranean region

In regard to material wealth the Mediterranean area has not been lavishly endowed by Nature. Many of its countries have ever been and still remain sparsely peopled; and even in the richer districts close settlements are seldom possible except where rivers or springs or artificial supplies of water mitigate the summer drought. But in antiquity the compulsory clustering of the population on the most eligible sites was not without its attendant benefits, for it favoured the growth of cities and fostered the social and political aptitudes which urban life engenders. The natural tendency to city life among the Mediterranean peoples also facilitated the organisation of the Roman Empire.

2. Italy

The climate of Italy

In comparison with other Mediterranean countries Italy is on the whole a favoured land. Its climate conforms to the general Mediterranean type, but exhibits several local variations. The winter of peninsular Italy is mild and open;[4] but the region north of the Apennines, being cut off by this chain from the warm sea winds, becomes frostbound like continental Europe. In the summer months the western seaboard of the peninsula is exposed to the occasional searing blast of the Sirocco, the *plumbeus Auster* of Horace. But these disadvantages are more than compensated by the comparative coolness and moistness of the Italian summer. At Rome or Florence the rainless season does not ordinarily extend over more than a month.

Its mountains

The physical structure of Italy is of the usual Mediterranean pattern. The Apennine range, which constitutes its backbone, does not rise to more than a moderate height: its tallest peak, the Gran Sasso, in the country of the ancient Piceni, falls slightly short of 10,000 feet. But it stands up boldly and imparts to the Italian landscape the usual clear-cut contours of Mediterranean scenery. The Apennines, like most other Mediterranean mountains, glut the rivers in winter and starve them in summer. On the other hand the Alpine chains on the northern border render the short summer drought of that region almost innocuous, for their perennial snow keeps the rivers comparatively well fed throughout the rainless season.

Relative fertility of Italy

Italy possesses a larger expanse of rich soil than most Mediterranean lands. From the Alps the northern plain receives not only a copious water supply, but a mass of fertilising detritus which the rivers deposit on the land during the winter floods. Along the western margin of the peninsula, from the Ciminian mountains of southern Tuscany to the bay of Naples, an intermittent line of volcanoes has covered the adjacent plains with a rich coating of lava-dust. Like all volcanic districts, western Italy has to pay a price for its high fertility. Although no earthquake comparable with that which destroyed Messina in 1908 is recorded in ancient history, minor tremors were often reported at Rome;[5] and in A.D. 63 the dormant giant of Vesuvius turned over in his sleep and caused a premonitory havoc at Pompeii. In A.D. 79 the first recorded eruption of the mountain utterly destroyed Pompeii and two neighbouring towns (p. 413). The volcanoes in southern Etruria and Latium at the northern end of the chain remained quiescent through all the centuries of Roman history, and their extinct craters formed attractive lakes, as Bracciano, Albano and Nemi, but in prehistoric times they rendered the lower valley of the Tiber unattractive for human settlement (p. 31). Yet the occasional disturbances and dangers in the volcanic borderland were atoned for by the richness of the soil.

The use and misuse of Italy's natural resources under Roman rule will require fuller consideration in subsequent chapters. It will suffice here to mention that while the eventual decline of cereal cultivation in Italy was due to political causes rather than to the lack of good arable land, the development of orchard industry and of ranching by the Roman landowners was in accordance with the country's natural line of growth. In particular, it may be observed that Italy has a natural abundance of *saltus* or summer pastures in the highlands, to serve as a complement to the winter grasslands in the plains. Taken as a whole, Italy has a lesser percentage of cultivable land than France or England (only 55 per cent of the surface was cultivated in the late nineteenth century, and the percentage may have been even lower in Roman times), but it has a lower ratio of waste or semiwaste districts than most other Mediterranean countries.

In regard to mineral resources Italy is not well endowed. But it possessed one important metalliferous area on the northern coast of Tuscany and in the adjacent island of Elba. The copper mines of the mainland and the extensive iron deposits of Elba went a long way to supply ancient Italy with its two most essential metals.

Populousness

Thanks to its combination of natural advantages, Italy is, next after the Nile valley, the most densely populated of Mediterranean lands. With an area only half that of the Spanish peninsula, it now carries almost double the number of inhabitants. In ancient times its relative abundance of man-power contributed in a large degree to its political ascendancy over its neighbours (pp. 121, 130).

Inland communications

In the matter of internal communications Italy is handicapped by its great length from north to south, and by the diagonal barrier of the Apennines, which impedes alike the passage from coast to coast and from the peninsula into the Po valley. Its rivers are for the most part too rapid and carry too variable a volume of water for purposes of transport. The facility of inland travel which the country came to enjoy under Roman rule was due in part to the artificial regulation of its water-courses, but more especially to the construction of the Roman highroads.

The Alps

The Alpine ranges which mark off Italy from the European mainland are a less formidable obstacle than the height of their peaks might suggest. On the north-eastern frontier of Italy a gap in the Carnic Alps provides a thoroughfare at a mere 2500 feet of altitude. In the central and western Alps the passes rise to 6000–8000 feet, yet on the outer side the river systems of the Rhine and Rhône give easy access to them. It has accordingly been affirmed that the history of Italy is the history of its invaders. This dictum, applied to ancient history, is not without a foundation of truth, for the Alps were repeatedly traversed by ancient armies, and where soldiers went, traders also were sure to find their way. Nevertheless for many centuries of early Italian history the Alps remained an almost insurmountable barrier. The comparative seclusion which they gave to Italy at the beginning of Roman history was a fortunate circumstance, for it enabled the Italians to mature their own civilisation without constant molestation from the ruder Transalpine tribes, until the day when they crossed the barrier and entered the European continent on their own terms.

The coast of Italy

The seaboard of Italy has long stretches of open roadstead and offers no such abundance of sheltered inlets as the neighbouring Greek peninsula. As is the case with all Mediterranean coast-lands, its river estuaries are positively dangerous to shipping, for the sea has no strong tides to scour away the fluvial deposits, so that their entrances are commonly blocked with banks of silt. Neither Po nor Tiber has ever been accessible to large vessels: under the emperors the port of Ostia at the Tiber mouth had to be refashioned at some distance from the river

(p. 357). Of Italy's best harbours, Genoa and Spezia are culs-de-sac in the Maritime Alps, and lay almost unused in ancient times; two other commodious basins, at Brindisi and Taranto, open on to the same hinterland and in antiquity effaced each other in turn. It was not until the Middle Ages that Italy became a great home of mariners and explorers. Yet the coasts of the peninsula were frequented from early days by seafarers of other nations, and its people soon came under the influence of visitors from overseas (Chap. 3). With the rise of the Roman Empire Italy inevitably became the focus of Mediterranean navigation.

Lastly, Italy possesses one geographical advantage, which is so obvious as to be often overlooked. Its central position in the Mediterranean marks it out to be the natural seat of any Mediterranean empire. Once the ancient Italians had been united under Roman rule, their overseas conquests were greatly facilitated by the commanding position of their country within the circle of Mediterranean lands.

Its central position

CHAPTER 2

The Early Inhabitants of Italy[1]

1. Stone Age Man

The Palaeo-
lithic Age

Some 200,000 years ago, near the end of the second interglacial period, man first appeared in Italy. He has left tangible evidence of his presence in the flint axes which are found throughout the country (especially near Chieti and at Venosa), and an actual settlement has been revealed just west of Rome at Torrimpietra. His successors of the Middle Palaeolithic Age have left skulls of the Neanderthal type at Saccopastore at the very gates of Rome and in caves on Monte Circeo. More advanced were the men of the Upper Palaeolithic of *c.* 10,000 B.C., who are represented for instance by a Cro-Magnon type of skull in the Fucino area. Although engravings of animals are found on cave-walls and on bone, and a Palaeolithic 'Venus' has turned up near Lake Trasimene, Italy can offer nothing like the spectacular art found in the caves of France and Spain: indeed its population must have been very sparse, continually on the move, hunting and gathering food where best it could, and life was 'poor, nasty, brutish and short'.

The
Neolithic
peoples

A great change occurred *c.* 5000 B.C. when Neolithic farmers began to replace the earlier hunters; they probably arrived by sea at Gargano in the heel of Italy from across the Adriatic and settled at Coppa Nevigata. With them they brought seed-corn and sheep and cows, they made pottery vessels and built huts, and thus could live more settled lives. By the Middle Neolithic this culture spread widely in south-east Italy and skeletal remains, which were buried in contracted positions, reveal that the people were of Mediterranean stock, short in stature and long-headed. Their pottery became more artistic, and while some may still have lived in caves, others lived in villages. These were revealed by the study of air-photographs taken by the Royal Air Force in 1943 in the Tavoliere, the plain around Foggia in northern Apulia. Here huts were grouped into compounds, each surrounded by a ditch, and these compounds were often united into a village, again with a surrounding ditch: the largest village enclosed a hundred compounds and an area of 500 × 800 yards.[2]

Thus the nomadic life of Palaeolithic man was replaced by Neolithic settlers who cleared the forests, cultivated the fields and raised domestic animals, but when the soil within easy reach of their villages was exhausted and their population increased they would move on to other virgin areas throughout the eastern and southern parts of the peninsula and indeed their pottery is found reaching northward to Emilia. As interchange increased in the Late Neolithic from *c.* 3500 B.C. their wares occur in Etruria and even in Malta, but after this period of great prosperity increasing desiccation led to the virtual abandonment of the Tavoliere and doubtless expedited their settlement in north and west Italy (including a settlement at Sasso di Furbara north of Rome). Gradually in this Late Neolithic Age external influences increased, coming from the south-west and north-west and reflecting the wider cultures of Neolithic western Europe in France, Spain and North Africa. In particular, material of a type found in a settlement near Brescia (at Lagozza di Besnate) spread down the Adriatic coast; its makers may well have brought with them knowledge of spinning and weaving which begins to appear about this time. Even more significant for the future, amid the stone tools shone the occasional glint of a piece of worked metal, albeit not of home manufacture.

2. Bronze Age Man

The Copper Age

Man's mastery over the working of metals was gained slowly. In the Alpine regions and the plain of the Po knowledge of copper began to infiltrate from Bohemia and Hungary, and stone tools were gradually supplemented by copper during a long transitional period known as the Chalcolithic or Copper Age. At the same time men with round heads ('Alpine Man') appear, as shown by surviving skulls: a new phenomenon pointing to warrior immigrants from central Europe. In Italy the culture of this Copper Age is represented in three main areas: in the Po valley (at Remedello near Brescia), in Tuscany (at Rinaldone) and in the province of Salerno (at Gaudo near Paestum). Thus it was widespread, but Neolithic groups of course still lived on, affected to a greater or lesser extent by new trends. Even in the Copper Age settlements this metal was far too rare to replace stone for most of the tools and weapons of everyday life: flint daggers and stone battle-axes long continued in use, and flint-workers still required supplies of obsidian from Lipari. To what extent Aegean influences affected the more southern settlements remains debatable.

The Bronze Age

When men discovered that by adding tin to copper they could produce an alloy which was easier to work and more durable than copper, they advanced into the Bronze Age, very roughly around 1800 B.C. in Italy. The two main cultural areas which emerged, one in the north, the other along the Apennines, must now be briefly reviewed.

Pile dwellings

First the north. We have already seen that a settlement flourished at Lagozza near Brescia as early as the Late Neolithic Age, but its nature was not described. It was in fact typical of a number of villages built on piles on the edges of lakes (*palafitte*) which are found by the northern Italian Lakes (Maggiore, Garda, etc.) and by the swampy rivers of the Po valley. These villages continued to flourish through the Copper into the Bronze Age, and their culture is often called Polada from a settlement on Lake Garda. They probably have some connection, obscure though it may be, with the later so-called Terramara settlements which were established in the Po valley in the Middle and Late Bronze Age.

When these latter settlements were discovered last century they were named from the 'black earth' (*terra marna*, a modern local dialectal phrase) which because of its rich nitrogenous matter was used by the local farmers as a fertiliser. Until some thirty years ago they figured large in modern accounts of early Rome because it was thought that some of their inhabitants may have spread southwards through Etruria and reached the site of Rome and that the regular layout of their settlements influenced later Roman ideas of the planning of towns and camps. Now, however, they are thought to be a more local group who settled in the middle Po valley somewhat later than once believed and who arrived in Italy from the area of the middle Danube in the north-east. The settlements, which are found in the modern provinces of Modena, Reggio Emilia, Parma and Piacenza, consist of villages of huts (usually circular) built on raised terraces or piles, sometimes surrounded by a ditch which would protect them against man and water. Outside lay other smaller *palafitte* which formed cemeteries where the ashes of the dead were buried in urns, incineration being a distinctive mark of this culture. It may be that climatic deterioration at the end of the second millennium B.C. led to increased building on piles and possibly even to the ultimate abandonment of the settlements.

These people, whom archaeologists have called Terramaricoli, brought with them significant skills and practices: a distinctive pottery, great ability in bronze-working (deriving metal supplies from the Austrian Alps), the custom of cremation and in all probability an Indo-European language or dialect. They were in the main agriculturists and stock farmers (cows, goats, pigs, sheep), though many continued to hunt (boar, deer and bear) and perhaps to fish; remains of flax, beans and two kinds of wheat have been found; cartwheels have been discovered and the horse was used for draught purposes. But besides importing goods from the north and thus forming a channel between Italy and the Danube, they became manufacturers and ultimately began to export their products southward into Apennine Italy, which was poor in metals.

Apennine culture

This brings us to the second main Bronze Age culture in Italy, once known as 'extraterramaricola' but now as Apennine Culture, which stretched along the mountain back of Italy from Bologna in the north to Apulia in the south; it reached its developed form about 1500 B.C. The people were semi-nomadic pastoralists who moved between more permanent winter settlements on lower ground (often only in caves by water courses), and summer pastures high in the mountains; such annual transhumance still continues today among the high mountainous areas. But by the twelfth century they had become somewhat more stable and practised some agriculture. They consisted of descendants of the Neolithic population, intermixed with some 'warriors' who may have come in small groups from overseas (from the Aegean world) and landed either on the west coast or in Apulia and who probably spoke an Indo-European language which would be spread more widely by their semi-nomadic life and which may well have been the ancestor of the later Umbro-Sabellian dialects spoken by Samnites, Sabines and other tribes of the central Apennines. They lacked the technological skill in metalwork of the northern Bronze Age folk, and unlike them, they buried their dead. As will be seen, their pottery has been found on the future site of Rome (p. 37).

Contacts between Terramara and Apennine folk

In the course of time peaceful contacts developed between the Terramara and the Apennine folk. Some of the latter seem to have moved north and settled in open villages near the Adriatic and the mouth of the Po; they perhaps brought with them bronze from Etruria. The Terramara people then worked the metal and exported the finished products not only back to Etruria but also down the Adriatic coast to the south of Italy where an 'Apennine' settlement near Tarentum (Scoglio del Tonno), which had traded with the Mycenaean Greeks until their collapse (see p. 16), played an important role. Thus from the beginning of the Late Bronze Age (c. 1200–1150 B.C.) the two main cultural areas in Italy began to draw much closer together, as seen at Pianello, a typical site inland from Ancona. Cremation and urnfields were introduced into many districts where inhumation had prevailed, but the old Apennine culture with its practice of inhumation persisted well into the Iron Age in much of central and southern Italy.

Mycenaeans in the west

Before tracing the merging of the Bronze into the Iron Age, we must glance briefly outside Italy whose Bronze Age culture had lagged far behind that of the Minoans and Mycenaeans in the eastern Mediterranean. These predecessors of the classical Greeks traded widely in western waters. Even before 1400 B.C. traces of Mycenaean influence have been detected in Sicily and the Aeolian Islands (Lipari), but thereafter Mycenaean traders not only visited southern Italy but some appear to have established a trading post at Tarentum, where they were active until their own world collapsed over two centuries later. From Tarentum they could extend their trade over the heel of Italy, to the Adriatic, to Sicily and Lipari and even to central Italy where they sought to obtain copper from Etruria. The extent of this trade is problematic, but Mycenaean sherds have been found around Syracuse and at Mylae in north-eastern Sicily, at Lipari, at Ischia and even at Luni in Etruria; the five from Luni date to c. 1250 B.C. Thus whether or not the name Metapa found on a Linear B tablet of Pylos should suggest that Metapontum in southern Italy at some time

came under the control of the kingdom of Nestor at Pylos in the Peloponnese, the extent of Mycenaean influence, both economic and cultural, in these western areas was considerable, and some trade with Greece even continued after the collapse of Mycenaean power, although the settlement at Tarentum itself was abandoned in the twelfth–eleventh century.[3]

Lipari Islands and Ausonian culture

The volcanic Lipari Islands (Aeoliae Insulae), 25 miles north-east of Sicily, occupied a key position in this area, both geographically for trade and archaeologically for the chronology of the Bronze Age. Thanks to their exploitation of their native obsidian the inhabitants flourished from Neolithic times onwards, but about 1250 B.C. the Middle Bronze Age huts on the acropolis of Lipari were destroyed by fire. They are covered by a layer containing pottery which is completely different from the earlier types and is closely related to that of the late Apennine phase in Italy (e.g. in the villages of Scoglio del Tonno and Coppa Nevigata).[4] This 'Italianisation' may well be reflected in the legend, recorded by Diodorus, that Liparus, son of the king of the Ausonians of central-southern Italy, occupied Lipari and founded a city there. The resultant cultural phase, which in consequence has been named Ausonian, flourished until c. 850 B.C. On Lipari (the other islands seem to have been abandoned) and also at Milazzo in Sicily we find a culture which represents a fusion of Apennine and Terramara, such as we have already seen in northern Italy at Pianello and elsewhere, with cremation prevailing. The cemetery found at Milazzo was in use c. 1050–850 (that at Lipari is earlier: c. 1150–1050) and closely resembles the 'urnfields' which are common in central Europe, in northern Italy (Terramara) and later, as will be seen, in central Italy. All this heralds the coming Iron Age and the Villanovans, while the later material from Lipari has close parallels with the earliest Iron Age remains from the Palatine and Forum at Rome.

3. The Iron Age and the 'Villanovans'[5]

Beginnings of the Iron Age

Both the process and dating of the merging of the Bronze into the Iron Age are obscure: only the result is clear, namely that ultimately much of northern and central Italy, as far south as Rome and even further, was occupied by a culture which archaeologists have named Villanovan, after a typical site discovered in 1853 at Villanova, some four miles east of Bologna. The only firm dates are provided by Greek evidence: the full flowering of the Apennine Bronze Age coincides with Mycenaean III A and B (*c.* 1400–1200 B.C.), that of the Villanovan Iron Age in Etruria with the beginning of Greek colonisation in Italy at Ischia and Cumae from *c.* 750 B.C. (see p. 16). The intervening gap has been filled differently by varied interpretations of the archaeological evidence: some would put the beginning of the Iron Age back to 1000, others find the transition about 900, while yet others by postulating Sub-Apennine and Proto-Villanovan periods bring down the Villanovan period proper to *c.* 800.

Urnfield and Proto-Villanovan culture

One factor in the problem is the chronological relationship between the cemeteries of the Villanovans and the 'urnfields' found north of the Alps. These *Urnenfelder* are large cemeteries where urns containing the ashes of the cremated dead are buried in the ground side by side, often numbering many hundreds. Wherever the practice may have started (Hungary-Transylvania?), it spread widely north of the Alps in the Rhineland, France and part of Spain. It also penetrated into Italy, probably over the Julian Alps, perhaps also from Illyria across the Adriatic. From the twelfth century such urnfields are found at Pianello in the north and at Timmari in Apulia in the south; then others, marked by a development both of the pottery and the *fibulae*, spread widely over Italy. While many archaeologists believe that the impulse to this so-called Proto-Villanovan phase came from central Europe, a few have argued that it was a development from Terramara or even only a local evolution of the Apennine culture. At the same time from the beginning of the first millennium greater skill in metallurgy was acquired, not only in bronze but in the new metal, iron, that was coming into use in two cultures, that of the Celtic Hallstatt period in Gaul and the Villanovan in Italy.

Villanovan culture

Villanovan culture falls into two main groups, one in the north around Bologna and a southern group in Tuscany and northern Latium, where settlers are found in the Alban Hills and at Rome where they occupied the Palatine and used the Forum as a cemetery. There were other outlying settlements, for instance at Fermo in the Marche near the Adriatic, and considerable settlements as far south as around Salerno. Even between the two main areas there were naturally local differences, but by and large their most distinctive feature was the use of biconical cinerary urns. These were covered by inverted pottery bowls by the northern group, more often with helmets in Etruria, while in parts of Etruria and in Latium urns modelled like huts replaced the northern type of ossuary. The urn was then placed in a round hole in the ground, sometimes enclosed by stones; in and around it were placed ornaments,

2.1 'Villanovan' biconical pottery urn for ashes, covered by a bronze helmet; from Tarquinii.

such as brooches, bracelets and razors, though not many weapons.

The northern Villanovans

The settlement at Bologna, the largest of the northern group which stretched eastwards to Rimini, was the key position astride the early trade-routes. It drew copper, and later iron, from Tuscany and in return exported manufactured metalwork and agricultural products: by the eighth century it had become 'the Birmingham of early Italy'. Increasing wealth brought social changes. Villages began to cluster together, though it may be too early to think of communities organised as towns (except

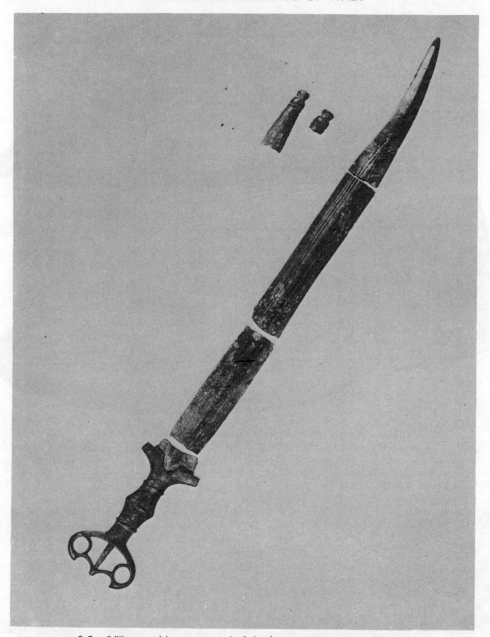

2.2 'Villanovan' bronze sword of the 'antenna' type; from Bologna.

perhaps in the case of Bologna itself); larger groups would be economically stronger and the *gens* was perhaps replacing the family as the unit of importance. Although few arms survive, military activity may have increased later in the sixth century, but there was apparently no 'warrior-class', at most a citizen militia. In this later period art came under 'orientalising' influences which probably derived from Etruria, where by this time, as will soon be seen, Etruscan civilisa-

tion had emerged. Indeed about 500 B.C. Etruscans themselves advanced north over the Apennines and founded Felsina on the site of Bologna, near to the Villanovan settlement; the two peoples remained aloof, but soon afterwards Villanovan culture died out and the area passed to Etruscan control.

The southern Villanovans ultimately developed differently from their northern counterparts. The huts in which they lived can be recon-

The southern Villanovans

11

2.3   Cinerary urn in the form of an Iron Age 'Villanovan' hut.

2.4   Shepherds' *capanne* by the Volturno river, resembling an Iron Age hut.

structed from the clay replica cinerary urns found in southern Etruria and south of the Tiber, while the foundations of three such huts have been found on the Palatine at Rome (see pp. 37 f.). These were cut into the tufa rock, roughly rectangular in shape, while the arrangement of the post-holes allows the wooden superstructure to be reconstructed, the walls consisting of wattle and daub. Remains of charcoal and ash attest a hearth inside the hut; fragments of cooking-stands, smoke-blackened household utensils and charred animal bones indicate the family meal and the life of the early Romans. Village-settlements grew out of clusters of these huts, and recent excavation at Veii in Etruria fifteen miles north of Rome reveals that several such villages might be built around a central strong-point on a hill, and then later fused into a unified town settlement.[6] The Villanovans perhaps had greater instinct to social development than has sometimes been allowed. At first they followed the custom of the northerners in placing their burial urns at the bottom of a pit (*pozzo*), but after 750 B.C. inhumation began to appear alongside cremation, the bodies being laid in trenches (*a fossa*). The objects put in the graves also became finer and included more imports, among them some Greek pottery, since now the Greeks were beginning to found colonies in southern Italy. In the seventh century in Tuscany inhumation became the normal form and the dead were laid in chamber-tombs cut into the rock. At the same time the funeral equipment becomes richer, with more imported Greek and Oriental objects, including gold and silver work, and iron becomes more common. These changes and the beginning of the orientalising phase in art appeared first among the settlements near the coast, and spread only slowly inland. In fact a transition from a Villanovan culture was taking place; villages were becoming wealthy cities and men were beginning to use the Etruscan language. Whether this was due to the arrival of another people, the Etruscans, from overseas or merely to the influx of new cultural influences will be considered later (see pp. 18 f.), but it is a striking fact that whereas the northern Villanovans retained their own culture until they died out, the southern culture north of the Tiber gradually became Etruscan. That south of the river, at Rome and in Latium, took a different course, as will be seen later.

4. The Peoples and Tongues of Italy

In historical times Italy presents a mosaic of peoples and tribes, some apparently autochthonous, others more recent settlers. It is impossible to analyse this agglomeration accurately, still less to trace their origins or define their languages, but something must be said about these problems, while the contribution of the Etruscans and Greeks to the life of Italy is reserved for the next chapter. First at the archaeological picture, then the linguistic.

In the mountains which rise up sharply from the coast of the Italian and French Rivieras lived *Ligurians* a Neolithic people, while the wild and backward mountaineers who inhabited the district in later times were known to classical writers as Ligures. Since they spoke an Indo-European tongue and archaeologists have discovered no cultural break in Liguria, they may well be descendants of Neolithic folk driven back into the mountains by some invaders (from the Lakes?) who imposed their Indo-European language on the natives.

In addition to the Villanovans, two other main groups of kindred cremating peoples are found in northern Italy in the early Iron Age: Golasec- *The Italian* cans around Lake Maggiore and in Piedmont *lakes and* and Lombardy, together with the Comacines *Venetia* around Lake Como, and the Atestines (or, in Roman terminology, the Veneti) around Este (ancient Ateste) in Venetia. Golaseccan culture, which persisted from about 900 B.C. until Roman times, appears to have enjoyed a different social structure from that at Bologna or Este, since, unlike them, it had a warrior class to judge from the chariots and arms found in the graves of some chieftains. During the fifth century trade developed with the Etruscan and Greek areas, to be followed by increasing Celtic penetration. The Atestines very probably came to Italy from Illyria under the impulse of the movement of peoples which caused the Dorian invasion of Greece. Their cemeteries, however, which also start about 900 B.C., provide little evidence of any sharp distinction between rich and poor. Their metalwork rivals that of the northern Villanovans at Bologna; in particular their pictorially decorated bronze buckets (*situlae*) provide splendid scenes of everyday life, as ploughmen, huntsmen, soldiers, chariotcers, boxers and banqueting. Inscriptions, some of which are found on offerings dedicated to a goddess named Reitia, show that they spoke an Indo-European language which was closely related to Latin but was written in an alphabet mainly derived from Etruscan script. In the fourth century this culture was so dominated by the invading Celts that, later, Polybius described the second-century Veneti as virtually indistinguishable from the Celts except in language; at that time they had come under Roman control, but they retained their language and customs until the Christian era.

The Picenes

Next, three groups of Iron Age peoples who practised inhumation. First, the Picenes, a war-like people as shown by their weapons and their *stelae* which depict battles by sea against pirates in the Adriatic. They lived around Ancona in the Marche. They perhaps comprised some invaders from Illyria who mingled with the indigenous population; their language, as recorded later, is Indo-European and akin to Illyrian. The contents of their tombs indicate wide trade, and post-1945 excavation within Ancona throws light on their domestic life and supplements the earlier evidence from the famous cemeteries of Novilara near Pesaro. Secondly there is the *Fossa grave culture* Fossa Grave culture in Campania and Calabria, named after its trench graves, which began in the final stages of the Bronze Age. An important settlement was founded in the tenth or ninth century on the hill of Cumae, at the foot of which its trench-grave cemetery was discovered. Long before it was superseded by the Greek *Cumae* colony at Cumae in *c.* 750 B.C., its traders were reaching north to Etruria and south to Calabria and Sicily, and Greek geometric pottery probably of the ninth century, has been found; at the same time the settlement shows traces of Villanovan influence. Some eight miles across the water lay the islet of Vivara, where an Apennine settlement had traded in Mycenaean wares, *Ischia* and the larger island of Ischia, where another Apennine village (on the hill of Castiglione) was followed on Monte Vico by a Fossa culture settlement like that at Cumae; this also, as at Cumae, was superseded by a Greek colony named Pithecusae (*c.* 760 B.C.). The Fossa settlements further south in Calabria are closely related to similar ones in Sicily, a fact which may be reflected in the Greek tradition (recorded by Hellanicus in the fifth century) that the people whom the early Greek colonists met in eastern Sicily in the late eighth century were called Siculi and had recently come from southern Italy.

Apulia

A third inhuming group is found in the heel of Italy in Apulia. In later times this area was inhabited by three tribes, the Daunians, Peucetians and Messapians. As suggested by Greek legend as well as by the occurrence of Illyrian tribal- and place-names in Messapia, the tribes were probably of Illyrian origin. With the founding of Taras and other Greek colonies in south Italy, the native populations increasingly came under their superior cultural influence, but these three Iapygian tribes continued to produce distinctive pottery, that of the Daunians (from *c.* 600 B.C.) being fanciful and even grotesque.

Indo-European dialects

No inscriptions exist to show what languages all these people spoke at the beginning of the Iron Age – nor in fact could they ever have existed, since before the time of the Greeks and Etruscans the inhabitants of Italy were illiterate.[7] However, later inscriptions and the languages spoken in Roman times indicate that the majority of their predecessors shared a linguistic group of Indo-European dialects. The tribes of the central Apennines used Osco-Umbrian or Umbrian-Sabellic dialects: Umbrian in the north, Sabellic ('Italic') dialects in the centre, and Oscan (the language of the Samnites) in the south. These people were probably descendants of the 'Apennine' culture, reinforced by some Indo-European-speaking peoples from overseas (cf. pp. 8 f.). Akin to, but quite separate from, this group of dialects was Latin, which was spoken by the peoples who occupied the plain of Latium to the east and south of the Tiber.

Their origin?

The Indo-European dialects in Italy probably originated from a common source, perhaps more immediately in the Danube area. But how did they reach Italy; by land or by sea? (as we have seen, Messapic in the south and Venetic in the north almost certainly were brought by Illyrians from across the Adriatic). Did their arrival involve the immigration of large numbers of people or did they spread more by infiltration? If they were due to mass movements, did the individual dialects arise before or after their speakers arrived in Italy? Despite the labours of comparative philologists, no agreed and sure answers can be given to these and similar questions.

Thus for the early history of Italy we have two strands of evidence, linguistic and archaeological; a third strand is provided by what the classical writers tell about these prehistoric days. Unfortunately the three sources cannot be neatly woven into a unified pattern, and as yet no firm correlation between linguistics and archaeology can be established. However, some theories may appear more reasonable than others.

The language of the Apennine people

The classic view held in recent times has been that two waves of peoples who spoke Indo-European dialects came down from north of the Alps: the first group, who cremated their dead, settled west of a line which ran from Rimini in the north to just south of Rome, and the second, the Sabellian-Italici, who buried their dead, settled east of this line. We will return to the first part of this view shortly, but the second part should probably be rejected: the supposed hordes of inhuming Italici have left no trace of an advance through north Italy. The Italic dialects therefore may well have spread from western or eastern parts of Italy among the 'Apennine' Bronze Age peoples, who retained their habit of inhumation. Nor need the new language presuppose mass immigration of invaders: a relatively small number of Indo-European speakers may have arrived and their tongue have infiltrated gradually. The process would have been facilitated by the practice of the Italic peoples, known from historical times, of the Sacred Spring (*ver sacrum*), whereby as tribes expanded in population the children born at a certain time were marked to be sent out to a new settlement when they grew up, thereby spreading both their customs and language further afield in central Italy.

The language of the Villanovans

Regarding those settled west of the Rimini-Rome line, namely the Terramaricoli, Villano-vans and Latins, the theory of their northern origin is still widely held, as also is the view that they spoke an Indo-European dialect (as the Latins certainly did). A much less probable view is that the urnfield culture reached Etruria not by land from the north but by sea from the east. Others again believe that the Villano-vans were autochthonous and that their culture was a native growth, based on Apennine culture which absorbed external (urnfield) elements which were brought perhaps both by land and sea but by numbers so small as not to effect a profound ethnic change in the country. Professor Pallottino, the proponent of this last view, also believes that the Indo-European dialects reached Italy in successive waves from across the Adriatic. However, amid a great variety of possibilities it is still a reasonable view that the Villanovans came into Etruria from the north, bringing with them an Indo-European dialect and urnfield culture, though they did not necessarily come in vast numbers. Thus the safest use of the word 'Villanovan' is to suggest a com-mon culture without implying an unduly rigid and unified racial and linguistic block.

Difficulties about the origin of the Villano-vans are matched by those which surround the reason for their end, which varied in different areas. In the north they were gradually absorbed by Etruscans, Celts and Romans, as will be seen; in Tuscany their culture developed into Etruscan civilisation and their tongue was super-seded by Etruscan; in Latium and Rome they survived as Latins.

Thus in the early Iron Age Italy was inhabited by a medley of peoples whose general level of *Italy in the* culture gave little promise of their eventual *Iron Age* leadership among the nations. Their material civilisation had not advanced, except in a few favoured districts, beyond that of a reasonably self-contained agricultural people; they were unacquainted with writing; their craftsmanship was competent but their art, though attractive, relatively rudimentary. Their social organisation varied; among the Villanovans villages were on the verge of becoming towns, while the tribes in the mountains of central Italy were probably much looser units. Later social developments, as they emerge into the light of history, will be examined below, but in general there was little to indicate the peninsula's future greatness. Not even the diviners of Etruria could have foretold that by the beginning of the third century B.C. the whole would have been united within the framework of a Confederacy led by Rome and have become a world power: still less that two or three centuries later a Roman Italy would be the unchallenged master of the western world from Spain to the Euphrates, from Britain to the Sahara.

CHAPTER 3

Greeks and Etruscans in Early Italy

1. The Greeks

At the beginning of the first millennium B.C. the Italic peoples had laid the foundations of a settled and ordered life, but their civilisation lagged behind that of the older seats of culture in the Nearer East. The next stages in the development of Italy were the result of increased contact with peoples from the Eastern Mediterranean.

Mycenaean traders

The Greeks of the classical age were not the first mariners to explore western waters: they had been preceded by Mycenaean traders who visited Sicily and southern Italy and perhaps even set up a permanent post at Tarentum (see p. 9). Some dim knowledge of these adventurous seamen may conceivably be reflected in the Greek legend that the survivors of an abortive expedition to Sicily, led by the Cretan king Minos, settled in southern Italy. But the link was broken by the fall of Mycenaean civilisation in the twelfth century: apart from some very tenuous links with the area around Tarentum, the visits of traders from the Aegean world were suspended for several centuries. In the meantime the exploration of the western Mediterranean was completed by the Phoenicians, who established colonies in North Africa, in Sicily and in Spain, and perhaps paid trading visits to the coasts of Tuscany. In the sixth century the trade of the Phoenicians with Italy was gathered into the hands of their colonists at Carthage (p. 115), who cultivated friendly relations with Tuscany. But the Phoenicians left singularly little trace of their visits to Italy, and they exerted no direct enduring influence upon its early civilisation apart from their indirect gift of the alphabet.[1]

The Phoenicians

A much closer and more fruitful contact was established between the Italic peoples and the Hellenic or (as the Romans came to call it) the Greek nation, which had been formed in the Aegean area after the Indo-European invasions. Stray finds of Greek 'geometric' pottery (with linear decorations) on the coasts of Apulia, of Campania and of Tuscany, show that the Aegean seafarers resumed intercourse with Italy not very long after 800 B.C. In the second half of the eighth and during the seventh and sixth centuries the Greeks made one chain of settlements in Sicily, and another on the southern and western coasts of Italy from Tarentum to the bay of Naples. From this base-line Greek traders carried their characteristic merchandise, bronze ware and the so-called proto-Corinthian, Corinthian and Attic varieties of pottery to central and northern Italy. One stream of traffic moved from Tarentum up the Adriatic coast, extending northwards as far as Hadria (near the Po estuary), and inland as far as the Apennines. Another proceeded from Cumae, the oldest permanent settlement of Greeks on the Italian mainland,[2] to Latium and Tuscany, and spread itself like a flood over the Tuscan inland. One such Greek trader was Demaratus, a noble of Corinth, who after his native city became subject to a tyrant (c. 655 B.C.) migrated to Etruria, taking with him workmen, potters and painters. He settled at Tarquinii where he married a noble Etruscan lady; their son is said to have moved to Rome and become king, ruling as the Elder Tarquin (p. 41). The story of Demaratus may well be true: it certainly illustrates the great volume of trade between Greece and Etruria which is also attested by archaeological finds.[3] Thus between 750 and 500 B.C. Italy became one of the chief markets for the Greek export trade.

Colonisation by the Greeks

But the influence of the Greek merchant and

3.1 Air-view of the Greek city of Poseidonia (Paestum) in Lucania. Note the surrounding wall. The two temples side by side in the centre (the so-called basilica and temple of Poseidon) were in fact dedicated to Hera. To the left (i.e. to the north) stands the temple of Ceres (in fact 'of Athene') of the late sixth century.

Influence of the Greek colonists

colonist went further than the mere exchange of goods. Greek settlers introduced into Italy the cultivation of the vine and the olive, which had hitherto existed there in a wild state only, and so took the first steps by which the country was converted into the 'garden of Europe'. Having acquired from the Phoenicians an alphabetic system of writing, the Greeks adapted it to the needs of Indo-European tongues, and they made a gift of this improved script to the Italic peoples, all of whom, directly or indirectly, took over their letter-signs from Cumae or some other Greek colony.[4] The bronzes and ceramic ware which the Greeks disseminated over Italy, the sculpture and architecture with which they decorated their cities, provided the natives with art-patterns which here and there found not unskilful imitators. The Greeks also gave Italy its first lessons in scientific war-craft, in the fortification of towns with walls of dressed masonry, and the decision of set battles by the shock-tactics of armoured spearmen.[5]

Nevertheless the Greeks accomplished far less in Italy than they might have achieved, had they applied their superior civilisation in a systematic manner to the penetration of the peninsula. With the quarrelsomeness that was their besetting sin, they frittered away their opportunities in mutual warfare between their several cities, or in civil dissension within each town wall. Under these conditions they scarcely advanced their political ascendancy beyond their original area of settlement, and their institutions of city-life at first found few imitators among the Italic peoples. In the political history of Italy the first chapter belongs, not to the Greeks, but the Etruscans.

2. Who were the Etruscans?[6]

Etruscan origins

The name 'Etruscans' was given by the Romans to their neighbours in the district now known as Tuscany; by the Greeks, even as early as the epic poet Hesiod, they were called Tyr-

3.2 Paestum. Temple of Poseidon (mid-fifth century) and, in background, the 'basilica' (mid-sixth century). Cf. 3.1.

senians or Tyrrhenians. But the origin of the splendid civilisation which flourished in Etruria from *c.* 700 B.C. is one of the most vexed questions of early Italian history. Although the Etruscans owed much to Greek influence, many of their institutions were not derived from that quarter. Were they native Italians, or were they immigrants, like the Greeks? The age-long debate on this controversial issue was opened about 450 B.C. when the Greek historian Herodotus reported the story that the Etruscans were an offshoot of the Lydians of western Asia Minor who because of a famine had set out (at an uncertain date) in quest of new lands. This version found credence among Roman writers, and was accepted by the Etruscans themselves. But another Greek author, Dionysius of Halicarnassus, pointed to the many divergences between the Etruscan and Lydian languages and institutions of his day (*c.* 30 B.C.) and concluded that the Etruscans must be of Italian origin.[7]

In more modern times a battle royal has been fought between the champions of autochthony and of immigration.

Two of the weightiest arguments for the indigenous character of the Etruscans are drawn from the location of their cities and from the development of their cemeteries, together with the contents. Their towns for the most part replaced a former Villanovan settlement on or close by the same site: this process can be seen most clearly at Veii, just north of Rome. In Etruscan cemeteries the successive types of tomb appear to develop out of each other in a continuous series, and the style of their furniture exhibits a similar unbroken progression. Thus at Tarquinii, perhaps the oldest Etruscan city, Villanovan cremation burials in urns (*a pozzo*) were supplemented and superseded (*c.* 750–700 B.C.) by inhumation in trenches (*a fossa*), with an increasing richness of the buried objects; then inhumation became normal, with chamber-

Were the Etruscans autochthonous?

tombs cut in the rock; painting, sculpture and ceramics flourished, and imported Greek and oriental objects increased. Etruscan civilisation had arrived without, it may be argued, any major break.[8]

To such arguments those who believe in Herodotus would reply that to build cities where only villages had existed presupposes new skills and administrative talent of a different order from those shown hitherto by the Villanovans. Further, although the cemeteries show no abrupt break, they do indicate a change in the disposal of the dead, a matter of deep feeling among primitive peoples and not lightly to be undertaken. Also if the immigration was gradual and spread over a considerable period (and few scholars today believe in vast hordes of Etruscans descending like locusts on the shores of Etruria in one mass movement) then one would expect the change in burial customs to be gradual. Even apart from any specific resemblance between some tombs in Etruria and Asia Minor, Etruscan civilisation as a whole seems more eastern than Italic: the luxury of the Etruscans, their love of feasting, music and dancing, of games, jewellery and bright colours, and many of their religious practices, especially their science of divination by means of the liver of sacrificed animals, have eastern parallels. Lastly, their language is of crucial significance. By general agreement it is non-Indo-European. The Autochthonists would argue that therefore it is the survival of a very early pre-Italic tongue, but it happens that on the island of Lemnos in the Aegean there survives the inscribed tombstone of a warrior, and the language of the inscription has links both with Etruscan and with tongues of Asia Minor, while the historian Thucydides tells us that the pre-Greek population of Lemnos was Tyrrhenian. Thus it is very tempting to see in Lemnos a stage of Etruscan migration from the East.[9]

Despite the attempted help from physical anthropologists in examining skulls and bones, and of medical biologists in studying blood-groups, the problem remains. Recently, however, emphasis has moved from an apparently insoluble problem to the undeniable fact that Etruscan civilisation, as it is known to us, developed on Italian soil, and so the problem is often now posed as one of formation rather than of origin: what elements in Italy and from overseas combined to create the culture?[10] Stress is laid on not viewing the Etruscans in their early days as a clear-cut and closely knit unit, but rather upon analysing their racial, linguistic and cultural aspects, all of which may have separate lines of origin. As various elements were fused in the crucible during the so-called 'orientalis-

3.3 Engraved back of bronze mirror from Vulci, *c.* 400 B.C. It depicts the seer Calchas examining a sacrificial liver (hepatoscopy). The Romans later had recourse to this Etruscan method of divination.

ing' phase in the early seventh century, it is clear that the basic population of Etruria was still of Villanovan origin and that it was adopting new ideas of burial and social organisation and increasingly importing Greek and oriental wares which were gradually imitated by local artists. But unless we are prepared to forget Herodotus, we still want to know whether all this was the result of the upsurge of native talent under eastern cultural influences, spread by trade and probably by the settlement in Italy of some foreign artists, or whether the change was so fundamental as to justify belief in the impact of foreign occupation.

If the speed with which city-life and culture suddenly emerged in Etruria — and not, be it noted, in other Villanovan areas in Italy — suggests the influx of a relatively small number of men with administrative skills and the power to organise large labour forces, then the process may reasonably be imagined on the following lines (*imagined*, however, since the evidence is still too contradictory to allow more than hypothetical reconstruction). In the turmoil and dislocation of peoples in the eastern Mediterranean

3.4 Terracotta sarcophagus from Caere, *c.* 500 B.C. Husband and wife recline on a banqueting couch. Women had far greater social freedom in Etruscan than in Greek society.

which resulted from the collapse of the Hittite and Mycenaean empires, many peoples from Asia Minor drifted westward. Some of these 'Peoples of the Sea' tried to raid Egypt in the twelfth century, but hieroglyphic inscriptions of Ramses III record their expulsion; later it is possible that some arrived in Lemnos and others on the coast of Etruria. They would be warrior-bands, with few womenfolk, but bringing with them their language, and their experience in war, administration and the arts of city-life; their numbers may not have been large and their arrival spread over a considerable period of time. In Etruria they would find a Villanovan population which lived in villages, spoke an Indo-European tongue and cremated its dead. They imposed themselves as a conquering aristocracy and intermarried with the Villanovans. Their language and burial habits gradually predominated; they encouraged the subjugated Villanovans to clear the forests, drain the land and build cities; further, by exploiting the mineral wealth of the country, they developed an overseas trade which brought many of the luxurious products of the East. Thus by the early seventh century we find an Etruscan nation, born on Italian soil; but it must be remembered that not all scholars would define its parents in the same terms as those suggested above.

3. Etruscan Civilisation

The land of Etruria

The central area of Etruscan civilisation lay between the river Arno in the north, the Tiber in the east and south and the Mediterranean in the west. Into it were thrust the lower slopes of the Apennines. The northern part comprised fertile alluvial valleys, plains and rolling hills of sandstone and limestone where cities such as Clusium, Cortona, Perusia and Faesulae grew up; such was their attraction that the sites continued to be occupied through to modern times. Southern Etruria on the other hand, where the earliest settlements are found, was a volcanic zone, whose tufa rock has worn into peaks and plateaux, separated by deep valleys and gullies; here cities, such as Tarquinii, Vulci, Caere and Veii, are found on hills which rise where rivers or streams meet, amid a wild landscape which in part still retains something of its primitive appearance. Much of the land was covered by forest and wild macchia. The Villanovans, as pioneers, had begun to penetrate into this formidable barrier and gained enough land for cultivation, but wider occupation resulted in the 'Etruscan' period from engineering skill shown in land-reclamation, drainage, forestry and road-building. Even so, the settlers had to choose for their homes various pockets of land which were often separated from one another by physical barriers which made communications difficult. Thus geography, as also in Greece, led to the emergence of city-states, each with its individual characteristics, and made wider political union more difficult. The basis of life was agriculture, supplemented by hunting and fishing, but the mineral wealth of the country, especially its copper and iron, were quickly exploited. Thus nature afforded mineral wealth which provided building-stone for cities and raw materials for export in exchange for foreign luxuries, while the land was fertile

enough to support a large population. But in addition it needed man's co-ordinated labour and his technical skills to produce a rich civilisation.

The foundation of cities

Etruscan cities had to be founded in accordance with religious practice, laid down in Ritual Books, and in particular each city had to be surrounded by a sacred boundary (*pomerium*) in order to secure the population within from all unseen dangers without. It is probable that rules for the plan and orientation of the temples may have led to some symmetry in the layout of public buildings from an early date, but the rough nature of many sites will have precluded the careful grid-system of street-planning which was certainly adopted later: it is seen most clearly at an Etruscan colony founded *c.* 500 B.C. at Marzabotto near Bologna (p. 26). The later Roman grid-system, used in camps and colonies, may have been influenced by Etruscan practice, which, however, was not quite the same, since it was not based on the axial crossing of two main streets (the *cardo* and *decumanus*), but on a pattern of alternating wider and narrower divisions (such as are found in many Greek cities in the west from *c.* 500 B.C.). Most of the cities seem to have relied on the strength of their natural position for long, but from *c.* 400 B.C., when the power of Rome began to rise on their southern horizon, they were fortified by walls of dressed stone. Their temples were more square than Greek ones, with a wide frontage; the front half had a colonnaded portico, the back comprised three shrines (*cellae*) for three deities, or one *cella* with two flanking wings (*alae*). Only the foundations were of stone; the main framework was of wood which was covered with gay multicoloured terracotta ornamentation. Small private houses were generally rectangular, of mud-brick, laced with timber, built on stone or pebble foundations; larger houses had upper storeys, with flat or gabled roofs. The houses (*domus*) of the rich aristocracy can be reconstructed from the interior appearance of the stone chamber-tombs, which were decorated like houses and reflect something of their elegant and luxurious construction. They are the forerunners of the *atrium* (central courtyard) type of house which later Romans used and developed (p. 192).

Tombs

The cemeteries underwent a continuous development, as has been seen, from simple pits and trenches to rock-cut family tombs with vaulted roofs and frescoed walls. The tombs were built in rows of streets so that the cemeteries literally resembled 'cities of the dead' (*necropoleis*), as revealed by the spectacular cemeteries at Caere. The dead were usually buried, but on some sites, especially in northern

3.5   Large burial tumulus at Caere.

3.6   Interior of the Tomba della Cornice at Caere. The wall imitates the façade of an Etruscan house with doors and windows.

3.7   Terracotta statue of Apollo from Veii, made by the artist Vulca or his school, *c.* 500 B.C. A master-
piece of Etruscan art.

and inland Etruria, cremation was practised.
The more elaborate tombs, often themselves
shaped like houses, were equipped with a sumptuous furniture which vividly illustrates the
luxury and artistic taste of the Etruscan nobles.
The pottery found in these burials consisted in
part of a native ware of black polished clay (*bucchero*), but their chief ceramic contents were fine
Greek vases, of every type from 'geometric' to
Attic, in immense quantities. The metal ware
of bronze and gold was mostly of native workmanship, but of high quality. Among the keep-

sakes of bronze were toilet-cases and mirrors
with incised decorations which plainly betrayed
Greek influence; the gold filigree ornaments
were less dependent on foreign models and in
craftmanship equalled the finest Greek work.
The jewellery and metalwork were widely
exported, even to Celtic lands. Two masterpieces
are the Capitoline wolf in Rome and the Chi-
mera of Arezzo. Although sculpture in stone,
which could be practised only where local stone
was suitable, fell far below Greek achievements,
the Etruscans excelled in sculptured terracotta

Art

which was brightly painted and widely used to cover the wooden structure of temples and even for life-size statues, as the Apollo of Veii. The gaily coloured wall-paintings in the tombs, especially those at Tarquinii, display great *joie de vivre* but also some grim figures of the underworld; in general they throw a vivid light on Etruscan life, showing scenes of banqueting, dancing and music, horse-racing, wrestling, hunting and fishing. All Etruscan art derived ultimately from Greek and Oriental inspiration, but it developed an individual character all of its own.

Religion The Etruscans believed that their religion had been revealed to them in early days by seers; this teaching, the *Etrusca disciplina*, which defined religious practice, was enshrined in a number of books of ritual. The *libri fulgurales* interpreted thunder and lightning, which were believed to portend events in man's everyday life, while the *libri haruspicini* instructed professional *haruspices* in the art of divination based on the inspection of the entrails of sacrificed animals. The Romans later often appealed to Etruscan *haruspices* to interpret omens which they themselves failed to understand. The books also dealt with founding cities, consecrating temples, matters concerning war and peace, and thus all public and private life was dominated by what the Ritual Books had foreseen. The names of many Etruscan deities are known, although their precise functions are sometimes obscure; they were soon assimilated to Greek gods. Etruscan religion was, or at any rate became in its later phases, gloomy and cruel, unlike most Greek and Italic cults. This repulsive trait is illustrated by the scenes in tomb-paintings which depict the torments of the departed at the hands of the demons of the underworld. For the appeasement of their divine fiends the Etruscans seem to have offered up human sacrifices; a common method of dispatching their victims was to set them to kill each other off in duels, which served as the models for the gladiatorial contests in Rome.

The social and political organisation of the Etruscan city-states was rigid and aristocratic. *Political* In early days they were ruled by kings (*lucu-* *organisation* *mones*) who were surrounded with great pomp. The king wore a robe of purple and a golden crown, carried a sceptre, sat on an ivory throne, and was escorted by retainers who carried an axe in a bundle of rods (*fasces*), eloquent symbols of the ruler's right to execute or scourge.[11] When Etruscan kings occupied Rome they left as a legacy to the later Republican magistrates many of these trappings of office. During the sixth and fifth centuries the power of the kings was

3.8 Etruscan wall-painting from the tomb of the Leopards at Tarquinii, probably early fifth century. It illustrates the Etruscans' love of music and dance.

challenged and then superseded by that of the nobles; before this happened some kings possibly had tried to bolster up their waning power by reorganising the city's institutions in order to strengthen the military potentiality of a middle class as a counterweight to the nobility, as seems to have been attempted in Etruscan Rome, where the army was reorganised (p. 52). When the monarchy fell some military adventurers may have gone on the warpath in an attempt to establish personal power, but were soon reduced to the level of their fellow nobles, and the cities were administered thereafter by local aristocracies. The latter exercised their power through magistracies which were normally annual, but the detailed functions of the *zilath*, the *maru* and the *purthne* are hidden from us.

The cities were autonomous states, but they were linked in a League of Twelve Cities and had a federal sanctuary at the Fanum Voltumnae near Volsinii (Voltumna was their chief god), where leaders of the cities met for common cult and games. Whether this became a strong communal bond or whether federal ties were held loosely is uncertain, but clearly the cities did develop some feeling of national unity which on occasion resulted in joint League action. However, local loyalties often overruled federal considerations and this failure to establish real unity of purpose through an effective confederation was ultimately to prove fatal to the cities when they came into conflict with Rome.

The general picture of the social structure given by our sources is that of a powerful and rich aristocracy and an immense body of clients, serfs and slaves, but the gap may have lessened slightly when during the sixth century the Etruscans adopted the Greek military formation of a closely-knit battle-line (phalanx) of heavily armed soldiers (hoplites). The citizen body comprised families or clans, a gentilician system, with a strong feeling for family and a recognition of a position of the mother as well as of the father within it. Little is known about the serfs and slaves who worked the land for their overlords, but the opulent culture and private lives of the nobles are partly revealed by the great richness of the archaeological remains.

3.9   Bronze statuette of an Etruscan warrior.

3.10   Funerary *stele* of Avele Tite of Volaterrae, of the sixth or fifth century, depicting the dead man, with his name inscribed on the border.

4. Etruscan Expansion

Expansion southward

Etruscan culture, and to a more qualified extent political control, soon spread beyond Etruria itself. Some Etruscans advanced southward over the Tiber into Latium, where they occupied Rome and other centres (p. 41). Others penetrated further, either by land or sea or both, into Campania where they established themselves at Capua (*c.* 650 B.C.?), Nola and Pompeii among other places. This expansion into a Greek sphere of influence led to conflict, the more so because of a wider clash of interest at sea where Greek penetration into western waters limited the spread of Etruscan direct control. As we have already seen, the Greek cities of southern Italy provided the Etruscans with new markets for their metals, and a vast network

Etruscans and Greeks

3.11 Air-view of Capua, perhaps founded by the Etruscans. In the central lower part the Roman (Etruscan?) rectangular city-planning is still preserved. At the top, a Roman amphitheatre.

of trade developed especially in Greek pottery (p. 23). But a new phase started when the Phocaeans of Asia Minor established a colony at Massalia (modern Marseilles) *c.* 600 B.C. This was a direct challenge to the Carthaginians, who were defeated in a naval battle, recorded by Thucydides, in an attempt to keep the Phocaeans out of this area: the resultant Phocaean thalassocracy pleased the Etruscans no more than it did the defeated Carthaginians. When the Phocaeans moved nearer the shores of Etruria by settling at Alalia in Corsica (*c.* 560 B.C.), the Etruscans and Carthaginians soon made common cause and met the intruders in a naval engagement off Alalia *c.* 535; while the Etruscans gained control of Corsica, the Carthaginians took over Sardinia.[12]

Encouraged perhaps by these events the Etruscans launched an attack on Greek Cumae, which had remained independent (524 B.C.), but they were repelled through the energy of the Cumaean Aristodemus. Soon Etruscan influence in Latium weakened (pp. 55 f.) and when Tarquinius was driven from Rome the other Latin cities were encouraged to seek freedom and appealed to Cumae for help. Once again Aristodemus was the hero of the hour: he helped to rout the Etruscans at Aricia (*c.* 506), with the result that the Latins could cut communications by land between Etruria and Campania. Some years later, in 474, Cumae, either threatened by the Etruscans or taking the initiative against them, appealed to Hiero of Syracuse, who had recently smashed at Himera a Carthaginian attempt to occupy eastern Sicily. At a naval battle off Cumae the allies broke Etruscan sea-power: the Greeks regained the freedom of the seas around Naples, and the Etruscan cities in Campania were isolated by sea as well as by land.[13] In the event neither victors nor vanquished in Italy enjoyed independence in Campania for long, since Sabellian tribes began to descend from the mountains (p. 87) and by 420 both Etruscan Capua and Greek Cumae had succumbed.

Cumae

With their hold on the south loosening, the Etruscans began to expand northward over the Apennines into the valley of the Po (*c.* 500 B.C.) where they exerted influence for over a century. The chief colony was founded alongside the old Villanovan settlement at Bologna and was named Felsina; it soon became a prosperous city of farmers, industrialists and merchants, importing large quantities of Greek vases. These came directly from Spina at the head of the Adriatic which became the chief port for Greek goods, especially Athenian vases; it was a Greek settlement in which the Etruscans secured a strong foothold. The third important Etruscan foundation was at modern Marzabotto, some seventeen miles south of Felsina, commanding the valley southward over the Apennines. It is of great interest because it was a new foundation (*c.* 500 B.C.) and it has not been built over since: thus it provides us with our best evidence for a late Etruscan city and its street-planning. The extent of Etruscan settlement beyond the area

Expansion northward

3.12 Inscribed sheets of gold leaf found in 1964 between two temples at Pyrgi, the port of Caere. The left-hand one is in Etruscan, the right in Phoenician. They contain a dedication by Thefarie Velianus, ruler of Caere, to the goddess Uni-Astarte, and date from *c.* 500 B.C.

of these three cities is problematic and the view that they spread over the northern plain as far as the Alps is not supported by archaeological evidence, while the tradition that they founded a League of Twelve cities here, as in Etruria (and allegedly in Campania), is open to doubt. Etruscan trade certainly extended north of the Po, but large-scale settlement is improbable.

Celtic attacks But trade rivals soon appeared: Celtic tribes were tempted to move over the Alps and occupy the northern plain of Italy. The movement may have started in the fifth century, but it only became threatening after *c.* 400 when they began to sweep all before them. The final attacks fell on Marzabotto and Felsina, the latter being overwhelmed *c.* 350: on the burial *stelae* we see the horsemen of Felsina matched against naked

Gauls. Thus Etruscan power north of the Apennines was smashed and the northern plain became what the Romans called Gallia Cisalpina. Nor was Rome itself immune from these Gallic invaders (p. 73).

Despite ultimate repulse in north and south the Etruscans at the height of their power had gathered into their hands all the richest portions of the country, and they held sway over a territory far exceeding that of any Greek city or native canton. At the same time they gained control of the seas on either side of Italy, so that they could impose their terms of admission upon the Greeks.[14] Their ascendancy on the western sea was commemorated by the name of 'Mare Etruscum' or 'Tyrrenum' (from the Greek name for the Etruscans), which it retained

*Influence
of the
Etruscans
on the
Italic
peoples*

throughout antiquity. The wider range of the Etruscan conquests enabled them to exercise a more extensive and enduring political influence than the Greeks. To the Etruscans rather than to the Greeks was due the incipient urbanisation of Italy. The Etruscans not only founded cities of their own on conquered territory, but they set the example of town-building to their subject peoples. A movement of population from villages to towns took place under Etruscan influence in Latium and Campania, and even in the hill-country of Umbria on the slopes of the northern Apennines. Another lasting result of the Etruscan ascendancy in Italy was the dissemination of the Etruscan alphabet, which was received in Umbria and (with some important modifications) in Latium, and was adopted, in preference to its Greek prototype, among the Oscan-speaking populations of the southern Apennines.

*The failure
of Etruscan
imperialism*

But the Etruscans had overrun Italy rather than secured it with a firm hold; they had overawed rather than conciliated or assimilated the subject populations.[15] Moreover, they failed to preserve unity among themselves. For all their rigid organisation, the governing aristocracies of the cities could not prevent armed risings of the unprivileged serf or artisan populations. Neither could the several cities achieve any durable harmony among themselves. The Etruscan conquests, therefore, were not the product of a concerted drive across Italy, but the isolated results of haphazard thrusts by individual cities or private war-bands, and no effective organisation was formed to defend these gains. To these causes of weakness might perhaps be added the progressive enervation of the Etruscan ruling classes under the corrupting influence of over-abundant wealth. But leaving aside this reason – and we need not take at face value the highly coloured accounts of Etruscan debauchery in Greek and Latin writers – we can find a sufficient explanation for the early failure of Etruscan imperialism in the deficiencies of Etruscan statecraft.

After 500 B.C. the political destiny of Italy passed out of Etruscan hands (p. 55), and a concurrent regression in their material welfare and artistic proficiency foreboded the eventual extinction of the peculiar Etruscan culture. From this date the Etruscans require no more than incidental notice, as the centre of political power and culture moves across the Tiber to Latium and Rome.

PART II

The Roman Conquest of Italy

CHAPTER 4

Latium and Rome

1. The Geography of Latium

Extension of Latium

Latium, the cradle of Rome, consisted originally of the coastal plain from the mouth of the Tiber to the Circeian promontory, and its adjacent foothills. In the south its habitable zone was narrowed by the Pomptine marshes and by the Mons Lepinus, a spur from the Apennines extending toward the sea. On its northern and western border the lower valleys of the Tiber and of its tributary the Anio – the 'Roman Campagna' of the present day – formed a wider belt of open land. The centre of the region consisted of a group of volcanic hills, the principal of which, the Mons Albanus, rose to a little above 3000 feet.[1]

The soil of Latium

The plains of Latium were composed of a stout layer of alluvial clay overlaid with a thin coating of lava from the Alban volcanoes. This upper crust, being rich in plant-food and friable in texture and well provided with springs, gave the district a well-deserved reputation for fertility. But the hard pan of clay prevented the absorption of flood-water into the subsoil, so that the low-lying land was liable to become waterlogged.[2] At the dawn of Roman history the lowlands of Latium were kept in cultivable condition by systematic drainage, and in recent years a great reclamation scheme has at last won them back for intensive husbandry. But in the intervening centuries areas of insalubrious fenland were allowed to form near the coast.

The Latin hill country, despite progressive deforestation, still possesses fine woodland; in the early days of Roman history it was noted for its tall beech copses. On these pleasant uplands the villages of primitive Latium clustered most thickly. The remaining settlements were mostly built on the low but steep bluffs that jut out of the plains here and there.

Communications

Latium is cut off from the eastern face of Italy by an almost continuous ridge of high land. The only commodious road across the Apennine range, by way of the Anio valley and the Lacus Fucinus, extended along the northern border of the Latin territory. Coastal communications with the bay of Naples were impeded by the Mons Lepinus and the Pomptine marshes. On the other hand two low cols between the Alban Mount and the Apennine foothills provided gateways into the valleys of the Trerus and the Liris, and so gave an easy approach from Latium into Campania. Between Latium and Etruria the Tiber formed a strong natural boundary. Though not the longest of Italian rivers, the Tiber is one of the most voluminous, and even at its lowest summer level it is not easy to ford, except at a few easily guarded points. On this side lay the most vital frontier of Latium: if the Alban Hills formed the geographical heart of the country, the line of the Tiber was the natural seat of its political capital.

2. The Early History of Latium

The early population of Latium

The inhabitants of ancient Latium had no recollection of their immigration into the country. Roman writers, in a vain endeavour to conciliate this native tradition with the random speculations of Greek historians, made the Latins into a conglomerate of Aborigines, Ligurians and Sicels. In the light of modern research they appear as one of the youngest of Italian peoples. Continuing volcanic activity may have made Latium unattractive to man during the Chalcolithic and Bronze Ages, but it was not entirely uninhabited in these centuries, as once was thought. However, sporadic finds of 'Apennine' material suggest only sparse population and do not prove a link with the Iron Age when the population suddenly increased to an extent which suggests settlers from outside. From Rome southward to Terracina there spread a culture, now known as Latial, which closely resembled the Villanovan culture of Etruria.[3] These people lived in huts which can be reconstructed from the clay replicas which some groups used as cinerary urns in place of the biconical type employed in the north. They are found at Rome and in settlements in the Alban Hills, although apparently the archaeological evidence no longer supports the belief that the latter were slightly the earlier arrivals. Apart from an 'Apennine' substratum, the new elements were reinforced by representatives of the inhuming Fossa culture (p. 14) who perhaps came from southern Italy.[4] This new mixture marks the beginning of the Iron Age in Latium

from c. 800 B.C., and early local variations tended to merge into a common culture. After some 150 years conditions began to change again when the Etruscans started to expand into Campania.

Thus Latium became a land of self-supporting herdsmen and tillers of the soil, living in villages (*vici*) which relied for protection on their hilly positions, strengthened possibly by wooden palisades. From surviving lists of Latin communities in ancient writers the number of early villages has been put at about fifty, while the *Prisci Latini* ('Original Latins') are given as thirty.[5] But however numerous these small *populi* were, the sharing of a common language would make them conscious of a degree of unity, which would be stronger if memories of a common tribal origin lingered on among any groups. They were probably organised on the basis of clans (*gentes*), but as a social unit the *gens* was displaced by the *familia* or household within which the *paterfamilias* or eldest living male held an almost absolute dominion. Beside *vici* there were *pagi*; in some cases these may have been only the extended areas in which the inhabitants of each *vicus* carried on their pastoral or agricultural work; in other cases the inhabitants of various *vici* may have held a *pagus* in common and were thus linked up in cantons. *Vici* might also be grouped together in several cult-associations, of which the most notable were formed for the worship of Jupiter Latiaris on the Alban Mount, of Diana at the Lacus Nemorensis (Lake Nemi), and of Venus (originally a goddess of gardens) at Lavinium. In these religious federations the Latins possessed the framework of a political union, but they were long in forming a real political league. By virtue of its proximity to the sanctuary of Jupiter, the village of Alba Longa (near Castel Gandolfo, on the west side of the Alban Lake) enjoyed a religious primacy among the Latin communities, but it was never the political capital of a Latin state.

About 650 B.C. a new era opened for Latium with the coming of the Etruscans: the whole area became subjected to Etruscan influences, but Etruscan culture did not drive its roots very deep since Latium remained essentially Latin-speaking. The Etruscans encouraged agriculture (rock-cut drainage channels in the Tiber valley and on the southern slopes of the Alban Hills reflect the same technique as that of southern Etruria). They also fostered industry and commerce, promoted synoecisms, and thus swept the whole area into a wider world. But since Greek ideas were also reaching Latium from the south, it is not always easy to determine whether a Greek idea arrived direct or via the

Prisci Latini

Etruscan influences

2. ROME'S NEIGHBOURS

Etruscans: was the alphabet for instance, an indirect gift of the Etruscans or a direct gift of the Greeks from the south? It is equally difficult to assess the political aspect: where and when do Etruscan features represent definite Etruscan rule? Etruscan rulers certainly occupied Rome during the sixth century and during that period a collection of villages became a united city with one of the largest temples in Italy crowning its Capitoline hill. There is no certain evidence for Etruscan rule over other cities, but their influence should not be minimised nor their general dominance questioned.

Praeneste

Praeneste (modern Palestrina) seems to have been of Latin (and Sabine?) origin, but it was soon Etruscanised. Two famous tombs, the Bernardini and Barberini, contain a princely treasure of gold and bronze ware which resembles that of a similar tomb at Etruscan Caere of *c.* 650 B.C. Although one *may* have contained a gold fibula bearing an early Latin inscription ('Manios made me for Numasios'), these tombs may well have been those of Etruscan nobles, and Praeneste may have been a key point in the Etruscan advance into Latium: it commands the route to the Liris valley. Further, its flourishing bronze industry continued to prosper until Roman times. The names of

Tusculum, Velitrae and Tarracini seem to link these cities with the Etruscans, but there remains little direct evidence. However, the earliest treaty between Rome and Carthage of *c.* 509 B.C. (p. 48) suggests that the Etruscan rulers of Rome may have exercised some control over the coastal cities of Ardea, Antium, Circeii, Terracina and perhaps Lavinium.

A great gift of Etruria to Rome, and probably to Latium also, was the temple, a new architectural form. The coloured terracotta decorations of the temples which were built at Satricum, Velitrae and Lanuvium are virtually indistinguishable from those in Etruria, though they also resemble many in Campania. In fact a considerable area of central Italy was developing a common culture, based on Etruscan and Greek ideas, the latter modified by the Etruscans or else coming from direct Greek contacts. The latter channel has been emphasised by a recent discovery: in 1959 a series of thirteen massive archaic stone altars was found at the Latin city of Lavinium (Practica di Mare) some sixteen miles south of Rome. One altar had a bronze tablet inscribed in archaic Latin to Castor and Pollux (see p. 580). Whereas it has often been thought that the cult of the Dioscuri (Castor and Pollux) reached Rome from Etruria, the

Temples and altars

4.1   Archaic stone altars at the Latin city of Lavinium.

route may now appear to have been from the south. But in general in the seventh and sixth centuries Latium was closely linked with Etruria. By 500 B.C. the original fifty or more communities had been reduced by a process of absorption into some ten or twelve, the largest of which, Praeneste, Tibur and Tusculum, long dealt with Rome on equal terms.[6] But Etruscan rule in Latium was not of long duration and far from universal, while its influence on Latin culture was no more than sporadic. The history of Latium was not bound up with that of Etruria, but with the annals of its own foremost city, Rome.

3. Rome. The Site of the City

The situation of Rome Rome was situated on the borderland of Latium and Etruria, at a distance of 15 miles from the Tiber estuary. At this point the combined activities of the Ciminian and Alban volcanoes threw up a ring of hillocks to a height of 200–300 feet above sea-level, and of a 100 feet or more above the surrounding plain.[7] The western arc of the ring consisted of two isolated ridges on the right bank of the Tiber, the Janiculan and the Vatican. The eastern arc, on the left bank, formed a continuous stretch of high ground from which four spurs, the Quirinal, Viminal, Esquiline and Caelian, projected into the river valley. *The hills of Rome* Within the circle three inner bluffs, the Capitoline, Palatine and Aventine, guarded the passage of the Tiber. Of the central hills the

Capitoline, which was the smallest in extent, stood detached on every side. The Palatine was separated by a deep-cut valley from its southern neighbour, the Aventine, and by a similar depression from the Quirinal on the north; on the north-eastern side it was connected with the Esquiline by a land-bridge, the so-called Velia. Through the rim of volcanic upcast the Tiber cut itself a new bed. Avoiding the Quirinal by a sudden westward bend, the river left a wide piece of open ground, the site of the Campus Martius; by a return curve it approached close to the three inner hills, and in this reach its channel was bisected by an island which facilitated crossing by a ford or bridge.

In this position Rome enjoyed a unique combination of natural advantages. *Dominant position of Rome* A city of the Latin plain, it stood in a fertile territory which, under proper cultivation, was capable of maintaining a large population for its size. Its hills partly raised it above the reach of the inundations to which the Tiber valley is peculiarly exposed. In the Tiber itself Rome possessed an easy approach to the sea and a potential avenue of foreign commerce. At the same time it commanded the most convenient passage of the stream in its lower reaches, and thus held a key position on the main line of travel along the western face of Italy. From this double advantage of easy progress along and across its river Rome derived a similar ascendancy to that which nature has bestowed on London and Paris. Finally, Rome lay in the heart of Italy, at equal distances from its northern and southern extre-

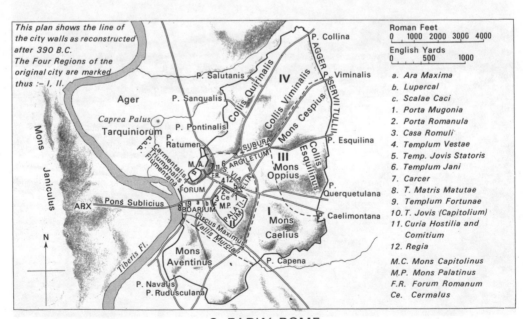

3. EARLY ROME

4.2   Island in the Tiber which facilitated crossing by ford or bridge.

mities. In a word, it was Italy's natural centre of communications.

4. The Origins of Rome. The Traditional Story

The native legend of Romulus

The origins of Rome became a fruitful subject of speculation even before the city had given clear signs of its future importance, and an endless variety of foundation-legends was composed in its honour.[8] The starting point of the native tradition was the creation of a founder 'Romulus' out of the name of the city. Round this lay-figure a tissue of folk-tales was woven, so as to give it a human and heroic semblance. Romulus was fitted out with a twin-brother Remus[9] and was affiliated to Mars, the tutelary god of Rome. The story grew up that, as an unwanted child born out of wedlock, he was cast forth into the Tiber but was saved for Rome by Providence which directed the river to swirl him ashore, a wolf to suckle him[10] and the shepherd Faustulus to rear him, hard by the site of his future city. Out of the rest of the indigenous legend it will suffice here to recount that Romulus, grown to manhood, founded a settlement on the Palatine, while Remus made an abortive attempt to colonise the Aventine, and that he provided wives for his settlers by raping the women of a neighbouring Sabine community on the Quirinal (cf. p. 39).

The tale of Romulus in its native version had come into existence not later than the fourth century B.C.; and the fact that in 296 a bronze statue of a wolf suckling human twins was set up in the Forum shows that by then the main outlines of the legend were familiarly known at Rome.[11]

But Roman tradition was brought into competition with a multitude of rival stories of Greek origin. The Greek story-telling faculty supplied mythical founders to all cities that lacked an authentic record of their creation, and to some whose genesis was a matter of history; its range of invention did not stop at the frontiers of the Greek world, but extended to foreign towns in which it happened to take an interest. In the fifth and fourth centuries Rome had already attracted sufficient attention among Greek men of letters to become the subject of a whole repertory of foundation-tales.[12] In these alien versions the heroes of Greek legend, already the creators of innumerable towns, were requisitioned to be the founders of a 'barbarian' one. The somewhat shadowy figure of the Arcadian chieftain Evander was invoked for no better reason than that the name of the Palatine hill recalled that of his native place, Pallanteum. The Greek mythologists naturally did not forget Odysseus, for the scene of several of his adventures had been located by Greek tradition in Italy.[13] In one legend Romus, the son of Odys-

The Greek legend of Aeneas

seus by Circe (the enchantress of the Circeian promontory), became the founder of Rome; in another, a second son of Odysseus by Circe created the neighbouring town of Tusculum. But the principal Greek contribution to the foundation-story of Rome was the introduction of the Trojan warrior Aeneas into it.[14] Greek legend had busied itself with Aeneas since the seventh century, when the Sicilian poet Stesichorus traced the Trojan hero's wanderings to the west, perhaps to his native isle and even to Italy. At any rate the story of Aeneas was well known in Etruria in the late sixth century: from Veii come votive statues (which imply a cult) of Aeneas carrying his father Anchises in flight from Troy, while at least seventeen vase-paintings (525–470 B.C.) depict the scene, and nearly as many show Aeneas in battle. In the fifth century a Greek writer, Hellanicus, made Aeneas the founder of Rome,[15] but for a century or two after the Etruscan period Aeneas does not appear to have been much regarded at Rome, perhaps because he was linked with the Etruscans, now Rome's enemies. Soon after 300 B.C. a historian named Timaeus created a new problem by bringing the foundation-date of Rome down to 814 B.C. (in order to synchronise with that of Carthage) or 370 years later than the reputed date of the fall of Troy, which was fixed at 1184 by the scholar Eratosthenes in the second half of the third century. But at this stage Greek speculation ran dry; it was left to Roman writers to blend native and foreign elements into one authoritative version. The Greek tradition was known at least in its outlines to King Pyrrhus of Epirus (p. 94), who fancied himself as a descendant of Achilles in conflict with the progeny of Aeneas.

By 300 B.C. the story of a Trojan landing in Latium had been accepted in native tradition, for relics of Trojan origin were exhibited to Timaeus in the temple of Venus at Lavinium. Before the First Punic War the same tale had found credence in Rome, for in 263 the Romans gave favourable terms of alliance to the Sicilian city of Segesta, on the ground of common descent from Troy. At the end of the third century the process of bringing the Roman and Greek versions into harmony was carried further by the pioneers of Roman literature, the historian Fabius Pictor and the poets Naevius and Ennius. In the revised form of the foundation-legend Romulus ousted Aeneas and the gap between

The Roman form of the Aeneas legend

4.3 Terracotta statuette of Aeneas rescuing his father Anchises from Troy. Of the early fifth century B.C., it comes from Veii, thus demonstrating that the legend of Aeneas was known there at that time.

the two was bridged. This was achieved by adapting the story to allow the interpolation, between Aeneas and Romulus, of a line of kings at Alba Longa; in this remodelling process Cato played a leading part (p. 60). Briefly, when Aeneas landed in Latium he was welcomed by King Latinus, whose daughter Lavinia he married. After founding a city named Lavinium in her honour,[16] Aeneas died and was succeeded by his son Ascanius (or Iullus), who founded Alba Longa. After him twelve kings reigned at Alba, the last of whom, Numitor, was the father of Ilia (or Rhea or Silvia), who became the mother of Romulus and Remus; they in due season founded Rome. The Alban king-list thus made possible a reconciliation between Romulus and a Latin origin and Aeneas and a Trojan origin of Rome. The chief point of divergence among the early Roman writers lay in the various dates which they assigned to the birth of Rome. While Ennius went back beyond Timaeus to the neighbourhood of 900 B.C., Fabius advanced it to 748, and another early historian, Cincius Alimentus, to 728 B.C.[17] About the middle of the second century Fabius's estimate was confirmed on the dual authority of Cato and Polybius, and a century later the date 753, proposed by the scholar Varro, became canonical. In the Augustan age final shape was given to the received version by Virgil and Livy. Virgil's chief personal contribution to the legend was the episode of Aeneas and Dido.[18]

5. The Origins of Rome. From Village to City

The starting-point of any modern discussion on the origins of Rome must be the record of archaeological discovery on the site.[19] In common with other places exposed to the action of the Latin and Etruscan volcanoes, the territory of Rome was only very sparsely populated until the first millennnium B.C. Except for a few vestiges of a Neolithic settlement on the Aventine, the first traces of human tenancy belong to the Chalcolithic period, and some Apennine pottery of the Bronze Age has come to light in the Forum Boarium which suggests a settlement on one of the neighbouring hills around 1500 B.C.[20] But there is no certain evidence of continuity with later times.

A fresh start was made in the early Iron Age when small villages of shepherds and farmers, living in wattle-and-daub huts, spread over the Palatine, Esquiline, Quirinal and probably the Caelian Hills; they disposed of their dead on the slopes and valleys between.[21] Overcrowding in the villages led some of the inhabitants to move down the slopes, early in the seventh century, and well before the end of that century they were able to build huts on the site of the future Forum Romanum, which by then they had drained and made habitable. One, perhaps slightly the earliest, village was on the Palatine, a height which commanded the Tiber and could easily be made defensible, yet was comparatively

Iron Age settlements at Rome

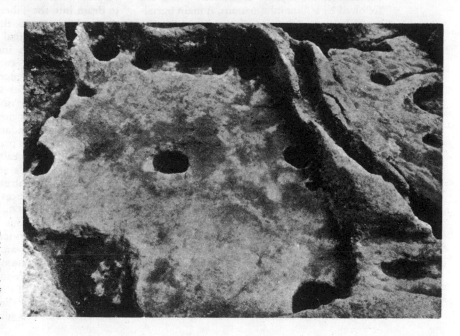

4.4 Foundations of an Iron Age 'Villanovan' hut on the Palatine hill at Rome, of the mid-eighth century B.C. Note the post-holes, porch at top of picture and drainage channel between two huts.

4.5 Reconstruction of such a hut. Cf. 2.3 and 2.4 above.

roomy and not too inaccessible from the landward side. Here under the later House of Livia an early cremation-burial was found and also the foundations of three huts cut in the tufa rock. Here too in historical times was preserved the Hut of Romulus *(casa Romuli)*, indicating that later Romans believed this hill to have been the heart of primitive Rome. On the Esquiline hill, on the other hand, the tombs are almost exclusively burials *a fossa*, while on the Quirinal the earliest are *a pozzo* cremations which are followed by *a fossa* inhumations. A main burial-ground was on the site of the Forum at the foot of the Palatine: here both cremation and inhumation burials are found, but with cremation dominant in the earliest tombs. These cremations almost certainly are the burials of the Palatine community, and the inhumations those of the occupants of other hills; they extend from the eighth to the early sixth century. On the Capitol, despite its dominant position, no traces of early settlment have yet come to light; this steep and narrow bluff was well suited to be an *oppidum* or temporary refuge and may have served as such rather than as a permanent habitation.

The inhabitants of these villages were essentially similar to those of other Iron Age settlements in Latium: those on the Palatine resembled the 'Villanovans' of the Alban Hills, while material from the Esquiline finds its parallels at Tivoli and southern Latium. Despite some individual characteristics in their pottery, they all clearly shared the same culture. This was basically Latin though some scholars associate the inhumations with the Sabines, whom the later Romans believed to have formed a substantial element in the early population. Thus the early settlers may have been reinforced by others from the central Apennine regions, to whom the valley of the Anio offered an easy avenue into the Tiber basin (p. 31).

The Palatine, Esquiline and Quirinal communities were at first quite distinct; indeed the marshland of the Forum, through which the surplus water of the outer hills made its way to drain into the Tiber, interposed an effective physical barrier to the amalgamation of the Palatine and Quirinal groups. A very general picture of how an incipient coalition of the villages developed can be gleaned from the archaeological evidence and from later religious customs. The former suggests that during the seventh century the isolation of the villages was beginning to break down; their products were becoming more standardised, partly through the emergence of more professional craftsmen; the distribution of wealth was widening (the remains of a man's armour and chariot were found in a *fossa* tomb of *c.* 650 on the Esquiline); and external influences increased, more particularly from *c.* 625 B.C., when Etruscan *bucchero* and metalwork from Veii and Caere appear, together with Etruscan imitations of Greek proto-Corinthian and Corinthian pottery. Though the inhabitants still lived in huts, their cultural desires were increasing.

At the festival of the Lupercalia the Luperci used to run round the Palatine in a ceremony of purification; this suggests an original isolated

The isolation of the villages decreases

Septi-montium

settlement on that hill. But another festival which also survived into historical times was called the Septimontium; the *septem montes* were not the well-known Seven Hills of Rome but the original elements of three groups, namely the Palatine (comprising the heights known as Cermalus, Palatinus and Velia), the Esquiline (= Oppius, Cispius and Fagutal) and the Caelius. This suggests that the first stage in the formation of the city was the union of these communities, even if the Septimontium proves nothing more than an association of villages for a common religious worship.

The 'City of the Four Regions'

The next stage appears to have been a union of the enlarged Palatine community with that on the Quirinal; it also is reflected in later recorded religious practice. The Salii, dancing warrior-priests, were divided into two groups, the Salii Palatini and Salii Collini (= of the Quirinal), and the Luperci were divided into two groups which also seem to represent the Palatine and Quirinal. This 'twin city' (*urbs geminata,* as called by Livy, i. 13) was organised into four regions, as is shown by a religious procession of the Pontifices and Vestals who used to visit twenty-seven (or twenty-four) shrines of the Argei in four regions of the city, namely Palatine, Caelius, Esquiline and Quirinal.[22] Here is a union of four areas, and since the procession went round each separately, the rite may possibly go back to a period when the four villages were separate communities. Although the Capitoline hill (and the Aventine) were probably excluded, the area was roughly coextensive with the four urban 'tribes' or city wards of the Republican period and so has been named the City of the Four Regions. It also corresponds roughly to the area within the *pomerium,* a ritual furrow made by a plough drawn by a yoked bull and cow to mark off the area of an augurally constituted city. This spiritual boundary, which the Romans shared with the Etruscans (p. 21), was not necessarily strengthened at this stage by an inclusive defensive rampart. Nor indeed is there definite evidence for the separate fortification of the earlier villages: they may have relied for defence on the steep hillsides, possibly reinforced with wooden palisades, while there *may* have been some earth walls across the Oppius, Cispius and Quirinal.

Etruscan elements appear

This stage in Rome's growth heralds the transition to the Etruscan city. In the last quarter of the seventh century not only was Etruscan pottery reaching Rome (p. 48) but also Etruscan ideas: huts, which now superseded the final Forum burials, began to give place to houses with tiled roofs. This archaeological evidence coincides in a remarkable manner with the literary tradition of the Romans that the first Etruscan king, Tarquinius Priscus, gained the throne of Rome in 616 B.C. Henceforth Rome had become an Etruscan *urbs* rather than scattered *pagi* and entered the ambit of Etruscan civilisation. But before this flowering of early Rome is described we must see briefly what the later Romans themselves recalled about their early rulers.

Romulus and the Sabines

To the mythical Romulus was attributed the creation of several of Rome's institutions, including the Senate, but discussion of these is better left until they have emerged a little more clearly into the misty dawn of history.[23] He is also said to have tried to increase the number of his citizens by two methods: he established an asylum on the Capitoline where all outlaws could find refuge and acceptance; this story reflects the later generosity of Rome in extending its citizenship. The other story is the rape of the Sabine women. Romulus attracted to Rome many Sabines and other neighbours by a splendid celebration of a festival in honour of Consus (the god of the granary or storehouse); his men then seized the women for themselves. In reply Titus Tatius, king of the Sabine town of Cures, attacked Rome and captured the Capitoline through the treachery of Tarpeia. In the resultant battle the Sabine women intervened: peace was made and the Romans and Sabines became one people, Romulus reigning on the Palatine and Tatius on the Capitoline. After Tatius's death Romulus ruled the community alone until he was taken up to heaven in a chariot by Mars.

Such stories naturally have no historical foundation, but they raise many problems. The joint rule of the two kings was probably invented as a precedent for the later division of authority between the Republican magistrates, the consuls. But what about the Sabines? While the tradition that Sabines conquered Rome and exercised a political ascendancy over the Romans is best set aside, some gradual Sabine infiltration is indicated by the infusion of a small Sabine element into the vocabulary of the Romans, and the reception of a few specifically Sabine deities among their state cults. These deities included the mysterious Quirinus whom the Romans identified with both Mars and the deified Romulus, and the word may be linked with the Quirinal and also with Quirites, the name by which the Romans sometimes called themselves.[24] Much is to be said for the view which identifies this Sabine element in Rome with the inhuming peoples who had occupied the Quirinal and Esquiline in early days. If this is accepted, the legend of Tatius may reflect a general, though not specific, historical truth.[25]

King Numa

Romulus, the warrior-king, who was believed to have given Rome many of her military and political institutions, was said to have been succeeded by Numa Pompilius, a priest-king who organised the religious life of the community by establishing regular cults and priests (*flamines, pontifices, Salii* and the Vestal Virgins and by reforming the calendar, correlating the lunar and solar year by introducing a twelve-month in place of a ten-month year (p. 52). Numa's name and alleged Sabine origin may well be historical,[26] but it is hazardous to attribute to the traditional date of his reign (*c.* 700 B.C.) any specific institution: some of his 'reforms' are certainly earlier (thus the Salian priests had armour of Bronze Age type), while the reform of the calendar may belong to the Etruscan period a century later. Robbed of his historical accretions, Numa becomes a very shadowy figure, but he need not disappear completely into thin air: he could well be a strong and respected leader who contributed to the process of unification.

Tullus Hostilius

The third king, who traditionally reigned from 673 to 642, was Tullus Hostilius, an aggressive warrior who repulsed an Alban invasion and then destroyed Alba Longa and transferred its population to Rome. Both his name, which is Latin, and his destruction of Alba may be accepted: the Iron Age settlement at Alba, which was perhaps very slightly older than the one at Rome, gradually disappears, although there is no archaeological evidence for a catastrophic sacking *c.* 650 B.C. The name of the Alban commander, Mettius Fufetius, may also be historical: he had been appointed as a magistrate to succeed the dead king, and Mettius is the Latin form of an Oscan magistrate called *meddix*. The later Senate-house at Rome was known as the Curia Hostilia and attributed to the king; this is possible, although it might have been built by members of the Hostilian *gens* a century or two later. However, as the Hostilii did not reach the consulship or become prominent until the second century, long after the establishment of the Curia and of Tullus in the regal canon, at least his name and perhaps his building suggest history rather than legend.

Ancus Marcius

Much the same reason suggests that Ancus Marcius, Hostilius's successor, was a historical figure: the Marcii did not reach the consulship until 357 B.C., long after the name had been incorporated in the list of kings. Nor, incidentally, would the Romans have falsely inserted a plebeian name into the list (the Marcii were plebeians). Although Ancus did not found a colony at Ostia at the mouth of the Tiber, as tradition describes, he almost certainly gained control of the salt-pans there south of the river. The Etruscans controlled those on the north bank as well as the crossing of the river at Fidenae above Rome, but the Romans began to wish for their own supply of salt which they could trade to the hill tribes in the east. Hence the occupation of Ostia. But the salt also had to be brought over the Tiber, and so the tradition that Ancus built the first bridge at Rome is most reasonable. Further this bridge, the Pons Sublicius, was made entirely of wood (*sublica* means a 'pile'); this suggests antiquity and also a probable connection with the *pontifices*, whose name means 'bridge-makers' (*pons, facere*). The report that Ancus incorporated the Janiculum hill in Rome is exaggerated, but he may well have established a bridgehead on it to protect the salt route and his new bridge. Finally, it was during his reign, which ended traditionally in 617, that Tarquin came to Rome. But that story belongs rather to Etruscan Rome.

CHAPTER 5

Rome in the Period of the Kings

1. The Kings and Tradition

In the sixth century Rome edges a little further into the brighter light of history, though much still remains obscure. In this chapter we shall look very briefly at what the later Romans believed to have been the history of that century and what tradition, combined with archaeology, tells of the amazing growth of the city and its buildings. Thereafter we can turn to the economic, religious, social and political institutions of Rome from early times down to the end of the sixth century and finally consider the fall of the monarchy and the establishment of the Roman Republic.

The literary tradition The Romans began to write their history only about 200 B.C., as will be described in the next chapter. Thus living some three centuries after the regal period even these early annalists would not always find it easy to differentiate between fact and fiction, although they had some reliable material to draw upon (pp. 57 ff.). Further, since their works are now lost, our main sources are two writers, Livy (i–ii. 15) and Dionysius of Halicarnassus (i–v), both of whom wrote some 200 years later – that is, half a millennium after the end of the monarchy. So it is not surprising that the surviving literary tradition presents many problems and has evoked diverse interpretations.

The Tarquins The three pre-Etruscan kings were followed by Lucius Tarquinius Priscus (traditionally 616–579 B.C.), Servius Tullius (578–535) and Tarquinius Superbus (534–510). It is clear that, however hard the later Roman tradition tried to disguise the fact, the Tarquins were Etruscan rulers: their name alone denotes this. Although the name Lucius may reflect a misunderstanding of the Etruscan title of Lucumo, and Priscus

and Superbus are later additions, Tarquin is Etruscan (cf. the Etruscan city of Tarquinii). Since many similar actions are attributed to both kings, some scholars would regard them as reduplicated forms of one historical figure, but in view of the probable duration of the Etruscan period in Rome, both Tarquins may be retained. Later Roman writers may have found uncertainties in the surviving tradition as to whether some acts were to be attributed to the one or the other: hence the resultant confusion, since in handling their material they did not all reach the same conclusions.

Tarquinius Priscus Tarquinius Priscus, son of Demaratus (p. 16), whether he came from Tarquinii or (as a family tomb possibly suggests) from Caere,[1] gained control peacefully. He is said to have established Games and a system of drainage at Rome: since these are both typically Etruscan interests, the tradition may be accepted. His alleged addition of a hundred members to the Senate, who were called *minores gentes*, reflects the fact that he encouraged many Etruscan families to settle in Rome, as is shown by the existence of several Etruscan family names among the titles of the tribes established by his successor Servius (e.g. Papiria, Voltinia); these newcomers would strengthen his power.

Servius Tullius Servius Tullius traditionally was Tarquin's son-in-law and secured the throne through the boldness of his wife Tanaquil. His name, which is Latin and later was used only by plebeians, supports his historicity: a fictitious king would have received a patrician name. There was, however, an Etruscan tradition, known to the later Roman emperor Claudius, that Servius was in fact an Etruscan named Mastarna. This view gains some support from a surviving Etruscan painting of *c.* 300 B.C., but the story is a compli-

5.1   Wall-painting from a tomb at Etruscan Vulci. It shows Mastarna liberating Caeles Vibenna. See p. 581.

cated one;[2] on balance it would seem that, while both peoples had a strong reason for claiming Servius, he is more likely to have been a Latin. However, even if a Latin king was sandwiched in between two Etruscan Tarquins, Etruscan influence will nevertheless have continued at Rome during the middle of the century.

His achievements   Servius is credited with three outstanding achievements. He reorganised the state on a timocratic basis by creating new military units and property classes; many recorded details of this reform may have been introduced later (pp. 53 ff.), but the essential elements probably go back to Servius. Thereby he both enfranchised many men whom trade and industry had attracted to Rome under Etruscan rule, and he strengthened the monarchy vis-à-vis the nobles by appealing to the middle class, who could supply legionary hoplites for the army; at the same time he may have checked the increasing exclusiveness of the nobility. Second, he is said to have protected the city by building an encircling stone wall: although this probably exaggerates his construction, he did not neglect the defences (p. 45). Third, on the Aventine hill, a plebeian quarter of the city, he established the cult of Diana, having persuaded some neighbouring Latin towns to allow the building of a common federal sanctuary at Rome: this will represent an attempt to assert Rome's political

leadership in Latium, perhaps at the expense of Aricia, an older centre of the League.[3]

Tarquinius Superbus   Servius is said to have been murdered by the younger Tarquin (the son or more probably the grandson of Priscus), who was instigated by his ambitious wife, Tullia, Servius's own daughter. The literary sources dress up the second Tarquin in the guise of a typical Greek tyrant, but his essential historicity should not be questioned. In Rome his building-schemes included the temple of Jupiter Capitolinus and the Cloaca Maxima (p. 44), which beside drawing on workmen and artists from Etruria provided employment for many at Rome; abroad he extended Roman influence in Latium and concluded a treaty with Gabii (p. 54). The story of his downfall will be recorded later (pp. 55 f.) after a consideration of the growth of Rome during the regal period, including not least the extraordinary development of the public buildings of the emergent city which owed so much to the Tarquins.

2. The City[4]

The Forum   The Etruscans perhaps provided the stimulus which provoked the scattered villagers to greater unity; they certainly provided the architectural and engineering skill which produced the new buildings of the city of Rome. The heart of the new city was the Forum, which became usable only when properly drained. After a disastrous flood c. 625 B.C. the bed of the Forum brook was dredged (by Tarquinius Priscus?), while the main drain was attributed to the second Tarquin and belongs to c. 570. Both these works were open drains, since the surviving cappellacio work of the Cloaca Maxima dates to after 390 B.C. Over the top of the older graves and huts a pebble floor was laid for the new civic centre, and huts were replaced by houses of sun-dried brick with tiled roofs during the early sixth century. The most famous of the regular streets, which were now planned, was the Via Sacra, which followed the course of a stream and led between the Regia and the temple of Vesta; it continued to the Capitol, while the Vicus Tuscus led on from the Forum to the Cattle Market (Forum Boarium) near the Tiber. This Vicus was a district where Etruscans, perhaps largely craftsmen and traders, lived and in it stood a statue of the Etruscan god Vortumnus.

The Regia   In the Forum on the north side of the Via Sacra where later the Regia stood, originally there were huts which were replaced during the sixth century by a temple precinct; the antefixes of one of two temples belong to c. 550–525 B.C.

5.2 Terracotta moulded reliefs from Regal Rome (first half of sixth century?). Warriors, charioteers and winged horses.

Recent excavation suggests that the Regia itself dates only from *c.* 500; if this is accepted, it cannot have been the dwelling of a king (one account associates it with Numa), but will have been the residence established at the beginning of the Republic for the priest who took over the sacral duties of the former kings, the *rex sacrorum* (though later the building was transferred to the Pontifex Maximus).[5] On the opposite side of the Via Sacra was the early temple of Vesta, rounded like one of the primitive huts; *Temple of Vesta* votive deposits, which include early Greek pottery, suggest a date of *c.* 575–550 B.C. At the north-west end of the Forum was the Comitium, the later assembly-place of the Roman people; its political use may be contemporary with its first pavement, but beneath this was a gravel surface of *c.* 575 B.C. Nearby under the so-called *Lapis Niger* Lapis Niger are the remains of a shrine *(sacellum)*, which later had an altar flanked by two bases holding statues of lions and was held to be the tomb of Romulus; a covered *aedicula*, dedicated to a primitive but unknown deity, goes back to about 570. Near the north corner of the Forum was the sanctuary of Volcanus, an altar in an enclosed area which formed a platform from which the king could address the people.

A similar pattern of development took place *Forum Boarium* in the other Forum, the Boarium, as revealed by excavations around the Church of Sant'Omobono: by 575 B.C. earlier huts were destroyed and a floor was laid down, while an open-air sanctuary had been established. This was followed about the beginning of the fifth century

5.3 Another terracotta, showing a Minotaur and two felines.

by two temples built on a platform with altars in front of each. These are probably temples of Fortuna and Mater Matuta, which were attributed to Servius Tullius; if too late for him, he may well have been associated with the preceding precinct. Considerable quantitites of Greek pottery, dating from *c.* 570 to 450, together with terracotta plaques depicting horses and charioteers have been found.

The Capitoline temple

    The Capitoline hill had curiously been neglected hitherto, but the Tarquins included it within the city and built on its southern side a great temple to Jupiter Optimus Maximus, making it the religious centre of the city. Traces of other early buildings have been found, together with a *bucchero* bowl inscribed with one of the three Etruscan inscriptions discovered in Rome. But the temple of Jupiter was the crowning architectural glory of Etruscan Rome; traditionally vowed by Priscus, it was virtually finished by Superbus and dedicated in the first year of the Republic. Only parts of its stone foundations and fragments of its terracotta antefixes and tiles survive. Jupiter occupied the middle of three *cellae*, Juno and Minerva the

5.5 Terracotta antefix of a temple on the Capitol, in the form of a female head with archaic smile.

side ones. His cult statue in terracotta was made by a master Etruscan sculptor, Vulca from Veii. Some 180 feet wide, 65 high, with three rows of six columns, 8 feet in diameter, forming a *pronaos* in front of the *cellae*, the temple was of imposing size, while the gaily coloured painted terracotta, which covered its wooden superstructure, its figured friezes and the figure of Jupiter in a quadriga towering over the pediment delighted the eye.

    The religious importance of the new temple was great. Under the Etruscans the Romans first began to see the vaguer spirits in which they believed (p. 48) in the form of men and women and to build temples to house them in place of the earlier rustic altars. Further, Jupiter the Best and Greatest became the state-god of the whole community, while Vulca's statue of him gave the worshippers a glimpse of Etruscan art to match his statue of Apollo at Veii. This new cult was linked with an Etruscan ceremony of holding a triumph which Rome now adopted. After a solemn procession which ended at the temple the triumphator, the king in regal times, sacrificed on the Capitol to the god whom he had represented in the procession (p. 51). He then descended to the Circus Maximus in the valley between the Palatine and Aventine, and there the Roman Games were held in the god's

5.4 Terracotta head of a statue of Minerva from the Forum Boarium, perhaps originally the acroterium of a temple. Late sixth century.

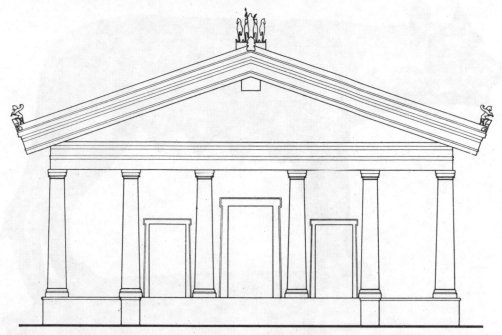

5.6 Reconstruction of the façade of the temple of Jupiter on the Capitol, showing the form of Etruscan temples. Resting on stone foundations, much of the superstructure was made of wood, covered with gay multicoloured terracotta ornamentation.

5.7 Detail of 5.6.

honour. These Games were ascribed to Romulus, but they accord with the Etruscans' love of horse-racing and were no doubt elaborated, if not started, by the Tarquins, who built the first wooden stands for the spectators.[6]

Was sixth-century Rome encircled by a stone wall built by Servius, as tradition holds? The existing 'Servian' Wall belongs in the main to the fourth century; although some archaeologists would assign some parts made of *cappellacio* tufa to Servius, this is far from certain. More probably he constructed the earthwork (*agger*) which runs across the Viminal and adjacent hills to block the heads of the valleys leading into Rome. Thus, like contemporary Ardea, regal Rome may have been protected only by its natural position and by an *agger* and ditch.[7]

The 'Servian' Wall

Thus under Etruscan rule Rome became a united city, with public buildings which could vie with those of the older cities of Etruria. Fragments of temple friezes give us tantalising glimpses of the life of the times: banqueting scenes, horsemen, chariots and chariot-races, strange feline beasts and minotaurs, while the quantity of imported Greek pottery shows that the cultural level of the life of the upper classes had advanced far beyond that of their predecessors, who less than a century before were living in huts.

5.8   Bronze statue of the Capitoline Wolf, perhaps the work of the Veientine school, *c.* 500 B.C. Figures of the twins, Romulus and Remus, were added during the Renaissance.

5.9   The so-called 'Servian' Wall of Rome, attributed traditionally to the Regal period, but more probably built after the sack of Rome by the Gauls in 390 B.C.

5.11 Bronze figurine of a ploughman from Arezzo in Etruria. The group illustrates the essentially agricultural basis of life in early Italy.

5.10 Early earthworks at the Latin town of Ardea. They show the kind of *agger* that protected the exposed parts of Rome in the Regal period.

3. Economic Conditions under the Kings

The territory of Rome, which at the end of the regal period covered some 350 square miles, originally did not extend over more than some 60 square miles — a lesser area than that of many of its later colonies. From the list of deities and festivals in the Roman state-calendar (p. 48) it appears that an appreciable part of Rome's earliest wealth lay in its flocks and herds. But until the Roman conquests extended into the Apennines, the lack of suitable summer pasture must have prevented the pursuit of a pastoral economy on any large scale. The inclusion of a vintage festival in the calendar shows that viticulture was not wholly neglected; but vineyards were not yet common in central Italy, and the olive had probably not been introduced into the neighbourhood of Rome. The greater part of the cultivable land was under the plough or hoe, *Early Roman agriculture* and the staple crop was a species of wheat named *far*, which produced a husky grain, more suitable for boiling into porridge (*puls*) than for bak-

ing into loaves, but was hardy and prolific. Under these conditions it may be assumed that the yield of the Roman land was high according to the standards of the day, and that a relatively large population subsisted on it. While the pasture-land remained for the most part undivided, it is probable that from the beginning of Roman history the arable land was held in severalty.[8]

Although the early Romans were predominantly an agricultural people, Etruscan influence and occupation gave a great stimulus to their industrial and commercial development. *Early Roman industry* The scale of the transformation of the physical city, which has just been described, clearly had fundamental economic consequences: thus, for instance, consider the labour involved in quarrying, transporting and building up the stone required for the massive foundations of the temple of Jupiter, which covered almost an acre of ground. Further, the technical skill of the Etruscans in clay and metal set an example for Roman craftsmen to imitate, and the labour guilds which are attributed to the regal period are quite credible, namely bronze-smiths, potters, goldsmiths, carpenters, dyers, leatherworkers, tanners and flute-players. The growth of a ceramic industry is attested by the finds of terracotta revetments of the sixth century in many parts of the city. In the field of bronzework the famous statue of the Wolf of the Capitol is pre-eminent, but unfortunately its precise date and authorship are doubtful. If, as well may be, it belongs to the late sixth century and to the school of Vulca of Veii (p. 44), it will have provided a very high standard for native Romans to admire and seek to attain.[9] But in fact we cannot say how many of the products

Commerce

of industry were due to Romans, how many to immigrant Etruscan artists.

Roman tradition is silent about trade in the regal period. For currency cattle still did duty, or lumps of copper *(aes rude)* weighed in the balance. But the wide freedom of contract and bequest conceded in the law of the Twelve Tables of 450 B.C. indicates that the Romans had long passed out of the stage of domestic economy. Material evidence for overseas commerce survives in the quantity of Greek pottery found on the site of the city. Fragments of at least 306 vases survive for the period 575–500 (and only 26 before that date), and 203 of them belong to 530–500 B.C., while no less than 255 are Athenian. It is significant that Attic imports to the six chief cities of Etruria during 530–500 are on average, as represented by surviving evidence, almost exactly the same in number as those which reached Rome.[10] It is abundantly clear therefore that overseas trade played an important role in sixth-century Rome. It is extremely likely that Etruscan Rome had a formal treaty with the great trading-power of the western Mediterranean, Carthage (since the so-called first treaty between Rome and Carthage which was made at the beginning of the Republic, see p. 65, was probably a renewal of an earlier agreement). This is made even more probable by what is now known from the Pyrgi inscriptions (Pl. 3.12; p. 27) about the very close contacts between Carthage and Etruscan Caere: the Tarquins of Rome will not have wished to lag behind the city from which they themselves probably derived. The imports were presumably paid for in salt from the pans at the Tiber mouth, timber from the upper valleys of the Tiber and Anio, and perhaps some slaves acquired in war. With the growth of Roman trade we may connect the beginning of a new settlement on the Aventine, under which the first river wharves were built, and an institution of a fair at the sanctuary of Diana on that hill (p. 42), where merchants from other Latin towns could meet traders from overseas.

4. Early Roman Religion[11]

Popular religion

In the early Roman community religious usage clearly reflected the agricultural basis of the people's life. Each household worshipped the protectors of its home and its livelihood: the Lares, who kept general guard over house and land; the Penates who watched over the grain-store; Vesta, who fanned the glow in the Hearth-fire; Janus, who guarded the door; Jupiter, the arbiter of sun and rain; Mars, who stirred the plants to life in spring; and a host of other powers that aided or hindered the work of herdsman or husbandman, or guided the members of the family through the critical stages of birth and childhood, wedlock and death.[12] In his devotions the peasant hardly looked beyond the practical needs of day-to-day life. His idea of the powers *(numina)* whom he addressed was so hazy that he could not envisage them in any clear shape and was not always sure of their sex; his conception of the next world was so dim that he could think of the dead *(manes)* only in a collective sense. His acts of worship consisted of a simple invocation and libation of milk or (more seldom) of wine, an offer of a cake or a sacrificial animal, on an altar of turf. Magical spells were occasionally practised by him, but formed no regular part of his ritual.

The religion of the state, as exemplified by the calendar of official festivals (the so-called calendar of Numa), was in large degree a duplication of the private cults. The city of Rome gave public worship to Vesta, to the Lares and Penates, and to other guardians of fields and flocks, with ceremonies that did not differ substantially from those of the individual household. But certain of the rustic deities were transformed in the state cult into protectors of the community as a whole in all its activities. Mars The state cults turned the tide of battle in Rome's favour; Janus mounted guard over the city-gates; above all, Jupiter became the general watcher over Rome's welfare. During the sixth century, moreover, the official religion was elaborated under Etruscan influence. Deities were regarded more anthropomorphically, and if gods were fashioned in the image of man, they needed housing in temples and to be provided with cult-statues. The Romans did not indeed give a ready welcome to new deities from Etruria. But their earliest temples and cult-images were of Etruscan type, and the great sanctuary of Jupiter, Juno and Minerva on the Capitol was copied from Tuscan models. Though their practice of ascertaining the will of the gods by observing the flight of birds and the feeding of chickens was probably of Italic rather than of Etruscan origin, it was no doubt in imitation of Tuscan ritual that the taking of such *auspicia* was made into a necessary preliminary of numerous acts of state, and the code for the interpretation of the *omina* became so complicated as to require a special board of consulting experts *(augures)*.

At the close of the regal period the official Roman religion had acquired those permanent Characteristics of Roman religion characteristics which no intrusive influence of later centuries was ever able to obliterate. It combined the practical give-and-take attitude of the Italian peasant with the ceremonial formalism of the Etruscans. The Roman state cults were in the nature of contractual acts, by which the magistrate bargained for certain benefits, or abstention from certain torts, on the part of the deity, in consideration of certain services, which were graduated according to a comprehensive tariff and performed with punctilious exactitude: *Do ut des* (I give that you may give). Of all ancient religions it was the least emotional. The official Roman mind admitted a feeling of vague awe (*religio* in its original sense) in the presence of the deity, but it deprecated any *superstitio* or unchecked display of emotion as out of place in an act of worship, just as it would have frowned on cheers or groans before the praetor's tribunal. It was equally the most meticulous and conservative in its ritual. Even in the emancipated and irreverent days of the later republic ceremonial taboos inherited from the Stone Age were observed with an outward scrupulousness that bordered on the absurd. Encased in this strait-jacket, Roman religion never became, like that of the Greeks, the foster-mother of art, music and literature; though it possessed some resemblances with the religion of the early Israelites, it never could produce a comprehensive and satisfying code of conduct: it produced only priests, not prophets. Yet for all its hardness and seeming selfishness, it was not lacking in social value. Negatively, it was singularly free from those extravagances of lust and of fear which emotionalism in ancient religion usually carried in its train: temple prostitutes were entirely unknown in the state worship, and human sacrifices were of the utmost rarity. Positively, in emphasising the principle of reciprocal service between man and god, it also fostered the idea of mutual obligation between man and man. Again, within each Roman family the traditional religion strengthened the feeling of partnership in a common cause: in early Rome weddings in patrician families were usually consecrated by a religious ceremonial (*confarreatio*), and husband and wife shared the duties of the household ritual. Lastly, the *pax deorum*, or covenant with the gods, which it was the primary object of Roman ritual to maintain, imparted to the early Roman a sense of security which reinforced his inborn doggedness and could make him invincible in his fixity of purpose.

Its conservativeness

5. Social and Political Groupings[13]

The patrician nobility and the plebs

The social structure of early Rome was that of a free community with an inner circle of aristocratic houses. In the city the artisans and traders were their own masters, and the slave population was limited to a few debtors whose servitude was neither hereditary nor irrevocable. In the countryside the peasantry were not tied to the soil,[14] and they usually were the owners of a small plot. But the *plebs* or mass of the people in city and country gradually became distinct from the privileged class of the *patricii*; later in the sixth or perhaps early fifth century the citizen body definitely hardened into the two sharply divided 'orders' of patricians and plebeians (p. 64). The origin of this social division is not to be found in any diversity of race, but in a progressive differentation of wealth which had commenced before the foundation of the city. A limited number of families, in whose hands the larger estates were held, had gradually acquired a hold over the lesser peasantry, among whom the subdivision of land had been carried so far that they were driven to eke out their livelihood as labourers or part-tenants in the service of their wealthier neighbours. This economic nexus was reinforced by a social bond between the patrician and his 'client'. The patron gave economic support to the client and assisted him in obtaining his rights against third parties. In return the client gave field labour, military aids (p. 52), and occasional contributions of money, like those of a medieval vassal to his overlord.[15] These mutual obligations, though not enforceable by law, were sanctioned by custom and religion and were handed on from generation to generation, so that for many centuries the relation between patron and client remained one of the strongest links in Roman society.

The social organisation of the early Roman community, as that of other Italic peoples, was based on a 'gentile' pattern. The *gens*, clan or group of families, was marked by a common name: in addition to his personal name (*praenomen*) a Roman would always bear that of his *gens* (the *nomen* proper). Gentile solidarity long remained a powerful force among the ruling families of Rome; but the *gentes* never officially formed part of the machinery of government, although they had considerable influence on the development of law and religion. As a social unit the *gens* was replaced by the *familia* or household which at all times remained a miniature state within the state. The patriarchal organisation which was common to all peoples of Indo-European stock was maintained at Rome longer than elsewhere in its pristine rigour. The *paterfamilias*, having acquired his wife by simple arrangement with the bride's father, assumed *manus* or complete disciplinary control over her, and he wielded a similar despotic authority over his sons, of whatever age, and over his unmarried daughters. Although the arbitrariness of his

The gens

The family

power was mitigated in actual practice by customary safeguards against abuse, such as the institution of a 'family council' *(consilium familiae)* to try offences of a serious nature, and by the discipline of the family religion, for many centuries his omnipotence within the family circle was unrestrained by law. Roman husbands might put their wives to death, and fathers might sell their children into slavery, without committing a crime.

*The three tribes*In early times the Roman people were divided into three tribes *(tribus)*, the Ramnes, Tities and Luceres; if these names are Etruscan, the tribes will be a fairly late creation, but they may be Etruscanised forms of pre-existing Latin names.[16] These tribes were probably originally ethnic rather than local groups, but little is known about their political functions; they were later replaced by new local tribes (p. 53). For political purposes the citizen body was grouped into thirty *curiae*. These may have been primitive groups of *gentes* associated for common defence, but they became local units of families who at first at any rate were neighbours.[17] The members of each *curia* met occasionally to witness adoptions and testaments and to decide *The* curiae disputed cases of legitimacy. Thus the *curiae* controlled admission to the citizen body; but the *curiones* who presided over them had no executive duties except a few religious formalities. They were probably the elements of the earliest military organisation and certainly of the oldest Roman assembly. Meeting in joint convention (Comitia Curiata) they constituted the original Roman folk-moot. The chief function of the assembly was to ratify the choice of a new king by a *lex curiata de imperio*, by which it bound itself to obeys his commands (but it had little choice as to the ruler himself, who had already been nominated by an *interrex* and ratified by the Senate). The Comitia Curiata might also be convoked at the king's discretion to confirm a sentence of death upon a citizen or to pledge its loyalty in a war or other political crisis. But it could not meet, except at the king's writ; it had no power, or only a restricted opportunity, of discussion; and its method of voting was probably by mere acclamation. The Comitia Curiata was therefore little more than a sounding-board which made the people's voice audible but not necessarily effective.

*The Senate*A more authoritative position was held by the *Senatus* or Council of Elders, an assembly of all the notables who had a customary claim to receive the king's summons. These were the *patres*, the heads of the leading *gentes* which became known as the patrician *gentes*. The tradition that Romulus enrolled exactly 100 senators and that by the end of the regal period these

had been increased to 300 cannot be accepted literally,[18] but it indicates a gradual increase in the number of senators; this increase may be reflected in the phrase *patres conscripti*, by which the Senate as a whole became known.[19] This council was a merely advisory body, whose pronouncements had no binding force. But its collective opinion inevitably gained in weight from the personal importance of its members. Moreover, at the death of a king his sovereignty passed back into its hands, and an *interrex* was appointed to conduct the election of a new monarch. But when a distinction had developed between the more privileged (patrician) senators and the others (whatever their origin), only a patrician could be an *interrex* and only patrician senators had the right of electing him and also of giving assent *(auctoritas patrum)* to the resolutions of the Comitia. Further, when an interregnum occurred, 'the auspices returned to the *patres*' (Cic. *ad Brut.* 1.5.4) and so the patricians maintained an exclusive monopoly of ᵗhis piece of religious machinery (p. 48). Again, outside the Senate, the major priesthoods, the *flamines*, were confined to patricians who also controlled several cults as well as the auspicial rights.

6. The Monarchy

*The king-ship. Its powers*Our knowledge of the powers and functions of the kings depends for the most part not upon contemporary evidence but upon the conception of these which was held by later Roman jurists, annalists and historians who had to fill the gaps in their own knowledge by arguing back from later institutions. This suggests the need for caution in accepting statements of detail. But while, for instance, the conception of regal power, as well as its outward trappings, may well have been somewhat different under the earlier Latin kings as contrasted with their Etruscan successors, nevertheless the general picture of the monarchy which the ancient sources present is doubtless reliable. It appears that the monarchy at Rome was a trust rather than a family possession. It was not exercised by dynastic right, but was conferred by the Senate and people without regard to family claims. The Roman kings made no pretence to divine descent, nor to any special communion with the gods, save by the right of taking the *auspicia*. Yet the trust conferred upon them invested them with almost despotic power. The royal *imperium* or right of command was unlimited in range, and could be enforced by the sanction of capital punishment. The plenary power of the kings was reflected in their outward insignia. They, or at any rate the later kings,

5.12 Painted plaque from Caere, showing a ruler seated before the statue of a goddess. Note the folding ivory seat, like the later *sella curulis* used by Roman magistrates. His clothing resembles the short Roman toga (*trabes*). his upturned shoes are typically Etruscan.

5.13 The Roman *fasces*.

were clad in purple, administered justice sitting on an ivory chair on a chariot (called *sella curulis*, after the chariot, *currus*), and were attended by lictors bearing the *fasces* or bundles of rods and axes, the visible symbols of their *imperium*. On their return from a successful war they rode at the head of their army in a 'triumphal' procession to the temple of Jupiter on the Capitol. This triumph may originally have involved a ceremonial purification of the soldiers and the city. Under the Etruscan kings its external form was elaborated: the *triumphator* wore the purple and gold garments of Jupiter, while his face was painted vermilion like that of the god's statue in the Capitoline temple; he stood in a four-horse chariot which was escorted on a fixed route through the city by his army, which shouted 'Io triumphe'.

Triumphs remained a feature of public life throughout Roman history; in the later Republic they became even more gorgeous and emphasised the personal glory of the general, while under the Empire they became the personal monopoly of the emperor himself, as of the king in early days.[20]

As executive head of the state the king had a threefold competence. He was charged with the maintenance of the *pax deorum*. But he delegated the more onerous religious ceremonies, such as the state cults of Jupiter, Mars and Quirinus (a somewhat shadowy counterpart of Mars), to special officiators (*flamines*), whom he selected from the patrician families, and the most exacting of all, the tending of the eternal fire of Vesta, to six daughters of leading families, who gave thirty years of their life to this never-ending task and lived in maiden seclusion for the term of their office. The king committed the duty of preserving and expounding the general law of state ritual (*ius divinum*) to a college of five *pontifices*, and the interpretation of omens to a board of three *augures*. Like the officiating priests these delegates of the king were nominated by him out of the patrician families; but they had few regular duties, and could only express their opinion at the king's special request. Apart from some minor sacri-

Religious functions of the kings

ficial rites the king in person discharged no regular religious duty save that of fixing the year's calendar. In fact the creation of a new calendar (the pre-Julian calendar) was attributed to Numa: he established a twelve-month calendar in place of the older ten-month one (March to December) which tradition had assigned to Romulus. This reform, however, which almost certainly belongs to the regal period, should more probably be assigned to the Etruscan kings. The adoption of a twelve-month calendar helped to correlate the lunar with the solar year, which had to be brought into further adjustment by the periodic insertion of an 'intercalary' month of 22/23 days (this latter device may have been elaborated, or even created, at the time of the *decemvirs* in 450 B.C.).[21]

Military functions

In the second place the king represented the community in its foreign relations. He made treaties, decided on questions of peace and war, levied troops and money, and took the field as *imperator* or general plenipotentiary. Lastly, the king made and declared the law. The rules of civic intercourse, however, were regulated by use and wont rather than by statute, and it is probable that the royal laws were mainly confined to the sphere of religious ritual.[22] The king's jurisdiction was restricted by the concurrent authority of the *paterfamilias* over his household; and his interference in the disputes between private citizens was limited to the appointment of *arbitri* who made an award in his name, but left the execution of it in the hands of the successful suitor. On the other hand the Roman king, as guardian of public security, freely exercised large powers of penal justice. His criminal jurisdiction extended particularly to two fundamental offences against the community: treason and unjustifiable homicide. Such 'capital' cases, involving exile or death (sometimes by hurling from the Tarpeian Rock, a cliff of the Capitol), he delegated to specially appointed officials, *duoviri perduellionis*, to deal with cases of treason, and *quaestores* (later *quaestores parricidii*) to investigate murder.[23] Though he might allow the revision of a capital sentence by the Comitia Curiata this act of grace lay entirely in his own discretion. The efficacy of the king's criminal justice is shown by the total absence of the blood feud in early Rome. The practice of private war, which proved so difficult to eradicate in the cities of early Greece and in medieval Europe, had been abolished at the very beginning of Roman history.

Judicial functions

Apart from the levying of money (in weight of copper) for purposes of war or public works, the king exercised no financial functions of any importance. The small revenue which he required for ordinary administration accrued to him in the form of rents from public domains (consisting of pastures and forests), from customs dues, from licences for the monopoly of salt, and from fines on public offenders. The surplus funds, which never amounted to a substantial sum, were deposited in a strong room (*aerarium*), later, at any rate, under the custody of regularly appointed *quaestores*.

Revenue

In comparison with other ancient communities at a similar stage of development, Rome in the regal period possessed a strong and active government. The salient feature of its early constitution lay in the exercise of *imperium* by the king, which gave him not only full powers of military discipline in the field of war, but an unlimited right to enforce his will and punish recalcitrants in time of peace. The *imperium* was subsequently circumscribed and made less arbitrary in its incidence, but it was always preserved as an attribute of the head magistrates at Rome. The drastic right of coercion which the Roman community conferred upon its executive was one of the clearest expressions of that practical turn of mind which made them realise that 'His Majesty's government must be carried on', and that political discipline is prior, in fact if not on paper, to political liberty.

7. Military and Political Developments

The earliest Roman army consisted of a general levy which was raised from the aristocratic landowners through the *gentes* and *clientelae*. It was based on the three tribes, each of which provided 1000 infantry commanded by a *tribunus militum*, together with three squadrons of 100 horsemen (*equites* or *celeres*) each under a *tribunus celerum*. Each of the three corps of 1000 comprised ten groups or centuries, corresponding to the ten *curiae* of each tribe. The infantry was probably equipped with long body-shield and throwing-spear; the tactics were doubtless somewhat rough and ready, approximating to the early 'heroic' stage in the growth of the armies of other city-states. But despite analogies with Greek cities and medieval knights and despite much modern controversy, there does not appear to be conclusive evidence that the cavalry at Rome was restricted to the patricians.[24] Rather, the *equites* may have provided the king's bodyguard and not have played a leading role in military tactics: a reliable but fragmentary literary source, known as the *Ineditum Vaticanum*, records that cavalry was not important until the Samnite Wars of the fourth century.

The early army

A radical change in the organisation of the army and in many other aspects of Roman public life was attributed to Servius Tullius. The

The army reform by Servius

army reforms may be dealt with first.[25] Servius is said to have doubled the number of soldiers and levied them on the basis of wealth, of new tribes (in place of the three old ones), and of 'centuries' (in place of Thousands). Thus the new levy (legio) comprised 6000 infantry, organised in sixty centuriae.[26] The cavalry were also increased, perhaps to six centuries (sex suffragia); alternatively, the sex suffragia could have been introduced earlier by Tarquinius Priscus, and Servius's increase then will have been of twelve new centuries of equites (making eighteen in all, i.e., comprising sixty turmae, each of thirty equites, corresponding to the sixty centuries of the legion).[27] This reorganisation probably went hand in hand with the adoption of hoplite tactics, now well established in Greece and Etruria, although some historians would date the change much later.[28] With this new battle-line new equipment was needed: the round shield (clipeus), fastened to the forearm, and the sword (a bronze clipeus has been found in a tomb on the Esquiline, dating to about 600 B.C.). Thus there is good reason to believe what the ancient sources almost unanimously tell us, namely that the mid-sixth century saw radical military reforms.

The accounts of the reforms which the ancient authorities ascribe to Servius are encrusted with many details which are clearly reflections of later developments and cannot go back to the sixth century. In consequence many modern critics have assigned the reforms to various periods in the fifth century and even the fourth century, but more recently an increasing body of historical opinion supports the view that the essence of the reforms does belong to the regal period although admitting that many details are added from a later stage of development. In consequence the principles of the reforms are described in this chapter.[29]

The growth of trade and industry had attracted many men to settle in Rome, but while these immigrants helped to promote economic prosperity they did nothing to strengthen her military might: since they were not citizens, they were not liable for service in the army. The need to draw on this new reservoir of manpower suggested the desirability of incorporating the newcomers in the citizen body, but to have drafted them into the existing curiae, closely knit family groups, would have given offence; hence a new structure was required. The three old tribes (Tities, Ramnes and Luceres) were abolished and twenty new tribes were created. Four were city tribes (urbanae) and took their names (Sucusana, Esquilina, Collina and Palatina) from the chief hills in each of the four regions into which Rome was now

The new tribes, urban and rural

in effect divided. In addition the population of the countryside (ager) was enrolled in sixteen rural tribes; they were mainly named after gentes (e.g. Aemilia, Cornelia, Fabia), perhaps taking over the names from the still earlier pagi. Thus residence, not birth or ownership of property, was made the basis for this new census of the settled population of Rome which was now incorporated into the citizen body by means of the new tribes.[30]

But Servius went further. From the military standpoint not all the new citizen body was of equal value: clearly the poor man could not guard the city with sticks and stones as well as the richer man with spear and sword. Thus in the census the landholders were divided into five classes, graded according to the equipment they could provide; the lowest class probably possessed only two (or two and a half) iugera of land, the first perhaps a minimum of twenty.[31] Those whose property fell too low for inclusion even in the fifth class were registered together 'by heads' as capitecensi or proletarii. Thus this new system, based on wealth, was timocratic and was not altogether dissimilar from the reformed constitution which Solon had introduced at Athens in 590; it is by no means impossible that the Romans were aware of what had recently been done at Athens. Further, the tribal reorganisation at Rome had much the same object as that later introduced at Athens by Cleisthenes, who wished to incorporate the new resident aliens who had settled in the city without a head-on collision with the older aristocratic clans.

The five classes

With the abolition of the old three tribes based on Thousands went the introduction of the Hundreds (centuriae) as subdivisions of the five new classes. In each class half the centuries comprised men of military age (iuniores, aged seventeen to forty-six) and half elders (seniores, forty-seven to sixty). But the number of centuries in each class varied: eighty in the first class, twenty in classes two, three and four, and thirty in the fifth, i.e. a total of 170 centuries of combatant infantry, half juniors. Below were five (or six) centuries of unarmed men, who served as armourers, smiths, trumpeters and the like (i.e. the capitecensi), while at the other extreme above the first class were the eighteen centuries of equites. Thus in all there were 193 centuries.

The 'centuries'

The primary purpose of the reform was military. The centuries were the units for recruiting, and the junior centuries of the first three classes probably formed the infantry of the line of the legio.[32] But from it grew a political Assembly-by-centuries, Comitia Centuriata, whose military origin was reflected in that it was summoned to meet by trumpet and it assembled in the Field

The Comitia Centuriata

of Mars, Campus Martius, outside the *pomerium* of the city. The people continued on occasion to meet by *curiae* in the Comitia Curiata, but gradually the *curiae* were replaced as administrative units by the tribes, and the Centuriate Assembly became more important than the Curiata. The method of voting was that each century recorded the majority vote of its members. Then the centuries voted in order of precedence: first those of the *equites* and then those of each of the five classes. But since the centuries of cavalry and the first class numbered 98 (18 + 80), they had a majority in the total of 193 centuries and thus, if they voted the same way, they could outvote the rest: in fact the voting stopped as soon as a majority was reached. But if the rich could thus outvote the poor, it must be remembered that it was on them that the main burden of fighting and financing the wars fell.

The date of its creation

How early did a political assembly based on the centuries begin to function? A *terminus ante quem* is provided by a reference to the *comitiatus maximus* in the Laws of the Twelve Tables of the mid-fifth century (except for those scholars who identify this assembly with the Curiata). Thus its genesis may reasonably be assigned at least to the beginning of the Republic, while a regal date is extremely probable (whether from the first with a quintuple class division or only a simpler structure must remain hypothetical). If then the Comitia Centuriata did meet under the kings, it perhaps voted on the king's proposals for peace and war and also approved the leaders he appointed, but it will have lacked the right to initiate business. Only gradually did it acquire the fuller powers that it enjoyed in later times.

Effect of the reform

Besides strengthening Rome by increasing the army Servius seems to have sought to strengthen the power of the monarch against increasing pressure from the nobility, by supporting the middle class who formed the backbone of the new army. Thereby he probably slowed down the process by which the nobles by claiming more religious, social and political privileges for themselves were beginning to form a separate class, the patriciate. However, in this he was not fully successful, since he himself was killed. But though his successor is said to have maintained his rule for another quarter of a century, the days of the monarchy at Rome, as at other Etruscan cities, were numbered.

8. Rome and her Neighbours

Intertribal usage. Ius Fetiale

Rome's early relations with her neighbours were governed by a rudimentary code which was common to other Italic peoples. This bound her not to make war on her neighbours without at least a formal justification, or without due notice given. A primitive procedure, which was perhaps first applied in minor disputes such as alleged theft of cattle or other property, came to be used in more serious territorial quarrels with other peoples. A college of Fetiales was appointed by the kings to preserve and expound these rules of intertribal and international behaviour.[33] Four Fetiales were sent to demand restitution (*rerum repetitio*). If at the end of thirty days this was not forthcoming, the envoys returned to the enemy and solemnly called on the gods to witness that their case was right (*testatio deorum*). Then after the Senate had decided on war and the people had confirmed this a messenger was sent to hurl a magical spear into the enemy's territory in order to counter his power (*indictio belli*). Thus the gods were invoked to witness that Rome's war was 'just'. This procedure shows that the normal status between Rome and her neighbours was peace, not war, and that Roman custom, at least in theory, did not recognise mere aggression or territorial covetousness as legitimate causes for war. The existence of Fetial priests in other Latin towns and even among the Samnites suggests that a basis might exist for the emergence of an international code.

Nevertheless Roman tradition represented all of the kings, except Numa, as engaged in frequent and almost monotonously successful warfare. But while many of these alleged conquests were nothing but anticipations of victories gained in the republican period, Rome did steadily extend her territory and her influence during the seventh and sixth centuries. Under the pre-Etruscan kings Rome had advanced into the Alban Hills and destroyed Alba Longa, as already said (p. 40); she also gained control of the salt-pans at the Tiber mouth at Ostia (p. 40). The territory north of the Tiber was dominated by the Etruscan city of Veii, while in the north-east Fidenae blocked Roman advance. The Romans will have gained control of the east bank as far as the Anio (defeating, e.g., Collatia) and probably a few miles further north, but Fidenae and Nomentum are unlikely to have succumbed. Gabii, just south of Collatia, was defeated by the second Tarquin, who then made a treaty with it, establishing 'isopolity', equality of rights, between the two cities. This treaty was written on the ox-hide covering of a shield which was preserved until the time of Augustus in the temple of Semo Sancus on the Quirinal.[34]

Extension of Roman territory

Treaty with Gabii

To how many other Latin cities Rome extended this new policy during the regal period is uncertain, but in the first treaty with Carthage, which Polybius ascribes to the first year of the Republic, Rome spoke for the cities of the Latin coast who were 'subject' to her (i.e. Ardea, Antium, Circeii, Tarracina and perhaps Lavinium) and for those who were not.[35] The former were probably *socii*, subject allies, who, like Gabii, had recognised Roman leadership in individual treaties. Rome's claim to speak for the Latins 'who were not subject' implies that she was speaking for a league of which she claimed to be leader. By destroying Alba Longa she had already wrested from Alba the leadership of the League centred on the cult of Jupiter Latiaris (p. 32), but it is uncertain how membership of this early League was related to that of a League based on a shrine of Diana at Aricia which met at Lucus Ferentinae and became the chief Latin centre from the sixth to the fourth century.[36] We have already seen (p. 42) how Servius Tullius tried to centralise, or at least to imitate, the cult of the Arician League by building a temple of Diana on the Aventine. Later Superbus married his daughter to Mamilius of Tusculum, hoping perhaps thereby to secure control of the League through Mamilius, its leader (dictator). The interrelationship of the various Leagues and the date when they became of political as well as of religious importance escape us, but under the Tarquins Rome seems to have enjoyed alliances with many coastal towns of Latium as far as some sixty miles south of Rome and to have claimed to act as spokesman for members of the Arician League. Finally, Etruscan Rome was known further afield and had a treaty with Carthage if, as is probable, the treaty recorded by Polybius is the renewal of an earlier one (p. 48).

But while Rome thus acquired considerable territory (perhaps some 350 square miles) in Latium and a man-power far exceeding that of any other Latin town, her kings never exercised any general dominion over Latium, and at the end of the period of monarchy there was as yet no sure indication that Rome would one day advance its frontiers far beyond the Tiber basin.

9. The End of Etruscan Rome

Etruscan rule at Rome, according to tradition, came to a dramatic end in 510 B.C. with the expulsion of Tarquinius Superbus, but its demise should be seen in a wider context: the downfall of Etruscan power in Latium, the history of Lars Porsenna, the gradual cessation of Etruscan influences at Rome, and the establishment of a Republican constitution.

First, the outline of the traditional story. The rape of Lucretia, wife of Tarquinius Collatinus, by Sextus, son of Tarquinius Superbus, provoked a conspiracy of nobles under the leadership of L. Iunius Brutus against the misrule of Superbus. While Sextus fled to Gabii, where he was killed, his father and two brothers found refuge in Caere.[37] At Rome the monarchy was replaced by two annually elected consuls, one of whom was Brutus. With help from Veii and Tarquinii Superbus met the Romans in an indecisive battle at Silva Arsia and thereafter secured the aid of Lars Porsenna of Clusium.[38] Porsenna

then marched on Rome, but (and here we move into the realm of legend) failed to capture the city, thanks to the defence of the Tiber bridge by Horatius (and two companions who had Etruscan names); later he called off the siege of the city, impressed by the bravery of the Romans exemplified in the exploits of Mucius Scaevola and Cloelia.[39] Thus Livy, but Tacitus and other later Romans knew better: Porsenna captured Rome, where he is said to have banned the use of iron weapons, in the same way that the Philistines tried to keep down the conquered Israelites. Indeed since he did not restore Tarquinius, Porsenna may well have been attempting to replace him. However, his stay in Rome was brief. Other Latin cities were encouraged by Rome's example to seek freedom from the Etruscans and with help from Aristodemus of Cumae (p. 26) they defeated at Aricia the force,

led by Porsenna's son Arruns, which he sent against them (*c.* 506). This engagement is of historical and historiographical importance. In the first place the victorious Latins could now cut the land communications between Etruria and Campania, while Aristodemus strengthened his rule at Cumae. Second, a fairly long account of these operations is preserved by Dionysius of Halicarnassus (vii. 5–6), which he derived probably from a local history of Cumae or at any rate from a source other than the Roman annalistic tradition; thus the chronology of the fall of the monarchy at Rome, as preserved in Roman tradition, is roughly confirmed by an independent Greek tradition, and this is important.[40]

Tarquinius Superbus next found refuge with his son-in-law, Mamilius Octavius of Tusculum, who had persuaded the Latins, according to Roman accounts, to support the cause of the exiled king and to fight the Romans at Lake Regillus. In fact Tarquin probably was not the cause of that battle: rather the Latins, who had co-operated successfully at Aricia, were organised in a League from which Rome was excluded, and the two rival groups clashed (p. 70). Soon afterwards in 496 Tarquin died at

Cumae where Aristodemus had granted him a final refuge.

Tarquinius Superbus

In the belief of the Romans their monarchy ended in 510/509 in a bloodless but forcible revolution, and the odium which for many centuries to come attached to the very name of *rex* in Rome is clear proof that the monarchy ended by becoming deeply unpopular. Thus although the story of the expulsion of Tarquinius Superbus was eventually overlaid by the Roman annalists with a mass of fictitious details, some of which were plainly borrowed from the classical stories of wicked despots in Greek literature,[41] we need not doubt that the second Tarquin made himself odious by tyrannical practices and that his fall was encompassed by a conspiracy of nobles, while in a wider context it may be regarded as an episode in the collapse of the Etruscan dominion in Italy.

Gradual decline of Etruscan influence

But although the outline of the traditional story is acceptable, we must not fall into the error of supposing that Etruscan influence came to an abrupt end in Rome in 510. In this very same year the tyrant Hippias was expelled from Athens and we know that this did not lead to the ejection of all his supporters. So at Rome there was no wholesale expulsion of Etruscans who had settled in the city. A political revolution did not involve an immediate cultural one. Thus Etruscan art still flourished in Rome for another half-century; Greek pottery continued to be imported, although on a declining scale; there was much temple-building (p. 64); and even some magistrates with Etruscan names were elected to office. Thus the fall of Tarquin may have been followed by a few decades which might be called sub-Etruscan, marked by the activities of men like Porsenna.[42] In these disturbed times, when control of many other Etruscan cities was passing from kings to oligarchs, ambitious nobles, with bands of clients, could strive for power, as may be exemplified in the story of how the clan of the Fabii and their clients fought against Veii at the Cremera in *c.* 475 (p. 117).

Alternative explanations of the end of monarchy

Finally one basic problem must be faced, although its complexity forbids more than brief mention here. Many historians, not satisfied with the traditional story, have tried to find other explanations of the end of the monarchy at Rome and do not accept the view that it was abruptly replaced by a Republic and two annually elected magistrates. There are those who believe in evolution rather than revolution: by analogy with other cities (e.g. Athens) some suggest that the authority of the king declined and was gradually transferred piecemeal to three magistrates. Others, who accept an abrupt ending, do not accept the sudden creation of a dual consulship in 509 as an anti-monarchical safeguard: it will have evolved from earlier prototypes, e.g. auxiliaries of the king, or praetors. Others again have postulated a period between monarchy and two magistrates of equal authority: during this interim one magistrate (or a college of magistrates in which one predominated) exercised control, e.g. a dictator, *magister populi* or *praetor maximus*.[43]

Date of the Republic

All such theories involve rejecting or tampering with the authority of the Fasti, the list of Roman magistrates which starts with the first consuls of the Republic (p. 58). Thus according to one well-known view (that of K. Hanell), 509 was the first year of the new cult of Jupiter Capitolinus and not the first year of the Republic, and thus the lists of the first half of the fifth century represent not the consuls but eponymous magistrates of the new cult. This view has been accepted by the archaeologist E. Gjerstad, who retains the traditional length of the reigns assigned to the kings; he therefore brings the period of Etruscan rule in Rome from *c.* 616–510 down to *c.* 530–450 B.C.[44] Since this theory involves transferring to the regal period many events which tradition assigns to the early Republic (e.g. the Struggle of the Orders and the treaty of Cassius) it produces a telescoping and dislocation on a scale which is not acceptable. Such theories deserve mention here if only to give a glimpse of the difficulty of interpreting evidence which can lead able scholars into such mutually contradictory views, as well as to illustrate that early Roman history is today a very lively arena of debate. But many will feel that it is better to stick to the essential reliability of the Fasti (although admitting that they are not free from some errors and falsifications) and to the outline of the traditional account. Radical departure from what the later Romans themselves believed is liable to create more difficulties than it solves.

CHAPTER 6

The Sources for Early Roman History

1. Documentary Records

So far reference to the sources of our knowledge of Rome's early history has been made mainly in regard to specific points rather than in any systematic manner. It may be well therefore at this point to break away from the story of Rome's growth in order to consider briefly what evidence survived until Roman writers wanted at the end of the third century B.C. to tell the history of their city, what use they made of the evidence available to them, and to what extent we can today supplement their knowledge.

Fact and fiction

Our evidence derives from the surviving literary sources and the results of archaeological research, supplemented by knowledge of the languages of early Italy (p. 14) and by what can be deduced about religious practice from the survival of some festivals and ritual into later times (e.g. of the Luperci and Argei; p. 37). Knowledge of the earliest history of Italy is very largely derived from archaeological research, which every year adds a little more information. The nature of Etruscan civilisation and the outward appearance of early Rome and other Italian towns has been revealed largely by the spade, and the result often strikingly confirms the later literary tradition which can thus be tested and controlled at many points. Thus the main lines of Italy's first progress from savagery to civilisation now stand forth clearly. But an analysis of the foundation-legends of Rome has shown that while they incorporated some historic facts, they were mainly a product of imagination. The traditional history of Rome down to the third century B.C. stands on a somewhat better footing, but the authentic records on which it was based were supplemented with much free play of fancy. Hence the problem of reconstructing the actual course of events out of the traditional version is one which modern scholars have solved in widely different ways.

Documentary sources for the period of the early Roman monarchy are almost wholly lacking. During the excavations of 1899 under the Lapis Niger in the Roman Forum (p. 43) a broken stone pillar was brought to light inscribed in archaic Latin and containing a fragment of what is probably a ritual law. Whereas the accompanying votive deposit goes back to the early sixth century (p. 43), the inscription is generally dated either to the later part of that century or to the first half of the fifth. It contains the word *recei* (= *regi*, probably meaning 'to the king'). This is tantalising: it looks as if it refers to a king of the regal period, but it might equally well apply to the *rex sacrorum* of the early Republic.[1] The texts of a few treaties, of which copies had been set up in temples or other public places, survived at any rate to the first century B.C. and were known to the historical writers of that age, e.g. the treaty with Gabii (p. 54) and the Foedus Cassianum (p. 66). But it may be assumed that under the kings few written records were drawn up, and that next to nothing of these was preserved to the time when literary composition began at Rome.

The Lapis Niger

The documentary material for the first two centuries of the republican period requires a somewhat fuller discussion.

(1) *The Code of the Twelve Tables*. – This collection was made about 450 B.C. (pp. 66 ff.). Its original text soon perished; but since the Code remained in force for many centuries copies of it were continually kept in circulation, and considerable fragments have been preserved in quotations by a succession of Roman writers

The Twelve Tables

6.1 Lapis Niger Inscription. This archaic Latin inscription, found under a black stone in the Roman Forum, dates to the later sixth or early fifth century B.C. The lines are written alternately from right to left and from left to right. The first lines:

    quoi hoi . . . .
    . . . sakros es-
    ed sor . . . .
    . . . ia. ias
    regei ig

from the age of Cicero. These extracts, it is true, are couched in a modernised idiom. But if their verbal form underwent progressive alteration, there is no reason to suppose that their substance was not accurately handed down: the surviving remnants of the Code reflect precisely such a condition of society as our other sources of information would lead us to presuppose in fifth-century Rome. The fragments of the Twelve Tables are therefore of fundamental importance for reconstructing the history of the early republic.[2]

Their authentic character

Early statutes

(2) *Individual Statutes.* – Measures enacted by the Popular Assemblies *(acta populi)* were engraved in later centuries on tablets of bronze and lodged in the temple of Saturn (which did treble duty as a sanctuary, a treasury and a record office). But it is probable that little or

no legislation was passed by the people before the fourth century (p. 80 f.). Moreover the custody of the documents in the Roman record office was notoriously lax, and it is not unlikely that some of the early documents were damaged or lost outright in succeeding centuries.[3] Copies of treaties were sometimes, as in the regal period, exhibited in public places, and a few of these survived intact to the end of the republican age. But in general it may be doubted whether the writers of the later republican period had any accurate knowledge of the early republican laws mentioned by them. The actual texts of the laws were seldom quoted by them, and then only in small excerpts.

(3) *Resolutions of the Senate.* – From 449 B.C. onwards copies of *senatus consulta* were, according to Livy, delivered to the aediles of the plebs for storage in the temple of Ceres on the Aventine.[4] In the last two centuries of the republican period they were deposited in the temple of Saturn. However, there is no evidence that our literary sources made use of early *senatus consulta*.

(4) *Executive Records.* – The memoranda of business transacted and rules of procedure *(commentarii)* which Roman magistrates and priests drew up for reference were collected on rolls *(libri magistratuum, pontificum)* and were preserved. Some were kept in the family archives of the individual office-holders, others were (at least in later times) handed over for depositing in the Aerarium or perhaps in any offices which the respective boards of magistrates might have. One item of business which was of especial value for the writing of history was the census returns. Statistical information about the numbers of the citizen body and of their assessed property was amassed from an early period, and extracts from these *censorum tabulae* were often made by the Roman historians. The figures quoted by them are credible and consistent, although those previous to 300 B.C. remain under dispute.[5]

(5) *Consular Fasti.* – During the later Republic there were available to would-be historians lists of the chief magistrates of Rome from the beginning of the Republic onwards; these were in the form either of books or inscriptions. They were contained in a publication, known as the Annales Maximi, by Mucius Scaevola, Pontifex Maximus in 130 B.C. (see below, p. 61), while Cicero's friend Atticus compiled a *liber Annalis*. They were also published in calendars: thus a copy of the Fasti with notes was set up in the temple of Hercules Musarum, erected by M. Fulvius Nobilior *c.* 187, while the earliest surviving calendar, with consular and censorial Fasti, comes from Antium and dates to *c.* 70 B.C. Then at the end of the century

Year-lists of the consuls

Augustus set up an official list on the inner walls of the triumphal Arch of Augustus in the Roman Forum: this comprised the Fasti Consulares, recording the names of all the chief magistrates from the beginning of the Republic, and the Fasti Triumphales, naming all the magistrates and pro-magistrates who had obtained triumphs since the time of Romulus. The very considerable surviving fragments are now known as the Capitoline Fasti, because they are preserved in a museum on the Capitol. Nevertheless, despite their impressive grandeur, these Fasti are second-hand compilations from literary sources and have no independent documentary value. They are as reliable or unreliable as the literary records.[6] We must now enquire therefore how these lists came to be formed in the first place and how accurate they are.

The Tabulae Pontificum

At the beginning of the republican era the Pontifex Maximus took over from the king the duty of drawing up the calendar of religious festivals and the court days for the ensuing year – that is, the days on which it was right *(fas)* or not right *(nefas)* to transact public business. He set up this list, which was written on a whitened board *(tabula pontificum)*, in the Regia. At some point (perhaps from the beginning) he added the names of the chief magistrates of the year and began to widen the content by including day-to-day events of the years which might have a sacral connexion, as dedications of temples, wars, triumphs, famines, eclipses and prodigies. The old calendar of *dies fasti* and *nefasti* received definite publication by Cn. Flavius in 304 B.C. (p. 79), while the annual wooden tablets themselves were kept in the Regia and could be inspected. Thus these Tabulae Pontificum would provide at least a skeleton of contemporary history for those interested in Rome's past, and so about 130 B.C. Mucius Scaevola decided to make them more easily accessible by publishing the entire series in book form,

The Annales Maximi

which became known as the Annales Maximi. Since it comprised eighty books, some scholars have argued that Scaevola must have added more material from the pontifical archives, but in fact he may well have merely reproduced the content of the tablets, which may have grown fairly full of daily events in more recent years, while of course we have no idea as to the length of Scaevola's 'books' which could have been relatively short.[7]

The starting-date of the Tabulae

How far back did the Tabulae Pontificum go? Cicero expressly says *(de orat.* ii. 12.52) that they went back to the beginnings of the Roman state. The general antiquity behind this vague remark may be accepted, even though they may not have been made public before *c.* 300 when popular demand became vocal. But did the early

records survive? In 390 Rome was sacked by the Gauls, but it may well be that the temples and the archives and records kept within them escaped desecration in the Gallic catastrophe.[8] Further, Cicero says *(de Rep.* 1.25) that the first observed (and not merely computed) eclipse, recorded in the Annales Maximi (and by Ennius), was 'about 350 years after Rome was founded'. This will probably have been the eclipse of 21 June 400 B.C. (354 years is 'about 350').[9] This would take the Tabulae back to *c.* 400, although it might be argued not further, since Cicero implies that earlier eclipses mentioned in the Annales were based on backward calculations from 400 rather than recorded by contemporary evidence. Thus we may believe that there was a continuous record from *c.* 400, but that does not exclude the possibility that some fifth-century material survived. In fact a recent editor of Livy finds very early material in passages of Livy referring to 463 and 431 B.C. and concludes 'that a number of *tabulae*, although not a complete set, survived from the period 509–390 (especially 460–390) and contained much more variegated material than is usually assumed (cf. iii. 7.6: iv. 30.5–7), and that their edition, so far from amounting to an imaginative fabrication of early history, consisted of an attempt to relate the scattered and isolated fragments into a consecutive narrative'.[10]

The reliability of the Fasti

The authenticity of the consular Fasti for the third century onwards is not doubted, but how far are they reliable for the fifth and fourth? One line of attack upon their essential accuracy (few would maintain that they are *entirely* free from error or falsification) was made by pointing to the existence in the lists of 509–445 B.C. of consuls with plebeian names while the general tradition is that plebeians were excluded from this office until 367: these entries, it is argued, must therefore be later forgeries due to the family pride of some great plebeian families. But one would expect the names of the families which were important in the later Republic to have been interpolated, whereas some of the names (e.g. Volumnii, Minucii, Genucii) represent families of little distinction at that time. Further, families which were plebeian later may well originally have been patrician: even some of the kings had names which later were plebeian (Pompilius, Hostilius, Marcius, Tullius). Also it is not quite certain that the tradition is correct in asserting that no plebeian held the consulship before 450.[11] Thus the alleged presence of plebeians can scarcely stand as an objection and it is not unreasonable to suppose that the Fasti are substantially sound from the beginning of the fifth century and that, despite some later inventions, a reliable list of names is to be found. The Fasti are important if only because they served to date all transactions at Rome, both public and private, and were universally used by the Roman annalists as a chronological framework.

The dates of early republican history, as fixed by the consular Fasti, have been proved to be fairly well in accord with the authentic chronology of the Greek historians. The discrepancy never exceeds eight years, and at points is narrowed down to two or three years.[12] In the following chapters accordingly the traditional dates have been retained, because for most purposes they are sufficiently near the mark, and none of the modern substitutes have found general acceptance.

Conclusion about early documents

To sum up. It appears that the documentary material for the earliest days of the Republic, which survived into the later Republic and (via literary sources) to modern times, comprised the year-lists of consuls, the first treaty with Carthage, the *foedus Cassianum* and the Code of the Twelve Tables; that few if any texts of fifth-century laws were stored in the Roman archives; that the texts of fourth-century statutes may not in all cases have been accurately preserved; and that the Tabulae Pontificum doubtfully provided much material before *c.* 400 B.C. (and some would say not before *c.* 300).

2. Oral Tradition

For events preceding the third century the only supplementary material available to the Roman historians consisted of folk-tales and the traditions of the ruling families. The conventional story of early Rome is full of pictorial or dramatic episodes which have all the air of being derived from folk-stories (the suckling of *Folk-legends* Romulus and Remus; the rape of the Sabines; the combat of the Horatii and Curiatii; the villainies of Tarquin the Proud; the treason and repentance of Coriolanus; the self-immolation of Mettius Curtius; the geese that saved the Capitol from the Gauls).[13] These legends throw valuable light upon the folk character of the early Romans, but like all such tales they do not deserve to be taken at face value. Some appear to be pure inventions; others are plainly tricked out with fictitious detail, sometimes with help from Greek stories; others fit badly into the general context of Roman history.

The traditions of the noble houses

The traditions of the Roman aristocracy contained much trustworthy information, and would constitute a valuable source of knowledge about early Rome, if they had reached us intact. The ruling families of the republican era cherished the record of their claims to privilege with jealous care. In the reception-hall of each nobleman's house the waxen images of his ancestors were set up, and brief records of their careers were inscribed on *tituli* underneath them.[14] In early days the exploits of distinguished ancestors were also commemorated in songs at banquets, and in his *Lays of Ancient Rome* Macaulay tried to reconstruct the kind of ballad that was sung. But while this tradition may be accepted, it is unlikely that the practice continued after the fourth century; hence, while it *could* have influenced the oral historical tradition, the content of these songs is unlikely to have been available to the Roman annalists.[15] Unfortunately the early surviving authentic material was subsequently overlaid with a tissue of deliberate fiction, when upstart families that had joined the circle of the nobility after the Conflict of the Orders set the example of adorning their pedigree with dubious titles of honour.[16] The aristocratic tradition therefore needs even more careful sifting than the popular legends, for its embroideries are more artful and less easy to detect.

3. Literary Sources

With the rise of Latin literature at the end of the third century B.C. the conventional story of Rome's past began to receive definite shape. About 200 B.C. the historians Fabius Pictor and Cincius Alimentus, and the poets Naevius and Ennius, cast the existing traditions, popular and aristocratic, into literary form. Their work, and that of the later historians, is discussed in more detail later (pp. 196 ff.), but here we must take a general glance at the way they treated Rome's early history.

The early Roman annalists

The earliest Roman annalists all wrote in Greek, partly in order to explain Rome to the Greek world, and partly perhaps because historiography was a Greek form of literature which no writer had yet attempted to imitate in Latin.[17] They recounted the legends of the Regal period but probably did not elaborate their accounts of the first two centuries of the Republic: thus Fabius Pictor hastened on to deal with the First Punic War and his own times in more detail. The earliest historian writing in Latin was Cato; the first three books of his *Origines* dealt with the origins and earliest history of Rome and other Italian cities, and since his fourth book dealt with the First Punic War, he too seems to have dealt very summarily with the early Republic. His example was followed by the 'early' annalists, as Cassius Hemina and Calpurnius Piso (consul in 133), who began to reconstruct Roman history on a slightly fuller scale: Piso's history reached 158 B.C. in book 7. Then came the publication of the Annales Maximi by Mucius Scaevola: this gave a definitive arrangement to the material, made it much more easily accessible, and perhaps even considerably elaborated it. Thereafter annalists wrote for a wider public and on a larger scale, using the traditions (partly oral) preserved in the great families and applying rhetorical methods. Thus Cn. Gellius devoted twenty books to the events of 500–300 B.C., which the more sober Piso had covered in two.

The later annalists: their methods

With the annalists of the age of Sulla, especially Valerius Antias and Licinius Macer,[18] historiography reached its lowest level. They amplified their accounts by continual recourse to free invention. As was only to be expected, they extended *ad infinitum* the list of Roman successes in the field of war, and added to the glory of the families in whose interest they wrote by recording fictitious battles and captures of towns and swelling out enemy casualty lists to monstrous proportions. Another characteristic device of the later Roman annalists, which plainly reflects the legal bent of the Roman mind, was to invent episodes of earlier history to serve as precedents and justifications for the institutions and ceremonies of their own day.[19] Yet another favoured expedient was to fill out the narrative by simple reduplication. Where tradition was obscure or discrepant about the time of a campaign or a law, the annalists would relate the incident twice over.[20] In order to expand the scanty record of the conflict between Patricians and Plebeians they projected episodes from the struggle of Optimates and Populares in the last century of the Republic backward into the fifth or fourth century, relating them by anticipation with slightly altered names and circumstances.[21] By these means the received version of early Roman history was recast into a more voluminous and impressive form; but the air of precision which it acquired from its new wealth of detail was wholly delusive.

Definitive shape was given to the early history of Rome towards the end of the first century B.C. by the Roman annalist Livy and by the Greek man of letters Dionysius of Halicarnassus.[22] Both these writers abstained from further falsification, but neither of them succeeded in purging the record of its previously embodied fiction. Livy made but a perfunctory attempt to sift his materials; Dionysius took no little trouble to collate the work of his predecessors, but was at a loss how to apply any helpful criticism to it. The two standard ancient historians of early Rome hardly made a begin-

ning of reconstructing it on a scientific basis.

Greek and Etruscan writers

Other Greek writers, and indeed Etruscan sources, may be mentioned. As early as the fifth century, as we have seen (p. 35), some Greek historians, named by Dionysius of Halicarnassus (i. 72–3), referred to foundation-legends of Rome. They include writers as famous as Hellanicus, Theopompus, Aristotle and Callias (the historian of Agathocles), while Theophrastus (fourth century B.C.) has a puzzling story about an abortive Roman attempt to colonise Corsica.[23] These writers were not of course directly concerned with Rome's history. This may have been sketched lightly by Hieronymus of Cardia, but Timaeus (died after 264) was the first Greek who really appreciated the significance of Rome's rise to power, which he dealt with in his history of Sicily and again in his work on Pyrrhus.[24] In addition there may well have been incidental references to early Rome in such works as the Chronicle of Cumae (p. 55) which provides so valuable a background to the history of Latium about 500 B.C. We can only guess also at the use Roman historians may have made of Etruscan sources, both literary and pictorial, which will occasionally have impinged on Roman affairs, as witness the François painting of Tarquin the Roman (p. 581). Whether or not any Republican writer turned to Etruscan sources, at least the emperor Claudius did: he discovered in Etruscan sources a king of Rome named Mastarna, neglected hitherto by Roman historians, but known to us in the François painting: Claudius identified him with Servius Tullius (p. 41). Roman historians, writing under the Empire, as Tacitus, learned (from Etruscan sources, mediated through Claudius's Etruscan history?) that Porsenna had in fact captured Rome (p. 55).[25]

One other Greek writer deserves mention – Diodorus Siculus, who lived in the first century B.C. His world history included Roman affairs, though often in a somewhat summary fashion. The mythical period was handled in the first five books, while the next five survive only in fragments: however, we have the next ten which cover the years 479–301 B.C. Besides a chronological table which provided a list of consuls, Diodorus probably used as his chief source one of the earlier annalists, as Fabius Pictor, and thus perhaps preserves a better tradition than Livy or Dionysius of Halicarnassus, who used first-century annalists.[26]

In view of the imperfections of our record the reconstruction of events which is offered in the early chapters of this book should be read with considerable reserve. It does not claim even approximate certainty.

CHAPTER 7

The Conflict of the Orders.
The First Stage

1. The First Republican Constitution

The revolution which ended the monarchy at
Rome was effected, like all such movements in
the early history of ancient city-states, by the
nobles and for the nobles.[1] The Roman Republic
was therefore first constituted as an aristocracy.
About 500 B.C. the patrician *gentes*, which at
Rome that time numbered about fifty, contained less
becomes an than one-tenth of the free population.[2] But their
aristocratic wealth and power of patronage, and their *esprit*
republic *de corps*, intensified by the practice of intermarriage, gave them an unchallenged preponder-
ance. They did not indeed dispute the ultimate
sovereignty of the people. Under the new constitution the commons were periodically convened
in the Comitia Centuriata to ratify important
acts of state, and to act as a court (*iudicium*
populi) for capital cases.[3] But the decisions of
the Comitia (in other than judicial matters)
were now made subject to the approval of the
Senate as a whole, or more probably of its patrician members alone (*patrum auctoritas*). The
Comitia was further tied by the bonds of clientship which attached many of its members to
the patrician families and debarred them from
voting against the wishes of their patrons.

In accordance with the usual practice of city-
states emerging from monarchy the functions
of the Roman king were put into commission,
but were not yet parcelled out among different
departments. The royal prerogative passed virtually intact into the hands of two magistrates,
who at first carried the name of *praetors*
('leaders') but at a later date adopted the colour-
The consuls less title of *consuls* ('colleagues').[4] The two consuls (if, in accordance with the usual practice,

we may use by anticipation the more familiar
name) held office for one year only, and as each
had equal authority (*imperium*) and the same
range of functions as his partner, either possessed in fact an unlimited power of veto over
the other. To this extent the sovereignty of the
consuls was less absolute than that of the kings.
But in actual practice the head magistrates usually shared out their duties amicably, or at least
refrained from mutual interference; therefore
while their power lasted it was in effect monarchical. Of the trappings of royalty, the kings'
successors did not assume the full purple toga
save on festival-days or when granted a triumph.
But they wore a purple border round their
garments (*toga, tunica praetexta*); they retained
the ivory chair of state (*sella curulis*) and, most
significantly, the twelve lictors and *fasces*.[5] They
continued to exercise the king's personal command in war, and the importance of their military duties increased progressively as the range
of Roman warfare grew wider. They assumed
the same disciplinary power over the citizens,
subject only to the custom of allowing appeals
against sentences of death or exile, or so later
Romans believed.[6] They delegated penal jurisdiction as before to quaestors, of their own
appointment.[7] The quaestors also retained custody of the aerarium, which was permanently
established in a recently constructed temple of
Saturn in the Forum.[8]

In religious matters alone the consuls did not
inherit the functions of the king. These were
transferred to a *rex sacrorum* for whom an *The* rex
official residence (Regia) was provided in the sacrorum
Forum (p. 42), but his activities were strictly *and*
limited and in fact he was soon overshadowed Pontifices

by the Pontifex Maximus.[9] Indeed the nobles, in creating the office, which was for life, may have sought to prevent a religious successor to the king from dominating the priesthoods which they themselves held. Thus the major part of the religious functions of the king came into the hands of the Pontifex Maximus, who took charge of the calendar, nominated the Flamines and the Vestal Virgins (while the other religious colleges mostly became co-optative), and exercised a disciplinary jurisdiction over his nominees.[10] But in the main the function of the pontifices remained advisory, and the sphere of action of the other priests was confined as before to ritual.

The royal powers of which the consuls became the depositaries were jealously conserved within the narrow circle of the aristocracy. The consuls were elected by the Comitia Centuriata, while the Comitia Curiata was invited to confer the *imperium* upon them, as it had been formerly bestowed upon the kings. But the choice of candidates was limited: they were proposed by the senators from their own number, and no doubt the outgoing pair of consuls had much influence upon their selection. The plebeians may not have been legally excluded from seeking office, but during the early fifth century the patricians in practice gained an increasing control which became almost exclusive. Thus under this system the consular office remained securely in the hands of the noble families. Among the patrician *gentes* a small inner ring who secured the lion's share of consular places appears to have formed at the very outset of the republican period, for the chief magistracy fell again and again into the hands of men carrying the name of Aemilius, Cornelius, Fabius, and (after 450) Claudius. But alongside these recurrent names the lists of the early consuls contain many others which are seldom or never repeated. The aristocratic ideal of sharing out power equally within the privileged circle was fairly well realised under the early Republic. Under the similar systems by which the state priesthoods were appointed all the high religious offices likewise remained in the possession of the nobility.

The ruling families

But the chief citadel of patrician ascendancy was the Senate. Under the republican constitution, it is true, the Senate continued to be a merely consultative body; it could not meet except at the pleasure of a magistrate, nor discuss any business beyond that which the convener laid before it. Yet in actual practice the consuls were more dependent on the Senate than the king, for the brevity of their term of office did not allow them to acquire the experience which would accrue to a monarch reigning

The Senate

for life. It may also be assumed that the Senate had a large share in fixing the respective spheres of duty of the head magistrates, and influenced their choice of successors, just as it had previously guided the discretion of the *interrex* in appointing a new king. Under the new constitution the Senate in effect developed from an advisory into a supervisory organ. But while it gained in authority, it became more rigidly aristocratic. The customary obligation of selecting the members of the Senate from the noble houses, which had formerly restricted the king's right of nomination, became increasingly binding upon the consuls; plebeians were not excluded but their influence in the assembly would be small since the patrician senators organised themselves into a privileged group. At the same time the prescriptive right of senators to retain their seats *ad vitam aut culpam* became unassailable. Under the early Republic, therefore, the Senate came under close control of the patricians.[11]

The organisation of the dual magistracy, by its collegiality and limitation of tenure to one year, might seem adequately to guard against any resurgence of monarchy. But divided command might prove hazardous when external pressures demanded quick military action, as happened when Rome had to face the Latin League and then other enemies such as the Aequi and Volsci (see the next chapter). To meet such emergencies, and the increasing risk of divided counsels in the field of war, an emergency officer was created: the *magister populi*, later called dictator. Recourse to this device may well have been made as early as *c.* 500 B.C., as tradition records. It was arranged that at times of agreed crisis a consul might at short notice nominate a dictator who would in turn nominate a *magister equitum* as his chief subordinate. The officer thus appointed united in his person the joint powers of the two consuls, whom he overshadowed but did not replace; he was required to abdicate his power as soon as the crisis was over, or at the latest after six months.[12]

The dictator

2. Economic Conditions

The political revolution which ended Etruscan monarchy at Rome did not change the city's social and economic structure in the twinkling of an eye. As we have seen (p. 56), the decline of Etruscan influence was gradual, and times were disturbed. Some of the leading Etruscans left in Rome may have supported the plebeians against the landed Latin nobility, and a few men with Etruscan names even held the consulship occasionally until 487 (and again in some years between 461 and 448). At one point the Etruscan Porsenna seized Rome temporarily, while the story of the clan of the Fabii, helped by their clients, fighting at the Cremera (p. 71) suggests that the stricter military organisation which Servius Tullius had imposed gave place on occasion to more 'heroic' battles of an earlier type. Further, as will be seen in the next chapter, Rome was involved in increasing struggles with her neighbours. But not all aliens were hostile. In 504 the Sabine Attius Clausus migrated with all his clan to Rome where he was admitted to the patriciate and his people received Roman citizenship; they were settled on land beyond the Anio. His Roman name was Appius Claudius and from him sprang one of Rome's most famous *gentes*; thus from early times Rome showed both generosity and self-interest in extending her citizenship to others.[13]

Appius Claudius

The new Republic doubtless tried to maintain earlier trade contacts, but very gradually her commerce and industry declined. Greek pottery continued to be imported, but the quantity was less than in the late sixth century (a similar decline is noted in cities in Etruria). Then about 450 a dramatic change occurred when commercial connexions with Athens were spectacularly reduced: only two Attic Red Figure vases assignable to 450–420 B.C. have been found at Rome, in contrast with fifty-three during the years 500–450, and this trade did not begin to revive until *c.* 400.[14] Building activity in Rome continued for a while on a striking scale: a temple to Saturn in 496, to Mercury (the god of commerce, be it noted) in 495, to Ceres, Liber and Libera on the Aventine in 495, to the Dioscuri in the Forum in 484, and to Dius Fidius in 466; that of Ceres is expressly said to have been decorated by Greek artists. Then suddenly this burst of activity died down. Clearly therefore about half a century after the establishment of the Republic, Rome was beginning to face increasing economic difficulties.

Economic decline only gradual

Further, in the Roman state, where exposure of infants was discouraged and private war was banned by the magistrates, the ravages of foreign campaigns did not suffice to keep the population stationary. Under the monarchy annexations of conquered territory and a nascent industry and commerce provided additional subsistence. But in the first half of the fifth century the extension of the Roman frontiers was brought to a standstill, and the productivity of the land was reduced by frequent enemy forays, which not only impeded cultivation, but entailed the neglect of the *cuniculi* on which the drainage of the Tiber valley depended. To avert a famine, the republican

Population and corn shortages

government was repeatedly compelled to make special purchases of grain in Etruria, Campania or Sicily.[15] We hear later (*c.* 440) of corn-distributions made by two individuals, Sp. Maelius and L. Minucius, but details of the stories told about them are suspect.[16] So too are the traditional accounts of demands made for the distribution of public land to needy peasants. Spurius Cassius, consul for the third time in 486, is said to have made such a proposal and to have been killed for aiming at personal power. An outstanding leader (p. 66), he probably championed the interests of the people, but little confidence can be placed in his alleged agrarian proposals, which were probably attributed to him after the revolutionary tribunates of the Gracchi.[17]

Under these conditions even the patricians were reduced to a life of severe simplicity, and a single bad season might plunge the peasantry into debt. But in early Rome, as in all ancient communities where lenders were few and could make their own terms, rates of interest were high, and the penalties for insolvency were merciless. Under one common form of contract (known to the Romans as *nexum*) the lender was empowered to levy execution upon a defaulter without recourse to a court of law; and in cases where the creditor left the settlement in the hands of a judge (appointed by the consul on the lender's application), he would as a rule obtain from the court the same unmitigated powers of distraint.[18] Failure to repay the borrowed seed-corn or stock therefore meant eviction for those who could pledge sufficient land as security, and loss of liberty to the rest. Among the smaller peasantry many no doubt obtained loans under more humane conditions by attaching themselves to a patron; some of the *nexi* succeeded in paying off their liability by personal service. But it was a not uncommon fate for Roman freemen to end their days in permanent duress, or to be sold away in the market 'across the Tiber' to an Etruscan or Greek slave-dealer. Another grievance of the commons lay in the general severity of punishments inflicted upon public offenders, and in the powers of summary conviction which the consular *imperium* (whether exercised in person or by delegation to the quaestors) carried with it.

Distress of the peasantry

Bondage for debt

3. The Plebeian Counter-organisation

Out of such grievances and difficulties arose the 'Conflict of the Orders', a class struggle between patricians and plebeians which lasted over two centuries. These two classes have already been mentioned, but a close definition is more diffi-

Patricians and plebeians

cult. A distinction between the haves and the have-nots, between the economically, socially and politically privileged and under-privileged, existed no doubt from early times, but when is it legitimate to speak in precise terms of patricians and plebeians, defined as rival groups? The remote past or not until the fifth century? Scholars have argued for either of these extremes. It may well be that economic differences deepened during Etruscan rule and that one of the purposes of Servius Tullius's reforms was to check the increasing self-conscious power of the *patres* by giving the middle class greater military value as a counter-weight. With the ending of the monarchy the nobles were able to extend their growing monopoly of political and religious rights to include the whole operation of the state; at the same time each of the great families will have organised its bands of clients for politics and war. To this overshadowing menace those plebeians who were dissatisfied with their aristocratic patrons or had none became more self-conscious of their common interests and began to organise a concerted resistance which was soon embodied in a very efficient organisation.[19]

The Conflict of the Orders

The history of the struggle was related by the later Roman annalists with a deceptive amplitude and accuracy, but much of the detail which they furnish will not bear critical examination. A modern reconstruction of the Conflict must prune away much dramatic embellishment with which the Roman writers sought to enliven their story. It must also discard fictitious statutes that were not derived from documentary sources, but were invented by legally minded historians, who assumed that all the acknowledged rights of the *plebs* in later times were based on some specific act of legislation. Nevertheless, despite many retrojections into this distant past of many aspects of agrarian and political quarrels of the later Republic between Optimates and Populares, the basic outlines of the story are clear. At these we must now look, but it should constantly be borne in mind that these internal struggles were not contested *in vacuo* but against a wider background of often fierce wars with Rome's neighbours, and the two areas of tension closely inter-reacted upon each other.

The most distinctive feature of the Conflict is that the plebeians entered it as an organised body. Their methods were not those of random agitation or mob violence, but of collective bargaining and preconcerted resistance. A nucleus for a separate plebeian organisation was at hand in the small trading community which had gathered on the Aventine hill.[20] This community included merchants from Greece, some

The plebeian organisation.

of whom had no doubt witnessed the overthrow of the landed aristocracies in their native towns and the establishment of more or less democratic constitutions. The activity of the Greek traders on the Aventine is reflected in the erection of a temple to the givers of grain and wine, Ceres, Liber and Libera, who were in reality nothing but the Greek deities Demeter, Persephone and Dionysus in a transparent Italian guise; it was decorated by Greek artists and had Greek priestesses, drawn from Naples and Velia (Elea, the centre of the Eleatic philosophers). We may ascribe to the same influence the gradual transformation of the wardens or 'aediles' of the temple into political officers. These functionaries assumed a summary jurisdiction of the commercial disputes within the trading community of the Aventine, and when the Conflict of the Orders began their sanctuary formed the earliest rallying-point for the *plebs*. Thus while patrician families, as the Fabii, maintained traditional ties with Latium and Etruria, the plebeian community had contacts with Magna Graecia and Sicily, where many new ideas of political reform, of personal liberty and indeed of written codes of law were to be found.

The 'aediles'

Yet in a community like Rome in the fifth century, which was reverting to the condition of a self-contained agrarian state, the mercantile elements were insufficient in numbers or wealth to carry through a political revolution. If the plebeian townsmen gave the first impetus to the class war, it was the rustic *plebs* that was chiefly instrumental in carrying it to a successful finish. In this respect the Conflict of the Orders at Rome differed from the class struggles of the typical Greek city-state or of the medieval towns. Another point of diversity from the conditions of the middle ages was that the medieval device of refusing to pay taxes previous to the redress of grievances was not open to the Roman *plebs*. The patrician government of the early Republic had even less need of a large revenue from taxation than the kings. In war-time a *tributum* or tax on landed property was occasionally levied; yet the necessity for such special imposts was not sufficiently frequent to furnish the *plebs* with a serviceable lever for extracting concessions. But if the plebeians were not heavily taxed, they were being called upon to render an ever-increasing due of military service.

Taxation and conscription

The details of the earliest efforts made by the plebeians must remain obscure. It is noteworthy that a high proportion of non-patrician consuls are found in the Fasti of 509–486 B.C., many with names of Etruscan origin, from *gentes* as the Larcii, Junii, Cassii, Menenii, Tullii and Sempronii; thereafter these families disappear from the Fasti for many a year, several for ever. While some of these men may have co-operated with the patricians, others helped the plebeian cause, but all were gradually squeezed out: the Fabii were firmly in the saddle after 486, holding one consulship every year from 485 to 479. However, Roman tradition placed the first plebeian assult on privilege in 494, the year before the plebeian leader Sp. Cassius in his second consulship concluded a very successful treaty with the Latins, while in 485, the year after his third consulship, he was condemned to death when a Fabius was a consul. The *plebs* were not strong enough to save him: the aristocracy, led by the Fabii, triumphed, but their victory spurred on the plebeians to improve their organisation against increasing patrician monopoly.

Spurius Cassius

The method by which the plebeians sought to implement their demands was a general strike *(secessio)*; they threatened to withdraw from Rome, which needed their military services. Five such secessions are recorded between 494 and 287, although not all may be historical. By this means they ultimately obtained recognition for the officers whom they appointed and for the Assembly in which they met to discuss their needs. The First Secession was traditionally in 494 when the plebeians withdrew to the Mons Sacer (some three miles north-east of Rome) or else to the Aventine, until they were persuaded to return by Menenius Agrippa whose parable of 'The Belly and the Limbs' is said to have convinced them that they were a vital part of the State. A compact was reached by which their officers, the tribunes, were recognised: though later historians regarded this *lex sacrata* as a law which affirmed the sacrosanctity of the tribunes, it was probably an oath which established the plebeians as a sworn confederacy, dedicated to the struggle against the patricians.[21] If, however, this first secession is rejected as unhistorical, the tribunes may have been first recognised in 471 (see below).

The First Secession

The origin of the *tribuni plebis*, whether military or tribal, is less important than their later development.[22] In assuming the burden of regular military duty the plebeians became more conscious of their own value to the state, and acquired habits of discipline and co-operation which enabled them to assert their rights more effectively. The leadership which they required in their political warfare was supplied by the more substantial landowners who stood outside the privileged circle but might hold subordinate commands as *tribuni militum*. As self-appointed *tribuni plebis* these 'squires' became the spokesmen of the plebeians and undertook to refer their grievances to the consuls or Senate. So

The tribuni plebis

too there is doubt about the stages by which their numbers were increased from two to ten. More important is their power, which was not legal but sacrosanct: the *plebs* bound itself by oath *(lex sacrata)* to hold its officials sacrosanct, inviolable, which in practice meant that it pledged itself, by physical force if necessary, to defend them against attempts at arrest or intimidation by patrician magistrates. The basic right claimed for them was to help a plebeian against the arbitrary exercise of a consul's (or dictator's) *imperium (ius auxilii)*. A tribune asserted a right to constrain *(coercitio)*. Lacking *imperium* himself, a tribune was not technically a magistrate, but he acquired the right to consult the *plebs* and to convene its meetings *(ius agendi cum plebe)*. Whatever the nature of earlier plebeian gatherings, a meeting was soon developed, organised on a tribal and territorial basis, known as the Concilium Plebis Tributum. At first it lacked constitutional authority, but the patricians were gradually forced to take note of it until in 471 a law *(lex Publilia)* recognised its constitutional existence.[23] Thus the plebeians now had the right to meet and to elect their officers by tribes.

4. The Twelve Tables

Since a main object of the plebeians was to obtain fuller security of person and property they began to agitate for a written code of law to define their obligations and risks, and to prevent arbitrary aggravations of customary penalties on the part of patrician magistrates. This demand was first voiced by a tribune Terentilius Harsa (his name is probably authentic) in 462, but ten years of effort were required before the patricians gave way. Then in 451 ten commissioners *(decemviri)*, all patricians, were appointed to reduce the existing customary law, both public and private, into definite and permanent shape; while they were at work the regular constitution was temporarily suspended, or at any rate they dominated the State. A mass of legend later gathered round their actions. Since they had not finished their work at the end of the year but had produced only ten tables of law, they were followed by a second decemvirate, of whom five were plebeians, Appius Claudius being the only member of both commissions. Encouraged by him, they added two more tables of what Cicero calls unjust laws, acted oppressively and refused to resign. Appius Claudius in particular played the tyrant; the most famous episode was the killing of Verginia by her own father to save her from Appius's lust. Amid this disorder the

Codification of the law

plebeians seceded for a second time, the decem-virs abdicated, constitutional government was restored, ten tribunes were appointed and L. Valerius Potitus and M. Horatius Barbatus were elected consuls for 449. Much of the detail and indeed possibly the whole account of the second decemvirate should be rejected.[24] But the basic achievement is beyond question, and it would seem that since the decemvirs did not go as far as the plebeians wished, the latter seceded and forced the decemvirs to give place to more radi-cal legislators, namely Valerius and Horatius. The decemvirs themselves doubtless were all patricians, for these alone could speak with authority on the subject of Roman law, and they probably remained in office without change of membership until after publishing the Twelve Tables they were forced to give place to more progressive forces. It may equally be assumed, in the light of the actual remains of their work, that their terms of reference did not go beyond the standardisation or at most the interpretation of current usage, and did not include the making of fresh law.

The code of the 'Twelve Tables'
The code of the 'Twelve Tables' was a com-prehensive document, embracing both public and private life.[25] In the sphere of private law it regulated, in however tentative a manner, the rights and duties attaching to the family and to individual property, and the limits and modes of self-help in defence of those rights. In the domain of public affairs it defined offences against the community, and it laid down a few fundamental rules of the constitu-tion. Being intended to formulate rather than to rectify existing usage, it naturally contained some incongruous provisions. On the one hand it preserved some fossil survivals of a more primitive society. It countenanced retaliation for assault, in cases where compensation in money was refused; it provided penalties

Archaic features
against witchcraft (such as the spiriting away of other men's harvests); it regarded punishments for public offences in the light of expiations to an irate deity; it apparently authorised the joint creditors of an insolvent and unsaleable debtor to carve up his body (or property) in proportionate shares, 'more or less'.[26] On the other hand it took a relatively advanced standpoint in conceding a wide range of liberty to the individual, while it insisted firmly on public order. In the matter of family law it sanctioned, under certain conditions, the emancipation of wives and children from the autocracy of the *paterfamilias*. Under its provi-sions a son might be made free by a fictitious sale into slavery and redemption, twice repeated; a woman might become married by simple *usus* (cohabitation without any religious

solemnisation), without passing into the *manus* of her husband, so that on her father's death she became her own master (*sui iuris*). In a similar vein of liberality it conceded the right of association for purposes of trade,[27] and it allowed freedom of bequest in regard to mov-able chattels. At the same time it safeguarded the community against abuses of personal liberty. It forbade the insanitary custom of burying the dead, and the dangerous practice of cremating them, within the city walls, and it prohibited provocative displays of luxury or emotion at funerals. Above all, it set a ban on the taking of life except by sentence of a competent court.

Provisions for freedom in private life and for public order

The constitutional laws contained in the Twelve Tables were surprisingly scanty, but they affirmed the right of appeal from any sen-tence and any court to the popular assembly, and in particular they reserved the final pro-nouncement in a case of death or exile to the *comitiatus maximus* (which most probably signi-fies the Comitia Centuriata).

The right of appeal to a Popular Assembly

The code of the Twelve Tables was never repealed: indeed some of its statutes remained in force to the end of Roman history. In course of time Romans learnt to take a sentimental pride in it, and not without reason. Taken as a whole, it was the law of an orderly but not unprogressive community. To the oppressed ple-beians who had called for its enactment it not only gave the general security of written rules, but it safeguarded them comprehensively against arbitrary judicial sentences. These ordi-nances, moreover, were framed in a terse and accurate diction which gave promise of the future sovereignty of the Latin language in the domain of European law and administration.

General merits of the code

Yet the Tables left a number of contentious points unsettled. The rules of procedure for all civil actions had been published, but the set form of words in which pleadings were to be conducted (*actiones*) remained the secret of the patrician pontiffs for many years to come (p. 79). Further, while the Tables conceded a right of appeal against judicial decisions, they nowise curtailed the *imperium* of the consuls in execu-tive matters, such as conscription for military service. Above all, they contributed but little to the alleviation of economic distress. In the interests of the insolvent debtor they provided that execution of a court order against him should be stayed for thirty days; they required the creditor who held him in duress to give him adequate subsistence and not to overload him with chains; and they prescribed a further interval during which the prisoner was to be given the opportunity of raising the amount of his ransom before he was sold into permanent

Its deficiencies

slavery. But while they mitigated the consequences of insolvency, they provided no remedy for the conditions which plunged men into debt. Finally, the code contained a provision which was calculated to sharpen the contrast between patricians and plebeians by drawing a permanent line of cleavage between them. By placing a legal ban, where previously nothing more than a private convention had existed, upon intermarriage between the two orders, it definitely converted the patriciate into a closed caste. This statute was originally included in a supplementary table – the code in its original form having been limited to ten sections – so as to suggest a deliberate reaction at the eleventh hour against the previous attempt at conciliation.

5. Plebeian Advances

The Twelve Tables were published, but the plebeians still suffered economic hardship, while their leaders were still subject to political and increased social discrimination. Thus after a second secession they extracted further advantages which were promulgated in laws passed by *The Valerio–* the new consuls of 449. These Valerio–Horatian *Horatian* laws were clearly regarded as an important land-*laws* mark in the struggle of the Orders, but their details are controversial. Here we may note what may be regarded as probable interpretations of their contents, which concerned *plebiscita, provocatio* and *sacrosanctitas*.[28]

First, however, it must be noted that a new *The Comitia* form of Assembly came into being about this *Tributa* time, if not earlier: the Comitia Populi Tributa, which is not to be confused with the Concilium Plebis. The organisation of the latter was based on tribes and was seen to be much less cumbersome than the Comitia Centuriata, which met by centuries (193 units as against some twenty tribal groups). Thus for business of lesser importance the whole people *(populus)* decided to meet by tribes, while they continued to meet by centuries for important affairs, as the election of consuls. Thus the Comitia Centuriata and the Comitia Tributa comprised the same people meeting in differently organised groups, while the Concilium Plebis Tributim consisted of the plebeians alone.[29]

According to Livy (iii. 55.1) the Valerio–*Plebiscita* Horatian laws gave the resolutions of the *plebs (plebiscita)* the force of law; since this victory was not achieved until 287, clearly Livy's statement needs qualification. Perhaps the most likely explanation is that in 449 all measures carried by a tribal system of vote (i.e. *plebiscita* in the Concilium Plebis and *leges* in the Comitia

Populi Tributa) were made valid, subject to ratification by the *Auctoritas patrum*. Thus any legislation approved by the patricians, even if not initiated by them, became law. (It may be convenient to note here that this patrician right to veto legislation was probably cancelled in regard to the Comitia Tributa by the *lex Publilia* of 339, and in regard to the Concilium Plebis by the *lex Hortensia* of 287.)[30]

A second law dealt with *provocatio*, appeal *Provocatio* to the Roman people by a victim of a magistrate's *coercitio* (this was the right of all magistrates with *imperium* both to compel citizens to obey their orders and to inflict punishment). The sources suggest that *provocatio* was the subject of legislation in 509, under the Twelve Tables and again in 449. The end of the process was in 300 when a legal right to appeal against a capital sentence imposed within the city was granted to every Roman citizen by a *lex Valeria* (p. 79), but the details of the earlier stages remain obscure, though something was apparently done in 449 to extend the citizen's opportunity of appeal against magisterial oppression.[31]

A third law enacted that the *caput* of any man who harmed the tribunes or aediles should be *Iovi sacrum* – that is, the offender should be *Sacro-* put to death and his goods consecrated to Ceres, *sanctitas* Liber and Libera. Thus probably the tribunes' rights, which hitherto had been based on a *lex sacrata* sworn by the plebeians, now were confirmed by law; possibly it was at this time that their numbers were raised to ten. A fourth law, somewhat surprisingly, enacted that resolutions of the Senate *(senatus consulta)* should be stored in the temple of Ceres under the care of the aediles (p. 58) who already probably acted as custodians of the plebeian archives. From temple officials the aediles became plebeian officers, duly elected, two annually, by the Concilium Plebis, to act as assistants to the tribunes; their functions increased, and included seizing the victims of the tribunes' *coercitio* and municipal administration. On occasion they applied the revenue accruing from fines to public works, such as paving the streets of the Aventine quarter.

In 445 patrician social and political privileges came under fire. A tribune, C. Canuleius, forced through a measure which allowed intermarriage *Inter-* between plebeians and patricians, thus reversing *marriage* the recent law of the Twelve Tables. Since children were to be enrolled in their fathers' *gens*, henceforth the sons of plebeian women could become patricians. No doubt intermarriage long remained extremely rare, but a principle had been established. Then a radical change was made in the highest magistracy: in place of two

Military tribunes with consular power

consuls three (later up to six) 'military tribunes with consular power' *(tribuni militum consulari potestate)* were elected most years for a long time to come (in twenty-two years between 444 and 367 B.C. consuls, not military tribunes, were chosen); plebeians were eligible, and one of the first board of 444 was a plebeian. The reason for this innovation was given by some authors whom Livy read as military, by others as political. Rome was faced by enemies on several fronts (see next chapter), and this increase of high commands might give greater flexibility to meet the threats. Alternatively, it is suggested that the patricians saw that their monopoly of the consulship was threatened and so devised a compromise by transferring some of the old functions of the consuls to a new and exclusively patrician magistracy, the censorship. The difficulty about this second explanation is that apparently some plebeians had already held the consulship (p. 63), but nevertheless the patricians may have acted in order to forestall an increasing infiltration into this chief magistracy.[32]

The censors

Two censors were appointed in 443, and thereafter at somewhat irregular intervals, varying between three and twelve years, but later they held office every five years; their period of office was fixed in 434 at eighteen months. Their primary function was to relieve the consuls and take over from them the maintenance of the *census* or roll of citizens, placing each man in his appropriate class, century and tribe; they also made up the list of men liable for cavalry service. As time went on they acquired very wide supervisory authority in the state (p. 82).[33]

One other junior magistracy was developed, the quaestorship. Quaestors, who had been assistants of the kings (p. 52), became helpers of the consuls, by whom at first they were probably appointed. After 447 B.C. two were elected annually by the tribal assembly, while in 421 their number was raised to four and the office was opened to plebeians. In 409 three out of the four were plebeians. Their functions were largely financial and they did not receive *imperium*, so that the patricians might at first regard the admission of plebeians as a small concession, but it was a plebeian gain.

Quaestors

To sum up. During the fifth century the plebeians had made considerable advances. In civil law the two Orders were equal, although the patricians retained sole knowledge of the forms of procedure. Socially, intermarriage was legalised, if rare in practice. The plebeian institutions were recognised, although not dominant; the power of the tribunes was particularly significant. The plebeians were winning their way into some of the magistracies. The patricians, however, retained their leadership in the Senate and Assemblies, and in the field of religion. In the later part of the century the plebeians' pressure slackened; they were less united since the richer and more ambitious men had been attracted by the glittering prize of the military tribunate, while many of their leaders were engaged in the wars against Aequi, Volsci and Etruscans. If Concordia was not yet a present deity, at least she might seem more propitious.

Plebeian gains

CHAPTER 8

The Early Wars of the Republic

1. Rome and Latium

Rome and the Latin League

Etruscan power in Latium had collapsed with the defeat of Porsenna's forces at Aricia, and Rome was freed not only from the Tarquins but also from the vanquished Porsenna (p. 55). The new Republic in its treaty with Carthage had boldly reasserted Rome's claim to considerable control in Latium (p. 55): this the now victorious Latins would not recognise, and so conflict soon followed. Their League, from which of course Rome was now excluded, presumably corresponded to the old federation of Diana at Aricia which met *ad caput Ferentinae* and whose members are recorded by Cato (pp. 55 and 584). The alliance which had been so successful against the Etruscans was now turned against Rome, and Tusculum may have regained the leadership which she had apparently held before Rome had overshadowed her. The cleavage led to a trial of strength at Lake Regillus (496).[1] Since this lake lay in Tusculan territory Rome may have taken the initiative: having shaken off Porsenna, she was now ready to contest the leadership of Latium. The battle lived long in Roman memory, and was embellished by the many patriotic legends; the most famous was the divine intervention of Castor and Pollux, the great Twin Brethren and horsemen gods, on Rome's behalf. The issue, however, was probably left open. Nevertheless a temple to Castor and Pollux was dedicated in the Roman Forum some ten years later, and a parade of horsemen (Transvectio Equorum), which took place on 15 July during the later Republic and was revived by the emperor Augustus, long commemorated the battle and the divine epiphany.

The battle of Lake Regillus

By these mutual quarrels the Latins brought upon themselves persistent attacks by the adjacent peoples of the central Apennines. Among these tribes the pressure of population upon subsistence, which was periodically relieved by the compulsory emigration of the younger men (p. 15), and the need of winter pasture for the herds, was a cause of repeated encroachments upon the Latin lowlands. In the fifth century the Tiber valley was continually exposed to their inroads.

The incursions of the mountain tribes, which were an even graver menace to the neighbouring Latin towns than to Rome, compelled the Latin League to compose its quarrel with the Romans. About 493 a treaty, of which the text remained on view in the Forum until the first century B.C., the so-called *foedus Cassianum*, was entered into by the Romans on the one hand, and the collective Latin federation on the other. By this compact a common army of defence was formed, to which each party pledged itself to contribute an equal contingent while each was to receive an equal share of the spoils; whichever side summoned the other's aid took command of the combined forces.[2] A supplementary convention was made shortly after (*c.* 486) by the Romans with the small canton of the Hernici in the upper valley of the Trerus, so as to impede communications between the Volsci and the Aequi. This early application of the principle of 'divide and rule' was to prove very valuable.

Treaty (foedus Cassianum) between Rome and the Latins

The Hernici

2. Sabines, Aequi and Volsci

Of the joint wars waged by the triple alliance of Romans, Latins and Hernici against the mountain peoples only a little authentic record has survived. In Roman tradition the part

Early colonies

played in these conflicts and in the subsequent colonial settlements was almost lost out of sight. The chief interest of the wars lies in the settlement of colonists drawn jointly from Rome and from Latin towns at places decided upon probably by the League after consultation with Rome. They were established on territory gained or recovered from the Volscian and other invaders, and they reflect one of the beneficial results of the Cassian treaty and its clause giving equal shares of the spoils of victory to both partners. Later Roman writers might try to disguise the fact of their joint foundation by referring to them as *coloniae Romanae,* but a more accurate title is Priscae Latinae Coloniae. Any Roman who enrolled as a member of such a colony ceased to be a Roman citizen and became a citizen of a new independent community which was admitted into the association of other sovereign Latin states, namely the Latin League. These Latin colonies were the prototypes of a characteristic instrument of empire which the Romans brought into systematic use in the later stages of their conquests. Some fourteen had been founded before 338 B.C., but the history of the early settlements is uncertain: Cora, Signia, Velitrae and Norba may have been founded in the 490s against the Aequi and Volsci, but they may have changed hands more than once in the border warfare of the times which was marked by raids and counter-raids.[3]

Rome had to keep a wary eye on many fronts. To the north of the city was a potential Etruscan menace, while in the north-east were the Sabines. But the edge of a Sabine attack was blunted at the outset by the wise concession of receiving the Sabine chieftain Appius Claudius into the Roman community (p. 64). About 460 another Sabine chief, Appius Herdonius, is said to have stolen by night into Rome and occupied the citadel on the Capitol. But his band of marauders, left without reinforcements, was driven to surrender after a short siege. A notable feature of this *coup de main* was the assistance which the Romans received in the siege operations from an auxiliary corps of Tusculans.[4]

The Sabines

A more persistent pressure was maintained by the southern neighbours of the Sabines, the Aequi. Passing at will through the territory of Praeneste (which stood aloof from the Latin League), these invaders established themselves on the col of Mt Algidus, between the basins of the Anio and the Trerus, and fortified it as a base for incursions into either valley. The chief incident in the Aequian wars was a campaign in which a Roman force sent to dislodge the garrison of Mt Algidus was caught in a trap, but was extricated betimes by a relief force under L. Quinctius Cincinnatus (c. 460).[5]

The Aequi

But the most formidable enemies of the Romans and Latins were the Volscians. From the valley of the Liris this tribe moved across the Mons Lepinus to the edge of the coastal plain of Latium. From this position they more than once obtained possession of Antium and other towns of the Latin seaboard, and occupied the adjacent hill-side towns as far north as Velitrae. Roman tradition retained a vivid recollection of a Volscian invasion, led by a renegade Roman noble, Cn. Marcius Coriolanus, by which the city itself was threatened. Though the details of the Roman legend – the domestic disputes that led to Coriolanus's exile, and the pleadings of his mother Veturia and his wife Volumnia, which caused him to stay his hand – have no historical value, we may believe that, with a Roman traitor to show them the way, the Volscians at some time in the early fifth century pushed their advance as far as the Alban Mount.[6]

The Volsci

In the second half of the fifth century the Roman armies at last turned the tide of the border wars. After a decisive battle at the Algidus Pass (431) the Aequi were definitely dispossessed of Mt Algidus. Towards the end of the century the Volsci had been thrust back from the coastal plain and, although some uncertainty exists about the traditions, Latin colonies may have been established at Antium (467), Ardea (442) and Labici (418).

Roman successes

3. The Conquest of Veii

After the battle at Aricia (p. 55) the Etruscans definitely retired beyond the Tiber, retaining little or nothing on the left bank save the bridgehead at Fidenae, where the city of Veii maintained a garrison. The Veientanes seem to have involved Rome in something more than mere border-raiding in 483–480. At any rate in 479 the Romans, apparently without support from their Latin allies, made an attempt to gain Fidenae, this last corner of unredeemed Latium. But on the banks of the Cremera rivulet (which flows down from Veii into the Tiber opposite Fidenae) they sustained a heavy reverse, in which a detached corps drawn from the gens Fabia and its clients was cut down to the last man.[7] Half a century after this disaster the reformed Roman army, fresh from its victory at Mt Algidus, renewed the attack upon Fidenae. In a pitched battle hard by, the Roman commander A. Cornelius Cossus slew with his own hand Tolumnius, king of the Veians (c. 426). The panoply which Cossus stripped from his royal opponent was set up by him in the shrine of Jupiter Feretrius (a diminutive neighbour of

Fidenae

the great temple of Jupiter Capitolinus), where the emperor Augustus was apparently still able to decipher its dedicatory inscription.[8]

The siege and capture of Veii

For some twenty years the Romans remained content with this prize. But about 405 they entered upon a war which aimed at nothing less than the subjugation of Veii. This struggle, which marked the first definite step in Rome's career of world conquest, was remembered in Roman tradition as a turning-point in the military history of the city, and the siege of Veii which ended it was magnified into a ten years' investment (405–396), a Roman counterpart to the Greek leaguer round Troy. In actual truth the investment of Veii strained Rome's resources to the utmost. The besieged town was not inferior in size to Rome, and its situation on a steep rock, with ravines and running water on three sides, rendered it almost impregnable. Of the other Etruscan towns, Caere maintained a neutrality that was distinctly friendly to the Romans, and the federal assembly of twelve Tuscan cities, which had little experience of combined political action, declined Veii's call for help. But two minor states of southern Etruria, Capena and Falerii, and the powerful city of Tarquinii gave assistance, and individual volunteers came in from the laggard towns. Nevertheless the Romans, with the help of some Latin contingents, beat off the rescue parties and maintained the blockade through a winter campaign. In 396 the Roman general M. Furius Camillus carried Veii by assault.[9] He set a bad example to future victors in Roman siege-warfare by giving his troops licence to massacre the townsfolk and sell the survivors in slavery. Thus Veii was struck off the roll of Etruscan cities, while Rome was enriched with a large haul of loot, and acquired a fertile domain which nearly doubled the total extent of its territory. A considerable portion of the conquered land was allotted in holdings of generous size to the poorer citizens. From the spoils a golden bowl was dedicated to Apollo at the sanctuary of Delphi – Rome's first offer to repay its debt to Greece.

4. The Siege of Rome by the Gauls

In the fourth century the history of Rome was nearly terminated under conditions which foreshadowed its final downfall in a distant age. After the turmoil caused by the movements of the Bronze and Iron Age people Italy was again visited by fresh invaders. These were a people who now enter for the first time into the full light of history, the Celts.[10]

Among the warriors of the Bronze Age Urn-field cultures, which had spread from the Upper Danube to the Rhine, the Rhône, the Seine and Low Countries (p. 10), new ways of life began to appear *c.* 650 B.C. in Bohemia and Bavaria: chieftains were buried on waggons in wooden chambers under massive tumuli with iron spears and swords. Whether these new features of iron, inhumation and waggon-burial, derived from foreign settlers or only from foreign influences (including Etruscan?), is not certain, but it was this culture which developed into what we call Celtic. About a hundred years later these Celts were importing Greek pottery which came up the Rhône from Massilia. One of their most famous burials is the princess of Vix, whose body on its waggon was surrounded by Greek and Etruscan vessels including the well-known magnificent bronze *crater*, some 5 feet high. Celtic trade with Massilia was later superseded largely by trade from northern Etruscan centres as Felsina and Marzabotto.

The Celts

These early contacts tempted the Celts to move south over the Alps into the northern plain of Italy, perhaps during the fifth century and led by the Senones. Their penetration may at first have been peaceful, but by 400 B.C. they were being bitterly resisted.[11] Successive tribes overpassed each other like waves in a rising tide. The Insubres halted in Lombardy where the town of Melpum (near Milan) fell to them *c.* 396 and formed their chief settlement. The Boii proceeded beyond the Po and gave their name to Bononia (Bologna); the Senones advanced to the south-eastern edge of the plain of northern Italy. In their eastward course the Gauls stopped short at the Adige and did not enter Venetia. Further south Etruscan Marzabotto (p. 27) was sacked, perhaps by the Boii; here a Gallic cemetery has been found, containing iron swords typical of the La Tène period, while the invaders seem to have settled for a short time in the ruins of the town that they had destroyed. Felsina (Bononia) apparently held out until about 350: on the burial *stelae* of the men of Felsina we see them depicted on horseback in fierce struggle against naked Gauls. But in general the invaders probably met with little resistance: the inhabitants of the northern plain were neither numerous nor united enough to stem the tide. Henceforth the continental part of Italy received from the Romans the name of 'Cisalpine Gaul', which it kept to the end of the republican period.

Occupation of northern Italy by the Gauls

Once in possession of north Italy, the Gauls had an abundance of good land at their disposal. But in the Po valley the work of deforestation, begun by the earlier inhabitants, was far from complete, and the hard toil of land-improvement had little attraction for a people that had fallen

8.1 *Stele* from Felsina (Bologna) in northern Italy, *c.* 400 B.C. The lowest panel shows an Etruscan horseman fighting a Gallic soldier on foot. This illustrates the fierce struggles when the Gauls swept over northern Italy and expelled the Etruscan settlers.

into nomadic habits. Moreover, fresh relays of immigrants from France every now and then caused a renewal of unrest in Cisalpine Gaul. During the next two centuries central Italy remained exposed to incursions by unsettled Celts in search of loot or adventure.

Gallic attack on Rome

In 391 a miscellaneous host of Gauls under a Senonian chieftain, named (perhaps wrongly) Brennus, broke into Etruria and drew near to the town of Clusium. Unable to obtain assistance from the other Etruscans, the threatened city is said to have appealed to Rome, who had captured Veii while the Etruscan League looked on; the Senate then sent envoys to warn off the invaders and this remonstrance was accepted by the Gauls as a challenge. The story of the appeal to Rome is, however, somewhat suspect.[12] In the following year a reinforced army of Celts made a pounce on Rome and arrived within 10 miles of the city before it was brought to battle. On the banks of the Allia,

a small tributary of the Tiber, the Romans met the Gauls with their full levy and with contingents from some neighbouring Latin cities. The 'disaster of the Allia' long survived in the memory of the Romans as the black day *(dies ater)* of their early history. Unable to stop with their spears the first wild rush of the Gauls, who came like the Highlanders at Prestonpans, they found themselves overweighted at close quarters and out-reached by the Gallic longswords. The Roman line was crumpled up, and although part of the defeated army escaped by swimming across the Tiber and entrenching itself at the deserted site of Veii, the road to Rome now lay open.[13]

The battle of the Allia

Had the victors pressed on in pursuit, they would in all probability have carried everything before them. A brief delay on their part enabled the city folk to improvise a last refuge on the steep height of the Capitol, but the rest of the city lacked adequate defences (p. 45) to stem the tide.[14] The Gauls accordingly occupied the city without opposition. The systematic character of their devastation has been revealed by the layers of burnt debris which excavation has brought to light in the Forum and on the Palatine.[15] The Vestal Virgins and at least the flamen Quirinalis escaped with some cult objects *(sacra)* and found a refuge at Caere.[16] The Capitol was held under blockade for seven months, during which it received no assistance from Veii or the Latin cities, and its garrison was eventually driven by famine to capitulation, which it obtained on easy terms. The besiegers, who were more intent on plunder than on conquest, accepted a ransom of gold and drew off as suddenly as they had come.

Rome captured

The siege of the Capitol

The capture of the city and the siege of the Capitol became fertile themes for popular legend, many of which may not have lacked a kernel of truth. The traditional story told how the Gauls found the elderly senators sitting on their ivory seats like gods upon their thrones, awaiting their fate with quiet dignity, before they were massacred. It told too of a nocturnal scaling of the Capitol by which the defenders were almost caught napping but for a timely alarm from the sacred geese of Juno. It was said that when the ransom-gold was being weighed out and the Romans complained of false weights, Brennus threw his sword on to the weights with the words 'Vae victis' ('Woe to the conquered'). Finally, it related how Camillus, the captor of Veii, sent into exile by his jealous compatriots, returned with a tardily collected force of Latins and Roman fugitives at Veii, and twice defeated the Gauls on their way home; and it is recorded how this same hero dissuaded the Romans from a faint-hearted resolve to leave

Legends and facts

their homes and migrate to Veii.[17] But these edifying stories cannot obscure the fact that the Gauls had the Romans at their mercy, and that a more vindictive or pertinacious enemy might have stayed to kill or sell into slavery the entire population.

Rome freed by ransom

CHAPTER 9

The Conflict of the Orders
The Second Stage

1. New Discontents after the Gallic War

During the century that followed the Gallic invasion the Romans, while continuing to hammer out a compromise between the claims of the two Orders, also completed the main stage in the development of their republican constitution. But these internal developments were achieved against a background of severe external threats and wars which inevitably affected not only economic life but also the tempo of the pressure which the plebeians could exert upon the patricians. The wars themselves will be described in the next chapter.

Before the Gallic storm broke, the economic horizon had been brightened by a gleam of hope. The territory of defeated Veii had been annexed and was made available to the plebeians in individual allotments; soon afterwards it was formed into four new rustic tribes.[1] This not only secured new settlements for the Roman poor at no great distance from Rome itself, but it made Rome the largest city in Latium and automatically increased her military strength since the army was recruited from men who held landed property. After the Gallic invasion the economic distress, out of which the Conflict of the Orders had first arisen, again became acute. The devastations of the Gauls had borne heavily upon the smaller landowners. In the next thirty years, during which the Romans made good past losses rather than gained fresh ground, the distribution of new allotments almost came to a standstill. Neither did industry or trade afford the embarrassed plebeians relief, for throughout the fourth century these remained at a low ebb. At the same time the

Economic distress at Rome. The burden of conscription

burden of conscription grew more oppressive, as more and more of the lesser proprietors were drafted into regular military service, and the range and duration of the Roman field operations were extended. It is therefore no mere accident that the severest political conflicts of the fourth and early third centuries usually took place soon after the more exacting wars of the period. But the demand for economic remedies was now reinforced with a claim for political reforms round which the Conflict of the Orders revolved in its latest phases. This growing insistence on reforms of a political nature was due to the rising ambitions of the more well-to-do plebeians. These men, having already been admitted to the higher commands in the Roman army (p. 69), had acquired confidence in their own powers, and now aimed at nothing less than a general abolition of patrician privilege.

Renewal of the Conflict of the Orders

On the other hand the patricians, with equally firm leaders and a docile troupe of clients to vote as directed, fought every position inch by inch. The domestic history of Rome in the fourth century was therefore one of continuous class struggle. But the final success of the plebs was virtually assured through the growing disparity in the numbers of either party. Not that the positive increase of the plebeian community was in itself of decisive importance. In the fourth century such growth as the citizen body experienced was mainly due to the incorporation of Latin or Campanian cities, whose burgesses, if not formally disqualified from voting at Rome (p. 100), were practically debarred from exercising their suffrage by the distance which separated them from the capital. On the other hand the patricians suffered a progressive

Numerical
decline
of the
patricians

decline in their numerical strength. This decrease was partly due to their losses on the field of battle, of which they had always borne their full share: at the Allia alone their casualties must have amounted to a high proportion of their total muster.[2] But its principal cause was the self-imposed ban on intermarriage with plebeians, which was tantamount to a sentence of class suicide: it took more than the *lex Canuleia* (p. 68) to break down the social exclusiveness of the patricians in practice. It has been calculated that of the fifty-three patrician *gentes* whose names are recorded in the history of the fifth century only twenty-nine reappear in the fourth century.[3] By 300 the ratio of nobles to commons must have fallen to less than one in twenty.

The scales were further tilted against patrician privilege by the attitude of some individual noble families, which were induced by superior political foresight, or by motives of family ambition, to adopt a conciliatory attitude towards the plebeians. Some patricians might even befriend plebeian champions and help them to high military commands. Such co-operation had far-reaching effects and very gradually the older exclusive patrician governing class was forced to give place to a newer mixed patricio-plebeian nobility. Thus when disunion began to appear within their own attenuated ranks the patricians could no longer delay further accommodation with their opponents.

2. Economic Legislation

Though we should probably reject the story that M. Manlius Capitolinus, who thanks to the sacred geese had saved the Capitol in the nick of time, later gave up his property to redeem debtors from slavery and was killed as a would-be tyrant, nevertheless reform was desperately needed in the economic field. The plebeians made frequent and not altogether vain attempts to remedy distress by legislation. In 357 two tribunes fixed the maximum rate of interest at *unciarium foenus* ($8\frac{1}{3}$ per cent?); in 347 it was reduced by half; in 342 another law *(lex Genucia)* is said to have prohibited loans and usury altogether (probably a temporary measure which soon fell into disuse). In 352 a Commission of Five *(quinqueviri mensarii)* was set up as a state bank to help debtors in difficulty by taking over mortgages on adequate security. In 326 or 313 a *lex Poetelia* went far beyond the shy attempt of the Twelve Tables to mitigate bond-servitude and was so successful that the *nexum*, now radically altered, soon fell into disuse. Details are uncertain, but the law required in

Legislation
against
usury

The lex
Poetelia

all circumstances a judgment by a court of law to authorise enslavement before execution was carried out, thus eliminating the more primitive practice of self-help. It perhaps compelled creditors to accept any property which debtors might offer in payment, before distraining on their persons, while it may even have enacted that loans were to be made on the security of the property, not of the person, of the borrower. At any rate the *lex Poetelia* was a landmark: 'the liberty of the Roman plebs had, as it were, a new beginning; for men ceased to be imprisoned for debt', wrote Livy; while in Cicero's words 'The bonds of the citizens were released and thereafter binding for debts ceased'.[4] The application of these remedial statutes was facilitated in 304 by an aedile named Cn. Flavius, who published in convenient form the somewhat intricate rules for instituting a civil suit, as laid down by the Twelve Tables (p. 79).

A further restrictive act, which was carried in 367 by the tribunes C. Licinius Stolo and L. Sextius, allegedly after ten years of agitation for the restoration of the consulship (p. 77), limited the amount of public land *(ager publicus)* which any individual might hold; tradition gives 500 *iugera* (300 acres) as the maximum, but this may reflect later conditions. The law may also have included a clause which limited the number of sheep and cattle which could be kept on public pastures. The wings of the large patrician landowners, who sought to absorb more and more public land, were thus clipped.[5]

Control of
ager
publicus

The law of Licinius and Sextius was a step in the right direction, in that it liberated land for assignation in small allotments to the impoverished peasantry, which was the only lasting solution of the agrarian problem. Before 360 the total amount of land available for this purpose was inconsiderable, and the legislation of 367 could have been no more than a palliative. But after that date large tracts of territory were acquired by confiscation in the newly conquered parts of central and southern Italy. In regions where military considerations required a resettlement by Roman colonists, the patricians of their own accord assigned large blocks of territory for corporate assignation; in other districts the plebeian leaders demanded the distribution of land in *viritane* or individual allotments. On this latter principle the Pomptine level was repeopled with a Roman peasantry in 358, and in 318 a large tract in the country of the Volscians and in northern Campania (the *ager Falernus*) was disposed of in the same way. It has been reckoned that between 343 and 264 some 60,000 new holdings were created by colonisation and viritane assignation.[6] Of these allotments a certain proportion was reserved for

Land
assignations

Latins, but it is safe to assume that not less than 40,000 Roman families benefited by these distributions. In this manner the Roman conquests, which to a large degree were the cause of the economic crisis, brought their own remedy with them.

3. Plebeian Victories

While the poor plebeians were struggling against the dangers of enslavement and land shortage, the richer plebeians were seeking political power and began to demand access to all magistracies. In the face of similar pressure in the previous century the patricians had been forced to abandon the consulship, which they could no longer defend, and allow plebeians to hold the substitute office of military tribune with consular power, though not the new office of censor which they created in order to escape complete capitulation (p. 69). Now, fighting a rearguard action, they acted in a similar manner: they restored the consulship to which they were forced to admit plebeians but at the same time they channelled off some of the consuls' duties to a new magistracy, the praetorship, which was to be exclusively patrician.

The plebeians given access to the restored consulship

This resulted, it was said, from ten years of struggle. In 376 two tribunes, C. Licinius and L. Sextius, proposed the restoration of the consulship and that one consul should be a plebeian. During the agitation, which allegedly involved irregular elections and the election of Camillus to two dictatorships, the patricians in 368 increased the officials responsible for religious ceremonies from two to ten (*decemviri sacris faciundis*) and allowed half to be plebeians. Finally in 367 the Licinian–Sextian rogations, which included a land-law (p. 76), were passed, and L. Sextius was elected as plebeian consul for 366. The law probably enacted that one consul must be a plebeian, but since in seven years between 366 and 342 two patricians were elected, either the law was neglected or it made one plebeian consulship permissive. In the latter case obligation was probably enacted in 342, when L. Genucius carried several laws, including one about debt (p. 76).[7] Plebeian access to the consulship marked a decisive stage in the Struggle, and the aged Camillus, 'the second founder of Rome', lived long enough to vow a temple to Concord (Concordia Ordinum) in order to commemorate the equalisation of the Orders.[8]

One reason for the restoration of the consulship may have been to allow a greater unity of command in the military field than a larger number of military tribunes with consular power had afforded. In order to leave the consuls a freer hand for their increased military duties they were given a junior colleague in 366, the praetor, who might act as their delegate in any capacity, but whose primary duty was to supervise civil jurisdiction. The fact, however, that only patricians could hold the office suggests that class motives reinforced administrative convenience. The election of this consular deputy (who held the title which the consuls themselves had enjoyed in early days: p. 62) was naturally entrusted to the Comitia Centuriata that appointed the consuls. Further, in 367 the patricians created another exclusively patrician magistracy, namely two curule aediles, in order to supplement the plebeian aediles as supervisors of streets and markets.

The praetorship

Curule aediles

But in yielding over the consulship the patricians had conceded the principle of equality of office, with the result that the plebeians soon reached all the other magistracies. As soon as 366 it was agreed that in future curule aediles should be selected in alternate years from either Order. At the same time the curule aediles came to an understanding with the plebeian aediles (as the older pair continued to be called) in regard to a division of functions, so that henceforth the four aediles formed in fact, if not in strict law, a homogeneous magistracy. But a far more important prize was won by the plebeians in 356, when a distinguished soldier of their Order, C. Marcius Rutilus, was nominated to a dictatorship. In 351 the same plebeian leader was elected to a censorship, while in 339 the plebeian consul Q. Publilius Philo was named dictator by his colleague Ti. Aemilius and carried measures which included the obligation that one censor *must* be a plebeian. Two years later the praetorship was opened to the plebeians and the same Publilius became the first plebeian praetor (normally this office was held before, not after, the consulship). Finally, in 300 the tribunes Q. and Cn. Ogulnius carried a measure which raised the number of the pontiffs and augurs from four (or perhaps five for the pontiffs) to nine apiece, and stipulated that the additional members should be co-opted from the plebeian Order.

Other magistracies open to plebeians

Meantime in 339 Publilius, besides dealing with the censorship, had carried two other measures which helped the community as a whole rather than merely the careers of individuals. Henceforth the sanction of the Patres (*patrum auctoritas*) must be given beforehand to new laws proposed by a magistrate in the Comitia Centuriata before the voting. This practically abolished the patrician veto, but at the same time, since a magistrate proposing a law now had to discuss it before the Senate,

Publilius's laws

Publilius's enactment would increase the power of the Patres over the magistrates, as it decreased it over the people. Secondly, he is said to have made *plebiscita* binding on the whole people, but since this was not achieved until 287 his law probably cancelled the patrician right to veto legislation in the Comitia Tributa (p. 68). Thus the *populus* as a whole voting by tribes was freer to pass laws *(leges)* without patrician interference than were the plebeians when they passed *plebiscita* in their Concilium Plebis. This inferior status of *plebiscita* was finally removed, as will be seen (p. 79) in 287. Thus Publilius's laws seriously weakened patrician privilege, though they did not grant to the *plebs* unfettered powers of legislation.[9]

4. The Patricio-Plebeian Nobility

The Licinian–Sextian and subsequent legislation had profound effects upon the governing class: the main result was the supersession of the older patrician governing body by a new patricio-plebeian nobility which consisted of those patrician families that would co-operate with the plebeians and the successful plebeian leaders themselves. And this new body in time became as exclusive as the older patrician aristocracy. But the emergence of this coalition created discontent on both its wings: on one side was a small group of right-wing patricians who would not co-operate, on the other an urban proletariat which felt neglected by its leaders.[10]

New plebeian leaders

As the number of patrician families declined, so more plebeian families gained nobility by attaining the consulship. The number of successful plebeian *gentes* varied at different times. Immediately after 367 the Licinii, Sextii and Genucii predominated, and some patricians may have reacted against the new trend; however, these plebeian names soon disappear from public life, and after 360 the Popillii, Plautii, and Marcii come to the fore and co-operate with the patrician aristocrats. In the decade after 340 eight new *gentes* were admitted to the charmed circle, but then the numbers lessened until the last decade of the century when more *novi homines* were successful. A certain number of families from Latin and Campanian cities shared in this privilege of office: Tusculum gave Rome the Fulvii and Ti. Coruncanius and in fact more consular families than any other municipality. All Latins who settled in Rome permanently could claim Roman citizenship, but few will have had the wealth and position to follow the example of the Fulvii; the majority probably were poorer men who had no desire

or qualification for office, and many would be engaged in trade and small-scale industry, and being landless enrolled in the four urban tribes.

From about 349 B.C. Rome was developing contacts further south with the Greek cities of Campania and her commercial interests were increasing (pp. 88 f.). Thus others, beside Latin allies, were attracted to the city, including many *cives sine suffragio* (the so-called 'half-citizens'; pp. 90 f.) and foreigners, while the number of freedmen increased, since the manumission of slaves was becoming common. In 357 a government tax of 5 per cent was levied on manumission, and since 4000 lb. of gold had accumulated in the treasury from this source by 209 B.C., an average of some 1350 slaves may have been freed each year (though the extent of slavery may have been less in the fourth than in the third century). A freedman *(libertus)* could not be officially enfranchised, but his sons *(libertini)* could. Since most of these latter would be engaged in industry rather than in possession of land, they too would be enrolled in the four urban tribes. The political significance of enrolment in one of the four urban tribes *vis-à-vis* the rural tribes (which numbered twenty-seven in 312 B.C.) was that it restricted the value of the vote. Since vastly larger numbers of men were in the urban tribes in contrast to the relatively few in each of the rural tribes, and since each tribe recorded only one group vote, clearly the proportional value of the vote of a city-dweller was less than that of the countryman. Possession of land, however, enabled the landowners even though domiciled in Rome to be enrolled in rural tribes where they could exert considerable political pressure on the smaller numbers in each tribe.

Freedmen and the tribes

An attempt to improve the position of the urban population was made during his censorship in 312 by Appius Claudius, one of the outstanding personalities of early Rome. He proposed to distribute the landless (but not necessarily poor) urban population throughout all the tribes, allowing each man to register his property where he wished.[11] This would in fact give them an advantage over the rural population, into whose tribes they could infiltrate, and as they were on the spot in Rome to vote, they might outvote the few farmers who had time to leave their farms and make the journey to the city.

The censorship of Appius Claudius

This was only one item in a large reform programme which Appius Claudius introduced. As censor he admitted sons of freedmen into the Senate; they were, however, rejected by the consuls in the following year, while his tribal reform was in part reversed by the censors of 304 who confined at least all freedmen to the four urban tribes. He is said to have offended the nobility in revising the list of the Senate, a right which recently had been transferred to the censors from the consuls by a *lex Ovinia*. More lasting were his public works. He improved the water supply by building the first of the Roman aqueducts, which brought the water of the Sabine Hills to the growing city population, and he constructed one of the great military roads of Italy, the Via Appia between Rome and Capua, thus linking Rome more closely with this area of trade and industry.

Appius's policy

Appius Claudius was a man of immense distinction: he was twice consul, and once dictator, as well as censor, cultured, literary and expert in legal matters. What led this patrician to embark on radical reform? Various answers have been given. To Niebuhr he was the champion of patrician reaction against the new patricio-plebeian nobility. At the other extreme, to Mommsen he appeared as a democratic demagogue and would-be Caesar. More recently Garzetti has reacted against the portrait of a patrician demagogue and sees Appius as a moderate politician, bent on building up his own political following and *clientela*, hoping to succeed to the leading position which Publilius Philo had enjoyed. Staveley sees his career as an attempt to prepare the way for a change in the balance of the economy which would transform an essentially agrarian community into one in which agriculture and commerce played an equal part. But whatever the springs of his inner ambitions and his political aims, his internal policy should be seen against the background of external affairs. Just as Publilius had carried his reforms during the critical Latin revolt (p. 90), so Appius's censorship fell half-way through the Second Samnite War (pp. 90 ff.) at a time when Rome had recovered from her defeat at the Caudine Forks and was girding herself to bring the war to a successful end. At times of national need concessions might be more acceptable on the home front.

Cn. Flavius and the civil law

A substantial step forward in the equalisation of the Orders was taken in 304 when a magistrate's clerk (*scriba*) and son of a freedman, Cn. Flavius, was elected aedile and published a legal manual of phrases and forms of procedure (*legis actiones*) and posted up in the Forum a calendar of *dies fasti* and *nefasti*, court- and non-court days (p. 59). Two contradictory traditions record that he was acting with the help of Appius Claudius and alternatively that he stole the book from Appius, who had composed it. At any rate the result was significant: although the law had been published in the Twelve Tables, the nobles had more detailed, if not exclusive, knowledge of the precise and involved phraseology which was essential and thus they could block proceedings on technical grounds. Against this danger the people were now shielded by the *ius civile Flavianum*.

The right of appeal (provocatio)

In 300, the year when the plebeians won entry to the two priestly colleges (p. 77), they gained another major victory. The consul M. Valerius Maximus passed a law which defined and confirmed the right of appeal (*provocatio*) to the people against a magistrate's sentence of death or scourging in the city. Whatever the early development of *provocatio* (pp. 67, 68, 588), henceforth a magistrate was compelled to recognise such an appeal, and now even dictators were included.

The lex Hortensia legalises plebiscita

Another plebeian achievement was a *lex Maenia*, carried some time after 293; it extended to elections the clause of the *lex Publilia* of 339 which enacted that the sanction of the Patres (*patrum auctoritas*) must be given beforehand to legislative enactments (p. 77). But the crowning victory came in 287 just after the end of the Samnite Wars. Troubles about debt provoked a final secession and the *plebs* withdrew over the Tiber to the Janiculum. Q. Hortensius, a plebeian, was elected dictator and carried a law that resolutions of the Concilium Plebis (*plebiscita*) should have the force of law (*leges*) and bind the whole community. As with *provocatio*, so with *plebiscita* the traditional accounts of their earlier development are fraught with obscurities, but now the *lex Hortensia* gave the plebeians the right to pass laws which bound not only themselves but also the patricians. The sovereignty of the people was established and the Struggle of the Orders was ended. Yet though the way might now seem open for democracy, in fact the new patricio-plebeian nobility, which had replaced the earlier patrician aristocracy, was to retain control.

5. The Resultant Constitution

A practical constitution

The plebeians had established a state of their own within the framework of the patrician state and without real bloodshed the two had been merged into one. This extraordinary achievement, however, resulted in a rather confusing constitutional set-up, since the Romans were reluctant to scrap rather than to modify the old. The constitution was not written, as that of some Greek cities who entrusted the task to a law-giver, but was the result of a long period of trial and error. 'The reason of the superiority of the constitution of our city to that of other states', Cato is reported to have said, 'is that the latter almost always had their laws and institutions from one legislator. But our Republic was not made by the genius of one man, but of many, nor in the life of one, but through many centuries and generations.' In the same spirit Polybius wrote that the Romans did not achieve their constitution 'by mere thinking, but after many struggles and difficulties, always choosing the best course after actual experience of misfortune'.[12] The result was flexible but untidy, with no fewer than four overlapping assemblies of the people, while as the magistracies increased, their functions, and those of the tribunes, had to be more closely defined. It will therefore be well to look briefly at the picture that emerges.

Comitia Curiata

The old Comitia Curiata gradually faded into the background, surviving but insignificant. To the end of the republican period it was convened to witness wills and adoptions, and formally to confer *imperium* on consuls and praetors. In the first century its only attendants were the presiding official (usually a consul or Pontifex Maximus) and thirty lictors, who were commissioned to act as representatives of the thirty *curiae*.

Organisation of the Comitia Centuriata

The early history of the Comitia Centuriata, as we have seen (pp. 53 f.), is obscure, but the complex system of organisation had certainly evolved before the end of the Struggle of the Orders, even if its regal origin is rejected by some. It may be well to recall this here in schematic form (though without giving the monetary qualification for classification, since coined money had not yet been adopted):

Property class	Number of centuries	
Equites		18
Class 1	50 *seniorum* and 40 *iuniorum* =	80
„ 2	10 „ „ 10 „ =	20
„ 3	10 „ „ 10 „ =	20
„ 4	10 „ „ 10 „ =	20
„ 5	15 „ „ 15 „ =	30
Proletarii		1
Special craftsmen (*fabri* and *cornicines*)		4
	TOTAL	193

We have seen how the rich could outvote the poor. Though the constituent centuries of each class voted simultaneously, the votes of the classes were recorded in order of precedence, based on wealth.[13] If the Equites and the first class voted the same way, their votes totalled 98 (18 + 80) out of 193: thus a majority was obtained and the matter was finished. Further, the first vote of all was given by a *centuria praerogativa* which was selected by lot from the centuries of the Equites; this vote was then announced and could have considerable influence on the subsequent voters, since the Romans readily followed a lead, while superstition may have played its part. Another source of in-

equality, though affecting rich and poor alike, was that the *seniores* had an artificial advantage, in that eighty-five out of 193 centuries were allotted to them, although they numbered less than one-third of the citizen body. The Comitia Centuriata was the weightiest of the Assemblies. In jurisdiction it remained the court of appeal in capital cases. Its electoral duty was to choose the consuls, praetors and censors. And while the tribes took over much legislation, the Centuriata still legislated regarding the declaration of war and the signing of peace.

Comitia Tributa

The same people also met by tribes in the Comitia Tributa (p. 68). This had been designed partly for convenience since thirty-five tribes (the ultimate number) were easier to handle than 193 centuries. It gradually took over business in several spheres from the Centuriata. The presiding officers, who were the regular magistrates, included an increasing number of plebeians, who would tend to bring proposals before this tribal assembly, in which the influence of wealth and age, which prevailed in the Centuriata, gave place to the predominance of the smaller country landowners who formed the backbone of the tribes, in which rich and poor had an equal vote.

Apart from a *tribus praerogativa*, selected by lot, the tribes voted simultaneously, and the only notable disparity of voting power came from the inclusion of all the landless citizens in the four urban tribes. As the latter increased in number, so the vote of the individual diminished in value as compared with the relatively small number of members of the more numerous rural tribes. As has been seen (p. 78), Appius Claudius made some attempt to adjust the balance. But clearly the Comitia Tributa was a more democratic body than the Centuriata. It carried much legislation, it elected the curule aediles and quaestors and it heard cases on appeal when the penalty was only a fine.[14]

Concilium Plebis

The Concilium Plebis was organised on a tribal basis in the same way as the Comitia Tributa. There was no difference in the procedure of voting, but whereas the Tributa was convened by a consul or praetor, the Concilium was summoned by a tribune. Further, the Concilium omitted certain formalities such as the taking of auspices and of course patricians were excluded. Yet in actual practice the composition of the two tribal assemblies was similar, since the patricians probably did not often exercise their right of attendance at the Tributa. The functions of the Concilium were to elect tribunes and plebeian aediles, and especially to legislate which after 287 it could now do in the name of the whole state. The two tribal assemblies gradually became the main legislative organs, and while the Tributa heard cases on appeal involving fines (p. 80), some trials possibly still took place before the separate Concilium. With the gradual approximating of the two tribal meetings it is not always easy to distinguish the activity of each in certain cases, nor is this made easier by the fact that ancient writers habitually tended to ignore the distinction between them.

Control of the magistracies by the nobles

The two consuls had been forced to share their work with an increasing number of magistrates who had been created partly because of the growing amount of business, partly also with the unsuccessful object of trying to retain patrician privilege. But a magistracy was an *honos*, an unsalaried office. This meant that, whereas the plebeians had gained the right of entry, only the richer plebeians could go in. Further, though the magistrates were elected by the whole body of citizens (or more strictly by those who were in Rome at election time and troubled to vote), the elections could be manipulated in favour of a given class. Thus the new patricioplebeian nobility of rich landowners were able to hand down from generation to generation the tradition of office within their own families, and a *novus homo* who belonged to a family outside the governing circle found it increasingly difficult to gain a magistracy, especially the higher offices.

The magistrates

The number of magistrates was remarkably few: only two consuls, one praetor, four aediles, four quaestors, two censors at intervals, and, exceptionally, a dictator. The tribunes were active, but not technically magistrates of the · Roman people. The magistrates were helped at times by a board of senatorial advisers (*consilium*) and by numerous subordinates, such as lictors, clerks (*scribae*), messengers (*viatores*) and heralds (*praecones*). Later, other appointments were made: four prefects, to whom the praetor delegated the administration of justice in Campania in 318; police officers (*triumviri capitales*), appointed about 290; *duoviri navales*, chosen by popular election in 311. But more important than delegation of authority or the creation of minor magistracies was a method by which a consul or praetor was allowed to prolong his office (*prorogatio imperii*) and after the end of the year to act *pro consule* or *pro praetore*. It was first devised in 326 to meet specific military needs, when the Senate tentatively requested the tribal assembly to prolong the term of the former dictator Publilius Philo in order that he might be able to carry on the siege of Neapolis (p. 91). In 307 the Senate repeated the experiment in favour of another tried commander, Fabius Rullianus, but this time without troubling the Comitia to confirm its decision. From

'Prorogation' of offices

these beginnings the prorogation of high officials grew to be part of the regular administrative practice of the republic, and in the third century it became the recognised rule that such extensions of office should be at the sole discretion of the Senate.

The 'cursus honorum'

The various offices gradually arranged themselves in a definite hierarchy. The foundations of a political career would be laid in a term of military service, usually lasting from the seventeenth to the twenty-seventh year, and ending with the tenure of a military tribunate. Having served his military apprenticeship, an aspirant to political honours would sue for a praetorships was increased (p. 122), the tenure a tribuneship of the *plebs* to follow. If he proceeded to a higher magistracy, he might qualify for a consulate by a previous term of office as praetor; after 227, when the number of the praetorships was increased (p. 229), the tenure of this office became a necessary preliminary to the consulship. The censorship and dictatorship were ordinarily reserved for men of consular rank. The same office might be held for more than one term, and men of high ambition made a point of holding as many consulships as they could obtain. About 342 a *lex Genucia* (p. 590) was passed which prescribed an interval of ten years between successive tenures of the same magistracy; but during the major wars of the fourth and third centuries this measure was repeatedly suspended, so as to allow of some measure of continuity in the higher commands.

The consulship. Military duties

Of the individual magistracies, the consulate had been shorn of most of its routine duties and was tending to become an exclusively military office. But the ever growing scale of military operations, and the regularity with which victory was now coming to attend Roman arms, invested it with a peculiar glamour. A successful Roman general could look forward to a triumphal procession on his return to the city, and to a large share in the booty (but on the understanding that he should devote his prize money to the public benefit). Within the circle of the ruling houses the relative distinction of the individual families came to be reckoned by the number of consulates which their members had gained for them; and any military successes achieved by them were carefully recorded under the waxen busts of the family ancestors exhibited in the atrium of every noble house.

The praetors. Judicial procedure

The consuls' chief understudy, the praetor, had a narrow range of routine duties, for his jurisdiction was concerned with civil suits only; and in these his personal share was confined to the hearing of the preliminary pleadings, and to the issuing of general instructions to a *iudex*, or to a board of three or five *reciperators* (usually younger senators), who sifted the evidence and made the final award. A more important function of the praetor was that of publishing *edicta* or general ordinances, in which he laid down principles for the handling of cases on which statute law or common custom gave no clear ruling. A supplementary duty of the praetor was to nominate the *praefecti*, who administered jurisdiction and exercised a general supervision in Italian cities (p. 81). In addition, he acted as a general deputy of the consuls, convening the Senate in their absence, and sometimes even following them into the field.

The censorship

In the fourth and third centuries the censorship attained a position of peculiar authority. As an essentially administrative office, it was never invested with *imperium*; but derivatively it acquired a wide disciplinary jurisdiction. In distributing the citizens into their appropriate property classes, the censors took it upon themselves to take into consideration other qualifications than those of property, and to degrade into a lower class persons whom they could convict (after a brief informal trial) of bad citizenship in any form (cowardice in the field; misuse of public money; profligacy or cruelty in private life). These *notaë censoriae*, despite their lack of formal legality, were legitimised by the force of public opinion, so that a person rendered *infamis* by the censors was held as much in disgrace as if he had been sentenced in a regular court of law. A further quasi-judicial function of the censors accrued to them from the duty of drawing up the list of the Senate. Though restricted by the provisions of the *lex Ovinia* (p. 79) to appointing the 'worthiest men of every rank' (which came in practice to mean ex-magistrates in the first instance), they retained the right of not replacing on the roll former members whom they considered unworthy, so that their disciplinary power extended to the ruling families of Rome. But the exercise of these arbitrary powers could only remain tolerable so long as the entire citizen body imposed a high standard of duty upon itself, and so long as the censors themselves were men of exemplary discretion. The censors' office therefore came to be reserved for men who had completed the *cursus honorum*, and its conferment was a special testimonial to personal character.

Censorial 'notation'

Another derivative but increasingly important function of the censors lay in the domain of finance. On the one hand they took into their hands the arrangements for the collection of indirect revenue (which the Romans, in accordance with a common practice of ancient states, farmed out to *publicani*, or private contractors). On the other hand, they let out the contracts for public works undertaken at the state's expense, such as the construction of the great military roads.

The tribunate

But the most remarkable rise in status among Roman offices was that of the *tribuni plebis*. In its beginnings the tribunate had been an illegal institution, and its revolutionary origin was reflected in the fact that it never became a magistracy in the strict sense, for the tribunes always lacked the right to take the auspices, to wear a purple-edged toga, and to be attended by lictors. Yet however inferior they remained in outward dignity, the tribunes had by 300 attained a power without parallel among ancient states. In the last resort their unique position was derived from their opportunities of obstruction. By a persistent enlargement of their original *ius auxilii* on behalf of oppressed plebeians, the tribunes of the fifth and fourth centuries had brought the actions of all the magistrates, the resolutions of the Senate and the bills submitted to the various popular assemblies within the scope of their veto. Further, they had established an unquestioned prescriptive right to exercise this veto at discretion. By simply pronouncing the magic word *intercedo*, any of the ten tribunes became legally entitled to hold up any business of state (except for a few specified exceptions).

Unlimited right of veto

In actual practice, of course, this utterly irresponsible power could only have been secured by a judicious restraint in its use, and a readiness to compromise on the part of the patricians. At the end of the Conflict of Orders a *modus vivendi* was in fact arranged, by which the tribunes were transformed from leaders of opposition into instruments of government. Though they might not have a seat in the Senate, the tribunes received the right of putting motions to the House; by 216 they were even authorised to summon it and preside over its sessions. Without prejudice to their ultimate power of using their veto at will, the tribunes placed it at the general disposal of the Senate. Without sacrificing their rights of carrying laws and of conducting impeachments in the Tribal Assembly, they usually consulted the Senate before putting them to use.[15] Nothing illustrates better the Roman habit of slow but continuous movement from precedent to precedent than the manner in which the tribunes came by their power; nothing shows up more clearly the Roman aptitude for compromise than the new position which they took up in the state when the Conflict of Orders was ended and their original vocation was gone.

Accommodation between Senate and tribunes

While magistrates came and went one body remained: the Senate. The need for a permanent governing body which could make quick de-

The Senate

cisions at times of crisis and could deal with the increasing complexity of business, not least in foreign affairs, led to an immense increase in its authority. Though it could not legally legislate, its resolutions (senatus consulta) were generally obeyed. The average magistrate would carry out its wishes, since he would not dare to challenge the authority of a body composed of ex-magistrates, on which he himself would sit for the rest of his career. In fact the magistrates became the executive of a senatorial administration which claimed by right of custom alone to direct the policy of the state in all its important branches, especially in finance and foreign affairs. Only the actual declaration of war and the concluding of peace were left to the people, and even then the preliminary diplomatic negotiations had been conducted by the Senate, which could give the people a strong lead. However, the people were more ready to acquiesce, since it was they who elected the magistrates from whom the Senate was recruited. As members retained their seats for life, the Senate had a real claim to be a representative council which embodied all the experience of past and present. Its reverence for custom (mos maiorum) made it conservative and inclined to safe and moderate policies, but it was well designed to give a strong lead in times of trouble and by its collective wisdom to check any dangerous whims of the sovereign people. Its dignity, rather than its power, was indicated when Cineas reported to his royal master Pyrrhus (p. 95) that the Roman Senate was an assembly of kings.

6. Conclusion

Romans of the later republican period, looking back upon the Conflict of the Orders, could feel

a certain pride in the process by which patricians and plebeians had composed their differences and restored civic harmony. In reality, no doubt, the atmosphere of the struggle was less forensic than the traditional story would suggest, and we may assume that the antagonists did not always stop short at chicanery and threats. Yet the history of the Conflict sets forth in a clear light the fundamental good sense of the early Romans in matters of politics. Despite occasional mutinies and outbreaks of violence, the contending parties again and again closed their ranks in the face of a common enemy, and in the final resort, rather than engage in civil war, they compromised their quarrels. The plebeians displayed a rare patience and capacity for organisation; the patricians loyally accepted most of the reforms, once conceded, and played a conservative rather than a reactionary part. In comparison with the class-struggles of the Greek city-states and of the Communes of medieval Italy, or with the internecine wars of later Roman history, the duel between patricians and plebeians was almost a model of patriotic solidarity and forbearance. Moreover, if haphazard expedients of letting difficulties settle themselves by slow usage and prescription, rather than by formal legislation and definition, left the republican constitution in a singularly untidy condition, they none the less produced a stable system of government which gave the Romans a long respite from serious internal friction, and enabled them to throw their whole strength into the great military tasks of the third century.

Methods and results of the Conflict of the Orders

CHAPTER 10

The Latin, Samnite and Pyrrhic Wars

1. The Establishment of Roman Ascendancy in Central Italy

Rome refortified

Army reforms

In buying off the Gauls (p. 73), the Romans won a respite of 800 years for their city, until another Northman, Alaric the Goth, captured it in A.D. 410 (p. 551). But their defeat at the Allia so discredited them in the eyes of their neighbours that the Aequi, Volsci and Etruscans seized the opportunity to reopen war, while the Latins and the Hernici became doubtful or divided in their loyalty. The ascendancy acquired by Rome in 100 years was lost in a single campaign.

But the Romans with characteristic doggedness set to work to retrieve their losses; with equally characteristic sagacity they studied their own failure and drew profitable lessons from it. As in the case of Hannibal's invasion, a great disaster was the prelude to far-reaching victories. In anticipation of further Gallic inroads a solid stone wall some 12 feet thick and 24 feet high, backed in part by the earlier *agger* (p. 45) which was now raised to the same height, was constructed around the whole city, including the Aventine, a circuit of some 5½ miles; many impressive traces of this so-called Servian Wall survive (one greets the visitor to Rome as he leaves the main railway station). The masons' marks on the large blocks of tufa suggest that Rome may have employed a building staff of Greek contractors. The labour was supplied perhaps by the Roman army, although Veientine captives may have helped, since the stone was quarried from the Grotta Oscura near Veii.[1]

Walls alone, however, would not save Rome. The battle of the Allia had shown that a line of foot-soldiers armed in Greek fashion might be successfully rushed by a mobile enemy, and

that a phalanx of pikemen, once broken, could not cope with swordsmen. Both arms and battle-formation required changing, and this was done by a fundamental reform of the Roman field forces. The date is unfortunately uncertain: possibly it was due to the wisdom of Camillus immediately after the withdrawal of the Gauls or else later in the century when the Romans were operating in the rough hill-country of Samnium.[2] The heavy infantry was provided with a screen of slingers and javelin-throwers *(velites)*. In the main body of the legions (since the establishment of the Republic the legion had probably been divided into two legions; if not, the division was made now) the men of the front rank *(principes)* were rearmed with two throwing-spears *(pila)* and a sword apiece. The middle and rear ranks *(hastati and triarii)* for the time being retained their thrusting-spears *(hastae)*, but eventually the *hastati* were re-equipped on the pattern of the *principes* and the lines were rearranged so that the *hastati* formed the first line, the *principes* (despite their name) the second, and the *triarii* the third. They also exchanged the earlier round shield *(clipeus)* for the long *scutum*, which was four-cornered and slightly cylindrical.

The manipular formation of the legions

A more important innovation than this change of armament was made in the internal grouping of the legions which led to the supersession of the phalanx by a manipular formation. The centuries in each of the three lines were constituted into separate tactical units which allowed a more open order of fighting. Each unit carried a field ensign consisting of a bundle of straw *(manipulus)*, and at any rate in later times each maniple comprised two centuries and was commanded by the centurion of the right-hand century; the legion then comprised thirty

10.1   Latin soldiers carrying their dead comrade. The handle of the lid of a box (*cista*) from Praeneste. Probably fourth century B.C.

maniples, each of 120 men. On the field of battle the maniples of each of the three lines were drawn up with intervals between them; the maniples of the two rear lines each covered the gaps in the line in front. In the course of the action the maniples of the second line would be pushed up into the gaps of the first line, if necessary, and the maniples of the *triarii* would reinforce the front lines in the same way. These details have been mentioned at this point, but the time of their introduction, as well of the inception of the whole principle, remains obscure. Henceforth, however, the Roman legion combined compactness with elasticity in a remarkable degree.[3] It could fight in loose order or in serried ranks, as occasion might require, and the tactical independence of the maniples ensured that if the legion as a whole lost its cohesion, it did not dissolve into dust, but could rally round the intact maniples. This finally gave Rome the victory over her enemies in the fourth century, but, as will be seen (p. 129), even greater elasticity was needed before she could defeat Hannibal later. Finally, the political reform of the year 367, by which the

consulship was thrown open without reserve to plebeians (p. 77), provided the reorganised army with new leaders of ability and enterprise.

The new war-machine was not tested for a long time against the Gauls. Though they continued to make occasional inroads into peninsular Italy, extending their raids as far as Apulia, they mostly kept clear of Roman territory. In 360 the sudden irruption of a Gallic host into the Alban hill-country so unnerved the Romans that they tamely retired behind their new fortifications and there waited for the marauders to withdraw at their own leisure. In 349 they forestalled a further foray by calling up betimes the other Latins, and a second failure of nerve – this time on the part of the Gauls, who retired precipitately – ended the campaign without a battle.[4] Meanwhile the Gauls, having completed their occupation of northern Italy, began to acquire settled habits. In 331 the Senones, who had headed the invasions into central Italy, made their peace with Rome. Under the impression of the foray of 360 a special reserve fund was set apart in the treasury (*aerarium sanctius*) for use in similar emergencies, but no actual call

Intermittent Gallic raids

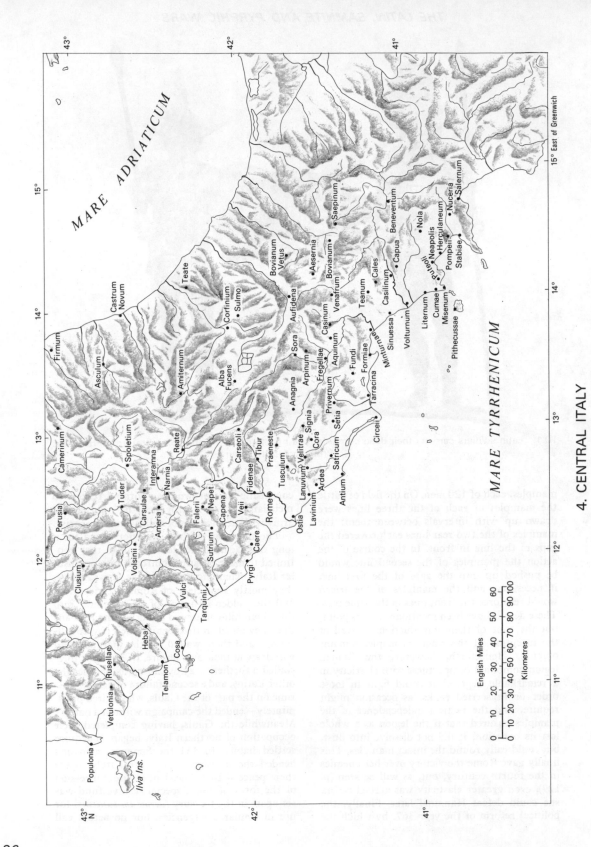

MARE ADRIATICUM

MARE TYRRHENICUM

43° N

42°

41°

43°

42°

41°

11°

12°

13°

14°

15°

15° East of Greenwich

Firmum

Asculum

Castrum
Novum

Teate

Corfinium
Sulmo

Bovianum
Vetus

Aesernia

Saepinum

Benev.

Nola
Neapolis
Herculaneum
Pompeii
Stabiae

Salernum

Nuceria

Capua

Beneventum

Cales
Casilinum

Puteoli
Cumae
Misenum

Pithecussae

Liternum
Volturnum

Sinuessa
Minturnae

Teanum

Venafrum
Casinum

Bovianum

Aquinum
Fundi
Formiae
Tarracina

Sora
Aufidena

Arpinum
Fregellae

Privernum
Setia
Circei

Anagnia
Signia
Cora
Satricum
Antium

Alba
Fucens

Amiternum

Reate

Carseoli
Tibur
Praeneste
Tusculum
Velitrae
Lanuvium
Ardea
Lavinium

Camerinum

Spoletium

Interamna
Narnia

Carsulae
Ameria

Nepet
Sutrium
Falerii
Capena
Veii

Rome
Ostia

Fidenae

Tuder

Perusia

Clusium

Volsinii

Tarquinii
Vulci

Pyrgi
Caere

Heba
Cosa
Telamon

Rusellae
Vetulonia

Populonia

Ilva Ins.

English Miles
0   10   20   30   40   50   60

0 10 20 30 40 50 60 70 80 90 100
Kilometres

4. CENTRAL ITALY

86

was made upon it until the Second Punic War.

Successes against the Etruscans

While the Gauls held their hand, the Romans beat off the attacks of their neighbours on each side of the Tiber and consolidated the gains made before 390. On the Etruscan front they defeated an attempt by Falerii and Tarquinii to recover the territory of their former ally, Veii, and made secure a new frontier line along the transverse ridge of the Ciminian mountains by establishing Latin colonies at Sutrium and Nepete. On the outskirts of Latium they brought the incursions of the Aequi to a dead stop in a single campaign (389). They threw back the Volsci, who had resumed their raids and carried them as far as Lanuvium, in a series of campaigns which ended about 380.

During the next decade or so the domestic disturbances which led to the Licinian reforms (p. 76) prevented the Romans from following up these successes. But after this pause they came to a final reckoning with the Latins. Collectively the Latin League appears to have refrained from an open breach with the Romans after 390, but its hold upon individual Latin towns was insufficient to prevent these from making war. About 360 the city of Tibur joined Praeneste (which had always stood out of the League) and the Hernici in a campaign against the Romans. Their defeat was followed in 358 by a fresh settlement of Latin affairs, in which the Romans

Reorganisation of the Latin League

preserved the outlines of the *foedus Cassianum* (p. 70), but in fact imposed a new treaty upon the League, so as to convert their former allies into dependants. In the reorganised League (into which Praeneste was now obliged to enter) the Romans permanently assumed military control, and the two annual *praetors* who replaced the previous federal dictator were but the subordinates of the Roman consuls. Antium was not incorporated in the League, but Rome annexed part of her territory and formed it into two new tribes (Pomptina and Poblilia: the latter was possibly in Hernician rather than Volscian territory); thus the number of tribes was raised to twenty-seven. The reconstituted League was at once tested in a hard-fought war with the Etruscans. In 359 the city of Tarquinii (encouraged perhaps by the fiasco of the Gallic raid in the previous year—p. 85) resumed hostilities, and three years later all the towns of the Etruscan League for the first time apparently made common cause against Rome. With all the forces of Latium at their disposal, the Romans beat off the combined Etruscan assault. In 353 they detached their former friend Caere by a grant of favourable terms;[5] two years later they overran the land of Falerii and Tarquinii, and constrained these cities to accept a forty years' truce (*indutiae*).

By 350 the Romans had acquired sufficient territory to appease their existing land-hunger (p. 75), and they no longer lived under the shadow of invasion. But their army had been

Motives for further conquest

refashioned into an instrument of conquest which the new plebeian leaders were ready to bring into use wherever a chance might offer — and opportunities for carrying the Roman arms further afield were never lacking. The Romans had not fully consolidated their supremacy in central Italy before they were drawn on into a lengthening chain of wars in the southern part of the peninsula.

2. The Oscan-speaking Sabellians[6]

In the fifth and early fourth centuries, while the Romans were gradually winning elbow-room for themselves, the Oscan-speaking populations of the southern Apennines had overrun the adjacent lowlands in all directions. Proceeding from the same pressure of overpopulation as was driving the Aequi and Volsci from the central Apennines into the plains of Latium (p. 71), their thrusts towards the southern coastal plains met with a more rapid success, for neither the precarious remnants of the Etruscans in Campania nor the scattered and mutually discordant Greek cities of the seaboard could offer them any determined resistance. Soon after

Migrations of the Sabellian peoples

450 Sabellians from the mountains were dominating the Campanian plain; in 423 they seized Capua and three years later they made Cumae, the pioneer of Hellenism in Italy, into an Oscan town. Further south they occupied the hill-country of Lucania between the western and the southern seas, driving the natives into the mountainous and barren 'toe' of Italy (which henceforth carried the name of Bruttium), and confining the Greeks to a narrow seaboard strip. In the mid-fourth century the Oscanised inhabitants asserted their independence of the Lucanians and became known as the Bruttii. On the eastern border of the Apennines the Sabellians won an outlet to the Adriatic on the northern side of Cape Garganus. In the south-eastern region the natives of Apulia and the Greek city of Tarentum held their ground more tenaciously; but by 350 the greater part of southern Italy had fallen into Sabellian hands.

If the success of an invasion be measured by the extent of ground occupied, the Sabellian conquests in the south of the peninsula were more impressive than those of Rome in central Italy. But they lacked the systematic character of the slower Roman advance. They had been

Their sporadic character

accomplished by disconnected bands of adventurers, stimulated by the practice of the Sacred

Spring (p. 15), rather than under the uniform direction of an organised state; consequently the diffusion of the Oscan peoples led to differentiation and eventual antagonism among themselves.

The Samnites

The residual population in the Apennine uplands – henceforth known as 'Samnites' – consisted of a hardy race of shepherds and crofters, living in villages rather than towns.[7] Although some large landowners doubtless existed, marked differences of wealth were comparatively small. Each valley or plateau constituted a *pagus* with an elective headman (*meddix*), whose duties were confined to leadership in war and a summary jurisdiction. The *pagi* were loosely gathered together in cantonal associations (Caraceni, Pentri, Hirpini and Caudini), and each of these *populi* formed a *touto*, led by a *meddix tuticus*. These in turn were grouped in a wider league with a central meeting-place at Bovianum Vetus, where the cantonal chiefs met on emergency to appoint a federal commander-in-chief and where a federal diet, and possibly an assembly, met. In the fourth century the Samnite homeland was still as densely inhabited as its mountainous character would permit, and no class dissensions or cantonal jealousies hindered prompt co-operation by the entire people. But the geographical isolation of the several cantons stood in the way of any closer political concentration. In the intervals between the federal wars individual bands would engage in private forays, or hire themselves out as mercenaries to the Greek cities of Italy and Sicily, in order to spend their winnings on costly armour and personal adornments. These soldiers of adventure brought the entire Samnite people into bad odour with its neighbours, yet the federation could not or would not restrain their licence.[8]

The Lucanians

The same political institutions and similar habits of life were preserved among the Sabellian settlers in Lucania; but the federation of Lucanian cantons formed a wholly separate state, and its troops stood under their own *generalissimo*. In Campania the Sabellian immigrants not only made themselves independent of their mother-country, but adopted widely different customs. Under the influence of the Etruscans and Greeks, whom they had not wholly dispossessed, they acquired an urban civilisation which contrasted sharply with the rustic habits of the Samnites. Though some of their younger men, with a touch of the old highland restlessness, went to seek their fortunes in foreign mercenary service, the Campanian Oscans in general settled down to the sedentary life of the lowlander. In the fourth century the Campanian towns, and especially the city of Capua, became the chief centres of industrial production in Italy (p. 106). The culture of their wealthy governing classes was a peculiar compound of Etruscan and Greek elements. The frescoed rock-chambers of the grandees, and the gladiatorial games in which the Campanians disposed of their captive Samnites, were borrowed from the Etruscans; but their industrial art followed Greek rather than Tuscan patterns. The Oscans of Campania also adopted the usual political institutions of city-states. Their regional league, of which Capua was the predominant partner, was a federation of towns, like that of the Latins or Etruscans. By 350 the Sabellian folk as a whole had ceased to form a homogeneous group: its constituent peoples were about to enter upon a period of internecine warfare.

The Campanians

Capua

3. The First Samnite War and the Great Latin War

The first political encounter between the Oscans and the Romans was of a friendly character. In 354 the Samnites offered the Romans a treaty which these accepted; the interests which both peoples had in the middle Liris valley were probably defined to their mutual satisfaction. Presumably this alliance was inspired by a common fear of the Gauls, and it is not unlikely that a Samnite contingent was included in the army which scared away the Gallic invaders of 349 (p. 85). But as the Gallic peril receded, the bond between Romans and Samnites was loosened.

Alliance between Romans and Samnites

In 343 the Romans, renouncing their amity with the Samnites, entered upon a contest with them, in the course of which the stakes were raised to nothing less than supremacy over southern Italy. Their change of front was induced by a rival offer of alliance from the Capuans, who were being molested by marauders from the Samnite country, and now sought to play off the Romans against them. Notwithstanding their recent treaty, the Romans opened hostilities against the Samnites on behalf of a state to which they were not bound by any previous political ties. The reasons for this sudden reversal of Roman policy are not wholly clear. But the natural antagonism between the settled communities of the plain and the cattle-reiving highlanders, and the prospects of economic benefit accruing out of an alliance with one of the richest cities of Italy, no doubt had their due effect upon the Romans; and it is not unlikely that the influence of new plebeian leaders intent on proving their military ability was exerted on the side of war.[9]

The Capuans invoke the Romans against the Samnites

In the same year a considerable Roman force

10.2 Sabellian warriors depicted on a tomb-painting at Paestum, the 'Tomb of the Warriors', early fourth century B.C.

The 'First' Samnite war

assisted the Capuans in driving the Samnites out of Campania. But the gains of the season were jeopardised in 342 by a mutiny among the Roman troops, who had not yet acquired the habit of prolonged service in distant fields and were in no mood to mount guard over Samnites on behalf of Capuans.[10] It was fortunate for the Romans that at this juncture the Samnites had their attention diverted to their southern neighbour, the city of Tarentum (p. 94), and so consented to the renewal of the previous treaty with Rome (341). But in coming to terms with the Samnites the Romans threw over their more recent allies in Campania. In answer to renewed Samnite forays the Campanians now made an alliance with a group of other Latin cities, who gave them support in beating back the raiders. On the other hand a call by the Samnites for Roman assistance against Tarentum was left unanswered. Rome's first adventure in southern Italy had a singularly inglorious ending, but it was highly significant: it showed that Campania was falling into Rome's sphere of influence.

The unwonted vacillation which the temporary paralysis of the military forces had imposed upon Roman policy not only alienated the Oscan peoples; it had the further effect of bringing to a head a gathering quarrel with the Latins. Under the terms imposed upon them in 358 the Latins had been called upon to supply contingents for wars (such as the Etruscan campaigns of 358–351 and the recent operations in Campania) in a Roman rather than a collec-

tive Latin interest. In 358 they had seen the Romans appropriate for themselves the Pomptine level recovered from the Volscians, and on this occasion the land-distributions to Roman citizens were not balanced by the establishment of new colonies for the Latins (p. 87). In 349 they had openly expressed their discontent by threatening to withhold their aid against the Gauls. The attitude of the Romans towards the Latins was reflected in the treaty which they made with Carthage, probably in 348.[11] The Carthaginians were required not to obtain any permanent foothold in Latium, and not to molest the towns which accepted Roman leadership, but they were left free to make slave hauls at the cost of the independent Latin cities (e.g. a town like Antium). In return, the Romans recognised an even wider Carthaginian trade monopoly than in their earlier treaty (p. 55): Roman traders were excluded not only from the western Mediterranean from the Gulf of Tunis to Cartagena in Spain, but also now from Sardinia and Libya where previously they had been allowed under certain conditions; Carthaginian Sicily and Carthage itself alone remained open to them. Thus Rome's general lack of interest in widespread commerce at this period is demonstrated.

The fiasco of the First Samnite War finally encouraged the Latins to send an ultimatum to Rome, in which they demanded a restoration of the previous parity of rights between themselves and the predominant partner (340).[12] Upon refusal of these terms the Latins con-

Restiveness of the Latins

Rome's treaty with Carthage renewed

firmed their alliance with the Campanians and made a league with their old enemies, the Volsci. But the Romans had by now restored order within their own ranks, and they received loyal support from the Samnites, who stood by the treaty of 341 in spite of their partner's recent tergiversations. While their adversaries were still collecting their contingents, the Roman armies effected a junction with the Samnite forces by marching across the territory of the Aequi into the central Apennines, and the combined forces, descending the valley of the Liris towards Campania, met and defeated the collective contingents of Latins and Campanians near Suessa Aurunca.[13] The Romans followed up this success with an offer of favourable terms to the Campanians, so as to break up the enemy coalition (340). Having detached the Campanians, they proceeded in the next two campaigns to defeat the Latins in detail, and they finally wrested from the Volscians the seaboard town of Antium, which had frequently changed hands in the previous border wars. A trophy of this war long remained on view in the Roman Forum, where the prows of the captured Antiate pirate cutters were affixed to the speakers' platform (which took from them the name of 'Rostra').

The settlement dictated by the Romans in 338 finally established their supremacy in central Italy. Their military control over the Latins was made complete by a systematic policy of isolation. The federation which had held the Latins together since the end of the Etruscan domination was broken up, and each city was obliged to enter into a separate convention with Rome. But Rome avoided driving Latin opposition underground by an enlightened policy of binding the conquered to herself by bonds of common interest and by stimulating their loyalty to a state of which they became members. Some peoples were to receive either complete or partial grants of Roman citizenship, thus becoming members incorporated in the State with the prospect that the so-called 'half-citizens' (i.e. those who had *citivas sine suffragio* or the private and not the public rights of citizenship) might one day be upgraded to full citizenship. Others remained or became Latin allies. Tusculum, Aricia, Lanuvium and two other towns were granted full citizenship, but retained their municipal governments (within a generation, in 332, a Tusculan noble had reached the Roman consulship), while in 332 two new Roman tribes (Maecia and Scaptia) were formed in Latium. The first towns *(municipia)* to receive *civitas sine suffragio* were those whose peoples did not speak Latin (Volsci, Aurunci and Campani), as Fundi, Formiae, Capua,[14] Suessula,

Cumae and soon Acerrae. This status was at first regarded as an honour by which Rome and the *municipium* exchanged social rights, but soon it came to be considered an inferior grade of Roman citizenship, especially since these *municipia*, although remaining separate *respublicae* with local autonomy, had to provide Rome with soldiers and were visited by Roman judicial prefects.[15] Thirdly, the other Latin cities and colonies retained their old status, being allies *(socii Latini nominis)* bound to Rome but not to each other. They retained their local independence, but were obliged to furnish troops to Rome whenever required, and suffered restrictions in regard to mutual trade and intermarriage. Cities of this class were the Latin colonies, Signia, Norba, Ardea, Circeii, Sutrium, Nepete and Setia. Other towns were allied to Rome on a different basis: thus Tibur and Praeneste were deprived of some of their territory, but, like Gabii and Cora, retained their Roman alliances. Fourthly, Antium received special treatment; after destroying its fleet the Romans then allowed the Antiates to enjoy their city, but a small colony of Roman citizens was sent to occupy part of their territory, where they could guard the seaport. This was a new type of colony, in which Latins were not allowed to share (p. 102), and as a partner to Antium a second *colonia maritima* was planted at Ostia, probably about the same time; traces of the walls of this *castrum* can still be seen.[16]

This general settlement had far-reaching consequences. It laid the foundation of a confederation which was ultimately to embrace the whole of Italy and which is described more fully in the next chapter. Rome's policy, by which her allies supplied troops to fight alongside the Romans in their common interests but were not subjected to taxation or tribute, generated a mutual interest and loyalty which secured for Rome the possibility of winning the hegemony of Italy. But before that was possible Rome had to come to terms with the Samnites, who controlled at least 6000 square miles of territory.

4. The Second Samnite War

After the campaign of 340 the Romans did not take the Samnites into any further consideration. Reckoning that they could henceforth dispense with their services, they ignored their allies in the settlement of 338, which had the effect of binding all the peoples of the western plain together against those of the mountains. In 334 they secured Capua against further Samnite raids by posting a Latin colony at Cales on the border of the Campanian lowland; in 328 they expelled the Volscians from the valley of the Liris and improved their communications with Campania by establishing another colony at Fregellae. Though not primarily intended as an outpost against the Samnites, Fregellae in effect barred their descent through the Liris valley into Campania, and all but completed the process of cutting them off from the western seaboard. In 334 the Romans gave offence to the Samnites by entering into a treaty with the Tarentines, while these were at war with their Oscan neighbours. The estrangement between the allies led on to open hostilities in 327, when the Samnites, having regained a free hand by concluding a peace with Tarentum, renewed their thrusts towards the western seaboard. In this year they took advantage of internal dissension in the small Greek town of Neapolis (Naples) to introduce a garrison into it. In answer to a protest from Capua, the Romans put Neapolis under siege and eventually stole it from the Samnites with an offer of propitious terms.[17] The scene was now laid for the first serious trial of strength between the two chief military powers of peninsular Italy.

In the Second Samnite War (326–304) the Romans were confronted with new problems which compelled them to make further reforms in their military methods and to seek alliances still further afield. While they could generally reckon on beating off the Samnite excursions into the coastal plains, they had to learn some hard lessons before they could venture with success into the mountain fastnesses of the enemy.

In the opening campaigns of the war operations on the western front soon reached a state of deadlock. The Samnites could not pass the Roman outposts in the valleys of the Liris and Volturnus, and the Romans would not venture to follow these streams upward into the heart of the mountains. In 325 a wide turning move was begun by a Roman force which traversed the central Apennines by way of the Lacus Fucinus and showed Roman arms for the first time on the Adriatic coast. On this expedition the Romans won over the Marsi and Paeligni in the central Apennine massif, and reduced by force the Vestini on the Adriatic seaboard, perhaps to prepare for an advance into Apulia. But before such a turning operation could be completed, a frontal attack on Samnium itself, attempted in a moment of impatience, brought the whole Roman offensive to a standstill. In 321 a Roman and allied force of 20,000 men set out from near Capua with the apparent intention of finding a short cut through the Apennines to Apulia. At the 'Caudine Forks' it was trapped in a combe between two mountain defiles and forced to capitulate. The price of

its redemption was a treaty by which the Samnites received possession of Fregellae and other Roman outposts, together with 600 Roman equites as hostages. The defeated Roman soldiers had to pass under a yoke of spears, wearing only their tunics: humiliated, they could then go free.[18]

To the Romans, however, the Caudine peace was merely a pause for reorganisation. In the next five years they made provisions for the increase of the ordinary infantry levy from two to four legions of 4200 men each. With an equal quota of soldiers from the allied states, the total Roman field army in a normal campaign was henceforth fixed at 35,000–40,000 men. If manipular tactics were introduced only as late as this (p. 85), no doubt the Roman army used the respite to practise their use. Further, two new tribes of Roman citizens were created from land that was lying idle: the Falernia in northern Campania and the Oufentina near the Middle Liris from territory confiscated from Privernum in 329.

In 316 the Romans repudiated their treaty (it is not known on what pretext) and in 315 resumed their attempts to take the Samnites in the rear by way of Apulia. Their plans were crossed at the outset by an enemy flying column which made a dash from Fregellae to the coast, so as to cut the Roman lines of communication with Capua. A reserve force was sent from Rome under Q. Fabius Rullianus to recover the coastal road to Campania, but was caught in the defile of Lautulae (near Tarracina where in 329 a Roman colony was established) and suffered a defeat scarcely less complete than that of the Caudine Forks. For a while the loyalty of the Campanians, who had held firm in 321, was shaken, and Capua actually changed sides. The Latins remained loyal and before defection could spread further the Romans, drawing heavily upon the remnant of their man-power, made good their casualties and recovered the lost ground. In 314 they drove the Samnites from Tarracina and received a hasty surrender from Capua; in the next two years they recovered the line of the Liris and strengthened it with a Latin colony at Interamna; two others were established at Saticula and Suessa Aurunca. At the same time they secured a permanent foothold in Apulia by capturing the Samnite stronghold of Luceria and establishing a colony on its site (314). Finally, they took in hand the construction of the most famous of their metalled highroads, the Via Appia, which provided an all-weather line of communications from Rome to Tarracina and Capua (312; p. 79).

The Samnites now seemed well held on every

Estrangement of the Romans from the Samnites

The Second Samnite War

The Romans gain access to the Adriatic

The disaster of the 'Caudine Forks'

Increase of the Roman forces

The disaster of Lautulae

The Roman recovery

The Via Appia

side except the south. But they won a long respite by a successful counter-offensive in the diplomatic field. In 311, the date at which Rome's armistice with Tarquinii and Falerii lapsed, they induced the Etruscans to a general mobilisation against Rome, and in the ensuing year they detached Rome's new allies in the central Apennines, the Marsi and Paeligni, as well as their old friends the Hernici. But the Romans, all the time retaining their hold on Campania and Apulia, systematically reduced the lesser rebels and fought the Etruscans to a standstill (311-304; below). The way at last was open for an invasion of the southern Apennine highlands in full force, when the Samnites, now dangerously isolated, sued for peace (304).[19] The Romans, rather than prolong the strain of a twenty years' struggle, left the Samnites in enjoyment of their full independence and contented themselves with their existing gains. In thus sparing their enemy they gave him the chance of trying another fall. Yet the Romans could enter upon the next Samnite War with the dice heavily loaded in their favour. In the recent war they had definitely detached the Campanian Oscans from their kinsmen, they had made secure the western seaboard as far as Naples, and they established a Latin colony at Sora (303) to guard the upper Liris valley; they had ringed in the Samnites on three sides. In 311 the Romans, perhaps influenced by their new Greek allies at Naples, established a small Naval Board, *duoviri navales*, and a little squadron helped to patrol the coast, while a Latin colony had been sent in 312 to occupy the offshore island of Pontiae.

In the interval between the Second and the Third Samnite Wars the Romans consolidated their gains by making or renewing alliances with the lesser tribes on the northern fringe of Samnium – the Marsi, Paeligni, Marrucini, Frentani and Vestini – and by establishing Latin colonies at Alba Fucens (303) and Carseoli (298), so as to control the main passage through the central Apennines where they were constructing the Via Valeria.

The Second Samnite War incidentally brought about an extension of Roman ascendancy in Etruria. In postponing their intervention in that conflict until the expiry of the armistice of 351, the Etruscans had missed their tide, for by then the Romans had the Samnites firmly held and could detach sufficient forces to assume the offensive on the new war front. In 310 Fabius Rullianus redeemed his previous defeat at Lautulae by a brilliantly daring march through the dense forest of the Ciminian mountains, by which he outflanked an advancing Etruscan army and drew it into central Tuscany.

End of the war. The Roman gains

Alliances with the peoples of the central Apennines

More victories over the Etruscans

A defeat in a set battle (possibly near Lake Vadimo) now sufficed to disintegrate the Etruscan league. In the next two years one city after another made separate terms with the Romans.[20] This debacle so far damaged the prestige of the governing aristocracies in the Etruscan towns that they could no longer maintain order within their own house and were repeatedly obliged to call in the assistance of the Romans to suppress insurrections by the serfs or urban artisans.[21] Though the Romans were content for the present to conclude alliances with the Tuscan cities on a footing of equality, they had in effect reduced the whole country to a condition of dependence.

The added prestige which these victories conferred upon the Romans also brought them into relations with the Umbrians – a hill folk who had formerly been pressed back from the western seaboard by the Etruscans and had more recently been losing their Adriatic outlet to the Gauls – and with the Picentes of the Adriatic coast, who had a similar reason for protective alliances against the Gauls. The Romans made treaties with the Picentine people and with several Umbrian cities – under Etruscan influence the Umbrians had separated into city-states. In order to prepare a passage to the Adriatic through Umbrian territory a Latin colony was planted at Narnia, near the confluence of the Tiber and the Nar (299).

Etruria becomes a Roman dependency

Alliances with the peoples of the northern Apennines

5. The Third Samnite War

While the Romans were thus engaged in extending their dominion from sea to sea, the Samnites sought compensation for their losses by pressing an alliance upon their Lucanian kinsmen, with whom their previous relations had generally been amicable. But the Lucanians, who probably desired a free hand to deal with their Greek neighbours at Tarentum (p. 94), refused these overtures, and when the Samnites attempted to gain their point by force they solicited Roman intervention (298). The Lucanian appeal came from a quarter in which the Romans as yet had shown no interest, but it offered them the opportunity of completing the encirclement of the Samnites and was therefore accepted. A relief expedition under L. Scipio Barbatus – the first representative of that family to enter into Roman history – drove the Samnites out of Lucania,[22] thus opening the round between the two chief military powers of Italy.

In the Third Samnite War the Romans at once carried operations into enemy territory. But their new obligations to the Lucanians had compelled them to extend their lines to such

The Lucanians invoke Roman aid against the Samnites

The Third Samnite War

a perilous length that in 296 the Samnites succeeded in a break-through at two points. While a lesser division made one of the customary forays into Campania (in reply Roman maritime colonies were settled at Minturnae and Sinuessa), the main Samnite army under Gellius Egnatius slipped past the Roman outposts at Alba Fucens and Carseoli and advanced across the Sabine and Umbrian country as far as the land of the Senones, collecting contingents from the peoples on its route of march.[23] This sudden coalition was further strengthened by the appearance of contingents from several of the Etruscan cities. In the following year (295) a crushing defeat sustained by Scipio, who had gone in pursuit of Egnatius, only to be overwhelmed by a combined force of Samnites and Gauls at Camerinum,[24] made the Romans aware of their danger. Calling the older men and the ex-slaves to arms for garrison service, they put together a field force of full 40,000 men under their tried veteran, Fabius Rullianus, and a new plebeian leader named Decius Mus, who brought the confederates to battle at Sentinum in northern Umbria. In this encounter more troops were engaged than in any previous action on Italian soil, and the fate of all Italy appeared to depend on its issue. The Roman forces all but gave way before an unexpected onslaught of Gallic chariots; but Decius rallied his wing at the price of his own life, and Fabius carried the day with a final charge by the Campanian horsemen.[25] With the destruction of the Samnite contingent and the death of their leader the hostile coalition fell to pieces. In the same year Fabius received the surrender of the Umbrian rebels and forced the Senones to come to terms by overrunning their territory. In 294 the Etruscan cities made their peace with Rome.

After the failure of Egnatius's grand scheme for the union of all Rome's enemies the Samnites were left exposed to invasion by Roman armies from several quarters. Though they beat off more than one attack, they could not prevent two of the new plebeian leaders, L. Papirius Cursor (who defeated their crack Linen Legion at Aquilonia in 293[26]) and M'. Curius Dentatus (290) from harrying their territory from end to end. In 290 they applied for peace: they were mulcted of some territory and had to become 'allies' of Rome, with all the obligations thereby entailed instead of remaining merely 'friends'.[27] They were now cut off on every side by a network of alliances which Rome had industriously spun round them, and by military barrages which left them scarcely a loop-hole of escape. On the Lucanian border the Romans established on land taken from them a Latin colony of unusually strong numbers at Venusia (291). For the

purpose of shutting off the Samnites securely from their recent allies in the north they annexed the territory of the Sabines, who were given Roman 'half-citizenship' (civitas sine suffragio);[28] thus Roman territory (ager Romanus) now stretched right across to the Adriatic Sea, on whose coast a Latin colony was settled at Hadria.[29]

During the long duel between Rome and Samnium the losers had observed their treaty obligations more scrupulously than their conquerors. In warfare they had shown equal courage and determination and had conducted their campaigns with an occasional flash of strategic inspiration. But they had lacked the Roman aptitude for systematic and ever-renewed attack, and for the methodical consolidation of ground won. Above all, by their predatory habits they had alienated their neighbours and facilitated the diplomatic victories to which the Romans largely owed their final success. On broad political grounds a Samnite defeat was in the general interest of the Italian peoples. An eventual Samnite victory (with further Gallic raids to follow) would have thrown Italy back into chaos; a peace dictated by Rome brought settled conditions of life.

The results of the Third Samnite War were for a moment jeopardised by a sudden return of the Senones, whom the campaign of Sentinum had checked but not crushed. In 284 (or 283) the Gauls renewed their invasions of Etruria by setting siege to Arretium. On the massive defeat of a Roman relief force several Etruscan cities renounced their allegiance, and the unrest spread momentarily to Samnium and Lucania. But the blaze that threatened was promptly stifled by Curius Dentatus, who led a Roman force directly into the invaders' own territory and defeated them in a battle which left them at his mercy. By way of avenging some Roman envoys whom the Gauls had murdered he turned their land into an utter desert. The ager Gallicus, as the Romans named the Senonian country, remained waste for fifty years, save only a coast strip where the Roman maritime colony of Sena Gallica was founded. By these excessive reprisals Curius prolonged rather than ended the Gallic war, for the neighbouring Boii, anticipating a similar fate, attempted to draw off the Romans by another incursion into Etruria (283).[30] Gathering Etruscan contingents on their way, the Boii arrived within some 50 miles of Rome, but were held fast and defeated near Lake Vadimo by P. Cornelius Dolabella, and a second invasion in the following year met with no better fortune. Hereupon they sued for peace, and obtained it on easy terms. Their Etruscan confederates carried on the struggle for a few more years, but eventually capitulated under lenient conditions. The only extension of territory with which the Romans rewarded themselves at this stage was at the expense of their former friend Caere, which was probably annexed in 273 with a grant of *civitas sine suffragio* (p. 87). The reason for this lucky escape of the Etruscans and Boii was that the Romans had in the meantime been called upon to face towards another front.

6. The War with Tarentum and Pyrrhus

Before the third century the Romans had hardly yet entered into relations with the Greek cities of the southern seaboard. To most of these their newly established ascendancy in southern Italy was welcome as giving them some guarantee of security against the Oscan marauders. But to the Tarentines it appeared as an intrusion into a sphere of action which they had reserved for themselves.

The city of Tarentum

Of the Greek towns in south Italy, Tarentum alone had enjoyed continued prosperity. Its wealth was primarily based on its pastures, which produced the best fleeces in Italy. Tarentine industry made the wool into fine cloths, and dyed these with purple from the mussel-beds in its harbour. In the fourth century the city became a centre of ceramic manufacture, and its trade up the Adriatic was being extended into the valley of the Po and even across the Alps.[31] Under a moderate democracy it achieved a measure of political stability unusual in a Greek city-state; it could put into the field an army of some 15,000 men, and it possessed the strongest of Italian navies. In the period of the Samnite wars the Tarentines supplemented their citizen forces by taking into their pay sundry captains of adventure whom the Greek homeland was at that time producing in profusion. With these reinforcements they could not only hold the Oscan raiders at arm's length, but could aim at an extension of their frontiers into the Apulian downlands.

At the time of the First Samnite War the Tarentines took into their service a Spartan king named Archidamus, who eventually perished in a battle against the Lucanians, but for a time kept these enemies in play and put even the Samnite people on their guard. In 334, the year in which Alexander the Great started out on his eastern campaigns, they engaged his brother-in-law, King Alexander of Epirus, who was bent on similar adventures in the west. In a few rapid campaigns Alexander beat off Lucanian, Bruttian and Samnite raiders from the territory of the Greek cities, and in anticipation of more

Early relations with Rome

extensive conquests he obtained the neutrality of the Romans by a convention which pledged them not to come to the assistance of their Samnite allies (p. 91). But the Tarentines, suspecting the growth of Alexander's ambitions, presently withdrew their support and left him to be defeated and slain by the Lucanians. During the Second Samnite War the passage of the Roman armies into Apulia began to cause concern to the Tarentines, which found expression in a vain attempt at mediation between the belligerents (*c.* 314). The rebuff with which the Romans met this proposal, and their establishment at Venusia after the Third Samnite War (p. 93), definitely estranged the Tarentines. The latter had invited further help from the Greeks, but neither Cleonymus of Sparta in 303 nor Agathocles, tyrant of Syracuse, in 298 had achieved much for them.

The ill-feeling at Tarentum against Rome was brought to a head in 282. In that year the Romans sent a force at the request of the Greek city of Thurii on the Gulf of Otranto to relieve it from the attacks of the Lucanians, and commissioned a small patrol fleet to render support. This expedition was resented by the Tarentines as an infraction of the agreement with Alexander of Epirus, by which the Romans had engaged themselves, *inter alia*, not to send their ships into the Gulf. In the eyes of the Romans this treaty had apparently been rendered obsolete by the lapse of time; but it had never been formally abrogated.[32] Without waiting for explanations, the infuriated Tarentines mobilised army and fleet, sank several of the Roman ships, and drove the relief force away from Thurii. With an Etruscan and Gallic campaign still on their hands, the Romans showed unusual readiness to pocket the insult. But the Tarentines rejected their simple request for compensation, for they had in the meantime secured the services of another Epirote king, whose army was reputed more than a match for that of Rome.[33]

Disputes about spheres of influence

The Tarentines force a war

King Pyrrhus of Epirus was the last of the race of military adventurers which the age of Alexander had bred in profusion among the Greeks. A complete misfit in his own world, which had wearied of knight-errantry, he sought a new outlet for his energies in the west and hastened to the aid of the Tarentines with a seasoned force of 25,000 men. Since the military prestige of the Greeks now stood at its zenith, and Pyrrhus was accounted the best captain of his day, his entry into the lists put the Romans to a severe test, and their victory over him was remembered with particular pride. Unfortunately the accurate record of the Pyrrhic war which was kept by contemporary Greek his-

King Pyrrhus of Epirus called in against the Romans

10.3 Clay dish from Campania, showing an Indian war-elephant with tower. It almost certainly depicts one of Pyrrhus's elephants.

and the winners' casualties were dangerously severe.

The victories of the Epirote king merely served to convince him that the war against Rome could only be won by attrition, and that his reserves might not outlast those of the enemy. After the battle of Heraclea he had conducted negotiations with the Roman ambassador C. Fabricius about the ransom of prisoners, and the somewhat ostentatious gestures of friendliness which his agent Cineas had then made on his behalf at Rome had been met by the Senate with like courtesy. To these discussions the king annexed a formal offer of peace, on the condition that the Romans should abandon all southern Italy – a proposal which the Senate rejected after a rousing speech by the aged Appius Claudius, who had been one of the organisers of victory in the Second Samnite War, and was loth to see his life's work wasted. After Asculum Pyrrhus made new overtures, in which he demanded nothing more than freedom for the Greeks, and perhaps some guarantee of indemnity for his Oscan allies,[37] but once again after negotiations the Senate refused his terms. This resolute attitude of the House was inspired by the visit of an envoy from the Carthaginians, who suspected that Pyrrhus might be planning an attack upon them in the interests of the Sicilian Greeks, and accordingly made an offer of naval and financial aid to the Romans, in the hope that they might keep the king in play. At first rebuffed, the Carthaginian ambassador, Mago, on a second visit to Rome met with success and an agreement was reached.[38] But Pyrrhus, although he failed to buy off the Romans, realised the fears of the Carthaginians in breaking off his unhopeful Italian campaign and seeking a more promising field of adventure in Sicily.

In the three years of Pyrrhus's absence the Romans beat his Oscan allies out of the field and pressed so hard upon the Samnites, who in effect were engaged in a Fourth Samnite War from 283 to 272, that in 276 they sent him an urgent message of recall. The king threw up his Sicilian enterprise, which had followed the pattern of his Italian campaigns – beginning with victory and ending in deadlock – and hastened back to Italy, but with forces sadly depleted. He laid a well-conceived plan to surprise and destroy a Roman consular army under the veteran Curius Dentatus near Beneventum; but Curius repelled his attack in open battle, thus allowing the other consul to come up, and in so doing he won the entire war. Checkmated by this threatened concentration of superior Roman forces, Pyrrhus cut his losses and slipped back to Epirus. He posted a garrison in Tarentum, but left his Oscan allies defenceless, and

Negotiations between the Romans and Pyrrhus

The Carthaginians offer aid to Rome

The battle of Beneventum

torians was overlaid in Roman tradition with the usual tangle of patriotic fiction, and our surviving accounts are not to be trusted in detail.[34]

Undeterred by Pyrrhus's reputation, the Romans brought him to battle at Heraclea, on the Gulf of Otranto, with a force of only 20,000 men (280). In this action the Roman legions successfully withstood the highly trained but somewhat unwieldy pikemen of Pyrrhus's heavy infantry. But the cavalry was thrown into disorder when the Epirote corps of elephants was thrown in – for untrained horses could not be brought to face these unfamiliar beasts – so that Pyrrhus's horsemen were enabled to take the Roman infantry in flank and put it to rout.[35] The king's victory, though bought at a high cost, was sufficiently decisive to enlist on his side the other Greek cities and to win over the Lucanians and Samnites.[36] In the hope of causing further defections from Rome, Pyrrhus made a progress through Campania and Latium and penetrated to Anagnia or perhaps even to Praeneste. But these regions remained loyal to Rome, and he won no fresh allies; with the reserve Roman levies crowding in upon him he was obliged to fall back upon south Italy.

In 279 Pyrrhus advanced into Apulia with a force augmented to 40,000 or 50,000 men, where he was met by a reinforced Roman army of equal strength. At the battle of Asculum Pyrrhus's elephants again prepared for a victory after a hard-fought action, but the Romans made good their retreat to their fortified camp,

The battle of Heraclea

The battle of Asculum

if he ever had thoughts of returning to Italy with a second Greek force he soon lost them out of mind. Shortly before his death in 272 the king recalled the remnant of his troops from Tarentum, and to secure a safe retreat the garrison made over the town to the Romans. In the same year the Roman field armies completed the subjugation of the Samnites, Lucanians and Bruttians.

Definite reduction of southern Italy by the Romans

Rome now had to organise her relations with many peoples in southern and central Italy. With the Greek cities of the south she made alliances by which they, unlike the other allies, provided ships rather than troops: these *socii navales* included cities like Velia, Heraclea, Thurii, Metapontum, Croton and Locri. Even Tarentum was granted allied status, although it was punished by having to offer hostages and to receive a permanent Roman garrison in its citadel. If any other cities received similar garri-

Allies and colonies

sons, they probably did so voluntarily, as guardians against either the Bruttian tribes or overseas invaders. The Brutii were deprived of half their forest-land but retained some autonomy. The Lucanians merely had to accept a Latin colony at Paestum (273). Rhegium, which had been temporarily seized by a garrison of Campanian troops who were Roman citizens, was stormed (270).[39] Apulia and Messapia were reduced to alliance (267–6), while the Sallentini in the heel of Italy were defeated, and land confiscated from Brundisium later (244) received a Latin colony.

Rome's grip on the south was thus secure. She now finally settled accounts with the Samnites who had been on the warpath since 283. Their League was broken up, leaving only cantonal or tribal divisions which individually became allies of Rome; in the heart of their land Latin colonies were planted at Beneventum (formerly called Malventum) in 268 to watch the Hirpini, and Aesernia in 263 to guard against the Pentri. Further north a Latin colony was sent to Cosa (273) to overlook Etruria, while another on the coast at Ariminum (268) secured the *ager Gallicus*.[40] The Picentes, who rebelled, were reduced in 268 and were incorporated as Roman *cives sine suffragio* (Asculum Picenum alone received a treaty of alliance) and they were supervised by a Latin colony at Firmum (264). The Sabines were considered sufficiently loyal to be raised from half to full citizenship in 268. Thus by 264 Roman supremacy was recognised in every corner of peninsular Italy.

Final settlement with the Samnites; Latin colonies

But the war against Pyrrhus did more than mark the end of one stage in the Roman conquests: it foreshadowed their extension to a wider field. Not only had the treaty with Carthage been renewed, but in 273 King Ptolemy II of Egypt offered and obtained an agreement with Rome; this was not a formal treaty but a grant of *amicitia*, a gesture of diplomatic courtesy which did not commit anybody to anything. But it implied that the Roman Republic was now gaining recognition as one of the 'Great Powers' and might before long play a leading part in Mediterranean politics.[41]

Wider horizons: friendship with Egypt

CHAPTER 11

The Roman State in the Third Century B.C.

1. The Roman Constitution. Apparent Defects

After the war with King Pyrrhus the history of Rome advances to a new stage. Its scene, henceforth extends from Italy to the whole of the Mediterranean. At this point of transition the structure of the Roman state and the conditions of life of its people call for a brief survey.

The first impression made by the Roman political system after the Conflict of the Orders is one of chaos. As in the case of the modern British constitution the rules of government were not summed up in a comprehensive code, nor even in any loose aggregate of single statutes, but consisted to a large extent of unwritten usages which had tacitly gained acceptance by virtue of long observance. In the absence of any methodical attempt at co-ordination the medley of laws and customs by which the Roman state was administered remained full of anomalies and offered countless opportunities of friction and even of deadlock.

One embarrassing consequence of the piecemeal procedure by which the plebeians had asserted the principle of popular sovereignty was the multiplication of popular assemblies which stood in no fixed legal relation to each other. The survival of the obsolete Comitia Curiata, which went on functioning like a fifth wheel on a coach, was a quite harmless incongruity. But the simultaneous yet uncorrelated action of the Centuriate and Tribal Assemblies, together with the Concilium Plebis, all of which could discharge electoral, legislative and judicial functions with customary rather than statutory definition of their spheres of competence, harboured manifold possibilities of conflict.

Apparent chaos of the Roman constitution

Co-ordinate popular assemblies

Another potential source of confusion lay in the lack of a sufficiently clear-cut division of labour in the executive branch of the government. This lack of definition was all the more perilous because of the accepted principle that among officials of equal rank any one might veto the action of any other. But the most extravagant feature of the Roman constitution lay in the almost unlimited right of obstruction which any of the ten tribunes might exercise against any other official.

Risk of executive deadlocks

2. The Working of the Constitution

Despite all these possibilities of breakdown the constitution of the third century 'marched' sufficiently well to carry the Roman people through a most critical stage of its history. Its practical success was partly due to the comparatively simple character which the administration preserved, notwithstanding the rapid territorial expansion of the Roman state. The Roman community was still of a homogeneous agricultural type, and the city of Rome, though by now the largest of all Italy (containing perhaps 100,000 inhabitants),[1] did not yet call for an elaborate commissariat or police supervision. Neither did the state finances require any expert management. It is true that public expenses were mounting under the stress of more distant and continuous wars, entailing the payment and partial equipment of the troops[2] and the construction of military roads; and that the revenue was being swelled by the proceeds of these wars in the form of booty and of rents from confiscated lands. Nevertheless the sums involved were not

Simple character of the government

yet sufficient to necessitate a scientific system of budgeting. In the warfare of the period any commander who had received the ordinary training of a regimental officer in his youth could still reckon to win his battles against any Italian enemy.

Besides, the Roman administration possessed one co-ordinating agency which went a long way to maintain harmony among the magistrates, and, through them, between the Comitia. Year by year the Senate arranged the *provinciae* or spheres of competence of those officials who could not come to an agreement; not infrequently it anticipated possible misunderstandings by prescribing the duties of magistrates at the outset of their term. In an emergency the Senate had a choice of ways and means for bringing a self-willed member of the executive to heel. To overawe a refractory consul it might induce his more acquiescent colleague to nominate a dictator over his head; after a victorious campaign it might penalise him by refusing to sanction the expenses of a triumph. But its most potent remedy against executive anarchy was of a homoeopathic order. To checkmate an obstructor the Senate would invoke his colleagues to obstruct him. This device was particularly effective in dealing with self-assertive tribunes bent on applying their veto without strong popular support. In such a case the Senate could generally persuade one or more of his colleagues to veto the vetoer into political paralysis.[3]

Control by the Senate

But the chief safeguard of Roman politics in the third century was the general atmosphere of goodwill, in which each social order and each branch of the government showed its readiness to co-operate with the rest. This spirit of reasonableness appears both in the willingness of magistrates and Comitia to follow the directions of the Senate, and in the discretion with which the Senate avoided any set conflict on an issue on which the people had strong feelings.[4]

General goodwill

The Roman constitution of the middle Republic, however, had other merits besides that of tolerable smoothness in its working. In a rough-and-ready yet practically effective way it achieved a fair compromise between the opposite ideals of political discipline and political liberty. On the one hand it maintained intact the *imperium* of the chief magistrates in the field of war; and it allowed an adequate power of *coercitio* to the other magistrates, all of whom were entitled to punish disobedience with a summary fine. On the other hand it upheld, and by means of the tribunes enforced, a universal right of appeal to a popular assembly against magisterial sentences; serious criminal cases, and particular those involving death or exile,

normally ended in a popular trial. Roman magistrates refrained from making arrests inside a citizen's domicile, and so far as possible they avoided detentive custody. In consequence – for penal imprisonment was practically unknown in the ancient world – the Roman citizen was in little danger of losing his personal liberty by a magistrate's action.[5] In the middle Roman Republic the writ of habeas corpus ran hard and fast, and the boast *civis Romanus sum* was full of practical significance.

The 'liberty of the subject'

The Comitia of the middle Republic played an effective and essential, if somewhat intermittent, part in the government. With a membership of several thousands they were unfitted to discuss public questions in detail. Unlike Greek popular assemblies (*Ecclesiae*) which met to discuss and vote, the Roman Comitia in fact did not possess the right of debate, but met merely to listen to the directions of the presiding magistrate and then to vote. Any discussion was confined to one or more preliminary public meetings (*contiones*), at which speeches were delivered on the issue to be voted upon in the subsequent Comitia. The speakers, however, were the presiding magistrate and the men whom he called to his tribunal: he could summon any citizen and compel him to speak. Those summoned would normally be well-known men and though the president might throw open the debate to all citizens he was not compelled to do so; thus the ordinary Roman citizen had little chance to express his opinion in words. Since, however, the magistrate often summoned men known to oppose the measure at issue, some freedom of discussion existed, but only at a high level: the average Roman had to be content with his vote.[6] Therefore they never claimed the initiative in bringing forward new measures, but left it to the appropriate magistrate to summon them at his discretion. But in the third century the membership of the Comitia was still drawn for the most part from the yeoman peasants of the neighbouring countryside, who had sufficient economic independence and adequate knowledge of the general outlines of current politics to give an intelligent personal vote. In deciding on peace and war they might be lured to adventurous courses by the prospect of new land allotments after a successful campaign; yet since they took the risks as well as the profits of the fighting they did not cast their vote in the irresponsible spirit of an exempted person. Furthermore, the marshalling of the citizens into centuries or tribes at formal vote-taking assemblies was a partial check upon the play of herd-impulse. But the chief contribution of the Comitia to the success of the Roman government was in the exercise of an independent

The contio

Effectiveness of the Comitia

An open aristocracy

judgment at the yearly elections of magistrates. The electors, it is true, still gave a general preference to the candidates from certain distinguished families with a proud record of public service. Hence the fall of the legal barriers which had excluded plebeians from the higher magistracies did not lead to an immediate inrush of office-holders from the lower order; promotions of new plebeian families to the consulship came by fits and starts rather than in a steady flow. The Licinii and Sextii relapsed into comparative obscurity, and in the next hundred years only some ten plebeian *gentes* (notably the Plautii and the Marcii) definitely established themselves among the ruling houses at Rome.[7] But if the door to the magistracies had not been flung wide open, it now admitted an appreciable number of worthy new entrants. Moreover the new elements which penetrated into the governing circles at Rome were derived not only from the leading plebeian families of the capital, but from the ruling houses of the neighbouring Latin and Italian towns. In the middle Republic Tusculum gave to Rome the Fulvii and the Porcii, and a few Etruscan and Oscan families made their way into the Roman aristocracy. But the successful newcomers were soon absorbed into the reigning oligarchy, so that the earlier exclusiveness of the patricians was now replaced by that of a patricio-plebeian nobility.

Procedure in the Senate

Under the electoral system of the middle Republic, accordingly, the magistracy became fairly representative of the best talent in the Roman state. Furthermore, since a magistracy now conferred almost automatically a seat in the Senate, this body in turn became a reservoir of political ability, and the great majority of its members had received a training in executive responsibility. The procedure at senatorial sessions was little tied down by regulations; but a custom which was seldom infringed prescribed that the presiding official (usually a consul, occasionally a praetor, dictator or tribune) should give the right of speech in accordance with seniority of rank, so that the debates were regularly opened by the *censorii* and passed on from these to the *consulares* and *praetorii*. Consequently the junior grades *(tribunicii, aedilicii* and *quaestorii)* were seldom called upon to speak, for as a general rule the sense of the House had been made sufficiently clear, and a division, if necessary, could safely be taken before their turn arrived.[8] The preponderance which this order of discussion gave to the oldest members tended to make the Senate over-cautious and dilatory. But if the House cultivated no long views and exercised no wide play of imagination, it had a saving sense of what was practically

possible, and in times of crisis it did not shrink from giving a strong lead.

3. The Roman Conquest of Italy

Causes of Roman supremacy

The establishment of Roman supremacy in Italy was an event to which ancient history offers no parallel: in no other case did a city-state acquire a dominion of like extent or of equal stability. The cause of this unique achievement is partly to be sought in the geographical position of Rome, which enabled its military forces to operate on inner lines and to keep its adversaries divided. The story of the wars of the fifth and fourth centuries again and again illustrates the advantage of the Romans in being able to dispose of separate antagonists in detail. The only instances of concerted operations against Rome by enemies on different fronts date from the Second and Third Samnite wars, by which time Roman man-power had grown sufficiently to be a match for any hostile coalition.

Roman man-power

But the Romans owed their success in a less degree to their natural advantages than to their superior warcraft and statecraft. The Roman army which conquered Italy was no more than a city-state militia whose strength lay almost entirely in the heavy infantry of the legions. The mounted men had become little more than scouts and flank-guards; the light infantry were incapable of independent manœuvring; the commanders were not sufficiently trained to attempt combined operations with different arms. The war against Pyrrhus revealed what the encounters with Hannibal subsequently demonstrated with crushing force, that the Roman legions were not yet on a level with armies trained up to the best Greek standards. But in comparison with the other Italian levies the Roman forces had several decisive advantages. The man-power supplied by the largest city of Italy and a densely populated suburban area was utilised to the utmost; and the citizen levies were heavily reinforced with drafts from the allied states (p. 104). The Roman reserves were therefore amply sufficient to repair even such disasters as those of Lautulae and of Heraclea: indeed Pyrrhus's officers complained that the king's victories had no more effect than the cutting off of the Hydra's heads.[9] But Rome's battalions, besides being the biggest of all Italy, were also the best. Unlike most of their adversaries, who regarded warfare half in the nature of a sport, the Romans looked upon it as a business operation, requiring careful preparation and methodical execution. They submitted themselves to a more rigorous drill and a stricter discipline than their neighbours. In the field the

Military discipline

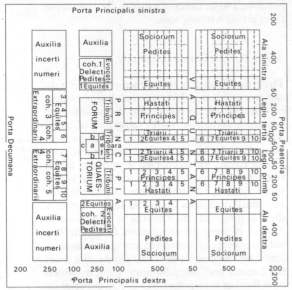

Porta Principalis sinistra

| Auxilia incerti numeri | Auxilia
coh.1
Delecti
Pedites
1 Equites | Sociorum
Pedites

Equites | Sociorum
Pedites

Equites |

Porta Decumana · Extraordinarii · Porta Praetoria · Ala sinistra · Ala dextra · Porta Principalis dextra

PRINCIPALIS · VIA · QUINTANA · VIA · PRAETORIA

FORUM · QUAES-TORIUM · Tribuni · Evocati

Legio tertia · Legio prima

Hastati / Principes / Triarii / Equites / Pedites / Sociorum

5. PLAN OF A ROMAN CAMP, ACCORDING TO POLYBIUS

Scale of Pedes: 0 200 400 600

a. Praetorium   d. Tribunal
b. Praefecti   e. Praesidium
c. Quaestor   f. Augurale

a

b

c

11.1   Alba Fucens, a Latin colony founded in central Italy in 303 B.C. (a) The site within the walls. (b) A corner of the walls. (c) The Via Valeria, running through the town.

imperium of the commander stood unrestricted, and offences such as breaking the ranks in battle or dozing off on sentry duty were visited with the death penalty; misconduct by entire units was occasionally punished by the method of decimation, which entailed the execution of every tenth man (drawn by lot). But the most distinctive feature of Roman warcraft was the application with which it studied the results of its past operations, and its readiness to learn from an enemy, even from a beaten one. The fruit of these continuous experiments appeared in the equipment of the legions, which became the best balanced of all armaments carried by ancient infantry, and in their manipular formation, which was equal to any emergency in a straightforward infantry battle (pp. 84 f.).[10]

As the range of Roman field operations extended to more distant regions, three further instruments of victory were created, the military road, the field camp and the colony. The Via Appia and the Via Latina (a slightly older but less frequented road, which followed the valleys

11.2 The walls of Signia, an early Latin colony; the walls are probably fourth century B.C.

11.3 Air-view of the centre of the Latin colony at Cosa, founded in 273 B.C.

of the Trerus and the Liris) provided two alternative lines of communication with Capua, and became the first strands in a network which eventually covered the whole of Italy. Though less elaborately paved and embanked than the later Roman trunk roads the original Appian and Latin Ways were all-weather routes, which enabled the Romans to throw their forces at any season into Campania or the Samnite borderland. While the roads enhanced the strategic mobility of the Roman troops, the marching camps which they were required to construct at the end of every day in the open field increased their tactical security. The value of these entrenchments was demonstrated after the battle of Asculum, when the prepared position behind the defeated Roman army preserved it from destruction by Pyrrhus's pursuing cavalry. Although the nature of the ground available led to minor variations, camps were laid out according to 'drill-book' pattern: this meant that every man knew beforehand his precise job and the position of his quarters, so that no time was lost in building the camp, a valuable factor when in enemy territory. The layout is described in detail by Polybius (vi. 27 ff.), writing in the second century, while the general accuracy of his account is shown by the excavation of some camps which the Romans built during the wars in Spain (pp. 145 f. and Pl. 14).

Roman roads and camps

Lastly, the *coloniae* consolidated the ground won in battle and prepared for a further advance. These settlements usually consisted of some 4500 to 6000 men, who were in most cases provided jointly by Rome and the Latin cities (*coloniae Latinae*), but in some instances mainly by Rome (*coloniae Romanae*).[11] While the colonies subserved an important object in appeasing the land-hunger of the Roman and Latin peasantry (p. 71), their primary purpose was to guard strategic points such as river-crossings (Fregellae, Interamna), the exits of mountain-passes (Alba Fucens, Ariminum), natural road-centres (Aesernia, Venusia), or convenient landing-places on the coast (Antium, Sena Gallica). Their importance as bases for the penetration of hostile territory, or as outworks to hold up an enemy invasion, was abundantly proved in the Samnite and Pyrrhic wars. By the middle of the third century the network of these fortresses, which at that time numbered some twenty-five or thirty, still showed gaps here and there, but it was spread over the whole of peninsular Italy.[12] Colonies, no less than camps, were laid out with military precision. After a decision had been reached, technically by the people but in practice by the Senate, on the need for a colony of a certain size at a certain place, three commissioners were appointed to

Latin and Roman colonies

Founding a colony

plan and inaugurate the settlement. The land around the urban centre (the *territorium*), which might amount to 50 square miles, was carefully surveyed from a central point (where an instrument called a *groma* was set up). It was then divided into squares of land (*centuriae*), each of some 200 *iugera* (125 acres). This delimitation (or centuriation) was based on two main roads (*decumanus* and *kardo*) which crossed at right-angles and thus formed the basis for a grid-system. The actual allotments assigned to individuals consisted of parts of a *centuria* and varied in size. Some of the outlying colonists would live on their allotments, but many more would live in the town which was built at the centre of the territory. This too was laid out like an army camp. Where the ground permitted it was rectangular, with a gate in each wall and a chess-board street-plan; the public buildings resembled those at Rome: forum, temples, a Curia for the local Senate (*ordo*) and a basilica. The formal pattern, although adapted to local needs, remained standard for centuries: thus, for instance, it is reflected in the symmetrical grid-system in the imperial colony at Timgad in North Africa (p. 470). The foundation of the early colonies, sometimes in partly hostile country, was a semi-military operation: the *coloni* were enrolled in Rome and then marched in military formation under a standard (*vexillum*) to the site, which was marked out by a bronze plough in accordance with Etruscan ritual (*Etrusca disciplina*). The actual building was presumably done by the colonists themselves and would be a task for months if not years; no doubt they slept more soundly at night when the wall had reached a defensible height.

Strong as the Roman army was, it could never have conquered Italy without the continuous co-operation of other Italian peoples. The readiness with which these made common cause with Rome was a tribute alike to the prowess of Roman arms and to the general good reputation of Roman statecraft. The claim made by Romans of a later age, that the wars of their ancestors had been fought in defence of themselves or of their allies,[13] may be accepted as broadly true. Though the land-hunger of the peasantry and the military ambitions of individual leaders undoubtedly influenced Rome's policy, it cannot be said that its conquests were the result of systematic aggression. In some of the early Roman wars the issue hung on some honestly debatable point, such as an uncertain frontier line (as in the earlier Etruscan wars), an ill-defined sphere of influence (in the war against Tarentum), or an elusive question of suzerainty (in the Great Latin War). But a recurrent feature in the campaigns of the fifth

Causes of Rome's wars

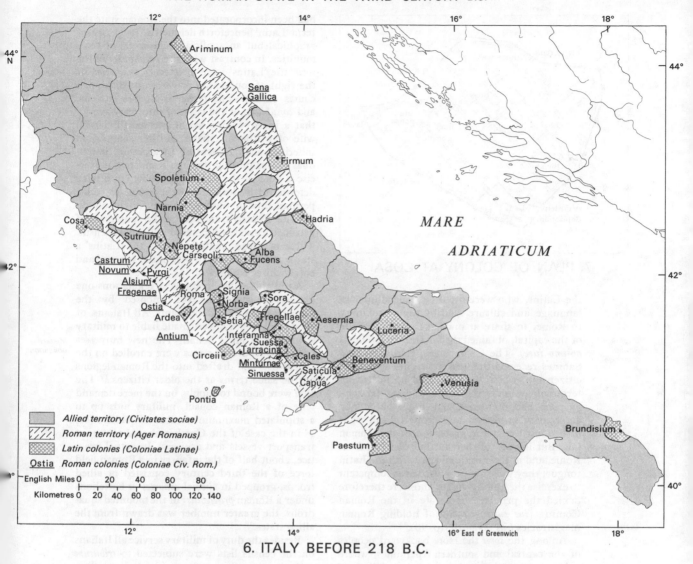

6. ITALY BEFORE 218 B.C.

Allied territory (Civitates sociae)
Roman territory (Ager Romanus)
Latin colonies (Coloniae Latinae)
Ostia Roman colonies (Coloniae Civ. Rom.)

English Miles 0 20 40 60 80
Kilometres 0 20 40 60 80 100 120 140

and fourth centuries was that the Romans fought the battles of the settled and normally pacific populations of Italy against the more roving and predatory ones, or against the alien Celtic nomads. On the whole, therefore, the Romans appeared in the light of protectors rather than of oppressors.

4. The Political Organisation of Italy

In their political settlement of Italy the Romans did not adhere to any hard-and-fast scheme of treatment, but felt their way from case to case by the same empirical method which they had applied to their domestic politics. After the Roman conquest the Italians were divided into two broad classes, those who had been incorporated into the Roman state, and those who were bound to Rome by the looser tie of a treaty. The former category comprised in general the peoples of Latium, of Campania and southern Etruria, and of the Sabine country; the latter contained the more outlying communities in northern Etruria and Umbria, in the Apennine highlands and in the south of Italy. Of the total area of peninsular Italy one-fifth, with a population of about one million inhabitants in the third century, was Roman territory; the *socii*, as the communities bound by treaty were called, numbered about two million souls.[14]

Within either of these main groups there was considerable variety in the status of the individual communities. Among the annexed peoples

Annexation, and association by treaty

103

7. PLAN OF COLONY AT COSA

Degrees of Roman franchise

the Latins, who were fitted by their affinity in language and culture, and by their proximity to Rome, to share at once in the political life of the capital, obtained the full franchise *(civitas optimo iure)*. The Campanians, Etruscans and Sabines received the 'private' rights of Roman citizenship, which were summed up in Roman terminology under the heads of *provocatio, commercium* and *conubium,* and might be defined as security of person and property and right of bequest under the protection of the Roman law. But in view of their further distance from Rome, and of their unfamiliarity with the Latin tongue, they were not yet regarded as competent to exercise the 'public' rights, and were therefore denied the privilege of a vote in the Roman Comitia *(ius suffragii)* and of holding Roman magistracies *(ius honorum)* (p. 90).[15]

Tribal and urban units

Among the *socii* the more backward peoples of the central and southern Apennines, where urban centres of population were still rare, entered into collective treaties with Rome which bound the entire canton (of Marsi, Paeligni, Hirpini, etc.). But wherever city life had developed the Romans made a separate compact with each individual town. The total number of treaties negotiated by the Romans with the *socii* thus rose to 120 or 150.[16]

The nomen Latinum

Within the category of *socii* a hybrid subgroup was constituted under the name of *nomen Latinum.* This 'Latin denomination' consisted of a few of the original Latin communities *(prisci Latini)* which had avoided incorporation after the Great Latin War – notably Praeneste and Tibur – and of the so-called 'Latin colonies' (p. 90), which formed small enclaves of settlers from Rome and the lesser Latin towns in every region of Italy. Since most of the cities of Latium

had been incorporated into the Roman state the term 'Latin' henceforth denoted no longer a geographical but an artificial legal group of communities. In contrast with the remainder of the *socii,* the 'Latins' were granted *commercium,* or the right of conducting private suits in Roman courts on the same terms as Roman citizens, and *conubium,* or the right of intermarriage (so that a Latin woman might become the lawful wife of a Roman citizen and her sons would inherit Roman franchise). In addition, individual Latins passing through Rome might exercise a vote in the Tribal Assembly (in a tribe determined by lot), and if they came to reside permanently in the capital they might obtain the full Roman franchise by the simple act of getting themselves registered at the next census. These privileges conferred upon the 'Latins' a status approximating to that of the annexed and enfranchised Italians.

Privileges of the Latins

Amid this wide diversity of regulations one unvarying condition was imposed by the Romans upon their dependants. All Italians, of whatever category, were made liable to military service on Rome's behalf. The new burgesses of the incorporated states were enrolled on the census lists and drafted into the Roman legions on the same terms as the older citizens.[17] The *socii* were bound to supply, on the mere demand note of a Roman consul, military aids up to a stipulated maximum number of soldiers (or, as in the case of the Greek seaboard towns, of transport vessels and cruisers). In actual practice, about half of the infantry in a Roman field force of the third century consisted of allied troops, grouped in special *cohortes* or battalions under a Roman *praefectus*; of the mounted squadrons, the greater number was drawn from the allied states.[18]

Military obligations

Besides the duty of military service all Italians on the census lists were subjected to *tributum* and all other Roman taxes (the Italian allies, however, remained free from Roman taxation). For the enforcement of the Roman state's demands in men and money, four additional quaestors *(quaestores Italici* or *classici)* were stationed at various points in the annexed territory. For the hearing of the more important lawsuits, both civil and criminal, in the more distant of the incorporated states, the praetor at Rome nominated a number of *praefecti* or deputy-judges, who went on circuit in some of the outlying districts.

Taxation of Roman citizens

In addition to the burden of conscription which they carried the *socii* suffered restrictions in their freedom of intercourse. Since their treaties obliged them 'to have the same friends and enemies as Rome' they were forbidden to enter into political relations with any other state.

Restrictions upon the socii

Limits were also prescribed to their commercial intercourse, though we may doubt whether these prohibitions were effectively enforced.

Apart from the above-mentioned exactions and restrictions the Italian dependants scarcely felt the weight of Rome's arm. The *socii* retained their full rights of local self-government, and their constitutions were left untouched:[19] indeed the Romans had little reason to interfere with the local administrations, for most of the Italian states were ruled by landowning aristocracies whose interests were naturally bound up with those of the Roman governing class. The use of the local dialects and the observance of the traditional cults were not discouraged in any way, and the number of local coinages actually increased under Roman rule.[20] The allied states even remained at liberty to receive as residents persons who had been driven into banishment from Rome: some of these exiles went no farther than Tibur or Praeneste, and were allowed to dwell there unmolested. The *socii* paid no taxes to Rome; they were not placed under the regular supervision of Roman officials; and they were not called upon to accommodate Roman garrisons, except as a special war measure in rare cases.

Self-government of the socii

The incorporated communities, as we have seen (p. 104), received regular visits from the *quaestores Italici* and the praetor's deputies. In a few communities all local magistrates were temporarily abolished as a punishment for rebellion, and the entire administration devolved upon a Roman *praefectus*.[21] But in general the Roman agents supervised rather than supplanted the local governments. In the incorporated towns of Latium municipal aediles, praetors or dictators continued to function. At Capua two annual officials, who retained the Oscan name of *meddix*, carried on the administration in their native dialect. In the so-called 'Roman colonies' (which were reckoned as part of the Roman territory) a rudimentary local administration was set up; and similar arrangements were made for certain lesser settlements of Roman citizens, the *fora* or villages of crofters who took up allotments along the new military roads (probably with obligation to keep these under repair), and the *conciliabula* or hamlets which served as administrative centres for the more scattered settlers on land allotted by *viritane* or isolated assignation. In these smaller communities jurisdiction was partly reserved for itinerant justices appointed by the Roman praetor.

Municipal organisation

On first impression the Roman organisation of Italy would appear to have been vitiated by a fundamental injustice. The dependants of Rome were bound to render military aids, yet

Disability of Rome's dependants

none of them, save a few Latin communities which had received the full Roman franchise, had a voice in determining peace and war. The military obligations of the Italians, it might be argued, entitled them to some measure of representation in the Roman Senate and Comitia, or, better still, in a newly constituted federal parliament. For such a federal congress the Romans could have found ready-made models in Greece; indeed the rudiments of a larger federal body were to be found in such ancient Italian institutions as the Latin and Samnite Leagues. Yet the idea of creating a confederacy to comprise all peninsular Italy does not appear to have been so much as considered in the third century; and in view of the difficulties of communication in the country before the completion of the Roman road system, and of the diversity of Italian dialects, such a scheme would probably have proved impracticable at this stage.

Besides, whatever theoretic disabilities the Italians suffered under the Roman settlement were outweighed by the solid benefits of their association with Rome. In return for military service they shared the fruits of the Roman victories. All alike received their quota of the booty; those who had obtained Roman franchise and the allies of Latin status were entitled to participate in the new colonial settlements. The Roman supremacy gave the Italians such a degree of security as they had never yet possessed, and could never have realised except under Roman leadership. It conferred upon them a triple guarantee against Gallic invasions from the north, against the recrudescence of internecine wars within the peninsula,[22] and against internal revolutions (for the local governing aristocracies could count, in an emergency, on assistance from Rome against domestic insurgents).[23]

Benefits of the Roman supremacy

Security

Again, provided that they discharged the few obligations which the Romans laid upon them the Italians were left substantially free. They were not subjected to jealous supervision, to petty chicanery or to financial exploitation. Lastly, the Italians could look forward to an eventual admission into closer partnership. After the Great Latin War the Romans had set a new example in statesmanship by receiving defeated enemies into their state on equal terms with themselves. In 268 they promoted the Sabines from the status of *cives sine suffragio* to that of full franchise. These acts implied a promise of a wider diffusion of Roman citizenship.

Prospects of enfranchisement

Under these conditions the Roman settlement found general acceptance in Italy, and Roman rule became firmly established. The consequences of Rome's rise to dominion in Italy will

Union of Italy

appear more fully in the following chapters. In securing for their own use the man-power of Italy the Romans acquired an indispensable instrument for their world-conquests. In bringing the congeries of peoples who inhabited the peninsula into one political system they prepared for the birth of an Italian nation which survived the Roman empire and became the pioneer of modern European civilisation.

5. Economic Conditions in Rome and Italy[24]

The momentous political changes which transformed the map of Italy in the fourth century were not accompanied by any corresponding developments in the economic life of the country. The Romans in particular were so much absorbed in their career of conquest that their latent capacity for other occupations was hardly yet drawn out. While their city was becoming a political capital, it lagged behind several of its dependent towns in point of wealth. Such economic progress as Italy experienced in this age was in large measure due to the Greeks in the south of the peninsula and to their Oscan pupils in Campania. An improved breed of wheat *(frumentum)*, which they introduced from overseas, now gradually displaced the native Italic *far*, and baked bread began to supplant the customary dish of porridge. The use of silver or bronze coinage, which became common among the Greeks of Sicily and Italy after 550, spread in the fifth century to Etruria; but it was not until about 300 that any considerable number of Italic communities set up their own mints; in the remoter mountain districts the custom of payment *per aes et libram*, by weighing lumps of copper on a balance, still persisted. Among individual Greek cities Cumae was eclipsed by the Oscan invasion, but Tarentum became the chief trading-place of the peninsula (p. 94). North of the Tiber the Etruscans retained their proficiency in metal and ceramic industry. Their export of bronze work beyond the Alps was interrupted by the Celtic invasions; but their armourers and ironworkers found good markets in Italy, and notably in Rome itself. In Latium the goldsmiths and silversmiths of Praeneste surpassed themselves in the decoration of caskets and mirrors. In the fourth century the potters of Campania and Apulia imitated (with indifferent success) the fine painted vases of Attica; at the same time Capua grew into a centre of bronze manufacture whose wares were exported to Carthage and as far as the Black Sea.

Economic development of Italy

Backward condition of Rome

In the fifth and fourth centuries Roman economy tended to revert to the self-contained stage. The citizen community was almost wholly engaged in agriculture of the traditional subsistence farming type. The ruling families derived their modest wealth from the land; distinguished senators were not too proud to reside on their estates and supervise the farm-work in person, or even to put their own hands to the plough. A solitary casket of incised bronze work, whose inscription proclaims its Roman provenance, is hardly sufficient evidence of a regular bronze industry in the city.[25] The extreme paucity of Greek pottery in Roman tombs after 450 (although the amount began slowly to increase again in the fourth century) suggests that imports into Rome were now being restricted to articles of first necessity, such as grain in seasons of shortage. Among the Greek cities which kept up the overseas trade of Rome Cumae ceased to figure, and Syracuse declined in importance after 350, but Massilia established closer relations with Rome and probably became its chief importing agent. The lack of Roman interest in foreign commerce is plainly betokened by the terms of the fourth-century treaties with Carthage (pp. 55 and 89), in which the integrity of the Latin coast is jealously safeguarded against foreign occupation, but the claims of Carthage to set up a trading monopoly in the western Mediterranean are frankly conceded. The seaboard colonies of Ostia and Antium were intended to protect the coast-lands against military encroachments rather than to open up an overseas trade; at Antium the Roman settlers looked on while the remainder of the native population carried on their practice of piracy.

The tardiness of Rome's economic development is also reflected in the history of its coinage. In early days values were reckoned in terms of oxen and sheep *(pecus,* hence *pecunia,* money) and bronze was weighed out in rough lumps *(aes rude)*; gradually, and more particularly in the north, bronze bars made their appearance, to be followed by rectangular pieces of cast bronze bearing distinctive devices (so-called *aes signatum)*. In 289 B.C. the Romans established *triumviri monetales* to supervise an official mint. This new mint began (or continued) the production of *aes signatum* (which was money but not coinage, since each piece lacked a mark of value and had to be weighed) and also initiated the issue of real coins, circular bronze *asses (aes grave)*, weighing a pound and marked 'I' (one *as*), together with subdivisions of the pound. The earliest libral *as* was probably the one with the heads of Janus and Mercury on its two sides; it was followed by other series, culminating at Rome in the Janus/prow series which remained the normal type of Roman bronze *asses* through-

The first Roman coinage

11.4   Libral bronze *as, c.* 235 B.C. *Obv.* Janus. *Rev.* Prow of ship.

11.5   Early Roman silver, *c.* 269 B.C. *Obv.* Head of Hercules. *Rev.* Wolf and twins.

11.6   Silver *quadrigatus, c.* 235 B.C. *Obv.* Head of young Janus. *Rev.* Quadriga driven by Jupiter, holding a lightning-bolt. ROMA.

11.7   Silver ·*denarius, c.* 211 B.C. *Obv.* Head of Roma. *Rev.* The Dioscuri, Castor and Pollux.

out the republican period. The war against Pyrrhus, which brought Rome into closer contact with southern Italy, where silver coins had long been used by the Greek cities, led her to produce in a southern mint two issues of silver coins, marked ROMANO(RUM) as a war measure which ended with the occupation of Tarentum. Then in 269 the mint officials in Rome produced a silver coinage with the same legend and bearing the types of Hercules/wolf and twins, to be followed during the First Punic War with an issue depicting Roma/Victory (both with corresponding bronze, while the old *aes signatum* gradually disappeared and struck bronze began to replace the cast *aes grave*). Four silver issues, marked ROMA, soon followed (with bronze); the last of these, *c.* 235 B.C., showed a Young Janus/Victory in a chariot (*quadriga*) and became known as a *quadrigatus*; by this time, if not earlier, the Janus/prow *aes grave* bronze type had been adopted. Thus if early Rome was slow to make use of coins, the exigencies of war with Pyrrhus and Carthage led her to a rapid and diverse development of this new medium of exchange, once she had taken the plunge. Roman soldiers on service in southern Italy, and also traders, would benefit; Rome would gain prestige by moving into the circle of states which provided their citizens with this 'civilised' method of exchange.[26]

6. Architecture and Art[27]

In general appearance the city of Rome underwent little change between the end of the regal period and the third century. Wars and internal tensions distracted energies from urban embellishments. One main change came after the Gauls had demolished the city in 390, namely the vast and impressive new wall that *City* girdled it (p. 84), but the rest of the rebuilding *buildings* was haphazard. The poor continued to live in small houses, often of wattle-and-daub, the wealthier families in *domus* of the *atrium* type (pp. 192), but as yet without gardens or peristyles. Apart from the Forum area the town was probably a sprawl of narrow winding unplanned lanes, with perhaps some higher tenement buildings (p. 192) beginning to appear towards the end of this period. The sides of the Forum were flanked by *tabernae*, small shops with open fronts, behind which some of the nobles had town houses. Public utilities were not completely overlooked, as shown by the new aqueduct constructed in 312 by Appius Claudius (p. 79). This Aqua Appia was largely underground and less than a mile in length, but in 272 it was followed by the Anio Vetus, an aqueduct of 40 miles, which brought an excellent supply of water from the Sabine Hills. Also after 350 several new temples were erected from the proceeds of the sale of war-booty, in fulfilment of vows made before battle by victorious Roman commanders.[28] In 338 the consul Maenius built balconies on the upper floors of some of the Forum *tabernae*, whence its life, and especially public ceremonies such as the funeral of the great families, could be observed. Further embellishment followed shortly afterwards when the orators' platform (henceforth Rostra) was decorated with the 'beaks' *(rostra)* of the ships captured from Antium (p. 90).

Town-planning of colonies

Early Rome, as also presumably many another Latin hill-top settlement, had grown largely in a shapeless and unplanned manner. That had been unavoidable, but when the Romans came to make new settlements they could apply their essentially orderly minds to a fresh creation and make use of later Etruscan and Greek ideas of town-planning. Their earliest citizen maritime colony, Ostia, was a rectangular *castrum* with neat ashlar walls which can be dated to the second half of the fourth century. Similar walls survive at other colonies, as Minturnae, Fundi and Pyrgi, and above all at Cosa (273) where they stretch for nearly a mile. So too impressive stretches of wall survive at other towns of this period (Circeii, Signia, Cora, Arpinum, Norba, Aletrium); construction varied, whether ashlar or polygonal, according to the availability of stone rather than according to period. Thus Rome and her allies strengthened themselves against attack, for instance the threats of the Volsci, just as the Etruscan cities had built walls against Rome's advance. Within these cities the streets were generally laid out on a grid-system, so unlike Rome itself, not only when the ground was flat (as at Minturnae), but even as far as possible on a hill site, as Cosa which with its temples and other buildings dramatically reveals to us the order imposed by the founders. At the same time these new colonies had to be bound together with a network of roads; a new start was made when Appius Claudius linked Rome and Capua with a paved way (p. 79), and increasingly in the third century the Romans began to use basaltic lava on massive foundations instead of gravel for their road surfaces: many an impressive stretch of these military ways survives.[29]

Sculpture

Roman sculpture of the early Republic was largely confined to the cult-images in the temples, which were made of terracotta or of stone, according as an Etruscan or a Greek artist was employed. From the later fourth century Rome was brought into direct contact with the later Greek culture of Campania and southern Italy, and many Greek statues reached the city as war-booty. With some of these the Forum was adorned; thus, curiously, statues of Pythagoras and Alcibiades were placed in the Comitium, although a more Roman monument was set up near by in 296, namely a group of the Wolf and the Twins. 'Portraits' of kings and early republican heroes were also set up in this period (they are reflected in some coin-types of the first century B.C.); these were not of course accurate portraits, but were in fact influenced by the contemporary early Hellenistic idealising portraiture. Real portraiture, with 'warts and all', was the product of the second century B.C. onwards, deriving from a combination of this tradition with the early Roman practice of patricians of displaying in their homes and in family funeral parades the wax *imagines* or masks of their ancestors. These were generalised representations rather than literal death-masks, but when this influence fused with the Hellenistic practice realistic individual portraiture was born (p. 194).

Painting

A branch of art in which the Romans showed early interest and promise was fresco-painting (a Greek accomplishment in which the Campanians also were proficient pupils). The pictorial decorations of the temple of Salus, which was dedicated in 303, were believed by later ages to be the handiwork of a Roman nobleman, Fabius 'Pictor'. Another group of frescoes, executed in 272 and 263 to commemorate victories in the Pyrrhic and First Punic Wars, may be regarded as the forerunners of the pictorial sculpture of the first two centuries A.D. Similar historical scenes were of course depicted on the Etruscan wall-paintings of the François tomb at Vulci (p. 42), but only one fragment survives from Rome: some roughly executed war scenes in a fourth-century rock-tomb on the Esquiline in three superimposed registers. Another form of third-century art which does survive is revealed by the coins-types (p. 107), which owe much to Greece. If the *aes grave* appears coarse this is due partly to the nature of the casting process, since the treatment of the heads of deities and the animals depicted is in the Hellenising style. These central-Italian pieces may have been made by local pupils of Greek masters, but the silver issues which Rome produced, both 'Romano-Campanian' and the output of the Roman mint in silver and struck bronze, became increasingly neat and attractive.

Coins

7. Social and Religious Life

The legislation of testamentary bequest by the Twelve Tables, and the growing prevalence of

Slavery

marriage by *usus* (p. 67), introduced slight modifications into the family life of the Romans. But so long as the self-contained economy of the Romans persisted the austerity of their patriarchal custom was scarcely relaxed. The institution of a special tax on manumissions in 357 is evidence that by then the influx of slaves into Rome had attained sufficient proportions to provide an appreciable new revenue. But servile labour as yet played no important part in Roman economy, and it hardly entered into the Roman household. Of the persons reduced to slavery, a considerable number was sold away 'across Tiber' to Etruscan masters.

In the fifth and fourth centuries the outward transformation of Roman state-religion, which had begun under the later kings, was continued under Greek or Etruscan influence. Temples with cult-images continued to replace the rude altars of an earlier age. The ritual of the Etruscan *haruspices* (p. 24) was summoned to reinforce the augural lore, and sons of Roman noblemen were sent to Tuscany to study the *disciplina Etrusca* in matters of religion. In 264 a member of a rising plebeian house, D. Iunius

Influence of Etruscan and of Greek religion

Brutus, introduced into Rome the Etruscan and Campanian custom of exhibiting gladiatorial contests at the obsequies of an important personage. Greek influence is evident in the institution of state cults of Ceres (p. 65), of Castor and Pollux and of Hercules, all of which were derived directly, or through the mediation of other Latin cities,[27] from Hellenic prototypes, and of Aesculapius, who was imported in 293 from the Greek homeland to stay a pestilence. The reception of most of these worships was made in deference to the 'Sibylline books', a collection

The 'Sibylline books'

of oracles which had been brought to Rome under the last Tarquin, or perhaps in the early days of the Republic, and had been placed under the special care of a new body of priests, the *duoviri sacris faciundis*, who consulted the prophecies at the Senate's direction on the occasion of unusual religious portents. They were responsible for introducing many new Greek cults, particularly to distract public attention at times of difficulty. Thus in 496 during a famine they recommended the introduction of the cult of Liber, Libera and Ceres, and in 433 during a plague the foundation of a temple of Apollo, while during the crisis of the war against Veii in 399 they advised that the *pax deorum* (the right relation with the gods) could be restored only by introducing a new ritual whereby statues of six gods reclining on couches at meals were displayed *(lectisternia)*, i.e. the gods were invited to partake in a sacrificial feast. The ceremony was of Greek origin, but may have come more immediately from Etruria (Caere?). The

patrician *duoviri*, increased to ten in 367 when half were plebeians, continued to supervise all foreign cults, especially the *Graecus ritus*.

But the ancient Italic religion of the home and of the fields and flocks remained wholly untouched by these exotic influences. Besides, the introduction of foreign usages into the Roman state cults was carefully supervised. While the ruling families at Rome were willing to admit that foreign deities deserved a welcome for favours which they alone, or they best, could bestow, they admitted them only on condition of their allaying rather than exciting popular emotion; cults and beliefs which savoured of *superstitio* or primitive self-abandonment were jealously kept out of bounds. It is significant that when the Sibylline oracles were brought to Rome they were confided to the keeping of a responsible board of officials, and that the pontifices were at pains to prevent the circulation of private collections of prophecies. Under such conditions ceremonies might be multiplied and rituals elaborated, yet no new ferment of a more imaginative and exacting religion was allowed to disturb the mental composure of the Roman people.

Control by the Pontifices

A dignified national pride was also encouraged by two occasional public ceremonies: triumphs and the funerals of illustrious men. The elaboration of triumphal processions under the Etruscan kings has already been mentioned (p. 51). In later times this honour was granted to certain victorious generals (qualification included at least 5000 enemy dead). In the procession the *triumphator* and his army were accompanied by the magistrates and senators, together with the spoils of war, sacrificial animals, musicians and others. Starting from the Campus Martius they passed through the Forum Boarium, circled the Palatine, proceeded through the Forum along the Sacred Way and so ascended the Capitol where the general offered thanks and sacrifice to Jupiter Optimus Maximus. During this mixture of religious and military ceremony Rome made holiday: the temples were thronged, incense smoked on every altar, and flowers adorned all the shrines. More solemn spectacles were provided by the funerals of men of state. The body was carried in procession to the Forum, followed by members of his family and by a procession in chariots of men who impersonated the dead man's illustrious ancestors; they wore these men's *imagines* (which were normally kept in the *tablinum* of the family home: p. 108) and also the robes and insignia of office appropriate to the rank of the ancestor each represented. On arriving at the Rostra the corpse was set upright for all to see, and the 'ancestors' sat on ivory

Triumphs and funerals

thrones; then the son or another relative delivered a funeral oration in praise of the dead man and each of his ancestors. By this means every generation was reminded of the glorious exploits of earlier days, and the practice impressed the Greek Polybius not only as extraordinarily striking but also as an inspiration for the younger generation to emulate the past. Thus was preserved the *mos maiorum*.

8. Early Roman Literature[31]

Funda-
mental
merits of
the Latin
language

The distrust of exuberance in emotion which cramped the development of Roman religion also delayed the birth of a Latin literature. Yet the materials for such a literature lay close at hand. Like all Indo-European tongues, the Latin language was equipped with a rich apparatus of inflexions which made it into a suitable vehicle for a free and varied expression of mental life. In the fourth century the Romans, endowed with a finer ear than their Etruscan or Oscan neighbours, began to smooth down the asperities of their consonantal system and to differentiate more sharply their vowel-sounds. Their native capacity for terse and accurate formulation of legal concepts was already revealed in the code of the Twelve Tables.

The germs of a national Roman literature may be found in the ballads sung at the banquets of Roman nobles (p. 60), in the epitaphs

inscribed on the tombs of notable men,[32] and in the *tabulae pontificum* (p. 59). Here were the starting-points of Roman epic and history. For a Roman drama no rudiments existed as yet, save in the *versus Fescennini*, the rough improvised banter which was exchanged at harvest festivals, at weddings and triumphs,[33] and was sometimes cast into the form of the so-called 'Saturnian' metre, with a ponderous accent-rhythm like that of Anglo-Saxon poetry. But the foundations of a dramatic literature had been laid among Rome's neighbours. In 364 trained Etruscan actors performed at a Roman public festival.[34] Before the end of the fourth century the Romans had imported from Campania the charades known as *fabulae Atellanae*, in which stock characters such as Maccus, the clown, Bucco, the fool, and Dossennus, probably the sharp-witted hunch-back, the prototype of Pulcinello and of Punch, were presented by masked players. From these beginnings it was a comparatively short step to Roman drama and satire.

Early
Italian
drama

Lastly, the growing importance of the popular assemblies in the fourth century gave increasing scope to the art of the public speaker. The speeches of the censor Appius Claudius were deemed worthy of preservation and still found readers in the days of Cicero. The emergence of a Latin literature was a slow process; yet by the fourth century the Romans had given some indication that in a future day their pen would be as good as their sword.

Roman
oratory

PART III

The Conquest of the Mediterranean

CHAPTER 12

The First Punic War and the Conquest of North Italy

1. Sources of Information

The sources of Roman history become more plentiful

The year 264, which marks the beginning of Rome's overseas conquests, may also be taken as the point at which Roman history emerges from shadow-land into daylight. By this time documentary materials for the writing of history had begun to accumulate (pp. 57 ff.), and the earliest Roman annalists, writing at the end of the third century, could obtain information about the First Punic War from actual eye-witnesses.

Of our surviving sources of information for the period 264–133, which constitutes the main stage in Rome's career of foreign conquest, the Greek historian Polybius and the Roman annalist Livy have a special claim on our notice. Polybius was a leading politician of the Achaean League who incurred the suspicions of the Romans during their wars in Greece and suffered deportation to Italy in 167 (p. 160). By a rare piece of good fortune he made the acquaintance of Scipio Aemilianus, the most notable Roman general of his day, and became his friend and travelling-companion. The insight which he was thus able to obtain into Roman warcraft and statecraft compelled him to acknowledge that the nascent Roman Empire had come to stay. By way of driving this unpalatable but necessary truth home to his countrymen he wrote a general political history of the Mediterranean lands from 264 to his own time, tracing out their coalescence into a single political unit under Roman control; a universal history, he believed, could now for the first time be attempted, thanks to the unity which Rome had introduced into world affairs. This work,

Polybius

of which considerable portions have been preserved, is our principal authority for the middle period of the Republic.[1] For the years 220–167 we also possess an unbroken account from Livy (books xxi–xlv). In these books Livy fulfilled most successfully what he regarded as his chief task, which was not so much to construct a minutely exact record of the march of past events as to provide living and inspiring exemplars of Roman courage, constancy and fair dealing. It is through Livy's work that the spirit of the heroic age of Roman history may best be appreciated.[2]

Livy

2. The Carthaginian State[3]

After the conquest of peninsular Italy the Romans possessed as much land as they could cultivate effectively, and as large a circle of dependants as they could conveniently control with their existing machinery of government. Their interest in overseas trade, which to them was an accidental result of conquest rather than its antecedent object, had scarcely yet been awakened. Yet they had hardly completed the subjugation of the Italian peninsula when they launched out into an endless succession of overseas adventures.

Early commencement of Rome's foreign conquests

Rome's first antagonist outside Italy was the city of Carthage. Founded early in the eighth century by Phoenicians from Tyre, in a commanding position at a meeting-point of Mediterranean trade-routes, Carthage was marked out by nature to be a centre of commerce.[4] But it won its place in world history by its political

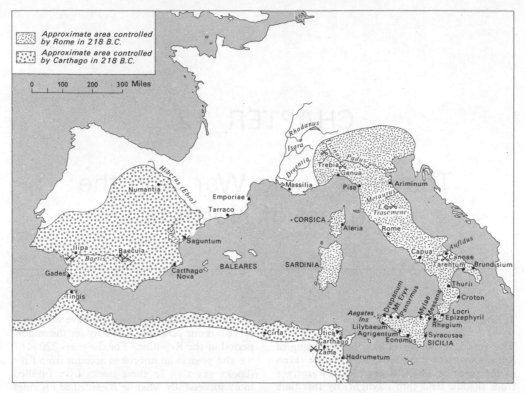

8. THE PUNIC WARS

12.1   The site of Carthage; view taken from the Byrsa hill, looking over the ancient harbours and across the Gulf of Tunis.

Trade wars between Greeks and Carthaginians

and military aptitudes, in which it excelled all other Phoenician cities. About 600 it took the lead among the Semitic communities of the western Mediterranean in their secular warfare against rival traders and colonists from the Greek lands. In a series of wars lasting over three centuries the Carthaginians succeeded in ejecting the Greeks from the greater part of the Spanish coasts, and in reducing their hold upon the islands of the western Mediterranean to a precarious tenancy of the eastern part of Sicily.[5]

At the time of their first clash with the Romans the Carthaginians had acquired an empire comprising the coastlands of North Africa, of southern Spain, of Sardinia and Corsica, and of western Sicily. Their city was the largest and richest in the western Mediterranean.[6] Its wealth was not derived primarily from agriculture. Though the Carthaginian or, to use the common Roman term, the 'Punic' aristocracy took pride in the highly farmed estates which it had laid out in the fertile valley of the Bagradas (mod. Medjerda), the cultivation of the interior was left in the hands of the native Libyans, who had to pay a high taxation, perhaps a quarter of their crops.[7] Though the Carthaginians showed the usual Phoenician aptitude for textile manufactures and purple-dyeing, they lagged behind the Greeks in general industrial proficiency; their ceramic and bronze ware was mass-produced so that good-quality ware was largely imported from Greece or (since the fourth cen-

Carthaginian commerce

12.2   Carthage; walls in foreground and siege bullet.

tury) from Campania. Punic commerce was also restricted to a definite sphere; it scarcely penetrated the interior of continents, and its ramifications in the Levantine seas were limited.[8] But it acquired a virtual monopoly in the western Mediterranean and the Atlantic. In the fifth century Punic explorers opened up a lucrative traffic in Cornish tin, and in gold and ivory from West Africa.[9] By this time Carthage had become the general *entrepôt* for the metal trade of the West. Additional revenues accrued to Carthage from the contributions levied upon the vassal Phoenician cities in the western Mediterranean, and from the rents imposed upon the Libyans of the Punic hinterland.

The Carthaginian army and fleet

On these ample resources the Carthaginians built up a military establishment which proved a match for all comers until they met the Romans. The war fleet, on which the citizens presumably gave personal service,[10] was equipped and navigated by expert shipwrights and seamen; in the third century it had definitely wrested the control of the western seas from Syracuse and Tarentum. The foreign-service armies of Carthage after the fourth century contained hardly any citizen troops, but were recruited from a medley of conscripts from the African hinterland, of auxiliary contingents hired from the chieftains of the free native states of Numidia (mod. Algeria), and of mercenaries swept together from all corners of the western Mediterranean. Such heterogeneous collections of men were naturally not easy to keep in hand, and they had performed but indifferently in the warfare against the Greek cities of Sicily. But the command of these forces was held by officers who made a special profession of military service, and so gained a wider experience than the annually changing Roman consuls.

The Carthaginian government

The Carthaginian government was an oligarchy of wealthy merchants, which has been aptly compared with the aristocracy of medieval Venice. The chief magistrates were two shophets (Latin *suffetes*), who were elected annually on a basis of birth and wealth; they did not hold military commands, which were in the hands of separately elected generals. The effective organs of administration were a senate with an inner council of thirty leading nobles, and a high court of 104 judges, also drawn from the ruling families. The aristocracy humoured the commons to the extent of consulting them on highly important or debatable questions, of buying from them the principal offices of state, and of leaving in their hands the petty charges and perquisites. At the same time it kept a jealous eye on its professional generals, and took ample precautions against attempts at military revolutions. The stability of the Carthaginian constitu-

tion was much admired by Aristotle, Cicero and other writers.

Tenacious but cautious foreign policy

In its foreign relations the Punic government pursued the same tenacious but cautious policy by which the Venetian republic built up its empire. Though it never scrupled, if necessary, to defend its mercantile interests by force of arms, it none the less avoided war where peaceful methods availed, and it never resorted to hostilities without some definite gain in view. In Africa it annexed no more than a portion of Tunisia and Tripoli, embracing in all some 20,000 square miles. In its relations with the Italian states (where its trade connexions were not extensive) it relied upon diplomacy to remove in advance the causes of a possible clash. In the sixth century it had come to amicable terms with the Etruscan seaboard towns. As soon as the Romans acquired an extensive sea-front along the Latin coast, it offered them successive treaties (pp. 55, 58). In 279 it supplemented these pacts with a military alliance against Pyrrhus, and, although neither party actually gave armed support to the other, it is not unlikely that the Romans drew a subsidy in money from their confederates (p. 95).

Early relations with Rome

In spite of these friendly overtures the Romans harboured a suspicion that the Carthaginians might seek to control the Italian coasts in the same manner as they dominated the seaboard of Spain and Sicily. In each of their treaties they had stipulated that the Carthaginians must not take any permanent foothold on Italian soil. Between 350 and 270 they had established a chain of coastguard colonies from Etruria to Campania: Roman colonies at Ostia, Antium, Tarracina, Minturnae and Sinuessa, and Latin colonies at Paestum and Cosa (p. 96). In 311 they had commissioned a flotilla of cruisers to patrol the Italian coast (p. 92), and in 267 they had specially charged the new *quaestores Italici* or *classici* with the supervision of naval defences.[11] Nevertheless as late as 264 a clash between Rome and Carthage was nothing more than a remote contingency. It required a very peculiar concatenation of aggravating circumstances to bring about the First Punic War.

3. The Affair of Messana

By a not unnatural yet fatal oversight no attempt had been made in the afore-mentioned treaties to define exactly the respective spheres of the contracting parties in Sicily, where the Romans as yet had no important interest, political or commercial. Because of this gap in the covenant an unforeseen situation arose at Messana, a city whose commanding position on the straits that carry its name had made it into a long-standing object of contention between Carthaginians and Greeks. In 264 Messana was suddenly thrown into the political market.[12] Since *c.* 288 it had been in the hands of a corps of discharged Campanian mercenaries who went by the name of 'Mamertines' (sons of Mars). Some twenty-four years later it was put under *siege by king Hiero of Syracuse, the most power-* ful of the remaining Greek states on the island.

Messana besieged by Hiero of Syracuse

The capture of Messana by Hiero would probably have entailed the wholesale execution of the garrison, for the Mamertines were no better than a Grand Catalan Company who lived by systematically plundering or blackmailing the rest of Sicily. In this extremity the Mamertines accepted an offer of help from an expectant Punic flotilla, whose admiral thereupon induced Hiero to call off his attack. But as soon as they were rid of Hiero, they cast about for means of ushering out their Carthaginian guest, who was outstaying his welcome, and resolved to offer themselves as allies to the Romans, upon whom they could make a claim on the ground of common race. In extricating themselves from their scrape the Campanian adventurers contrived to set Romans and Carthaginians by the ears.

Invocation of Carthage and of Rome

Roman policy

The appeal of the Mamertines raised substantially the same issue at Rome as the call for help from the Campanians of Capua in 343 (p. 88), except that this time the appellants lived outside Italy. Were they to assume new and possibly indefinite obligations by taking sides in a dispute that did not concern them directly? On the one hand the acquisition of Messana by the Carthaginians would furnish them with a potential base for attack upon Italy, and their presence in that city could not be simply ignored. Further, such an advanced post might threaten the commercial interests of Rome's Greek allies in southern Italy. On the other, to say nothing of the disreputable character of the appellants,[13] it was to be feared that a Roman intervention in Sicily might be resented by the Carthaginians as a trespass upon their preserves, and thus might lead on to a war for which there was otherwise no clear warrant.[14] In the Senate opinions were so evenly balanced that it weakly referred the matter to the Comitia without any positive recommendation.[15] The voters in the popular assembly, who still felt the need of rest after the great effort of the Pyrrhic war, showed equal hesitation at first, but were eventually won over to action by the presiding consuls, who represented to the commons that an expedition to Sicily might bring in large 'benefits', i.e. military reputations for the commanders and booty for the troops. The Comitia, it is true,

at first went no further than to order a relief expedition to Messana, and the Roman detachment which was sent to carry out these instructions fulfilled them without any shedding of blood, for the Punic commander lost his nerve at the unexpected appearance of the Romans and tamely withdrew from the city. But the Carthaginian government had no intention of being bluffed in this fashion out of its claims upon Messana. It forthwith sent an expeditionary force to recover the lost prize, and it succeeded in bringing Hiero back into the field, this time against the Roman interlopers. On the other hand the Senate reinforced the small corps of occupation with a consular army. Thus the scuffle round Messana drew on the Romans and Carthaginians into formal war.

Roman intervention in Messana and collision with the Carthaginians

For this drift into hostilities both parties may be considered equally responsible. Had either of them, instead of attempting to steal a march upon the other, made an offer of fresh negotiations a durable compromise should not have been difficult to arrange. An agreement by which the Carthaginians kept Messana but conceded the freedom of the Straits to Rome and Syracuse and their allies might have offered a fair basis for a lasting peace.[16] On the other hand both parties may be acquitted of using the affair of Messana as a pretext for a predetermined war. The collision which brought on the First Punic War was wholly accidental.

Responsibility for the war

4. The Growth of Roman War-aims

Before the Roman reinforcements could reach Messana the city had been placed under siege by two separate forces from Carthage and from Syracuse. On his arrival the consul Appius Claudius had no difficulty in driving a wedge between these unaccustomed and somewhat mistrustful allies, who presently withdrew their troops in different directions. In thus making sure of Messana the Romans attained their original war object. But they were lured on by their first easy success to an ill-judged offensive against Hiero. In 263 a strong Roman army under the consul Manius Valerius invaded the king's territory and drew lines of siege round Syracuse. Faced by the immensely strong fortifications of the city, against which more than one Punic army had dashed itself to pieces, Valerius's attack was bound to fail. But the consul made amends for his military error by a notable diplomatic success in detaching Hiero from his unnatural alliance with Carthage. In return for a small indemnity Hiero was left in possession of a narrow but fertile and populous territory in eastern Sicily, extending from Cape

The Romans come to terms with Hiero

Passaro to the neighbourhood of Mt Etna, and was admitted to an alliance on equal terms with Rome.[17]

With Messana in their hands and the king of Syracuse on their side the Romans had completely cut off the Carthaginians from the Straits. Nevertheless the Punic government made a second and greater attempt to make good its losses. It prepared to throw a new army of more than 50,000 men across to Sicily, using as its base the Greek city of Agrigentum on the south coast, with which it had a long-standing mercantile connexion. To stifle this Carthaginian counter-attack the Romans in 262 advanced across the whole breadth of the island and put Agrigentum under siege. After a hard-fought campaign during which the investing army was in its turn half blockaded by the Punic reinforcements, they stormed and sacked the city. By this feat of arms they so overawed the Carthaginian leaders that these never again ventured to engage Roman armies in set battle. At the same time they satisfied themselves that it lay in their power to expel the Carthaginians from Sicily altogether. The capture of Agrigentum was therefore a turning-point in the First Punic War. Henceforth the Romans frankly allowed their policy to be dictated by military ambitions, and in this spirit they set themselves new war objects which in 264 had been far from their minds.[18]

The siege of Agrigentum

The decision of the Romans to conquer the whole of Sicily cost them twenty years of further warfare. An indecisive campaign of small successes and reverses in 261 made them realise that a long war of exhaustion lay before them, unless they could supplement their land operations by naval action. At this time the Carthaginian battle-fleet consisted of some 120 quinqueremes, galleys propelled by fifty or more large oars, each of which was worked by five rowers, and containing a complement of 120 marines. Against these the Romans had nothing to hand save a few cruisers, and the naval contingents which they could exact from Tarentum and the other coastal towns of Italy by the terms of their treaties were quite inconsiderable. But they now resolved to build and to man out of their own resources a fleet of quinqueremes slightly outnumbering that of Carthage.[19] The challenge which they threw out to the more practised Punic navy was not quite so foolhardy as might appear at first sight. In ancient naval warfare the advantage of superior manœuvring power was severely limited by the lack of efficient artillery, in the absence of which the final decision could only be won by ramming or boarding. Every ancient sea-fight therefore tended to resolve itself into a land-battle on

The Romans prepare a war-fleet

planks, in which the marines rather than the rowers settled the issue. It was nothing unprecedented that a land-power should take to naval warfare: at that very moment a king of Macedon was improvising a fleet with which he drove the more experienced Egyptian navy out of the Aegean Sea. None the less the Romans had reason to look back with pride upon their quick decision to become a naval power.

In 260 the completed Roman battle-fleet, some 140 strong, fell in with a Punic squadron of 130 ships off the north coast of Sicily near Mylae. The Carthaginians, thinking to make an easy prey of the Italian landlubbers, rushed in pell-mell upon them, only to find themselves held fast by newly invented boarding-bridges or grappling-irons (*corvi*) and involved in a hand-to-hand tussle on unfavourable terms.[20] In the end they broke away with a loss of fifty vessels. The action of Mylae, for which the Romans rewarded their admiral, C. Duillius, with a commemorative column in the Forum,[21] gave them the command of the Sicilian waters for several years to come, for the Punic government, with unaccountable supineness, made no immediate attempt to recover its naval ascendancy. On the other hand the Romans, somewhat bewildered by the completeness of their victory, wasted it in operations, not altogether unsuccessful, but wholly indecisive, against the Carthaginian colonies in Corsica and Sardinia (259). In the meantime the Roman land forces in Sicily had carried all the towns in the centre of the island, but had not come within reach of the three main Punic strongholds at Panormus (mod. Palermo), Drepana (Trapani) and Lilybaeum (Marsala).

Battle of Mylae

5. The Invasion of Africa

In 256–255 the end of the war drew within sight, but was again lost to view. Having learnt the futility of striking at the wings of the Carthaginian empire, the Romans prepared to deliver a blow at its heart. Some fifty years previously a despot of Syracuse named Agathocles had defended himself against the Carthaginians by invading Africa, and had all but succeeded in reducing Carthage itself (310–306). With the object-lesson before them, the consuls Atilius Regulus and Manlius Vulso set out for Africa in 256 with a fleet raised to 230 galleys. Near Cape Ecnomus, off the south coast of Sicily, they fell in with the Carthaginians, who had made a belated effort under the threat of invasion and brought their numbers almost to the level of the Romans. In this encounter the Punic admirals experimented with a plan which Hannibal and Scipio subsequently carried out with

Battle of Cape Ecnomus

success in the land-battles of the Second Punic War. While the Carthaginian centre drew on the Romans by a feigned retreat, they prepared an enveloping movement on both flanks. The Roman centre actually went into the trap; but the wings held up the enclosing attacks of the enemy by resolute grappling and boarding, and the centre, after extricating itself by a clean break-through, returned to the original scene of action, where it crumpled up the Punic left wing against the coast.[22]

The battle of Ecnomus, the hardest-fought of ancient naval actions in western waters, gave the Romans an unopposed landing in Africa. Here Atilius Regulus, who had been detailed with a mere 15,000 men to hold a base for next year's offensive, gained such rapid successes against the hastily levied Punic militia that he was emboldened to advance his winter quarters within one day's march of Carthage. The campaign of 256 had virtually won Sicily for the Romans, as the Carthaginians, beaten out of the field and distracted by a native rising in their hinterland, entered into peace negotiations with Regulus. The latter, however, by laying down conditions (including the evacuation of Sicily) such as only an utterly defenceless enemy could have accepted, goaded the Carthaginians into a characteristic rally at the eleventh hour. With the assistance of a Spartan *condottiere* named Xanthippus they equipped and drilled their home-defence force according to the best Greek methods, and in the spring of 255 they brought Regulus to battle in the valley of the Bagradas. In this action Xanthippus rehearsed Hannibal's tactics at Cannae. Pinning down the Roman centre with his infantry and elephants, he enveloped both their wings with his horsemen. The invading army was virtually destroyed, and their commander was taken prisoner. A counter-attack which the Carthaginians made with their refitted fleet was less fortunate, for in an action off Cape Hermaeum against the Roman navy they sustained losses which crippled their sea-power for the next five years. But the victorious Roman fleet, which had come to reinforce Regulus for his second campaign in Africa, could do nothing further than pick up the survivors of the land campaign and transport them back to Italy. On the way home, moreover, it was caught in a storm, in which more than 250 vessels (including some 100 captured Carthaginian ships) foundered, and was reduced to a mere eighty sail.

6. Later Operations in Sicily

At the end of 255 the Romans seemed no nearer success than before Mylae. But they had by now

grasped the importance of sea-power so firmly that by another effort, surpassing all their previous exertions, they forthwith replaced all the lost ships. The reconstructed fleet, however, instead of being used to convoy fresh expeditions to Africa, was directed to co-operate with the army in Sicily for an attack upon the remaining Carthaginian fortresses. The first-fruits of this amended policy were gathered in 254, when the city of Panormus was carried in a joint assault, which found a weak point in the defences on the sea front. In spite of this success the Romans contented themselves in 253 with a raiding expedition to the coast of Tripoli which yielded no other result than further casualties by storm. For the first time in the war the Romans faltered, and two uneventful years passed, in which each side waited upon the other. In 250 at last a Carthaginian commander, with a sudden flash of enterprise, attempted to recover Panormus, but in a battle outside the gates he was heavily defeated and lost the whole of his elephant corps.[23] This victory so reassured the Romans that in the following year they resumed their offensive against the Punic strongholds in western Sicily. Their attack upon Lilybaeum was their first notable attempt at scientific siege-craft (in which the officers of King Hiero no doubt gave them the necessary lessons). But even with Greek aid they failed against the superior resourcefulness of the defenders.

The danger to Lilybaeum, moreover, roused the Carthaginians to refit their long-neglected fleet and to put their superior seamanship to better use. In 249 the consul Claudius Pulcher, who was stationed with 120 sail off Lilybaeum, made a dash into the port of Drepana, where the new enemy squadrons were being concentrated; but the Punic commander, Adherbal, with rare presence of mind defiled out of the harbour, and drove ashore Claudius's ships as they doubled back in pursuit, capturing most of them.[24] A few days later the other division of the Roman fleet, under the consul Iunius Pullus, was herded by the Carthaginian admiral Carthalo towards the coast by Cape Passaro and left to be destroyed by a rising south-westerly gale, while the Punic ships doubled round the headland into sheltered water. By land, however, Iunius then managed to seize the city of Eryx and the temple of Aphrodite on the mountain behind Drepana, thus commanding all roads leading to the city. But after the two successes of the Carthaginians by sea, which left Rome virtually without a navy, they negotiated with their adversaries about an exchange of prisoners; if they went further and sounded the Romans about possible peace negotiations, nothing came of it.[25] But the Romans were wil-

12.3   Mount Eryx in western Sicily, important in the later stages of the First Punic War.

ling to recognise a *de facto* armistice, since they had for the time being reached the limits of their man-power and financial strength.

From 248 to 242 the Carthaginians obtained one last lease of naval power and ample leisure to prepare a decisive counter-attack upon their exhausted adversary. In 247 they conferred the chief command in Sicily upon a young officer named Hamilcar Barca, who subsequently won fame as an attacking general. Hamilcar made *Hamilcar* several raids upon the Italian seaboard, which *Barca's* obliged the Romans to establish some more pro- *guerrilla* tective colonies; among these coastguard *attack* stations Brundisium presently grew into a commercial port and eclipsed its neighbour Tarentum. In Sicily Hamilcar seized in succession two natural strongholds, Mt Hercte near Panormus,[26] and Mt Eryx by Drepana, from which he conducted a successful guerrilla attack against the Romans, so as to relax their hold upon the besieged towns in the west of the island. But he was not supplied with sufficient troops to attempt a decision in set battle, nor with enough ships to venture a descent in force upon Italy.

By 242 the Romans had nursed their resources to the point of recovering the initiative. With the help of a forced loan upon its own members, and of a special call for materials upon the arsenals of the Etruscan cities, the Senate contrived to fit out 200 new lighter galleys to complete the investment of Drepana and Lilybaeum. By a crowning example of false economy the Carthaginians had in the meantime laid up their ships and dispersed their crews. Unable to reorganise their navy in time to save the fortresses, they hurried out a relief fleet which was little better than a scratch force. Against this ill-found armada the Roman admiral, Lutatius Catulus, fought the last action of the war near the Aegates Islands off Drepana, *The battle* gaining a victory as complete as it was easy *of the* (March 241). With Lilybaeum and Drepana *Islands'* now past all hope of rescue, and the way open for a new invasion of Africa by the Romans, the Punic government accepted peace on the enemy's terms. The terms proposed by Lutatius on the spot seemed too lenient to the Roman Comitia, which tightened them up and increased the proposed indemnity: the Roman people had not declared war from aggressively imperialistic motives, but in making peace they were determined to secure adequate compensation for their losses. The Punic government was forced to abandon all claims to Sicily and undertook to pay a substantial indemnity (3200 Euboic talents = 1600 cwt of silver) within ten years. Thus Rome's war-effort resulted in the acquisition of an annual revenue, an overseas province, Sicily, which marked the first step in the creation of a Mediterranean empire,[27] and finally a navy which dominated the western seas.

7. The First Punic War. Conclusion

The First Punic War was a conflict of giants, during which each side repeatedly sent armies of 50,000 and fleets of 70,000 or more men into action. Its long duration may be explained by the fact that the Carthaginians deliberately tried to convert it into a war of exhaustion, while the Romans endeavoured to force the issue, but were continually held in check. For their setbacks the Romans were themselves largely responsible. The effect of their early naval victories was nullified by Regulus's over-confidence and by the Senate's premature despair in the invasion of Africa. In the later stages of the war successive Roman admirals threw away their fleets through faulty seamanship, so that the total losses of the winners in ships (not less than 600) and seamen exceeded those of the losers. But the failures of the Romans were more than made good by their abundant man-power (the fruit of their successful organisation of Italy), by their nerve in capturing and recapturing the initiative, and by their readiness to learn the enemy's game in order to beat him at it. On the other hand, the continual economy of effort on the side of the Carthaginians both delayed their defeat and made it certain in the end. Their policy of half-measures was correctly imputed by their adversaries to their mercantile habit of 'peddling' war (as Ennius put it) and of weighing gains and costs too nicely. But it must be borne in mind that their lack of trustworthy man-power obliged them to limit their risks, while the Romans could afford to pile loss upon loss.

Causes of the Roman victory

The effect of the Roman victory was to draw the Republic irrevocably into the wider field of Mediterranean politics.[18] It opened the eyes of the Romans to those profits of empire on which the Carthaginians had long fixed their gaze, and it gave them a nearer acquaintance with that Hellenic culture of which Syracuse was the most brilliant exponent in the western Mediterranean.

8. The Seizure of Sardinia and Corsica

The settlement of 241 was put to the test in the very next year when the mercenaries whom Hamilcar had brought back to Africa to be paid off broke into open mutiny over a quarrel about

The mutiny of the Punic mercenaries

their wages and fomented an insurrection among the Libyan natives.[29] The Carthaginians, taken unawares, were virtually placed under siege, and they could not have extricated themselves without reinforcements of fresh mercenary troops from overseas, for which they were dependent upon Roman goodwill. In the first instance the Romans gave them every facility (possibly even to hire new forces in Italy), and they refused an offer from the disloyal Punic garrison of mercenaries in Sardinia to hand over that island to their keeping. But in 238 a sudden turn of fortune in Africa, where, after long hesitations, Hamilcar was given the chief command and completely restored Carthaginian sovereignty, caused a brusque change of attitude in Rome. In the same year a second overture from the Punic mercenaries in Sardinia, who had exposed themselves to attacks by the natives of the island, was accepted by the Romans, who sent a force to occupy the Carthaginian stations on the south-western coast. Heaping insult upon injury, the Romans met a protest from Carthage with a declaration of war and refused an offer of arbitration.[30] For the moment the Carthaginians had no option but to submit to the Roman conditions of peace, which required them not only to abandon their claims upon Sardinia, but to surrender Corsica and to pay an additional indemnity (1700 talents). The motive of the Romans in grabbing Sardinia and Corsica is not altogether clear. The strategic value of these islands was as slight as that of Sicily was great, and their natural resources — which in the case of Sardinia at least were considerable — were never fully developed by them. Their sharp practice may have been inspired by a false calculation of future profits, but its main object, no doubt, was to take precautions against a change of Carthaginian policy under the influence of Hamilcar. In any case, the seizure of the two islands completely belied Rome's reputation for fair dealing, and it fostered rather than stifled the spirit of revenge at Carthage.[21]

The Romans occupy Sardinia

The Romans demand Corsica

9. The Last Gallic Invasion

Pending the next trial of strength with Carthage the Roman armies found employment in the suppression of native risings in Sardinia and Corsica — a task which provided a quick succession of cheaply won triumphs for the Roman commanders — and in a new Gallic war, the greatest of those fought on Italic soil. After their encounters with the Romans in the early part of the third century (pp. 93 f.) the Gauls of northern Italy showed a disposition to settle down to a more peaceful mode of life. During the Pyrrhic and First Punic Wars they did not take advantage of Rome's preoccupation to resume their raids into Etruria. Their quiescence may partly be explained by their opportunities for mercenary service in the Carthaginian forces during the First Punic War. But the end of that war was followed by unrest in northern Italy. It is true that an isolated movement by the Boii in 236 was arrested by the mere appearance of a Roman army at Ariminum. For the moment the Romans could afford to celebrate their easy success by closing the temple of Janus in the Forum – a ceremony which was only sanctioned at times of complete peace in the Roman dominions, and was therefore of extremely rare occurrence – and by throwing open for settlement part of the land taken from the Senones fifty years before (p. 93) and since left waste. During the next few years Rome's attention was directed to the Adriatic (p. 123). But in 225 a general coalition of Gallic tribes, assisted by mercenaries from Transalpine Gaul, collected a force, estimated at 70,000 men, to overrrun the peninsula. The Romans, however, with all central and southern Italy to draw upon, and more than willing co-operation of their dependants against such an enemy, rapidly mobilised a force of not less than 130,000 defenders. The invaders succeeded in breaking into Etruria by an unguarded pass in the western Apennines and made their way as far as Clusium. But converging Roman armies presently shepherded them towards the Tuscan coast, and another expeditionary force, which had been recalled from Sardinia and made an opportune landing near Pisae, cut off their retreat. At Telamon, a point on the coast of central Etruria, the Gauls made a last stand, fighting back to back against the Romans closing in upon them from two sides; but failing to break through – for the Romans by now had learnt to disarrange the first terrible charge of the enemy by concentrated javelin fire, and then to outfence them at close quarters – they were cut down almost to the last man.[32]

The alarm caused by the inroad of the Gauls decided the Romans to end their forays once for all by conquering northern Italy. In making this resolve they committed themselves to overrunning and colonising a territory nearly as large as the peninsula. Yet the Roman armies accomplished their task in three sweeping campaigns, during which they made short work of some isolated and irresolute attempts at defence by the separate Gallic tribes. In 224 they subdued Cispadane Gaul; in 223 C. Flaminius crossed the Po, dismantled his bridges, and defeated the Insubres; in 222 M. Claudius Marcellus revived the old duelling warfare in slaying

an Insubrian chief at Clastidium by his own hand. By 220 the Romans had received the submission of all the Gallic tribes except the Taurini of Piedmont and a few of the lesser sub-Alpine peoples. In the same year they established Latin colonies at Placentia and Cremona to control the passages of the middle Po; and Flaminius, now promoted to a censorship, made arrangements for the construction of Rome's Great North Road (the so-called Via Flaminia) as far as Ariminum. About this time a parallel road, the Via Aurelia, was built along the coast of Tuscany to Pisae, and naval stations were established at Luna (Spezia) and Genua.[33] By their acquisition of the northern plain and of the chain of islands in the Tyrrhenian sea the Romans had extended their dominion almost to the limits of the present state of Italy.

During these years the home front had seen some changes. In 241 two new rural tribes were created to incorporate the Picentes and Sabines, thus bringing the total of tribes to thirty-five, a number never increased (hereafter any new citizens were enrolled in one of the existing tribes). The Comitia Centuriata was reformed, probably at the same time, in order to correlate the centuries and tribes and perhaps to make it somewhat more democratic (p. 80). Further, the middle class and poorer peasants found a champion in Gaius Flaminius, a plebeian and a *novus homo* who later won the consulship (223) and thus nobility. As tribune in 232 he proposed that part of the *ager Gallicus* taken from the Senones (p. 121) should be divided into small allotments for poor citizens. This met with bitter senatorial opposition, so he carried the measure in the plebeian assembly. The suggestion, deriving from the hostile aristocratic tradition, that this measure caused the beginning of 'the demoralisation of the people' and also hastened the Gallic invasion of 225, may be dismissed. He also was the only senator to support a measure, proposed by a tribune, Q. Claudius, that prohibited senators from possessing ships of sea-going capacity: they must concentrate on their landed estates rather than be allowed to develop private commercial interests which might pervert their political judgments.[34] New fields of administration, however, were opening up abroad for them. In 227 Sardinia-and-Corsica was constituted as Rome's second province while the administration of Sicily, which had been governed by a quaestor, was changed. The number of praetors was raised to four in order that each year one might go as governor to each of the two overseas provinces. The nature of the 'provincial' government thus instituted is discussed in Chapter 18.

Renewed Gallic unrest

Invasion of Etruria

Battle of Telamon

The Romans counter-invade northern Italy

New Roman roads

Constitutional developments

Flaminius and the Senate

10. The Illyrian Wars[35]

Illyrian piracy

The Romans were gradually compelled to extend their gaze over the troubled waters of the Adriatic, and to become responsible for the protection of the Adriatic trade-routes, which had previously been under the care of the Tarentines. This obligation became urgent after the First Punic War, when the scattered tribes of Illyria were united under a line of rulers who organised piracy as a regular state industry and whose realm stretched from Dalmatia in the north down to the coast opposite the heel of Italy. The Senate, however, took no action until 230, when it went so far as to remonstrate with the reigning queen, Teuta.[36] The matter would no doubt have ended there, had not Teuta compassed or connived at the murder of one of the Roman envoys. In answer to this direct challenge the Senate sent the two consuls of 229 with an army and with the fleet which had won the First Punic War to sweep Teuta's subjects off the Adriatic. Distrusting her prompt offer of submission the Romans established a protectorate over the Greek towns (as Corcyra, Apollonia, Dyrrachium and Issa) and tribes on the east side of the Strait of Otranto.[37] These states were left free, without taxes, garrisons or governors; they were not bound to Rome by formal treaty, but became 'friends' (*amici*). The only link was a moral one, which arose from the *beneficium* of their liberation; they must show Rome practical gratitude, while Rome was morally engaged to maintain their liberty.[38] Thus Rome had secured a potential foothold east of the Adriatic and developed a new diplomatic method of extending her *clientela* to Greek cities. Further, as these operations were of benefit to the trading communities of the Greek mainland, where

The First Illyrian War

Roman influence in Greece

many might regard Rome's first step across the Adriatic with suspicion, the Senate dispatched envoys to Athens, Corinth, Achaea and Aetolia to report on their result (228). Although this mission ended in nothing more than an exchange of courtesies, the Corinthians, by admitting the Romans to the Isthmian Games, recognised them as part of the civilised world.

The Roman broom, however, had not swept the Adriatic quite clear. In 219 a Greek adventurer, Demetrius of Pharos, who had deserted from Teuta to the Romans and had in consequence been confirmed as an *amicus* of Rome in his little principality (an island off the Dalmatian coast), resumed his buccaneering expeditions. If he had reckoned on immunity as a result of Rome's possible embroilment with Hannibal over Saguntum in Spain (p. 125), he was soon undeceived. The Senate, temporising over affairs in Spain, sent to the Adriatic a second armada under the consuls of 219, who duly smoked out the pirate's nest. Demetrius fled to Philip of Macedon, and the consuls, anxious at the news that Hannibal was now actually besieging Saguntum, another 'client' of Rome, made a quick settlement on the same lines as that of ten years before. The outbreak of the Second Punic War in the following year obliged the Romans to put Greece out of mind, at least until the shadow of Philip of Macedon began to fall across their path. In any event the problem of the Adriatic pirates was a local one: taken by itself it could not have led to a permanent Roman engagement in Greek affairs, nor is there any evidence that the Senate before the Illyrian wars had any imperialistic eastern policy or during the 220s sought any lasting involvement in the Greek affairs.[39]

The Second Illyrian War

CHAPTER 13

The Second Punic War

1. The Carthaginian Conquests in Spain

Hamilcar's expedition to Spain

While the Romans were advancing their frontiers from Apennines to Alps the Carthaginians were making an unexpected recovery from their recent disasters. After the suppression of the revolts in Africa, Hamilcar, whose influence was now paramount at Carthage, obtained a commission to extend the Punic dominions in Spain, by way of compensation for the territory lost to the Romans (237). The interest of the Carthaginians in the Iberian peninsula had hitherto been confined to the trade-routes along its southern coast and to the mines of Andalusia: their position in Spain might be compared to that of the early East India Company in Madras or Bengal. Like Clive in India, Hamilcar gave a new turn to his state's policy. In the remaining nine years of his life he laid the foundations of a Punic empire, which his son-in-law Hasdrubal (228–221), who established an impressive new base at Carthago Nova (New Carthage; modern Cartagena), and his son Hannibal (221–218) extended to the Ebro and the Sierra de Toledo.

Iberians and Celts

The early population of Spain consisted of a pre-Indo-European Tartessian–Iberian stratum into which from *c.* 900 B.C. several waves of Celts began to penetrate. The latter mingled with the Iberians to produce a mixed race of Celtiberians in the north and north-west (Aragon and Castile), one of their principal settlements being at Numantia. In the south the kingdom of Tartessus had flourished in the first half of the first millennium, rich in its native silver- and copper-mines and trading with Phoenicians, Carthaginians, Greeks and (in tin) with Cornwall. About 500 B.C. it disappears

from our view, to be replaced by the Iberians (who may indeed have been the same stock as the Tartessians, although they spoke a different non-Indo-European language). At any rate in the south in the fifth and four centuries the Iberians displayed a widespread common culture, stimulated by Punic and Greek imports, and formed tribal monarchies.[1] On the central plain, however, they scarcely reached the agricultural stage by the third century. The tribal units were split up into numerous small clans, each of which clustered round its hill-top stronghold and constituted a miniature state of its own. The lack of cohesion among the Spaniards greatly facilitated the task of the Punic commanders, who played off one clan or tribe against another and achieved their conquests by diplomacy as much as by force of arms.

The primary object with which Hamilcar and his successors launched out on a new policy in Spain, and the reason with which no doubt they justified it to their countrymen, was to find fresh sources of revenue to make up for the recent war losses. Since their conquests embraced the richest parts of the peninsula, and the yield of the mines was greatly increased under direct Punic exploitation, the finances of Carthage were soon restored to prosperity. The Punic generals also secured the man-power of the peninsula for the service of Carthage. The Spaniards of ancient times were distinguished by their great powers of physical endurance, and their finely tempered thrusting swords, worthy ancestors of the Toledo blades of the Middle Ages, were unsurpassed among ancient weapons. Under their own leaders Spanish soldiers were dangerously impatient of discipline, but under Carthaginian commanders they

Punic recruitment in Spain

13.1   *Obv.* Head of Melkart (Heracles), probably with features of Hamilcar Barca. *Rev.* Carthaginian African war-elephant. Minted at New Carthage in Spain.

2. The Affair of Saguntum

On the death of Hasdrubal in 221 the command in Spain devolved upon Hamilcar's son Hannibal. Although he was only in his twenty-fifth year Hannibal had already won the complete confidence of the troops, and he had inherited from his father a general distrust or even hatred of Rome. This feeling was inflamed by an incident at Saguntum. A quarrel of the Saguntines with a neighbouring tribe which was subject to Carthage led to political disturbance in Saguntum and to an appeal by one party to Rome to arbitrate (probably *c.* 221). The Romans decided in favour of the appellant party, which was put in power with some loss of life among the Punic faction. Here, Hannibal might think, were the Romans, intervening in the internal affairs of a city just as earlier they had interfered in Messana: now was the time therefore to take a firm stand. Whatever his real intention, the Saguntines felt themselves threatened and more than once appealed to Rome. At last Roman envoys visited Hannibal in his winter headquarters in New Carthage (220/19) and ordered him to keep his hands off Saguntum. But he merely denied their *locus standi* in the affair,[5] and when the Roman delegates carried their message to Carthage the Punic government upheld the action of the general.[6] Though a section of the Carthaginian aristocracy headed by a politician named Hanno, stood for permanent good understanding with Rome, and was inclined to look to Africa rather than to Spain as a field for further expansion, the brilliant exploits of Hamilcar and his successors had rendered this peace party impotent. Hannibal, well aware of Roman commitments in Illyria (p. 123), decided to act. In the spring of 219 he moved against Saguntum, which refused to surrender, relying on Roman help; though Roman *fides* was involved, this help never came and Saguntum fell after a bitter siege of eight months. But early next year news of extensive fresh armaments by Hannibal convinced the Senate, now freed from the Illyrian War, that he was planning some major campaign beyond the Ebro. Accordingly it now addressed to Carthage a peremptory demand for the surrender of Hannibal. When the Punic government stood firm against this provocative ultimatum and bade the Roman envoy to give them either peace or war, he chose war: the deadly gift was accepted (March 218).

It is clear that Hannibal had deliberately precipitated war at a moment which he regarded as favourable to himself. The legal position is both complicated and unclear, since it depends on a number of uncertain factors, such as the

Hannibal in command

Troubles in Saguntum

Saguntum appeals to Rome

Hannibal besieges Saguntum

Rome and Carthage at War

Hannibal's motives

were capable of being trained into excellent infantry. The military resources of Spain were systematically exploited by Hamilcar and his successors. In the districts under Punic rule they levied troops by conscription; from the Castilian plateau they raised additional recruits of Celtiberian race – the flower of the peninsula's fighting stocks – by voluntary enlistment. Out of these materials, with a stiffening of seasoned African troops, the Punic generals built up a larger and better land army than Carthage had yet possessed.

Hamilcar's activities long escaped the attention or interest of the Romans. In deference to a protest from the Greek city of Massilia, which had long been on friendly terms and perhaps on a basis of formal alliance with Rome, and now feared the loss of its outposts on the eastern coast of Spain, the senate made a passing attempt to sound Hamilcar's intentions (231). But its envoys accepted at face value his evasive reply, that he was casting about for fresh sources of revenue to pay off the Carthaginian indemnity to Rome.[2] In 226 a second embassy was reassured by a promise on the part of Hasdrubal not to cross north of the Ebro in arms: the Romans apparently offered no *quid pro quo* (unless there was a 'gentleman's agreement' that they would not interfere south of the river).[3] During the next six years the Senate was too much engrossed in the war against the Gauls and later against the Illyrians to pay further heed to Carthaginian movements in Spain: with one significant exception. Saguntum, a native town in the plain of Valencia south of the Ebro, felt itself threatened by the Carthaginians and asked for Roman help. The Romans promised protection and received Saguntum into its *fidem,* possibly without a formal treaty (perhaps *c.* 223).[4]

The 'Ebro treaty'

13.2   View of Saguntum, looking westward, with a Roman theatre in the foreground. The medieval walls and castle probably correspond in general to the ancient city which Hannibal stormed in 219 B.C.

precise content of the Ebro treaty and the temporal relation of it to the Roman agreement with Saguntum.[7] But even if he violated no treaty with Rome by attacking Saguntum, Hannibal had been warned that its capture would be regarded as a *casus belli*: yet he persisted, and his action provided the proximate cause of the war.

Causes of the Second Punic War

But what were the underlying causes? Polybius finds three: Hamilcar's hatred of Rome, Punic bitterness at Rome's seizure of Sardinia, and the successes of the Barcid generals in Spain. To Polybius the Hannibalic War was a war of revenge, based on the hatred of the Barcid family for Rome, as exemplified in the anecdote (which may well be true) that Hamilcar had made his nine-year-old son Hannibal swear an oath of eternal hatred to Rome. This view, how-

ever, in its extreme form, is often doubted. It presupposes that the generals in Spain were building up an army with the precise purpose of challenging Rome once again, whereas the object of their empire-building may have been defensive and merely aimed at winning compensation for the loss of Sicily and Sardinia.[8] Nor do the Romans seem to have been unduly alarmed at what was happening in Spain: so far from planning a pre-emptive strike, such as their action regarding Sardinia might have seemed, they were content with half-hearted negotiations, and even this probably only at the instigation of their friend Massilia. They had Gauls and Illyrians on their mind more than Carthaginians. But though Hannibal may not have nurtured from boyhood a deliberate purpose to re-engage the Romans, he must have long envisaged the possibility of a future clash and was determined to be ready. He knew that Rome's intervention in Messana had lost Sicily for Carthage, and Rome's intervention to 'protect' the Punic mercenaries had led to the loss of Sardinia, so that when he saw Rome intervening in Saguntum he refused to risk further bullying from Rome and preferred war. He may indeed have lulled the Romans into a sense of false security since he had not made any serious attempt to build a new fleet, without which they may have thought that he would not pose a serious threat. But he had determined to stake

13.3   Probable portrait of Hannibal.

his chances on an altogether new strategy, in which naval operations were to play no vital part, and on this point, as on the general question of war or peace, he had carried his government with him.

3. Hannibal's Invasion of Italy. Cannae[9]

In consequence of their inattention to the march of events in Spain, the Romans miscalculated the readiness of the Carthaginians for war. Assuming that the Second Punic War would be little more than a continuation of the First, the Senate commissioned an army and fleet to strike directly at Carthage, and a slightly lesser force to hold Hannibal in Spain. But Hannibal crossed the Roman plans at the outset with a rapid move which gave him the initiative through the most critical stages of the war. With a view to cut-

Hannibal marches upon Italy

ting off the inexhaustible supply of Roman man-power at the fountain-head before it could be brought into full play, he staked his fortunes on an invasion of Italy – an audacious plan, but the only one that appeared to him to offer any prospect of final success. His expeditionary force probably numbered considerably less than 50,000 men; but long years of warfare in Spain had welded its diverse elements into a coherent corps of expert campaigners, and Hannibal had won their loyalty so completely that he could make unlimited demands upon their courage and endurance.

While the Romans were collecting their forces Hannibal advanced as far as the Rhône and forced its passage (either near Beaucaire–Tarascon or further north beyond the Druentia, modern Durance) in the face of native opposition. He was sighted by patrols of the Roman expeditionary force on the way to Spain, but he gave his opponents the slip in order to reach Italy, if possible, with an intact army. In cross-

Crossing of the Alps

ing the Alps (most probably by one of the passes of the Mont Cenis or the Mont Genèvre group)[10] he had to fight his way to the summit against the resistance of the mountain tribes, and on the descent he suffered heavy losses on ice-chutes rendered doubly treacherous by premature falls of fresh snow. On his arrival in the Po valley he had but 26,000 men left, yet with these he carried northern Italy in a two months' campaign. On the bank of the Ticinus he fought his first action with the consul P. Cornelius Scipio, who had doubled back from France to Italy by the sea route and moved forward again with the garrison forces of the Po valley to meet the invaders. Though the action on the Ticinus was a mere skirmish of advance guards, it showed up so plainly the superiority of Hannibal's light

African horse over the indifferent Italian cavalry that Scipio abandoned the Transpadane plain and fell back upon the Apennine foothills near Placentia. In this position he was joined by his colleague, Sempronius Longus, the intended invader of Africa, who had meantime been recalled from his base in Sicily, and reached north Italy in time for a late autumn campaign. The combined Roman forces now crossed the swollen river Trebia and threw their whole weight into a frontal attack upon Hannibal.[11] As soon as they had become closely engaged, they were taken in flank and rear by Carthaginian forces held in concealment. With their retreat cut off by the flooded stream the Romans saved little more than 10,000 men, who broke through the enemy centre, out of a force of some 40,000. After this disaster the Romans withdrew all their forces from northern Italy, except the garrisons of the newly founded colonies at Placentia and Cremona, and the Gauls, who had hitherto been inclined to wait upon the issue, flocked to join Hannibal.

Battle of the Trebia

In 217 the Romans, resigning themselves to a defensive attitude, posted one consular army at Ariminum to hold the line of the Via Flaminia, and a force of some 25,000 men under C. Flaminius at Arretium to cover Etruria. With his forces swelled by Gallic reinforcements, Hannibal stole through an unguarded Apennine pass,[12] slipped round the defence corps at Arretium and drew it after him to Lake Trasimene in central Etruria. As his pursuers defiled between the lake and the adjacent mountains without a previous reconnaissance, he assailed them in flank and rear from his coverts behind the foothills, so that the greater part of the Roman army perished in the pass or in the lake.[13] Among the fallen was Flaminius, whose vigour and restricted ability to reconnoitre in face of Hannibal's superior cavalry had made him a somewhat easy victim.

Battle of Lake Trasimene

The victory of Lake Trasimene gave the invaders an open road to Rome, yet it was singularly barren in results. The city could now no longer be captured by a *coup de main* as in 390, and it could not be put under effectual siege so long as the investing force lacked a neighbouring base of supplies. But not a single town of central Italy threw open its gates to the Carthaginians. Hannibal accordingly swerved aside from Rome and staked his last chance on raising rebellion in southern Italy and completing the work which Pyrrhus had left half-finished. But among the southern Italians he met with no better welcome. As he moved from Apulia to Campania and back into Apulia, he was shadowed by a new Roman army under a veteran campaigner named Q. Fabius Maximus, who

The Romans adopt 'Fabian' tactics

127

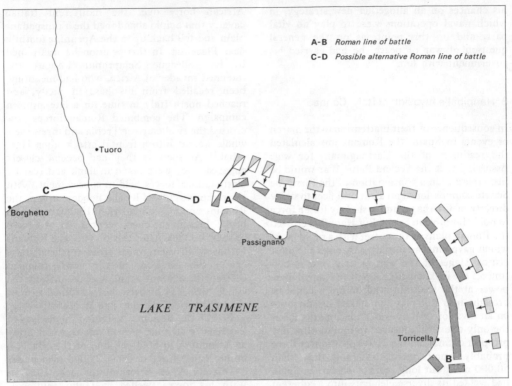

A-B *Roman line of battle*

C-D *Possible alternative Roman line of battle*

Tuoro

C *Borghetto* D A

Passignano

LAKE   TRASIMENE

Torricella • B

9. BATTLE OF LAKE TRASIMENE, 217 B.C.

had been appointed dictator by the unusual procedure of a popular election. Fabius obstinately
refused to hazard his hastily levied troops in a
pitched battle. Though he momentarily
cornered Hannibal in Campania by seizing all
the mountain-passes on his rear and flank, he
was dislodged from his position by Hannibal's
latest recruits, a weird army of two thousand
oxen, who were driven by night towards
Fabius's camp with lighted faggots tied to their
horns, and drew off the bewildered garrison
from one of the adjacent passes. Yet by his mere
presence Fabius heartened the allies of Rome
to keep their gates closed against the invaders.
Though impatient critics dubbed him 'Hannibal's lackey', the poet Ennius with better
discernment immortalised him as 'the man who
singly saved the state by patience'. At the end
of 217 Hannibal had not won over or conquered
a single city of peninsular Italy, where he
remained a mere intruder.

But in 216 the Romans played into the
enemy's hands. Instead of waiting in true
Roman fashion to study their adversary's warcraft and readapt their own methods to it, they
resolved to smother his superior skill under a
sheer mass attack in a straightforward infantry

combat. They raised their field army to not less
than 50,000 men and transferred its command
from Fabius to the two consuls, L. Aemilius
Paullus and C. Terentius Varro, neither of
whom had previous experience of Hannibal's
tactics. Against this force Hannibal could put no
more than 40,000 men into line, yet he
humoured his opponents by offering them battle
on a bare plain near the Apulian town of Cannae, where the Romans had nothing to fear from

Battle of Cannae

13.4 View from the hill of Cannae, overlooking
the plain and the river Ofanto (Aufidus). The
precise site of the battle in which Hannibal
defeated the Romans in 216 B.C. is uncertain.

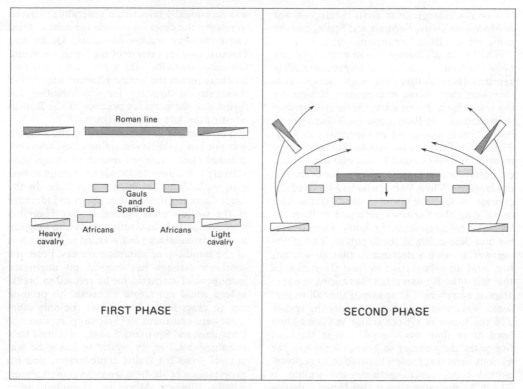

Roman line

Gauls
and
Spaniards

Heavy
cavalry

Africans

Africans

Light
cavalry

FIRST PHASE

SECOND PHASE

10. BATTLE OF CANNAE, 216 B.C.

hidden reserves.[14] In this open position the Romans made no other use of their superior numbers than to deepen their infantry line so as to increase the weight of its impact upon Hannibal's front. Hannibal, on the other hand, starved his centre of troops and instructed it to fall back before the enemy's charge. While the retreat of the Punic centre drew on the enemy infantry and shepherded it, as it were, into the slaughtering pen, the light troops on the Carthaginian wings took it in flank, and the cavalry, which had driven the Roman horse off the field, closed in on the rear of the Roman centre.[15] At a cost of barely 6000 men Hannibal virtually annihilated the Roman forces compressed within this ring of steel. The battle of Cannae was a unique instance of a complete encirclement of a numerically stronger army by a weaker one. This seeming miracle was accomplished by a brilliant application of the Greek tactical principle of co-operation between a containing and a striking force, and by the excellent battle-discipline with which Hannibal's containing corps bent without wholly breaking, while his striking corps reined in from the pursuit of the routed Roman cavalry and returned in the nick of time to the main scene of action.

4. The Roman Effort after Cannae

The weeks that followed upon the catastrophe of Cannae were the supreme testing-time of the Roman Republic. Having lost 100,000 men in the recent battles the Romans were further weakened by defection on the part of their dependants in southern Italy. These hitherto staunch allies were beginning to make up their minds that Hannibal had come to stay, and they made peace with him the more readily as he had promised not to impose forced levies upon them. With the exception of the Roman and Latin colonies and of the Greek cities of the coast, practically the whole of southern Italy was lost to Rome. The most serious blow was the secession of Capua, which was won over to the Carthaginian side by the prospect of taking Rome's place as the first town of Italy. Since Capua at this time was the chief industrial centre in the country, its alliance with Hannibal, besides providing him with comfortable winter quarters, gave him an excellent base of supply.[16] Lastly, several powers outside Italy, which had been watching the conflict with interested neutrality, now prepared to throw in their weight on the side of the winners, and Rome would have

Secessions in southern Italy and Capua

129

to face the emergence of fresh theatres of war in Macedon, Sicily, Sardinia and Spain, and the consequent calls on her man-power.

The battle of Cannae left an enduring mark upon the Romans, who never forgave the Carthaginians their victory; yet in the actual crisis they kept their nerve in exemplary fashion. By the lead which it now gave, the Senate justified its ascendancy in Rome, and the Roman people proved itself worthy of its supremacy in Italy. The spirit of the Senate may be illustrated from its attitude to the consul Varro, who was a political upstart and personally unwelcome to the ruling families. When Varro, who had survived the carnage of Cannae and had done good service in rallying the fugitives, returned to Rome to lay down his command, the Senate thanked him for 'not despairing of the Republic'. This greeting was at once a declaration that all was not lost, and an exhortation to close the ranks. In this spirit the Roman people submitted to unexampled sacrifices.[17] It answered the call to personal service so readily that before the end of 216 the losses of citizen troops at Cannae had been more than made good, and in the next five years the number of Roman legions in the various theatres of war was raised to an unprecedented total, reaching twenty-five legions in 212.[18] At the same time it shouldered a double rate of property tax (*tributum*); the wealthier families contributed slaves for service in the army or fleet, and advanced money or supplies on a mere promise of future reimbursement; and the troops did not press for arrears of pay.[19] Even so, the government could not meet the costs of a gigantic army and a strong navy in permanent commission. The coinage had to be depreciated, so that the *as* gradually declined in weight; and the troops on service overseas had to be left to fend for themselves.[19] Yet not a voice was raised in favour of peace. By an exemplary display of severity the men who had straggled away from the field of Cannae were punished with a term of twelve years' unbroken service in Sicily under humiliating conditions; lest peace proposals should originate out of negotiations for the redemption of prisoners it was decided to leave the Roman captives unransomed.

With equal patriotism the Romans agreed to sink their domestic differences. In the opening years of the war Roman strategy had been somewhat embarrassed by bickerings between the senatorial class, who inclined as usual to a cautious policy, and the commons, who clamoured for more resolute action. After Cannae the conduct of affairs was tacitly left in the hands of the Senate, and although the claim of that body to influence the consular elections was occasionally resented, it generally contrived to reserve the chief commands for men of tried merit (notably Fabius Maximus; Q. Fulvius Flaccus, another veteran of the Gallic wars; and Claudius Marcellus, the victor of Clastidium). By these means the Senate achieved a unity and continuity of direction for which neither the forms nor the previous practice of the Roman constitution had made provision.

The example of firmness set by the Romans was not lost on their remaining allies, who contributed their increased quotas of troops with scarcely any demur and made no attempt to bargain with Rome for higher privileges. In the event Cannae proved one of the most indecisive of the world's great battles. It gave Hannibal a secure foothold in southern Italy and long immunity from attack; but it failed to relieve him of the handicap of inferior numbers. From the southern Italians he received no important increment of strength, for he refused to break, indeed could not afford to break, his promise not to exact forced levies, and the only allies who were consistent in their support were the Lucanians and Bruttians. So long as central Italy remained solid in its loyalty to Rome he was cut off from his Gallic confederates, and his expectations of aid from overseas proved almost wholly illusory. Moreover Hannibal never obtained a further chance of reducing the odds against him in another great battle, for Fabius and the officers of his school, with the Senate's consistent approval, adopted 'Fabian' tactics and refused to engage in any but minor actions with limited risks; they contented themselves in general with guerrilla operations, so as to prevent the enemy from settling down to siege tactics against the remaining loyalists in southern Italy.

5. Sequel of the War in Italy

The stand made by the Romans after Cannae virtually decided the Second Punic War. The two contingencies on which Hannibal's chances of success depended, the crippling of Roman man-power by losses in battle or defections of allies, and the breaking of Roman morale under the impact of successive defeats, were not realised. From this point the remorseless pressure of Rome's superior numbers assured the final result of the Second, as of the previous, Punic War.

The subsequent campaigns in Italy do not need detailed description. For the most part they consisted of marches and counter-marches, interspersed with lesser engagements, in which Hannibal endeavoured to lure Roman armies

The Senate's call for unity

The Roman war-effort

Control of war-policy by the Senate

Loyalty of central Italy

Roman man-power tells

Hannibal gains Tarentum;

into fresh traps, but seldom met with any notable success. After three uneventful campaigns mainly in Campania he carried the city of Tarentum except the citadel by treason (212), thus acquiring a second rich base of supply. But this isolated gain was outweighed by the loss of Capua in the following year. While Hannibal's main force was detained near Tarentum, the consul Q. Fulvius Flaccus mobilised every available man for a counter-attack upon the seceding Campanians. He invested Capua with a ring of trenches which Hannibal was unable to break through on his return from Tarentum. As a last resort Hannibal attempted to raise the siege by making a forced march with a flying-column upon Rome, in the hope that the Senate might be stampeded into recalling Fulvius from Capua. But although he pitched his camp within 3 miles of the city and caused great alarm among the townsfolk, the Senate realised that Hannibal's approach was a mere feint and left Fulvius to carry on in his trenches. Shortly after *but loses Capua* this futile demonstration Capua was starved into surrender (211). Though it remained a large centre of industry it was punished by extensive confiscations of territory and the transference of its entire municipal administration into the hands of Roman *praefecti*. The reconquest of Capua, and the reduction of many lesser places in Samnium and Apulia, were followed in 209 by the recovery of Tarentum, which succumbed for a second time to treason and paid for its unwilling defection by a systematic plundering. After the recapture of these key positions the Roman armies began to close in upon the dwindling Punic forces in Lucania and Bruttium.

Hannibal's only remaining chance in Italy now depended on his receiving a large reinforcement from outside. In 207 this hope appeared likely for a moment to be fulfilled. After several years of indecisive campaigning in Spain (pp. 133 f.) his brother Hasdrubal received orders to risk the loss of that country for the sake of a decision in Italy. Making an unopposed passage through Gaul and across the Alps Hasdrubal *Hannibal reinforced from Spain* arrived in northern Italy with an intact force, which he augmented with a large Gallic contingent. At the same time Hannibal prepared to join hands with his brother at some point in central Italy. But the Romans counterbalanced the Punic reinforcement by a mobilisation second only to that of 211. In addition they had the advantage of operating on inner lines, and an accidental stroke of good fortune, which threw Hasdrubal's messengers into their hands, enabled them to turn defence into attack. While Hannibal, left uncertain of his brother's line of march, was marking time in Apulia, the consul C. Claudius Nero, who held the chief com-

13.5   Probable portrait of Hasdrubal Barca.

mand in southern Italy, slipped away with a flying-column to join his colleague Livius on the northern front. Hasdrubal, who had been advancing along the Adriatic coast, endeavoured in his turn to give the Romans the slip by swerving off along the Via Flaminia, but he was eventually cornered and brought to battle against the superior forces of the two consuls on the banks of the river Metaurus.[20] Nero, observing *Battle of the Metaurus* that the Gauls on Hasdrubal's left wing had no intention of moving forward from the strong defensive position which they occupied, stole round the rear of Livius's lines with a strong detachment, which he threw upon the enemy's right flank. Under this side-thrust the Punic army was completely rolled up, and Hasdrubal himself fell fighting.

The victory of the Metaurus was celebrated at Rome with almost hysterical rejoicings, which showed how severe the previous strain had been. After this great deliverance the Senate seemingly lost interest in Hannibal, who was allowed to retire unmolested into the mountain fastnesses of Bruttium, and there to maintain himself for four further years.[21] The Roman field *Hannibal remains in Italy on sufferance* forces were gradually reduced, and Nero, who had proved himself a proficient pupil of Hannibal, was given no further opportunity of measuring himself against his instructor.

6. The War in Greece and Sicily

Although no important naval actions were fought in the Second Punic War, the ascendancy of the Romans at sea was an essential factor in their ultimate victory.[22] In the whole course of the war the Carthaginian government never equipped a fleet of more than 130 battleships. The Romans, on the other hand, fitted out 160 battleships in 218, and despite other calls on *Ascendancy of the Roman fleet* their resources in subsequent years always maintained a sufficient margin of superiority to deter the enemy from trying his fortunes in a set fight on any large scale (for the battle off the Ebro see p. 133). Though the Roman fleet failed to intercept some Punic convoys to Sicily and Spain, it achieved the more important task of preventing the dispatch of any considerable reinforcements from Africa or Spain to Italy, and of holding at arm's length Hannibal's ally, king Philip V of Macedon.

Treaty between Hannibal and Philip V of Macedon

The relations of the Roman Republic with king Philip will be more fully discussed in Chapter 15. In 215 this ambitious monarch, who had been carefully watching the progress of the Second Punic War with a view to his intervention at a critical point, engaged himself by a treaty with Hannibal to co-operate and give him some help.[23] Had this promise of help been fulfilled Philip might well have turned the scales against Rome, for as a general he was little inferior to Pyrrhus, and he disposed of a considerably stronger army. But the appearance of a Roman squadron in the Adriatic sufficed to render his treaty abortive, for Philip possessed no ships strong enough to oppose the Roman men-of-war (214). To make assurance doubly sure the Roman admiral, Valerius Laevinus, landed a small force on Philip's side of the Adriatic and fomented a domestic war against him in Greece (Chapter 15). So little influence had the 'First Macedonian War' on the greater conflict in Italy that in 205 Philip agreed to peace in consideration of some trifling territorial concessions.

The Roman fleet checks Philip

A more serious danger to Rome arose from another Greek participant in the Second Punic War. In Sicily king Hiero of Syracuse entered the war as a zealous ally of the Romans, who received timely gifts of corn and money from him. But after his death in 215 his crown passed to a young and inexperienced grandson named Hieronymus, who let himself be excited by the Carthaginian triumph at Cannae, and by the seductions of Punic agents, who promised him half of Roman Sicily in return for his co-operation. Before he could render material aid to his

Syracuse won over by the Carthaginians

13.7 Hiero of Syracuse.

new confederates Hieronymus was murdered, and the republican government which replaced him reversed his foreign policy. But the Carthaginians still had a strong following in Syracuse, and their party regained the upper hand at the news that a Roman expeditionary corps under Claudius Marcellus had proceeded at once to warlike measures, capturing the frontier post of Leontini and sacking it with over-hasty severity. Marcellus's carnage at Leontini was answered by the Syracusans with a counter-massacre of Roman partisans and a renewal of Hieronymus's alliance with Carthage (213).

In a vain attempt to stifle the war which he had conjured up Marcellus at once put Syracuse under siege by land and sea. But under Hiero the formidable defences of the city had been strengthened with new artillery that outranged the Roman catapults, and with powerful cranes that could drop gigantic weights upon the Roman warships, or lift the lesser craft out of the water. These machines were a by-product of the genius of Archimedes, a citizen of Syracuse who had been called away from his studies in pure mathematics, as the Florentine Michelangelo was summoned from his paintings, to apply himself to the invention of war-engines. By these devices the Roman assault was baffled at every point, and Marcellus's operations were reduced to an ineffective blockade.[24] In the meanwhile the Punic government, with Hannibal's consent, had fitted out a force of some 30,000 men, which eluded the Roman patrols and established a base at Agrigentum. A further atrocity on the part of a subordinate Roman commander, who outdid his chief in a precautionary massacre of the inhabitants of Enna, had the effect of driving one Sicilian town after another into alliance with Carthage, so that in the winter of 213–212 Marcellus, like the Athenian Nicias in 414–413, was 'more besieged than besieging'. But the Roman general never relaxed his hold; and he did not wait, like Fulvius at Capua, for famine to accomplish his work for him. In a night surprise he eventually

Siege of Syracuse. The war-engines of Archimedes

13.6 *Obv.* Probable portrait of Mago, Hannibal's brother. *Rev.* Carthaginian warship.

carried the outer defences of Syracuse. Re-inforcements from Carthage hurried to the relief of the city; but the Punic army was destroyed by the swamp-fever which haunted the southern outskirts of the town, and a squadron of 130 galleys – the largest Carthaginian fleet of the Second Punic War – flinched from an encounter with a Roman force of 100 vessels. The city was finally delivered to the Romans by a traitor (211). Marcellus gave the troops licence to loot, and thus became responsible for the death of Archimedes, who was run through by a Roman soldier in a casual scuffle. In 210 Agrigentum was handed back to the Romans by mutinous Carthaginian auxiliaries, and the rest of the island made a rapid submission.

Capture and plunder of Syracuse

Sardinia and Corsica, albeit an important factor in the genesis of the Second Punic War, played but a minor part in its military operations. In 215 a fresh outbreak of revolt in Sardinia encouraged the Carthaginians to send a small force to recover the island. But the Romans, who looked to Sardinia to furnish the supplies of corn, which they could no longer obtain from Italy or Sicily, sent sufficient troops to make a quick end of the rebellion and of the Punic expedition.

Abortive rising in Sardinia

7. The Scipios in Spain[25]

Although the Romans had failed to hold Hannibal in Spain they nevertheless persevered in their original purpose of extending the war into that country. This resolute policy was initiated by P. Cornelius Scipio, a general whose insight and enterprise foreshadowed the achievements of his more famous son and namesake. Though Scipio, on discovering that he was too late to prevent Hannibal from reaching Italy, returned in person to organise the defence of the Po valley (p. 127), he sent his two legions on to Spain under the command of his bróther Gnaeus (218). From his base at Emporiae (Ampurias), a Massilian colony under the foot of the Pyrenees, Gnaeus at once applied himself to the conquest of the eastern seaboard. He quickly seized Tarraco (Tarragona) and thwarted an attack by Hasdrubal, Hannibal's brother. In 217 Hasdrubal approached the Ebro with land and sea forces. Though outnumbered, Scipio's ships (thirty-five against forty) won a victory off the mouth of the Ebro and thus both prevented a break-through by Hasdrubal and smashed Punic sea-power on the Spanish coast.[26] He was also strengthened by the arrival of his brother Publius with reinforcements; together they advanced over the Ebro and camped near Saguntum (traces of their camp survive). In 215

Operations of the Elder Scipios in Spain

Hasdrubal, also reinforced from Carthage, made a final attempt to break through to join Hannibal in Italy. This counter-offensive was shattered in an action at Dertosa on the Ebro, where the Romans won an orthodox victory by a quick and clean break through the Carthaginian centre, which Hasdrubal had left weak in order to entrap his adversaries, as Hannibal had done at Cannae. By 211 the Scipios had advanced over the Ebro and gained Saguntum, which they could now use as a base for further advance; they could now aim at the complete expulsion of their opponents from Spain. Unfortunately for them Hasdrubal had again received fresh troops, while they themselves were weakened by wholesale defections on the part of their Celtiberian allies, and had to divide their forces in order to ease the strain on their commissariat.[27] While Publius advanced to the upper courses of the Baetis (Guadalquivir) against one Punic army, Gnaeus met Hasdrubal in the hinterland of New Carthage. Both armies were defeated and the two brothers died with the greater part of their forces. The Romans had to fall back to the line of the Ebro and hold it if they could.

Their defeat and deaths

Although the career of the Scipios ended in disaster, their campaigns in Spain contributed materially to the Roman victory in the Second Punic War. During the most critical years of that conflict they had not only prevented the passage of reinforcements to Hannibal, but had diverted to Spain successive drafts of African troops, which might have had a decisive influence on the war if they had found their way to Italy after Cannae. Though they were ill served by their native levies, they had at any rate undermined the loyalty of the Spaniards to the Carthaginians. Their final defeat, moreover, had singularly little influence on the course of events in Spain. At best the Carthaginians had missed their most hopeful opportunities of restoring Hannibal's ascendancy in Italy, for the simultaneous recovery of Capua and of Syracuse by the Romans had left them with sufficient reserves to cope with Punic reinforcements from Spain. In actual fact the Carthaginian commanders put their victory to no better purpose than to retrieve their recent losses in the peninsula. In 211 and 210 they recovered the lost ground to the south of the Ebro, but made no serious attempt to carry the line of that river against the attenuated Roman defences.

Value of their strategy to the Romans

In 210 the Senate sent a new army to Spain, and by an unwontedly bold decision it conferred its command upon an ex-aedile of twenty-five years, the son of the P. Scipio who had fallen in 211. The choice was that of the people in

The Younger Scipio. His personality

Comitia, who thus elevated a young man who had been neither praetor nor consul and who thus became the first *privatus* to be invested with proconsular *imperium*, a significant foreshadowing of the basis of the later military authority of the emperors of Rome. But the choice was soon justified since Publius Cornelius Scipio proved to be one of the greatest soldiers of antiquity, and has even been called by a leading modern military expert 'a greater than Napoleon'. He appears to have possessed a genuine belief in his direct communion with the gods, especially Jupiter, as well as a magnetic power of conveying his supreme confidence in himself to others.[28] At the same time he had a keen sense for practical details and readiness to take lessons in warcraft from his adversaries. He rivalled the victories of Hannibal by adapting Hannibal's methods to the service of Rome.

13.8   Hieronymus of Syracuse.

Scipio seizes New Carthage

In 209 Scipio resumed his father's offensive with a sudden move, whose well-calculated audacity matched that of Hannibal's march to Italy. On the report that the Carthaginian armies had drawn away into the interior of Spain, he made a sudden dash along the eastern coast and pounced upon New Carthage which he seized by a sudden assault by land and sea.[29] By this brilliant stroke he deprived the Carthaginians of their chief arsenal and of the revenues from the neighbouring mines, and he acquired for himself a secure base for an advance into Andalusia, the lack of which had been fatal to his father. But he did not seek to engage the enemy in pitched battles until he had exercised his troops in new tactical movements derived from Hannibal's school, and rearmed them with the finely annealed Spanish sword. He also resumed, with notable success, his father's policy of winning over the native chiefs, so that the Punic dominion was widely undermined.

Battle of Baecula

In 208 Scipio advanced and brought Hasdrubal to battle at Baecula (modern Bailen) near Castulo. Using a screen of light troops and one line of infrantry to hold Hasdrubal's centre, he sent his remaining legionaries up the two sides of the hill on which the enemy stood. Thus outflanked, Hasdrubal managed to break off and withdraw the bulk of his troops. Scipio had won a striking success, though not an overwhelming victory, which he owed to the training he had recently given his men in independence of manoeuvre; hitherto no Roman army, stereotyped in its traditional three lines, could have shown such flexibility. Hailed as king by his Spanish allies, he declined the honour, but he may have been greeted by his troops as *imperator*; if so, this was the first example in Rome's history of an honour that was to become customary for victorious generals. Hasdrubal realised that if ever he was to bring help to his brother in Italy, he must do so at once, before the Carthaginians were finally reduced to the defensive in Spain.[30] He therefore stole away across the Castilian plateau and gained France by the western end of the Pyrenees. In this long and arduous march he was left unmolested by Scipio, who perhaps discounted Hasdrubal's chances in Italy and at any rate saw that his duty lay in Spain, where he had been sent; his decision assured final success in the peninsula. In effect Hasdrubal had delivered Spain into the hands of the Romans. Though his successor, Hasdrubal, the son of Gisgo, had made up his numbers with Spanish recruits, he had few seasoned troops left to oppose to Scipio's highly trained force. In 207 the Punic general avoided battle and left Scipio to carry on a war of sieges. In 206 he took the risk of a set fight (perhaps under orders from the Carthaginian home government, which could no longer look to Hannibal to obtain a decision in Italy). At the battle of Ilipa (near Seville), in which some 48,000 Romans and Spanish allies engaged over 50,000 Punic troops, Scipio refined on the tactics employed by him at Baecula by using his light troops and horsemen to carry out a highly complicated double-outflanking movement, while his centre of inferior troops successfully held the main troops of the enemy. During the action he completely destroyed the enemy flanks, and he pursued the remnants of the defeated army with such vigour that the Carthaginians were left without any field forces in Spain. An illness of Scipio, which gave rise to a rumour of his death and a consequent outbreak of disorder among his troops, both Spanish and Roman, somewhat delayed the final expulsion of the Carthaginians from Spain. But before the end of the year Scipio led his reconstituted army to Gades and received its surrender. At the end of 206 Spain had been finally lost to Carthage.

Battle of Ilipa

8. The War in Africa[31]

Scipio carries the war into Africa

In the course of his Spanish campaigns Scipio had prepared for an expedition to Africa by diplomatic overtures to several of the Numidian chieftains who stood in loose alliance with Carthage. On his return to Rome where he had been elected consul for 205 he applied for a commission to carry the war into Carthaginian territory. His demand was refused in the first instance by Fabius in a Senate which was still afraid of making any heavy draft upon the defence forces in Italy so long as Hannibal held his ground there, and recoiled from imposing fresh levies. Its reluctance to cast further burdens upon the Italians was not devoid of good reason. In Rome itself the last reserve funds in the *aerarium sanctius* (p. 85) had been broken into, and twelve favoured allies of Latin status had withheld their aid since 209 on a simple plea of *non possumus*. But Scipio appealed over the heads of the senators to the people, and he carried the Comitia with him by playing upon its desire to retaliate upon the Carthaginians for the devastation of Italy — a motive which smouldered on at Rome for many years to come. Foreseeing that its hand might be forced the Senate eventually authorised Scipio to take over the two legions which had been sent in disgrace to Sicily (p. 130), together with any volunteers whom he might collect. Scipio, who was never loth to be hailed as popular hero, but disdained to become a demagogue, accepted this compromise.

In 205 the new expeditionary force went no further than Sicily, where it received a rigorous training in the tactical methods of Baecula and Ilipa. In 204 Scipio landed his force on African soil near Utica, but found the Carthaginians ready for him. When threatened with invasion the Punic government had the nerve to maintain its first line of defence overseas. While it left Hannibal to keep the Romans in play in Lucania and Bruttium it commissioned his surviving brother Mago to raise fresh troops in the Balearic isles and to make a naval descent on northern Italy. Though Mago effected a landing at Genua, he received so little support from the Cisalpine Gauls that, after two years of virtual inactivity and a final hopeless foray into the Po valley, he fell back upon the coast (205–203). But a second line of defence had been prepared against Scipio in Africa. A new army had been levied in the Carthaginian hinterland, and the most powerful of the Numidian rulers, Syphax, had atoned for previous changes of front by finally throwing in his lot on the Punic side. Scipio, for his part, had won over a chieftain named Masinissa, who possessed a small principality

Syphax and Masinissa of Numidia

in eastern Numidia. As a leader of light horse in the Spanish campaigns Masinissa had taken a hand in the destruction of Cn. Scipio's army in 211. His accession to the Roman side was destined to have an important influence on the course of the war, but for the moment he could bring to Scipio no other reinforcement than a troop of mounted retainers, for he had recently been expelled from his dominions by his more powerful neighbour Syphax.

In 204 Scipio was held fast by the joint forces of Syphax and the Carthaginians. From this impasse he extricated himself in the following spring by a carefully planned surprise that recalled his dash upon New Carthage. Having lulled the suspicions of his adversaries during the previous winter by pretending to entertain an offer of peace negotiations he suddenly broke off the discussions and delivered a night attack

13.9 Probable portrait of Scipio Africanus. Silver coin minted at New Carthage in Spain after his victory there.

upon the camps of Hasdrubal and Syphax, in which their armies were destroyed by fire and sword. This cheaply won victory, it is true, had little immediate effect, for Syphax and the Carthaginians repaired their losses with fresh levies, which included a stray corps of Celtiberian mercenaries. Scipio suddenly pounced on this hastily collected force who had to offer battle on the 'Great Plains' (Campi Magni) in the valley of the Bagradas. In this engagement he applied a new refinement of his envelopment tactics, by holding back the second and third lines of his legionary infantry (the *principes* and *triarii*) and then sending them to the right and left of the *hastati* in the front line, who thus acted as a screen to the enfilading columns.[32] The manoeuvre succeeded so well that the Celtiberians in the Punic centre were cut down to the last man, and Syphax was so enfeebled that a Roman flying-column was able to expel him from his capital at Cirta (Constantine) and install Masinissa as joint king of Greater and Lesser Numidia (203).

Scipio's successes in Africa

13.10   Masinissa.

After these disasters the Carthaginians were reduced to sue for peace; but they insured themselves against its failure by recalling Hannibal and Mago from Italy (the latter died on the voyage home). The terms imposed by Scipio, which included the cession of Spain, the reduction of the Punic navy to twenty warships and an indemnity of 5000 talents, were accepted at Carthage and ratified by the Senate and Comitia at Rome. But the return of Hannibal, who brought back some 15,000 seasoned veterans from Italy, incited a party at Carthage to break off the armistice before the peace conditions could be implemented. Hostilities were therefore resumed, and the scene was prepared

for a trial of strength between Hannibal and Scipio.

In the summer of 202 the rival leaders met at a site some distance from Zama Regia.[33] Either army numbered from 35,000 to 40,000 men. Hannibal had collected a large elephant corps, but his infantry was of unequal value, and the loss of Numidia left him unusually weak in regard to his mounted troops. Scipio's forces were uniformly well trained, and he delayed engaging the enemy until his Italian cavalry had been reinforced by a strong Numidian contingent under Masinissa. Hannibal opened battle with a mass attack by the elephants, who were either driven off by the Roman screen of skirmishers, or raced uselessly down the lanes which the legionaries had formed by drawing up their maniples in columns, instead of the usual quincunx order. After this episode Scipio sought to envelop Hannibal by the manœuvre which he had applied at the Great Plains; but his adversary had countered this move beforehand by drawing up his infantry in three successive detachments. The rear line comprised his veteran troops from Italy and was held some distance back from the two front lines, thus acting as a kind of reserve; if the Romans outflanked Hannibal's two front lines, they would still find

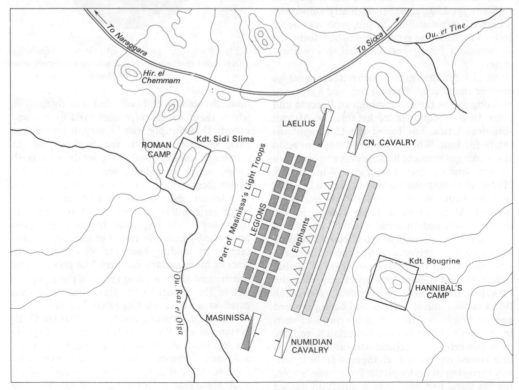

11. BATTLE OF ZAMA, 202 B.C.

the third line facing them. A slight lull enabled both sides to reorganise their lines, which were probably extended; they then renewed the engagement in a purely frontal attack which finally resolved itself into a deadlock.[34] In the meantime, however, Scipio's cavalry brigades, the Italians under C. Laelius and the Africans under Masinissa, had driven off the Punic horse; breaking off the pursuit at the right moment, they turned in upon Hannibal's rear. The battle of Zama thus ended like Cannae, but with the Carthaginians inside the circle of iron. The Punic army suffered such utter destruction that Hannibal, who was among the few survivors, insisted upon a speedy peace. Scipio accorded the same general terms as in 203, but doubled the indemnity, cut down the Punic fleet to ten ships, and deprived Carthage of the right of waging further war without Rome's consent. Masinissa was rewarded for his services by a gift of all African land 'held by him or his forefathers'. These terms were ratified on both sides in 201.

Roman victory and peace

9. Conclusion

The Second Punic War might be described as the 'World War' of ancient times, because of the wide range of its operations, and by virtue of the intensity and persistency with which both sides threw their strength into the tussle. It was marred by many brutalities, the Romans in particular being guilty of indiscriminate plundering and massacre in the towns recovered by them; but it was lighted up by the great personalities of Hannibal and Scipio Africanus. Of these two leaders, Hannibal possessed the more original genius. Though he avowed himself a disciple of Pyrrhus in his application of Greek tactics, he displayed a skill and precision all his own, and at Cannae he accomplished the most amazing feat of arms in ancient history. His capacity for leadership is set forth in a clear light by the fact that he exposed a motley army of race-alien conscripts and mercenaries to all manner of danger and hardship without provoking a single mutiny. His only notable deficiency was in siegecraft,

Hannibal and Scipio as war-leaders

in which he was plainly inferior to Alexander and Caesar. Though Roman tradition took vengeance on him by representing him as a monster of cruelty and perfidy there is nothing in his record to show that he did not respect the accepted usages of ancient warfare. Scipio for his part was an imitator of Hannibal: in all his big battles he followed the general lines of the Punic plan at Cannae. But he varied the details of Hannibal's tactics with unfailing ingenuity, and he ended by beating his master at his own game. He trained his army to a standard far higher than that of any other Roman force of conscripts, and he stood out among the Roman generals of his day by his humanity no less than by his military talent.[35]

In the Second Punic War the Carthaginian government displayed a far greater resolution and tenacity than in the First. It had strangely neglected to build up its navy, and it showed poor judgment in sending to Spain reinforcements which, if they could have reached Hannibal betimes, might have decided the issue of the war in all its theatres. On the other hand, after each defeat in Spain and in Africa it was unsparing in its efforts to remake its armies. But the principal heroes of the war were the Senate and people of Rome, and the Italians who stood by them. The main problem of the Second Punic War was whether Hannibal's superior military skill could be nullified by Rome's greater man-power and by the development of tactics which would enable the Romans after Cannae to face him again in a pitched battle with any hope of success. It was the doggedness and the readiness for personal sacrifice of the Romans and their allies that defeated Hannibal's calculations and turned the scales against him. Fabius's tactics provided the opportunity of recovery until the army trained in Scipio's new tactics was ready. This army, however, even if it defeated Hannibal in Italy, might end the war but it could not humble Carthage itself. This could be accomplished only by a successful invasion of North Africa, and it is Scipio's achievement to have forced this strategy through against political opposition at home and then to have vindicated it in the field. Well did his fellow Romans call him Scipio Africanus.

The 'home-fronts'

CHAPTER 14

The Conquest of the
Western Mediterranean

1. Rome's Expanding Dominance

Rome unifies the Mediterranean area

Although the Second Punic War was fought by the Romans in defence of past conquests it brought them extensive new acquisitions, and finally established their supremacy in the western Mediterranean. At the same time their copious man-power and military efficiency led them, often somewhat reluctantly, to action in the eastern Mediterranean. The result was that in little more than half a century they were the dominant power throughout the whole Mediterranean area, into which they introduced a unifying ecumenical influence for the first time in history, a process on which the contemporary Greek historian Polybius pondered with amazement.

Brief outline of events

The story of how between 200 and 133 B.C. the Romans reached this unparalleled position forms the theme of the next three chapters, but since we shall trace separately their expansion in various regions over considerable periods of time, it may be well here just to erect a few signposts in order to indicate the chronological interrelation of some of their major actions. Although in the first decade or so of the second century the Romans consolidated their grip on Cisalpine Gaul and on the Ligurian tribes to the north-west and had to face some hostilities in Spain which they had annexed as two provinces at the end of the Hannibalic War, their main effort was directed to the Hellenistic world in order to check the ambitions of Philip of Macedon and Antiochus III of Syria. By 194 they had defeated Philip in the Second Macedonian War and had withdrawn their forces from Greece where it had been fought. Scarcely was this confrontation over when they were drawn into a contest with Antiochus, who had invaded Greece: the Romans drove him out and then for the first time Roman armies crossed into Asia Minor, where the king was defeated and humbled. Over twenty years later a third struggle with Macedon led to the defeat of Philip's son Perseus in 168 and the abolition of the monarchy in Macedon, which the Romans divided into four republics. Rome still refused to undertake direct rule in the Balkans, which she now clearly dominated. Meantime in Spain, after some intermittent disturbances, Rome became involved in a series of long-drawn-out struggles with Celtiberian and Lusitanian tribes (154–133) who were harassing the two provinces. While these were dragging on Rome again intervened in Greece where a pretender to the defunct Macedonian throne upset the peace (Fourth Macedonian War). He was quickly crushed by another Roman expeditionary force, while Roman determination to establish order in southern Greece led to the destruction of Corinth (146). After four Macedonian Wars Rome at last turned to direct rule and established Macedonia as a Roman province. Meantime the coast of Italy had been protected by Roman action in Istria and Dalmatia. During the final struggle with Macedon Rome had at the same time (in 149) become engaged for the third time with her old enemy, Carthage, after a relatively peaceful co-existence for half a century. The quarrel ended with the destruction of Carthage in 146 and the establishment of a

Roman province of Africa (roughly modern Tunisia). From the time when Rome had first humbled the two great Hellenistic monarchies of Macedon and Syria, she naturally dominated the lesser kingdoms and cities of the Hellenistic world. Thus she extended her influence and patronage over various peoples who were often at loggerheads among themselves: a policy of 'divide and rule' was inevitably easy. In particular she often intervened in the interminable quarrels between Egypt and Syria and in the internal feuds of various Ptolemaic kings, while in Asia Minor she had constant diplomatic relations with the republic of Rhodes, the kingdom of Pergamum and peoples such as the Bithynians, Galatians and Cappadocians. Here the scene changed radically in 133 when Attalus, king of Pergamum, bequeathed his kingdom to the Romans who accepted the legacy and created the province of Asia. Thus whereas at the end of the Hannibalic War Rome had added Spain to her older provinces of Sicily, Corsica and Sardinia, now more than fifty years later she annexed Africa and Macedonia and took over Asia. Her power was now beyond serious threat or challenge, but its acquisition resulted in vast problems not only of administration but of cultural and economic pressures: could a city-state rule an empire and could the *mos maiorum* successfully meet the challenge of new and often revolutionary ideas? But before we consider the results of conquest we must now first follow out the process of Rome's expansion in detail.

2. The Final Reduction of Cisalpine Gaul

In peninsular Italy the recovery of the districts which had gone over to Hannibal was all but completed before his departure. Those regions of Lucania and Bruttium which Hannibal had retained to the last made an immediate surrender after his return to Africa. Capua lost its municipal self-government, and the Bruttians were left for an indefinite period as *dediticii*, without any treaty rights, and with only such autonomy as Rome chose to concede to them on grounds of administrative convenience. Tarentum was allowed to renew its treaty with Rome, and in general the political status of the southern Italians was not disturbed. But the rebel communities were punished by drastic reductions of territory. One half of the Bruttian peninsula and the whole of the domain of Capua were converted into Roman *ager publicus*. The area thus acquired was far too vast for complete repopulation with Romans or Latins; but a chain of colonies was founded in 194–

Roman land-confiscations in southern Italy

192 along the south-west coast from the mouth of the Volturnus to the Strait of Messina. Of these settlements the only one that attained more than local importance was Puteoli, a station between Cumae and Neapolis, which eventually became the principal port of southern Italy.[1]

In northern Italy the Second Punic War was succeeded by ten further years of fighting. During that war the Cisalpine Gauls had given so little support to the Carthaginians that a force of two legions had generally sufficed to hold them in check. Left to their own resources at the conclusion of peace they endeavoured to forestall Roman retribution by a belated but vigorous offensive. In 200 the Insubres, Cenomani (round Verona), and Boii jointly attacked the river fortresses of Placentia and Cremona, which previously had suffered nothing worse than a loose blockade, and they carried and destroyed Placentia. Here their progress ended; but in the next two years they held their own against the inadequate Roman detachments sent to round them up. In 197 two consular armies delivered a convergent counter-attack upon the Gauls. While one division crossed the Apennines near Genua and made a drive down the Po valley, the other advanced beyond that river and defeated the main levy of the Cenomani and Insubres on the banks of the Mincio near Mantua. A second victory gained in the ensuing year near Lake Como by M. Claudius Marcellus (son of the hero of Clastidium: p. 22) obliged the Insubres and Cenomani to sue for peace. These two tribes were left in possession of their land, but they were probably bound by their treaties to render occasional military aids to Rome.[2] The Boii were left over for a later reckoning, for in 195–192 no serious attempt was made to reduce them. But in 191 they were finally defeated by P. Cornelius Scipio Nasica (a son of Gnaeus Scipio and cousin of Africanus). In the settlement of accounts with Rome they were now charged compound interest, for they were required to surrender one half of their territory. The dispossessed Boii drifted away to the Danube regions, where the name of Bohemia remains as a record of their last settlement. The long duration of the war in northern Italy was partly due to the Romans' need of rest after the Hannibalic War, partly to their new commitments in Spain and the East (Chapters 15, 16), which prevented them from maintaining continuously a large army in northern Italy.

Of the territory taken from the Boii a considerable portion was reserved for colonial settlement. In addition to the older fortresses

Final reduction of northern Italy

of Placentia and Cremona, which received fresh drafts of settlers, three new colonies were founded: a Latin colony at Bononia (189), and Roman colonies at Mutina and Parma (183). Of these cities Bononia, which was the Roman successor of a Villanovan, an Etruscan and a Gallic town, was lavishly endowed with an estate of more than 600 square miles. But most of the surrendered land was disposed of in *viritane* assignations. These individual allotments clustered most thickly in the Po valley and along the new Roman roads. They were constituted as *fora*, with partial powers of self-government.[3]
The Roman settlements in northern Italy were connected with several new military roads, of which the most important ·was the Via Aemilia Lepidi (called after Aemilius Lepidus, consul in 187, who arranged for its construction). This highway (whose name survives in the modern district of Emiglia) continued the Via Flaminia from Ariminum to Placentia; over part of its course it ran on a raised causeway, as the adjacent land was exposed to inundation. The intensive resettlement of northern Italy brought about its rapid assimilation. Travelling through the Po valley some fifty years after its final reduction by the Romans, the Greek historian Polybius observed that the roadside districts were already Italianised, and although the name of 'Gallia Cisalpina' remained in official use, in the ordinary parlance of the first century the sub-Alpine lands were included under the term of 'Italia'.

Colonies and roads in northern Italy

Romanisation of northern Italy

3. The Ligurian Wars

Apart from the establishment of naval outposts at Genua and Luna (Spezia) before the Second Punic War (p. 122), and the clearing of the pass from Genua to the Po valley in 197, the Romans were slow to set foot on the territory of Liguria (the Italian Riviera and its hinterland). This region, the most barren and impenetrable of all Italy, had been left by successive invaders of Italy since the Bronze Age in the hands of a primitive population, who seemed to Roman observers of the second century to be little better than savages. But the need to protect the cross-roads from the west coast to Cisalpine Gaul, and to secure maritime communications from Italy to Spain against the pirates in the Gulf of Lions, obliged the Romans to take possession of Liguria. In 187 the consul C. Flaminius supplemented the Via Flaminia, which his father had constructed, by a trans-Apennine route from the Arno valley to Bononia. From 186 to 180 the Senate regularly commissioned two consular armies to reduce the

Campaigns in Liguria

native strongholds and to secure the Roman lines of communication. In these campaigns, conducted with heavy infantry in unfamiliar country against light-footed skirmishers, the Roman forces repeatedly suffered reverses, or won victories to no purpose. But by persistent attacks they succeeded in occupying the mountain-glens one by one, or in starving out the populations. In 181 L. Aemilius Paullus first made his mark by forcing the tribe of the Ingauni (to the west of Genua) into submission; in 180 two proconsuls subdued the Apuani (between Genua and Luna) and deported 40,000 of them to Samnium. Although Liguria continued for some time to be a favourite ground for Roman triumph-hunters – in 173 a consul named M. Popillius even went so far as to attack an unoffending tribe for the sake of taking booty off them – its pacification was now substantially complete.

The Ligurian Wars occasioned a sympathetic rising on the part of the Corsicans, who no doubt were confederates in their piratical pursuits (181). This revolt was promptly suppressed; but a more serious rising by the Sardinians kept a consular army under Ti. Sempronius Gracchus occupied for two years (177–176). Gracchus made Sardinia safe for the Romans by carrying off a large part of the population into slavery. But the Roman occupation of the two islands was even now scarcely extended beyond the seaboard.

Corsica and Sardinia

The conquest of Liguria was not followed by any systematic Roman settlement, though the outpost at Luna was reconstituted as a Roman colony in 177. The highroad to Genua (Via Aemilia Scauri), which offered special difficulties of construction because of the rugged nature of the Riviera coast, was not completed until 109.[4]

At the other extremity of northern Italy the Romans stood in continuously friendly relations with the Illyrian tribe of the Veneti. But occasional inroads by mountain peoples from the Alpine borderlands determined them to establish a large Latin colony on the site of Aquileia, from which the passes through the Julian and Carnic Alps could be readily observed (181). This station also served to watch the Istri, who shared the piratical habits of their Illyrian kinsmen further south. In 178 the consul A. Manlius Vulso, who had been sent to overawe a confederacy of Istrian cantons, went beyond his instructions in making a preventive attack upon them. The war in this quarter opened with the usual Roman defeat in an unexplored country, but two campaigns sufficed for the final reduction of the Istrian peninsula. No further colonies were founded

Subjugation of Istria

in this region, but an infiltration of private Roman settlers gradually converted it into an integral part of Italy.

4. The Spanish Wars, 197–179 B.C.

The conquests made by the Romans in Spain during the Second Punic War were primarily intended to deprive the Carthaginians of a base of attack upon Italy. It was therefore an obvious postulate of Roman policy that the Punic government should not be allowed to recover its foothold there. This object might have been *Annexation* accomplished without a permanent occupation *of Spain* of the country, if it had been possible to set *by the* up strong native principalities. But the *Romans* experience of two generations of Scipios had warned the Senate not to trust the competence or the enduring loyalty of any native chieftain. An additional reason for retaining the recent Spanish conquests in Roman hands was furnished by the mineral wealth of the country, which had contributed materially to the helping out of the Roman finances in the last stages of the war, and promised to be a substantial source of revenue for the future. In 197 therefore the Senate made arrangements for the regular administration of the conquered territory in Spain by converting it into two new provinces, Hispania Citerior and Hispania Ulterior, and providing for the annual election of two additional praetors to govern them. At this time Hither Spain comprised little more than the eastern seaboard of the peninsula as far as (and inclusive of) New Carthage; Further Spain was roughly co-extensive with modern Andalusia.

In appointing officers of the rank of praetor to administer the Spanish provinces the Senate assumed that their pacification was almost com- *Roman mis-* plete; in this belief it reduced the garrison of *government* each province to a small corps of 8000 Italian *in Spain* auxiliaries. But in the very year in which the provinces were constituted warfare in Spain was renewed, and it was not until 133 that Roman rule became firmly established. The protracted Spanish wars of the second century arose partly from the exactions of the Roman governors, which a people unaccustomed to any sort of political discipline could not easily tolerate. During the Second Punic War the Spaniards had at first welcomed the Romans as deliverers from the Carthaginian yoke; but as soon as they began to realise that they were exchanging one overlord for another, they wavered in their loyalty. After the departure of Scipio and the relaxation of the strict discipline which he had imposed upon his troops, the oppressive charac-

ter of Roman rule soon became apparent. Even the Phoenician towns of Gades and Malaca, which had been accorded special treaties as a reward for their ready surrender, had to complain that the guarantees of municipal liberty accorded to them were not being respected.[5] But the commonest cause of disturbance lay in the habitual unrest of the peoples who had been left unconquered by the Carthaginians and for the present remained outside the sphere of Roman rule, the Lusitanians in the western part of the peninsula and the Celtiberians of Castile and Aragon. The Romans in Spain found themselves in the same position as the pioneers of the British dominion in India, who were driven to the expedient of making new conquests in order to safeguard previous ones. But as the Roman armies penetrated further into Spain *Difficulties* they were beset with all the peculiar difficulties *of cam-* under which invaders of that country have *paigning in* always laboured. Their unfamiliarity with the *Spain* hinterland made them easy victims of ambuscades, which were laid in the concealed watercourses of the plateaux or in the forests, with which Spain was then more richly provided than at the present day. The long marching distances in a country with double the expanse of Italy, and the peril of starvation in its extensive steppe-lands, presented new problems which Roman warcraft did not readily overcome. The elusiveness of the Spaniards, who possessed all their modern descendants' aptitude for guerrilla war, prevented the Romans from obtaining pitched battles except under the natives' own conditions.[9]

It is not possible to give more than a general account of the Roman wars in Spain, because of the wide gaps in our ancient sources and their lack of topographical detail. In 197 hostilities *Risings* began in the extreme south of Spain, where the *of the* tribe of the Turdetani rose in revolt and received *Spaniards* the support of Malaca and other Phoenician *against* towns. In the same year another rebellion broke *Rome* out at the opposite end of the peninsula, between the Ebro and the Pyrenees. Between these two foci of insurrection the Celtiberians, whom the Turdetani enlisted for mercenary service, formed a connecting-link. Against such a widespread movement the inadequate Roman garrisons could make little headway until 195, when the Roman forces were increased to a total of some 50,000 men, and one of the consuls, M. Porcius Cato, was sent to take supreme command. This hard fighter stamped out the insurrection in the north, and he opened up a new line of communications between the two provinces by following the course of the river Salo (a tributary of the Ebro) towards the sources of the Tagus. In 194 the Turdetani were defi-

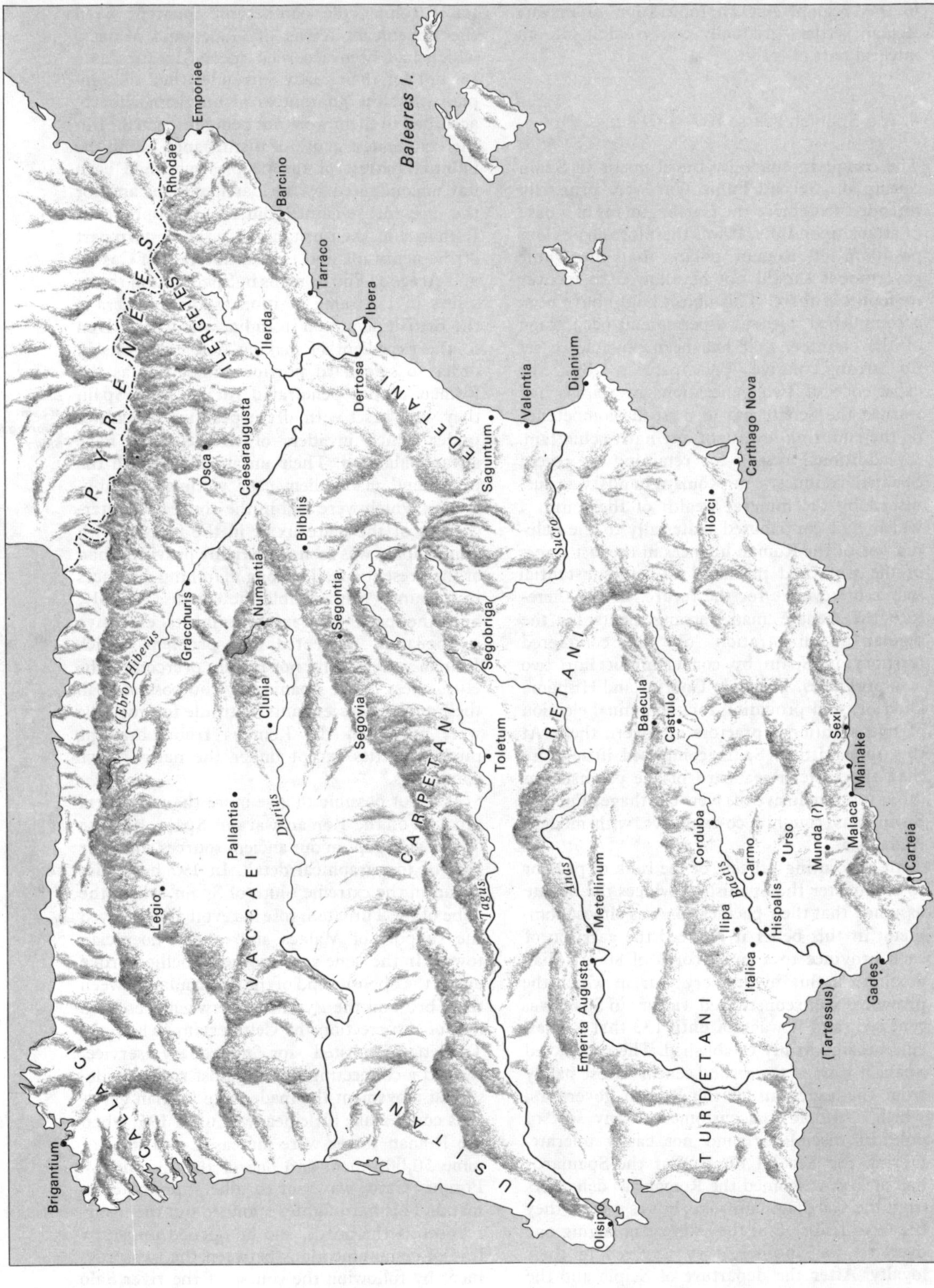

Baleares I.

Emporiae
Rhodae
Barcino
Tarraco
Ibera
Dertosa

P Y R E N E E S

I L E R G E T E S

(Ebro) *Hiberus*
Osca
Caesaraugusta
Ilerda

E D E T A N I

Valentia
Dianium
Saguntum
Sucro

Carthago Nova
Ilorci

Bilbilis
Gracchuris
Numantia
Segontia

C A R P E T A N I

Segobriga
Toletum

O R E T A N I

Clunia
Segovia

Baecula
Castulo

Sexi
Mainake
Malaca

V A C C A E I

Pallantia
Durius
Tagus

Corduba
Munda (?)
Carmo
Urso
Carteia

Legio

L U S I T A N I

Anas
Baetis
Metellinum
Ilipa
Hispalis

G A L L A E C I

Brigantium

Emerita Augusta
Italica

T U R D E T A N I

(Tartessus)
Gades

Olisipo

12. SPAIN

The Celtiberian and Lusitanian Wars

nitely reduced to submission by the praetor Scipio Nasica (the future victor over the Boii)—p. 139. But the Celtiberians, whom Cato had vainly attempted to buy over or to bring to a set battle, carried on the war, and in the same year the Lusitanians joined in. In the next twelve years the only notable Roman success was the occupation of New Castile (the territory of the Carpetani and Oretani) by two armies converging from the Ebro valley and from the south (193–192), and its renewed subjection after a rebellion (185). In the latter campaign the two praetors defeated a combined force of Celtiberians and Lusitanians in one of the few set encounters of the war. They achieved their victory by a double outflanking movement in the Scipionic style, in which their native auxiliary troops took a prominent part. Four years later the praetor Fulvius Flaccus gained a similar success over another army of Celtiberian invaders in New Castile. These actions prepared the way for a combined drive against the Celtiberians, which the pro-praetors Sp. Postumius and Ti. Sempronius Gracchus (the future pacifier of Sardinia) carried out in 179. While Gracchus moved from the south-east through New Castile, Postumius advanced northward from the river Guadiana into the territory of the Vaccaei (in the middle basin of the Douro). Thus caught in front and rear, the Celtiberians sued for peace and became tributary to Rome. Their submission was followed by a general settlement, which gave the Romans control of the whole peninsula with the exception of its Atlantic seaboard. This pacification was in large measure due to the personal ascendancy of Gracchus, who gained the confidence of the Spaniards as no Roman had succeeded in doing since the departure of Scipio Africanus. As the latter had left a settlement of veterans at Italica in the Baetis valley (p. 147) so Gracchus founded Gracchuris on the Upper Ebro as a centre of Roman civilisation.

The Celtiberians submit

5. The Spanish Wars, 154–133 B.C.

From 179 to 154 the Spaniards observed the terms of Gracchus's settlement; but successive Roman governors endangered it by acts of oppression, and the complaints addressed by the sufferers to the Senate were met with little more than promises. In the meantime, too, a new generation of Celtiberians and Lusitanians was growing up which wanted its war. Thus another twenty-year round of campaigns was opened in 154, during which the two last-named tribes took it in turns to keep the Romans in play. An invasion of Further Spain by the Lusitanians

Renewed risings

in 154 was followed next year by a Celtiberian rising. In 153–152 the consul Fulvius Nobilior attempted a direct invasion of Old Castile from Aragon by the valley of the Salo (modern Jalon) and forced his way as far as Numantia, a small but well-built town which was the key to the upper basin of the Douro. Here he lost a battle through a panic among a small corps of elephants which the Numidian chieftain Masinissa had sent to his assistance, and his was the first grave in the cemetery of Roman reputations at Numantia. His advance to the citadel of the Celtiberian land nevertheless achieved a moral effect, for his successor, the consul M. Claudius Marcellus, was able to conclude a fresh agreement with the Celtiberians. The policy of conciliation which Marcellus adopted in regard to the Spaniards stood in opposition to the wishes of the Senate; but he successfully overrode his home government and gave Hispania Citerior eight years' respite from war (151–143).

The peace with the Celtiberians left the Roman governors free to concentrate against the Lusitanians, who had gained repeated successes against the Roman forces in Further Spain and in 151 inflicted a severe defeat upon the praetor Servius Sulpicius Galba. In the same year Marcellus's successor, L. Licinius Lucullus, made an unprovoked attack upon the Vaccaei of the middle Douro valley, where he reduced the town of Cauca to surrender at discretion and massacred part of the capitulants. Though Lucullus did not commit a formal breach of faith, he set an example of sharp practice which was followed by later governors impartially after victory and defeat, and in the long run stiffened rather than broke the resistance of the Spaniards. In 150 Lucullus went to the assistance of Galba and inflicted such losses upon the Lusitanians that they sued for peace. Galba, who conducted the negotiations, lured a large number of the Lusitanians away from their homes by an offer of better land in other regions; having thus isolated them, he used the same short way with them as Lucullus with the Vaccaei. But far from making the peace safe by this wanton perfidy, he incensed the Lusitanians to a renewal of war.

Roman atrocities in Lusitania

In their last struggle against Rome the Lusitanians were captained by a born guerrilla leader named Viriathus, who rose from the calling of a herdsman to a position of almost royal authority. From 146 to 141 Viriathus won an almost unbroken series of victories over five Roman commanders and made repeated incursions into the Roman provinces. His sweeping successes encouraged the Celtiberians to take the field once more (143), so that after ten years of fighting the Romans seemed as far off as ever from

The Spanish guerrilla campaign under Viriathus

13. PLAN OF NUMANTIA

a settlement. In 141 Viriathus manoeuvred the consul Fabius Maximus Servilianus into a position from which there was no escape, but he spared his opponent in return for a treaty, in which the freedom of the Lusitanians was acknowledged by the Romans. In thus putting his trust in the plighted word of a Roman he was violating his own precept, for he had previously warned his tribesmen against any understanding with the compatriots of Galba: presumably the strain of a continuous guerrilla operation was beginning to tell upon his people. Fabius's compact was ratified at Rome by Senate and Comitia. Nevertheless in 140 his successor, Servilius

Caepio, persuaded the Senate to disavow it, in order to recommence hostilities with the Lusitanians. In this new campaign Viriathus outmanoeuvred Caepio, yet was driven to a capitulation through the desertion of his own troops. Caepio took the opportunity to cap his previous treachery with another profitable perfidy, for he bribed Viriathus's agents to murder their chief in his sleep. Left without a capable leader, the Lusitanians shortly after made their submission (139). With the annexation of Lusitania the extension of the Roman dominion in Spain was brought to a close for the time being. In 137 Caepio's successor, D. Iunius Brutus, made a

Murder of Viriathus

144

raid into Galicia as far as the river Minho, but attempted no permanent conquests apart from fortifying Olisipo (modern Lisbon); the Roman frontier in western Spain was drawn for the present along the line of the Tagus.

In Hither Spain the Celtiberians were driven from the field in a rapid campaign (143–142) by the consul Q. Caecilius Metellus, an officer who had gained experience in dealing with rebellion in Macedonia (p. 160), so that his successors had nothing left to do but to reduce a few outstanding cities. Of these, however,

Numantia defied the Romans for nine years. Its military population did not exceed 8000, but its position between two rivers flowing in deep ravines was one of great natural strength, and the forest belt which surrounded it was a ready-made trap for investing forces.[7] In 141–140 Metellus's successor, Q. Pompeius, was himself put under siege in his camp by the defenders of the city. Nevertheless he induced them to sign a treaty and even to pay an indemnity. As soon as he had pocketed the fine Pompeius went back upon his bargain, and he found the Senate

The campaigns around Numantia

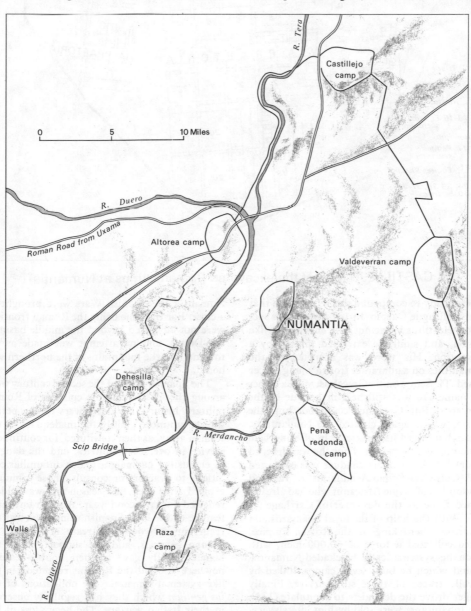

14. SCIPIO'S SIEGE OF NUMANTIA, 133 B.C.

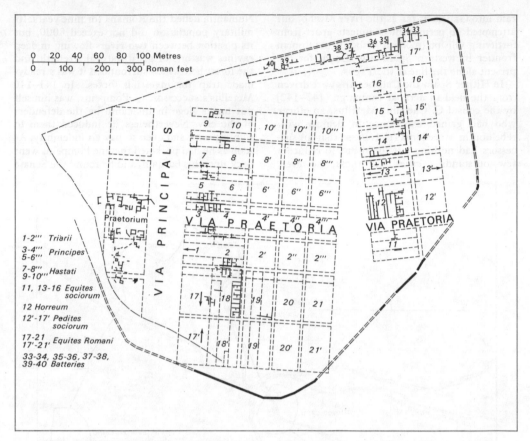

1-2''' Triarii
3-4''' Principes
5-6'''
7-8''' Hastati
9-10'''
11, 13-16 Equites
sociorum
12 Horreum
12'-17' Pedites
sociorum
17-21 Equites Romani
17'-21'
33-34, 35-36, 37-38,
39-40 Batteries

15. CASTILLEJO (one of the excavated Roman camps at Numantia)

Capture of Numantia by Scipio Aemilianus

no less ready to compound this felony than that of his colleague Caepio. In 137 Pompeius's successor, Hostilius Mancinus, was ensnared in like fashion, and similarly extracted himself by a convention. His word was accepted by the Numantines on a guarantee from a young officer named Ti. Sempronius Gracchus, whose father and namesake was still held in honour by the Spaniards. But Gracchus could not bind the Senate, which again cheated the Numantines, although it salved its conscience by offering them Mancinus as a scapegoat. Thus the war dragged on until 134, when its conduct was entrusted to P. Cornelius Scipio Aemilianus, a grandson by adoption of Scipio Africanus who had already earned fame as the destroyer of Carthage (p. 149). With the help of the loyal Spaniards and of various client kings in the Roman Empire, Scipio collected a force of 60,000 men, with which he systematically blockaded Numantia, around which he built seven camps, linked by a wall; traces of these still survive. Finally hunger drove the defenders to capitulate (133). The inhabitants were sold by him into slavery, and the town was destroyed. With the fall of

Numantia the Spanish Wars were brought to a close. For the time being the Roman frontiers were not advanced beyond the middle basin of the Douro, and no attempt was made as yet to penetrate the mountains of the northern seaboard.

The Spanish Wars of the second century were among the least creditable episodes of Roman military history. No other wars of the period showed up more plainly the inadequacy of the Roman army, as then consituted, for continuous service in overseas countries, and the dangers of entrusting campaigns under unfamiliar conditions to praetors or consuls whose command expired after their first season and was seldom renewed for a second year. An extraordinary feature of the later Spanish campaigns was the recurrent disavowal of treaty obligations by Roman generals, and the support which the Senate usually gave to their double-dealing: nowhere else did the Romans repudiate in the like systematic manner the obligations of the *ius gentium* which they had regularly observed in their Italian warfare. The heavy loss of life which attended the Spanish Wars reacted upon

Roman breaches of faith

the course of politics at Rome. It stirred up a passing gust of resentment in the Roman citizen body (p. 202), and it contributed to a more deep-seated discontent among the Italian allies. But if the conquest of Spain revealed unsuspected weaknesses in the Roman military system, it also reinforced the lesson of the Punic wars, that the Senate disposed of a sufficient man-power to reduce all its adversaries by sheer exhaustion, and would not recoil from engaging it, if necessary, in a prodigal manner.

In Spain no systematic attempt was made to follow up the Roman conquest by colonisation. But in a few instances discharged soldiers who had become acclimatised by long service and (we may surmise) had taken native wives, were permitted to settle down near the scene of their campaigns. In 206 Scipio Africanus pensioned off some of his veterans with grants of land at Italica (near Seville), which was constituted as a town of Italian pattern as was Gracchuris (p. 143).[8] In 171 a Latin colony made up of like elements was founded at Carteia (near Gibraltar). A mixed population of Roman veterans and of Lusitanian captives was settled at Valentia about 138, and the town of Corduba was probably composed of similar ingredients (152 B.C.). Round these centres the romanisation of southern and eastern Spain made an early start.

Roman settlements in Spain

6. Rome, Carthage and Numidia

Of all the problems which confronted the Romans after the Second Punic War the question of their future relations to Carthage was the simplest, and yet it was the least successfully handled. While the terms of the peace of 201 destroyed the former trade monopoly of the Carthaginians they imposed no particular disability upon Punic commerce. Under these conditions Carthage was able to resume its place as the mercantile capital of the western Mediterranean. At the same time it obtained a rising revenue from the African hinterland, where the Punic landowners introduced a more intensive system of cultivation.[9] While the city's fund of wealth was being replenished, its administration was amended by Hannibal, who used his unabated influence with the Carthaginian people to make the government accountable for the money handled by it. In 191, or ten years from the end of the war, the defeated state was able to offer immediate payment of forty further instalments of its indemnity; in the same year, and on several later occasions, it contributed large consignments of corn as free gifts for the Roman expeditionary forces in the eastern

Economic recovery of Carthage

Mediterranean. Carthage, it is true, did not long enjoy the benefit of Hannibal's honest statesmanship. His political opponents took vengeance by accusing him before the Roman Senate of collusion with Rome's enemies in the eastern Mediterranean (pp. 162 f., 165) and soliciting a Roman embassy to lay complaints against him before the Carthaginian council (195). On the arrival of the Roman commissioners Hannibal at once sought safety in flight, and the Punic aristocracy resumed its former ascendancy. But the ostentatious deference of the Carthaginian government to Rome's ill-authorised interference gave plain proof that all thought of *revanche* had passed out of its mind.

Exile of Hannibal

But if the Romans had every reason to be reassured about the attitude of Carthage, another former enemy of that city used all means in his power to keep alive their suspicions. By the peace of 201 Rome's former ally Masinissa had been made king over an undivided realm of Numidia. During the next half-century he applied himself indefatigably to the development of his enlarged dominion.[10] With a standing army of 50,000 men at his back, he reduced the border chieftains to submission and gave Numidia an unwonted security against raids from the steppe-lands of the interior. Under the more settled conditions which his strong rule created he induced the inhabitants of the fertile sea-border to forsake their semi-nomadic habits and to bring their cultivable lands under the plough. But Masinissa's restless energy, like that of Tsar Peter, was not wholly absorbed in the business of internal development; his ultimate ambition was to form an empire comprising the modern territories of Algeria, Tunisia and Tripoli. Under cover of the treaty of 201, which deprived the Carthaginians of the right of self-defence, he proceeded to appropriate by progressive encroachments the Punic dependencies on the seaboard of North Africa, and to lop off pieces of the Tunisian hinterland. In reliance on the same treaty, which placed at least a moral obligation upon the Romans to defend Carthage against attacks by a third party, the Punic government sent protest after protest to the Senate. But Masinissa was on his guard against these claims for redress. No only did he outdo the Punic government in his proofs of loyalty to Rome, sending consignments of corn to the Roman expeditionary forces in the east and auxiliary troops or elephants to the armies in Spain, but he lost no opportunity of keeping alive the latent fear of Punic reprisals in the minds of the Senate. By these devices he contrived to turn successive arbitral awards by the Romans in his favour.[11] In 150 at last the Carthaginians, unable to

Masinissa's strong rule in Numidia

His aggressions against Carthage

obtain justice from Rome, took their cause into their own hands and made open war upon Masinissa. Their improvised forces fared ill at the hands of the trained levies of the Numidian king, who seized the opportunity to extort another corner of Tunisia, including part of the fertile Bagradas valley, as the price of peace. At this stage the dominion of Masinissa extended from the borders of Mauretania as far as Cyrenaica and closely enveloped the territory of Carthage, now reduced to a mere 5000 square miles.

The defeat of the Carthaginians in the campaign of 150 ought assuredly to have revealed to the Romans from what quarter, if any, they ought to apprehend danger. There had indeed always been in the Senate a party which deprecated the continuation of the Second Punic War into peacetime, and this group had the powerful support of the Scipios. In 195 Africanus had made a vain attempt to shield Hannibal against his own compatriots. In 152 a Roman commissioner named P. Scipio Nasica had for once compelled Masinissa to disgorge a slice of filched Punic territory, and two years later he spoke in defence of Carthage before the Senate. But the spectre of Hannibal still haunted Rome. Nurses told fractious children that Hannibal was coming to fetch them; politicians conjured up the same dread name to throw the Senate into a thoroughly un-Roman panic. The enemies of Carthage, moreover, were aided by the powerful advocacy of the veteran M. Cato. This formidable character scorned illicit gain but disdained no respectable means of enrichment, and it has been argued that he and some other senators may have been influenced by hopes of economic advantage from the complete ruin of Carthage. This is most improbable; more likely his predominant motive was honest if misguided fear.[12] As a soldier in the Second Punic War, he had felt the weight of Hannibal's arm; on a recent embassy to Carthage he had been perturbed by the symptoms of its renewed material prosperity. Exploiting to the utmost the fact that in resorting to arms the Carthaginians had committed a technical infraction of the peace of 201 he denounced them as inveterate treaty-breakers, and reinforcing a weak argument with obstinate iteration, he wound up every speech in the Senate with the monotonous refrain that Carthage must be destroyed. Under the weight of this mass attack the Senate capitulated to Cato. In 150 it sent an embassy to Carthage with orders to protest against the city's recourse to arms, but to withhold all information as to legitimate means of redress against Masinissa. In 149 it procured from the Comitia a formal declaration of war, and the consuls led an expeditionary force to Africa. Under this menace the Carthaginians made a formal surrender (*deditio*) as a desperate bid for peace. On first demand they gave hostages and surrendered all their war-material (inclusive of 2000 catapults). But as successive instalments of the Roman blackmail were paid the consuls raised the terms of ransom. Their final statement of conditions required the Carthaginians to abandon their town and betake themselves to some inland site in Tunisia. To a people which derived its livelihood from the sea and placed all its pride in its ships this demand was a sentence of communal extinction. By a sudden revulsion of sentiment the threatened people turned from abject submission to frenzied defiance. While the consuls were completing their unhurried war-preparations in Sicily the whole population of Carthage worked feverishly at the defences of the city and the replenishment of the military and naval arsenals. At the same time the government improvised a new field army. No assistance was forthcoming from the neighbouring town of Utica (always a lukewarm ally of Carthage) or the other Phoenician settlements in Tunisia, all of which made an early peace with Rome; but a considerable force was levied (presumably by promises of high pay) among the Libyans of the hinterland. On the other hand Masinissa adopted the unfamiliar part of an onlooker. Having overplayed his hand in his intrigues at Rome against Carthage, so that the Romans now seized his destined prey for themselves, he gave vent to his chagrin by withholding support from them.

Attitude of the Romans to Carthage

Cato's call for strong measures

The Roman ultimatum

Punic war-preparations

7. The Third Punic War

Thanks to the eleventh-hour effort of Carthage the Third Punic War, instead of being a mere military execution, lasted through four hard-fought campaigns.[13] In 149–148 the Romans drew their lines round the city, but could make little headway against its massive fortifications and the determination of its defenders, who had found in Hasdrubal, the head of their war-party, a resourceful tactician and engineer. Neither could they establish an effective blockade; indeed their own supply-columns were seriously hampered by the Punic guerrilla bands in the hinterland. The siege operations made no appreciable progress until 147, when the people, against the wishes of the Senate, expressed its impatience by conferring a consulship and the high command in Africa on a junior officer who had returned to Rome to stand for an aedileship and was in no way technically qualified for the consulship. The new general, P. Cornelius Sci-

The Third Punic War

pio Aemilianus, was a son by blood of Aemilius Paullus, the victor of the Third Macedonian War (p. 159), and a grandson by adoption of Scipio Africanus.[14] Inheriting the traditions of two great military houses he had made his mark, where others had failed, in the campaigns of 149–148; in 147–146 he won a reputation second only to that of his elder namesake, though he owed his success to sheer driving power rather than to brilliant strategy. Pressing the attack against a garrison which never lost heart, but was being gradually overborne by hunger, he broke through the outer wall, and in a week of hard street-fighting mauled his way to the citadel, where the surviving inhabitants, a mere 50,000, made their surrender. This remnant was sold into slavery; the city was razed to the ground, and its site was doomed by exhaustive imprecations to utter desolation.

Scipio Aemilianus captures and destroys Carthage

The ghost of Hannibal was now laid but the Romans would not let the territory of Carthage pass out of their hands. The remaining hinterland of the city was constituted into a Roman province under the name of 'Africa', and the frontier of the new province was delimited by a continuous trench, the *fossa Scipionis*. The Phoenician cities of the seaboard were rewarded for their desertion of Carthage with a guarantee of municipal freedom and an increase of territory; Utica in particular inherited a large share of the trade of Carthage. It is noteworthy than when a large part of North Africa lay open to Rome the new province was limited to the diminished territory which Carthage had controlled in 150. Rome had clearly acted from what she believed to be political necessity or expediency, not from any desire for territorial expansion: Carthage must be destroyed, but Roman commitments must be kept to the minimum, while the rest of the area could be left in the hands of native client states. Thus Rome's predominance was assured at the minimum cost of direct administration, although a larger province would have produced more revenue from taxes.

The Roman province of 'Africa'

Three years before the fall of Carthage king Masinissa died at the age of ninety. After a temporary partition between three of his sons, his realm was reunited under his eldest son Micipsa. This ruler had neither the opportunity nor the ambition to extend the Numidian boundaries still further, but contented himself with carrying on his father's work of internal development.

Death of Masinissa

A retrospect of the Punic Wars will impose the conclusion that they were largely of Rome's making. In the first war Rome struck the first blow; the second war was in effect the outcome of Rome's seizure of Sardinia and Corsica; the third war was a case of sheer persecution. In the actual conduct of the wars it is not easy to strike a balance between the combatants on the score of military ability and firmness of purpose. If the Carthaginians injured themselves by undue economy of effort in the first war they made amends by the determination with which they fought out the second war and by the blind heroism of their last stand against Rome; their triple defeat was due in greater measure to their inferior man-power than to lack of skill in the use of their limited resources.

The Punic Wars. Retrospect

But if the Punic Wars are to be judged by their broad results we must not grudge the Romans their victory. Whatever its deficiencies Roman imperialism at any rate did not exclude the idea of a partnership between members of the empire, even though the relationship tended to become one of patron and client. Carthaginian imperialism was definitely based on exploitation of the subject peoples. The lack of trustworthy man-power under which the Carthaginians laboured was the nemesis of their short-sighted policy towards their dependants: Rome won the Punic Wars by the willing assistance of the Italians, the Carthaginians could not even reckon on their Phoenician kinsmen. It was equally in the interest of ancient civilisation that Rome rather than Carthage should survive. Punic culture hardly progressed beyond technical inventiveness. The art of the Carthaginians produced little but indifferent imitations of objects imported from abroad. Their literature consisted mostly of practical manuals; of historical composition only a few lines have survived, of poetry there exists not a trace. Their religion, in which nature-deities and tutelary gods of the city were associated and partly fused in the usual manner of ancient city-states, could rouse them to heroic sacrifice, but it was tainted with a gloom and cruelty which made it an incubus rather than an inspiration. It is true that in the age of the Punic Wars the mind of the Romans was scarcely more awake to the amenities of life. Yet the germs of a higher civilisation had been laid in them, and in due time bore such fruit as a thousand years of political ascendancy and material prosperity would not have produced at Carthage.[15]

The Imperialism of Rome and Carthage; their respective cultures

CHAPTER 15

The Macedonian Wars

1. Early Contacts between Rome and Greece

At the same time as the Romans were rounding off their possessions in the western half of the Mediterranean they were laying the foundations of a dominion in its eastern basin. Their principal antagonists in the eastern Mediterranean were the Greeks. Between 800 and 500 B.C. the Greek people had occupied by sporadic colonisation the greater part of the Aegean seaboard and of the Black Sea coast. Their inability to combine their numerous city-states into a durable confederacy had been a bar to further expansion, and in the fourth century it had facilitated their conquest by king Philip II of Macedon. But by virtue of their superior culture the Greeks soon absorbed their half-civilised masters, and in the political sphere they came to play the part of allies rather than of subjects to the Macedonians. It was in partnership with the Greeks that Philip's son Alexander overthrew the Persian Empire (334–325); and although the principal dynasties established on the ruins of that dominion were Macedonian, yet as a soldier of adventure, as an administrator, as a civilian settler, it was the Greek that reaped the chief fruits of Alexander's campaigns. In the third century the eastern Mediterranean had virtually become a Greek lake. But it had ceased to be under a unified political control. After the death of Alexander in 323 his empire was split up into a number of succession-states, of which only three were at all comparable in resources to the Roman Republic of the third century. Of the three first-class powers in the 'Hellenistic' world (as the Greek world after Alexander is usually called) the dynasty of the Ptolemies

ruled over Egypt, Cyrene, Cyprus, the greater part of Syria, and a chain of maritime stations in the Levantine and Aegean seas; their capital was established at Alexandria, the greatest of Alexander's colonies in the East. The Seleucids, whose residence was at Antioch in northern Syria, held the eastern provinces of Alexander's empire and the southern half of Asia Minor. The Antigonids became kings of Macedonia and overlords of Thessaly, and exercised a somewhat fluctuating ascendancy over the rest of the Greek homeland. Despite quarrels these three kingdoms on the whole managed to maintain a balance of power and a considerable degree of stability.[1]

After the completion of his conquests in the east Alexander received a multitude of deputations from the peoples of the Mediterranean in his new capital at Babylon; from Italy envoys of the Bruttians, the Lucanians and the Etruscans visited his court. These missions, moreover, were not mere formalities, for many may have feared that Alexander might turn his arms westward in order to subdue Carthage and Italy, under pretence of assisting the western Greeks against their enemies.[2] Among the envoys to Alexander a Roman delegacy is said to have been present; but this statement rests on very doubtful evidence.[3] In any case the Romans did not enter into serious political contact with the Greek populations of the eastern Mediterranean until the war with Pyrrhus (pp. 94 ff.). After their victory over the king, however, they entered into friendly relations with Ptolemy II of Egypt (p. 96). Then followed their more direct contact with the Greek world in the Illyrian Wars which ended in 218 (p. 123).

2. The First Macedonian War

In 215 a new turn was given to the relations between Rome and the Greek world by the alliance of Philip V of Macedon with Hannibal (p. 132). In view of the part which this monarch played in drawing the Romans irrevocably into Greek politics, his position within the circle of Greek states will require explanation.[4] After the death of Alexander the union of Greek states which had been founded by his father, Philip II (p. 150), fell to pieces in the general ruin of his empire. Its place was partly filled by two sectional confederacies, the Achaean League in Peloponnesus and the Aetolian League in central Greece. But in 224 the predecessor of Philip V, Antigonus Doson, reunited the Greeks of the homeland in a second Hellenic confederacy, from which the Aetolians and the Athenians were the only notable absentees; and in 221 Philip succeeded him as

15.1   Philip V of Macedon.

Macedonian ascendancy in Greece Proper

captain-general of the League. The new king employed the first years of his reign in consolidating the confederacy. In 217, when all Greece was being startled by the news of the battles at the Trebia and the Trasimene Lake, and was divining the need to close the ranks against the as yet uncertain winner of the Second Punic War, he was instrumental in bringing about a general pacification of the Greek homeland. If Philip had continued to maintain a united Greek front in an attitude of vigilant neutrality it is extremely doubtful whether the Romans, with all their other commitments in the western Mediterranean, would have intervened any further in the affairs of the Greek world. But Philip, whose rising

The ambitions of Philip V

ambition rendered him impatient of a merely expectant policy, lent a willing ear to the promptings of the fugitive Demetrius of Pharos (p. 123), who for obvious reasons wished to bring Philip to blows with Rome. In 216 the Macedonian king went so far as to make a surreptitious attempt to restore Demetrius at Pharos, to prepare a fleet of light ships and to

acquire an outlet on the Adriatic for himself; but at the mere rumour of the advent of a Roman fleet he abandoned the enterprise.

· In the following year, however, Philip was emboldened by the Roman disaster at Cannae to enter into a compact of mutual assistance with Hannibal (p. 132). The king made no express stipulation in this treaty for anything more than the expulsion of the Romans from their protectorate in the eastern Adriatic. Whether or not he had the ulterior hope of gaining a foothold in southern Italy, and perhaps of reviving the schemes of king Pyrrhus for conquests in the west, the treaty at least secured him against a Roman war of revenge.

Treaty with Hannibal

As an incident of the Second Punic War the 'First Macedonian War' was of very slight importance (p. 132); and its immediate effect upon the relations of Greeks and Romans was of no great moment. In 214 the admiral Valerius Laevinus disembarked a small Roman force at Apollonia on the Illyrian coast to keep Philip in play; in 212/211 he negotiated alliances with the Aetolian League, which had a tradition of enmity against Macedon, and with Attalus I of Pergamum.[5] This king was ruler over a small but prosperous territory in north-western Asia Minor, which had detached itself from the dominion of the Seleucids; with a view to extending his possessions in the Aegean area at the expense of Macedon, he now came to terms with Laevinus. The bond thus formed between Rome and Pergamum was to have far-reaching future consequences, but its immediate results were trifling. After a series of desultory campaigns in the Greek homeland the First Macedonian War died of inanition. Its Greek participants made peace with Philip in 206; the Romans, after sending out reinforcements under Sempronius Tuditanus as a demonstration of Roman strength, followed suit in 205. By his treaty with Rome which was negotiated at Phoenice, the Macedonian king acquired a frontage on the Adriatic seaboard between the rivers Aoüs and Apsus (the district of Atintania). On the other hand he had thrown away the leadership of a united Greek homeland; and he had opened an account with Rome, of which the final settlement was yet to come.

The First Macedonian War

Roman alliance with the king of Pergamum

3. The Overtures of Pergamum and Rhodes to Rome

After the First Macedonian War Philip turned from the Adriatic, where his hopes of further expansion appeared to have been frustrated, to the Levant. In 203 he concluded a secret treaty

Philip's aggressions in the Aegean area

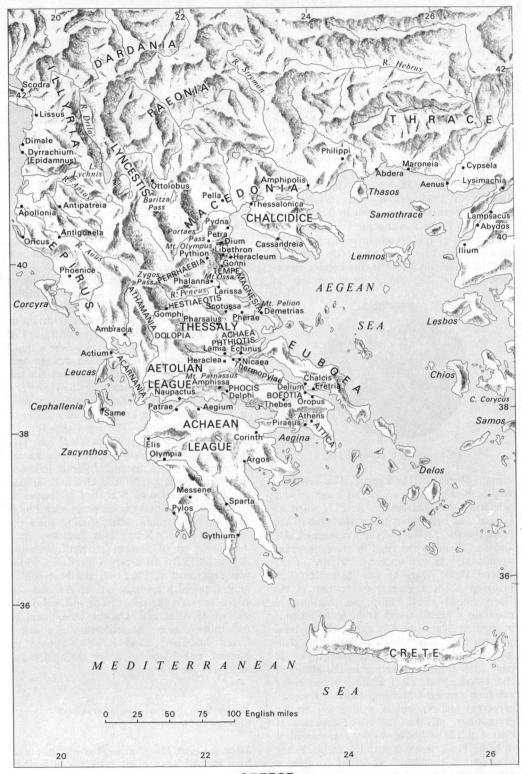

GREECE

with the Seleucid king, Antiochus III, who had invited him to make a joint attack upon the boy-king Ptolemy V of Egypt and to partition his overseas dominions. With a newly created fleet the Macedonian king carried several outposts of the Ptolemies in the Aegean area (202–201). But in this war he forfeited the remnant of his popularity with the Greeks through the indiscriminate attacks of his admirals on Aegean shipping, and through his wholesale enslavement of the inhabitants of towns captured by him — a practice which the relatively humane war-code of the Hellenistic Greeks no longer tolerated. Philip's barbarous methods of warfare drew upon him the active hostility of the city-state of Rhodes, which had extensive trading interests in the Aegean area and was always ready to engage its well-found war-fleet for the protection of its commerce. The Rhodians, further, had little difficulty in persuading Attalus of Pergamum to enter the field once *Pergamum* more against Philip. In a naval campaign, *and Rhodes* fought off the west coast of Asia Minor in 201, *solicit* the allies foiled a determined attack by Philip, *Roman aid* but the Pergamene king suffered heavy casualties. In order to redress the balance Attalus now resolved to enlarge the coalition against Philip by renewing his friendship with Rome. His embassy to the Senate was accompanied by a deputation from the Rhodians, who had hitherto watched the intrusion of the 'barbarians' into Greek politics with an unfriendly eye, but in their present embitterment against Philip no longer disdained to sue for alien assistance (201).

The Greek envoys reached Rome at a moment when the Republic stood in sore need of a respite from its exertions in the Second Punic War, and in any event had almost too many commitments in the western Mediterranean. Besides, Philip had at least kept the *The Senate* terms of his peace with Rome, and a formal *decides on* justification for declaring war upon him was *intervention* not ready at hand. Although the Senate for its part had not forgotten the opportunity which Philip had found in Rome's difficulty after Cannae,[6] it had not sought war a year before when some Aetolian envoys had asked for help against Philip: it had in fact sharply rebuffed them. Why then did it advocate war in 201? The most likely explanation is that the Rhodian and Pergamene envoys revealed the existence of the Syro–Macedonian pact. Thus the Senate suddenly became aware of the fact that Antiochus was behind Philip and so it decided to strike at Philip before the kings began to cooperate. Near the end of the year P. Sulpicius Galba, who had campaigned in Macedonia from 210 to 206, was elected consul for 200

with Macedonia as his province. But when in 200 he summoned the Comitia Centuriata to pass a formal declaration of war upon Philip, on the plausible though legally invalid ground that he had attacked the allies of Rome,[7] the commons, taking a shorter view than the Senate, voted solidly against war piled on war. But when Sulpicius some time later returned to the charge with a bullying speech, in which he warned them that they must fight Philip in Macedonia or in Italy, they sanctioned a preventive attack upon the king. In the meantime Athens had been attacked by Philip's allies, the Acarnanians, and Cephisodorus, an envoy sent by Athens to Rome to add his voice to those of the other appellants, possibly arrived just before the Comitia had finally decided upon war. In any case Rome could now extend her protective patronage over the cultural centre of Greece. Soon afterwards Roman envoys, sent to Philip, delivered their message in the form of an ultimatum, which bade him indemnify Attalus and the Rhodians and required him to abstain in future from any act of war against any Greek state. This 'Monroe doctrine', being calculated to reduce Macedon to the status of Carthage, and being addressed to the king by a power whose interference in his affairs at this juncture must have seemed a mere impertinence, was naturally repudiated by him.

In strict legality the Romans had no *locus* *Roman* *standi* in the quarrel between Philip and his *rights and* Greek antagonists, and the king could declare *interests in* with some show of reason that they and not *the East* he were the aggressors. From the standpoint of immediate expediency it may be doubted whether the preventive war which the Romans fastened upon Philip was necessary. In all probability Philip, left to his own devices, would have had his hands full in the Aegean area for many years to come, and Antiochus would certainly not have been his ally in a second attack upon Rome. But this is not how the situation appeared to a Senate shocked by what the Rhodian and Pergamene legation had revealed. Philip alone might not seem unduly formidable, but Antiochus had recently returned from following the footsteps of Alexander the Great in a victorious campaign to 'India' (i.e. the Kabul valley), reducing Parthia and Bactria (212-206). The two kings together might seem to pose a very real threat to Roman interests. Thus the dominant cause of the Second Macedonian War was the Romans' defensive imperialism, the desire to humble their old enemy Philip now that he appeared so threatening and to establish a protectorate over Greece in order to keep him out.[8] From a broader point of view it may be asked whether the Romans might not in the long run have made their empire more solid and durable by confining it to the western Mediterranean. Yet in view of Philip's past record it is not surprising that the Senate should have regarded him in the same light in which Hamilcar and Hannibal viewed the Romans after the seizure of Sardinia and Corsica, or that it should have taken advantage of the Pergamene and Rhodian offer to force a precautionary war upon him.

4. The Second Macedonian War

Rome's allies in the Second Macedonian War

In view of the people's reluctance to declare war upon Philip the Senate did not venture to order extensive levies for service against him. The total number of Roman and Italian troops engaged in the Second Macedonian War scarcely exceeded 30,000, and most of these were new recruits, for the veterans of the Punic War were exempted from military duty in the East. The fleet which was commissioned to operate in the Aegean Sea was on a correspondingly reduced scale. As a supplement to this barely adequate force the Senate made an attempt to form a general coalition of Greek states against Philip. But its envoys met with a cool reception, for the part which the Romans had played in the First Macedonian War had brought them little credit in the eyes of the Greeks. The only city to accept the Roman invitation without demur was Athens, which had recently become embroiled with Philip, and Athens had long ceased to be of any account as a military power. In 199 the Aetolians resumed hostilities against Macedon, and in 198–197 the Achaean League, under severe pressure from the Roman fleet, gave some belated assistance. Roman agents were also sent to incite the Dardanians, a predatory tribe on the northern outskirts of Macedon, to resume their habitual incursions into that country. The advantage which the Romans obtained from this ill-assorted coalition proved almost negligible; and they were hardly better supported by Attalus and the Rhodians, who were content to leave the hard fighting to their Italian confederates.

Isolation of Philip

On the other hand Philip had so far alienated Greek sympathies that only a few of the lesser states espoused his cause. The only substantial aid that he received was from Thessaly, a country which had long been linked with Macedon in a personal union. From his partner Antiochus, who stood under no formal obligation to assist Philip, and was busy else-

where feathering his own nest (p. 161), the Macedonian king derived no help at all. His total military forces were therefore merely equal to those of the Romans, and his fleet was so hopelessly outmatched that it was at once reduced to a passive part. But the Macedonian army was drawn from the same hardy and loyal peasantry which had conquered the East for Alexander; man for man it was no whit inferior to the Roman legions.

Ineffective Roman campaigns in Albania

The campaigning season of 200 was already well advanced when the Roman forces took the field.[9] In this year they accomplished little more than to establish a base at Apollonia. But their mere landing in Illyria was sufficient to recall Philip from his expeditions in Asia Minor and to thrust him back upon the defensive. In 199 the ex-consul Sulpicius planned a combined drive by land and sea against Philip. But the Roman and allied fleets, whose part it was to reduce the seaboard towns of Macedon, accomplished next to nothing. The Roman legions, following the track of the future Via Egnatia (p. 159), threaded the difficult passes through the mountains of the Balkan watershed and forced a line of defence beyond Lyncestis (modern Monastir), where Philip was ready to receive them, but did not venture to engage them closely. But before the invaders could debouch on the central plain of Macedon, lack of supplies compelled them to fall back upon Illyria. They had, however, won the support of Aetolia.

Roman advance to Thessaly

In 198 the Macedonian king, rightly divining that the Romans would not again follow the line of the Via Egnatia, but might attempt the valley of the river Aoüs, in order to join hands with the Aetolians in Thessaly, moved forward to occupy a defile on this route not far from the Adriatic coast. Here he successfully held up a new Roman commander, the consul T. Quinctius Flamininus, for several weeks. Abortive negotiations ensued, but failed when it became clear that Flamininus's intention was to drive

15.2 Flamininus. Gold coin minted in Greece in his honour.

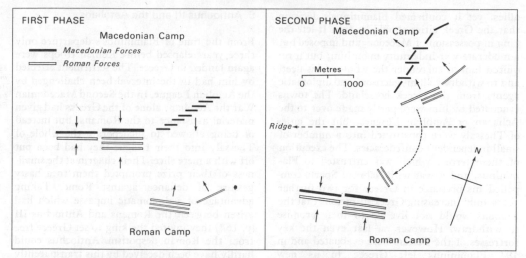

17. BATTLE SKETCH OF CYNOSCEPHALAE, 197 B.C.

Battle of
Cyno-
scephalae

Philip completely out of Greece. Finally a traitor in his camp led the Romans round his position by a mountain track. Philip made haste to extricate his army, and did not halt on his retreat until he reached the pass of Tempe on the border between Macedon and Thessaly. Flamininus was thus able to occupy Thessaly and to establish contact with the Aetolians; he also won the support of the Achaean League. But he did not venture to attack the difficult frontier line of Macedon in the face of Philip's intact forces.

Flamininus again turned to diplomacy and met Philip at Nicaea in Locris. But although Philip was more conciliatory than before, he refused to abandon the three fortresses he held in Greece at Demetrias, Chalcis and Acrocorinth, the so-called three 'Fetters of Greece'. Thus after two indecisive campaigns it appeared as if the Romans might have to win the Macedonian War, as they had won the Punic Wars, by sheer weight of numbers. But in 197 Philip, lacking the necessary reserves for a war of attrition, determined to stake his fortunes on a pitched battle. Advancing across Thessaly with 25,000 men, he was making for the open ground in the valley of the Enipeus, when his scouts discovered Flamininus's army, in slightly superior force, moving in a parallel direction on the reverse side of an intermediate line of downs, the ridge of Cynoscephalae. With prompt decision the king initiated and won a race for the heights, and as the former of his two divisions of heavy infantry reached the summit he flung it down the opposite slope against the Romans. The Macedonian 'phalanx', a ponderous mass of pikemen with spears about 20 feet in length, crashed into the left wing of

the Romans and put it to rout by the sheer momentum of the charge. But Flamininus saved the day by a counter-attack with his intact right wing and his Aetolian auxiliaries upon the second Macedonian division, which had scarcely breasted the hill and was not yet closed up in battle formation, so that it broke up on first contact with the enemy. The action as a whole remained undecided until on the victorious Roman right wing a military tribune (whose name is not recorded) detached the maniples of the second and third lines in his legion and turned in with these upon the rear of the successful Macedonian division. By this happily inspired move he finally won the day for Rome, for the densely arrayed pikemen on the Macedonian right wing could not swing round in time to face an attack in flank and went down helplessly before the swords of the legions.[10]

Legion
versus
phalanx

The battle of Cynoscephalae delivered the whole of the Greek homeland into the hands of the Romans, and encouraged them to assume the role of general arbiters of its destiny. The pretext which they had invoked in 200 to force a war upon Philip — concern for the liberties of the Greek cities — had in the meantime developed into a standing article of Roman policy. The tentative peace offer by Philip early in 198 had been met by Flamininus with a significant demand: the king was not only required to keep his hands off the free Greek cities, but was enjoined to restore to full liberty those Greek states which at that time stood under his rule. In 196 the Senate, to whom Flamininus referred Philip's second request for peace, took upon itself to dictate a general settlement of Greek affairs without consulting its

The settlement of Greece by Flamininus

allies, yet it confirmed Flamininus's decision that the Greek cities should be free. It left the king in possession of Macedon, and imposed but a moderate war-indemnity upon him; but it required him to surrender the whole of his fleet, and to withdraw all his garrisons and diplomatic agents from the Greek homeland. The towns evacuated by him were partly made over to the Achaean or Aetolian Leagues, but the cities of Thessaly were constituted into a number of small independent confederacies. The execution of these terms, which was entrusted to Flamininus, and a war with Nabis of Sparta compelled his presence in Greece for two further years amid increasing Greek suspicions that the Romans would not live up to their promise to withdraw. However, at last even the key fortresses of the Fetters were evacuated and in 194 Flamininus left Greece to its new freedom—under carefully chosen municipal aristocracies—and withdrew all his troops to Italy.

Evacuation of Greece by the Roman troops

The evacuation of Greece by the Romans after the Second Macedonian War proves beyond doubt that they had as yet no intention of making permanent conquests in the eastern Mediterranean. On the other hand there is no need to look for a strain of quite un-Roman sentimentalism in their attitude towards the Greeks. Though educated Romans had by now learnt to admire Greek civilisation, and Flamininus frankly appreciated the many compliments which the Greeks showered upon him, neither he nor the Senate ever thought of sacrificing Roman interests to an abstract phil-Hellenism. The conferment of freedom upon the Greek cities was simply an extension of the policy of clipping Philip's wings which had in the first instance drawn the Romans into Greek politics. But if from the Roman point of view Flamininus's settlement of Greece was simply a matter of expediency, from the Greek standpoint it appeared an act of extraordinary generosity. When the Roman general announced the liberation of Greece to the multitude assembled at Corinth for the Isthmian Games of 196, he received an ovation such as the Greeks had never accorded to one of their own compatriots.[11] It may, however, be contended that the Romans would have been better advised to extend their occupation of Greece over a somewhat longer term, or at any rate to set up a system of supervision by resident commissioners, until the liberated cities had proved their capacity to stand on their own feet. In the event the Romans found it no more possible to withdraw permanently from Greece than from any other country which their legions had visited.

The motives of Roman policy in regard to Greece

Greek ovations to Flamininus

5. Antiochus III and the Aetolians

From the time of Flamininus's departure only three years elapsed before Roman troops were again landed in Greece. The settlement effected by him had in the interval been challenged by the Aetolian League. In the Second Macedonian War the Aetolians alone of the Greeks had given material assistance to the Romans; but instead of being allowed to incorporate the whole of Thessaly into their League they had been put off with a mere slice. Their chagrin at the smallness of their prize prompted them to a hasty gesture of defiance against Rome. Taking advantage of a diplomatic impasse which had arisen between the Romans and Antiochus III (p. 162) they invited the king to set Greece free from the Roman despotism. Antiochus could hardly have been deceived by this transparently hollow pretext, but in consideration of Aetolian support against Rome he assumed the superfluous part of Greek liberator. In 192 he landed at Demetrias (a city on the Gulf of Pagasae which the Aetolians had seized on his behalf by a *coup de main*) with an advance guard of 10,000 men, and proceeded to overrun Thessaly. But his reception in Greece was of the chilliest. The Greek cities, unaware as yet that Rome's gift of freedom might become a source of embarrassment, and rightly suspicious of his attempt to outbid Roman liberality, withheld all military support from him; the Achaean League may even have declared war upon him and received a treaty on equal terms (*foedus aequum*) from Rome. Further, the Aetolians soon began to repent of an alliance in which each partner was merely intent on using the other for his own ends. Worse still, his former accomplice Philip, who had not evacuated Greece for the benefit of an interloper from Asia, not only stood by the settlement of 196, but took sides openly with the Romans who had granted him an alliance.

Estrangement of the Aetolians from Rome

The Aetolians invite Antiochus of Syria to occupy Greece

To the Romans, who had urgent military tasks on hand in the western Mediterranean, the prospect of a renewal of war in the east was unwelcome. The Senate therefore took no further step in the first instance than to send Flamininus to disarm the Aetolians by diplomatic methods. But when Antiochus invaded Greece it took exaggerated alarm, in the belief that he might use that country as a stepping-stone to Italy. It therefore mobilised a force of over 20,000 men, which the consul M'. Acilius Glabrio embarked for Greece in 191. Glabrio made an unopposed march across Greece to Thessaly, from which Antiochus at once fell back to the pass of Thermopylae. Here the consul was held up for a while, for in the narrows

A new Roman expedition

his attacking columns were an easy prey to the king's catapults. But on the chance of history repeating itself he detached a flying-column to follow the mountain path by which the Persian monarch Xerxes had turned the pass against its Spartan defenders in 480. The Roman circumventing force, which was placed under the orders of the ex-consul Cato, now serving as a subordinate officer under Glabrio, met with the same good fortune as the Persians of old, for an Aetolian corps, on which Antiochus had relied to protect his flank, hardly even delayed the Roman column's progress. Antiochus extricated himself from the defile, but suffered the total loss of his army in the retreat.[12] After this fiasco he evacuated his remaining positions in Greece, leaving his disloyal Aetolian allies to make what terms they could with the victors.

Battle of Thermopylae

The Aetolians indeed had little to hope for from the Romans: they had previously met Flamininus's conciliatory overtures by informing him that they would presently continue the discussions in their camp on the banks of the Tiber! Their request for terms of peace in 191 was answered by Glabrio with a point-blank demand for unconditional surrender, and when they elected to take their chance in a war of sieges, the Roman general prepared for a systematic attack upon their strongholds. But Glabrio's successor in 190, the consul L. Cornelius Scipio, the brother of Africanus, granted an armistice to the Aetolians, so as to release the Roman troops for service against Antiochus who decided to fight on in Asia Minor against a Roman counter-attack (p. 163); and a second expeditionary force, which the consul M. Fulvius Nobilior brought from Italy in 189, was not put to use, for the new commander was induced, through the good offices of the Athenians, to grant terms to the Aetolians. But Fulvius took good care to reduce the League to impotence by confining it almost wholly within the limits of Aetolia proper and conferring independence upon its accessory members. In a formal treaty the Aetolians bound themselves to have the same friends and enemies as Rome and to 'preserve the empire and sovereignty (*maiestas*) of the Roman people without fraud'. Thus they surrendered all hope of any independent foreign policy and at the same time were shown that Rome understood her clients to have undertaken a moral obligation which was now specifically included in the legal treaty. Thus amputated, Aetolia ceased to be a disturber of the Greek peace.

Surrender of the Aetolians

6. The Third Macedonian War

In 188 the Roman troops for a second time evacuated Greece, and seventeen further years passed before the next military intervention. But in this interval the friendship of the Greek states towards Rome showed signs of cooling off, and relations between the Republic and Macedon once again became strained. After the Aetolian War Philip, who had co-operated wholeheartedly with the Romans, was allowed to retain under his own rule a number of Thessalian towns recovered by him from Antiochus, including the fortress of Demetrias. In the next decade he busied himself with the internal development of Macedonia and the strengthening of its northern frontiers. By fresh taxation, by developing the mines, and by settling many Thracians in Macedon he strengthened his country's man-power and economic resources. But although this may have seemed suspicious to Rome, he made no attempt to undermine the Roman settlement in Greece. Disputes about the status of individual Thessalian towns, some of which Philip was compelled to surrender a second time, threatened to provoke a fresh crisis; but a visit to Rome by the king's younger son, Demetrius, who found favour with several of the governing families of the Republic, gave hope that the relations of the two states might be placed on an amicable footing. Demetrius's diplomatic success, however, roused the suspicions of his elder brother Perseus, who scented danger to his own prospects of succession. By playing on the king's hasty suspicions Perseus contrived the execution of the younger prince on a highly doubtful charge of treason. Under a quick revulsion of feeling Philip next prepared to disinherit Perseus in favour of a prince of a collateral line; but by his premature death in 179 he put Perseus in possession of the crown.[13]

Further negotiations between the Romans and Philip V

The new king was by temperament as cautious as his father had been impetuous. Nevertheless, as the supplanter of Rome's friend Demetrius, he had condemned himself to live under a cloud of suspicion, which ended by bursting over his distracted head. At the outset of his reign he applied himself to carry on his father's policy of internal development in Macedonia. But an ominous accumulation of treasure and enrolment of additional troops raised doubts as to his ultimate intentions. These doubts were confirmed by Perseus's alliances with Thracian and Illyrian chieftains, and by his somewhat ostentatious interference in the affairs of the cities of the Greek homeland. In Greece an economic crisis, whose ultimate causes were to be sought in the conquests of

Accession of Perseus. Roman suspicions

15.3   Perseus of Macedon.

Alexander and the eastward displacement of the Greek world's economic centre of gravity, came to a head in the second century, during which the tension between creditors and debtors became increasingly acute. In befriending the bankrupt classes the Macedonian king gave the impression of fomenting social revolutions in order to undermine the Roman settlement of Greece. Further, some Romans might read sinister political implications into Perseus's marriage to Laodice, daughter of the Syrian king Seleucus IV (who had succeeded Antiochus III) and that of his sister Apame to Prusias II of Bithynia. Lastly, Perseus had neighbours who sedulously kept the Senate apprised of his doings and cunningly put the worst construction upon them. The chief informant against him was Eumenes II of Pergamum, who carried on his father Attalus's feud with Macedon, and lost no opportunity of representing Perseus to the Senate in an unfavourable light.

Intrigues by Eumenes of Pergamum

In view of Perseus's fundamental caution, it is hardly to be doubted that the Romans could have disarmed him by a frankly conciliatory or an openly intimidating policy. But the Senate persisted in taking half-measures, to which Perseus made a like reply. It sent repeated commissions of inquiry which could neither incriminate nor exculpate the king, but merely served to deepen distrust on either side. In 172 it lent a willing ear to a carefully studied denunciation of Perseus, which King Eumenes in person delivered before it,[14] and took ready offence at a blustering rejoinder by an unskilful Macedonian agent. At this stage the Senate overcame its hesitations and forced a war upon Perseus by the same methods as it had used against Philip in 200. On the pretext that the king had attacked some Balkan chieftains who had been admitted into alliance or 'friendship' with Rome, it sent a demand for reparations, and on refusal of these it induced the Comitia to sanction war (171).[15] But whereas the Senate followed a clear policy in regard to Philip,

A drift into war

it drifted rather than drove to a rupture with Perseus.

The Third Macedonian War, like its predecessor, resolved itself into a duel between the two protagonist states. In answer to the overtures which the king had made to the cities of Greece he could at the least count on a more benevolent neutrality than had been accorded to his father. In 171 the Greeks were recoiling from the somewhat boisterous gratitude which they had shown to their Roman liberators in the days of Flamininus; and the debtor classes were becoming restless under the new condition of political tranquillity which cut off all hope of a social revolution. But lack of timely financial support from Perseus, and above all the memory of Cynoscephalae, held back most of the states from overt assistance to Macedon. In the event Perseus received some ineffective help from a few cities of Boeotia, from Epirus (now a federal republic) and from an Illyrian chief named Genthius. The Romans for their part had offers of support from their old allies, Pergamum, Rhodes and the Achaean League, but drew sparingly upon them. Thanks to the excellent internal administration of Philip and Perseus, Macedonia had made such a good recovery from the previous war that it could now put some 40,000 men into the field. The Romans slightly outnumbered Perseus and held complete control of the seas, but hardly knew how to derive advantage from their maritime superiority.

The allies on either side

The same irresolution which had marked the negotiations before the Third Macedonian War characterised its first two campaigns. In 171 Perseus ventured himself into Thessaly and gained a handsome victory in a cavalry action near Larissa against the vanguard of the Roman army under the consul P. Licinius Crassus. The king was so flustered by his success that he followed it up with overtures for peace. The Romans, rendered intractable by defeat, rejected this and several later offers by Perseus, but were well-nigh reduced to helplessness by bad discipline among the troops, by faulty cooperation on the part of the fleet, and by the natural difficulties of the Macedonian frontier. Licinius never attempted an attack in force upon Perseus, and his successor, Hostilius Mancinus, failed in an endeavour to enter the valley of the Haliacmon by the Volustana pass across the frontier range. While the consular armies were held fast in Thessaly the king easily repelled a subsidiary Roman force in Illyria; but he missed his chance of an offensive in Greece. In 169 a more resolute consul named Q. Marcius Philippus successfully made a perilous march of eleven days' duration across the densely wooded shoulder of Mt Olympus, and by his mere

Roman set-backs in Thessaly

appearance on Macedonian soil he so unnerved Perseus as to cause him to abandon the entire frontier line. Fortunately for the king, Marcius's army was too exhausted to advance.

In the fourth year of the war the Roman attack was at last driven home by the consul L. Aemilius Paullus, a veteran of the Spanish and Ligurian wars. With a better disciplined army Paullus made good his footing on the Macedonian plain and drew Perseus at last into a set battle at Pydna. The action of Pydna, like that of Cynoscephalae, developed out of an affair of outposts, which encouraged the king to hurl his heavy infantry at the half-prepared Romans. The phalanx, charging in one massive corps of 20,000 men over level ground, flung back the Roman front and gave Paullus, as he afterwards avowed, the most terrifying impression of his lifetime. Yet the Roman line, instead of being broken by the shock, fell back in good order towards higher ground, while the phalanx, carried away by its own momentum, jerked itself asunder. Into the gaps thus formed, and round the flanks of the Macedonian column, the Romans thrust themselves maniple by maniple, and with their swords made short work of the disordered pikemen.[16] The battles of Cynoscephalae and Pydna finally demonstrated the advantage which the elastic manipular formation possessed over the rigid Macedonian phalanx – the superiority of tempered steel over cast iron. The second of these encounters left Macedonia without an army and without a king. The Macedonian cities capitulated at once to Paullus's invading forces, and Perseus surrendered himself after a vain attempt at flight.

In 168 a second Roman force was sent to Illyria, where it captured Genthius after a whirlwind campaign. In the following year Paullus received orders to carry out a military execution against the people of Epirus. By a ruse recalling the massacre of Glencoe he fell simultaneously upon all the towns and villages of the country and made a haul of 150,000 prisoners, who were sold off into slavery. Since Epirus had rendered no effective aid to Perseus, this kidnapping expedition strained to the utmost the ancient usages of war.[17]

7. The Fourth Macedonian War

The atrocities perpetrated in Epirus by the Senate's order illustrate the spirit in which that body devised the new settlement of Greece after the Third Macedonian War. While it was still minded to leave the Greek states free, or rather refused to burden itself with their government, it was determined to deprive them of all power

Battle of Pydna

Surrender of Perseus

The Roman slave-haul in Epirus

for further mischief. A ruthless political purge followed: allegedly anti-Roman leaders, denounced by their pro-Roman fellow citizens, were deported in considerable numbers (p. 160). Further, the Senate not only deposed Perseus (who was interned for the rest of his life in the small country town of Alba Fucens), but it deported all the royal officials. Thus left without any governing body, Macedonia was carved up into four separate republics (extending in a line from west to east), in each of which a parliament of representatives from the various towns or villages took over the administration. Severe restrictions were placed upon intercourse between the four sections and upon their trade with the rest of Greece.[18] On the other hand the Senate made no attempt to exploit the modest economic resources of the country. The land-tax, henceforth payable to the Roman treasury, was reduced by half, and the royal gold and silver mines were closed for a term of ten years. To the Romans this settlement might seem reasonable or even generous, but it violated the Macedonians' sense of nationhood. A similar experiment in political surgery was made in Illyria, where Genthius's kingdom was dissected into three federal republics. The tribute imposed upon Illyria was on the same moderate scale.

By this excess of precautions Roman statecraft deprived the Macedonians alike of the power to harm their neighbours and to protect themselves. In 150 the militias of the several republics proved themselves unable to deal with an adventurer named Andriscus, who had rallied a royalist party on the pretence of being a son of Perseus, so that he succeeded for a moment in reuniting Macedonia under a stolen crown. In the 'Fourth Macedonian War', which Andriscus now imposed upon them, the Romans made an even worse beginning than in the previous wars, for a small detachment sent in haste to hold the usurper in check met with a heavy defeat, and Thessaly was overrun by Andriscus's bands (149). But in 148 a stronger Roman force under Q. Caecilius Metellus expelled the pretender from Macedonia and ran him down in Thrace.

The campaign against Andriscus, insignificant in itself, occasioned an important change of Roman policy in regard to the Greek states. In 148 the Senate, realising that gifts of liberty tempered by military executions could bring no lasting peace to the Greek world nor liquidate Roman commitments in that region, resigned itself to the annexation of Macedonia.[19] For the defence of the new province, into which Epirus and Thessaly were incorporated, alliances were made with several Thracian chiefs, and a high road, the Via Egnatia, was constructed from

The partitioning of Macedonia

Macedonia overrun by a pretender. A Roman force sent to defeat him

Annexation of Macedonia as a province

Apollonia to Thessalonica – the only good road in Albania until the second Italian occupation of the country in 1916. But no systematic attempt was made as yet by the Romans to penetrate the Balkan hinterland, or to attach it to themselves by diplomatic ties.

Roman interventions in Dalmatia

Occasional Roman interventions were also required in the new Illyrian protectorates, which were unable to cope with raids by land and sea on the part of the neighbouring tribes of Dalmatia. In 155 a Roman punitive force cleared the coast of lower Dalmatia; in 129 an expedition was directed from Aquileia against the more northerly tribes on the Carso. Through these operations the entire Adriatic coast was brought under Roman control. Presumably Illyria and Dalmatia were placed under the general supervision of the governor of Macedonia.[20]

8 Rome and the Greek Homeland

In leaving the towns of the Greek homeland free from all regular control, whether by Rome or by some form of Greek federal government, the Senate was almost inviting a recrudescence of those quarrels between cities or factions which had at all times been the bane of the Greek city-state. Among the feuds which agitated Greece most persistently in the second century was a dispute between the Achaean League, which had extended its authority over all Peloponnesus in 192, and the city of Sparta, which resisted incorporation or stood out for a special measure of local autonomy. This issue became a frequent subject of reference to the Senate or to Roman commissioners on tour in Greece. The decisions made from time to time by the Senate or its agents were doubtless given in good faith, but being usually based on a somewhat perfunctory hearing of the parties, and an incomplete understanding of the case, they failed to effect a durable settlement. Indeed the pro-Roman statesman of the Achaean League, Callicrates, in 181 advised the Senate to support the pro-Roman at the expense of the patriotic parties in the various cities, and Polybius remarked that a new era in Graeco-Roman relations ensued whereby Rome tended to support those who appealed to her authority, whether right or wrong.[21]

Roman arbitrations between Greek states

The restlessness of the Greek cities was aggravated by a sudden and high-handed interference in their internal affairs after the Third Macedonian War. In Aetolia Roman commissioners gave military aid to the partisans of the Republic in carrying out a judicial massacre of the friends of Macedon. After a vain attempt to institute a similar Bloody Assize in Achaea they deported 1000 of its leading citizens to Italy, on the pre-

Deportations from Achaea

tence of reserving them for trial in a calmer atmosphere. Despite repeated protests from the Achaean League the Senate detained the prisoners for fifteen years without granting them an opportunity of meeting their accusers. Among these hostages – for such in effect they were – the historian Polybius had the good fortune to be received into the circle of the ruling families (p. 113); but 700 others eventually died from the effects of their confinement. The liberation of the remnant in 150 came too late to mitigate the embitterment of their long internment. Besides, any good effect which their release might have had was nullified three years later, when the Senate humoured the recalcitrant Spartans by authorising them to leave the Achaean League. In the following year the Senate offered to reopen negotiations on the subject; but in the meantime the rising current of feeling against Rome, reinforced by an agitation for social revolution among the industrial and commercial proletariat at Corinth, had led to the appointment of a dictator named Critolaus, who frustrated all attempts at accommodation. In 146 Critolaus threw out a direct challenge to Roman authority by over-running central Greece with an extemporised army, but he was easily routed by Caecilius Metellus, who came down upon him from Macedonia. Later in the year the consul L. Mummius, with reinforcements from Italy, destroyed a reserve levy of Achaeans, which fought gallantly against hopeless odds in a final encounter near Corinth.

The Achaean League appeals to arms; and is defeated

After the Achaean War the Romans still left central Greece and Peloponnesus outside the sphere of provincial administration, and they contented themselves with a temporary payment of tribute by way of a war-indemnity. But they guarded against further disorder by dissolving the Achaean League into its component city-states, and by authorising the governor of Macedonia to interfere, whenever necessary, on behalf of the public peace. In the other Greek towns they restored the rule of the wealthier classes, and they made Corinth safe against social revolution by razing it to the ground and selling its inhabitants into slavery.[22]

A new Roman settlement of Greece. Destruction of Corinth 146 B.C.

The events leading up to the Achaean War and the destruction of Corinth, which followed it, showed up in a grim light the forcible-feeble character of Roman policy in regard to the Greek states. They virtually closed the long and often glorious chapter of Greek political history, and they frustrated all attempts at Greek political union by reducing the country once more to a mere aggregate of small city-states. But the settlement of 146 brought to the Greeks an enduring peace such as they had never been able to establish of their own free will.

The end of Greek political history

CHAPTER 16

The Roman Wars in Asia in the Second Century

1. The Origins of the War against Antiochus

Until the second century B.C. Asia remained wholly outside the sphere of Roman politics. The eventual intrusion of the Republic into Asiatic affairs was, in no less degree than its intervention in European Greece, an unpremeditated adventure.

16.1 Antiochus III, the Great, of Syria.

Conquests of Antiochus III

Rome's earliest antagonist in Asia was the Seleucid king, Antiochus III. In the opening years of his reign this monarch had restored the crumbling authority of his dynasty on the Asian continent; his victorious progress across Persia and Bactria to the frontiers of India (209–204) had earned him the title of 'Great' among the Greeks, and a reputation second only to that of Alexander. In fulfilment of the 'partition pact' which he had entered (probably on his own initiative) with Philip V of Macedon (pp. 151 f.), he had been engaged since 203 in appropriating the Ptolemaic possessions in Asia. In 201–200

he had acquired southern Syria and Palestine; in 197 he had carried the southern seaboard of Asia Minor and the southern half of its western coast, where he made the city of Ephesus into a second capital. In 196–195 he reasserted a somewhat shadowy claim to the Thracian Chersonese (Gallipoli peninsula) which had been held by his ancestor Seleucus Nicator, by capturing some Ptolemaic stations on the European side of the strait. Unlike Philip, Antiochus was a diplomat no less than a soldier. He took care not to have more than one enemy at a time, and he was generally willing to compromise on unessential details. After the conquest of Palestine he had secured his winnings by a marriage alliance with Ptolemy V; during his campaigns in Asia Minor he respected the integrity of Rhodes and Pergamum, and even called off a demonstration against the latter at Rome's request (198). Yet his conquests in western Asia Minor could not but cause apprehension to the rulers of Pergamum, for their realm had been constituted by secession from the Seleucids, and it was no doubt the ultimate object of Antiochus to recover it for his house. In 196, therefore, Eumenes II, who had recently succeeded Attalus I on the throne of Pergamum, resolved to call the Romans to his assistance, as his father had invoked them against Philip.[1]

Eumenes of Pergamum invokes the Romans against Antiochus

The king of Pergamum opened the diplomatic game by advancing two pawns, the city-states of Smyrna and Lampsacus, which had of late enjoyed full independence, but were now being threatened with reconquest by Antiochus.[2] The application of these two towns to the Senate furnished a test case to determine whether the

Romans were prepared to extend their newly assumed patronage of Greek municipal liberty to the cities of the Asiatic continent. The Senate merely went so far as to refer the envoys of the two appellant towns to Flamininus, who was then engaged in the settlement of European Greece (p. 156). Yet this instruction sufficed to bring about the deadlock between Rome and Antiochus for which Eumenes had been working. In reply to the agents of Antiochus, who came to Corinth to forestall Flamininus's remonstrances, the Roman general not only required the king to keep his hands off all the free Greek cities in Asia, but ordered him to evacuate all Greek towns recently acquired by him from Ptolemy, and forbade him to set foot on Europe. These terms constituted as direct a challenge as the Roman ultimatum to Philip in 200. But Antiochus, who at this stage had no intention of jeopardising his recent gains in a war with Rome, patiently argued his case at a conference with Flamininus's agents at Lysimachia (on the Gallipolli peninsula). He proved that his interest in the Greek cities of Asia Minor and in the Gallipoli peninsula, being based on previous possession, had a better legal foundation than Flamininus's sudden concern for them, and by producing the text of a recently signed treaty with Egypt, he completely stultified the Roman general's intervention on Ptolemy's behalf (196). With these retorts he disarmed Flamininus so effectively that the Roman commander in the next two years tamely allowed Antiochus to occupy the Gallipoli peninsula, and in withdrawing his troops from Greece in 194 Flamininus signified that he did not apprehend a war with the Seleucid king in the near future.

Ineffective Roman protests

Other Romans were less sanguine, the more so since in 195 news came that Hannibal, evading the trap set for him at Carthage (p. 147), had found his way to Antiochus's court at Ephesus. Their alarm was not unnatural, since Hannibal was rumoured to be planning a fresh invasion of Italy with a Seleucid army. In consequence Hannibal's conqueror, Scipio Africanus, was elected to a second consulship for 194. He urged that Macedon should be made a consular province and that Roman troops should be left in Greece a little longer as a barrier against Antiochus: to denude Greece of all Roman troops would leave a dangerous vacuum into which the king, with Hannibal behind him, would be drawn. But the Senate followed Flamininus's advice and Greece was evacuated. Measures, however, were taken to protect the coast of Southern Italy with a chain of new colonies (p. 139), and three years later, on the actual outbreak of war with Antiochus, the

Hannibal at the court of Antiochus

Senate detailed considerable forces to prevent his landing. But these precautions proved superfluous, for Antiochus had no desire for a fight to a finish with Rome, and he was not blind to the dangers of engaging his army in Italy.[3] The cool reception which he offered to Hannibal did not entirely allay Roman suspicions, yet it dissuaded the Senate from any hasty diplomatic move against the king.

In 194 Antiochus sent an embassy to Rome to settle all outstanding points and negotiate a treaty of friendship. The Senate now modified the terms previously laid down by Flamininus and he offered to the king's envoys in secret session (he could not in public proclaim this abandonment of earlier Roman claims to protect *all* the Greeks) an option of renouncing his claims on the free Greek cities of Asia or on the Gallipoli peninsula, and he gave a hint that Rome would be content with his withdrawal from Europe. This proposal, which gave to Antiochus all that was worth contending for, might well have been made the basis of a durable peace. But the king's envoy, sacrificing the substance to the shadow, insisted on preserving his precarious foothold in Europe, and thus prevented an immediate settlement. The Senate, it is true, offered to continue negotiations in 193 at Ephesus;[4] but here again the king's ministers played their cards unskilfully, and delegates from Lampsacus and Smyrna, whom the Romans admitted to the discussions at the instance of Eumenes, contrived to wreck the conference by calculated obstruction. The Roman envoys for their part did nothing to widen the breach, but the failure of the parley at Ephesus incited the king to a fatal false step. In the ensuing winter he accepted the summons of the Aetolians to liberate the Greek homeland and prepared for a descent in force upon Europe (p. 156). His object in occupying Greece was probably nothing more than to embarrass the Romans and to pick up a new counter for his diplomatic game. But it is not surprising that the Romans, mistaking Antiochus's move for an attempt to overthrow their recent settlement of Greece, and for a first stage in an advance upon Italy itself, should have answered it with a declaration of war. The 'War against Antiochus', with which the Romans made their entry into Asia, was the least deliberate of all their great military undertakings. It came upon them because, not having formulated any clear-cut policy in regard to Antiochus and not being convinced by his probably genuine expressions of a desire for peace with themselves, they met the king with half-measures which led him on to overplay his hand.

Breakdown of further negotiations

Antiochus's false step in Greece

2. The First Roman Campaign in Asia

The fiasco of Antiochus's expedition to Greece has already been described (p. 156). Delays in the mobilisation of his main force and lack of support from the Greek cities left him with barely sufficient strength to protect his bases; the negligence or ill-will of his Aetolian allies exposed his army to destruction at Thermopylae. At the end of 191 he evacuated European Greece and prepared to hold Asia Minor against the Roman counter-attack. His first line of home defence was a navy of seventy battleships (to say nothing of a hundred cruisers), which he had raised from the coastland towns of Asia Minor. With these numbers his admiral Polyxenidas (a Rhodian renegade) was hardly a match for the Roman fleet of eighty battleships under C. Livius, which was dispatched somewhat tardily to Aegean waters in the summer of 191; and he was definitely inferior to the combined squadrons of Livius and of Eumenes, who could furnish some twenty-five additional ships of the line. He had also to reckon with the navy of the Rhodians, who had hitherto stood aloof from the war, but eventually renewed their alliance with Rome, in order to secure the freedom of the Aegean Sea and the Dardanelles. Unable to prevent the junction of the Romans and Pergamenes he took the risk of attacking them near Cape Corycus before the arrival of the Rhodians. He was beaten off with severe loss by the Romans, who successfully used grappling-irons and boarding tactics. But the season was now too late for the allies to follow up their advantage.

In the winter of 191–190 Antiochus raised his fleet by fresh construction to a total of ninety battleships. He also commissioned Hannibal, whom he had hitherto treated with polite distrust, to equip another squadron in Phoenicia. In the following spring Polyxenidas further reduced the odds by a surprise attack upon the Rhodian fleet at Samos, which he all but destroyed. But this victory was offset by an action fought off Side (in southern Asia Minor), where a second Rhodian fleet, under an admiral named Eudamus, disabled the numerically stronger Phoenician navy under Hannibal. The maritime war was definitely decided by a battle off Myonnesus (near Cape Corycus), which arose out of an abortive attempt by Polyxenidas to surprise the combined fleets of Eudamus and the Romans. In this engagement, while Eudamus checked an attempt by Polyxenidas to envelop the allied line, the Roman admiral L. Aemilius Regillus broke the enemy centre. The action of Myonnesus, the last notable victory of a Roman fleet over a foreign enemy, secured to the allies the command of the seas and prepared for the Roman army's passage into Asia.

While the naval campaign was being fought out the Roman army was engaged on a long march from Greece to the Dardanelles. It now stood under the nominal orders of L. Scipio, the younger brother of Africanus and consul in 190; but the effective command was in the hands of Africanus himself.[5] After a rapid journey through Macedonia, where Philip provided it with escorts and supplies, it crossed the Strait unopposed, for after his naval defeats Antiochus had withdrawn all his troops into Asia Minor. Thus for the first time a Roman army set foot in Asia. Its numbers, however, had not been materially increased by fresh drafts, and even with the addition of a small Pergamene contingent it scarcely exceeded 30,000 men. Against this force Antiochus had mobilised the entire field army of his kingdom to the number of 72,000, the largest muster which the legions had yet confronted. But this levy lacked the uniformity and cohesion of the Roman or Macedonian army; though the contingents (mostly Oriental) of which it was composed were individually of high value, they were insufficiently trained for combined action. With a just appreciation of the real odds against him, and a growing aversion from a war into which he had stumbled against his own wish, Antiochus offered to the Scipios to concede all the points on which he had stood in previous negotiations, and to pay one-half of the Roman war expenses. But L. Scipio, on the advice of his brother, required the king to pay the entire costs of the Roman campaigns, and to evacuate not only the debatable coast-lands of Asia Minor, but all his possessions in the interior of that country. This demand was plainly unacceptable to the king, for the interior of Asia Minor was held by him on the valid ground of continuous possession, and it was a cardinal point of Seleucid policy to maintain a sea-front on the Aegean. Unable to procure peace at a reasonable price Antiochus offered a mid-winter battle to the Romans on a piece of open ground near Magnesia-ad-Sipylum. In this action he reverted to the tactics of Alexander's age, which Philip had abandoned to his cost at Cynoscephalae. Using his infantry and elephants as a defensive wing to fix his opponents he staked his chances on a massed attack by his excellent Persian horsemen, of whom he took command in person. With this striking-force he enfiladed and put to rout the Roman left wing, but he let himself be carried too far in the pursuit, and so lost touch with the rest of his troops.[6] On the other wing the initiative was taken by King Eumenes, who shared the effective command of the Roman

Antiochus's preparations against a Roman counter-attack

Naval warfare in the Aegean

Naval defeat of Hannibal

Battle of Myonnesus

The Romans invade Asia Minor

Abortive negotiations between Antiochus and Scipio Africanus

Battle of Magnesia

forces with the ex-consul Cn. Domitius Aheno-barbus – for Scipio Africanus was prevented by illness from directing the battle. After a preliminary encounter, in which his slingers disposed of Antiochus's scythed chariots, Eumenes charged the unhandy armoured horsemen who constituted the enemy's left flank-guard, and by this quick thrust he spread confusion through the whole of the opposite left wing. Notwithstanding the loss of its flank cover the Seleucid centre, consisting of a phalanx of 16,000 heavy infantry, stood its ground valiantly, and might have saved the whole battle for Antiochus, had he reined in betimes and returned to the main action.[7] But eventually the elephants, whom he had posted in the intervals of his phalanx-columns, were stampeded by the Roman javelins and made gaps in the heavy infantry, into which the Roman legionaries penetrated. With the disruption of its centre the entire Seleucid army was dissolved into fragments and destroyed in detail.

3. The First Roman Settlement of Asia

Antiochus evacuates Asia Minor

After this catastrophe Antiochus agreed to peace terms, roughly those previously offered by the Scipios under which Syria would have been left humbled but not completely crushed. The terms, arranged under an armistice, were referred to Rome, where the Scipios' political opponents had got the upper hand and ungenerously sent out Cn. Manlius Vulso to supersede L. Scipio and to impose much harsher terms on Antiochus. He had already agreed to an indemnity of 15,000 talents (the largest that Rome ever extracted from a beaten enemy), but now he had to surrender all his fleets except ten ships and his war-elephants. As well as evacuating all territory to the west of Mt Taurus he now had to agree not to make war in Europe or the Aegean; he could resist attack by any such peoples but must not have sovereignty over them and must not procure allies from the regions from which he had been excluded.[8] Thus the Senate, unlike the Scipios, determined to exploit the victory to the full and to tie his hands in all relations with his neighbours. There was little chance for Syria to maintain a prosperous national life, and the weakening of the central power would hasten the breaking up of the state, with the result that Rome would be drawn further into eastern affairs, contrary to her present desires and policy.

In 188 Manlius joined ten senatorial commissioners at Apamea and there the final treaty was signed. The settlement was completed by division of the spoil among the victors. The territories ceded in Asia Minor were shared out between Eumenes and the Rhodians. The latter received Lycia and Caria (the south-western edge of Asia Minor, as far as the river Maeander); the rest of Seleucid Asia Minor, together with the Gallipoli peninsula, was assigned to Eumenes, whose realm henceforth comprised a wide belt of land extending diagonally from the Dardanelles to Mt Taurus. Of the Greek cities, on whose behalf the Romans had professedly entered the war, the greater number remained independent, but those which Eumenes could claim on the ground of previous possession, were handed back to him.[9] The Pergamene ruler was the chief gainer by the war, and it can hardly be doubted that it was he who suggested to the Romans the expulsion of the Seleucids from Asia Minor. The Romans pocketed the war-indemnity, but kept none of the conquered lands for themselves; and in 188 they withdrew all their troops from the eastern Mediterranean.

Territorial gains of Eumenes

This anabasis was one which the Romans could probably have avoided by a more clear-headed diplomacy. The penalty which they finally inflicted upon Antiochus was out of all proportion to his offence; and its consequences were ruinous to Greek civilisation in the Near East, for the loss of military man-power, of wealth and of prestige which the king suffered entailed the defection of his easten provinces and their reversion to a purely oriental culture. The settlement of 188, it is true, demonstrated what had lain implicit in all the earlier negotiations, that the Romans were not seeking territorial aggrandisement in Asia. Yet their first interference in the affairs of this continent had been on such a scale, and had achieved such far-reaching results, that they could no more disentangle themselves from it than they could abandon their hold on European Greece.

Roman policy in Asia

The war against Antiochus brought the Romans into contact with several states in Asia Minor that lay beyond the fringe of its Greek principalities. In 189 L. Scipio's successor, Cn. Manlius Vulso, conducted a punitive expedition against the predatory tribes on the southern mountain-border, and made a systematic attack upon the fastnesses of the Galatians, a Celtic people from the Danube lands, who had occupied the central plateau of Asia Minor a century before, and from that point had repeatedly raided the western coast-lands. During his progress Vulso blackmailed the peaceful communities no less than he plundered the warlike ones; but in reducing the Galatian strongholds he conferred a lasting benefit upon the populations of the adjacent seaboards. We may surmise that Vulso's anabasis was suggested to him by

A Roman raid in Galatia

Eumenes, who certainly derived the chief benefit from it. On the other hand the Romans let off with a trifling fine king Ariarathes of Cappadocia, a minor dynast of eastern Asia Minor, who had sent a contingent to assist Antiochus at Magnesia. In this act of leniency we may again· discern the influence of Eumenes upon Roman policy.

4. The Romans in Asia Minor down to 129 B.C.[10]

Occasional Roman interventions in Asia Minor

After the peace of 188 king Eumenes, whose territorial acquisitions involved him in frequent border disputes with his neighbours, repeatedly invoked Roman aid, but received no more than occasional diplomatic support. In 186 Prusias I of Bithynia (in north-western Asia Minor) engaged in war with Eumenes, but was overawed by the Senate's emissary Flamininus into an early peace. The Senate's intervention in this instance was no doubt due to the fact that Prusias had enlisted Hannibal to take command of his fleet. In the negotiations with king Antiochus the Romans had required that the Carthaginian leader should be surrendered to them, but Hannibal had slipped away betimes and eventually found shelter at Prusias's court. A second demand for his extradition which Flamininus now made, was eluded by Hannibal taking poison (183). In the year of Hannibal's death a more general war broke out between Pharnaces of Pontus (in the north of Asia Minor) and a combination of all the neighbouring kings. On behalf of this coalition Eumenes once more solicited Roman intervention; but the Senate made no move until 180, and its envoys tamely allowed themselves to be argued into silence by an adversary with a bad case. So far as Rome was concerned the matter ended there, and the allies were left to settle accounts for themselves with Pharnaces, which they did by defeating him decisively in the ensuing year. On the other hand the Romans kept up their reputation as champions of municipal liberty when the cities of Lycia protested against unfair exactions by their new Rhodian overlords. By a disposition of the Senate the complainants were emancipated from Rhodian control (177).

At the end of the Third Macedonian War the extension of Roman authority to every part of the eastern Mediterranean was made manifest by a long train of embassies from kingdoms and cities, which came to solicit the Senate's favour or to deprecate its displeasure. Despite these reassuring displays of submissiveness the same mood of irritable suspiciousness, which henceforth dictated Roman policy in regard to Euro-

pean Greece, affected its dealings with the Asiatic states. In 168 the Rhodians, intent on protecting their Aegean trade and presuming upon their well-deserved reputation as peacemakers in Greek quarrels, had the temerity to tender their services as mediators between Perseus and the Senate. Though their envoys had received their instrùctions before the battle of Pydna the news of the victory outpaced them on the way to Rome; consequently their offer of intercession was misconstrued as an attempt to shield Perseus and to cheat the Romans of the fruits of their success. Though a proposal by a praetor with an eye to a lucrative military commission, that war should be declared incontinently on Perseus's accomplice, was defeated at the instance of Cato (who stood for fair play to all states except Carthage) the Senate despoiled the Rhodians as effectively as if they had been defeated in a naval counterpart to Magnesia. It withdrew from them their recent acquisitions on the Asiatic mainland, and it struck a blow at their trade in the Aegean area by converting the island of Delos in the Greek archipelago into a free port.[11] By these measures it so improverished the Rhodians that their war-fleet had to be laid up, and the patrolling of the Levantine seas, which it had faithfully discharged for a hundred years, fell into abeyance. Although the Senate so far relented as to grant Rhodes a formal treaty of alliance in 165/4, its peevish resentment at the false step taken by the Rhodians in 168 created a condition of growing insecurity in the eastern Mediterranean, and eventually a danger to Rome itself (p. 250).

Punitive measures against the Rhodians

A similar ill-humour was vented by the Romans on their ally Eumenes, though the Pergamene king was let off with a mere humiliation and escaped material loss. Their displeasure sprang from a suspicion that Eumenes had been meditating a similar intervention on behalf of Perseus on the eve of Pydna. Despite the detailed rumours affirming his collusion with Perseus it is hardly credible that Eumenes, the instigator of the Romans against the Macedonian king, should have suddenly interceded on his behalf. The Senate for its part betrayed its lack of conviction by some quick changes of front. In 167 it made an abortive attempt to suborn Eumenes's brother Attalus as a pretender to the Pergamene crown, and when Eumenes prepared to visit Rome to plead his case in person it refused him permission to land in Italy. On the other hand it asserted its authority against the Galatians, who had resumed their incursions into Pergamene territory as soon as it became known that Eumenes was under a cloud, and it turned a deaf ear upon Prusias II of Bithynia, who came

Roman displeasure with Eumenes

to Rome to play the good boy and to tell tales against his neighbour. After the death of Eumenes in 159 the Senate openly took sides with his brother Attalus II against Prusias, and put pressure upon the latter to break off a war which he was levying upon the Pergamene ruler. In 149 it sent envoys to restrain Attalus from supporting Prusias's son Nicomedes in a rebellion, but made no further protest when Attalus set Nicomedes upon his father's throne.

Notwithstanding some inconsistencies and errors Roman policy in Asia Minor broadly achieved its object. It engaged Rome's resources as sparingly as possible, yet on the whole it maintained the Republic's prestige. But the success of this policy depended in large measure on the co-operation of the Pergamene dynasty, which combined the ability to keep its own house in good order and to serve Roman *The king-* interests.[12] In 133 the Attalid house was ex-*dom of* tinguished with the death of Attalus III, who *Pergamum is* left no heirs and solved the problem of the suc-*bequeathed* cession by bequeathing his kingdom to the *to Rome* Roman people. The value of the king's gift was somewhat diminished by a clause in his will which stipulated that Pergamum and other Greek cities of his realm should in future be exempt from tribute. But the revenues from the extensive crown lands, and perhaps also from the factories in the ownership of the Attalids, were a sufficiently powerful inducement to the Romans to accept the legacy and to take over the administration of the Pergamene territory.[13]

The responsibilities which Attalus's bequest carried with it were at once brought home to the Romans both in their domestic affairs (where the effects were catastrophic: p. 205) and abroad. In the year of the last king's death an illegitimate son of Eumenes, Aristonicus by name, raised an insurrection. At first he appealed to the nationalist feelings of the Greek *The Roman* cities of Asia Minor and their desire for indepen-*campaigns* dence, but as this hope faded he relied more *against the* on the native population of the interior. There *pretender* was much social discontent which he could *Aristonicus* divert to his cause: serfs on the Pergamene crown lands and slaves in the factories, apart from the help he received from rebellious Greek cities and a corps of discharged mercenaries. Out of this motley mass he created a serviceable army, but as his cause flagged on the seaboard he held out hopes of social betterment and proposed to found a Utopian state called the City of the Sun (Heliopolis), where all men should be free and equal. At first the Romans merely asked the kings of the adjoining principalities to prevent the rebellion from spreading, but in 131 a Roman force had to be sent to hunt him down.[14] The Roman troops, as so often in a

guerrilla campaign on unfamiliar ground, bought their experience with an initial defeat, which resulted in the capture and death of their commander, the consul P. Licinius Crassus; but in 130 his successor, M. Perperna made short work of Aristonicus. In the following year the consul M'. Aquilius definitely constituted the kingdom of Pergamum into the province of 'Asia'. His settlement showed *The province* an anxiety to reduce Roman commitments in *of 'Asia'* Asia to the lowest point. In order to relieve his troops from the troublesome task of policing the interior, Aquilius made over its eastern borderlands to the kings of Pontus and Cappadocia, and he gave the tribes of the southern mountain border, whom the Pergamene kings had sought to control by means of military colonies, the questionable boon of liberty. In the same spirit of abstinence he relieved from taxation all the Greek cities which had stood out against Aristonicus. It was not until after some years that the Romans came to look upon the new province as a financial milch-cow (p. 208).

5. Relations with Syria and Egypt

By the peace of 188 the Romans had mutilated the Seleucid kingdom so effectively that there was no danger of a Perseus succeeding a Philip in this monarchy. The Senate therefore gave no more than occasional attention to its affairs. The decline of the monarchy was temporarily arrested by an erratic but vigorous ruler named Antiochus IV Epiphanes, who met an attempt on the part of Ptolemy VI to recover Palestine by invading Egypt and setting siege to Alexan-*Antiochus IV* dria (169–168). Nowithstanding their 'friend-*of Syria* ship' with Egypt (p. 96), which they had *invades* renewed on its hundredth anniversary in 173, *Egypt; but* the Romans at first let the siege take its course. *withdraws* But as soon as the victory over king Perseus *at Rome's* at Pydna set its hands free, the Senate inter-*bidding* vened decisively. Its envoy, C. Popillius Laenas, presented to Antiochus a point-blank command to call off his attack, and when Antiochus proceeded to argue the matter he drew a ring round the king with his stick and bade him give his answer before he stepped out of the circle. Antiochus, who had a just appreciation of Roman might – he had been a hostage at Rome, and in his light moments he instituted an imitation aedileship at Antioch and canvassed the townsmen for it in the style of a republican candidate – submitted to this 'hold up' and evacuated Egypt without further demur. After the death of Antiochus IV the Senate, acting presumably in accord with the late king, sent three commissioners to administer the realm on behalf of his boy successor (163). The senatorial agents seized the opportunity to enforce rigorously some neglected clauses of the peace of 188, by causing all their ward's warships to be burnt and his elephants to be hamstrung. This belated act of vigilance cost the life of the chief commissioner, the ex-consul Cn. Octavius, for Antiochus's subjects, infuriated at the sight of the mutilated elephants, murdered him in a riot. In the meantime, however, the Senate had seemingly lost interest in its own dispositions. When *Roman interventions in Syria* a rival claimant to the throne, Demetrius I, escaped from Rome, where he was being detained as a hostage, and displaced Antiochus's son, it acquiesced in the accomplished fact.[15] On the intercession of a friend of the new king, Ti. Sempronius Gracchus, it recognised his title, and when Demetrius sought to atone for the death of Octavius by sending the alleged assassins to Rome for punishment it disdained to take action against them. Yet the Senate had not forgotten its grudge against the runaway. *Treaty with Judas Maccabaeus* In 161 it embarrassed him by conceding a treaty to Judas Maccabaeus, the leader of an insurrection against the Seleucids in Palestine, so as to hold the shadow of intervention over Demetrius's head.[16] For the time being the Senate did not carry the implied threat into effect; but in 152 it encouraged another pretender to the Seleucid throne, Alexander Balas, to supplant the king whom it had recognised.

With the accession of Balas the Seleucid monarchy passed into an era of chronic civil war, in the course of which it lost most of its remaining possessions and was reduced to the status of a third-class power. The Jews, who had risen against an ill-advised attempt by Antiochus IV to replace the worship of Jehovah at Jerusalem by the cult of Zeus Olympius, but *Decline of the Seleucid monarchy* had since been reduced to submission by Demetrius, now obtained their autonomy, and their complete independence not long after (150–129). At the same time the last of the continental provinces of the Seleucids, Mesopotamia and Babylonia, were taken from them by the Parthians (on whom see pp. 255 f.). This progressive decomposition of the Seleucid kingdom freed the Romans of any lurking fear of an attack from that quarter. After 150 the Senate paid no further attention to its affairs.

The relations of the Romans with the Ptolemies in the second century were characterised by the same spasmodic interventions which marked their attitude to the other Greek monarchies. But the kings of Egypt, who had been the first Greek rulers to cultivate friendship with the western Republic, were as careful as the Attalids or the Seleucids after Antiochus III

not to risk any serious act of disobedience to it. At the time of Antiochus IV's invasion of Egypt two brothers, Ptolemy VI Philometor and VII Euergetes Physcon, were rival claimants to the throne. An attempt to patch up the dispute by instituting a joint rule soon broke down, and a long-drawn-out quarrel between *Abortive Roman interventions in Egypt* the two Ptolemies ensued, in which each contestant took it in turn to reign at Alexandria and to go on his travels. In 164 the elder brother presented himself before the Senate in rags and obtained a decree of restitution but no material assistance. In 163 Ptolemy VII, who had meanwhile been dethroned by the Alexandrians and relegated to Cyrene, laid his claim before the Senate, which modified its previous award by transferring Cyprus to him, but did not help him to obtain possession. In 154 the younger brother published a testament, in which he bequeathed Cyrene to the Roman republic in the event of his demise without issue – an act of calculated generosity which found more than one imitator among Hellenistic kings.[17] He followed up this manifesto by a second visit to Rome, in order to exhibit to the Senate some knife-marks on his body as evidence that Ptolemy VI was conspiring against him. The Senate was sufficiently impressed to vote the petitioner back to Cyprus; but it left the enforcement of this decree to the neighbouring vassal-kings in the East, who of one accord pretended to have heard nothing. Eventually the two brothers came to an amicable understanding, by which Ptolemy VI retained Egypt and Cyprus and the younger brother contented himself with Cyrene.

After the death of Ptolemy VI in 145, the Egyptian dominions were reunited under the surviving brother; but a fierce triangular dispute now broke out between him and his two successive queens, in the course of which he again lost and recovered his throne. In answer to the complaints which it received against the king, the Senate sent no less a person than Scipio *Visit of Scipio Aemilianus to Egypt* Aemilianus to investigate the state of Egypt (c. 140). The stern republican general showed his disdain for mere monarchs by obliging Ptolemy VII, who was absurdly fat – his subjects called him Physcon ('Puffing Billy') – to bustle about on foot behind him. But the report which Scipio made on his return to Rome was not sufficiently damaging to the king to stir the Senate to action. The flames of the domestic war in Egypt were left to burn themselves out by slow degrees without further intervention from Rome. Nevertheless the prestige of the Republic remained unabated: at the end of the second century senators engaged on private journeys up-Nile could count on being escorted like royal personages.[18]

The establishment of a Roman empire in the

Causes of Rome's easy successes in the East

eastern Mediterranean was even more the product of a chapter of accidents than the Roman conquests in the West. Its ultimate cause is to be sought in the chronic dissensions of the Greek states, which continually invited or even demanded Roman intervention. In the face of a united Greek front the Romans could hardly have forced an entry into the eastern Mediterranean: in all probability they would never have embarked on such an enterprise. The divisions within the Greek ranks presented the Roman legions with a series of relatively easy successes and made it unnecessary for them, except in the case of Macedon, to repeat their initial victory. In the West the enemies of Rome returned to the charge again and again; the Greek states of the East, despite their greater material resources and higher military prestige, capitulated after three set battles.

CHAPTER 17

The Government of the Roman Provinces

1. The Client States and Kings

Haphazard
formation
of Rome's
overseas
empire

By the middle of the second century B.C. every state in the Mediterranean, except Mauretania and a few Balkan principalities, was held to Rome by some kind of political tie. Of this ring of dominions and dependencies it might be asserted, as it has been said of the British Empire, that it was acquired 'in a fit of absent-mindedness'. As a result of the unpremeditated character of most of their conquests the Romans had no ready-made plan for their control, but gradually evolved their rules of administration by trial and error; and they never reduced their empiric practices to a cut-and-dried system. Nevertheless the main lines of their methods of government had been laid down before the end of the second century.

Roman
alliances

Of the two methods by which the Romans had attached the Italians to themselves, annexation and alliance, the latter was the one which they applied by preference to overseas countries in the third and second centuries.[1] But the nature of the alliance varied greatly. It might be negotiated between equals, but even then it took different forms. An early example of a formal treaty (*foedus*) is that concluded between the young Republic and Carthage (p. 70), but her relations with Massilia were on a different basis. Although Rome and Massilia had been friendly for centuries they probably were not originally linked by a formal treaty (this may date from after the First Punic War); diplomatic exchanges led merely to a formal 'friendship' (*amicitia*), as in the case between Rome and Egypt in 273. Alternatively Rome might negoti-

ate not from nominal equality but from superior strength and regulate the position of a dependant by a punitive treaty which limited his armaments and restricted his political intercourse with other states. The terms imposed upon Carthage in 201 and upon the Aetolians in 187 conformed to this type (p. 157). But given the disparity in power between Rome and the other Mediterranean states, alliances on an equal basis were bound in practice to become one-sided. One of Rome's earliest treaties with a smaller power outside Italy was that made with the Mamertines, who surrendered Messana into the trust (*fides*) of the Romans and in turn received an alliance (as, for example, in Italy Thurii had done in 282): the stronger partner then helped to repel the Carthaginian intruder (p. 117). Soon afterwards, in the First Punic War, some Sicilian cities voluntarily joined Rome and were declared 'free' (*civitates liberae*) but apparently without a formal treaty, i.e. free from tribute, garrison and any legal obligation to their 'ally'. But if their freedom was in theory unlimited, they had incurred a moral obligation, and the weaker depended on the stronger. In fact by surrendering in *fidem populi Romani* they became dependent on Rome's goodwill (*beneficium*) and their status was that of clients *vis-à-vis* a patron. Indeed as long as the Romans shaped their foreign policy on the general principle of avoiding entanglements overseas so far as possible, they showed no eagerness to enter into agreements carrying a definite obligation of assistance at the other party's call.

This principle of association without treaty was extended east of the Adriatic after the First

'Friends' of Rome

Illyrian War when Rome established a 'protectorate' over cities such as Corcyra, which became her *amici*, while in the Second War the fate of Demetrius of Pharos showed what would happen to a 'friend' who became too independent (p. 123): a client must show gratitude and loyalty. When Rome extended her protection to Saguntum (p. 125) she may have followed the same procedure of avoiding a formal treaty and merely have received the city less formally into her *fides* which carried with it moral but not legal obligations. Reluctant to become involved in Greek affairs the Romans limited their direct obligations in the First Macedonian War to such necessary but temporary treaties as that with the Aetolians in 212/211, and settled matters in the final peace treaty of Phoenice in 205 in such a manner that they were left with many *amici* but no treaty-bound allies in the Greek world.

From protection to domination in Greece

Thereafter Rome might perhaps have peacefully co-existed with Philip, with perhaps a balance of power in the Hellenistic tradition – but Philip's aggressions soon upset any such prospect, and Rome decided to take the appellant Greek states under her protection without even the formality of a treaty; there was now little question of equality between allied partners, but Rome's *amici* had become her clients.[2] In 200 the Romans merely required Philip to stop attacking Greeks, but they soon went further and in 198, through Flamininus, announced that Philip must evacuate all Greece. Then followed the proclamation at the Isthmian Games when Flamininus announced 'the freedom of the

Greeks': they were to be free *amici* of Rome, who finally withdrew her troops so that Greece could enjoy that freedom, which was now underwritten by Rome. Rome's claim to protect all Greeks soon led to difficulties with Antiochus, though Rome at one point was cynically willing to sacrifice the Asiatic Greeks and keep out of Asia if Antiochus would keep out of Europe. But the king refused and in consequence was humbled in war. In the final settlement at Apamea the Romans abandoned their claim to have fought for the freedom of the Greeks: many were left subject to Eumenes and Rhodes. In Greece itself Rome's policy of protection finally had to give way to one of domination, and the direct administration of Macedon as a Roman province was undertaken (p. 159).

The concept of *amicus* proved fruitful and was widely extended. This type of agreement was concluded with Masinissa, who became Rome's watch-dog over Carthage, and it was subsequently extended to most of the dynasts of Asia Minor. Such clients kings were, at least from the second century, formally enrolled as *amici populi Romani* and their names recorded in a *tabula amicorum* at Rome. As already seen, these compacts were little more than 'gentlemen's agreements'; they did not explicitly bind the contracting parties to render mutual aid, but left it to their discretion to give active assistance or to remain benevolently neutral. In practice the Romans drew with increasing frequency upon the military resources of the client kings, but they habitually avoided engaging the legions

The client kings

Diplomatic and military aids

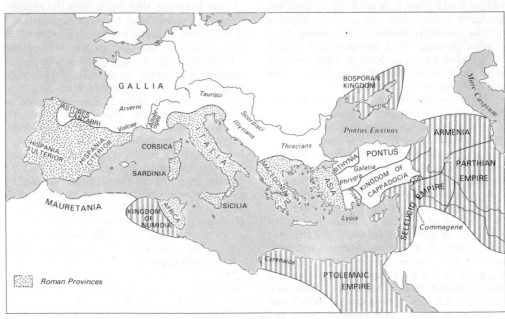

18. ROMAN EMPIRE *c.* 133 B.C.

on behalf of their overseas allies. They requested the Numidian kings to furnish contingents in the Third Punic War, and although Masinissa stood aloof, his successor Micipsa provided auxiliary troops. Similarly in 101 the Senate issued a general proclamation to the dependent states in the eastern Mediterranean to lend a hand in the suppression of piracy (p. 213). More frequently the allied kings made offers of help unbidden: Masinissa and Micipsa repeatedly sent troops and elephants to assist the Romans in Spain, and there was a general rally of rulers in Asia Minor against the pretender Aristonicus. Diplomatic aid was often asked of the Romans by their clients, but was not always given with alacrity and did not meet with invariable success. The Romans for their part resented such offers of assistance, as the Rhodians and King Eumenes discovered to their cost. Altogether, the bond of *amicitia* was a singularly loose one, and its vagueness at times gave rise to awkward misunderstandings. Yet it had the merit, from the Roman point of view, of securing the neutrality, if not the active assistance, of the allies, without committing the Republic too deeply in return; and to the allies the mere prestige of an agreement with Rome, though it might not have the backing of Rome's military power, was a substantial asset.

2. The Status of the Provincial Communities

The formation of 'provinces'

The system of alliances with *socii* and *amici* satisfied the Romans so far that in the eastern Mediterranean it remained in use for several centuries. In the western lands, on the other hand, their usual method was to incorporate conquered territory in the Roman state, and this procedure was eventually extended to the eastern dependencies. The first Roman *provincia*, as annexed districts outside of Italy came to be called, was Sicily; Sardinia and Corsica were joined together to make up a second province; Spain was divided into a third and fourth. In all these cases the chief concern of the Romans was to safeguard regions taken by them from the Carthaginians against recapture. Military security was also the main reason for annexing Macedonia and the African dominion of Carthage after the Third Punic War. A secondary motive for acquiring provinces, which gained in strength in the later days of the Republic, was the desire to draw a revenue from them. The annexation of the Pergamene kingdom subserved a financial interest, and in the appropriation of Spain and later of Gallia Narbonensis similar considerations cannot have been entirely absent.

The general outlines of the provincial constitutions were settled by the Senate; since 146 at the latest its regulations for each province were issued collectively in a code known as the *lex provinciae*.[3] The Senate's charter was ordinarily based on a report by a commission of ten of its leading members, at the head of whom stood the general who had finally reduced the country to submission. The details of administration which fell outside the scope of the *lex provinciae* were left to be filled in by successive governors of a province. On taking up his duties a governor would publish an 'edict' containing the supplementary regulations which he intended to apply during his term of office. Like its prototype, the praetor's edict at Rome (pp. 81 f.), a provincial edict would set forth the principles according to which the governor proposed to administer law in his court; but it might contain a wide variety of additional details, such as the restrictions imposed from time to time upon the local governments. In practice the provincial edicts tended to become stereotyped: one governor would simply take over the greater part of his predecessor's code; in cases of doubt he might borrow from the edict of the praetor at Rome, or from that of some exemplary governor of another province.[4]

The provincial charters

Since the territories converted into provinces had for the most part come into Roman hands by way of conquest, their inhabitants generally stood at the outset in the condition of *dediticii* or capitulants, and therefore enjoyed no rights save such as their captors chose to concede, and these concessions were liable to be revoked at any moment. A few specially favoured communities, which had been bound to Rome by a previous alliance, retained their treaty rights and neither paid tribute nor were brought under the jurisdiction of the Roman courts (*civitates foederatae*). Of the sixty-five cities of Sicily Messana and two others preserved their privileged status, and Massilia remained nominally an allied state after the annexation of Gallia Narbonensis.[5] A somewhat larger number of communities was exempted, by a revocable law or resolution of the Senate, from taxation and military occupation, and received a guarantee of self-government (*civitates liberae et immunes*). The majority of the communities in any province possessed no legal guarantee of their status; but the Romans made it a general practice to entrust to the provincials a generous measure of local self-government. Wherever the process of urbanisation had been carried far enough, and municipal governments with a sufficiently long experience of administration were to be found, the Romans left local affairs in the hands of these; in the more backward districts they

Status of the provincial communities

Local self-government

left local administration in the hands of tribal chieftains. Though the Romans usually required the provincial cities to impose a property qualification for municipal office they did not interfere in local politics without a valid excuse, such as disloyalty, anarchy or bad financial administration. On the other hand the question of conferring Roman citizenship upon the provincials was not even considered in the third or second century. So long as the enfranchisement of the *socii Italici* appeared outside the pale of practical politics, *a fortiori* that of the extra-Italian communities was not to be thought of.

3. The Provincial Governors

The Roman governor

No set rules were framed at first for the appointment of provincial governors. Probably it was left to the consuls to nominate, on the Senate's advice, any two persons qualified to act as their deputies in Sicily and Sardinia. But from *c.* 227 the government of these two provinces was regularly entrusted to two new praetors, who were elected annually, like the praetors who remained at Rome, by the Comitia Centuriata; and in 197 another two additional praetors were instituted for Hither and Further Spain. If a province was in a disturbed condition and likely to become the scene of military operations on a large scale, a consul might be appointed by special arrangement in place of the praetor; on this principle Hither Spain frequently obtained a consular governor. After the constitution of Macedonia and Africa as provinces the practice of creating new magistrates *ad hoc* was abandoned, and regular recourse was had to the device of *prorogatio*, which now developed out of a temporary expedient into a permanent institution. After 146 it became customary to prolong the term of office of all the consuls and praetors, after a year spent in Rome, as governors of provinces with consular or praetorian rank (*pro consule, pro praetore,* from which expressions the titles of 'proconsul' and 'propraetor' were eventually coined). The Senate determined annually which provinces should be held in the ensuing year by men of consular or praetorian standing respectively. In times of emergency it might apportion particular provinces to individual magistrates; but ordinarily it was left to the consuls and praetors to select their several provinces by mutual arrangement or, failing agreement, by drawing lots. The usual term of a provincial governor was of one year; but where military exigencies required the continued presence of an officer of tried capacity – and in Spain this was a not uncommon contingency – his tenure of office

Appointment by 'prorogation'

might be prolonged to a second or even a third year.

The primary duty of the governor was to defend his province against foreign enemies and domestic disturbers; but in normal times his most onerous duty was that of jurisdiction. It would fall to him to hear cases of treason and other serious crime; those in which a Roman citizen was involved as plaintiff or defendant; and disputes between parties from different parts of the province.[6] The governor's court was not permanently established in any one city, but moved about from district to district; eventually each province was divided into a fixed number of circuits (*conventus*) with a separate assize centre.

Roman jurisdiction

The only regular assistant of the governor was a quaestor, who served as his receiver of revenue and paymaster. In order to maintain the requisite tale of quaestors the number of these magistrates was increased *pari passu* with the constitution of each new province. But a governor usually kept in his train one or more *legati*, whom he appointed, subject to the Senate's approval, as his deputies general. He also generally had an entourage of personal friends (later, a *cohors* of *comites*), including young political aspirants, who might be entrusted with minor executive duties, while he could draw upon the services of 'minor civil servants' (secretaries (*scribae*) and the like).[7] In districts where Roman citizens had taken up their domicile it became the custom for the governor to invite the more prominent of their number to a seat on his bench as advisory members, and to appoint them to examine questions of fact in civil trials, like the *iudices* and *reciperatores* of the praetor's court at Rome.

The governor's staff

4. Conscription and Taxation in the Provinces

It was a fundamental point of difference between the provincials and the Italians that the former were not liable to the same degree to military service, but were subject to regular taxation. Conscription was applied to the more backward tribes who could make little or no payment to Rome in the form of taxes: in the Spanish wars native contingents were habitually enrolled on the Roman side. In cases of emergency the governor might order a general levy of local militias, and the *civitates foederatae* were obliged by their treaties to render occasional military aid.[8] But the Romans did not impose personal service on the provincials in the same systematic manner as in Italy. Distrusting their loyalty or fitness for military duty under the rigid Roman standards of discipline, they

General absence of conscription

drafted Italian troops into the provinces for the ordinary business of maintaining order and defending the frontiers.

Taxation was not imposed by the Romans upon the *civitates foederatae*, nor upon the more favoured of the *civitates liberae*, to whom fiscal immunity as well as self-government had been conceded. But all states which had not received special exemption were made tributary. On the legal justification for this tribute the Romans were slow to formulate any clear-cut theory. According to Cicero the provincial taxes were a kind of war indemnity levied upon conquered peoples.[9] The same author suggested an alternative explanation when he described the provinces and their revenues as 'so to speak the property of the Roman people', as though by the mere act of annexation the Romans had acquired title of ownership thereof; but his qualifying phrase, 'so to speak', really shows that he did *not* consider them as Roman property, and the principle in question never became part of Roman law.[10] The more valid explanation, that the tribute imposed upon the provinces was a form of compensation to the Romans for garrisoning and administering them was not, to our knowledge, formulated before the time of the emperor Vespasian.[11]

Roman theories of taxation in the provinces

In their methods of taxation the Romans did not follow any set scheme, but so far as possible retained the fiscal system of the previous government, so that the imposts varied considerably from province to province. In accordance with the usual practice of ancient states the principal levy fell upon the owners of arable and plantation land (*tributum soli*). In most provinces the land tax was a fixed sum of silver (*stipendium*), representing a quota of the value of an average harvest; but in Sicily, Sardinia and Asia the established custom of taking a tithe (*decumana*) of varying annual amount on the actual harvest was preserved. In Sicily and Sardinia the tithe was delivered in grain; in Asia it was commuted into a payment of money. Beside the *tributum soli*, a poll tax (*tributum capitis*) was imposed on Africa in 146 and thereafter was probably levied in all the provinces. These direct taxes were supplemented by indirect *vectigalia*. Thus a fixed amount fell on each head of cattle grazing on public land (*scriptura*). Tolls (*portoria*) were levied at a low flat rate at harbours on goods entering or leaving a province.[12] Further revenue accrued in the form of rent from the tenants of former public lands or royal domains, which under Roman rule became corporate property of the Roman people, and of royalties from the lessees of mines or quarries.

The Roman imposts

For the business of gathering in these imposts from the individual taxpayers the Roman governor's staff was totally inadequate. Where the tax consisted of a fixed quantity its exaction was left in the hands of the local authorities, each of which was bound to pay over to the Roman quaestor the lump sum at which it was corporately assessed. The local governing bodies usually transferred the work of collection in detail to companies of private contractors, who paid in advance the agreed total of each tax and recovered the sum thus expended, together with their trading profit, from the individual taxpayer. In Sicily the equitable regulations devised by King Hiero for the levying of the corn tithes were preserved unaltered under Roman rule.[13] The Sicilian tax-farmers were mostly drawn from the native population, and their operations were controlled by the municipal magistrates. In Asia the collection of the land-tax was transferred from the officials of the Pergamene kings to contractors at Rome, where the contract was sold by the censors. These *publicani* paid the stipulated sum-total of the impost directly into the Roman treasury and recouped themselves in the province by means of their trained staffs of collectors (p. 208).[14] By virtue of the larger amount of capital at their disposal the Roman tax-farming companies were able to displace the native collectors in other provinces; but they never obtained a complete monopoly of this business.

Methods of collection

Tax-farming

In addition to the regular imposts described above the provincials were liable to find billets, provisions, fuel and fodder for the governor's staff and his troops. The quantity of such requisitionings was limited by successive Roman statutes or resolutions of the Senate, and fair rates of payment were prescribed for the grain delivered for the governor's use. Finally, in Sicily and Sardinia the Roman state reserved to itself the right of pre-emption of additional quantitites of corn (not exceeding a second tithe on the harvest) for the population of Rome or for the armies on foreign service. For this contribution in excess the provincials were remunerated at full market rates.

Additional requisitions

Further economic burdens in the form of restrictions on commerce were imposed on particular provinces or for certain periods. In Sicily and Sardinia the Romans assured themselves of a plentiful supply of grain for their own uses by limiting its exportation to other countries than Italy.[15] But there is no evidence of any systematic attempt on the part of the Romans to hamper the economic activities of the provincials for the benefit of Italian traders.

Few commercial restrictions

In the western provinces, where coinage had been relatively scarce before the Roman conquest, additional mints were opened by several

Provincial coinage

towns of Sicily and Spain, but these mostly restricted themselves to the emission of copper pieces on the Roman standard. In the eastern Mediterranean many of the existing municipal mints remained active, and no attempt was made by the Romans to impose a uniform weight-standard upon them. In Asia the large silver pieces known as *cistophori* continued to be issued in large quantities by Pergamum and Ephesus, and maintained themselves by the side of the Roman money as a general provincial currency.

Few Roman colonies in the provinces

The provincials were not required, except in rare instances, to surrender land for allotment to Roman colonists. In countries where detachments of Roman troops on active service were stationed, an influx of Italian settlers was not considered necessary for military security. In southern and eastern Spain a few settlements of Italian veterans, who had become acclimatised to the country through long years of service, were authorised (p. 147). On the territory of Carthage the Senate refused to sanction the colony at Junonia (p. 207), but it tolerated the colonists' informal occupation. In Gaul it consented reluctantly to the constitution of a colony at Narbo (p. 211). In the eastern provinces not a single Roman colony was founded before the time of Caesar.[16]

5. The Defects of Roman Rule in the Provinces

Discontent at Roman rule

Roman rule in Italy gave general satisfaction; in the provinces it caused widespread discontent. The ultimate reason for this difference lay in a fundamental disparity between the condition of the Italians and of the provincials. While the Italians rendered military aid to Rome the provincials paid tribute. In the eyes of the Romans accordingly the provincials became a source of gain, and as they lost the habit of bearing arms they had no effective means left of asserting themselves against abuses of Roman power. Under these conditions they became victims of many forms of financial exploitation, in which Roman officials and private residents participated with equal zest.

Money-making by Roman governors

The example of illicit exactions in the provinces was set by the governors themselves. The process, however, was gradual, and over 150 years intervened between the acquisition of Sicily and the unbelievably corrupt governorship of Verres. Polybius bears witness to a general probity in early days, though he admits a deterioration of the Roman character in the second century, and it is probable that excesses increased after the Roman acquisition of Asia. Until then, in general, public exploitation of the provinces is hard to find: it was the individual that was mainly guilty. Roman magistrates on duty outside of Italy were provided with kit-money and journey-money. In the event of a successful war they were entitled to hold back for themselves a generous share of the booty. Nevertheless Roman noblemen, who made it a point of honour to render public service at home without any monetary reward, learnt to look upon their terms of office in a province as a heaven-sent occasion for personal enrichment. Indeed, as the financial burden of public life in Rome grew more onerous (p. 178), provincial governorships inevitably came to be regarded as an indispensable resource for recovering past expenses and providing for future costs. Needless to say the lead which governors gave in extorting money was eagerly followed by the subordinate members of their staff, who also had their careers in Rome to keep in mind. The ingenuity of Roman officials in extracting unauthorised payments out of the provincials was inexhaustible. One of the commonest forms of money-making was the traffic in exemptions from the burdensome obligation to provide billets for the troops and from the liability to furnish grain and means of transport. The sale of justice by governors, and of access to the governors by their underlings, was another source of illicit profits. The collection of compulsory 'benevolences', for the ostensible purpose of providing the governors with crowns of honour, or with the means of giving a special entertainment to the Roman people on his return home, was also a frequent method of enrichment.

Extortion by publicani and usurers

While these official depredations went on, Roman residents in a private station took advantage of the prestige attaching to their nationality, and of the connivance of rapacious or weak governors to search the pockets of the natives. The most persistent among the private pilferers were the Roman *publicani* or tax-farmers, who had an obvious interest in collecting more than their due, and sometimes did not wait to assure themselves of the connivance of the governor before they fleeced the tax-payers. In collusion with other Roman capitalists the *publicani* also used their funds to buy up grain at low prices after harvest, in order to retail it at famine figures in areas of shortage, or to make advances of cash to hard-driven provincials at rates of interest that might rise to 4 per cent per month or more. For the collection of their debts the Roman usurers could generally count on assistance from the governors, some of whom even put soldiers at the disposal of financiers intent on squeezing blood out of stones.

While the Romans overpaid themselves for their services in keeping the peace and defending the frontiers of the provinces they were not always successful in discharging these services efficiently. In most of the provinces the standing garrisons were cut down to the point of danger; the governors often lacked experience in warfare under the local conditions, and their term of office was usually too short to provide them with the necessary training. In some districts (notably in Macedonia) the frontiers were habitually unsafe, and instances will come to our notice in which provinces were overrun by foreign enemies from end to end.

Insecurity of the frontiers

Against this misrule voices were raised from time to time by natives or by Roman residents, but so long as the protests were not carried beyond the four corners of the province the governor could safely disregard them. Some of the more unscrupulous of the governors were not content merely to ignore complaints, but imprisoned or killed their critics with or without the semblance of a trial. Cases were even on record in which governors put to death Roman citizens, in defiance of a law (carried in 199 by the tribune P. Porcius Laeca), which expressly affirmed their right of appeal outside Roman territory.[17]

Ineffective protests against Roman misrule

6. Attempts at Reform

The defects of Roman provincial administration were not allowed to escape the attention of the government at Rome. Protests against the prevalent abuses were carried from time to time to the Senate collectively and to individual members of the ruling class. The cause of the oppressed peoples was taken up by several of the military leaders who had assumed an obligation of patronage in regard to the provinces pacified by them. The Spaniards could always count on the advocacy of a Sempronius Gracchus, the Allobroges of Gallia Narbonensis on that of Fabius Maximus and his descendants.[18] The most redoubtable champion of injured provincials in the second century was M. Cato, who combined a personal sense of responsibility to provinces in which he had held office, an impartial interest in straight dealing, and a discerning eye for a suitable stick to beat a political opponent. The Senate in its corporate capacity also showed some concern for the oppressed natives, and it was not blind to the dangers which might recoil upon its own head if Roman magistrates on duty overseas were to form a habit of setting themselves above the law.

Champions of the provincials at Rome

From time to time individual champions of the provinces initiated prosecutions before the Popular Assembly against particularly flagrant offenders, and the Senate issued new regulations for the protection of the provincials. In 171, on receipt of complaints from the Spanish provinces against rapacious governors, it directed a praetor to constitute a court of *reciperatores* for the assessment of damages. In this case, it is true, the injured parties received no tangible compensation, for the culprits evaded restitution by retiring from Rome; but the action of the Senate was tantamount to a sentence of exile upon them. In 170 a more drastic procedure was adopted against an ex-praetor named Lucretius Gallus, who had ill-treated Rome's allies in Greece during the Third Macedonian War. At the instance of the Senate two tribunes impeached him before the Tribal Assembly, which imposed a heavy fine upon him.[19] In 149 the same Assembly acquitted a far worse offender, Sulpicius Galba, who had both plundered and massacred the Spaniards (p. 143), and had drawn upon himself the fulminations of the nonagenarian Cato. Galba outmanœuvred his opponents by the time-honoured Greek device of exhibiting his family to the court in tears and tatters. This fiasco, however, led to the transfer of cases of provincial maladministration from the Popular Assembly to a special tribunal. In the year of Galba's acquittal the tribune L. Calpurnius Piso carried a law by which prosecutions for extortion were made over to a permanent court consisting entirely of senators, whose decision was placed beyond the reach of an appeal to the people and of a tribune's veto (*quaestio de rebus repetundis*).[20] At some later time (but certainly before 86 B.C.) a second special court of the same type was set up to deal with cases of malversation of public money (*peculatus*). Like the *reciperatores*, of which they were a development, these tribunals were strictly speaking a civil court and possessed no competence beyond that of assigning simple damages to the plaintiff; but an order of simple restitution would have the same force as a sentence of exile, unless the culprit could pay the award out of his own pocket.

Action against guilty officials

The quaestio de rebus repetundis

These remedial measures were an honest but not a whole-hearted attempt to grapple with the problem of provincial misgovernment. The institution of the standing jury-courts marked an important stage in the history of Roman jurisdiction, but it failed to put a stop to extortion in the provinces. The initiation of prosecutions in a jury-court was attended with some difficulty, for while there was no lack of Roman citizens to come forward as prosecutors – some acting out of public spirit, some from a desire of self-advertisement, others again in pursuit of a political feud – the collection of incriminating

Ineffective-ness of this court

evidence was liable to be impeded by a governor with a guilty conscience or (after the culprit's departure) by a complaisant successor; and it might require a formidable mass of adverse testimony to counteract the effects of the panegyrics which peccant governors sometimes contrived to extort from their victims. Besides, if the senatorial juries were free from the herd impulses that might beset the Popular Assembly, they were by no means exempt from a bias in favour of defendants drawn from their own political class. The hazard of a condemnation by a *quaestio perpetua* was therefore not sufficiently great to deter the more resolute offenders. The question of provincial reform was not to be solved by any simple remedy, and an adequate combination of protective measures was not carried into effect until after the fall of the Republic.[21]

Dangers of generalising about Roman rule

Yet if accounts are balanced we may hesitate to conclude that the general condition of the Roman provinces was worse than under their previous rulers. In judging Roman provincial administration we must bear in mind 'the privilege which Evil has over Good, of getting itself more talked about'. Our information concerning this administration is mostly derived from historians who naturally reported at greatest length the most scandalous cases of misrule, and from Cicero, who gained his most notable forensic triumph as a prosecuting barrister in a particular *cause célèbre* (pp. 243 f.). We are therefore

prone to judge Roman provincial rule by the single example of Asia, which became the favourite field of the Roman fortune-hunters, or by the unique maladministration of a C. Verres in Sicily. The admission of Verres's prosecutor, that hitherto Roman rule had been popular in Sicily, is sufficient proof that a Verres was the exception rather than the rule. While we must admit that the provincials were exposed to a harassing uncertainty, never knowing what the next change of governor might bring, we may doubt whether avaricious or feeble magistrates outnumbered energetic and upright ones; and given a moderately efficient administration the provincials could not have had much to complain about. The general provisions of the provincial charters were not oppressive; the normal rates of taxation were moderate and in some instances stood at a lower level than under the previous régime; and a liberal amount of local self-government was conceded to the natives. Lastly, after allowance has been made for occasional disorders or foreign invasions in this district and that, it remains broadly true that under Roman rule the provinces passed from a condition in which warfare was a normal experience to one in which it was a rare incident. On this ground alone it may be believed that on the whole the compensating advantages of Roman rule in the provinces outweighed its attendant evils.

Benefits of the Roman rule

The Pax Romana

CHAPTER 18

Domestic Politics in the Second Century

1. The Popular Assemblies

Reactions of the Roman conquests on domestic politics

The expansion of the Roman Empire in the third and second centuries B.C. was not only rapid and continuous, it was also unpremeditated and to some extent undesired. The Romans were carried along without any clear perception of the responsibilities involved in their new acquisitions, and they were slow to observe and control the inevitable reactions of their conquests upon their domestic affairs. In fact they were caught unprepared in much the same way as the modern world has been taken by surprise by the Industrial Revolution and by the changes of the last hundred years in methods of communication. The domestic history of the later Republic is largely a record of successive crises resulting from this failure of adaptation to a quickly changing environment.

Final organisation of the Tribal Assembly

Of the transformations which the Roman body politic underwent in the third and second centuries the most fundamental related to the Popular Assemblies. The alterations in the structure and procedure of the Comitia during this period were not in themselves far-reaching. Until the middle of the third century the number of the tribes was augmented from time to time, so as to keep pace with the extensions of Roman territory. After 241, when their total was raised to thirty-five, no further increase in their number took place, and new citizens were henceforth distributed among the existing tribes, with the result that the tribes gradually lost their primary local significance and became merely administrative units. At this period the constitution of the Tribal Assembly received its final shape.[1]

At some time after the completion of the tribal organisation, probably between 241 and 218, a change was made in the constitution of the Comitia Centuriata where the centuries and tribes were correlated. The number of centuries in the first class was reduced from eighty to seventy, so that two centuries (one of *seniores* and one of *iuniores*) were assigned to each of the thirty-five tribes. If, as seems probable, the total number of centuries remained 193 the ten centuries taken from the first class must have been redistributed among some or all of the other four, but the method of this redistribution remains uncertain. At the same time the eighteen centuries of Equites lost the privilege of providing the *centuria praerogativa*, which hereafter was chosen by lot from the first class. No formal alteration was made in the ratings of the several classes, except that the property qualification of the fifth class was reduced from 11,000 to 4000 asses (perhaps early in the second century). But a further lightening of the *as* from two ounces (sextantial) to one (uncial), which probably took place about the time of the Gracchi, had the automatic effect of lowering the qualification for every class. The purpose of this reform of the Comitia Centuriata, apart from administrative convenience, remains uncertain. Dionysius of Halicarnassus says that it was to make the assembly 'more democratic'. This would be true of the effect in so far as the voting would have to continue slightly further down the timocratic scale before a majority was reached,

Reconstitution of the Comitia Centuriata

but in fact the nobles strengthened rather than relaxed their hold upon affairs in the later third century.[2]

Change in the 'personnel' of the Comitia

But the reforms in the constitution of the Comitia were of slight importance compared with the changes in the personnel of the voters who attended them. With the expansion of Roman territory and the progress of Roman colonisation the number of country voters continued to rise. But as the distance which separated them from the capital grew ever longer, their opportunities for putting their suffrages to use became less frequent. Moreover, the increase in the country vote was counterbalanced by a rapid growth of the urban population, through the influx of dispossessed peasants, and of slaves from foreign lands who eventually received their personal freedom and therewith the Roman franchise and the *ius suffragii*. In the Tribal Assembly, it is true, the voting power of the freedmen was reduced by their confinement to the four 'urban' tribes, but in the Comitia Centuriata it had equal value with that of the free-born.[3] On the other hand free-born immigrants into Rome who already possessed the franchise remained enrolled in the rustic tribes, and no doubt controlled their corporate vote, except on those rare occasions when the country residents flocked into Rome to attend the Comitia.

Dependence of the urban voters

The urban voters of the second century were a sorry substitute for a sturdy suburban peasantry which had stood out successfully against the patricians in the Conflict of the Orders. The ex-slaves were tied by the bond of clientship to their former masters, and the immigrant population in general, whether formally attached to a patron or not, was economically dependent on the wealthier classes. Furthermore, as Rome completed the transition from a city-state to an empire-state, its politics attained a degree of complexity which almost removed them from the grasp of the plain citizen. Small wonder, then, that the urban voters fell into a state of dependence on political 'bosses'.[4]

Direct and indirect bribery

The opportunity which thus presented itself to the governing families of capturing the urban electors and, through them, the entire Popular Assemblies was not allowed to pass by. The purchase of votes by candidates for office became so common in the second century that two additional statutes *de ambitu*, which were carried in 181 and 159 by champions of old-fashioned rectitude, remained dead letters. A collective system of bribery was introduced by the Senate, which took advantage of the frequent donations of corn from Carthage and Numidia (p. 147), and of occasional gluts in Sicily or Sardinia, to make gratis distributions of food to the urban proletariat. From private fortunes or the proceeds of provincial taxation special distributions (*congiaria*) of wine and oil were provided on occasion.

But the principal means by which the ruling houses influenced the electorate was by keeping it amused with a constant succession of public entertainments. Before 220 the only regular public games in Rome were a one-day festival known as the *Ludi Romani*. In that year a second holiday, the *Ludi Plebeii*, was instituted. During the dark days of the Second Punic War the Senate appointed three further festivals, in order to keep up the spirits of the people, the *Ludi Apollinares* (212), *Megalenses* (204) and *Ceriales* (before 202). In 173 a sixth public entertainment, the *Ludi Florales*, was introduced. The duration of each of these festivities was subsequently extended to five, seven or even fourteen days,[5] and the Senate voted increased appropriations for them. In addition to the sums provided out of public funds, contributions were habitually made out of their private pockets by the individual magistrates (praetors, curule and plebeian aediles) who presided over these festivals. The official *ludi*, in which circus races and dramatic performances played the principal part, were supplemented with gladiatorial contests and beast-hunts, which individual noblemen exhibited as a private speculation. For instance at the Games given by M. Fulvius Nobilior in 185 'many actors from Greece came to do him honour, and athletic contests were introduced for the first time in Rome. The hunting of lions and panthers formed a novel feature' (Livy, xxxix. 22).

Amusements for the urban population

To the end of the republican period the theoretical sovereignty of the Popular Assemblies was preserved intact, indeed was never called into question. About 150 a partial substitute for the obsolete *patrum auctoritas* was provided by two statutes, the *lex Aelia* and the *lex Fufia*, establishing, or more probably confirming, the right of any curule magistrate or tribune to disband all (or only legislative) assemblies of the people on the simple declaration that he had witnessed an unfavourable omen.[6] But there is no evidence of this new method of veto being put to systematic use before the first century. Until then the need to resort to it seldom arose, for the individual and collective patronage which the aristocracy exercised over the urban voters gave it a sufficient hold upon the Popular Assemblies. In the course of the second century the ultimate control of Roman politics, which the commons had secured for themselves during the Conflict of the Orders, was slipping out of their hands.

Indirect veto on popular legislation

2. The New Nobility

The growing impotence of the Comitia left a virtually irresponsible power in the hands of the Roman nobility; and this power came to include, in practice, the faculty of filling up its ranks at its own discretion. In the fourth and third centuries the admission of plebeians into the magistracy and the Senate had produced a slow but constant infiltration of new families into the governing class. In the Second Punic War plebeian Fulvii and Claudii Marcelli had shared the chief military posts with patrician Fabii and Cornelii. By 179 the Senate was composed of plebeians to the extent of nearly three-quarters,[7] and in 172 plebeian candidates carried both the consular places, an achievement which they often repeated in later years. In the third and second centuries the old hereditary aristocracy had been replaced by a new aristocracy of office, to which the distinguishing name of *nobiles* came to be applied. Since admission to the ranks of *nobiles* depended on election to the consulship it always remained theoretically possible for a *novus homo* to gain entrance into them, but in actual fact the 'nobility' became as much of a closed caste as the patriciate. In consorting with the patricians the ennobled plebeians had absorbed the exclusive spirit of the older families: they hauled up behind them the ladder by which they had climbed into the charmed circle, and combined with the patricians to keep newcomers out of the higher magistracies. From the time of the Punic Wars the door forced open by Licinius and Sextius began to swing back. From 264 to 201 not more than eleven *novi homines* attained the consulship; between 200 and 134 the consulship all but passed into the possession of some twenty-five families, and only five new names were added to the consular *fasti*.[8]

By virtue of their monopoly of high office the *nobiles* retained control of the Senate, in which the members of consular and censorial rank exercised a preponderant influence (p. 99); and the Senate was the instrument by which they directed Roman policy. The position of almost unchallenged authority which the Senate had attained in the Second Punic War was confirmed and extended in the course of the second century. The consolidation of its power was an inevitable result of the overseas conquests, which added greatly to the scope and complexity of Roman administration and emphasised the need of a co-ordinating body to gather up its manifold threads into a single hand. Since the Senate alone possessed the necessary breadth and continuity of experience for this task, its guidance became positively indispensable to the magistrates and to the Popular Assemblies. In questions of war and peace, of contracting treaties or of constituting new provinces, its word was as good as law; and it was the body to which foreign powers, provincial communities and Italian dependants alike carried their suits. It frequently apportioned provincial and military commands among the individual magistrates (p. 98), and in taking from the Comitia the right of extending their offices by a 'prorogation' (p. 172) it assumed a valuable means of patronage. At the same time it asserted a tighter control over Roman finances, which had now attained such a scale and complexity as to pass out of the sphere of executive routine into that of parliamentary policy. In making lavish appropriations for games and festivals it kept the urban population under a due sense of obligation. By its power to vote ample or meagre supplies for provincial governors, to lengthen their tenures of office for a further term or to cut them short, to grant or refuse the expenditure incidental to a triumph, it gained additional holds on the magistracy. Finally, the Senate's authority was enhanced by two successful usurpations, through which it acquired the right of suspending the operation of laws or of declaring them null and void (if enacted without due regard to existing law), and discretion to appoint extraordinary judicial commissions with unlimited punitive powers.

In the second century the Roman constitution reverted in effect to a rigidly aristocratic type. A nobility which enjoyed no statutory privilege, like that of the old-time patriciate, had constituted itself as an exclusive governing caste by the simple process of controlling the elections so as to monopolise the higher offices and acquire a commanding influence in the Senate. Upon this class fell the double duty of directing the foreign conquests and of adapting the constitution to the needs of the Roman Empire. For such a task, however, it was not well fitted: indeed it is doubtful whether any kind of governing body at this period could have brought the right mind to it. The innate bent of Romans, whether gentle or simple, was to advance by slow steps in politics and not to make any sudden or sweeping change in established usage. This method of progress by cautious experiment had plainly justified itself in past centuries, for the machinery of government which it had evolved had stood the searching test of the Punic Wars. It was therefore only to be expected that the Romans of the second century should have become as complacent about their constitution, and as slow to realise the need of a more resolute policy of reconstruction, as Bri-

Control of the elections by a few families

Constitution of a new nobility

Preponderance of the nobiles in the Senate

Growth of the Senate's power

Senatorial patronage

Inadequacy of the new nobility

Excessive conservatism

tons have recently been for similar reasons. But the conservatism which was common to the Romans in general was intensified within the ruling class, which lived largely on its own past and excluded from its ranks new men and new ideas. The domestic history of Rome after 200 B.C., though not wholly devoid of reforms, was in the main a record of missed opportunities and of belated half-measures.

3. Political Groups at Rome

Rivalries and ideals of the nobility

Although real power in the Senate rested, as has been seen (p. 179), in the hands of a relatively few families, within this governing circle competition for the highest offices was keen and often bitter. This did not result in the emergence of party politics in a modern sense, since the electorate did not normally vote for candidates who represented certain policies either for home or foreign affairs. In general the nobles were elected as the result of the strength of their personal and social backing; through the patronage which they exercised on behalf of their clients' personal, economic, social, legal or political interests, they built up groups of supporters through whom they tried to control the elections. High office was the legitimate aim and indeed the duty of the nobles according to the social standards of the day; '*virtus*, in the Republican noble, consisted in the winning of personal pre-eminence and glory by the commission of great deeds in the service of the Roman state'.[9] The leading members of the noble families thus struggled for *fama, gloria, auctoritas* and *dignitas*, and keen rivalries resulted.

Political groupings, but not parties

In the first instance a noble would rely on the support of his family and then of his *gens* as far as he could carry it with him. Then other families might be won over by marriage alliances, by patronage or by political compacts (*amicitiae*). Such personal and unofficial groupings undoubtedly existed and continued to remain personal in the sense that they did not develop into political parties, but modern historians have reached varying conclusions when attempting to define in detail their composition, interrelationships and permanence. Some dismiss them as brief kaleidoscopic groupings and changes, others see them as merely the supporters of an individual, while others again suppose that some group loyalties might survive the political eclipse or death of a leader and that patterns of similar family groupings might survive for longer periods owing to the strong ties of family and the conservatism of the Roman character.[10] At any rate Livy describes the keen

electoral contests every year in the late third and early second centuries, while rivalries might be fought out not only at the hustings but be carried over to the courts of law in 'political' trials. Thus Cato, himself the object of forty-four impeachments in the course of his career, was ever on the look-out for a pretext to invoke the law against his adversaries. In general the familiar comparison between second-century Rome and England under Walpole and the Pelhams places the Roman nobles in their proper light.

The rivalry between Scipio Africanus and Cato

No attempt can be made here to follow the political intrigues of families as the Aemilii, the Cornelii, the Porcii, the Fulvii, the Postumii and the Popillii in the early second century, but the culmination of one bitter quarrel may be mentioned, that between Cato and the Scipos. It presents, however, two features which are not perhaps quite typical of the average political struggle: a *novus homo* was fighting one of the oldest patrician families and the depth of Cato's personal hatred may have been more marked (private relations away from the hustings may not always have been so strained, and *per contra* political *amicitiae* did not always involve personal friendship). Further, although major political issues occasionally affected the electorate (as, for instance, when Scipio stood for the consulship for 205 with the declared intention of carrying the war into Africa), normally they took second place to personalities and personal loyalties. But between Cato and Africanus there was a deep dividing-line: their attitude towards Greek culture. Africanus was an ardent phil-Hellenist in his private life, while Cato wished to stem the tide of Greek ideas which was flooding Rome and to maintain untainted the *mos maiorum*. This clash clearly affected their attitude to domestic policy, while it also spread over to foreign affairs. Cato wished to have as little to do with Greek affairs as possible, while Scipio was ready for resolute action in the East: he may not have approved of such hurried action against Philip V in 201 as did other senators, but he was certainly eager to take preventive measures, by force if need be, against Antiochus. The quarrel of these two individualists well illustrates the lengths to which public life might be split by personal animosities.

Cato attacks the Scipios

In 187 Cato instigated two tribunes, both named Petillius, to interrogate L. Scipio in the Senate about a sum of 500 talents which he had held back from the first instalment of King Antiochus's war indemnity in order to pay his troops. Knowing that the attack was really levelled against himself, Africanus intervened and disdainfully tore up Lucius's account-books, thus asserting that his brother was not answerable. The technical matter was in fact a question of definition: was the money booty (*praeda*), which was at the general's disposal, or state funds? Cato, thus thwarted in the Senate, found another tribune, C. Minucius, to raise the matter before the people and imposed a fine and a demand for surety on Lucius when he refused to account for the money. When Lucius was threatened with imprisonment, Africanus persuaded another tribune, Ti. Sempronius Gracchus, to intervene, and Cato, having obtained his object of discrediting the Scipios, allowed the matter to rest. But in the year of his censorship (184) he was emboldened to attack Africanus himself before the people. The charge may even have been treason, arising from Africanus's alleged ambiguous dealings with Antiochus (among other things Antiochus had released Scipio's own son without ransom before Magnesia). Such a charge was fantastic, but it was adequate for Cato's purpose. Africanus diverted the enemy's fire by an appeal to his past services to his country and the trial broke down. Sheer force of personality had saved Africanus but, now old and tired, he decided to withdraw from Rome to Liternum where he died the next year. In the political field Cato had triumphed and forced Hannibal's conqueror into self-imposed exile.[11]

Death of Scipio Africanus

Struggles within the nobility did not seriously affect the Senate's controlling position, but a more serious threat might come from military leaders who were tempted by the plenitude of their power on foreign service, and by the deference paid to them by dependent peoples, to set themselves above the Senate's authority. During the Hannibalic War legal restrictions against holding the consulship twice within ten years and other safeguards had perforce been abandoned. The most striking example was Scipio Africanus, who for ten years (210–201) held supreme command successively in Spain, Italy and Africa, the hero of a devoted army. But when peace came he made no attempt to face his fellow senators except as an equal.[12] An ominous sign of disobedience, however, was the frequency with which Roman generals began to embark on quasi-private wars without senatorial warrant. In 189 Manlius Vulso exceeded his instructions in attacking the Galatians (p. 164): and minor campaigns were undertaken at various times in Liguria and Illyricum by commanders acting on their own responsibility, who on occasion (as M. Popillius in 173) flouted direct senatorial orders and by political wire-pulling managed to escape if not trial at least condemnation. These escapades foreshadowed the days when Roman armies would be mobilised against the Senate itself.

Disregard of senatorial orders by military leaders

4. The Executive

In the second century the duties of the Roman government were approaching a stage of complexity at which the services of a trained professional executive could no longer be dispensed with. In recognition of this fact a permanent body of accountants and secretaries was attached to the treasury and to the bureaux of the chief magistrates. But this staff was recruited in part from ex-slaves and formed a class wholly distinct from the magistracy. Additional praetors and quaestors were instituted for the administration of the provinces,[13] and after 150 proconsuls and propraetors were appointed for the same purpose (p. 172). But no increase took place in the higher executive staff at Rome, and no attempt was made to prolong the terms of office of the home magistrates. The Roman aristocracy clung obstinately to the ideal of unpaid half-time service by men born rather than apprenticed to exercise authority. In order to check any potential threat from unduly ambitious magistrates after the Second Punic War it brought back into operation the fourth-century law prescribing a ten years' interval between two successive tenures of the consulship, and from *c.* 197 the praetorship was made a necessary qualification for the consulship. In 180 the aristocracy procured the enactment of a general regulating act, the *lex Villia Annalis*: hereafter minimum ages were fixed for the curule magistracies (probably 36 for curule aediles, 39 for praetors and 42 for consuls). The quaestorship, with a minimum age of perhaps 25, became a customary, if not compulsory, prerequisite to an official career, while a biennium was prescribed between each magistracy and the next one above. Thus the *cursus honorum* was regulated to hold back ambitious young men.[14] The levelling policy which the Roman aristocracy pursued within its own ranks is further illustrated by the practical abolition of the dictatorship during the Second Punic War after its tenure by Fabius Maximus (pp. 127 f.).[15]

Additions to the Roman magistracy

Regulation of the cursus honorum

In 153 a slight administrative change was effected. In order to facilitate the arrival of the consul at the Spanish seat of war in good time for the campaigning season, his entry into office was advanced from 15 March to 1 January,[16] which thus became the beginning of the Roman official year.

Beginning of the official year

5. Reforms in the Judicial System

The sphere of government in which the ruling class of the third and second centuries showed the greatest enterprise was jurisdiction. About 242 the extension of Rome's political ascendancy to all Italy and the neighbouring islands had brought about a sufficient increase of commercial intercourse, and consequently of litigation on cases of contract or tort, to render necessary the appointment of a second praetor, the *praetor peregrinus*. Henceforth the new praetor tried cases between foreigners; the original praetor, or *praetor urbanus* (as he came to be called), retained charge of suits between citizens and perhaps at first dealt with those between citizens and aliens.[17] The increase in the number of actions to which aliens were parties had an important effect on the development of Roman law, for the cases which they brought to the courts of the two praetors were often of a character for which the existing *ius civile*, as prescribed in the Twelve Tables and in subsequent statutes, did not make provision, so that the praetors had perforce to borrow elements of law from elsewhere. In their courts accordingly the *ius civile* began to be overlaid with the *ius gentium*, a composite code pieced together out of the current usage of surrounding states, and out of the praetors' own conceptions of equity.[18] In the application of non-Roman law, moreover, neither of the praetors was fettered by the rigidity of procedure which the *ius civile* prescribed in the initiation of lawsuits, but was left free to use his own discretion in conducting the preliminary hearing and in formulating his instructions to the *iudex* or *recuperatores*. The advantages of this 'formulary' procedure became so manifest that a *lex Aebutia*, whose date may be placed near 150, authorised its introduction into the court of the *praetor urbanus*. Thus the praetors' bench became an instrument for the continual expansion and remodelling of Roman private law.

In the domain of criminal jurisdiction the safeguarding of the citizens against harsh penalties was carried several steps further by a series of statutes of the early second century, all of which stood to the credit of members of the Gens Porcia. In 199 the tribune P. Porcius Laeca gave the right of appeal in capital cases to Romans in Italy and the provinces; in 198 or 195 M. Porcius Cato prohibited the scourging of citizens without appeal; in 184 the consul L. Porcius Licinus safeguarded them from summary execution on military service.[19] By 150 the infliction of the death penalty upon citizens had fallen into general disuse. In cases where a citizen had been proved guilty of a capital crime the custom arose of deferring sentence, so that the culprit might make a timely escape from Rome. After his retirement to a safe

The praetor peregrinus

The ius civile and the ius gentium

Extension of the right of appeal

distance the court would solemnly prohibit his return on pain of being 'deprived of the use of fire and water': by this legal subterfuge the death sentence was commuted into one of banishment.[20]

In view of the general reluctance of Roman magistrates to inflict severe sentences on citizens, recourse to the Popular Assemblies as courts of law might not be very frequent, but in the first half of the second century not a few leading public men were arraigned by prosecuting tribunes on political charges before *iudicia populi* (capital trials came before the Comitia Centuriata, while the tribal assemblies dealt with those which involved only fines). But an important step towards the supersession of popular jurisdiction was taken in 149, when the tribune L. Calpurnius Piso carried his bill for the institution of the *quaestio perpetua de rebus repetundis* (p. 175). In outward form the tribunal resembled that of the praetors' civil courts. It was ordinarily presided over by a magistrate of praetorian rank,[21] and the jury of senators who pronounced sentence were known as *iudices*, like the delegates of the *praetor urbanus*. But under subsequent supplementary statutes it adapted its rules of procedure to the requirements of a criminal court, and in its re-formed shape it eventually served as a pattern to other new courts for the trial of criminal offences (p. 236).[22] But the benefit of these reforms in criminal jurisdiction was confined to citizens. Aliens and slaves had to take their chance of a trial by summary procedure before the tribunes, aediles or *triumviri capitales*. While the Roman criminal courts became almost squeamish in their dealings with citizen culprits they might sentence a non-citizen to death after a perfunctory hearing.

Introduction of trial by jury

6. Financial Administration[23]

The overseas conquests raised the revenue and expenditure of the republic to an altogether new level. Since 264 the Romans took the fullest advantage of the fact that its chief victims in war were states possessing large stocks of gold and silver; the indemnities collected by them attained a total to which ancient history offers no parallel save in the hauls made by Alexander in the treasure-houses of Persia. These windfalls were supplemented by a regular inflow of tribute from the provinces, of royalties from the Spanish mines, and of rents from the public land, which had been greatly augmented by confiscation after the Second Punic War. With these resources at its command the Roman government was able to issue a copious silver coinage,

Windfalls from the Roman overseas conquests

which presently became the principal currency in the western Mediterranean; and after 167 it had no further need to levy a land-tax (*tributum*) on Roman citizens.

Rise of expenditure

But the expenditure of the Republic rose in proportion. The initial costs of the wars that opened up these fresh sources of revenue laid a heavy mortgage upon the new income. From the Second Punic War the Roman treasury inherited a dead-weight of loans due for repayment, and although the *tributum* or land-tax was refunded in part only, the special advances made by contractors for munitions and transport were reimbursed in full. During the first half of the second century the Republic rarely had fewer than 100,000 men on active service; for all of these it had to find provisions, for the citizen troops, amounting to somewhat less than half the total, it had to provide pay. These war expenses, swelled by occasional distributions of bounty-money, absorbed the greater part of the additional intake. From the income that remained over after meeting the costs of Roman armaments large grants (*ultro tributa*) were made from time to time for the construction of military roads, or for public works at Rome, and substantial sums were appropriated for the amusements of the urban proletariat. The average surplus of revenue over expenditure was therefore so slender that by 157 the total funded reserve amounted to little more than 25,000,000 denarii,[24] less than one-half of the maximum sum laid by at Athens in the days of Pericles.

Lax financial administration

The lack of trained administrators was nowhere more apparent than in the financial management of the later Republic. Though the Senate maintained a general supervision over the whole field of income and expenditure, it drew up no detailed budget and it did not subject to any close scrutiny the accounts of the magistrates. The censors gave but passing attention to financial matters; the quaestors likewise were mere birds of passage, and possessed so little experience that they were quite unable to control the permanent subordinate staff.[25] In financial affairs the republic ended as it had begun, by living from hand to mouth.

7. The City of Rome

Growth of the city of Rome

In the third and second centuries the city of Rome was transformed from a large market town to a cosmopolitan capital. After the Second Punic War its outward appearance and sanitary condition were much improved by new public works (pp. 192 f.). But these constructions were the haphazard product of individual censors, who by their personal energy obtained the necessary grants of public money, or of occasional war-winners who applied their share of the spoil to the adornment of the city. The general upkeep of streets and houses was left in the hands of the aediles, mere transient functionaries, and ill provided with technical assistance. For lack of expert supervision new aqueducts soon became choked with calcareous deposits. The timber shanties which Roman 'jerry builders' ran up to meet the rapidly growing need for housing accommodation were apt to catch fire like so much tinder. The importation of food supplies for the urban population had become so large and so difficult an undertaking as to require a special board of control, such as many lesser Greek cities had instituted; yet it was left to the unregulated activities of private trade. Worst of all, in a town that was filling up with a large population of slaves and was attracting to itself broken men of all kinds, no trained police, such as Alexandria possessed among Hellenistic cities, was provided. Before the end of the second century Rome needed the services of a separate municipal council and executive. But the dissociation of municipal from imperial government was not even thought of, and the city received but passing attention from a Senate absorbed in problems of empire.

Lack of a competent municipal government

The problem of public order

8. Italy

Closer contact of Romans and Italians

In Italy a new political problem was raised by a century or more of military association between the Romans and their allies. During the Second Punic War the Italians had mostly stood by the Republic in its most searching ordeal; in the second century they had provided more than half of the troops that won the Roman Empire overseas. Besides, the close contact of Romans and Italians on joint military service, and the broadcasting of colonies on the Italian countryside, had set in motion a process of assimilation between them. A stray notice in Livy, which records that in 180 the city of Cumae asked leave of the Roman Senate to adopt Latin as its official tongue in place of Oscan, indicates that the cultural influence of Rome was extending far beyond the immediate environs of the city;[26] and the Latin literature of the second century offers eloquent testimony to the proficiency of Campanians, Apulians and Umbrians in the Roman language (p. 194). The time was undoubtedly ripe for the admission of the Italian allies to Roman citizenship, or to a more equal partnership in a federation of

Rise in status of some Italian communities

Italian states. Thus in 188 three towns on the borderland of Latium and Campania, Arpinum, Formiae and Fundi, received full Roman franchise in exchange for their previous *civitas sine suffragio*; and it may be assumed that most of the other cities possessing the half-franchise received similar promotion not long after, for their claim to citizenship was never mentioned in the agitation for Roman franchise towards the end of the century (p. 209). Italian allies as well as citizens received shares in the *viritane* assignations of land in Cisalpine Gaul, and it is probable that they also participated in some degree in the colonisation of northern Italy.

No general grant of franchise

But the Roman government no more than nibbled at the problem of Italian franchise. It had no desire to bestow citizen rights upon large masses of men whose votes they would not be able to control like those of the urban proletariat. Still less was it prepared to share the plums of office at Rome with *novi homines* from the Italian municipalities. Therefore nothing was done at this stage to improve the status of the *socii Italici*. A slight diminution of their privileges was even suffered by the allies of Latin status. In 187 the Latin cities were faced with a serious loss of population through the number of their citizens who had settled at Rome and claimed Roman citizenship there, while at the same time their quota of conscripts to the Roman army remained undiminished. They therefore asked Rome to repatriate these emigrant settlers, and although such an act would infringe the *ius migrationis* of the individuals concerned, a praetor's edict ordered 12,000 Latins already registered as Roman citizens, to surrender their franchise and leave the city. About the same time the Senate enacted that *every* Latin who came to Rome to settle must leave a son behind him in his town of origin (hitherto this restriction had applied only to colonies founded after 265). Ten years later a similar request to that made in 187 was repeated by Latin cities and more men were repatriated by senatorial decree, and an attempt was made to close all means of evasion of the law. True, these measures were made at the request of the Latin authorities themselves, but they involved hardship and the infringement by Rome of rights granted.[27] A similar disposition to override the treaty rights of the allies was shown in 186, when the Senate, intent on extirpating a network of illicit societies that had spread over Italy (p. 198) authorised the consuls to apprehend and put to death members of these conventicles on allied territory.[28]

Infractions of treaties with the allied communities

In the second century the quota of soldiers levied on the allies was frequently raised so as to exceed that of the citizens; yet their share

Curtailment of their share in the profits of conquest

in the spoils of victory was curtailed. Since 177 their portion in the movable war-booty was reduced to half of the citizens' allowance, and after about 180 no further Latin colonies were founded. The disparity between burgesses and allies was accentuated by the maintenance of the Roman commanders' full *imperium* over the allies, while the right of appeal from their sentences of capital punishment was accorded to Roman soldiers (p. 182).

High-handed conduct of Roman magistrates

In view of the Senate's depreciatory attitude towards the Italian allies it is small wonder that individual Roman officials sometimes treated them in cavalier fashion. The practice of collecting contributions from allied towns for the aediles' games at Rome became so common that even such a conscientious politician as Sempronius Gracchus obtained large sums from them and in 179 the Senate found it necessary to issue a general ban upon such extortions. A more serious abuse was introduced when itinerant Roman magistrates, instead of hiring lodgings and other necessaries with the journey-money provided for that purpose by the Senate, began to demand free entertainment. The example of such blackmail was given in 173 by the consul L. Postumius at the expense of the Praenestines. In several towns the local magistrates were ill treated because they had not been prompt enough in clearing the municipal bath for the use of a Roman official or his wife. The Latin colony of Cales went so far as to prohibit the townsmen from entering the public bath during the stay of a Roman magistrate in the town.

9. Foreign Affairs. The Army

The problems of foreign policy and of provincial administration which confronted the Roman government in the second century have been discussed in previous chapters (14–17). The errors in foreign policy, as we have seen, were mostly due to ignorance or indifference about overseas affairs rather than to sinister intent on the part of the Republic. Information from abroad generally reached the Senate in the form of petitions and complaints presented by envoys with some special cause to plead, or of reports by itinerant Roman commissioners who were liable to have dust thrown into their eyes during their somewhat perfunctory tours of inspection. The wide range and the complexity of Rome's foreign relations now made it difficult for the Senate to maintain a clear and consistent foreign policy without a permanent corps of residents or liaison officers to instruct it with a continuous supply of authentic in-

Lack of a diplomatic service

formation. But no steps were taken to create a regular diplomatic service; and indeed, with the progressive reduction of client states into provinces, the need for such a service gradually became less imperative.

In military matters the Roman government proved itself strangely unheedful of some of the most striking lessons of the Punic Wars. Regardless of the vital services rendered by the Roman seamen in these conflicts it progressively reduced its naval establishments, and after the Third Macedonian War it dispensed altogether with a regular fleet. Unmindful of Cannae and Zama, it again neglected its cavalry and made shift with auxiliary contingents from the dependent kings or the more warlike provincial populations. Forgetting that the Second Punic War had been won by quasi-professional commanders, and all but lost by amateurs, it reverted to the practice of annual transfers of the leadership between consuls or praetors, and made but occasional use of the expedient of *prorogatio*, so as to retain a general of proved ability. The Roman forces were fortunate in not being called upon to meet an opponent of the calibre of Pyrrhus or Hannibal, and their most worthy antagonist, the Macedonian army, was ill provided with horsemen. But if the legions escaped serious disaster in set battles they repeatedly suffered defeats when engaged on difficult or unexplored ground, where inexperienced commanders habitually led them into ambuscades. In the warfare of the second century it almost became an axiom that a series of initial reverses must precede the final victory, and eventual success was bought by the slow method of trial and error.

But the most ominous feature in the warfare of the second century was the increasing reluctance of the Roman recruits to perform their military obligations. In the eastern campaigns, it is true, the prospects of a rich booty attracted large numbers of semi-professional soldiers who re-engaged themselves voluntarily. On the other hand Roman officers in Spain had recurrent difficulties in raising fresh drafts. The example of evading duty was set by the nobles themselves, despite their statutory obligations to serve in ten campaigns before presenting themselves for election to a political office. Not a few contrived to avoid enrolment in the cavalry troops, in which sons of senators were expected to spend at least five seasons, by securing a more or less honorary position on the general's staff. The *cohors praetoria* of Scipio Aemilianus at Numan-

tia numbered no fewer than 500 men, though this particular general no doubt kept his aides-de-camp suitably employed. In 151 the consul L. Lucullus even had difficulty in finding volunteers to hold the subordinate commands in his Spanish campaign. Small wonder then that the rank and file held back. In order to assist enrolment the minimum property qualification for service was reduced from 11,000 to 4000 asses. Roman soldiers received exemption from the penalty of scourging and the right to appeal to the Comitia against sentences of death (p. 182). But these concessions failed to satisfy the troops, and other more dangerous relaxations of discipline were extorted by them from their commanders. In the early stages of the Third Macedonian War common soldiers received extended furloughs, or took them without asking, in order to engage in petty trading behind the lines; bazaars of sutlers and prostitutes were allowed to form close by the Roman encampments. The first duty of strict commanders, such as M. Cato, Aemilius Paullus or Scipio Aemilianus, was to send these civilians packing and to put the soldiers through a supplementary course of drill.[29]

The diminishing efficiency of the Roman armies in the second century conveyed the plain lesson that the half-time militia which had served admirably for the purpose of seasonal warfare in Italy was unsuited for protracted campaigning in overseas countries. The protection or further extension of the Empire's frontiers urgently required a professional army of soldiers engaged on a voluntary basis. But city-state tradition, and a long record of past successes with conscript forces, stood in the way of this essential reform.

But the symptoms of a forthcoming crisis long went unobserved. Shortly before 133, on the eve of the actual revolution, the Greek friend of Scipio Aemilianus, the historian Polybius, commended the Roman constitution on account of its excellent system of checks and balances, and remarked on the high standard of probity among the governing nobility.[30] For the time being Rome's prestige in the whole Mediterranean stood unshaken, and the benefits of the Roman peace gave adequate compensation for the burdens of Roman imperialism. The stability of the Roman government had not yet been seriously threatened, and there still was ample time for the Republic to set its house in order.

CHAPTER 19

Roman Society in the Second Century

1. Agriculture[1]

The conquests of the Romans in the third and second centuries left as profound a mark on their private life as on their political institutions.

The confiscations of land after the Second Punic War and the ensuing campaigns in Cisalpine Gaul almost doubled the extent of the Roman territory. In Cisalpine Gaul, and to a lesser degree in southern Italy, a large proportion of the land thus acquired was distributed to Roman or allied settlers in holdings of 5–30 acres. Thanks to this mass-creation of new *Condition of* allotments, the havoc of the Hannibalic War *the small* among the Roman peasantry was more than *proprietors* made good. These small proprietors adhered for the most part to the cultivation of cereal crops by traditional methods. Since they grew mainly for their own consumption they had little to fear from the competition of better-equipped neighbours or of exporters from overseas countries. On the other hand the exigencies of military service abroad compelled many smallholders to neglect their homesteads. At the same time the importation of slave labour into the Italian countryside (p. 187) diminished the peasants' opportunities of eking out their living by wage-labour on the adjacent large estates. Besides, while the struggle for a livelihood on the land was becoming harder, the lure of Rome, where subsistence was cheap and amusements cost nothing (p. 178), grew more insistent. Soon after 173, the date at which the distribution of confiscated land was discontinued, the number of smallholdings underwent a slow but steady decline.[2]

The salient feature in the agricultural economy of the second century was the growth *Growth of* of relatively large estates, with areas exceeding *relatively* 100 acres and sometimes rising to over 300. The *large estates* increase in the number of these was in large measure the result of the overseas conquests. Roman magistrates, who had amassed warbooty or had made profits out of a provincial governorship, and the rising class of tax-farmers and contractors, seized every opportunity of enlarging their estates, for these were the only safe fund in which they could invest their winnings; to the aristocrats land was a traditional form of property, while to the new business men it offered social respectability as well as security of investment.[3] They purchased the plots of the smaller peasantry as these began to drift away from the country; they leased large tracts of the undistributed public domain; they took up waste lands which the censors were willing to let off at a peppercorn rent to lessees with sufficient capital to stock and redeem it. The *possessores*, it is true, were to some extent restricted by a statute, the *lex Licinia* of 367 (p. 76), which was possibly reaffirmed later; it set an upper limit of 300 acres to the amount of public land which any one person might occupy.[4] But the provisions of this act lent themselves to evasion by fictitious leases to bogus tenants, and it is doubtful whether it was ever enforced with any consistency.

The owners and lessees of the large estates looked to these not merely to preserve but to increase their profits: in the words of Cato, a *Improve-* good landlord ought to sell more than he *ments in* bought.[5] To this end they began to introduce *cultivation* scientific methods of husbandry according to the precepts of Greek experts on agriculture. They ameliorated the cultivation of cereals by introducing rotations of crops with restorative courses of leguminous plants in place of biennial fallows; they prepared the soil with deep-cutting ploughs and grew from specially selected seed-corn; they threshed the grain with spiked sledges of Carthaginian pattern (*plostella Punica*). But improved methods of arable culture could not yield any appreciable increase of profits. The only market in Italy for the mass-production of grain was Rome, and imports from overseas kept pace with the growing requirements of the capital.[6] In northern Italy an actual over-production of corn reduced its price to absurdly low rates. The cereal crops on many of the large estates were therefore restricted to the amount required for local consumption, while the open fields were in large measure replaced by plantations, which under scientific cultivation could be made to produce a far higher rate of profit; the richest land was converted into vineyards, the poorer tracts into olive-groves. Before the end of the second century Italian olive-oil was being sold in Greece, and Italian vintage wine was beginning to fetch high prices among Roman connoisseurs. But the principal areas of olive-culture always remained confined to Campania and Apulia, and the vineyards were not extended to northern Italy until a later period.[7]

Orchard industry

In the lowlands the none too plentiful water-meadows were supplemented by artificial irrigation. But a far wider extension of the pastoral industry took place in Etruria and still more on the downlands of southern Italy, where the system of seasonal migration between summer and winter grazings was organised on a right royal scale: at the change of seasons as many as 1000 head of sheep might be driven over a distance of 100 miles. By means of such mass-migrations the costs of tending the herds were reduced to the lowest point, while the clip and the hides, if not the meat, of the grazing-animals gave a good return. Ranching was therefore considered the most profitable pursuit for a capitalist landowner, and it was probably the source of the largest fortunes derived from the land under the later Republic.

Ranching

These large estates of over 300 acres (500 *iugera*) are generally referred to in modern works as *latifundia*, a word which is not found in any surviving Latin text before the first century A.D. and is too vague. It does in fact apply to two very different establishments, namely the ranch and the large-scale mixed farm. The former involved stud-farms for sheep and horses and transhumance from summer to winter grazing-grounds; the latter generally came into being through the linking up of separate properties, a process which was accelerated by the dis-

Latifundia and mixed farming

turbances resulting from the civil wars of the last century B.C. Alternatively of course a large landowner might hold smaller properties in different parts of the country, and while his separate farms might not qualify as *latifundia*, his aggregate would put him in the class of *latifondisti* in the Italian sense of the word, 'absentee landlord'. Beside the large estates, of varied nature, were the medium-sized (80–500 *iugera*) estates and the smallholdings. The former included, among other estates, the vineyard of 100 *iugera* and the oliveyard of 240 *iugera*, which were given by Cato as examples of the new intensive enterprises of the second century. The smallholdings of 10–80 *iugera* which had predominated until the end of the third, continued into the second and later centuries.[8]

2. Slave Labour on the Land[9]

The new uses to which the Italian land was being put in the second century raised a problem of labour for which a satisfactory solution was never found. Though capitalist farming might reduce the number of workers required to each square mile, in the aggregate it had need of larger quantities of labour than it was possible to recruit on demand from the free population of Italy. In southern and central Italy, where the estates of the wealthy Romans were mostly to be found, the countryside had been most heavily devastated during the Hannibalic War, and subsequent colonisation had not sufficed to make good the decline in the numbers of the peasantry. In addition the wars of the early second century continually kept 100,000 Italians (mostly of the peasant class) on military service abroad. But while these wars depleted the ranks of the free land-workers, they filled the gaps with a servile population recruited from prisoners of war. The capitalist landowners were not slow to turn this fresh supply of labour on to their estates; indeed they not only absorbed the greater number of the war captives, but stimulated the regular slave-trade of the Mediterranean regions into unwonted activity (p. 213). Compared with free wage-earners, slaves offered several advantages to the capitalist cultivator. They were not liable to be called away on military duty; they could be subsisted on the coarsest fare and held to their work incessantly. In the handling of their servile workers the Roman landlords exhibited their characteristic aptitude for organisation. Wherever slaves could be put to work in gangs they were distributed into regular squads under a foreman, and each labourer was carefully selected, in accordance with his physique and mentality, for his

Lack of free cultivators

Their replacements by slaves

Organisation of servile labour

particular task. Among the servile workers men were not lacking who could be entrusted with skilled operations such as vine-dressing: even the bailiffs who had charge of the entire estate were habitually recruited from the same class.

Nevertheless the labour of slaves never completely ousted that of free wage-earners. The seasonal business of harvesting the grain and of picking the grapes and olive-berries required a larger number of hands than could find regular employment on the estate; for these operations itinerant troops of hired workers had to be called in. Moreover, the disadvantages inherent to slave labour were not long in showing through. The early Roman slave-masters frankly treated their staff as mere 'vocal instruments', and relied upon the fear of punishment by scourging or chaining as a sovereign inducement to work. *Discontent of the slaves* The food and clothing of the slaves, though adequate in quantity, were of the coarsest type; their sleeping-quarters often consisted of underground chambers. Their work, besides being unending, was monotonous; opportunities of family life were denied to all except the bailiff; and their chances of eventually ransoming themselves out of their slender *peculium* or pocket-money were remote. Under such conditions the thought of rebellion was never far from the minds of the slaves, and although Italy escaped a servile war on a large scale in the second century it was frequently agitated by minor risings. But the principal weapon of the dissatisfied slave was passive resistance or petty insubordination. He grew even with his master by pilfering his property or handling it negligently; as soon as the foreman's eye was turned he slackened his stroke of work. On not a few estates the bailiff himself conspired with the *Their labour inefficient* staff so as to reduce the output of labour to a plausible minimum. It therefore required constant personal attention on the part of the owner – which few of the capitalist landlords had leisure or inclination to bestow – in order to maintain work on the estate at a profitable level of efficiency. At best the labour of slaves was economical for so long only as their initial cost of purchase remained low.

Thus in the second century Italy underwent a gradual economic revolution. Land became an *The agricultural revolution* object of speculation to be exploited for profit, worked often by slave labour, managed by a *vilicus* and owned by an absentee capitalist who lived in Rome or some other city. These new large estates, which drove so many small farmers off the land, were given over to pasturage and stock-farming or the cultivation of the vine and olive. Mixed farms could be quite profitable in Latium and Campania, and Cato's handbook was written for men who would invest in a mixed estate of 100–300 *iugera* (66–220 acres) which could provide the neighbouring town with oil, wine, fruit, vegetables, meat and wool. These farms, combined with the larger ranches, might represent the best use to which some parts of Italy could be put.[10] But there was a darker side to the picture, since few small farmers could afford to change from corn-growing to other forms of production. Hence free men were forced off the land; some might turn to commerce overseas, others may have migrated to the Po valley in the north, but thousands drifted to Rome and other cities where no work could be found for them.

3. Industry and Commerce

Italian industry underwent relatively few changes in the third and second centuries. In *Few changes in manufacturing industry* Rome the building handicrafts received a stimulus from the application of war-spoils to the construction of new public works; but the influx of war-wealth did not give rise to a general increase of manufactures. Craft workers and labourers contributed but little to the growth of the urban population, and such new industry as sprang up remained in the hands of small masters. But there was no great Industrial Revolution to stimulate trade and industry, and this was due to a considerable extent to the perennial problem of the cost of transporting goods by land. Though the road system of Italy was improving, few of the rivers of Italy lend *Transport costly* themselves to the transport of industrial or natural products, and the cost of transport by land was crippling: Cato shows that to move an oil-press weighing 4000 lb. by an ox-team increased the original cost of the press by some 2·5 per cent per day. Further, it was slow and technically inefficient: horses were harnessed with a collar around the throat which half-choked them (a hard collar around the chest was not invented before the middle ages), and though oxen fared better a team could move at only 2 miles an hour; mules were used as pack-animals and according to Varro, who bred them at Reate, extensively for vehicular transport, though probably mainly for lighter loads. Transport by sea was very much cheaper, but it was often hazardous and would not help people far inland. These drawbacks, combined with a restricted internal market due to the poverty of the masses, prevented any spectacular expansion of industry, which tended to remain in the hands of craftsmen who worked in small shops and often sold their products direct to the consumer.[11] Among the older seats of Italian industry Tarentum never recovered from its losses in the Hannibalic War. On the other hand Capua remained a thriving town, notwithstanding the political degradation which it had suffered (p. 131); by the side of its ancient industries in pottery and bronze were new manufactures of furniture and perfumery were established there. In the second century Campania definitely outstripped Etruria as the industrial centre of Italy. Puteoli diverted part of the Tuscan iron industry to itself, and Pompeii rose to affluence by the sale of its textiles.

In the wake of the Roman flag a considerable volume of new trade was attracted to Italy, but its movement was singularly one-sided. Apart from the bronzes of Capua and the olive-oil of the Campanian *latifundia*, the exports of Italy were insignificant. On the other hand Rome now imported large quantities of grain from Sicily, and took most of the produce of the Spanish silver-mines. The capital itself, together with the new *latifundia*, absorbed a regular influx of slaves from Delos, which became the collecting-point of the human cargoes destined for the Italian market. This overplus of imports over exports was the medium by which the Mediterranean lands paid toll to their new master.

Increase of imports from the provinces

It has already been observed that Roman policy was not directed to commercial objects. The Roman nobility took so little personal interest in overseas trade that in 218 it allowed a law[12] to be passed which prohibited it from possessing ships of sea-going capacity; still less was it concerned to establish a mercantile monopoly for those of lesser rank. The settlements made by the Senate with the conquered and allied peoples showed the same disregard for trade. These treaties did not as a rule confer any special privilege upon Roman or Italian men of business;[13] in the Roman provinces the merchants of Italian origin had no advantage except that of easier access to the court of the governor. After the Second Punic War the Senate even shook off the responsibility which it had previously assumed of protecting Italian traders against pirates. Under these conditions the general carrying trade of the Mediterranean remained in the hands of Greeks and Phoenicians. The traffic of Carthage passed over to Utica and Gades, that of Corinth and Rhodes to Delos and Alexandria. Italian merchants established themselves in considerable numbers at Delos; some bold spirits followed the seamen of Gades across the Atlantic in quest of Cornish tin; others carried the wine of their country to Gaul and the Danube lands. But the majority of Italian residents at Delos – despite the name of 'Romans' which the Greeks fastened upon them – came from Campania and the Greek cities of the south rather than from central

Disregard of the nobility for commerce

The carrying trade in foreign hands

Italy;[14] and the principal port by which overseas products flowed into Italy was Puteoli, a town which, notwithstanding its status as a Roman colony, had a predominantly Greek or Campanian population. The station of Ostia at the Tiber mouth was still relatively undeveloped.

But if the Romans were slow to engage in general mercantile activities, they rapidly acquired such a proficiency in the handling of money that in their financial operations they left the Greeks and Orientals far behind them. The concentration of this branch of business in Roman hands was a natural result of the wars of conquest, which had the effect of accumulating the Mediterranean's stocks of gold and silver at Rome. The wealth of capital which Roman money-lenders and tax-farmers held at their disposal gave them an advantage over their competitors which sometimes amounted to a monopoly (p. 208). But the success of the Romans in money-dealing was largely due to their better organisation. The Roman *publicani* carried the practice of dividing risks much further than the Greek tax-contractors. They not only combined in partnerships in order to raise the funds required, but they associated in their enterprise the general Roman public, on the principles of the modern joint-stock company. With the capital thus subscribed in many small contributions or shares (*partes*), the active partners (*socii*) would bid for a tax, and if successful would enter into a contract with the censors, which was signed by a trustee-in-chief (*manceps*) and underwritten by a number of acceptors (*praedes*). The actual gathering of the revenue from the individual tax-payers was undertaken by slaves or freedmen under the supervision of a manager (*magister*).[15] The Roman tax-farming associations also maintained a special intelligence service, so that they might calculate to a nicety the prospective intake of any impost and adjust their bid accordingly. For this purpose they kept trained messengers who could cover 50 Roman miles (44 English miles) in a day. The companies of *publicani* enjoyed the privilege, which at this period was denied to all other business partnerships at Rome, of incorporation as legal personalities which survived the death or retirement of the individual associates. Thus, in the absence of the creation of an adequate civil service, these men helped the State to collect taxes, undertake the construction of public works and buildings, and develop the provincial mines.

Though the *publicani* no doubt made short-term loans out of the tax-money exacted by them, the business of usury was mostly in the hands of individuals who might be termed *negotiatores*, a word which covered both these

Roman proficiency in money-dealing

Organisation of the tax-farming companies

Money-lending

great Roman capitalists and the more humble Italian traders who spread through the Mediterranean world. The money-lenders also resorted to the provinces for their main sphere of operations. It Italy their opportunities were restricted by the fourth-century legislation against the taking of interest (p. 76),[16] in the provinces they might be limited by the governor's edict to a mere 12 per cent, but they found borrowers (such as hard-pressed tax-payers) willing to offer 24 per cent or even 48 per cent. Since ancient industry consisted mainly of manufacture in the literal sense, and required no expensive machinery, it absorbed comparatively little loan capital. But advances were commonly made to shipowners for the purchase of cargoes on the security of their vessels. This branch of usury remained largely in the hands of Greeks or Orientals, but Roman companies also entered the business, and the investing public took up shares in it.[17]

Banking techniques

For the settlement of debts the Roman financiers adopted from the Greeks the technique of payment by book entries in lieu of cash transfers. Under the later Republic it was usual for Roman persons of means to keep a current account with a banker, and to finance their private transactions by bankers' orders or by letters of credit.[18]

The profits accruing to the Romans directly from their conquests, and indirectly from the capitalisation of their war gains, raised them to a level of material prosperity exceeding that of any other Mediterranean people. The soldiers were paid off with handsome war-bonuses, and often received a land allotment into the bargain.

Acquisition of large fortunes

The senatorial class derived wealth from the proceeds of their war-booty, from the administration of provinces, and from the scientific development of their *latifundia*. The fortune of P. Licinius Crassus (consul in 131), who was estimated to possess a hundred million sesterces, was no doubt exceptional at this stage of Roman history. But it is noteworthy that Aemilius Paullus, the victor of Pydna, was reckoned a man of modest means, although he possessed one and a half million sesterces, a sum which any nobleman of the fourth or third century would have regarded as princely.

The 'Equester Ordo'

But the outstanding feature of the period under review was the rise of a new bourgeoisie, the Equites or Equester Ordo, which took the lead in capitalistic enterprises of all kinds, whether of land improvement, of building or of traffic in goods and money.[19] The term Equester Ordo, which originally had been applied to the men performing mounted service in the army and voting in the *equitum centuriae* (p. 80), was subsequently extended to all those citizens whose wealth qualified them for service on horseback.[20] Finally, probably in the second century, it came to denote all persons possessing not less than 400,000 sesterces who stood outside the ranks of the governing aristocracy. In the second century the number of these Equites was sufficient to constitute them as a distinct social class. The Equites were essentially those whose way of life separated them from the possibility of becoming senators: their interest was private finance, not public office. But increasingly the term included a great variety of people. Some indeed came from the same social background as the senators; wealthy enough to compete for office in Rome and with the right family connexions they nevertheless preferred the quieter life of country gentlemen on their estates around the towns of Italy to the hurly-burly of Roman politics. Others of this class turned to finance as opposed to politics, and their status enabled them to increase their wealth still further. Of these the *publicani* were the most outstanding, and those who had not sprung from a landed background soon tried to cover this up by investing their gains in real estate. When clashes began to occur between the Senatorial and Equestrian Orders it was these *publicani* who were primarily involved. Finally the word Equites came to embrace the increasing number of private *negotiatores*, large capitalists and men of more modest means, whose financial qualification was accepted by the censors at Rome. Later, however, as will be seen, the term came to be used even more loosely.

Attendant economic evils

But against this solid prosperity must be set the growth of a parasitic proletariat in Rome, the replacement of free peasants by slave labourers, and the exploitation of the overseas dependencies. The Roman Empire still had far to travel before it attained an economic equilibrium.

4. Roman Private Life

Effects of Greek culture on Roman life

Increasing wealth and closer contact with the Greek world produced a manifold change, though it fell short of a revolution, in the outward manner of Roman life. Though the Romans still remained faithful to the toga as the distinctive Italian garb, they adopted the Greek fashion of clean shaving, which Scipio Africanus is said to have introduced. Among the townsfolk baked bread took the place of porridge as the staple article of diet. In the houses of the wealthier citizens meals were now prepared by professional cooks and served on silver plate. The informal after-dinner potations of the earlier Romans gave way to the more elaborate

Greek drinking-bouts under the direction of a *magister bibendi*. These innovations in Roman private life naturally drew protests from those who had a meticulous regard for the *mos maiorum*. Its foremost defender, Cato, inveighed against Greek luxuries and frivolities as an eighteenth-century English squire might have vented his wrath on French kickshaws and capers.[21] The champions of the established order succeeded in carrying a series of sumptuary laws (beginning with the *lex Oppia de Luxu Feminarum* in 215) which became progressively more strict and comprehensive. But in the absence of any regular police supervision or of any widespread public disapproval, these statutes remained ineffective. Indeed there was as yet little call for alarm at the current changes of fashion. In adopting some of the amenities of Greek civilisation the Roman governing class did not hastily abandon its homely native traditions; and the Equites, in true bourgeois fashion, were more eager to acquire riches than to enjoy them. The only serious misuse of wealth at Rome in the second century lay in the bribery, direct and indirect, of the urban proletariat, by means of which the nobility maintained its political ascendancy (p. 178).

An incidental result of the Second Punic War was that in not a few well-to-do houses the male line became extinct and the family estate was concentrated in the hands of women, whose increased opulence gave rise to a growing luxury in dress and ornament. The authors of the Roman sumptuary laws naturally did not forget this appalling extravagance in their repressive legislation, and in 169 a tribune named Voconius carried a measure to limit the amount of real estate that might be devised to female heirs. But while the sumptuary laws were simply disregarded, the *lex Voconia* was evaded by nominal transfers of land to collusive trustees. Further, though Roman law still required a 'tutor' to represent a woman *sui iuris* in the courts and to countersign her documents, it connived at the choice of mere men-of-straw for these formalities, so that unattached women became in fact free to manage their property as they pleased. It is probable that women also received or took full liberty to attend the various public spectacles on the same terms as men. In the richer households the daughters were now considered worthy to receive a higher education similar to that of the sons. In the middle of the second century the intellectual élite of Rome foregathered in the salon of Cornelia, the daughter of Scipio Africanus and wife of Sempronius Gracchus.

Another effect of continuous military service on Roman social life was a growing disregard for the marriage-tie, which manifested itself in an increase of celibacy and an incipient tendency to dissolve marital unions on political or financial rather than on moral grounds. The advice which the censor Metellus Macedonicus gave to the Roman burgesses in 131, that they should submit to matrimony as to a necessary evil in order to keep up the numbers of the population, was hardly calculated to check the spread of celibacy. But as yet the loosening of the marital laws did not assume serious proportions.

The most radical change in family life at Rome consisted in the increase of domestic slavery, which progressed *pari passu* with the extension of servile labour on the land. While the wealthier Romans drafted their barbarian war-captives to their *latifundia* they retained in their town houses the Greek slaves, many of whom were unfitted for the rough and monotonous work of the farm, but readily adapted themselves to the conditions of domestic service. The Greek captives not only performed the menial functions of the great households, but held quasi-professional positions as secretaries, teachers and physicians; and the women slaves found additional occupations as spinsters and websters.

In comparison with the condition of the rural slaves the lot of the *familia urbana* was an enviable one. Since custom required that the establishments of the richer families should be staffed on a generous scale the task of each domestic was seldom heavy; the secretaries and other brain-workers might be virtually as free as the house-tutors and confidential clerks of more modern times. The household slaves, moreover, had the opportunity of catching the master's eye and of earning special rewards for good service. They might obtain permission to enter into a quasi-matrimonial union (*contubernium*), which once conceded was seldom revoked; or they might earn a liberal allowance of pocket-money (*peculium*), with which a thrifty slave might be able to ransom himself before the prime of his life was spent. As a freedman, it is true, the former domestic was frequently indentured to render specified services to his previous master, under pain of forfeiting his newly won liberty. On the other hand he was often provided with a small fund by gift or loan, so as to set him up in a business of his own.

The domestic slaves, it is true, had to accommodate themselves to the caprices of wanton or cruel masters, and their servitude might be an apprenticeship in the arts of the sneak and the sycophant. The slave-owners for their part were exposing themselves to new temptations:

Sumptuary laws

Improved status of women

Increase of celibacy

Growth of domestic slavery

Privileges of the familia urbana

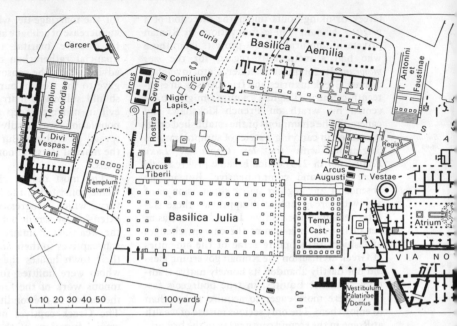

19. PLAN OF

Influence of Greek house-slaves

with a staff of submissive agents to gratify their every desire they stood in danger of losing their habits of self-help and self-control. But the virus of domestic servitude was a slow-acting one, and it needed several generations before it made any serious inroad on the traditional Roman virtues. On the other hand household slavery was one of the principal channels by which Greek culture was transmitted to Rome. As a confidential secretary or house-tutor the Greek war-captive imparted to his master's family that close and constant contact with a maturer civilisation which enabled it to be absorbed beyond skin-depth. Horace's well-known line, 'Graecia capta ferum victorem cepit', is more accurate than appears on the surface: it was the Greek captive that took Rome prisoner.[22]

Roman private life in the second century should not be judged exclusively by the household of a Cato, whose somewhat grim but thoroughly sincere affection for his wife and son were the redeeming features of an unlovely character. Yet the Roman family was more successful than any other Roman institution in withstanding the shock of a rapidly changing environment.

5. The City of Rome

In the third and second centuries the city of Rome outstripped all the towns of the West in size, and came to rank with the Hellenistic capitals of Antioch and Alexandria. Its growing population now sought accommodation in large tenement blocks *(insulae)*, which were let off in flats or by single apartments; the cheaper domiciles of this kind were hastily run up in lath-work. For the private mansions of the more opulent families dressed stone, with an internal coating of stucco, now came into general use. The ordinary plan of the second-century town-house at Rome may be recovered from the contemporary remains at Pompeii, where the original Italian 'atrium' was converted into an ante-room for receptions, and the principal living-rooms were grouped round an inner court of Greek type, the 'peristyle'. Wealthy Romans adopted the custom of repairing during the hot season to a 'villa' in the country. But these holiday abodes still retained much of the simplicity of the ordinary farm-house: the residence of Scipio Africanus at Liternum (near Naples) astonished later generations by the scantiness of its appointments.

Private dwellings

Tenements and 'peristyle' houses

The face of the city was greatly changed by the numerous public works constructed with private funds by the various war-winners, and with public money by the censors. Among the private dedications votive temples were still the commonest form of memorial. In the construction of these shrines Greek marble now came into use (the first was a temple to Jupiter Stator dedicated by Q. Metellus in 146), but stuccoed

Public buildings

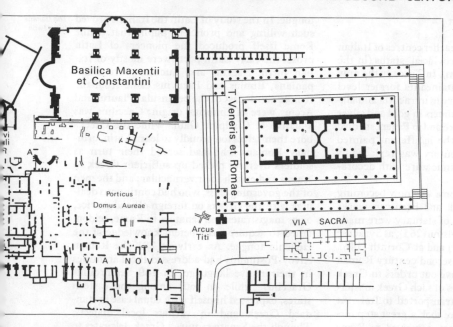

Basilica Maxentii
et Constantini

T. Veneris et Romae

Porticus
Domus Aureae

Arcus
Titi

VIA SACRA

VIA NOVA

MAN FORUM

tufa or travertine remained the norm, while the old Etrusco-Italic ground-plan maintained itself tenaciously in Roman temple architecture. Greek influence was more manifest in the numerous new *basilicae* or public halls which replaced the old rows of shops along the Forum and did double duty as markets and as courts of justice. The first of these purely Greek buildings, the Basilica Porcia, was erected, oddly enough, by Cato (184); a second basilica was constructed jointly by the censors Aemilius Lepidus and Fulvius Nobilior in 179, and a third by Sempronius Gracchus in 170. In 193 a large market-hall and granary, the Porticus Aemilia, was built on a quay of the Tiber, south of the Aventine; if this is correctly identified with an imposing surviving building, it provides evidence for the possible first use of concrete, a building-material which was before long to revolutionise Roman architecture.[23] A typically Roman form of monument, the 'triumphal' or, better, the commemorative arch *(fornix)*, began to appear early in the second century: L. Stertinius celebrated victories in Spain by erecting two in Rome in 196, to be followed by Scipio Africanus in 190, while Fabius Maximus celebrated his Gallic victory in the same way in the Forum in 120. In deference to the people's imperious appetite for amusements the censor Flaminius began the construction of a new circus in the Campus Martius (220). On the other hand a lurking prejudice against a too exact imitation of Greek institutions stood in the way of the construction of a stone theatre, so that the dramas of Plautus and Terence had to be performed in temporary wooden structures.

To match the extensive building of highways in Italy (p. 140) the streets of Rome were repaved with flags of hard lava from the Alban Mount, and in 179 Aemilius Lepidus laid the foundations of a stone bridge (completed in 142), to supplement the old trestle bridge which had hitherto carried all the traffic within the city. But nothing was done to widen or straighten the streets. The old Via Sacra from the Velia to the Forum was still the only commodious road for vehicular traffic, and the Forum, with its narrow and irregular area of a 100 yards by 50, was not enlarged to meet the growing needs of public life. On the other hand the sanitation of the city was well cared for. In addition to constructing the Basilica Porcia, Cato commemorated his censorship by carrying out a thorough repair of Rome's drainage-system. In 144 the praetor Q. Marcius Rex provided for the construction of Rome's first high-level aqueduct, the Aqua Marcia, which conveyed the city's purest supply of water from the head of the Anio valley over a distance of 36 miles. In general the public works of the second century reflected the traditional preference of the Romans for solid and useful rather than showy architecture.

Paving; draining; water-supply

6. Roman and Italian Art

Decline of Italian art-centres

In the third century the earlier centres of Italian art began to sink to a 'provincial' status (in the modern sense of that term). In Tuscany the only branch of art that maintained its former level of proficiency was statuary in terracotta and alabaster. The school of artificers in gold and silver which had flourished there and in Praeneste died out. In southern Italy the indifferent painted pottery of the fourth century was replaced by an equally mediocre ceramic ware with decorations moulded in relief.

Mass-importation of Greek sculpture

On the other hand Rome was now becoming a vast museum of Greek and Etruscan works of art. Memorable hauls of statuary were made at the Tuscan town of Volsinii (265), at Syracuse (210), at Tarentum (209) and at Corinth (146). Towards the end of the second century Roman connoisseurs began to give out orders to Greek statue-factories for copies of such Greek masterpieces as had not been transported to Italy. At the same time portraiture took a great step forward. Late Hellenistic art, conveyed to Rome and Italy by immigrant Greek portraitists, combined with the older native traditions of the *imagines* (p. 108) and Etruscan portraits of their dead, stimulated the 'verism' of the numerous heads, busts and statues in bronze, stone and marble which abounded in the last century of the Republic. For the decoration of temples and public buildings painting continued to be in greater demand than sculpture; but nothing survives by which Roman pictorial art in the second century can be judged.

Portraiture

7. Early Latin Poetry[24]

Rise of a Latin literature

The period of the great foreign wars was also that which gave birth to Roman literature. The conquests of the third and second centuries imparted to the Romans a pride in their past achievement and a confidence in their power to conquer new worlds which broke down their native reticence. Within the aristocratic class they created a small but influential group of men with sufficient wealth to lend their patronage to nascent authors, and with sufficient leisure to cultivate their own pen. The foremost family of Rome, the Cornelii Scipiones, admitted literary men of humble and even of servile origin into its company in the so-called 'Scipionic Circle' which Aemilianus formed around himself.

At the same time the extension of the Roman Empire raised Latin to the position of a universal language in Italy and imposed upon the Romans the duty of learning Greek as a second tongue. In the study of Latin the Italians proved such willing and proficient pupils that, while Rome itself produced the pioneers of Latin prose, the early Latin poets were mostly of Italian birth. Naevius and Lucilius were Campanians; Ennius and Pacuvius came from the remote south-east of the peninsula; Plautus and Accius were of Umbrian origin; Caecilius was a native of Cisalpine Gaul. While the Greeks bore themselves too proudly to learn Latin, ordinary Romans who had served their turn as soldiers overseas picked up sufficient Greek to season and enrich their vernacular; and the men of the governing class, who had continuous dealings with the Greeks on foreign official service, or as magistrates and senators in Rome, seldom failed to acquire a competent knowledge of the Hellenic tongue. As early as 281 the Roman envoy Postumius had addressed the Tarentines in their native language; in 160 Sempronius Gracchus, while on tour among the eastern states, expressed himself with equal ease in standard Greek and in various local dialects. Though the Senate required Greek delegates to address it through a Latin interpreter it drafted resolutions intended for publication among the Greeks in their own idiom.[25] Even Cato, who inevitably protested against such an innovation as the study of a foreign language, found it necessary for the discharge of his public duties to acquire a knowledge of Greek. Another hardbitten soldier, Aemilius Paullus, reserved for himself the library of King Perseus as his share of the Macedonian booty. For those who could not afford a house-tutor enterprising teachers opened schools, in which Greek letters and the chief works of Greek literature were studied. By 150 practically every Roman who wished to pass for an educated person was bilingual. This widespread study of Greek by the Romans improved their ear and gave them a sense for the finer points of linguistic usage; at the same time it provided them with a wide range of models of literary form and style.

The Italians learn Latin

The Romans learn Greek

The influence of Greek on Latin literature was nowhere more apparent than in its earliest productions. The first Latin author, Livius Andronicus, was actually a Greek from Tarentum, who was brought captive to Rome in 272 and repaid the subsequent gift of freedom by rendering Homer's *Odyssey* into 'Saturnian' verse (perhaps an accentual metre) in his adoptive tongue; it long remained a Roman schoolbook. He also adapted into Latin several Greek plays, the first being performed in 240 B.C. In 207 he was commissioned to compose a Processional Ode for a ceremony of purification of the State. This was followed by the establishment of an Academy or club for literary

Translations of Greek classics

19.1 A scene from a comedy.

men on the Aventine. Ennius, the composer of the first Latin classic, was also a prolific translator of Greek classics.

The Latin drama

The nascent Latin literary drama did not seek its models in the native Italian charades and the *fabulae Atellanae* (p. 110), but in Greek tragedy and comedy. It was performed, as in the Greek cities, at certain of the public festivals (at the Ludi Romani, Plebeii, Apollinares and Megalenses), and the presiding aedile selected the playwrights. The early Roman dramatists did not wholly ignore native tradition. Naevius staged the story of Romulus and the victory of Claudius Marcellus over the Gauls (p. 122), Pacuvius a tragedy bearing the name of *Aemilius Paullus,* and Accius two plays entitled *Brutus* and *Decius* (presumably the hero of Sentinum — p. 93). Among the Roman comedies a whole class took its subjects, if not from Rome itself, from the neighbouring Latin towns where the scenes were often laid, and provided what were, in all but name, skits on Roman manners *(fabulae togatae).* Yet the prevalent custom, alike in tragedy and in comedy, was to adapt Greek originals. Indeed the Roman dramatists never succeeded in emancipating themselves sufficiently from their Greek prototypes. While the

elder of the surviving Latin comedians, T. Maccius Plautus (254–184), foisted characters taken from Italian life into a Greek plot with the audacious incongruity of an Elizabethan dramatist, his successor, P. Terentius Afer (an emancipated African slave, *c.* 190–159), followed his Greek models far more closely. It is not surprising that while Plautus's plays, being racy of the soil, carried their audiences with them and were frequently reproduced in later days, the more finished and more exotic work of Terence achieved no more than a half-success on the stage. The other second-century dramatists, Accius, Caecilius and Pacuvius, are little more than names to us; but at least one of them, the tragedian Pacuvius (*c.* 220–130), shared with Plautus the good fortune of frequent revivals in the first century.

Plautus and Terence

A typically Italian feature of Plautus's plays was the mordant raillery of the dialogue. This vein of robust banter found expression in a new type of literature, which although not unknown to later Greek literature was peculiarly congenial to the Roman temperament. This was *satura,* a 'medley' of different matters (occasionally with prose interspersed in the more normal verse). The first practitioner was Ennius, whose

Roman satire

195

Lucilius

saturae were a general commentary on life, not least its follies and vices, in the form of narrative, anecdote, fable or dialogue. This poetic form was developed by C. Lucilius (*c*. 180–100), a friend of Scipio Aemilianus, who aimed his shafts with impunity at his pet aversions in Roman society, not least at the political opponents of his patron Scipio.

Naevius

The literary work of Naevius (*c*. 270–200), which included tragedies and comedies as well as historical plays *(fabulae praetextae)*, also contained some political commentary, which led to a personal clash with the Metelli. But even more important was his first Latin epic, the versified history of the First Punic War. Its style is sometimes vigorous, sometimes matter-of-fact, but the poem had considerable influence on Ennius and Virgil. A skilful blending of Greek and Roman traditions was achieved by Naevius's

Ennius

successor, Q. Ennius (*c*. 239–169). He was born in Messapia where Greek, Oscan and Latin cultures mingled and, correspondingly, he claimed to have three hearts. He served in the army in Sardinia whence he went to Rome under the patronage, it is said, of Cato. In Rome he gained the further patronage and perhaps the friendship of more famous men, including some Scipios and Servilii, but especially M. Fulvius Nobilior, consul of 189, whom he accompanied on his campaign to Aetolia and whose exploits he celebrated in verse. He borrowed from Homer the hexameter verse and a true poet's play of imagination, but took for his subject the *Annales* of Rome, a running history of the city, in which the periods of the kings, of the Pyrrhic and of the Punic Wars received the fullest treatment. Ennius adapted the hexameter to the less tripping but more stately rhythm of the Latin tongue; and he gave to the Roman people a national poem which was above all things a glorification of Roman character. The gist of the *Annales* was contained in the well-known line, 'moribus antiquis stat res Romana virisque' ('on her ancient customs the Roman state stands firm, and on her men').

8. Early Prose Literature[26]

The first Roman historians

In prose literature history was the natural starting-point for authors of Roman nationality. The first two writers of prose annals, Fabius Pictor and Cincius Alimentus, lived at the time of the Second Punic War and, like most early historians of Rome, took an active part in the political events of their day: Fabius was a senator who was sent to consult the Delphic oracle after Cannae, while Cincius was praetor in 210 and was captured by Hannibal. Both men composed general histories of the city from its foundation, but they dwelt, like Ennius, at greater length on the period of the kings and on the events of the third century, and passed lightly over the earlier history of the Republic. Strangely enough, their works were written in Greek. Their choice of a foreign idiom may have been due in part to diffidence in handling their mother-tongue; but its main reason probably was that they might convey their message not only to the educated Roman public – who by this time could read Greek – but to the growing number of Greeks who were acquiring an interest in the affairs of the West, and to provide a rejoinder to those Hellenic writers who had recorded the Punic Wars from the Carthaginian point of view. (p. 600). Though Fabius's work

Fabius Pictor

will have owed something to the primitive priestly annals, its spirit was more akin to Hellenistic historiography than to the pontifical tradition. Its purpose was political and didactic. Fabius wished to relate the moral qualities of the Romans to their history; thus, for instance, he was concerned to discuss the responsibility for the Hannibalic War in particular as well as to explain Rome's moral code in general and not least its expression in senatorial policy. His example of writing in Greek was followed up in the early second century by a few more senators, probably of less stature as historians.

Cato

The most notable advance in historical writing at this time was the *Origines* of Cato, who preferred to use and mould his mother-tongue and thus to address primarily his fellow Romans and Italians. Despite his narrow nationalism, this work, however, is in the Greek tradition, as that of Fabius had been; even its title was equivalent to *Ktiseis*, the founding of cities, which was a Greek form of historiography. In this work Cato devoted two books out of seven to the early history of Italy in general, then passed rapidly on to his own time where his treatment was selective and polemical; by including some of his own speeches and by his bitter attitude to his opponents in this part of his work he approached political autobiography and self-justification. In general he was not wholly content to rely on tradition or the narratives of his predecessors, but supplemented this ready-to-hand material with occasional documentary research. Cato's total contribution to literature was immensely wider: beside publishing over 150 of his speeches, he wrote encyclopaedic works on rhetoric, medicine, military matters, law and not least his surviving *De agricultura*. His style of speech was blunt, vigorous and vivid, his prose terse and simple. Not without reason has he been called the father of Latin prose.

Soon, perhaps under Cato's influence,

The early annalists

other Romans had started treating the history of Rome from the beginning down to their own day in annalistic fashion, based on the pontifical annals (pp. 58 f.). Thus the *Annales* of L. Calpurnius Piso, consul in 133, came down to 146 B.C. in seven books, while those of L. Cassius Hemina were on much the same scale. The treatment was sober and more reliable than that of their contemporary Cn. Gellius, who wrote a very much longer work: this expansion may have been due partly to the easier accessibility of material after the publication of the *Annales Maximi,* but partly to elaboration and even invention designed to entertain the readers. The first Roman historian to take for his subject a shorter period and to study it in a more intensive manner was Coelius Antipater (*c.* 120); his account of the Second Punic War was probably a work of considerable historical value.[27]

At the end of the second century the Romans had not yet completed their literary apprenticeship; but they had already produced a richer and more varied output of writings than any Mediterranean people except the Greeks and the Israelites. In concurrence with the schoolmasters they had in the main standardised the spelling and grammar of Latin, and had gone a long way to make it a suitable vehicle of literary expression. The compilers of the Twelve Tables had proved that Latin lent itself to terse and precise statement; the poets of the second century showed that it could also be shaped into a melodious and flexible tongue.

The standardising of the Latin language

9. Science and Philosophy

The Romans were not too proud to become the pupils of the Greeks in the domain of literature; but they conceived a somewhat arrogant disdain of Greek dancing, gymnastics and music. In particular, the latent Italian genius for music remained as yet completely undeveloped; in the opinion of a Roman crowd the purpose of an orchestra was to make as loud a noise as possible at a popular merry-making.[28]

Lack of Roman appreciation for music

A congenital lack of speculative imagination among the Romans stifled their interest in natural science, save for narrowly utilitarian purposes. The obvious practical advantages of keeping the calendar true to the sun induced them to study the Greek systems of time-reckoning. In 191 they introduced a more accurate rule for intercalating additional months into their official calendar. In 159 they awakened to the fact that a sun-dial which they had brought back from Sicily in 263 would mark the hours inaccurately at Rome, and adjusted it to their latitude; and about the same time they imported

Lack of interest in natural science

their first water-clocks from Greece. In 168 a nobleman named C. Sulpicius Gallus startled the Roman forces on the eve of the battle of Pydna by predicting a lunar eclipse, but his astronomical lore remained a mere oddity. Though Greek physicians began to take up their domicile at Rome from the time of the Second Punic War the study of medicine struck no roots there; no doubt the custom of relying on slaves as house-doctors prevented it from acquiring its proper status.

In one branch of social science the Romans of the second century showed a characteristic proficiency. At the same time as they were extending their legal system to include the *ius gentium* (p. 182), they were applying themselves to the methodical study of their substantive law, out of which eventually rose the distinctive Roman science of jurisprudence. The first juristic treatise in Latin was a commentary by Sex. Aelius Paetus (consul in 198) on the Twelve Tables, and on the *legis actiones,* or procedure for initiating suits.

Proficiency in jurisprudence

In regard to the mental and moral sciences, on which visiting Greek scholars from time to time gave specimen discourses, the Romans were caught between two minds. Conundrums of logic and of metaphysics they curtly dismissed as unpractical, and therefore positively harmful. They were quicker to grasp the value of a considered ethical doctrine. But they resented the somewhat barren scepticism of the Academic school because of its subversive and unsettling tendency. Still more did they mistrust the Epicureans, whose cult of pleasure, however refined, and detachment from active social life, seemed the very negation of the Roman *mos maiorum.* The earliest comers among the Greek philosophers were accordingly banished as intellectual and moral anarchists (173 and 161). But one Greek school, that of the Stoics, found even greater favour among educated Romans than among Greek intellectuals, for its moral code was eminently congenial to the Roman temperament.[29] Unlike the other Greek doctrines the Stoic rule commended a life of action and encouraged participation in public affairs. Its main postulate, that the world was a theatre for the display of human will-power, and that the difficulties of human life were literally 'trials', appealed directly to Roman stubbornness and self-respect; on the other hand its lack of ready sympathy with human suffering gave no shock to Roman pride. The chief Stoic teacher of the second century, Panaetius of Rhodes, became the personal friend of Scipio Aemilianus. He adapted the more rigid values of early Stoicism to the practical needs of Roman life, and from his day the exponents of the Stoic

Distrustful attitude to Greek philosophy

Influence of the Stoic system upon the Romans

system were usually received with favour among the Roman governing class. In this philosophic intercourse between two nations the Romans gave as well as received. From the Greeks they obtained a reasoned justification of their traditional code of behaviour, and a cosmopolitan outlook which placed a wholesome check upon the natural arrogance of a conquering people. To the Greeks they imparted some of their practical common sense: it was partly due to Roman influence that the Stoic sage stepped down from his pinnacle of moral perfection and became content to trudge along the road to full proficiency.

10. Religion[30]

The state-religion and alien rites

As the impact of foreign influences upon the Roman world became more powerful the Roman state-religion deliberately guarded itself against them. During the Punic Wars, it is true, the Senate sanctioned the introduction of alien rites in order to put new heart into the people. In 249 and 207 it appointed special festivals of appeasement (*Ludi Tarentini*) to the Greek underworld deities, Dis and Proserpina; in 216 it fulfilled the injunction of a Sibylline oracle which bade it bury alive a Greek and a Gaulish couple – 'sacrum minime Romanum', as Livy justly remarked. But the predominant note of the new ceremonials was one of gaiety. In 217 the Italian thanksgiving festival of the Saturnalia was converted into a Greek merrymaking festival *sans gêne*, during which all doors stood open and masters changed parts with slaves. The decorously dull ritual of various Roman state cults was diversified with processions, circus games and dramatic performances, in which the significance of the original act of worship became almost obliterated. The elaborate cheerfulness of the Greek ritual was no doubt adopted in the first instance as the right tonic for nerves frayed by a long-drawn-out war; subsequently it served the purpose of keeping the urban proletariat amused and duly grateful to its noble patrons. In 204 an Oriental deity, the Phrygian nature-goddess Cybele or Magna Mater, was officially brought to Rome. By the good offices of King Attalus of Pergamum a Roman deputation was able to bring home from her sanctuary at Pessinus a black fetish-stone, like the Ka'aba of Mecca, in which the goddess was deemed to reside; an orgiastic type of ritual, such as hitherto had been quite foreign to Roman practice, was performed in her honour.

Notwithstanding these war-time concessions the general policy of the governing class was to prevent any rapid intrusion of alien influences into Roman religion. Though elements of Greek ceremonial were incorporated into official Roman cults, the former practice of adopting new Greek gods into the circle of Rome's patron deities was almost discontinued. The only notable newcomer from Greek lands was Venus of Mt Eryx in Sicily (217). The ritual of Cybele was admitted only under the most stringent safeguards, and no Roman citizen was allowed to officiate at her worship. Though the official Sibylline oracles might be consulted at moments of crisis by order of the Senate, private prophecies were suppressed with jealous care. In 242 the Roman government went so far as to urge the allied city of Praeneste to close down the lot-oracle of its patron goddess, Fortuna Primigenia. Illicit attempts to introduce exotic worships of an exciting and unnerving character were punished with a heavy arm. The masterful energy with which the Senate stamped out a secret cult of Bacchus in 186 has already been noted (p. 184). What was primarily objected to was the accompanying crime and immorality which the cult engendered throughout southern Italy on such a scale as to threaten public order. Thus the Senate did not completely ban all practice of the cult, but brought it under such tight official control that it could not again become a public danger.[31] The same vigilance against *supersititio* or religious over-excitement appears in the zeal and promptness with which the portents and prodigies announced from time to time to the pontifices were expiated.

Exclusive attitude to new cults

The watchfulness of the Senate over foreign worships illustrates its concern to preserve the calm good sense of traditional Roman religion. But the religious policy of the Roman nobles shows up no less plainly their readiness to exploit religion as an instrument of their class ascendancy. The subordination of the *res divina* to political convenience was implied in the conversion of the public festivals into mere amusements, and was affirmed with almost cynical frankness by the Aelian and the Fufian laws (p. 178), which virtually sanctioned the abuse of divination to suit political exigencies.[32] This view of religion as a useful trace-horse for helping to pull the political cart was a more powerful solvent of any sincere spirit of worship than the open ribaldry with which Plautus and Terence, in the holiday mood of Greek comedy, caricatured respectable deities like Jupiter, or the *jeux d'esprit* of Ennius, in which he reaffirmed the Epicurean doctrine that the deities lived in a world apart and took no heed of men.

Exploitation of religion in the interest of politics

An expulsion order by which the *praetor peregrinus* of 139 banished from Rome all astrologers and members of the Jewish sect shows that by then the city was becoming a missionary

Expulsion of Jews and astrologers from Rome

field for the religions and the philosophies of the Near East. But at this stage the leaven of Oriental thoughts and faiths had hardly begun to work among the western peoples.

In the history of Roman civilisation there is no more important period than the second century B.C., when the Republic, in becoming a world-state, was confronted with the choice between the traditional Italic ways of life and the cosmopolitan, but predominantly Greek, civilisation of the eastern Mediterranean. Like western Europe in the age of the Renaissance the Romans had to decide whether to eat of the fruit of the knowledge of good and evil. Characteristically enough, they made a compromise; they adopted Greek culture, but their imitation was selective; the Italic stock was preserved, but was quickened by grafting with Greek shoots.[33] Of the many pupils of Greece the Romans were the most proficient; they were not too proud to learn, and they learnt with their eyes open. In the second century, accordingly, the Republic raised itself to the level of a 'culture-state', and it prepared for the diffusion of a distinctively Roman civilisation in western Europe.

Rome becomes a 'culture-state'

PART IV

The Fall of the Republic

CHAPTER 20

Tiberius and Gaius Gracchus

1. Tiberius Gracchus. His Political Aims

Progressive disorder after 133 B.C.

The period of comparative calm through which Roman domestic politics had moved since the end of the Conflict of the Orders was brought to a close in 133 with the tribunate of Tiberius Gracchus. The following century was a period of almost continuous internal disorder, in the course of which the republican constitution was progressively disjointed and paralysed.

The storm that blew up in 133 was preceded by some premonitory squalls due in part to the irritation caused by the severe conscription of the Spanish Wars. In 151 men resisting the levy appealed to the tribunes, who went so far as temporarily to imprison the consuls who were refusing exemptions; the procedure was repeated in 138. Such defiance of magisterial and senatorial authority and the popular action of the tribunes foreshadowed the greater clash which was to come in 133. Further, in 139 a tribune named A. Gabinius made an attempt *Previous symptoms of unrest* to secure a greater degree of independence for the Comitia by means of a bill which substituted the ballot at electoral assemblies for the previous system of voting by open declaration. In 137 another tribune, L. Cassius Longinus, extended the ballot to judicial assemblies of the people. These laws, however, may not have had much practical effect, for the hold of the aristocracy upon the urban proletariat was so firmly established by now that minor reforms of this kind could not free the Comitia from their tutelage. The first really formidable attack upon the privileges of the nobles was made by Tiberius Gracchus, the prime mover of the Roman revolution.

As the son of the elder Sempronius Gracchus, a powerful noble who had been censor and twice consul, and of Cornelia, the daughter of Scipio Africanus, Tiberius seemed hardly the man to head a list of Roman demagogues. As an officer in the Third Punic War he had been first over the wall of Carthage. At Numantia he had conducted the negotiations by which the army of Hostilius Mancinus was saved from destruction; but the influence of his brother-in-law Scipio Aemilianus had helped to shield him from the discredit which that capitulation subsequently brought upon Mancinus (p. 146). With such an ancestry and such a personal record, Tiberius had merely to observe the Roman nobleman's ordinary code of 'good form', and his career was assured.[1]

Tiberius Sempronius Gracchus. His antecedents

The motives which led Tiberius to seek reform and ultimately to force it through against the opposition of his own order are not clearly revealed in the ancient sources, which are in general anti-Gracchan in origin. Thus he has been depicted in various guises, from an altruistic social reformer to would-be tyrant. But even those who regard him as a genuine reformer are not united in their interpretation of his motives or aims. Did he turn demagogue because of the treatment he received in the Mancinus affair? Was he a young man ambitiously seeking to advance his career within the traditional framework of factional politics? Did his Greek tutor Diophanes and the Stoic philosopher Blossius of Cumae instil in him ideas of Greek political theory and Hellenistic views of social justice? Was his main concern to get the small independent farmer back on the land in the interests of Italian agriculture, or of ridding Rome of her unemployed, or (through concern at potential military dangers) of increasing the number of landowning peasants who would

Tiberius's motive for land-reform

be available for the army? At the very least he was clearly disturbed by the economic situation and sought a cure for some of the current ills.

On his way to Numantia he had noted the dearth of small peasantry in Etruria, a land of large estates tilled by servile workers. In Spain he had observed the deterioration of the Roman soldiery, and he had sought its cause in the decline of the Italian yeoman class. An even more compelling proof of the dangers of slave-cultivation had been offered to him by a recent insurrection in Sicily, where the servile population had risen *en masse* in 135 against its Greek and Roman landlords. This revolt gave reason for alarm, not only because of the large number of slaves under arms – their forces were estimated at not less than 60,000 – but because of the aid which they received from the lesser free proprietors, and of the remarkable powers of leadership revealed by their self-constituted captains, the Syrian Eunus and the Cilician Cleon.[2] The indifferent Roman army that was sent in the first instance to repress the rebels met with the usual early disasters, and it was not until 133–132, when the fall of Numantia released some of Scipio Aemilianus's well-trained troops for service in Sicily, that the island was pacified.[3] The uprising in Sicily coincided with some outbreaks in Campania which apparently necessitated the appointment of two consulars with special *imperium* to deal with them in 133; it may have helped to stimulate the revolt of the Pergamene serfs under Aristonicus (p. 166). It was with a view to combating some of these evils that Tiberius became a land-reformer and a revolutionary politician.[4]

A slave-rising in Sicily

2. The Gracchan Land Law

Tiberius's land act

Elected tribune for 133, Tiberius brought forward a bill for the creation of allotments mostly out of the large area of public land which the Republic had acquired after the Second Punic War. Of this territory he offered to leave in the hands of the existing occupiers a portion of 500 *iugera*, i.e. 300 acres apiece (the maximum) which in strict law might be taken up by a single tenant (p. 76), and perhaps an additional 150 acres for each child; the residue he proposed to distribute to smallholders in parcels of varying size.[5] He imposed upon the new allotment-holders a small quit-rent, and a promise not to alienate their plot for a certain term of years. By way of compensation for the disturbed tenants, some of whom had effected considerable improvements on the land occupied by them, he conceded to them possession in perpetuity, free of rent, of the land left in their hands.

If meant as a contribution to Roman military reform Tiberius's land law was totally inadequate. As a means of checking the decline in the numbers of the free cultivators it could have no more than a transient effect. So long as Italian peasants were liable to be called away from their fields for long spells of military service overseas, or were lured to Rome by the artificial attractions in which that city abounded, no mere entail on their holdings could have attached them securely to the countryside. But as a palliative measure his proposal could hardly have been better conceived. It did not infringe on any legal vested right, and it treated the existing occupants of the public land with reasonable consideration, safeguarding them against any further loss of territory. Above all, it was not in the least a revolutionary measure in itself, but merely resumed, after a brief interruption, the traditional Roman policy of land settlement. A bill, probably not unlike that of Tiberius, had but recently been brought forward by Scipio Aemilianus's friend C. Laelius (*c.* 145), though he had not persisted in the face of opposition from the sitting tenants.[6] With resistance from this quarter Tiberius had equally to reckon; on the other hand he had an assurance of support from some leading members of the nobility, including his father-in-law Appius Claudius Pulcher, the Princeps Senatus (the senior member on the roll of the House, and the first to be consulted at a *rogatio*), P. Licinius Crassus, the wealthiest Roman of his day, and P. Mucius Scaevola, a famous jurist, who was consul in the year of Tiberius's tribunate, and probably helped him to draft his bill. With such powerful support Tiberius was far from being a lone reformer.

Its merits and deficiencies

Support from prominent noblemen

If Tiberius had followed the established practice of submitting bills to the Senate before presenting them to the Popular Assembly, it is by no means certain that his agrarian measure would have been flatly rejected by the nobles. There is no warrant for asserting that the Senate had made up its mind against him beforehand; and in any event this body alone was competent to discuss and adjust those points of detail in the bill which subsequently forced themselves upon Tiberius's attention. Tiberius, however, chose to follow the solitary and distant precedent of C. Flaminius, whose land law had been carried in 232 without previous consultation of the Senate (there were, however, certain areas of legislation, e.g. concerning citizenship, where tribunician bills might be put to the people without prior senatorial discussion). In taking this short cut he may have had nothing more in view than to save time in a situation which he

Tiberius omits to consult the Senate

regarded as urgent: assuredly he did not intend to proclaim a novel constitutional doctrine. Yet his impatience precipitated a constitutional crisis. Whatever individual senators might think of the merits of his bill, as a body the House was bound to resent the slight which the tribune, however inadvertently, was putting upon it. It therefore had recourse to the recognised procedure for curbing a refractory official, a veto by another official. When Tiberius's measure was about to be read to the Concilium Plebis, a fellow tribune named M. Octavius imposed silence upon the clerk.[7] But Tiberius, far from accepting this rebuff, adjourned the meeting, perhaps for two or three weeks, and prepared for a trial of strength with the Senate.[8] The constitutional impasse which he was facing was unprecedented. At the instance of some cooler heads, it is true, he agreed to discuss the situation with the House; but tempers had by now risen to such a point that the attempted parley merely added fuel to the flames. Tiberius thereupon reassembled the Concilium, which duly voted to depose Octavius from office since he persisted in his constitutionally unconventional veto; his actual removal from the tribunal involved some slight physical brawling but not serious violence. In adopting this short way with a dissenting colleague, Tiberius himself took a course which was wholly unprecedented,[9] but for the time being he had the support of all the land-hungry citizens and could use their votes to overbear opposition. Without further protest from the Senate Octavius was replaced by a more amenable tribune, and the agrarian bill was carried into law. To give full effect to the measure, a permanent commission was set up, of which Tiberius himself, his younger brother Gaius, and Claudius Pulcher were the original members, and this executive commission was invested with judicial powers to decide all disputes arising out of the redistribution of land.[10]

3. The First Senatorial Reaction

The Senate then tried to thwart Tiberius by refusing all but nominal financial aid to the commissioners, who required it in order to help the new settlers stock their allotments. But fortunately at this point news came that Attalus had died (p. 166) and made the Roman people his heirs. Tiberius immediately introduced a bill, or announced that he would do so, to make some of this wealth available for his settlers and threatened to by-pass the Senate and bring the matter of settling Attalus's kingdom before the people.[11] Even Tiberius's friends in the Senate

could not be expected to accept this double challenge to the Senate's recognised authority in financial and foreign affairs. However, he had got the funds for his settlers.

The agrarian commission now got to work, and allotments were made in various districts of Italy, but especially on the outskirts of the central and southern Apennines. But Tiberius henceforth lived under a threat of reprisals by the nobility. To safeguard himself against impeachment and his legislation against annulment he offered himself for a second tribunate;[12] but in so doing he raised yet another constitutional issue. Election to the same magistracy in two successive years was expressly forbidden by a recent statute, the *lex Villia* of 180 (p. 181);[13] and although it was not quite certain whether the tribunate, not being technically a magistracy of the whole Roman people, came under the scope of this measure, no instances could be quoted of its repeated tenure by one person since the Conflict of the Orders. At this stage, moreover, Tiberius found his supporters melting away from him. The other tribunes and the urban protelariat, who had been carried along by the fervour of his first appeal, eventually lost interest in a cause that was of no personal concern to them, and the rustic voters, who had previously flocked to Rome in his support, were busy with the harvest. Had the nobles now allowed events to take their course they might have defeated Tiberius and recovered their ascendancy by strictly lawful methods. But in the heat of the discussions about the legality of his candidature a brawl broke up the electoral assembly meeting on the Capitol, and some over-zealous senators lost their heads. Led by the ex-consul Scipio Nasica, they marched out of the temple of Fides, where the Senate was meeting, to the assembly on the Capitol. Making a rush at Tiberius they clubbed him and some 300 of his supporters to death.

Tiberius's ill-considered disregard of senatorial prerogatives and his attitude to the tribunate had offended most senators and driven a few to resort to bloodshed in civil strife, from which Rome had been free for nearly 400 years. But of all persons who initiated a revolution, Tiberius Gracchus was perhaps the most conservative, although some of his actions might appear to nervous contemporary opponents (more sharply than to some modern interpreters) directed on a course which might lead to a personal ascendancy or *regnum*. His land-law was almost a model of compromise; the liberties which he took with the constitution, once he had made his first false step, were practically forced upon him by way of self-protection;

The Senate has recourse to a tribune's veto

Tiberius obtains the deposition of the obstructing tribune. His land bill is enacted

The bequest of Attalus

Land assignations in Italy

Tiberius seeks re-election to the tribunate

He is killed by lynch-law

Tiberius not a deliberate revolutionary

and they were as nothing compared with the example of political murder set by Scipio Nasica. Indeed Tiberius marked rather than made the beginning of the Roman civil wars.

Reprisals against Tiberius's supporters

The lynching of Tiberius was followed by quasi-legal proceedings on the part of the Senate against his principal supporters. In 132 the consul P. Popillius was directed to hold an assize, at which men who at most had talked of violence were sentenced to death. On the other hand the worst offender, Scipio Nasica, was made safe against a dose of his own medicine by an honourable exile, in the guise of a diplomatic mission to the newly constituted province of Asia where he soon died. In 131 another political murder was threatened, when a tribune named C. Atinius, who had a personal grievance against the censor Metellus Macedonicus, attempted to improve upon Nasica's methods by hurling his enemy from the Tarpeian Rock; but his colleagues intervened in a body, and for the time no further violence was committed.

The land assignations are continued

While the Senate proceeded with ruthless severity against Tiberius's partisans at Rome, it took no steps to thwart his land-commission. With P. Licinius Crassus, father-in-law of Gaius Gracchus, to replace Tiberius, the triumvirs carried on with their task; and the consul Popillius, the president of the Bloody Assize, apparently not only co-operated with it, but boasted publicly of his collaboration.[14] Thus the senatorial nobility made it clear that its opposition had not been directed against the land-law as such, but against the methods by which it had been forced through.

Re-election to the tribunate is made legal

In 131 the nobles again adopted a conciliatory attitude when a tribune named C. Papirius Carbo completed the series of the *leges tabellariae* by introducing the secret ballot at legislative assemblies of the people. At the instance of Scipio Aemilianus, who had meanwhile returned from Spain and resumed his post as watchdog of the constitution, they defeated an attempt by Carbo to authorise re-election to the tribunate; but after Scipio's death they probably allowed Carbo's measure to be carried by some other tribune.

4. The first Italian Franchise Bill

Scipio Aemilianus and the Italians

Many of Rome's allies were already feeling aggrieved by her attitude towards them (p. 184) when some had to face the additional impact of Gracchus's agrarian law which affected those who were holding land in excess of the legal limit. They would be reluctant to hand over the surplus for distribution to the unemployed in Rome, while some border territories may also have been in dispute.[15] To champion their cause the allies turned to Scipio Aemilianus. On the general question of agrarian reform he presumably shared the half-hearted yet not unfriendly attitude of his friend Laelius (p. 204). But on grounds of constitutional propriety he had repudiated Tiberius's actions and remarked that 'if Tiberius intended to seize the state, he was killed justly', a compromise assessment. Moreover, as a former military chief who owed his victories no less to his Latin and Italian auxiliaries than to the Roman legionaries, he felt obliged to defend their interests. Accordingly in 129 he induced the Senate to transfer the settlement of disputes in respect of land held by non-citizens from the Gracchan triumvirate to one of the consuls, who in the event conveniently went off to Illyricum.[16] This will have eased tension for the Italians, while the commissioners continued to devote their activities to land held by citizens, and it seems with good effect: the census figures of 125 B.C. (c. 395,000) were some 75,000 higher than those of 131 B.C., and this rise almost certainly reflects the work of land-settlement.[17] But Scipio's patronage of the Italians, together with the fact that he had opposed Carbo's bill about re-election to the tribunate, increased his unpopularity with the urban mob, and one morning he was found dead. Although at the time, and later, various eminent people were suspected of his murder, probably no crime was involved; although suicide is just possible, a natural death is more likely.[18]

His death

Fulvius Flaccus and Italian enfranchisement

Deprived of their patron, many of the allies gradually went to Rome to agitate concerning the more general question of their enfranchisement, which had long become overdue. They met with no success: a tribune, Iunius Pennus, in 126 passed a law, against which Gaius Gracchus spoke, to prevent non-citizens settling in Rome and to expel any who had done so.[19] However, their cause was taken up by one of the consuls of 125, M. Fulvius Flaccus, who was one of the land-commissioners. He proposed that all allies who wished should receive Roman citizenship, while the rest should be given the right of appeal against Roman magistrates. But the Roman nobility was not willing to face the creation of a mass of voters who stood outside their *clientela* and might prove unmanageable. The Senate therefore forced Flaccus to abandon his reform by sending him off to Gaul to help Massilia against an attack by the Saluvii (p. 210).

The revolt of Fregellae

Thus a most statesman-like bill, which would have saved Rome from the tragedy of the Italian War in 90 B.C., was thwarted by senatorial conservatism. However, despite the overwhelming odds against it, one Latin colony, Fregellae in the Liris valley, refused to accept political defeat and openly revolted from Rome. The days of her independence were short, since no other Latin towns joined her: the city was besieged and then destroyed, the inhabitants being moved down from their hill-site to the plain where a colony was established at Fabrateria. The Senate had been lucky to escape so lightly. But the efforts of Tiberius and Flaccus were but a prelude to a more sustained assault delivered by Gaius Gracchus in 123–122: it was in these years that the ascendancy of the Senate was for the first time put to a serious test.

5. The Social Reforms of Gaius Gracchus

Gaius Gracchus

The younger of the Gracchi was but twenty-one years of age at the time of his brother's tribunate. But he took his seat on the land-commission at its inception, served as quaestor in Sardinia in 126, and gave support to the reforms of Carbo and Flaccus with a weight of utterance that revealed the future statesman. Foreseeing their danger from this quarter the nobles endeavoured to cut short his career by prosecuting him on various trumped-up charges; but he cleared himself without difficulty and was returned tribune for 123.

His power of oratory

Gaius Gracchus was a man of wider imagination and of deeper passions than his brother, and as a public speaker he exerted a power second only to that of Cicero. At the outset of his tribunate he took his popular audiences by storm and intimidated the Senate into immediate acquiescence. He was re-elected tribune for 122 without opposition, so that for a year and a half he remained the uncrowned king of Rome. He made use of his spell of sovereignty to carry a programme of legislation of such comprehensiveness as no other tribune produced.[20]

Gaius's land and colonial bills

As the heir of his brother's social ideals Gaius reaffirmed the agrarian act of 133, removing whatever limitation Scipio Aemilianus had placed upon the commissioners. In order to facilitate the marketing of the produce from the new allotments he made provision for the construction of new secondary roads in Italy; these would give employment and also help the rural electorate to travel more easily. To help cultivators who preferred a corporate settlement and at the same time to stimulate industrial revival Gaius carried a supplementary bill for the foundation of colonies at Tarentum, Capua and some other sites. Some of the colonists were to come from the middle classes, who had sufficient capital to promote the industries which were languishing in these towns. His most notable colonial scheme, perhaps not mooted until 122, was for a transmarine settlement on the terri-

tory of Carthage which had become Roman domain land in 146. A fellow tribune named Rubrius proposed that the colony should be named Junonia and be assigned to some 6000 settlers with large allotments of 200 *iugera* each in absolute ownership; some non-Roman Italians may have been included among the colonists. Overseas colonisation, essentially a Greek idea, was a novel move in Roman policy.

Gaius's corn law

But Gaius despaired of converting all the needy folk of the capital into peasants. For the relief of those who preferred to take their chance in Rome he brought forward a law for the regulation of the city's corn-supply. The cost of grain at Rome was liable to sharp fluctuations, and years of glut, in which Sicily and Africa unloaded their surplus upon Rome, were followed by seasons of high prices.[21] No adequate storage accommodation had been provided at the capital, and the private speculators, in whose hands the trade in grain resided, had no interest in maintaining prices at a uniform level. With a view to stabilising the commerce in cereals, Gaius made provision for the purchase of the overseas crops in bulk by the state and for delivery at public warehouses in Ostia; and from this store he enacted that a fixed monthly ration should be sold on demand to any Roman citizen at a fixed price of $1\frac{1}{3}$ *asses* a *modius*, which was slightly below the market-rate. Though control of the corn trade was nothing unusual among the Greeks – it had been practised at Athens since the fifth century and at Alexandria the Ptolemies had instituted a special 'minister of cheapness' – Gaius's experiment in state socialism was sharply criticised at Rome. His scheme imposed a fresh burden, albeit not a heavy one, on the treasury, and its tendency must have been to encourage a further drift of population from the country to the capital. Yet as a palliative measure it was well conceived, and it should be held distinct from subsequent corn-laws framed by unworthy imitators, whose object was nothing more than mass bribery.

The philanthropic legislation of Gaius was rounded off with a statute which mitigated the harshness of military conscription by prohibiting the enrolment of recruits before the customary age of seventeen, and by providing clothing for the troops.

6. The Political Legislation of Gaius Gracchus

His law against judicial usurpations

But Gaius's programme went far beyond the limited objects of Tiberius. Unlike his brother he was by intent and not merely by accident a political reformer. The earliest of all his measures was an attack upon the illegal but hitherto unchallenged practice by which the Senate had authorised the consul Popillius in 132 to constitute a special tribunal with powers of capital punishment (p. 206). This usurpation of the people's sovereign rights was now declared a punishable crime, and by a retrospective application of the new statute Popillius was impeached before the Tribal Assembly and driven into exile. This measure may have been supplemented by a rather mysterious law 'ne quis iudicio circumveniatur', which perhaps precluded senators from misusing their judicial powers against the people.[22]

Reform of the quaestio *de rebus repetundis*

Gaius's main judiciary law was directed against the abuses which had crept into the jury-court for the trial of provincial governors on the charge of extortion. The natural sympathy which jurymen drawn exclusively from the Senate felt for culprits of senatorial rank had of recent years resulted in the acquittal of men whose guilt was patent or at all events generally assumed. Gaius's judicial statute, which was probably moved by Acilius in 122, abolished the senatorial juries altogether and transferred the court *de rebus repetundis* into the hands of the equestrian order; at the same time he drew up the rules of procedure so as to load the dice in favour of the prosecution.[23] In this law Gaius for the first time gave political recognition to a social class which had acquired considerable economic importance since the age of the foreign conquests (p. 189). Though the precise definition which he gave to the *equester ordo* in his judiciary statute is not known,[24] it is clear that in actual practice the juries *(iudices)* of the court *de rebus repetundis* were predominantly drawn from that section of the Order which derived its wealth from tax-farming and other financial operations. This group had interests in the provinces which were not unlikely to bring them into conflict with the governors. While the *publicani* in their capacity as tax-collectors had an obvious interest in gathering as much revenue as possible from the provincials, it was the duty of the governors to protect these against illegal exactions, and, if not a few governors were unduly complaisant to the Roman financiers, others were not lacking who refused to sacrifice the tax-payers to them. The transference of the court for extortion from senatorial to equestrian juries therefore had the effect of providing a tribunal which might be predisposed to condemn rather than to acquit.

Transference of the juries to the Ordo Equester

This judicial law of Gaius was described by himself as a dagger which he had fixed securely in the flank of the Senate, and indeed it showed up plainly the touch of vindictiveness that vitiated his disinterested zeal as a reformer. In

Defects of this measure

recognising that the Equites were entitled to a larger share of political power he initiated a reform which subsequently bore good fruit. If in place of his judicial measure he had carried legislation to open up effectively the magistracies and the Senate to the Equestrian Order, he might have infused into the Roman government some much-needed new blood from the most industrious and enterprising class of the community.[25] The actual effect of his judicial law was that he hampered the Senate without improving it and gave to the Equites power without responsibility.

A minor enactment of Gaius against senatorial jobbery related to the method of staffing the provinces. In order to prevent the Senate from taking into account personal likes and dislikes in its annual selection of two consular provinces for the outgoing magistrates of that rank, it provided that in future the selection must be made before the actual election of the consular pair to whom the provinces thus chosen would fall due. Since the elections of magistrates in the later Republic were normally held six months before their entry into office, the effect of this regulation was that the Senate was obliged to make its choice of consular provinces at least eighteen months beforehand. A curious provision, by which this law was rendered immune against the tribunician veto, shows in what light Gaius regarded this former safeguard of popular liberties.

Regulations for provincial appointments

The fundamental contradiction in Gaius's legislation was again revealed in a law which regulated anew the taxation of the newly created province of Asia. By this measure the exemptions from tribute which the Senate had accorded to the cities of the former kingdom of Pergamum, in accordance with a request in the testament of Attalus III, were withdrawn from all except perhaps a few favoured towns. Of the provincials' rights in general Gaius was an outspoken champion; but the need to compensate the treasury for losses of revenues consequent upon his corn-law and colonial schemes obliged him to cancel some of their covenanted rights. In this same law Gaius also played (unwittingly, we may believe) into the hands of the Roman financiers. Instead of leaving the collection of the tribute of Asia in the hands of the several municipalities, he provided that the rights of tax-gathering in all the cities of the province should be put up for auction at Rome, so that in effect he created a monopoly for the Roman tax-farming companies. In making this regulation Gaius no doubt assumed that the Roman *publicani* would make more advantageous tenders to the treasury for the privilege of farming the consolidated revenues of the

Financial regulations for the province of Asia

entire province. Apparently he did not observe the risk of handing over the provincials to these powerful Roman corporations, or he turned a blind eye upon it.

The activities of Gaius did not end with the drafting and enacting of his large and varied code of new laws, for he doubled the part of legislator with that of minister-general. In addition to his duties on the land-commission he personally supervised his scheme of road-construction, and in 122 he went on a visit to Africa in order to prepare for the foundation of his colony at Junonia. In the execution of his measures he displayed the tact of a professional administrator, to the surprise of those who could see nothing in him but a demagogue.

Gaius's administration of his own laws

7. The Second Senatorial Reaction

In 122 Gaius was associated in the tribunate with M. Fulvius Flaccus, who had not disdained to step down from his consular rank in order to resume his work as a reformer. He now revived in a modified form Flaccus's bill for the enfranchisement of the Italians. To the allies of Latin status he offered full citizenship, to the remainder he gave the Latin rights as a half-way house to complete enfranchisement.[26] But this, the most statesmanlike of all his measures, proved the first step towards his downfall. During his second term of office the support which he received from Flaccus was offset by the insidious sapping and mining which another colleague, M. Livius Drusus, carried out against him in collusion with the Senate. Not venturing as yet to oppose him openly Drusus sought to outbid Gaius in popularity with a rival block of laws whose object was to prove that Short, not Codlin, was the people's friend. He amended Gaius's agrarian law by relieving the allotment-holders of the rent imposed upon them. He improved upon Gaius's colonial projects by proposing a mass-foundation of no less than twelve settlements in Italy, each of 3000 men, to which the very poorest citizens were to be admitted. He took the wind out of Gaius's sails by offering to the Latins absolute exemption from execution or scourging at the hands of Roman military commanders, thus placing them in a better position than Roman citizens, who merely possessed a right of appeal against such punishments. Though no effort was made to establish the new colonies, which indeed never existed except on paper, Drusus's measures were carried into law, and due credit was bestowed upon him.

In the meantime, too, the spell of Gaius's oratory was working itself out. His inflammatory

Gaius's act for the enfranchisement of Italy

The counter-legislation of Livius Drusus

eloquence had produced a magical effect on first impression, but repetition damped its explosive power. The assembly to which Gaius presented his franchise bill was therefore no longer steadfast or undivided in its loyalty. The contents of the bill, however much attenuated in comparison with Flaccus's previous measure, were as unpalatable as ever to the Roman voters; and the consul C. Fannius (a renegade from the Gracchan movement) appealed quite frankly to their instinct not to spoil a good thing by making it too common. Finally, lest fear should prevail upon the assembly where reason failed, the Senate instructed the consuls to prohibit any of the allies (except perhaps the Latins) from appearing within five miles of Rome on the day of the poll. Under these conditions Drusus was probably emboldened to oppose the franchise bill with a direct veto, and Gaius lacked the assurance to prepare for him the fate of Octavius. At any rate the bill was defeated.

Gaius's waning popularity

After the defeat of the franchise act commons and nobles combined to get rid of Gaius altogether. While he was away from Rome, engaged in delimiting the territory of his new colony in Africa, persistent rumours were circulated in Rome that he was encroaching on the cursèd site on which the city of Carthage had been built, that hurricanes charged with the wrath of heaven had whirled away some of the trespassing boundary-marks and that 'wolves' (presumably jackals) had grubbed up the rest and carried them far out of reach. There is reason for believing that Gaius had actually been at pains to avoid the banned area; but while he was absent in Africa he could not clip the wings of a false rumour, and on his return he could no longer catch it up.[27] Back in Rome he met with a serious reverse: in the summer of 122 the electors refused him a third tribunate, thus exposing him to reprisals at the hands of the governing class. The aristocracy lost no time in launching their counter-attack. After the expiry of his second term of office the Senate instructed a new tribune, M. Minucius Rufus, to propose the formal annulment of the *lex Rubria*, by which the colony of Iunonia was to be constituted. But in the event the issue between Gaius and the Senate was fought out with other weapons.

Religious objections to the colony at Carthage

In order to oppose Minucius's action Gaius unwisely gathered a group of friends together, and one of the servants of the consul L. Opimius was killed in a scuffle. This was Opimius's opportunity: he persuaded the Senate to pass a resolution which declared that the state was in danger, and charged the consuls and other high magistrates 'to see to it that the republic take no harm'. By this motion, which sub-

The senatus consultum ultimum

sequently was known as the *senatus consultum ultimum*, and by repeated use became stereotyped into a set form, the Senate in effect promised its moral support to magistrates proceeding by summary executive action against those endangering the state. On the strength of this exhortation Opimius called the senators and Equites to arms, and Gaius reluctantly agreed to Flaccus's desire to resist by force. The Gracchans therefore occupied the Aventine, but after vain negotiations they were overwhelmed and both Gaius and Flaccus were killed. Without waiting for further instructions Opimius made wholesale arrests among Gaius's followers and executed them after a perfunctory trial; in all, it is said, over 3000 perished.

Military execution against Gaius and his adherents

The Gracchi brothers are among the most tragic figures in Roman history. Both of them were admittedly men of high probity and sincere patriotism, and their measures were for the most part excellent examples of that conservative reform which, if applied betimes, preserves a constitution by adapting and rejuvenating it. But in spite of their fundamental moderation both in turn were carried away in the excitement of the political fray, and made tactical errors which had the effect of raising passions and exposing them to merciless retaliation. At first sight indeed it might appear as if their efforts had been in vain; and their careers certainly conveyed the lesson that no reformer of the later Republic could succeed in the long run by invoking the Popular Assembly against the Senate. The days were past in which a determined plebeian yeomanry backed up reforming tribunes with a persistence that knew not defeat. The urban proletariat now predominating in the Comitia was but a broken reed to lean on: though it contained volatile elements which might cause it to flare up temporarily against the Senate, its fires quickly rendered down and left the impending revolution less than halfbaked. Henceforth political leaders who worked through the people (*populus*) rather than through the Senate became known as Populares, while the traditional oligarchy claimed to be the Best Men, the Optimates, but the Populares gradually found it necessary to set their power on a more solid basis than that of popular favour.[28] Nevertheless the Gracchi left an enduring mark on Roman history. For a time, however brief, they had thrown the Senate completely out of action, and their fleeting success made a greater impression than their eventual failure. Their example incited many more Populares to try a fall with the Senate; and in the end the Populares gained their point by turning against the Optimates the weapon of physical force with which Scipio Nasica and Opimius had

Reasons for the failure of the Gracchi

Importance of the precedent set by them

won the first disastrous victories of the Roman civil wars.

8. The Conquest of Narbonese Gaul

During the Second Punic War Transalpine Gaul had figured only as a land of passage. In the early part of the second century it did not engage the attention of the Romans, who were content to confide their overland communications with Spain to the safe keeping of their trusty allies at Massilia. But eventually the Massilians took the initiative in soliciting Roman intervention against invaders from the hinterland whom they were unable or disinclined to repel singlehanded. In 154 they called for assistance against Ligurian raiders on their stations in the French Riviera. The Senate at first tried the effect of a simple remonstrance, but when the Ligurians replied by insulting the Roman envoy it sent an army under the consul Opimius to drive them off. For a further thirty years the Romans made no attempt to gain a foothold in Transalpine Gaul; but in 125 a second call from the Massilians had the effect of drawing them on into new adventures.[29]

The Massilians solicit Roman aid in Transalpine Gaul

In answer to renewed complaints about the Ligurians the consul M. Fulvius Flaccus led an army across the western Alps (by Mont Genèvre), so as to take the Ligurians in the rear. After a campaign against the marauders of the seaboard district, he turned inland in order to subdue another Ligurian tribe between the Durance and the Isère (124). In the following two years the Ligurians of the French Riviera were definitely reduced by C. Sextius Calvinus, who established a small settlement (*castellum*) of Roman veterans at Aquae Sextiae (Aix) to protect the hinterland of Massilia. But these excursions into the interior of Gaul involved the Romans with another enemy, the Celtic tribe of the Allobroges, who dwelt in the Alpine foothills between the Isère and the Rhône. The Allobroges embroiled themselves with the Romans by refusing to surrender a fugitive Ligurian chieftain; at the same time they were denounced as peace-breakers by another Celtic tribe, the Aedui of Burgundy, who had long maintained trade relations with the Massilians and were now introduced by them to the Romans. In 121 the proconsul Cn. Domitius Ahenobarbus fought the first Roman battle against the Transalpine Gauls in the neighbourhood of Avignon. With the help of an elephant corps, which as usual proved irresistible on first acquaintance, he crushed the resistance of the Allobroges. This victory gave the Romans control of the whole left bank of the Rhône as far as Geneva; but

Campaigns against the Ligurians and Allobroges

an appeal by the defeated people to their neighbours in Auvergne brought the most powerful of the Celtic tribes, the Arverni, into the field against the Romans. The engagement which finally decided the fate of Mediterranean France was fought at the confluence of the Rhône and the Isère, between an unwieldy army under the Arvernian king Bituitus and a much smaller force under the consul Q. Fabius Maximus. Of this battle little is known except that it ended in a Gallic disaster, as the bridges which the Arverni had thrown across the Rhône broke under the weight of their retreating masses. The story ran in Rome that Fabius had slain 120,000 Gauls with a loss of fifteen on his side! The pacification of southern France was completed by Domitius, who had stayed on in Gaul after the expiry of his term as Fabius's subordinate, but resumed the chief command on the latter's return to Italy. After the manner of the Roman generals in Spain, Domitius violated a safe-conduct which he had promised to Bituitus for the purpose of a peace negotiation and sent him as a prisoner to Rome; the Senate became a partner in his perfidy by keeping Bituitus captive (120). The Arverni nevertheless concluded peace, and Domitius further acquired (by conquest or, more probably, by cession from the Arverni) a tract of land on the right bank of the Rhône, the modern Languedoc and upper Garonne valley, inclusive of the towns of Nemausus (Nîmes) and Tolosa (Toulouse). The districts conquered in the campaigns of 125–121 were ultimately constituted into a new Roman province (within which Massilia

Defeat of the Arverni

Annexation of Gallia Narbonensis

remained an independent allied state). From the Rhône to the Pyrenees Domitius constructed a highroad, to which he gave his name, and on this route a colony of Roman veterans was established at Narbo.[30]

The extension of the Roman dominion into France was, like the annexation of Sicily, the result of an afterthought. In either case an initial defensive operation on behalf of a third party lured the Romans by its successful accomplishment to enlarge their objectives and acquire fresh territory for themselves. For the time being the Romans were content to control no more than the Mediterranean face of Gaul. But a formal alliance with the Aedui, which they now concluded, gave them opportunities for further interventions in the affairs of the hinterland; and the open frontier of Gallia Transalpina or Narbonensis (as the new province came to be called) on its western and north-western sides was a standing incitement to them to carry on the conquest of Gaul to its natural boundaries on the Rhine and the Atlantic.

Roman alliance with the Aedui

In 123 the Roman conquests were rounded off by the reduction of the Balearic Isles which had become a haunt of pirates since their evacuation by the Carthaginians in 206. They were reduced by Q. Caecilus Metellus, who assumed the *cognomen* of Balearicus and left behind two settlements (towns, not colonies, but probably containing some veterans) at Palma and Pollentia in Majorca. The islands were placed under a *praefectus* appointed by the governor of Hispania Citerior.[31]

Conquest of the Balearic Islands

CHAPTER 21

Marius and the New Roman Army

1. The Restored Senatorial Government

The senatus consultum ultimum is declared legal

After the death of Gaius Gracchus and the massacre of his partisans the senatorial aristocracy returned to power unopposed. In 120 a doubtful constitutional point was settled in its favour, when L. Opimius was prosecuted in a popular court by a tribune for putting citizens to death without a trial, but overawed the people into granting a sentence of absolution. His acquittal virtually legalised the Senate's Emergency Decree and gave it confidence to make regular use of this weapon in domestic crises. In truth, so long as Rome lacked a properly constituted police force the *Senatus Consultum Ultimum* was not only a justifiable but a necessary means of defence against armed attacks upon the government.[1]

The restored régime of the Senate

In the following decade the Senate accepted the main results of Gaius's legislation, just as it had previously tolerated Tiberius's land commission. Gaius's scheme of corn distribution was modified in the interests of the treasury, but was not totally abolished. The bill of Minucius, which was the occasion of Gaius's downfall, was formally carried into law, and the colony of Iunonia was not constituted; nevertheless the land-commission was allowed to make *viritane* settlements on the territory of Carthage. In 118 or soon afterwards the Senate offered opposition to the bill of an unknown tribune for the foundation of a colony at Narbo (p. 211). But a speech by a young free-lance noble named L. Licinius Crassus, which established his reputation among Roman orators, and, we may suspect, the influence of the Equites, who no doubt had an interest in the colony, overcame its objections.[2]

The scheme for a colony at Capua fell into abeyance, but settlements were probably made at Tarentum and on other Italian sites in accordance with Gaius's law. About 121 the land-acts of Tiberius and Gaius were amended by a supplementary law permitting allotment-holders to sell their allotments, some of which may gradually and illegally have passed back into the hands of capitalist investors. But in the long run no prohibition could have tied to the land those settlers who could not obtain a living from it; in all probability the amending act was an agreed measure. Not long after (probably in 119) the land-commission, which had attained the limit of its usefulness, was abrogated, and the titles of the sitting tenants on public land (i.e. those holding up to the maximum of 500 *iugera*) were confirmed. In 111 a general consolidating act was passed, by which the system of *possessio* was abolished, all the public domain in Italy, except a few reserved territories, was converted into private property, and every class of landholder, alike in Italy and in Africa, was safeguarded against unsettlement.[2]

Final settlement of Italian land tenures

The affair of the Vestal Virgins

In 114 a passing squall blew up in consequence of a religious portent, the death by lightning of a Vestal Virgin, which roused the dormant superstitions of the multitude. A tribune named Sex. Peducaeus seized this opportunity of affirming the competence of the Tribal Assembly in regard to religious matters. By means of an overriding law of the Assembly he had the case taken out of the hands of the pontifices and transferred to a special court of inquiry (presumably consisting of Equites). The presiding judge, a former censor named L. Cassius Longinus, who was famous for his use of the question 'Cui bono?' ('to whose advantage?'), imported the methods of the Star Chamber into this trial, and so procured the condemnation of three Virgins on a charge of unchasity. But this display of severity did not suffice to calm the passions of the multitude, which was not appeased until the Senate consulted the Sibylline oracles and by their direction authorised the sacrifice of a Greek and a Gallic couple, as in the dark days after the battle of Cannae.

The Metelli and Scaurus

During this period the Caecilii Metelli appear to have been the dominant family; members held many consulships and gained military reputations. Thus Metellus Balearicus (p. 211) was censor in 119, an office held in 115 by his cousin C. Metellus, who had protected the northern frontier of Macedonia by defeating a Thracian tribe, the Scordisci, on the lower Save; he adopted the *cognomen* of Delmeticus. The Scordisci were again checked by C. Metellus Caprarius (112–111), while M. Metellus established order in Corsica and Sardinia (115–112). Linked with the Metelli was M. Aemilius Scaurus, who married the daughter of Delmeticus. He was a member of the *haute noblesse* who combined an appearance of old-fashioned *gravitas* with an open mind for political novelties. His policy was more particularly directed towards a good understanding with the Equestrian Order, to which he was probably bound by commercial ties; the Metelli too perhaps showed more sympathy to the Equites than to the Die-Hard senators.[4]

Gaius Marius

One of the clients of the Metelli was C. Marius, who came of a good municipal family from near the hill-town of Arpinum in Volscian country, whose citizens had received full Roman franchise in 188. After a distinguished military début at Numantia he was encouraged by the Metelli to try his chance of a political career at Rome, where he reached the tribunate in 119 and showed some independence by opposing a scheme to extend the corn-distribution, while at the same time he tried to check the intimidation of voters. This involved him in a quarrel with the Metelli, and he only just secured a praetorship for 115. Thereafter he may have interested himself in business, since he had Equestrian contacts. At some point (c. 111?) he made a useful link with a noble family by marrying a Julia, an aunt of Julius Caesar. A *novus homo* had to create a faction, since he was not born into one, and Marius sought political help wherever he could find it. Soon he was apparently reconciled to the Metelli, since he served as legate to Metellus Numidicus in Africa (p. 215).[5]

2. Affairs in the Eastern Mediterranean

For a little while the tension between the political orders was again relaxed. But in the closing years of the second century a series of military disasters gave rise to a fresh outburst of popular anger against the aristocracy and brought into the field against it Marius, an opponent more dangerous than either of the Gracchi.

No further interference with Egypt and Syria

In the eastern Mediterranean the Republic had for the time being no serious commitments. In Egypt and Syria the round of dynastic wars grew ever more fast and furious, but Roman intervention was neither invited nor offered. In Asia Minor the rich but narrow territory of Pontus was transformed into the centre of a Black Sea empire by the restless energy of Mithridates VI (120–63). Soon after his accession this ruler, half-Persian and half-Greek by descent, accepted a call for help from the Greek cities of the Crimea which could no longer resist the pressure of the Scythian and Sarmatian tribes in their hinterland, and he accomplished his work of rescue so thoroughly that he assumed control over the entire north coast of the Black Sea. Through these conquests he gathered the trade of that sea into his hands and acquired a valuable recruiting area. This sudden rise in Mithridates's power boded no good to Rome. At his accession the Senate had revoked the grant of the Phrygian borderland which it had made in 129 to his father (p. 166), thus sowing the seeds of a determined enmity.[6] But Mithridates, who knew how to bide his time, made no move in reply until he had consolidated his recent gains.

Mithridates VI of Pontus

At the end of the second century the pirates and slave-raiders of the eastern Mediterranean, whom the declining Rhodian navy could no longer hold in check (p. 165), began to conduct their operations on such a scale that the client-kings made protests to Rome. In 102 the Senate sent a detachment under the praetor M. Antonius to occupy some patrol stations on the coasts of Pamphylia and western Cilicia, where the corsairs had established their principal bases. This move was backed up later by the passing of a law to mobilise resources for a concerted drive against them, but not much apparently came of it (p. 612). Since the losses inflicted by these bandits fell mostly upon Greek merchantmen, while the gains from the slave trade (in which the pirates took a large hand) were shared by the owners of the Italian *latifundia*, the Roman government were content to impose upon the corsairs a certain discretion in the pursuit of their calling.[7]

Measures against piracy in the eastern Mediterranean

In 96 the territory of Cyrenaica, which the

*The king-
dom of
Cyrene is
bequeathed
to Rome*

childless King Ptolemy Apion had bequeathed to Rome (thus confirming the tentative bequest of his father Ptolemy VII – p. 167), became escheat to the Republic. The Senate promptly sent a quaestor to collect the revenues from the crown lands, but for twenty years it omitted to provide a governor and garrison for the country, so that the Greek cities of the coastland were left to arrange a makeshift administration for themselves. It was clearly determined to limit its administrative responsibilities.

3. The War against Jugurtha. The First Phase

*Numidia
after the
death of
Masinissa*

In North Africa the Romans had insured themselves against Carthage by fostering the growth of Numidia; after the destruction of that city they had left Masinissa's successor Micipsa in the enjoyment of all his father's dominions. The new ruler carried on Masinissa's policy of fostering agriculture in the coastal regions, and he made his capital, Cirta (modern Constantine), into a centre of the grain trade where Italian and Greek merchants took up their residence; but he abandoned his father's military ambitions, and he scarcely used his army except in support of the Roman expeditions in Spain and southern France (pp. 146, 210). Yet he laid the seeds of future trouble by an ill-judged attempt to put the monarchy into commission at his death. Unable to choose between his two sons, Adherbal and Hiempsal, and an adoptive child named Jugurtha, he made arrangements for a joint rule by the three brothers. In a state where no fixed laws of succession obtained and illegitimacy was not a serious bar, the wisest expedient would no doubt have been to select Jugurtha as sole ruler, for this prince had inherited a large measure of Masinissa's vigour and ability, and in the camp of Numantia, where he had served with distinction, he had ingratiated himself with many of the Roman nobles. Shortly after Micipsa's death in 118 Jugurtha got rid of Hiempsal, who had gone out of his way to pick a quarrel, by assassinating him, and he drove Adherbal out of his rightful portion. The fugitive came to Rome to plead his cause, and thus opened a 'Numidian question' which troubled the Republic for the next ten years (*c.* 116). The Senate decided upon a new territorial division between the two survivors, and a commission under L. Opimius arranged a partition by which Adherbal received the eastern and richer half of Numidia. On the face of it this was a fair compromise; but now that Jugurtha had tasted blood he could no longer

*Jugurtha
usurps the
regal power*

be restrained by a mere show of Roman authority. After an uneasy truce he resumed war against his brother and penned him up in his residence at Cirta (112). The defence of this city, which occupied a commanding site on a high tongue of land within a river-loop, was stiffened by a corps of Italian residents, who encouraged Adherbal to hold out, in confident expectation of succour from Rome. But the Senate, loth to engage the Roman armies in Africa at a time when several European frontiers were in danger (pp. 217ff.), took no further step than to send two successive embassies to remonstrate with Jugurtha. The Numidian prince played the envoys with evasive politeness until Cirta fell into his hands; had he but persevered in the policy of eluding rather than defying Roman authority, he might even yet have induced the Senate to acquiesce in his usurpation. But in the hour of victory he wreaked a savage vengeance on Adherbal, and his troops, perhaps getting out of hand, massacred the Italian residents. After this atrocity the Senate was constrained to overcome its hesitations, for fear that the Numidian affair should be taken out of its hands. The Roman proletariat, stirred up by a free-lance tribune-elect named C. Memmius, who hinted that a good many senators were in Jugurtha's pocket, was again becoming restive; and it may be assumed that the Equites, who had interests to protect and casualties to avenge in Africa, pressed for a more resolute policy. Jugurtha's apologies were therefore not even heard, and a punitive expedition was fitted out.

*Massacre of
Italians at
Cirta*

*The Senate
is forced to
make war
upon
Jugurtha*

In 111 the consul L. Calpurnius Bestia began the operations against Jugurtha with a vigorous incursion into Numidia, only to find that with his heavy infantry he could make no impression upon the nimble Numidian horsemen.[8] With a sudden change of mind he accepted an offer of negotiations from Jugurtha and granted him an armistice which appeared to save the face of the Republic while ridding it of a troublesome war. But this convention had the opposite effect of letting loose the storm which had been brewing at Rome since the massacre at Cirta. Returning to the charge Memmius induced the Tribal Assembly to vote a safe-conduct to Jugurtha, so that he might give king's evidence at Rome against the senators who were believed to have fingered his money. But the tribune's gesture turned out to be a false move. As soon as Jugurtha was presented to the Tribal Assembly and invited to give information, a colleague of Memmius interposed his veto, and the people accepted this way out of a course which threatened to involve the good name of Rome in an prece-

*Difficulties
of warfare
in Numidia*

*Abortive
peace
negotiations*

dented scandal. At this juncture Jugurtha might still have snatched a tolerable peace out of the fire, had he not capped Memmius's blunder by setting bravos on to a cousin and possible rival named Massiva, who had fled betimes from Numidia to Rome. By this new crime he irretrievably coiled a rope round his neck; though he was allowed to depart from Rome, which he is alleged to have dubbed as 'a city for sale', he had forfeited his last chance of a friendly accommodation. Among all classes in Rome it was now agreed that no terms short of unconditional surrender should be granted to him.

Failure of a new offensive

In 110 the consul Sp. Postumius Albinus, with a force of some 40,000 men, rushed into another offensive against Jugurtha, but accomplished even less than his predecessor. After an ineffectual wild-goose chase he returned to Rome on some constitutional pretext, leaving his troops in charge of his brother Aulus, who took it upon himself to resume operations in a winter campaign. The new commander's plan, which aimed at seizing Jugurtha's chief treasure-castle at Suthul (near Calama, on the table-land of northern Numidia), was in itself not ill conceived, for with the loss of his paychests the king would not be able to keep together his regular forces, which were indispensable as a stiffening element in his loosely compacted army. But after a vain attempt to carry Suthul by a *coup de main* he was tempted into another will-o'-the-wisp pursuit of the king in person. By this time the rigours of a winter campaign amid heavy rains had so undermined the discipline of his unseasoned army that Jugurtha was able to carry its encampment in a night attack and force it to surrender. Still hoping to compromise his dispute with the Republic the king spared the lives of the defeated legions, but he allowed himself the luxury of making them defile under a yoke of spears, in imitation of an obsolete Roman ceremony.

Capitulation of a Roman force

Popular indignation in Rome

The news of Aulus Albinus's fiasco raised another wave of indignation at Rome against the whole nobility. A successor of Memmius named C. Mamilius instituted by a law of the Tribal Assembly a special court to investigate recent cases of aristocratic corruption. Though the presidency of the court was confided to Aemilius Scaurus, who had been on Calpurnius's staff in Africa, the jurymen were derived from the Equestrian Order. Mamilius did not repeat the mistake of summoning Jugurtha, but without the king's prompting the court satisfied itself of the guilt of several leading senators. Though nothing is known of the fate of Aulus Albinus, his brother Spurius, Calpur-

Judicial proceedings against the nobles

nius Bestia and even Opimius were sent into exile. It is open to doubt whether any of these men had handled Jugurtha's money, for the conduct of all three can be explained without imputations of dishonesty. But with each decade the reputation of the ruling class for financial probity was wearing thinner, and the charges of bribery at Jugurtha's hands had been repeated so often that they came to be accepted as proven. Nevertheless, once the Senate's critics had made an example of corrupt practices, they were content to leave to that body the more difficult task of carrying on the war.[9]

4. The War against Jugurtha. Metellus and Marius

In 109 the African army was taken over by the consul Q. Caecilius Metellus, the nephew of Metellus Macedonicus. The new commander temporarily retrieved the reputation of the aristocracy for military proficiency. He accomplished the preliminary task of restoring discipline among the demoralised Roman troops so thoroughly that in the ensuing campaigns they fought with admirable steadiness and patiently executed forced marches in the torrid African summer. But since the best infantry could not bring Jugurtha's light horse to battle, Metellus resumed the policy of attacking the king's strongholds. He carried several fortified towns, including the capital city of Cirta,[10] and in the valley of the river Muthul he beat off a determined attempt by Jugurtha to surprise his marching columns. Towards the end of 108 after another engagement he reduced Jugurtha to an offer of submission. But he could not obtain the personal surrender of the king, who was too wary to put his head into the proffered noose; and a scheme to hoist Jugurtha on his own petard by suborning Numidian assassins against him met with no more success than it deserved. Eventually the Numidian king repaired his losses by hiring auxiliary troops from the Gaetulian tribes on his southern border, and by making alliance with Bocchus, the king of Mauretania (Morocco), whom he won over with an offer of territorial concessions.

Metellus gains successes over Jugurtha

but cannot drive him to surrender

By 108 public opinion at Rome, where the difficulties that beset Metellus were not properly understood, again became restive, and its impatience was now exploited by a less petulant and more calculating agitator than Memmius or Mamilius, namely C. Marius, whom Metellus had appointed as one of his deputy-generals in Africa. His services in the Jugurthan War, and a stray prophecy by a seer at Utica, kindled

Popular feeling is stirred up by Marius

Marius receives the command against Jugurtha from the Comitia

his hopes of a consulship and an independent command. In 108 he extorted leave from Metellus to sue for the consulship at Rome, but not without a sharp struggle. On his arrival in the city Marius did not scruple to foment the prevalent irritation against the nobles or to belittle his own chief. In quick succession the Comitia Centuriata elected him consul, and the Tribal assembly, overriding a resolution of the Senate to prolong Metellus's proconsulship for a further year, appointed him to take command on the African front. This encroachment by the people upon the Senate's traditional right of military patronage was no doubt intended as a mere gesture of impatience; yet it created a dangerous precedent, and in the event proved an important step towards the overthrow of the Senate's authority. Another change in established military usage was made by Marius in preparation for next year's campaign. Conscription and the levies had become increasingly unpopular: although the length of compulsory service may have been reduced from an earlier twenty

Marius's recruits

campaigns, a peasant who had to leave his farm for only six years abroad would often return to face ruin unless compensated by sufficient booty and donatives – and these depended largely on whether he served in a rich or a poor country. To meet the need for men the State had to some extent modified the qualification for enlistment, which had normally been limited to members of the five classes: the minimum census qualification had been lowered (possibly in 214 and *c.* 171). This meant that poorer men could be called up, and at the time of crisis even *proletarii* (men below the five *classes*) had been enrolled. Marius, however, went much further and enrolled *proletarii* as volunteers on a large scale, thus establishing as a normal practice what had hitherto been very exceptional. The far-reaching effect of this makeshift expedient may not have been fully realised by Marius himself at the time, but it was to become ever more apparent: the legions increasingly contained more *proletarii* (conscription kept up their numbers where voluntary enlistment failed) and these men looked to their generals for support after their period of service.[11]

Marius's first task in Africa – the training of this new type of recruit to the high standard of a Roman legionary – was accomplished by him with signal success. Though he made the most rigorous demands on the fortitude of the troops, he tempered his severity with a rough *bonhomie* which seldom failed in its appeal to Italian soldiers. The promises which he had lavished at Rome, that he would make a speedy

Marius's victories over Jugurtha

end of the war, were soon proved to be delusive: indeed his strategy was merely that of Metellus on a bigger scale. But with larger forces at his disposal he was able to penetrate Numidia more thoroughly. In 107 he cut through to Jugurtha's southernmost stronghold at Capsa and destroyed it. In the following year he continued systematically to reduce other Numidian fortresses and made a bold advance to the river Muluccha, full 600 miles to the west of the Roman province; there he captured the king's chief treasure-house, an achievement comparable with Scipio Africanus's storming of New Carthage. This last success compelled the Numidian king and his Mauretanian ally to stake their last chance on pitched battles. During Marius's retreat from the Muluccha they twice delivered a desperate assault upon his marching columns, and at the second encounter (near Cirta) they all but overwhelmed

21.1 Reverse of a *denarius,* minted by Faustus Sulla, the dictator's son, *c.* 56 B.C., depicting Bocchus kneeling before Sulla.

the Roman army; yet on both occasions they were eventually driven off with heavy loss.

The exemplary steadiness of the Roman troops in these engagements virtually decided the Jugurthan War. Bocchus, who had previously received overtures from Metellus and had played with the idea of changing sides, now made up his mind that the Romans were the winners and opened underhand negotiations. Marius, who knew that his bluntness of speech disqualified him as a diplomat, left the bargaining in the hands of his quaestor L. Cornelius Sulla, a member of an impoverished patrician family who had shown promise as a soldier in the recent battle. Sulla conducted the discussions with admirable tact and sangfroid. At the risk of driving Bocchus back into alliance with Jugurtha, and of himself being delivered to the Numidian king, Sulla declared that Bocchus could only earn the friendship of the Republic by an act of perfidy towards his partner, by handing over Jugurtha to Roman custody.[12] After long parleys Bocchus

Surrender of Jugurtha by Bocchus to Cornelius Sulla

overcame his hesitations and obediently kidnapped Jugurtha, who was brought to Rome to
be executed in 104 like any common criminal.
As a recompense for his treachery Bocchus
received from the Senate a large slice of
Jugurtha's dominions; the eastern portion of
Numidia was made over to a half-brother of the
late king named Gauda, an insignificant person
who kept his realm free from further adventures. The province of Africa remained, as
before, a narrow enclave in Numidian territory;
the Roman treasury collected no indemnity,
and the only gain from the war accrued to the
Equites, who were able to resume their trade
in Africa without further molestation.

Political importance of the Jugurthan War

The Jugurthan War was one that could
probably have been avoided altogether by a
firm display of Roman power at the outset, or
could have been brought to an early, lasting
settlement by accepting Jugurtha's capitulation
after the first campaign. The hesitancies of the
Optimates, and the clamour of the Populares
for Jugurtha's head, saddled the Roman army
with a burdensome war of a 'colonial' type.
The difficulties of the African expedition were
increased by the strange negligence of the
Roman commanders in not providing themselves with an adequate mounted force – it was
not until 106 that any considerable body of
horse was recruited by them (it was led by
Sulla). The eventual success of the Roman
forces was a handsome testimonial to the
versatility of the legions, which once again
proved that under competent leaders they
could be trained to almost any military task.
But the chief significance of the Numidian War
lay not so much in its military aspects as in its
reactions upon the political situation at Rome.
Although the Populares showed no greater
understanding of the Jugurthan problem than
the nobles, and merely used it as a stick to
beat the Optimates, their leader gained the
credit for its final solution, and his victory
raised him to a quasi-dictatorial position in the
capital.

5. The Invasion of the Northmen

The impatience of the Roman public at the
slow progress of the Jugurthan War was partly
due to tidings of a new danger on the northern
frontiers of the Empire. Towards the end of
second century central and western Europe
were thrown into temporary confusion by the
migrations of two tribes, the Cimbri and Teutones, who had been driven out of their homes
in Jutland and Frisia by inroads of the sea, like
those which changed the face of Holland in

Migrations of the Cimbri and Teutones

the twelfth and thirteenth centuries.[13] After
long years of wandering along the Elbe and
Danube, the Cimbri and Teutones were deflec-
ted by the resistance of the Balkan populations
towards the Italian borderland. In 113 they fell
in with a Roman force under the consul Cn.
Papirius Carbo, who had been sent to bar their
further advance. Unwilling as yet to measure
their strength against Rome the Northmen
gave an undertaking to fall back from the
Italian frontier; nevertheless they were
attacked by Carbo, who anticipated an easy
triumph over a multitude encumbered with a
large baggage-train. The Cimbri and Teutones
beat off his assault at Noreia (near Ljubljana),
but they did not resume their march towards
Italy. Like the Germans who eventually destroyed the Roman Empire in western Europe,
they were half frightened at their victory over
a giant whom they had for this once caught
napping, but could hardly hope to resist when
he was fully awakened. After a four years' trek
round the northern outskirts of the Alps they
invaded eastern France, bringing with them
reinforcements from the Tigurini and other
Celtic tribes in Switzerland or southern
Germany.[14] Near the borders of Gallia Narbonensis they encountered a second Roman
army under the consul M. Iunius Silanus. Still
distrusting their chances in battle they made
a request for land within the Roman borders
and an offer of mercenary service under the
Roman standards (109). Such terms, presented
to Roman emperors of another age often met
with glad acceptance; but the Senate, to whom
the application of the Northmen was referred,
disdained their assistance. By way of proving
their military worth the Cimbri and Teutones
attacked Silanus and broke his army at the
first onset.[15] For a second time they did not
press on in pursuit; but the Tigurini, detaching themselves from the main body, raided the
Roman territory on the west bank of the
Rhône, and caused a rebellion among the
Volcae Tectosages (in the Languedoc). In 107
another consul, L. Cassius Longinus, allowed
himself to be lured by the Tigurini into
Gascony and to be killed in an ambuscade;[16]
his lieutenant, C. Popillius Laenas, was
released only on condition of his men being
passed under the yoke. In the following year
the voluntary retreat of the Tigurini from the
Roman province gave the consul Q. Servilius
Caepio the opportunity of reducing the Tectosages and of looting their chief sanctuary at
Tolosa. The treasure appropriated — later
rumour estimated it at the fantastic sum of
100,000 lb. of gold and 110,000 lb. of silver
— disappeared mysteriously on the way to

Indecisive successes over Roman frontier corps

Campaigns in southern Gaul

217

Rome, so that Caepio came under suspicion of having embezzled it.

After two years of roving in central France the Northmen returned with further reinforcements and now hesitated no longer to overstep the Roman boundary. The Senate took this invasion with due seriousness. With the end of the Jugurthan War in sight it ordered a large fresh levy and sent the consul Cn. Mallius Maximus with these new drafts to join hands with Caepio. Before such a concentration of forces the Cimbri and Teutones stayed their advance and made fresh overtures for an amicable concession of land, which was again refused. But Mallius, a *novus homo* like Marius, was entirely lacking in Marius's self-assurance. He failed to maintain discipline among his men, who converted their camp into a bazaar, and although as consul he was the superior of the proconsul Caepio, he could not prevail upon his subordinate to obey orders. Caepio condescended to rejoin Mallius on the left bank of the Rhône, but he refused to co-operate loyally with the consul, so that the invaders, giving battle near Arausio (modern Orange), were able to hurl back the Roman forces, section by section, against the river. Though we need not accept the estimate of 80,000 Roman casualties in this engagement, undoubtedly this was the most disastrous Roman defeat since Cannae.

Battle of Arausio

The way to Italy now stood clear to the Northmen; but the prestige of Rome still overawed them. The Teutones resumed their travels in Gaul, while the Cimbri moved off to try their fortunes in Spain, thus giving the Republic a respite of three years to prepare for the final trial of strength. During this interval Marius, whom the people appointed to the command on the northern front immediately after his return from Africa, electing him consul five times (104–100), trained another proletarian army. By way of inuring his troops to the hardships of war he imposed upon them a fatigue-task that foreshadowed the great public works of the imperial army, the excavation of a canal as a by-pass to the silted Rhône estuary.[17]

The Northmen fail to follow up their victory

In 102 the Northmen, after some rough handling by the Celtiberians of Spain and the Belgae of northern Gaul, reunited for a conclusive attack upon the Romans. With belated audacity they may have planned a converging advance upon Italy on three fronts; at any rate Rome had to face a threefold attack.[18] While the Teutones proceeded by the direct route through southern France, the Cimbri retraced their steps along the northern edge of the Alps in order to enter Italy by the valley of the Adige, and the Tigurini, fetching a still wider compass, proposed to invade Venetia by way of the Julian

The Northmen plan an invasion of Italy

Alps. These dispositions threw the brunt of the Northmen's assault in 102 upon the main Roman army under Marius's personal command in the Rhône valley. For the greater part of the year Marius allowed the campaign to drag on, so as to harden his own troops and take full measure of the enemy; but once he saw his way clear he struck with the boldness of a Scipio. Leaving the Teutones to defile past him towards the coastal road he overtook them again by a side-road and engaged them on a site near Aquae Sextiae (modern Aix), where a narrowing valley would give a defeated army no room for retreat. Of the battle of Aquae Sextiae no satisfactory account survives.[19] But it is clear that Marius invited the Teutones in Hannibalic fashion to attack him until the moment came for launching a reserve force on to their rear. Hardly an enemy escaped from the rout, so that Marius's soldiers made a haul of prisoners exceeding all previous captures.

Battle of Aquae Sextiae

While Marius was lying in wait for the Teutones in France, the defence of Italy was committed to Q. Lutatius Catulus, a nobleman more versed in letters than in warfare. Catulus took up a position in the narrow valley of the upper Adige which left him with a difficult line of retreat. At the sight of Cimbric detachments escalading the surrounding mountains in order to work round his flanks he hurriedly withdrew his wavering troops to the south bank of the Po. Fortunately the invaders, intent on enjoying the harvests and vintages of the rich sub-Alpine plains, made no serious attempt to cross that river or to capture the neighbouring cities. Once more, therefore, Marius was given time to retrieve the Roman losses. In 101 he joined hands with Catulus, bringing the combined Roman forces to a total of 55,000 men. As in the previous season, he held his hand a long while before he struck, so that the midsummer heat of Lombardy might sap the vigour of the Northmen. Eventually he met them on the open site of the Campi Raudii, near Vercellae. This encounter appears to have been a soldiers' action, in which the Roman troops outstayed the enemy, as in the battles of old against the Gauls, and ended the day in a slaughter and slave-haul rivalling that of Aquae Sextiae.[20] In the same year Cornelius Sulla drove off the Tigurini in the eastern Alps. Thus the northern peril dissolved as if by magic.

Battle of Vercellae

The terror inspired by the Cimbri and Teutones caused ancient writers to exaggerate their numbers and their military prowess. In the course of their long wanderings they had continually improved their discipline and equipment, but they always remained slow in their movements, and if they failed to carry a battle at the first onset they ceased to be formidable. They were scarcely a match for their Celtic and Spanish adversaries, and their repeated victories over Roman forces showed up the urgent need for reform in the Roman military system. But if Marius's final triumphs somewhat flattered his reputation as a tactician they revealed in the clearest light his talent as an organiser of victory. In throwing open the *Voluntary* legions to proletarians on terms of voluntary *enlistment* enlistment, and training his recruits up to the standard of regular soldiers, Marius took the decisive step in converting the Roman army *Marius's* from a conscript militia into a standing force *army* of professional warriors. The Roman legion of *reforms* the first century differed from its predecessors in its equipment and organisation. All ranks alike were armed with pilum and sword,[21] the division into three lines of *hastati, principes* and *triarii* was abolished, and for tactical purposes the maniple was superseded by the cohort, ten to a legion, which was standardised at 6000 men. A good stiffening was given to the ranks by the presence of sixty centurions in each legion. The new-style legionaries were highly trained duellists, whose technique in cut-and-thrust was modelled on that of the gladiatorial schools, and they developed an *esprit de corps* which was foreign to the old-time militia; this regimental loyalty was symbolised in the legionary standard, a silver eagle. Further, Marius made the army more mobile by making the men carry their own entrenching-tools and other equipment; as a result they became known as 'Marius' mules' (*muli Mariani*), but they were less dependent on the baggage-train and could construct their temporary marching-camps at speed. By these reforms Marius not only won his own victories, but prepared for those of his more famous successors.

The migrations of the Cimbri and Teutones caused a temporary unsettlement on other European fronts. In the Balkans the Scordisci (in modern Yugoslavia), who had stayed the advance of the Northmen down the Danube, were emboldened to make incursions on their own account into Roman territory, as we have seen (p. 213). In 114 they inflicted a severe defeat *Minor* upon the consul C. Porcius Cato and carried *campaigns* their raids as far as Delphi. The consuls of 113 *in the* and 112, Metellus Caprarius and M. Livius *Balkans* Drusus (the former antagonist of Gaius Gracchus), drove the invaders back upon the Danube, but it was not until 101 that the praetor T. Didius restored a durable peace in the Balkan lands.

and in Spain In Spain the successful defence of the Celtiberians against the Cimbri similarly encouraged them to try conclusions once more with the Romans, and the Lusitanians again took the field in concert with them. Of the campaigns in Spain little is known, except that T. Didius earned a second triumph by reducing the Celtiberians (93), and that P. Licinius Crassus, after traversing Lusitania from end to end, occupied the harbour of Brigantium (modern Corunna) in the north-west of Spain.[22]

Lastly, the concentration of Roman troops on the northern frontiers gave another opportunity for a servile rebellion in Sicily. In this *A second* province the larger estates had of recent years *servile war* been partly restocked with free men kidnapped *in Sicily* and reduced to slavery by the pirates of the eastern Mediterranean. In 104 a decree of the Senate called upon all provincial governors to make search for persons thus detained and to restore them to freedom; but in Sicily the influence of the slave-owners had prevented its effective enforcement. The kidnapped men thereupon took their cause into their own hands, and carried with them the rest of the slaves (103). The revolt was headed by two leaders, a Cilician named Athenion and one Salvius, who took the high command with the insignia of a Roman magistrate and called himself King Tryphon. These chieftains organised the rising in the same methodical manner as Eunus and Cleon in the previous outbreak (p. 204), and for three years the Roman governors were left with insufficient troops to make definite headway against them. In 101, however the arrival of Marius's lieutenant, M'. Aquilius, with a detachment of the army from Aquae Sextiae brought the war to a close.

6. Saturninus and Marius's Sixth Consulship

In Rome the Northern Peril again set in motion *Popular* those forces of oppostion to the senatorial aristo- *anger at the* cracy which the Jugurthan War had evoked. In *defeats by* 106 the consul Q. Servilius Caepio, in an *the Cimbri* endeavour to make capital out of a revulsion of sentiment following the excesses of the Mamilian commission (p. 215), carried a bill by which some control of the court *de rebus repetundis* was handed back to senators: all courts were now probably to be empanelled from both Equites and senators.[23] But Caepio had missed his tide. In the same year a new current of hostility to the Senate set in, because of the failure of its representatives in the Cimbric Wars. The passing of a Roman army under the yoke at the hands of the Tigurini (p. 217) so inflamed public opinion that an impeachment for *perduellio* (treason) which a tribune directed against Popillius, the officer responsible for the capitulation, ended in a vote of condemnation by the Tribal Assembly. In 105 the news of the disaster of

Marius reappointed general

Arausio raised up a storm which took five years to blow itself out. In this and the four ensuing years the Comitia Centuriata re-elected Marius to five successive consulships without asking the Senate to suspend the *lex Villia* (p. 181), which declared such a practice illegal, or inviting it to prolong Marius's office by *prorogatio*; and the Tribal Assembly, taking yet another senatorial privilege into its hands, appointed him commander on the northern front, as it had previously nominated him to take charge of the war in Africa.

In 104 a tribune named Cn. Domitius, who had failed to secure co-optation to the college of augurs through the opposition of Aemilius Scaurus, prosecuted the Grand Old Man on the charge of contravening the augural ritual. In this obviously vindictive accusation he met with no success; but he carried a bill by which the right of co-optation by the various priestly colleges was reduced to a mere *congé d'élire*, and the effective choice of new members was transferred to a special popular assembly of seventeen tribes selected by lot.

Further judicial proceedings

The main impact of the people's anger, however, was borne by Servilius Caepio, who was rightly singled out as the person chiefly responsible for the catastrophe of Arausio. The Tribal Assembly interfered to deprive him of his proconsulship, and a tribune named Cn. Servilius Glaucia made a side-attack upon him by procuring the repeal of his recent judiciary law and handing the court *de rebus repetundis* back to the sole charge of the Equestrian Order.[24] The unfortunate Caepio managed to escape serious penalty at the hands of a special inquiry concerned with the disappearance of the Tolosan gold (pp. 217f.), but in 103 he was condemned for Arausio by the people, while his colleague Mallius was exiled by a plebiscite.[25]

Saturninus

Behind these prosecutions was a tribune named L. Appuleius Saturninus. This personage, appointed *quaestor Ostiensis* in the previous year, when the slave-war in Sicily was causing a shortage of grain in Rome, had been relieved of his functions by a senatorial decree which transferred the control of corn-transport to the more experienced hands of Aemilius Scaurus. To avenge what he considered a personal slight Saturninus sought election to the tribunate of 103 and became the greatest popular agitator since Gaius Gracchus, though his eloquence appealed to the eye rather than to the ear. Because the charge of *perduellio* – hostility to the State – was not particularly suitable for offences such as Caepio and Mallius had allegedly been guilty of (namely, military negligence leading to defeat), Saturninus therefore established a new permanent court (*quaestio*) to deal with the

His law de maiestate

new crime 'derogation to the majesty of Rome' (*maiestas populi Romani imminuta*). The charge of *maiestas* was in itself a criminally vague indictment, under cover of which any unpopular person might be brought to court. In subsequent impeachments it was habitually misused as a makeweight or a substitute for more definite indictments.[26]

In two further measures Saturninus revealed himself as a social reformer of the Gracchan type. He reintroduced Gaius's system of monthly corn-distributions at the same moderate price[27] – an expedient which in times of scarcity at least had not a little to commend it. To provide for those of Marius's soldiers who had a claim to a pension after the Jugurthan War he carried a bill that conferred upon them capacious allotments of 60 acres apiece in the province of Africa. But Saturninus's legislation was less remarkable for its objects than for the systematic violence which he applied in order to force it through. After a first successful venture in turning a mob upon a colleague who had vetoed his allotment-law, he made habitual use of knuckles and sticks and stones in political battles. It 102 he defeated an attempt by the censor Metellus Numidicus to remove him from the Senate by setting the rough elements of the city population upon him; in the next year he called upon the riffraff to break up the Tribal Assembly, before which he was being accused of having insulted the envoys of King Mithridates (p. 230). In the same year he facilitated his own re-election to the tribunate by hiring bravos to murder one of his competitors.

Saturninus's recourse to mob-violence

In his second tribunate Saturninus again lent his services to Marius. After his victory over the Northmen Marius enjoyed a personal ascendancy such as no Roman had exercised since the days of Scipio Africanus. Had he now set himself to create a New Model state to match his New Model army he could without doubt have carried a larger programme of reform than either of the Gracchi. But Marius was as devoid of political ideas as Africanus, and the self-assurance which never deserted him on the battlefield failed him disastrously in the Senate-house. His main thought on his return to Rome was to find land for his discharged soldiers and he left it to Saturninus to carry the necessary legislation. In 100 B.C. Saturninus brought forward a bill to provide allotments for the veterans on land in southern France which the natives were deemed to have forfeited by not defending it against the Cimbri; another bill authorised the foundation of colonies in Sicily, Achaea and Macedonia.[28] Whether an attempt was made to provide a military command for Marius against the pirates must remain uncertain.[29] In anticipa-

Marius enlists Saturninus to procure pensions for his soldiers

tion of a senatorial counter-attack Saturninus appended to his agrarian bill an oath of obedience to its terms which every senator was obliged to swear on pain of exile.[30] By this device he disarmed senatorial opposition for the time being; but he met with resistance from another quarter. In the colonial law provision had been made for allotments to Latins and Italians (who had contributed their full share to Marius's victories), and for the conferment of full Roman franchise upon a select number of them.[31] These entirely equitable clauses had the effect of bringing back the urban proletariat to the side of the nobles, so that the very ruffians who had formerly lent their fists to Saturninus now used them against him, and it required all the assistance which the tribune could derive from the expectant veterans to defeat the town mob in a battle fought in the Forum with legs of chairs and tables.

Saturninus carries his measures by force

After this excusable display of force Saturninus again stooped to assassination for personal ends. In order to rid his confederate Servilius Glaucia, who although praetor was illegally suing for the consulship of 99, of an inconvenient competitor, he procured the death of the ex-tribune C. Memmius by means of a band of bravos. By this wanton act he forfeited his alliance with Marius, whose soldierly sense of discipline asserted itself against mere murder. Observing their estrangement the Senate was emboldened to renew its declaration of emergency by-passing the *senatus consultum ultimum*, and to summon Marius to exercise his consular powers for the safety of the State. In obedience to this call Marius penned up Saturninus with an improvised force on the Capitoline hill and drove him to capitulate. Before the Senate could decide on the tribune's fate an angry crowd broke into his place of custody and claimed him as the next victim of mob law; with him perished Glaucia and several other agitators.

Saturninus breaks with Marius, and is suppressed by him

In using Marius to rid them of Saturninus the nobles simultaneously reduced him to a state of paralysis. Unable to take a new line of action for himself, he looked on helpless while the Senate perhaps declared Saturninus's legislation

The Senate regains control

null and void in whole or part, on the valid ground of its having been carried by violence.[32] To hide his confusion Marius quitted Italy for the East after a time (98), leaving the Senate once more in full possession of the political field.[33]

At first sight Saturninus appears as a very inferior imitator of the Gracchi; yet he wielded a weapon which in more steady hands was destined to play a decisive part in the overthrow of the senatorial aristocracy. In the riots of 100 B.C. the most ominous feature was the intervention of Marius's soldiers. This incident revealed that the new army, which had proved itself the saviour of the Republic, might in turn become its destroyer. Composed mainly of proletarians without a stake in the country, and serving continuously with the colours for long terms of years, it gave its loyalty to the officer who enlisted and led it rather than to the Senate and people. Luckily for them when the crisis came Marius hesitated. Whether from lack of political ability or ambition, or from an innate respect for law and order, he made no serious attempt to use his troops as a means to a personal domination. Future army commanders were to prove more ambitious and less scrupulous. The collision between Marius and the Senate over the provision of land-grants for his veterans also raised in an acute form the question of pay and pensions for the new army. Had the nobles promptly acknowledged the professional soldier's claim to an assured livelihood and bound him to themselves by the nexus of cash and land-allotments, they might have retained their hold on the Roman army. In relinquishing to the generals the duty of making material provision for their troops the Senate in effect played into the generals' hands, and brought nearer the day on which Roman commanders would use their forces as if they were private armies. Moreover, now that the Tribal Assembly was usurping the Senate's previous sole right of making military appointments, the latter lost its surest guarantee of the generals' loyalty to it. In the last decade of the second century the nobility lost more ground than in the age of the Gracchi.

Political importance of the new professional army

The Senate fails to secure control of the professional army

CHAPTER 22

The Italian Wars, 91–83 B.C.

1. The Tribunate of Livius Drusus

Agitation for the franchise

The stormy opening of the first century B.C. was followed by an interval of calm, or rather of stagnation, in which the senatorial aristocracy let its new lease of power run itself out without any serious attempt to set its house in order. The only notable reform of this period was a resolution passed by the Senate in 97 against human sacrifices, by which it strengthened its hands against a recurrence of popular outcries such as that of 114 (p. 213). While the government was taking its siesta a crisis which had been gathering in the last thirty years came upon it unawares. The demand of the Italian allies for the Roman franchise, which the Senate had eluded but by no means silenced in the days of Fulvius Flaccus and Gaius Gracchus, was raised again in a more menacing tone. In the Jugurthan and Cimbric Wars the allies had contributed their full share to the Roman victories, and the career of Marius, who came from an obscure country town – albeit from one which happened to have been raised to full Roman status – showed once for all that Italians were no less fit to exercise high command than Romans in the narrow sense. In 100 their expectations had been raised by Saturninus's colonial act (p. 220), and large numbers of Italian stalwarts had flocked to Rome to clamour or to scuffle on behalf of this measure. But Saturninus's law was allowed to lapse, and those of his followers who stayed on in the capital to continue the campaign of intimidation were condemned under a law brought forward in 95 by the consuls L. Licinius Crassus and Q. Mucius Scaevola, which set up a *quaestio* on aliens who were claiming to be citizens. This measure com- mended itself even to the more conciliatory among the senators (including the two consuls who gave their name to it) as a justifiable precaution against renewed rioting, but coming at this juncture it could only add fuel to the flames of discontent.

Reform programme of the younger Livius Drusus

In 91 an eleventh-hour attempt to forestall the coming rebellion was made by a nobleman named M. Livius Drusus, a son of Gaius Gracchus's former antagonist, who held a tribunate in that year. The younger Drusus was spiritually a descendant of Tiberius Gracchus rather than of his adroit and opportunist father. Though an avowed supporter of senatorial government he was thoroughly in earnest about reforms which to his mind had become urgent. In hopes of inducing the Popular Assembly to swallow an unpalatable powder Drusus began by offering it a few spoonfuls of jam. In the first place he revived his father's colonial law and sponsored a corn-law. To meet the costs of these measures he brought forward a third bill for the debasement of the silver coinage with an eighth part of copper, but this proved abortive.[1] Drusus then turned to his real programme of reform. Of his two major measures the first to be promulgated was the outcome of a recent judicial scandal in the court *de rebus repetundis*. In 92 an equestrian jury had pronounced an ex-consul named P. Rutilius Rufus guilty of extortion in the province of Asia. Having previously rendered valuable service to Marius in the training of his new armies Rutilius had recently aided the proconsul of Asia, Q. Mucius Scaevola, in drawing up a model edict, and had proceeded with unflinching severity against the agents of the Roman tax-farming companies, who were recklessly abusing the powers placed into their hands by Gaius Gracchus (p. 208). In defence of their profits the *publicani* prevailed upon the Equestrian Order to make an example of model governors, and Rutilius, being a *novus homo* and lacking powerful connexions, was selected as the scapegoat. The condemnation of Rutilius was rendered all the more sensational by the uncompromising dignity of his defence, which came to be compared with that of Socrates, and by the acclamations of his alleged victims in the province of Asia, where he went to spend his exile as an honoured guest. His case gave definite proof that Gaius Gracchus's reform of the court *de rebus repetundis* had been a change for the worse: instead of guilty men being acquitted, innocent men were being punished.

Abuse of judicial power by the Equites

To prevent a recurrence of either of these abuses Drusus devised an ingenious compromise by which control of the court was either shared between senators and Equites or 300 Equites were to be enrolled into the Senate which would then provide the *iudices*.[2] If Drusus's proposal was the latter scheme, it was even more a reform of the Senate than of the court for extortion. It proposed to draft into that body a class of men of abundant personal ability and enterprise – qualities in which the governing aristocracy was becoming dangerously deficient – while it imposed upon them a much-needed sense of responsibility. Nevertheless Drusus's bill met with a chilly reception on all sides. The Equites were more angered by the certainty of lessened gains than allured by the chance of seats in the Senate. Among the senators there probably were not a few individuals who had an indirect interest in the financial speculations of the Equites, and the nobility as a whole was loth to buy back its judicial privileges at the price of a heavy dilution with new peers. In order to secure the passage of the measure Drusus had to fall back upon the methods of Saturninus and to sweep away his opponents by force. After this dubious success Drusus produced his most important project, which aimed at nothing less than the conferment of full Roman franchise upon the Italian allies. But the mere promulgation of this bill sufficed to revive the bloc which had previously defeated Gaius Gracchus. Senators and Equites closed their ranks in opposition, and the urban voters rallied to their side. Moreover Drusus had been gravely compromised by the precipitancy of some of his Italian supporters. 'Committees of Action' were being set up in various allied towns, and a Marsian chieftain named Q. Poppaedius Silo actually started out for Rome with an armed force, though on second thoughts he was induced to turn back. That Drusus should have

Drusus's judiciary legislation

Rescinding of his law

His association with Italian agitators

countenanced this premature coup is hardly credible: indeed he gave warning to the consul L. Marcius Philippus, who had throughout been his most persistent opponent, of a plot for his assassination. None the less Philippus affected to believe in Drusus's complicity with Poppaedius, and the fact that this chieftain had been his guest-friend gave colour to this supposition; and it is probably no injustice to Drusus to assume that a large posse of Italians was numbered among his supporters who had employed force on behalf of his judicial bill. In this highly charged atmosphere Philippus procured from the Senate a declaration that the laws already carried by Drusus were null and void on the ground of unconstitutional procedure.[3] By means of this pronouncement he virtually killed the franchise bill before it was put to vote. But some over-zealous supporter of the consul marred his victory, as Scipio Nasica had spoilt the success of the Optimates against Tiberius Gracchus, by taking Drusus's life with a poniard. As a further measure of insurance against fresh franchise acts a tribune named Q. Varius carried a bill for the trial of persons suspected of collusion with the Italians before a special court of equestrian jurors. Though Aemilius Scaurus, who was summoned before this commission, browbeat his prosecutor with a few proud words in the manner of Scipio Africanus, several lesser senators were driven by it into exile. But a recoil, like that which sent the authors of the Jacobin Terror to the guillotine, presently made Varius into a victim of his own law.[4] The attempt of the Equites to make party capital out of Drusus's downfall soon fell into abeyance, for all classes at Rome were now called upon to close the ranks against a peril such as the republic had not faced since the Hannibalic War.

Assassination of Drusus

2. The Rebel Italian Confederacy

While the Varian commission carried on its vendetta against the partisans of Drusus, the Italian Committees of Action, abandoning the hope of amicable concessions, were organising a war-coalition to extort the franchise by force. A Roman delegation which the Senate appointed to visit the chief centres of disaffection and, if possible, to appease the allies, had the opposite effect of precipitating hostilities. In the Picenian city of Asculum a Roman agent, named C. Servilius, so provoked the townsmen with his ill-timed threats and scoldings that they replied with a massacre of all resident Romans. This outrage wrecked in advance a final attempt by a deputation of allies to reach an accommodation with the Senate. In the winter of 91–90 both sides made open preparations for war.[5]

The Italian malcontents prepare for war

Outbreak at Asculum

The rebel Italian confederacy

At the outbreak of hostilities in 90 the rebel coalition hardly extended beyond the mountain-cantons of the central and southern Apennines and the central strip of the Adriatic coastland. The core of the confederacy consisted of the Vestini, Picentes, Marrucini and Frentani along the Adriatic seaboard, the Marsi and Paeligni in the central Apennine massif, the Samnites, Hirpini and Lucanians in the southern highlands. The revolt never spread to northern Italy, and it scarcely touched Etruria and Umbria. Latium and the Greek cities of the coastland held by the Romans throughout, and for the time being the Apulians and the Campanians stood in with them. Within the insurgent area there also remained loyal enclaves, where the inhabitants were bound by economic ties to Rome, or the local aristocracies stood in a relation of clientship to the ruling families of the capital.

22.1 Coin issued by the Italian allies in the Italian War, showing their representatives swearing an oath of mutual loyalty round a standard.

Its organisation

But if the rebellion remained restricted to the poorer mountain land of the peninsula, it was supported by some of its best fighting stocks. The insurgent battalions were stiffened with veterans from Marius's armies and were officered by leaders who had been *praefecti* of the auxiliary contingents. Further, the rebel cantons achieved a greater measure of co-operation than might have been considered feasible in view of their previous lack of political intercourse. They combined to constitute a secessionist confederation, whose seat of government was established at Corfinium, the chief place of the Paeligni, which formed a natural centre of communications within the insurgent area. To this meeting-place (which they renamed 'Italia') the constituent peoples sent 500 delegates to form a federal senate. While each of the twelve cantons (*populi*) selected its divisional leader the senate appointed the two commanders-in-chief; and the same body (or an inner committee) controlled the levying of troops and of financial

aids.[6] The confederate government, it is true, was not able to concert a complete unity of war-aims. Within the insurgent area the more northerly tribes, which had by now adopted Latin as their official tongue, fought consistently for the attainment of the Roman franchise. The Samnites, on the other hand, who still retained their Oscan dialect, eventually enlarged their objectives and aimed at nothing less than complete independence.[7] Nevertheless the Italian senate contrived to place some 100,000 men into the field and to find money and supplies for them. Since none of the mountain-cantons could have possessed any large stocks of funded wealth, the success of the confederacy in financing a war on such a scale was a very notable achievement.

The rebel field forces

At Rome the Senate was given a free hand to direct operations without intereference from

22.2 Coin of the Italian Confederacy, showing the Italian bull oring the Roman wolf. Inscription in Oscan letters: Vitelliu = Italia.

the Tribal Assembly, and it showed no lack of energy in its counter-measures. It supplemented the levies of citizens and loyal allies with auxiliary corps of Gauls (probably for the most part from Transpadane Italy), of Spaniards and Numidians and it enrolled ex-slaves for patrol service at sea. By these means it raised at least fifteen legions and a total force of some 150,000 men. But it allowed political considerations to dictate its choice of generals. It withheld the high command from Marius, and in order to make this refusal appear the more plausible it similarly disappointed two other winners of previous wars, P. Licinius Crassus and T. Didius. These three veterans, together with seven other officers of less distinction, were attached as *legati* to the two consuls, L. Iulius Caesar and P. Rutilius Lupus, to whom the supreme control of the Roman troops was entrusted, although neither of them had sufficient military experience for such a task.

Roman counter-preparations

3. The Italian War

The surprisingly scanty records of the Italian War do not provide us with sufficient material to piece together a coherent account of its operations.[8] In general, its course ran like that of the American Civil War of 1861–5. The Confederates, being more fully prepared and served by more capable generals at the outset, had the better of the early exchanges, but were unable to inflict any crippling blow upon their opponents, whose superior resources told with increasing force in the later stages of the conflict. Like other wars between former allies, it was waged with much bitterness, and the slaughter was disproportionately heavy.

General character of the Italian war

In 90 the Confederates, catching the Romans not more than half-prepared, maintained the initiative over the greater part of the field. But whether they mistrusted their own strength, or counted on intimidating rather than overwhelming their opponents, they did not play for a quick decision, but adopted a strategy of exhaustion. Instead of rapidly concentrating forces at Corfinium and putting maximum weight into the drive which they made at Rome itself along the line of the Via Valeria, they attempted to dislocate the enemy defence by capturing its centres of communication, and to extend the revolt by incursions into the Italian lowlands.

Strategical errors of the insurgents

In view of the wide area of operations both sides divided their front into two sectors with a separate commander-in-chief. In the northern zone Rutilius Lupus was confronted by the Marsian chief Poppaedius Silo; in the southern sector L. Caesar stood against the Samnite C. Papius Mutilus. On the southern front the Confederates detailed a strong force to invest the colony of Aesernia, which cut off free contact between the Samnites and the Marsi. After two field battles, in which the besiegers beat off successive endeavours by L. Caesar to disengage the beleaguered fortress, Aesernia fell into their hands. Meanwhile Papius in person broke into Campania, whose manpower and wealth in munitions of war made it a particularly valuable prize to the insurgents. He readily won over Pompeii, Nola and other towns of southern and central Campania, but L. Caesar drove him back from Capua, the chief arsenal of the Romans in southern Italy. Other Confederate leaders made successful raids into Apulia and Lucania, where they carried several of the larger towns and the colony of Venusia went over to them.

Early successes of the insurgents in southern Italy,

In the northern area the territory of the Marsi and the line of the Via Valeria formed the principal theatre of war. Here the rebels tried to thrust past the Latin colonies of Alba Fucens

and in central Italy

and Carseoli on the Via Valeria to strike at Rome itself. They laid siege to the colonies and defeated the Roman relief armies in two battles, in the earlier of which the commander-in-chief, Rutilius Lupus, lost his life. But these defeats were made good by Marius, in whose hands the forces on this sector were eventually united: and it is doubtful whether the Confederates ever carried Alba Fucens. In the Picentine territory the initiative was taken by a Roman *legatus* named Cn. Pompeius Strabo, who had raised a considerable force on his private estates in that region and directed it at once against the city of Asculum, which he eventually succeeded in putting under blockade. Despite occasional setbacks the Romans appeared to be holding their own more fully in the central Apennine region than in the south, until some rebel detachments stole their way into Umbria and Etruria. Apparently these intruders did not capture any towns, but their mere presence on the lines of communication to northern Italy was a serious threat to the Romans, for Cisalpine Gaul had become one of their chief recruiting-grounds. The war in Italy was also a cause of grave financial embarrassment at Rome. The losses which it inflicted on landowners compelled many of these to borrow at ruinous rates. The strain which it imposed upon the state finances drove the Senate to authorise the sale of portions of the public domain.

Spread of the rebellion

At the end of 90 it had become clear that the Romans could not afford to let the rebellion spread any further. The Senate therefore instructed the consul L. Caesar to bring forward a bill conferring franchise possibly only upon all those Italians who had remained loyal to Rome, but more probably also upon any who laid down their arms.[9] By this law, which had the effect of giving full Roman status to the Etruscans and Umbrians, and to the allies of Latin status, the area of the revolt was definitely circumscribed, so that henceforth the process of attrition worked more in favour of the Romans than of the Confederates. But once the ice had been broken by the *lex Iulia* the passage of supplementary franchise acts offered no great difficulty. In 89 two tribunes, named M. Plautius and C. Papirius, carried a supplementary law after which the grant of full citizenship was probably available to every unenfranchised freeman in peninsular Italy and in Cispadane Gaul.[10] In the same year Pompeius Strabo, now raised to the consulship, rewarded the semi-Celtic population of Transpadane Gaul by promotion to the Latin status.[11] But a real and serious limitation was imposed on the scope of the new legislation because the new franchise-holders had to be enrolled in a manner that ensured

The Romans concede the franchise in successive instalments, that their collective voting power should always be inferior to that of the older citizens: they were confined to eight (new?) or ten of the old thirty-five tribes.[12] This piece of gerrymandering, instead of serving as a safety-valve, merely led to a renewal of agitation, and created the occasion for civil war within Rome itself (p. 227).

but the war continues

In selecting commanders for the campaign of 89 the Senate again took political considerations into account. It rewarded the services of Marius, who more than anyone else had turned the tide of defeat in 90, by transferring his forces to one of the new consuls, L. Porcius Cato, a comparatively untried man. This general shared the fate of his predecessor, Rutilius Lupus, while engaged in a frontal attack upon the Marsic territory by way of the Via Valeria. But his colleague, Pompeius Strabo, while maintaining the investment of Asculum, made a successful drive from the Adriatic through the land of the Vestini and Paeligni, which gave him possession of Corfinium and brought him on to the rear of the Marsi – an ancient forerunner of Sherman's 'march to the sea'. Leaving a corps to complete the reduction of the Marsi in conjunction with Cato's army Strabo returned to the siege of Asculum. This city became the rallying-point for all available forces, both Roman and rebel, in the northern sector. In a battle where 60,000 Italians are said to have faced 75,000 Romans Strabo foiled a Confederate effort to disengage Asculum. The inhabitants of that town held out until the end of the year, but after its surrender the rebellion in the northern zone was rapidly stamped out.

Suppression of the revolt in central Italy by Pompeius Strabo

On the southern sector the army of L. Caesar was taken over by L. Cornelius Sulla, who opened his campaign with a decisive victory in southern Campania over the Samnite forces under Papius Mutilus. After this success he was free to recover all the ground lost in Campania and to make a systematic sweep of Samnium as far as Bovianum Vetus, where the Confederates had set up their parliament after the fall of Corfinium. Though Bovianum fell into his hands he was eventually held in check by the Marsian general Poppaedius Silo, who had escaped from the northern seat of war and rallied the broken forces of Papius. The rump of the Confederate senate continued its sessions until the ensuing winter at Aesernia, which Sulla failed to recapture. But the death of Poppaedius Silo in an encounter with a subordinate commander, Q. Metellus Pius (probably at the beginning of 88), ended the war as a war. Though a few rebel towns held out, and Samnite or Lucanian detachments remained at large during the next two years, they owed their reprieve

Victories of Sulla in southern Italy

to nothing else but the civil discord which had broken out meanwhile in Rome.

It is hardly fanciful to say that to the Romans the Italian War was a struggle for actual existence, for in the exasperation of a fiercely fought series of campaigns a victorious rebel confederacy would almost certainly have gone beyond its original war objects. It may therefore be claimed that Rome's victory saved the Mediterranean lands from a relapse into chaos. The enfranchisement of Italy, which was its most enduring, albeit involuntary result, hastened the amalgamation of Romans and Italians into a single nation, and it gave Rome a new supply of administrators, who eventually took their full share in the service of the empire. But its benefits were not realised in time to prevent the downfall of the Republic. On the other hand victors and vanquished alike suffered ruinous losses in men and wealth, and the armies to which the Roman government owed its success became even more of a menace to it than Marius's soldiery after the Cimbric Wars. The Italian War marked a further stage in the divorcement between the civil and military power in the Roman state; in the long run Rome paid heavily for its tardiness in meeting the just claims of its Italian allies.

Results of the Italian War

4. The Tribunate of Sulpicius Rufus

The embers of the Italian War were still glowing when domestic discord was revived in Rome. The first clash took place in 89 between money-lenders who exacted payment of debts swollen with heavy interest, and borrowers who invoked the obsolete fourth-century legislation against usury (p. 76). The debtors prevailed upon the *praetor urbanus* A. Sempronius Asellio to reapply this antiquated code, but the creditors exercised self-help against the magistrate himself by lynching him while he performed a religious office in the Forum. Although the Senate made a determined attempt to bring the murderers to book, no informants came forward and no trial was held.[13]

In 88 all the outstanding questions of domestic politics were brought to an issue by a tribune named P. Sulpicius Rufus. As a former associate of Livius Drusus, Sulpicius had inherited a tradition of disinterested reform, and his oratorical powers marked him out for leadership by constitutional methods. But he shared Drusus's ill-fortune in making several enemies at once, and he let himself be carried much further along the path of violence. His programme of legislation included a bill to distribute the newly enfranchised Italians among all the pre-existing

Reform programme of Sulpicius Rufus

thirty-five tribes, perhaps his main object; a measure to unseat all senators owing sums above the moderate amount of 2000 denarii; and a proposal to transfer the command in the impending war against Mithridates from Sulla (whom the Senate had formally appointed) to Marius. The first of these laws was a laudable attempt to secure fair play for the new citizens and remove from them a disability which affronted them quite gratuitously; the second law was probably brought forward in the interests of the Equites, who stood to gain most by a prompt settlement of debts among the nobility; the third measure, which was constitutionally improper and unjustified on military grounds, was plainly intended to win Marius's political support.

The command against Mithridates is transferred from Sulla to Marius

Having carried its distrust of Marius to perilous lengths in the Italian War the Senate naturally passed him over as a candidate for the command against Mithridates. His successful rival was a scion of an impoverished patrician family which had not attained high office for two centuries. Disdaining to ingratiate himself with the inner ring of the nobility Cornelius Sulla had had to wait long for the consulship which he assumed at last in 88, and his eventful promotion over the head of Marius was not an act of favour but a due reward of merit. But Marius, who had accepted the slights put upon him during the Italian War with unwonted acquiescence, did not abandon his claim to an eastern command with equal forbearance. Ever since his victory over the Cimbri he had harboured hopes of another high command, and after his sixth consulship he had visited Asia Minor, as if to cast an eye upon a prospective theatre of war. In 88 Marius was half-forgotten by the people to whom he had once been a hero; but he could still count on the support of the Equites, who knew by past experience that he would protect their interests better than a senatorial representative, and it was no doubt through their good offices that Sulpicius now became his spokesman.

Rivalry between Marius and Sulla

The programme of Sculpicius called forth all the latent antagonisms which had lain buried during the Italian crisis; and it was both defended and defeated by organised violence. In a first attempt to circumvent it by constitutional means the Senate, instead of resorting to the time-honoured device of a fellow-tribune's veto, authorised the consuls to proclaim a *iustitium* or general suspension of public business, as though the Gauls were once more outside the gates. But Sulpicius, who is said to have provided himself with an organised escort of young stalwarts from the Equestrian Order, his so-called 'anti-senators', and could draw at need upon his Italian

Sulpicius carries his laws by force

supporters in the capital, met the Senate's chicanery by open force. Amid the rout of the Optimates a son of Sulla's colleague Q. Pompeius Rufus was killed, and Sulla himself only escaped a like fate by a prompt capitulation to Marius. In return for Marius's protection the consuls cancelled the *iustitium* and allowed Sulpicius's measures to be carried into law. In 88 Marius carried his point by the same weapons with which he had defeated the Senate in 100; but in the event his agent Sulpicius was disarmed as thoroughly as Saturninus before him, and Marius was more nearly involved in his downfall.

5. The Capture of Rome by Sulla and by Cinna

For the moment Sulla had been reduced to a plain consulship. But where his ambitions were concerned constitutional scruples weighed upon him even less than upon Marius. Though legally deprived of the six legions which had fought under him in the Italian War and had been detailed to serve with him against Mithridates he still held them by the bond of his personal authority, for he had endeared himself to them by a jaunty and devil-may-care manner, which appealed to the new professional soldier more forcibly than the old-time Roman *gravitas*. He hastened to their quarters in Campania and invited them to follow him in a march upon Rome. Had the troops refused, Sulla would have been liable to summary punishment as a rebel in arms. But they abetted his felony and made him master of the city before Marius and Sulpicius could collect a force of defence.[14]

Sulla leads an army against Rome and captures it

Sulla utilised his victory in this, the first civil war of Roman history, to rescind Sulpicius's legislation and to insure himself against future attacks. At his bidding the Comitia Centuriata set a price upon the heads of Sulpicius and of Marius, and it accomplished a radically reactionary change in the Roman constitution. It arranged that all business submitted to the people should go to itself (the Comitia Centuriata), while nothing was to be brought before the people without previous senatorial approval. Thus both the Comitia Tributa and the Concilium Plebis were by-passed.[15] Sulla also carried an emergency measure for the relief of debtors, which seemingly reduced the maximum rate of interest to one-tenth. Though he did not interfere with the consular elections he constrained one of the successful candidates, L. Cornelius Cinna, to abjure all intentions of tampering with the new political settlement. Lastly he attempted to disarm his former war-colleague, Pompeius Strabo, by transferring the command which he

Sulla recovers his command, and outlaws Marius

still held in the central Apennines to Pompeius Rufus. As soon as he had completed these precautionary arrangements Sulla drew off his forces and left Italy to take its chance during the next four years.

The *coup d'état* of Sulla had seemingly entrenched the senatorial aristocracy in an impregnable position. Sulpicius was presently hunted down and put to death, while Marius had several hairbreadth escapes from his pursuers and finally found a precarious refuge in Africa.[16] But Sulla's example of insubordination proved more potent than all his safeguards against its repetition. He had not long left Rome before another general appealed to his soldiers against constituted authority. When Sulla's colleague, Pompeius Rufus, called upon Pompeius Strabo to surrender his command the dispossessed leader incited his troops to kill the intruder out of hand. His act of defiance went unpunished, for the Senate did not venture to call him to account.

In 87 the consul Cornelius Cinna, a noble of undistinguished family who had come to the fore in the Italian War, promptly absolved himself from his oath of fealty to Sulla and reintroduced Sulpicius's redistribution bill in favour of the Italians. In the inevitable battle in the Forum the Italian forces on whom he was relying suffered defeat at the hands of the urban proletariat, whom the other consul, Cn. Octavius, had rallied in defence of the existing order, and the Senate procured a sentence of outlawry against him.[17] But the ex-consul, taking a leaf out of Sulla's book, invoked military force against the violence of the mob. He went the rounds of Latium and Campania, calling back the discontented ex-allies to arms, and at Capua he seduced a Roman army to make common cause with the Italians over whom it was standing guard. On his way back to Rome with his

strangely assorted levy he joined hands with Marius, who had meanwhile landed in Etruria with another unofficial force recruited among his old soldiers in Africa, and was swelling his numbers with slaves from the neighbouring *latifundia*.

After the events of the previous year the march of Cinna and Marius upon Rome could not take the Senate wholly by surprise. The fortifications of the city were hastily strengthened by Octavius,[18] new levies were ordered among

the loyal populations of Italy and Cisalpine Gaul, and a call for aid was sent to Pompeius Strabo, whose army could no doubt have made a quick end of Marius and Cinna if it had taken the field against them without delay. But Strabo lost precious time in haggling for a second consulship as the price of his assistance, and

although he eventually came to the rescue of Rome, the issue had by then been settled. In the meantime Cinna and Marius had drawn a cordon round the city and sent a force to intercept the new levies from Cisalpine Gaul. The beleaguered garrison was reduced by dearth and pestilence (to which Strabo succumbed soon after his arrival),[19] and eventually threatened to melt away by desertion. Towards the end of the year (87) Octavius was reduced to surrender at discretion.

The re-entry of Cinna and Marius into Rome was marked by such scenes as had often followed a party victory in the Greek city-states, but had hitherto been unknown and hardly conceivable among the Romans. The leading members of the aristocracy were systematically put to death, sometimes after the semblance of a trial, more often by mere murder, and their heads were exhibited in the Forum. The chief instruments of this carnage were a *soldatesca* under the orders of Marius whose resentment of past injuries now found expression in a blind blood-lust. The terror was eventually ended by Cinna, who had at first deferred to Marius, but subsequently turned his more disciplined troops upon Marius's savages and destroyed them. For the ensuing year Cinna and Marius declared themselves consuls without the formality of an election, but a few days after his entry upon his seventh consulship Marius fell ill and died. By this timely decease he salvaged his own reputation and gave Rome a respite from civil war.

6. The Rule of Cinna

Under the rule of Cinna, who now became the virtual dictator of Italy, some attempt was made to clear up the disorders out of which the civil war had arisen. Sulla's legislation was swept away, and censors were elected for 86 to carry out the registration of the new citizens. Either at this time or in 84 they were registered in all the thirty-five tribes, as Sulpicius had enacted. This liberal action by Cinna was a great stride forward: for the principle of equality between the new citizens and the old was now established beyond recall.[20] The relief of debtors was accomplished, on a far more generous scale than in Sulla's recent law, by a new measure in the name of L. Valerius Flaccus, the successor of Marius in the consulship, which remitted three-quarters of all outstanding obligations. On the other hand the financial interests were appeased by reasserting the old official exchange-rates of silver and gold, and a better system of control over the moneyers' operations. While this reform was of special benefit to the money-dealers of the Equestrian Order, it was also received with acclamation by the population of the capital, which had suffered from the recent uncertainty of Roman coin-values.[21]

The ensuing three years (86–84) were a period of tranquillity, in which the Senate regained at least a nominal control of public affairs. Yet during this interval Rome and Italy lived under the shadow of a third civil war. Year after year the consular elections were either not held or were reduced to a mere formality, for Cinna reappointed himself for 85 and 84, and selected his colleague Cn. Papirius Carbo by personal nomination.[22] In keeping the consulship to themselves, Cinna and Carbo retained in their hands the right of levying troops and, by implication, the decision between peace and war. But unconstitutional though some of Cinna's actions may have been, nevertheless he was leader of the legitimate government in Rome and many of the nobles co-operated with him, while Sulla, outlawed by the government, was now in Greece and could appear, with his army and personal supporters, as standing against the

Military autocracy of Cinna and Carbo

Sulla outlawed; abortive negotiations for his restitution

Republic. Cinna was apparently ready for compromise, for a policy of *concordia,* but when in 86 Flaccus was sent to the East against Mithridates,[23] neither he nor his successor could gain Sulla's co-operation (p. 232). Then after his victories in Greece, and still more after he had made peace with Mithridates and had the resources of the East at his disposal, Sulla could threaten the government in Rome; the Senate began to waver and tried to negotiate with him. Cinna, however, was ready to face the risk of war and even shipped some men across the Adriatic, but while he was waiting at Ancona his men mutinied and killed him (84). The nobility now began to go over to Sulla's cause, but none the less Carbo, now sole consul, continued the impressment of troops, and in the event Sulla was left with no option but that of keeping his forces together or of running his head into a noose. In this atmosphere of preparations and counter-preparations the negotiations with the Senate were broken off, and in 83 the Roman civil wars began in earnest.

CHAPTER 23

The Temporary Monarchy
of Cornelius Sulla

1. Events in Asia Minor to 88 B.C.

Aggressions of Mithridates in Asia Minor

While the Romans were emerging from the Italian War, only to plunge into their first civil wars, they also became involved in a conflict with their most formidable enemy in the eastern Mediterranean, King Mithridates VI of Pontus. This masterful ruler, whose restless ambition could not be wholly absorbed in the development of his Black Sea empire (p. 213), became intent on enlarging his territories in Asia Minor. In pursuit of this policy he ran continuous risks of collision with Rome, for all his neighbours in Asia Minor were bound by treaty with the Republic and had a claim on its assistance. Mithridates realised that he was scarcely a match for the undivided strength of Rome, and took care to avoid a direct affront upon it; but he banked heavily on the Senate's distractions with other troubles and its growing reluctance to add to its commitments overseas.

Temporising policy of the Senate

In 104 the king of Pontus took advantage of Rome's absorption in the Cimbric War to occupy Galatia and Cappadocia. So long as the Northern Peril hung over its head the Senate turned a blind eye on the affairs of Asia Minor. Its policy, it is true, did not find favour with the Equites, whose lucrative financial operations in the province of Asia made them eager for fresh conquests in the East, nor with Marius, whose desire to measure his strength against Mithridates was not first formed in 88 (p. 221). In 103 his henchman Saturninus endeavoured to precipitate a war by insulting the king's envoys in Rome. In 98 he went on a tour of inspection in Asia Minor (on pretence of fulfil-

ling a vow to Cybele at Pessinus in Phrygia), but he was invested with no official authority and had to be content to admonish Mithridates at a private interview.

The king remained in undisturbed possession of Cappadocia until Nicomedes III of Bithynia, who had been an accomplice in his aggressions but had since quarrelled with him about the spoils, directed a complaint to the Senate. Having no other war on its hands at this moment the Senate decided to order Mithridates to withdraw from Cappadocia, and to support the claim of a Cappadocian noble, named Ariobarzanes, to the throne. The task of installing the king was given to Sulla, who had been sent as proconsul to Cilicia in 96, probably with the main purpose of dealing with the pirates.[1] Sulla carried out his mission, but in the process clashed with some troops of Tigranes, the new king of Armenia, who had overrun Sophene. Sulla then went on to the Euphrates where he accepted an offer of friendship from an envoy from the great Parthian empire, which thus made its first official contact with Rome, a contact that foreshadowed centuries of intermittent warfare. Mithridates accepted the situation for the moment, strengthened by a link with the powerful Armenian kingdom: Tigranes became his son-in-law. He could afford to wait a while.

Sulla in the East

Mithridates' apparent compliance with Roman protests

The outbreak of the Italian War gave the king a new opportunity, which he seized with both hands. In 91 or 90 he expelled Nicomedes's successor and namesake from Bithynia, and he reoccupied Cappadocia in conjunction with Tigranes. The Senate, however, took up this challenge with unexpected vigour, for as soon

23.1   Sulla. A Roman *denarius*, issued *c.* 54 B.C.

New aggressions by Mithridates. A Roman commissioner forces a war upon him

as the tide of the Italian War had turned it sent M'. Aquilius, the winner of the Second Slave War in Sicily, to reinstate the two kings, and it instructed L. Cassius, the governor of Asia, to put his troops at Aquilius's disposal. With less forbearance than Sulla Aquilius at once directed the Roman forces, together with contingents from Asia and Galatia, to eject the intruders from Cappadocia and Bithynia. Again Mithridates withdrew without a battle; but if the Senate could restrain the king it could not control its own commissioner. For his services in restoring Nicomedes Aquilius had stipulated a fee which the Bithynian king could not pay on the spot. He therefore pressed his client to raise funds by raiding Pontus and levying a toll upon shipping in the Bosporus. His injunction was faithfully obeyed by Nicomedes, who feared his friend more than his foe (89). Again Mithridates offered no resistance, but contented himself with remonstrances. But after two successive rebuffs from Aquilius his patience at last gave out, and once he made up his mind that the Romans were determined to fix a war upon him he struck first and struck hard.

Misjudging the king's past compliance for weakness Aquilius had planned an invasion of Galatia in 88 with such few Roman troops as the governors of Asia and Cilicia could supply,

Mithridates sweeps all Asia Minor

and the unwilling militias of the Greek towns in these provinces. But Mithridates, taking the field with a larger and more practised army, swept Aquilius and Nicomedes out of Bithynia: then turning southward he ended the campaign with a drive through the province of Asia, where the towns readily came over to him on a promise of relief from taxation for five years. Apart from a few places on the south coast and the city of Rhodes, which successfully stood a vigorous siege, he carried Asia Minor in a single whirlwind invasion.

After this easy triumph Mithridates threw his habitual caution to the winds. In the hope of expelling the Romans from the province of Asia once for all, and of attaching its inhabitants

to himself by the bond of a common blood-guilt, he gave orders for the simultaneous massacre of all the Italian residents. Though no reliance can be placed on the recorded casualty-lists — the most cautious estimate gave the enormous total of 80,000 victims — it is certain that most of the Asiatic cities carried out the king's command with a will. These 'Asiatic Vespers' are the most compelling proof of the unpopularity of Roman rule in the provinces under the later Republic. But it must be remembered that from the time of Gaius Gracchus Asia had been the principal hunting-ground of the Italian fortune-seekers, official and private; conclusions drawn from this province should not be applied without reserve to the rest of the Roman Empire.

The 'Asiatic Vespers'

2. The First Mithridatic War[2]

But Asia Minor was becoming too small for Mithridates. Under the same pretence of liberating the Greeks from their Roman oppressors which had already served him well in Asia, he now prepared for an invasion of Europe. Using a diplomatic offensive as his spear-point he promptly won over Athens, where his agent Aristion led a revolution against an unpopular oligarchy and established himself as a despot. In the wake of Aristion his admiral Archelaus made a descent on Delos, where all the Italian residents were put to the sword, and occupied Piraeus (the port of Athens). From this base he carried all southern and most of central Greece. In the absence of reinforcements from Italy, where Sulla's expeditionary force was being detained for other ends (p. 227), the Roman troops from Macedonia could do no more than defend Thessaly against Archelaus.

Mithridates overruns Macedonia and Greece

In 87 Sulla made a belated landing in Greece with an army of five legions, perhaps 30,000 men. These forces proved barely sufficient for the simultaneous investment of Athens and Piraeus, to which Sulla at once proceeded. It was not until early in 86 that he broke into Athens (where famine had done its work) and forced Archelaus to evacuate Piraeus after a fiercely contested siege that left the town in permanent ruins. While Archelaus kept Sulla pinned in Attica the main Pontic army was advancing through Thrace and Macedonia, and threatened to take the Romans in the rear. It was fortunate for Sulla that this force was more intent on consolidating the ground won in the Balkan lands than on co-operating with Archelaus in Greece. Eventually both sides concentrated their strength for a set battle at Chaeroneia, on a narrow plain between the spurs of the Boeotian mountains.[3] In this engagement Archelaus,

Sulla's belated arrival in Greece

Siege of Athens

231

who had assumed the chief command on Mithridates's behalf, led his troops in a style that recalled the great antagonists of Rome in the third century. With the advantage of numbers on his side he directed his scythe-chariots and infantry to keep the Roman centre in play, while his mounted men rolled up the Roman flanks. But Sulla, divining Archelaus's intentions, held a mobile corps in reserve, and he threw it into action with such good judgment that he succeeded in holding up the Pontic horse on both wings. With a final counter-attack on the disordered left flank of the enemy he converted the battle into a rout, in which Archelaus's army was virtually destroyed. The disaster to Mithridates's forces, however, was repaired by the arrival by sea of a reinforcing army, which engaged Sulla at the neighbouring site of Orchomenus. Here Archelaus found an open plain where he could give full play to his horsemen, but Sulla cramped his attack by digging trenches to protect the Roman flanks. The action was decided in the centre, where the Pontic scythe-chariots, recoiling upon their own line, threw it into confusion, and Sulla, repeating Eumenes's manœuvre at Magnesia (p. 164), put the enemy to flight with a well-timed cavalry charge. Pursuing the fugitives untiringly, the Roman general stormed their camp and made an end of Mithridates's expeditionary force.

Battles of Chaeroneia and Orchomenus

The campaign of 86 gave Sulla an open road through Macedonia into Asia. In the following year he made a slow advance towards the Dardanelles, while his lieutenant, L. Licinius Lucullus, scoured the Levant for naval aids, which he had great difficulty in collecting. In the meantime a counter-offensive in Asia had been opened by a second Roman force under the consul L. Valerius Flaccus, which Cinna had sent out in Sulla's wake. Even if, as Sulla probably falsely claimed, Flaccus had secret orders to turn against him, Flaccus could hardly have persuaded his troops to cross swords with Sulla's men, fresh from their victory at Chaeroneia. In the event he marched straight to his province of Asia, but on the way through Bithynia he was killed in a mutiny instigated by his *legatus* C. Flavius Fimbria, who now assumed command. In 85 Fimbria invaded the province of Asia, plundering the Greek cities on his way, yet keeping his Grand Catalan Company well in hand in the face of the enemy. After an easy victory over a reserve Pontic army, which he caught by surprise on the banks of the Rhyndacus, he expelled Mithridates from his residence at Pergamum, and would have taken him prisoner if Sulla's lieutenant, Lucullus, who was passing close by with his flotilla, had co-operated to cut off the king's retreat by sea. Though

The Roman counter-attack in Asia Minor

Mithridates escaped capture, he had been fought to a standstill, and his only remaining resource was to beat down Sulla and Fimbria in a Dutch auction of peace conditions. In the summer of 85 Sulla crossed the Dardanelles with the aid of Lucullus's squadron and negotiated a peace with Mithridates at Dardanus (near Troy). With Italy in the hands of his personal enemies, he could not afford to use up his troops in prolonging the war in Asia. Shortly after his victory at Orchomenus he had offered terms to Archelaus, which Mithridates accepted without substantial alteration at Dardanus. The king agreed to evacuate all conquered territory in Asia Minor, to surrender his Aegean fleet, and to pay a moderate indemnity. In return he was recognised as king of Pontus and ally of Rome.

The treaty of Dardanus

As soon as the peace was signed Sulla caught up Fimbria, who had retired inland to Thyatira, and by his simple proximity overawed the rival commander's smaller force into wholesale desertion. Fimbria took his own life; his troops were left under Sulla's *legatus*, L. Licinius Murena, to hold down the province of Asia. In this country the early hopes evoked by Mithridates's first overtures had given way to bitter disillusionment. The heavy drain of the war in Greece upon his resources had compelled Mithridates to break his word to the natives of the province by imposing severe taxation and conscription; and the sporadic revolts which this harsh treatment provoked had been repressed by him with the utmost rigour. The cities of Asia therefore submitted readily to Sulla. Nevertheless they were held strictly to account for the 'Asiatic Vespers'; although cities which had remained loyal to Rome (as Rhodes) were rewarded, others now lost their freedom and became liable to regular taxes collected by the *publicani*, as well as being plundered. In addition Sulla demanded of the province the enormous sum of 20,000 talents (the cost of the war and five years' arrears of taxation). The unfortunate provincials had to borrow from exploiting Roman business-men, and suffered further from increasing pirate-raids: indeed while Sulla himself was on Samothrace, pirates carried off 1000 talents worth of booty from the island.[4]

Sulla's settlement in the province of Asia

After Sulla's departure from Asia a renewal of the war was threatened by an escapade on the part of Murena, who undertook an incursion into Cappadocia and Pontus on the pretext that Mithridates was rearming (83–82). The king beat back Murena no less successfully than he had formerly repelled Aquilius; but when Sulla, to whom he had made a prompt appeal, disavowed his lieutenant's action, he stayed his hand and ended the 'Second Mithridatic War' on the

The 'Second Mithridatic War'

previous terms. As a sop to Murena Sulla allowed him to celebrate a triumph.

Lenient treatment of Mithridates by Sulla

The First Mithridatic War, like the conflict with Jugurtha, arose out of an impulsive action by a king who appreciated the power of Rome and had no wish to measure his strength against it, but was eventually carried away by his ambitions and resentments. Had Mithridates appealed in 89 to the Senate against Aquilius, as he subsequently referred Murena's case to Sulla, the war might have been not only postponed but avoided altogether, for the senatorial government again and again proved that it desired no further commitments in Asia. The terms of settlement which Mithridates received stood in startling contrast with the treatment meted out to Jugurtha, but in signing the peace of Dardanus Sulla was looking over his shoulder towards Italy.

3. The Homecoming of Sulla

Sulla's return to Italy

While Sulla was settling the affairs of Asia Carbo prepared against his return by holding a general levy in Italy, which produced some 100,000 recruits. But these troops, being mostly untrained and not more than half-willing, were not fit to take the field at the beginning of 83, when Sulla made an unopposed landing at Brundisium. As soon as he set foot in Italy other members of the aristocracy who had been outlawed after his departure flocked to his standard. Metellus Pius, a son of Metellus Numidicus, who had fought with distinction in the Italian War, rejoined him from Africa, and M. Licinius Crassus, a son of the consul of 97 (p. 219), returned to him from Spain. But Sulla's most valuable recruit was a son of Pompeius Strabo. This youth, who had been molested but not seriously endangered by Cinna, raised three legions among his father's old soldiers in Picenum and put this force at Sulla's disposal. With these reinforcements Sulla's army, now augmented to more than 50,000 men, began its second march upon Rome. To check his advance Carbo had sent forward two armies under the consuls L. Cornelius Scipio and C. Norbanus. But these commanders had so little confidence in their soldiers that they gave Sulla a free road as far as Campania. Here each consul in turn offered battle, but Norbanus was heavily defeated, and Scipio saw his legions charmed away from him with promises of higher pay.

Easy victories over Carbo's troops

A severe winter brought the campaign of 83 to a premature close. Carbo profited by this respite to repair his recent losses with fresh levies. In southern Italy he rallied to his cause the Samnite cantons, whom Sulla had but half-

A rally by Carbo

defeated in the Italian War. His colleague in the consulship, a son of Marius, lured his father's veterans back to the standards by the magic of his name. The Marian forces of 82 were far more battle-worthy than the ill-conditioned levies of the preceding year. The funds for the upkeep of Carbo's armies were raised by rifling the temples at Rome.

At the outset of 82 the war-front extended from Campania to the northern Adriatic, and the initial disposition of the rival armies was not unlike that of the opening year of the Italian War. But the war-zone was quickly narrowed down by a sweeping northward move on the part of Sulla, who broke away along the line of the Via Latina towards Praeneste. Near this town he outfought the younger Marius so completely as to drive him to seek refuge behind its walls and to clear the way to Rome for himself. He did not, however, enter the city in time to forestall a leave-taking massacre among the nobility by the retiring Marians, whose principal victim on this occasion was the model governor of Asia, Q. Mucius Scaevola. Hardly pausing to take possession of Rome Sulla hurried on to Etruria, where Carbo was stationed with his reserve forces. Despite a check sustained by him near Clusium Sulla's northward march virtually decided the campaign. While he drew Carbo's reserves the remaining Marian forces, left unsupported, were crumpled up by Sulla's lieutenants. While Crassus and Pompey broke through from Picenum into the Tiber basin Metellus entered the plain of northern Italy and stove in the Marian left wing near Faventia. With enemy armies closing in on all sides, and his own supporters melting away by desertion, Carbo lost his nerve and fled from Italy. The Marian troops in Etruria now surrendered or dispersed, but a few resolute units cut their way through to join hands with a belated Samnite levy. Their combined force, estimated at 70,000 men, made a determined attempt to disengage Marius in Praeneste, and when it was beaten off by Sulla (who had returned to take charge of the investment), it endeavoured to lure away the besiegers by a sudden pounce on Rome, in imitation of Hannibal's march from Capua (p. 131). Dividing his force Sulla doubled back to Rome with a mobile column, and offered battle under its walls outside the Colline Gate. His own wing was almost overpowered, but made a final rally, while Crassus carried all before him on the right flank. The fight for Rome ended in the destruction of the last Marian army; the Samnites fell to the last man, for those few who surrendered were subsequently butchered in cold blood by Sulla's orders. The fall of Praeneste and the death of the young Marius

Sulla recaptures Rome, and corners Carbo

Carbo's Samnite allies make a rush on Rome

Battle of the Colline Gate

followed soon after. A few cities defied Sulla's siege-forces for some months, and in Etruria Volaterrae was not starved out until 79; but the 'Battle of the Colline Gate' put the final issue beyond doubt.

Sulla recovers the western provinces from the Marian nominees

The last actions of the civil war were fought in the western provinces, where Sulla's lieutenants dispossessed the governors appointed under the influence of Cinna or Carbo. In Spain an old officer of Marius, named Q. Sertorius, who had served with distinction in the Cimbric and Italian Wars, was easily driven out of the peninsula by the stronger forces of Sulla's deputy, C. Annius. Sicily was rapidly cleared by Pompey, who ran down Carbo in one of the neighbouring islets and put him to death (81). In Africa, where Marius's colonies provided a good recruiting-field, Cn. Domitius Ahenobarbus, Cinna's son-in-law, had raised a considerable force and received substantial support from a Numidian chieftain named Iarbas, who had supplanted Gauda's son Hiempsal. He was quickly overmastered in 80 by Pompey, who brought with him a force of some 35,000 men. In the same campaign Pompey restored Hiempsal to his throne, thus laying the foundations of a lasting friendship with the Numidian dynasty. By the end of 80 the Marian party had been dislodged from its last places of refuge, and the entire Roman Empire was at Sulla's disposal.

4. Sulla's Settlement. The Proscriptions

The first use to which Sulla put his victory was to exercise reprisals against the defeated party on a scale which left the Marian atrocities far behind them. The massacre of the captured Samnites was followed by a long train of isolated murders, in which the chief and the lesser captains alike took vengeance on their private enemies. On a remonstrance which Metellus Pius ventured to address to him Sulla undertook to impart more method into his killing, but killed all the more relentlessly. He posted up from time to time lists of names, with a declaration that the men thus 'proscribed' were outlaws and that a price would be paid for their heads. He lingered over the task of selecting his victims with maddening deliberation, issuing supplementary notices again and again, and extending the reign of terror far into the following year. This novel system of mass-murder was directed with particular vindictiveness at the prominent members of the Equestrian Order, who had consistently abetted the Marian leaders, and offered an additional incentive to reprisals by reason of their wealth. The executions at Rome were reproduced on a minor scale in such Italian

The 'proscriptions' of Sulla

towns as had shown sympathy with the Marians, and the territory of the Samnites was given over to Sulla's soldiery to devastate from end to end. The total number of persons despatched by Sulla's head-hunters amounted to several thousands.[5] From the slaves of the murdered men Sulla recruited a corps of 10,000 stalwarts, whom he emancipated in his own name and retained at call as a private bodyguard (the Cornelii). As a final safeguard against a resurrection of the Marian faction he debarred the sons of the proscribed from all public offices.

The ruthlessness of Sulla's proscriptions was matched by the rapacity of his financial exactions. In order to redeem the lavish promises of pay and pensions which he had made to his troops he had recourse to the rough-and-ready expedient of confiscating the estates of the persons on his proscription lists. There were no doubt plenty of cases in which men who had taken no part in politics suffered death on the score of their wealth alone. In addition to these individual spoliations Sulla confiscated large tracts of land from Italian cities held guilty of collusion with the Marians; in particular the towns of Etruria and northern Italy now experienced a loss of territory similar to that which had befallen the southern Italians after the Second Punic War. The land thus appropriated was used to provide at least ten colonies for perhaps 120,000 discharged soldiers.[6] Further supplies of money, which he used to reward his personal associates, were raised from the cities of the Empire and the allied kings, among whom Sulla collected benevolences and held a traffic in privileges and immunities.[7]

Confiscations in Italy

Both the cause and effect of this land-resettlement programme are highly significant. It was largely forced upon Sulla by the needs of the troops. Following Marius's reforms the armies were increasingly dependent on their personal commanders to secure their future well-being on demobilisation, since many were landless men with no farms to which to return. Sulla was compelled to make even more brutally clear what Marius himself had already shown, that a link between commander and army threatened the security of the Republic: he must get land for his men. Further, the settlement of so many men led to major social and economic upheavals. In the process no doubt many large estates were broken up, while the moving around of numerous families would help to produce a more uniform culture. Yet not all the new colonists would settle down happily or make good farmers: some would be ready either to come to the help of Sulla if ever he were in need, or indeed to follow other emergent leaders who offered more excitement than the farm could provide.

Their cause and effect

5. Sulla's Constitutional Legislation

Sulla is appointed dictator rei publicae constituendae

The sheer violence and mockery of constitutional forms with which Sulla consolidated his power at Rome presented him in the light of a mere military adventurer, of a Marius without Marius's hesitations. Yet Sulla fully realised the need of setting the Roman government once more on a legal basis. On his return to Rome the Senate obediently gave a retrospective sanction to his past acts (the proscriptions, as such, seem to have been the subject of a *lex Cornelia*). Sulla then bade the Senate appoint its senior member, L. Valerius Flaccus (consul with Marius in 100), as *interrex,* and instructed Valerius to carry through the Comitia a law to revive the obsolete office of dictator and confer it upon Sulla for the novel purpose of redrafting the republican constitution (*legibus scribundis et reipublicae constituendae*). This office was not limited to six months, but was held at Sulla's pleasure since he could resign if and when he wished. The new dictator was attended in the city by twenty-four lictors and was free from the checks which curbed ordinary magistrates. In January 81, after celebrating his triumph over Mithridates, he turned to his reforms, showing a similar regard for constitutional forms, since his code of laws, when completed, was submitted to the Comitia for ratification.

Sulla's earlier career

The result of Sulla's legislation was to reinforce the authority of the Senate, but hitherto he had followed a career that was very different from that of an orthodox Optimate.[7] He came from an old patrician family, but for generations its members had failed to gain consulships. His father was said to have lived in poverty and obscurity, conditions which the sources may exaggerate. Sulla himself, after a slow start, was helped to a public career with legacies from his stepmother and a mistress. As quaestor he had distinguished himself by the capture of Jugurtha (p. 216), and he again served under Marius in the German Wars. The two men became bitter enemies, but this quarrel may date not from the end of the Jugurthine War, as generally believed, but at least some ten years later and certainly before 91 when Sulla's client, King Bocchus, dedicated on the Capitol statuary showing the surrender of Jugurtha to Sulla.[8] Sulla was now ready to seek a consulship after the hard-won praetorship which he had held as far back as 97; the Italian War provided the stepping-stone to office in 88. A marriage to Metella, the widow of Aemilius Scaurus, brought him closer to the nobility, while the attempt by Marius and the popular party to deprive him of the Mithridatic command drove him to extreme action. Thereafter as a victorious army commander and absolute dictator he was freer from political pressures,[9] but whatever his earlier feelings may have been, he now saw that Rome's only hope for peace and order lay in a strengthened Senate. And one streak in his enigmatic character was an innate desire for order and efficiency in public, if not in his private, life. Further, with orderly government restored, he could return to *otium cum diginitate* and to his private pleasures.

By virtue of his dictatorial power Sulla carried a programme of legislation even more comprehensive than that of Gaius Gracchus. In regard to the Popular Assemblies he did not revive the drastic measure by which he had virtually abolished the Concilium Plebis in 88 (p. 227). But he resuscitated the Senate's right of veto upon its legislation. Apart from this revival of the *patrum auctoritas* Sulla made no alteration in the constitutional rights of the Senate; but he added considerably to its members. In the first instance he introduced 300 new members into it – *a fournée de pairs* which more than made up for the losses caused by the civil wars and proscriptions. For the future he provided that seats should be assigned, *ex officio*, to all ex-quaestors. Since the number of the quaestors was now fixed at twenty (p. 236), the ultimate effect of this rule would probably be to maintain the normal membership at about 500.[10] One of Sulla's objects in filling out the ranks of the Senate was no doubt to provide a larger number of persons qualified to sit in the jury-courts, whose service he made much more onerous (p. 236). But since his new peers were all recruited from the Equestrian Order Sulla in effect carried out Livius Drusus's policy of a partial amalgamation between the Equites and the senatorial aristocracy. Furthermore, since it may be assumed that the Equites to whom he gave promotion were not drawn from the financiers at Rome, who were his special aversion, but from the 'country members' of the Order who filled the chief positions in the Italian municipalities, Sulla's reform of the Senate had the result of drafting a large Italian element into it.[11] We may therefore detect in Sulla's measure the germs of those cardinal reforms by which Augustus subsequently drew the municipal aristocracies into the service of the empire. But Sulla provided no means of ensuring that his *novi homines* should pass on to the higher executive offices. In the event, therefore, the senatorial nobility succeeded in retaining their chief magistracies in its own hands, and in resuming control of the Senate.

Increase of the Senate's numbers

Admission of Italians to the Senate

In resuscitating the *patrum auctoritas* Sulla struck a direct blow at the tribunes, who thereby

Restrictions on the powers of tribunes

lost their unrestricted power of carrying laws in the Tribal Assembly, and an indirect one at military adventurers like Marius, who could no longer have recourse to tribunes to procure for them by legislation the commands refused to them by the Senate. But his attack on the tribunate did not end here. He abolished or curtailed the tribunes' right to prosecute before the Tribal Assembly; he placed restrictions (of uncertain scope) on their veto, depriving them of it in criminal cases; by a further act of precaution he debarred them from holding a praetorship or other high office.

Apart from the drastic diminution of the tribunes' powers, Sulla made no fundamental change in the magistracy. To provide for additional chairmen of the jury-courts he raised the number of the praetorships from six to eight; to keep pace with recent increases in the number of the provinces he brought the quaestorships up to the total of twenty.[12] A somewhat more important measure regulated anew the *cursus honorum*. By this act Sulla removed the absolute veto on a second consulship, but he revived the older rule prescribing a ten years' interval between two tenures (p. 181). Henceforth no man was to be quaestor before the age of thirty, praetor before thirty-nine and consul before forty-two; thus the rise of ambitious young men was slowed down. Sulla managed to do without the censorship, although probably not abolishing it; its most important function, that of *lectio Senatus*, was redundant since the Senate was now automatically filled by ex-quaestors. Pro-magistrates were not so easy to control as magistrates, but Sulla encouraged (without probably embodying it in law) a practice that had been developing more recently, namely that praetors and consuls should remain at home during their year of office and go overseas as promagistrates in the following year, while the Senate by deciding which provinces should be allocated to proconsuls and which to propraetors could keep some control on potentially dangerous men. Sulla also passed a treason law (*de maiestate*) to regulate the activities of promagistrates in their provinces, in particular forbidding them to leave their provinces or make war beyond the borders without authorisation from the Senate or people: there must be no repetition of escapades like those of Aquilius and Murena in Asia Minor. While trying to curb potentially dangerous threats to the senatorial government from tribunes, magistrates and pro-magistrates, Sulla gratified the harmless aspirations of those who coveted dignity without power by increasing the number of the pontifices and of the augurs to fifteen each; at the same time he restored to either college

Magistrates and pro-magistrates

the full right of co-opting its new members (p. 220).

On his return to Italy from the East Sulla made it known at once that he had no intention of revoking the recent grants of Roman franchise. The Italian question, which had bedevilled Roman politics for the past forty years, was closed, and Sulla had no wish to re-open it. He kept this promise in all cases except those of a few towns like Volaterrae, which had held out obdurately against him; and the disabilities which he put upon these were quietly allowed to lapse after his death. Once they felt assured of retaining their Roman status many Italian towns voluntarily remodelled their constitutions, so as to adapt them more closely to the Roman pattern; not infrequently they invited a Roman patron to draft a new municipal charter for them.[13]

Remodelling of municipal constitutions in Italy

Sulla did not acquire any new provinces for Rome in the East; but he probably constituted one on Italian soil by detaching Cisalpine Gaul from peninsular Italy and providing it with a garrison and governor. In view of the recent enfranchisement of the Cispadane part of Cisalpine Gaul the reduction of this district to the status of a province was a constitutional anomaly. Its practical justification lay in the need of a permanent defence force in the sub-Alpine regions. The necessity for such a measure had been shown some ten years previously when a band of marauders from Raetia adventured itself as far as Comum (at the southern end of Lake Como) and put the town to sack. The total number of Roman provinces was thus raised to ten, of which seven (Sicilia, Sardinia et Corsica, Hispania Citerior, Hispania Ulterior, Africa, Gallia Transalpina and Gallia Cisalpina) were situated in the western Mediterranean, and three (Macedonia, Asia and Cilicia) in the East. Thus Sulla showed no desire for conquest or to extend the Empire.[14]

Northern Italy is made into a province

In the domain of jurisdiction Sulla completed the transference of the more important criminal cases from the Popular Assemblies to special jury-courts. Since the institution of the *quaestio de rebus repetundis* in 149 several other courts had been appointed on the same pattern; under Sulla the number of the *quaestiones* was raised to seven, and their competence was extended so as to cover the whole range of higher crime.[15] At the same time a new regulative law was issued for each of the older courts. In all the *quaestiones*, old and new, the jurors were appointed from the ranks of the Senate, and the Equites were completely excluded from the higher jurisdiction at Rome.

Extension of trial by jury

The reforms of Sulla in financial administration were of very small consequence. He

Finance

slightly eased the burden on the treasury by abolishing the public sale of corn at low prices; and he made an ill-advised attempt to restrict private expenditure by sumptuary laws, which he promptly stultified by his own extravagant mode of life.

Sulla resigns his dictator- ship

Sulla remained dictator for the unprecedented term of three years. But he gradually became less dictatorial in manner and ended by effacing himself altogether from public life. In 82 he unceremoniously put to death a distinguished officer, named Q. Lucretius Ofella (or perhaps Afella), who had defied him by standing for the consulship against his regulations. In 80 he invited a trial of strength with Pompey by refusing him a triumph on his return from Africa; but when Pompey stood by his demand and significantly delayed the disbandment of his troops the dictator humoured his lieutenant with a show of good grace. When Pompey further asserted his independence by supporting the candidature of M. Aemilius Lepidus (on whom see p. 240) for the consulship of 78 against Sulla's express wish, his only rejoinder was a mild and ineffective remonstrance. In 79 Sulla resigned his dictatorship and withdrew to a country estate in Campania, so as not to embarrass the restored government of the Senate by his formidable presence.[16] In the following year he died without having seen Rome again.

6. Sulla's Place in Roman History

Personality of Sulla

Sulla stands in a line with Scipio Africanus and Caesar as one of the outstanding figures of the Roman Republic. His personality is the most baffling of the three. By nature indolent and inclined to the habits of the *bon vivant* he was capable of unsparing hard work. His aristocratic composure seemed equal to any crisis, yet he could outdo Marius in acts of vindictive savagery. Like Africanus and Caesar he had a mystic strain which expressed itself in an unshakable faith in his own luck, a belief which he openly proclaimed in 82 by the adoption of the cognomen 'Felix'. Yet his career was that of a detached and self-contained cynic.

Of his eminence as a soldier there can be no question. In his campaigns he showed the same boldness of initiative, the same fertility of resource, the same uncanny influence over his troops as Africanus and Caesar. As a politician he ended a career of unscrupulous self-advancement with a resolute act of self-abnegation. His period of dominance could be called *Sullanum regnum*,[17] yet he did not take the decisive step of attaching his 'client-army' to himself on a permanent footing. His abdication from the dictatorship puzzled Caesar, and has often been blamed by modern critics, yet it was hardly a matter for surprise. Despite its many and various failures the Roman Republic of his day still possessed a prestige that raised it far above the kingdoms of the earth, and a return to monarchy as a standing institution was hardly yet within the range of practical politics, nor indeed was it probably desired by Sulla himself.

Reasons for his abdication

In restoring the Republic Sulla buttressed up the ascendancy of the Senate. Not that he had any intimate connexion with the inner circle of the senatorial nobility or showed special concern to hand back the control of the State to them: the object of his legislation was nothing more or less than practical efficiency as he understood it. But, like many practical men and most Romans, he was lacking in constructive imagination. He took no wide or far-seeing view of the Republic's needs, but limited his field of reforms to matters arising directly out of his experience. The two cardinal failures of Sulla lay in his omission to take adequate measures for a regular infusion of fresh blood into the senatorial aristocracy, and to devise efficient safeguards against further military usurpations.

Object of his reforms

True, he made a start in the right direction. Since Gaius Gracchus the Equites had enjoyed political power without responsibility; now they were deprived of their control of the courts where they had exercised this power; thus the 'two-headed state', which the antiquarian Varro recognised as a result of Gracchus's reform, now reverted to its earlier monocephalous form. At the same time many of the more responsible Equites had been drafted into the Senate. Thus Sulla showed himself conscious of the fact that for the creation of a more competent governing class an excellent field of recruitment lay at hand in the municipalities of Italy. But the means whereby the Italian aristocracies could best have been drawn into the service of the Republic escaped him. It would no doubt have been too great an innovation to convert the Senate into a House of Representatives with a definite number of seats attached to each Italian town or district, although working models of representative institutions could have been found in the Greek federal republics. But a relatively simple reform, and one which was brought into actual if belated operation under Augustus (p. 327), would have been to give to the Italians a more effective share in the annual elections of magistrates by opening polling-stations in their several towns.[18] Though under this system the Roman nobility would no doubt have continued to carry the greater number of candidates for high office, the resultant infusion of *novi*

His failure to make the Italian vote effective

homines might have been sufficiently strong and steady to impart a new energy and a wider outlook to the Senate. At any rate it is inadmissible to assert that in Sulla's day the Republic was past praying for, and that an attempt to salvage it by resolute constitutional experiments could no longer have borne fruit.

An improvement in the personnel of the Senate might in itself have gone far to render it immune against military *coups d'état*. The creation of a special corps of officers, with no political careers to advance and no political axes to grind, probably lay too far from the traditions of the Republic to come within the range of practical reforms. On the other hand if Augustus succeeded in attaching the professional soldiery

to his house by enlisting them on fixed terms and guaranteeing their pay and pensions, it should not have been impossible for Sulla to achieve as much on behalf of the Republic.

Sulla missed a unique opportunity of setting the republican constitution in order while there was yet time. In the long run his own example of successful military usurpation proved more effective than the inadequate remedial measures which he devised against a recurrence of his offence. Yet his political deficiencies weigh less heavily in the scale than those of the senatorial nobility in general, for it was their habitual short-sightedness which threw the Republic's machinery of government out of gear and made careers like that of Sulla possible.

His failure to safeguard Rome against further military coups

CHAPTER 24

The Fall of the Restoration Government[1]

1. Prospects for the Seventies

The Republic in need of peace

In the Restoration period that followed the dictatorship of Sulla the foremost need of the Roman Republic was to rest and recover from the convulsions of the previous ten years. The greatest danger of the moment lay in the possible recrudescence of the civil wars that had recently paralysed the senatorial government. In view of this peril the restored senatorial aristocracy was more than ever averse from military adventures abroad, with their concomitant military usurpations at home. Nevertheless the years after the death of Sulla were an age of recurrent warfare. The hostilities were largely an aftermath of the troubles of the preceding decade; but fresh conflicts arose on borderlands of the Empire where frontiers were still ragged and undefined. Sertorius was in revolt in Spain, Thracian tribes were pressing on the frontiers of Macedon (p. 278), piracy was rampant and demanded drastic measures, and Mithridates started once again on the warpath. In the handling of these wars, which are described mainly in the next chapter, the Senate often displayed a timidity which had the effect of aggravating them, and of provoking domestic reactions, like those of the Jugurthan War, by which its ascendancy was once more undermined. A few consequential adjustments were made. As part of the drive against the pirates Cyrene was annexed as a Roman province (p. 250), and when the Romans accepted the legacy of the kingdom of Bithynia on the death of its king in 75/74 they upset the balance of power in Asia Minor and precipitated a series of wars which was in the

Renewal of warfare

sixties to lead to major reconstruction in the East.

In domestic politics, even more than in foreign affairs, the period of the Restoration appeared to hold a promise of tranquillity after a succession of storms. The internal feuds of the previous age had lost their sharp point. The newly enfranchised Italian voters belied the fears of those who imagined that they would flock to Rome to swamp the Popular Assemblies. The urban proletariat was still capable of flaring up in a moment of crisis, but took little interest in the ordinary course of politics.[2] The Equestrian Order had lost its most resolute leaders in the proscriptions of Sulla; those of its members who were drafted into the Senate were speedily absorbed into it, and never constituted a separate faction within its ranks. The ordinary routine of administration fell back by common consent into the hands of the aristocracy, who continued to monopolise the highest offices and to dominate the Senate.[3] Above all, a new generation of Romans was growing up in a postwar mood of loathing for the massacres and atrocities of the age of Marius and Sulla, and fervently hoping that its horrors would not be repeated.[4] But this pacific sentiment was not accompanied by any firm resolve to take efficient steps against their recurrence. Least of all did the restored nobility read aright the lessons of the past fifty years. Engrossed in the maintenance of its collective class-privileges, or in the pursuit of internal rivalries between its various coteries, it made no attempt to carry on Sulla's work of reconstruction, but drifted along from one crisis into the next.

The Senate resumes control at Rome, but lacks a policy

2. The Rebellion of Lepidus and its Aftermath

The Senate's ability to discharge the most important of all its duties, to hold military adventurers in check, was tested immediately after Sulla's death, when one of the late dictator's officers, a member of the high nobility named M. Aemilius Lepidus, took the field to enforce a repeal of his former chief's acts.[5] Elected consul for 78 with the indifference of Sulla, who rated his capacity for mischief too cheaply or the Senate's capacity for self-help too highly (p. 237), Lepidus brought forward in 78 a programme which included the restoration of the tribunate to its former status, renewal of the sales of cheap corn and restitution of the dispossessed Italians to their estates. The insincerity of his agitation was sufficiently evident from the *Attempted military coup by Lepidus* fact that he had been among the foremost to buy up at knock-down prices the property of the proscribed, and indeed his whole past career marked him as a mere groper in the political lucky-bag. But the Senate, instead of opposing him squarely, played into his hands. In the vain hope of buying off his ambitions at a reduced price, it gave him a commission to quell a local uprising in the neighbourhood of Faesulae in Etruria, where some of the evicted landowners had anticipated their legal reinstatement by forcibly expelling the colonists of Sulla. Once out of the Senate's reach Lepidus made common cause with the rebels and fomented another revolt in northern Italy by the agency of M. Iunius Brutus. The Senate made a belated attempt to coax the ringleader back to Rome: but he now put forward the significant condition that he should be allowed to stand for a second consulship for the following year, and in anticipation of the Senate's refusal he began to move in upon Rome with the insurgent troops from the Arno valley early in 77. The senatorial government was obliged to make another Declaration of Emergency, *Senatus Consultum Ultimum*. Fortunately for it the veterans of Sulla, who had an obvious interest in checking Lepidus's propaganda, made a prompt rally round the proconsul Q. Lutatius Catulus, and round Pompey, to whom the Senate had unwisely given a special grant of *propraetorian imperium*. In northern Italy Pompey drove Brutus into Mutina and obtained his early surrender on terms. Contrary to his later wont he sullied his victory by dishonouring his *Defeat of Lepidus* promise to spare Brutus's life. Meanwhile Lepidus made a dash for the capital, but was defeated by Catulus in a battle at the Milvian Bridge near the Janiculan Hill. Though he escaped pursuit, he died shortly after in Sardinia, and his principal followers betook themselves to Sertorius (p. 241). In staking his chances on a mass rising of discontented Italians Lepidus showed less than his usual gambler's cunning. But if his revolution was never more than a forlorn hope his opponents' indecision almost gave it an undeserved victory. The Senate's handling of this crisis boded ill for its success in dealing with more formidable antagonists.

The rising of Lepidus was followed by a few years of comparative calm, during which the nobles took the edge off some lesser discontents by judicious, if reluctant, concessions. The main political issue was restoration of the full powers of the tribunes. After agitation for this in 76, a conciliatory consul of 75, C. Aurelius Cotta, *The tribunate and senatorial administration* who had been a friend of the younger Drusus, carried a measure by which tribunes were relieved from their vexatious disability to proceed to higher magistracies. But this more liberal senatorial attitude did not last long, and agitation for complete restoration of the tribunes' powers continued. The Senate's reputation was certainly not enhanced during these years by a number of scandals in the law-courts where senatorial juries were on occasion guilty of flagrant corruption, but more serious threats developed from the repercussions of its handling of foreign affairs. Pompey, to whom the Senate had rashly made a special grant of *propraetorian imperium* to help in the crushing of Lepidus's forces, deliberately delayed disbanding his army and suggested to the Senate that he should be sent to help Metellus in his struggle against Sertorius in Spain. Though young Pompey had held no regular magistracy, the crisis in Spain persuaded the Senate weakly to capitulate, and Pompey was given a proconsular command as Metellus's colleague. This was just the kind of action which Sulla had hoped could be avoided. So too if Sulla had intended that consuls should remain in Italy and without armies (p. 236), his plan soon broke down: M. Aurelius Cotta and L. Licinius Lucullus, the consuls of 74, were given commands in the East to deal with Mithridates (p. 251), while M. Antonius (late Creticus) was invested with a special proconsular *imperium infinitum* to deal with the pirates. Owing to piracy corn was scarce and expensive, so the consuls of 73, M. Terentius Varro and C. Cassius Longinus, were forced to carry a law to safeguard the corn-supply of Rome by a preemption on the annual surplus of Sicily, and to distribute grain at reduced rates to some 40,000 recipients.[6] In the following year prospects might look a little brighter: Sertorius had been defeated in Spain and Mithridates had been driven out of Pontus, but in Italy the slave-revolt of Spartacus (p. 242) necessitated granting Crassus a special command. And the ambitions of Crassus were matched by those of the vanquisher of Sertorius, Pompey the Great.

3. The War against Q. Sertorius[7]

Sertorius rallies the Marian party in Spain

Even before the death of Sulla the embers of the civil war blazed up again in Spain, where the Marian leader Sertorius recovered his foothold soon after the recall of the forces that had expelled him (p. 234). A man of rough breeding but commanding personality, he acquired an authority over the Spaniards such as no native chief possessed, so that they flocked to his standard to fight a Roman's battles, and in spite of his training in legionary warfare he proved himself an adept at the Spaniards' own guerrilla warfare. In 80 Sertorius raised a rebellion among the Lusitanians, by which a further nine years' round of Spanish wars was opened. In 79 and 78 Sulla's colleague Metellus Pius, whom the dictator sent to stifle the Lusitanian rising, attempted to round up Sertorius from the line of the middle Guadiana, but his antagonist broke through the net.[8] In 77 Sertorius received a reinforcement of fugitives from the abortive rebellion of Lepidus in Italy (p. 240), whose leader, M. Perperna, he joined with his own lieutenants to form an opposition Senate.

His conquests in Spain

Henceforward he was strong enough to contain Metellus in southern Spain, while his mobile columns overran the central and northern plateau as far as the Pyrenees and occupied most of the eastern coast. In Osca, at the foot of the Pyrenees, he founded a high school, where the sons of the Spanish chieftains whom he kept as hostages were given a training in Latin letters. On the eastern seaboard he came into touch with the flotillas of the pirates (p. 250), and by their mediation he later (probably 76/75) made a compact with King Mithridates, who gave him financial and naval support in return for a loan of Italian drill-masters.[9] He also fomented local risings in southern Gaul, and he was credited at Rome with the intention of marching upon Italy and conducting a second Hannibalic war.

The campaigns of Pompey against Sertorius

The death of Sulla broke off the personal feud which had originally driven Sertorius into the opposite camp and stood in the way of a political reconciliation. In view of Sertorius's clean record in the civil wars – he had boldly stood up against the extremists of his party and had taken no part in the Marian massacres – the Restoration government could have made an honourable end of the Spanish War by offering him reinstatement. But with a misplaced loyalty to Sulla's memory the Senate carried on the con-

flict. At the end of 77 it sent heavy reinforcements to Spain under its best general, the still youthful Pompey. In 76 and 75 the main scene of operations in Spain lay along the east coast, from which Pompey, following the strategy of the Scipios in the Second Punic War, sought to dislodge Sertorius. In 76 he endeavoured to nip his adversary between his main force advancing from the Ebro, a detachment which he had sent by sea to New Carthage, and the army of Metellus marching in from Andalusia. But the division from New Carthage was held fast by Sertorius's lieutenants, and though Metellus succeeded in defeating L. Hirtuleius, the ablest of Sertorius's subordinates, he did not arrive in time to lend effective aid. In the meantime Pompey, engaging Sertorius single-handed, sustained a humiliating defeat near Lauro. In 75 Metellus definitely recovered southern Spain for the Senate by a crushing victory over Hirtuleius near Segovia, in which he applied on a small scale the tactics of Cannae. After this success he again marched east to take Sertorius in the rear; but once more Pompey would not wait for his partner, and in consequence lost a second battle near the river Sucro and later fought an indecisive action near Saguntum. At the end of the year Sertorius still held the best part of the rich coastlands near Valentia, while Pompey and Metellus were hard put to it to victual their large armies in a depleted country. But in reply to a querulous letter[10] the Senate sent Pompey fresh supplies, and it fitted out a fleet which effectively cut off Sertorius from his allies on the high seas.

His defeats at the hand of Sertorius

With their forces now augmented to more than 50,000 men, Pompey and Metellus proceeded to a campaign of sieges on the Celtiberian plateau, which had become Sertorius's chief recruiting-ground. Though still outmanœuvred from time to time by Sertorius and forced to abandon the investment of Pallantia, they recovered one stronghold after another in 74 and 73, so that the remaining enemy forces were steadily edged into the Ebro valley. Finally the authority of Sertorius over his Italian officers was gradually weakened, especially if a law which granted a pardon to Lepidus's former associates was passed as early as 73.[11] In 72 one of these refugees, M. Perperna, who had consistently failed Sertorius in battle and could not forgive his chief for winning victories while he but sustained defeats, murdered him and usurped his command. By this act of treachery Perperna simply played into the hands of Pompey, who made short work of him, and thus brought the long war to an abrupt end.

Eventual defeat and murder of Sertorius

In his duel with Sertorius Pompey did not increase his military reputation; indeed he

Pompey's settlement of Spain

achieved less than Metellus, though the latter received scant credit for his compensating victories. But in his settlement of Spanish affairs he redeemed a reputation for cruelty which he had incurred in his previous campaigns. He gave a pardon to all of Sertorius's officers except Perperna, and by destroying the correspondence of Sertorius, which had fallen into his hands, he stifled a campaign of prosecutions in Rome. The terms which he accorded to the Spaniards brought back early prosperity to the rich country on the eastern and southern seaboard and gave him a reputation which stood his family in good stead after an interval of thirty years (p. 275).[12] But in fighting Sertorius to a finish the Senate threw away a fair chance of winning back to Rome a general of outstanding ability; and it paid for its victory by a defeat at the hands of its own commander (*see* § 5).

4. The Slave-war in Italy

The rebellion of Spartacus

In 73 Italy became the scene of a far more desperate encounter than the rebellion of Lepidus. A band of gladiators, led by a man of Thracian origin named Spartacus, who had gained military experience in the auxiliary forces of the Roman army, broke loose from their barracks at Capua and called the rural slaves to liberty. His ranks were joined by many thousands of runaways, including a large contingent of Thracians and Gauls, of German survivors of the Cimbric Wars, and of herdsmen from the *latifundia* of southern Italy, who habitually carried arms for the defence of their flocks. In 73 they defeated with ease some hastily levied defence corps; in the following year they beat off in succession the armies of both consuls and of the governor of Cisalpine Gaul; and between their victories they traversed the length of Italy, plundering the country estates to their hearts' content. But the very completeness of their success proved their eventual undoing. Although the way lay open to their native lands beyond the Alps, and Spartacus (who had no illusions about the outcome of a slave-war fought to a finish) urged them to take their chance before it was too late, the rank and file would not consent to forgo the sudden delights of licence and rapine in Italy. While the fugitives drifted aimlessly about the rich countryside, Sulla's former lieutenant, M. Crassus, was collecting a force of some 40,000 men and putting it through a rigorous course of drill.[13] After a checkered campaign in southern Italy, and a vain attempt to elude Crassus's pursuit by hiring ships from a flotilla of corsairs at the Straits

Its suppression by Crassus

of Messina, Spartacus was finally rounded up in Apulia, where he died with most of his men in a hard-fought battle (71). Of the surviving slaves, 6000, whose masters could not be found, were exhibited on crosses set up like telegraph posts along the whole length of the Via Appia.

The War of Spartacus was the last formidable slave-revolt of which we have a record in ancient history. It had at least this good effect, that it educated the more thoughtful Roman landowners to treat their slaves more leniently, or to substitute free for servile labour (p. 300). On the other hand the headlong courage of the fugitives and the circumspect leadership of Spartacus reinforced the lesson of the Sicilian slave-wars, that servitude made a sad waste of human talent. Moreover, if the rising in Italy did not bring lasting ruin to the countryside, it helped to precipitate a political crisis in the capital.

Effects of the revolt

5. Pompey's *coup d'état*

While Crassus was running down the last of the fugitive slaves Pompey brought back his victorious forces from Spain and took part in the man-hunt. On the pretext of being absorbed in this necessary occupation he was able to keep his army in being and to make political capital out of it. The career of Pompey was determined by two conflicting forces. As a man of few constructive ideas and of fundamentally conservative outlook, he had little personal ambition beyond a distinguished military record and the honourable position of *princeps* or leading personage within the governing class – substantially the same ideal as that attributed to Scipio Aemilianus.[14] But he was the son of Pompeius Strabo, a military adventurer who had used his army as an instrument of personal advancement (p. 228), and the pupil of Sulla; and at the age of twenty-five he had not hesitated to play off his soldiers against his own master (p. 237). After the rebellion of Lepidus he had contrived a significant delay in disbanding his forces, and his subsequent appointment to high command in Spain was made in compliance with this veiled threat. Pompey's discomfitures in Spain, for which he sought to foist the blame on to the Senate (p. 241), ended by driving him into political opposition. In 73 he opened negotiations with a tribune named C. Licinius Macer (the annalist), with a view to rescinding certain inconvenient articles of Sulla's constitution. On his return to Italy in 71 he manœuvred his troops within striking distance of Rome, and from this commanding position he sprang upon the Senate a request for leave to stand for a consulship, notwithstanding the *lex Annalis* of

The ambitions of Pompey

597
POMPEJUS MAGNUS
d. 48 f. Kr.

24.1   Head of Pompey.

he lacked the nerve to throw in his life after his purse. Distrusting his chances of success against Pompey he played for safety by making common cause with him and confronted the Senate with a claim to share Pompey's privilege. Thus left defenceless the Senate conceded the double demand of the two war-leaders, and the Comitia duly elected both of them to the consul- *Pompey* ship of 70. The election, it is true, had scarcely *and Crassus* been completed before Crassus repented of a *obtain* bargain which in effect condemned him to play *consulships* second fiddle to Pompey and the tension between the two consuls became so acute that neither would take the first step in disarming. But a fresh civil war was averted by an eleventh-hour reconciliation. The two rivals dismissed their forces and co-operated for the rest of their term in carrying through fresh legislation.[16]

The rise of Pompey to the consulship was embarrassing in its rapidity. Knowing nothing of the rules of the Senate, in which he had not yet obtained a seat, he was obliged to beg the scholar M. Terentius Varro for a memorandum on the duties of a chairman. He left one of his new laws in charge of the praetor L. Aurelius Cotta, who carried it through the Popular *They reform* Assembly. This measure provided that the jury- *the jury-* courts, which Sulla had transferred back to the *courts* Senate, should in future be shared in equal pro- portions between these and the Equites, together with the next wealthiest class, the so-called *tribuni aerarii*. In the interval since Sulla's dictatorship the senatorial juries had again acquired a bad reputation for indulgence to malefactors of their own order, and a *cause célèbre* which came before the court for extortion in the summer of 70 gave point to current criti- cisms. A former governor of Sicily named C. Verres, who had plundered his province with an effrontery that admitted of no concealment or palliation, had been denounced at Rome by the almost unanimous voice of the Sicilians, who confided their case to an aspiring young bar- rister named M. Tullius Cicero.

The prosecutor of Verres was sprung from the municipal aristocracy of the small Volscian city of Arpinum, which had also given birth to Marius. Cicero's ambition to rise to the highest positions in Rome was no less intense *Cicero's* than that of Marius; but instead of seeking pro- *Verrine* motion through military service, he staked his *orations* chances on success at the Roman bar, which had by now become sufficiently important to provide a new avenue to political distinction. Combining a rare agility of intellect with a rigorous training in rhetoric, jurisprudence and the liberal arts, he rapidly came into notice as a pleader and a man of letters. Shortly before the death of Sulla he had caused a mild sensation

Pompey's Sulla. Coming from a man who had not yet *threat of a* stepped on the lowest rung of the *cursus honorum* *military coup* this claim was even more inadmissible than Lepidus's demand for a second term of office in 77; and the Senate had fair warning that Pompey would use his consular power to its own detriment.

At this juncture the fate of Rome was com- mitted to the hands of Crassus, whose well- trained army was a fair match for Pompey's men.[15] Had Crassus now taken heart to assume the part of Catulus against Lepidus he might at one blow have made Sulla's constitution safe, and have won for himself the position of *prin- ceps*, which he coveted no less ardently than *Crassus* Pompey. But Crassus's ambition was tempered *joins in with* with an inveterate strain of cautiousness. A reso- *Pompey* lute speculator in the field of finance, in which he had acquired unprecedented wealth (p. 302),

243

by confronting in the courts one of the dictator's most influential favourites.[18] In 70 he set the seal of his reputation by winning the suit of the Sicilians against Verres. He collected so much damning evidence, and presented it with such effect, that Verres's counsel Q. Hortensius, a consul-elect and hitherto the unrivalled leader of the Roman bar, threw in his brief, and Verres betook himself into exile. But although justice was done in this instance, the trial of Verres cast an ugly light upon the political methods of the restored aristocracy, and the impression made by the case was heightened when Cicero, coupling oratory with journalism after the Greek fashion, gave his *Actiones in Verrem* to the general public in book form.

The admission of the *tribuni aerarii* to the jury-panels indicates that one object of the *lex Aurelia* was to arrange a more equitable distribution of jury-service, which was a burden as well as a privilege. But the law did little or nothing to improve the quality of Roman justice; in cases of a political complexion the reformed *quaestiones* could no more be trusted to return an impartial verdict than their predecessors. It is probably no injustice to Pompey to suggest that his chief reason for sponsoring Cotta's law was to assure himself of the political support of the Equites.

Deficiencies of the remodelled jury-courts

Another business which the consuls effected by proxy was the revision of the Senate-lists. A pair of censors named L. Gellius and Cn. Cornelius Lentulus, the first to be appointed since 86, performed this duty with unprecedented severity, expelling no fewer than sixty-four members.[19] We need not doubt that their victims consisted mostly of the more unworthy of Sulla's recent nominees. But the personal insignificance of the censorial couple, both of whom had recently suffered defeat at the hands of Spartacus, suggests that they were acting under orders. Both of them subsequently held commands under Pompey, no doubt in acknowledgment of service rendered.

Purgation of the Senate

But Pompey and Crassus brought forward in person the most important measure of the year, which restored to the tribunate all the powers held by it before the restrictive legislation of Sulla.[20] In this act we may discern the real object of Pompey's *coup d'état*. After his quarrel with the Senate in 73 he could no longer count on patronage from this source. But since he had no intention of closing his military career at the age of thirty-five, he was driven to follow the example of Marius in looking to tribunician legislation for his commissions. In 'unmuzzling' the tribunate, it is true, he had no immediate campaign in view. In the East Lucullus was at that moment carrying all before him, and public

Pompey 'unmuzzles' the tribunate

opinion at Rome was not yet ripe for drastic action against the pirates. But when Pompey declined the usual proconsular term in a province, he did so merely that he might be at hand in Rome to seize any future chance of an important command. He had not long to wait, for in 67 the raids of the corsairs upon the corn-supply of Rome created an irresistible demand for adequate military action against them. A tribune named A. Gabinius, acting on a hint from Pompey or divining his purpose, framed a bill to confer upon him an overriding command in the Mediterranean Sea (p. 251). The nobles, led by Catulus, offered opposition as best they could, and a tribune named L. Trebellius interposed his veto at the polling. But the Senate had already cut the ground from under its feet by creating a similar post for M. Antonius in 74 (p. 250); and in any case the people of Rome, with the spectre of famine over it, was not in the mood to listen to counter-argument. Trebellius withdrew his brave but bootless veto at the last moment, and Gabinius's bill was passed over the Senate's head.

The lex Gabinia

Another measure of Gabinius, by which the command against Mithridates and Tigranes was withdrawn from Lucullus and bestowed *ad interim* upon Acilius Glabrio, was no doubt intended to prepare for its final devolution to Pompey (p. 253). Early in 66 the tribune C. Manilius presented to the Tribal Assembly the bill which gave Pompey his general commission to settle the affairs of the Near East.[21] This project was no less unpalatable to the nobles than the *lex Gabinia*. But if it did not rouse the enthusiasm of the people in the same measure it received strong support from the Equites, who had been taken aback by the effects of their agitation against Lucullus, and now resumed their more familiar part as upholders of a strong foreign policy. Their case was set forth with engaging candour by Cicero, who had often defended the interests of the *Ordo Equester* in the courts, and now came forward as their spokesman in high politics. The *lex Manilia* was therefore carried, and it would seem as if the second test case between tribunes and Senate went almost by default. From this time the aristocracy ruled but on sufferance, and under a constant apprehension of renewed military usurpations.

The lex Manilia

The Senate on sufferance

6. Crassus, Caesar and Catiline

After Pompey's departure to the East an uneasy feeling came over his former opponents, who realised that the Gabinian and Manilian laws had placed the Republic in the hollow of his

Crassus's feud with Pompey

hand, and remembered Sulla's homecoming from a previous Mithridatic war. In the face of this risk the Senate had no policy save to wait on events; but Crassus, whose feud with Pompey had been suspended rather than ended, set about to insure himself against reprisals. His first thought was to try to counter Pompey's great influence in Spain and then perhaps obtain a foreign command for use as a bargaining asset, or, if necessary, as a base of operations against Pompey. In 65 he took advantage of a sudden vacancy in the governership of Hither Spain to press upon the Senate the appointment of his agent, Cn. Calpurnius Piso. The choice of Piso, who was a young reprobate with no visible qualifications for the post, had all the appearance of a bad joke; but Crassus, who had used his wealth to buy up impecunious members of the House, as eighteenth-century borough-mongers bought up parliamentary constituencies, exercised enough influence to carry his point, and Piso went to Spain as *quaestor pro praetore*. His stay in the province, however, was cut short by the dagger of a Spaniard whom he had affronted, and Crassus made no attempt to find a substitute for him.

His intrigues to acquire military power

Crassus's next move was to gain control of Egypt by means of a bill to be passed in the Tribal Assembly, by which the kingdom of the Ptolemies was to be converted into a Roman province and an agent of Crassus was to be sent to take over the annexed territory. With Egypt in his grasp Crassus might meet Pompey on less unequal terms, and his delegate, a young nobleman named Gaius Iulius Caesar, had better personal qualifications than Piso. This project of Crassus was legally defensible, since the reigning monarch, Ptolemy XI (Auletes), held his throne by a questionable title, and the Roman Republic could claim Egypt for itself on the strength of a testament (of doubtful authenticity) by a former king; it was economically attractive since the Ptolemies possessed a large funded treasure. Nevertheless his bill was rejected. Its defeat was mainly due to Cicero, who had assumed a watching brief on behalf of Pompey and spoke against Crassus's proposal.[22]

Proposed annexation of Egypt

After this second set-back Crassus enlisted a new supporter in L. Sergius Catilina, a scion of an old but impoverished patrician family, who had served Sulla with equal zeal in the civil wars and in the proscriptions, and resolved to stick at nothing in order to win the coveted prize of a consulship. In 66 he offered himself as a candidate, but was not allowed to stand (on the ostensible ground that he was an undischarged prisoner in a trial before the *quaestio de rebus repetundis*). In retaliation he laid a plot to murder the successful candidates as they

Candidature of Catiline for the consulship

entered on their consulate in 65; but he observed so little secrecy in his preparations that his plan was easily frustrated.[23] Though his guilt was patent he escaped prosecution through the influence of Crassus, and in 64 he was admitted to the competition. But the patrician, who regarded the consulship as his birthright, now found himself running against a *novus homo* who was striving with equal determination to break into the preserves of the aristocracy, M. Tullius Cicero.[24] In any event Cicero could count on the votes of the Ordo Equester, and on those stray suffrages which were awarded frankly on personal merit. In addition he set himself to win the support of the nobles, on whose ground he was trespassing, by playing upon their latent fears of further dirty work on the part of Catiline, or of a political coup by Crassus. Though Catiline was not engaged at this stage in any definite conspiracy the alarmist speeches of Cicero were not without effect upon the aristocracy. The *novus homo* was returned, with one C. Antonius (a brother of the admiral M. Antonius) as his colleague. Though Crassus's intentions in helping Catiline to the consulship are not altogether clear, it seems likely that his object was to have at his beck and call a man who would not hesitate to use his consular power to mobilise Italy against Pompey, as Carbo had impressed it in 83 against Sulla.

Rival candidature of Cicero

Election of Cicero

After the elections of 64 Crassus discarded Catiline and fitted another string to his bow. In 63 he instructed a tribune, P. Servilius Rullus, to introduce a harmless-looking bill of the Gracchan type for an extensive redistribution of land in Italy and the provinces. The hidden purpose of this measure was to concentrate in the hands of the allotment-commissioners all territories upon which Pompey might wish to lay hands for the benefit of his soldiers, so that he would be obliged to purchase them on Crassus's terms. But this subtle intrigue was unmasked by Cicero soon after his accession to the consulship,[25] and the bill was withdrawn before it was put to the vote. After this last rebuff Crassus made no further attempt to insure himself against Pompey. Though Crassus undoubtedly did not desire a civil war, and was aiming at a bargain with Pompey rather than a battle, he was playing with a fire that might easily have passed out of his control. The victory of Cicero over him was therefore something more than a personal triumph.

Crassus's attempt to corner the public lands

The year of Cicero's consulship also marked the advent to high office of C. Iulius Caesar. Like Sulla and Catiline, Caesar was sprung from a patrician family which had long dropped out of the inner circle of the nobility.[26] For his political advancement he had hitherto put his

The early career of Julius Caesar

chief trust in his considerable powers as an orator and a demagogue. Not that he had as yet any clear-cut political programme. Of recent years his heavy debts had driven him into a somewhat compromising association with Crassus, and his occasional theatrical gestures of opposition to aristocratic misrule suggested to most observers nothing more than the antics of a notoriety-hunting young lordling.[27] But in *His advent to high office* 63 he snatched for himself the office of Pontifex Maximus, by collusion with a tribune named T. Labienus, who carried a bill to transfer back the choice of the High Priest to a special electoral body of seventeen tribes (pp. 220, 236); and in the same year he was elected praetor. He had now finished sowing his wild oats and was emerging as a responsible statesman.

7. The Conspiracy of Catiline

Catiline's programme of novae tabulae Undeterrred by the loss of Crassus's patronage Catiline persisted in his suit for the consulship. At the elections of 63 he staked his chances on a programme of *novae tabulae* or a general cancelling of debts. With this policy he was making a general bid for the votes of peasants with mortgaged farms and of ruined financial speculators; but his appeal was principally directed to a large and growing section of the nobility who had lived beyond their means, and in return for financial relief would equally support a Crassus in the Senate (p. 244) or a Catiline at the polls. But if Catiline could count on support from his own class he did not rally any compact mass of rural voters, and the *Ordo Equester*, as constituting the creditor class, stood almost solid against him. The balance was definitely *Its defeat by Cicero* turned in his disfavour by his former rival Cicero, who honestly shared the conviction that *novae tabulae* was tantamount to fraudulent evasion. By a repetition of the alarmist tactics which had answered so well in the preceding year he again contrived Catiline's defeat at the elections.

Catiline's conspiracy Unable to reach the consulship by constitutional means Catiline resolved once again to cut his way through by force. In the autumn of 63 he planned a *coup de main* in Rome, with the help of a few ruined men and rejected suitors for office like himself, and of a posse of disgruntled Sullan colonists in northern Etruria, who were engaged to march upon the capital on the day appointed (27 October).[28] Of this *The first phase* plot sufficient details leaked out to justify the Senate in proclaiming a state of emergency (21 October), and Cicero in picketing the city with improvised patrols. For the moment Catiline was held in check; but for a second time he was not brought to book. With a shrewd suspi-

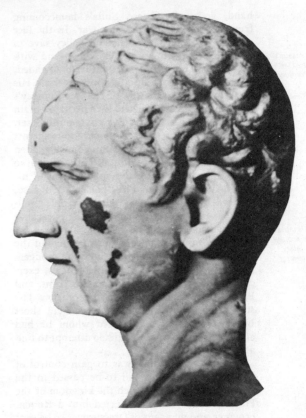

24.2 Bust of Cicero.

cion that the Senate would not protect him if he were subsequently to be attacked for overstraining his consular powers, Cicero left Catiline at large, on the chance of his obtaining more conclusive evidence about his plans. But Catiline profited by his immunity from arrest *The second* to concert a second attack on a far wider front. *phase* The gist of his revised scheme was to distract the government's attention with minor risings in every part of Italy where discontented elements could be roused to take up arms, and with systematic looting and incendiarism in Rome, while he marched upon the city with an army from Etruria. To this new plan, which did not remain secret for long, Cicero replied with precautionary mobilisations of troops. But *Cicero's* the consul still lacked evidence to warrant im- *'Catilinarian* mediate proceedings against Catiline in person; *orations'* and a cleverly calculated speech (known as the First Catilinarian), by which he endeavoured to feel the pulse of the Senate, left him more perplexed than ever (8 November).[29] On the following day Catiline, who had listened imperturbably to the consul's denunciations in the Senate, left Rome without let or hindrance to muster his forces in Etruria.

Catiline's accomplices reveal the plot

But the associates whom Catiline had detailed to make preparations in Rome had not patience enough to wait for his return. With a singular lack of discretion they initiated some visiting envoys from the Gallic tribe of the Allobroges into their secrets, in a wild expectation that these might despatch auxiliary troops from Gaul to Etruria. The Gauls passed on their information to Cicero, who seized the ring-leaders without delay and confronted them with evidence which the whole Senate accepted as conclusive (3 December).[30] Two days later he reassembled the Senate in order to obtain its consent for the summary execution of his prisoners – a procedure which he considered

Debate in the Senate concerning their punishment

necessary to the Republic, as a salutary example of firmness in the face of rebellion, but danger-ous to himself, for it was a matter of doubt whether a consul, acting under the Declaration of Emergency, could legally kill without trial Roman citizens who were not actually in arms or an immediate source of danger.[31] In this debate one senator after another pronounced in favour of immediate action, until Caesar cast doubts on the constitutional propriety of this course and made the strange counter-proposal that the prisoners should be detained for life. Since it may be regarded as certain that neither he nor Crassus had any sympathy with Cati-line's accomplices – both of them had passed on information about the plot to Cicero – his amendment was probably intended as nothing more than a protest against a revival of the massacres and proscriptions of Sulla's age. Yet to lodge men permanently in gaol without the sentence of a court was almost as gross an infrac-tion of a Roman's *Habeas Corpus* as to put them

Caesar versus Cato

to death out of hand, while its deterrent effect was far more problematic. Nevertheless Caesar completely turned the tide of the discussion, until a tribune-elect named M. Porcius Cato, a great-grandson of Scipio Africanus's redoubt-able antagonist, controverted Caesar with all the stubborn self-assertiveness of his elder namesake and rallied the Senate to its earlier opinion. In the event Cicero obtained the Senate's moral authorisation and executed the prisoners on the same day.

While Catiline's associates in Rome were engaged in cutting their own throats, his emis-saries in Italy accomplished nothing more than to collect scattered groups of rebels, who began to melt away after the executions on 5 December. Thus left to his own resources Cati-

Defeat and death of Catiline

line lost whatever chance he might have pos-sessed of repeating the march of Cinna or of Lepidus upon Rome, and his only salvation now lay in flight from Italy. But he was headed off by one army under Q. Metellus Celer in an attempt to cross the Apennines, and threw him-self and his remaining supporters away in a hopeless attack upon a second pursuing force under M. Petreius near Pistoria.

The eventual fiasco of Catiline's rising was partly due to the indiscretions of his supporters at Rome, but in greater degree to the fact that Italy had now settled down and had no desire to revive the feuds of Cinna's and Sulla's days. Even though Catiline had momentarily gained possession of Rome he would merely have played the part of a diminutive Carbo to Pompey's Sulla, for Pompey would certainly not have mis-sed the opportunity of returning to Italy in the role of a Saviour of Society, and the final issue between him and Catiline could never have been in doubt. Yet Cicero's vigilance and energy saved Italy from the risk of another sanguinary,

Cicero's hour of triumph

if transient, period of civil conflict, and the com-plimentary title of *pater patriae*, which Catulus proposed to confer upon him in the Senate, did no more than reflect a genuine and general feel-ing of gratitude towards him. The fear inspired by Catiline was also revealed in a new law pro-viding for distributions of cheap corn to the urban proletariat on a far more liberal scale. It is significant that this measure was presented to the Assembly by Cato, a sound financier and determined enemy of corrupt practices.

8. The *Concordia Ordinum* of Cicero

In 63 Cicero had attained the goal of his per-sonal ambitions and had become the man of the hour. In the following years he made his only

Cicero attempts to forestall new revo-lutions, with the support of Pompey

practical attempt at constructive statesmanship. Having rallied against Catiline all the more solid elements in the Roman state that stood to lose by civil disorder, he conceived a more permanent 'Concord of the Orders' or 'of all Good Men', and more particularly strove for an enduring reconciliation between the senatorial nobility and the *Ordo Equester*. In this coalition he natur-ally reserved for himself the position of acting manager, but he cast Pompey for the part of figure-head. Though Cicero's programme was a merely conservative one, and his ideal of 'dignified tranquillity' (*otium cum dignitate*) was woefully inadequate to the needs of the Re-public, it had at least the merit of offering a guarantee against further political convulsions, which indeed was at this moment the Republic's most urgent necessity. Further, the sharp divi-sion between the two orders had softened con-siderably since Sulla had drafted so many men of non-senatorial origin into the Senate, while senators were taking over an increasing share in financial activities, even in the public contracts; thus we know that in 59 B.C. Caesar, to be followed later by Vatinius, held shares (*partes*, presumably unregistered ones) in a public company.[32] Moreover, the idea of setting up Pompey as the defender of the constitution was less fantastic than might appear at first sight. On his return to Italy at the end of 62 Pompey belied all the gloomy prognostications about his homecoming by disbanding his troops as soon as he landed at Brundisium, and at his first meeting with the Senate he addressed it with studied courtesy. His craving for military glory had at last been satisfied, and the part of Scipio Aemilianus, which Cicero had assigned to him, now seemed adequate to his relenting ambitions.

Pompey's home-coming. His overtures to the Senate

But Pompey's gesture of reconciliation was ignored by those who stood most to gain by it. With perverse obstinacy the Senate refused the reasonable demands which he laid before it. Led by Lucullus and Crassus, who seized this occasion to pay off old scores, and by Cato, who would not allow himself to forget Pompey's past record as a revolutionist, it put off from session to session the ratification of his settlement of the Near East, and it dallied provokingly with the urgent business of providing land for his soldiers, whose excellent conduct during the campaigns had given them an undeniable claim to the customary rewards. When Pompey sought to turn their flank by employing a tribune to introduce a land law before the people, the nobles continued their obstruction in the Forum. Here the urban voters, forgetful as ever of their former hero, gave Pompey such indifferent support that he withdrew his bill and waited on events. He could, to be sure, have carried his point by reassembling his troops and repeating the *coup d'état* of 71; but whether increasing age had strengthened his scruples or weakened his nerve, he accepted his double rebuff with unwonted forbearance.

The Senate rebuffs Pompey

Pompey accepts defeat

9. The First Triumvirate and Caesar's First Consulate

The Senate might venture to flout Pompey as though he were a spent force; but it made a fatal mistake in applying the same treatment to Caesar. After a propraetorship (62) and a year of provincial administration in Further Spain Caesar returned to Rome in 60 to sue for the consulship. Cicero, who was quick to recognise in him a man of outstanding power, played with the fancy that Caesar too might be trained into a defender of the established order. Though

Caesar's campaigns in Further Spain

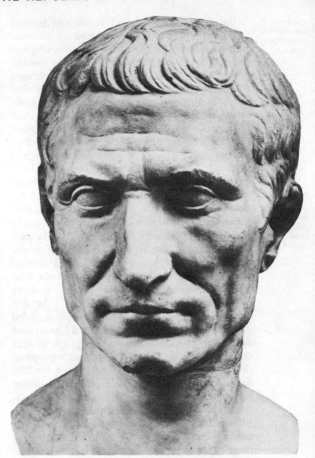

24.3   Bust of Julius Caesar.

Caesar in his salad days had made some noisy demonstrations against the Restoration government, and could at no stage of his career have acquiesced in a mere attitude of *otium cum diginitate*, he had at any rate given no clear sign as yet of any unconstitutional ambitions, and the idea of winning him to the cause of the *Concordia Ordinum* was by no means chimerical. But the Senate was less anxious to convert him into a 'Good Man' than to pay off old scores against him. It denied him the triumph which he claimed for some minor victories in northwest Spain. Worse still, in anticipation of his election to the consulship, it made an extraordinary disposition by which the consuls of 59, instead of taking up the usual provincial appointments, were to stay on in Italy as 'commissioners of forests and cattle-drifts', a routine office of third-rate importance.[33] This last decision was nothing less than a declaration of war upon Caesar, who had discovered his military talents in Spain and was determined to test them more thoroughly on a wider field.

The Senate refuses further military commands to Caesar

He at once retaliated by offering an alliance to Pompey, with a view to joint action against the Senate. Though Pompey had hitherto had no more than passing relations with Caesar[34] he accepted his overtures and took the hand of his daughter Julia into the bargain. Caesar also sought the support of his former patron Crassus, and of Cicero, whose oratorical ability he recognised as a valuable political asset. Crassus renewed his partnership, if only to safeguard himself against Pompey; but Cicero, conquering his chagrin at the ruin of the *Concordia* by the folly of the nobles, refused to abet Caesar in an enterprise which threatened to lead him astray into the path of revolution.

Caesar forms the 'First Triumvirate' with Pompey and Crassus

The 'First Triumvirate', as the political *amicitia* between Caesar, Pompey and Crassus is commonly called, was unmasked at the beginning of 59, when Caesar entered upon his first consulship. He at once brought forward a land-act, by which he provided for Pompey's veterans and also made a modest attempt to draw off from Rome some of its superfluous population.[35] After a vain attempt to secure a discussion of his bill in the Senate he submitted it to the Popular Assembly, and when his colleague L. Calpurnius Bibulus, assisted by several tribunes and by Cato, used and abused every device of constitutional obstruction against it, he brought in a detachment of Pompey's old soldiers, who swept away opposition by physical force and secured the passage of the law.[36] By this display of determination, which sufficed to bring home to the nobles their helplessness, Caesar cleared

Caesar's land acts

He overcomes opposition by force

the field for a wide programme of supplementary legislation, which was submitted partly in his own name, and partly in that of his henchman, the tribune P. Vatinius. He obtained ratification for Pompey's settlement of the Near East, and supplemented it with some unblushing sales of privileges to dependent kings, among whom Ptolemy Auletes bought recognition from the Roman people in consideration of an enormous bribe to Caesar and Pompey. Caesar also found time to carry two genuine measures of administrative reform. He strengthened the law against extortion in the provinces, and he provided for the official publication of authentic texts of all acts of the Popular Assemblies and resolutions of the Senate – a somewhat belated effort to instruct the citizen body in current political events.[37] Lastly Caesar realised the main object of the Triumvirate by obtaining for himself, through the agency of Vatinius, the governorship of Cisalpine Gaul and of Illyricum for a term of five years, reckoned from 1 March 59.[38] Later in the year he took advantage of a sudden vacancy in Narbonese Gaul to secure this province into the bargain. This additional grant came to him from the Senate, which foresaw that if it did not offer Narbonese Gaul to him, he would help himself by means of another tribunician law. Thus Caesar redeemed his promises to Pompey and procured for himself a provincial command after his own heart.[39] But in reintroducing the weapon of physical force into domestic politics at Rome he laid the train of a new civil war.

The lex *Vatinia. Caesar appointed to Gaul*

CHAPTER 25

The Wars of Lucullus, Pompey and Crassus

1. The Campaigns against the Pirates

Organised piracy in the Mediterranean

Shortly after the death of Sulla the Senate was called upon to grapple more seriously with the problem of the pirates of the Mediterranean, whose activities of recent years had attained such a scale as to threaten vital Roman interests. At the instigation of Mithridates, who saw in them useful auxiliaries to his own navy, and of a new class of political refugees whom the upheavals of the 80s had set adrift in East and West, the corsairs began to build light battle-ships in place of cutters, and to organise themselves into fleets that did not shrink from attacking or blackmailing entire towns. Further, as their power grew, they took less care to avoid offence against the Roman Republic. They held to ransom Roman citizens of distinction;[1] they infested the western seas, which they had previously left unfrequented, and they made alliance with Sertorius in Spain.

The Senate's first reply to the pirates was to resume and extend the occupation of their bases in southern Asia Minor which it had commenced in 102 (p. 213). In 78 the ex-consul P. Servilius opened a methodical attack by land and sea on the corsairs in Lycia; in 76 he smoked out Pamphylia; in the following year he reduced the inland border of western Cilicia as a preliminary to a combined drive against the remaining robber-castles in this region.[2] But before he

Roman operations against pirate haunts in Asia Minor

could deliver his final assault he was recalled, and the outbreak of the Third Mithridatic War in 74 (p. 251) necessitated a redistribution of the Roman forces in Asia Minor.

Meanwhile the pirates scattered over the Mediterranean in quest of new bases, so that the Senate was driven to take fresh protective measures. In 74 it took part of the African coastland out of their hands by establishing a garrison at Cyrene, which was now definitely constituted as a Roman province after twenty-two years of indeterminate autonomy.[3] In the same year the Senate revived the scheme for a simultaneous operation on many fronts which had been put forward before (p. 213). To this end it conferred a special command upon the ex-praetor M. Antonius (whose father had fought the Cilician pirates in 102 – p. 213), with unlimited powers of requisitioning ships and ship-money, in every country of the Mediterranean seaboard. This revised plan eventually produced quick results; but it was marred at the outset by the ineptitude of Antonius, who was at a loss to organise a concerted set of movements against his ubiquitous enemies. In 74 and 73 he partly cleared the western seas, thereby rendering material assistance to Pompey in his campaigns against Sertorius. But before his task in the West was completed he transferred his fleet to the Aegean area, where he suffered defeat in Cretan waters at the hands of a pirate battle-squadron (72), and died shortly afterwards. His fleet was thereupon disbanded, and the policy of attacking the corsairs on a wide front was discarded for the time being.

A combined naval drive against the pirates results in a fiasco

The following years mark the highest point of the corsairs' power. In 69 they sacked the harbour of Delos and ruined it for ever. But the chief scene of their activities was the coast of Italy, which they waylaid from Brundisium to Ostia. They carried off two praetors on coast-

The pirates hold up the corn-supplies of Rome

guard duty; they cut out a consular fleet (presumably in 68, under Marcius Rex) at Ostia; they intercepted the corn-supplies of Rome. In reply to this direct challenge the Senate took no further steps than to send a punitive expedition under the ex-consul Q. Metellus against the Cretan bandits. After two hard-fought campaigns (68–67) this commander subdued the entire island, which was thereupon converted into a Roman province. But meanwhile the threat of famine at Rome had driven the people to wrest the direction of the pirate war out of the Senate's hands. In 67 the Tribal Assembly reconstituted the *imperium infinitum* of Antonius and entrusted it to Pompey (p. 244).

A new combined drive is organised by Pompey

With all the resources of the Mediterranean at his disposal Pompey recruited a fleet of 270 warships and 100,000 legionary infantry.[4] Out of these forces he formed a special mobile squadron for his personal use; the rest he distributed in thirteen divisions over the whole of the Mediterranean and Black Seas; and in two well-synchronised moves he swept these waters from end to end. Closing the strait between Sicily and Africa with a strong cordon, he scoured the western seas in forty days; at every point the enemy was driven off the water into the arms of expectant pickets on the adjacent coasts. By a similar combined movement he shepherded the Levantine corsairs to their last refuge in western Cilicia, where strong infantry detachments demolished their castles with the help of a siege-train. In three months Pompey

Pompey sweeps the seas clear

was able to report all clear, and although piracy raised its head here and there, it ceased to be a general menace until new civil wars replenished its forces. Pompey crowned his success by the leniency with which he treated his captives. The greater number were set up by him as honest peasants or traders in Cilicia or on other coastlands which they had previously depopulated. But if the pirate war ended in a brilliant Roman success, the earlier handling of it by the Senate was marked by more than the usual amount of vacillation; and the Senate's failure recoiled upon it in the form of another constitutional crisis (p. 244).

2. Lucullus's Conquests in Asia Minor

During the wars against Sertorius and the pirates the Romans became indirectly involved with King Mithridates, whose good relations with them scarcely outlasted the lifetime of Sulla. In 78 the Senate had the opportunity of coming to a clear understanding with him, when he requested it to ratify the treaty of Dardanus; but it shelved his application on the weak pre-

text of stress of other business, and thus created an atmosphere of mutual suspicion like that which preceded the Third Macedonian War. In anticipation of a new conflict Mithridates engaged some Marian refugees to redrill his army on the Roman pattern, but he refrained from any overt act of hostility until 74, when he made a sudden invasion of the Roman territory in Asia. This abrupt offensive was partly intended to bring relief to his hard-pressed allies in Spain and on the high seas, partly to forestall a Roman occupation of Bithynia, which the childless King Nicomedes IV had recently devised to the Republic. In accepting Nicomedes's bequest the Senate probably had nothing more in view than to increase the Roman revenues, as in the similar cases of Pergamum and Cyrene. But from Mithridates's standpoint the conversion of Bithynia into a Roman province conveyed a new threat, for henceforth the Romans would have complete control of the Black Sea entrance and could double-lock the Dardanelles and the Bosporus against him.[5]

Mithridates rearms

The Roman annexation of Bithynia leads to a new war

At the outbreak of the Third Mithridatic War two Roman legions, the relics of Fimbria's former army, were stationed in the province of Asia; but these were caught off their guard, so that the king was able to overrun Bithynia without opposition. At Chalcedon, the only town that could be prepared for a siege, he cut out a hastily levied fleet of 100 ships, which the consul M. Aurelius Cotta, appointed to Bithynia, brought to the relief of the city, and destroyed it completely. Thus the whole brunt of the war fell upon Cotta's colleague L. Licinius Lucullus, who by intrigue had secured appointment to the provinces of Asia and Cilicia (74).[6]

Mithridates overruns Bithynia

After his victory at Chalcedon Mithridates sent his fleet on into Aegean waters, in order to foment a new rebellion in Greece; with his land forces he invaded the province of Asia and laid siege to Cyzicus, its gateway on the Sea of Marmara. A gallant stand by the Cyzicenes gave time to Lucullus to concentrate the scattered Roman detachments in Asia and Cilicia and to bring up a relief force of 30,000 men. Though Lucullus would not venture an assault upon the Pontic trenches he succeeded in cutting Mithridates's communications so effectively that starvation reduced the besiegers sooner than the besieged. In midwinter 74–73 the king attempted to draw off his troops by detachments, but their retreat was delayed by swollen rivers, and all save a few who were picked off by the Pontic fleet were overtaken and destroyed in the Roman pursuit. In the spring of 73 Lucullus followed up this success with a naval victory off Lemnos, in which a flotilla hurriedly raised among the Greek cities of Asia

Lucullus's counter-attack. Destruction of Mithridates's army and fleet

defeated a Pontic squadron under an officer from Sertorius's army named M. Marius. Having won a passage into the Sea of Marmara, he laid a scheme to bottle up the remnant of the royal fleet in the deeply recessed Gulf of Nicomedia and to cut off the retreat of the king. A delay on the part of Lucullus's vice-admiral gave Mithridates time to escape before the trap was closed; but his fleet had no sooner regained the Black Sea than it was crippled by a storm. The way at last stood open for an invasion of Pontus.

Lucullus invades Pontus

In the autumn of 73 Lucullus made a dash through Galatia into the valley of the Lycus, in the heart of Mithridates's realm. This overhasty advance brought disaster upon him, for he could neither bring the king to battle nor capture his fortresses. After a second winter under canvas he became involved in a troublesome guerrilla action round the fortress of Cabira, during which his communications with the province of Asia were cut. With the assistance of a Galatian chieftain named Deiotarus, who brought up a timely reinforcement of cavalry, he eventually gained the mastery over the Pontic horse. A panic among the king's raw levies turned his retreat into a rout, and Lucullus, catching up the fugitives at a little distance from Cabira, made a carnage of them. Mithridates again eluded his pursuers by a hair's-breadth, but he was left without an army or a kingdom. His son Machares, whom he had placed in charge of his European dominions, declared against him, and his kinsman the king of Armenia, with whom he sought refuge, held him virtually as a prisoner.

Battle of Cabira

The *dèbácle* of Cabira left the Romans free to reduce the fortified towns of Pontus at their leisure, a task which they completed in 70. In the meantine Lucullus, leaving the greater part of the siege operations to his lieutenants, returned to the province of Asia, where a financial crisis called for his intervention. Condemned by Sulla to a fine of 20,000 talents (p. 232) the cities of Asia had paid the Roman treasury by borrowing from private Roman moneylenders at a high rate of compound interest. Under this cut-throat scheme their debt swelled up in snowball fashion to the stupefying total of 120,000 talents, under which the cities fell into bankruptcy. By scaling down their obligations to 40,000 talents and arranging for the repayment of this amount by instalments Lucullus removed the deadlock and set the province back on the path to prosperity.[7] His debt-settlement earned him enduring gratitude among the Asiatic cities, which instituted special festivals in his honour; but it also drew upon him the undying resentment of the Roman

Lucullus's debt-remissions in the province of Asia

financiers, who lost account of their real gain over their paper losses.

3. The Campaigns of Lucullus in Armenia

By the end of 70 all Asia Minor was at Rome's disposal, and the Mithridatic Wars had been seemingly fought to a finish. Yet Lucullus, rightly judging that nothing was settled so long as Mithridates was not dead or in Roman hands, determined to obtain his surrender from the king of Armenia, even at the cost of another war.

Consisting of a high plateau intersected by steep mountain-ranges, and remote from the main lines of communication in the Near East, Armenia had hardly entered the world's history until Tigranes raised it to momentary importance. This ruler, on coming to the throne *c.* 100, at once followed the example of his father-

The aggressions of Tigranes of Armenia

25.1 Mithridates of Pontus.

in-law Mithridates in delivering nicely timed attacks upon his neighbours. After his earlier check by Sulla (p. 230), in 78 he overran Cappadocia; he snatched the western corner of Mesopotamia from the Parthians (p. 256) and he expelled the last feeble representatives of the Seleucid monarchy from Syria and eastern Cilicia, so that by 83 his frontiers extended to Mount Lebanon. Apart from Sulla's earlier warning his attacks upon Roman allies had not so much as drawn a remonstrance from the Senate. Though Tigranes had withheld active assistance from Mithridates against Lucullus, he now stood firm against the demand for his surrender. But the Roman general would take no denial. In 69 he crossed the Euphrates and invaded Armenia.

Lucullus forces a war upon Tigranes

In undertaking this new expedition Lucullus was assuming a double risk. He had no commission from the Senate to make war upon Armenia, and he had no more than 16,000 weary and half-willing soldiers to oppose to Tigranes's far superior forces. Nevertheless he

Battle of Tigranocerta

made a direct march upon the fortress of Tigranocerta, which the king had built as a gate of entry into Mesopotamia, and drew his opponent to wage a battle in its defence. Though heavily outnumbered — on first view of the Romans Tigranes is said to have exclaimed that they were 'too few for an army, too many for an embassy' — Lucullus attacked without hesitation and obtained the victory in a few minutes' fighting. Observing that the king had misplaced the most serviceable part of his force, a troop of mail-clad horsemen, in an unsupported position on the right flank, he swung in upon it and sent it hurtling into the Armenian centre. This manœuvre recalled the movement by which King Eumenes had won the battle of Magnesia (p. 164), and it gave Lucullus a success as complete and far more speedy, for the unsteady Armenian infantry at once broke into disorder and was ground to dust in the Roman pursuit.[8] By this feat of military judo, which placed Lucullus in the foremost rank of Roman tacticians, Tigranes's empire was brought down like a house of cards, and Tigranocerta fell into the hands of the Romans, who used it for their winter quarters.

Lucullus marches through Armenia

In 68 Lucullus became involved in a difficult pursuit in the wake of the retreating Armenian forces. By the advice of Mithridates, who had at last been admitted to his host's counsels, Tigranes drew the Romans on by a continual retirement towards his capital at Artaxata, situated far north in the valley of the Araxes. After routing the two kings Lucullus struggled along within striking distance of Artaxata, when he was brought to a standstill by his own men. From the outset of his command the old soldiers of Fimbria and Sulla, accustomed to spells of licence and plunder between campaigns, had murmured against the unremitting strictness of his discipline. In 68 the rigours of a march across the Armenian highlands, followed by the first blizzards of an Armenian autumn, snapped the frayed bowstring: like Alexander's veterans in the Punjab, Lucullus's troops stoutly refused to advance any further. This mutiny, it is true, checked rather than dashed Lucullus's hopes. Evading Tigranes by an unexpected swerve along a more easterly route (past Lake Van) the Roman general made good his retreat to Mesopotamia and wintered with an intact army at Nisibis. While he fell back from Artaxata Mithridates returned to Pontus and opened a guerrilla attack on the Roman lines of communications; but a detachment from the now pacified province of Asia held him back. Had Lucullus now received from Rome his long-overdue reinforcements, he might even yet have checkmated both the kings.

Mutiny of his troops

But in 67 the remainder of his army fell, or rather was deliberately picked, to pieces. Instead of obtaining fresh drafts Lucullus was actually despoiled of what troops he had left. At Rome his unauthorised attack upon Tigranes exposed him to censure, and his settlement of the debt question in the province of Asia raised an outcry against him among the financiers. The Senate humoured his critics so far as to detach from him the provinces of Asia (in 69) and Cilicia (68), leaving to him Bithynia and the command of the Roman field forces. In 67 the concentration of all the spare military resources of the Empire in the hands of Pompey cut off all sources of fresh supplies. Finally, the new commander-in-chief against the pirates cast his eye upon Asia Minor as a future field of campaigning for himself. The same tribune who procured Pompey's commission against the corsairs (p. 244) also carried a law transferring the province of Bithynia and the command against Mithridates to the consul M'. Acilius Glabrio. In view of Glabrio's insignificance, it can scarcely be doubted that he was simply sent out to hold the fort for Pompey. We may likewise detect Pompey's hand behind a senatorial resolution or, more likely, another law, by which Lucullus's veterans were authorised to take their leave there and then.

Lucullus is attacked on his 'home front'

A further blow befell Lucullus when his lieutenant C. Triarius let himself be drawn into a battle with Mithridates on unfavourable ground and sustained a heavy defeat near Zela (67). In the midst of this general ruin Lucullus fought on gamely. Hurrying back from Nisibis to Pontus he restored his line of communications and prepared to spring upon Tigranes while he advanced to join hands with Mithridates. But at this juncture the remnant of his field force began to melt away. The Fimbrian veterans, having got wind of the licence for their discharge, disbanded themselves incontinently, and the new governors of Cilicia and Bithynia, to whom Lucullus turned for assistance, found excuses for staying in their provinces. With a mere skeleton force he made a stand in the valley of the upper Halys, where neither of the kings ventured to close in upon him; but he could not prevent them from regaining full possession of their dominions. At the end of 67 the warfront in Asia Minor bore an ominous resemblance to that of 74.

Lucullus retreats into Asia Minor

In the ensuing spring the contingency which Lucullus had foreseen as far back as 74,[9] that Pompey might dispossess him of his command, was realised. A law brought forward at the beginning of 66 invested Pompey with a general commission against all the enemies of Rome in Asia, and authorised him to effect a general

Lucullus is replaced by Pompey

253

settlement of affairs in the eastern Mediterranean (p. 244). The new commander-in-chief, whose final operations against the pirates had opportunely brought him to Cilicia, was wintering in that province with the greater part of his army. On receipt of his fresh commission he moved forward to the Halys and sent Lucullus home.

Reasons for Lucullus's ill-success

The apparent failure of Lucullus was due in far greater measure to his ill-fortune than to his personal mistakes. As a general he redeemed his over-bold strategy by his outstanding tactical ability. Though he helped himself to the spoils of victory with more than the usual *sans-gêne* of a Roman triumphator, he was by no means ungenerous to his soldiers. The substance of his troops' complaints against him was that he imposed a severer discipline than Sulla and lacked his predecessor's personal magnetism. But the main reason for his eventual set-back was that his home front turned against him, as it had turned against Sulla.[10] Besides, if the war-map of 67 showed little improvement on that of 74, Lucullus was none the less the real winner of the Pontic and Armenian Wars. By his campaigns he had so reduced the military resources of the two kings that their defences against Pompey were nothing more than façades.

4. Pompey's Settlement of the East

In 66 Mithridates lost the support of Tigranes, who was called away to form a new front against an invading army from Parthia (p. 256). Outnumbered and outmatched by Pompey's well-found force of more than 50,000 men he fell back into the valley of the Lycus, where he endeavoured to keep the Roman general in play by the same guerrilla strategy as he had formerly applied in those regions against Lucullus. But Pompey hemmed in his opponent with a wide chain of field fortifications, and the king's attempt to break out of this ring ended in a disaster similar to that of Cabira. At a site near the future town of Nicopolis (which Pompey subsequently founded to commemorate his victory) the Romans caught up and slaughtered the last Pontic army. Mithridates, as usual, broke through the cordon, and slipping past Pompey's patrol squadrons in the Black Sea he regained the Crimea, which he speedily recovered from his unfaithful son Machares. With unabated energy the exiled king raised fresh troops among his European subjects (65–63). It was credibly rumoured that he was planning to march up the Danube, sweeping the Balkan peoples into his army after the manner of an

Pompey's pursuit of Mithridates

Battle of Nicopolis

25.2 Tigranes of Armenia.

Attila, and with this medley of contingents to break in upon Italy from the north-east. But the inhuman severity of his conscriptions and exactions caused a rebellion, of which his own son Pharnaces took the lead. Brought to bay in his citadel at Panticapaeum, he took his own life (63).

Meanwhile Pompey, leaving the pursuit of Mithridates to another occasion, had turned from the field of Nicopolis towards Armenia. Here he received the prompt submission of Tigranes, who had beaten off the Parthian invaders, but now lost his nerve at the approach of the Romans. Pompey therefore had time to round off his campaign with an uncalled-for attack upon the Albanians, an inoffensive nomad folk near Mt Caucasus, under whose shelter he spent the winter (66–65). In the following spring he negotiated with Parthia (p. 256) and turned westwards through the land of the Iberians (modern Georgia) to the Black Sea in order to catch up Mithridates, but on finding the entrance into Russia barred by the impassable spurs of Caucasus he retraced his steps towards the Caspian Sea. It is not clear whether his object was to find a new water-frontier for the Roman Empire in Asia, or to explore a trade-route from the Black Sea to the Farther East. He did not complete his march to the Caspian, for his troops were now showing signs of exhaustion, but ended an unprofitable campaign with a retreat to Pontus.

Submission of Tigranes

Campaigns in the Caucasus lands

In 64 Pompey occupied himself with the restoration of order in Syria, where the perpetual feuds of the last Seleucid princes had brought on general anarchy. In 63 he started out on an expedition against the kingdom of the Nabataeans in northern Arabia, who had taken advantage of the growing weakness of the Seleucids to encroach upon Syria and occupy Damascus. Since the Nabataean territory lay astride the overland routes from the Arabian ports to Syria and Palestine, and its capital Petra was a centre of the spice and perfume trade, its reduction promised at once to safeguard Syria and

Pompey starts out for Arabia,

to give the Romans control over a highly profitable line of traffic. But on the way from Antioch to Petra Pompey swerved aside into Palestine, and lost the Nabataean enterprise completely.[11]

After the conclusion of the treaty between Judas Maccabaeus and the Senate in 161 (p. 167) and its renewal in 134 the Jews had not only asserted their independence against the Seleucid monarchy, but had enlarged their territory at its expense, until it attained approximately the same frontiers as under Kings David and Solomon. But since 67 a quarrel over the succession between two brothers, John Hyrcanus and Aristobulus, had kept the country in a state of civil war. In 64 both claimants referred their suit to Pompey, who decided in favour of the elder and weaker brother, Hyrcanus. After some hesitation Aristobulus, who was in possession of Jerusalem at the time, withdrew his claim. But his partisans in the city disavowed his surrender and refused to admit Pompey's officers. To this act of defiance Pompey made reply by turning in from Transjordania and capturing Jerusalem after a three months' siege.[12] With this operation he brought his conquests in the East to a close.

but is diverted to Judaea. Siege of Jerusalem

In the intervals between his campaigns and in the following year Pompey was occupied with the political settlement of the Near East, which he carried through on his own initiative, unhampered by the customary senatorial decemviral commission.[13] He dealt gently with Tigranes, who was left in possession of Armenia and had part of his conquests in western Mesopotamia confirmed to him. He conceded to Pharnaces his father's dominions in Europe, and he allowed the king of the Nabataeans to retain Damascus. On the other hand he excluded the dynasty of Mithridates from Asia Minor; he detached from Judaea all its recent acquisitions except Galilee, Idumaea and a border strip of Transjordania, and deprived Hyrcanus of the royal title, leaving to him only the office of High Priest. Finally, he took Syria out of the hands of the remaining Seleucid princes, on the valid ground that these had virtually ceased to govern. Of the territory thus withdrawn from the native rulers he attached eastern Pontus to the dominion of Deiotarus of Galatia (who in 52 further obtained the title of king from the Senate at Pompey's instance); western Pontus he annexed to the province of Bithynia. The Seleucid territory, together with the districts separated off Judaea, he constituted into a new province named Syria. At the same time he enlarged the province of Cilicia by appending to it the previous no-man's-lands along the seaboard of Asia Minor as far as Lycia and the interior up to the central plateau.

Pompey's settlement of the Near East

New provinces

Thus the eastern Mediterranean was to be guarded by a string of Roman provinces: Bithynia et Pontus, Asia, Cilicia and Syria, with outliers at Crete and (in 58) Cyprus. Guarding the eastern frontiers of the provinces was a medley of native client-kingdoms who as friends or allies of Rome enjoyed peace and considerable internal freedom in return for handing over control of their foreign policy to Rome. Thus Rome's eastern horizon now reached to the Euphrates: beyond lay the Parthian Empire, but Rome might feel secure as long as Armenia remained friendly and Commagene (under Antiochus I) continued to safeguard the crossings of the upper Euphrates in Rome's interests.

In the provinces created or enlarged by him Pompey resumed the policy of the Hellenistic kings in fostering the growth of towns. It is estimated that in Asia Minor and Syria he founded or restored some forty cities, whose inhabitants were supplied by the refugees of the recent wars, and by the populations forcibly transplanted by Tigranes to Tigranocerta. On the other hand he reverted to Gaius Gracchus's practice of cancelling the immunities of the more privileged towns of Asia Minor, among whom Rhodes and Cyzicus were perhaps the only two to retain their fiscal independence. A small annual tribute was also imposed upon Judaea by way of war-indemnity.[14]

Foundation of towns

The triumph celebrated at Pompey's homecoming was one of unparalleled splendour, and his fame as a conqueror put that of Lucullus into the shade. His military laurels were earned somewhat cheaply, for none of his wars, except the initial campaign against the pirates, had put his military skill to a severe test. But his political settlement was of lasting importance. It consolidated Roman authority in the East; it brought to the treasury a huge windfall of war spoils, and it raised the annual revenue of the republic from fifty to eighty-five million denarii. In return for these exactions the peoples of the Near East received a measure of security such as they had not enjoyed since the conquests of Alexander. The pacification of Asia Minor was all but completed; Syria was redeemed from anarchy; and the Levantine coasts, the greater part of which now stood under direct Roman rule, were made tolerably secure against piracy.

Pompey's achievement

5. The Campaign of Crassus against the Parthians

Although Pompey settled the other problems of the Near East, he raised a new question which was to trouble successive Roman governments for three centuries, the relations of Rome to

Parthia. This monarchy was founded *c.* 250 B.C., when a band of invaders from the grass-lands of central Asia established itself on the northern edge of the Persian plateau (in the district to which the name of Parthia properly belonged). After the battle of Magnesia the Parthian chieftains gradually wrested the whole of Persia from the decrepit Seleucid monarchy, and by the end of the second century they had advanced their western frontier to the Euphrates. Shortly before 100 they opened relations in the borderland of Ferghana with the Chinese empire, where a vigorous line of rulers was at that time extending its authority over the Tarim plateau in central Asia. In the early part of the first century dynastic disputes and new inroads from the steppe-lands temporarily enfeebled the Parthians, and gave Tigranes of Armenia his opportunity of wresting western Mesopotamia

Growth of the Parthian kingdom

25.3   Orodes II of Parthia.

from them. But about 70 B.C. King Phraates III restored order within his dominions and prepared to recover his lost provinces.

A common distrust of Mithridates and Tigranes had brought Rome and Parthia into friendly relations as early as the mid-90s, when a Parthian king proposed an alliance to Sulla, then acting as governor of Cilicia (p. 230). Though both the Pontic and the Armenian kings sought to win over Phraates in 66 the Parthian ruler took sides with Pompey, on the understanding that he should recover possession of all the lost ground in western Mesopotamia. But after the capitulation of Tigranes Pompey went back on his promise by partitioning the disputed territory between the rival kings. By this uncalled-for change of front he laid the seeds of a long-lived feud between two powers which were by nature complementary rather than antagonistic. A further affront was put upon the next Parthian king, Orodes II, in 56 when Pompey's former lieutenant Gabinius, returning to the East as proconsul of Syria, gave support to a claimant to the Parthian crown. Gabinius, it is true, did not engage his army on behalf

Pompey creates an 'Armenian question' between Rome and Parthia

of the pretender, who was in consequence promptly crushed by Orodes; but his action gave either power an adequate excuse for making a preventive war upon the other. But the actual outbreak of war was hastened by the personal ambitions of the veteran M. Crassus, who became intent in his later years on winning military laurels to match those of Pompey and Caesar, and seized an opportunity of acquiring for himself the governorship of Syria and a free hand to deal with Parthia (p. 266). After raiding Mesopotamia and a winter spent in making forced requisitions upon the temple at Jerusalem and other sanctuaries in Syria, he crossed the Euphrates in 53, with the object of marching upon Seleucia-on-Tigris, the commercial capital of Babylonia at that time, and (we may believe) of annexing the Land of the Two Rivers.[15]

Crassus forces a war on Parthia

Parthia was a loosely compacted monarchy, whose kings – known collectively as the Arsacids – left the outlying provinces of their realm in the hands of vassal princes and conceded a large measure of self-government to the Greek cities of Babylonia. The Parthian army was an aggregate of contingents raised by the king in person on his own domains, and of the semi-private levies of his chief vassals, which sometimes took the field, like the baronial hosts of the Middle Ages, as independent units. The infantry, composed of poorly trained serfs from the estates of the great landowners, was of little account, but the mounted forces were exceptionally strong. The Parthian nobility provided a corps of heavily armoured cuirassiers, whose chargers were specially bred for weight and strength – the prototypes of the mail-clad medieval cavalry; their retainers were exercised to skirmish on horses of Arab type and acquired a special skill in discharging their arrows while engaged in a feigned retreat.[16]

The Parthian army

Crassus had under his command not less than 35,000 men. But his army consisted almost wholly of legionary infantry, and apart from a small contingent of horsemen which his son Publius, a former lieutenant of Caesar (p. 261), had brought from Gaul, his mounted troops were of little value. He had looked to Tigranes' successor, Artavasdes, to make good his deficiency, but could not agree with him as to the route of the march and did not wait to come to terms. Taking a short cut across the steppe-land of western Mesopotamia, he had reached the neighbourhood of Carrhae, when he fell in with an experimental Parthian army of 10,000 mounted archers, reinforced with a few cuirassiers, but unencumbered with infantry. While the other Parthian troops under Orodes himself made a front against the Armenian king this small but select corps, under a vassal ruler

Battle of Carrhae

of the Suren family, sought out the legions and found them on an open downland ideally adapted to cavalry manœuvres. Selecting their own range the archers steadily shot down the helpless Roman infantry, replenishing their quivers from a special corps of 1000 Arabian camels which Surenas had organised; and the cuirassiers destroyed the Gallic horsemen, and killed their leader P. Crassus (the general's son), when these were sent forward to disengage the legions.[17] The survivors of this carnage fell into such a state of demoralisation that, although the Parthians did not press them closely on their retreat, they compelled their commander to enter into a capitulation. Crassus was killed off-hand by a Parthian officer in a casual scuffle, and his army was carried off into captivity. A bare 10,000, breaking away in detachments, regained the Roman frontier.

At Rome the news of the disaster was received with unwonted apathy. Since the attack upon Orodes had been in the nature of a private speculation on the part of Crassus, its failure did not challenge Roman pride in the same manner as the defeats at Cannae and Arausio; and the chaotic condition into which the republican government had fallen at that time (pp. 266 f.) prevented the prompt dispatch of reinforcements. Fortunately for Rome the Parthian king was more alarmed by his victory than his enemies by their reverse. In apprehension of a revolt on the part of Surenas – for the army with which this general had won the campaign was mostly made up of his personal retainers – the king put him to death, and in so doing deprived himself of his only capable commander. Though the Parthian armies had no difficulty in recovering the lost provinces of Mesopotamia from Artavasdes, they made no serious attempt to counter-invade Syria until 51, when Crassus's former quaestor, C. Cassius, beat them off with the reformed fragments of the defeated army. Orodes did not even take advantage of the civil war in which the Romans became engaged in 49, but came to an informal understanding with Pompey which enabled him to denude the Roman frontier of its remaining defences. Thirty years elapsed before a formal peace was signed between Rome and Parthia; but in the meantime the war had died of inanition.[19]

Failure of the Parthians' counter-attack

CHAPTER 26

Caesar's Conquest of Gaul, and the
Breakdown of the First Triumvirate

1. Gaul and its People[1]

Caesar's Cisalpine command

In making first choice of Cisalpine Gaul for a provincial command Caesar was partly guided by political necessities. No other province could offer him equal facilities for keeping an eye on the march of events in the capital and forestalling the manœuvres of his political opponents. Whenever he could safely leave Transalpine Gaul Caesar spent his winters in his Italian province, performing the routine duties of a governor and receiving visits from his agents and associates in Rome. But he was no less alive to the military opportunities which Cisalpine Gaul offered. Since the Italian War this province had become one of the principal recruiting areas for the Roman armies, and its Alpine border provided a wide base for new conquests. The inclusion of Illyricum in his proconsular command, and the disposition of his troops at the beginning of 58, when three of his four legions were stationed at Aquileia, indicate that his original plan of operations may have been to extend the Roman frontiers north-eastward beyond the Carnic Alps where he might come into contact with the expanding empire of Burebistas, king of the Dacians, who lived in what is now Romania. In the event, however, the province of Transalpine Gaul, which he had received by an afterthought, became the starting-point of his campaigns.

Transalpine Gaul. Land and people

Transalpine Gaul was a country more richly endowed by nature than Italy. The manifold resources of its soil and its excellent internal communications marked it out as the seat of a powerful independent state. But its destiny in antiquity was to become the annexe of a Mediterranean country and a land of passage between the Inner and the Outer seas. Its population consisted of a shadowy substratum of 'Ligurians' (p. 13); of the Celts, who entered Gaul from southern and western Germany in the first half of the first millennium, under pressure of Teutonic migrations from the Baltic seaboard (p. 72); of Iberians who passed from Spain into Gascony and Languedoc during the fifth or fourth century; and of Belgae, a mixture of Celts and Germans who crossed the Rhine and occupied the districts north of the Seine and Marne *c.* 200 B.C. Among these constituents of the Gallic people the Celtic element predominated. Except in Aquitania (south-western Gaul), the Celtic language was in general use and the governing class was of Celtic stock.

Gallic civilisation

The civilisation of the Gauls was more advanced than that of any European people beyond the Mediterranean border. Though the cultivation of the vine had not yet extended beyond the Mediterranean coast-lands, intensive agriculture was practised in many districts of Gaul: several improvements in the ordinary process of tillage which eventually reached the Roman world were of Gallic origin. Among the Gallic industries textile and ceramic manufactures were still awaiting development; but from the beginning of the first millennium the Celtic peoples had become highly proficient in metallurgy, and Gallic swords had no rivals except those of Spain. From the sixth century, when the Greek colony of Massilia was founded near the Rhône estuary, trade began to follow the river valleys of Gaul; after 300 the traffic in British tin was largely gathered into the hands of the Veneti of Brittany, who transported it across the Channel, and of other Celtic tribes who forwarded it to Massilia or Narbo. From the third century Greek coins and native imitations obtained a widespread currency; after 200 Roman denarii and copies thereof came into use. By the time of Caesar carriage-roads had been made to supplement the waterways, and the trading-centres along them were growing into permanent towns. Writing was as yet unknown in Gaul, except among the priestly colleges of the Druids, who made secret use of a Greek script. But the Gauls had their native ballads, which were sung by professional bards at the banquets of the nobles, and cleverness of speech was counted among them as second only to prowess in war.

Political organisation The political organisation of the Gallic states was essentially aristocratic. The common people, many of whom stood in a position of clientship to the governing class, was kept in a position of political nonage. Kingship still prevailed among the Belgae, but in central Gaul it had disappeared after 100. The ruling nobility was divided into several branches. The Druids formed an influential professional corps, which had gathered into its hands a jurisdiction concurrent with that of the secular tribunals; they exercised a formidable right of religious excommunication; they executed criminals and war-captives. But they never assumed the direction of state-policy. The secular nobility not only provided the flower of the Gallic armies, but furnished its annual magistrates and its governing councils. By the first century the Gauls had made far greater progress towards national unity than their Spanish neighbours. Some fifty *Incipient unification* separates tribes could still be counted, but among these the more powerful were in process of absorbing or reducing to vassalage the lesser units. Towards the end of the second century the Arverni of central Gaul had established their dominion from the Atlantic and the Pyrenees to the Rhine. After the collapse of their ascendancy, which was shattered by the Roman conquests in Narbonese Gaul (pp. 210f.), the Suessiones of the Seine basin temporarily extended their sovereignty into Britain. A nucleus of a national confederacy had already been created by the Druids, who held courts of voluntary arbitration on the plain of Chartres and composed disputes between litigants from all parts of the country.

But the Gauls had not attained a sufficient degree of political stability to render themselves secure against foreign invasion. While the lesser aristocracies met in council and made good laws in defence of public order, the more powerful nobles engaged in 'Wars of the Roses' with private armies of retainers. Rivalries between the various tribes were sometimes carried to such *Inter-tribal feuds* a length that one Gallic state would invoke foreign aid to defeat another. The Gallic armies had good equipment, and their cavalry, which was supplied by the nobles and their retainers, was superior to that of the Italians. But the infantry was ill-trained and discipline was scarcely stricter than among the chivalry of Crécy and Agincourt. The defects of the Gallic *Gallic warfare* fighting forces had been exhibited in the comparative ease with which the Romans had wrested the southern coast-lands from them, and by their general helplessness during the Cimbric invasions, when the Belgae alone succeeded in keeping out these unwelcome guests. In the first century Gaul still presented a promising and remunerative field of conquest to any enterprising neighbour.

At the time of Caesar's appointment to the two Gauls a repetition of the Cimbric invasions in a more dangerous form was threatening his *Pressure of* Transalpine province. By 100 B.C. Germanic *the German* peoples had begun to intrude upon the ancient *peoples* home of the Celts between the Main and the *upon the* Danube, and in this region a confederacy of *Gauls* nomadic tribes known as the Suebi was preparing for a further advance into France and western Switzerland. While the shadow of this invasion was cast over Gaul the Arverni and the Sequani (between the Saône and the Rhine) called upon the Suebi to fight their battles against their neighbours on the lower Saône, the Aedui. The Suebic chief Ariovistus, a man born out of his time, and the prototype of the German chieftains who eventually carved *Systematic* themselves principalities out of the decaying *conquests* Roman empire, duly assisted the Sequani to *by Ariovistus* overcome the Aedui; but he retained part of his allies' territory in Alsace as the fee for his services and set to work to repeople it systematically with German settlers (*c.* 65–60). At the same time as Ariovistus was building his bridgehead on the left bank of the Rhine, the Helvetii, a Celtic tribe which had recently been pressed back from southern Germany into Switzerland, and now anticipated a further thrust against it by the Suebi, prepared to migrate across the territory of the Aedui in quest of a new home near the Atlantic seaboard. Information of these movements had been laid before the Senate by the Aedui, who invoked Roman *The Aedui* aid by virtue of their long-standing treaty of *invoke* friendship (p. 211). But the Senate gave them *Roman aid* nothing better than empty promises, and it stultified even these by entering into relations of *amicitia* with Ariovistus, who was wily enough to bid against the Aedui for Roman favour.

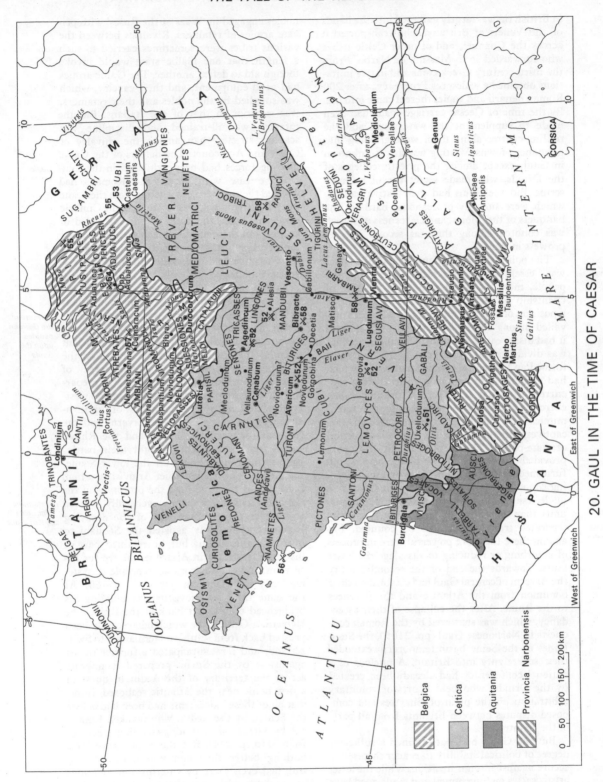

20. GAUL IN THE TIME OF CAESAR

Belgica

Celtica

Aquitania

Provincia Narbonensis

0   50   100   150   200km

2. Caesar's Advance to the Rhine and the Channel

At the outset of 58 Caesar was still lingering near Rome when news was brought that the Helvetii, after a previous false start, were about to cross the Rhône near Geneva (a village in the territory of the Allobroges), and to traverse the Roman province on the way to western France. With the legion that was stationed in the Transalpine province he hastened to the threatened point and headed off the invaders. But the Helvetii found an alternative route across the Jura and the land of the Aedui, who renewed their solicitations for Roman assistance. In answer to their call Caesar at first went no further than to cry halt to the Helvetii and demand hostages from them. But when the Helvetii refused these terms and resumed their march he advanced across Aeduan territory to meet them with his four original legions (which had now been concentrated along the Rhône) and two newly enrolled ones. Near Bibracte (modern Autun) he was counter-attacked and all but defeated through the failure of the Aeduan horse to protect the flank of his advancing infantry; but his legionaries pulled the battle round. After this encounter the remnant of the Helvetii complied with Caesar's injunction to return to their homes.

Caesar repels the Helvetii from Aeduan territory

The vigour with which Caesar had bundled back the Helvetii opened the eyes of the Gallic chieftains at large. Deputations from all parts of the country now joined the Aeduan leader Divitiacus in requesting his aid against Ariovistus, whose inroads had left the Gauls alarmed but helpless. Their appeal put Caesar into a false position, for he was the author of the senatorial resolution which recognised the German chief as a friend of the Roman people.[2] He therefore made two successive attempts to come to an understanding with Ariovistus, requiring nothing else of him than that he should restore the hostages taken from the Aedui and transfer no more of his countrymen to Gallic soil. But Ariovistus repudiated Caesar's claim to speak for the Gauls and openly avowed his intention of extending his conquests to the Atlantic. His jaunty manner was not without effect upon the Roman army, which fell into a panic when it received orders to move forward to the Rhine. But Caesar shamed his men out of their fears, and made them face up to the Suebi in a set battle at the foot of the Vosges (near Cernay). In this action the Germans, who were indifferently equipped and mounted, but surpassed the Romans in strength and agility, held their own until Caesar's lieutenant, P. Crassus, the son of the triumvir (his subsequent death at Carrhae

Appeal of the Gauls to Caesar against Ariovistus

Caesar expels Ariovistus from Gaul

has already been recorded, p. 257) threw in the Roman reserves on his own initiative. The rout of the Suebi, once begun, extended as far as the Rhine; their confederacy fell to pieces, and a long period of security set in for the Gauls along the middle and upper Rhine.

At the end of 58 Caesar had discharged his obligations in Transalpine Gaul and was free to transfer his troops to his Cisalpine province. But at this stage he abandoned whatever schemes he might have formed for conquests on his Italian frontiers and committed himself to the subjugation of all Transalpine Gaul. In quartering his legions for the winter at Vesontio (Besançon) he virtually annexed the territory of the Aedui and Sequani, and conveyed a warning to all the other Gauls which these were not slow to heed. Except that under Caesar's leadership events in Gaul moved much faster, the situation in that country now resembled conditions in Spain during the second century; in either case the natives had borrowed one foreigner to expel another, only to find that they had merely exchanged masters.

Caesar definitely plans a conquest of Gaul

The first reply to Caesar's notice of annexation came from the Belgae. In 57 a coalition of all the Belgic tribes except the Remi (near Reims) took the field against Caesar, who advanced with an augmented force as far as the Aisne. The 'battle of the Aisne', which was never delivered, was decided by masterly inaction on the part of Caesar, who had ascertained that the Gallic army was too unwieldy for its ill-organised supply corps, and simply waited for it to disperse for lack of provisions. Once the Gallic retreat began Caesar pressed the pursuit in this direction and that, and in a lightning campaign reduced the greater part of what is now northern France. His operations were greatly assisted by a powerful siege-train, which overawed rather than actually battered the Gallic towns into submission. In the extreme north of Gaul a lesser coalition headed by the Nervii (of Hainault) offered a more stubborn resistance. On the banks of the Sambre Caesar let himself be surprised by their tribal levy and all but lost his army in a confused and desperate hand-to-hand encounter. Thanks to their higher battle-discipline, and to Caesar's exemplary presence of mind in extricating them out of their disorder, the legions eventually turned the tables upon the Nervii. After this hard-won victory the reduction of the Belgae was all but completed within the same year. While Caesar was engaged in the north of Gaul, a detachment under P. Crassus made an easy progress along the western seaboard from Normandy to the Garonne and received the submission of the peoples of this coast with scarcely a blow struck.

Caesar's campaign against the Belgae

His battle against the Nervii

Caesar's aggressions in western Gaul

Crassus's unprovoked attack upon the peaceful Atlantic populations proved beyond all doubt that Caesar was now aiming at nothing less than the complete annexation of Gaul. It also revealed his plan of campaign: he was ringing off the inland in order to subdue it at his leisure.

At the end of 57 Caesar gave out, and possibly believed, that all Gaul had been pacified. But after the first shock of surprise many of the Gallic tribes recovered their breath and ventured on a new trial of strength. In 56 the Atlantic peoples, led by the Veneti of Brittany, reasserted their independence and prepared to reduce Caesar to a stalemate by retiring to their strongholds on the tidal estuaries, which were inaccessible by land except at ebb tide. But Caesar took the Veneti in rear with a fleet which he had hurriedly built on the Loire. His light galleys of Mediterranean type, it is true, at first could neither run down nor outmanœuvre the stout oceangoing craft of the Gauls, with their wide spread of canvas. But the resourcefulness of the Roman admiral D. Brutus, who improvised scythes on long poles to cut the enemy rigging – the counterpart of Duillius's 'crows' in the First Punic War (p. 118) – and a providential calm which left the Gallic ships motionless, put the Veneti at the mercy of the Roman boarding-parties. The rebellion of the Veneti was punished by Caesar with wholesale executions and enslavements. In the same season P. Crassus continued his march from the Garonne to the Pyrenees and reduced the small and weak Aquitanian tribes without any serious struggle. Towards the end of 56 Caesar occupied all the northern seaboard between Brittany and Flanders, but he was checked by the autumn floods in this as yet ill-drained region.

Naval campaign against the Veneti

3. Caesar's Forays into Germany and Britain

In 55 Caesar was momentarily thrown on the defensive by an incursion of two German tribes, the Usipetes and Tencteri, into northern Belgium. Expelled from their homes in southern Germany by the Suebi, these peoples had been drifting in search of new land like the Cimbri and Teutones, but once on the Rhine they put their arms at the service of Gallic tribes, which seized the opportunity of employing them against Caesar. At a meeting between their leaders and Caesar near the confluence of Rhine and Meuse negotiations were opened; but Caesar took advantage of a presumably accidental infraction of the armistice by a German detachment to arrest the chieftains in his camp, to fall upon their unsuspecting followers, and to hunt down the entire horde to the last woman

Caesar massacres two migrant German tribes

and child. He followed up this massacre with an invasion of Germany. The trestle-bridge which his soldiers threw across the Rhine (in the narrow and swift reach of the river near the Lorelei rock) in ten days seemed to presage a permanent occupation of the right bank. But after a brief foray, in which he failed to bring the Suebi or any lesser German tribe to action, or to collect any profitable booty, he retraced his steps and broke up the bridge. Any passing thought which he might have had of safeguarding Gaul by conquering Germany was now laid aside, and the Rhine was definitely fixed by him as the new Roman frontier.

Caesar's reconnaissance across the Rhine

In the latter half of 55, and again in 54, Caesar made similar exploratory expeditions across the English Channel.[3] A pretext for this invasion was afforded by the intervention of some British tribes in the recent revolt of the Veneti; but Roman interest in Britain was largely of an economic order, for the island was reputed to be rich in pearls and precious metals. In Caesar's day the Celtic immigration into Britain, which had been in progress for at least 500 years, had brought it within closer reach of European civilisation. In the English lowlands the use of iron, the practice of agriculture, textile industry and the construction of framed timber houses had been introduced. In the south-eastern districts, where Belgic tribes had established themselves shortly before Caesar's coming, the iron bars that had previously served as currency were being replaced by coinages of Gallic type. But Britain's reputation for riches was not based on this solid but slow development. It was partly derived from the ancient trade in Cornish tin, which for many centuries had been conveyed by sea to Gades, and more recently had been sent overland to Narbo or Massilia (pp. 258 f.), and partly rested on its mere remoteness, for ancient venturers, like those of early modern times, habitually sought Eldorado just beyond the verge of the known world.

Britain. Its development since the Celtic immigration

Its reputed wealth

In the campaign of 55 Caesar took but a small force of his legions with him, and hardly achieved more than to secure a landing-place on the east coast of Kent; he was in fact in real danger for a short time until he could rebuild his fleet, which had been wrecked by storm on the exposed south coast. But in 54 he returned with five legions and made a stay of two to three months, during which he was engaged in some hard fighting. His principal opponent was a chieftain named Cassivellaunus, who ruled over a principality in Middlesex and Hertfordshire and had recently laid the foundations of British imperialism by subduing the neighbouring tribe of the Trinovantes in Essex. Though he easily defeated the Britons in battle

Caesar's abortive invasions of Britain

and captured Cassivellaunus's stronghold (probably at Wheathampstead, in the upper Lea valley),[4] he could not shake off their guerrilla activity, while his fleet again suffered severe losses by tide and wind. Moreover, his only booty was cattle. The campaign ended with the submission of Cassivellaunus; but it is more than doubtful whether the stipulated hostages and tribute were ever delivered.

4. The Final Reduction of Gaul

Although Gaul had remained quiet in 55 and 54, discontent had been simmering over the requisitions and plunderings of the Roman armies and the compulsory levies of auxiliary troops which Caesar had latterly imposed upon the chieftains. In the ensuring winter Ambiorix, king of the Eburones (in the Ardennes), inveigled a detachment of one and a half legions out of its winter cantonments near Liège into a defile like the Caudine Forks and there destroyed it. This disaster led to sporadic rebellions in northern Gaul, and another legion under the command of Q. Cicero (brother of the orator) was closely beset in its camp by the Nervii. But Caesar relieved Cicero by a forced march from his quarters at Samarobriva (Amiens), and in the summer of 53 he reduced the insurgents one by one.

Risings in northern Gaul

The real trial of strength, however, was yet to come. After a winter spent in Cisalpine Gaul (53–52), Caesar was recalled beyond the Alps to meet an adversary of equal rank. The severity with which he had repressed the previous year's risings had stiffened rather than broken the spirit of resistance among the Gauls, and the tribes of central France, which hitherto had stood aloof, now put themselves at the head of a more formidable rebellion. This movement was directed by an Arvernian chief named Vercingetorix, who had revived the kingship in his own tribe and was acknowledged as commander-in-chief of a bloc of insurgent peoples between

Central Gaul is united and organised by Vercingetorix

Loire and Garonne. With rare discretion Vercingetorix stinted his levies in order to maintain their quality, and he imposed a Roman strictness of discipline upon them. The Gauls had at last produced an army and a leader that could meet Caesar on even terms.

On his return from Italy in the spring of 52 Caesar found himself almost cut off from the main body of his troops, which had been cantoned in north-eastern Gaul. He drew Vercingetorix away from his line of communications by a sudden irruption through the snow-bound Cévennes into Arvernian territory, and thus cleared his path to the Seine valley, where he concentrated his forces. Reverting to the attack he crossed the Loire and set siege to Avaricum (modern Bourges). Here Vercingetorix attempted to starve out the investing army, after the manner of Lucullus at Cyzicus (p. 251); but before the Roman commissariat had quite given out the attackers broke into the city and replenished their supplies. From Avaricum Caesar pushed on to Gergovia, in the heart of the Arvernian country (near Clermont-Ferrand), but in an attempt to carry the fortress by a *coup de main* his troops got out of hand and were hurled back with considerable loss.

Caesar invades Vercingetorix's land, but suffers a defeat at Gergovia

After this setback, which broke the spell of Caesar's invincibility, all the Gallic tribes except three declared themselves against him; even the Aedui made common cause with the rebels. Caesar's position was now all the more critical, as he had sent back four legions under T. Labienus to northern Gaul. For a second time he eluded Vercingetorix and rejoined Labienus, who had meanwhile won a complete but ineffectual victory over a coalition of lesser insurgents near Lutetia (modern Paris). After this reunion Caesar stayed long enough in northern Gaul to replace his absconding Aeduan horsemen with volunteers from the nearest German tribes, out of whom he improvised a serviceable cavalry by providing them with Gallic mounts in place of their native ponies. He had scarcely completed this reorganisation, when an impending attack by Vercingetorix upon Gallia Narbonensis obliged him to retrace his steps for the defence of the province. For the moment all the work of the past six years seemed wasted. But a battle near Dijon, where Vercingetorix attempted to waylay the retreating Romans, but was himself roughly handled by the German substitute cavalry, gave back the initiative to Caesar.

General revolt of Gaul

Caesar beats off Vercingetorix's attack

After this reverse Vercingetorix committed the fatal mistake of retiring behind the walls of a hill-city named Alesia (modern Alise).[5] Whether his intention was to gain breath and re-form under its shelter, or to apply the 'ham-

The Siege of Alesia

26.1   Probable portrait of Vercingetorix. Roman *denarius* of 48 B.C.

mer and anvil' strategy of holding the enemy under the fortress-walls, while a Gallic relief force took them in the rear, he played once for all into Caesar's hands. Applying to the best advantage the Roman legionary's proficiency in the art of entrenchment, Caesar invested Alesia with a double line of earthworks, whose complexity baffled both the besieged garrison and the mass levy which the other Gallic chiefs brought to the rescue of Vercingetorix. Caesar's defences were strained to the utmost in a final battle with the relief force, but they held firm until Alesia was starved into surrender. After the capture of Alesia some irreconcilables maintained a sporadic resistance in the far north and south, on the chance that they might outlast Caesar's term of command in Gaul, and they severely frayed Caesar's patience in a series of sieges and man-hunts which lasted to the end of 51. But after the capitulation of Vercingetorix the independence of Gaul was irretrievably lost.

Surrender of Vercingetorix, and end of the Gallic resistance

26.2 Gallic trophy, with inscription CAESAR; Roman *denarius* issued in 48 B.C.

Caesar spent the last year of his proconsulship in conciliating his former enemies. For the time being he left the tribal governments practically undisturbed, and the tribute which he imposed was little more than nominal. On these terms the Gauls made an early and a lasting peace with him. In 49 he could safely withdraw the greater part of the Roman forces and enrol Gallic auxiliaries to fight his personal battles in a civil war.

In conquering Transalpine Gaul Caesar added to the Roman dominions a country twice as large as Italy and far more populous than Spain. Like the British in India, he owed his success in large measure to the dissensions among the natives: except in the campaign of 52, he could always count on Gallic auxiliaries, and his mounted troops consisted almost wholly of 'friendlies'. Yet even in the severely matter-of-fact account of the Gallic Wars which survives in Caesar's own Commentaries, the Roman con-

Reasons for Caesar's victories

quest of Gaul appears as one of the outstanding feats of ancient warfare (p. 309). As a general Caesar made fewer tactical innovations than other famous commanders of ancient times. Like all Romans of the republican period he relied almost exclusively on his infantry to win his battles – a preference which was indeed largely justified by the extraordinary versatility of the legionary of the first century. His chief advance in technique upon his Roman predecessors lay in the fuller use which he made of his engineering resources, whether in attacking fortresses or in throwing up defensive field-works. What chiefly marked him out as one of the great captains of antiquity was the carefulness of his preliminary organisation – unlike many other Roman commanders in a strange country, he never walked into a 'Caudine Fork'; the unshakeable nerve with which he accepted the inevitable hazards of warfare – he freely admitted that war is largely a matter of chance;[6] and, above all, his rapidity in seizing and remorselessness in exploiting an opportunity offered by Fortune: in his pursuit of a broken enemy he was as unsparing of foe or friend as Alexander or Scipio Africanus. His unfailing energy and self-control, coupled with his complete frankness towards his officers and men, and his ungrudging recognition of merit, gave him an influence over his troops such as none but Scipio Africanus equalled among Roman commanders.

His military genius

Caesar's record in Gaul was marred by one inexcusable piece of sharp practice (p. 262), by exhibitions of terrorism which often defeated their own object, and by unprovoked attacks upon the peoples of the western seaboard. Yet on the whole his policy in Gaul was a typically Roman opportunism, which took proffered chances rather than pursued a set purpose of aggression. His campaigns against the Helvetii and Ariovistus in 58 might be honestly described as defensive. The crux by which his policy should be judged consists in his occupation of north-eastern Gaul in the winter of 58–57, an act whose implications Caesar must surely have foreseen. Was Caesar justified in taking the watch over the Rhine frontier out of the hands of the Gauls? After the defeat of Ariovistus all danger of a deliberate conquest of Gaul by Germans had been postponed for centuries. On the other hand Gallic disunion was a standing temptation to German marauders, and ever since the breakdown of the empire of the Arverni in the second century the Gauls had shown little disposition to put their house into better order. With the Cimbric Wars in his memory Caesar could plausibly and perhaps cogently argue that the peace of Gaul was a near concern of the Romans. Like many other

Caesar's conquest of Gaul. Was it justified?

264

Roman conquests his annexation of Gaul was neither strictly necessary nor a mere private speculation for his own profit.

Though it may be contended that the Gauls benefited no more by their forcible subjugation than if the maturer Roman culture had come to them by peaceful penetration, the compulsory contact between Gauls and Romans that followed Caesar's conquests was undoubtedly beneficial to both peoples.[7] For Caesar his term of command in Gaul was the turning-point of his career. The war-booty which he appropriated not only sufficed to pay off his enormous private debts, but enabled him to buy political services in Rome on a scale comparable to that of Crassus. He held at his beck and call an invincible army that was ready to follow him anywhere. Above all, it was as proconsul of Gaul that he 'found himself' and brought into full play his latent powers as a soldier and administrator. From this point Caesar's actions betoken a leader who is serenely conscious of his superior genius and regards himself as a Man of Destiny.

Effects of the conquest

5. The First Crisis in the Triumvirate

During Caesar's absence in Gaul the domestic history of Rome almost reduced itself to that of the Triumvirate.[8] The senatorial nobility, it is true, continued to secure most of the high magistracies for its own candidates, and it could still strike at its opponents in the courts of law. But the ultimate decision on all questions of importance henceforth rested with one or other of the three *principes*. The usefulness of such an overriding control over the short-sighted and vacillating administration of the Senate was now becoming more evident: at the end of the 50s even Cicero admitted the need of a 'rector' to give an occasional masterful turn to the helm.[9] Yet the Triumvirate was ill adapted to the exercise of a statesmanlike supervision: being based on nothing more than a temporary and evanescent community of interests, it was continually hampered by mutual suspicions among its three partners and was never free from the danger of falling to pieces.

Precarious character of the First Triumvirate

With a shrewd foreboding that Pompey and Crassus could not be trusted to play their appointed part in safeguarding him against reprisals by the nobility, Caesar had secured the services of a disreputable but talented adventurer named P. Clodius, who became for a year and a half the uncrowned king of Rome. Appointed tribune for 58,[10] Clodius ingratiated himself with the urban proletariat by means of a law substituting free gifts of public corn for the previous sales at reduced prices. But the

The legislation of Clodius in Caesar's interests

chief instrument of his autocracy was a trained and permanent army of expert scufflers, to which he gave the semblance of legality by formally enrolling its members in harmless-looking *collegia* or artisans' clubs. Clodius was thus responsible for two unhealthy developments in public life: his unwise introduction of a dole hastened the demoralisation of the people, while his organisation of the roughs led to gang-warfare and ochlocracy. Having established his authority on a secure basis such as neither Gaius Gracchus nor Saturninus had possessed he carried without opposition a supplementary programme to the legislation of Caesar and Vatinius. As a precaution against the abuse of omens by obstructive magistrates – a practice which Caesar's colleague Bibulus had recently carried *ad absurdum* – he repealed the Aelian and the Fufian laws (p. 178) and limited the right of religious obstruction to augurs and tribunes.[11] With the double object of gratifying a private feud and of depriving the nobility of its ablest spokesman he drove Cicero from Rome with a bill of doubtful legality but unquestionable efficacy, which 'deprived of fire and water any person guilty of killing a citizen without a trial' – an obvious allusion to the ex-consul's summary proceedings against Catiline's accomplices.[12] In a third bill he again killed two birds with one stone by deposing the king of Cyprus (a younger brother of Ptolemy Auletes, who had hesitated to follow the Egyptian king's good example of buying recognition from the triumvirs), and by sending Cato away from Rome with a commission to take over the late monarch's treasure. Ptolemy committed suicide. By an act of naked aggression Cyprus was added to the province of Cilicia, and the king's property enriched the Roman treasury by 7000 talents so that Clodius got funds to finance his corn-dole – but if he had hoped that Cato might have lined his own pockets and thus exposed himself to prosecution on his return Clodius was in this disappointed.[13]

Banishment of Cicero

Thus far Clodius had served Caesar well. But in the hour of his omnipotence he lost his head and prepared for his own downfall by turning his bands upon Pompey. Taken aback by this gratuitous assault Pompey for some time submitted to a siege in his own house. But eventually he beat Clodius at his own game by forming an opposition army of ruffians under another free-lance politician named T. Annius Milo, and by calling his veterans to his aid. In summer 57 Clodius was deposed from his *royaume des gueux* and reduced to relative innocuousness. The end of his reign was marked by his failure to obstruct a law sponsored by Pompey, which authorised Cicero's return from exile, and by

Clodius attacks Pompey

His eventual defeat, and the recall of Cicero

the triumphal reception accorded to the orator at his homecoming.

In asserting himself against Clodius Pompey recovered an ascendancy at Rome such as he had not enjoyed since his consulship. In 57 he received by common consent a commission to relieve Rome of a sudden and severe shortage of grain – a task which he discharged with a flash of his old-time energy. In the following winter he declined the command of an expedition to reinstate Ptolemy Auletes, who had *Pompey's* bought recognition from the triumvirs only to *ascendancy* suffer expulsion at the hands of his subjects. To Pompey a police operation of this kind could have offered little attraction. Yet his friends and his foes alike assumed that he was secretly covetous of a new military command, and this belief brought him into open collision with his col- *His quarrel* league Crassus, whose resurgent military ambi- *with Crassus* tions prompted him to compete for the Egyptian commission. This renewal of the ancient feud between Pompey and Crassus was a signal for an assault upon the Triumvirate from two quarters. Cicero, who still nursed the hope of detaching Pompey to the side of 'all good men', sought to drive a wedge between him and Caesar by proposing the suspension or partial repeal of Caesar's land legislation (p. 249), no doubt on the chance that Pompey might be willing to jettison Caesar's measures if only his personal interests in them were safeguarded.[14] At the *A crisis in* same time a nobleman named L. Domitius *the Trium-* Ahenobarbus came forward as a candidate *virate* for the consulship of 55, and gave notice that, if elected, he would introduce a bill for the recall of Caesar from Gaul at the earliest possible moment.

6. The Conference of Luca and the Dictatorship of Pompey

The Con- But whatever chances Cicero and Domitius *ference of* might have had of splitting the Triumvirate *Luca. Caesar* were thrown away by their precipitancy in *restores the* showing their hand. At the time when they *Triumvirate* opened their campaign (March 56) Caesar had not yet left his winter quarters in Cisalpine Gaul, but was stationed at Ravenna, a mere 200 miles from Rome. After a preliminary meeting with Crassus, who had hastened to post him up about the situation in the capital, he summoned Pompey to a conference at Luca, the southernmost town in his province. At first Pompey hesitated, and the fate of the coalition hung in the balance; but eventually he repaired to Luca. Here the three partners patched up their quarrels and disposed of the Roman Empire for years to come.[15] In anticipation of their coming

to terms and restoring their joint autocracy an expectant crowd of more than a hundred senators flocked to Luca to solicit their sovereign patronage.

From Luca Pompey and Crassus returned together to Rome to implement the resolutions taken at the conference. A polite warning sufficed to deter Cicero from proceeding with his attack upon Caesar.[16] Domitius persisted in his candidature, but Pompey and Crassus headed him off by entering the field against him, and with the help of some soldiers whom Caesar sent on furlough in autumn 56 to hold the Campus Martius for them, they were duly returned to *Caesar's* a second joint consulship. In 55, they fulfilled *command* their part of the bargain struck at Luca by carry- *in Gaul is* ing a law to prolong Caesar's proconsulship in *prolonged* both the Gauls for another 'quinquennium', the terminal date apparently being fixed at some point in 50 or early 49.[17] The passing of the *lex Licinia Pompeia* was strongly resisted by the aristocracy, but Pompey on this occasion did not hesitate to use violence to fulfil his promises to Caesar. In return for their services a tribune named C. Trebonius procured proconsular commands for Pompey and Crassus, to run concurrently with Caesar's commission until November 50. Crassus chose for himself the province of Syria (p. 256); Pompey took the two Spains, but by a special dispensation (for which his corn-commission was offered as an excuse) he exercised his proconsular authority by deputy, so that he might remain in person near Rome. The reinstatement of Ptolemy was *Pompey and* effected in the same year by A. Gabinius, then *Crassus* acting as governor of Syria, at a mere hint from *obtain* the triumvirs. The principal result of the con- *military* ference of Luca was that Caesar was assured *commands* of sufficient time to complete the conquest of Gaul, but conceded parity of armament to his partners, and to Pompey the sole control of affairs in the capital.

In 54 and 53 the Republic drifted into a condition of virtual anarchy. Once he had discharged his obligations to Caesar Pompey left events to take their course. But he remained none the less an incubus upon the Senate, which dared not move freely during his presence at Rome. In the absence of any serious political issues its members indulged in an intensified scramble for high office. Bribery was practised on such a scale that loan-money could only be obtained at doubled rates of interest, and the *Growing* tribunes' veto was misused with such persistency *anarchy* to obstruct the elections that the years 53 and *and disorder* 52 began with an interregnum. To moderate *in Rome* the ardour of candidates the Senate passed a resolution that in future ex-magistrates should not proceed to their provinces until five clear years had elapsed from their tenure of the magistracy; but this palliative was a totally inadequate remedy for the prevailing confusion.

The chronic disorder at Rome culminated early in 52 in an affray between the retinues of Milo and Clodius, in which the latter was killed, and in an unprecedented outbreak of rioting, in the course of which Clodius's ruffians, reinforced by all the unruly elements in the capital, burnt down the Senate-house and other buildings in the Forum. In this intolerable situation the Senate passed an Emergency Decree, by which Pompey was charged with the restoration of order. A hasty levy of troops in Italy and a few whiffs of grapeshot sufficed to drive the riff-raff under cover. But the need of remedial legislation to prevent a recurrence of the recent troubles had now become apparent to all. The Senate therefore went on to recommend that Pompey should be elected 'sole consul', and under this title the people invested him with a virtual dictatorship, such as Sulla had held, *rei publicae constituendae*. Armed with these exceptional powers Pompey carried stricter laws against bribery and breaches of the peace, which he applied retrospectively and with impartial severity against Milo and other agitators.[18] These measures sufficed to keep Rome quiet until the next civil war.

In the same year Pompey confirmed by legislation the resolution of the Senate prescribing a five-year interval between a magistracy and a promagistracy. But in view of his own assumption of such power at Rome Pompey had to consider the reaction of Caesar, who was expecting a second consulship in 48 (with a further military command to follow). Pompey therefore arranged for the ten tribunes to carry a joint measure dispensing him from a personal canvass, so that he might, if necessary, carry on his work in Gaul up to the commencement of his second consular term. To discourage other candidates from soliciting similar favours he subsequently obtained from the Popular Assembly a reaffirmation of the general statute requiring the personal presence of candidates at the hustings; but lest this supplementary act should be misapplied to the prejudice of Caesar's candidature he added a postscript to it in his own handwriting to the effect that it did not override the law of the ten tribunes. These favours to Caesar, however, were offset by a resolution of the Senate prolonging Pompey's command in Spain for a second term of five years (presumably reckoned from some point in 52). In the course of the summer Pompey took as his consular colleague, his new father-in-law, Metellus Scipio.

Rioting after the death of Clodius

Pompey is commissioned to suppress the riots

His remedial legislation

7. The Second Crisis in the Triumvirate

In 54 the premature decease of Caesar's daughter Julia, who had won Pompey's affection in a remarkable degree, removed the only bond of sentiment between Pompey and his partner; and in the following year the death of Crassus at Carrhae removed a possible counterpoise to Pompey within the Triumvirate. Nevertheless Pompey for the time being gave no sign of disloyalty to Caesar. In 53 he obliged the latter with the loan of one of his Spanish legions; in 52 he showed due regard to his partner's interests in his legislation. But the accumulation of extraordinary powers in one man's hands during this year gave the impetus to a political campaign against Caesar, into which Pompey was drawn half-reluctantly. Since 59 a group of resolute Optimates, among whom M. Cato and L. Domitius were the leading spirits, had been nursing their revenge upon the founder and ringleader of the Triumvirate. After Domitius's abortive attempt to procure Caesar's premature recall from Gaul (p. 266) Cato had demanded that he should be handed over to the Usipetes in retribution for his perfidy toward them. (p. 262). In 54 the Optimates were successful in a prosecution of Pompey's henchman Gabinius on a charge of extortion in Syria, and this minor triumph suggested a hopeful method of attack upon Caesar himself. Yet so long as they had no armed force behind them Caesar's would-be prosecutors possessed no sure means of compelling his attendance at court. The investment of Pompey with a dual command in Spain and in Italy, however, inspired Caesar's enemies with a new plan of campaign. The recent riots in Rome had brought about an emergency coalition between the Senate and Pompey. Why should this alliance not be extended to other objects? Pompey, it was assumed, must be jealous of Caesar's victories in Gaul, and apprehensive of his ambitions for the future. Accordingly the extremists in the Senate, who had made a virtue of refusing co-operation with Pompey in 61, now saw fit to prolong their fortuitous alliance with him until they should have got rid of Caesar. In the next two years their scheme was slowly brought to fruition.

Early in 51 Caesar, scenting danger in the new alignment of interests at Rome, sent a request to the Senate for a further prolongation of his command in Gaul to the end of 49, so as to close the gap between his proconsulship and his second consulship (due to begin on 1 January 48), and to leave his enemies no time to prosecute him.[19] This proposal was rejected by the House at the instance of consul M. Claudius Marcellus, a determined enemy of Caesar,

Attempts to detach Pompey from Caesar

A 'diehard' group in the Senate plans to prosecute Caesar, with Pompey's concurrence

Abortive attempts to curtail Caesar's command

and Pompey maintained a silence which the extremists took as a sign of encouragement. In May 51 Marcellus made a counter-proposal that Caesar's term be curtailed so as to expire on 1 March 50, on the plea that the reduction of Gaul was now complete. But his motion met with a chilly reception and Pompey now spoke out in defence of the *lex Licinia Pompeia* of 55, which Marcellus was virtually impugning. All further attempts by the extremists to draw Pompey on were eluded by mysterious silences or evasive replies on his part.

Pompey stands for strict justice to Caesar, and no more

On 1 March 50 the consul C. Marcellus (a cousin of Marcus) again pressed for Caesar's early recall, and Pompey now declared himself in favour of giving Caesar no less, but also no more, than his legal due. But the motion was vetoed by a tribune named C. Scribonius Curio, a bankrupt young nobleman whom Caesar had bought at an enormous price to defend his interests.[20] On the other hand the Senate humoured the extremists so far as to call upon Caesar and Pompey each to surrender one legion for service against the Parthians. Since Pompey, as expected, asked for the return of one of his legions from Spain, which he had lent to Caesar in 53, the net result of this square deal was that Caesar lost two legions.[21] After their arrival in Italy the troops handed over by Caesar were kept there at Pompey's disposal, on the pretext that the situation on the Parthian front had cleared in the meantime. But in a renewed debate on Caesar's term of office Curio outflanked Marcellus by insisting that Pompey's extraordinary double command in Spain and Italy should not be allowed to run on beyond Caesar's term in Gaul. This proposal was on the face of it entirely reasonable, and it received a hearty welcome from all those who dreaded civil war and saw in joint disarmament the best guarantee against its recurrence. Put to the vote on 1 December, Curio's motion was carried by 370 votes against 22. To the extremists, however, this solution was wholly unacceptable, for without Pompey's forces to bring him to court and see that strict justice was done they feared that Caesar might still evade punishment.

Curio (on Caesar's behalf) proposes the joint disarmament of Caesar and Pompey

In the game of constitutional chicanery the extremists had been definitely outplayed. But on the next day Marcellus appealed to Pompey to ignore constitutional scruples and to 'save the Republic' by mobilising his troops in order to bring immediate pressure upon Caesar. After some hesitation, which we need not regard as feigned, Pompey allowed himself to be overpersuaded. From this moment the die was as good as cast, for Caesar replied by summoning

Caesar's enemies, defeated in the Senate, invite Pompey to put pressure upon him

his legions from France to his winter quarters near Ravenna, and the remaining negotiations were like those of two men covering each other with firearms. At the eleventh hour Caesar made several earnest attempts to reach a compromise. Late in December he offered to surrender Transalpine Gaul at once and his other province on the day of his election to a second consulship (presumably in summer 49). But when Pompey showed signs of entertaining this offer Marcellus remained obdurate. On New Year's Day 49 Caesar repeated Curio's proposal of joint disarmament, but Pompey himself now declared that he expected the Senate to stand firm. Interpreting this hint as a command the House rejected Caesar's offer and proceeded to nominate L. Domitius to Transalpine Gaul and an ex-praetor to the Cisalpine province, with orders to take over at an early date (presumably before summer 49); to the veto of M. Antonius, who had succeeded Curio as Caesar's spokesman, it replied with threats against his person. In the next few days Cicero, who had just returned from a term of proconsular duty in Cilicia, reopened negotiations with two complementary proposals, that Caesar should retain Illyricum but not Cisalpine Gaul, and that Pompey, instead of disarming, should go to Spain.[22] But the extremist party, now headed by the consul L. Cornelius Lentulus, cut these discussions short. On 7 January the Senate, still under pressure from Pompey, passed the Decree of Emergency, and handed the Republic to the care of consuls and proconsuls, which meant, in effect, to Pompey. Three days later Caesar was apprised of this resolution, which was tantamount to an ultimatum bidding him surrender himself to his enemies. For one anxious hour he reflected in solitude; finally he made his reply by crossing the Rubicon (the frontier stream) and invading Italy.[23] Hoping against hope that he might at least curtail the fighting by fresh negotiations (preferably with Pompey in person) he made six further overtures in the course of the next eighteen months; but some of these advances were rejected by Pompey himself, others by the escort of extremists that stood guard over him.[24]

Abortive attempts at negotiation between Caesar and Pompey

The Senate, under pressure from Pompey, orders Caesar's early recall

Caesar invades Italy

From the point of view of formal law Caesar was the person mainly responsible for civil war. In 59 he had laid himself open to prosecution by using physical force for political ends. His demand for an additional extension of his proconsulship in order to evade impeachment was unconstitutional and set a bad precedent. Lastly, in crossing the Rubicon he committed high treason. On the other hand the privileges which Caesar demanded were no more irregular than the position actually held by Pompey in regard to

Unconstitutional action on both sides

Spain. Furthermore, in calling upon Pompey to put military pressure upon the Senate and in overriding M. Antonius's veto at the beginning of 49, the enemies of Caesar in their turn became guilty of violating the constitution of which they were the champions.

The civil war not of Caesar's direct making. Responsibility of his enemies

On broader grounds it may be confidently said that the civil war was not of Caesar's direct making. Surveying the stricken field of Pharsalus in 48 Caesar exclaimed: 'It was their doing; but for the support of my army they would have requited my services by pronouncing sentence upon me.'[25] This remark contains the gist of the whole case. Caesar in 49, like Sulla in 83, was offered the choice between self-defence and political extinction. Had he returned to Rome to stand his trial there can be no doubt that the jurors would have been given no option but to condemn him. That he should thus put his head into a noose was hardly to be expected; and had the Senate been given a free hand in 49, it is all but certain that it would have voted as solidly for an accommodation with Caesar as in 50 it had pronounced for disarmament all round.[26] Therefore the twenty-two extremist senators who insisted on Caesar's immediate recall were in fact insisting on civil war. To them the feud with Caesar had become a higher object than the welfare of the State.

The part played by Pompey in the genesis of the civil war is difficult to judge, because of his hesitations and tergiversations, which sorely perplexed his own contemporaries. There is no adequate reason for accusing Pompey of petty personal motives in siding with Caesar's enemies; but neither is it possible to affirm that with his eyes open he gave his allegiance to the State rather than to his political ally. The Spirit of Irony in 49 decreed that he who had the power to mobilise or to disarm, and therefore more than any other man had the whole issue of peace and war in his hands, knew least of all which way to turn, and finally deferred to his worst advisers.[27]

Pompey's vacillations

In essence the civil war was a struggle for personal power, prestige and honour, with no real constitutional issues at stake between the contenders. Caesar frankly admitted that 'his *dignitas* had ever been dearer to him than life itself', while Pompey could be branded by Tacitus as 'more secretive, not better' (occultior, non melior').[28] The origin of the war, as both Cicero and Cato recognised, lay in the formation of the First Triumvirate, which was a turning-point in the history of the Free State. Thus too Asinius Pollio, a supporter of Caesar, started his history of the great civil war with the year 60, the consulship of Metellus and Afranius. Three men, supported by armed force, by the urban populace and by many Equites, imposed their wills on the Senate. In 59 Cicero felt that he had lost freedom of speech, *auctoritas* and *dignitas* and that the State was at the mercy of dynasts, *principes*, who contended for *potentia* and *dignitas*. These were the values which they set above the constitution and which kept them on a collision course until the crash of 49 B.C.

The struggle for personal power

CHAPTER 27

The Rise of Caesar to Supreme Power[1]

1. The Campaigns of 49 B.C.

Pompey's apparent and Caesar's real superiority

When 'the die was cast', at the crossing of the Rubicon, it might seem on first view as if Caesar had thrown two aces against Pompey's double-six. The total field force at his command fell short of 50,000 men, and not more than one legion was stationed with him at Ravenna. On the other hand Pompey had at his disposal the entire resources of the Roman Empire outside Gaul. But while Caesar's soldiers were seasoned veterans and ready for a rapid concentration on the war front, his rival's army was hardly yet in being. In Italy Pompey had hardly any trained troops save the two legions recently handed over by Caesar (p. 168); the rest were recruits who for the moment lay scattered over the whole of the peninsula. In view of their unreadiness the precipitancy of Caesar's enemies in forcing a crisis at the beginning of 49 is hard to explain, except on the ground that they lent too willing an ear to the stories of discontent in the Caesarian ranks, which Caesar's former lieutenant Labienus, now a renegade in Pompey's camp, had been spreading, or that they did not foresee Caesar's midwinter march.

The first week of the campaign of 49 virtually decided the fate of Italy. Taking the fullest advantage of Pompey's backwardness Caesar advanced with bewildering rapidity and seized two of the principal Apennine passes into Etruria without a blow being struck. Without delay Pompey fell back from Rome to Capua; but whatever hopes he might have had of playing for time in southern Italy until he could

Caesar's march to Brundisium

collect a serviceable field force were dispelled by Caesar's remorseless progress down the east coast of the peninsula and the rapid arrival of his remaining legions from Transalpine Gaul. Pompey's plans were further disarranged by L. Domitius, who made an unauthorised attempt to intercept Caesar's vanguard at Corfinium, only to find himself encircled by the enemy legions converging upon him in unexpected

27.1 Pompey.

force.[2] After this miniature 'Sedan', in which Domitius capitulated with three legions, the Italian campaign resolved itself into a race for Brundisium, which was won by Pompey. Masking his embarkation with great skill Pompey drew off the whole of his remaining forces, amounting to some five legions, and shook off the pursuit of Caesar, who had no ships to follow him across the Adriatic. Thus Caesar's attempt to end the war without a battle was foiled, and Pompey was left at leisure to reconstitute his

Pompey draws off his forces

army for a second campaign. Yet in two months' time Caesar had carried all Italy with scarcely any loss to his side.

The remainder of 49 was spent by Caesar in securing his rear, previous to a fresh advance against Pompey. Returning to Rome from Brundisium, he endeavoured to capture the machinery of government for his own uses. But most of the higher magistrates and the leading senators had left the city with Pompey. Caesar found a praetor named M. Aemilius Lepidus to convoke the remnant of the Senate on his behalf, but this rump would not take the risk of authorising him to fight against Pompey or even to treat with him. For the present Caesar *Caesar's* made no further attempt to place his power on *return to* a constitutional basis, and it was by mere right *Rome* of conquest that he broke into the treasury, which his flustered adversaries had not wholly emptied when they evacuated the city. Neither did Caesar make much use of his opportunities of enrolling additional troops in Italy. Though he incorporated in his army most of the troops captured from Pompey, to the end of the civil war he put his main trust in his veterans from Gaul. But Caesar was at any rate able to belie the rumours which his enemies had assiduously spread, that he was a mere revolutionary, bent on rapine and blackmail. His soldiers had observed an exemplary discipline, and the campaign of early 49 had been marked by none of those horrors that had attended the struggle between Marians and Sullans. There had been no proscriptions.

Caesar's successes in the second campaign of 49 were marred by one serious reverse. In Africa the governor P. Attius Varus had declared against him, and the Numidian king, Juba I, was his personal enemy.[3] Underrating the *Defeat and* strength of his adversaries on this front Caesar *death of* conferred the command against them upon the *Curio in* ex-tribune Scribonius Curio, who lacked mili- *Africa* tary experience, and gave him an army that contained many former soldiers of Pompey. Encouraged by a preliminary success, which he owed to a surprise landing near Utica, Curio made a hasty dash into the valley of the Bagradas in pursuit of a Numidian force, which drew him into an ambuscade. In this disaster Curio himself was killed, and two of the Caesarian legions were destroyed. His failure to secure Africa in the campaign of 49 had an important bearing on the later stages of the civil war, and for the time being it deprived Rome of one of its sources of corn-supply. But a food crisis in the capital was averted by the speedy capture of Sicily and Sardinia, which the Pompeians abandoned without a struggle.

The principal operations in the second cam-

paign of 49 were conducted in Spain, where *Caesar's* Pompey's deputy-governors, L. Afranius (a *whirlwind* veteran of the eastern wars) and M. Petreius *campaign* (the conqueror of Catiline), commanded a *in Spain* serviceable army of five legions. To insure himself against the double risk of Afranius and Petreius reinforcing Pompey or invading Transalpine Gaul Caesar in person led a force of six legions against them. He found the Pompeian army firmly entrenched in a prepared position at Ilerda in the valley of the Sicoris (a tributary of the Ebro), which he could not hope to storm without heavy losses, and he got into serious difficulties through shortage of supplies and the spring flooding of the river. Eventually he managed to dislodge his adversaries by means of his Gallic cavalry, which succeeded in cutting off their supplies; he headed off their retreat to the Ebro by sustained hard marching; he finally compelled their surrender by throwing up field-works round a steep but waterless hill on which they had taken refuge. In forty days he completely disposed of a large and not unpractised force under two capable commanders. By this dazzling feat of arms he overawed the remaining Pompeian forces in Spain, led by Varro, to a speedy capitulation. On his way back to Italy Caesar received the surrender of Massilia, which had been induced by a detachment of Pompey's fleet to make an isolated and futile stand against him, and had been reduced to extremities by his lieutenants D. Brutus and Trebonius, after some resolute fighting by land and water.

Shortly before Caesar's return to Rome the praetor Lepidus had obtained authorisation *Caesar's* from the Popular Assembly to nominate him *position is* to a dictatorship. This office was perhaps limited *legitimatised* in scope and was designed (as dictatorships had often been in the fourth and third centuries) to allow him to hold the elections (*comitiorum habendorum causa*). Armed with this emergency authority Caesar conducted the consular election for 48, at which he was both returning officer and successful candidate. After carrying some emergency legislation and holding his first dictatorship for only eleven days, he gave up the office; for the time being he was content with the consular office.

2. Dyrrhachium and Pharsalus

While Caesar was consolidating his position in Italy and the West Pompey had fixed his head- *Pompey's* quarters at Thessalonica. Though he failed to *war-* obtain active assistance from the Parthians he *preparations* received from them a promise of benevolent neu- *in the East* trality. On the strength of this assurance he

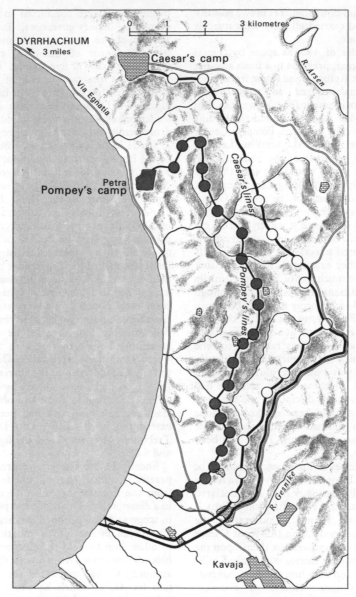

21. POMPEY AND CAESAR AT DYRRHACHIUM

Caesar, eluding Pompey's fleet, crosses the Adriatic

withdrew the Roman garrisons from the eastern frontiers, so as to make up a total force of eleven legions. From the dependent peoples of the east he collected a strong corps of horse and a fleet far outnumbering the few ships of Caesar. At Dyrrhachium on the Adriatic seaboard he formed an advanced base for the recapture of Italy in the following campaign.

But Pompey was not given the choice of battle-ground. Early in 48 Caesar carried the war to the east side of the Adriatic. For lack of transport he was compelled to throw his troops across in two relays, thus doubling the risks of destruction by winter storms or by Pompey's patrols. But he slipped across unscathed with the first division, and after a hairbreadth escape from a Pompeian blockade squadron M. Antonius rejoined him with the second instalment.[4] Though Pompey meanwhile had concentrated his forces at Dyrrhachium, he would not venture to expose them in a pitched battle against the more seasoned troops of Caesar, and therefore failed to crush the two enemy divisions before they had joined hands. With

Attempted siege of Pompey at Petra. Defeat of Caesar

a combined force of seven legions at hand Caesar now endeavoured to make a quick end to the war by investing Pompey in a field position at Petra (close to Dyrrhachium). But the siege of Petra took a different course from that of Alesia. Though Pompey was hard put to it to find forage for his cavalry he was able to replenish his other supplies by sea; on the other hand Caesar was compelled by shortage of food to detach all but the bare minimum of troops required for the blockade. Making skilful use of his inner position and of his naval transport Pompey eventually crumpled up one of Caesar's attenuated wings. The besiegers' position had now become all the more precarious, because shortly before this reverse their transport had been destroyed in a successful cutting-out operation on the part of Pompey's eldest son, Cn. Pompeius. Fortunately for Caesar his adversary's reluctance to engage his immature troops too closely enabled him to disengage from Dyrrhachium and to slip away to the cornlands of Thessaly, where he found provisions for his half-starved men. In the meantime, however, the strategic initiative had fallen into the hands of Pompey. Had the victor of Dyrrhachium now embarked a corps for the reconquest of Italy, nothing could have prevented him from repeating Caesar's walk-over in 49.

Caesar's retreat to Thessaly

But rightly judging that his true objective was Caesar himself, Pompey followed his opponent to Thessaly. Since he still distrusted his chances in open battle he used his superiority in cavalry to cut off Caesar's supplies for a second time and to wear him down before closing in upon him. But the retinue of Roman nobles in his camp, over-elated by their sudden good fortune, counted the victory as already theirs, and had fallen to quarrelling over their respective shares of the bear's skin. Again putting pressure upon Pompey, as in the critical days of December 50, the Optimates over-persuaded him to stake everything on a quick finish. On an open site near Pharsalus he drew up a battle-line of 35,000 to 40,000 men, against which Caesar could put no more than 22,000 into the field.[5] His plan, like that of Antiochus III at Magnesia, was to use his infantry to contain Caesar's front, and his powerful mounted force to take him in flank and rear. The massed cavalry easily overbore Caesar's horse, but was held up by a flank-guard of picked infantrymen, whom Caesar had instructed to handle their *pila* as modern infantry uses its bayonets. By this simple manoeuvre Caesar's select cohorts turned the tide of the battle, for the Pompeian horsemen, instead of circling round the obstacle, broke into premature flight. As soon as he had brought the enemy attack to a standstill Caesar

Pompey over-persuaded to force a decision

Battle of Pharsalus

threw in his remaining reserves, with an effect no less devastating than that of the final advance at Waterloo. The Pompeian infantry at once followed the horse in flight, and the disorder was aggravated by a failure of nerve on the part of Pompey, who at first left the rout to take its own course and, when the pursuers began to break into his camp, rode off like Persian King Darius from the onrush of Alexander's men. The Pompeian remnant which managed to escape from the camp found a momentary refuge on the adjacent heights, but here they were cut off by the untiring Caesarians, who completed their victory, as at Ilerda, by ringing off the fugitives with entrenchments. At a loss of not more than 1200 men he killed not less than 6000 Pompeians and captured 24,000.

3. The 'Bellum Alexandrinum'

Caesar in pursuit of Pompey

After the battle of Pharsalus many Pompeian officers in command of detached forces and most of his admirals surrendered to Caesar. But in Greece and the Balkans a group of irreconcilable nobles, who had made good their escape or had been stationed on Pompey's lines of communications, collected the debris of his army and embarked it at the Adriatic ports for Africa. Had Caesar retraced his steps from Thessaly and prevented this concentration Pharsalus

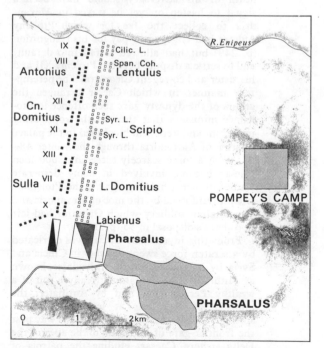

22. BATTLE OF PHARSALUS, 48 B.C.

would no doubt have been the last serious action of the civil war. But he went off in pursuit of Pompey, who had fled with a few personal companions to Egypt, seemingly with a vague hope of entrenching himself there as the self-invited guest of the young king, Ptolemy XII (son of the recently deceased Auletes). Caesar's anxiety to capture the disarmed and helpless Pompey was certainly not due to any vindictiveness against his adversary, whom he always chose to consider as the well-meaning but irresolute dupe of the extremist party among the nobles. He possibly intended to preserve Pompey by an act of calculated generosity, in the not unreasonable hope that he might renew a partnership, in which his former associate would serve as a dignified figure-head, while he gathered all effective power into his own hands.

Murder of Pompey in Egypt

But Caesar's schemes were crossed by the ministers of Ptolemy, who got rid of their embarrassing visitor by murdering him out of hand. For Pompey this piece of foul play was perhaps a kindness in disguise. Though his last two campaigns had shown that his military judgment was as clear and sound as ever, in the field of politics he had virtually become the prisoner of the nobles who drew him into the civil war, and if Caesar had brought him back to Rome he would probably have been doomed to spend the rest of his life in a gilded cage if he had deigned to survive. For Caesar the death of his adversary should have been a signal to hasten on yet he stayed in Alexandria to collect the fee for which Ptolemy Auletes had engaged to pay for his recognition (p. 249) but had allowed to fall into default, and to settle a dispute between Ptolemy XII and his sister and co-regent Cleopatra. The peremptory manner in which Caesar arranged the affairs of the dynasty gave such offence to Ptolemy's ministers that they set the royal army upon him and kept him blockaded in the palace quarter of Alexandria through the winter 48–47. With a force scarcely exceeding 3000 men Caesar became involved in many desperate rounds of street-fighting against the Ptolemaic troops, reinforced by the mob of Alexandria and some Italian soldiery which Gabinius had left at Auletes's disposal in 55 (p. 266).[6]

Caesar's delay in Egypt

Caesar besieged in Alexandria

From this investment Caesar was extricated by a scratch force swept together in Cilicia and Syria by a reputed son of Mithridates, known as Mithridates of Pergamum (really a son of a wealthy Pergamane), and by Antipater, the minister of Hyrcanus at Jerusalem. In the spring of 47 Mithridates threaded his way past the frontier-gate of Pelusium to the apex of the Delta, where Caesar, eluding the patrols of Ptolemy, joined hands with him. A few days

A relief force frees Caesar

afterwards the 'Bellum Alexandrinum' was ended in a pitched battle near one of the western Nile arms, in which the royal camp was stormed by Caesar's troops and Ptolemy XII met his death. The late king's crown was transferred by Caesar to his younger brother, Ptolemy XIII; but the effective ruler of Egypt henceforth was the co-regent Cleopatra, who had gained Caesar's favour during the siege of Alexandria. Whether rumour or truth, he is said to have spent two months with her on a holiday tour up the Nile.

His settlement of Egypt

In summer 47 Caesar began his return journey to Rome. On the way through Palestine he rewarded Antipater's services by bestowing upon the Jewish people a reduction of tribute.[7] From Syria he proceeded to Asia Minor, where he conducted a lightning campaign against Pharnaces, son of Mithridates. This prince, whom Pompey had left in possession of his father's European dominion, reoccupied Pontus during the campaign of Dyrrhachium. After Pharsalus Caesar had sent a detachment under an officer named Cn. Domitius Calvinus to expel the intruder; but Pharnaces, taking up a position near Nicopolis, defeated all attempts to dislodge him. His success against Domitius emboldened him to cross swords with Caesar himself, and even to deliver an uphill attack upon him – a manoeuvre which even Caesar's veterans might have found too difficult for them. The second battle of Zela (for the first, see p. 253) was nevertheless a hard-fought contest, and the placard which Caesar exhibited at his subsequent triumph, containing the telegraphic message *veni vidi vici*, did scant justice to Pharnaces's soldiers. Yet this engagement sufficed to end Caesar's five-day war in Asia Minor. After a new settlement of that country, in which the Galatian king Deiotarus, a former supporter of Pompey, was required to cede the eastern half of his realm to Mithridates of Pergamum, Caesar at last was free to return to Rome.

Caesar's grants of privileges to the Jews

Settlement of Asia Minor

In 48 the government of the capital had at first been carried on by the consul P. Servilius, in conjunction with the Senate. After Pharsalus Caesar was nominated to a second dictatorship, this time probably with fuller powers 'rei gerundae causa' and for a year from October 48; he appointed M. Antonius as his Master of the Horse.[8] No elections of magistrates were held for the following year, so that Antony, acting as Caesar's viceroy, exercised a temporary autocracy.

Antony as Caesar's viceroy in Italy

Servilius and Antony in turn were called to suppress disorders instigated by indebted young noblemen who had been disappointed by Caesar's financial arrangements in 49 (p. 277), first Caelius Rufus and then Cornelius Dolabella.

Antony finally quelled these riots by bringing troops into action in the Forum. His over-severe methods of repression brought him into temporary disfavour with Caesar, who transferred the Mastership of the Horse to Lepidus. A more serious danger arose from the defiant temper of Caesar's Tenth Legion (his 'crack regiment') and other veteran troops whom he had sent home after Pharsalus. These men, who were only too conscious of their past services and now considered themselves indispensable, stood out for larger bounties or earlier pensions, and ended by marching upon Rome to enforce their demands. But Caesar, arriving from Asia Minor in the nick of time, overawed them with a curt order to 'get out of uniform' – a piece of bluff which instantly reduced the mutineers to submission.[9]

Mutinies in Caesar's army

4. Thapsus and Munda

Rally of the Pompeians in Africa

Caesar stayed in Rome no longer than was necessary to conduct belated elections of magistrates for the last three months of 47 and to reduce the city to order. His second dictatorship probably ended in October, but he retained proconsular *imperium* and was elected to his third consulship for 46. After easing the economic situation, rewarding his followers and pardoning many Pompeians who submitted, at the end of the year he embarked for a midwinter campaign in Africa, which would bear no further postponement. In this province the remnants of the Pompeian forces had been pieced together into ten new legions, to which King Juba brought a reinforcement of four Numidian legions trained by Italian drill-masters, and the cavalry of the Pompeians alone had been raised to a strength of 15,000. With a somewhat untimely regard for the rights of seniority, the Pompeians had conferred the command of the Roman forces upon Q. Metellus Scipio, the father-in-law of Pompey, who deferred too readily to the ferocious but incompetent Juba; but his chief lieutenant, Labienus, was of all pupils of Caesar the most likely to beat the master at his own game.

For Caesar the African war was a race against time. He therefore took the risk of transporting his troops by instalments in the intervals between the winter gales. With his vanguard he obtained a precarious hold on the coast strip near Lepcis Minor. On a foraging expedition near Ruspina he was surprised and all but enveloped by a strong cavalry division under Labienus; but he promptly rearranged his force in a back-to-back formation and struggled through to the shelter of the adjacent hills without any serious loss. After the arrival of his later convoys, which brought his numbers up to a total of eight legions, he sought to entice his adversaries into a pitched battle. His opportunity came to him during the siege of a city called Thapsus, which was situated on a headland in the Tunisian coast and was connected with the hinterland by two corridors on either side of a wide lagoon. He allowed himself to be cut off on this tongue of land; but in making this apparent sacrifice he drew Metellus Scipio on to a position in the northern corridor where he could not decline battle, and by the headlong rapidity of his attack he broke into the enemy line and rolled it up before it had completed its formation. During the pursuit Caesar's troops got out of hand and refused to give quarter, so that the encounter at Thapsus ended in a carnage far worse than that of Pharsalus, and all the leading Pompeian officers except Labienus perished in the rout or shortly after.[10] The last notable casualty of the African campaign was M. Cato, who had been left in charge of the Pompeian garrison at Utica. After the catastrophe of Thapsus, Caesar's most implacable enemy eluded his mercy by taking his own life. Cato's suicide, which obtained undeserved notoriety and almost set a fashion, was a tribute to the Stoic philosophy to which he had become an addict. His scholastic training exalted to a Utopian level the attributes which he had inherited from his famous ancestor, heroic personal integrity and inhuman unforgivingness.[11]

Battle of Thapsus

Suicide of Cato

Like the English Civil War the conflict between Caesarians and Pompeians burnt itself out in a final blaze, which was started by a son of the defeated leader. The younger Cn. Pompeius, profiting by the good name left by his father in Spain (p. 242), and by the odium excited since 49 by a tyrannous Caesarian governor, had been engaged there after Pharsalus in raising new forces. After Thapsus he was reinforced by refugees from Africa under Labienus and his younger brother Sextus. Eventually his army grew to thirteen legions, most of which, however, were composed of native recruits.

Final Pompeian rally in Spain

After a summer spent in Rome Caesar took the field against the sons of Pompey with eight legions, and conducted his fourth winter campaign of the civil wars in the south of Spain. Unable to draw his opponents by laying siege to their strongholds he took the unusual risk of accepting combat on ground which compelled his legions to deliver their attack uphill. The action of Munda (between Seville and Malaga) was one of the hardest fought of Caesar's battles; but in the end the tenth legion overthrew an enemy flank, and the horsemen of the

Battle of Munda

Mauretanian king, Bogud, took the disordered wing in the rear. Though Sextus Pompeius lived on to wage new wars with Caesar's successors no other Pompeian officer of note survived the disaster of Munda, and the Pompeian troops were slaughtered indiscriminately. In March 45 Caesar had become the undisputed master of the Roman Empire.

Military interest of the civil war

The war between Caesarians and Pompeians was unique among the conflicts of ancient history in its range, which covered the entire Mediterranean, in the general high level of its manœuvring and fighting, and in the decisiveness with which great generals and soldiers beat good ones. In this contest the legions of Caesar proved themselves the most efficient infantry of ancient times, and their commander exploited to the utmost their tactical skill and their superhuman endurance in marching and entrenching. In no other war of antiquity, fought between two armies of approximately equal equipment, did the victors destroy the losers so completely and at such slight loss to themselves.

5. Caesar's Measures of Reconstruction

Caesar resumes Sulla's task of reconstruction

Caesar's victory in the civil war imposed upon him a task of reconstruction similar to that which Sulla had taken up but left half-completed. His first problem was to fix his terms to the defeated party. On this question Caesar's policy was plainly dictated to him by his own past record. In his earlier career at Rome he had lost no opportunity of denouncing Sulla's reprisals upon the vanquished Marians. From the time when he re-entered Italy with his invading legions he was at pains to show that he had no intention of repeating Sulla's methods. The first few weeks of his campaign in 49 proved to the Italian peasantry that they need fear no confiscations or plunderings. In this year and the next the captured enemy troops were either dismissed unscathed or enrolled in new Caesarian legions. After Pharsalus all the adherents of Pompey who sought Caesar's mercy without delay received it ungrudgingly, and not a few of them were advanced by him in their political careers. M. Brutus, who had fought at Pharsalus, and C. Cassius, one of Pompey's best admirals, were promoted to praetorships in 44. Cicero, who had passed the first year of the war in an embarrassed and self-questioning neutrality, but had joined Pompey in 48 from a sudden impulse of misplaced loyalty, was granted a free pardon.[12] After Thapsus, it is true, the obduracy of the surviving Pompeians was punished by outlawry and confiscations of

His clemency to the defeated Pompeians

property. But individual exiles for whom special intercession was made were reinstated, and a pardon was given to such a determined enemy of Caesar as M. Marcellus, the consul of 51. Caesar's policy of indulgence was amply justified by its results. It was all the more welcome for being unexpected, and it made as deep an impression as Sulla's opposite policy of frightfulness had done. The erection of a temple to the 'Clemency of Caesar' was the most sincere of all the compliments which Senate and people paid to him in return.

A scarcely less urgent and far more exacting task was to repair the machinery of the Roman government, which had been thrown out of gear by a century of inept handling and by many forcible interferences with the men at the wheel. When the battle of Thapsus brought the end of the civil war within sight Caesar was elected to a third dictatorship *rei publicae constituendae causa*, in accordance with the precedent set by Sulla, but for a fixed term of ten years. During the brief interludes between his campaigns Caesar was unremittingly engaged on the work of reconstruction, and the number and variety of his measures, enacted or projected, left those of Gaius Gracchus and of Sulla far behind them. There was scarcely a department of administration on which Caesar did not leave an enduring mark.

His energy as a reformer

In the days of Caesar the city of Rome probably had a population perhaps not greatly short of a million inhabitants.[13] The rapidity of its growth had created a serious state of overcrowding in its central quarters; and the difficulties of maintaining order among the urban proletariat had proved too great for the senatorial government. Caesar's contributions to the architectural history of Rome will be considered in a later chapter (p. 304); here it will suffice to mention that the scheme for decongesting and reconstructing the centre of the city, which successive emperors carried out in the next two centuries, originated with him. Caesar hardly touched the problem of public security in the capital. His only contribution to its solution was a half-measure prohibiting all private clubs, except *bona fide* associations of artisans and traders, and religious conventicles such as the Jewish synagogues. On the other hand he was the first, and indeed the only Roman statesman to deal effectively with the question of the idle proletariat. With one resolute swing of the axe he reduced the number of recipients of free corn from 320,000 to 150,000; for 80,000 of the disqualified recipients he made provision by sending them to his new colonies overseas. To ensure a more regular supply of corn he made plans for the excavation of a commodious arti-

Problems in the administration of Rome

Curtailment of the corn distribution

ficial harbour at Ostia to replace its inadequate open roadstead.

A war-time measure of equal benefit to Rome and to Italy was enacted by Caesar on his return to Rome in 49 from the campaign of Ilerda. With a view to mitigating the hardships arising from a financial panic and the consequent abrupt calling in of all outstanding debts he arranged an equitable accommodation between lenders and borrowers.[14]

Public works in Italy

Caesar's concern for the material welfare of Italy was expressed in an abortive and probably unenforceable law, requiring all citizens of means to invest part of their estate in Italian land, and in a series of more practical schemes for new public works. His most ambitious projects provided for the drainage of the Pomptine marshes and of the Lacus Fucinus, a large mountain-tarn in central Italy. Though none of these enterprises was carried out in his lifetime, most of them were brought to fruition under the early emperors. A statute requiring graziers to employ not fewer than a certain quota of free herdsmen should not be regarded as a step towards the abolition of rural slavery, but as a measure of insurance against servile revolts.

Enfranchisement of the Transpadanes

On his return to Rome in December 49 Caesar carried a bill – whether in his own name or in that of some praetor or tribune is not certain – to confer full franchise in lieu of the Latin status on the people of Transpadane Gaul.[15] This constitutional reform he had advocated from the beginning of his political career; after his campaigns in Transalpine Gaul he lost no time in carrying it into effect, in recognition of the valuable service which his Transpadane soldiers had rendered. Caesar's interest in the removal of constitutional anomalies is also shown in two statutes which he drafted for the regulation of municipal government in Italy. In one of these acts he prescribed uniform rules for the municipal *cursus honorum* and admission to the local senates; in the other he made arrangements for the more accurate and punctual performance of municipal census operations.[16]

New rules for municipal government in Italy

The condition of the provinces had engaged Caesar's attention from the outset of his career. As a political debutant in 77 and 76 he had attracted passing attention upon himself by prosecuting (albeit without success) two of Sulla's most rapacious governors; as consul in 59 he had tightened the law relating to extortion. After Pharsalus he reduced the taxation of Asia and perhaps of other eastern provinces, which had suffered heavily from the requisitions of Pompey's officers, and transferred the rights of collection from Roman tax-farmers to the municipal governments. But it is not certain whether

Reductions of provincial taxation

these concessions were intended as anything more than temporary palliatives in distressed areas.[17] In Asia and Sicily he substituted a land-tax of fixed amount for the tithe previously imposed – a permanent reform which probably was of more benefit to the Roman treasury than to the taxpayers. A positively retrograde measure, by which he limited the term of ex-praetors in the provinces to one year and that of ex-consuls to two, was clearly not inspired by solicitude for the natives, but by fear of ambitious governors bent on crossing their Rubicon.

With these incidental innovations Caesar hardly touched the fringe of administrative reform in the provinces. Nevertheless his dictatorship was a period of fundamental importance in the history of the provinces, because at this time the first clear gaps were made in the barriers which had hitherto separated the provincials from the Italians. Though the nobility had not been able to prevent a considerable emigration of Italian peasants and traders (p. 299) it had discountenanced their corporate settlement abroad, and only in rare cases had it sanctioned the constitution of colonies on foreign soil.[18] Caesar, on the other hand, kept the tide of emigration flowing in a double current. He drained off to the provinces the superfluous proletariat of Rome, and he pensioned off the greater number of his old soldiers with grants of provincial land – only for a favoured few did he reserve allotments on Italian soil. To all these overseas settlements he gave the status of Roman or of Latin colonies,[19] and he accorded similar privileges to some of the older groups of Italian residents abroad. It is estimated that not fewer than twenty colonies were constituted by him in the provinces, and that more than 100,000 Roman citizens received new homes from him in foreign parts. In Spain his principal foundations were Hispalis (modern Seville) and Tarraco (Tarragona); in Gaul, Arelate (Arles), which received a large slice of confiscated territory from Massilia, and Lugdunum; in Africa, Carthage, where Caesar provided for a large settlement of Roman proletarians on the site laid under a curse by Scipio Aemilianus. Although the greater number of Caesar's colonies were situated in the western Mediterranean some experimental settlements were made in the oriental provinces; but among these Corinth alone, which was like Carthage a proletarian colony, attained any importance.

Colonisation in the provinces

The primary object of Caesar in planting his colonies outside of Italy was a financial one – provincial land cost him less than Italian soil. But it may safely be assumed that he also had in view the contribution of Italian settlers to the romanisation of the overseas lands inhabited

Romanisation of the provinces

Grants of Roman franchise to provincials

by them, and gave active encouragement to this tendency. He also broke new ground in making gifts of Roman franchise to provincials who had earned this privilege by services to the Republic or by voluntary acceptance of Roman culture. Since the time of Marius Roman generals had made occasional grants of Roman citizenship to auxiliary troops, and the Senate had given *de facto* recognition to this practice; but such enfranchisements had remained few and far between. Caesar, on the other hand, made lavish use of his right to reward military service with citizenship, for he enfranchised *en masse* an entire legion (the *Legio Alaudae*, so called from the lark's crest on its helmets), which he had recruited in Narbonese Gaul. But he was not content to admit to Roman citizenship, by a side door only, however widely flung open. He made provision by legislation for the future enfranchisement of all medical practitioners and high-school teachers taking up their domicile in Rome, and he conferred Roman or Latin status by statute upon the burgesses of several provincial municipalities. The first towns to receive full Roman franchise were Gades and Olisipo (modern Lisbon) in Spain. Several cities of Gaul and of Spain, including Tolosa (Toulouse), Vienna (Vienne) and Avenio (Avignon), obtained *ius Latii*, and all the towns of Sicily were raised to Latin status. Besides enrolling in the Senate many *novi homines* from the municipalities of Italy Caesar admitted to it some notables of Cisalpine and Narbonese Gaul. Caesar's policy of gradually breaking down the distinction between Italians and provincials, and of converting the Roman Empire from a military dominion into a mere commonwealth, was his most important contribution to Roman statesmanship, and on this question he gave a lead which his successors could not ignore.[20]

6. Caesar's Foreign Policy. Miscellaneous Reforms

Raids and counter-raids in the Balkans

Though Caesar is not known to have formulated any definite policy in regard to the Roman frontiers he laid plans for their extension on several sectors. The first danger point to which his attention was drawn was in the Balkans. In the previous half-century these had been the scenes of many sanguinary raids and counter-raids. In 75–73 C. Scribonius Curio (the father of Caesar's associate) had threaded the Vardar valley into Serbia and had carried Roman arms to the Danube. In 72–71 M. Lucullus had supported his brother's campaign in Asia Minor by devastating Thrace and the Black Sea border. But at best the policy of 'butcher and bolt' was

no adequate substitute for the rectification of the haphazard and highly vulnerable boundaries of Macedon and Illyria. Caesar, who had foreseen the need of extending the Roman frontiers in the Danube region as early as 58 (p. 258), detailed some of his troops after Pharsalus to repress the incursions of the Delmatae (of Bosnia) into the Adriatic coastlands. An expedition which A. Gabinius (the former lieutenant of Pompey, whom Caesar had recalled, together with other political exiles) conducted against them in 48–47 ended in disaster; his successor, P. Vatinius (the tribune of 59), held the Delmatae in check, but did not break new ground against them.

Growth of a Dacian empire. Caesar plans a preventive attack

But a more serious enemy than the Dalmatian raiders arose in the region of the lower Danube. Here a chieftain named Burebistas had established a military autocracy over the Dacians, a people of Thracian stock that inhabited modern Romania and Transylvania, and had founded an empire extending from the eastern Alps to the Black Sea. Though Burebistas threw open his dominions to Greek and Roman traders, he derived much of his revenue from pillage, and his forays extended to the borders of Macedon and of Illyria.[21] Had Caesar lived to resume his foreign conquests, he would have led an expedition against the Dacian emperor, perhaps in 44 in order to safeguard communications with the East during the grand campaign which he was planning against the Parthians; alternatively, Burebistas might have been contained for the moment and dealt with later on after the return from the East.

Caesar's projected invasion of Parthia

Though King Orodes had never followed up his victory at Carrhae with any show of vigour he had offended Caesar by his agreement with Pompey during the civil war, and in 45 he gave support to a mutinous governor of Syria. Taking to heart the lesson of Carrhae Caesar fitted out a corps of 10,000 horsemen and an auxiliary force of archers to reinforce his legionary troops on the Parthian expedition;[22] instead of invading Babylonia he intended to strike through Armenia at Parthia proper; and he was allowing himself no less than three years (44–42) to carry the war to a conclusion. A rumour was spread that Caesar had planned to return from the East by way of Russia and Germany, conquering half of Europe in his stride;[23] but this story may be set aside as a mere embroidery upon his real schemes. In southern Russia he allowed Pharnaces to retain his throne. After the death of this ruler, who was supplanted *c.* 45 B.C. by his son-in-law Asander, he commissioned Mithridates of Pergamum to expel the usurper and add Pharnaces's possessions to his kingdom in Pontus, but he gave Mithridates no military sup-

Caesar's lavish expenditure

port. Had Caesar been able to carry out his schemes of further conquest he would no doubt have advanced the Roman frontier to the Danube; we do not know where he would have fixed the Roman boundaries in the East.

As a financier Caesar was less ruthlessly predatory than Sulla, but his methods were not essentially different. His lavish entertainments of the Roman populace (including a four-day triumph in 46 over the Gauls, Pharnaces, Juba and Ptolemy XII, and in memory of his victory at Munda in 45), the handsome bounties and pensions which he provided for his soldiers, and his extensive schemes of new public works, involved a heavy capital expenditure; and a permanent new burden was laid by him upon the treasury when he raised the yearly pay of the troops from 120 denarii (a rate which had been in force for at least a century and was scarcely adequate for a professional army) to 225 denarii.

and extensive confiscations

On the other hand Caesar did not increase the rates of the regular imposts; neither did he make the existing revenue go further by drastic reforms in administration. For his additional requirements in money he had recourse to special exactions and requisitions, which in the long run would have drained the taxation-fund, but yielded a prolific revenue for the time being. He not only confiscated the estates of Pompeians who delayed their surrender after Pharsalus (p. 276), but imposed heavy fines upon the African and Spanish towns that had shown sympathy with his adversaries. After his return to Rome from the East he raised large sums by sales of privileges to dependent kings and cities, and by collecting 'benevolences' from his wealthier subjects.

Issue of a gold coinage

By these expedients he not only cleared himself of his debts, but accumulated a fund of 175,000,000 denarii in the treasury and of 25,000,000 on his personal account. From the plentiful stocks of precious metals in his possession he made the first regular emission of gold coins at Rome, the *aurei* or equivalents of 25 denarii.

Miscellaneous measures

The long tale of Caesar's administrative reforms ends with some miscellaneous measures of varying degrees of importance. To the fiasco of Sulla's sumptuary acts Caesar added another which proved equally abortive – a unique example of merely stupid legislation on his part. He devised a premature project for the codification of Roman law, an undertaking which had to wait 500 years for its consummation. He disqualified the *tribuni aerarii* from jury service (p. 243). He gave the first public support to popular education at Rome by planning a public library under the charge of Rome's greatest scholar, M. Terentius Varro (p. 310). Finally, he rectified the Roman calendar, which had fallen

Reform of the calendar

into a state of chaos before the civil war, by adding sixty-seven days to the year 46, and by introducing a solar calendar based on the calculations of Sosigenes, an Alexandrian man of science. With a slight modification introduced in 1582 by Pope Gregory XIII and not adopted in Britain until 1752, this calendar is still in use at the present day, and therefore represents the most lasting of Caesar's reforms.

In the rare intervals between his multifarious political activities Caesar found time to compose two notable literary works, his *Commentaries* on the Gallic and Civil Wars (the latter unfinished), and a couple of pamphlets known as the 'anti-Catones', in which he replied disparagingly to a eulogistic memoir of Cato by Cicero – a posthumous reprisal more worthy of Sulla than of himself.

7. Caesar's Constitutional Position

When Caesar became *dictator rei publicae constituendae causa*, it was generally believed that, however much his reforms might alter the details of Roman administration, they would not destroy the general framework of the republican constitution. His autocracy, however prolonged, was not expected to outlast the crisis out of which it had arisen. After his return from Africa in summer 46 it began to be surmised that he

Caesar's accumulation of offices

27.2   Julius Caesar, dictator.

might not follow the example of Sulla in abdicating his emergency powers. Occasional remarks of his, in which he called the Republic a 'mere name without a substance', and dubbed Sulla an ignoramus for resigning his dictatorship, might be disregarded as mere *boutades* that reflected nothing but a passing mood. But his actions began to give substance to his words. Although his dictatorial powers invested him with ample authority to carry through his work of reconstruction he assumed a bewildering assortment of additional offices and insignia.[24]

Inter alia, he held a consulship in 48, 46, 45 and 44, and a *praefectura morum* with censorial powers in 46–44. In 44 he accepted the *sacrosanctitas* of a tribune. In the new calendar he allowed the month 'Quintilis' to be renamed 'Iulius'. He adopted from the Hellenistic kings the custom of placing his portrait on his coins.[25] He allowed his statues to be set up, one even in the temple of Quirinus (the deified Romulus), while another showed him with a globe beneath his feet; thus the sharp line which the Roman pontifices had hitherto drawn between the *res humana* and the *res divina*, became blurred. Caesar's growing disregard for republican usage is also shown in his arbitrary treatment of the magistracy. His action in raising the number of aediles from four to six, of praetors from eight to sixteen, and of quaestors from twenty to forty might suggest on first impression that he intended to give more scope and a wider range of functions to the republican executive. Yet in 47 and 45 he made no arrangements for the election of officials (other than tribunes) for the current year until summer or autumn, and he virtually appointed all the higher magistrates in advance by his personal recommendation.[26] While the ordinary magistracies were in abeyance, the routine business of administration, so far as it was discharged at all, was gathered in the hands of Caesar himself or of his Master of the Horse. In 45 Caesar took a further step towards monarchy in appointing eight *praefecti* to assist the Magister Equitum Lepidus during his absence in Spain – the forerunners of the future imperial executive.

His disregard of republican usage

To the end of his life Caesar showed respect for the Senate so far as to submit his decisions to it for information; but he did not invite it to assist him in forming them. His deliberations on important matters of state were held in private, and to these he did not summon men like Cicero who were steeped in the senatorial tradition.[27] His chief confidants were two persons of equestrian standing, L. Oppius and C. Cornelius Balbus, the latter of whom was a native of Gades and became a Roman by an afterthought.

His manner becomes more autocratic

Lastly, Caesar's break with republican tradition was foreshadowed by a growing imperiousness of manner and an occasional display of petty tyranny on his part, especially during the last months of his life. In earlier days he had heaped coals of fire on the poet Catullus by replying to his scurrilities with an invitation to dinner, but during his dictatorship he punished the satirical side-hits of the mime-writer, D. Laberius, by obliging him to act one of his own parts at a public performance – a galling insult to a Roman *eques*. His lack of *civilitas* was perhaps due to nothing more than his long absence from the Forum and continuous exercise of the military *imperium*; but in a society where freedom of speech had been habitually carried to the point of licence, his curt and repressive bearing suggested an autocracy in the making.[28]

On 14 February 44 the suspicions of a coming revolution were converted into certainty when Caesar assumed a new dictatorship which was to be not merely of indefinite but of perpetual duration.[29] Other honours were voted to him by an obsequious Senate. On public occasions he was to wear a triumphal robe and a laurel crown, and sit on a gilt chair instead of the magistrate's *sella curulis*. Antony was appointed as his priest (*flamen*), perhaps rather in Caesar's honour than for his worship, thus falling short of the establishment of an official cult. A temple, however, was to be erected to his Clementia.[30] Such innovations, which were hardly compatible with any kind of republican usage, increased the suspicions of his enemies if not of his friends that he had come to destroy, not to reconstruct, the Roman Republic.

His dictatorship made perpetual

Caesar, on the eve of his Parthian expedition, is unlikely to have worked out the precise position which he would occupy on his return. He is unlikely to have coveted the invidious title of *rex*: with its association with the Tarquins of old it would have given great offence to Romans and would not in fact have added to his powers. But his enemies (and possibly even some of his admirers, who did not know his mind) might fear or suggest that he was moving toward this hated title. When early in 44 he was hailed as *rex* he shrugged off the embarrassment by a feeble jest ('my name is Caesar, not King'; Rex was a Roman *cognomen*). Two tribunes removed a diadem (the symbol of royalty) which had been placed on Caesar's statue and said that he had threatened to punish anyone who spoke of him as king. Then at the Lupercalia on 15 February he refused a diadem offered to him by Antony and ordered an entry to be made in the Fasti that he had declined royalty. If it is believed that Caesar did seek the title, then the Lupercalia episode will have been staged so that if the crowd urged him on he would have accepted the diadem. But more probably he was trying to put an end to rumours by a public renunciation. However, a Sibylline oracle was discovered which was interpreted to mean that the Parthians could be defeated only by a *rex*, and so a motion was to be put to the Senate that he should adopt the royal name outside Italy. His enemies were thus cornering him.

The title of rex

The impression made by Caesar's usurpation of power was by no means wholly unfavourable.

Widespread acquiescence in his domination

In Rome voices might hiss at the name of *rex*; but the urban proletariat in general had no roots in Rome's past and little regard for republican tradition; it judged political actions by their material results, and tried by this standard Caesar's domination had every prospect of gaining its approval. The collective opinion of the Senate was equally accommodating. Once the chief guardian of republican tradition, the House was being gradually transformed into a passive instrument of Caesar's will. Its membership, now raised to the unwieldy number of 900, consisted largely of Caesar's nominees, comprising junior army officers, centurions and prominent municipal figures. Many of the senior senators habitually absented themselves from its sessions. Indeed the Senate had virtually egged Caesar on to assume a crown by the number and the extravagance of its complimentary decrees, and shortly before Caesar's death its members bound themselves by oath to defend his person at the risk of their own lives.

Resentment among a group of senators

Yet there remained individual senators who resented Caesar's usurpation fiercely. To Cicero, who had long suspected Caesar's intentions, but had been willing to give him the benefit of the doubt, the dictator was henceforth 'the tyrant', and this opinion was widely echoed among the members of the governing class. But every educated Roman was familiar with the edifying stories of tyrannicide in Greek literature, and from the time of the Gracchi political murder had found practitioners and apologists at home. Further, Caesar almost invited attempts upon his own life by his deliberate refusal to protect it by special measures. Though rumours of conspiracies had reached him from time to time he disdained to surround himself with a service of spies, and shortly before his death he dismissed his personal bodyguard – a picked corps of Spanish horsemen.

The conspiracy of Brutus and Cassius

The need of striking the blow for freedom quickly became apparent when Caesar declared his intention of leaving Rome for his projected military campaigns on 18 March. A group of sixty to eighty champions of the Republic accordingly laid a plan to assassinate him at a session of the Senate on 15 March. The originator of this plot, C. Cassius, and its figurehead, M. Brutus, were pardoned Pompeians, but the majority of their accomplices were former officers of Caesar. The conspiracy naturally included men with personal grievances against the dictator, and adventurers who hoped for a better career under a restored Republic. Yet several of the ringleaders, such as D. Brutus and C. Trebonius, who had sided with Caesar in the civil war and still stood high in his favour, jeopardised their personal prospects by joining

27.3 *Obv.* Marcus Brutus. *Rev.* Two daggers and a *pileus* (the cap worn by ex-slaves to celebrate their liberation); EID(ibus) MAR(tiis), the Ides of March. Struck by M. Brutus to pay his troops, 43–42 B.C.

the plot, and we need not doubt that the predominant motive of the confederates was a desire to serve the Republic according to their lights. Though vague rumours leaked out about the conspiracy, these were not sufficient to turn Caesar back from the place of meeting on the Ides of March – a lounge attached to a stone theatre built by Pompey. Unarmed and unattended, for the senators forgot their oath to protect him and made a bolt for their own lives, Caesar was quickly despatched under a rain of dagger-thrusts.

The Ides of March

8. Caesar's Personality and Achievements

Amid a nation whose political successes were more due to high average capacity than to a profusion of genius Caesar stood out with a colossal stature. Endowed with a vitality which after years of unending toil showed scarcely any sign of flagging, and with a versatility which gave him an easy mastery with sword and pen and tongue, he applied his talents with a swiftness of decision and a directness of aim that set him on a level with Alexander as a supreme man of action. The *Caesariana celeritas*, at which his contemporaries marvelled, was no more evident in the pedestrian prowess of his soldiers than in the workings of his own mind. Moreover, the consciousness of possessing these exceptional powers gave Caesar a sovereign self-assurance which cast a spell on friend and foe alike.

Caesar's many-sided genius

Yet if Caesar compelled general admiration he did not win many friends. Unlike other heroes of history, he had no sense of a religious or philanthropic mission. His driving power, so far as it was not merely egoistic, was rather a liking for abstract efficiency than a burning desire to benefit his fellow men. An efficient

Pontifex Maximus, he took little interest in religion, save as a field for antiquarian study (in the manner of his contemporary, Terentius Varro) or as a handy pawn in the political game of chess (like most other Romans of the governing class). The only guiding hand which he felt behind him was that of Venus or Fortune, which to him, as to Sulla, was little more than a projection of his own self-confident ego. Though he was generous and frank in his appreciation of other men's services it is difficult to detect in him a vein of that natural kindliness which endeared Alexander even to those who feared him. His matrimonial record resembled that of Sulla or Pompey or many another Roman noble in its unblushing utilitarianism; his *affaire* with the Princess Cleopatra was but a passing incident. His subordinates gave him strict obedience, but did not open their minds to him. Therefore, while the unanimous verdict of antiquity proclaimed Caesar a great man, not a few saw in him a 'great bad man', and regarded him mainly as a destroyer.[31]

His essential egoism

But to the student of history his personality is less important than his achievements. Caesar's capacity for 'getting things done' is nowhere more apparent than in the quantity and the range of his administrative reforms. The work which he accomplished in 46 and 45 went farther and cut deeper than the sum total of new legislation in the generation after Sulla. With rare exceptions his measures were informed by practical good sense, and they set a new standard of administrative efficiency to his successors.

Caesar's achievements as a reformer

The final issue, however, on which Caesar's reputation depends is whether he was justified in usurping autocratic power. On this question no final judgment is ever likely to be passed.[32] It is a not uncommon view (to which Cicero gave free expression in his last writings) that from the time of his entry into politics Caesar had decided to make himself king. But the actual facts of his career militate against this. The theory that he was inspired by eastern models of monarchy is equally difficult to maintain. The Hellenistic rulers of Caesar's own day were anything but an inspiring example, and Caesar's

His usurpation of autocratic power – was it justified?

own experience of ruler-craft was gained almost entirely in Rome itself and in the western provinces. It seems more likely that the germs of his ambition were laid in his long term as a virtual autocrat in Gaul, and were brought to maturity during the dictatorship which was thrust upon him as a necessary consequence of the civil war.

But whatever the precise motives for Caesar's usurpation of power a broad justification for it may be found in the history of the Republic since the time of Sulla. The first dictator *rei publicae constituendae* naturally and rightly set himself to mend rather than to end the Republic. It was the failure of his attempt at reconstruction which gave Caesar reason to think that the Republic might be past mending. Leaving aside all minor issues we may hold that the crucial test of the restored senatorial government of the period after Sulla was whether it could control the chiefs of the professionalised army. Its failure to establish some sort of 'Concordia Ordinum' against the use of physical force in politics may be regarded as its death-warrant. On this ground Caesar had good cause to try a new system, by which the chief war-lord should assume political responsibility in his own person.

Definite failure of senatorial government

Caesar has often been accused of making his transition from Republic to monarchy too abruptly. If there is any ground in this criticism it should not be sought in the fact that he provoked a successful conspiracy against his life, for it would have been an easy matter for him to protect himself against 'tyrannicides' by the simple expedient of retaining his bodyguard. A more serious problem is whether he was not throwing old institutions on the scrap-heap before he had provided efficient substitutes. In the event of his life being spared could he have organised a new imperial executive and have carried the new régime beyond the experimental stage? This question hardly admits of a definite answer. But in any case the chaos that followed his death is no proof of failure in his statesmanship. The responsibility for this falls on those who cut short his work of reconstruction before it had been completed.

Was Caesar over-hasty?

CHAPTER 28

The Second Triumvirate [1]

1. The Interim Administration of Antony

The Ides of March end in chaos

The tyrannicides had planned the murder of Caesar well, but they had planned nothing more. Their calculation had gone no further than this, that the forcible removal of the dictator Caesar would have the same effect as the voluntary abdication of the dictator Sulla, and that on the release of the brake the machinery of senatorial government would automatically resume work. But the senators, before whose eyes Caesar had been killed, stampeded out of the council chamber, not knowing where the next blow might fall. On the chance of rallying the fugitives by a demonstration of popular enthusiasm the conspirators sallied out to spread the glad news in the Forum; but they found the place of assembly almost deserted, and from the few bystanders they drew but the faintest of cheers. Completely baffled, and in growing apprehension for their own safety, they withdrew to the Capitol under the escort of a band of gladiators. The candle which they had lit was guttering ignominiously.

In retiring to wait upon the course of events the conspirators let the initiative pass into the hands of Caesar's chief assistants, M. Aemilius Lepidus and M. Antonius. At the time of Caesar's death Lepidus, who was about to take up the governorship of Gallia Narbonensis and Hispania Citerior, had at the gates of Rome a legion of recruits waiting to proceed to Gaul. Without delay he brought a detachment of these troops into Rome and prepared for an attack upon the Capitol. But before the assault was delivered he allowed the conduct of affairs to be taken out of his hands by his more capable colleague Antony, and a few days later he with-

Mark Antony takes charge

drew to his province. M. Antonius was, like Sulla and Caesar, a member of an ancient family, which of recent years had achieved no more than moderate distinction; his father had made an inglorious ending to his career in the war against the pirates (p. 250). After a dissipated youth, during which he acquired an incurable habit of reckless spending, he found his true vocation as a lieutenant of Caesar in Gaul. His burly limbs and boisterous good humour, which a sudden gust of passion would sometimes eclipse but could never extinguish, endeared him to the troops, and his resourcefulness in the field commended him to Caesar, who promoted him to be his chief deputy in the civil war. After the campaign of Munda the passing misunderstandings between him and his chief (p. 275) had been cleared away, and in 44 he was Caesar's partner in the consulship. In fear for his own life – indeed the tyrannicides had debated whether he should share Caesar's fate – he spent the Ides of March in hiding. But in the following night he improvised a private bodyguard, and he secured Caesar's state papers, which the dictator's widow, Calpurnia, willingly entrusted to him; on the ensuing day he took over the control of affairs from Lepidus. His experience as a general warned him to reconnoitre before engaging in action. Therefore he held back Lepidus's soldiers and convened the Senate for the next day. At the same time he came to terms with his former enemy, P. Cornelius Dolabella, a worthless but engaging young man, whom Caesar had pardoned for his escapades during the civil war (p. 274), and had somewhat weakly nominated as his successor in the consulship after his intended departure from Rome. Though Antony had previously intrigued

Antony as Caesar's vicegerent

His conciliatory policy

against Dolabella's nomination, he now allowed him to take over the fasces of Caesar.

On 17 March the senators made unwonted good use of the freedom of speech which Antony conceded to them, and came to a number of wise decisions. They carried the proposal of Cicero that the conspirators should receive an amnesty – an equitable compromise which for the time being averted fresh civil war. They accepted Antony's offer that he should submit for their approval the numerous memoranda of official appointments and orders on the treasury which Caesar had jotted down but had not yet made public, a suggestion which had the merit of setting the wheels of government into motion with the least possible delay.[2] Lastly in the same spirit of conciliation, they voted a public funeral for the dead dictator. This last resolution, it is true, almost had the effect of rescinding the previous amnesty. The sight of Caesar's body and blood-stained toga, the recital of his will (in which his great-nephew, Octavius, was named as chief heir, with D. Brutus as a contingent heir, and every Roman citizen was left 300 sesterces, together with a gift to the Roman people of Caesar's fine gardens beyond the Tiber), and a *laudatio* by Antony, which probably lost nothing for being brief, combined to stir the assembled crowds to frenzy, and the tyrannicides, who had come down from the Capitol after 17 March, now fled from Rome to escape lynching.[3] The most ominous feature of this mob-outburst lay in the attitude of Caesar's old soldiers, who were honestly angry at the murder of their chief, and apprehensive of losing their promised pensions. But the two consuls vigorously, if somewhat tardily, repressed the rioters with a hastily collected military force, and overthrew an altar which some of Caesar's admirers had set up for his worship in the Forum.

Until the end of April 44 Antony persevered in his policy of conciliation. He made no attempt to prevent those of the tyrannicides whom Caesar had previously appointed to foreign commands from proceeding to their provinces; among those who now benefited by his indulgence D. Brutus took possession of Cisalpine Gaul and Trebonius of Asia. On behalf of M. Brutus and Cassius, who were wandering about Italy in a forlorn condition and would not venture to return to the city, he procured a special dispensation from their judicial duties as praetors. He drafted a number of Caesar's veterans away from Rome by means of a new agrarian law, which provided allotments for them in Italy. In deference to the Senate's resentment at the manner in which Caesar had misused the dictatorship he carried another

measure by which that office was abolished root and branch. On behalf of himself and Dolabella he made no demand beyond two good proconsular provinces, a claim which the Senate met by assigning Macedonia to Antony and Syria to his colleague.

The entente between Antony and the Senate saved Rome from impending chaos after the Ides of March, and it gave apparent proof that the republican constitution could and would be restored. But its success was jeopardised from the outset by Antony's traffic in privileges and immunities, for which he obtained a fictitious authorisation by producing forged *acta* of Caesar, and by the cool disregard with which he ignored or evaded the Senate's attempts to set a check upon his expenditure. Moreover, at the end of April the situation was given a new turn by the arrival in Italy of Caesar's adoptive son and heir, C. Octavius.

2. The Philippics of Cicero and the War of Mutina

C. Octavius was descended from a municipal family of the Volscian town of Velitrae, which had but recently passed from equestrian to senatorial rank, but had become connected with the Julian *gens* by the marriage of his grandfather with a sister of Caesar. In 46 the dictator had made acquaintance with his grand-nephew; in the following year he had sent him to Apollonia in Epirus to begin his military training, and had altered his will in favour of the young man. At the news of Caesar's death Octavius, who was but eighteen years of age, had no definite reason for believing that he would be called upon to assume the dictator's political heritage, but shrewdly suspecting that he might have been remembered in his will, he returned to Italy to watch his own interests. On discovering that he was Caesar's heir-in-chief and had been adopted as his son, he proceeded to Rome, where he took the name of C. Iulius Caesar Octavianus, and visited Antony (as Caesar's trustee) to claim his share of the dictator's estate. Antony, who had dissipated Caesar's private fortune as rapidly as the public funds, tried to bluff the young suitor out of his rights by an ostentatiously rude refusal, but merely succeeded in drawing out his fundamental quality of pertinacity. In May 44 a duel began between Antony and Octavian (as modern scholars call him from this date), in which the latter attempted, not without success, to steal the sympathies of Caesar's old soldiers from Antony by the magic of his new name, and effectively played upon their resentment at Antony's indul-

---

Antony agrees to an amnesty for the conspirators

His funeral speech over Caesar

He represses riots

He concedes provincial commands to several conspirators

He embezzles public money

Caesar's grandnephew, C. Octavius

Octavius becomes Caesar's heir. His change of name

Quarrel
between
Antony and
Octavian

gence towards Caesar's assassins. For the present Antony did not retaliate directly upon Octavian; but he sought to safeguard himself against future attacks by means of a law which gave him a five years' command in Cisalpine and Transalpine Gaul in lieu of Macedonia, and authorised him to transfer Caesar's legions from Macedonia to his new provinces (June 44). By this *lex de permutatione provinciae* he hoped to protect his home front after his departure from Rome in the same manner as Caesar after his first consulship. In August the feud between him and Octavian was temporarily suspended under pressure from some of Caesar's former officers, who shared the view commonly held by Caesar's old soldiers that their interests would be betrayed if Caesar's son and Caesar's chief lieutenant were to come to blows. This attitude of the Caesarian troops repeatedly acted as a brake on the two protagonists, but it retarded rather than prevented the final trial of strength between them, and in this instance the reconciliation between Antony and Octavian was of brief duration.

Antony
quarrels with
M. Brutus
and Cassius

In July 44 Antony became involved in a dispute over a very trifling issue with M. Brutus and Cassius. At this time the two chief conspirators broke their silence in order to object to the provinces assigned to them for the ensuing year – the Senate had earmarked Crete for Brutus and Cyrene for Cassius – and to demand more important commands for themselves. To this wholly unreasonable demand Antony replied with random menaces which led Brutus and Cassius to believe that the amnesty of 17 March would no longer protect them. Overcoming their long hesitations they resolved to arm in self-defence, and abandoned Italy, like Pompey in 49, in order to recover it from the East.

Antony
offends
Cicero

In September a still more gratuitous quarrel embroiled Antony with the veteran statesman Cicero. Though Cicero had taken a leading part in the senatorial debate on 17 March, he had since then fallen into a somewhat premature state of despondency about the future of the Republic, and had again retired from active participation in public life. On 1 September Antony chose to take offence at his abstention from a not particularly momentous meeting of the Senate. On the following day Cicero reappeared in the House and in the absence of Antony delivered his so-called *First Philippic*, a speech whose conciliatory intent was spoilt by a jarring undertone of criticism. Its effect was to irritate Antony into a violent rejoinder, which in turn startled Cicero into his last great political effort.

The First
and Second
Philippic

For the moment the orator found no opportunity of retaliating; but he prepared at leisure the pamphlet known as the *Second Philippic*, in

which he branded Antony as an unprincipled adventurer who shared Caesar's traitorous ambitions but lacked that great criminal's self-restraint. Further, he convinced himself of the truth of his accusations and took the role of a new Demosthenes in defence of liberty and civilised living against brutal military dictatorship.

Octavian
and Antony
prepare for
war

In October Antony broke his armistice with Octavian by trumping up a charge of assassination against·him.[5] This ill-judged attack drove Octavian to make his supreme cast of the dice. While Antony was preparing to transfer the Macedonian legions to Italy, his rival took the hazard of calling Caesar's veterans to arms and of inciting the legions to defection. Though Octavian had no legal authority to levy troops and was inviting upon his head the punishment of a brigand, his kinship with the dictator and the magic name of Caesar which he now bore loaded the dice in his favour. Several thousands of old soldiers, who had received settlements in Campania, rallied to his standard; of the four legions recalled from Macedonia two eventually went over to his side and the temper of the remainder became so uncertain that Antony, after summoning the Senate to declare Octavian a public enemy, did not venture to put the motion to the vote (28 November). For the moment,

Antony
attacks
D. Brutus

indeed, neither antagonist would take the risk of striking the first overt blow. Octavian merely shadowed Antony, and the latter diverted his troops to Cisalpine Gaul which he had decided to take over from D. Brutus without waiting for the end of the year.

Left without support D. Brutus could not have stood his ground against Antony for long. But he received instructions from Rome to hold firm. After Antony's departure for northern Italy Cicero returned to the city and launched his crusade in defence of the Republic. He opened his oratorical campaign on 20 December with the *Third Philippic*, and in quick succession he delivered to Senate or people eleven further calls to action. In attempting to convince his audiences that Antony was aiming at a military dictatorship he set himself the hardest task of his life, for he had scarcely any real evidence to support his case, and the Senate was as little disposed to quarrel with Antony in 44 as to fix a war upon Caesar in 50. Yet by the cumulative force of his invectives he carried his point and attained a power such as he had never wielded in the prime of his life.

Cicero forms
a coalition
to save the
Republic
against
Antony

On 20 December Cicero carried a resolution in the Senate by which D. Brutus was authorised to stay on in his province until further notice. On 1 January 43 he unfolded his full purpose in the *Fifth Philippic*, in which he urged that

Octavian
receives a
commission
from Cicero

all the recent legislation of Antony, and in particular the measure by which he claimed possession of Cisalpine Gaul, should be annulled on the pretext of having been carried by force, and proposed that Octavian should be formally enrolled as an ally against Antony, with the rank of propraetor. For the time being the Senate declined to rescind Antony's laws or to break off relations with him; but it sent him an injunction to keep his hands off Cisalpine Gaul, and in anticipation of his refusal it not only gave Octavian a legal commission but ordered the new consuls, A. Hirtius and C. Vibius Pansa, to raise additional troops.

D. Brutus besieged in Mutina

Meanwhile Antony closed in upon D. Brutus and penned him up in the town of Mutina. But he did not press the siege closely, and in reply to the Senate's demands he offered to evacuate Cisalpine Gaul at once, and Transalpine Gaul at the end of five years, provided that his laws were allowed to stand, and that the pay and pensions due to his troops were guaranteed to them.[6] The moderation of these terms, which recalled Caesar's offer to the Senate at the end of 50 (p. 268), was so evident that Cicero was hard put to it to explain them away. But the effects of his crusade were now showing through. In Italy recruits were coming in briskly for the defence of the Republic: Hirtius and Pansa, though former comrades in arms of Antony, did not hesitate to take the command against him; and the Senate, instead of testing Antony's sincerity by further negotiations, annulled his legislation and proclaimed a state of emergency (February 43).

Battle of Mutina

After the rejection of his peace offer Antony drew tighter the blockade round Mutina, with a view of starving out Brutus before the relief armies were ready to take the field. But Brutus was still holding out in April, when Hirtius and Pansa joined hands with Octavian near the beleaguered city. After a preliminary encounter at Forum Gallorum, in which the consuls beat off an attack upon their marching columns,

Defeat and retirement of Antony

Antony sustained a serious defeat outside Mutina. Hastily withdrawing his troops from their entrenchments, he retreated by forced marches across the Apennines into southern France.

At Rome the news of Antony's retirement fostered the illusion that the campaign was definitely won, and the Senate now took the extreme step of declaring him a public enemy. But Antony's supposed flight was the winning move of the war. By drawing clear of Mutina he succeeded in effecting a junction with the reinforcements which his lieutenant, P. Ventidius, had been recruiting in Picenum; by continuing his march into France he was able to win over to

his side the governors of Gaul and Spain. In 43 Lepidus was stationed in Gallia Narbonensis with an army of seven legions, which included some of Caesar's best troops. Two other armies of considerable strength lay in Hispania Ulterior and in Gallia Comata (the newly conquered part of Gaul) under two former officers of Caesar, C. Asinius Pollio and L. Munatius Plancus. To all these commanders Cicero was posting dispatch after dispatch, exhorting them to hold fast by the Republic. But each in turn, when confronted by Antony, deserted to him. To Lepidus, who was disposed to haggle over terms, Antony conceded a formal equality in rank; but in effect he became the sole commander of a composite force of twenty-two legions. Re-entering Italy in the late summer of 43 Antony occupied Cisalpine Gaul without opposition. The coalition which had outfought him at Mutina had melted away, and D. Brutus, left unsupported, made an unavailing attempt to escape to the army of his namesake in Macedonia (p. 289). His army deserted him on the march, and he was put to death by a brigand chief in the Carnic Alps.

Antony joins hands with Lepidus in Gaul

He returns to Italy with overwhelming force

3. Octavian's *Coup d'État* and Pact with Antony

By a strange sequence of accidents Hirtius was killed in action at Mutina and Pansa died of his wounds shortly afterwards, so that Octavian was able to gather into his hands the whole of the relief army. But Octavian would not and could not combine with D. Brutus, the assassin

28.1 Mark Antony

of Caesar. At his first appearance in public life he had come forward to avenge no less than to inherit Caesar, and in his disputes with Antony he had made capital of the latter's supineness in regard to the tyrannicides. He therefore disregarded an instruction from the Senate to join hands with Brutus and to resign

28.2   Octavian.

28.3   Lepidus.

Octavian's false position as the ally of D. Brutus

to him the chief command, well knowing that though he might constrain himself he could not induce his troops to obey this order. The rift thus opened was widened by a succession of slights from the Senate, which had been cajoled in the first instance by Cicero's eloquence to side with Octavian against Antony, yet could not fail to discern that in the long run Octavian might prove the more dangerous enemy of the Republic. In a vain attempt to undermine his influence with his army it treated him with studied disdain, and with better excuse, but more disastrous results, it failed to provide from the depleted treasury the exorbitant sums which Octavian had promised in bounties to his soldiers. In July 43 Octavian decided to escape from his false position by forcing an open rupture with the Senate. In making a sudden and quite preposterous request for one of the vacant consulships he presented a demand which was almost certain to be refused. Cicero indeed, who had always stifled his latent distrust of Octavian, would have humoured him even at this stage, but the Senate rejected his ultimatum. Hereupon Octavian ended his long inaction by marching his troops upon Rome, which he entered without opposition. The battle of Mutina hastened on rather than averted the military dictatorship against which Cicero had struggled with heart and soul.

He breaks with the Senate

He occupies Rome by a military coup

Octavian, not yet twenty years old, was now in a strong position to face the rival army commanders. This position he owed to his courage and political skill: by appealing to the *plebs* and veterans he had raised a private army and built up a faction of friends which included three knights, Q. Salvidienus Rufus, M. Vipsanius Agrippa and C. Maecenas, to whose help he was to owe much. He now lost no time in throwing a veil of legality over his usurpation by instituting consular elections, at which he was returned in company with his second cousin, Q. Pedius. In order that his personal position might be made completely above reproach Octa-

He revokes the conspirators' amnesty

vian's adoption as Caesar's son was confirmed by a *lex curiata*.[8] His first consular act was to carry through the Popular Assembly a bill to rescind the amnesty of the previous year, and to institute a special court for the trial of Caesar's assassins, all of whom were duly declared outlaws. At the time when these sentences were passed the two murderers inchief stood at the head of powerful armies (p. 289), so that in forcing a rupture with them Octavian made another civil war inevitable. But by his next act he put an end to the existing civil war. His feud with Antony was as yet not so much an affair of principle or of vital interests as of personal pride, and this sentiment he was usually ready to sacrifice to political expediency. As soon as his relations with the Senate became strained he had made secret overtures to his antagonist, and further discussions were carried on through the mediation of Lepidus. After his return to Rome Octavian annulled the sentence of outlawry on Antony, and he followed up this offer of peace by meeting him and Lepidus at Bononia. At a conference recalling the conversations of another triad at Luca (p. 266) the three Caesarian chiefs agreed upon a common future policy.

Overtures to Antony

Conference at Bononia

Returning to Rome with combined forces Antony, Lepidus and Octavian placed their power on a regular footing by means of a law which a tribune named P. Titius hastily carried through the Tribal Assembly. By this act they were appointed *triumviri rei publicae constituendae consulari potestate* for a term of five years. From this titulature it might be inferred that the object of their special commission was to wind up a state of war, after the manner of Sulla and Caesar. In point of fact it was intended to give them an absolutely free hand in prosecuting further wars of their own making, and it threw the rule of the Senate and ordinary magistrates permanently out of gear. While the fiction of popular election was still upheld the

Constitution of the 'Second Triumvirate'. A military autocracy

higher magistrates became virtually the nominees of the Supreme Three and functioned, or enjoyed their sinecures, under their orders. The Senate was similarly packed with their adherents and did little more than register their good pleasure. It validated all their public acts in advance and reconfirmed them at the end of each year by an oath of allegiance. In support of their arbitrary policies the triumvirs exercised unlimited rights of conscription and taxed the Roman Empire à merci.[9] While they avoided the banned title of 'dictator', they were in effect a commission of military dictators of the original type, with this important difference, that they were bound by a less narrow time-limit.

Definite extinction of the Roman Republic

The 27th of November 43, the day on which the *lex Titia* was passed, may be taken as definitely marking the end of the Roman Republic. Its abolition was no less complete and its process of extinction far more painful, than if Caesar had lived to consolidate his monarchy. A faint hope of its revival after Caesar's death appeared when the play of chance, rather than the forethought of the conspirators, brought about a temporary *entente* between the Senate and Antony. So far as Antony had a predecessor it was Pompey rather than Caesar. As a man of purely military ambitions he had no desire to enter upon the full heritage of Caesar, with its burdensome entail of multifarious administrative duties. But he was not altogether unfitted to play the part of Lord Protector for which Cicero had once cast Pompey, and if he had held fast to his original policy of conciliating the friends of the Republic, he could in all probability have held Octavian in check. But his quarrel with Cicero doomed the *entente*, and with it the Republic. When the Senate at Cicero's instance cast out Antony and set up Octavian, it took King Stork in exchange for King Log. Though Octavian was destined in the event to become the champion of law against force, at the age of twenty he was still unfitted for this task; for the time being he was carried along by the troops on whose shoulders he had hoisted himself. His rise to power led naturally to the *coup d'état* of July 43, out of which the Triumvirate sprang by a logical process.

Cicero's last crusade for the Republic

4. The Proscriptions and the Campaign of Philippi

Renewal of Sulla's proscriptions

The first practical demonstration of the new dictatorship was a wholesale political massacre. Three hundred senators and two thousand Equites were pricked off on a list of suspects and delivered to the head-hunters. A few of the victims eventually obtained a pardon, a great many more found refuge outside of Italy; but the slaughter was on a scale recalling that of Sulla's proscriptions, and it had even less excuse.[10] The reason for this massacre is partly to be sought in a genuine feeling of nervousness with which the murder of Caesar infected his successors for many generations to come. But the masters of forty-three legions had small need to take fright at the disarmed remnants of the republican party. The real driving power behind their proscriptions was probably the necessity to raise without delay the enormous sums of money which both Octavian and Antony required to redeem their lavish promises to their troops.[11] In the event, however, the confiscated estates of their victims, consisting mostly of land, proved almost as unsaleable as the assignats of the French Revolution, so that the triumvirs had to have recourse to additional taxation. In the first resort they endeavoured to fasten the entire burden of the new imposts upon the wealthy women of Rome; but they deferred to the protests of a lady named Hortensia (the daughter of Q. Hortensius, Cicero's chief forensic rival), who delivered a public speech from the Rostra on the text of 'no franchise, no taxation!'[12]

Confiscations and taxations

The most notable victim of the triumvirs was Cicero, who had burnt his boats on the day when he published the *Second Philippic*. The murder of the orator closed a career whose later stages were clouded by disappointment. His first triumphs in the courts and on the hustings, and the intoxicating success of his *annus consularis*, were succeeded by a long period of political eclipse and the final fiasco of his crusade against Antony. But his last failure brought into relief his self-sacrificing loyalty to the republican constitution and gave him a better-earned place than Cato on the list of ancient Rome's martyrs. His incapacity for detailed constructive reform would probably have prevented him under any circumstances from becoming the saviour of the Republic in any definite sense; but the flash of insight with which he divined the need of a 'rector' for the Roman government, as the only practical alternative to a military despotism, was not without its effect in guiding the policy of the first Roman emperor.[13]

Death of Cicero

His political insight

Another early measure of the triumvirs was to build a temple and institute a state-cult in honour of *divus Iulius*. This decree of apotheosis came as a natural sequel to the appearance of a comet in July 44, which Octavian had promptly hailed as an epiphany of the murdered dictator. Thus on 1 January 42 B.C. Octavian became the son of a god (*divi filius*).

The Triumvirate of Antony, Lepidus and Octavian was, to an even greater extent than the partnership of Caesar, Pompey and Crassus, an unstable equilibrium of conflicting elements. But its associates took precautions against a collision of interests by defining their respective spheres of power on geographical lines. While they retained Italy as a common possession, so that each of them was free to levy troops and station his own legions there, they shared out the man-power and the revenues of the western provinces between them. In the original division Antony took Gallia Comata, Lepidus received Gallia Narbonensis and the two Spanish provinces, and Octavian was promised Sicily, Sardinia and Africa. The reconciliation between Antony and Octavian was confirmed by the betrothal of the latter to Antony's stepdaughter Claudia. But for the time being the chief bond of union between the triumvirs was the need to reconquer the eastern provinces from M. Brutus and Cassius.

When Brutus absconded from Italy he repaired in the first instance to Greece, where he gathered round himself the stray survivors of the campaign of Pharsalus and formed a corps of officers out of the young Romans engaged in study at Athens. His recruits included a son of Cicero, who was more given to dissipation than to scholastic pursuits, but proved himself an able adjutant of Brutus in the field, and the son of a freedman named Q. Horatius Flaccus, who in later years laughed at himself for his sudden and evanescent burst of military ardour. With this improvised force he confronted an outgoing governor of Macedonia and took over his province (which had been legally assigned to a brother of Antony, C. Antonius). By a similar piece of bluff he won over the troops of P. Vatinius in Illyricum, who had got out of hand during an illness of their commander. In the winter of 44–43 he spread desertion among a corps recently landed by C. Antonius at Apollonia, and captured it after a short siege. Finally, in February 43 he received from the Senate the legal status of a proconsul of Macedonia and Illyricum. For a victory over a Thracian tribe named the Bessi he was hailed by his troops as *imperator*. Had Brutus followed up these successes by joining hands with his namesake in Cisalpine Gaul in the summer of 43 he would have had a reasonable chance of disarming Octavian and securing northern Italy against the return of Antony from Transalpine Gaul. But despite the admonitions of Cicero, who was incessantly urging him to this course, he moved off to Asia Minor to meet Cassius.

In the meantime Cassius had returned to Syria, where he had left a good reputation by his successful defence of the province after the battle of Carrhae (p. 257). Finding a desultory

war in progress between some mutinous troops of Caesar and several loyal divisions which had been sent to restore order, he made a happy ending to it by persuading all the belligerents to take service under him. In taking command in Syria he was usurping the place of Antony's colleague Dolabella, who had been legally appointed to govern this province in 44 (p. 284), and left Rome towards the end of 44 to take possession. On the way to Syria Dolabella made a surprise attack on another tyrannicide, C. Trebonius, who had held the province of Asia since 44, and put him to death. For this kidnapping exploit he was declared an outlaw by the Senate, and Cassius received a commission to make war upon him with the Syrian armies. The duel between Cassius and Dolabella was decided by the desertion of the Roman army of occupation in Egypt, which Dolabella had summoned to his aid. With this reinforcement Cassius was able to pen up his antagonist in the Syrian port of Laodicea, which he captured after a short investment. To escape Trebonius's fate Dolabella committed suicide (summer 43). After the fall of Laodicea Cassius co-operated with Brutus in taking possession of all Asia Minor. By the end of 43 the two arch-conspirators had acquired control of all the eastern provinces, and the allegiance of all the dependent monarchs except Queen Cleopatra. Like Pompey in the campaign of Pharsalus they disposed of a powerful fleet and of a serviceable if somewhat heterogeneous army, and by dint of merciless requisitioning they had provided themselves with ample sinews of war.[14]

Underrating the strength of Brutus and Cassius, Antony had arranged in the first instance that he should conduct the war against them single-handed, while Lepidus kept guard over Italy, and Octavian undertook a minor naval campaign against Sextus Pompeius who was opposing the triumvirs (p. 292). But finding himself unable to cross the Adriatic in the face of the enemy fleet he summoned Octavian to his aid.[15] The combined forces of the two Caesarian chiefs broke through the blockade and advanced without opposition as far as Macedonia. But here they were held fast by the joint armies of Brutus and Cassius, which had entrenched themselves in an impregnable position at Philippi, and the tyrannicides' fleet played havoc with the Caesarian supply-convoys in the Adriatic. In a situation not unlike that of Caesar before Ilerda (p. 271) Antony forced Brutus and Cassius out of their entrenchments by constructing field-works between them and their naval base of supplies. In the 'First Battle of Philippi' he defeated the divisions of Cassius, who took his life in a fit of premature despair;

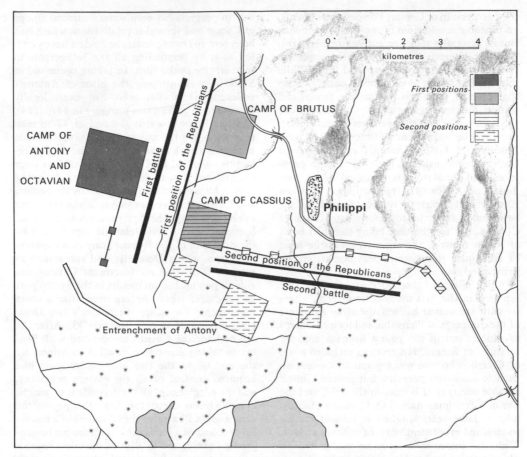

23. BATTLE OF PHILIPPI, 42 B.C.

The double battle of Philippi

but his success was rendered abortive by Brutus's victory over Octavian's wing. Some three weeks later Antony tempted Brutus to a second engagement, which the Caesarians won outright. Brutus in turn took his own life; the greater numbers of his high officers were executed after capitulation; his troops were incorporated in the Caesarian forces. Of the republican forces the fleet alone survived the disaster of Second Philippi.

Political incompetence of Brutus and Cassius

Of the two chief tyrannicides Cassius has been made to suffer by the desire to find a foil to the 'honourable' Brutus; and Brutus's addiction to philosophy has prompted the belief that he was a purblind doctrinaire. In executive ability and in practical worldliness Brutus was a fair specimen of the obsolescent Roman nobility of the Republic:[16] in this limited sense the petulant description of him as 'the last of the Romans' contains a core of truth. But if neither he nor Cassius could restore the Republic after the Ides of March, still less could they have succeeded after the proscriptions, in

which the old governing class had been almost extinguished. A republican victory at Philippi would have settled nothing; the Caesarian victory paved the way for a durable reconstruction of the Roman Empire.

5. The Wars of Perusia and Brundisium

The despoiling of Lepidus

The campaign against Brutus and Cassius had hardly been ended, and the need of a united Caesarian front dispelled, than the triumvirs began to play odd man out. The two active confederates, Antony and Octavian, took the first step towards a new monarchy by squeezing out their sleeping-partner Lepidus. On the pretence that he had anticipated them in disloyalty and was intriguing with Sextus Pompeius, they despoiled him of his provinces and fobbed him off with a promise of Africa, contingent upon his disproving the charges against him. Octavian took Spain from him; Antony helped himself to Narbonese in addition to Transalpine Gaul, but surrendered Cisalpine Gaul, which was treated henceforth as an integral part of Italy.

Though Octavian was the chief gainer by this redistribution of territory the ascendancy of Antony within the Triumvirate was now at its height. As the victor of Philippi he could virtually dictate his terms to Octavian, who had been little more than an onlooker in that campaign. In rearranging the spheres of work within the Triumvirate he reserved for himself an attractive occupation in the East; he relieved Lepidus of all active duties,and he saddled Octavian with a bailiff's job in Italy.

The ascendancy of Antony

The task assigned to Octavian was to pension off some 100,000 soldiers, whose services were no longer required after Philippi. For this purpose the triumvirs had earmarked the territory of eighteen cities in various quarters of Italy, selected on no apparent principle. The confiscations of land which Octavian carried out in 41 were more extensive than those of Sulla, and coming on top of the proscriptions they intensified the odium in which he was held at this time in Italy. To be sure, he had kept sufficient troops in hand to stifle any rebellion; but he was hard driven by Antony's masterful wife Fulvia and by his brother L. Antonius (consul in 42) who made Octavian's difficulty into Antony's opportunity. These intriguers pretended, on the one hand, to share the indignation of the evicted Italians against Octavian; on the other they reassured the discharged soldiers with promises of far more handsome bounties from Antony out of the spoils of the gorgeous East, and they used the same bait to steal Octavian's active troops from him. But the effect of their ingenious propaganda was ruined by their precipitancy in making open war upon Octavian before they had obtained Antony's consent to such a step. In autumn 41 L. Antonius concentrated the troops which he commanded in his brother's name at Praeneste and made a dash upon Rome, where he promised to the people that Antony would restore the Republic on his return, and obtained authority (probably in the form of a *Senatus Consultum Ultimum*) to wage war against Octavian. But Octavian's troops stood firm by him in the hour of crisis, and while L. Antonius was carrying out his *coup de théâtre* in Rome, his adversary made sure of his communications through northern Italy with Spain, to which country he had recently sent the major part of his legions under an officer named Q. Salvidienus. At Octavian's summons Salvidienus returned to Italy, and in conjunction with another friend and agemate of Octavian, M. Vipsanius Agrippa, who won his spurs in the campaign, penned up L. Antonius in the Etruscan hill-city of Perusia.

Octavian's renewed confiscations in Italy

L. Antonius and Fulvia attempt to discredit him

L. Antonius attacks Octavian

But the decision in the Perusine War, as in the campaign of Mutina, lay with the legions from Gaul.[17] At the outbreak of hostilities L. Antonius had called upon Antony's vicegerents in Gaul, P. Ventidius and C. Asinius Pollio, to reinforce him with their powerful armies. These two officers entered Italy on the heels of Salvidienus and eventually advanced within a few miles of Perusia; but they neither attempted to hinder Salvidienus's march nor made any serious effort to relieve the beleaguered city. Since they did not hold their commission from Lucius they declined to engage Octavian's forces until they had received authorisation from Antony; meanwhile they tamely withdrew to the Adriatic coast to await his orders, leaving L. Antonius to be starved into surrender (winter 41–40). Octavian further damaged his reputation by executing the unoffending senate of Perusia; but he treated L. Antonius with calculated generosity. But Perusia was not the only gift of Ventidius and Pollio to Octavian. While they continued to mark time on the Adriatic coast Octavian sent part of his victorious troops to occupy Gaul, whose depleted garrisons capitulated without resistance to his emissaries. By this lucky gamble he gained control over all the western half of the Roman Empire in Europe.

He fails to receive expected reinforcements from Gaul

Siege of Perusia. Surrender of L. Antonius

It now remained for Octavian to balance accounts with Antony. In 41 Antony had disregarded the call for help from his over-zealous partisans in Italy. In 40 he made a belated return to the West, and when Octavian's commander at Brundisium refused him admission, he landed troops close by and put the town under blockade. Octavian replied with a counter-concentration of forces, and the third civil war in Italy since the death of Caesar began. But neither the soldiers nor the officers had their hearts in their work. Messages passed between the troops from camp to camp, and Antony, who was more disposed to blame his brother and wife for making war without consulting him than Octavian for resisting them, accepted the latter's protests that he had acted in strict self-defence. By the mediation of some confidential friends, among whom the wealthy Etruscan landowner C. Cilnius Maecenas figured as the representative of Octavian, the triumvirs came to an understanding. Antony retained control of all the eastern provinces, but left Gaul and Spain in Octavian's hands and ceded Illyricum to him into the bargain. Lepidus, who had recently been allowed by Octavian to proceed to Africa, was confirmed in possession of that province. On the model of the First Triumvirate the two chief partners supplemented their political pact with a dynastic alliance. In place of Fulvia, who had

Mark Antony returns to Italy. The 'War of Brundisium'

The 'Peace of Brundisium'

28.4 Octavia.

Antony marries Octavia

died at an opportune moment, Antony took the hand of Octavian's sister Octavia. Thus civil war had been averted, and the consequent relief and hope is probably reflected in Virgil's Fourth Eclogue, which foreshadows the birth of a child who would bring in the Golden Age, most probably the hoped-for offspring of this new dynastic marriage.[18]

6. Octavian's War against Sextus Pompeius

Sextus Pompeius gains control of Sicily and the western Mediterranean

Before he returned to the East Antony made an attempt at a final settlement between the Caesarian leaders and a surviving republican champion, Sextus Pompeius. This son of Pompey, who had maintained himself in Spain with the remnants of the army of Munda, had been reinstated in his citizen rights after the death of Caesar, and during the War of Mutina he had been commissioned by the Senate to take command of the remains of Caesar's navy as *Praefectus Classis et Orae Maritimae*. After the fall of the Republic he had been placed on the list of the proscribed; but in the meantime he had taken possession of Sicily with Caesar's ships, and he retaliated upon the triumvirs by organising an excellent salvage service along the Italian coast which picked off many other refugees.[19] In 42 he beat off with ease an attack which Octavian made upon him with an improvised fleet before the campaign of Philippi (p. 289); after that he took over the greater part of the surviving fleet of the republicans, and in the following year he enlisted many of the victims of Octavian's expropriations in Italy. In 40 he put pressure upon Octavian by intercepting the grain-supplies of the capital. Disregarding an indirect overture by Octavian, who now took to wife a kinswoman of his named Scribonia, Sextus gave support to Antony in the War of Brundisium, in the course of which he added Sardinia to his possessions. Despite the efforts of Antony to include him in the negotiations at Brundisium he was not admitted to the

peace-treaty; but in the following year he reduced Rome to such a state of famine that Octavian was compelled to negotiate with him. At a conference near Misenum, in which Antony acted as peacemaker, Octavian agreed to repatriate Sextus and the other refugees, and to recognise him as proconsul of Sicily and Sardinia (with the Peloponnesus thrown in by Antony), on the simple condition of his calling off the blockade of Rome and revictualling the capital. But these conditions were not strictly observed by any of the parties concerned, and Octavian promptly made a wreck of the Treaty of Misenum by receiving the island of Sardinia from a traitorous vice-admiral of Sextus. At the same time he divorced Scribonia – on the very day on which she gave him his only child, a daughter named Julia – and married a lady named Livia, who already had one son (the future emperor Tiberius) from her former husband, Tib. Claudius Nero, and was expecting another (Nero Claudius Drusus).

The Treaty of Misenum; its prompt infraction

The fight to a finish in which Octavian and Sextus now engaged ran a course not unlike that of the First Punic War. In 38 Octavian made for Sicily with two converging squadrons from the Etruscan ports and from Tarentum, but mistimed his movements, so that Sextus,

Octavian attacks Sicily in a naval war

28.5 *Obv.* Sextus Pompeius. MAG(nus)PIUS IMP(erator) ITER(um). *Rev.* Heads of Pompey the Great and his son, Gnaeus Pompeius, face to face. PRAEF(ectus) CLAS(sis) ET ORAE MARIT(imae) EX S(enatus) C(onsulto).

operating on inner lines round the Strait of Messina, was able to defeat the attacking fleets in detail. He incurred further losses by exposing one of his divisions to a storm, which cast up his ships on the coast of Bruttium. This fiasco was followed by renewed disorders in Rome and a spread of unrest over Italy, where Octavian's forces had to be parcelled out for patrol service.

Agrippa builds a fleet

To repair his losses Octavian now invoked the aid of Antony and recalled his lieutenant Agrippa from a command in Gaul. Overlooking the fact that Octavian had embarked upon the war against Sextus in disregard of his express warning, Antony returned once more from the East and met his partner at Tarentum. With a sudden change of mind Octavian at first evaded an interview with Antony, but by the mediation of Octavia a new accord was eventually reached. In return for a reinforcement of 120 warships, which Antony placed at his colleague's disposal, Octavian promised to furnish him with 20,000 Italian troops. At the same time the Triumvirate, which had in strict law expired at the end of 38, was renewed to the end of 33.[20] While the conference of Tarentum was dragging along, Agrippa was engaged in constructing a new fleet and patiently training its crews on the Lake of Avernus, which he had converted into a naval harbour (the 'Portus Iulius') by cutting a channel between it and the Bay of Naples.[21] Octavian's preparations for a second offensive consumed the whole of 37; but Sextus made no use of this respite for a counter-attack upon Italy.

Conference at Tarentum. Antony lends ships to Octavian

The campaign of 36 opened with a further reverse for Octavian, for in an attempt to execute a converging attack upon Sicily with three separate armaments he dislocated the entire plan of operations by a heavy defeat which the squadron under his personal command sustained off the east coast near Tauromenium. But Agrippa made good a foothold on the northern shore and eventually joined hands with Lepidus, who had meanwhile landed a detachment at Lilybaeum. With the enemy armies closing in upon his main base at Messana Sextus was obliged to stake his last chance on a set battle, which was delivered at Naulochus, near the Strait. This action was both the largest and most decisive of ancient naval encounters in western waters. Each side put 300 ships into line; Sextus had the better turn of speed, but Agrippa, who had chief command of Octavian's fleet, discounted this advantage with an improved grapnel for boarding operations. In the event all except seventeen of Sextus's vessels were captured or driven ashore. Sextus in person escaped to Asia Minor, where Antony would no doubt have given him a friendly welcome, had

Battle of Naulochus

he not embarked on a foolhardy filibustering expedition into Phrygia, which ended in his capture and execution by one of Antony's subordinates.

Octavian's attack upon Sextus was unprovoked and far from glorious; yet its successful termination marked a turning-point in his career. With 500 to 600 warships and 45 legions at his disposal he had so far outdistanced Antony with his armaments that his partner could no longer catch him up. Further, he now laid the foundations of a new régime based on consent rather than force. The war against Sextus had at least the merit of bringing a durable peace to the western Mediterranean, and the pertinacity with which Octavian fought it to a decision impressed the Italians, who began to look to him as the restorer, not of the old republican liberties, which now seemed too much to ask for, but of orderly government;[22] and Octavian for his part showed a new disposition to cultivate public opinion. After the surrender of Sextus a mutiny among his troops, who clamoured for higher rewards or a speedy discharge, gave him a sharp reminder that military despotism was in itself a form of servitude. To escape thraldom to his troops he cast about henceforth for the support of the general body of citizens. The first sign of his change of heart was given after Sextus's capitulation, when Lepidus made a belated attempt to assert himself by claiming Sicily as his own perquisite, but was promptly deserted by his troops and disarmed. Octavian, who naturally deprived Lepidus of his triumviral powers, nevertheless spared his life and even allowed him to retain the dignity of Pontifex Maximus (which Antony had procured for him shortly after Caesar's death). On his return to Rome the Senate conferred upon him the inviolability of a tribune, a useless but sincere compliment, and in a similar spirit Octavian gave an undertaking to restore the Republic in due course.[23]

Octavian's military ascendancy

His aversion from military despotism

Abortive rising by Lepidus

Having disposed of all his Roman rivals in the western Mediterranean Octavian next employed his troops in a war in the Balkans, which was a prelude to the most important of his later foreign conquests. In this quarter no serious danger threatened at the time from the Dacians, whose formidable king Burebistas had meanwhile died; but the Dalmatian coast-strip still lay exposed to the raids of the hinterland tribes, which Caesar's officers had not definitely subdued. In 35 and 34 Octavian systematically reduced the Adriatic border peoples from Aquileia to Salona, capturing their chief strongholds, which lay on steep hills at the further end of winding wooded valleys. In 35 he completed the season's operations with a transverse march

Octavian's campaigns in Illyricum

across the coastal range into the basin of the Save, where he reduced the fortress of Siscia and prepared for an eventual thrust forward to the Danube. At the same time his fleet finally swept the Adriatic clear of corsairs.[24] At the beginning of 33 a new turn in his relations with Antony compelled him to postpone his plans of conquest in the Danube lands.

7. Antony in the East

Antony receives submission of the eastern provinces; meets Cleopatra

After the battle of Philippi Antony made a tour of the eastern provinces, where he exacted indemnities from the unfortunate inhabitants for their unwilling submission to the exactions of Brutus and Cassius. These fresh requisitions were intended to provide the sinews for a war with the Parthians which he was preparing to prosecute as Caesar's military heir. With a view to taking toll of the still unexhausted treasures of the Ptolemies he summoned Queen Cleopatra to his presence. At the time of Caesar's death Cleopatra was paying a prolonged visit to the dictator in Rome, presumably for the purpose of strengthening her somewhat precarious hold on the throne of Egypt. Caesar had enrolled her among the 'Friends of the Roman People', placed her statue in the temple of Venus Genetrix, and installed her with her infant son in a house on the Janiculum. After Caesar's murder she lost no time in returning to Alexandria, where she made away with her brother and consort, Ptolemy XIII. In 41 she went to meet Antony in Cilicia, and induced him to spend the winter in Alexandria. But at this stage the political relations between the triumvir and the queen were perhaps stronger than any personal bond: in return for Cleopatra's subsidies Antony hunted down and executed her younger sister and rival Arsinoe. In the spring of 40 he left her and did not see her again or the twins she bore him for the next four years.

Preparations for a Parthian War

The War of Brundisium and other political crises in the West compelled Antony to make several prolonged stays in Italy, and retarded his preparations for the invasion of Parthia. In the meantime King Orodes, with more than his usual enterprise, made a preventive attack upon Roman territory. He entrusted his forces to his son Pacorus and to a Roman refugee Q. Labienus, a son of Caesar's lieutenant and later adversary, who had been sent to the Parthian court by Brutus and Cassius to win the king's alliance or friendly neutrality. Entering Syria at the head of a foreign army Labienus won over to his side the greater number of the Roman garrison, which consisted largely of old soldiers of the tyrannicides, and carried the entire prov-

28.6 *Obv.* Q. Labienus. Q. LABIENUS PARTHICUS IMP(erator). *Rev.* Parthian horse; bow-case. This coin was struck by Labienus to pay the Roman troops whom he had enrolled after his invasion of Syria with Parthian troops.

ince but for a few towns on the coast (40 B.C.). Later in the same year he similarly overran Asia Minor, while the forces under Pacorus broke into Palestine and carried off its ruler Hyrcanus.[25] At the end of 40 the Roman Empire had lost most of its Asiatic possessions. In the following two years, however, reinforcements sent by Antony under Ventidius swept the invaders back as fast as they had come. Labienus evacuated Asia Minor without a serious struggle, and the Parthians were driven from Syria after two battles (the second at Mt Gindarus near Antioch), in which their heavy cavalry rashly closed with the legionaries instead of relying on their horse-archers. These successes were not followed up by Ventidius, who let himself be bribed to inaction; but in 37 another general of Antony, C. Sosius, recaptured Jerusalem from the partisans of Parthia. The place of Hyrcanus was taken by his minister Herod, who had ingratiated himself with Antony and Octavian during a visit to Rome in 40, and had persuaded them to confer the title of king upon him. While Antony's lieutenants recovered the lost provinces the Parthian realm was distracted by a change of rulers and a series of precautionary massacres by the new king, Phraates IV.

The Parthians overrun Asia Minor and Syria,

but are driven off by Antony's lieutenants

Herod becomes king of Judaea

In 36 Antony at last got off the mark. Adopting the plan of Caesar, he took with him a strong contingent of horsemen and light infantry,[26] and instead of striking at Babylonia he decided to make for the Persian plateau by way of Armenia. After a circuitous journey by the valley of the Araxes he arrived with unspent forces in Media Atropatene (modern Azerbaijan), and set siege to its chief town Phraaspa (near Tabriz). But although he beat off all attempts by the Parthians to relieve the city, he was not able to reduce it for lack of his artillery train, which a flying Parthian column had intercepted

Antony's invasion of Parthia; a 'campaign of 1812'

on its way through Armenia by a more exposed route. In autumn 36 Antony found himself in a similar position to that of Napoleon after the burning of Moscow. Having neither provisions nor shelter for the bleak winter of northern Persia, he abandoned the siege and fell back through Atropatene and Armenia. By resolute leadership he made good his retreat with the greater part of his force, but he lost some 22,000 legionaries.[27] His army was unfit to resume operations until 34, and in this year he contented himself with overrunning Armenia and dethroning its king, Artavasdes, whom he held responsible for the loss of his siege train in 36. In 33 he advanced once more to the borders of Atropatene, whose vassal-king had meanwhile rebelled against Phraates; but a gathering of fresh storm-clouds in the West obliged him to turn back. Carrhae still remained unavenged, and Antony had missed his opportunity of emulating Caesar and eclipsing Octavian.

Cleopatra gains ascendancy over Antony

The year 36, which was a turning-point in Octavian's upward career, also marked the first stage in Antony's downfall. Though he escaped the Parthian pursuit, he was taken prisoner on his return by Cleopatra. Having sent his wife Octavia back to Italy in the previous year, he had been joined in Antioch by Cleopatra. Hitherto the queen's influence over him had been of the same transient character as in her previous affair with Caesar. But the fiasco of the Parthian invasion, by depleting his war-funds and sapping his self-reliance, made him more dependent on her financial assistance and more susceptible to the flatteries with which she laid siege to his heart. From this time she gradually reduced him to be an instrument of an un-Roman policy.

The growing influence of Cleopatra over Antony was demonstrated on his return to Alexandria (autumn 34) when he celebrated a 'triumph' for his Armenian victory and staged a pageant in the Gymnasium, where he and Cleopatra, robed as Isis, sat on golden thrones, together with their own three children and Caesarion. Antony declared *urbi et orbi* that Caesarion (Ptolemy Caesar) was the legitimate son of Julius Caesar; this was a direct challenge to Octavian, the adopted son and now declared a usurper.[28] This lad of thirteen was now proclaimed King of Kings, and his mother Cleopatra was named Queen of Kings; together they were to rule Egypt and Cyprus. Under them the three children of Antony and Cleopatra were to govern parts of the East, whether Roman territory, client-kingdoms or even the lands of foreign kings. Alexander Helios (the Sun), aged six, received Armenia, Parthia and Media, his twin sister Cleopatra Selene (the Moon) got Cyrenaica and Libya, while the two-year-old Ptolemy Philadelphus obtained Syria and Cilicia. These 'Donations of Alexandria' were commemorated and advertised by an issue of coins which displayed Cleopatra's portrait and named her 'Queen of Kings and of her sons who are kings'; on the other side was Antony's portrait and the legend 'Armenia devicta'. Had all these transfers of territory been carried into effect, the result would have been to form an empire within the Roman Empire, and in all probability to disintegrate the Roman dominions into two rival states. Antony's complaisance to Cleopatra, if not actually treasonable (he himself had kept in the background as donor rather than recipient), might easily be construed as such.[29]

The 'Donations of Alexandria'

8. The War of Actium

The ascendancy which Cleopatra gained over Antony not merely placed him in a false position in regard to general public opinion at Rome, it also drew upon him the personal enmity of Octavian. Until 33 the unstable equilibrium between the two confederates had always been restored by mutual concessions. Antony had repeatedly given way to Octavian on outstanding issues; after the conference of Tarentum he had not even pressed for the remission of the 20,000 legionaries whom Octavian had promised but failed to send. Conversely, Octavian obliged Antony in 36 by staging a triumph to celebrate a pretended victory over the Parthians. But three years later Octavian deliberately prepared a break with his partner. The cause of the rupture lay in the dynastic policy of Cleopatra, which required that Antony should be not only her lover, but her husband. Her efforts did not

Octavian's definite estrangement from Antony

28.7 *Obv.* Antony. ANTONI(us). ARMENIA DEVICTA. *Rev.* Cleopatra. CLEOPATRAE REGINAE REGUM FILIORUM REGUM, 'Queen of kings and of her sons who are kings'. This coin, struck by Antony, *c.* 32 B.C., admits the claim of Cleopatra's children to hold sub-kingdoms under the sovereignty of their mother.

meet with immediate success for Octavia was as good a wife to Antony as Julia had been to Pompey: after the death of Antony she took under her protection his children by Fulvia and Cleopatra. Antony therefore did not formally divorce her until 32. But after 35 he refused to see Octavia and in 33, if not already in 37, he consented to become Cleopatra's Prince Consort by Greek dynastic law, although such a marriage was not valid under Roman law.[30] This affront to Octavia may be regarded as the turning-point in the relations between the triumvirs. Octavian, who habitually sacrificed family sentiment to considerations of policy, might have condoned the super-session of Octavia by another Roman wife; but her rejection in favour of an alien seducer hurt his Roman pride.

In 33 Octavian entered upon an open campaign of recrimination with Antony with the intention of compromising him in the eyes of the Romans. In this war of words, however, Antony at first held his own. He showed up Octavian's past acts of disloyalty towards himself, and he capped his adversary's offers to restore the Republic with a similar promise in his own name

But at the end of 33 the Second Triumvirate reached its legal end. Whereas Antony kept the title and acted as if still in office, Octavian abandoned the title and presumably the powers.[31] At a meeting of the Senate on 1 February 32, the consuls C. Sosius and Cn. Domitius, who were friends of Antony, would have proposed a vote of censure upon Octavian, had not a tribune interposed his veto. At a subsequent session of the House Octavian spoke in his own defence, and he had the satisfaction of driving the consuls, and with them 300 senators, out of the city. But the flight of Sosius and Domitius was not so much due to Octavian's counter-arguments, as to his menacing action in surrounding the Senate-house with an armed retinue. The dissident senators left Italy to join Antony. Octavian had now cut off his retreat, but in the absence of any strong expression of public feeling he did not venture to proceed any further against Antony.

In summer 32 the news of Octavia's divorce and the publication of Antony's will, whose contents and place of deposit two deserters from Alexandria revealed to Octavian, at last turned the tide. Though the will disclosed nothing new, except Antony's avowal that he wished to be buried at Cleopatra's side, it reaffirmed the legitimacy of Caesarion and completed the process of converting public opinion in Italy which was further shocked by a rumour that Antony intended to make Cleopatra queen of Rome and

28.8 *Obv.* Galley, with rowers; standards placed by the prow. ANT(onius) AVG(ur). IIIVIR R(ei) P(ublicae) C(onstituendae). *Rev.* Three military standards. One of a series of coins struck by Antony for the use of his navy and army before the battle of Actium.

to transfer the seat of Roman government to Egypt. The municipalities of Italy, and then many in the western provinces, proceeded to take an oath of allegiance (*coniuratio*) to Octavian personally, thereby proclaiming themselves the *clientela* of an individual party leader, a *dux*. Octavian later described this as a personal mandate to proceed against Antony, and claimed, doubtless with a substantial measure of truthfulness, that the movement had been spontaneous.[32] Octavian was elected consul for 31 and obtained a formal declaration of war against Cleopatra, who had crossed with Antony and his forces to Greece. No overt measures were taken against Antony, beyond depriving him of a prospective consulship for 31, but since the Triumvirate had now expired, he became in the eyes of the law a mere *condottiere* in the employ of the enemy queen. Octavian's diplomatic triumph was late in coming, but when it came it was complete.

In the final encounter between Antony and Octavian the latter had a material as well as a moral advantage. In the strength of his infantry Antony was fairly matched with Octavian if he disposed of thirty legions, mostly recruited from men of Italian stock. But he was definitely inferior to Octavian at sea. Though

Octavian's military advantage

he had raised the total number of his fleet to some 500 sail Octavian probably had close on 600 ships of approximately equal tonnage, and his high admiral, Agrippa, was the greatest naval tactitian in Roman history. Moreover, the presence of Cleopatra in Antony's camp – for the queen in true Ptolemaic fashion had insisted on taking the field in person – was resented by many of Antony's officers, and further weakened their waning loyalty to him.

At the end of 32 Antony had moved forward as far as Greece. The site of his advanced base, on the commodious bay of Actium, was well chosen; but difficulties of supply compelled him to distribute his forces widely. Octavian's troops meanwhile lay concentrated near the harbours of Brundisium and Tarentum. In 31 Agrippa was first off the mark with Octavian's fleet. He failed in an attempt to cut out Antony's ships by a surprise attack at Actium, but from his bases at Leucas and Corcyra he succeeded in intercepting the enemy reinforcements and supply columns. At the same time Octavian's army entrenched itself on the bay and harassed Antony's communications by land. In this campaign of attrition Antony's effectives were being steadily depleted by disease or desertion. Towards the end of summer he attempted to extricate his remaining forces by a retreat to Asia Minor. On 2 September 31, he issued out of the bay with a fleet reduced to barely 200 galleys, in the hope of giving his adversaries the slip. His plan of escape was not ill founded, for

Agrippa's naval guerrilla action against Antony

(contrary to the ordinary practice of ancient naval battles) he had taken his ships' canvas aboard and intended to sail away before the brisk sea breeze which springs up in the Ionian Sea on summer afternoons. Antony's scheme was so far successful, as he eluded the attempts of Agrippa to draw him into a set battle. But whether his fleet got out of hand in the preliminary skirmishing, or, as seems more likely, disaffection had spread among his officers, his order to hoist sail was badly obeyed. Cleopatra's well-found squadron of sixty vessels broke clean through, and Antony slipped away in her wake with a few more ships. The remainder of his fleet became involved in a confused fight, but the larger part apparently found their way back into harbour.[33]

Antony's attempted retreat. The fiasco of Actium

In the actual engagement no mass attacks seem to have been delivered, and Agrippa inflicted no crushing losses. Yet the battle of Actium had no morrow. The breakaway of Antony in the wake of Cleopatra suggested to his suspicious followers that he had deliberately deserted them, and furnished them with a valid excuse for deserting him. The intact remnant of his fleet at Actium capitulated to Octavian at once, and the army followed suit not long after. Antony and Cleopatra made good their escape to Egypt, for Octavian's pursuit was checked by a mutiny among the troops sent home for disbandment after the battle, which obliged him to return to Italy. But when he resumed the pursuit Antony's detachments everywhere made a prompt surrender, and in the summer of 30 Octavian crossed the strong frontier-line at Pelusium without opposition. With their retreat cut off on all sides – for the king of the Nabataean Arabians had burnt the Ptolemaic Red Sea fleet in a surprise attack – Antony anticipated execution, and Cleopatra avoided exhibition at a Roman triumph, by taking their own lives.[34] This simplified Octavian's position: he was not primarily seeking the lives of his two opponents, but rather the treasures of the Ptolemies. A few of Antony's officers, including two surviving murderers of Caesar, were put to death; but Octavian's subsequent claim that he had spared all his victims in the civil wars possessed some semblance of truth in this instance.[35] Cleopatra's children by Antony were allowed to survive, but Caesarion, as a possible claimant of the Ptolemaic throne, was removed. Having accomplished the extinction of the Ptolemaic dynasty Octavian converted Egypt into a Roman province under a prefect responsible to himself, and carried off the royal treasure which Cleopatra had recently replenished by confiscations and by the seizure of hitherto untouched temple funds. His victory was the

General desertion of Antony

Suicide of Antony and of Cleopatra

Octavian's victory complete

a Cleopatra
b Antony
c Octavius
d Caelius

Wall OCTAVIAN'S CAMP
Wall
ANTONY'S MAIN CAMP
Preveza
Agrippa
Gulf of Preveza
Cleopatra
Arruntius
Octavian
Harbour of Actium
ANTONY'S FIRST AND THIRD CAMP

24. BATTLE OF ACTIUM, 31 B.C.

most complete in the long series of Roman civil wars, and it was the most profitable.

9. Review of the Second Triumvirate

The best that can be said of the Second Triumvirate is that it was too bad to last. It was ruinously wasteful in men and wealth, and it rested on nothing firmer than a precarious balance of essentially antagonistic ambitions. Its eventual collapse was a foregone conclusion, and the real point at issue was, which of the confederates would survive the inevitable process of weeding out?

Of the three associates the eldest, Lepidus, was in a false position from the outset, and was plainly predestined to an early disappearance. Despite his rapid promotion by Caesar, he lacked the leadership and the prestige among the troops which was essential to success in an age of military revolutions.

Reasons for Antony's failure

Antony, on the other hand, combined high military talent with self-reliance and the art of winning his way to the hearts of the soldiers. In the triumviral game of *écarté* he seemingly held the best cards and should have been the winner, but for the lure of the Parthian War and of Cleopatra. His preoccupation with eastern affairs condemned him to lose touch with public opinion in Italy, which not even a triumvir could afford to neglect in the long run; his attachment to Cleopatra deprived him of the goodwill of his troops, which was his last and best asset.

The queen who stole Antony from the service of Rome was Rome's most dangerous opponent since the days of Mithridates; and she shared with Hannibal the honour of having her character most sedulously blackened by Roman propagandists. As an almost pure-blooded Macedonian she exhibited all the virile energy that distinguished the princesses of this race; but to this common trait of the Macedonian ruling houses she added a diplomatic finesse which was her most formidable weapon. Her ambition was

Cleopatra. Her gifts and ambitions

to restore the Ptolemaic kingdom to the dimensions which it had possessed under its early rulers, and to provide a series of appanages for the other members of her family. But however legitimate this object might be in the eyes of a Ptolemy it was bound to lead to a conflict with Rome. Though Cleopatra read Antony like a book she miscalculated the force of opinion in Italy and among Antony's own troops. In the event she destroyed her dynasty and dragged down Antony with her.[36]

Octavian: his good fortune and good qualities

The junior partner, Octavian, had the initial advantage of the prestige which the name of Caesar gave him among the soldiery. He had long tried to identify himself with Italy's greatest need, that of peace and security: as early as 36 the inscription on a golden statue set up in the Forum proclaimed that order had been restored by land and sea. This was true regarding the West, from which he had eliminated his two colleagues and all rivals, but in so doing he was splitting the Roman world into two. And while Antony increasingly leaned towards eastern traditions Octavian could foster his sincere respect for Italian tradition and thought. Thus this revolutionary leader was enabled more easily to identify his own cause with that of his country, and he could gradually appeal not only to ambitious new men but also to more aristocrats of the ancient families. His Italian outlook was enhanced when after his Illyrian campaign he and his friends began to provide the city with new buildings, good water and cheap food, and by expelling astrologers, banishing eastern rites, and repairing old shrines and temples to remind Romans of their older traditions. Further, Agrippa organised victory for him, and Antony played into his hands. But if his success over Antony was largely a gift of fortune his personal qualities of patience and pertinacity enabled him to take his chances at the right moment; and in the second act of his life they enabled him to consolidate his victory as neither Sulla nor Caesar had succeeded in doing.

CHAPTER 29

Roman Society in the First Century

1. Changes in Roman Agriculture

From the political standpoint the century following the tribunate of Tiberius Gracchus was the most revolutionary in Roman history. From the economic point of view it was a period of gradual development rather than of abrupt transitions.[1]

Land assignation in Italy

The most notable event in the agricultural history of the later Republic was an extensive change in the ownership of land, both in Italy and in some of the provinces. In Italy the resumption of land-settlement from the time of the Gracchi resulted in an unprecedented transfer of titles. It has been estimated that 50,000–120,000 allotments were provided on Italian soil by Sulla, 50,000–80,000 by Caesar, 120,000–170,000 by Octavian. But the disturbance created by these assignations was less violent than the huge number of the colonists might suggest. It may be assumed that many of the military settlers, having become unfitted by continuous campaigning for the work of the husbandman, left the former owners in actual possession as rent-payers with a virtual fixity of tenure. Others sold their plots to enriched traders, who were as eager as ever to convert their winnings into real estate. The process of breaking up large holdings by colonisation was

The small proprietors hold their own

therefore counteracted by a tendency to re-assemble them under a new proprietor. But there is little evidence at this period of a rapid growth of large estates or of a steady squeezing out of the smaller peasantry. In one respect the small proprietors of the first century were better off than those of the preceding age, in that they were no longer called upon to perform long spells of compulsory military service. The scanty followings which adventurers like Lepidus and Catiline were able to muster in the Italian countryside may be taken as a sign that discontent among the peasantry was waning.

In the provinces considerable tracts of land passed into the hands of men of Italian birth. Roman capitalists took the opportunity of good bargains in overseas land which still awaited development or had depreciated in times of political disorder. They acquired large areas of crop-land in Sicily and especially in northern Africa; and it was no doubt on the large estates of the new Italian landlords that the vine and the olive were propagated in Spain. But the transfer of provincial soil into Italian possession was chiefly effected by the assignation of small or moderate-sized holdings to military pensioners. The old soldiers of Marius were settled in Africa, and probably also in Narbonese Gaul. Caesar paid off most of his troops with Gallic or Spanish land. In 43 L. Plancus founded a veteran colony under the Senate's direction at Lugdunum (modern Lyon); and Octavian again had recourse to Narbonese Gaul to provide for the soldiers disbanded after Actium. Civilian settlements of small owners were made by Caesar at Carthage and Corinth and in Spain. In addition we may assume a drift of evicted proprietors from Italy to various provinces. The large scale on which transmarine emigration from Italy took place is demonstrated by the extensive recruitment of Italian soldiery in the provinces during the civil wars of the later first century. Metellus Scipio raised several legions (no doubt somewhat diluted with native elements) in Africa, and the younger Cn. Pompeius in Spain; the elder Pompey and Antony replenished their forces with large drafts from the Italian residents in the East.[2]

Settlement of Italians in the provinces

The supply of labour for the large estates

Labour on the large estates

in Italy continued to be met by the importation of slaves. It is true that the servile revolts in Sicily, and still more the War of Spartacus in Italy itself, had shown up the danger of large concentrations of unfree workers on the countryside, and the more observant landlords were beginning to realise that the whip and the chain were not productive of the best results. In the first century accordingly Italian landowners partly replaced their slave staffs by free tenants known as *coloni*, who paid a rent (usually in money) in return for the use of the land and the stock. L. Domitius, the antagonist of Caesar, had several thousands of *coloni* on his estates (mostly in Etruria); and it is probable that in northern Italy the system of cultivation by free men was prevalent at all times. But in peninsular Italy the use of *coloni* did not as yet pass beyond the experimental stage. The foreign wars and the slave trade still supplied an abundance of unfree labour, the greater part of which continued to be absorbed on the land. The normal practice of good landlords, as embodied in the agricultural treatise of M. Terentius Varro, was an improvement on that of Cato, in that it prescribed the hope of rewards rather than the fear of punishment as the proper inducement to hold the farm-hands to their work; but it still took an adequate supply of servile labour for granted. On the other hand Sicily was the only province in which cultivation by slaves was predominant. Elsewhere the Roman landowners had recourse to *coloni* or to free wage-workers.

Experiments with free tenants

Better treatment of slaves

In Italy the methods of cultivation underwent comparatively little alteration. The capitalist landowners extended and improved the orchard husbandry which had been introduced in the second century. Before the end of the first century the best Campanian vintages, such as those of the Ager Falernus and Mons Massicus, ranked on a level with the choicest wines of Greece. Rougher brands of north Italian growth were produced for export to Gaul and the Danube lands. After the opening up of the Near East by the Roman armies the acclimatisation of oriental fruits and plants on Italian soil was carried out by enterprising landlords. On behalf of Lucullus it might be claimed that his greatest triumph was the transplantation of the edible cherry and the apricot from Armenia. The Greek writer Dionysius of Halicarnassus (c. 40 B.C.) commented admiringly on the garden cultivation of Italy, and with pardonable exaggeration Varro likened the country to one great orchard.[3] In the neighbourhood of Rome and of the populous districts of Campania market-gardening, poultry-farming, bee-keeping and the cultivation of flowers were pursued intensively, and might yield handsome profits.

Prosperity of orchard industry

But this scientific husbandry was on the whole confined to the more productive lands or to the vicinity of the largest markets. The small peasantry on the less fertile or the more remote territories adhered to the traditional methods of cultivation. Moreover, as the wealthier Romans became more engrossed in the duties and pleasure of town life, they abandoned the personal supervision of their estates to their bailiffs. Their visits to the country became less like tours of inspection and more like summer holidays; and considerable tracts on their estates were converted into pleasure-grounds with avenues of planes and hedges of box-wood, or into hunting-preserves. The landlords of Varro's age were losing that single eye to profit which characterised the elder Cato. On the other hand in several of the western provinces the new Roman proprietors introduced more intensive methods of cultivation. Africa and Sicily (until the governorship of Verres) increased their grain production so as to cover the rapidly increasing needs of the city of Rome. In southern and eastern Spain and in southern Gaul the development of the orchard industry may also be ascribed in large measure to the Italian immigrants.

Absenteeism of the large proprietors

2. Manufactures and Trade

Outside Italy industrial activity in the first century stood at a low ebb. In the eastern Mediterranean the continuous drain of wealth, consequent upon the civil wars and the plunderings by Roman officials and traders, disorganised manufactures for the time being. In Italy the copper mines, which had once been a principal source of Etruscan riches, were now nearing exhaustion, and the gold-washing industry on the western Alpine border was deliberately kept within narrow limits by the Senate.[4] On the other hand the last century of the Republic was a period of considerable building activity. In Rome the spoils of war were applied on a larger scale than ever to public works (pp. 304 ff.). Under the influence of Gaius Gracchus a new spurt was made in road-building (p. 207). In the first century the wealthier citizens began to spend lavishly on their residences in Rome, and rebuilt their country villas to match the luxury of their town houses. So also many Italian towns were enjoying prosperity. For example, some of the best public and private buildings at Pompeii belong to the years 133 to 90, while the city soon recovered again after the setback inflicted upon it by its capture by Sulla in 90 and subsequent colonisation. The importation of skilled Greek craftsmen (partly as prisoners of war) brought new prosperity to two ancient Italian

General stagnation of manufacturing industry

industries, ceramics and bronze-founding. About 100 B.C. Capua extended its manufacture of bronze ware (notably of cooking-utensils, wine-jugs and lamps) to supply northern Europe as well as Italy. The Etruscan town of Arretium produced good imitations of a type of Greek pottery with embossed ornaments, the so-called 'Samian Ware', and created a widespread vogue for this kind of table-ware. But the distribution of wealth in Italy remained too unequal to permit the rise of a large and varied manufacturing industry. It appears equally true of the first as of the second century, that none of its great fortunes was derived from manufactures.

Arretine pottery

The commerce of the Mediterranean suffered alike from the political convulsions of the later Republic and from the scourge of piracy. In its western countries such extensions of trade as fall within this period were mainly due to the enterprise of the Italian bourgeoisie. The new and urgent business of providing Rome with corn was taken up by Italian merchants, who organised exportation from Sicily and Africa. As early as 113 the Numidian town of Cirta contained a considerable group of Italian residents (p. 214). In 46 the Italian trading community virtually controlled the city of Utica, and no fewer than 300 men of business were to be found in the relatively small town of Thapsus. The exportation of Italian wine and bronze ware to Gaul and the Danube lands was carried on by itinerant Italian merchants.[5] By the middle of the first century the growth of Latin literature had created a book trade and publishing business at Rome (p. 310). In the eastern Mediterranean the commercial activity of the Italians was at its highest in Asia Minor. A serious blow to Italian trade in the Aegean area was inflicted by the ruin of the emporium at Delos, which never recovered from the devastations which it suffered in 86 and 69 (pp. 231, 250). The trade formerly carried on by the Italian residents on this island fell into the hands of Alexandrian and Syrian merchants, who opened depots at Puteoli for the supply of the Roman market from the Levantine centres of production. Within their own waters the Levantines maintained an unbroken monopoly: neither at Alexandria nor at Rhodes was there an Italian trading community of any importance.[6]

Importation of grain into Italy

Exportation of wine

The Levantine traders hold their own

The Roman business world continued, as before, to concern itself by preference with money-dealing.[7] The farming of provincial taxes, which had been conducted on a relatively modest scale before the time of Gaius Gracchus, henceforth assumed much larger dimensions, and each new annexation in Asia increased the turn-over of the *publicani*. The Roman usurer broke fresh ground in front of the tax-gatherer.

Increased dealings of Roman tax-farmers and money-lenders

In Rome itself the opportunities of profitable money-lending were restricted by the lack of a market for state loans. The Roman government habitually paid its way out of current revenue, or raised funds by requisitions and confiscations. In the eastern Mediterranean the financing of commercial enterprise remained in the hands of Greeks and Syrians. On the other hand provincial cities and dependent kings now began to have habitual recourse to Roman usurers to pay off their debts to the Republic. Though the loans to semi-bankrupt communities in the East were highly speculative, and remissions had sometimes to be made, with more or less of good grace, to positively insolvent debtors, the high rates of interest demanded (usually from 24 to 48 per cent) gave sufficient cover for contingencies: indeed, the net profits that accrued were so substantial that even Roman nobles who had a reputation for integrity to maintain, such as Pompey and M. Brutus, were tempted to questionable transactions with the kings and cities of the East.[8] Of the strictly reputable banking firms, which provided funds for legitimate trading purposes or conducted the ordinary business of the great Roman households, much less is heard. But the correspondence of Cicero illustrates at many points the services which the banker T. Pomponius Atticus could render to a solvent but unbusinesslike client in paying and collecting his debts.

With the first century the age of the millionaires at Rome may be said to begin. The triumvir M. Crassus, whose real estate alone was reputed to be worth 50,000,000 denarii, had more than twice the wealth of his ancestor P. Crassus, the richest Roman of the Gracchan period (p. 190). But these huge fortunes were concentrated in a dangerously small number of hands. No doubt there was much exaggeration in the remark of Marcius Philippus (consul in 91), that only 2000 citizens possessed any property; yet the men of wealth formed an insignificant minority in comparison with the 320,000 proletarians who were in regular receipt of free corn *c*. 50 B.C. The corn-distributions, it is true, together with the lavish bribes which aspirants to office paid to the electors, and the time-honoured system of clientship, provided effective means of social insurance. Though slave revolts and civil wars might shake the countryside of Italy, there was little danger of a general proletarian rising in the capital, save at occasional moments of shortage in the food supply. Nevertheless the wealth of the Roman nabobs rested on a very unstable basis. Extortion and cut-throat usury exposed them to reprisals such as those of the 'Asiatic Vespers' in 88, in which many fortunes as well as many lives were lost. In Italy the civil wars

Roman millionaires. Crassus

Insecurity of these large fortunes

gave sudden opportunities of rapid enrichment. The colossal profits made by Crassus were chiefly in the form of unearned increment on landed property, which he had bought at knock-down prices at the time of Sulla's proscriptions and held against the rise in values which followed upon Sulla's settlement;[9] and we need not doubt that similar fortunes were acquired under the Second Triumvirate. Yet the men who enriched themselves by one political convulsion were marked down for expropriation in the next.

3. Standards of Living[10]

Growth of luxury at Rome

The accumulation of wealth at Rome in the first century was reflected in a far more opulent style of life. The traditional simplicity of Roman manners lingered on in some great houses, notably among the members of the Equestrian Order. The private expenditure of Atticus was on the scale of a *petit bourgeois,* and Crassus, the richest Roman of them all, was a man of unassuming habits. But the nobles as a class abandoned their former customs of dignified frugality, and imposed upon themselves an ostentatious standard of spending in private no less than in public life. In addition to a town residence – preferably on the Palatine Hill, which now became the fashionable quarter – they built themselves a separate 'villa' on each of their country estates and at the seaside resorts which were springing up along the west coast, especially the Bay of Naples. Cicero, who was not a man of abundant wealth, possessed a residence on the Palatine which cost him 750,000 denarii, and at least eight country-houses. Some

Private houses and 'villas'

of the villas, it is true, were mere places of rest on routes of habitual travel; others, with a full equipment of ball-playing rooms, baths and libraries, surpassed the palaces of Hellenistic kings in their appointments. The furnishings of these mansions were in keeping with their architecture. The old restrictions on the amount of a senator's dinner-plate were frankly disregarded, and absurd prices were paid for decorations and articles of vertu. Dinner-menus were elongated and diversified, and vintage wines were laid in store. Domestic staffs became highly specialised in their functions. Only in dress and toilet did some of the old severity of personal habit survive: the tendency to discard the cumbrous toga and boots with solid uppers save on ceremonial occasions, and to adopt the more convenient Greek mantle and sandals, was a concession to comfort rather than to mere ostentation. Among the governing aristocracy expenditure not infrequently outran all regular sources of income. The liabilities of Caesar and

Indebtedness

Curio at one time ran into millions,[11] and it was the nobles who, as a class, had the greatest interest in bankruptcy acts.

At the other end of the social scale conditions for many of the urban populace were very grim. In Rome the population numbered not fewer than three-quarters of a million, with a high proportion of freedmen and perhaps 100,000 slaves. The poor were crowded together in a small built-up area, with a density seven or eight times that of a modern English town. They lived in tenements, often 70 feet high and jerry-built, which lacked adequate light, heat and cooking facilities; they were not connected with the public sewers or with the aqueducts, so that water had to be carried in; furniture will often not have exceeded a stool and a bed. If a man's house did not fall down (Cicero tells how in 44 two tenements he owned collapsed and cracks had appeared in others, while the tenants and the mice had fled), it might suffer from fire or flood: fires were frequent and there was no fire brigade, while the Tiber frequently overflowed. Further, rents were high and debts accumulated. Hunger often threatened, especially when war or piracy interfered with the supply of corn: true, since 58 there had been free corn-distributions, but the dole, even if providing a bare subsistence for a man, certainly did not cover the needs of his wife or children. To these miseries unemployment must be added. High costs of transport forbade the building up of industry to cater for overseas markets and there was a limit to what the local population needed. Some temporary relief was offered by the need for casual unskilled labour, seasonally for harvesting in the countryside and intermittently for helping in the construction of public works in the city or at the docks or for transport. True, there were large numbers of shopkeepers, artisans and traders in regular employment, but there were also many men who must have wondered where the next family meal was coming from. Abortion and infanticide, especially of female infants, must have been common. Against this picture of misery and squalor must be set the fact that slums throughout history have unfortunately been a frequent feature of all urban life, while the Mediterranean climate and the outdoor life that it made possible will have ameliorated conditions at least in the summer months.[12]

The poor of Rome

A noticeable feature of the last half-century of the Republic is the growth of violence. Poverty must have encouraged crime and have helped to provide the gangsters whom politicians increasingly employed (although before the days of Clodius and Milo popular leaders had relied perhaps less on the urban *plebs* than

Violence

on supporters drawn from the countryside and from their armies, which had been recruited in the country). While lack of a police force prevented the checking of violence in the city, the countryside of Italy was far from immune, thanks not least to the effects of the series of civil wars. Here many stories are recorded of brigandage, the expropriation of farms while the owners were on military service, kidnappings, and attacks by armed herdsmen. In 78 the consul Catulus apparently passed a law proscribing armed violence, which was later supplemented by a *lex Plautia*, but humble men may often have found it difficult to gain legal redress.[13]

4. Social Life

In the first century the Roman aristocracy lost the rustic character which still adhered to it in the days of the elder Cato, and was becoming as urbanised as the French *noblesse* of the *ancien régime*. In midsummer, when the air hung heavy in the streets of the city, high society would frequent the fashion resorts along the Bay of Naples (chief among them Baiae and Puteoli), or would scatter to the foothills of the Apennines.[14] Men of country breeding might return to their native haunts to collect their thoughts and regain possession of their souls: Cicero would betake himself to the mountains of Arpinum to recover his peace of mind, or to his Tusculan villa on the edge of the Alban hills to engage in concentrated literary work. But the appreciation for fine landscape or of rural solitude which the Romans of the Ciceronian age expressed was that of visiting townsmen, to whom the city's stir and bustle is indispensable for everyday life, and the routine of a country squire would seem appallingly dull. The city of Rome offered a continuous round of entertainment – the cut-and-thrust of political strife in Forum and Senate-house, the morning levee where clients came to pay respects and seek advice, the dinner-parties, the causeries of the literary dilettanti, and the exchanges of highly spiced gossip among the men and women of the world.

Roman high society takes country holidays;

yet is essentially urban

In the society of the later Republic women moved with complete freedom.[15] They owned a considerable amount of wealth in their own names and managed it at their own discretion. They received enough education to hold their own in social life; behind the scenes some of them exercised no slight influence on politics. Clodia, the sister of P. Clodius, was the queen of the most dashing social circle of her day. Cicero confided his political anxieties to his wife Terentia; Brutus needed the admonitions of his masterful consort Porcia (a daughter of M. Cato)

Women in society

before he braced himself for his last great adventure in the East. The emancipation of women was accompanied by a relaxation or even a frank abandonment of the traditional code of family solidarity. The tying and severing of matrimonial knots as a means of acquiring wealth or useful political connexions was elevated by the Roman nobility to a fine art. In the pursuit of political promotion matches were made and unmade with the utmost unconcern for its effects on family life. Sulla had five wives, Pompey five, Caesar four, Octavian three. Women as well as men could indulge in gallant adventures without serious harm to their reputation, and Caesar's remark that 'his family must be above suspicion' was no doubt hailed as the joke of the season. In short, the prevailing tone among the Roman aristocracy was one of recklessness, as though it foresaw the coming deluge, but banked on the survival of the Republic in its own time. Yet its profligacy was tempered by a new *urbanitas* and *humanitas* of intercourse, on which educated Romans could henceforth pride themselves in a hardly lesser degree than their Greek teachers.

Marriages and divorces

Roman humanitas

For the urban proletariat the round of amusements was extended by further public festivals, of which the two most notable were the *ludi Sullanae victoriae* and the games instituted by Caesar after Pharsalus in honour of his tutelary deity, Venus Genetrix. The triumphs of the leading military men were celebrated with interminable pomp. The procession in which Pompey displayed the spoils of his eastern conquests took two days to defile through the Via Sacra; Caesar entertained the people with three triumphs on successive days in 46, and with a fourth celebration in 45. Though gladiatorial contests were not yet admitted to the calendar of state functions, private performances at the cost of candidates for office were given with such frequency that the training of fighters for hire became a regular form of business enterprise: at the games which Caesar gave in 65 (the year of his aedileship) 320 pairs of combatants were exhibited. During his dictatorship Caesar varied the usual procedure of these contests by staging a *naumachia* or imitation naval battle on a large pond constructed for the purpose. The blood-lust of the populace was also stimulated by a great increase in the number of *venationes*, at which wild animals from the remoter borders of the Empire were pitted against each other or against professional huntsmen. Pompey gratified Roman playgoers by building a permanent theatre in stone. The dramatic performances were often the occasions for impromptu demonstrations by the spectators, which politicians used as a means of feeling the public pulse.[16]

Circus games

Gladiatorial shows and beast-hunts

29.1   Roman Forum to the east, looking from the Capitol. Arch of Septimius Severus in left foreground. In distance, at top of picture, Arch of Titus and Colosseum.

5. Architecture and Art

Public works at Rome

Under the later Republic the city of Rome outstripped all other Mediterranean towns in the size of its population, which now may have approached the million mark. Of the war-winners of this period neither Marius nor Lucullus left any notable monument of himself, but Sulla, Pompey and Caesar executed important new public works. Sulla reconstructed the temple of Jupiter Capitolinus, which had been burnt down in 83, and planned a *tabularium* or new Record Office, on the brow of the Capitoline Hill, with an arcaded gallery on its topmost tier, thus linking the Forum with the Capitol as an architectural unit; it was erected in 78 by Lutatius Catulus. In the Forum Sulla rebuilt the Senate-house to accommodate its enlarged membership, and repaved the western end of the open area.[17] To Pompey Rome owed its first stone theatre in the Campus Martius and an adjoining portico

New buildings by Sulla, Pompey and Caesar

(in which Caesar met the Senate on the Ides of March). Before the end of his term in Gaul Caesar began the construction of his chief architectural monuments, the Basilica Iulia and the Forum Iulium. The Basilica was a covered hall at the south-west end of the old Forum; the Forum Iulium was an enclosure, to the northwest of the old Forum, with surrounding galleries and a temple of Venus Genetrix at one end. Both these buildings served in a dual capacity as commercial exchanges and as courts of law. Caesar also provided the funds with which L. Aemilius Paullus (a consul in 50, who observed a friendly neutrality to him) restored the Basilica Aemilia of his second-century ancestor (p. 193) after its destruction in 52 (p. 267). During his dictatorship Caesar similarly made provision for the reconstruction of the Senate-house, another victim of the disorders of 52, and for the erection of a large covered enclosure for voters at the Popular Assemblies (Saepta Iulia).

The Forum Iulium

29.2 Roman Forum, looking to the west.

His work in the old Forum aimed at introducing a greater measure of axial systematisation such as was seen in the piazza of the Hellenistic cities and in a modified form in Italy at Pompeii and in colonies such as Cosa and Alba Fucens.

On the other hand the censors of the later Republic no longer kept up the practice of making improvements or effecting repairs out of occasional surpluses in the treasury; and the senatorial government remained blind to the need of controlling the vast building operations which the rapid growth of the urban population entailed. While the aristocracy was appropriating the Palatine Hill as a select residential *Random* quarter the poorer inhabitants of the city were *growth of* being huddled together in crazy matchwood *the poorer* tenements of many storeys, whose rents soared *quarters* as high as the buildings themselves – height made possible by the increasing use of concrete. On the other hand the outskirts of Rome now began to be laid out with pleasure-grounds in Hellenistic fashion. The gardens of Lucullus and

Sallust in the north, of Maecenas in the east, and of Caesar across the Tiber provided a loose *Suburban* chain of parks around the city. *parks*

The outward appearance of Rome was enlivened with the introduction of brighter building materials. For construction of a durable but inexpensive character architects had recourse to concrete with facings of wedge-shaped stones. But for the more decorative kinds of work they brought into use the handsome cream-coloured limestone of Tibur nowadays known as 'Travertine'; for columns or panelling they employed white or coloured stones from Greece, Asia Minor and Numidia, and, from Caesar's day, *Use of* the white marble of the quarries at Carrara *marble and* (Luna) in northern Italy. In matters of detail, such *'Travertine'* as the increasing use of columns and pilasters, *stone* the buildings of the later Republic betrayed Greek influence; yet their plans adhered to the Italian types. The stone theatres which now sprang up in Rome (the first was built by Pompey in 55) and in the country towns (at Pompeii

29.3 Forum of Julius Caesar.

one such building was erected in the second century, another after the time of Sulla) followed Greek plans in general; but whereas Greek theatres were fitted into the solid rock of hillsides, Italian architects made the bold experiment of constructing the auditoria in masonry supported on vaults. The 'amphitheatres', with a continuous ring of seats round an oval arena, were of purely Italian type. The amphitheatre at Pompeii was built for the veterans of Sulla's colony.

Buildings in Italy

While the city of Rome was drawing all the wealth of the Mediterranean to itself, other towns in Italy acquired new buildings, though on a more modest scale. Surviving buildings of this period include two temples at Cori, two others at Tibur (Tivoli), many villas (including an earlier one under Hadrian's villa near Tibur), and a great temple-complex of Jupiter Anxur

on the hill above Tarracina with its imposing surviving platform. A notable reconstruction of the sanctuary of Fortuna Primigenia was made at Praeneste after the civil war of 83–82 B.C. The approaches to the temple, which was situated at the summit of a steep hill, were laid out in terraces after the manner of the Acropolis of Pergamum.

Finally, mention should be made of two tributes by Greeks to the growing skill of Roman architects and to the fact that the Roman version of Hellenistic architecture was even winning its way into the Greek world itself. The Syrian king Antiochus IV (175–163) commissioned a Roman, Decimus Cossutius, to rebuild the Olympeion at Athens, while Strabo extols the Roman architecture of Caesar's time in Nicopolis, a suburb of Alexandria, which outshone the Hellenistic buildings.[18]

Roman architectural skill

29.4   Temple of Mater Matuta at Rome, probably after 80 B.C. rather than Augustan.

Roman collectors of Greek 'Old Masters'

Roman plastic art derived much benefit from close acquaintance with Greek models.[19] Dilettantism in Greek sculpture was now becoming a fashionable foible among the Roman aristocracy. Fantastic prices were being offered for

29.5   Temple of Hercules at Cori, late second century B.C.

Greek 'Old Masters'. Since the supply was obviously limited a demand for good copies arose. Greek statues and other works of art were reproduced largely by Greek artists for rich Roman patrons, and a flourishing new industry grew up. But in sculpture, as in architecture, the Italian artist was an independent pupil; while he acquired the refinements of Greek technique he retained his preference for the traditional Italian subjects. He made no attempt to rival the cult-images of the Greek temples, but exercised his skill in the typically Italian genre of portrait statuary. Surviving examples of the first-century portraiture, such as the familiar busts of Cicero in the Vatican Museum and of Pompey at Copenhagen, combine a Greek smoothness and roundness of execution with the inherited realism of Roman art (p. 194). A growing desire for decorated sculptured monuments was answered by adorning sarcophagi with sculpted mythological or battle scenes. This new develop-

Portrait statuary

ment is linked with a desire to commemorate public events, such as victories, and it led on to the historical reliefs which were to become a striking feature of Roman art under the Empire.

Pompeian frescoes

The pictorial art of the first century is illustrated by some scattered frescoes from private residences in Rome, and by a group of house-remains at Pompeii. These remnants show that the painters of the period usually broke their field into several small panels, but that they filled these in with naturalistic figures and landscapes, and had acquired proficiency in setting these against their background so as to produce an illusion of depth in space.

Coinage

Of the late republican metal-work it is difficult for us to form an idea except through the copious coinage of Roman denarii. Although some of the silver coins of the first century betray a rather rough workmanship, many issues were of remarkably fine execution, especially from 66 to 55. The effigy of Caesar is rendered very carelessly, but the heads of Antony, Octavian and Lepidus on the triumviral coinage exhibit the characteristic Roman talent for portraiture. In general it may be said that Roman art under the late Republic was completing its apprenticeship, that it was successfully applying Greek refinements of technique to Italian types and subjects, and was leading up to its climax of achievement under the early emperors.

6. Latin Literature. Poetry

Roman education and the study of Greek at Rome

In the school of language and letters the Romans of the later Republic proved such proficient pupils that they outstripped their Greek teachers and established Latin as one of the classical literatures. Roman society was now at one in admitting that an intensive study of Greek was an indispensable requisite of a good education. After a 'primary' stage at which he learned to read and write, a Roman boy from about twelve to fifteen studied at a 'grammar' school where he was taught *grammatike*, which consisted of language and literature. Here he had a teacher for Greek and another for Latin, and pupils were often grounded in Greek before studying their mother tongue; then they proceeded simultaneously with both. They were taught the correct use of words with some reference to style, although the latter fell rather within the next stage of education which embraced rhetoric. They read and memorised Greek and Latin 'classics', including Homer and Greek tragedy, comedy and lyric, while Horace as a boy, under the threat of the cane of his master Orbilius, studied Livius Andronicus and

says that the Romans learned by heart such authors as Ennius, Naevius, Pacuvius, Accius, Afranius, Plautus, Caecilius and Terence (before very long Horace himself and Virgil were to become the two chief 'school' authors).[20] After this stage, in order to put the finishing touch on their education young Romans went to study at the Greek university towns. Both Cicero and Caesar attended courses of rhetoric at Rhodes; Cicero also studied philosophy at Athens, and sent his son there for the same object. Others attended the classes of Greek rhetoricians who took up their residence at Rome, and a strange ordinance by the censors of the year 92, by which Latin schools of rhetoric were temporarily compelled to close down, gave the Greek courses an artificial impetus. In the first century a knowledge of Greek among the Romans of the governing class could be assumed as a matter of course, so that an interpreter was no longer required when Greek envoys were allowed to address the Senate in their own tongue. Greek phrases and quotations came as naturally from the lips of Cicero or Caesar as French from educated Britons and Germans in the eighteenth century. Caesar, Cicero and Octavian even found time to compose Greek plays or histories – which they had the good sense not to publish.

Quotations in Greek

On the other hand, the Latin language was now gaining ground at an even faster rate than Greek. In Italy (inclusive of Cisalpine Gaul) it was rapidly ousting the local dialects and was being taught at every school. It was being carried by emigrants to the western provinces and was beginning to establish itself in the Mediterranean lands as a second universal tongue. At the same time the accidence and orthography of Latin were being standardised by grammarians, and in the written language at least a uniformity like that of the 'common speech' of the Greek world was established.[21] Further, in the last century of the Republic Latin acquired, in addition to its native clearness and terseness, a musical rhythm and a flexibility of syntax which made it a suitable vehicle for almost every mode of literary expression. Yet its chief writers, however much they might borrow Greek elements of form and thought, usually impressed a peculiarly Italian character upon their work.

Latin becomes a second universal tongue

The early promise of Roman poetry was not fulfilled in one of its principal branches.[22] Though the theatre had firmly established its hold on the favour of the Roman public, the plays sank back to the level of mere amusements. The blame for this relapse falls mainly on the playgoers. The cosmopolitan rabble which now filled the auditorium at Rome lacked the intellectual stamina to follow out a drama with a

Decay of the Latin drama

The 'mime'

carefully constructed plot. Though the best of the older plays were occasionally reproduced at festivals, even Plautus had to be cut to hold the flickering attention of later audiences. In the first century literary drama was definitely replaced on the Roman stage by the 'mime' which henceforth held unbroken sway in the theatres. The mime was a short sketch with scenes taken from daily life, as in the old Atellane farce, which itself continued at Rome (temporarily in a more literary form in the Sullan period). At its best, the mime gave scope for clever delineation of character and smart repartee, and in the hands of two contemporaries of Caesar, the ex-slave Publilius Syrus and the knight D. Laberius, it momentarily rose to the level of literature. But its plots were usually attenuated to mere love-affairs, and the libretto was subordinated to an accompaniment of rowdy music and suggestive dancing.

Epic poetry. Lucretius

Epic poetry in the strict sense of the word suffered an eclipse after Ennius, whose *Annales* seemed destined to remain an unapproachable classic. In an age distracted by civil conflicts the glow of pride which the national wars against Pyrrhus and Hannibal had kindled was becoming dulled, and a new epic on Rome's past could hardly have rung true. On the other hand the age of the Restoration produced one of the two great didactic epics of ancient times, the *De Rerum Natura* of T. Lucretius Carus (c. 94–55). Little is known of the author of this poem, save that he turned away in disgust from the political strife of his times to find solace in the philosophical doctrines of Epicurus. His epic provided a complete abstract of Epicurus's system; its sixth book summarised the history of man in a *légende des siècles*, wherein the idea of continuous progress first found clear expression. But Lucretius was no more a mere copyist than Milton, the English poet whom he most resembled. His hexameters, no less sonorous but more rhythmical than those of Ennius, were the counterpart to Cicero's prose. He argued passionately that the gods do not intervene in the affairs of this world which is governed by the mechanical movement of atoms, and that man should not fear death since he does not survive it. The awe which Lucretius felt for Nature, despite his atomistic physics, and the truly religious earnestness with which he denounced conventional morality and the traditional mythology that reflected it, were certainly not derived from Hellenistic Greece, but were a sublimation of old Italian traits.

Reflective poetry. Catullus

The age of the Restoration also overcame the shy pride of Roman tradition to the point of producing the first Latin poetry of the self-revealing type, the sonnet, elegiac and epigram.

The most notable of the pioneers of this genre, C. Valerius Catullus, was a native of Verona in Transpadane Gaul, who obtained admission to high society at Rome and burnt his wings in the flame of a boyish passion for the *belle dame* Clodia, sister of P. Clodius, the Lesbia of his poems. By assiduous practice in translating the highly finished *vers d'occasion* of the Hellenistic writers he attained an effortless ease in manipulating the various lyric metres; but he threw to the winds the conventionality of his Greek models and gave reckless utterance to each up-welling emotion – a gust of anger at Caesar's high-handed politics, a surge of joy over the scenery of Lake Garda, the transports and the anguishes of young love. The effusiveness of Catullus was no more typically Roman than the spontaneity of Burns was characteristically British; yet it was not inappropriate to an age in which established conventions were breaking down and the mantle of Roman *gravitas* was wearing thin.

7. Latin Prose Writers

The later annalists

Historical composition received a stimulus from the stirring events of the Gracchan period and remained a prolific branch of Latin literature.[23] The older type of compact chronicle, of which L. Calpurnius Piso (consul in 133) produced the last example, was superseded by more voluminous histories extending into twenty or more volumes. A certain Cn. Gellius eked out his narrative into at least fifty books (p. 197). No fewer than three of these larger works were written concurrently c. 70 B.C. by C. Licinius Macer, Claudius Quadrigarius and Valerius Antias. Despite their greater compass, these histories did not embody much serious research. Literary padding and free invention of a patriotic or partisan character accounted for much of their additional bulk. The newer annalists, moreover, differed from those of the third and second centuries in having little personal experience of politics; of the above-named trio Licinius Macer (a tribune in 73, who played a minor part in opposition to the Restoration government) was the only one with any extensive knowledge of practical affairs. The dependence of Livy on the later annalists is a main reason for the difficulties of reconstructing early Roman history (p. 61).

Caesar's war-histories

But the more typical historical work of the later Republic was the monograph on a limited period or subject. The surviving specimens of this class are the *Commentaries* of Caesar on the Gallic and Civil Wars, and the *Bellum Catilinae* and *Bellum Iugurthinum* of C. Sallustius

Crispus. The writings of Caesar had an apologetic as well as a historical purpose, and their title shows that their author regarded them as materials for historical treatises rather than as histories in themselves. But their bare and rock-ribbed narrative still serves as a show-piece of Latin lucidity, and their substantial accuracy of fact has been established beyond reasonable doubt.[24] The works of Sallust – a partisan of Caesar who ruined his career by scandalous extortion, yet took up his pen to expose corruption elsewhere – exhibit two Roman characteristics, terse expression and mordant criticism, in the highest degree. But his unconcealed bias against the governing Optimates and his carelessness in handling his facts make him fall far short of his model, the Greek historian Thucydides. His reputation would no doubt stand higher if we possessed his *Histories*, a longer and maturer work on the period 78–67.[25]

Sallust

The increasing importance of the individual in the politics of the later Republic was reflected in the growth of a biographical literature, which had its beginnings, significantly enough, in the days of the Gracchi. The most notable of these Lives were the memoirs of several leading public men, among whom were included Aemilius Scaurus, Rutilius Rufus, Q. Catulus, Sulla and Cicero. These autobiographies were no doubt apologetic in character. Allied to them was a frankly polemical literature of pamphlets, which were as plentiful in Ciceronian Rome as in Stuart or Hanoverian England.[26] Among the by-products of historical literature the chonological works of Atticus and Cornelius Nepos, though hardly ranking as serious works of research, were of some importance in finally fixing the conventional dates for early Roman history. The antiquarian researches of Cato were continued on a larger scale in the *Antiquities* of M. Terentius Varro, which embodied a mass of patient investigations on early Roman institutions.[27] The nucleus of a history of Roman literature was contained in the various writings in which Cicero sketched the growth of oratory at Rome. These treatises, which combined wide learning with a keen and sympathetic appreciation of Cicero's predecessors, take a high place in the surviving historical literature of Rome.[28]

Memoirs and pamphlets

Roman antiquities

Under the later Republic Roman oratory enjoyed conditions as favourable as Attic eloquence in the days of Demosthenes, and attained a similar standard of achievement.[29] On the one hand the technique of public speaking was now being reduced to a fine art, which aspiring orators acquired by taking lessons from Greek rhetoricians or by an apprenticeship (*tirocinium fori*) with an approved Roman practitioner. On the other the prizes of eloquence in Roman public

The climax of Roman oratory

life were never greater. Though the atmosphere of the Senate-house was generally too cool to sustain the higher flights of oratory, the Popular Assembly, now composed of a volatile urban proletariat, answered readily to the touch of a skilled public speaker, and the jury-courts offered a new and wide field to the forensic pleader. The list of great Roman orators began with Gaius Gracchus; in the next generation it included M. Antonius (grandfather of the triumvir) and L. Crassus (*cos.* 95) who served as patterns to the youthful Cicero. In the decade after Sulla Caesar made a promising debut as a public speaker, but he left the field to an extreme partisan of the Restoration government, Q. Hortensius. After the trial of Verres (p. 243) Hortensius lost the first place to Cicero, who remained by universal consent the supreme master of Roman eloquence. To a modern reader the speeches of Cicero often appear laboured and turgid; but to a Roman ear the music of his carefully constructed periods made an ever-fresh appeal. His subtle irony, which often escapes the modern critic, delighted the ancient audiences; and the hard-hitting invective, which nowadays gets taken for mere barn-storming, carried along hearers who dearly loved a stout fighter. But the chief secret of Cicero's as of Demosthenes's success was his versatility. He was a master of many styles, and with his keen psychological flair he seldom failed to strike the appropriate note. Despite the occasional emergence of 'opposition' schools of style it was Cicero who fixed the norms of classical Latin prose.

Cicero

Though the Roman Republic never instituted an efficient postal service, communication by private messengers (and especially by the trained couriers of the tax-gathering companies) was sufficiently well organised to render possible a brisk exchange of missives, and letter-writing became a minor literary art, which we can still study in the voluminous correspondence of Cicero. It is in the main due to the survival of Cicero's letters that our knowledge of life under the later Republic is more vivid and varied than that of any other period of Roman history. Lastly, though the patronage of Roman nobles still counted for much among literary men,[30] it became less indispensable, as publishing-houses were set up at Rome and enabled Latin authors to reach a wider circle of readers. The fame of Cicero was enhanced in no small degree by his friend Atticus, whose trained slaves multiplied copies of the orator's works for the general market.

Cicero's correspondence

8. Science and Philosophy

Despite a smattering of mathematics which was imparted, in imitation of Greek curricula, in some of the higher Latin schools, the Roman mind remained as unappreciative as ever of natural science; only the solitary genius of Lucretius showed any deep interest in the works of Nature. Though a senator named Nigidius Figulus succeeded in casting a correct horoscope of the future emperor Augustus, Caesar had to have recourse to an Alexandrian scholar to rectify the Roman calendar. But Roman writers applied scientific methods to the study of language. L. Aelius Stilo (c. 100 B.C.) analysed the mechanism of the Latin tongue, and Varro composed a complete treatise (which survives in parts) on the Latin grammar and vocabulary. While they made due allowance for the inevitable anomalies of any living tongue the Roman grammarians standardised written Latin sufficiently to qualify it as a medium of intercourse for half the Roman empire.

Latin grammar

In the field of jurisprudence the theorists of the later Republic followed the practitioners in imparting greater elasticity to the legal system of Rome. While the practitioners tempered the *ius civile* with the *ius gentium*, framed equitable rules of evidence for the jury-courts and increasingly used the more flexible formulary system, which had been introduced by the *lex Aebutia*, in place of the earlier *legis actio* procedure (p. 182), the theorists provided a rational basis for the actual law by borrowing the Stoic doctrine of a universal 'natural law'. Among the chief legal authors of the first century we may mention Q. Mucius Scaevola (consul in 95), who wrote a complete treatise on the *ius civile*, and a friend of Cicero named Servius Sulpicius Rufus, who published a commentary on the praetors' edict. In the Ciceronian age many of the jurisconsults began to come from a different social class, namely the Equestrian Order or even men of humbler stock.[31]

Jurisprudence

Philosophical studies began to enter into the curriculum of well-educated Romans of the later Republic, though always kept subordinate to the linguistic and rhetorical training. The Stoic school, whose chief exponent, Posidonius of Apamea, exercised a wide influence in the Restoration period, still made a strong appeal and counted Cato and M. Brutus among its adherents. Several prominent Romans, including Caesar and his murderer Cassius, made a perfunctory and ineffective study of Epicureanism; others, like Cicero, struck a rough-and-ready compromise between conflicting doctrines.[32] Of Latin philosophical writers Lucretius surpassed all others in understanding

Philosophy

and strength of conviction. Popular philosophy was represented by the *Menippean Satires* (so called after a Hellenistic prototype) of Varro, which appear to have been short and racy essays on topical problems. But the most enduring Roman contributions to philosophy were the treatises in which Cicero expounded and criticised the principal Greek doctrines for the educated layman. While these works laid no claim to originality they conveyed the essence of the Greek systems in easy and lucid Latin, and pointed them with illustrations from Roman life and history: whenever Cicero cast a dissertation into the form of a dialogue, he used Roman personages, such as Scipio Aemilianus and his circle, as interlocutors. These works, which include *De Officiis*, *De Finibus*, *Tusculanae Disputationes*, *De Senectute* and *De Amicitia*, not only made the substance of Greek philosophy more widely available to his fellow countrymen, but exercised a great influence on later history, both during the Renaissance and the French Revolution, not to mention Tully's *Offices* in eighteenth-century England.[33]

Cicero's expositions of Greek doctrine

9. Religion[34]

The religion of the Roman world under the later Republic passed through an apparent state of stagnation, or even of decay. While the cults of the homestead retained their old-time vitality (of which the family altars in the houses at Pompeii and Delos offer visible proof), the worship of the State-gods was undergoing ossification. No further deities of any importance were admitted into the official pantheon; while the *ius civile* was being expanded in the light of a wider experience, the *ius divinum* was becoming stereotyped. But the fixity in the outer form of the State religion was of less consequence than the change in its inner spirit. In the second century the *pax deorum* had become a conspiracy between the State-gods and the governing aristocracy for the maintenance of the latter's ascendancy; in the first century it was further perverted to the selfish uses of individual politicians, who misused the elaborate code of divination for their personal advancement or the discomfiture of personal enemies. Under such conditions the official worships lost much of their remaining hold on the Roman people. From the point of view of the ordinary citizen their chief function was to provide him with amusements at the public festivals.

The state religion is subordinated to personal politics

The government of the later Republic maintained with considerable success the policy of discouraging the propagation of new worships by private initiative. In 139 it evicted the first

Oriental cults

Jewish immigrants into Italy for proselytising. In the first century it tolerated the synagogues set up by Pompey's prisoners of war from Palestine, and it did not formally proscribe the cult of the Egyptian deities Isis and Sarapis, which entered Italy *c.* 100 B.C.; but it banned these foreign gods from the city to its outer precincts and in 58 destroyed altars to Isis on the Capitol. So long as the Oriental element of population in Italy remained relatively small, these police measures proved effective, and the influence of eastern deities was as yet of no great account. On the other hand the ban which Antony placed on the worship of the dead Caesar in 44 was lifted two years later, when the triumvirs instituted an official cult of *divus Iulius* (p. 288); a comet, which appeared during games in Caesar's honour, was thought to be his soul received in Heaven, and he was now officially enrolled among the gods of the Roman State. The great

Caesar-worship

personality of Caesar made the Greek practice of offering divine homage to human beings, dead or alive, appear less strange to the Roman mind. But for the time being man-worship did not strike deep roots in Italy.

An interest in stars, however, had long flourished. A belief in astrology received some respectability when the philosopher Posidonius

Astrology

assessed it as a branch of astronomy. He linked on to Stoicism a belief that all parts of the universe were united by an all-embracing power ('sympatheia'). Thus many educated and rationalist Romans found in astronomy a link between human causality and the cosmic laws that governed the movement of the stars, while many others approached astrology in a less scientific and more emotional manner. Thus despite the scepticism of men such as Lucretius, Cicero and Caesar, astrological belief was widespread during the late Republic. It was also denounced by P. Nigidius Figulus, the learned praetor of 58 B.C., who championed another form of belief that was gaining ground in Rome, namely the teaching of Pythagoras, with its belief in the transmigration of souls.[35]

Thus however little regard Romans of the ruling class might have for any kind of formal worship, they could not dispense with religion altogether. Lucretius, the prophet of Epicurean atheism, could not abjure his faith in a governing Providence. Varro gravitated to Stoic pantheism; others toyed with the Pythagorean doctrine of the transmigration of souls, which Posidonius had quite illogically grafted on to the Stoic doctrine of impersonal immortality. Cicero derided popular mythology and seercraft; yet he wrote a treatise in proof of deism, and after the death of his favourite child Tullia he seriously thought of erecting a shrine in her honour. Among his contemporaries receptivity to religious ideas was dormant rather than dead.

Interest in religion not dead

PART V

Consolidation of the Roman Empire

CHAPTER 30

The Settlement of Augustus. Rome and Italy[1]

1. The First Settlement, 29–23 B.C.

Popularity of Octavian on his return from Egypt

On his return to Italy in the summer of 29 Octavian enjoyed a personal ascendancy such as neither Sulla nor Caesar had ever possessed. He had the entire military strength of the Empire at his disposal; he came back with the prestige of a victor in a foreign war, with the odium that inevitably attaches to success in civil strife largely forgotten, and he brought with him the treasure of the Ptolemies, which not only enabled him to pay off the troops without recourse to further confiscations, but left him with a surplus for distribution to the people of the capital. In the reshaping of the constitution, which was his next task, he had a freer hand than either of his predecessors, and the republican susceptibilities of the Romans, which Sulla had humoured, and Caesar had defied to his cost, weighed far less heavily upon him. It was now full thirty years since the republican government had been in anything like normal working order; the memory of the days of liberty (as then understood) was becoming faint, and the nobles who had been the most active guardians of the republican tradition had been severely reduced in numbers and corporate strength by the civil wars and proscriptions.[2] Above all, Octavian was now acclaimed as the Prince of Peace who had terminated a period of domestic strife, of massacres, confiscations and dragonnades exceeding all previous terrors in Roman history. The welcome which he received in 29 was like that which Charles II experienced in 1660 after eleven years of military rule in England, or Napoleon on his return from Marengo, after as many years of revolution.

But in one matter Octavian had no choice. He could offer no guarantee of peace in the future, except by retaining the armed forces of the empire under his undivided control. His prestige among the troops was now so high that he could answer for their good behaviour; but if he were to abdicate his military power or to share it with others, there was every reason to fear that ambitious military officers might again turn their soldiery upon the civil authorities or upon each other. Fifty years of civil war and revolution had created a tradition within the Roman army which none but Octavian could break; therefore it was his duty no less than his right to keep the entire military *imperium* in his own hands.

His duty to retain control of the army

Under such conditions Octavian might have proceeded to set up an absolute monarchy in 29 with far greater chances of success than Caesar in 44. Nevertheless, instead of advancing along the line of least resistance, he attempted to recross his Rubicon. The promise which he had made in 36, that he would eventually restore the Republic (p. 293), was more than a tactical move in a diplomatic game: his own inclination and experience now turned him in that direction.[3] He had none of the robust health and abundant energy that prompted Caesar to carry the whole world on his shoulders. Though he contrived to eke out his life to the age of seventy-seven, repeated illnesses gave him warning that he must ration his work and pass on some of his responsibilities. By natural sentiment he was a genuine believer in the *mos maiorum*, and a conservative both in and out of politics.[4] True

Octavian goes back on his past

30.1 Statue of Augustus, found near Porta Prima in Rome in the ruins of a villa belonging to Livia. Augustus is represented as *imperator*, but the cuirass depicts the restoration of peace: in the centre the Parthians restore the lost Roman standards, while they are flanked by the figures of pacified Gaul and Spain. Above, the powers of the sky, Sol, Aurora and Caelum, usher in the new era, while below, with Apollo and Artemis, is Mother Earth with cornucopia.

His genuine republican leanings

enough, in the struggle for power he had been a revolutionary leader who had led his followers to victory, but with the elimination of all rivals he could identify his followers with the State and claim that his power rested on universal consent. This he bluntly proclaimed later in his *Res Gestae:* 'per consensum universorum potitus rerum omnium'. Further, he knew that he had bought success at the price of a humiliating dependence on his own soldiery. Accordingly Octavian did not cling to autocratic power like Caesar; but neither did he completely abdicate it like Sulla. He worked his way to a compromise, in which his guiding principle was to reserve for himself the military and foreign policy of the Empire and a general supervision over the civilian administration, but to leave over the details of civilian government to two privileged classes of public servants, the *senatorius ordo* and the *equester ordo*: he aimed at doubling the inevitable part of warlord with the freely chosen role of 'rector' in Cicero's sense.

His attempted division of power

Since the expiration of the triumvirate Octavian had rested his power on a makeshift basis, relying on the moral, though not constitutional, support of the oath of allegiance taken by Italy and the western provinces; from 31 onwards he held the consulship. While he was still busy in the East in 30 a grateful people offered him many honours, including full tribunician power (he had received tribunician sacrosanctity in 36), but for the present he declined this offer, or if he accepted he made no practical use of it.[5] He was granted the right to judge cases on appeal, and to create new patrician families whose numbers had been weakened by the civil wars. He officially used the *praenomen* Imperator, and was greatly pleased when the Senate decreed the closing of the temple of Janus which symbolised the restoration of peace.

His constitutional position since 32 B.C.

By August 29 Octavian had returned to Rome and celebrated a triple triumph for the conquest of Illyricum, the victory at Actium and the annexation of Egypt. Already he was tackling

The years 29 and 28 B.C.

30.3 Agrippa, wearing a rostral and mural crown.

the vast task of settling great numbers of his veterans in colonies (p. 340), ultimately reducing his sixty legions to twenty-eight. The restoration of order at home was symbolised by the fact that when he held his sixth consulship in 28 with his friend Agrippa, both consuls remained in Rome throughout the year for the first time for twenty years; further, by edict he proclaimed an amnesty and annulled any illegal orders that he had given during the civil wars. He was also concerned to lay the foundations of a revised Senatorial and Equestrian Order. He obtained for himself and Agrippa a special grant of censorial power; they revised the Senate (perhaps in 29), placing Octavian's name at the head of the list as Princeps Senatus, and took a census of the whole people in 28. They purged the Senate of some 200 members, expelling some of the more disreputable men who had crept in during the triumviral period (rather than old Republicans or Antonians). The Senate was thus reduced from 1000 to 800.

The process of deflation was continued in 18, when he cut the membership down to 600, and was completed by a less drastic revision in 11 B.C.[6] For the filling of vacancies in his purified Senate Octavian brought back into full force the Sullan system of automatic recruitment from ex-quaestors; but he restricted the right of suing for the quaestorship to members of a limited *senatorius ordo,* and he made admission to this order dependent on certain indispensable qualifications — personal integrity, the fulfilment of a term of military service, and the possession of sufficient property (with a minimum of 800,000, subsequently raised to 1,000,000 sesterces) to ensure economic independence. Octavian himself could give the laticlave (that is, the broad purple stripe on the tunics worn by men of senatorial birth) to young men of non-senatorial birth, who could then seek one of the minor offices known as the vigintivirate which would qualify them to stand for the

The Senatorial and Equestrian Orders

30.2 Augustus.

quaestorship. Thus a certain number of men of equestrian stock turned to an official career and some new blood was infused into the Senate. For entrance into the *equester ordo* similar rules were laid down; the property-qualification remained, as before, at 400,000 sesterces. In practice the two orders came to be recruited in large measure from the governing classes of the Italian *municipia*, with a slight infusion of men of Italian origin from Roman colonies in Gaul and Spain. The *senatorius ordo* tended to become a hereditary body, as indeed Octavian meant it to be. It naturally included all the survivors of the old governing families; yet its membership was drawn from a far wider area than that of the republican nobility, and it was continually replenished with *novi homines*.

By the beginning of 27, when he would enter on his seventh consulship, Octavian judged the time ripe for further settlement. He may have been hastened to this decision by the realisation that he must have no rivals in the military field when M. Licinius Crassus, grandson of the triumvir, had claimed the honour of *spolia opima*, a claim which Octavian had not allowed.[7] Thus early in January he suddenly announced in the Senate that he was renouncing all his powers and provinces and placing them at the free disposal of Senate and people. Consultation with senior members and friends must have paved the way for this remarkable move and for its sequel. With apparent reluctance he then agreed to undertake the administration of a large *provincia*, consisting of Spain (except perhaps the south which now or in 16–13 became a separate senatorial province), Gaul and Syria, for a period of ten years, possibly with proconsular authority.[8] Further, he was and continued to be consul. Other honours followed: in the Senate-house a golden shield proclaimed his 'valour, clemency, justice and piety', while his door-posts were decorated with laurel and lintel with oak because he had saved the lives of Roman citizens (*ob cives servatos*). More important he received the name Augustus and abandoned that of Octavian (the month Sextilis was also renamed August, but this change may not have been made until later). The significance of his new name defies exact analysis. It had a religious flavour, conveying that its holder had been inaugurated in all due form in his new charge and had commended himself to gods as well as to men; it also sharply distinguished him from Octavian, the triumvir and military despot.

In the new sharing-out of power the Senate received back into its hands the supervision of Rome and Italy, and of one-half of the provinces. By the original partition it resumed control of Sicily, Sardinia and Corsica, southern Spain (henceforth known as 'Baetica'), Illyricum, Macedonia, Achaea (or Greece Proper, which was now constituted as a separate province), Asia, Bithynia, Crete and Cyrene (which were combined into a single province), and Africa. In subsequent rearrangements it surrendered Sardinia and Corsica, and Illyricum; but it obtained Cyprus and Gallia Narbonensis in compensation. Few of its members continued to serve as jurors in the criminal courts in the three panels (*decuriae*), each nearly 1000 strong, which consisted mainly of members of the Equestrian Order who had to share this privilege with persons possessing the lower property-qualification of 200,000 sesterces. But the Senate as a body was constituted as a court of law for the first time in its history. At some time between 23 B.C. and A.D. 8 it was authorised under the presidency of the consuls (Augustus could of course attend) to try cases of political crimes or ordinary crimes in which senators were involved. Thus provincial governors accused of extortion would come before the Senate, while if any provincial wanted merely to sue a governor for restitution instead of on a capital charge, a smaller committee of the Senate was set up *ad hoc*. Under the eye of the Senate the various grades of magistrates resumed their previous routine, and the government of the 'senatorial' provinces reverted to the ex-consuls and ex-praetors (henceforth all called proconsuls). The number of magistrates was again fixed on a similar scale to that of the later Republic; but the age-limit for the quaestors was lowered to twenty-five, and for the consuls to thirty-five.

The prerogatives which Augustus (as we shall henceforth call him) reserved for himself do not admit of exact definition. They were not gathered together in a single comprehensive act, but were parcelled out into a series of separate grants. In 27 and the following four years he continued to hold successive consulships, and either by a special grant of an *imperium proconsulare*, or by an extension of his *imperium consulare* beyond Italy, he retained all the provinces which he had not handed back to the Senate. This *imperium* Augustus was authorised to exercise by the agency of acting governors in the several provinces, who received his directions from Rome. Thus Augustus could claim with some degree of truth that the ancient form of the Republic was restored. Instead of a dictator, it had a *Princeps Civitatis* who was *primus inter pares*, and although he was commander-in-chief of the armed forces, there were still three independent proconsuls in Illyricum, Macedonia and Africa with armies under their command.

2. Augustus's Second Settlement

Threats to Augustus's authority

For nearly three years Augustus now absented himself from Rome, perhaps judging that the new state would settle down better with time to adjust its outlook, undisturbed by his presence. First he held a census in his province of Gaul and then proceeded to campaign in north-west Spain (p. 334), where he was taken ill. He returned to Rome in 24, but trouble developed the next year, that of his eleventh consulship. M. Primus, governor of Macedonia, was accused in the court of *maiestas* with having made war on the Thracian Odrysae without orders, and was condemned for treason after Augustus had denied that he had given any such order. Then a conspiracy against Augustus's life was discovered, led by a republican named Fannius Rufus, while a Varro Murena, probably Augustus's consular colleague, was implicated.[9] No sooner was this crushed than another crisis blew up: Augustus was nearly carried off by a dangerous illness. He gave his signet-ring to his friend Agrippa and some state documents to the consul who had replaced the treacherous Murena.

The settlement of 23 B.C.

On his recovery Augustus's first thought was to resign office altogether; eventually he came to a new understanding with the Senate. On 1 July he resigned the consulship which he had held continuously since 31, and henceforth resumed it only on rare occasions. In relinquishing this office he rid himself of various routine duties which were taking toll of his physical powers; at the same time he gratified the members of the Senatorial Order, who still coveted the consulship as the highest distinction in public life and were as resentful as ever of the continuous occupation of this office by one person.[10] To make up for the loss of authority which this surrender involved Augustus's powers were increased both at home and abroad. He was now granted, or more probably brought into active use, the full *tribunicia potestas* which he had hitherto allowed to remain dormant (p. 317). By virtue of this power he convened the Senate, presented legislation to the people, and exercised a general criminal jurisdiction. As a supplement he acquired the right of submitting motions to the Senate by written message, which the House bound itself to discuss in priority to any other business. Though in practice he did not make great use of his tribunician power, he made much display of it and numbered the years of his reign by it, starting from 23. Further, it was popular and it compensated Augustus for the loss of control over civilian affairs inherent in the consulship; Tacitus called it 'the title of the highest eminence in the state'

Tribunicia potestas

(*summi fastigii vocabulum*). In the second place, when he abandoned the consulship, Augustus still retained his *imperium* as governor of the provinces he had received, and this grant was renewed at intervals of five or ten years (in 18, 13 and 8 B.C., and again in A.D. 3 and 13). This *imperium* was now (as it may have been since 27: p. 318) proconsular and could not continue to be held by a proconsul within the city of Rome. A second limitation was that it was only equal to that of any other proconsul in the provinces. Therefore Augustus's *imperium* was now modified in two ways: he could retain it in the city and it was made *maius*, 'greater', so that Augustus could now override the governors of all the provinces and exercise a potential *imperium* over the whole Empire and the whole army. In practice he very seldom called into play this *imperium proconsulare maius*, and used it very tactfully when he did.[11] The area of his provincial command was slightly modified in 23: he transferred Gallia Narbonensis and Cyprus to the Senate; all additional provinces created after 23 needed military protection and were included in his sphere of power. Thus, in 23 were forged the two main constitutional bases of the Principate: tribunician power and proconsular *imperium*.

Imperium proconsulare maius

Augustus further retained or resumed the right which he had exercised as triumvir, of influencing the election of magistrates: he could nominate (*nominare*) candidates by receiving or rejecting their names, but the consuls also had this right. He could canvass for and commend (*commendatio*) candidates whom he favoured. Either procedure would tend to leave a mere *congé d'élire* in the hands of the Comitia, whose electoral freedom was further limited by a reform later in the reign (p. 321).[12] Augustus at this stage, if not previously, assumed the right to nominate the jurors for the *quaestiones*. He continued or renewed the practice of the triumviral period, by which all incoming magistrates swore an oath to observe all his *acta* or ordinances, past or future. Lastly, he obtained special authority to conclude treaties with foreign powers, without submitting them to Senate or people for ratification.

Rights of nomination to the magistracies

The effect of the revised constitution of 23 was that Augustus's position became more sharply differentiated from that of the regular magistrates, and assumed more of an overriding character such as Cicero had prescribed for his ideal 'rector'. But in its essential features Augustus's scheme of government was fixed in 27 when he claimed that he had 'handed back the Republic to the authority of Senate and people', and that he had reduced himself to the status of a magistrate who surpassed his colleagues in

The 'restoration of the Republic'

auctoritas alone.[13] On inscriptions and coins, and in the literature of the day, his settlement was hailed as a 'restoration of the Republic'. This assertion was not mere make-believe, but contained a foundation of truth. From 27 B.C. Augustus was technically an elective official who held his power by gift of the Senate and people, and subject to the sovereignty of the laws. Taken singly, the constituent elements in his prerogative were for the most part covered by precedents from the history of the later Republic.

Republican precedents

Successive consulships had been held by Marius; proconsulships in several provinces and over long terms of years had been accorded to Lucullus, Caesar and Pompey; and Pompey had set an example of governing provinces by proxy. The right of nominating candidates for office had once been inherent in the power of consuls or other returning officers (p. 63); admission to the Senate and the *equester ordo* had formerly been at the discretion of the censors.

During the winter of 23/22 floods and famine led to some rioting in Rome, and Augustus was asked to accept an annual and perpetual consulship, a dictatorship, a censorship or a curatorship of the corn-supply: he contented himself by taking, as Pompey in 57, only the *cura annonae*. He then went to the East (22–19) and further disturbances occurred in Rome, especially in 19. On his return he was granted the

Further honours in 19 B.C.

right to sit between the two consuls of the year and to have twelve lictors, and according to Dio Cassius he was granted consular powers for life. This latter statement has caused much debate. If true, it would explain the basis of some of Augustus's subsequent actions in Rome and Italy, but on the other hand it may be an exaggerated misunderstanding of some specific right enjoyed by a consul and granted to him (e.g. a right to appoint a Prefect of the City).[14] In any case it may suggest that he had given up rather too much in 23 and now responded to popular demands to strengthen his position. In general he kept the Senate informed of his own decisions and consulted it on questions of high policy. He encouraged free discussion, and on minor points he submitted with good grace to adverse resolutions. Though he suppressed publication (but not the redaction) of the *acta senatus* he allowed the continuance of the official gazette (*acta diurna*) for the general public.

His plain style of life

In deliberate contrast with the monarchical style of Caesar, Augustus was at pains to maintain the outward semblance of a republican magistracy. He wore the purple-edged toga of a curule officer and carried no insignia except those of a consul. The modest *Domus Augusti* (or 'house of Livia') on the south-eastern edge of the Palatine resembled the mansion of a noble

rather than the palace of a king in size and appointments.[15] Though Augustus maintained a bodyguard, he made his custodians as inconspicuous as possible; to all comers he was 'citizen-like' in his bearing. The select company of *amici Caesaris* who had unrestricted right of entrance to his household did not differ essentially from the *cohortes* of the republican grandees. Lastly, the comprehensive title of *princeps* or 'first citizen' under which he summed up his position was wholly in keeping with republican usage; it had served at various times to describe the personal ascendancy of Pompey and of other republican leaders.

But however much Augustus's prerogative might recall the republican magistrates in this detail or that, in its totality it was incompatible with republican usage. The wide range and the continuity of his functions, and the magnitude of his powers of patronage, were essentially monarchical. Of his individual attributes his *imperium proconsulare* and his *maius imperium* over the senatorial provinces were sufficient in themselves to raise him far above the status of a republican official. By virtue of this extended *imperium* he controlled the entire armed forces of the state and a large proportion of its revenues. Every Roman soldier continued to take the oath of allegiance to him and to look to him for his material rewards, as in the days of the Triumvirate, and all acting commanders of Roman armies were his subordinates.[16] Augustus never surrendered the power of the sword; in the last resort he could, *de facto*, exercise the power of life and death over all the inhabitants of the Roman Empire. Herein lay the ultimate insuperable difficulty of reconciling Augustus's theory of government with his practice: his enlarged *imperium* fastened upon him an essentially arbitrary power such as no republican official had wielded, except in a brief emergency. In effect the *princeps* was swallowed by the *imperator*, and the name of 'emperor', by which the modern world usually designates Augustus and his successors, indicates the real essence of his position.

Augustus's power of the sword

But the power of the sword which Augustus kept in his hands carried with it the control of foreign policy and, in a large measure, of financial administration. The permanent master of the legions had the last word on every question of peace and war. It was in recognition of this plain fact that the Senate conceded to Augustus the right of concluding treaties in his own name, and that foreign powers diverted their embassies from the Senate to the emperor. Again, the master of the legions, being also their paymaster, was obliged to appropriate for himself a share of the public revenue, which in effect

Control of foreign policy

gave him a determining voice in questions of taxation.

Furthermore, the general powers of supervision which Augustus had taken into his hands were brought into such frequent use that they became in fact a part of his regular prerogative. In the senatorial provinces, it is true, the active exercise of his *maius imperium* appears to have been confined to rare occasions. On the other hand his intervention was again and again solicited in the affairs of the capital, where the new *senatorius ordo*, whether from lack of experience or by a sheer failure of nerve, failed to provide a better administration than that of the republican nobility. In recognition of its own incapacity the Senate gradually withdrew the various administrative services of Rome from the magistrates under its direct control, and transferred them to new officials nominated *ad hoc* by the emperor (no doubt with the Senate's nominal concurrence). By this process responsibility for the welfare of the capital was permanently fixed upon the emperor. Similarly the Senate made such sparing use of its powers of legislation, that this function also devolved upon the emperor, who either brought forward bills in his own person (by virtue of his tribunician power), or initiated measures which were carried in the name of a consul or other magistrate.

The very vagueness of Augustus's prerogative further tended towards an imperceptible increment to his powers from precedent to precedent, as with the tribunes in the earlier period of the Republic. In particular, the emperor's jurisdiction grew by this piecemeal method. Once Augustus was recognised as the supreme power in the state, the habit of 'appealing unto Caesar' sprang up spontaneously, and the emperor found himself saddled with a general appellate jurisdiction which proceeded not merely from the provinces under his direct control, but from the senatorial provinces, and from Rome and Italy. Though Augustus delegated many of the cases thus submitted to him he did not deny his competence, so that the imperial court of appeal gradually established itself as a regular part of the constitution.[17]

During the early part of his principate in so far as Augustus influenced magisterial elections he did so mainly by indirect methods (p. 319), and this no doubt continued to be true at any rate in regard to candidates for the consulship. But at all times it is probable that if he let his wishes be known, his favoured candidate would be likely to be successful. In A.D. 5 the consuls carried a *lex Valeria Cornelia* which amended the procedure for the election of praetors and consuls in the Comitia Centuriata. An additional group of ten centuries, designated in honour of Augustus's grandsons as 'centuriae C. et L. Caesaris', and derived from senators and all the equites enrolled as jurors, made a preliminary choice (*destinatio*) of candidates to be presented to the Comitia Centuriata. Their choice, although not binding, would normally be followed by the whole Comitia in its votes, as earlier it had often taken a lead from the *centuria praerogativa* (p. 80). The effect of the reform, which was modified early in Tiberius's reign, was to enhance the dignity more than the political power of the upper classes and to diminish still more that of the people.[18]

Lastly in 12 B.C. the death of Lepidus created a vacancy in the office of Pontifex Maximus, which was offered to Augustus and accepted by him with less reluctance than most of his other supplementary functions. The Pontificate, however, added more dignity than power to the emperor's position. When finally in 2 B.C. he received the title of Pater Patriae, he was officially designated the father of the state which he had so widely reformed.

3. The New Executive

To carry out the multifarious duties which Augustus partly took and partly had thrust upon him, he instituted a special executive of his own, which expanded under his successors into the most extensive bureaucracy of ancient times. For the administration of the provinces of which he was the titular proconsul he appointed acting governors under the name of *legati Augusti pro praetore* or (as in Egypt) of *praefecti*;[19] and to these he attached a staff of *procuratores* as his financial agents (p. 342). In Rome he discharged his responsibilities by means of a civil service under the supervision of *curatores* or *praefecti* functioning singly or in boards. These 'imperial' officials (as we may call them, to distinguish them from the surviving republican magistracy) were recruited from the Senatorial and the Equestrian Orders, on the general principle that governorships of provinces and high military posts should be reserved for senators, while the civilian functions were mostly confided to persons of equestrian rank. Unlike the older magistracy the new officials carried on their work from year to year, after the fashion of the permanent executive staffs in the Hellenistic monarchies, and received a generous salary in return for their services. Many functionaries, indeed, left the emperor's service after some ten years of duty in order to return to their native places; and those who desired to vary their experience by holding an occasional magistracy under senatorial control could always count

Marginal notes (left column):
Powers transferred back to Augustus by the Senate

The administration of Rome

Legislation

Augustus's appellate jurisdiction

Elections

Marginal notes (right column):
Augustus appointed Pontifex Maximus

The new imperial executive

Its professional character

upon obtaining the necessary leave. But not a few of the imperial officials made a life's career of their administrative work, and most of them served long enough to acquire some measure of special skill in their duties. The gradual substitution of a professional public service for the amateur magistracy of the republican period was one of the most far-reaching, though perhaps the least sensational, of all the constitutional changes initiated by Augustus: it put into the hands of the emperors a far more powerful executive machine than the Senate ever possessed.

Augustus's secretariat

In addition to the functionaries recruited from the Senatorial and Equestrian Orders Augustus held at his disposal a large staff of ex-slaves of his household who served as his accountants and secretaries.[20] Though these assistants were technically his private servants they discharged a wide range of public duties and formed the nucleus of a large and important branch of the executive.

The praetorian cohorts and prefects

To the end of Augustus's reign the new executive remained in an inchoate and imperfectly organised condition. But a potential chief of the imperial staff was available in one or other of the two *praefecti praetorio*. These officials held command of the *cohortes praetoriae*, a corps of nine battalions, each 500 (possibly 1000) strong, of picked soldiers, who did double duty as the emperor's guards and as his orderlies.[21] In addition to their strictly military duties, the *praefecti praetorio* carried out the miscellaneous functions of imperial aides-de-camp. A masterful personality in this position might become in effect a vizier or might aspire to the imperial succession. In anticipation of this office growing over the emperor's head Augustus entrusted it to none but men of equestrian rank, and he divided its functions between two officials of equal standing; but this practice was not strictly followed by his successors.

The Consilium Principis

Lastly, though Augustus did not form a Privy Council after the pattern of the Hellenistic monarchies, he laid the foundations of such a body. Between 27 and 18 B.C. he instituted a committee of the Senate, consisting of the two consuls, of one representative apiece from each of the other colleges of magistrates, and of fifteen private members selected by lot, for a period of six months, to prepare the agenda and expedite the business of the whole House; it would also help Augustus to take the pulse of the Senate more privately. In A.D. 13, however, he virtually killed this useful body by changing its nature: he appointed as permanent counsellors three members of his own family; the ordinary members, now twenty, were probably not appointed by lot, while Augustus himself

had the power to co-opt any of his *amici*; further, it lost its probouleutic character and Augustus carried out its recommendations without submitting them to the Senate. A senatorial committee was thus changed into an imperial council. In addition to this regularly constituted committee Augustus also convened from time to time informal *consilia* of assessors in judicial cases, according to the ordinary custom of the republican magistrates. From these two sources the formal *Consilium Principis* was eventually derived.[22]

Ambiguities of Augustus's constitution

The discrepancy between political theory and practice in Augustus's constitution became the cause of many misunderstandings between the emperors and the Senate, and the uncertainty of their mutual relations placed a severe strain upon both parties. Yet the barest justice requires us to admit that Augustus did not intentionally hoodwink the Roman public in order to abstract political power out of its pocket and to appropriate it surreptitiously for himself. At the worst his scheme was an honest attempt to compromise between the grinding despotism which was the Triumvirate and the chaos which was the Republic. Moreover, for all its incidental defects, the vagueness of Augustus's constitution had this great merit, that it conformed to the sound Roman tradition of making political transformation by slow and gradual steps. Augustus, in fact, exhibited the same kind of statesmanship as those earlier Romans who settled the Conflict of the Orders by a succession of small concessions and compromises; and he

Its essential merits and long duration

achieved equally lasting results, for his scheme of government survived in essentials for more than two centuries. Lastly, however little he restored the Republic, he at any rate salvaged two of its most salutary principles, that political power is a trust to be exercised for the benefit of the ruled, and that the task of government should be widely shared between those possessing political ability.[23] In having the courage to make the great refusal of eschewing absolute despotism Augustus deserved well of the Roman Empire.

4. The City of Rome

Augustus lived on for some forty years after the settlement made by him in 27 B.C., so that he had ample time to bring his system into full working order. The rest of this chapter and the next will review the results of his long reign.

Rome under the Triumvirate

In the city of Rome the great building scheme of Caesar had suffered serious interruption during the Triumvirate, when funds for its completion were sadly lacking. At the same time the paralysis of the ordinary administration, and the preoccupation of the triumvirs themselves with high military policy, had reduced the capital to an even worse state of chaos than under the dying Republic. Crime went almost unchecked, and the triumvirs hardly interfered on behalf of public order, except now and then to repress the rioting of crowds half mad with famine.

A promise of better administration had been given in 33, when Agrippa stepped down from his quarter-deck to assume the homely office of aedile and carried out its duties with exemplary vigour, making personal inspections of all the public property and adventuring himself up the Cloaca Maxima in a boat. On his return from Egypt and the East, Augustus at once carried out urgently a programme of repairs to the more dilapidated temples. In subsequent years he applied large sums from his private revenue to further reconstruction, to the completion of Caesar's unfinished buildings, and to new public works; and he encouraged his chief military officers, among whom Agrippa again proved himself a zealous assistant, to devote their share of the war-booty to the adornment of the city. He took no effective steps to ease the congestion in the centre of the town; but he checked it by a regulation imposing a limit of 60 feet to the height of tenements. In the Forum he dedi-

Augustus's public works

30.4   The arched Cloaca Maxima, discharging into the Tiber.

cated a new temple to the deified Caesar in 29 B.C., and near by was built a new Arch of Augustus on whose walls were inscribed the Fasti, to remind Rome of her past heroes. North of this old Forum and over against that of Julius Caesar, which he completed, Augustus at great expense bought land to build a new Forum Augusti. In the centre of its back-wall stood the temple of Mars Ultor which he had vowed at Philippi when Caesar was avenged: it too proclaimed the glorious past with statues of the *triumphatores* and *elogia* which recalled their careers and achievements. On the Palatine Augustus built a temple to Apollo which he had vowed in 36. There was much building in the Campus Martius, where a portico was named

The Forum Augusti

in honour of his sister Octavia and the ever-impressive theatre after his nephew Marcellus. Here too his friend Agrippa laid out a park, and built baths and the original Pantheon (the present building is the work of Hadrian). Then near the Tiber were two great memorials: the Mausoleum which Augustus began as early as 28 B.C. for members of his family and ultimately himself and on the pillars of which was later inscribed his official testimony, the *Res Gestae*, to be matched by one of the noblest monuments of Augustan art, the Ara Pacis Augustae, the Altar of the Augustan Peace. Further, he instituted a permanent Board of Works (two praetorian or consular *curatores operum publicorum*) to enforce the new building regulations and to

30.5 Forum of Augustus, with temple of Mars Ultor, vowed at Philippi and consecrated in 2 B.C.

30.6 The theatre of Marcellus. Built by Augustus in memory of his nephew Marcellus. It held from 10,000 to 14,000 spectators. In the Middle Ages it was used as a fortress and residence.

maintain existing structures under repair. Augustus's boast, that he had found Rome a city of (unbaked) brick, and left it a city of marble, was an exaggeration, but it could be applied with some truth to the monumental centre.[24] In sum, Augustus's building programme in its quantity and quality, in its range and opulence, was an amazing achievement.

Water-supply

After the battle of Actium Agrippa took personal charge of the water-supply of Rome. In 19 B.C. he constructed a short but copious new aqueduct, the Aqua Virgo, and erected the 'Thermae', an elaborate bathing establishment in the later Greek style, combining the modern swimming-pool and Turkish bath. After his death, in 12 B.C., his technical staff of 240 trained slaves was placed on the public pay-list,

and the control of water-mains was permanently made over to an imperial board of three *curatores aquarum*, the chief being a consular.[25] Before the end of Augustus's reign water was available for most of the houses in Rome. For the problem of coping with the recurrent floods of the Tiber the emperor found a partial solution in the widening of its bed (in A.D. 15 five *curatores riparum Tiberis* were created).

The curator aquarum

Another public service for which Augustus created a special staff was the extinction of fires in the capital. Despite the facility with which the matchwood tenements in the narrow streets of the city could be set ablaze no regular provision had yet been made for dealing with conflagrations.[26] In 26 the emperor's attention was drawn to this deficiency by the action of an

Dangers of fire in Rome

30.7   Mausoleum of Augustus. Built in 28 B.C., it was the burial-place of several members of the imperial family beside Augustus himself.

ambitious aedile named M. Egnatius Rufus, who improvised a private fire-brigade, and took such credit to himself for his enterprise as to convey an implied taunt to Augustus. The emperor took up the challenge, but contented himself at first with half-measures. In 21 he placed a force of 600 public slaves at the disposal of the aediles; in 7 B.C. he called upon the tribunes and praetors and a body of lesser magistrates, the *vicomagistri*, to assist the aediles, and he mapped out the city into fourteen regions (*regiones*) to each of which a special corps of firemen was assigned. In A.D. 6 he realised at last that the fire-service required the unremitting attention of a professional expert. He appointed a permanent officer of equestrian rank named the *praefectus vigilum*, and provided him with a brigade of 3500 firemen, all freedmen, in seven cohorts,

Augustus's fire-brigade

each of which took charge of two urban regions. Though this reform did not put Rome beyond the reach of big conflagrations it was a considerable step in the right direction.[27]

The praefectus vigilum

During the war with Sextus Pompeius Rome had lived continuously under the shadow of famine, and after this struggle it had to reckon with a permanent reduction of supplies from Sicily. Fortunately Africa and Numidia were still increasing their production, and by stimulating the growth of wheat in Egypt Augustus was able to draw four months' rations from that quarter. But there remained the problem of organising the provisionment of Rome so as to ensure an adequate service of transport and distribution. Towards the end of his reign the emperor concluded a series of experimental reforms by appointing a permanent commis-

Corn-supply

The praefectus annonae

sioner of equestrian rank, the *praefectus annonae*, to charter the necessary shipping, to store the imported food, and to punish private dealers attempting to make a 'corner' in supplies.[28] The first prefect, C. Turranius, a former governor of Egypt, proved the worth of his services by holding his post for thirty years. Though supplies still fell short under some of Augustus's successors he laid down the lines on which Rome was eventually made safe against famine.

Free corn-distributions maintained

On the cognate question of the doles of public corn for the proletariat Augustus's original plan was even bolder than Caesar's. In the hope of checking the influx into the capital from the countryside he contemplated the complete abolition of free distributions. But on second thoughts he recoiled from this too heroic measure and fell back on the inadequate expedient of pruning the list of recipients (which had increased again under the triumvirs) to 200,000 (between 5 and 2 B.C.). At the same time he introduced an improved system of control and distribution. In the matter of public entertainments Augustus frankly accepted the republican nobles' policy of keeping the urban proletariat amused. He left the old-established *ludi* (circus races and dramatic performances) in the hands of the aediles and praetors, but he provided additional diversions out of his own purse. In particular the exhibition of gladiatorial contests at Rome, which had by now established themselves firmly in the popular favour, became almost an imperial monopoly. The first permanent amphitheatre in the city was built in Augustus's reign by one of his lesser war-winners, T. Statilius Taurus.

Increase of public amusements. Gladiatorial contests

The cohortes urbanae and praefectus urbi

In the most pressing of all problems of municipal reform Augustus advanced a long way beyond the tentative measures of Caesar. To repress the chronic disorder and rioting in the capital he not only reaffirmed Caesar's ban on unlicensed *collegia*, but he took the decisive step of providing the city with an adequate police force. For the suppression of petty crime the seven cohorts of *vigiles* were brought into requisition, and their prefect took over the summary jurisdiction of the *triumviri capitales* (p. 591). For the protection of the public peace he made permanent the office of the *praefectus urbi* for a consular and equipped him with three *cohortes urbanae*, each 1000 strong, and organised in military fashion.[29] In case of need the urban cohorts could be reinforced by the nine *cohortes praetoriae*. Henceforth the mob of Rome was kept well under control. Demonstrations at the public festivals were sternly suppressed, and the rioting which had been such a perturbing factor in the politics of the later Republic became a very rare incident.

5. Italy

Organisation of Italy

In Italy — a country which now included Cisalpine Gaul[30] (p. 291) — Augustus had less occasion to show a reforming hand. The governments of the 474 separate municipalities had by now become sufficiently standardised and brought into conformity with the central administration at Rome. As a supplementary measure to Caesar's census regulations Augustus divided Italy into eleven administrative regions; but these played a very subordinate part in the government of the country.

Augustus's colonies in Italy

In addition to the settlements of veterans which he had made during the Triumvirate Augustus established several military colonies after the battle of Actium, including Ateste (modern Este), Augusta Praetoria (Aosta) and Augusta Taurinorum (Turin).[31] To make effective the voting-power of magistrates in these new foundations he set up local polling-stations in them, and made arrangements for the ballot-boxes to be conveyed to Rome for the counting of the votes. But this experiment, which might have been of appreciable service to the Republic a hundred years earlier, came too late to have any practical influence on the course of politics. A far more important innovation was the incorporation of large numbers of young men from the leading municipal families into the Senatorial and Equestrian Orders at Rome.[31] By this gradual but far-reaching process the latent administrative ability of Italy was at last brought into full use, and the Italians became in the fullest sense the partners of the Romans in the government of the Empire. It was probably no mere coincidence that one of the consuls of A.D. 9, M. Papius Mutilus, bore the same name as the commander of the Samnites against the Romans in the Italian War of 90–89 B.C.

Italians participate more fully in the administration of the Empire

Public works in Italy

Augustus extended to Italy the policy of applying the spoils of war to public works. In view of his concern about the corn-supply of Rome it is strange that he did not carry out Caesar's plans for the improvement of the harbour at Ostia. But the emperor gave subventions for building purposes to many individual towns, and he undertook, in association with several of his leading generals, to carry out a thorough repair of the road system, which had received little attention since the days of Gaius Gracchus. Augustus paid out of his own purse the costs of reconstructing the Via Flaminia; the thoroughness of his work is still attested by the imposing ruins of the high-level bridge

The curatores viarum

at Narnia. To ensure more timely repairs in future, the emperor created in 20 B.C. a permanent board of senatorial *curatores viarum* of praetorian rank, who were made responsible for the maintenance of the main highways. The roadside towns were henceforth saddled with part of the expense of maintenance; and they were required in addition to hold in readiness relays of carriages and horses for the *cursus publicus*, a new state-post which Augustus instituted, no doubt on the model of the Ptolemaic courier-services.[33] Despite its name the *cursus publicus* was confined to the use of official messengers and a few other privileged persons. This one-sided arrangement gave rise to many complaints; yet on balance the Italian country towns were the chief gainers by the road improvements under the new Ministry of Transport.

Suppression of brigandage

But Augustus's principal gift to Italy was greater public security. During the second Triumvirate, with its sudden demobilisations and wholesale expropriations, the countryside had become infested with vagabonds who readily turned to brigandage and kidnapping. A special force of *carabinieri* was formed by the emperor (probably by virtue of his early consular authority) to patrol the country districts. A greater and more permanent cause of insecurity was removed when Augustus extended the Roman frontier beyond the Alpine chain and thereby gave Italy two centuries of respite from incursions by foreign raiders (Chapter 31). During the reign of Augustus Italy as a whole made a rapid recovery from the disorders of the triumviral period; but its northern regions in particular profited by the establishment of the imperial peace. It is more than an accident that the ascendancy which northern Italy has exercised almost continuously in the medieval and modern history of the country dates from the time of Augustus.

6. Social Legislation

So long as the Roman emperors had to look to Italy to supply them with soldiers and administrators it remained a matter of practical importance to maintain the vitality of the Italian stock. Under the stress of the civil wars and political convulsions of the first century the population of the country had suffered heavy losses, and the general unsettlement of the period, with its consequent weakening of the old traditions of Italian family life, had caused

Temporary increase of celibacy

a notable increase in celibacy and sterile marriages. An unpleasant by-product was the activity of fortune-hunters who toadied to the unmarried or childless rich. With the restoration of

political security the decline was not merely arrested but reversed. A rough indication of the rise in the population of Italy during the reign of Augustus is afforded by the census returns of 28 B.C. and A.D. 13, registering a total increase in the citizen-body of nearly a million.[34] When allowance is made for the considerable growth in the burgess-population in the provinces, these figures show plainly enough that the decrease during the preceding decades in Italy had been made good. Nevertheless Augustus, throwing aside his habitual caution, would not wait for time to provide its own remedy, but sought to speed up the process of repopulation by a series of laws.

Augustus's legislation to encourage marriage

Following upon some tentative ordinances at the beginning of his reign, which he soon withdrew, Augustus used his tribunician power in 18 B.C. to carry a *lex Iulia de maritandis ordinibus*.[35] This proved so unpopular that in A.D. 9 he employed the consuls M. Papius and Q. Poppaeus to modify and complete this new code; it is not easy to distinguish the precise content of each. These measures enacted that all celibates above a certain age who did not marry, and all widowers below a specified age who did not re-marry, were in varying degree debarred from receiving inheritances or legacies (except from close relations) and from attending the public games. Similar penalties were imposed upon married but childless persons, while to those who had children, especially three or more, quicker advancement in their public careers was offered. The *lex Iulia* also, while recognising the validity of marriage between free-born and freed in general, debarred senators and their descendants from marrying freedwomen. A more striking innovation was contained in the *lex Iulia de adulteriis coercendis* (probably of 18) which made conjugal unfaithfulness a public crime as well as a private offence. After a husband had divorced a suspected wife, he (or the woman's father) could prosecute her and her lover; if this was not done within sixty days, any accuser could bring the charge before a newly established jury-court. In certain circumstances the husband might even kill the lover. Persons convicted of adultery became liable to banishment to some small island: conniving husbands were also threatened with penalties.

Its partial failure

Augustus's marriage-code was the least successful of his reformatory measures. While it produced a crop of vexatious accusations by professional informers it proved of little avail against the real offenders. Not only were its provisions evaded by legal subterfuges, such as fictitious weddings, but it was never enforced in any consistent manner. It created many hard cases which had to be met by special exemptions. A common form of dispensation was a grant of the *ius trium liberorum*, which accorded all the privileges of persons having fulfilled all their marital obligations to others who had not complied with the laws. Among the recipients of this benefit were the poets Horace and Virgil, the empress Livia (whose family was limited to two sons), and the very consuls Papius and Poppaeus in whose name the final statute *de maritandis ordinibus* stood. Though Augustus's marital legislation was never rescinded, it soon fell into abeyance.

The ius trium liberorum

Augustus was concerned, not only to increase the numbers of the Italian stock, but also to prevent its too rapid dilution with alien elements. To this end he inspired two consular laws (the *lex Fufia Caninia* of 2 B.C. and the *lex Aelia Sentia* of A.D. 4) against the indiscriminate emancipation of slaves, which of late had become prevalent among masters bent on showing off their liberality, or on reducing their economic responsibilities by throwing unproductive workers on the public dole. Testamentary manumission was limited by the first law, manumission *inter vivos* by the second. In another statute the *lex Iunia (?Norbana*; either 17 B.C. or A.D. 19) he put a check upon emancipation of slaves without fulfilment of the proper formalities – a practice which had no doubt been adopted to evade the tax on manumissions – by prescribing that freedmen not duly certified as such should not receive the full Roman franchise, but the status of 'Latins'; they became known as Latini Iuniani.

Laws to check the emancipation of slaves

Needless to say, Augustus maintained the restrictions debarring freedmen from the *cursus honorum* in Rome or the Italian municipalities. But he gave them compensation by inventing some minor offices which were wholly or mainly confined to their class. In Rome he created the *vicomagistri*, parish functionaries who assisted in the fire-service and had charge of the *ludi compitalicii* (local circus performances). In many Italian and some provincial towns he encouraged the parallel institution of the *Seviri Augustales* (or *Augustales* in short), colleges of six minor officials, mostly of freedmen status, who took control of the cult of Augustus and some of the public entertainments. The *Augustales* were expected to subscribe freely to the festival funds out of their own pockets; but wealthy freedmen (of whom there were many) willingly paid for their footing on a higher rung of the social ladder.[36]

Offices for freedmen

The Augustales

7. The Ludi Saeculares

In regard to the state religion Augustus displayed more than his usual reforming zeal. The systematic repair of disused temples, which he undertook in 28 B.C., was a prelude to the resuscitation of many half-forgotten ceremonies. As Pontifex Maximus he carefully supervised the worship of Vesta; he revived, after a long intermission, the cult of a primitive field goddess, the 'Dea Dia', by the obsolescent college of the Fratres Arvales; he made a fresh appointment of a Flamen Dialis, whose post had been left vacant since 87 because of the absurd and obsolete taboos with which it was hedged in. The emperor's religious policy was perhaps best summed up in his performance of the Ludi Saeculares, an expiatory ceremony which was due to be held at the end of every hundred years (reckoned from an uncertain date). On the authority of a convenient Sibylline oracle the emperor anticipated the next centenary by a premature celebration in 17 B.C., and he transferred the principal act of worship from the deities of the nether world to Apollo and Diana.[37] By these alterations in the ritual he converted the Ludi Saeculares into a ceremony of thanksgiving for the passing of a period of danger and the opening of an age of tranquillity. The festival, to which all Italy had been invited, lasted three days. Its main episode was a rite in front of Apollo's new shrine on the Palatine, at which a chorus of youths and maidens sang the *carmen saeculare* composed for the occasion by Horace, and the consummating sacrifice was offered by Agrippa and Augustus in person.

Augustus renovates the state religion

The Ludi Saeculares

Augustus's religious revival was neither the product of mere antiquarian dilettantism nor an attempt to exploit religion in the interests of his dynasty (he adopted a very restrained attitude towards any popular desire to establish divine honours for him in Rome: p. 348). It was an honest endeavour to revive the *pax deorum* of an earlier age and to re-establish the former serene belief in the state-protecting deities of Rome. Among contemporary poets his sentiment was more truly echoed in the genuinely patriotic odes of Horace's third book than in the withering phrase of Ovid, '*expedit esse deos*'. But the emperor's religious outlook had the typical limitations of the old-fashioned Roman: it was narrowly bound up with the official worships and aimed at little more than the preservation of Rome's political ascendancy. It is characteristic of his attitude that, while he provided for the preservation of an authentic text of the Sibylline oracles, he destroyed all collections of unofficial soothsayings that he could lay hands on. Although favourable to the

Augustus's religious conservatism

Jews, in general he disapproved of foreign cults, both the Druidism of the North and Isis of the East. It was the Roman gods who had given him victory at Actium against the monstrous deities of Egypt, and to them and to the western tradition he remained loyal.

The writers

In this widely based attempt to improve the moral standards of Roman life, especially among the aristocracy, Augustus received immense help from the writers of his day, especially Horace, Virgil and Livy, who focused men's attention on the older simpler days of early Rome and the qualities of the men who had made her great. This literary help came from men whose work was encouraged by his patronage, but that is

not to say that Horace and Virgil were mere court poets, echoing their master's voice. Rather, they were men of independent mind, expressing their genuine feelings: that these chimed in with the hopes and aspirations of Augustus for his age was indeed fortunate. Their work is discussed below (pp. 394 f.); here it is sufficient to note that the Augustan restoration received immense stimulus not only from the skill of his artists, architects and builders but also from the natural co-operation of two of the world's most outstanding poets, together with a prose-writer worthy of Rome's imperial greatness.

CHAPTER 31

The Roman Empire under Augustus

1. The Roman Frontiers

Augustus's foreign policy

After the civil wars Augustus had a free hand to reshape the foreign policy of Rome as thoroughly as he had reconstructed its internal administration. With all the armed forces of the Empire at his permanent disposal, he had ample means to resume and to extend Caesar's schemes of conquest. Public opinion at Rome, which had but recently hailed him as the bringer of internal peace, presently urged him to fresh wars against foreign enemies, including Britain and Parthia. The emperor perceived that by advancing the Roman frontiers he might strengthen the defences of empire at some points and open new avenues of trade at others. He realised the need of finding employment for the troops, so as to turn their thoughts from fresh civil wars, and he was not loth to provide opportunities of military distinction for the younger members of his family. On the other hand Augustus could not be blind to what the Senate of the later Republic had clearly seen, that foreign expeditions were a seed-bed of military usurpations. For fear that the glamour of popular applause might turn the heads of his subordinate commanders he reserved the honour of a triumphal procession to the members of his own household.[1] He recalled in disgrace the first prefect of Egypt, C. Cornelius Gallus, who had flattered a harmless vanity by setting up statues of himself in his province, together with a boastful trilingual inscription at Philae (dated 29 B.C.).[2] Further, Augustus was acute enough to grasp that Rome had reached the turning-point in its history, at which foreign warfare would in general embarrass rather than relieve the public finances. Beyond the existing boundaries of the Empire there were hardly any states left with accumu-

Further conquests no longer lucrative

lated stocks of gold and silver or wide tracts of good soil to repay the costs of conquest. Between these conflicting considerations the emperor for a long time pursued an opportunistic foreign policy, which scarcely differed from that of Caesar or of the republican Senate. But towards the end of his reign he definitely called a halt to Rome's territorial expansion and expressly laid it down as a maxim for his successors, that they should keep the Roman Empire within the boundaries which he had provided for it.

2. Africa and the Red Sea

Frontier re adjustments in Africa and Egypt

In northern Africa the frontiers of the Roman province, which supplied the capital with much corn, needed the protection of a legion stationed after A.D. 6 at Ammaedra near Theveste, though the province itself, with Carthage restored as a colony, was peaceful enough. Augustus made shift with its ill-defined frontiers towards the inland. In this direction the proconsul L. Cornelius Balbus (a nephew of Caesar's former confidant) held the coastlands against the raiding parties of the nomadic Garamantes by occupying the oasis of Djerma (19 B.C.); soon afterwards P. Sulpicius Quirinius checked the Marmaridae south of the province of Cyrene, and in A.D. 5–6 Cornelius Lentulus defeated the Gaetulians south of Mauretania. In Egypt the unfortunate Cornelius Gallus had pushed forward the frontier to the First Cataract, but in 25 the queen of the Ethiopians (whose title was Candace), attacked Roman troops in this area, and carried off booty which included statues of Augustus himself. A punitive expedition, led by C. Petronius, advanced as far as Nabata but did not reach Meroe, the southern capital of Ethiopia. After an attack on a Roman garrison left at Primis had failed, the Candace finally submitted: her envoys met Augustus in Samos in 22 B.C. She ceded some territory south of the First Cataract which became the frontier-line for the next 300 years.[3] While this was guarded by Roman forts, the prefect of Egypt had the command of three, but after *c* A.D. 7 only two, legions. For the protection of traffic between Egypt and Arabia Augustus maintained the Ptolemaic picket-service from the Nile to the Red Sea ports, and replaced the Ptolemaic patrol fleet on the Red Sea with a Roman force.

An abortive expedition into Arabia

Augustus's readiness to engage his armies where some definite commercial advantage offered was exemplified by his Arabian expedition of 26–25 B.C. To secure for Alexandrian traders the freedom of the Strait of Bab-el-Mandeb and unimpeded access to the Indian and Somali coasts, which the Arabs had hitherto barred in the interests of their commercial mono-

poly, he directed the Egyptian prefect, C. Aelius Gallus, to invade the kingdom of the Sabaeans (in Arabia Felix, the Yemen behind Aden). With reinforcements from the neighbouring kings of Judaea and of Nabataean Arabia, who no doubt expected to share the profits of the new eastern trade, Gallus advanced from the Nabataean port of Leuce Come as far as Mariba. But in his six months' march through the desert he sustained heavy losses on account of sickness, and at Mariba lack of water compelled him to raise the siege. Nevertheless the Sabaeans were overawed into accepting a relation of *amicitia* with the Roman Empire and conceding a free passage to the Strait.[4] A subsequent attempt by the Sabaeans to go back upon this arrangement was answered by a naval raid upon Aden, in which the Roman fleet destroyed that station (*c.* 1 B.C.) The emperor's interest in the commerce of the Indian Ocean is also illustrated by the reception which he gave to successive embassies from Hindu rajahs (26 and 20 B.C.). These mis-

Embassies from India

31.1 The Gemma Augustea. In the top zone Augustus is seated near Roma. *Orbis Romanus* holds a crown above his head. To the left are young Germanicus, and Tiberius, with Victory, stepping from a chariot. In the lower zone Pannonian prisoners are man-handled, while Roman soldiers erect a trophy.

sions were certainly intended for something more than an exchange of empty compliments.[5]

3. Asia Minor and the Euphrates

In the eastern policy of Augustus the chief problem lay in his relations with the kings of Parthia and Armenia. In Armenia the throne which Antony had held in reserve for Cleopatra's child had been seized in 33 by Artaxes, a son of the deposed king Artavasdes (p. 295), who avenged his father by a massacre of all Romans in the country. After the battle of Actium and the capture of Egypt Augustus had a unique opportunity of paying off this score and of settling accounts at the same time with Parthia. He had a powerful army close at hand, and the Parthian king Phraates was at that moment involved in a protracted war with a pretender named Tiridates. But the emperor had no intention of reviving the plans of eastern conquest which had brought Crassus and Antony to grief, and he reckoned that the essential object of restoring Roman prestige in the East could be adequately achieved by the slow but safe and inexpensive methods of diplomacy. For the time being he took no notice of Artaxes, and he gave no more than moral support to the rebel Tiridates. Ten years later, however, Augustus seized a new chance of interference when a malcontent party in Armenia wished to replace Artaxes with his brother Tigranes, who had been brought up in Rome and was willing to hold power as a Roman vassal. The emperor now sent his stepson Tiberius to crown Tigranes in the Armenian capital and a mere show of force on Tiberius's part sufficed to dispose of all opposition (20 B.C.). Artaxes was assassinated and by a simple threat of invasion Tiberius further obtained from the Parthian king the surrender of all his Roman prisoners and all the captured ensigns. On the strength of these effortless successes Augustus

Augustus's eschews war with Parthia

Diplomatic mission of Tiberius to Armenia. Recovery of Crassus's ensigns

proclaimed that he had 'conquered' Armenia and driven the Parthian king down upon his knees, and thus effectually silenced the clamour of those impatient spirits who called for a war of revenge in the East.[6]

After the death of Tigranes (c. 6 B.C.) Armenia again fell under Parthian ascendancy; yet the emperor made no serious attempt to recover the lost ground until his grandson Gaius Caesar reached a sufficient age to take charge of a Roman army. In 1 B.C. Gaius Caesar repeated Tiberius's exploit by imposing another well-disposed prince (Ariobarzanes by name) upon the Armenian throne, and in overawing a new Parthian monarch, Phraataces, into acquiescence with this settlement. The Parthian party in Armenia, it is true, attempted resistance against Gaius, and not long after his departure it expelled the Roman nominee; and although in the last ten years of his reign both Armenia and Parthia fell a prey to further internal troubles, the emperor allowed events in the East to take their course.

Gaius Caesar's mission to Armenia

The dealings of Augustus with Armenia and Parthia might be described as a half-hearted compromise between a resumption of Caesar's and Antony's plans of conquest and a frank abandonment of Armenia to Parthian overlordship. But the latter course, which was ideally the best solution of Rome's eastern problem, might have given serious offence at Rome; the former was a gamble for a stake of very doubtful value. In the event Augustus secured the Roman frontier against invasion, and made adequate amends for past Roman defeats without any heavy expenditure in men and money. When he had the recovered standards placed in his new temple to Mars Ultor in his Forum, he might well feel that his policy of compromise had been justified.

Half-success of Augustus's eastern policy

In Asia Minor there remained a small focus of disorder in the mountain fastnesses of Mt Taurus, whose reduction neither Servilius Isauricus nor Pompey (pp. 250, 251) had completed. Some check upon the unruly tribes of this region was imposed by the Galatian king Deiotarus and his successor, Amyntas. After the death of Amyntas in 25 B.C. Augustus annexed Galatia and took over responsibility for the peace of the central plateau. At first he took no further measures than to establish a military colony at Antioch-in-Pisidia. But at some date between 12 B.C. and A.D. 1 he commissioned the governor of Galatia, P. Sulpicius Quirinius, to seek out the principal robber folk, the Homonadeis, in their lairs on the high border-lands towards Cilicia. After several laborious campaigns Quirinius finally pacified this district by transplanting the inhabitants to the adjacent plains.

Suppression of brigandage in Asia Minor

31.2 Coin of Augustus, showing a kneeling Parthian handing over a captured Roman standard. SIGN(is) RECE(eptis).

A chain of new colonies, chief among them Lystra, was founded to serve as advanced bases to the main depot at Antioch.[7]

4. Western Europe

The final pacification of Spain

By jettisoning Caesar's plans of conquest in Asia Augustus was better able to secure and extend his gains in Europe. In Spain he finally reduced the peoples of the northern and north-western mountain border, upon whom Caesar had first tested his military talents (p. 248). These campaigns involved the Roman forces in a hard and merciless warfare lasting from 26 to 19 B.C., for the principal tribes of the north, the Cantabri and Astures, proved no less stubborn than the Celtiberians in the second century.[8] The task of pacifying Spain was completed by Agrippa, who transferred the mountain peoples to the Castilian plateau and established a military station at Castra Legionum (modern Leon). Colonies of veterans were established at Emerita (Merida) and Caesaraugusta (Saragossa), and three legions were left in the peninsula, which was divided into three provinces, Lusitania, Tarraconensis and the more peaceful Baetica, which was left to senatorial administration.

In Gaul Caesar had done his work so thoroughly that after his death no considerable rebellion took place. In Aquitania, the district where Caesar had least shown his hand, minor campaigns were fought by Agrippa in 39 and by M. Valerius Messala in 30. But Augustus's task in Gaul was administrative rather than military. During his reign some twelve new towns were founded in various parts of the country by the transmigration of the inhabitants from the old Celtic hill-cities into the plain. But it is probable that in all these cases the *deductio in plana* was made by the free will of the Gallic population, which expressed its confidence in the Roman peace by abandoning its natural strongholds. Gaul was divided into four provinces, the southerly Narbonensis being handed over to senatorial administration. Under Augustus the other Tres Galliae were administered by one governor, with legates in each province. Here the cantonal system of *civitates* was recognised and it remained so strong that often the names of tribes rather than of towns survived—thus Lutetia, the centre of the Parisii, is now known as Paris. In 27 B.C. Augustus himself supervised the taking of a census, while Agrippa developed the road-system based on Lugdunum (modern Lyons), which was the political and commercial capital of the Three Gauls. Here in 12 B.C. sixty-four tribes built an Ara Romae et Augusti as a cult-centre

Minor campaigns in Gaul

and focus of loyalty; it was administered by a Concilium Galliarum. The security of Gaul was guaranteed by the legions stationed on the Rhine (p. 336).[9]

A journey to Gaul and Spain which the emperor undertook in 27–26 B.C. gave rise to rumours that he was about to invade Britain – an enterprise for which public opinion at Rome had conceived a passing fancy. But Augustus fell back upon or, more probably, never departed from Caesar's final decision to leave Britain to its own devices, for the characteristic reason that a conquest and occupation of that country would produce an unfavourable balance-sheet. Later in his reign he received an appeal from some fugitive British chieftains, but he refused them active assistance. A pretext for invasion might no doubt have been found in the growing power of the dynasty of Caesar's former antagonist Cassivellaunus, whose son (or grandson) Tasciovanus and the latter's son Cunobelinus extended their sovereignty over most of south-eastern England. But Augustus rightly judged that Gaul was in no danger from the British chieftains, whose aim, in fact, was to remain on friendly terms with Rome and to develop commercial intercourse with the continent. To this end Tasciovanus transferred his residence to Prae Wood above Verulamium (St Albans) *c* 15 B.C., and Cunobelinus (Cymbeline) followed up the conquest of the Trinovantes in Essex by establishing his capital at their chief town, Camulodunum (modern Colchester) *c.* A.D. 9. Later he conquered Kent. Under the impetus which these two rulers gave to overseas trade the principal cross-Channel routes came into regular use, and Londinium, hitherto a cluster of disconnected hamlets, began to assume its historic role as the connecting-link between Britain and the rest of Europe.[10] With this peaceful penetration of Britain Augustus had good reason to be satisfied.

The rising power of Cunobelinus in Britain

Camulodunum and Londinium

Augustus refuses to interfere

On the other hand Augustus seriously contemplated a departure from Caesar's policy in regard to Germany. For some thirty years after Caesar's death the Rhine frontier had proved itself an adequate barrier against German invasions of Gaul. In 38, or possibly during a later stay in Gaul *c.* 20 B.C., Agrippa effected a peaceful settlement of a land-hungry tribe, the Ubii, on the left bank, near the future city of Cologne. In 29 a raid by the much attenuated tribe of the Suebi (now settled in Suabia) was repelled without much difficulty. In 17, however, a more determined foray by the Sugambri and other peoples of the middle Rhine resulted in the loss of a Roman legionary standard. Although this inroad remained an isolated episode (the so-called *clades Lolliana*), it served as an excuse

New German raids into Gaul

for a systematic counter-invasion of German territory by the Romans. Augustus's forward policy in Germany was primarily intended to put Gaul beyond the reach of German attacks. Its ulterior intention, we may conjecture, was to establish a new frontier (presumably along the Elbe), so as to cut off the sharp re-entrant angle between the Rhine and the upper Danube (to which latter river the Roman boundary had previously been advanced – p. 336). It was probably also no mere accident that about this time Augustus's reorganisation of the Roman army had been completed (pp. 338 f.), and that his stepsons, Tiberius and Drusus, had reached a sufficient age for the conduct of a major campaign.

31.3 The elder Drusus, brother of Tiberius. NERO CLAUDIUS DRUSUS GERMANICUS IMP(erator).

The expeditions of Tiberius and Drusus into Germany

In 12 B.C. and the ensuing three years Drusus overran western Germany in a series of rapid forays, which carried the Roman arms as far as the Elbe. In connexion with these operations his fleet sailed out of the Rhine and the Zuyder Lake through a specially constructed canal into the North Sea, and opened up relations with the seaboard tribes of the Batavi and Frisii, who were enrolled as allies on condition of supplying auxiliary contingents to the Roman army. The accidental death of Drusus on his return from the Elbe in 9 B.C. terminated the first stage of the Roman invasions. His place was taken by his elder brother Tiberius, who consolidated the previous gains by transplanting refractory populations to Gaul (8–7 B.C.). In 5 B.C. a general named L. Domitius Ahenobarbus discovered a new line of advance into Germany from the upper Danube by the valley of the Saale and made a reconnaissance beyond the Elbe; he erected an altar to Rome and Augustus by the river.[11]

In A.D. 4 and 5 Tiberius resumed his summer marches across Western Germany. In the second of these campaigns he carried out a skilful combined operation of army and fleet, so as to relieve the soldiers from carrying a heavy luggage train through a difficult and little-known country.

About this time the Roman fleet also explored the Jutish coast as far as Cape Skager. In A.D. 6 Tiberius planned another converging movement, whose object was to reduce the Marcomanni, the only notable German people this side of the Elbe that lay outside the reach of the Romans. Success would mean that the defence of the Elbe could be linked with that of the newly conquered Danube by the establishment of a frontier from the Baltic to the Black Sea which could run along the line of the modern cities of Hamburg, Leipzig, Prague and Vienna, and then along the Danube to the Black Sea. After the campaigns of Drusus the Marcomanni had been withdrawn by their ruler Maroboduus from the lower Main to Bohemia, where they conquered or displaced the remnant of Rome's ancient antagonists, the Boii (p. 139). Though Maroboduus had been careful not to give offence to the Romans, he aroused their suspicions by introducing Roman equipment and some semblance of Roman discipline into his army, which was reputed to number about 75,000 warriors. Tiberius therefore opened a preventive attack upon him with two large forces. One army under his personal leadership advanced northward from Carnuntum (modern Petronell) on the middle Danube, while the other followed the Main in an easterly direction. The two arms of the Roman pincers had nearly closed upon Maroboduus when a serious revolt in Pannonia and in Tiberius's rear (p. 337) compelled him to release his prey. The German king, however, made no counter-attack, and Roman ascendancy in the Rhinelands remained unshaken.

Tiberius's invasion of Bohemia

Since 12 B.C. Germany, to the north of the Main and to the west of the Elbe, was being gradually reduced to the status of a province. Lacking urban centres and taxable wealth, it could not yet be brought within the framework of ordinary provincial administration, and no permanent Roman camps were established in it except a few forts along the ordinary marching routes. But the trans-Rhenane country was regularly patrolled by Roman troops, and systematic attempts were made to win over the native leaders. While German chieftains tended the altars set up for the worship of the emperor (p. 341) in the territory of the Ubii and on the Elbe, their sons served in the Roman auxiliary forces; and the folk appeared to be submitting to Roman rule without demur. But at the end of his reign the ageing Augustus undid the work of his stepsons by sending out an unsuitable governor, P. Quinctilius Varus, who had no previous knowledge of conditions on the northern frontiers. Varus incited a revolt among the Germans by a premature attempt to impose taxation

Incipient pacification of Germany

and to introduce Roman methods of jurisdiction among them. In A.D. 9 a young chieftain of the Cherusci (on the middle Weser), named Arminius, who had served in the Roman forces and had been admitted to the *equester ordo*, organised a rebellion, in which he turned his knowledge of Roman warfare against his teachers. Enticing Varus into unfamiliar country between the Weser and the Ems, he virtually annihilated a Roman force of some 20,000 men in the Teutoburgian Forest.[12] Reinforcements were hurried to the Rhine, and in the remaining years of Augustus's reign under Tiberius and his nephew, Nero Claudius Drusus (afterwards called 'Germanicus'), who took over the chief command in A.D. 12, the reconstituted Roman armies not only held the line of the river, but made retaliatory raids into German territory. There is little doubt that the Romans could have recovered all the lost ground. But the *clades Variana* had so shaken Augustus that he made no serious effort to retrieve it; before his death he appears to have abandoned any thought of a frontier beyond the Rhine.[13] A narrow area along the river was divided into two districts, Upper (southern) and Lower (northern) Germany, with the division near Coblenz. Each was permanently garrisoned by four legions, commanded by consular military legates; they were military zones, not provinces, and the governor of Belgica took responsibility for their civil administration. The legions were quartered in camps at Vetera (modern Xanten: a double camp), Novaesium (Neuss), Bonna (Bonne), Moguntiacum (Mainz: double camp), Argentorate (Strasbourg) and Vindonissa (Windisch in Switzerland). Although the camp buildings were constructed of wood – stone was not used until the Claudian period – it was a powerful defence.

5. The Danube Lands

At the end of Augustus's reign the boundaries of the Empire in western Europe remained substantially where Caesar had left them; in central and eastern Europe they had been completely redrawn. On these sectors the frontiers urgently needed a comprehensive rectification, and although Augustus attacked this problem in his usual piecemeal fashion, he solved it in an enduring manner.

Despite the long-standing connexion between Italy and France there existed as yet no safe and commodious line of land communications, except by the Mt Genèvre pass, where Pompey had constructed a military road at the time of his campaigns against Sertorius. In 35–34 the approaches to the St Bernard passes were partly cleared by Valerius Messala, who conducted expeditions against the predatory tribe of the Salassi; in 25 his work was completed by Terentius Varro Murena, who systematically rounded up the Salassi and sold them off into slavery. A high road was now built across the Little St Bernard, which, like the Great St Bernard, was guarded by a military colony at Augusta Praetoria (modern Aosta). In 14 B.C. the coastal frontier strip was finally cleared of Ligurian highwaymen, and was constituted into the diminutive province of Alpes Maritimae under an equestrian *praefectus*. The Mt Cenis route was left in the hands of a trustworthy native chieftain named Cottius, but a detachment of Roman troops was held at his disposal at the border town of Segusio (modern Susa).

The safeguarding of the north Italian plain against the incursions of the Raeti (an Illyrian people who inhabited the central and eastern Alps) was achieved once for all in the single campaign of 15 B.C., in which Augustus's stepsons, Tiberius and Drusus, won their spurs and the remodelled army was first tested in action. While Tiberius ascended the Rhine valley from the neighbourhood of Basle to Lake Constance, Drusus passed from the valley of the Adige into that of the Inn and the Danube, and their lieutenants searched out the lesser Alpine defiles. The two brothers completed the season's work by occupying the country of the Vindelici, a mainly Celtic tribe between the Rhine and the upper Danube, so as to extend the Roman boundary to the latter river.[14] The territory overrun in this campaign was at first attached to Gallia Belgica, but not long after it was constituted into a separate province with the name of Raetia; the natives were made safe by deportation and conscription. Two legions, stationed possibly near Augusta Vindelicorum (modern Augsburg), were withdrawn *c.* A.D. 9; and the province was guarded by the Rhine armies, and governed by an equestrian prefect. Though Raetia was not much used by the Romans as a passageway to the upper Danube, its reduction greatly added to the security of Italy.

A projection of the Roman frontier from the line of the Save, which had been reached in 35 by Octavian (p. 293), was undertaken about 16 B.C., in consequence of a raid by the Celtic tribes of Noricum (modern Styria) and Pannonia (Austria and western Hungary) into Istria. Noricum was easily overrun, and a native dynasty was allowed to remain in power for the time being; but at some later stage (probably under Claudius) the country was converted into a province. The reduction of Pannonia required four years of hard fighting (12–9 B.C.) under

The clades Variana

Augustus abandons his conquests in Germany

Pacification of the Alpine border of Italy

Tiberius and Drusus conquer Raetia

Roman advance to the upper Danube

the leadership of Tiberius; indeed the systematic disarmament and wholesale enslavements with which Tiberius concluded his campaigns were not sufficient to keep the Pannonians in subjection. In A.D. 6 a rebellion, whose cause may be found in the heavy requisitions of Tiberius for his expedition against Maroboduus (p. 335), threw all his previous successes into jeopardy. A Pannonian chieftain, Bato, acting in concert with a Dalmatian leader of the same name, rose in Tiberius's rear while he was engaged in Bohemia, and a Dalmatian mobile column made a dash for the Italian frontier. The magnitude of this revolt, which was accompanied by a wholesale massacre of Roman residents, brought back to Italy a memory of the Hannibalic and Cimbric Wars and threw the emperor into a momentary panic. But Tiberius, with prompt support from the Roman troops in the Balkans, soon averted the danger of invasion. While one of his lieutenants made a hurried retreat from Bohemia, so as to head off the Dalmatians from Italy, he fell back to a central position at Siscia on the Save and held up the main Pannonian attack. In A.D. 7 reinforcements from Italy and Asia Minor, which brought up the Roman forces to a total of nearly 100,000 men, enabled Tiberius to resume the offensive. Two campaigns, in which the rebel districts were systematically ravaged by separate Roman columns, brought about the surrender of the Pannonians. In A.D. 9 Germanicus won his first laurels by forcing the Dalmatian Bato to a capitulation. After this conclusive trial of strength both the

The Pannonian Revolt

defeated peoples definitely accepted Roman rule. Pannonia, which had hitherto been attached to Illyricum, was now constituted as a separate province, and Illyricum was shortly afterwards renamed Dalmatia. For the present the Roman legions were retained at Poetovio on the Dráva, but an advanced base was established at Carnuntum on the middle Danube.[15]

The annexations of Raetia, Noricum and Pannonia completed a process of advancing the Roman frontiers to the Danube which had been begun on the lower reaches of that river immediately after the battle of Actium. In 29 a raid by the Bastarnae (a trans-Danubian tribe to the east of Dacia) brought home to Augustus the insecurity of the existing Macedonian frontier. He therefore assigned some of the legions left over from the campaign of Actium to a grandson and namesake of the triumvir, M. Licinius Crassus, and instructed him to reach out for a better line of defence. With these reinforcements Crassus not only bundled the Bastarnae back beyond the Danube, but accomplished a systematic reduction of the Moesian and Thracian peoples bordering the river (in modern Serbia, Bulgaria and Romania) (29-28 B.C.). The Thracian tribes were for the present left under their own kings, but the Moesians of Serbia were incorporated into Macedonia. After a rising in 11–9 B.C., which was repressed by troops from Galatia, the principalities of northern Thrace were absorbed into the kingdom of the Odrysae (on the Aegean border), whose rulers had been in alliance with Rome for two centuries. For

Advance of the Roman frontier to the lower Danube

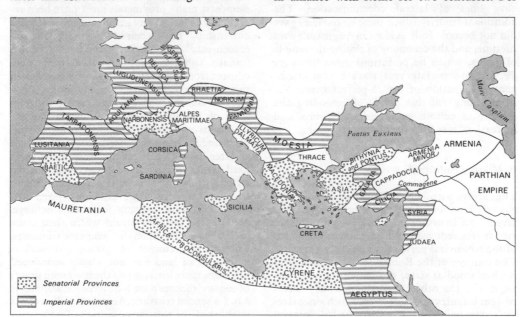

25. ROMAN EMPIRE AT THE DEATH OF AUGUSTUS

the defence of the Danube a separate province of Moesia was constituted c. A.D. 6, extending from the borders of Pannonia to the northern extremity of the Thracian kingdom.[16] Towards the end of his reign Augustus initiated the policy of controlled settlement of land-hungry trans-Danubian tribes in Moesia by admitting some 50,000 homeless Dacians across its borders.

Augustus's extensions of Roman territory

In making the Roman boundary coterminous with the Danube Augustus made a greater addition to Roman territory than any Roman conqueror before or after him, and he established a new frontier line whose vital importance was abundantly proved in later Roman history. The newly annexed Danubian lands brought less economic profit to the Romans than Gaul, but they proved an even more valuable recruiting area.

In southern Russia Augustus disposed by diplomatic methods of a problem which had remained outstanding since the death of Caesar. In this district the usurper Asander had driven off Caesar's nominee, Mithridates of Pergamum (p. 278), and after his decease in 17 B.C. his widow Dynamis had taken his place. Augustus restored Roman authority by inducing Dynamis to a marriage alliance with his vassal-king Polemo in eastern Pontus, after whose death (8 B.C.) Dynamis ruled alone during the rest of her life (until A.D. 7–8).

Augustus's frontier system

In the event the conquests of Augustus gave the Roman Empire an almost uniform extension round the Mediterranean basin and a nearly unbroken ring of easily defensible frontiers — oceans, deserts and rivers, whose valleys gave easy lines of lateral communication. The additional security which these boundaries gave did not become fully evident in Augustus's own lifetime, and the ceremony of closing the temple of Janus, which he performed three times (in 29, 25 and some later year) was at best an intelligent anticipation of future perfect peace. Yet in the long run his policy of extending the Empire to certain well-considered limits, and no further, was fully justified by its results.

6. Military Reforms[17]

The army with which Augustus redrew the Roman frontiers and made them secure was largely an instrument of his own forging. In size it was reduced from the ruinous standards of the triumviral period to those of Caesar's day. The number of the Roman legions, which after Actium stood at sixty, was cut down to twenty-eight. On the other hand the auxiliary forces of light infantry and horsemen, which since Caesar's day had become a more or less integral part of the field armies, were placed on the

Augustus's army establishment

regular establishment. It has been calculated that at the end of Augustus's reign the Roman army numbered from 250,000 to 300,000 men, of whom half served in the legions and half in the auxiliaries. This force was barely numerous enough to hold a frontier line exceeding 4000 miles, and it did not suffice for major operations on more than one front at a time.

Augustus not only upheld the Roman state's right to levy troops by compulsion, but extended it to the provinces. After the *clades Variana* enrolments were made in the population of the capital, and it became a regular practice to supplement the auxiliary troops with drafts from newly conquered territories such as the Danube lands. But in the main the voluntary system of recruitment, which had plainly justified itself since the time of Marius, was maintained. It is true that Italy was now showing the combined effects of the decline in the number of its free cultivators and of excessive enrolments in the period of the civil wars. But its northern districts at least continued to be one of the principal recruiting grounds of the legions; and the *collegia iuvenum* or cadet corps, which were now instituted or revived in most Italian towns, provided an adequate supply of officers for the entire army.[18] The legions consisted of Roman citizens only, but additional recruiting fields were found in southern Gaul, southern Spain and wherever men of Italian stock had settled, or the natives had acquired a tincture of Italian culture. In the East the legions had a greater admixture of non-Roman elements; many provincials must have been recruited who lacked any genuine claim to Roman citizenship, but received it unofficially on enlistment.[19] Volunteers for the auxiliary units (usually cohorts of 500 or 1000 men) were enlisted from non-Romans in the less Romanised regions of the Empire, notably from Gallia Comata and the wilder parts of Spain, and from some of the allied peoples, among whom the Thracians and Batavi supplied strong contingents under their own officers.

Recruitment in the provinces

The 'auxiliary' units

After 14 B.C. enlistments were made for a fixed term, varying from twenty years in the legions to twenty-five in the auxiliary forces. In actual practice, however, time-expired men were often kept waiting for their discharge, because of the heavy strain which their claim to pensions cast upon the emperor's finances. Though the custom of giving old soldiers allotments of land was not wholly abandoned it became more usual to pay them off with grants of money reckoned on a generous scale, and in A.D. 6 a special treasury (Aerarium Militare) was established for this purpose (p. 342). The cash bonus for a private soldier was 3000 denarii,

Enlistment for fixed terms. Regular pay and pensions

equivalent to thirteen years' pay; a thrifty ex-centurion might even rise to the financial status of an *eques*. The auxiliaries no doubt were less well paid (perhaps only 75 denarii against the legionaries' 225) and it is not certain whether they were entitled to pensions; but it gradually became the rule to reward them with Roman franchise at the end of their service.[20]

The more regular terms of enlistment made it possible to keep the individual units, if not at unvarying strength, at any rate in continuous existence. The legions, which since Caesar's days had tended to become fixed units, received permanent serial numbers and distinctive titles;[21] like British regiments, they formed their own traditions and developed a strong *esprit de corps,* which found expressions in a healthy mutual rivalry. Furthermore, the total number of the Roman military forces was maintained at a sufficiently steady level to facilitate their more scientific distribution. In keeping with Augustus's foreign policy, the greater number of the legions was concentrated near the Rhine and the Danube (8 and 7 respectively); other districts which received strong garrisons were Syria (3), Spain (3) and Egypt (2). Everywhere else the Roman forces were reduced to a bare minimum. A mere 5000 were stationed in Asia Minor, and 3000 in Judaea; for the security of southern and central Gaul a picket of 1200 men at Lugdunum (modern Lyon) was considered sufficient. At the frontier stations the encampments, though still constructed of earth and timber, began to be laid out and furnished as permanent quarters for their garrisons.

The prestige which Augustus had acquired as a war-winner, and the more certain conditions of remuneration which he had introduced, enabled him to restore the old-time severity of discipline in the army. But the troops were not merely taught to dread the centurion's stick; they were trained to take a pride in their regiment and to conceive an almost religious reverence for its colours. Delays in demobilisation sometimes gave rise to open complaints, but the defiant arrogance of the age of the civil wars was for the time being laid aside.

In deference to republican tradition Augustus did not create a complete professional corps of officers, but reserved most of the higher posts to the members of his own family, or to men of consular or praetorian standing, whose experience might be administrative rather than military. But the centurions, who continued to be drawn from the rank and file, and were transferred from one post to another by a carefully graded but complicated system of promotion, were highly trained professionals.[22] In addition, the *praefecti fabrum* (chief engineers) and the

The legions become permanent units

Distribution of the frontier forces

Restoration of discipline

praefecti castrorum (quarter-masters), whose position in the Roman army became increasingly important, were regular officers.

Though Actium was the last naval battle in Roman history Augustus was the creator of the first regular fleet under Roman colours.[23] In the Mediterranean Sea he maintained squadrons of cruisers to repress piracy and patrol the routes of the corn-fleets, and he established two main naval arsenals at Misenum and Ravenna, with subsidiary stations at Forum Iulii (modern Fréjus), Alexandria and Seleucia in Syria. River flotillas for the transport of troops and provisions were stationed on the Rhine and Danube. The original complements of the ships at Misenum and Ravenna contained some slaves taken over from the service of Sextus Pompeius; but in general the crews of the imperial fleets were recruited from freeborn provincials (among whom Dalmatians and Thracians provided particularly strong contingents), and the officers were mostly drawn from the same source. The terms of service were similar to those of the auxiliary troops.

Creation of regular Roman fleets

7. The Provinces

In the days of Augustus the Roman Empire contained at least 70,000,000 inhabitants, and perhaps was approaching the 100,000,000 mark.[24] Some three-quarters of this population were in the provinces, whose number had risen by the end of Augustus's reign to twenty-four or twenty-five. Apart from the new provinces formed by conquest several others were constituted by the partition of existing provinces whose territories had proved unmanageably large, or by the annexation of dependent kingdoms. In regard to the dependent kingdoms Augustus followed the same opportunistic policy as the Senate of the republican period. He made it a general rule to leave the native dynasties in possession; but where the security of the frontiers or the internal peace of the monarchy seemed to demand a change of system, he converted them into provinces. When King Bocchus of Mauretania died without making arrangements for the succession (25 B.C.) the emperor did not annex his realm – in which Rome as yet had hardly any interests – but made it over to a son and namesake of the Numidian King Juba; this learned young man had been brought up in Italy and had married Cleopatra Selene, the daughter of Antony and Cleopatra. But at the same time he deprived Juba of Numidia, which he incorporated into the province of Africa. In Judaea he gave his entire confidence to King Herod, who combined capacity to control, if not

Population of the Roman Empire

Annexation of dependent kingdoms: Egypt, Galatia, Judaea (after the death of Herod)

conciliate his subjects, with great energy in fostering the material development of his realm and unquestioning loyalty to Rome.[25] After Herod's death in 4 B.C. he allowed his three sons to divide his kingdom; but in A.D. 6 he deposed the eldest, Archelaus, at the request of the Jews themselves, and constituted his portion, Judaea and Samaria, into an imperial province, which was governed by a *praefectus* (later named *procurator*) with judicial authority (*ius gladii*) and in command of a few local troops; he resided in Caesarea, not Jerusalem. Of Herod's other sons, Herod Antipas ('that fox' of the Gospels) retained Galilee (until A.D. 39), Philip ruled the outlying parts for thirty-seven years. Egypt and Galatia, as we have seen (pp. 297, 333) were annexed near the beginning of Augustus's reign.

Partitioning of provinces

The partitioning of existing provinces was confined to the European portions of the Empire. The territory of Hispania Ulterior was divided into the senatorial province of Baetica and the imperial province of Lusitania (p. 334). Gallia Comata was split into three provinces, Aquitania, Lugdunensis and Belgica (p. 334). Achaea and Epirus were detached from Macedonia and received a separate governor as a senatorial province (27 B.C.).

Augustus's tours of inspection

The interest which Augustus took in the provinces was made manifest by the prolonged tours of inspection which he undertook in order to study their condition. In 27–24 he visited Gaul and Spain; in 22–19 he went the round of the eastern provinces; in 15–13 he revisited Gaul. Similarly in 23–21 and again in 17–13 Agrippa was appointed by him to be inspector-general of the eastern provinces.

Local self-government encouraged

Augustus carried on the excellent republican traditions of respecting local customs and conceding a large measure of self-government in the provinces. In the three new Gallic provinces the existing cantonal organisation was not disturbed. In Judaea strict instructions were issued to the governors not to offend the religious susceptibilities of the inhabitants; the troops were for the most part quartered at Caesarea, a new foundation of Herod with a large Gentile population, and detachments on duty at Jerusalem left their ensigns behind them. In the eastern provinces local bronze and small silver coins were allowed to circulate alongside the imperial money; in Gaul and Spain native bronze pieces continued to be struck. On the other hand the relations of clientship which larger Gallic cantons had exercised over smaller ones were dissolved. In Gallia Narbonensis, where urban development has proceeded further, the cantonal governments were replaced by municipal ones. In this and several other provinces some cities

had large territories 'attributed' to them. In Africa the 'county' attached to Cirta extended towards the coast for nearly fifty miles; in Gallia Narbonensis Geneva, a fair-sized town in itself, was a tributary of the distant city of Vienna (modern Vienne), and Nemausus (Nîmes) controlled twenty-four dependent communities.

Growth of towns fostered

Urban life in the provinces was also fostered by the numerous settlements of veterans made since the Triumvirate. It has been estimated that no fewer than forty colonies were established in the provinces between 43 and 30 B.C., and more than forty during the reign of Augustus. The emperor's most notable foundations included Vienna and Nemausus in Gaul; Barcino (Barcelona), Caesaraugusta (Saragossa) and Emerita Augusta (Merida) in Spain; Antioch and Lystra in Asia Minor; Carthage and Corinth (in fulfilment of Caesar's plans) in Africa and Achaea.

Colonisation in the provinces

By a bold and somewhat premature experiment Augustus established some twelve Roman outposts on the coast of Mauretania, inclusive of Tingis (modern Tangier).[26] But in general his settlements were situated in regions already colonised by Caesar, so as to reinforce the effect of the earlier settlements.

The most urgent administrative problem for Augustus in the provinces was to check the alarming drain on their wealth, which had been proceeding at an accelerated pace since the death of Caesar. The eastern provinces in particular had been bled white by the exactions of Brutus, Cassius and Antony, and with the drying up of their taxation fund the whole Roman Empire was being threatened with insolvency. In the objects and rates of provincial taxation, which were not unreasonable in themselves, the emperor made little change. With a view to the better apportionment of the fixed taxes he instituted a census in some, perhaps in all, of the provinces, and he made provision for a recount at the end of every fourteen years.[27] He probably introduced the system of taxation which prevailed later, namely the abolition of the republican differentiation between the fluctuating tithe and the fixed *stipendium* (p. 173), and the substitution of two direct fixed taxes; these were *tributum soli*, levied on all occupiers of land, and *tributum capitis* (a poll-tax in Egypt and some backward regions, but perhaps elsewhere a tax on other forms of property, which clearly must have been taxed under one category or the other). All provincials, including Roman citizens and the *liberae civitates*, had to pay the land-tax, with the exception of a few towns that enjoyed the *ius Italicum* (i.e. the exemption enjoyed by Italy itself;[28] those who had *immunitas* (as well as the Roman citizens) were probably immune from the *tributum capitis*. Indirect

Reform of provincial taxation

taxes included *portoria* (dues up to 5 per cent on goods that crossed certain frontiers); a tax (which also applied to Italy: p. 329) on manumission and on the sale of slaves; and grain for the governor and his staff. The direct tax was generally collected in the first instance by the local communities, whether cities or tribes. In the imperial provinces an imperial procurator of equestrian status, largely independent of the governor, was in overall charge; in the senatorial provinces the quaestor was responsible, but in some of them *publicani* continued to act as middlemen. Further, imperial procurators looked after the emperor's private property and estates (e.g. *saltus*) even in senatorial provinces and so could keep an eye open for possible abuses. The indirect taxes were still let out to *publicani*, but the contractors were now carefully watched.

Augustus's choice of acting governors

But in the long run all questions of administrative reform in the provinces resolved themselves into the more careful selection and more effective control of the governors. In the provinces of which he was titular proconsul Augustus chose his governors, *legati Augusti pro praetore* (ex-consuls or ex-praetors) for the important provinces, equestrian prefects for Egypt and minor provinces (as Judaea), with due regard to their individual capacities. Though he did not lay down any fixed term of service it would appear as if the usual period was from three to five years, which gave the officials time to learn their duties thoroughly. The emperor paid his governors and other agents fixed salaries on a generous scale, so as to rob them of all excuse for private money-making. Lastly, by improving the road systems in the provinces[29] and extending the *cursus publicus* or imperial post (p. 328) to them, he was able to keep in continuous touch with his subordinates and check their mistakes before serious mischief was done.

The cursus publicus

Little change in the senatorial provinces

In the senatorial provinces the governors continued to be selected in a somewhat haphazard fashion from the ex-consuls or ex-praetors — the provinces of Africa and Asia being usually reserved for men who had been *consules ordinarii*; and in view of the long waiting-list of ex-magistrates the term of each proconsul's office seldom exceeded one year. The Senate probably followed Augustus's example of providing fixed salaries for its governors, but it had no means of control over them such as the *cursus publicus* gave to the emperor.

Occasional instances of flagrant misgovernment under Augustus's rule are recorded. One of his procurators in Gaul, a freedman named Licinus, made himself notorious by his extortions, and a proconsul of Asia, Messalla Volesus, was alleged to have executed no fewer than 300 accused persons on one day (he was later condemned by the Senate). The senatorial provinces in particular did not reap the full benefit of Augustus's reforms. Yet we may find in his improved methods of administration one of the chief causes of the unmistakable advance in material prosperity that set in among the provincials during his reign.

Roman franchise given sparingly

While Augustus went well beyond Caesar in his administrative reforms, and unhesitatingly followed his example in sending Roman colonists to the provinces, he was somewhat more conservative in regard to their enfranchisement. He conceded to his time-expired auxiliary troops the franchise which he could not in justice withhold from them; and in Spain he promoted a small number of native towns to the status of Roman *municipia*.

On the other hand Augustus sought to create a new bond of loyalty among the provincials by playing upon their religious sentiments.[30] From the time when the Romans first entered Greece as conquerors the Hellenistic populations had expressed their gratitude or fear by setting up here and there altars to the goddess *Roma* or to individual Roman generals. Similar homage had been paid to Caesar in Greek towns, and after Actium the worship of Augustus became widespread in the Near East. In 29 B.C. the cities of Asia went a step further in combining to offer him a temple at Pergamum in the name of the whole province. Augustus accepted the gift on condition of the Goddess *Roma* being cojoined with him in the cult; he sanctioned the institution of similar cults in other eastern provinces; and eventually he took the initiative in introducing them into the western Mediterranean. In 12 B.C. his stepson Drusus dedicated an altar of *Roma et Augustus* at Lugdunum; in 2 B.C. L. Domitius established a similar cult on the banks of the Elbe; other altars were set up at Tarraco, at Oppidum Ubiorum (modern Cologne) in the territory of the Ubii, and probably also at Nemausus. By the end of his reign, or not long after his death, an altar or a temple of *Roma et Augustus* had been set up in most of the Roman provinces (though curiously not in Gallia Narbonensis or Africa). In connexion with this new worship Augustus instituted provincial *concilia*, or parliaments of deputies elected by the several cities or cantons, which met once a year at the chief town of the province to choose a high priest of *Roma et Augustus* and to conduct the festival in their honour; eventually there was hardly a province that lacked its *concilium*, or had not joined with other provinces in forming one.[31] Though it is hardly credible that such ceremonies could induce feelings of loyalty which had not already sprung up of their

Cult of Roma et Augustus in the provinces

The provincial concilia

own accord they certainly helped to fix and regulate those sentiments in all parts of the Empire. It is noteworthy that not only in the Greek lands, where king-worship was of old standing, but in Gaul and Germany, where it had hitherto been unknown, the leading men eagerly accepted the office of high priest.

8. Financial Administration[32]

Augustus's aptitude for finance

Of all the tasks of reconstruction that awaited Augustus the reorganisation of the Roman finances was probably that to which he brought the greatest natural aptitudes. A bourgeois by origin he had a better understanding than Caesar, the scion of the *haute noblesse*, of problems of ways and means, and he appreciated more clearly the necessity of weighing policy on the balance of revenue and expenditure. Besides, a reform of the haphazard methods of Roman finance was now becoming urgent. On the one hand Augustus had a large civil and military staff to provide for; on the other the limits of revenue expansion by conquest were within sight, and the emperor had set his face against further plundering and requisitioning within the empire.

Aerarium and fisci

True to his general policy of disturbing existing institutions as little as possible. Augustus made no fundamental change in the position of the *aerarium*. Though he insisted that its management should be taken out of the inexperienced hands of the quaestors and transferred to persons of praetorian rank he did not claim any direct control over it for himself. It continued to receive the taxes from all the provinces, and from it Augustus, like any other magistrate, could draw funds on the recommendation of the Senate. Presumably the Senate would automatically vote him an appropriate grant each time his control of his group of provinces was renewed; he must also have drawn direct from the *aerarium* for other expenses such as for maintaining the praetorian and urban cohorts. For his provinces, however, he would not in practice need to move much actual cash, since from republican times each province had had its own treasury (*fiscus*), into which the taxes were paid and from which the governor could draw in order to pay his troops. Thus generally only accounts of balances would pass between each province and the *aerarium*. Nevertheless the *aerarium* often ran into financial difficulties, and was helped by Augustus out of his own private funds, his *patrimonium*; he claimed to have paid to the *aerarium*, to the Roman plebs and to his discharged veterans no less than 600 million sesterces.

Augustus had abundant private sources of revenue to draw upon, a source which is generally called his *patrimonium*, but sometimes (and this has caused much confusion) his *fiscus*. His victory over Cleopatra gave him possession of the largest stock of gold and silver in the Mediterranean lands. In Egypt he also confiscated the extensive private domains of Cleopatra and her favourites, and in Asia Minor he took over several large estates which Antony had appropriated for himself.[33] From these private domains, whose exploitation was supervised by a special staff of bailiffs (who shared the name of *procuratores* with the collectors of taxes in the imperial provinces), the emperor drew a substantial additional income. His private purse was also filled by a large number of windfalls in the shape of legacies, which amounted to the grand total of 1,400,000,000 sesterces. Out of this revenue Augustus was not only able to meet his household expenses, but to pay part costs of his public administration or to subsidise the Senate.

Accounts of all the money that came into Augustus's hands must have been kept in Rome by a staff of trained accountants of his own domestic staff, many being freedmen or even slaves and working under the unremitting personal supervision of the emperor. The first chief accountant (*a rationibus*) known to us is a certain Antemus who served Tiberius. Augustus must have made a general survey of the accounts of the whole Empire, but how often he published this is uncertain: he did on two occasions, in 23 B.C. and at his death in A.D. 14, and perhaps more often. If he did not provide a comprehensive survey he may have published a yearly balance-sheet (*rationes*) of a more limited nature.

The aerarium militare and new taxes

The state revenue had to be augmented not merely by Augustus's generosity but also by further taxation. This was rendered even more necessary by his decision in A.D. 6 that the financial burden of providing for retired soldiers should no longer seem to depend on his personal generosity but should come direct from the State. He therefore created a new fund, the *aerarium militare*, which he started off with a gift of 170 million sesterces; in the future it was to be maintained by the revenue from two new taxes that he introduced, a sales-tax of 1 per cent (*centesima rerum venalium*) and death-duties of 5 per cent (*vicesima hereditatum*). The new treasury was administered by three ex-praetors. Now that the loyalty of the army to Augustus had been tested over so many years it was possible to cut the undesirable personal link between men and their commander which had bedevilled Roman political life since the days of Marius. Augusuts did not impose further

Coinage

burdens on the provincials. Except in Gallia Comata, where he exacted a far heavier tribute than the mere token payments demanded by Caesar, he refrained from increasing direct taxation in the provinces.

Like other military *imperatores* Augustus in his triumviral days had minted coinage, and he continued plentiful gold and silver issues in Asia, Spain and, perhaps after 23, at Rome. But in 15 B.C. he established an imperial mint at Lugdunum, which from 12 B.C. was the sole source of gold and silver coinage. The senatorial mint at Rome, under the *triumviri monetales*, thus issued only copper (*asses* and their submultiples) and orichalcum (*sestertii* and two-*as* pieces). In effect the senatorial mint became a sub-office for the provision of small change, but it clung to this privilege throughout the lifetime of the Empire and proclaimed this right by putting the letters *SC* (issued as the result of a *Senatus Consultum*) on all its coppers. Further, Augustus realised the propaganda value of pictorial coinage, which could be appreciated even by the illiterate. In the twenty-five years after Actium he issued silver with no less than 400 different types which displayed some of the outstanding achievements of his reign (e.g. the recovery of the standards from the Parthians) and some of the ideas which he wished to instil into a renewed people.[34]

As the result of his financial measures Augustus bequeathed to his successors a solvent treasury and a financial system which was not indeed equal to any heavy strain, but could meet ordinary calls upon the public purse out of legitimate and not unduly heavy taxes.

9 The Succession

The problem of a successor

Augustus's last duty to Rome was to provide it with a successor to his own position. Though in strict law he was not entitled to assume that the extraordinary magistracy which he held would not lapse after his death, in fact nothing was more certain than that his place would need to be filled. On this question of the succession the emperor carried his habitual slowness in coming to decisions almost beyond the limits of safety. On one point, indeed, his mind was

Augustus's dynastic policy

fully made up: he was determined that the imperial power should, if possible, remain in his own household. In itself this resolve was not inconsistent with republican usage, for a hereditary succession to high office had been the avowed ambition and the habitual practice of the senatorial nobility. But unfortunately Augustus had no son: however within the emperor's family more than one suitable suc-

31.4 Head of Livia, wife of Augustus, as personifying Pietas. Coin struck under Tiberius, her son.

cessor to his power could be found. But Augustus persistently hesitated to make a final selection among his field of candidates, and the eventual choice of the next emperor was made by the play of chance rather than by his own act.

Hesitation between rival candidates

Until 23 B.C., it is true, the question of the succession appeared to have been settled in advance. So long as his daughter Julia was unmarried, and his stepsons Tiberius and Drusus were mere boys, Augustus had no option but to look beyond his family circle, and here the claims of his friend Agrippa were irresistible. Accordingly, when the emperor stood at the point of death in 23, he handed his signet ring to Agrippa. On his recovery he procured for Agrippa an *imperium proconsulare* over all the imperial provinces, a privilege which appeared to mark him out as the next emperor.[35] Yet in the same year a marriage which Augustus arranged between Julia and his nephew C. Claudius Marcellus (a son of his sister Octavia by her first husband), was accepted by Agrippa as a hint that he was to be passed over, and although Agrippa took his supersession in good part, he deemed it politic to leave Rome on a mission of inspection in the eastern provinces. But he had scarcely started on his travels when the sudden death of Marcellus gave him possession of the field once more. On Agrippa's return to Rome in 21 he was remarried to the widowed Julia; in 18 he was invested with a *maius imperium* over all the senatorial provinces of the East – a prerogative which was prolonged for another five years in 13 B.C. and perhaps was extended to the western provinces – and with the *tribunicia potestas* (also prolonged in 13), so that he became virtually the co-regent of Augustus; finally, his two eldest sons by Julia were adopted in 17 by the emperor under the names of Gaius and Lucius Caesar. By these arrangements the succession appeared to have been regulated for the present generation and the next. But the death of Agrippa in 12 B.C.,

Agrippa

C. Marcellus

31.5 Gaius and Lucius Caesar, the grandsons of Augustus, each holding a spear and shield. These coins were issued frequently between 2 B.C. and A.D. 9 or 10.

Tiberius

before his sons had reached manhood, diverted the emperor's favours to his stepsons Tiberius and Drusus, who had recently distinguished themselves in command of the Roman armies. In 11 B.C. Augustus required Tiberius (much against his stepson's will) to renounce his wife, a daughter of Agrippa by an earlier marriage, in order to become the third husband of Julia; and he married Drusus to his niece Antonia, a daughter of Antony and Octavia. The choice between these two candidates was made in 9 B.C. by the death of Drusus, which left Tiberius for the moment as heir-apparent. In 6 B.C. the claims of Tiberius to the succession seemed to have been recognised once for all when the emperor procured for him a grant of *tribunicia potestas*. But in the same year Tiberius insisted on leave of absence, and for the next seven years he lived at Rhodes in complete retirement. The reason for this prolonged self-banishment lay in the significant marks of favour which the emperor was now beginning to show to the adolescent sons of Agrippa.

Caius and Lucius Caesar. Retirement of Tiberius

In 5 B.C. the emperor resumed the consulship in order to introduce C. Caesar to public life. In this year he obtained for him the honorary headship (as *princeps iuventutis*) of the cadets of the Equestrian Order; and he appointed him to be consul in A.D. 1 at the absurdly early age of 20. At three years' interval L. Caesar was promoted to the same honours. In the meantime the voluntary absence of Tiberius was turning into an enforced exile, and although he received permission to return to Rome in A.D. 2, he was debarred from further political activities. But the hand of death once more upset the emperor's calculations. The premature decease of L. Caesar in A.D. 2, and of C. Caesar two years later, reduced Agrippa's family to his widow Julia, to a daughter of the same name, and a young son named Agrippa Postumus. In contrast to his father the younger Agrippa had

a defiant and intractable character which disqualified him for the succession, and the two Julias eventually became the centre of the town's scandal. In 2 B.C. Augustus relegated the elder Julia, by virtue of his *patria potestas*, to the island of Pandateria (near Naples); in A.D. 7 he sent her daughter to a similar place of exile and banished Agrippa Postumus to the island of Planasia (near Elba). By the elimination of Agrippa's kin Tiberius was left as the only possible heir to Augustus, for in A.D. 7 Drusus's son, Nero Claudius Drusus (afterwards known as Germanicus), had not yet come of age. After the death of C. Caesar accordingly Augustus adopted Tiberius and restored his tribunician power (A.D. 4). In A.D. 13, when the aged emperor's strength showed signs of failing, he procured a law by which Tiberius was invested with an unlimited *imperium proconsulare* and thus became his co-regent.[36] By a chapter of accidents the tangle of the succession had been straightened out. Moreover, whatever Augustus's shortcomings in his dynastic policy, he had been at pains to give each of his potential heirs in turn a thorough training in the art of government. In this respect Tiberius was perfectly qualified to carry on Augustus's work, and the first and most important succession between emperors took place almost without a jolt.

Tiberius becomes co-regent

10. Summary of Augustus's Principate

The outstanding achievements and events of this period have now been surveyed, but it may be well to link them up in a closer chronological framework, if only to emphasise the very gradual way in which Augustus handled the problems that emerged from year to year. He had no rigid or doctrinaire plan, but proceeded in a practical pragmatic way, working cautiously to the best solution.

In 27 'the Republic was restored', with Augustus as *princeps civitatis* and consul VII with command of a great province and direct command of four-fifths of all the legions. The claim of M. Crassus for the *spolia opima* and a triumph no doubt made him conscious of the remaining fifth; hence Crassus was denied the greater honour. Reconstruction was carried further when Augustus restored the Via Flaminia as far as Ariminum at his own expense and persuaded other generals to take responsibility for other roads. Rome itself was adorned by Agrippa's Pantheon. After his election to his eighth consulship Augustus considered it more politic to leave Rome to settle down without his daily presence; he went off to Gaul, where he held a census and planned its reorganisation,

27–24 B.C. The first settlement

and then on to Spain. During his absence the luckless Cornelius Gallus, who had been recalled from Egypt, was accused of treason by the Senate and committed suicide; this alleged threat is not likely to have worried the Princeps unduly. His attempt to secure order in Rome by appointing Valerius Messalla Corvinus as Prefect of the City in 26 was not a success, since Messalla soon resigned. In Spain Augustus campaigned in the north-west (but found time to write to Virgil asking for a specimen of the *Aeneid*). In this same year (26) the ill-fated Arabian expedition was launched, while Polemo was recognised as ruler of Pontus. In 25 Augustus was ill at Tarraco, and in Rome the temple of Janus was closed for a second time: but prematurely, since fighting flared up again in Spain in 24, 22, 19 and 16. However, the end was foreshadowed by his settlement of veterans at Emerita and the reorganisation (probably at this point) of Spain into three provinces. He was still not well enough to reach Rome for the wedding of his daughter Julia to his nephew Marcellus, a marriage which he had doubtless planned with a view to providing Rome with a new Princeps, since he had no son of his own. Some provincial changes were made: on the death of Amyntas his kingdom of Galatia was annexed as a Roman province, Juba was moved to Mauretania from Numidia which was added to Roman Africa, the Candace attacked southern Egypt and thus provoked Petronius's Ethiopian expedition, while in the north Terentius Varro Murena reduced the Alpine Salassi and founded Augusta Praetoria. In 24 Augustus had at last returned to Rome, as consul for the tenth time, and the Senate honoured not only him but also his young relatives who had fought in Spain. Marcellus was given praetorian rank, with permission to stand for the consulship ten years before the legal age, and was made an aedile, while Augustus's stepson Tiberius was given the right to hold office five years in advance and was made a quaestor.

Some threatening storm-clouds arose in 23. Primus was condemned for treason, and Caepio and Murena were charged with conspiracy. Further, Augustus was gravely ill and, anticipating death, gave his papers to the consul Piso and his ring to his friend Agrippa: a somewhat ambiguous indication of his hopes for the future. However, fortunately for Rome, he recovered, but decided that a fresh settlement was necessary. He resigned the consulship, thus pleasing the nobles and conserving his own health, and accepted a readjustment of his power, which henceforth rested essentially upon *tribunicia potestas* and *imperium proconsulare maius*. Agrippa was sent off to the East with proconsular

23–19 B.C. The second settlement

imperium, which probably extended through the provinces of Augustus, who handed back Gallia Narbonensis and Cyprus to the charge of the Senate. Before the year was out he suffered a serious setback to his plans for the future, when his son-in-law Marcellus died. Troubles in Rome in 22 led to popular demands that he should be given further powers, but he refused and went off on an administrative tour of the East, starting in Sicily. In 21 he went on to Greece, while Agrippa returned to Rome to represent Augustus and to keep order. Augustus now turned less equivocally to Agrippa as a future helper: he was married to the widowed Julia. In 20 Augustus regulated affairs in Asia and visited Syria, but the year was marked by his diplomatic triumph of the recovery of the lost standards: Tiberius installed a king on the Armenian throne and war with Parthia was averted. Meantime Agrippa proceeded to Gaul and then (19) to Spain. But Rome was restless in Augustus's absence and disturbances occurred: only one consul was elected, since the people insisted on keeping the other place vacant for Augustus. Further, Egnatius Rufus, who earlier as aedile had won popularity by organising a private fire-brigade, insisted on standing for the consulship, although not technically qualified; rioting followed, but before Augustus returned Rufus had been accused of treason and executed. Augustus crossed over from Greece with Virgil, but the poet died soon after landing in Italy. The Princeps was back in Rome on 12 October which was declared an annual holiday, while an altar was dedicated to Fortuna Redux (Fortune the Home-bringer). He also received some further constitutional power, whether full consular *imperium* or not remains uncertain. His two stepsons also were honoured: Tiberius was given praetorian rank, and the younger brother Drusus received the right to hold magistracies five years before the legal age.

In 18 B.C. while securing for his fellow-helper Agrippa a grant of *tribunicia potestas* for five years and a continuation of his *imperium* (now probably *maius*), Augustus had his own proconsular *imperium* renewed for five years. He now felt that the new order had settled down sufficiently both for further reform and celebration. He reduced the Senate to 600 members (by means of *censoria potestas*?), and started his moral reforms, introducing in person laws relating to marriage, adultery, electoral corruption and luxury. Then in 17 came the staging of the Secular Games to symbolise the New Age. The future also looked more secure, since Agrippa and Julia now had two sons, Gaius Caesar, aged three, and Lucius Caesar, aged one. Augustus might hope that, if he died soon

18–12 B.C. Consolidation of the Principate

Agrippa, who was now in the East, might hold the fort until his own grandchildren were old enough to succeed. Hitherto the eastern and western frontiers of the Empire had demanded most attention, but in 16 there was unrest in the North and North-east. Taking Tiberius with him, Augustus went to Gaul, since the German Usipetes and Tencteri were giving trouble. In Gaul he reorganised the finances and no doubt planned the great thrust to the Danube which was one of the most significant results of his reign. Noricum was annexed and in 15 Tiberius and Drusus reached the Danube and reduced Raetia and the Alps. Thus Rome had now advanced along the length of the Danube from Vienna westwards to Lake Constance. The next year the little province of Alpes Maritimae was organised. Meantime Augustus had set up an imperial mint in Lugdunum (15) and was settling colonies for veterans in Gaul and Spain. In 13 he was back in Rome, where one of the great monuments of Augustan art, the Ara Pacis, was erected in his honour, and where he dedicated the theatre of Marcellus. Agrippa also was back and had his tribunician power granted for another five years and his proconsular imperium (now certainly *maius*) extended for five years. Tiberius was rewarded for his northern campaigns with the consulship, but trouble was brewing in Pannonia; Agrippa was sent, but died early in 12. This was something of a blow to Augustus's dynastic plans; his grandsons were growing up, but meantime he must rely more on Tiberius. However, more immediately Tiberius and his brother Drusus were needed elsewhere. The former went to Pannonia, while Drusus who dedicated the altar at Lugdunum to *Roma et Augustus*, started the first of four years of campaigns across the Rhine. In Rome Augustus at last gained an honour which he had avoided seizing: the former triumvir Lepidus, who was still Pontifex Maximus, died, and by succeeding to the office Augustus now became the official head of Roman organised religion.

11 B.C. – A.D. 4

In 11 B.C. Tiberius for dynastic reasons was forced to divorce his wife, and to marry Julia, knowing that he was being used merely as a stop-gap. However, he had to hurry back to Dalmatia (which the Senate handed over to the emperor) to meet the Pannonians. His campaigns ended in victory in 9, and Illyricum and Pannonia were organised; to the east Moesia was under control, even if not organised strictly as a Roman province. The Romans had thus reached the whole length of the Danube, from Switzerland to the Black Sea. Meanwhile Drusus was engaged on another major project, the conquest of western Germany as far east

as the Elbe. It can scarcely be doubted that Augustus was planning then to conquer the Marcomanni in Bohemia and link an Elbe with a Rhine frontier. In 11 Drusus reached the Weser (Visurgis) and in 9 the Elbe, but he died as the result of an accident. Since Tiberius was now free he was sent to carry on until 7. In Rome the Ara Pacis was dedicated in 9, while in 8 Augustus received an extension of his proconsular *imperium* for ten years, and perhaps now the month Sextilis was officially named after him, August. He held his second census and in 7 organised Rome into the fourteen *regiones*. But in 8 he had lost his friend Maecenas, while Horace also had died. Tiberius, who had defeated the Sugambri in Germany, was in 6 B.C. granted tribunician power for five years, but he declined an invitation to go to settle the Armenian question and, feeling overshadowed by the young princes, Gaius and Lucius, he retired to Rhodes. In 5 Augustus resumed the consulship (his twelfth) in order to advance these boys in public life: Gaius was to be consul in five years (when he would be twenty); he was also made a pontifex and received the title of *princeps iuventutis*. In 4 Herod the Great died; his kingdom was not annexed but divided between his three sons. Then in 2 B.C. Augustus received a title which he might consider that by this time he had earned: he was acclaimed the Father of his Country, Pater Patriae, by Senate, Equestrian Order and *plebs*. If a shadow was cast by his need to exile his profligate daughter Julia, it was balanced by seeing his younger grandson Lucius join his brother as *princeps iuventutis*. The dedication of the temple of Mars Ultor in his Forum would bring back memories of a world long changed. The future seemed assured: in 1 B.C. Gaius Caesar received proconsular *imperium* to deal with Armenia and Parthia, and entered on his consulship in the East in the following year (A.D. 1). Then in A.D. 2, while he was reaching an agreement about the Armenian throne, tragedy struck. His brother Lucius died at Massilia and two years later he himself died in Lycia. Augustus's dynastic plans lay in ruins.

Augustus was thus forced to turn to his stepson Tiberius, who had returned to Rome from his self-imposed exile in Rhodes in A.D. 2, but had received no renewal of his powers which ended in 1 B.C. Now after the death of Gaius Caesar Augustus adopted Tiberius as his son and secured for him tribunician power and proconsular *imperium* for ten years; however, he insisted that Tiberius adopt Germanicus alongside Tiberius's own son Drusus II. Tiberius was then sent off to the Rhine frontier, where the next year he advanced to the Elbe and planned

A.D. 4–9. Difficult years

the conquest of the Marcomanni. At home in 4 Cornelius Cinna Magnus, a grandson of Pompey, was accused of conspiring, but was pardoned. In 5 the *lex Valeria Cornelia* introduced a new system of magisterial election. In 6 Augustus made two important contributions to Rome's well-being, by establishing the *aerarium militare* and organising the Vigiles; he was also concerned with the corn-supply, although the two consulars whom he appointed were later superseded by a *praefectus annonae*. Provincial changes comprised the annexation of Judaea, with the assessment of Quirinius, and the transfer of Sardinia to Augustus because of brigandage; Cornelius Cossus, proconsul of Africa, had to protect Juba of Mauretania against the Gaetulians, and for his victory received the triumphal ornaments. In the North, however, a major disaster broke: the revolt in Pannonia and Illyricum. A hasty agreement with the Marcomanni left Tiberius free to cope with the emergency. This he did and after some critical fighting returned to Rome in victory in A.D. 9. However, that year was marked by the even greater disaster inflicted upon Varus's three legions in the Teutoburgian Forest by Arminius. To meet the new demands Augustus had to put pressure to get recruits, but finally with a new army Tiberius again returned to the northern front, where with Germanicus he 'showed the flag' for the next two years. But all hope of the permanent conquest of western Germany and occupation up to the Elbe had to be abandoned, and the defence of the Rhine was organised on the basis of a permanent occupation force of eight legions.

A.D. 12–14. The end

The ageing Augustus was severely shaken by the *clades Variana*, and the tempo of events began to slow down. In 12 Tiberius and Germanicus were on the Rhine frontier, where Tiberius left his adopted son to return for a triumph. Augustus leant ever more heavily on Tiberius and when in 13 his own *imperium* was renewed for ten years Tiberius received tribunician power for ten years and proconsular *imperium* equal to that of Augustus; he was in fact virtually a co-regent. Together they conducted a census, which was completed in 14. Then Tiberius was about to start back to Illyricum but was recalled by news of Augustus's illness and reached him in time to receive his final instructions before he died on 14 September A.D. 14 at Nola. Thereafter Tiberius's son Drusus read to the Senate four documents which Augustus had drafted: directions for his funeral; a final draft of his *Res Gestae*, which he had recently brought up to date from 2 B.C.; statements about the troops and finance; and advice to Tiberius and the public. This last itself is interesting: they were advised to restrict

manumissions and the granting of citizenship, to entrust public business only to men of tried ability, and above all to keep the Roman Empire within the bounds which Augustus had established for it. Then on 17 September by decree of the Senate Augustus was declared divine, and his widow Livia, whom in his will he had named Augusta, became the priestess of his cult.

11. Conclusion

The reign of Augustus was as much the turning-point of Roman history as Roman history was the pivot of ancient history in general. Yet the central figure in Roman history was one of its least heroic personages. Augustus had none of the immense vitality, the wide imagination and the quick decision that distinguished Caesar. Neither was he carried along by any strong sense of a religious mission. His piety, though sincere, was that of the old-fashioned Italian type which might sustain but could not compel.[37] It is noteworthy that in the *Res Gestae* or summary of his achievements, which he caused to be inscribed on the portals of his Mausoleum, he nowhere represented himself as the chosen instrument of a divine purpose. He possessed little of that personal charm with which some of the world's successful rulers have made up for their natural deficiencies.

Augustus not a heroic figure

If we seek to explain how such an unimpressive person could leave such a deep mark on history we must in the first place make a liberal allowance for the element of luck. In his first mad gamble for power Augustus enjoyed the support of Caesar's old soldiers. During the Triumvirate Antony played into his hands, both as a colleague and as an enemy. At this period and in the early years of his reign Augustus was well served by his fighting man and first minister, Agrippa, and his confidential adviser, Maecenas. Finally, he had forty years of unopposed power, during which his political system had time to be well tested and amended in its details.

His good fortune

But over and above his good fortune Augustus possessed two personal qualities which in a statesman outweigh all others. On the one hand he was remarkably candid to himself as to his own limitations. He was content to take one step at a time, and then to pause until he could see his way more clearly. He did not keep in his own hands, but willingly delegated to others, tasks for which he had no skill or leisure. On the other, once he had decided that a given task was in his power, he pursued it with steadfast determination. He refused to be discouraged

His statesmanlike qualities

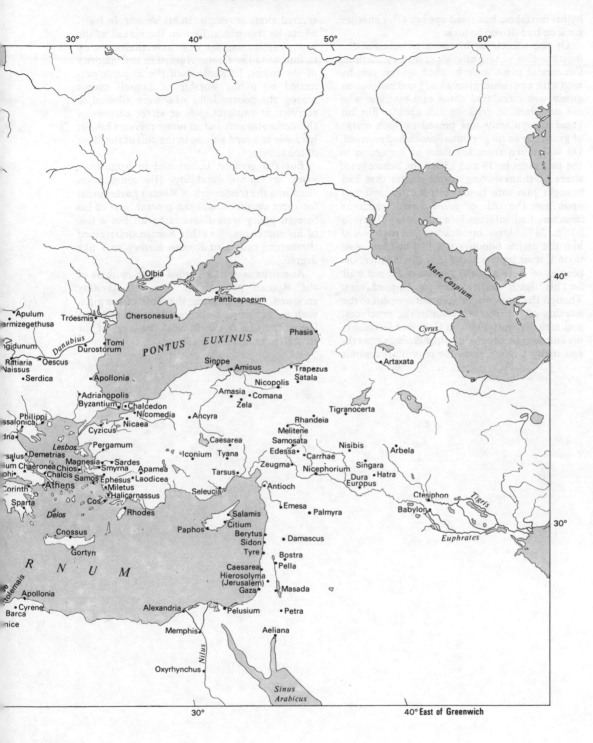

PONTUS EUXINUS

Mare Caspium

Olbia

Panticapaeum

Chersonesus

Phasis

Apulum
armizegethusa

Tróesmis

Cyrus

Artaxata

Tomi
Durostorum

Danubius

Ratiaria
Naissus

Oescus

Sinope

Amisus

Trapezus
Satala

ngidunum

Serdica

Apollonia

Nicopolis

Tigranocerta

Adrianopolis

Amasia

Comana

Byzantium

Chalcedon

Zela

Rhandeia

Philippi
ssalonica

Nicomedia

Ancyra

Melitene

Nicaea

Nisibis

Arbela

na

Cyzicus

Caesarea

Samosata

Lesbos

Pergamum

Iconium

Tyana

Edessa

Carrhae

Singara

Zeugma

Nicephorium

Dura
Europus

Hatra

salus

Demetrias

Smyrna

Apamea

Tarsus

um Chaeronea

Magnesia

Sardes

Chios

ohi

Chalcis

Samos

Ephesus

Laodicea

Corinth

Athens

Miletus

Halicarnassus

Seleucia

Antioch

Ctesiphon

Tigris

Sparta

Cos

Emesa

Palmyra

Babylon

Délos

Rhodes

Cnossus

Salamis
Citium

Paphos

Berytus
Sidon

Damascus

Euphrates

Gortyn

Tyre

Bostra

R   N   U   M

Caesarea
Hierosolyma
(Jerusalem)
Gaza

Pella

Masada

tolemais

Apollonia

Cyrene
Barca

nice

Alexandria

Pelusium

Petra

Aeliana

Memphis

Oxyrhynchus

Nilus

*Sinus
Arabicus*

40° East of Greenwich

by his mistakes, but tried one key after another until he had fitted the lock.

His popularity

Of the success of his work he received the most conclusive testimonials in his own lifetime. Occasional plots were hatched against him by men with a personal grievance,[38] and malevolent gossip was circulated about him by those who did not dare to criticise him openly. But his general popularity was proved by such marks of gratitude as no previous Roman had received. On his return from his tours of inspection in the provinces in 19 and 13 B.C. the Senate voted altars of thanksgiving to the deities that had brought him safe home. In 2 B.C. it conferred upon him the title of *pater patriae*, which its members had informally accorded to Cicero in 63 (p. 247). After his death it willingly voted him the divine honours which it had bestowed upon Caesar by command (p. 288). Further, the peoples of Italy and the provinces did not wait for his death before they worshipped him. Though the emperor gave encouragement to the

Spontaneous character of emperor-worship

worship of *Roma et Augustus* in the provinces, and actually initiated it in Gaul and Germany, his cult was in the main a spontaneous growth, and many cities besides the provincial capitals erected altars or temples in his honour. In Italy, where he frowned at first on the spread of the new worship, temples were nevertheless set up to him or to the *Genius Augusti* in the majority of the towns. In Rome itself the emperor permitted no public worship of himself except among the poorer folk, who were allowed to sacrifice in small chapels at street corners to the *Lares Augusti*; but in many privates houses his *Lares* received a share in the cult of the *Lares* of the family.

But the greatest testimonial to Augustus's work lay in its durability. His constitution remained the framework of Roman government for three centuries, and the general lines of his foreign policy were followed by all but a few of his successors. No other Roman determined the future course of Roman history to a like degree.

Augustus may be regarded as an epitome of the Roman people. He was not lavishly endowed, yet by making the most of his gifts, such as they were, he achieved a great and lasting work. This is also in brief the story of the Roman nation.

CHAPTER 32

The Julio-Claudian Emperors.
Internal Affairs

1. Tiberius (A.D. 14–37)

The first fifty years after the death of Augustus was a period of transition, during which his system of government gradually became hard-set. The four emperors whose reigns fill this half-century formed a dynasty (the so-called 'Julio-Claudian' dynasty), for all of them were related by blood to Augustus or to his third wife Livia (see pedigree, p. 574). This hereditary transmission of power was due to the unique personal ascendancy of the first emperor, and to the strong bond of allegiance by which the Roman army was attached to his family. After the extinction of his line the elective character of the Roman monarchy reasserted itself, and no later dynasty of emperors lasted for more than two generations.

32.1   Tiberius.

Tiberius Claudius Nero, or Tiberius Caesar Augustus, as he styled himself after his accession, was a son of Livia by her first marriage, born in 42 B.C., and the adoptive son of

Dynastic succession after Augustus's death

Augustus.[1] In his personality he furnished a classic example of Aristotle's tragic character – a man of good parts with one flaw, which by the play of circumstances vitiates his entire life. He brought to his task as emperor a stern, not to say defiant, sense of duty – 'Let them hate me, provided they approve of what I do' (*oderint dum probent*) was his motto – and a proved all-round proficiency as a soldier and administrator. But he was beset with an inborn diffidence in his own powers, which imposed upon him a cold and reserved manner, and by a reflex action made him suspicious of other men. This congenital distrustfulness was aggravated by the erratic dynastic policy of Augustus, in which he seemed to figure like a mere pawn on a chessboard, and by the knowledge that he had become the heir of Augustus by necessity rather than by choice. He therefore accepted the imperial power as one who enters upon an uncongenial office, and he ended by conceiving a positive loathing for his position.[2] At best, indeed, the succession to Augustus was bound to be a somewhat thankless task. The benefits of the new order were beginning to be taken for granted, and enthusiasm was giving way to ennui. But Tiberius's position was rendered doubly difficult by continual misunderstandings with those around him. From the Senate he received outward deference, but he doubted the sincerity of its professions and increasingly he found that the genuine co-operation that he desired became more difficult to achieve.[3] Further, some individual senators plotted against him, or at any rate toyed with the idea of conspiracy, as Scribonius Libo Drusus in 16 and C. Silius in 24.[4] But

Personality of Tiberius

His distrustfulness

the chief cause of his growing embitterment lay in his own family, with which he was constantly at feud, and in his false confidant and evil genius, L. Aelius Seianus.

In adopting Tiberius and devising the succession to him, Augustus had stipulated that the future emperor should in his turn adopt his nephew Germanicus and arrange the next succession in his favour. Although Tiberius had a son of his own by his first wife, Drusus II,

32.2   Germanicus. GERMANICUS CAESAR TI(berii) AUG(usti) F(ilius) DIVI AUG(usti) N(epos).

Domestic quarrels

he acquiesced in this condition, and after the death of Augustus he gave no sign of going back on it. Drusus II was a popular figure at Rome, but he lacked the campaigning experience of Germanicus and was no such favourite among the troops as his cousin and brother-in-law. At the beginning of Tiberius's principate mutinies broke out among the troops on the Danube and Rhine, less for political reasons than from discontent about terms of service. While Drusus quelled that in Pannonia, Germanicus dealt with the Rhine armies. There was a risk that the men might try to support Germanicus in an effort to supplant Tiberius, but Germanicus remained loyal, brought the troops to heel and then launched an attack over the Rhine in western Germany which developed into three years of hard campaigning (14–16: see p. 370). If he was hoping to resume Augustus's plan of an Elbe frontier he was disappointed when Tiberius, true to Augustus's policy (*consilium*) of not advancing the frontiers of empire, recalled him, judging rightly that enough had been achieved to keep the Rhine frontier safe. Embittered though he may have been, Germanicus could not justifiably complain since Tiberius allowed him a magnificent triumph in 17, gave him *maius imperium* over all the eastern provinces, and shared a consulship with him in 18. However, he judged it wise to keep an eye on this rather vainglorious young man and so appointed Cn. Calpurnius Piso, who had been consul with himself in 7 B.C., as governor of

Germanicus and Agrippina

Syria where he could watch Germanicus. After installing a new king in Armenia (pp. 368 ff.), Germanicus went on to Egypt, illegally since no senator could enter Egypt without the emperor's permission; there he received a rapturous welcome since he relieved a corn-shortage. On returning to Syria he died soon afterwards, convinced that he had been poisoned by Piso (A.D. 19).[5] This scandal precipitated a crisis in the imperial family. Though no serious evidence of foul play was brought forward his widow Agrippina (a daughter of Agrippa and of Julia, the daughter of Augustus) convinced herself that Tiberius had poisoned him, and henceforth she waged a relentless vendetta against the emperor.[6]

32.3   The elder Agrippina. AGRIPPINA M(arci) (SC. Agrippae) F(ilia) MAT(er) C(aii) Caesaris Augusti. The daughter of Agrippa and mother of Caligula. Coin issued under Caligula.

Tiberius at first betrayed no open resentment. Indeed Germanicus's death opened the way to the principate for his own son Drusus, who held the consulship with him in 21 and received tribunician power for the next year. Further, the succession might seem secured even for another generation, since Drusus's wife, Livilla, had borne him twins. Then came a blow in A.D. 23: Tiberius's son Drusus died, a natural death as it seemed at the time. Tiberius then recognised Agrippina's children, Nero and Drusus III, as heirs apparent. But the feud was kept alive by the emperor's *praefectus praetorio*, L. Aelius Seianus. The son of a professional administrator who had held the praetorian prefecture at the beginning of the reign, Seianus was quickly promoted to his father's office, and as adjutant-general to the emperor he made himself so indispensable that Tiberius, to make up for distrust of others, gave him an almost blind confidence. For his own ends Seianus roused the emperor's suspicions against Agrippina's family and against several prominent senators who stood in her favour. Whether Agrippina actually attempted to hasten the end of Tiberius in order to assure the succession of one of her sons, or

Intrigues of the praefectus praetorio, Seianus, against Agrippina's family

planned to become empress herself by a second marriage with a senatorial usurper, are questions that admit of no answer. But in view of the influence which the widow of Germanicus could exercise over the troops her hostile attitude to the emperor certainly laid her open to accusations of conspiracy. After the death of his mother Livia, who had hitherto prevented an open breach, Tiberius struck out in self-defence. In 29 he procured from the Senate a sentence of banishment against Agrippina and her son Nero; in the following year he sent the other son Drusus after them.[7]

The object of Seianus in removing Agrippina's family was to clear the field for himself as the successor of Tiberius. Though only of equestrian rank, he was connected by marriage with the old republican nobility, and the ascendancy which he had gained over the emperor stimulated his ambitions. In 23 he had made himself virtually master of the city of Rome by concentrating the whole of the praetorian cohorts (who had hitherto been dispersed in billets) in a large camp on its eastern outskirts.

Ascendancy of Seianus In 26 he had induced Tiberius to prolong indefinitely a stay on the island of Capri, so as to keep him out of full touch with events at the capital. As military commands on the frontiers fell vacant, he contrived to get them filled with his own nominees. His hopes increased when he was given proconsular *imperium* and nominated to be joint consul with Tiberius for 31. But Tiberius would give Seianus no definite promise of the succession, and in 31 a message from Antonia, the widow of the emperor's brother Drusus, who revealed to him the intrigues of Seianus against Agrippina and her family, opened his eyes to the minister's ultimate

His sudden disgrace and execution intentions.[8] Awakened to his danger Tiberius improvised a swift and crushing counter-conspiracy, which was long remembered as a classic example of diamond-cut-diamond. While he kept Seianus in suspense with half-promises of more honours to come, the emperor secretly instructed Sutorius Macro, the *praefectus vigilum*, to assume command of the praetorian cohorts and to steal them away from Seianus with the offer of a special bounty; he could also count on the support of the *vigiles*. At a meeting of the Senate on 18 October the presiding consul, Memmius Regulus, read a portentously long letter from Capri which left Seianus guessing and indeed hoping to hear that he had been granted tribunician power, until the last paragraph denounced him roundly as a traitor. Nobody raised a hand or a voice in defence of the accused, for the *vigiles* patrolled the streets, and the Guards remained invisible in their camp. On the same day the Senate passed

formal sentence, and the former favourite was executed. In his fall he brought down with him many of his adherents, who were found guilty of complicity in a merciless assize after the ringleader's death. A Parthian shaft from Seianus's widow, who gave out that her husband had removed Tiberius's son by poison,[9] completed the emperor's disillusionment. Still unable to overcome his distrust of Agrippina and her sons Tiberius put them to death or drove them to suicide. Agrippina's third son Gaius, who was considered too young to be dangerous, escaped his brothers' fate, but he was kept a virtual prisoner in the emperor's place of retreat at Capri.

Tiberius's distrust deepened

The morbid distrustfulness of Tiberius not only played havoc with his family life, but also acted as a drag upon his administration. Though quite capable of acting promptly as well as of thinking clearly, he sometimes let himself be caught between two minds. In such cases he would simply shelve the business in hand, or he would leave the decision thereon to the Senate. This might be interpreted as shuffling off responsibility on the Senate or as a genuine desire to make it take its full share of responsibility, but the result was that he often added to its embarrassment by the ambiguity of his instructions, which left the House in perplexity as to his intentions. His evasions and tergiversations saddled him with a reputation for hypocrisy which was ill-deserved, but scarcely to be wondered at.[10]

Tiberius's hesitations in administration

Tiberius suffered grievous shock by the revelation that his seemingly loyal friend had plotted against him and had even murdered his son Drusus several years before. Thereafter he adopted a much sterner approach to accusations of treason, many of which he had dismissed lightly in earlier days.[11] Even then they had been on the increase, partly because the crime of *maiestas* was ill-defined, partly because there was no public prosecutor at Rome and so the way was open for private gain or private revenge. Taking advantage of the emperor's suspiciousness, politicians in pursuit of personal feuds, or fortune-hunters who coveted the customary fee for a successful information (one-quarter of the condemned man's estate) laid accusation of treason. This dangerously vague charge, of which much wrongful use had been made in the political trials of the later Republic, was revived under Tiberius, in order to encompass the ruin of men who at the most had been indiscreet or disrespectful towards the emperor. It is true that in these trials, which were usually held at public sessions of the Senate, the accused persons were given the opportunity of speaking in their own defence; that Tiberius allowed the Senate to acquit, and even to institute counter-

Trials for maiestas in the Senate. Tiberius gives undue latitude to informers

proceedings against an obviously mischievous prosecutor; that he sometimes spoke in favour of the accused or stopped the trial with his tribune's veto; and that several prisoners threw away their lives prematurely by committing suicide. True, even after the fall of Seianus, seven accused persons were acquitted in 32, while of nine known to have perished Tacitus implies that only two were innocent. Yet if Tiberius's reign did not end in a savage and uncontrolled Reign of Terror, it hardly admits of doubt that death-sentences were passed upon innocent men, and if Tiberius did not deserve the reputation for vindictiveness which these trials fastened upon him he cannot be exonerated from all blame, for if he had put his foot down firmly he could have made an end once for all to vexatious prosecutions.

Tiberius's retirement to Capri

In the last ten years of his reign Tiberius absented himself permanently from the capital; after his retirement to Capri a failure of nerve kept him a prisoner there to the end of his life. His long seclusion on that lonely island gave rise to a crop of stories which represented the septuagenarian emperor as sunk in a condition of monstrous debauchery, but such gossip deserves little credence, since it is not supported by any first-century evidence, nor is it made more likely by the fact that he lived to be 77 and enjoyed the company of scholars, jurists and men of letters as well as of astrologers. A serious aspect of his absence was the increasing dependence of the Senate upon him, since it might often hesitate to act until his wishes were known. Though he still guided the administration with occasional dispatches he postponed the appointment of new officials and let the pay of the troops fall into arrears. Finally, at the emperor's death in 37, no definite choice had been made of a successor. By the deaths of Drusus II and of the two eldest sons of Germanicus the field of selection had been narrowed to Germanicus's youngest son Gaius and to the emperor's grandson Tiberius Gemellus. Tiberius evaded a decision between these two candidates by naming them as his heirs in equal parts, and by detaining Gaius at Capri he denied him the opportunity of acquiring experience in the duties of an emperor.

Tiberius's principate

Various aspects of Tiberius's policy are discussed later, but it may be well here to consider them together. The civil administration down to 23 or 26 was excellent, as is conceded even by Tacitus who was no admirer of Tiberius. He upheld and even increased the judicial, electoral and legislative functions of the Senate, but it was one of the tragedies of his reign that his well-intentioned efforts to co-operate with the Senate gradually broke down, partly from

defects in his character, partly through undue subservience by the Senate. He showed great moderation in style, avoiding the use of Imperator as a *praenomen,* twice refusing the title of Pater Patriae, and avoiding the consulship, which he held only three times in order to honour a colleague (Germanicus in 18, Drusus in 21 and Seianus in 31). The growth of treason trials, which at first he deprecated, was encouraged by his increasing fears for his personal safety. His financial policy was moderate: it avoided extravagance and was liberal when necessary. His foreign policy also was successful and adhered to Augustus's advice (Chap. 33). He wisely rejected Germanicus's dream of establishing an Elbe frontier and recalled him when he judged that Roman power had been sufficiently demonstrated beyond the Rhine to ensure the peace of that area. The fighting in Africa, Gaul and Thrace was of a minor nature. He made slight adjustments in the East, while dealing tactfully with Armenia and Parthia: when three client-kings died, he made Cappadocia and Commagene Roman provinces, and incorporated Cilicia into the province of Syria. Thus as under Augustus Tiberius had rendered the Empire outstanding service as soldier and administrator, so as *Princeps* he provided by wise administration a period of peace and stability which allowed the system time to take deeper root, marred chiefly by faults which arose from the increasing isolation into which the disloyalty of friends and the misunderstanding of senators drove him.

2. Caligula (37–41)

The uncertainty in which Tiberius had left the succession was soon resolved after his death. The praetorian prefect Macro, whose favour had been won by Gaius at Capri, at once submitted his name to the Senate. If necessary he would no doubt have summoned the praetorian cohorts to prove that might was right, but the Senate accepted his nominee without demur.

32.4 Caligula.

Caligula's promising début

Gaius Caesar, or Caligula – as his father's soldiers had nicknamed him after the boots of army pattern which he wore as a small boy in Germanicus's camp – was received at Rome with general acclamations: as a prince of Germanicus's line, he would afford, so every one imagined, a welcome relief from the stern and suspicious régime of Tiberius.[12] The young emperor at first gave promise of fulfilling the wildest hopes of the Romans; he abolished the sales-tax; he paid at double rates a bounty which Tiberius had promised to the praetorian cohorts; he regaled the populace with circus-shows and beast-hunts; he adopted his cousin Tiberius Gemellus; he recalled exiles and repressed informers; and he gave renewed personal attention to the government. Caligula had reigned only a few months when he suffered a serious illness; he recovered, but emerged as a megalomaniac and tyrant.[13] He put many men

His tyranny

to death without the pretence of a trial, including Tiberius Gemellus and Macro. He encouraged delation and treason-trials; he imposed new taxes and wasted the reserves which Tiberius had accumulated; he ignored or humiliated the Senate; he held the consulship each year (except in 38); he transferred the elections back to the people. Further, he sought honours which amounted virtually to deification and seemed to be turning the Principate into an absolute monarchy. His foreign policy (see Chap. 33) was hardly less disastrous. He upset matters in the East and drove Judaea and Mauretania to the point of revolt. He made what appears to have been a wild thrust into Germany, though its purpose and result may have been misrepresented by a tradition hostile to him, as also may have been the case when in 40 he drew up troops on the English Channel and then at the last moment called off an invasion of Britain. Such manœuvres certainly did little to enhance Roman prestige.

His conduct both at home and abroad, and especially his executions of prominent citizens, provoked several conspiracies, in which senators of old republican lineage co-operated with military officers. In 39 the commander of the legions on the Upper Rhine, Lentulus Gaetulicus, laid a plot, the object of which apparently was to set up a member of the old republican nobility, M. Aemilius Lepidus, in Caligula's place. The

Summary executions, followed by conspiracies

detection of this scheme provoked further executions, and two sisters of the emperor, Agrippina II and Julia, who were suspected of complicity, were sent into exile. But Caligula was caught in a vicious circle. The repression of one plot gave rise to another, until the disloyalty spread to the praetorian cohorts. In 41 a tribune of the Guards named Cassius Chaerea, smarting

under a gratuitous affront from the emperor, trapped him in a quiet corner of the palace grounds and dispatched him under a rain of dagger-blows.

3. Claudius (41–54)

After the murder of Caligula some of the guardsmen, who stayed on to plunder the palace, found the uncle of the dead emperor, Tiberius Claudius Drusus, crouching for concealment behind a curtain. Instead of sending him after Caligula they saluted him as a brother of their former favourite Germanicus and carried him off to their camp, where he was pressed to accept the imperial power from them. On recovering from his fright Claudius not only gave his consent, but held the soldiers to their allegiance by the promise of a special bounty.

32.5 Claudius. Coin of Claudius, showing the praetorian camp, where Claudius was received. IMPER(ator) RECEPT(us).

This was the first of many transactions by which the seat of Augustus was bought and sold in the camp market. In the meantime the Senate, forgetting Claudius and assuming the line of Augustus to be extinct, had considered, only to dismiss, the idea of restoring the Republic in good earnest, and had begun to debate on the choice of a new emperor from its own ranks. Its discussions were cut short by the Guards, who forced their nominee upon it. After a brief

The Guards force the Senate to make Claudius emperor

show of resistance the Senate conferred the imperial power upon Claudius.[14]

On his accession Claudius was over fifty years of age, yet he had taken no part in public life. He was handicapped by a congenital infirmity, which gave him a clumsy gait and an uncouth appearance, and made him slow and distrait in his mind.[15] In the judgment of Augustus and Tiberius these defects definitely disqualified him from political service, so that they left him to while away his time as an antiquarian and literary dilettante. Caligula fetched him out of his study, but only to make a court buffoon of him. On his accession the ugly duckling of Augustus's family strove to make up for lost time by a painstaking devotion to his new duties. Further, he disclosed an unsuspected fund of novel ideas, as though his literary studies had carried his imagination beyond the somewhat narrow range of thought of the first two emperors; his wider outlook on the grant of Roman citizenship and on the Empire harked back beyond Augustus to Julius Caesar. His historical studies, in which Livy is said to have encouraged him when young, had been wide; he had written twenty books on Etruscan history and eight on Carthaginian (both in Greek), forty-one on Augustus (whom he much admired and who had admitted his intelligence), a defence of Cicero and eight books of autobiography. He realised that much of Rome's achievement was due to her ability to introduce change and reform without sacrificing essential traditions, and he was proud of his country's past. He wanted to rule well and in many respects he fulfilled his desire.

Claudius's disabilities

Yet in the end perverse Nature overbore the emperor's good intentions. In the midst of his work his mind would wander or simply cease to function; his trials often ended in erratic decisions, or in adjournment while the judge slumbered on the bench. Claudius therefore had constant need of a prompter to help him out or to conduct him back to the point at issue, and as his malady gained upon him with advancing age he became more and more dependent on his mentors. But whereas Augustus and Tiberius had chosen their political confidants from the chief men of the Senatorial and Equestrian Orders, Claudius found them within his own household. The earlier emperors, it is true, had recruited their secretaries and accountants from their domestic staff, and in this respect they had merely followed the established practice of the ruling houses under the Republic, but they had restricted their assistants to routine work. Claudius, on the other hand, sought their guidance on questions of high policy and of appointments to the chief executive posts. In the later years of his reign no Roman of high rank possessed influence equal to that of Callistus, the *praepositus a libellis* (examiner of petitions), of Narcissus, the *praepositus ab epistulis* (chief secretary), or of Pallas, the *praepositus a rationibus* (chief accountant), all of whom were emancipated slaves. The influence of these freedmen, which increased the personal power of the *Princeps*, was greatly resented among the members of the two ruling orders as an affront to Roman tradition, and indeed their complaints were not without substance, for Claudius's domestics converted the palace into a bazaar where offices and favours were trafficked at premium rates. That Pallas and Callistus, who began their careers without a penny, should have died richer than the triumvir Crassus is a sufficient commentary on their salesmanship.

His dependence on his advisers

The emperor's freedmen

But if the monstrous regiment of freedmen excited the deepest disgust at Rome it was actually less pernicious than that of the last two of Claudius's four wives, Valeria Messalina and the younger Agrippina (whom he had recalled from exile soon after Caligula's death). Messalina was an unbridled voluptuary, whose licentiousness could not be satisfied by the ordinary intrigues of a corrupt court; Agrippina had inherited the masterful temperament of her mother, the wife of Germanicus, and exhibited an undisguised lust for power. Both these empresses were quite unscrupulous in the means by which they sought to gratify their fancies, and both used their influence with the emperor to remove those who stood in their way. They exploited the insouciance of Claudius or played upon his fears of conspiracy, which indeed were not wholly groundless. In the second year of his reign the governor of Dalmatia, Camillus Scribonianus, had combined with a nobleman named Annius Vinicianus in a plot recalling that of Lentulus Gaetulicus in the previous reign. In 48 another nobleman, C. Silius, was tempted by Messalina's infatuation for him to covet Claudius's place, and he would probably have carried his point, had not the freedman Narcissus summoned the Guards betimes to execute summary justice upon both, while Claudius stood dazed. These and several lesser conspiracies kept the emperor in such a state of alarm that he caused all visitors to the palace to be searched, and gave a ready ear to the charges brought by his wives. The insecurity which Romans of high rank felt in the later days of Claudius was even greater than in the Terror under Tiberius, for his victims were tried behind closed doors, or executed out of hand.[16]

Claudius's wives: Messalina and the younger Agrippina

More conspiracies and executions

By his marriage with Messalina Claudius had

a daughter Octavia and a son Tiberius Claudius, surnamed Britannicus after the emperor's victories in Britain (p. 373), who became heir apparent. But the claims of Britannicus were crossed by his stepmother Agrippina, who was determined to supplant him in favour of her own son by a previous marriage, L. Domitius Ahenobarbus. In A.D. 50 Agrippina induced the unsuspecting Claudius to adopt her child (who was hereupon named Nero Claudius Caesar), and to betroth him to Octavia. But the transfer of Britannicus's heritage had not been definitely accomplished when Claudius died suddenly (A.D. 54). Agrippina, however, had already come to an arrangement with the praetorian prefect Afranius Burrus, who now presented Nero to his troops and secured their allegiance with the customary promise of a bounty. The Senate for the third time in succession confirmed the choice of the praetorian cohorts. The promptness with which Agrippina filled the vacancy caused by her husband's death gives apparent support to the prevalent belief that she had poisoned him; but it is an open question whether she made or took her opportunity.[17]

Agrippina secures the succession for Nero

If during his last four years, Claudius's powers were failing and he was unduly dominated by his wife and freedmen, this subservience had not existed earlier, at any rate to a like degree, although hostile sources asserted it. Sufficient imperial enactments survive in inscriptions and papyri, which bear the imprint of Claudius's own mind and style, to show that he personally played his part in administration.[18] Further, he should be given full credit for skill in choosing good servants, whether palace freedmen or generals for the forces. His principate started well: he cancelled Caligula's acts, allowed exiles to return and dropped treason-trials in the Senate. Towards the Senate he tried to follow a policy of co-operation on Augustan lines; he showed it outward respect, used *senatus consulta* frequently, and held the consulship only four times, although his revival of the censorship in 47–48 offended senators.[19] He also tried to ensure that it worked efficiently; this involved some encroachments on its activities, including greater opportunities for Equites, but above all the creation of his new centralised administration with its new departments, run by freedmen, led to greater governmental efficiency at the expense of the Senate. This new bureaucracy was needed to deal with the growing complexity of business which the emperor had to handle, not least in the field of finance. Equally unpopular was the personal interest that Claudius took in jurisdiction, where he also aimed at greater efficiency as well as equity. A less pleasant aspect

Claudius's adminis tration

was when he judged criminal cases himself *intra cubiculum principis*. More popular were his public works, as the great harbour works at Ostia, the Aqua Claudia at Rome, the draining of the Fucine Lake and his new roads (e.g. continuing the Via Valeria as the Via Valeria Claudia to the Adriatic). In religious policy he was conservative, but tolerant to foreign cults where he regarded them as harmless to older Roman ideas. Thus in 47 he celebrated the Secular Games, to coincide with the eight-hundredth anniversary of the foundation of Rome; he followed Tiberius's sensible and restrained attitude towards emperor-worship (he told the Alexandrines that he did not want a high priest or temples, 'since I do not wish to be offensive to my contemporaries'); but he decreed the complete suppression of Druidism, and although he restored freedom of worship to the Jews throughout the Empire, he nevertheless in 41 denied the Jews in Rome the right to hold meetings (other than those of their synagogues?) to stop proselytising and later in 49 expelled them because of some disturbance, while he took a strong line with the restless Jews in Alexandria.

Claudius felt that the time had come when Augustus's advice about not extending the Empire might be modified. For varied reasons he added no fewer than five new provinces: Mauretania (two provinces), Britain, Thrace and Lycia (see the next chapter). In the north the Frisii and Chauci were checked, and a colony was established at Cologne, named Colonia Agrippinensis in honour of Claudius's wife. Noricum was entrusted to an equestrian procurator in place of a *praefectus*, and control of Achaea and Macedonia was restored to the Senate. Judaea, which Claudius had given back to his friend Herod Agrippa, was allowed to revert to provincial status on Agrippa's death in 44, but Commagene was restored to its king, Antiochus IV. Claudius was less jealous than Augustus of the rights of Rome and Italy, and tried to raise the status of the provinces by generous grants of Roman citizenship and municipal rights, and even by opening the Senate to more provincials from Gaul. Thus his provincial policy was imaginative and in line with Rome's more liberal traditions.

Claudius and the Empire

4. Nero (54–68)

The new emperor was the antithesis of his mother and of his paternal ancestors, a headstrong line of aristocrats, of whom Caesar's former antagonist, L. Domitius (pp. 266 f.), might serve as a type.[20] By nature an amiable child,

Nero a weakling, and a dilettante

32.6 Nero.

whose passions or fears needed to be roused before he would resort to harsh measures, he lacked staying power, and his robust frame concealed a weak will. A dilettante to his fingertips, he amused himself with gymnastics or horse-racing, with music, painting and literary composition.

At the outset of the reign of Nero, who was but sixteen years of age at his accession, his mother Agrippina became involved in a struggle for the regency with Burrus and the prince's tutor, L. Annaeus Seneca, the foremost man of letters of his day (pp. 396 f.). Though Burrus and Seneca owed their advancement to Agrippina, they asserted themselves against her attempt to exercise an undisguised domination in political affairs such as no Roman woman had as yet ventured to claim for herself. In this conflict they carried with them the young emperor, who soon tired of his mother's admonitions to 'be a king' and to live laborious days.[21] Agrippina, who loved power more than Nero, sought compensation in a sudden affection for Britannicus; but so long as Burrus commanded the praetorian cohorts, her chances of a successful military coup in favour of her stepson were slight, and the sudden death of Britannicus in 55 removed the only possible rival to the emperor. That Britannicus was a victim of foul play is hardly open to doubt;[22] but it is uncertain whether the murder was planned by Nero himself, or who his accomplices were. After this rebuff Agrippina resigned herself to the part of a dowager; but three years later she brought on a new conflict by interceding on behalf of Nero's consort Octavia against his paramour, Poppaea Sabina. The wife of one of Nero's boon companions (the future emperor Otho), Poppaea had set herself to win the emperor's own hand, and in all probability it was under her influence (and with the connivance rather than the active support of Seneca and Burrus) that he was induced to clear the path to his remarriage by taking the life of his mother. The murder was carried out by the admiral of the fleet at Misenum, a freedman named Anicetus. After an abortive attempt to drown her in a collapsible boat on the Bay of Naples,[23] Anicetus broke into her residence and had her crudely battered to death. The emperor, who felt little remorse but had a lively fear of public opinion, was helped out by Seneca with the pretence that Agrippina had plotted against the emperor, an explanation which those who knew of her past were half prepared to believe (A.D. 59).

The emperor's first impulse after the death of his mother was to give free rein to his artistic ambitions. In 59 and 60 he instituted two new festivals, the Iuvenalia (to celebrate the first clipping of the imperial beard) and the Neronia, in which contests of charioteering, music and dancing were held on the model of the Greek national games. At these functions he gave a public exhibition of his 'celestial voice'; the paid claque which he had prudently organised was scarcely needed.

During the ministry of Seneca and Burrus the government of Nero followed a cautious but efficient administrative routine. The emperor's pranks as yet did not give rise to serious scandal, and outside his own family he had spilt hardly any blood. But the death of Burrus in 62, followed by the retirement of Seneca, whose position at court now became insecure, marked a turning-point in Nero's reign. In the same year Nero got rid of his wife Octavia, whose divorce he had delayed while Seneca's influence endured. Having elicited from his handyman Anicetus a false confession of adultery with Octavia he banished her and shortly afterwards put her to death. His subsequent marriage with Poppaea had little effect upon the character of his reign. But one of the two praetorian prefects whom he appointed in place of Burrus, Ofonius Tigellinus, proved Nero's evil genius, for it was under his influence that the government was perverted into an irresponsible despotism on Caligula's model.

In his quest for novel amusements Nero now broke into a mad gallop of open profligacy that might have brought blushes to the cheek of Messalina. At the same time his fondness for horse-racing and musicianship became a consuming passion, to which the public interests were frankly sacrificed. The emperor culminated his career as a virtuoso of circus and opera by a tour through Greece in 67–68, during which he collected a bouquet of 1800 crowns at the classic festivals of the land of the Muses. His imperious showmanship not only caused him to neglect urgent public business, but involved him in a riotous expenditure which threw the state finances into grave embarrassment (p. 362).

His quarrels with Agrippina

Murder of Britannicus

Murder of Agrippina

Nero's exhibitions of artistry

Good administration by Burrus and Seneca

Evil influence of Tigellinus

Nero's artistic tour in Greece

Lastly, in the later years of Nero the terror of previous reigns was renewed. In order to raise new revenue by confiscation, and to stifle rising murmurs of discontent. Tigellinus played upon the emperor's fears and induced him to unleash the professional informers, whom Burrus and Seneca had held in check. Under Tigellinus's régime a few personages of high standing were accorded the privilege of an open trial before the Senate, but the charge of *maiestas* was now expanded to cover every manifestation of independence. A notorious case in 66, when an ex-consul and Stoic philosopher named P. Paetus Thrasea was condemned to death for an occasional veiled criticism of the emperor, surpassed the worst abuses of the law of *maiestas* under Tiberius (two other leading Stoics also suffered, one death, the other exile). More commonly, however, the accused received a curt order to commit suicide without the chance of offering a defence. Among those who were compelled to take their lives at short notice were Nero's former minister Seneca, and C. Petronius, a versatile writer (p. 397) and the organiser of the court's amusements, whose educated taste and pretty wit excited the jealousy of the more coarse-grained Tigellinus.

Nero's hand was especially heavy upon men of wealth,[24] and upon the survivors of the republican nobility whose pedigree seemed to mark them down as possible pretenders. But his victims also included some of the poorest and least formidable inhabitants of Rome. In 64 a great conflagration swept the centre of the town for over a week and consumed some of its most crowded quarters. This disaster was beyond doubt the result of accident; and the emperor deserved some credit for the vigorous measures of relief which he instituted for the homeless, and the rules which he laid down for the more scientific reconstruction of the devastated areas (p. 365). On the other hand Nero forfeited whatever goodwill he might have earned by appropriating for his own use some 120 acres of the burnt-out region between the Palatine and Esquiline hills, and laying them out as a pleasure-ground, in which a sumptuous new palace, the Domus Aurea, was erected for him. The cry therefore went up that he had fired Rome of set purpose in order to obtain at reduced prices the building-land which he coveted, and it was rumoured that he had celebrated the occasion by singing an aria on the burning of Troy.[25] The emperor, taking fright, cast about for a scapegoat, and Tigellinus helped him out by laying hands on the members of the newly formed Christian community in the capital.[26] An unknown number of victims was condemned on a mere profession of faith, and burnt or otherwise tortured to death.[27] Nevertheless the populace persisted in its belief that Nero was the real culprit, while his ruthless cruelty excited pity for the victims and thus increased his unpopularity.

Finally, Nero put to death without trial several of his military commanders on the frontiers, among whom his former generalissimo on the Euphrates front, Cn. Domitius Corbulo (pp. 369), had long enjoyed his special confidence.[28] By these precautionary executions the emperor fomented rather than stifled treason, for they were an encouragement to the others to get their blow in first. Nor did he have to wait long (p. 402).

In A.D. 54 young Nero had made a modest start. He promised to end secret trials and to respect the Senate and senators and allowed his predecessor to be named Divus, thereby himself becoming *divi filius*. Although he held a consulship in 55, 57 and 58, he declined the offer of a perpetual consulship in 58. He was content that policy should be guided by Seneca and Burrus and aimed at the well-being and economic prosperity of the Empire. Although Trajan's praise for the *quinquennium Neronis* may have had another application, it does help to emphasise that the early years of Nero's Principate witnessed good administration.[29] Financial policy was prudent, the food-supply was safeguarded, depopulation in Italy was checked by colonisation, and Nero even played with the idea of abolishing all indirect taxation. These happier days did not survive the year 62 when deterioration set in: treason-trials started again. Financial strains developed, arising from Nero's extravagance, the fire in Rome and the debasement of the coinage. His public display of his artistic talents and his increasing concentration on them at the expense of public duties, combined with his increasing employment of freedmen, Greeks and Orientals in high positions, united to heighten the growing animosity of Senate and people. Further hatred was engendered in Stoic circles, and finally Nero unwisely turned against some of his army commanders.[30] As conspiracies developed so did his cruelty, autocracy and megalomania. The last was reflected in the magnificent pageant in 66 when he crowned Tiridates in Rome, and was worshipped by him as Mithras, and by his triumphant progress through the festivals of Greece (including a crown of victory at a race in Olympia, although he had fallen from his chariot and had not completed the course), while his gift of 'freedom' to Greece was more theatrical than meaningful. Lastly, foreign affairs became more threatening as his reign advanced (see the next chapter). True, he made few pro-

A new reign of terror under Tigellinus

The great fire of Rome

Execution of the Christians in Rome

Gradual deterioration

vincial changes (the Alpes Cottiae were made a small procuratorial province, and eastern Pontus was incorporated in Galatia) and his ambitious schemes for campaigns in the Caucasus area and in Abyssinia did not mature, but there were three serious rebellions. That of Boudicca in Britain was crushed only after the province had been overrun; whatever the nature of Nero's Armenian policy it led to the defeat at Randeia; thirdly, the raging fire in Judaea was not quenched until after his death. Thus in general Nero during his later years tarnished the brighter hopes of his earlier reign: this was also the tragedy of his three predecessors.

5. Constitutional Developments

At the death of Augustus his system of government had won general approval, and a restoration of the Republic, even in a limited sense, was henceforth out of the question. On his accession Tiberius gave the Senate an opportunity of revising the imperial prerogative, and in view of his lack of self-confidence it may be assumed that his apparent reluctance to step into the place of Augustus was more than a formal challenge to the House. But the Senate, 'making a rush into servitude', insisted on maintaining Augustus's prerogative undiminished, and it cut off all retreat for itself by conferring Tiberius's powers upon him for life. Henceforth Augustus's prerogative was voted *en bloc* to each new emperor without any restrictions of time. After the murder of Caligula the Senate, exasperated by his tyranny, toyed with the idea of restoring the Republic, but was soon forced to reject it as impracticable.

Tiberius receives Augustus's powers undiminished

If the good results of Augustus's monarchy prevented any reaction against it, they also stood in the way of any rapid advance beyond it. Each new emperor deemed it politic to promise that he would tread in Augustus's footsteps. But the tentative and inchoate character of Augustus's constitution invited and almost compelled modifications of it on points of detail. Under the next four emperors a process of constitutional development went on, by which effective political power was still further concentrated in their hands.

Further centralisation of power

During Tiberius's reign one of the sheet-anchors of the republican consitution was slipped when the election of magistrates was transferred from the Popular Assemblies to the Senate; under Augustus the Comitia's voice had been almost smothered (p. 321), but now the people had merely to rubber-stamp the Senate's decision. In the reign of Tiberius the legislative functions of the Comitia also fell into abey-

The Comitia fall into disuse

ance, and no serious attempt was ever made to revive them, although later emperors now and then, as the fancy took them, submitted their measures to the people for confirmation. The common citizens could still give expression to their political opinions by organised clamour at the public festivals (which the emperors were not unwilling to use as a sounding-board), or by posting up pasquinades on the walls of Rome.[31] But their constitutional powers, which indeed had become almost farcical in the last days of the Republic, were to all intents and purposes abolished.

No formal change of any consequence was made in the functions of the surviving magistrates. In 47 Claudius resuscitated the long-defunct censorship, in order to number the citizens and revise the Senate-lists. In thus assuming the right to enrol senators directly (instead of appointing them by the indirect method of nomination to a magistracy), he created a precedent which eventually had important effects (p. 410); but for the time being no further *lectiones senatus* took place. But while the position of the magistrates remained to outward appearances as before, their sphere of competence was being insensibly restricted by the encroachments of the new professional executive.

Claudius's censorship

Of all the republican institutions the Senate showed the greatest vitality. Under the Julio-Claudian emperors it not only retained the rights left to it by Augustus, but had its range of functions enlarged. It continued to supervise the magistrates in Rome and in the Italian municipalities,[32] and the proconsuls in the more peaceful provinces. It was frequently consulted by the emperors on general questions of policy and of fresh legislation. As we have seen, Tiberius was at pains to elicit from it a free expression of opinion – in one division he was left in a minority of one! – and only under Caligula and in the later days of Nero was its liberty of speech endangered. Tiberius transferred to the Senate the choice of the annual magistrates, which he withdrew from the Comitia, thus endowing it with powers which it had never claimed under the Republic. These powers, it is true, were exercised subject to the emperor's overriding right of nomination or commendation (p. 319), but Tiberius made sparing use of these. He did not commend more than four men for the twelve praetorships, and *commendatio* was not at first employed for the consulship, though it was extended to this office before the end of Nero's reign. The emperor could also 'nominate' candidates, thereby giving them moral but not legal backing; he apparently nominated twelve candidates for the praetorship, but since four places were already pre-

The Senate receives full electoral powers

empted by his commendation, the Senate was left free to choose eight from the twelve or from any nomination accepted by the presiding magistrate. Under the standing rule by which ex-quaestors passed *ex officio* into the Senate this assembly now in effect became a co-opted body.

Tiberius also further developed the judicial functions of the Senate as a high criminal court of law (p. 318). In this capacity its competence extended to all cases in which the accused was a personage of high rank – a member of the ruling family, of the equestrian class or of its own order. In entrusting these new duties to the Senate, Tiberius no doubt intended to devolve prosecutions of an invidious character upon its shoulders. But even in cases of a political complexion he gave the Senate a free hand to find its own verdict, and in trials which did not directly affect the emperor (such as impeachments of provincial governors for extortion) it habitually exercised an unfettered judgment.[33]

On the other hand the Senate's administrative business was cramped by the fiscal reforms of Claudius (p. 362), which gave the emperor more control over the *aerarium*. Moreover, for every occasion on which the House took an independent line in debate there were several on which it refused to commit itself. If the emperor attended in person senators would hang on his every word and gesture in order to ascertain his views and echo them; if he absented himself they found excuses for coming to no decision at all.

For advice on the more important questions of public policy the emperors were driven to rely on their personal confidants. The Consilium Principis which Augustus had created (p. 322) does not formally seem to have survived Tiberius's withdrawl from Rome to Capri in A.D. 26. On the other hand the emperors relied increasingly on the *amici Caesaris*, men of various backgrounds who had been summoned to act as assessors in a judicial inquiry or for general consultation; the *amici* should not be rigidly divided into two categories in accordance with the nature of their advice, whether judiciary or non-judiciary. But the emperor's court – that is, the emperor assisted by his advisers, which was a high court parallel to the Senate with its new judicial functions – became increasingly important.

Under Tiberius the professional executive which Augustus had instituted underwent no rapid extension. The only notable development during his reign was the increasing importance of the *praefectus urbi* after the emperor's retirement to Capri. In this period the City Prefect acquired a regular jurisdiction in criminal cases

(by standing delegation from the emperor). On the other hand a great development in the imperial executive took place under Claudius. The number of the *procuratores* who collected taxes and rents on the emperor's account was considerably increased, and their powers were enlarged by the transfer of jurisdiction in questions involving imperial finance in senatorial provinces from the proconsul to imperial procurators. Efficiency was increased in Italy by the establishment of a *procurator aquarum*, a *procurator ad ripas Tiberis*, a *procurator portus Ostiensis*, and a *procurator de Minucia* (the last, not certainly Claudian, helped the Praefectus Annonae with the distribution of the corn-dole at the Porticus Minucia in Rome). More important were the administrative departments which he set up (p. 356), with their freedmen heads: *ab epistulis, a rationibus, a libellis*, and *a studiis*. In enlarging the functions of the professional executive Claudius no doubt acted on the advice of his freedmen, who brought to their own work a professional training and were not born in the Roman tradition of unpaid amateur service in public affairs. From this point of view his reign is an important link in the transition from a republic to a centralised monarchy.

Under the Julio-Claudian dynasty the imperial household began to take on the appearance of a royal court. Caligula and Nero lived in a luxury that would have scandalised Augustus, and the younger Agrippina's robes of state might well have shocked Livia. The claims of these two emperors to semi-divinity and their consequent behaviour contrast vividly with the simple personal life of Augustus in his modest house on the Palatine, so unlike the vast Golden House which Nero regarded as a worthy setting for his genius. Though their domestic staff did not yet include personages of high social rank in the office of a Lord Chamberlain or Chief Steward, the menial functionaries attached to the palace grew into a veritable army. The *liberti* and *servi Caesaris* comprised not only the personal attendants of the imperial family, but a considerable number of skilled industrial workers, who carried out constructional repairs, refurnished the imperial wardrobes, and went some way to convert the imperial household into a self-contained economic unit.[34]

Lastly, Claudius effected a minor usurpation which had a curiously far-reaching result. Though this emperor, unlike his two predecessors, had never been adopted into the *gens* Iulia, but remained in the Claudian *gens* to the end of his life, he assumed the *cognomen* of Caesar, which had hitherto been peculiar to the Iulii.[35] His example was followed by later

The Senate becomes a high court of law

The Senate shirks responsibility

Development of the Consilium Principis

Growth of the imperial executive

Increase of the palace retinue

emperors, so that these came to be known collectively as the 'Caesars'.

6. Finance

Under the successors of Augustus his financial system underwent a natural development towards greater centralisation in the hands of the emperors. Tiberius, however, made no encroachments on the powers of the *aerarium*, and pursued a careful financial policy. He increased the imperial revenues by terminating concessions to mining companies whose properties were transferred to the management of imperial procurators. In 33 he alleviated a crisis which had arisen from a shortage of currency, by establishing a loan-fund of 100,000,000 sesterces from which debtors could borrow without interest. His concern for sound finance was occasionally carried to the verge of parsimony. In his refusal to spend large sums on public amusement he set a good, indeed too good, an example. But his too tender regard for the newly established *aerarium militare* (p. 342) tempted him to continue Augustus's dangerous policy of delaying the dismissal of time-expired soldiers — an expedient which led to a brief but alarming mutiny of the Rhine and Danube armies in the first year of his reign. Yet in the face of actual distress Tiberius gave prompt and generous relief. His concessions to the victims of fires and earthquakes were not limited to Italy but enjoyed also by provincial cities in distress; he was equally open-handed in giving subventions to senatorial families who had fallen on evil days. At the end of his reign the total surplus of assets in the emperor's balance-sheet is stated to have amounted to *c.* 2,700,00 sesterces, say five or six times his annual revenue;[36] but in view of the heavy liabilities of the emperors in times of active warfare this accumulation of funds cannot be considered excessive.

Tiberius's sound finance

Surplus in the Treasury

Tiberius's savings were dissipated in three years by the riotous extravagance of Caligula. Taxation, which had been slightly lowered under Tiberius, was aggravated by several new imposts. Foodstuffs, which had hitherto been exempt from the tax on sales, no longer escaped their quota, and percentages were taken from the earnings of porters and prostitutes. An incidental but enduring innovation of Caligula's reign was the transference to Rome of the chief imperial mint, which Augustus had established in Lugdunum (p. 343).

Extravagance of Caligula

Caligula's new taxes were remitted by Claudius, under whom the treasury was again made solvent, and some anomalies and incoherencies inherited from the financial system of Augustus

Financial reforms under Claudius

were ironed out, so that Claudius and his servants gained greater control.[38] Although he probably did not establish a centralised *fiscus* in Rome (i.e. a Treasury where he kept public money), the imperial provincial *fisci* (p. 342) were more carefully organised through the development of the office of *a rationibus*. The accounts of his vast personal fortune (*patrimonium* or *fiscus*), namely the *ratio patrimonii*, were kept by a *procurator a patrimonio*, while Claudius appointed a *procurator vicesimarum hereditatum* to administer the inheritance tax; his procurators also, as we have seen, secured more financial authority in senatorial provinces. When Claudius received the right to appoint quaestors to administer the *aerarium*, clearly his influence over it increased. In fact he may not have been accountable for monies he drew from it, since any formal vote of funds to the emperor would be made at his accession without time-limit. The chief credit for this administrative overhaul may well belong to the freedman Pallas, whose fortune of between 300,000,000 and 400,000,000 sesterces was not wholly unearned. Its effect was reinforced by the gradual increase in the revenue of the newer imperial provinces as the economic development of these progressed. The emperor's purse therefore soon recovered from the raids which Caligula had made upon it.

The *aerarium*, however, began to fall into low water, so that an adjustment was made in the early part of Nero's reign, when he claimed to be aiding the state treasury to the tune of 60,000,000 sesterces annually, probably by surrendering the grain tribute to the *aerarium*. In return for these concessions two imperial prefects (ex-praetors) replaced quaestors at the *aerarium* in 56. Nero's most famous financial move was his proposal to abolish all the indirect taxes (*vectigalia*) in the Empire, which were collected by the hated *publicani*; the scheme was dropped, perhaps because it would presumably have involved some increase in the direct taxes which would have been more unpopular than the checking of publicans would have been popular. At first this moderate financial policy allowed Nero to provide special bounties for the victims of natural calamities, in accordance with the best traditions of Tiberius. But under the régime of Tigellinus the imperial finances, which were embarrassed not only by Nero's extravagance but also by the results of the great fire, were plunged into bankruptcy. To meet the mounting deficits Nero did not reimpose Caligula's taxes, but he relapsed from Augustus's high standard of probity in the issue of coinage. He added an alloy to the silver and reduced the metal content of both gold and silver by

Nero's finances

a tenth or less; this brought them into a better ratio with each other and with a fine new series of *aes* coinage that he also initiated in 64 (including some of the finest ever produced in Rome: Nero was not an artist for nothing). This depreciation was not a good precedent, but it was less serious than the steady drain of precious metals to the East in payment for luxury goods. But neither this expedient nor the confiscations of rich men's estates (p. 359) sufficed to check the drain on the treasury. At the end of Nero's reign the pay of the troops had fallen into arrears, and the loyalty of the Roman army, which had scarcely wavered since the days of Augustus, was fatally undermined.

7. Rome and Italy

Under Tiberius the city of Rome scarcely had a history. The only new public buildings of any note were a temple for the worship of *divus Augustus* and the new barracks for the Guard, at Castra Praetoria, built in brick-faced concrete. The emperor made no addition to the new municipal services of Augustus, except by the institution of a permanent Tiber Conservancy Board (the *curatores alvei Tiberis*). He gave a special bread subsidy (for the benefit of those not on the free list) in A.D. 19, which was a year of high prices, and in 36 he provided a relief fund for the victims of a conflagration on the Aventine. But he disdained to curry favour with the populace by a lavish supply of public entertainments. In this respect he was so niggardly that a speculative impresario gave a display of gladiators in the neighbouring village of Fidenae; unfortunately the stands collapsed under the weight of the assembled multitudes, and 50,000 persons were reported killed or injured. Tiberius's best contribution to the welfare of the capital probably lay in his rigorous maintenance of public order. But the emperor showed poor judgment in reverting to the futile

The curatores alvei Tiberis

Tiberius's police measures

32.7   Porta Praenestina (Maggiore). These two monumental arches carried the Aqua Claudia and the Anio Novus over the Via Praenestina and the Via Labicana. They were incorporated by Aurelian into his city-wall as a fortified double gateway.

eviction orders of the republican administration. In A.D. 19 he expelled, by means of a senatorial resolution, all Jews and votaries of Isis who were without Roman franchise. By an arbitrary act of conscription he impressed 4000 Jewish freedmen, and sent them on special service to the unhealthy station of Sardinia.

For the security of Italy Tiberius maintained Augustus's special police for the suppression of brigandage, which was virtually stamped out under his reign. Though he once expressed to the Senate a somewhat superfluous concern at Rome's dependence on grain from overseas, he deprecated any government action to stimulate the productivity of Italy. His policy of *laissez-faire* received seeming justification in 33, when the Senate called upon all persons of substance to invest two-thirds of their capital in Italian land. The sudden calling in of the debts which

Laissez-faire in Italy

followed this measure precipitated the financial crisis, mentioned above, which was not allayed until the emperor provided a special loan-fund out of his own chest.

Caligula left a solitary monument of good sense in a pair of new aqueducts, the Aqua Claudia (with a channel of 30 miles) and the new Anio Novus (with a length of 55 miles), which his successor completed. The special concern of Claudius was for the corn-supply of the capital, which Augustus's new organisation had failed to make perfectly secure, because of the losses attendant on the transportation of the grain from Egypt and Africa and the difficulties of using the Tiber estuary, which was becoming blocked with accumulations of silt. Claudius's engineers circumvented the harbour-bar by constructing a new outlet to a point about two miles north of the old river-mouth. At the entrance

Caligula's new aqueducts

Claudius makes a new harbour at Ostia

32.8   Porta Tiburtina. The outer side. The earlier Augustan arch was incorporated in the Aurelian Wall as a gateway. Honorius added a second outer arch and rectangular towers.

to the new cut they excavated a capacious basin of some 200 acres, with two gigantic break-waters of hydraulic cement, and a lighthouse in the channel between these two arms.[38] As a further inducement to shippers to engage in the grain trade, he undertook to indemnify them for losses sustained on the open sea — an almost unique example of commercial insurance in ancient times.

For the better enforcement of order among the sailor rabbles of the harbour-towns Claudius enrolled two additional *cohortes urbanae,* which he stationed at Puteoli and at *Portus Augustus,* as the rebuilt town of Ostia at the new Tiber mouth was officially called. In 49 another futile expulsion order was launched by him against the Jews of the capital, whether or not because of a clash about the new emerging religion of Christianity remains uncertain (pp. 400 f.).

Claudius drains the Fucine Lake

Claudius left his mark on the countryside of Italy by carrying out Caesar's scheme for the draining of the Fucine Lake into the valley of the Liris. This undertaking absorbed the labour of 30,000 men for eleven years. Its results hardly repaid the expenditure incurred, for the land reclaimed was partly lost again through the choking of the outlet channel. To the costs of the excavation should be added the heavy loss of life in a gigantic *naumachia* (sea-fight) on the lake, with which the emperor celebrated the completion of the borings. For this combat 20,000 condemned men from all the municipalities of Italy were saved up.

Nero added many buildings to the capital, even in the early part of his reign, to which belong the start of a temple to the deified Claudius (finished by Vespasian), a great Provision Market, the Macellum Magnum, on the Caelian (56–57), a gymnasium for Greek games (61 or 62), and his notable Baths (Thermae Neronianae). Then, like London in 1665–6, the capital was visited by plague and fire in successive years (64–65). Nero not only rebuilt burned buildings, as the venerable temple of Vesta and the Circus Maximus, but planned the rebuilding of the city on more scientific lines in contrast with its earlier haphazard growth: a rectangular street-system and blocks of skyscrapers (*insulae*), with rules to ensure better spacing of the houses and the use of fireproof materials. The recurrence of similar, if less extensive, conflagrations raises a doubt whether these regulations were strictly enforced. Nero's best service to Rome lay perhaps in the maintenance of an excellent corn-supply. Apart from measures to help ship-owners he tried to secure a good supply by completing the Claudian harbour at Ostia and even planned a canal from Ostia to Lake Avernus (125 miles long) in order to improve access to Rome for seaborne goods, but like many of his grandiose projects the plan was abandoned at his death.[39] But while mindful of his public works, he undermined the popularity which these engendered by the greed with which he gratified his own architectural dreams. On the ground between the Esquiline and Caelian hills (where the Colosseum later stood) he started to build his vast Golden Palace (Domus Aurea) with its parks, lakes, colonnades and a colossal 120-foot-high statue of Nero himself, together with statues and works of art for which his agents ransacked Greece. This building was of considerable architectural importance (p. 387), but death overtook him before it was completed.

Nero's rules for the reconstruction of Rome

CHAPTER 33

The Roman Empire under the
Julio-Claudian Dynasty

1. Africa

The Roman frontiers tend to become fixed

With the notable exception of Claudius the successors of Augustus complied with his advice not to extend the Roman Empire beyond its existing boundaries. Tiberius, who had given ample proof of his military ability under the direction of Augustus, would not trust himself to wage war on his own responsibility, and the next three emperors were unfit to assume command of armies. But emperors who did not take the field in person had reason to fear that conquests achieved by other generals might lead to military usurpations, like those which had destroyed the rule of the republican Senate. Accordingly the warfare of the first half-century after the death of Augustus was mainly of a defensive character; in this period the Roman army began its transformation from a field force into a border garrison.

Annexation of Maure-tania

At the end of his reign Caligula caused a rebellion in Mauretania by putting to death its king, a son of Augustus's nominee Juba, named Ptolemy, on some trivial pretext. Under Claudius the revolt was suppressed, mainly by the services of C. Suetonius Paulinus (the future governor of Britain), who pursued the insurgents through the fastnesses of Mt Atlas to the confines of the Sahara (41–42). Claudius carried out the designs of his predecessor by converting the kingdom into two provinces, known respectively as Mauretania Caesariensis and Tingitana, from their capitals Caesarea (modern Cherchell) and Tingis (modern Tangiers), governed by equestrian procurators; both towns received colonies of Roman veterans. This some-

what premature annexation was not followed by any systematic opening up of the interior; but *praefecti* were appointed to supervise the tribal governments and to levy recruits for the Roman auxiliary forces.[1]

Another 'Jugurthan War' in Africa

In the province of Africa a Jugurthan War on a smaller scale was waged under Tiberius against a Numidian chieftain named Tacfarinas, who had deserted from the Roman forces and raided the Roman territory with nomad bands from the Sahara border. After four years of ineffectual campaigning (17–20) the Senate (in whose hands Augustus had, contrary to his general rule, left the frontier defence of Africa), requested Tiberius to take charge of the operations. The emperor's *legatus*, Iunius Blaesus, all but trapped Tacfarinas in a network of small field fortifications; but he shared the fate of Metellus Numidicus in being recalled before the final victory. Tacfarinas was finally put down and put to death by another imperial legate, P. Cornelius Dolabella, Seianus's uncle, in 24.[2] The only enduring consequence of this war was that Caligula permanently transferred the command of the African forces to an imperial officer, while leaving the civil administration in the hands of the senatorial proconsul. Africa now entered on a period of prosperity, as indicated by the number of public buildings that were constructed in Tiberius's reign at such places as Thugga and Bulla Regia; its corn also continued to be vital to Rome.

In 61–63 a detachment of praetorian troops carried out a reconnaissance up the valley of the Nile as far as the Sudd, the fenland on the White Nile, south of Khartoum, an area that was not rediscovered until 1839–40. The expedition, while perhaps partly pure exploration to discover the source of the Nile among other wonders, may have been a preliminary to a possible attack upon the king of Axum (Abyssinia), Zoscales, who was suspected of hostile intentions against Rome's subject-allies in south-western Arabia, and of a plan to place himself athwart the new Roman trade-route to the Indian Ocean (pp. 380f.). But after the death of Nero this project was abandoned.

2. Judaea[3]

In the eastern Mediterranean the chief area of disturbance under the early emperors lay in Palestine, where the Jewish population remained permanently restless under Roman rule. Under the terms of Augustus's settlement the Roman governors of Judaea had instructions to make allowance for the people's religious susceptibilities. At Jerusalem the High Priest, assisted by his council, the Sanhedrin, exercised the usual powers of local self-government and an unfettered religious jurisdiction. In recognition of these concessions the higher clergy and the larger landowners, who were strongly represented on the Sanhedrin, were generally acquiescent in Roman sovereignty and worked for a good understanding. But the Jewish people in general, whose latent antagonism to Gentiles had been awakened during the revolt of the Maccabees against the Seleucids (p. 167), clung to the hope that the day of deliverance from foreign rule might be at hand. The belief was rife that the promised Messiah would be a liberator like Samuel and David, and not a few sought to prepare the way for him by preliminary insurrections. Shortly after the Roman annexation in A.D. 6 armed opposition was offered to the Roman census officials, and bands of *sicarii* or knife-men, who disappeared into the desert when pressed hard by the Roman patrols, continually infested the country. In 40 a sudden reversal of Augustus's policy of religious tolerance on the part of Caligula, who ordered the Jews to set up his statue in the Temple at Jerusalem, all but caused a general rebellion in Palestine. Forewarned of the trouble that would ensue by the governor of Syria, P. Petronius, and by M. Iulius Agrippa ('Herod Agrippa'), a grandson of Herod the Great and a favourite at the Roman court, Caligula relented, then changed his mind, ordered the statue to be made and Petronius to commit suicide, but the emperor's timely death saved Petronius and prevented open revolt in Palestine. But the mere attempt to introduce emperor-worship there

Augustus's settlement of Judaea

Continued unrest in the province

Temporary kingdom of Herod Agrippa

strengthened the hands of the anti-Roman Zealots. A more happily inspired plan of Caligula, to install Agrippa on the throne of his grandfather, was rendered abortive by the premature death of the new king in 44.

As a province of no great military importance Judaea was entrusted to a governor of procuratorial rank, under the general supervision of the *legatus* of Syria. In their choice of procurators the emperors showed less than their usual perspicacity. The financial corruption of several procurators, and notably of Antonius Felix, a brother of Claudius's freedman Pallas (52–60), recalled the worst days of the Roman Republic. But the most serious fault of the Roman governors was the indiscriminate ferocity with which they repressed the recurrent disorders. Thus Pontius Pilate (26–36) had committed a series of blunders which culminated in the unnecessary massacre of some Samaritans on Mt Gerizim; true he was suspended and sent back to Rome by the legate of Syria, L. Vitellius, but such disciplinary action was not often exercised. Admittedly the governors had to face increasing social, political and religious unrest on a wide front, but nevertheless these Roman pogroms contributed more than anything else to bring about a state of war. In 66 an onslaught upon the Jewish residents by the Gentile population of Caesarea, which the procurator Gessius Florus allowed to take its course, led to a retaliatory rising at Jerusalem, which gave the upper hand to the 'Zealot' party. Overriding an attempt at mediation by Herod Agrippa II (a son of the former king of Judaea, who had received a small principality in Transjordania) the knifemen put the small Roman garrison under siege and massacred it after a capitulation on terms. At this stage the Jewish insurrection, which as yet was a mere mob-affray, could have been stifled with comparative ease if the Roman commanders had kept their heads. But the procurator Florus looked on quite helpless, and the *legatus* of Syria, Cestius Gallus, who presently brought up an army of some 30,000 men and began the investment of the citadel at Jerusalem, abandoned the siege through a sudden failure of nerve with the approach of winter, and made a disastrous retreat out of Palestine. After this fiasco the rebellion swept over the whole of Judaea and spread to Galilee and parts of Transjordania, and the various towns of Palestine became battlefields, in which Jews and Gentiles alike massacred whichever party was in the minority. At Jerusalem moderates and extremists combined for the moment to set up a war-administration, under whose direction the insurgent forces were organised and drilled.

But Nero made prompt amends for his past

The governors of Judaea at fault in their methods of repression

National Jewish rising under Nero

neglect of Jewish affairs. He conferred a special command upon an officer named T. Flavius Vespasianus, who was personally not in favour at court, but had a good military record, and was considered a safe man to place in charge of a large army because of his obscure origin. With a force exceeding 50,000 men at his back Vespasian systematically reduced Galilee in 67 and the Transjordanian lands in 68, so as to encircle the rebels in Judaea proper. At this stage he suspended his somewhat leisurely operations on the pretext that Nero, from whom he held his commission, had been deposed. But the Jews were no longer able to take advantage of their reprieve. The concord with which they had entered upon the war had not outlasted the first outburst of indignation against the Romans. At Jerusalem moderates and extremists came to open blows; on the war-front the resistance of the moderates became no more than lukewarm. The attitude of this party was reflected in the History of the Jewish War by Flavius Josephus, a young officer who played a prominent part in the early stages of the war, but made his surrender to Vespasian in 67, and was subsequently rewarded with Roman citizenship. At the end of Nero's reign the extremists retained the upper hand in Jerusalem, but Palestine as a whole had been recovered by the Romans. (For the sequel see pp. 415 ff.)

The antagonism between Jews and Gentiles, which was the more deep-seated cause of the Jewish War, also manifested itself in occasional riots in Levantine towns, where the Jewish residents came into collision with the Hellenised populations. These disputes usually arose out of attempts by the Greek element to deny to the Jews the special privileges which had been granted to them by the Hellenistic kings, and confirmed by Caesar (p. 274) and Augustus.[4] The chief centre of conflict was at Alexandria, where the large Jewish colony possessed its own Council of Elders and President, but claimed in addition citizen rights on a par with the Greek community. The latter, jealous of the Jews, had its own grievances (it perhaps lacked a Senate), and an anti-Roman element had grown up which, led by Isodorus and Lampon, was ever ready to face martyrdom in its nationalistic fervour: it produced its own literature which is often anti-Semitic and has been named the Acts of the Pagan Martyrs.[5] In 38 the Greeks seized the opportunity of denouncing the disloyalty of the Alexandrine Jews when these refused to accord to Caligula the divine worship which he demanded, and the prefect of Egypt, Avilius Flaccus, abetted attacks by Greek mobs upon the Jewish population. Flaccus was recalled and later put to death, while both Jews

and Greeks of Alexandria sent deputations to Caligula, the Jews being led by the philosopher and theologian Philo; Isodorus spoke for the Greeks. Caligula dismissed the Jewish deputation after pointing out that, although they might have sacrificed on his behalf, they had not sacrificed *to* him. On his accession Claudius issued two edicts, one confirming the privileges of the Alexandrine Jews, the other those of the Jews of the Dispersion. Nevertheless further disturbances broke out in Alexandria, and in 41 Claudius was approached by both sides, and his letter of reply survives in a papyrus fragment: in effect he knocked their heads together, warning them both to keep the peace in Alexandria, 'otherwise I shall be forced to show you what a beneficent prince can be when changed by just indignation'. He ordered the Greeks to be kind to the Jews, and the Jews to stop 'fomenting a general plague for all the world'.[6] In 53 a Greek deputation from Alexandria laid certain charges against Agrippa II before Claudius, but so far from succeeding, Isodorus and Lampon were condemned to death after insulting the emperor. In 66 the Alexandrian Jews were emboldened by the rebellion in Palestine to prepare violent action against the Greeks, but the Egyptian prefect, Tiberius Alexander, a renegade member of the Jewish community, used his troops to repress the assailants with ruthless severity. Apart from this abortive movement in Alexandria the Palestinian rebellion did not extend to the Jews of the Dispersion.

3. Armenia and Parthia

In Asia Minor occasional punitive expeditions were still required against the predatory tribes of Mt Taurus, but these dwindled to the scale of police operations. To facilitate the patrolling of the southern highlands the coast-land of Lycia and Pamphylia was constituted into a separate province in 43. A more important annexation was carried out in 17, when Tiberius reduced the kingdom of Cappadocia to a province, so as to strengthen the Roman frontier along the Euphrates. Commagene, in northern Syria, had an unsettled time; on the death of its king in 17 it was annexed by Tiberius. Caligula first restored it to King Antiochus IV and then deposed him, but Antiochus was reinstated by Claudius in 41 and reigned until deposed again by Vespasian in 72 (p. 422).

In relation to Armenia and Parthia the successors of Augustus carried on his policy of maintaining Roman authority with the smallest possible military effort. Their caution at times degenerated into sheer supineness; but it was

Reconquest of Judaea by Vespasian

Disputes between Jews and Greeks at Alexandria

Police operations in Asia Minor

Armenia and Parthia

matched by an equal irresolution on the part of the Parthian kings, so that if the Romans sometimes lost their ascendancy on the Euphrates they always ended by reasserting it. At the death of Augustus the Parthian ruler, Artabanus III, was not yet established firmly, and Armenia was in a state of anarchy. Yet Tiberius made no move until 18, when the Armenian nobility invited a prince from one of the lesser dynasties of Asia Minor to become king. The emperor appointed his nephew Germanicus, who had recently been sent on a tour of inspection in the eastern provinces, to confer the crown on the Armenians' nominee at Artaxata – a ceremony which Tiberius himself had performed forty years ago under very similar conditions (p. 333). The new king, Artaxes, reigned undisturbed until 35. At his death the Parthian king, Artabanus, who had acquiesced in the enthronement of Artaxes, but now sought to take advantage of Tiberius's senility, impelled one of his sons to seize Armenia for himself. The Roman dotard, however, requited this interference with a flash of unsuspected energy. He sprang upon Artabanus an adventurer from Iberia, named Mithridates, who beat the Parthian troops out of Armenia and secured the throne for himself; and he abetted a pretender of Arsacid blood, Tiridates, who temporarily drove Artabanus out of all his western provinces. The latter, it is true, presently recovered the lost provinces without opposition from the Romans, but he made no attempt to displace Mithridates in Armenia.

Mission of Germanicus

Tiberius recovers Armenia

Under the next two emperors the fruits of Tiberius's astute policy were wasted by sheer mismanagement. In summoning Mithridates to Rome and holding him in custody for no assignable reason Caligula made a present of Armenia to Artabanus, who occupied the country without resistance. Claudius at first succeeded in reinstating Mithridates with the help of a small Roman force, while Artabanus's successor, Gotarzes, was being kept in play by further dynastic dissension at home. But in 52 another Iberian adventurer, Mithridates's nephew Radamistus, invaded Armenia and treacherously killed his uncle, who was left in the lurch by the Roman garrison in his kingdom and received no support from the neighbouring Roman governors. In conniving at this act of brigandage the Romans played into the hands of a new and able Parthian king, Vologeses I, who helped the Armenians to get rid of the intruder Radamistus, and with their consent replaced him by his own brother, Tiridates (52–54).

Claudius loses Armenia

On the accession of Nero the Roman governor of Cappadocia, Iulius Paelignus, who had been chiefly responsible for the loss of Armenia, was replaced in 55 by an officer named Cn. Domitius Corbulo, who had served with distinction on the Rhine front (p. 371). The new governor's instructions were to offer negotiations to Vologeses, on the understanding that the Romans would recognise Tiridates, provided that he should formally receive his crown from a representative of Nero. On the refusal of Tiridates to accept this compromise Corbulo was authorised to invade Armenia with a largely increased army. After a year of hard training, which was necessitated by the habitually lax discipline of the Roman troops on the eastern frontiers, the Roman general made a bold march across the plateau of Erzerum into the valley of the Araxes.[7] In two rapid campaigns he captured and burnt Artaxata, and repeated Lucullus's march across the Armenian highlands to Tigranocerta (58–59). From this base he systematically overran Armenia during the next summer, so that Tiridates, who had in the meantime lost his brother's support because of a rebellion on the eastern borders of Parthia, evacuated his kingdom altogether. In 60 Corbulo settled the Armenian question for the time being by enthroning a prince named Tigranes, from the former royal family of Cappadocia.

The campaigns of Corbulo

In the following year the new Armenian ruler provoked Vologeses with a gratuitous raid into Mesopotamia. The Parthian king, who had by now recovered a free hand, retaliated by penning Tigranes up in Tigranocerta. To this challenge Corbulo, who had meanwhile been transferred to the more important province of Syria, replied by withdrawing Tigranes from Armenia and agreeing to reinstate Tiridates, on conditions of his acknowledging Roman suzerainty. Though these terms now proved acceptable to Tiridates, they were repudiated by Nero, so that a direct clash between Romans and Parthians was brought about. In the opening campaign of the Parthian War Corbulo remained studiously inactive in Syria, while the new governor of Cappadocia, L. Caesennius Paetus, endeavoured to rival his predecessor's exploits in Armenia (62). Advancing heedlessly through southern Armenia with a quite inadequate force Paetus allowed himself to be surprised by Vologeses at Rhandeia and headed off from his line of retreat, and in the absence of timely assistance from Syria he was compelled to surrender. By the terms of the capitulation the Romans evacuated Armenia, of which Tiridates now resumed possession (62–63). But it was now the turn of Paetus to be disavowed at Rome, while Corbulo received a somewhat undeserved promotion in being created generalissimo of all the forces on the Euphrates front. With an army raised by drafts from Europe to a strength of 50,000 Cor-

Abortive negotiations with Parthia

The Romans suffer a minor 'Carrhae'

369

bulo resumed his invasions of Armenia in 64, but he did not seriously engage his troops. The mere demonstration of Roman might brought a new peace offer from Vologeses, and Tiridates agreed to the demand that he should receive his crown from the emperor in person. In 65 and 66 the Armenian king journeyed to Rome, where he was solemnly invested by Nero in person and entertained right royally. The friendly relations thus established between Rome and the two eastern kingdoms lasted with scarcely an interruption for half a century. At Rome the temple of Janus was closed.

An Armenian king is crowned at Rome

In 64 Nero strengthened the Roman hold on the border-lands of Armenia by incorporating the kingdom of eastern Pontus into the province of Galatia. With this territory the Roman government took over the royal fleet and the duty of patrolling the farther end of the Black Sea. In the last years of his reign Nero resumed Pompey's plan of carrying the Roman frontier to the Caspian Sea by a permanent military occupation of the Albanian border-land;[8] but this project was never carried out, and after his death it again fell into oblivion. Fifty years of desultory warfare on the Armenian and Parthian front left the Roman boundaries substantially as they were. But from the time of Nero the Roman garrison along the Euphrates frontier was permanently increased at the expense of the Rhine and Danube sectors.

The Roman Black Sea fleet

4. The Danube Lands

In the Balkan regions the enlarged kingdom of Thrace which Augustus had formed (pp. 337 f.) was troubled under his successor by dynastic disputes, and by the inroads of Roman recruiting officers, who applied the methods of the press-gang in disregard of treaty rights. A revolt which this high-handed procedure caused in 25 was suppressed by the governor of Macedonia, Poppaeus Sabinus. In 46 Claudius ended this anomalous state of affairs by deposing the native dynasty and constituting Thrace as a province under a procurator. The northern part of the Thracian kingdom was attached to the province of Moesia, whose frontier was thus advanced eastward as far as the Black Sea.

Annexation of Thrace

The extension of Moesia formed part of a series of precautionary measures, by which the Romans met a recurrence of unrest in the region of the lower Danube. At this period a forward thrust by a nomadic folk from the central Asiatic grasslands, the Alans, was giving rise to a surge of peoples across the Russian steppe, so as to anticipate on a small scale the greater migrations of the fourth century, and was exerting pressure

Measures of defence on the lower Danube

upon the populations near the Danube estuary, which threatened to overflow into Moesia. About 62 a governor of Moesia, named Tib. Plautius Silvanus, relieved the strain on the Roman frontier by settling 100,000 expatriated Dacians on the southern bank of the Danube. As a further measure of security he annexed to his province a strip of territory in the Wallachian plain, to serve as a screen for the route along the Danube. Lastly, he contracted a system of alliances with the tribal chieftains of Moldavia and with the Greek cities of south-western Russia, in some of which he posted small Roman garrisons.[9] About this time a Roman detachment was also placed at the disposal of the dynasts of Crimea. In this region the settlement of Augustus had been overturned under Tiberius by a local chieftain named Aspurgus, who supplanted King Polemo (p. 338). The usurper was recognised by Tiberius, and he founded a dynasty which lasted to the fourth century. Apart from these movements on the Moesian border the Danube lands enjoyed half a century of freedom from war.

A Roman garrison in the Crimea

5. Germany

The reign of Tiberius opened with three years of heavy fighting in northern Germany, where the emperor's nephew Germanicus conducted a series of expeditions with the heavily reinforced armies of the lower Rhine. In 14 he made a preliminary foray into the basin of the Lippe, where he systematically devastated the land and butchered its inhabitants. In 15 and 16 he utilised the Rhine fleet to transport a division of his army through Drusus's canal to the Ems (Amisia), so as to join hands with the main divisions marching up the valley of the Lippe. In 15 the combined forces reached the scene of Varus's disaster and interred the remains of the fallen Romans; in 16 they advanced beyond the Weser and defeated the Cheruscan levies in two set battles, the first at Idistaviso near Minden. Germanicus now had hopes of completing the reconquest of western Germany in one further campaign. But Arminius succeeded in holding the north German tribes together, and the Romans sustained serious losses by battle and shipwreck. At the end of 16 Tiberius recalled his nephew, who had hoped to annex Germany as far as the Elbe.[10] Tiberius, however, allowed these campaigns not for the purpose of permanent conquest but rather as a show of force after which the tribes east of the Rhine would keep the area weak through their internal dissensions: the safety of the river-frontier did not demand far-spread occupation to the east.

The campaigns of Germanicus in Germany

Organisation of the Rhine frontier

Tiberius thus fell back on the scheme devised by Augustus (p. 336): eight legions in permanent camps and the two military zones of Upper and Lower Germany. A few outposts on the right bank of the middle Rhine remained in Roman occupation, but the forts on the Lippe were definitely abandoned. In 28 Tiberius made no move when the Frisii of the North Sea coast expelled their Roman *praefecti*. Apart from occasional punitive expeditions in retaliation for minor German raids (including a drive against the North Sea pirates in 47, in which Corbulo laid the foundations of his military reputation), the Roman armies on the Rhine front remained quiescent for half a century.

Inter-tribal war in Germany

Tiberius's policy of inactivity was justified by the early disruption of Arminius's war-coalition, and by the general renewal of internecine quarrels among the Germans as soon as the Romans relaxed the pressure upon them. In the year after Germanicus's departure Arminius led a coalition of nothern Germans against King Maroboduus and inflicted a heavy defeat upon him; but in 19 he was killed in a rising by his own tribesmen, who had followed him as a war-leader, but would not tolerate him as a king.

In 21 a passing wave of unrest spread over the Gauls, who had been suffering from increased taxation in connexion with the campaigns of Germanicus, and from the exactions of the usurers in the wake of the tax-gatherer.

Local risings in Gaul

Two noblemen who had won the Roman franchise, the Aeduan Iulius Sacrovir and the Treviran Iulius Florus, made secret preparations for a general uprising. But the rebellion went off at half-cock, and Roman detachments from the Rhine easily stifled the local movements which the two ringleaders attempted in their own cantons.[11]

Communications between Italy and the northern frontier were considerably improved by Claudius, who opened two new highroads across the Alps, the Brenner route to the Inn valley, and the Great St Bernard to the valley of the upper Rhône.[12]

6. The Conquest of Britain

Augustus's policy of non-intervention in Britain was followed by Tiberius as a matter of course. In 40 Caligula made a progress across Gaul and took personal command of a force which had been assembled at Gesoriacum (modern Boulogne), with the apparent intention of conducting it across the Channel. But he abandoned the projected invasion of Britain as abruptly as Napoleon in 1805.[13] Four years later, however, Claudius carried his predecessor's scheme into

Caligula's projected invasion of Britain

effect. The reasons which induced these emperors to resume an undertaking which Caesar and Augustus had renounced escape our knowledge. Invitations to intervene in British affairs were presented to them by several lesser chiefs who felt the growing power of Cunobelinus's dynasty: Amminius to Gaius and Verica to Claudius. Cunobelinus, who was succeeded by his two sons Caratacus and Togidubnus (40–43),

33.1 Tombstone of a Roman centurion (Colchester Museum). M. Favonius M(arci) f(ilius) Pol(lia tribu) Facilis > (= centurio) leg(ionis) xx (vicisimae). Verecundus et Novicius liberti posuerunt. H(ic) s(itus) e(st). (Marcus Favonius Facilis, son of Marcus, of the Pollian voting-tribe, centurion of the Twentieth Legion, lies buried here; Verecundus and Novicius, his freedmen, set this up.) The centurion wears a cuirass, belt, kilt, greaves and half-boots. He holds a centurion's staff (*vitis*) and his cloak is draped over his shoulder. With the tombstone was found pottery of *c*. A.D. 55.

ROMAN BRITAIN:
approximate Tribal Divisions

English Miles 0 25 50 75 100
Kilometres 0 50 100 150

CALEDONIAN
CONFEDERACY

(Cardean)
PINNA CASTRA
(Inchtuthil)
(Dalginross)
(Strageath)

DAMNONII
(Castledykes)
(Inveresk)
TRIMONTIUM
(Newstead)
VOTADINI
CARVETII SELGOVAE
BREMENIUM
(High Rochester)
BLATOOULGIUM
(Birrens) VERCOVICIUM
NOVANTAE (Housesteads)
(Glenlochar) PONS AELIUS (Newcastle)
CORSTOPITUM ARBEIA (South Shields)
LUGUVALIUM (Corbridge)
(Carlisle) BROCAVUM
(Brougham)

BRIGANTES
GLANNAVENTA
(Ravenglass)
ISURIUM
(Aldborough)
OLICANA PARISI
(Lancaster) (Ilkley) EBURACUM
BREMETENNACUM (York)
(Ribchester) PETUARIA
MAMUCIUM (Brough)
(Manchester) DANUM
(Doncaster) LINDUM
AQUAE (Lincoln)
DEVA ARNEMETIAE
CANOVIUM (Chester) (Buxton) CORITANI
(Caerhun) DECEANGLI CAUSENNAE
SEGONTIUM CORNOVII (Ancaster)
(Caernarvon) VIROCONIUM RATAE DUROBRIVAE VENTA
ORDOVICES (Wroxeter) (Leicester) (Water Newton) (Caistor)
MEDIOMANUM VENONAE I C E N I
(Caer Sws) (High Cross)
(Castle Collen) SALINAE DUROVIGUTUM DUROLIPONS
BREMIA (Droitwich) (Godmanchester) (Cambridge)
(Llanio) DOBUNNI LACTODORUM
ALABUM GLEVUM (Towcester) CATUVELLAUNI CAMULODUNUM
(Llandovery) (Gloucester) (Alchester) (Colchester)
DEMETAE VERULAMIUM TRINOVANTES
MORIDUNUM (St. Albans)
(Carmarthen) NIDUM SILURES CORINIUM LONDINIUM DUROBRIVAE
(Neath) ISCA (Cirencester) (London) (Rochester)
(Cardiff) (Caerleon) VENTA ATREBATES CALLEVA DUROVERNUM
(Caerwent) CUNETIO (Silchester) CANTIACI (Canterbury)
AQUAE SULIS (Mildenhall)
(Bath) BELGAE REGNENSES
VENTA
LINDINIS SORVIODUNUM (Winchester) NOVIOMAGUS ANDERITA
(Ilchester) (Old Sarum) (Chichester) (Pevensey)
ISCA CLAUSENTUM
(Exeter) DUROTRIGES (Bitterne)
DURNOVARIA PORTUS ADURNI
DUMNONII (Dorchester) (Portchester)

ICTIS
(St. Michael's Mount)

27. ROMAN BRITAIN: APPROXIMATE TRIBAL DIVISIONS

372

had created a powerful kingdom in south-east Britain, but it in no way threatened the security of Gaul.[14] Apart from a wish to improve Roman prestige after Caligula's fiasco, it is possible that the rumours of easily gotten riches that had lured Caesar to Britain gained a new lease of life under Caligula and Claudius: the prominent part which Claudius's freedman, Narcissus, took in organising the expedition suggests that quick returns were expected from it. But the predominant motive of Claudius probably was to obtain a military reputation for himself, so as to strengthen his somewhat uncertain hold upon the frontier garrisons.

Reasons for Claudius's invasion

In 43 an army of some 50,000 men under A. Plautius landed unopposed at Rutupiae (Richborough) in Kent, defeated Caratacus on the Medway and forced the passage of the Thames.[15] He then waited for the arrival of Claudius himself, who took part in the last critical stage of the campaign when the Roman troops defeated Caratacus in a set battle and captured his capital, Camulodunum (modern Colchester). While Claudius returned to Rome to celebrate a quickly earned success,[16] his lieutenants rapidly overran East Anglia and the south coast. Though the future emperor Vespasian had to sustain numerous battles in a westward march along the Channel, in other regions several chieftains made immediate submission. By 49 the Romans had reached the Severn estuary and the Wash, and Plautius perhaps, rather than his successor P. Ostorius Scapula (47–52), organised a military frontier-line (*limes*) based on the Fosse Way from Exeter to Lincoln.[17] To protect the new lowland province Ostorius disarmed all tribes south of the Fosse Way and intervened against the Brigantes, who occupied much of northern England, and against the Deceangli of Flintshire, advancing his troops to Uriconium (Wroxeter) in 49. He then turned to the Silures of south Wales with whom Caratacus had taken refuge, and established a legionary base at Glevum (Gloucester).[18] Caratacus managed to escape northwards but was defeated and was handed over to the Romans by the Brigantian queen Cartimandua; he was sent to Rome where Claudius treated his prisoner with due honour. Having thus strengthened the frontiers of the new province, Ostorius established a colony of veterans at Camulodunum, where the city was being developed as a provincial capital, with a temple to Claudius as the centre of the imperial-cult.[19]

Conquest of southern and eastern Britain

Conquest of the Midlands

After Ostorius's death in 52 Britain enjoyed comparative peace, though the Romans intervened to reinstate Cartimandua, who had been deposed by her consort. The next advance was made in 59 when Suetonius Paulinus, the con-

33.2 Triumphal arch surmounted by an equestrian statue between two trophies, celebrating Claudius's victory over the Britons.

queror of Mauretania (p. 366), decided to strike at Mona (the island of Anglesey), which was the centre of the Druids and formed a supply-base and refuge for all Rome's enemies. In 61 Suetonius crossed the Menai Strait and was busy felling the sacred groves and settling the island when news reached him that a rebellion had broken out in his rear. In East Anglia Roman tax-collectors and money-lenders were relentlessly exacting their dues from the tribe of the Iceni, who had recently been saddled with an indemnity for a minor rising; and a Roman procurator had confiscated the estate of the last king, under pretence of executing his will, in which the Roman emperor had been named part heir. At the same time the Trinovantes of Essex were complaining of encroachments on their land by Roman colonists established at Camulodunum. Under the leadership of Boudicca (Boadicea), the widow of the East Anglian king, the insurgents nearly engulfed the whole of the Roman garrison. They made short work of Camulodunum, which the settlers had not troubled to fortify; they drove back with heavy losses a legion under Q. Petillius Cerialis, which came to the rescue from Lindum (modern Lincoln); and though they could not prevent Suetonius from cutting his way back to Londinium they eventually carried this town and its neighbour Verulamium, for which the Roman governor could not spare a garrison. All the three towns were burnt to the ground by the insurgents, and their Roman or romanised inhabitants were massacred. But eventually the rebels played into Suetonius's hands by engaging him in battle on a site of his own choice, perhaps near Lichfield. Though the Roman force numbered only 10,000 to 15,000 men, by perfect battle-discipline it put the enemy host to complete rout, and the death of Boudicca, who had been the Vercingetorix of the revolt, left the Britons without a leader to rally them. A brief period of merciless reprisals followed, but on the advice of the more conciliatory new

The rebellion of Boudicca

A massacre in Londinium

33.3   Reconstruction of the Roman Palace at Fishbourne, Sussex.

Repression of the revolt

procurator, Julius Classicianus, Nero prudently recalled Suetonius, and under the next governors the English lowlands as far as the Humber and the Dee settled down under Roman rule. The kingdom of the Iceni and various minor principalities, whose chieftains had hitherto retained their title, were merged in the Roman province.

The extension of the Roman frontier across the Channel, and the warfare on the Euphrates front under Nero, necessitated a slight increase of the regular army establishment. But the troops required for these additional services were mostly found by drawing upon the forces quartered along the Rhine and the Danube and in Spain, where the Roman garrisons could now be somewhat reduced, while Nero was able to withdraw a legion even from Britain for service in the East.

7. The Provinces

New provinces

Under the Julio-Claudian dynasty the number of the Roman provinces underwent a considerable increase. Of the new provinces Britain alone was acquired by conquest. The two Mauretanias, Cappadocia, Thrace and the Alpes Cottiae (at the foot of Mt Cenis) were formed out of dependent kingdoms whose dynasties died out or were deposed. Raetia was detached from Gal-

lia Belgica under Tiberius or Claudius, and Pamphylia was separated from Galatia under the latter emperor.

The new system of administration which Augustus had devised for the provinces passed through a probationary period of a half-century, during which it was subjected to no important alterations. The general closing down of local mints in the western provinces under Tiberius was a measure of small practical importance, since their coinages had long been restricted to copper pieces. On the other hand the rebellions of the Jews, of Florus and Sacrovir in Gaul, and of Boudicca in Britain are evidence that the abuses which had crept into provincial government under the Republic had not been extirpated under the early emperors. A fresh ground for complaint was given to the provincials when Roman officials constrained them to undertake tax-collection and other public duties for which volunteers did not offer themselves. For the present this form of compulsion was mainly confined to Egypt, a land with a long tradition of forced labour; but it was the thin end of a highly destructive wedge.[21] The discontinuance by Augustus's successors of the first emperor's periodical tours of inspection in the provinces removed a wholesome check upon the Roman officials. A notable feature of provincial administration under the early emperors was that the worst mischief was usually

Deficiencies of the imperial administration

done by officials of subordinate rank, which suggests that insufficient care was taken in filling the lesser posts, or that a less vigilant control was exercised over them.[22]

Road construction

But the new sense of obligation towards the provincials which Augustus had inculcated by no means died out under his successors. The material welfare of the provinces was promoted by the construction of roads, which served the interests of trade no less than those of frontier defence. In the Danube lands Tiberius created a system of highways to match that of Agrippa in Gaul; and two new metalled roads across the Alps were built by Claudius (p. 371). During his stay in Greece Nero employed his praetorian guards in a laudable though unsuccessful attempt to cut a canal across the Isthmus of Corinth. Against the laxity of administration which attained its highest level in the later years of Tiberius and Nero must be set the vigour which these same emperors displayed at the outset of their reigns. Tiberius checked an over-zealous prefect of Egypt, who had sent more than the due amount of tribute to Rome by reminding him that 'a good shepherd should shear but not flay his flock'.[23] In 17 the same emperor came to the assistance of twelve cities of Asia Minor which had suffered severely from earthquakes, by remitting all their taxes for a term of five years. A vote of confidence in Tiberius's administration was passed in 15, when the provincial councils of Macedonia and Achaea petitioned him to transfer their territories from senatorial to imperial control. Tiberius acceded to this request, but Claudius handed back the two provinces to the Senate in 44. When complaints about the chicanery of the remaining companies of *publicani* reached the ears of the young Nero he boldly proposed the abolition of all indirect taxes; on second thoughts he issued a drastic ordinance to remedy the surviving abuses (p. 362). Above all, Tiberius and Nero encouraged the provincial parliaments to assume the part of watchdogs over the Roman officials. A regular procedure was instituted, by which deputies from the *concilia* collected incriminating evidence and presented it at Rome to the emperor or the Senate. In most of the recorded cases, which were especially frequent under Nero, the *concilia* obtained a sentence of exile or of expulsion from the Senate against the person denounced by them.

Solicitude of the emperors for the provinces

The concilia keep watch over the governors

Attitude of the emperors to provincial enfranchisement

The enfranchisement of the provincials received no fresh impetus from Tiberius, who merely maintained Augustus's practice of giving Roman citizenship to time-expired soldiers, and discontinued his predecessor's policy of founding Italian colonies on provincial soil. His successors, however, struck out a new line. Caligula

had spent his childhood with his father on the Rhine frontier; his sister Agrippina was a native of the Rhineland. Claudius was born in Gaul at Lugdunum, and as a student of Livy he realised clearly that the partnership of Rome and Italy, which had produced the Roman Empire, must be succeeded by a partnership of Italy and the provinces, if that empire was to be made durable. Of Nero's ministers, Seneca came from Cordoba in Spain, Burrus was probably a native of Vasio in southern Gaul. After the death of Tiberius the settlement of Italian veterans in the provinces was not resumed on any large scale. But under Claudius several colonies were constituted in Noricum and Pannonia, and two notable cities of Italian type were founded at the northern confines of the Empire, Colonia Claudia Camulodunum (modern Colchester) and Colonia Claudia Agrippinensis (Cologne) — the latter in memory of the birth of the younger Agrippina on that site. To Claudius a number of the native towns in Noricum and in Mauretania owed the gift of Roman franchise. The same emperor also used his authority as censor in 48 to place on the list of the Senate several chiefs from the tribe of the Aedui in central Gaul, and in answer to protests from the more conservative senators he unfolded his philosophy of empire in a speech whose text is in large part preserved.[24] Under Nero the Alpes Maritimae on the Italian border-land received the Latin franchise. Though Claudius and Nero felt their way step by step in true Roman fashion, and did not embark precipitately on the wholesale policy of assimilation, they definitely broke with the principle that the provinces should be kept on a lower plane than Italy.

Colonisation

Speech of Claudius on provincial franchise

8. Conclusion

On first impression the history of the Julio-Claudian dynasty reads like that of a line of crazy monarchs playing practical jokes upon a long-suffering population. Henry VIII (as popularly conceived), James I and Ludwig of Bavaria seem to confront us in ancient garb. The family of the Caesars presents itself as a model for the Borgias, and in their circle heads seem to fly off as fast as in Bluebeard's chamber. In fact the early Caesars were subject to a strain that warped the mind of each in turn. The flattery of courtiers and office-seekers was apt to turn the strongest heads;[25] recurrent plots or rumours of plots were calculated to unnerve the calmest courage; and none of Augustus's successors, except the first, had been trained for his task. The misdeeds of the Julio-Claudian emperors lent colour to the regrets of those who

First impressions of the Julio-Claudian dynasty

sighed for the Republic, and they showed up the wisdom of Augustus in endeavouring to salvage whatever could be preserved of the previous régime. How would the successors to an undisguised despotism have comported themselves without the restraints of a dying, but not dead, republican tradition?

Its redeeming features

Yet on closer inspection the early Caesars present themselves in a more favourable light. If exception be made of Caligula, whose reign was luckily too short to leave many enduring marks, all the early emperors had their redeeming features. Tiberius lacked neither ability nor a sense of duty; the groping wits of Claudius were illumined by flashes of insight; Nero was less a 'monster' than a weakling. Further, the seeming absolutism of the Roman emperors was tempered by several restraining agencies. The Senate, for all its obsequiousness, still acted in some degree as an organ of enlightened public opinion. The influence of the emperors' confidants, if exception be made of Seianus and Tigellinus, was on the whole beneficial. If Seneca and Burrus did not assert their authority sufficiently, at any rate they used it in the right direction. If Claudius's freedmen valued their offices for what they could get out of them, they gave fair value in return by their unquestionably able administration. Lastly, the new professional executive was getting into its stride. It was perhaps the greatest merit of Tiberius that he was no less judicious than Augustus in selecting his officials, and no less vigilant, in his early reign at least, in controlling them. After fifty years of training in a sound tradition the imperial executive was learning to carry out its routine efficiently, and on the whole conscientiously, without continual instruction from headquarters. Last but not least the early Caesars were generally successful in maintaining the *pax Augusta* at home and abroad.

Progress of the imperial executive

Taken as a whole, therefore, the age of the Julio-Claudian emperors was one of general contentment. However heavily the hand of the early Caesars weighed on their own family and on the high personages around them, the common people of Rome and Italy were none the worse for the change from Republic to monarchy, those in the provinces were appreciably better off. The prosperous bourgeoisie and the members of the Equestrian Order were almost to a man supporters of the new régime, and the rank and file of the Senatorial Order was habitually loyal. In the fifty years after the death of Augustus his system had taken firm root; after the death of Nero it was able to weather some heavy squalls.

General contentment under the early emperors

CHAPTER 34

Roman Society under the Early Roman Emperors

1. Agriculture[1]

Few changes in Italian agriculture

The age of Augustus and of the early Caesars constituted an epoch in the economic no less than in the political history of the Mediterranean lands. But in agriculture the transformations of this period were less far-reaching than in trade and industry. In Italy the wholesale confiscations and reallotments under the Second Triumvirate had brought about an extensive change in the ownership of land. The general effect of this redistribution was to break up the larger domains into holdings of moderate size, and the tendency for these to be reabsorbed into *latifundia* was to some extent checked by Augustus's policy of giving free loans to rural proprietors. The imperial domains and the estates of the wealthiest Romans were to be found in the provinces rather than in Italy. The typical Italian estate of the first century A.D. was a holding of medium size, in which the bourgeoisie of the period invested the profits realised in commerce or manufactures. Though the large

Growth of medium-sized holdings

ranches which were characteristic of the later Republic did not disappear, and much land was still held back for parks or hunting-preserves, the oft-quoted phrase of the elder Pliny, that 'the *latifundia* had been the ruin of Italy', was less true of his day than of the last two centuries B.C. The laments of the Augustan poets over the decay of the small peasantry which once had conquered and developed Italy were similarly out of date. In the remoter parts lesser proprietors still held their own, independently of all political vicissitudes.

When Augustus called a halt to Roman con-

quest and suppressed piracy and kidnapping within the Empire, he incidentally cut off the main sources for the supply of slaves to Italy, and thereby created a new labour problem for all the larger proprietors. Concurrently with this diminution in the supply of slaves went a clearer realisation that servile labour was dear at any price. On this point nothing could be more explicit than the verdict of an expert of Nero's age, L. Iunius Columella, whose treatise *De Re Rustica* (p. 397) was the most authoritative of Roman writings on agriculture.[2] According to Columella nothing but constant watchfulness by a competent bailiff and frequent personal visits by the owner of the estate could keep unfree workers up to a profitable standard of industry and care, and only by paying high prices could trustworthy slaves be procured. Under such conditions the experiments made under the Late Republic in the use of free tenants were carried a stage further; Columella recommended their employment for the outlying pieces of crop-land. Yet the same author had to confess that *coloni* were scarcely more trustworthy than slaves, and that tenants recruited from the towns were never satisfactory, being often mere rolling stones who could not settle down to steady work. The nemesis of slavery on the countryside was now declaring itself: in reducing the numbers of the peasantry it had depleted the reservoir of competent surplus labour. In default of a better alternative many Italian landowners had perforce to make shift with the servile staff at their disposal, and to eke this out with the occasional assistance of free wage-workers.[3] To some extent the ser-

Decrease of the slave trade

Increased cost of slave labour

Free tenants not a satisfactory substitute

vile stock was still replenished by traders who bought unwanted children or picked them up after exposure; but the main source of supply from the time of Augustus consisted of home-bred slaves.[4] Like the cotton planters after 1807, the Italian landlords under the early emperors had increasing recourse to female labour on their estates; for each child reared the women workers received a premium, and they could look forward to personal freedom as the slaves' *ius trium liberorum*. Though chained workers could still be found on Italian plantations, in general the treatment of the slaves was more humane and intelligent than in the days of Cato or even of Varro. Baths and hospitals (*valetudinaria*) were sometimes provided; suggestions and criticisms from the staff might be invited; and specially trustworthy slaves might take a lease of a farm on terms similar to those of a *colonus*. With these improvements the servile estates in Italy could still attain a tolerable standard of efficiency; under an expert landlord they might yield a handsome profit.

Improvements in the treatment of slaves

So long as the city of Rome laid the provinces under contribution for its supplies of wheat, the Italian countryside merely grew for its own consumption. Experiments were made here and there in rotations or in the raising of cash-crops; some enterprising landlords made use of wheeled ploughs with deep-cutting convex blades that overturned the sod, and the marling of clay soil was introduced from Gaul.[5] But in general it was the least fertile portion of the cultivable land that was left over for the growth of cereals, and the methods of tillage underwent no important alteration.

Improvements in crop-farming

In the pastoral industry the improvement of herds by selective breeding and the laying down of artificial meadows received more attention. An important addition to the forage plants of Italy was the *herba medica,* lucerne or alfalfa grass, an Oriental species that was well adapted to the dry summer climate of the peninsula. But the typical Italian ranching system, with its alternation of summer and winter grazings, had reached its maximum extension under the Republic, so that no further development in this branch of husbandry was to be looked for.

Artificial grasses

The growing demands of the capital for wine and oil were met, like its requirements in grain, by increased importation from the provinces. But the finer brands for the tables of the rich were supplied by Italy, whose products now competed on equal terms with the choicest Greek marks. In the days of Columella a vineyard was regarded as the safest investment and the readiest means of winning a fortune out of the land.[6] Campania still flowed with wine and oil; the region of the Alban Hills became a second

Expansion of viticulture

centre for the production of vintage wines; and the trade with the Danube districts led to an increase of viticulture in the Po valley and of olive-growing in Istria. On the whole the fears which writers at Rome expressed that Italy was becoming less productive were groundless.

Among the provinces Sicily, which probably had been overcultivated in the republican period, fell back in productivity, and some of the moderate-sized native wheat-farms made way for the large ranches under Roman proprietors, though some small-scale farming continued. The place of Sicily as the chief granary of Rome was taken by Africa and by Egypt. The cultivation of Egyptian wheat for export was restored by Augustus to the same high level as under the early Ptolemies. This result was achieved by extending the area under crops rather than by altering the methods of tillage, for the actual cultivation of the land remained in the hands of the native peasantry. Under the more settled conditions introduced by the Roman emperors much crop-land which had fallen derelict was resumed on lease by Egyptian tenants, and pressure was put upon them, if necessary, to take up as much land as they could cultivate. The introduction of cotton-growing into Egypt, which probably belongs to the period under review, was little more than a curiosity, the use of the cotton cloth being mainly confined to the native priesthood.[7] The export of foodstuffs from Syria and Asia Minor was limited to a few specialities, such as the wine of Laodicea (on the Phoenician coast) and the figs from the hinterland of Smyrna.

Decline of Sicily, and progress of Africa and Egypt, in corn-growing

On the European continent the cultivation of the land was as yet barely sufficient for local needs. On the other hand the border-lands of the western Mediterranean, whose development under Roman influence had commenced under the Republic (p. 299), now began to rival Italy in food-production. The volume of emigration to these regions had been greatly augmented by the numerous colonial settlements of Caesar and Augustus; and it may be assumed that a medium-sized farm, cultivated by free native tenants under the active supervision of the Roman proprietors, was the normal type of holding, though in Tunisia some large estates were formed, which Nero subsequently converted into imperial domains (p. 634). In northern Africa wheat-growing along the river valleys of Tunisia and in the Algerian coast-lands was intensified, so that these districts became one of the chief sources of supply for Rome. The principal products of the western Mediterranean lands, as of Italy, were wine and oil. Southern Gaul still remained the chief provincial centre of viticulture, though the eastern

Vines in
Gaul;
olives in
Spain and
Africa

and southern coast-lands of Spain also grew for export. But in these latter regions the olive was grown with more success than the vine; and in the drier areas of northern Africa, and notably in southern Tunisia, the same tree was acclimatised on land which had hitherto been arid steppe and resumed this character from the end of the Roman to the French occupation.

Water-
conservation
in Africa

The success of the Roman cultivator in the semi-desert tracts of Africa, where the summer drought lasts from six to seven months, was due to the systematic manner in which he trapped and conserved all available supplies of water. In the uplands barrages were constructed across the beds of streams; in the plains innumerable cisterns stored up the winter rain, and irrigation canals distributed the water over the widest possible area.[8] The enterprise of the Roman planter may also be illustrated from the successful transplantation of eastern or Mediterranean species to the north of Europe. Peaches were acclimatised in Belgica, and the cherry, which Lucullus had brought from Armenia to Italy (p. 300), was established a hundred years later in Britain.[9]

2. Industry and Trade

General
security
and free-
dom of
movement
in the
Roman
Empire

The benefits of the new system of government were nowhere more apparent than in the impetus which it gave to the commerce and manufactures of the Roman Empire. Never before had the Mediterranean lands enjoyed a like measure of security and freedom of intercourse. Under the Roman fiscal system customs duties were reduced to a minimum and levied at a simple flat rate. The liberty of economic enterprise under the Roman emperors may best be gauged in Egypt, where the monopolies imposed by the Ptolemies on all money-making activities, from banking to brewing, were abolished.[10] Though special permits were required for entrance into Egypt, and a curious regulation of Augustus prohibited senators from visiting it, restrictions on travel within the Empire were almost unknown: a merchant might traverse its length from the Euphrates to the Thames without being called upon to produce a passport. The rapid extension of the Roman network of roads, and the establishment of Roman camps and colonies on the outskirts of the Empire, opened up many new markets. On certain frequented stretches of the Mediterranean Sea, between Puteoli and Ostia, from Brundisium to Corcyra, regular sailings were instituted. Though artificial waterways seldom repaid the costs of construction under ancient technical conditions and contributed little to the

Improve-
ment of
communi-
cations

opening up of inland navigation, the natural river system was systematically exploited for commercial purposes under Roman rule. The Baetis (modern Guadalquivir) was navigated as far as Hispalis (Seville), the Rhine up to Cologne. On the Italian lakes and on every considerable stream of Gaul organised gilds of boatmen plied a regular trade. Lutetia (Paris), which had been nothing more than a tribal capital, began to attain importance as a river-port; Lugdunum became a miniature St Louis.[11]

Inland
water
transport

The early Caesars not only created material conditions favourable to industry and trade, but in the conduct of their foreign policy they took economic advantages more into consideration than the Senate of republican days. Augustus's Arabian expedition was frankly directed to commercial gain; his treaties with Parthia almost certainly made provision for trading facilities in the interior of Asia; and beyond doubt he discussed trading facilities with the envoys from India (p. 332). The emperors were not too proud to supplement their revenue by exploiting industrial properties. They acquired by purchase, inheritance or confiscation large mining fields in the provinces; in Italy they manufactured ceramic ware for the general market. The example set by the emperors was followed by men and women of high standing at Rome. One of the largest brick-factories of Rome, which contributed largely to the rebuilding of the city after the fire of 64, was in the possession of a leading senator named Domitius Afer (consul in 39 and a famous orator); a *grande dame* of Nero's reign, Calvia Crispinilla, acquired her fortune by the exportation of wine and oil.[12]

Interest
of the
emperors
in trade

Lastly, though the period of the Roman emperors was as barren in technical inventions as the preceding age, one isolated discovery gave rise to an extensive new industry. During the last half-century B.C. Sidonian craftsmen acquired the art of making glass vessels by blowing instead of moulding, so as to produce a lighter and more transparent ware which was suitable for table-services and for window-panes.[13]

Invention
of the
blowpipe for
glass-
making

Under such favourable conditions the range and volume of commerce underwent a notable increase, and several branches of industry attained a far larger scale of production. From an economic point of view the Roman Empire began to be transformed from a congeries of loosely connected units into an organic whole.

While the older ceramic industry of Arretium and the bronze manufactures of Capua were extending the range of their export markets (p. 381), new industries sprang up in the north and the south of Italy. The coarser kinds of earthenware (lamps and tiles) were made at

Industrial activity in Italy

Mutina and Aquileia. Pompeii in the south, Parma, Mediolanum (modern Milan) and Patavium (Padua) in the north, produced woollen goods of all grades. The Campanian cities introduced glass-blowing into Italy, and Rome began to supply its own enormous market, notably in the more specialised industries, such as papermaking and work in the precious metals.

The old-established manufactures of the Levant experienced a revival of prosperity under the early emperors. They not only maintained their hold on local markets, but supplied Rome with luxury wares and found new outlets in the farther East *(see below)*. The new glass industry prospered in Phoenicia and at Alexandria; a vogue for half-silk goods (with a linen warp) benefited Cos and other cities of Asia Minor. In the European countries the mining industry maintained its former importance. In Spain the silver deposits of Andalusia were becoming less prolific, but the lead from the same workings increased in value as the towns of the west followed the example of Rome in laying down water-pipes, and the discovery of tin mines along the western seaboard gave the Spanish peninsula precedence over Britain as the chief source of supply of that metal. In Gaul the ironfield of Liège was opened, to supplement the older workings in the Auvergne and Jura. The iron-mines of Noricum remained highly productive, and the varied mineral resources of Illyricum were energetically exploited after the Roman conquest. In addition to its long-established metallic industries, Gaul developed ceramic and textile manufactures. At Graufesenque in the Cévennes a red-glazed pottery with embossed reliefs began to be produced about A.D.[20] This Gallic *terra sigillata* (or 'sealing-wax' ware, as it was called from its colouring), being a good factory-made substitute for the costlier Arretine ware, presently attained an even greater vogue than its Italian prototype.

Growth of industry in the provinces

Terra sigillata in Gaul

34.1 Terra sigillata.

The foreign trade of the Roman Empire attained its maximum rate of expansion in the first century A.D. In Britain the Italian or Gallic merchant began a peaceful penetration half a century before the military occupation by the Roman legions.[14] Along the Rhine and upper Danube the emperors, intent on securing the Roman frontier by a policy of isolation, discouraged commerce across the border-land except at stated points. But in the days of Nero a new trade-route was opened by a Roman adventurer in quest of amber, who found his way from Carnuntum to the eastern Baltic and inaugurated a regular exchange of wares along this track. The exploration of the North Sea by the Roman fleets (p. 335) opened up a new waterway from the lower Rhine to Germany and Scandinavia, by which the bronze of Capua and other metal-ware was carried to these countries.[15]

Expansion of foreign trade

The discovery of Greek textiles of the Augustan period in Mongolia suggests at least an occasional interchange of wares along the trail from the Strait of Kertch past the head of the Caspian Sea; but it is as yet uncertain whether any of the Caspian routes came into regular use before the Byzantine age. During the reign of Augustus or soon after, the main trans-continental routes from the Euphrates to Seleucia (near Baghdad), and thence in one direction to Merv and north-west India, and to the Persian Gulf in another, were surveyed for the benefit of Mediterranean traders, and no doubt served to carry regular convoys between inner Asia and the coast of Syria.[16] But these land-routes were liable to be closed by unfriendly Parthian kings, and thus any silk or other goods in transit from China could not proceed along the old trans-Asian Silk Route from China further west than Bactra (Balkh, in Afghanistan) or Merv. Hence when they reached Bactra they were diverted and sent south-east through Begram and Taxila (where interesting finds have been made); from here they could be carried either through the valleys of the Indus to the Arabian Sea, or else (as the *Periplus* records) via Mathura (south of Delhi) and then south-westwards to the port of Barygaza (Broach), where they could be picked up by the regular sea-routes and brought to the West.[17] These sea-routes, which had hitherto been kept in the hands of Arab or Hindu middlemen, were now thrown open to venturers from the Mediterranean. Under Augustus (or somewhat earlier) a sea-captain named Hippalus (presumably an Alexandrian Greek) made the discovery that ships sailing east with the summer monsoon and returning with the anti-trade winds of winter could ply safely and punctually by the open-sea route between

The transcontinental road to China (See Map 33)

Hippalus discovers the 'law of the Indian monsoon'

Aden and India. Hippalus himself established a direct route to the Indus estuary; in the next fifty years other pioneers discovered similar short cuts to central and southern India; under Claudius or Nero occasional adventurers touched Ceylon or crept up the Bay of Bengal.[18] These explorations led to the growth of a regular traffic between the Mediterranean lands and India; in the days of Augustus or Tiberius 120 merchantmen would sail from the Red Sea port of Myos Hormos to India in a single season. The extent of this trade has been recently demonstrated by the quantity of Arretine ware (manufactured in Italy 30 B.C.–A.D. 45) excavated at Podouke (modern Pondicherry) on the east coat of India. These goods must have been landed on the west coast and carried across the southern tip of India by land (a route marked by hoards of first-century Roman coins), since sailing round Cape Comorin was treacherous and not attempted until the end of the first century. Before long the Indian trade attained such a magnitude as to give concern to thoughtful observers. For the luxury wares imported from *Luxury imports from India* the East – perfumes, spices, muslin and jewels – the Mediterranean traders at first made payment in gold and silver coins, thus causing a drain of specie out of the Roman Empire. In the days of Nero it was estimated that the annual adverse balance of the eastern trade amounted to 100,000,000 sesterces.[19]

Another new sea-route was opened along the eastern African coast, which occasional explorers pursued as far as Zanzibar; but the only considerable traffic in these regions was in the frankincense of Somaliland.[20] Apart from the abortive reconnaissance of Nero's emissaries on the upper Nile (p. 366), and Suetonius Paulinus's raid across Mt Atlas (p. 366), no attempt was made under the early emperors to explore the interior of Africa. The caravan trade to Tripoli remained in the hands of the oasis tribes and did not attain any importance. Neither did *Sailings from Spain to the Indies foretold* the occupation of Mauretania lead to a resumption of the former Carthaginian traffic along the western African coast. Finally, the confident forecast of Seneca, that Spain would soon be joined to the Indies by a transoceanic link,[21] did not tempt any ancient mariner to anticipate Columbus.

But the foreign trade of the Roman Empire *Growth of inter-provincial trade* grew no faster than the commerce between its component parts. The wine and oil of the Mediterranean lands went with (and sometimes before) the legions across the European continent. The vases of Arretium travelled to the Rhine and to Britain, to Spain and Morocco, and eastward as far as the Caucasus. The terracotta lamps which the firm of Fortis turned out

at Mutina by mass-production were exported to remote villages of northern Africa. The *terra sigillata* of Auvergne followed the Arretine ware in the western provinces and competed with it in Italy. The bronze pots and pans of the factory of Cipius Polybius of Capua have been found in the Black Sea regions, in Wales and Scotland. Glass from the Levant and from Campania was carried to Lugdunum, and thence to the Rhine and across the Channel.

A notable feature of the new inter-provincial trade was that it was by no means confined to luxuries. It included not only the fine Arretine ware and glass table-services, but cooking-vessels, tiles and common lamps, and the coarser brands of wine and oil. Trade in the Roman Empire was ceasing to be predominantly local, and it was broadening out into a regular exchange of the necessaries of life.

Under the emperors the old-established Roman trade in money was partly diverted into new channels. The massacres of Roman traders during the revolts of the Pannonians in A.D. 6, of the Gauls in 21, and of the Britons in 61, suggest that the cut-throat usury of republican *Usury in the provinces* days was still being practised in the provinces. But the general improvement in the condition of the provinces from the time of Augustus reduced the opportunities of sharks to prey upon them; and the tax-farming companies not only found their scale of operations diminished but *Tax-farming less profitable* their rates of profit curtailed. On the other hand the growth of trade and industry brought with it a greater demand for business capital, and thus gave scope for a new kind of money-lending at moderate rates for productive purposes.[22]

In trade and industry, as in agriculture, slavery died hard. In the provinces and the Italian *Free labour predominant in the provinces* country towns free wage labour predominated, but in Rome workers of servile condition were the more numerous.[23] The labour for the imperial mines was largely furnished by the courts of law, which commonly punished the heavier crimes by *damnatio ad metalla*. Among the urban slaves a considerable number rose to the position of foremen or managers in business. A high proportion of the persons engaged in manufactures and trade consisted of freedmen, and the wealthy bourgeoisie was constantly being reinforced by men for whom slavery had been a gateway to opulence.

Though the period of the early emperors probably produced fewer millionaires than that of *Relative advance of the provinces in wealth* the later Republic, its prosperity was more widely diffused and more solidly founded. A notable feature of the age was that while Italy remained affluent, the provinces were now taking their share of the new wealth. The Roman corn-fleets were manned by sailors of Greek or

Semitic stock. The pioneers of Indian Ocean navigation were mostly Greeks. The traffic of western Europe was largely in the hands of Gauls. Though the Jews as yet had little part in wholesale trade or in money-dealing, they throve in the cities of the Levant, and in Rome itself, as craftsmen and retail merchants. The slaves and freedmen engaged in productive business at Rome were largely of Levantine provenance.[24]

3. Urban Life

Growth of towns

The economic activity of the age was reflected in the growth of town life. Though the colonising policy of some emperors also contributed to this result the increase in the number and size of the municipalities was mainly due to the expansion of industry and trade. The city of Rome possibly nearly reached the million mark under Augustus. Puteoli remained the principal port of entry into Italy, but the new Ostia began to enter into rivalry with it. Among the many flourishing towns of northern Italy Patavium and Aquileia profited particularly by the increase of trade with the Danube lands: 500 burgesses of Patavium possessed the equestrian census. In the eastern Mediterranean Corinth and Ephesus maintained their share of the transit trade with the Levant. Antioch remained the chief terminus of the trans-continental routes through Asia. Alexandria derived the chief benefit from the new commerce with India. *Alexandria* With a population of 300,000 free inhabitants it was second only to Rome in size, and its material prosperity gave it compensation for its loss of status as a royal capital. In the west resurgent Carthage soon rivalled Utica as the chief place of export from northern Africa; and Gades, which equalled Patavium in the number of Roman *equites* on its burgess roll, acquired a new source of wealth in transmitting the agricultural produce of southern Spain to Rome.

34.2   An Italian hill-town. Relief found at Avenzano.

34.3 A Campanian harbour-town, with moles, triumphal arches and statues on columns. A wall-painting found at Stabiae.

Londinium

In Gaul Arelate, which had received from Caesar a large piece of the territory of Massilia (p. 277), displaced both this town and Narbo as the chief starting-point of trans-continental traffic, but was in turn outstripped by Lugdunum, whose site, strangely neglected before the time of the Second Triumvirate, marked it as the centre of trade in western Europe. In Britain another upstart town, Londinium, became the inevitable focus of the new continental traffic; in the days of Suetonius it already covered most of the area of the medieval city.[25]

With the transition from Republic to monarchy changes in social fashion at Rome passed out of the control of the aristocracy into that of the emperors.[26] Under Augustus, it is true, the remnants of the old nobility sought compensation for the detriment to their political power in an attempt to maintain their social

High society at Rome

influence intact. They not only kept up the ancient and honourable traditions of patronage, but they revived the frivolous tone of society under the late Republic, and pursued gallant adventures while Livia span and Augustus played parlour games with the young men of his family. But under Augustus's successors the old ruling houses lost this last remnant of their privilege. Their numbers were being still further reduced by death-sentences under the renewed reigns of terror, and by a barrenness of progeny which was often self-imposed; and their fortunes continued to crack under the strain of obligatory luxury.[27] It became nothing unusual for scions of noble houses to go cap in hand to emperors, or to solicit their attention by appearing on the stage and in the arena. Under Tiberius their corporate influence could no longer hold out against that of the court.

383

34.4 A Roman patrician, carrying the busts of his ancestors.

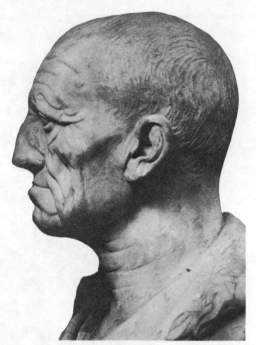

34.5   Portrait of an unknown Roman.

the high-born Roman had hitherto disdained, became fashionable accomplishments. While Seneca advocated celibacy or *mariages de convenance*, the court's open profligacy found as many imitators as in the days of Charles II.

With the fall of the Republic the Roman proletariat lost the entertainment which it had previously derived from the rough-and-tumble of politics. But the surviving republican magistrates – praetors, aediles or quaestors – still treated it to the usual round of games and shows on festival days, and the emperors charged themselves with the provision of additional diversions (most commonly gladiatorial contests), which were systematically organised by 'ministers of amusements' (*procuratores ludorum, munerum*). From the time of Augustus admission to the free places was more severely controlled by a system of tickets and women were relegated to the upper seats at gladiatorial games and beast-hunts. Among the various entertainments the popularity of the mime (p. 309) continued unabated; but chariot races and gladiatorial games, to which the Roman people had now become thoroughly blooded, became the absorbing passion. An additional stimulus was imparted to the chariot races when the jockeys conceived the brilliant idea of dividing themselves off into 'factions' with distinctive colours: spectators, who understood nothing of horses, 'followed' the red, green or blue colour and worked themselves up into a state of frenzy

Organisation of public festivals at Rome

Public interest in the circus games

Frivolity under Nero

Though Tiberius in person was even more careful than Augustus not to dictate to the nobles their private manner of life, the austerity and gloom of his environment spread like a pall over Roman society. But the same society eagerly joined in Nero's mad pursuit of amusement and threw off such remnants of reserve as the dying tradition of Roman *gravitas* had imposed upon it. In Nero's reign dancing and music, which

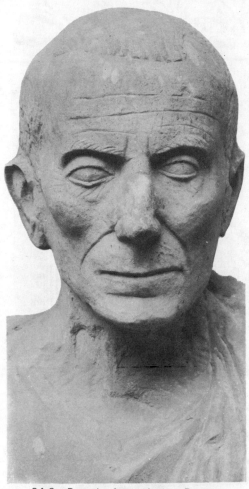

34.6   Portrait of an unknown Roman.

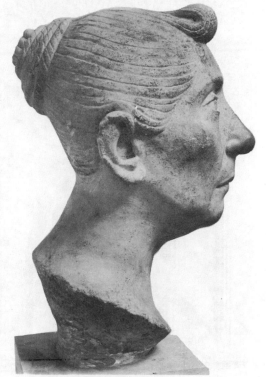

34.7   Portrait of an elderly lady.

general favour, but in western Europe and north-ern Africa the Roman colonies set the example of constructing amphitheatres, and many of the native cities followed suit.

4. Architecture and Art

Public baths

over it. The principal jockeys and gladiators were now to the Roman people what Scipio Afri-canus or Marius once had been, and their por-traits were reproduced on street-walls and drinking-cups and plates.[28] In the intervals between these events the proletariat could lounge its time away comfortably in the porticos and colonnades, which now began to adorn the main streets of the capital, and in the *thermae* (combined swimming-pools and Turkish baths), which sprang up in Rome like mushrooms from the time of Agrippa (p. 324).

Italian and provincial towns follow suit

In the municipalities of Italy and the prov-inces the ruling classes did not copy the frivolity of Roman society, but they imitated its ostenta-tion. The magistrates and Augustales (p. 329) paid their footing with public games and enter-tainments, or by building places of amusement. No town of any size in the Roman Empire even-tually lacked its bath or theatre. In the eastern Mediterranean gladiatorial contests did not find

The rapid growth of town life under the early emperors gave exceptional opportunities to the municipal architect, especially in the western provinces, where the numerous Roman colonies entailed much building on half-vacant sites, and native communities renovated their settlements on the Italian pattern. There was widespread demand for theatres, amphitheatres, circuses, baths and other public buildings, to match the splendid new buildings with which Augustus had adorned Rome itself (pp. 323 ff.). Under the general sense of security which the Roman peace now inspired town sites were transferred from hill-tops to the plains, and ring-walls were no longer considered indispensable. The towns of Gaul, alike in the centre and the south, still provided themselves with fortifications; but London and Colchester prematurely dispensed with this precaution. Nor did the towns of Spain and northern Africa lag behind in their building-programmes.

Municipal architecture

Ring-walls no longer indispens-able

34.8 *Bestiarii*, professional fighters of beasts, in the arena.

34.9 Chariot racing. A mosaic at Tunis.

34.10 Maison Carrée at Nîmes (Nemausus). A hexastyle pseudo-peripteral temple, standing on a tall podium, with frieze of acanthus scroll-work. It was erected during the lifetime of Augustus.

The temples in Italy and the western lands still conformed as a rule to the Italian plan; but many of them were now ringed with pillars ending in Corinthian capitals, after a new fashion of Greek architecture, and western builders were acquiring a Greek sense of proportion and care for details. Of all surviving Roman temples none shows a greater harmony of structure or delicacy of finish than the Maison Carrée at Nîmes, built by Agrippa in 19–12 B.C.[30] We may perhaps attribute to Agrippa a neighbouring monument, the magnificent three-storeyed bridge which carried an aqueduct to Nîmes over the deep valley of the river Gard. In one detail the Roman architects of the Augustan age went beyond their Greek models. They not only employed white marble (from Carrara) for their columns and revetting panels, but they made free use of coloured materials – yellow stones from Numidia, others with green streaks from Euboea or with purple veins from Phrygia. For this lavish use of costly materials Augustus himself set an example in the temple which he dedicated to Apollo on the Palatine, as a thank-offering for his naval victories. The portico of this splendid building was in Numidian stone, the shrine itself was of pure white marble.[31]

The Maison Carrée at Nîmes

The Pont du Gard

The remains of the residences built by the early emperors on the Palatine are not sufficient to convey an accurate idea of their architectural merits. Augustus's house (on the south-eastern edge of the Palatine) consisted of four blocks of apartments round a peristyle; Tiberius's mansion, on the opposite corner of the same hill, was considerably more pretentious, and Caligula added a wing to it. Nero's Domus Aurea linked the palace on the Palatine with imperial properties on the Esquiline and included new buildings and gardens which covered the valley between the Palatine, the Caelian and the Oppian, some 125 acres.[32] Remarkable for its scale, its wall-paintings and its circular dining-room with a revolving ceiling, it was even more significant for the future of architecture because of the new use of the shape of space within

The temple of Apollo on the Palatine

Imperial palaces

387

34.11 Pont du Gard. Between 20 and 16 B.C. Agrippa built an aqueduct to bring water to Nemausus from springs some 30 miles away. It was mainly trenched in the ground but had to cross the gorge of the Gardon. It was carried on the top of this impressive monument, 160 feet high, which at its first level served as a road.

a building at the expense of the function of the masonry masses that contained it. Another building which pointed to the future, especially to the Christian basilica, is the underground vaulted and arched hall near Porta Maggiore; it is probably Claudian in date and may have been the meeting-place for a mystery religion, perhaps Neo-Pythagoreanism. The house-architecture of the period is copiously illustrated from Pompeii, where there was much building activity, especially after an earthquake which damaged the town in A.D. 63. The wealthier inhabitants of Pompeii continued to reside in courtyard houses of one or two storeys (p. 192).

In Rome, Ostia and other cities, where space was more valuable, houses rose to a far greater height, and families of moderate means were content to take a flat in a block of four or more storeys. For the construction of the more durable houses burnt brick began to rival stone in Italy and the western provinces; but the brick core was commonly coated with a surface of stucco. In Italy and western Europe a system of central heating by terracotta pipes from an underground furnace ('hypocaust'), which originated in the public baths, was introduced into private residences and became a common feature of these.

Use of burnt brick

34.12   Amphitheatre at Nîmes. First half of the first century A.D.

Wall paintings

Wealthier houses were decorated with mural paintings, of which many survive at Pompeii. In the Augustan period the wall-surface was divided into a number of architectural features designed to produce an illusion of space; panels were often filled with pictures which were intended to suggest the open country outside. The walls of a room of the empress Livia in a villa at Prima Porta were covered with a lovely garden scene, with shrubs, birds, flowers and butterflies; very different were the ritual scenes from the House of the Mysteries at Pompeii. This style merged into one when the painted architecture became more elaborate, and the painted groups more panel-like. Then from *c.* A.D. 50 pictures, often impressionistic, were set in fantastic architecture, as in the Domus Aurea.

In the days of Augustus Roman portrait-sculpture showed peculiarly strong traces of Greek influence. In the splendid full-length statue of Augustus in the Vatican the emperor's features are rendered with due accuracy in essentials, but with a Hellenic refinement of detail. Under his successors the traditional realism of Roman portraiture gradually reasserted itself. The Medusa-like glance of Tiberius, the stuffy-looking cranium of Claudius, the flabby jaw and myopic contraction of the brows of Nero, were reproduced with unflattering fidelity. A notable development in Roman art took place under Augustus, when the sculptor replaced the painter in the reproduction of historical scenes on Roman architectural pieces. The finest early specimen of Roman historical relief was the decoration on the walls of the Ara Pacis, decreed in 13 B.C. (p. 324). The human groups on this monument are lacking in animation, as if over-conscious of their Roman *gravitas*; but the accessory scroll-work is executed with a delicacy rivalling that of the Erechtheum at Athens, and the skill with which the figures are made to

Portrait sculpture

The Ara Pacis

34.13 The Domus Aurea, Nero's palace, built after the fire of A.D. 64. It was a villa, with grounds covering some 125 acres, from the Palatine across the Forum and Velia as far as Mons Oppius.

34.14 Subterranean basilica outside the Porta Maggiore at Rome. The rich stucco decorations depict mythological subjects; the hall may have been the meeting-place of a Neo-Pythagorean sect.

stand out from their background recalls the best scenic sculpture of the Hellenistic Greeks.[33]

Of the minor arts of the period metal-work underwent the same development as sculpture. *Coin-portraiture* Portraiture on coins is copiously exemplified by the heads of the rulers, which appeared regularly on the obverse of all Roman money, and of other members of the imperial family, who were occasionally represented on the reverse. The idealising types of Augustus and Livia, and the realistic likenesses of the following emperors, represent the art of the Roman coiner at its best. Strangely enough, much of the choicest portraiture appears on the brass and copper pieces from the senatorial mint. A worthy parallel to the historical reliefs on the Ara Pacis may be seen on one of the few surviving specimens of Roman silversmiths' work, a cup from a villa at Boscoreale (near Pompeii), on which a triumphal procession of the future emperor Tiberius is embossed in high relief. The imperial family was also commemorated by the art of the gem-cutter, which may best be appreciated in the splendid 'Vienna cameo'.

34.15　Peristyle of a house at Pompeii.

34.16　A street in Pompeii.

34.17 Painting from the villa of Livia at Prima Porta, north of Rome. All four walls have landscape paintings, so that wherever anyone stood in the room he had a lovely vista of trees and flowers.

34.18 The Ara Pacis. Decreed in 13 B.C., the foundation stone of this altar was laid in 9 B.C. on the Campus Martius. Marble slabs were recovered in the sixteenth century and again relatively recently; the altar was reconstructed in 1938. The top right-hand panel shows the sacrifice of Aeneas and the temple of the Penates.

34.19   The Ara Pacis. This relief shows Terra Mater and the symbols of peace and plenty.

5. Literature. General Conditions[34]

Literary patronage

The first Roman emperor, appreciating the value of a trained public opinion, discharged the duties of a literary patron with discretion. He gave personal encouragement to the three outstanding authors of his day, to Livy, Horace and Virgil; he directed their efforts to further his own political schemes; but he allowed them great latitude in the performance of their tasks, and was at pains not to injure their self-respect. Augustus also gave effect to Caesar's plan of founding a public library at Rome, and confirmed the immunities which Caesar had conferred upon physicians and teachers but he made no attempt to control or aid public education.

The tradition of literary patronage which had established itself among the enlightened members of the republican aristocracy survived the fall of the Republic. Among the Augustan poets Virgil was launched on his career by *Maecenas* Asinius Pollio, and Tibullus by Valerius Messalla. But the greatest contribution ever made by a man of wealth and influence to Roman letters stands to the credit of Augustus's confidant Maecenas, who befriended Propertius, Horace and Virgil with princely liberality, and was the means of bringing the two last-named to the notice of the emperor. In the time of Augustus the fashion also set in of attending recitations by authors who read out portions of their unpublished works. Under the early emperors the reading public to which a Latin author had access was no longer confined to Italy, but extended over the western provinces. Literary talent was never more assured of a friendly welcome in the Roman world than in the period now under review.

Though the Augustan poets still showed a tendency to adhere too closely to Greek models in their early productions, Latin literature now rendered itself more and more independent of foreign influences. Literary aspirants abandoned the practice of finishing their training at the Greek universities, for the schools of 'rhetoric' (literary composition) established at Rome now met all their requirements, and the Latin masterpieces of the Ciceronian age provided them with excellent linguistic and metrical models. During the Augustan age national consciousness again ran strongly in Latin literature. But the spacious days of the first emperor were followed by a spell of boredom under Tiberius and of dissipation under Nero. Under these later rulers the glow of patriotism rendered down rapidly, and the individualistic strain, which had first become noticeable in the Ciceronian age, emerged more clearly.

Latin literature less dependent on Greek

The literary output under the early emperors was no less immense than in the later days of the Republic. Scribbling, whether by street urchins on the walls of Pompeii, or by members of the imperial family on *charta hieratica,* was a general habit. The works which demand our notice therefore cover a wide range of ground.

6. Latin Poetry

Though the theatre never had a wider vogue than under the Roman emperors, it never offered less scope to dramatic talent. Its performances were merely spectacular, and no work of literary merit was staged but for an occasional revival of a classic of the republican age. The only dramatic productions of the period that have survived are some juvenile tragedies of the 'Grand Guignol' type by Nero's minister Seneca, and an anonymous drama representing the sufferings of Nero's first wife, Octavia. Though Seneca's plays lacked neither wit nor force, they were put together without any knowledge of stagecraft and are only fit for reading.

Seneca's tragedies

At the beginning of the Augustan age erotic elegies of the Hellenistic type were composed by two minor bards, Albius Tibullus (55–19 B.C.) and Sextus Propertius (*c.* 50–15 B.C.). The flame of Tibullus was bright and clear, but not intense. The fires of Propertius burnt more fiercely, but required careful stoking; the glorious spontaneity of Catullus was absent from his verse.

Augustan elegiacs

The Italic vein of satire, which had trickled away since the days of Lucilius in mere lampooning, was quickened again to a strong flow by Q. Horatius Flaccus (65–8 B.C.). As a person of humble family, who had broken off a student's career in order to join the army of M. Brutus (p. 287), and had in consequence been reduced to the penurious calling of a scrivener, Horace at first discharged his vexation in impatient diatribes. When his fortunes were mended by Maecenas and Augustus, and by their generosity he became the proprietor of a comfortable farm in the Sabine hills, he improved upon Lucilius, both in the greater smoothness of his verse and in the franker *bonhomie* of his raillery: he learnt to laugh with his victims, not at them.

The Satires of Horace

The voice of Horace came back with a foggy echo in the works of A. Persius Flaccus (A.D. 34–62).[35] This writer improved upon Horace in ridding Roman satire of its last tinge of malice; but his knowledge was of books rather than of men, and his donnish horror of commonplace crabbed and blurred his style.

If Horace was the greatest of Roman satirists, it was chiefly by his later works, the *Odes,* that he earned his immortality. In these short sonnets he turned from the erudite Alexandrine writers, whom Tibullus and Propertius had followed, to the lyric poetry of early Greece, and he not only reproduced the studied simplicity of his models – an achievement which in an essentially economical tongue like Latin was not remarkable – but also captured their rhythm and melody: it was Horace who first established Italian as one of the world's singing languages. Yet Horace's *Odes* exhibited something more than mastery over the choice of words; they were a true index of the trend of feeling in the Augustan age, in that they marked a gradual return from studied indifference to a compelling interest in affairs of state, from potations and flirtations to the grand pageant of Roman history.

The Odes of Horace

Epic poetry of the miniature variety, which Catullus had introduced to Rome from Alexandria, was cultivated with the touch of a virtuoso by P. Ovidius Naso (43 B.C.–A.D. 17).[36] This most versatile of Roman poets composed various kinds of *vers de société* with unfailing dexterity; but he achieved his greatest success in recounting the familiar tales of Greek mythology, many of which he fixed in their final form. In his tripping elegiacs the Latin language took an unfamiliar air of nimbleness. But Ovid was the least typical of the Augustans. As the pet child of the frivolous high society of that age he frittered away his talent on graceful nothings, and his literary career was virtually ended in A.D. 8 when Augustus exiled him to Tomi on the Black Sea, perhaps on account of a compromising association with the emperor's daughter Julia.

If old Ennius had nothing to fear from Ovid he was superseded as the nation's poet by P. Vergilius Maro (70–19 B.C.).[37] Like most of his contemporaries Virgil first tried his pen in an Alexandrine *genre.* His *Eclogues* imitated the pastoral sketches of Theocritus without his Greek model's animation, but with the same frank delight in the summer scenes of Mediterranean lands. While his bucolic poetry in general anticipated the *Georgics* in their note of deep appreciation for the works of Nature, the *Aeneid* was foreshadowed in the prophetic tone of the fourth or 'Messianic' eclogue, a work of 40 B.C., in which he foretold the birth of a deliverer from the world's sufferings and with boyish enthusiasm described the golden morrow (p. 292).

Virgil. The Eclogues

In the *Georgics,* which was in outward form a didactic poem on husbandry, Virgil again took his subject from the Greek repertory, but he

The Georgics

handled it in a fashion all his own. Under the guise of practical (and highly competent) advice to crop-farmers and planters, to stock-breeders and bee-keepers, he sang a hymn in praise of country life. In this work we may find his soul enclosed. To the modern reader its principal charm lies in the pervasive sympathy with Nature, which to Virgil, as to Goethe and Wordsworth, made all living things akin. But with this sentimental trait Virgil combined a dour belief in the same defiant hard work by which the Italian soldier and peasant had laid the world at his feet; in this confession of faith Virgil was racy of the soil from which he sprang.

The Aeneid

If the *Georgics* was a song after Virgil's own heart, it also found favour with Augustus; and it was at the direct suggestion of the emperor that he went on to compose the epic poem on which his fame in antiquity chiefly rested, the *Aeneid*. This work, which was heralded as a challenge to the *Iliad* itself, achieved a pre-eminence in the Latin world that was scarcely inferior to the ascendancy of the Homeric poems among the Greeks. To be sure, the role for which he was now cast was not altogether congenial to him. Lacking the primitive man's joy of battle, he could not portray a hero of true Viking blood, or produce any honestly exhilarating scene of carnage: as a slaughterman his Aeneas is wholly unconvincing. But in literary craftsmanship Virgil left all previous epics behind. While he preserved the rich sonority of the Latin hexameter he diversified it by playing over the whole range of its rhythmic modulations. Above all, he constructed his story with an unerring sense of dramatic unity: through all the variety of incidents one increasing purpose runs, and all roads lead to Rome. To this grand climax of the birth of Rome, and of its rebirth under Augustus, everything is subordinated, even the personal attractiveness of his hero, whose *pietas* consists in obeying his fate rather than in compelling it, whose dutiful desertion of Dido stands in pointed contrast with Antony's treasonable loyalty to Cleopatra. While the *Aeneid* is rich in compassionate touches, which almost persuaded Dante to make Virgil a Christian, its dominant note is pride in Rome's past and a high sense of its future mission. As a patriotic poem Virgil's epic completely fulfilled its purpose; wherever Latin was spoken it found eager readers and justified to them the ways of Rome.

The *Aeneid* left no room for a further poem on the dawn of Rome. But the earlier epics by Naevius and Ennius had ranged over the historical even more than the legendary period of Rome's past. Reverting to their tradition, a writer of the Neronian age, M. Annaeus Lucanus (A.D. 39–65), commemorated the civil war between Caesar and Pompey in a poem called the *Pharsalia*. This topic was not ill-chosen, for while the issues of the war had become too remote to arouse partisanship, they were of enduring interest, and the personality of the winner clearly lent itself to treatment in the grand manner. In his method of work as well as in his subject Lucan stood in sharp contrast with Virgil. He was a product of the rhetorical schools which were now impressing their character upon Roman literature, and his appeal was not, as in the case of the Augustans, to his own literary conscience, but to the none too critical audiences that came to hear his advance readings. His epic was a string of detached episodes devoid of organic unity, or of insight into the controlling forces behind the actors in the scene, such as we find in the epics of Tolstoy and Hardy on the Napoleonic Wars. It relied for its effect on a sensational treatment of the horrors of war, and on a monotonous fusillade of epigrams. But its high spirit is infectious, and the vigour with which Lucan delineated Caesar, as a person possessed with a demon of energy that crashed through every obstacle, has a touch of Shakespearian downrightness.

The Pharsalia of Lucan

7. Latin Prose

Under the Roman emperors the study of oratory was pursued with a zeal worthy of a better cause. In the schools of rhetoric, which almost monopolised higher studies in Italy and the western provinces, declamation and disputation formed two main ingredients in the curriculum and oratorical ingenuity was cultivated to the point of perversity.[38] Specimens of the absurdly far-fetched theses which were pursued in these schools survive in the *Suasoriae* and *Controversiae* of the elder Seneca, an accomplished practitioner in the days of Tiberius, whose success did not upset his mental balance. But occasions for a practical exhibition of oratory had become disproportionately rare. Augustus's friend Valerius Messalla carried weight in the Senate by his eloquence on behalf of the new régime; in Nero's day Thrasea Paetus acquired a dangerous celebrity by his outspoken criticisms (p. 359). When the Senate became a tribunal for state trials, a lucrative but invidious career opened for those of its members who were willing to come forward as prosecutors; under Tiberius a speaker named Domitius Afer acquired great wealth and notoriety in this profession. But outside the Senate-house forensic oratory had little further scope; in the imperial courts pleadings were wholly technical, and the *pragmaticus* or attorney replaced the 'orator' of

Influence of rhetorical studies

Decline of practical oratory

republican times. The Rostra were silent, but for an occasional *laudatio*; and the atmosphere of the Senate, painfully conscious of its loss of sovereignty, was rarely such as to draw out the full powers of its speakers.

The History of Livy

Under Augustus the long series of general histories of Rome in annalistic form was virtually brought to a close by the monumental work of T. Livius, who covered the whole span from Romulus to Augustus in 142 books.[39] Unlike most of his predecessors in Roman historiography Livy was purely a man of letters, with a rhetorical rather than a practical training. Lacking a competent knowledge of legal and military details, and devoid, like most Roman writers, of historic imagination, he was largely at the mercy of his sources; and for the earlier centuries of Roman history he drew mainly upon the less trustworthy of the previous annalists (p. 309). The annalistic framework to which Livy adhered prevented him from bringing into clear view the play of cause and effect, or of throwing into proper relief the remorseless continuity of the growth of the Roman Empire. Nevertheless his work put all previous Roman histories into the shade. This primacy he owed in part to the swift but smooth current of his prose, which carries the reader along in the manner of Macaulay's *History*; partly to his keen sense of dramatic detail, which is particularly manifest in the fictitious yet strikingly apposite speeches that diversify his narrative. Above all, Livy was no less sensitive than the Augustan poets to the unique achievement of Rome; he shared the simple but alluring faith of Ennius, that the secret of Roman greatness lay in Roman character, and by insensible pressure he caused this conviction to sink into the minds of his readers. Though Livy's history was more read in excerpts than in the original, it travelled all over the Latin-speaking world, and as a missionary of empire it was second only to the *Aeneid*.

The secret of Roman greatness in Livy

Velleius Paterculus

The only other historical work of wide scope that needs mention here was the short primer written by M. Velleius Paterculus, a retired officer of the age of Tiberius. Not content to copy the military simplicity of Caesar's *Commentaries*, this old soldier attempted fine writing and acquitted himself creditably. His work carries little weight, except in the account of the German and Pannonian campaigns, of which he had been an eye-witness. The frank admiration which he expressed for Tiberius in these chapters throws significant light upon the attitude of the Roman army to Augustus's family.

For the history of the Republic the work of Livy was generally accepted as definitive. The more ambitious writers henceforth turned their hands to the more intensive study of brief periods of recent history. A good example of this kind of monograph had been furnished by Asinius Pollio, who used the leisure of his later life to produce an authoritative account of the Civil Wars from 60 to 42 B.C. — a work whose loss we have reason to regret.[40] In the days of Nero the elder C. Plinius Secundus wrote a detailed account of the German wars, and several other writers composed similar histories on the reigns of particular emperors. Since all these books were subsequently extinguished by Tacitus we can no longer judge them at first hand; but so much is clear, that they embodied much honest research.

Asinius Pollio's History of the Civil Wars

The writing of memoirs, which the grandees of the later Republic had brought into fashion, still flourished under Augustus and his successors. Augustus himself began, but did not complete, a book of reminiscences. Tiberius and Claudius composed personal Commentaries; the younger Agrippina, with scant discretion, divulged damaging secrets of court life. Among the military chiefs Corbulo described his campaigns on the Parthian front. The whole of this literature has perished beyond reconstruction.

Memoirs

We may probably ascribe to the period of Caligula and Claudius the only surviving historical romance in classical Latin, the *History of Alexander* by Q. Curtius Rufus. This work gave to the Roman public a sample of the highly dramatised tales of Alexander's life which had long ago ousted the authentic versions of his career in the Greek world. Written frankly to entertain, and with no tiresome regard for accuracy, Curtius's book achieved its purpose well and proved a starting-point of the medieval 'Alexander legend'.

Philosophical studies, which under the later Republic had shared the field of higher education with rhetoric, were now almost crowded out of the curriculum. The earlier poems of Horace and Virgil reflected a tendency to seek refuge from the misfortunes of the Second Triumvirate in Epicureanism. In their later works the Stoic creed, whose central doctrine of pride in self and fortitude was congenial to the more resolute spirit of the Augustan age, found more frequent expression, and the same school furnished the inspiration for the *Satires* of Persius. But the typical attitude of Roman intellectuals to philosophy continued to be an unsystematic eclecticism. This was the keynote of the chief philosophic works of the period, the *Sermones* (Discourses) and *Letters* of the younger Seneca. These were essays rather than systematic treatises, and they exhibited little of that power of consecutive reasoning which we find in Cicero's philosophic dialogues. The

Philosophical writings

The Sermones of Seneca

praises of a simple life on which Seneca expatiated did not ring quite true, for although his own tastes were ascetic, he had accepted a princely fee for his services to Nero and amplified his earnings by judicious investments. On the other hand his frequent exhortations to mercifulness and forgiveness gave genuine expression to his kindly if somewhat fibreless character, and they brought him celebrity in the Middle Ages, when the quite untenable belief was held that he was a pupil of St Paul. Seneca's enduring popularity among ancient readers was due to his sprightly and arresting style, which followed the rhetorical fashion of the period, but with the discretion of a true expert.

The novel of Petronius

While Seneca laboured to make men good, another confidant of Nero, C. Petronius Arbiter (p. 359), set them laughing by his realistic novel, the *Satyricon*, in at least sixteen books, which was in outward form a medley of different subjects in prose and verse like the *Saturae* of Varro (p. 310). The most complete surviving episode is *Trimalchio's Feast* (*Cena Trimalchionis*), a Gargantuan dinner party by a slave turned millionaire. Petronius's work recalls Aristophanes in its coarseness and in its uproarious yet good-natured ridicule; but its characters were genuine Italian figures of Nero's day.[41]

Technical manuals

Of the technical literature of the period we have already noticed the treatise on agriculture by Columella (p. 377), a highly competent manual which was not superseded until comparatively recent times. The handbook *De Architectura* by M. Vitruvius, a military engineer in the service of Caesar and Octavian, was a more amateurish work, but its influence on modern 'classical' architecture has been considerable. The grammatical studies of Varro were rounded off in the earliest Latin dictionary, the treatise *De Verborum Significatu* of Verrius Flaccus, the tutor of C. and L. Caesar. The study of Latin classics in schools brought into being a new literature of commentaries. The first notable example of these was the annotation of Cicero's speeches by Q. Asconius Pedianus, a contemporary of Claudius and Nero, whose surviving fragments prove that he possessed acumen as well as learning.

Commentaries on Latin classics

The comprehensive erudition of Varro was emulated in the days of Tiberius by A. Cornelius Celsus, the author of an encyclopaedia, whose extant volumes on medicine are a clear and competent summary of Greek medical knowledge, and by C. Plinius Secundus the Elder (A.D. 23–79). The latter's *Historia Naturalis* made a valiant attempt to systematise the chief known facts of natural science, of geography, and of the history of art. Its thirty-seven volumes drew upon

The Natural History of Pliny the Elder

2000 previous works by some 500 authors. Pliny was overwhelmed by the mass of his materials, and the Roman habit of treating natural science in a purely practical and empiric manner involved him in some grotesque errors. Yet his great work remains an invaluable quarry of materials for the student of Roman antiquities.

The best treatise on a scientific subject by a Latin author was probably the *Commentaries* of M. Agrippa, a systematic exposition of the geography of the Roman Empire, in explanation of a large map set up by him in Rome. This work appears to have combined the results of Greek geographic research and of Roman road-surveying. Its disappearance (except in the excerpts of Pliny) is a serious loss to us.

The map and geography of Agrippa

The age of the early emperors also witnessed a revival of Greek literature, which had fallen upon lean days under the later Republic. The erudite if not highly critical history of Rome by Dionysius of Halicarnassus has already been discussed (p. 61). The same scholar also wrote some estimable essays on the Greek classical authors; but in the field of literary criticism he was surpassed by an unknown writer, whose treatise *On an Elevated Style* was perhaps the best thing of its kind in ancient literature. In the days of Augustus and Tiberius the principal surviving work on ancient geography was composed by Strabo; under Nero a treatise on medicinal plants which remained standard until the sixteenth century was written by Dioscorides.

Contemporary Greek literature

Nevertheless from the time of Augustus Latin attained full parity with Greek as a world language, and Rome became the intellectual as well as the political capital of the Roman Empire. This pre-eminence was not admitted by the Greeks, but it was frankly acknowledged in the provinces of the West, where the Italian schoolmaster followed the soldier, and the Latin classics were studied on Roman methods. The fruits of this diffusion of Latin began to show under Augustus's successors, when the provinces made their first contributions to Latin literature. Domitius Afer was a Narbonese Gaul; the two Senecas, Lucan and Columella were Spaniards. The intellectual partnership thus formed between Italy and the western provinces was to be no less rich in enduring results than their political associations.

Latin attains parity with Greek

8. Religion

The age of Augustus saw the revival of one religion and the institution of another in the Roman world. The emperor made an attempt to breathe fresh life into the old state-cults, and he became

Renewed neglect of the state religion

the recipient of a new worship in his own person (p. 348). Both these religious movements were honestly inspired, but the wave of sentiment which created them was soon spent. As the crisis through which Augustus had guided the Roman world passed away the protecting deities of the state once again came to be simply taken for granted. Of Augustus's successors Claudius alone gave any personal attention to the state-religion, and his interest in it was purely anti-quarian: the renewed celebration of the Ludi Saeculares in A.D. 47, which he instituted at the eighth centenary of the city, was mere pageantry.

The feeling of gratitude to Augustus, which had given rise to his worship during his lifetime, remained alive for a while after his death (p.

Emperor-worship

34.20 Temple of Isis at Pompeii.

34.21   Wall-painting of a service at the temple of Isis.

329). Not only was the cult of *Divus Augustus* officially established at Rome and in the provincial capitals (where it replaced that of *Roma et Augustus*), but permanent temples were constructed in many towns of Italy and the provinces at the wish of the inhabitants. During the reigns of Tiberius and Claudius altars were set up here and there to these rulers, or to popular members of the imperial family, like Livia or Germanicus. But the enthusiasm which greeted the first emperor inevitably died down as the new order of things became established. Of Augustus's successors Caligula positively forced his worship upon his subjects, and Nero, in deference to his mother, requested the Senate to institute an official cult of *Divus Claudius* at Rome which was soon neglected. But Tiberius and Claudius (p. 357), with a shrewd perception that emperor-worship was ceasing to ring true, deprecated the setting up of temples in their honour;[42] and the deification of Claudius after his death was generally looked upon as a bad joke.[43] It is true that emperor-worship, once instituted, maintained itself with the usual tenacity of an established religion; but it soon became, like the cult of the older state-gods, a mere formality, or at most a gaudy social function.

But the attitude of suspense towards religious matters, which had been prevalent in the educated society of the later Republic, could not be maintained indefinitely; neither could the Roman world find a permanent substitute for one religion save in another. Philosophy was ceasing to be a widespread object of study, and in any case was coming to terms with religion. The virtually atheistic creed of the Epicureans was dying out; the more tenacious Stoic school was abandoning its original pantheism and was accepting a supreme personal deity. From the

Quest for new religions

399

time of Augustus, it is true, the highly impersonal doctrine of astrology, which had acquired a vogue in the eastern Mediterranean since the second century B.C., spread to Italy, where it made converts in high society and among the emperors themselves.[43] But astrology was merely fatalism in a quasi-scientific garb, a blind guide and a cold comforter; as a general substitute for religion it was simply inconceivable.

Astrology

Under the early emperors three religions could be singled out as holding the greatest promise for the future. In the Hellenistic world the ancient Egyptian nature-goddess Isis had been transformed by unknown hands into an essentially cosmopolitan deity, a universal mother and well-wisher of mankind, who repaid her worship and the observation of a few simple rules of life (such as an occasional fast) with happiness in this world and the next. Her elaborate and emotional ritual was conducted by a professional clergy, but her votaries, instead of merely looking on at the ceremonial, took an active part in it. The cult of Isis, and that of her male counterpart Sarapis, had a special attraction for mariners and merchants, who propagated it at every Mediterranean port. From Campania, where temples of Isis were built at Puteoli and Pompeii in the later years of the Republic, her cult spread to Rome. Though more than once banned from the capital by successive Roman governments, which disapproved of its noise and excitement, it was never long in re-establishing itself. In 43 B.C. the triumvirs somewhat unexpectedly decreed a state-temple in honour of Isis and Sarapis; under Augustus and Tiberius this resolution was simply disregarded, but it was carried into effect by Caligula.[45]

Spread of Isis-worship

The worship of Jehovah had become widely diffused over the eastern Mediterranean through the dispersion of the Jewish people in the Hellenistic period, and it had been introduced into Rome by the considerable Jewish colony which had been formed there in the last century of the Republic. The political revolt of the Maccabees against the Seleucids (p. 167) had entailed a revival of religious enthusiasm, and of missionary activity among the Gentiles. In the first century A.D. the cult of Jehovah had attracted to itself a considerable body of converts who regularly attended the synagogues, though they might not conform in all respects to the Jewish Law. It is not surprising that in a world of lowered ethical standards the lofty moral code and monotheism of Judaism should appeal to many better minds, even if some ceremonial features proved unacceptable.

Spread of the Jewish religion

During the last century B.C. the Jews in Palestine had been splitting up into sects: the pious Pharisees, the Scribes, the worldly Sadducees, the ascetic Essenes, and the Qumran community by the Dead Sea (perhaps Essenes), whose monastic life is revealed by their Scrolls and surviving buildings.[46] Thus the establishment of two new groups was a natural development, especially as the Jews continued to believe in the coming of a Messiah, a Saviour, a king in David's line who would 'restore again the kingdom to Israel' and usher in the kingdom of God. Thus about A.D. 27 John the Baptist emerged in the desert by the Jordan, calling for repentance and foretelling the coming of 'a mightier one'. Imprisoned by Herod Antipas, John was executed through the plotting of Herodias and her daughter Salome.

Jewish sects

These Messianic hopes were finally realised, in the belief of his followers, in the person and life of Jesus Christ, son of a carpenter of Nazareth in Galilee, in the reign of Tiberius. Jesus's conception of the kingdom of God and the Messiah soon outran that of John, from whom he had at first received baptism; there would be no earthly kingdom and no secular ruler. Rather, he gathered around himself a small group of followers to whom he explained the true nature of the kingdom and God's purpose of salvation for man. These disciples, and members of the Christian Church ever since, believed in his assertion that he was the Son of God. His teaching, combined with a ministry of healing, attracted such crowds that Herod Antipas feared political trouble, while the Jewish authorities became equally suspicious of Jesus and resented a new prophet who reinterpreted the Mosaic law and the old Israelitic ideal of 'righteousness' in terms of universal and undiscriminating love: God stood to all men as a father and called upon all men to be brothers. A turning-point came when the disciples realised that their Messiah would not fulfil their national hopes of an earthly kingdom, still less attempt by force to throw off the Roman yoke, but rather urged them to 'render unto Caesar the things that are Caesar's'. Jesus was resolved to continue his ministry. His entry into Jerusalem led to increased tension with the Jewish authorities. Finally after a preliminary investigation by the Jewish supreme court of the Sanhedrin on a charge of blasphemy he was handed over by them to the Roman governor Pontius Pilate on a charge that he was a rival to Caesar and was seeking the throne of David as 'king of the Jews'. Although Pilate 'found no cause of death in him' and was willing to release him, his fears of a mob-rising and political repercussions led him to give way to the cries of the Jews that Jesus should be crucified. This was carried out

Jesus of Nazareth

(c. A.D. 30), and attracted little attention at the time.[47]

The foundation of Christianity

If that had been the end there would have been no Christian Church and no Christian 'problem' to vex the Roman authorities for the next three centuries until they were finally overcome by it. The disillusioned disciples suddenly gained a new assurance that Christ's death had been followed by his resurrection. However the accounts of the empty tomb and the various appearances of their Risen Lord to different groups of the disciples are to be explained, the disciples themselves had no doubt that Jesus had 'risen from the dead' and was commissioning them to spread his teaching 'both in Jerusalem and in all Judaea, and in Samaria, and to the uttermost part of the earth'. These broken and disheartened men thus suddenly gained great courage, and their numbers quickly grew to 120, then 3000 and again to 5000. Led by Peter they continued to observe the Jewish law, but received into their number less orthodox elements when they converted some Jews of the Dispersion who had gone to Jerusalem for the feast of Pentecost. The Jewish authorities, finding that Jesus's followers instead of melting away were forming a new sect, decided to suppress it, as they had suppressed its founder.

Paul

The first victim was Stephen, who advocated a more liberal Judaism for propagation among the Gentiles: condemned by the Sanhedrin, he was stoned to death. By systematic persecution the Christian leaders were driven out of Jerusalem, some as far as Syrian Antioch where they and their followers were first called Christians. Among the fiercest of all the persecutors was a strict Pharisee, Saul of Tarsus, who was hunting down Christians with the blessing of the High Priest, until stopped by his extraordinary conversion while on the road to Damascus to persecute the Christians there. Using his Latin name Paul (he was a Roman citizen) the persecutor now became the champion of the faith and the Apostle of the Gentiles. As non-Jews (including the Roman centurion Cornelius) were baptised into the new faith, the problem arose whether Gentile converts must fully accept Jewish customs. It was solved when Peter accepted the more liberal policy of Paul, who now carried the Christian message through the Roman world, untrammelled by the confining shackles of Judaism. Christianity was thus to become a missionary and world-wide religion: 'this is a turning-point in history', wrote A. D. Nock, who also quoted Wilamowitz's assessment, 'Paul has unconsciously completed the legacy of Alexander the Great'.[48]

Paul's journeys in Asia Minor and Greece, as recorded in the Acts, were made possible by the *pax Romana*, while the existence of the *koine*, a Greek dialect that was common throughout the East, made his preaching intelligible. His arrival often led to disturbances, provoked either by the Jewish authorities or by men with vested interests in pagan cults who feared for their livelihood if Paul made too many converts (as happened at Philippi and Ephesus). Thus he was often subject to investigation or trial, when his Roman citizenship stood him in good stead: his judges included Gallio, the proconsul of Achaea; Claudius Lysias, the military tribune in command of the cohort at Jerusalem; Felix and Festus, the governors of Judaea; and King Herod Agrippa II. None of these men found him guilty of offences against Roman law, and interpreted the issues at stake as religious matters which concerned Jews alone. Finally, when accused of treason, he appealed to Caesar, and was sent by Festus to Rome, which he reached after shipwreck and other adventures. There he was kept for two years in free custody, but unfortunately the book of Acts breaks off at this point, and his fate is uncertain. There is a strong tradition that he died in the Neronian persecution.[49]

Jews and Christians in Rome

When Paul arrived in Rome he found there a Christian community already established, consisting probably of Gentiles as well as Jews. Its earlier history is not known. Any religion, like both Judaism and Christianity, which proclaimed a strong monotheistic belief was likely to encounter difficulties in a polytheistic society, where mutual acceptance of one another's deities was common form. Thus the Jewish community in Rome had twice been checked by Claudius (p. 357). On the second occasion, in 49, the emerging new religion of Christianity may have had some influence, since Suetonius records that a riot had been provoked 'at the instigation of Chrestus' (*impulsore Chresto*); this may imply internal trouble between the older Jewish community and an emerging Christian element.[50] The Christians were mostly humble folk, though it is possible (but uncertain) that the *externa superstitio*, with which a noblewoman Pomponia Graecina was charged in A.D. 57, was Christianity. Nor will the Christians have been popularly distinguished from the Jews, but this was changed by Nero's persecution (p. 359). Thereafter they were recognised as a sect apart, suspected of a general hatred of mankind and liable to persecution if the authorities so decided. The long war between the Roman State and the Christian Church had been declared, although its eruptions for a considerable time were only sporadic.

CHAPTER 35

The 'Year of the Four Emperors'

1. The Revolt Against Nero

Nero not generally unpopular

The misgovernment of Nero's later years did not bring about any sharp change of feeling in the provinces, where its effects were not immediately perceived. The people of Rome forgot its grudge against the emperor as soon as the traces of the great fire of 64 were removed. The Senate harboured resentment at the loss of many of its most prominent members, but so long as it was unsupported by public opinion or by military force it could make no overt move. But the soldiers who had made Nero emperor also had the power to unmake him.

The problem of military discipline

The tradition of strict military discipline which Augustus had restored to the Roman army had proved an adequate safeguard against civil war for half a century after his death. But signs were not wanting that the soldiers might get out of hand again: one good reason for Tiberius's diffidence in accepting the imperial power was that he felt himself 'holding a wolf by the ears'.[1] Within a few weeks of his accession the legions in Pannonia and on the lower Rhine, impatient at the delays in the disbandment of time-expired men after the disaster of Varus, broke into open mutiny; those on the German frontier offered to march upon Rome in order to set their leader Germanicus in Tiberius's place. Under Caligula the commander of the army on the upper Rhine, Lentulus Gaetulicus, had not waited for the troops to incite him to rebellion (p. 355); during the next reign Camillus Scribonianus had incited the Illyrian legions to break their oath (p. 356). In these two instances the soldiers either did not renounce their obedience or were soon won back to it. But the emperors did not read aright the lessons of these attempted insurrections.

Tiberius, who had won golden opinions by the solicitude which he had shown for the troops under his command before his accession, made no attempt to renew acquaintance with them in his later years by going the rounds of the camps. Except for Claudius's visit to the war-front in Britain, none of the next three emperors saw any active service, and Nero's only absence from Italy was on a theatrical tour. On the other hand the special 'donatives' which Augustus's successors bestowed upon the praetorian cohorts were in the nature of a danegeld, which advertised the dependence of the emperors on their household troops and at the same time excited the jealousy of the frontier armies. Finally, in letting the pay and pensions of the soldiers fall into arrears, Nero loosened their only remaining bond of loyalty; and in putting to death without trial several of his chief officers he inevitably turned the thoughts of the rest towards a preventive attack upon him.[2]

Emperors neglect the army

A premonition of revolt among the troops was given to Nero in 65 by the so-called 'Pisonian conspiracy', in which some twenty men of senatorial or equestrian rank made preparations for his assassination. The ringleader of this gang, C. Calpurnius Piso, was a wealthy scion of the old nobility who carried on in the style of a republican grand seigneur. But the real driving-force of the movement proceeded from Faenius Rufus, the colleague of Tigellinus in the command of the Guards, who was not content to perform all the duties of the office while Tigellinus carried off all the honours, and from several subordinate officers, whose professional pride rebelled against Nero's crazy bohemianism.[3] The procrastinations of Piso, and the craven zeal with which some of his accomplices turned king's evidence when suspi-

The 'Pisonian conspiracy'

cion fell upon them, ensured the failure of the plot, and not long afterwards Nero went on his operatic tour in Greece in his most carefree mood. But the prominence of the military element in the Pisonian conspiracy was an unmistakable danger-signal.

Rising of Vindex in Gaul

Nero had hardly returned to Italy from his triumphal progress through Greece when he received news that the governor of Gallia Lugdunensis, C. Iulius Vindex, had renounced his allegiance and was inciting his colleague in Hispania Tarraconensis, Servius Sulpicius Galba, to champion the 'human race' against the emperor (March 68).[4] Galba, who had been set thinking and hoping by a stray prophecy that a new emperor should come forth from Spain, and had but recently saved his life by intercepting a *lettre de cachet* from Nero to his own procurator, followed the lead of Vindex so far as to place himself 'at the disposal of the Senate and people'; but for the present he held back from overt military action (he had only one legion). In the meantime Vindex, without waiting to assure himself of effective support from Galba, hastily collected a large following in his own province. But his Gallic birth – he was descended from a line of Aquitanian chieftains – placed him in a false position. Though his gesture to Galba could only mean that his aim was simply to supplant Nero by a more acceptable emperor, his rising bore a superficial resemblance to that of Florus and Sacrovir (p. 371), and it was a signal to the legions of Upper Germany to repeat their march into Gaul.[5] At a meeting near Vesontio (modern Besançon) the commander of the Rhine army, L. Verginius Rufus, was half won over by Vindex; but the troops, taking matters into their own hands (so it was later alleged), fell upon the latter's Gallic recruits and made short work of them. After this debacle Vindex took his own life. His revolt had apparently been no more than a flash in the pan.

His suppression by the Rhine army

Yet Vindex applied the match to a couple of trains which presently set Italy ablaze. The army that had destroyed Vindex was infected by his disloyalty to Nero. Before it returned to its quarters from Vesontio it made an offer to its commander to continue its march to Rome and to set him up in Nero's stead. For the moment indeed the troops were held in check by Verginius, who had the nerve to refuse his chance. But the fuse was left burning.

The praetorian cohorts turn against Nero

The rebellion of Vindex also revived disaffection among the praetorian cohorts at Rome. At the first news from Gaul Nero was swayed about between spells of insouciance and fits of despair. The bad impression which his vacillations made upon the household troops was utilised by their new commander, Nymphidius Sabinus, who had inherited the jealousy of his predecessor Faenius in regard to Tigellinus, to spread the rumour that the emperor had fled to Egypt. Misled by this false but credible report, and by the promise of a huge donative which Nymphidius made to them in the name of Galba, they transferred their allegiance at a moment's notice to Nymphidius's nominee. Tigellinus, whose nerve failed him completely in his first real crisis, did not lift a hand to protect Nero, and the Senate, which in this instance required no prompting by the soldiery, not only deposed the emperor but sentenced him to execution 'in the old-fashioned way' (the military punishment of death by cudgelling). Deserted by all save a few of his domestics, the dethroned emperor after long hesitations was helped by a freedman to thrust his sword home (summer 68). Among other recorded 'last words' was his cry 'Qualis artifex pereo' ('what a loss I shall be to the arts'); this may reveal the mainspring of his life.

Nero's deposition and death

2. Galba

With the death of Nero the Julio-Claudian dynasty became extinct, and the hereditary principle of succession, which had been tending to establish itself among the Roman emperors, was overthrown. The imperial power was formally conferred upon Galba by the Senate, whom it

The Senate appoints Galba governor of Spain

35.1 Galba.

readily accepted as a distinguished member of its own order, and a new stage in the development of the Principate was reached: 'a secret of empire was revealed that a princeps could be made elsewhere than at Rome' ('evolgato imperii arcano posse principem alibi quam Romae fieri'). The news of his appointment was brought to him by his freedman Icelus in seven days of lightning travel from the capital. Galba, who had been giving himself up for lost since the overthrow of Vindex, at once set out for Rome to secure his prize. Before he could make good his position he had to dispose of two possible rivals in the provinces, who delayed the swearing in of their troops to him. In Africa the military commander Clodius Macer kept a free hand for himself, under pretence of acknowledging none but the authority of the Senate; but Galba got rid of him by the dangerously easy device of assassination. In Lower Germany the commander-in-chief, Fonteius Capito, was similarly removed by his own subordinate, Fabius Valens, without waiting for Galba's orders. A more serious obstacle was set in Galba's path by Nymphidius Sabinus, who suddenly repented of his choice of emperor. After the deposition of Nero, Nymphidius had lost no time in compelling the resignation of Tigellinus, and he was expecting to retain the undivided command of the praetorian troops. On hearing that Galba, before leaving Spain, had appointed a personal confidant, Cornelius Laco, to the post vacated by Tigellinus, he opportunely discovered or remembered that he was a natural son of Caligula – a claim to which the very obscurity of his origin gave a certain colour – and called upon the Guards to transfer their allegiance back to the house of Germanicus. But the soldiers for the present stood by their oath to Galba and dispatched the new pretender out of hand. For the moment Galba had obtained the allegiance of all the Roman military forces, and his journey to Rome was a simple walk-over.

Galba has a walk-over

On taking up his duties as emperor Galba applied himself to the two most urgent problems created by Nero's misrule, the rehabilitation of the finances and the restoration of discipline in the army. But he lacked or had lost the cool judgment which such a task required. At the age of 71 he was unequal to the physical strain of his new duties, and his sudden promotion had flustered rather than reassured him. He was also unfortunate in the choice of his advisers, some of whom, like his freedman Icelus, were rogues, while Laco proved as helpless as he was honest. In executing Nero's freedmen and political advisers (with the exception of Tigellinus) by the mere power of the sword, he recalled his predecessor's worst acts of tyranny. His economies caused more offence than they brought in revenue; and although the revocation of the large fortunes which Nero had squandered on his favourites was justifiable enough in itself, the new emperor stultified these confiscations by permitting his own confidants to help themselves freely to the public funds. Though he rewarded the Gallic tribes which had supported Vindex, he unwisely punished those which had remained loyal to Nero. He also acted with severity towards some marines whom Nero had enrolled as legionaries to oppose

Galba shows firmness, but scant discretion

him. His parsimony prevented him entertaining the people, who remembered the festivals of Nero. He displayed exemplary firmness but scant discretion in repudiating the promises which Nymphidius had made on his behalf to the praetorian troops. In recalling Verginius from his command in Upper Germany he committed another error of judgment, for Verginius alone had sufficient authority to hold the Rhine armies in check, and the generals whom Galba sent to replace him and Fonteius Capito – Hordeonius Flaccus in Upper Germany and A. Vitellius on the lower Rhine – were totally unable to restrain the soldiery. The effective command on the German front now fell into the hands of two divisional officers, Fabius Valens and A. Caecina, who did not share Verginius's misgivings about a march on Rome. Galba's combination of worthy intentions and unwise action provoked Tacitus's famous epigram, 'omnium consensu capax imperii nisi imperasset' ('by general consent capable of ruling – had he not ruled').

His necessary economies alienate the troops

On 1 January of 69 the legions of Upper Germany, acting no doubt at the instigation of Caecina, refused to renew their oath of loyalty to Galba; those of the lower Rhine promptly followed suit (p. 405). At the news of this defection Galba rightly judged that his only chance of stemming the insubordination would be to nominate a co-regent and prospective successor. Had he now associated Verginius with himself he might have retrieved his position and averted civil war, as Nerva did when under similar circumstances he called Trajan to his aid (p. 425). But the emperor allowed his confidants to direct his choice to a young and untried man named L. Piso Licinianus, who was acceptable to the Senate because he was descended on both sides from the republican nobility, but meant nothing to the troops. The appointment of Piso was not only quite useless as a means of overawing the Rhine armies; it also served as an incitement to the household troops to forestall the legions from Germany. In bestowing favour upon Piso Galba incidentally gave offence to one of his confidants, named M. Salvius Otho, the former governor of Lusitania, who had been the first army commander to proclaim his allegiance to the new emperor. That Galba should have passed Otho over was not indeed to be wondered at, since his only qualifications for the succession were that he had been a boon companion of Nero and the previous husband of the empress Poppaea. Still less could it be foreseen that this mere courtier would succeed where Nymphidius Sabinus had failed. Yet when Otho made overtures to the praetorians and gave the usual assurances of a donative, the guardsmen, knowing that they had nothing further to expect

He is repudiated by the Rhine forces

Conspiracy of Otho

Galba is murdered by his Guards

from Galba, resolved to take their chance of the pretender redeeming his promise more faithfully. On 15 January 69, the household troops acclaimed Otho emperor in their camp and marched in upon the Forum, where they unceremoniously lynched Galba without anyone raising a hand in his defence. His death was followed by that of Piso and his other associates.

3. Otho

Otho proclaimed emperor. He inherits Galba's difficulties

Otho's mad bid for power was met by prompt recognition on the part of the Senate and of most provincial governors. But in dispossessing Galba he inherited his predecessor's liabilities. To say nothing of Galba's financial difficulties, which the new emperor's spendthrift habits bade fair to aggravate rather than to remove, he had still to prove whether he could command troops as well as bribe them. With Galba's fate before his eyes Otho could not venture to impose strict discipline upon the praetorians: it required all his resourcefulness to check a berserk rush by the Guards upon the Senate,

35.2 Otho.

which they suspected quite groundlessly of designs upon the emperor. But his most formidable problem lay in the defiant attitude of the Rhine armies.

The Rhine armies proclaim Vitellius

When the legions on the upper Rhine took the initative in renouncing allegiance to Galba on New Year's Day they had no candidate of their own to set in his place, and their first thought was to invite the Senate or the praetorians to make a choice for them. But their hesitations were soon resolved by the troops in Lower Germany. On 3 January, 69, Fabius Valens, who had been left unrewarded for the murder of Fonteius Capito, induced the army of the lower Rhine to acclaim its own commander, A. Vitellius, as emperor, and the forces of Upper Germany promptly fell in with this decision. Their candidate was a quite insignificant person, and not more than half willing to

have greatness thrust upon him; but he had inherited a distinguished name from his father, L. Vitellius, the confidant of Claudius (p. 636). His name and his character alike commended themselves to Valens and Caecina, who were in search of a figurehead emperor to screen their usurpation of actual power. While Vitellius stayed behind to form a reserve army, Caecina and Valens at once moved off with the flower of the Rhenish armies, and the death of Galba did not stay their course. Otho, it is true, made an attempt to buy Vitellius off, a proposal which the latter repaid in like coin, and when these overtures failed each of the rivals laid an abortive plan to remove the other by assassination. In any event the officers and men of the Rhenish armies, now thoroughly confident in their power to impose their own candidate, would not have allowed themselves to be put off by the substitution of Otho for Galba.

War strengths of Otho and Vitellius

In the civil war which the Rhine armies thus forced upon Otho the aggregate strength of the Vitellians, amounting to some 100,000 men, was barely equal to that which the emperor had at his disposal. But theirs were the best seasoned of all the Roman armies; they had the highest *esprit de corps* and the most resolute leaders. Otho indeed had Suetonius Paulinus and Verginius Rufus on his council, but he did not give them the free hand which Vitellius accorded to his lieutenants. Though he displayed an energy surprising to those who only knew of him as a man-about-town, the emperor was as unnerved by his responsibilities as Galba, and could not make up his mind to any consistent course of action. Moreover, as with Pompey in 49 B.C., his troops were scattered over a wide area and could not be concentrated before summer.

The Rhine armies invade Italy

The plan of campaign of the Vitellians was of a boldness that recalled the greatest exploits of Lucullus or Caesar. Valens and Caecina were each to lead a corps of 30,000–40,000 men across the Alps before the winter snows had melted, and to effect a junction in Transpadane Italy. Valens's march lay through France and over one of the western passes; Caecina had to traverse Switzerland and to surmount the Great St Bernard. The difficulty of their enterprise was enhanced by the unruly behaviour of the troops towards the natives through whose territory they passed; among the Helvetii Caecina's force provoked a determined resistance, which it only overcame by cutting its way through ruthlessly. Nevertheless the Rhenish armies accomplished their march without serious loss or delay – an achievement ranking with Hannibal's or Napoleon's passages of the Alps – and their intact armies ultimately joined hands at Cremona. The venture of the Rhine forces might indeed have ended in disaster if Otho's troops had been at hand to receive them as they debouched from the mountains. But the praetorian cohorts and small details which he had at hand did not move out in sufficient time to occupy the exits of the passes.

Otho holds the line of the Padus

The division of Caecina, which was the first to emerge on the plain of northern Italy, made an attempt to force the line of the Po without waiting for the troops of Valens; but it was held up between Placentia and Cremona, where Otho's weaker force made a somewhat unexpected stand (the so-called battle of Locus Castrorum). With the arrival of Valens's division the Vitellians were for the moment in overwhelming strength; but the gradual arrival of the strong detachments from the Dalmatian, Pannonian and Moesian armies, whose advance guard had by now joined Otho, would bring his forces nearly up to parity. Moreover, if Otho succeeded in playing for time, the dog-day heat and the autumn vintages of Lombardy could be counted on to deteriorate the invaders from northern quarters, as formerly they had played havoc with the Cimbri (p. 218). But although Otho's advisers pointed out with all due force that his advantage now lay in protracting the issue the emperor could not bear the suspense of a long-drawn-out conflict. With a view to forcing an immediate decision most of his available forces advanced westwards from his headquarters at Bedriacum, and sought out the Vitellians near Cremona.[7] In a hard-fought soldiers' battle on ground interspersed with vineyards the Othonians bore up gallantly against superior numbers, until they were taken in the flank by a division of Batavian auxiliary troops, who ended the whole war by this opportune move. With its retreat cut off by the river Po, the defeated army was driven to surrender, and its capitulation so disheartened Otho that he committed suicide, possibly to save his country from further civil war. Still undismayed, the remnant of his forces invited Verginius to proclaim himself emperor and to carry on the campaign. But Verginius, who had declined to confront Nero with a victorious army, naturally refused to lead a forlorn hope against the triumphant Vitellians. The entire Othonian army therefore came to terms, and the Rhine armies continued their march to Rome without further opposition, plundering the Italian countryside as if it was enemy territory. At the news of Otho's death the Senate transferred the imperial prerogative to Vitellius without waiting for orders, and the provincial governors gave him allegiance, if only to prepare their next move at leisure.

First battle of Cremona

Otho commits suicide. Vitellius becomes emperor

4. Vitellius

After the battle of Cremona the Vitellian leaders attempted to make their victory secure by drastic measures of precaution against the defeated Othonians. The praetorian corps of the late emperor was disbanded, the Danubian legions, which had meanwhile arrived in Italy, were sent back to their quarters, and their best centurions were put to death. To all appearances the power of the 'German emperor', as Vitellius styled himself,[8] had been established on firm foundations. But of all the emperors whom the surge of civil war cast up Vitellius was the most inert and helpless. On his arrival at Rome – at a respectable distance behind Caecina and Valens – he gave himself up to an incessant round of dissipations which recalled those of Nero's later years, save that they lacked Nero's artistry. By ill-timed lavishness he plunged the Roman

Incompetence of Vitellius

35.3   Vitellius.

treasury yet further into bankruptcy, and condemned himself to disappoint his troops of the victory bonus which they expected as of right. The soldiery recouped itself by throwing off all pretence of discipline and giving itself up to the good cheer of Rome.

The sense of security into which the Vitellians had lulled themselves rested on the false assumption that they had once for all overawed the remaining military forces of the Empire. But their arrogant self-assurance served as an incentive to the armies on other fronts to measure their strength against the legions of the Rhine, and the execution of Otho's centurions drove the officers to meditate rebellion in self-defence. The first open challenge to Vitellius's authority was made in the eastern provinces, where forces hardly inferior to the Rhine armies had been accumulated since the outbreak of the Jewish war. Of the three chief officers in the East the prefect of Egypt, Tiberius Alexander (p. 636), was the first Oriental to attain a post of this importance in the Roman executive; but he would not venture to claim the imperial office,

Rivalry between the frontier armies

for which Italian birth was still considered an indispensable qualification. The governor of Syria, C. Licinius Mucianus, was a man of noble ancestry, but lacked ambition or nerve to play for heavy stakes. Reserving themselves for the part of king-makers, Tiberius Alexander and Mucianus put forward as rival to Vitellius the commander of the field forces in Palestine, T. Flavius Vespasianus. The son of a money-dealer of equestrian rank, Vespasian was scarcely less of a *novus homo* than Tiberius Alexander; but he had been incited by flattering prophecies, such as had once encouraged Marius, to aspire to the highest position.

The eastern armies proclaim Vespasian

On 1 July 69 Tiberius Alexander swore in his troops to Vespasian. A few days later Vespasian's own forces acclaimed him emperor without waiting for further orders, and all the governors and dependent kings in the East followed suit. Vespasian apparently had no great confidence in the issue of a battle, for he based his strategy on the doubtful chance of starving Rome into submission by cutting off its supplies of grain from Egypt. While he proceeded to Alexandria to organise this indirect attack, Mucianus made a leisurely march through Asia Minor towards Europe, taking with him an army of some 20,000 men, and raising additional forces on the way. In pursuing this painfully methodical strategy the eastern commanders were giving their somnolent adversaries time to pull themselves together. But the

Vespasian's leisurely strategy

issue of the war was taken out of the hands of either party by the legions of the Danube, which now for the first time assumed their historical part as the emperor-making armies *par excellence*. Though they did not at this stage possess a candidate of their own they could not resign themselves to a watching role between other contestants. In the spring of 69 they had moved in support of Otho, but had been outstripped by the rush of events in Italy; in the autumn campaign of the same year they forced the pace and stole a march on Mucianus. At the first news of Vespasian's proclamation as emperor the legions of Pannonia and Moesia threw in their lot with him and resumed the road to Italy. The prime movement in this enterprise did not come from the commander-in-chief, but from a subordinate officer in the Pannonian army named Antonius Primus — a Gaul from Tolosa and a protégé of Galba — who now played a part like that of Caecina or Valens in the Rhine forces.

The Danube armies support Vespasian and force the pace

In the late autumn of 69 Primus set out on a tear-away march to Rome, which was only surpassed in ancient Italian warfare by Caesar's swoop upon Brundisium in 49 B.C. Disregarding Mucianus's instructions to wait for the arrival

of the eastern legions Primus pushed forward into the plain of northern Italy. With a force which never exceeded 50,000 men[9] he was apparently exposing himself to a crushing defeat by the far superior numbers of Vitellius; but he found the Vitellians utterly unprepared. While the emperor himself lay absorbed in his amusements, Valens had fallen sick, and Caecina, believing that the demoralisation of the troops was past repair, deliberately held them back. Caecina's troops, it is true, made a better rally than their general had allowed for: when he proposed to them to desert to Primus in a body, they put him under arrest. Under new officers of their own choice the Vitellian soldiers prepared to make a stand on the line of the middle Po, where Otho had held them in the spring campaign of that year. A race for Cremona ensued, in which Primus started from Verona and the main body of the Vitellians from their previous quarters at Hostilia in the lower Po valley. The rival armies came upon each other by surprise between Cremona and Bedriacum, near the site of the Vitellians' final victory in the spring campaign. In the second battle of Cremona the Vitellians probably had superior numbers, and they fought with the utmost determination — their main body engaged without delay after a forced march of thirty miles; but under the more experienced leadership of Primus the Danubian troops eventually broke through and completed their victory in Caesarian fashion by storming the enemy camp. A carnage among the defeated troops was followed by the destruction of Cremona, where Primus's soldiery, now thoroughly out of hand, systematically looted the dwellings and set them ablaze. The sack of Cremona was merely the worst of the pillagings with which the rival armies of the civil wars in 69 marked their path.

Antonius Primus's dash into Italy

Second battle of Cremona

The second battle of Cremona was scarcely less decisive than its predecessor. Its first effect was to bring the governors of the western provinces, who had hitherto waited upon events, to declare themselves openly on Vespasian's side. A belated attempt by Valens to bring reinforcements for Vitellius from Gaul ended in his capture and execution. After these disasters the emperor roused himself so far as to send forward his praetorian cohorts and some other details — some 20,000 men in all — to hold the snowbound Apennine passes; but an epidemic of desertions had set in by then, so that on the mere approach of Primus the defenders deserted him. As a last resort he clutched eagerly at a straw held out to him by Mucianus, who was hastening at last to the war zone and had perhaps reached Italy by now.[10] In return for his abdication Vitellius was offered a safe retreat

Debacle of the Vitellians

407

and a liberal subvention. Through the mediation of Vespasian's elder brother Flavius Sabinus, whom Vitellius had not troubled to remove from his command of the urban cohorts at Rome, the terms of capitulation were agreed upon. But before they could be carried out the remnant of the praetorian troops, who were less elated than the emperor at the prospect of their compulsory retirement, took matters into their own hands. Setting upon Sabinus they drove him with a few followers to the Capitol and lynched him after a short siege, during which the temple of Jupiter again suffered destruction by fire.[11]

The reprieve which the praetorians gave themselves by breaking off the parley lasted but a few days. At the news of the attack upon the Capitol Primus made a dash for Rome, and although he arrived too late to rescue Sabinus he annihilated the Vitellians in a desperate combat which was begun in the suburban lanes and ended with the storming of the praetorian camp. The emperor himself attempted escape, but was detected and punished by a retaliatory lynching, although by a final act of courage he had endeavoured to shield Sabinus against the anger of the troops (December 69). The entry of the Danubian troops into the capital foreboded a new reign of terror, as in the days of Marius and Sulla. Although the Senate promptly met to invest Vespasian with imperial power, and his younger son T. Flavius Domitianus, who had escaped detection by Vitellius's troops on the Capitol, assumed the role of vicegerent, the city lay for some days at the mercy of the infuriated Danubian soldiery, whom Primus no longer troubled to restrain. Fortunately Mucianus now caught up the march of events. Hastening to Rome he displaced Domitian and overawed the troops, who returned obediently at his word to their stations on the frontier. On the arrival of Vespasian in Rome (in the summer of 70) Mucianus in turn effaced himself, and did not even claim to play Agrippa to Vespasian's Augustus.

5. Conclusion

The 'year of the four emperors', as A.D. 69 has been called, marked a temporary reversion to the conditions under which the Republic had been destroyed. Despite the professions which one pretender after another put forward, that he was the servant of Senate and people, or had come to avenge the last ruler but one, they were

without exception military adventurers, and all but the last of the series remained at the mercy of the soldiers to whom they owed their promotion. Though the civil wars began in a movement of protest against the misrule of Nero,[12] they soon became so devoid of political principle that the Senate played no part in them, save automatically to invest each successful usurper with the prerogative of Augustus.

But the civil war of 69 was more than a mere interlude between the Julio-Claudian and the Flavian dynasties. In the hope of gaining active support among the provincials, each emperor in turn extended the Roman franchise among them. Galba conferred Roman citizenship on several tribes of central Gaul; Otho bestowed it upon the Lingones in eastern Gaul; Vitellius made lavish grants of 'Latin rights', presumably in Spain and Africa. Though these donations were but expedients of the moment, and unsuccessful at that, the privileges thus conceded were allowed to stand, and the way was prepared for a wider participation of the provinces in Roman administration. Furthermore, the 'year of the four emperors' revealed two 'secrets of empire' to the Roman world. In the first place it showed that the seat of Augustus was not permanently reserved for members of the old republican nobility or of Augustus's 'senatorial order'. At the death of Nero the prejudice in favour of aristocratic descent was still so prevalent that Verginius Rufus and (on first thought) Nymphidius Sabinus held themselves disqualified by their obscure birth from becoming emperors and made way for Galba, who could trace his ancestry back to Jove and Pasiphae. The families of Otho and Vitellius could boast of no such pedigree, but they formed part of the new imperial aristocracy of office. On the other hand Vespasian was *ex senatus*, and his promotion to imperial power threw open the field of competition to a far wider range of candidates. Secondly, the campaigns of 69 disclosed that 'emperors could be made elsewhere than at Rome' — a discovery of which Tacitus grasped the importance, though he could not foresee its full consequences. Given this knowledge, and the rivalries among the several frontier forces, the danger was never remote that the soldiers might embark upon fresh rounds of civil wars. In 69, it is true, the troops soon became weary of a game with which they were not yet thoroughly familiar. But the events of that year gave warning that if once an army had broken its oath of loyalty to an emperor, it might make light of its engagements to all future rulers.

CHAPTER 36

The Flavian Emperors[1]

1. Personalities

Vespasian's origin

The founder of the 'Flavian dynasty', T. Flavius Vespasianus (71–79), was a fair representative of the new governing class which the early emperors had recruited among the bourgeoisie of Italy. Sprung from the Sabine hill-town of Reate of an equestrian family he turned to a senatorial career; he was suffect consul in 51, and served with distinction in Britain (43–44) and Africa (proconsul *c.* 63). Although he had incurred Nero's displeasure by falling asleep during one of the emperor's singing recitals, in A.D. 67 at the age of fifty-eight he was appointed to crush the Jewish revolt. His subsequent accession to imperial power was regarded almost as a portent, and his prospects of success in the work of reconstruction, which had proved too much for Galba, must at first have seemed highly problematical.

His merits as an administrator

The new emperor was an administrator rather than a statesman: of creative imagination he had scarcely a trace. Nevertheless he was peculiarly well fitted for his task, which was not so much to devise a new engine of government as to give the existing machinery a fresh

start after derailment. He was a man of indefatigable industry who spared neither himself nor his subordinates;[2] but he tempered his firmness with an imperturbable sanity and a disarming sense of humour. By the exercise of these opportune virtues he established his authority firmly, dominating both the Senate and the armies, and crushing all rebellions abroad. He thus gave the Roman world what most men desired, peace; and since he had two sons, he offered the prospect of sustaining order for a further generation at least. Like a second Augustus he might restore confidence in Rome's future after the shock of bitter civil war.

Titus, a general favourite

Vespasian's elder son, who bore the same three names as his father, but was generally known by his praenomen Titus (79–81), was one of the most lavishly endowed of Roman emperors, setting off a versatile intellect with a handsome presence and a winning manner. The 'darling of all mankind', he caught the world's fancy, as though the elder Drusus or Germanicus had come to life again. Like these two gallants he was cut off in his prime – 'whom the Roman people loved died young'. Cool observers, who remembered the similar

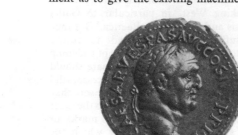
36.1 Vespasian.

36.2 Titus.

409

promising débuts of Caligula and Nero, wondered whether such amiability in a new emperor was a sign of ill omen. But his reign of two years was too brief to show its future trend.

Domitian, distrustful but despotic

The younger son, T. Flavius Domitianus (81–96), offered a striking contrast in outward manner to his brother, for he was as taciturn as Titus was expansive. In this trait he recalled Tiberius, on whose pattern he sought to model himself more closely by perusing that emperor's state papers and private memoirs. His natural reserve was confirmed by the slights which he experienced at the hands of Vespasian and Titus, for while both of these accorded to him consulships and other empty marks of honour, neither would trust him with military commands or other responsible offices. Enforced inaction turned Domitian sour and rendered him distrustful. But his diffidence, unlike that of Tiberius, never extended to himself; rather, his

36.3 Domitian.

early repressions made him more self-assertive, and when his brother's sudden death left the imperial power in his hands he exercised it in a frankly despotic fashion. He followed the example of Caesar in wearing the full purple toga of a *triumphator* even in the Senate; he was pleased when poets addressed him as *dominus et deus*, and may even have made unofficial use of the title himself; above all, he never put himself into the hands of a Seianus. His self-sufficing manner exposed his policies to

Domitian's ability

misconstruction and made him one of the most maligned of Roman emperors; yet it was in large measure justified by his abilities. If to him the state was a mere machine, at any rate he was an efficient driver. While he lacked his father's saving sense of humour, he inherited his industriousness and calm good judgment. Domitian completed the work of restoration which Vespasian had successfully begun.

2. Constitutional Changes

The constitutional powers which the Senate conferred upon Vespasian at his accession conformed throughout to the precedents set by Augustus and the Julio-Claudian emperors,[3] but they were subsequently enlarged in accordance with the set policy of the Flavian emperors. It was a change of appearance rather than of substance that Vespasian and Domitian held an almost continuous run of consulships, for these did not invest them with any effective additional power, and indeed were assumed by them for the first four or six months only of each year; their reiterated tenure of the consulate probably harboured no deeper design than to confer the mark of high nobility upon the upstart family of the Flavii Vespasiani.[4] A more far-reaching innovation was the revival of the censorship by Vespasian in 73, and its permanent occupation by Domitian from 84 or 85 to his death. In resuscitating this office the immediate object of Vespasian was to conduct a general numbering of the citizen body in Italy and the provinces; but the most important use to which he and Domitian put their censorial power was to create new senators by the process of direct nomination. The right of *adlectio*, which had been tentatively used by Claudius (p. 360), was resumed on a more extensive scale by Vespasian, and was habitually exercised by Domitian. The purpose of the Flavian emperors in nominating senators was not to pack the House with their adherents, as in the days of the Second Triumvirate; their aim was to draft into it men of tried ability (such as equestrian members of the administrative service) who were past the usual age for holding a quaestorship and qualifying for a seat in the normal manner. By this process the Flavian emperors gave wider effect to Claudius's policy of infusing the Senate with more men from the municipal towns of Italy and especially more men of provincial origin. Like Claudius, they used their censorial powers with discretion, restricting their field of selection to the more highly urbanised and Romanised districts of the Latin-speaking West, in particular to Gallia Narbonensis and to Hispania Baetica.[5] But they gave a sufficiently strong lead to future emperors to ensure that their policy of widening the area of recruitment for the Senate should be carried on. Though Domitian's successors did not formally assume the office of censor, they tacitly retained its power and used it to the same end. The epoch of the Flavians thus marks an important stage in the process by which the Senate, from being the preserve of the Italians, became representative of the entire Empire. Further, the members of the new aristocracy,

Revival of the censorship

Adlectio of senators

Admission of provincials into the Senate

which had been injected into the Senate, were not merely loyal to the emperors, but in the main sober and industrious men, like Vespasian himself, who proved good servants of the Empire. The irresponsibility of Nero's later years was succeeded by a period of greater conscientiousness (thus, for example, during the whole of Vespasian's reign only one trial for provincial misgovernment is recorded, and even then the accused was acquitted).

The Senate neglected by Vespasian

But while they modified the composition of the Senate Vespasian and Domitian did nothing to strengthen its position as a council of state. They regarded it merely as a panel from which they might choose individual members for their administrative service, rather than as a corporation with important collective functions. The attitude of the Flavians to the Senate was exhibited with almost brutal candour by Domitian.

and slighted by Domitian

While Vespasian consulted the House for form's sake and treated it with perfunctory courtesy, Domitian seldom summoned it except to impart information, and he mercilessly stripped away the illusion that it was the emperor's partner rather than his servant. He therefore earned the hatred of the Senate as no previous emperor had done, for while the heavy hand of Tiberius or of Nero had descended upon individual suspects in the House, that of Domitian rested on the House as a whole. Thus the co-operation between *Princeps* and Senate, to which Augustus had striven to give a semblance of reality, now suffered a severe set-back. In so far as it envisaged any real division of power rather than of function between the two partners it had always been a fiction, but a useful one: now it was brutally exposed.

Growth of the imperial executive

In the civil wars of 69 the value of the new professional executive had been set forth in a clear light. While emperors came and went the professional functionaries for the most part retained their posts and preserved a great measure of continuity in the administration. Under the Flavian emperors the executive officials were subjected to the same strict supervision as in the best days of Augustus and Tiberius: no emperor showed better judgment in selecting his administrators or more firmness in controlling them than Domitian. The supply of suitable candidates for an administrative career had now increased so far that the emperors had less need to confide public duties to their domestic staff. Hence, although the Flavians retained ex-slaves of proved merit in their service,[6] they transferred most of the secretarial and financial work which had previously been the special province of the freedmen to persons of equestrian rank. We may probably ascribe to Vespasian or to Domitian the creation of a

Equites replace freedmen

new official, the *iuridicus*, who relieved the governors in some of the larger imperial provinces of their jurisdiction among civilians.[7] The tendency for the professional executive to become differentiated into a military and a civilian branch is visible in this addition to the provincial staffs.

In regard to the succession Vespasian frankly treated the imperial office as a hereditary property. In order to remove all doubts as to his intentions, and to discourage inconvenient ambitions in other families, he instituted what was virtually a joint rule between himself and his elder son. Not content to associate Titus with himself in the consulate, the censorship and the *tribunicia potestas*, he appointed him sole commander of the praetorian cohorts and delegated to him a general right of control over the administration. Titus and Domitian also received the title of *Princeps Iuventutis*. Despite their distrust of Domitian, his father and brother recognised him without reserve as heir presumptive, in the event of Titus leaving no issue.[8] Domitian for his part executed two of his cousins, Flavius Clemens and Flavius Sabinus, on a charge of conspiracy (p. 424); but he destined one or other of Clemens's young sons to be his successor. Had Domitian not been cut off by a premature death the hereditary principle might have been definitely introduced into the Roman Empire under the Flavian dynasty.

Dynastic policy of the Flavian emperors

Since Vespasian could not claim, as had the Iulii, descent from gods and kings of Rome, nor even from the Divi who preceded him, he might have sought excessive honours, but the flattery of the ruler-cult was alien to his nature.[9] Although he believed in portents and prophecies his down-to-earth attitude to deification and emperor-worship is summarised in his half-amused remark when he was dying, 'Alas, I think that I am becoming a god' (*Vae, puto deus fio*. No less typically he struggled to his feet, since 'an imperator should die standing'). Nevertheless he knew well by then that his services to his country and the piety of his sons would ensure that after death he would become Divus. But in life, although he made no effort to check divine honours in the provinces, in Rome he was content, like Augustus, to be a *civilis*, a man. Titus, besides getting the Senate to consecrate his father, established a cult and temple near the Tabularium (completed by Domitian, the temple became that of Vespasian and Titus). He also secured the consecration of Domitilla, who is probably his sister rather than his mother. Further, he honoured his daughter Julia with the title of Augusta. His great popularity naturally secured his own consecration after his early death. Whereas he and his father

Emperor-worship

followed the moderation of Augustus and Tiberius, Domitian turned closer to the examples of Caligula and Nero, at least in the later part of his reign. Seeking to dominate all elements in the state, Senate, people and army, he welcomed the flattery of poets like Martial, who compared him with the gods (not always to their advantage), and he probably accepted greeting in the form of *dominus et deus*. Men had for long voluntarily taken oaths by the Genius of the *Princeps*, but Domitian now probably made this practice a test of loyalty: a suspect could be ordered to show his loyalty by sacrificing before the image of the emperor, and refusal might entail a charge of 'atheism'. This, rather than declaration of Christianity as such, will have formed the basis of the charge against any Christians who were executed during his reign. The evidence for any serious Domitianic persecution is very slight: even Ter-

tullian says Domitian soon changed his mind and recalled those whom he had exiled, but some Christians probably came under his ban on the spread of Oriental religions (Isis-worship being excepted) and the measures taken against proselytising Jews and judaising Gentiles.[10] In general his permissive attitude to flattery, which contrasts strangely with a strong streak of archaic harshness in his nature, emphasised the increasing autocracy of his position.

3. General Administration

In the city of Rome the Flavian rulers introduced a new 'Augustan age' of great building activity and extensive restoration including new Fora, temples, a palace and the Colosseum (p. 468). Domitian instituted a new festival of Jupiter Capitolinus on the model of Nero's

36.4   The Colosseum, with the temple of Venus and Rome in the foreground. The Amphitheatrum Flavium, generally known as the Colosseum, was begun by Vespasian and dedicated by Titus in A.D. 80. External view. It is elliptical and measures 180 metres long and 156 wide. It could contain an audience of some 45,000 to 50,000 spectators.

36.5   The Colosseum. Internal view. The masonry in the bottom right-hand side of the picture was below the wooden floor of the arena.

The administration of Rome

'Iuvenalia' (p. 358), and in 88 he conducted another jubilee celebration of the *ludi saeculares.* On the other hand the licence of Nero's reign was firmly suppressed. Domitian even insisted on the spectators at the games being properly dressed in a toga; and he made a short-lived attempt to bring the laws of Augustus *de maritandis ordinibus* into stricter operation. An attack of the plague in 79, followed by a second extensive fire in the centre of the city, showed up some remaining weak points in the government of the capital. On the other hand the supply of corn, which Vespasian went to intercept at Alexandria (p. 407), but stayed to reorganise, suffered no further interruption. Although an Egyptian squadron had probably formed part of the Roman navy since Augustus, Vespasian organised it as *classis Augusta Alexandrina* in order to secure the regular transportation of grain to Rome.

With the re-establishment of peace the traces of the civil war in Italy were soon obliterated, and Cremona speedily rose from its ashes. A great natural calamity befell the happy region of Campania during the reign of Titus. In 79 Mt Vesuvius, which had remained quiescent since the prehistoric age, broke into sudden activity and buried three cities, Herculaneum, Pompeii and Stabiae, under a rain of volcanic dust.[11] The greater number of the inhabitants, assisted by the fleet from Misenum, escaped in good time, and although the submerged

Italy. The destruction of Pompeii

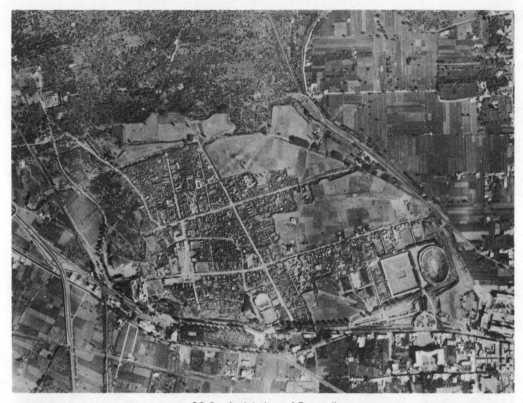

36.6   Aerial view of Pompeii.

towns were not rebuilt, the adjacent land was redistributed by an imperial commission and brought back into cultivation. An agrarian crisis under Domitian, arising out of an over-production of wine (p. 451), was solved in a rough-and-ready manner by renewing and reinforcing the Senate's policy of restriction (p. 626). The remedy swiftly prescribed by Domitian, an embargo on all new plantation in Italy, and the uprooting of half or more of the vineyards in the provinces, remained in force for two centuries, but it never became fully operative.

The financial chaos resulting from Nero's extravagance had been intensified to such a degree by the civil wars that the problem of balancing the state budget tested Vespasian's resourcefulness to the utmost. On his own reckoning it required at least 4000 million sesterces to set the state finances on a sound footing.[12] Vespasian drastically raised the rates of existing imposts and invented new sources of revenue with the ingenuity of a Henry VII. He increased, sometimes doubled, provincial taxation; he revoked the immunities from taxation which Nero had bestowed upon Greece; he resumed on behalf of the treasury most of the large estates in Egypt which earlier emperors had lavished

Vespasian restores the state finances

upon their friends. He set up commissions to delimit more strictly the public land in Italy and the provinces, so as to recover large pieces of territory which private landowners had surreptitiously incorporated into their holdings. We may probably ascribe to the same ruler a new code for the leasing of imperial *latifundia* and mining fields.[13]

In one respect Vespasian was more fortunate than his predecessors. Since he had not made extravagant promises of bounty money to his troops he contrived to settle with them at a comparatively slight cost to the treasury. In his personal expenditure he set an example of old-time frugality; and he did not connive at those pilferings by subordinates which had stultified the efforts of Galba at economy. By his resolute management Vespasian more than restored the imperial finances. He raised sufficient funds to carry out an extensive programme of new buildings and to inaugurate a policy of regular state subventions to higher education (p. 479), and he was able to give relief to the cities ruined by fires or earthquakes with the same liberal hand as Tiberius. It may be taken for granted that the additional taxation of his early reign was largely remitted before his death.

Under Titus, who lacked his father's capacity

Vespasian's liberalities

Prodigality of Titus

to say 'no', the treasury again suffered from leakages and it was burdened with a permanent new expenditure when Domitian, to ensure himself against fresh military mutinies, raised the annual pay of the legions from 225 to 300 denarii. But the same emperor slightly reduced the numbers of the army, and he refused to curry favour with the soldiers by paying them special donatives. The general administration of Domitian was so far successful, that he was able to follow his father's policy of judicious liberality to provincial cities and to effect a temporary improvement in the quality of the coinage, which had remained depreciated since the time of Nero.[14]

Domitian balances accounts

4. The Jewish War

The military history of the Flavian era falls into two distinct periods. In the first two years of his reign Vespasian was engaged in quelling rebellions which had broken out before his accession. In the warfare of his later years and of Domitian's reign the Roman legions broke fresh ground in search of better frontiers, or in making preventive attacks.

In Palestine the war of reconquest which Vespasian had carried to its final stage before the death of Nero was suspended by him in 68, on the ostensible ground that his commission lapsed with the emperor's decease, but with the real intention of keeping a free hand for himself. His entry into the field against Vitellius in 69 gave the insurgents a second year of respite. During this interval the Jews only partly healed their internal feuds and combined to repair the multiple lines of fortifications round Jerusalem. In 70 Titus, taking over his father's command, closed in upon the city, still weakened by fierce internal dissensions, and reduced it after a siege

Resumption of the Jewish War

36.7   Closer view of large theatre, Odeum and gladiatorial barracks at Pompeii.

36.8   A street in Herculaneum. The modern town can be seen above the ancient street.

of six months, which for sheer hard fighting recalled the investment of Carthage by Scipio Aemilianus. The defenders, even when reduced to the last extremes of famine, contested every position inch by inch, and when Titus carried the last two strongholds, the plateau of the Temple and the citadel, he occupied little else but a field of ruins. But the resistance in Palestine was not yet completely crushed: the three

Siege and destruction of Jerusalem

fortresses of Herodium, Machaerus and Masada held out, Masada until 73. This last stronghold, a residence and fortress of Herod the Great on a plateau rising sheer above the Dead Sea, withstood a final siege for six months, although surrounded by Roman walls of circumvallation, against the onslaught of 7000 legionaries and auxiliaries commanded by Flavius Silva, who

finally built a vast earth ramp on which to mount his artillery; the surviving garrison at length set fire to the buildings and, except two women and five children, committed suicide.[15] The settlement of Palestine was harsh. The surviving population of Jerusalem was mostly reduced to slavery, and a Roman legion, the Tenth, was permanently stationed on the site. The Sanhedrin was abolished, and the Roman procurator's court took over its criminal jurisdiction. The Temple, which had been burnt down in the siege — either by accident or more probably on Titus's orders — was not allowed to be rebuilt. A ban was set on proselytising to Jewish practices, and under Domitian at least this offence was systematically punished. The Jewish population throughout the Empire was

36.9   Masada. The Roman camps on the east side of the fortress, with the Dead Sea beyond.

called upon to pay as a new poll-tax for the service of Jupiter Capitolinus the two drachmae which they had been accustomed to pay to the temple at Jerusalem; this impost was levied by Domitian with inquisitorial rigour. The Jewish state ceased to exist, and the Saduccean party disappeared with the abolition of the Chief Priesthood. The Pharisaic party alone survived and concentrated its attention increasingly upon the study and inculcation of the Law in a centre which grew up at Jamnia.[16] On the other hand Rome still allowed all those born in the Jewish faith to remain free from Caesar-worship throughout the Empire. Meantime already in 68 the small Christian community in Jerusalem had escaped to Pella, and the destruction of Jerusalem henceforth meant greater freedom from its earlier cradle of Judaism for the new

36.10   Masada. The summit on which the fortress was built, showing the impregnable nature of the upper rock, which is the same on all sides. The height of the summit is 1700 feet above the Dead Sea.

36.11   Panel from the Arch of Titus which was erected in Rome after his death in A.D. 81. It depicts the spoils of Jerusalem (seven-branched candlestick, table for the shew-bread and trumpets) carried in Titus's triumphal procession.

religion as it spread through the Greek East. Titus, his settlement completed, returned to Rome for a glorious triumph, carrying off as trophies the golden table of shew-bread, the seven-branched candlestick and a roll of the Law. These symbols of the Jewish faith were duly represented on the Arch, which was later dedicated to Titus's memory in the Forum: on it, in Shelley's words, 'is sculptured in deep relief, the desolation of a city'. Desolation indeed might reign in Judaea, but at least it enjoyed peace for the next fifty years.

5. The Revolt of Civilis and Classicus

A second insurrection, which was the direct outcome of the civil war, broke out in 69 on the Rhine border. This movement originated with the Batavians of the lower Rhine region, who had rendered good service to Vitellius in the spring campaign of 69 (p. 406), but had since been aggrieved by a harshly enforced demand for additional troops in the ensuing summer. The rebellion was organised by a chieftain named Iulius Civilis. Like the Cheruscan Arminius (p. 336), the Batavian Civilis had re-

ceived Roman franchise after loyal service in the auxiliary forces; but a false charge of treason, which Fonteius Capito, the commander of the army on the lower Rhine, had sprung upon him about the time of Nero's death, turned him into an actual traitor. In autumn 69 the renewal of the civil war in Italy gave Civilis his opportunity. Acting in concert with Antonius Primus he declared for Vespasian, and in his name attacked the attenuated Vitellian garrisons on the lower Rhine; but he gave a hint of his ulterior purpose when he invited the independent German tribes to support his offensive. While Hordeonius Flaccus, who had been left in charge of the Rhine defences, stood irresolute at Novaesium (modern Neuss), Civilis secured the lower reaches of the river and laid siege to Vetera, the nearest legionary headquarters. Here Civilis sustained a temporary check, for his storming parties were held at a distance by the Roman camp artillery, and he was unable to prevent an energetic officer named Dillius Vocula, whom Flaccus had summoned from Moguntiacum, from cutting his way into the beleaguered fortress. But Vocula's effort was as inconclusive as the first relief of Lucknow in 1857. At the news of Vitellius's defeat in Italy

The rising of Civilis on the lower Rhine

418

The Roman garrisons depleted and demoralised

the discipline of the Roman troops, which had been lax throughout the campaign, broke down altogether. Flaccus, who had declared for Vespasian, was lynched by troops pretending loyalty to Vitellius. Vocula, returning to Moguntiacum, momentarily rallied its garrison (which had gone over to Vespasian), but he would not venture to take the field again. In the meantime Civilis, declaring himself openly as a rebel against Roman authority, resumed the blockade of Vetera.[17]

Rebellion in north-east Gaul

Early in 70 the tidings that the Capitoline temple at Rome had been burnt down (p. 408) caused a flutter among the Gauls, and emboldened some of the Druids to announce a forthcoming world-conquest by the Nordic peoples. Under the impression of these prophecies two chiefs of the Treviri, Iulius Classicus and Iulius Tutor, came to secret terms with Civilis. Resorting to the stratagem by which Ambiorix had formerly decoyed the lieutenants of Caesar from their camp (p. 263) Tutor and Classicus lured Vocula away from Moguntiacum by false promises of co-operation in a second relief expedition to Vetera. On the way to Vetera they removed Vocula by assassination and won over the bewildered soldiery to the service of an 'empire of the Gauls', of which Classicus was to be the ruler. By the same propaganda they also reduced the garrisons at Moguntiacum and Vetera, which were likewise incorporated into the imperial Gallic army. The fall of Vetera was an outstanding disaster in the annals of Roman military history, and the security of Rome itself was threatened. The entire line of the Rhine to Strasbourg or Basle had now been lost to the Romans, and the border tribes on the Gallic side of the river had mostly thrown in their lot with Classicus or Civilis.

The insurgents carry the line of the Rhine

But the landslide of rebellion, upon which Classicus and Tutor had counted among their own countrymen, never took place. At a congress which the other Gallic tribes held at Durocortorum (modern Rheims) the solicitations of the Treveri fell upon deaf ears, and the 'Gallic Empire' remained confined to the Rhine border.[18] Still less could the rebel Gallic leaders extend their control over Civilis and his German allies, whose eventual object was complete independence and, we may suspect, liberty to resume the plundering of Gaul. Their attitude to Classicus was revealed by a massacre which they committed among the troops from Vetera, in defiance of the terms of capitulation. The German and the Gallic armies eventually parted company, and neither party made preparations for Vespasian's counter-attack.

The rest of Gaul refuses support to the rebels

In summer 70 an army which Mucianus had formed from the remaining Roman garrisons in Europe took the field against the rebels under the command of a kinsman of Vespasian, Q. Petillius Cerialis. At the mere approach of Cerialis the legionaries in the 'imperial Gallic' army deserted back to the Roman side, and Moguntiacum fell back into his hands without resistance. From this position Cerialis recovered Augusta Trevirorum (Trier), the capital of Classicus, and in a hard-fought battle near this city he destroyed the Gallic Empire. After another stiffly contested fight near Vetera, where he met a miscellaneous German levy under Civilis, Cerialis drove the Batavians back upon their own territory. Here the Roman commander, who was ill-served by his fleet, found himself baffled by the intricacies of the Rhine and Meuse estuaries; but eventually he obtained the surrender of the Batavi by an offer of easy terms. In the following year Vespasian celebrated the termination of the Rhenish and the Jewish Wars by closing the temple of Janus.

Petillius Cerialis suppresses the risings

The revolt of Civilis and Classicus threw into relief both the strength and the weakness of the Roman Empire. On the one hand it gave proof that the Gallic people as a whole had become reconciled to Roman rule. Now that the Gauls had tasted the full benefits of Roman protection, and were being progressively accepted into partnership with their former conquerors, they were no longer in a mood for adventures which might end in the renewal of the German invasions.[19] On the other hand the warfare on the Rhine showed up in a clear light the dangers attendant on emperor-making by the Roman army. So long as this sport was confined to the household troops its effects did not reach far beyond the capital. But once the line regiments joined in, every Roman frontier was thrown into jeopardy, and every border tribe received, as it were, an invitation to take its chance against the depleted Roman garrisons. In 69, it is true, the troops did not stay away long from their proper quarters, and no permanent harm was done. But the rebellion in the Rhineland gave warning that if the game of emperor-making was to go on, it must be played under observation of a time-limit.

The Gauls reconciled to Roman rule

Emperor-making endangers the frontiers

As a measure of insurance against new civil wars, Vespasian entrusted the defence of the frontier to a large extent to other legions drawn from different parts of the Empire, and established a new legionary camp at Noviomagus (near Nijmegen), thus spreading out the legions a little more; the destroyed double legionary fortress at Vetera was replaced by a camp for a single legion about a mile away from the old station. To guard against further 'Sepoy rebellions', he moved the auxiliary troops from their native districts to distant frontiers, and

Reorganisation on the Rhine

transferred their command from native chieftains to Roman officers. He later decided to advance the Roman frontier east of the upper Rhine (p. 421).

6. Further Conquest in Britain[20]

Vespasian resumes the conquest of Britain

The peace which Vespasian celebrated in 71 lasted scarcely a year. A policy of foreign adventures, it is true, was no more congenial to him than it had been to Augustus, and the financial considerations, which had compelled the first emperor to call a halt in Rome's career of conquest, weighed even more heavily with the Flavian rulers. Yet Vespasian had the same interest as Augustus in occupying the troops on foreign expeditions, so as to efface the memory of the civil wars; and he had a clear strategic justification in advancing the frontiers in the half-conquered land of Britain. In this country the Romans made the same discovery as the Norman and Plantagenet rulers of a later day, that the English lowlands might be held more securely by taking in part of the adjacent hill-country.

Cerialis occupies Brigantia

The kingdom of the Brigantes in north Britain, stretching from sea to sea, under its client Queen Cartimandua (p. 373) had protected the northern frontier of the Roman province, but dynastic troubles necessitated Roman armed intervention under the governor Vettius Bolanus (69–71). More, however, was needed, and shortly after the reconquest of the Rhineland Vespasian appointed Petillius Cerialis to be governor of Britain (71). Advancing from his old quarters at Lindum (Lincoln), where he had commanded a legion under Suetonius Paulinus (p. 373), Cerialis advanced his legionary headquarters to Eboracum (York) and defeated the divorced husband of Cartimandua probably near the great hill-fort at Stanwick. He was helped by a pincer movement from Uriconium (Wroxeter) and the west, led by Agricola, legate of Legio XX. Cerialis's successor, Sex. Iulius Frontinus (74–78) then resumed the advance into Wales.[21] He moved Legio II Augusta from Glevum (Gloucester) to a new fortress at Isca Silurum (Caerleon) near the mouth of the Usk in the heart of the Silurian country, and built some forts on the southern Welsh coast (e.g. at Cardiff). He defeated the Silures, destroyed their stronghold in Llanmelin Wood and provided a new town for them at Venta Silurum (Caerwent), where they could be watched by the legion at Caerleon. He also built many roads and forts (e.g. around Brecon and in the upper Severn valley, as at Caersws). Nor did he neglect northern Wales; he started building a fortress at Deva (Chester) and turned against the Ordo-

Frontinus in Wales

vices, in whose territory he established some garrisons. Although he did not complete their conquest he laid down the pattern for the subjugation of the whole of Wales.

Agricola's governorship

Frontinus was succeeded in 79 by Cn. Iulius Agricola, who had already served in Britain on the staff of Suetonius Paulinus and as legate under Cerialis.[22] He thus knew northern Wales and lost no time in defeating the Ordovices and overrunning Mona (Anglesey). He established forts at Segontium (Caernarvon) and Caerhun, if Frontinus had not already done this. In 79 two parallel columns advanced from Deva and Eboracum, overrunning Brigantia, while the western division also cut off the Lake District. They reached the Tyne–Solway line (later occupied by Hadrian's Wall). Then in 80 the Lowlands of Scotland were conquered, the Tanaus (probably the Tay) was reached, and in 81 some forts were built from Bodotria to Clota (Forth to Clyde) very roughly on the line of the later Antonine Wall, and the whole position was consolidated. The advance, which Titus must have authorised, was now halted, perhaps with the intention of limiting conquest to southern Scotland. Thus in 82 the western flank of this area was conquered by an expedition across the Solway Firth to overawe Ayrshire and Galloway. Agricola, who had received a fugitive Irish chief, is alleged to have said that Ireland could be conquered by one legion, but he made no attempt to put his prophecy to the test. Domitian, who had succeeded Titus, was ready for further advance, so in 83 the Romans marched northwards through the plains of eastern Scotland, blocking the approaches to the Highlands on their left flank with forts at the exits of the glens. After beating off an attack they reached a point not far from Aberdeen, and a legionary fortress was started at Inchtuthil. In 84 the Caledonian tribes mobilised for a final effort which ended in their defeat at Mons Graupius, perhaps near the approaches to Inverness (a camp, apparently Agricolan, has been found at Auchinhove near the pass of Grange). Victory achieved, Agricola sent his fleet, which had rendered valuable support in the advance, to explore the Orkneys and to sail round the north of Britain to establish that it was an island. He then heard that Domitian had given him triumphal ornaments and that, after the unusually long period of six years' governorship, he was recalled. But extremely efficient military activity, with the concomitant construction of over 1300 miles of roads and at least sixty forts, is only one aspect of his governorship. The other was his policy of romanisation and education in the settled parts of the province. He encouraged urban development by the building of temples, Fora and town-houses (an inscription from the new Forum at Verulamium, dated 79, bears his name; Fora at London, Exeter and Cirencester are all Flavian), and he fostered the education of the sons of the leading men in the liberal arts. Thus, as Tacitus reports, 'the toga was seen everywhere'. Britain entered upon a period of accelerated economic development, and was for the first time brought fully within the ambit of continental European culture.

These conquests and the maintenance of peace in Britain had engaged four legions and perhaps some seventy auxiliary regiments, but because of trouble on the Danube (p. 422) Domitian transferred Legio II Adiutrix from Chester to Moesia (86–87). As it was not replaced, Legio XX had to be moved down from Inchtuthil to Chester. This in turn involved a reappraisal of the size of the province. Since the whole area could not be controlled by three legions, it was *The aban-* decided to abandon the legionary base at Inch- *donment* tuthil, which in fact had not yet been completed, *of northern* and with it occupation north of the isthmus. *Scotland* This abandonment of northern Scotland, which was not done in any hurry, lies behind Tacitus's remark that the conquest of Britain was completed and immediately let go (*perdomita Britannia et statim omissa*). The decision might seem to the historian, as to his father-in-law Agricola, a negation of all Agricola's work, and Agricola might attribute it to Domitian's jealousy, but it was based on considerations of the man-power of the Empire. A more justifiable grievance which Agricola had against the emperor was that Domitian gave him no further command or employment. Thus Britain, including the Lowlands of Scotland, was held by three legions, stationed on the confines of the English plain – II Augusta at Isca, XX Valeria Victrix at Deva, and IX Hispana at Eboracum – and the auxiliary cohorts which were distributed over Wales and garrisoned northern Britain as far as the Forth and Clyde.

7. The Rhine and Danube Frontiers

On the German frontier the Flavian emperors carried out a similar, if less ambitious, policy *Advance* of protective advance as in Britain. In order to *into* eliminate the sharp re-entrant angle of the *western* Rhine near Basle, and to hold the line of high *Germany* ground east of the middle Rhine, they took the Taunus Mountains and the Black Forest into their system of defences. This rectification of the boundary was begun by Vespasian (73–74), who annexed the Black Forest area (the Agri Decumates), bounded on the north and east roughly by a line from Strasbourg to Lake Constance. Domitian extended this to the Neckar and also dealt with the area to the north. After a series of raids by the Chatti (Hessians) on the middle Rhine, which were dangerous enough to warrant two retaliatory expeditions under the emperor himself (83 and 89), Domitian prolonged the forward zone beyond the north of the Main, thus enclosing the Odenwald and reaching the crest of the High Taunus. At the end of his reign the Roman *limes*, or frontier- *The new* road, ran from the neighbourhood of Bonn east- *limes* wards along the Taunus Mountains and then southwards down the Neckar valley to a point north of the Danube, where it met a similar *limes* extending along that river in front of Raetia. These roads were picketed at close intervals with wooden watch-towers which were connected by radial roads with the advance forts, as yet built only of earth, of the auxiliary cohorts; this advance line was supported by the legionary camps on the Rhine in their rear.[23] Within the area thus rendered secure by the Roman military occupation a mixed population of Celts and Germans made permanent settlements, and in the Black Forest area a new centre for the worship of the emperors was established at Arae Flaviae (Rottweil). Domitian formalised the administration by officially creating two provinces, Germania Superior in the south and Germania Inferior in the north under *legati Augusti pro praetore*, although their financial administration was still linked to Belgica under a *procurator provinciae Belgicae et utriusque Germaniae*. The establishment of this new frontier-system was a great achievement, which the ancient sources, hostile to Domitian, have treated in a very cavalier fashion; its full significance has been revealed only by the patient work of modern archaeologists. Its success is shown by the fact that Germany remained peaceful and Roman control of the left bank of the Rhine was not challenged until the third century, and Domitian was able to transfer two of the eight Rhine legions to the lower Danube where the point of serious danger now lay.

The civil wars of 69 did not bring the Roman frontiers on the Danube into any serious danger. A series of forays by the Suebi into Raetia was ended in 74 by the intervention of the troops from Upper Germany under Pinarius Clemens. *The Danube* In the winter of 68–69 a horde of heavily armed *frontier* Roxolanian horsemen from the Russian steppe crossed the frozen Danube for a raid into Moesia, but they were brought to grief by a providential thaw, in which the mud-bound invaders fell easy victims to the more handy Roman infantry. In autumn of 69 a projected raid by the Dacians was averted by the equally opportune advent of Mucianus with the legions from

Syria. In the next year Sarmatians defeated and killed the governor of Moesia, but were checked by his successor.

During the reign of Domitian a new danger arose from the reunion of the Dacian tribes, under the strong hand of a chieftain named Decebalus. This worthy successor of Burebistas (p. 278) reconstructed a national Dacian army and trained it in Roman fashion for a war of conquest, in which he probably intended to annex the kindred peoples of Thrace to his realm which lay in mountain-girt Transylvania. In 85 *The Dacian* Decebalus broke into Moesia in great force and *War* overwhelmed the legate of the province, Oppius Sabinus, perhaps near Adamklissi in the Dobrudja. Domitian hastened to the Danube with his praetorian prefect, Cornelius Fuscus, who brought up reinforcements from the middle Danube and drew off the invaders by an irruption into Dacia. But Fuscus, adventuring himself into unfamiliar mountain-land, involved the Roman forces in a fresh disaster (86).[24] In 88 another general, named Tettius Iulianus, renewed the invasion of Dacia and heavily defeated Decebalus in a set battle at Tapae. At this stage, however, Domitian broke off the Dacian War, since news came that L. Antonius Saturninus, commander of the two legions stationed at Moguntiacum, had revolted, while the Iazyges, Marcomanni and Quadi, hitherto pacific, began to threaten Pannonia. Domitian quickly arranged a peace with Decebalus on lines similar to the treaty between Nero and the Armenian king, Tiridates. Decebalus kept his territory intact and received a subvention from Domitian, but acknowledged himself a Roman vassal (89). Thanks to the loyalty of the governor of Lower Germany and the other legions on the Rhine, Antonius was crushed before Domitian arrived. From the Rhine Domitian went to Pannonia, but the course of operations against the Iazyges and other tribes is not clear, except that his timely peace with Dacia prevented a still greater concentration of hostile forces. In 92 further attacks on Pannonia developed and Domitian himself again went to the threatened front; some kind of peace was established.

Domitian's peace with Dacia was neither a Roman humiliation nor a Roman victory; the emperor did not add Dacicus to his titulature (he was already Germanicus), but it was a sensible agreement. Although he did not disarm Decebalus (in fact he lent him some Roman engineers to build defence-works), he fortified *The Danube* the Danube front against further attacks. He *frontier* concentrated a force of nine legions in a chain *strengthened* of camps along the river, extending from Vindobona (modern Vienna), Carnuntum and Aquin-

cum (Budapest) to Troesmis (not so very far from the Black Sea); five legions were stationed in Moesia and four in Pannonia. He partitioned Moesia into two separate provinces, Superior and Inferior. Lower Moesia was protected by the construction of a great earth *vallum*, with thirty-five forts about a mile apart, across the Dobrudja from Tomi to a point north of Rasova on the Danube. This considerable work of consolidation on what was now the most threatened frontier of the Empire, combined with his pacification of the Rhine frontier, is no small achievement by Domitian.

8. The East

After the fall of Jerusalem Vespasian made some successful provincial changes in the East which involved deposing the rulers of Lesser Armenia and Commagene. He put both Cappadocia and Lesser Armenia under the administration of the governor of Galatia (an arrangement which *Provincial* lasted until Trajan's day), thus creating a larger *changes in* unified command. This new province could *the East* guard the upper Euphrates, with a legion (XII Fulminata) at Melitene, and legionary troops at Satala where they could watch the Caucasian tribes to the north. Syria lost responsibility for Judaea after it had received its own governor and legion, and it was also deprived of Cilicia Campestris, which was made into a separate province with Cilicia Aspera, but it received Commagene (72). Syria's eastern frontier was now on the Euphrates from above Samosata to Sura; Samosata and probably Zeugma were held by legions. Thus two client-kingdoms had been eliminated, and two reorganised provinces watched the line of the Euphrates against any threats from Armenia or Parthia; in fact they were to secure peace for the next fifty years.[25]

The good relations which Nero had established between Parthia and Armenia remained undisturbed, but for a passing estrangement in Vespasian's reign. The Parthian king Vologeses, who had previously placed a large corps of archers at Vespasian's disposal for his campaign against Vitellius, suggested to him in 75 that *General* they should undertake a joint expedition against *good* the Alans, a nomad people who were making *relations* descents across Mt Caucasus into the Parthian *with* territory. But Vespasian would commit himself *Parthia* no further than to assist the vassal king of Iberia (modern Georgia) to fortify the exit of the Dariel Pass through Mt Caucasus,[26] and he declined to co-operate with the Parthians. Vologeses, already perhaps annoyed by the extension of Roman control over Palmyra, met this rebuff by a threatened invasion of Syria in 76, but was deterred by its governor, M. Ulpius Traianus (father of the emperor). This campaign was followed by thirty-five years of peace between Romans and Parthians.

9. The Provinces

Good administration of the provinces

For the Roman provinces the Flavian era was on the whole an age of uneventful prosperity. In 69 the provinces suffered from the heavy requisitionings of Vitellius's and Vespasian's armies, and during the reign of Vespasian they were severely taxed in order to clear off the deficits of the Roman treasury. But, more fortunate than in the civil wars of the later Republic, they escaped the havoc of actual battle; and they found compensation for the fiscal exactions of the emperors in the uniformly good administration which they experienced.

Vespasian confers 'Latin rights' on Spain

The Flavian emperors did not pursue a vigorous policy of colonisation in the provinces; but they carried their enfranchisement a considerable stage further. In connexion with the census which he held in 73–74 Vespasian made a concession of Latin rights to the entire Spanish peninsula (or possibly to Baetica alone), whose towns now provided themselves (if they had not done so before) with a constitution of Italian type.[27] The main purpose of this grant was no doubt to give recognition to the progress which Romanisation had made in Spain, and to draft the leading men of the Spanish towns into the administrative service of the Empire — an object whose attainment is proved by the number of Spaniards who entered the Senate under the Flavian dynasty.

10. The 'Opposition' to the Flavian Emperors[28]

By his services in putting the Roman world back into joint Vespasian earned a popularity such as only Augustus had surpassed among previous emperors. He was hailed as the *restitutor orbis,* and after his death the Senate willingly raised him to the rank of a *divus.* The personal popularity of Titus also brought him a somewhat cheaply earned deification. Nevertheless the Flavian dynasty encountered opposition from several quarters, and in the later years of Domitian the atmosphere became as thick with rumours of plots as in the later years of Tiberius and Nero.

The precautions which Vespasian had taken against a recurrence of civil wars proved so far effective that no serious military insurrection took place under the Flavian dynasty. In 79 A.

Military conspiracies

Caecina, who had played false to Vitellius ten years previously (p. 407), attempted to snatch the succession from Titus by the oft-tried device of seducing the household troops. But Titus, who was chief of the Guards as well as heir apparent, put the pretender to death out of hand. In 88 the commander of the army on the upper Rhine, L. Antonius Saturninus, made a foolhardy attempt to repeat the march of Valens and Caecina upon Rome, but having no more than two legions at his immediate disposal he was held up and defeated by another division of the Rhine forces under A. Lappius Maximus Norbanus (p. 422).

A philosophic fronde against Vespasian and Domitian

A form of opposition which was particularly irksome was offered by some obstructive philosophers of the Stoic and the kindred Cynic sects — the only two schools of Greek philosophy that retained any vitality at this period. Though the Stoics and Cynics were not bound by their own tenets to declare for or against any particular form of government, they made a virtue, and sometimes a fetish, of personal independence. If not particularly dangerous they appeared to many to be arrogant, with their claims to superior virtue. Their views varied widely from Stoics who disliked bad kings, but not monarchy as such, to Cynics who preached political anarchy. Some, tinged with memories of republican *libertas,* wanted merely to express dissatisfaction; others turned to conspiracy. This opposition goes back to Nero's reign when it had been found in literary and philosophic circles. Thus Seneca had praised the Stoic who opposed a tyrant, and Lucan had been deeply involved in the Pisonian conspiracy. After this a group of Stoic philosophers became suspect; Thrasea Paetus and Barea Soranus were condemned to death, and Paetus's son-in-law, Helvidius Priscus, was exiled. Under Vespasian leading members of this fraternity lifted up their voices once more against the emperor. So far as their opposition had any reasonable basis it seems to have been directed against Vespasian's dogged determination to treat the office of emperor as a hereditary possession; but their general attitude was one of obstruction rather than helpful criticism.[29] By their sheer insistence they broke down the patience of Vespasian, who issued an order of expulsion from Italy against them. Particularly galling was the conduct of Helvidius Priscus, who had returned under Galba and at first had even been friendly with Vespasian, but as his criticism grew harsher the emperor at first exiled him and then had him executed (?75). The less long-suffering Domitian twice (in 89 and 95) renewed his father's eviction order (which had been no more effective than a hundred others of the same kind), and caused the Senate to condemn on a charge of *maiestas* two members of their order who had written free-spoken biographies of Thrasea and Priscus.[30] But the bark of the philosophers was worse than their bite, and their opposition may be dismissed as a mere *fronde*. Among the wholly innocent victims of Domitian's decrees of expulsion were Dio Chrysostom and Epictetus, the two most distinguished Greek thinkers of their day (pp. 480, 482).

Trials for maiestas are resumed under Domitian

A more dangerous kind of opposition to the Flavian emperors took the form of conspiracies by groups of discontented senators, who resented the disrespectful attitude of Domitian to their order. These champions of liberty, as then understood, sought to recover it by the direct method of tyrannicide, though their aim was not to restore the Republic in any full sense, but to replace Domitian by a less despotic emperor. During the early part of his reign Domitian took no special precautions against assassination; but after the rebellion of Saturninus in 88 he gave free rein to the professional informers, whose appetite had been whetted by twenty lean years since the death of Nero, and the Senate was once more called upon to condemn its own members on charges of treason or *maiestas*. Many eminent men were condemned in the terror, though some, such as Agricola and Frontinus, found safety in retirement and lying low. Domitian's precautionary executions undoubtedly created an additional sense of personal insecurity among the senators, out of which arose fresh plots and aggravated repression. Caught in this vicious coil Domitian eventually fell a victim to a plot by his wife Domitia (a daughter of Domitius Corbulo), whom he had once divorced on suspicion of unfaithfulness, but had since received back into favour. Warned by the execution of the emperor's cousin, Flavius Clemens, on grounds of alleged conspiracy, Domitia felt herself reprieved rather than pardoned.[31] Under her instructions a palace domestic named Stephanus stabbed the emperor while he was reading a report on an imaginary conspiracy.

He falls a victim to a palace conspiracy

After the death of Domitian the Senate vented its hatred of him by 'condemning his memory' and ordering his name to be erased from all public monuments. The literary tradition of the following age, taking its cue from the Senatorial Order, persecuted him without mercy. Yet at the end of his reign the Roman world as a whole was no less contented and prosperous than at the death of Augustus.

His 'memory is condemned' by the Senate

CHAPTER 37

The 'Five Good Emperors'.
General Administration

1. Personalities[1]

The murder of Domitian was accomplished without the participation of the household troops, whose rank and file had been unshakeably loyal to the late emperor. But one of their commanders, Petronius Secundus, was in collusion with Domitia. After the death of Domitian he contrived to keep the Guards in check, while the Senate proceeded to make its first free choice of a successor. The imperial power was transferred to a senior senator, named M. Cocceius Nerva, who had not taken any prominent part in the opposition to Domitian, but had excited the emperor's suspicions and was probably privy to Domitia's plot.

The new emperor (96–98) was a man of somewhat undistinguished family, whose abilities as a jurist had raised him to high rank under Nero.[2]

He was well versed in administrative routine and did not lack personal courage; he treated a plot by a jealous competitor for imperial office, C. Calpurnius Crassus, with an insouci-

37.1 Nerva.

ance worthy of Caesar, not even troubling to punish his would-be assassin. But he was too advanced in years to guide the state firmly through a political crisis, and he had no prestige among the soldiers. The chief problem of his reign was whether he could keep the army under control. This question was brought to an issue in 97, when the praetorian troops, at the instigation of their second commander, Casperius Aelianus, demanded the execution of Petronius Secundus in atonement for the murder of Domitian. Though Nerva did not give way without a struggle he was eventually obliged to humour the soldiery. The new reign seemed to be shaping like that of Galba; but Nerva did not repeat Galba's final blunder. Realising the need to play off force against force he won the support of the commander in Upper Germany, M. Ulpius Traianus, by adopting him and making him co-regent.[3] Under the shelter of Trajan's legions Nerva ruled unmolested until his death a few months later (January 98), when Trajan succeeded him without opposition. Though Nerva's call to Trajan was an emergency measure it did more than avert a crisis: it set a new precedent for the regulation of the succession. The next three rulers, all of whom were providentially childless, or had outlived their sons, followed Nerva's example of adopting a man of tried ability and securing the reversion of their power to him. This method of transmitting the imperial office saved the Roman world for a century from further succession-crises and gave it a line of 'five good emperors'.

Trajan, the second emperor of this line (98–117), was first and foremost a military man who

37.2 Trajan.

37.4 L. Verus.

Personality of Trajan

commanded the respect of the soldiers, and had no need to humour or bribe them. But he showed no trace of Domitian's autocratic character; his tolerance and courtesy formed a welcome contrast with the overbearing manner of the last Flavian ruler, and the title of *Optimus Princeps*, unofficial at first but later conferred by the Senate, was a genuine expression of gratitude and relief. In selecting his successor Trajan passed over several of his chief military associates in favour of a distant relative named P. Aelius Hadrianus.[4] He delayed the formal act of adoption to the very last, and so gave rise to the rumour that Hadrian owed his elevation to a ruse on the part of his widow Plotina, who was alleged to have kept Trajan's decease secret until an official bulletin of a death-bed adoption had been safely launched. But various earlier marks of favour which Trajan bestowed upon the next emperor are sufficient proof that he had made his choice, and his selection showed true discernment.[5]

Adoption of Hadrian

37.3 Hadrian.

Hadrian's many-sided talent

Of all Roman emperors Hadrian (117–138) was the one who came nearest to Caesar in the versatility of his talent. He lacked Caesar's personal magnetism, and he possessed a gift of making enemies which was absent in Trajan; yet soldiers and civilians alike felt that his was a master hand. Two years before his death Hadrian adopted a young man named L.

Ceionius Commodus Verus, a person of precarious health and problematic abilities. The death of Verus in 138 (six months before that of his adoptive father) compelled Hadrian to make a second choice. On this occasion he played for safety by selecting a senator of high rank named T. Aurelius Antoninus.

Adoption of Antoninus 'Pius'

In character and abilities Antoninus (138–161) recalled Nerva, and the surname of 'Pius' which the Senate conferred upon him suggests a merely amiable personage.[6] But though of ripe age he was not too far past his prime, and the times in which he was called upon to rule were such as demanded or at any rate were not uncongenial to a Nerva. Following the precedent of Augustus (p. 352) Hadrian endeavoured to regulate the succession one generation ahead. He

37.5 Antoninus Pius.

required Antoninus to adopt a son and namesake of the lately deceased L. Verus, and one of Antoninus's own nephews named M. Annius Verus (and henceforth renamed M. Aelius Aurelius). Of the two candidates for the succession to which Antoninus's choice had been limited, the latter was rightly given the preference. M. Aurelius on his accession, it is true, insisted on his adoptive brother being invested with equal rights, so that until the death of the younger Verus in 169 the imperial power was held in commission. But the co-regent was such an insignificant person that he left all power and

Antoninus adopts M. Aurelius

responsibility in the hands of M. Aurelius, who to all intents and purposes ruled as sole emperor from 161 to 180.[7]

In the Flavian era the Stoic philosophy was providing ammunition for attacks upon the emperors. A hundred years later it directed the conscience of the emperor himself, and with the most fortunate results. By nature a recluse and an introvert, and better suited to the part of Hamlet than to that of Caesar, M. Aurelius was braced by his Stoic teaching to shoulder manfully the burden of his position, and he spared himself neither at home nor in the field of war. Of him it can be said much more truly than of another Stoic product, M. Brutus, that 'he was the noblest Roman of them all'.

Stoicism on the throne

37.6 Marcus Aurelius.

2. Constitutional Changes

In the period under review another vital question beside that of the succession was solved for the time being. The misapprehension between emperors and Senate, which caused mutual irritation under Domitian, gave way to an entente which was not seriously disturbed before the death of M. Aurelius. The emperors habitually convoked the Senate and kept it informed of their decisions. They submitted legislation to it for approval and peace treaties for ratification. Nerva, Trajan and Hadrian bound themselves by oath not to put a senator to death except by the Senate's own sentence after a free trial. From the time of Hadrian senators were permitted or encouraged, by a harmless concession to official vanity, to add the title of *vir clarissimus* (commonly abbreviated to v.c.) to their names.

Entente between emperors and Senate

The personal attitude of individual emperors naturally varied slightly. Nerva, as the Senate's nominee was obviously popular, as indeed was Trajan. In the Panegyricus, delivered by Pliny before the Senate on the assumption of his consulship in 100, the contrast between the despotism of Domitian and the forbearance of Trajan runs like a red thread. Trajan is hailed as leader

rather than master, his rule being a *principatus* not a *dominatio:* a similar line was taken by Dio Chrysostom in a sermon on kingship which he delivered before Trajan, while Tacitus could praise Nerva for reconciling *principatus* and *libertas*. Trajan showed great tact, consulting the Senate frequently, and mingling freely with senators socially; he avoided numerous consulships (completely during his last fourteen years, with only six consulships previously); and this great soldier was modest in the number of *salutationes* which he accepted (in contrast to a less warlike Claudius or a Domitian). Thus he gained the goodwill of the Senate, while recognising that it had lost its capacity for real government. Hadrian had an unfortunate start: the episode of the execution of the four consulars (see below) caused resentment in senatorial circles, but in general he showed a like moderation (he was consul only three times). However, his drive for efficiency in promoting the interests of the whole Empire, which he felt the Senate could not always adequately meet, led to increasing concentration of the administration at the Senate's expense. His reorganisation of the Imperial Council, of the bureaux and of the Equestrian Order, together with his creation of the four consular judges of Italy (see below), did much to annoy and weaken the Senate, although this was not his intention. But while the Senate missed Trajan's cordiality, outwardly good relations were maintained, though tensions developed towards the end of Hadrian's reign (*c*. 135) when he became increasingly irritable as the result of pain from an incurable illness. When he died, Antoninus had great difficulty in persuading the Senate to grant Hadrian divine honours (his success may explain his name Pius). Antoninus worked closely with the Senate and abolished the four consulars of Italy (though not the rest of Hadrian's reforms). His love of Italy, which contrasted with Hadrian's Greek interests and more cosmopolitan outlook, would appeal to many senators. But his real decisions were based on the advice of his *amici* and *Consilium*, not on the Senate's views. But although he allowed the Senate no further scope, he was deferential to it, careful of its dignity, and personally accessible. This harmony at the centre created a general feeling of well-being throughout the Empire, at least as expressed by the rhetorician Aristeides in his oration 'To Rome'. M. Aurelius showed equal goodwill to the Senate. Although he restored Hadrian's consular judges (now named *iuridici*) and increased the centralisation of administration, relations were harmonious.

But if the emperors of the second century were at pains to restore to the Senate a sense of partnership with themselves, they were equally careful to retain in their hands all the powers exercised by the Flavian dynasty. Though they did not formally assume the office of censor, they tacitly usurped the right of censorial *adlectio*. By this device Trajan and his successors intensified the policy of Claudius and the Flavians of introducing provincials of sufficient culture and wealth into the House; thus they brought in a quota of men from Africa and members from Asia Minor and other eastern countries, where the Greek-speaking populations were beginning to take a more active interest in the Roman administration.[8] By the end of the second century the Senate had become fairly representative of the Empire as a whole; but it was now of small practical importance, except as a panel for the recruitment of high imperial officials.

In cultivating better relations with the Senate the emperors of the second century dispelled that atmosphere of conspiracy which had poisoned the later years of Domitian. At the beginning and the end of Hadrian's reign, it is true, persons of high rank were executed on a charge of treason. In 118 four of Trajan's right-hand men, including his two chief military assistants, Cornelius Palma and Lusius Quietus (p. 439), were arrested by the praetorian prefect Caelius Attianus, and sentenced to death by Hadrian's followers in the Senate, in the absence of the emperor. The emperor showed displeasure at this precipitancy by removing Attianus from his post, although he had been Hadrian's guardian and had procured for him the allegiance of the Guards. In view of the fact that at the time

of their arrest the four ex-consuls were residing in widely separate parts of Italy, it may be assumed that they had not formed any actual plot, though they might have indulged in unruly talk. In 136 a brother-in-law of Hadrian named Julius Ursus Servianus was put to death on a charge of conspiring to make his grandson Cn. Pedianus Fuscus emperor.[9] In this case there can be little doubt that a real plot was formed. In 175 the vicegerent of M. Aurelius in the East, Avidius Cassius (p. 444), attempted to reproduce the career of Vespasian by having himself proclaimed emperor on a false rumour of Aurelius's death, but he obtained little support from his troops and was easily suppressed. In these rare conspiracies the ruling motive was personal ambition rather than political discontent.

The main feature of the Roman government in the second century was the further growth and more complete organisation of the imperial executive. This strengthening of the professional administrative service was mainly the work of Hadrian, whose mastery of administrative routine fitted him well for such a task.

To cope with the growing bulk of the imperial correspondence, Hadrian divided the secretariat into two separate departments for the Latin and the Greek dispatches respectively. To ensure the punctual conveyance of the imperial messages, he instituted a *praefectus vehiculorum*, who supervised the requisitioning of horses and carriages for the postal service in Italy. To speed up civil jurisdiction in Italy, he divided the country into four judicial districts and appointed to each of these an official of consular rank (*quattuoriri consulares*, entitled *iuridici* from the time of M. Aurelius), who took over the cases of trust and tutelage from the praetors at Rome and probably heard appeals from the municipal courts. A less happy idea of Hadrian was the commissioning of soldiers, on ostensible duty as foragers (*frumentatores*), to keep the provincial staffs under observation.

Under Trajan and Hadrian the freedmen of the imperial household were excluded from the public administration. Henceforth all the higher administrative posts that were not reserved by tradition for persons of senatorial standing were assigned to members of the Equestrian Order. Thus *Equites*, who since Domitian's reign had increasingly been replacing freedmen as heads of the great bureaux (*ab epistolis*, etc.), now gained a virtual monopoly of these posts, and at the same time the secretariats themselves were finally transformed from service in the emperor's household to government departments. Within the imperial executive the hierarchy of grades was defined more exactly, and regular 'promotion ladders' were set up. An outward mark of this more rigid organisation now appeared in the honorary titles which the imperial officials of equestrian rank began to append to their names – a practice which grew up in the later years of the second century. Officials of the third grade (e.g. the financial *procuratores*) henceforth styled themselves *viri egregii*; on rising to the next higher posts (such as the *praefecturae annonae* and *vigilum*) they became *viri perfectissimi*; those who rose to the summit of the equestrian career by appointment to the command of the household troops were transformed into *viri eminentissimi*. At the same time a distinction between civilian and military careers, which the republican tradition at Rome had consistently refused to recognise and early emperors had not drawn sharply, was established within the equestrian ranks of the imperial service. In the military branch of the service the imperial officials rose from the tribunate of a legion or the 'prefecture' of an auxiliary cohort to the governorship of a frontier province. In the civil section they took up a minor financial or judicial post in substitution for a military cadetship and ascended to the position of a *iuridicus* in a province, or to a high administrative function at Rome.

The Consilium Principis as the interpreter of Roman law

The reign of Hadrian also marks an important stage in the history of Roman law. Under this emperor the annual edicts of the praetors charged with civil jurisdiction at Rome, and presumably also the edicts of the provincial governors, were cast into final shape by a distinguished jurist named Salvius Iulianus. Thus the praetor's edict ceased to be a source of new law; it became a permanent code which the magistrates had to administer as it was, without alteration (when changes became necessary, they were made by the emperor and not by the praetors). Another old republican element in the development of law was the 'answers of the jurisprudents' (*responsa iurisprudentum*) which, unlike the old praetorian edict, fell short of creating law while at the same time strongly influencing the way the rules of law should be applied. The extent to which these *responsa* were purely informal, or on the other hand received some authorisation from Augustus and again perhaps by Hadrian, is extremely debatable ground.[10] All that we need note here is that the emperors on many matters, including legal, had been accustomed to consult their *amici*, who naturally included lawyers. Such councils were informal (the more formal *consilium principis*, which Augustus had established, had not survived Tiberius's reign: p. 322). Hadrian is thought by some to have reorganised his council as a new organ of government, but more probably he reshaped and adapted the old institution of *amici*, making more use of jurists in a council which became more regular and more professional than earlier. As the emperor himself gradually became the main source of law, so his need to summon more professional lawyers to his *consilium* would increase.[11]

Extinction of the Comitia

The second century also witnessed the final extinction of the Comitia as a legislative organ. Under Nerva the Tribal Assembly was resuscitated in order to pass the last of the long series of Roman agrarian acts; but under his successors it never met again for purposes of legislation. The place of the *leges populi* was taken once for all by imperial 'constitutions' or ordinances, whether in the form of general edicts (with or without the Senate's confirmation), or of rulings in answer to questions from the imperial officials. A notable feature of imperial legislation in the second century was its humane outlook and solicitude for the weaker members of the community. In this spirit the authority

Legislation by imperial ordinance

of Roman parents over their children and of masters over their slaves was whittled down: the interests of minors were safeguarded; the position of women and slaves in courts of law was approximated to that of free men.[12]

3. Municipal Government

In the second century the urbanisation of the Empire attained its furthest limits. The growth of city life at this period was in the main a natural process, for though Trajan constituted many colonies (especially in Thrace), the founding of new cities by government action fell into disuse soon after, and henceforth the line between *coloniae* and *municipia* or native cities became blurred. But the emperors readily conferred the status of a colony or a *municipium* upon urban centres of native growth, wherever these had acquired sufficient Roman or Hellenic culture to provide an administration of Italian or Greek type.[13] The statement that 'the Roman Empire was a federation of municipalities' never came nearer to being true than in the second century A.D.[14]

The growth of towns in the Empire reaches its climax

Though there remained much diversity of constitutional detail among the municipalities of the Roman Empire, their general political development was in the same direction as that of Rome in the second century B.C. Political power gradually became concentrated in the hands of ruling aristocracies, which were predominantly recruited from the local landowners, though enriched traders and industrialists would have less difficulty than at Rome in entering the governing circles.[15] They monopolised the local organs of government, namely the councils and magistracies. As a Senate (*curia*) of *decuriones*, varying in number with the size of the municipality, these town-councillors formed a council of the magistrates and very largely controlled the public life of their communities. Since wealth tended to remain in the same families they increasingly became a hereditary class. The local magistrates varied greatly in name in the Greek provinces (e.g. archons, strategoi, grammateis), but in the West the annual duumvirate became normal, with *duoviri quinquennales* appointed every five years for special duties (e.g. a census) and enjoying greater honour. Finances were sometimes in the hands of quaestors, and municipal priesthoods could be important. However, in many cities of the first and second centuries A.D. the *plebs* (i.e. the general body of burgesses) still exercised a real choice in the appointment of magistrates: the numerous surviving 'election posters' of Pompeii testify to a keen competition among candidates for popular favour. But the municipal senates eventually acquired the right of appointing the magistrates and of co-opting their new

The municipal aristocracies

members; as at Rome, the participation of the common people in public affairs was whittled down to organised clamouring.[16] In the first two centuries A.D. the ruling aristocracies on the whole proved themselves worthy of their privileges; they spent freely on public objects out of their private purses, and they kept alive an active and even self-assertive spirit of local patriotism. The avidity with which towns assumed (by imperial grant or by simple usurpation) such empty titles as *splendidissimum municipium*, and prominent citizens accepted statues and complimentary decrees, offered an easy target to satirists, yet it was a symptom of healthy municipal pride, albeit carried to excess.[17]

Their open-handedness

So long as the municipal aristocracies discharged their duties with tolerable efficiency the Roman government was well content to leave them a free hand. But in the second century the Roman officials were obliged to curtail the liberties of towns in two directions. In some districts, and notably in the eastern provinces, where the Greek populations kept up traditions of party strife, or came to blows with the Jewish residents, Roman intervention was now and then required in the interests of public order. Isolated municipalities also had difficulties in repressing brigandage on the outskirts of their territories, and Roman troops had to be sent to their assistance.[18] But the commonest failure in municipal administration related to the finances of the cities. In many towns the tradition of public munificence on the part of the governing families led to financial embarrassment or worse. Hard-and-fast rules were set up which required every entrant on a magistracy or new member of the local senate to pay a lump sum into the city treasury or to undertake some costly public work.[19] This system of compulsory contribution imposed an excessive strain on the less wealthy families, so that these began to withdraw from public affairs, and a dearth of suitable candidates for office set in where formerly there had been eager competition.[20] Again, while the obligation upon the public men to 'pay their footing' became inexorable, the form in which they made their donation was left too much to their own discretion. The natural tendency of citizens bent on currying public favour was to spend on objects of immediate gratification rather than for purposes of permanent utility. Though here and there a man of wealth invested his money in a market-hall or school or aqueduct, or undertook to repave and redrain his city, more frequently he half-wasted his funds on free dinners, theatrical entertainments and gladiatorial games. Lastly, the contributions of the ruling families came to be regarded by their townsmen as a substitute rather than a

Their administrative failures

Excessive demands on their purse

Incipient dearth of candidates for office

supplement to municipal taxation. Expenses which no public-spirited citizen took upon his shoulders were habitually met by borrowing, and not a few cities fell in consequence into a chronic state of indebtedness. If a useful public building such as an aqueduct was begun with funds supplied by private generosity, it might remain unfinished for lack of public revenue to complete its construction.[21] In the second century the financial embarrassment of many provincial towns became so grave as to require the intervention of the imperial government. In 109 Trajan appointed a special commissioner, Maximus, to remedy the financial disorders of the cities of Achaea. Two or three years later he sent the younger Pliny (C. Plinius Caecilius Secundus) on a similar errand to the province of Bithynia, with powers to overhaul the municipal accounts and to disallow injudicious expenditure.[22] The same emperor nominated *curatores* to take charge of the finances of individual towns, both in Italy and the provinces. The interventions of Trajan in municipal affairs were exceptional measures; but imperial control over local finances, once introduced, tended to become a regular practice. These representatives of the *Princeps* increased in number and activity under the Antonines, but before the third century are found in only a minority of cities.[23]

Municipal indebtedness

Trajan appoints financial controllers

The efficient working of the municipal system was in fact vital to the well-being of the Empire. By delegating to unpaid municipal magistrates and councils so much responsibility for administering their own local affairs the central government was enabled to limit the size and cost of the salaried civil service. When cities began to run into financial difficulties, whether due to inter-city rivalries or to wild unregulated competitive munificence on the part of local worthies, this became a matter of real concern to the imperial government at Rome.

4. Imperial Finance

While the emperors took steps to enforce economy upon the municipalities they loaded their own *fiscus* with new burdens. Their court expenditure remained on a modest scale, and they all followed the good example of Vespasian and Domitian in giving nothing away to favourites. But in their outlay for public purposes they were liberal and at times even lavish. Trajan reduced the customary donative to the praetorian cohorts at his accession, but the next two emperors bought their allegiance at an unnecessarily high price. Under Trajan (more probably than under Nerva) an important new experiment in public assistance was put into

Liberal expenditure by the emperors

37.7   Relief on the façade of the new Rostra set up by Trajan in the Forum. On the left Trajan makes an announcement, presumably about the *alimenta* which he is seen distributing on the right side, seated on a tribunal. A mother (Italia?) presents a child to him.

operation. This emperor made permanent loans of capital sums from the *fiscus* to Italian land-owners, on condition that they should pay interest at the moderate rate of 5 per cent into the chest of their municipality, and that out of the revenue thus accruing the municipalities should provide maintenance allowances for the children of needy families in their territory. These 'alimentary institutions' were progressively extended by Hadrian, Antoninus and M. Aurelius, and the service of this fund was placed on a permanent footing by Hadrian, who instituted a *praefectus alimentorum* to supervise the repartition and administration of the treasury grants.[24] By a similar act of judicious generosity Trajan made special provision for the distribution of free corn at Rome to 5000 needy children. Yet none of these emperors curtailed the indiscriminate feeding of the multitudes in the capital; indeed Trajan spent very large sums on additional distributions of cash, wine and oil to the people of Rome, and the *congiaria* of the next three emperors were even more profuse.[25]

The 'alimentary institutions'

Though Antoninus and M. Aurelius restricted expenditure on public works, their three predecessors carried out extensive building programmes in Rome which included Trajan's Forum with the Basilica Ulpia and his Column, and Hadrian's temple of Venus and Rome, the Pantheon and his Mausoleum (pp. 461 ff.). Nerva made provision for the repair of the Italian main roads, as also did Trajan, who improved communications between Rome and Brundisium by constructing a new highway across the Apennines to replace the old Via Appia beyond Beneventum. In addition he spent large sums on harbour works at Ancona, Centumcellae (modern Civita Vecchia), and especially at Ostia, where he increased the security of Claudius's port (p. 357) by adding an inner hexagonal land-locked basin to give protection against storms

Public works

(the surrounding town, some two miles from Ostia itself, was known as Portus). Hadrian in turn gave subventions with a free hand for public works in the provinces. Nerva transferred part costs of the imperial post from the roadside municipalities in Italy to the *fiscus*, and Hadrian similarly relieved the provincial towns. Lastly, under Hadrian and his two successors Vespasian's policy of bringing education under state patronage was revived. Not only were additional professorial chairs endowed in the provinces, but grants in aid were made to municipal schools.

Endowment of education

Nevertheless this increased expenditure was accompanied by slight reductions in taxation. It was probably nothing more than a matter of accounting that Trajan and Hadrian wrote off large amounts of tax-arrears as bad debts; in 118 Hadrian made a bonfire in the Forum of records of some 900 million sesterces' worth of such debts owed to the *fiscus*. But Nerva made a real inroad upon the revenue by confining the vexatious Jewish tithe to Jupiter Capitolinus to self-confessed Jews (p. 417), and Hadrian by conferring immunities upon importers of essential articles of consumption into Rome. Frequent exemptions from tribute were also accorded to towns that had been stricken by fires or other natural calamities. Despite these concessions to the taxpayers the imperial revenue normally sufficed to meet the higher expenditure. A heavy windfall accrued to the *fiscus* when Trajan brought back the accumulated treasures of the Dacian monarchy to Rome (p. 442), and the annual yield of the Dacian mines provided a substantial additional income to the emperors; thus after 107 he could launch out on many new public plans. But the buoyancy of the imperial finances was mainly due, as in the reigns of Augustus and Vespasian, to the general rise of the taxation fund under a régime of internal peace and sound administration.[26]

Reductions of taxation

Buoyancy of the revenue

The emperors of the second century maintained Augustus's system of taxation in its essential features, but modified it in various details. The direct imposts continued to be levied by the local authorities, but from the time of Trajan or Hadrian the responsibility for their collection was fixed on a special body of *decemprimi* selected from the senators or other notables of each community.[27] The raising of the indirect dues remained in the hands of private contractors, but the companies of *publicani* were replaced by individual collectors, who were residents in the district under their charge, and were no longer required to prepay the total amount of the tax. Under these conditions it was possible to limit the commission of the *conductor* to a lesser percentage; and imperial *procuratores* supervised their operations, so as to prevent illegal exactions. This procedure for the gathering of indirect taxes was adapted from the method of rent-collection which had gradually come into use on the imperial domains and was probably systematised by Hadrian. On these estates a *conductor* or tenant-in-chief sublet most of the land in small parcels to cultivating tenants (*coloni*) and levied their rents on behalf of the emperor. In return for these services the *conductor* was entitled to exact from the *coloni* a certain amount of labour on the 'home farm' under his direct exploitation. On each domain or group of domains a resident imperial procurator enforced the terms of the lease and adjudicated between the 'conductor' and the sub-tenants.[28]

For the hearing of disputes between taxpayers and the *fiscus* a special court of appeal was instituted at Rome by Nerva. The president of this court, the *praetor fiscalis*, was a magistrate of republican type, and had no interest in upholding the previous decision of the procurator's court; but from the time of Hadrian imperial officials named *advocati fisci* were appointed to present the case of the treasury both at Rome and in the provinces.

Under the financial system of the second century the *fiscus* remained unable to sustain any heavy additional burden. The wars of Trajan entailed heavy requisitions upon the provincials. To meet the deficits arising out of the Great Plague and the Marcomannic Wars (p. 443), M. Aurelius sold off the crown jewels and wardrobe and depreciated the coinage by 25 per cent.[29] But in less disturbed times the *fiscus* more than paid its way. Under Antoninus its surplus again rose to the sum of 2700 million sesterces, which it had not attained since the time of Tiberius.

Collection of taxes Conductores replace publicani

Conductores on the imperial domains

Financial stringency under M. Aurelius

5. The Provinces

An unpleasant sidelight is thrown upon the condition of the senatorial provinces by a series of trials before the Senate in the days of Trajan, which show that the proconsuls of these districts, if left to their own devices, were still apt to relapse into the tyrannous habits of the later Republic. These prosecutions further suggest that Nerva and Trajan were not sufficiently resolute in exercising their *maius imperium* to correct the negligence of governors of senatorial provinces. On the other hand the care with which Trajan supervised the provincial governors of his own appointment is copiously illustrated in the correspondence between him and his special commissioner in Bithynia (p. 430), the younger Pliny. We may even detect in his rescripts a trace of fussiness: the emperor appears a little too nervous lest the clubs of artisans in the Bithynian towns should develop into dangerous political cabals, and he seems excessively reluctant to modify the rulings of his predecessors, for fear of undermining imperial authority. But the dominant impression derived from his directions to Pliny is of a ruler no less considerate than strong. While Trajan insists on the fundamental importance of public order and sound finance he is prepared to make due allowance for local custom and is at pains to avoid anything suggestive of harsh or overbearing behaviour.[30]

The interest of Hadrian in the provinces was manifested by his systematic tours of inspection in the course of which he visited all but a few remote corners of his dominions. To say nothing of minor journeys he made a grand tour of the Empire in 121–125, travelling to and fro along the Rhine and Danube fronts, making an excursion into Britain, passing through Spain into Mauretania and Africa, and concluding his round with a long sojourn in Asia Minor and Greece. In 129–134 he made a similar progress through the eastern provinces as far as Egypt. Of the twenty-one years of his reign Hadrian spent more than half outside of Italy. Though his travels incidentally served to gratify his curiosity as a sightseer and to provide an outlet for his restless activity, their main purpose undoubtedly was to give him a first-hand acquaintance with provincial government in all the three continents. To supplement his own investigations he required his officials to furnish him with detailed reports on territories not visited by him.[31] By these means he acquired an unrivalled insight into the actual conditions of the various provinces, and was able to exercise a more effective control over his subordinates than any previous emperor.

The example of Hadrian was not followed

Maladministration in senatorial provinces

Hadrian's tours of inspection

His insight into provincial affairs

by Antoninus, who never left Italy, except possibly for a visit to the eastern provinces. On the other hand M. Aurelius frequently inspected the Danube lands in connexion with the Marcomannic Wars, and he devoted two years (175–176) to a general tour round the eastern Mediterranean. The provinces received more personal attention than ever before from the emperors of the second century.

The second-century emperors are of provincial origin

In the second century the enfranchisement of the provinces was carried within sight of completion. That Trajan and his successors should herein have followed the lead of Claudius and the Flavian emperors was not to be wondered at, for all of them had provincial blood in their veins. Trajan was born at Italica in southern Spain. As its name declared, this city was founded by immigrants from Italy (p. 147); but it may be assumed that on the distaff side the emperor was partly of Spanish race. Hadrian and M. Aurelius, albeit natives of Rome, were also of Spanish origin: Hadrian's family hailed from the birthplace of Trajan, and M. Aurelius's from the neighbourhood of Cordoba.[32] Antoninus was born at Lanuvium, but his place of origin was Nemausus in Narbonese Gaul. The process of enfranchisement by these emperors cannot be worked out in detail, but it is clear that they freely followed the example of the Flavian rulers in bestowing 'Latin rights' as a halfway house to full Roman status.[33] Presumably these grants were chiefly made in the Danube lands and in the eastern provinces. The final step of conferring full Roman citizenship upon all free men of the Empire, which was taken early in the third century, may be regarded as the enevitable sequel of the franchise policy of Trajan and his successors.

Enfranchisement of the provinces

CHAPTER 38

The 'Five Good Emperors'.
External Affairs

1. Foreign Policy

The last notable extension of the Roman boundaries beyond the limits fixed by Augustus took place in the reign of the warrior-prince Trajan. Under his successors the frontiers underwent rectifications here and there, but the further additions to Roman territory were insignificant. The area of the Roman Empire in the middle of the second century may be estimated at about 1,700,000 square miles. Before looking in more detail at the various changes that were made we may consider broader outlines of policy.

At the time of Nerva's death Trajan was serving on the Rhine, but so far from hastening to Rome he went to the Danube area where the Suebi had been giving trouble and Decebalus of Dacia was possibly threatening. He did not reach Rome until the spring of 99. He was thus personally well acquainted with the situation when he determined on a trial of strength with the Dacians. Whether the annexation of Dacia, *Advance* which followed his victory, was in his mind from *by Trajan* the beginning or was only decided later, the hallmark of the overall policy during his reign was an extension of the frontiers. Dissatisfaction with Domitian's settlement with Decebalus, fears of the king's aggressive intentions, or distrust in the strength of the river-frontier along the Danube, are all factors which may have influenced him. But, in addition, he enjoyed military life and, like Claudius, he may have thought both that a policy of foreign conquest at the beginning of his reign might strengthen his position in Rome and that in general the time had come to expand the frontiers in the interests

of security. In the East he annexed Arabia Petraea (106) and later became involved with the Parthians: his advance over the Euphrates resulted in the new Roman provinces of Armenia, Mesopotamia and Assyria.

Hadrian, who did not shrink from military action when he deemed it necessary and took important measures to strengthen the army, decided to revert to a generally defensive policy. He at once abandoned Trajan's new provinces *Withdrawal* in the East (apart from Arabia Petraea), and *and con-* even contemplated evacuating Dacia although *solidation* he did not do so. He hoped to secure peace by *by Hadrian* diplomacy, by strengthening the frontiers and by keeping the army alert, not least by his constant tours of inspection and his indefatigable personal care. Thus his conference of kings and princes of the East in 129 resulted in establishing a wall of vassals to protect the frontier. Where military action was needed he did not hesitate, but it was only taken if diplomacy was impossible. Where needed, the frontiers of the Empire were strengthened by physical barriers, especially in Germany and Britain. Whereas Domitian had relied more on spaced signal-towers, Hadrian built a continuous wooden palisade in Raetia and Upper Germany, and stone walls in Britain and Numidia. Close-spaced buildings guarded the lower Rhine, the middle and lower Danube, the upper Euphrates, and, where rivers were lacking, along desert frontier-roads (as from the Red Sea to the Euphrates) to control nomadic migrations across the frontier. This policy was successful in the short term and gave peace during Hadrian's reign, but there was a danger that the system might be found too static (like the Maginot Line) when the glamour of Trajan's demonstration of Roman power had faded and a less active emperor reigned.

The stay-at-home Antoninus Pius also aimed at defence and peace. Where fighting broke out (e.g. in Britain, Judaea and Africa) he quickly ended it, and where it threatened (as against Parthia) he relied primarily on diplomacy. His main contribution to the *limes* system was in Britain and Germany, where he advanced beyond the existing frontiers and established second lines (running through Lorch in Germany, and along the line from the Forth to the Clyde in northern Britain). Marcus Aurelius had to face a very different situation, since the weaknesses in Hadrian's system became apparent when the peoples beyond the frontiers began to attack in real earnest. At the beginning of his reign the Parthians seized Armenia and defeated two Roman armies. Although peace was ultimately established, the returning Roman troops brought home not only victory but the plague. About A.D. 166 Germans crossed the Danube and even invaded northern Italy. Much of the remainder of his reign had to be devoted to wars against Marcomanni, Quadi and Iazyges. His plan to advance the frontier by making two new provinces of Marcomannia and Sarmatia was checked by the attempted usurpation of Avidius Cassius and then abandoned by Marcus's son and successor, Commodus. Thus war had dominated much of the reign of the philosopher-king who desired only peace.

The new limes of Antoninus

2. Africa

On the African continent the Mauretanian provinces were the scene of recurrent petty wars. In this district the process of settlement had hardly been carried as yet beyond the coastal border, and the nomadic tribesmen of the uplands, some of whom had been apprenticed to disciplined warfare in the Roman forces, made occasional descents into the plains. During his visit to Mauretania in 123 Hadrian endeavoured to restrict these incursions by extending the area of effective occupation to the ledge of the Atlas plateau. But the inland tribes, reinforced by Gaetulian raiders from the not infrequent oases of the western Sahara (the modern Tuaregs), returned to the charge every

Raids into Mauretania

38.1 Lambaesis. The Praetorium or Headquarters of the Roman camp at Lambaesis in Numidia. From the end of the first century Legio III Augusta was stationed here. It was visited by Hadrian in A.D. 128.

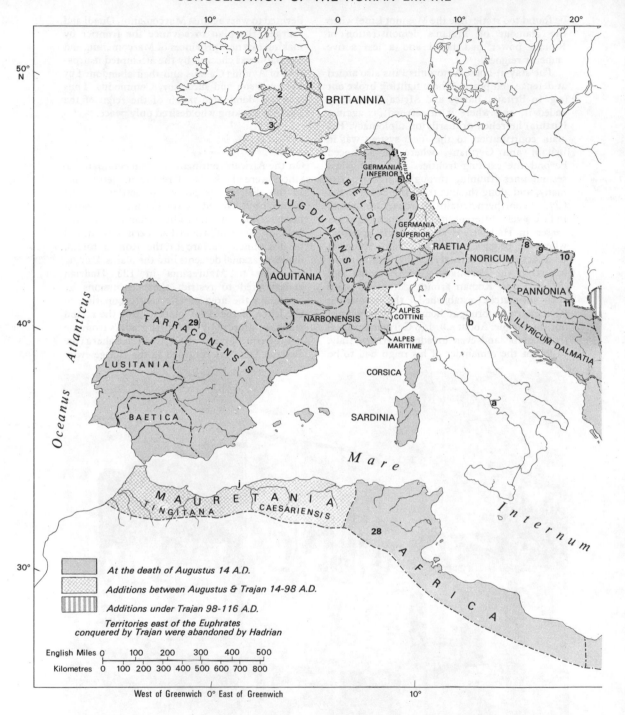

28. THE ROMAN EMPIRE FROM AUGUSTUS TO TRAJAN AND HADRIAN

Distribution of the legions and fleets c. A.D.120

LEGIONS

1 VI Victrix — *Eboracum (Britannia)*
2 XX Valeria Victrix — *Deva (Britannia)*
3 II Augusta — *Isca (Britannia)*
(3a) IX Hispana — *Destroyed in Britain or transferred to Noviomagus c. 119*
4 XXX Ulpia Victrix — *Vetera (Germania Inf.)*
5 I Minervia — *Bonna (Germania Inf.)*
6 XXII Primigenia — *Moguntiacum (Germania Sup.)*
7 VIII Augusta — *Argentorate (Germania Sup.)*
8 X Gemina — *Vindobona (Pannonia Sup.)*
9 XIV Gemina — *Carnuntum (Pannonia Sup.)*
10 I Adiutrix — *Brigetio (Pannonia Sup.)*
11 II Adiutrix — *Aquincum (Pannonia Inf.)*
12 IV Flavia — *Singidunum (Moesia Sup.)*
13 VII Claudia — *Viminacium (Moesia Sup.)*

14 I Italica — *Novae (Moesia Inf.)*
15 XI Claudia — *Durostorum (Moesia Inf.)*
16 V Macedonica — *Troesmus (Moesia Inf.)*
17 XIII Gemina — *Apulum (Dacia)*
18 XV Apollinaris — *Satala (Cappadocia)*
19 XII Fulminata — *Melitene (Cappadocia)*
20 XVI Flavia — *Samosata (Syria)*
21 IV Scythica — *Cyrrhus (Syria)*
22 II Traiana — *? (Syria)*
23 III Gallica — *Rapheneae (Syria)*
24 VI Ferrata — *Bostra (Arabia)*
25 X Fretensis — *Aelia Capitolina (Judaea)*
26 III Cyrenaica — *Nicopolis (Egypt)*
27 XXII Deiotariana — *Nicopolis (Egypt)*
28 III Augusta — *Lambaesis (Africa)*
29 VII Gemina — *Legio (Hispania Tarraconensis)*

FLEETS

a Classis Misenensis
b Ravennas
c Britannica
d Germanica
e Pannonica
f Moesica
g Pontica
h Syriaca
i Alexandrina
j Squardons in Mauretania

now and then. Between 144 and 152 the small Roman garrison was kept in play by continuous forays, and another series of raids took place between 170 and 176, in the course of which the marauders even made a descent on Spain. These tip-and-run raids, however, did not make any heavy call on the Roman defences.

The frontier of Africa is pushed forward

About 100 the frontier of the province of Africa, which had long remained stationary along the line of Lake Tritonis and Mt Aures, was carried westward and southward to the chain of the salt lakes. Under Trajan (probably) the headquarters of the solitary Roman legion in Africa were removed from Theveste to Lambaesis, where the best-preserved of Roman camps may still be seen. To Hadrian is probably due the inception of a vast system of frontier-works, known as the *Fossatum Africae*, which was gradually developed to guard the whole length of the southern flank of the Roman provinces in Africa as well as to promote and secure the development of economic resources.[1]

3. Armenia and Parthia

On the eastern border of the Empire extensive annexations were carried out by Trajan. The small Transjordanian principality which Herod Agrippa II. had held for nearly fifty years (p. 367) had, together with the principality of Emesa, already been incorporated into Syria by Domitian (*c.* 92). A more important acquisition was made by Trajan in 106, when he took over the kingdom of the Nabataean Arabs, whose position astride of the caravan-routes converging from the Arabian desert and the Red Sea to the Palestinian coast gave it a high commercial value. The Nabataean territory was constituted into a separate province of 'Arabia'; it included the Negev and probably the Sinai as its north-west part of the Arabian peninsula, but the territory of Damascus at its northern end was attached to Syria. From this city a fortified road was constructed via Bostra (now the headquarters of a legion) and Petra to Aelane on the Gulf of Aqaba.[2]

Annexation of Nabataean Arabia

Towards the end of his reign Trajan abolished the Euphrates frontier which Augustus had fixed and Nero refused to transgress.[3] This radical change of Roman policy in the East was provoked by a Parthian king named Chosroes. During the reign of Chosroes's elder brother Pacorus Trajan had consented to the conferment of the Armenian crown upon Pacorus's second son Axidares, in the expectation that his elder son Parthamasiris would succeed Pacorus on the throne of Parthia. In the event, however, the Parthian nobles, upon whom the choice of

Renewed Parthian interference in Armenia

the Parthian sovereign finally rested, passed over Parthamasiris in favour of his uncle Chosroes (112), and the new Parthian ruler, to insure himself against Parthamasiris, incited his nephew to seize Armenia by way of compensation (113). But although Parthamasiris obtained possession of Armenia he failed to dislodge Axidares from the remoter parts of the kingdom, and Chosroes in turn was assailed by a pretender in his eastern provinces. At the news that Trajan was meeting the challenge by a mobilisation of all his available forces in the East Parthamasiris offered to do homage to him on the same terms as Tiridates had arranged with Nero. For the time being the Roman emperor gave a non-committal answer, and when the Armenian king was admitted to an interview with Trajan near Erzerum he fully expected that he would save his crown for himself. But Trajan, who had learnt to distrust penitent vassals (pp. 441 f.), incontinently deposed Parthamasiris and declared Armenia a Roman province (114).

Trajan overruns and annexes Armenia

The annexation of Armenia may have been Trajan's original intention, and his motive may have been in part to guard the Roman frontier against the Caucasian tribes, including the Alans, who were moving southward; and some believe that he was far from unconscious of the economic possibility of exacting dues on the trade-routes of Mesopotamia. But in annexing Armenia he must have known that he was virtually committing himself to the strategic necessity of annexing Mesopotamia also, so as to cut off the deep re-entrant angle between Syria and Armenia. He continued (in 115?) his advance into Parthian territory, capturing Nisibis and Singara, and occupied northern Mesopotamia, whose vassal kings, left unsupported by Chosroes, made a feeble resistance or came to terms at once; Mesopotamia thus became a Roman province. After the construction (winter 115–116?) of a transport fleet on the middle Euphrates, the Roman forces moved into Media Adiabene, which became the Roman province of Assyria, and then made a parallel march in two divisions along each of the two Mesopotamian rivers, but united for a joint attack upon Chosroes's winter capital at Ctesiphon (on the Tigris, opposite Seleucia).[4] At the approach of the Romans the Parthian king fled precipitately, and Parthia could be called a Roman province. Thus the emperor had overrun the entire land of the two rivers, and he completed his progress by sailing down the Tigris to the Persian Gulf. But before his gains could be further consolidated widespread insurrections broke out to endanger his rear. Seleucia and other occupied cities rose in revolt, and in Judaea (p. 440) a rebellion, which had no doubt

Trajan reaches the Persian Gulf

been prearranged with the Parthian king, made an additional call upon Roman reserves (117). In an attempt to meet the threat Trajan sent his generals against the rebels, and at Ctesiphon crowned Parthamaspates, a son of Chosroes, as king of Parthia, thus abandoning Roman claims; as soon as the Romans withdrew, Chosroes expelled his son.[5] After a desperate attempt to reduce Hatra by siege Trajan safely regained the Euphrates, thanks to the services of his right-hand man, a Mauretanian chieftain named Lusius Quietus, who held the main line of retreat through central Mesopotamia. He led his forces back to Antioch (early 117), but illness and death soon overtook him.

Annexation of Meso-potamia

Trajan's annexations had at least the merit of disposing cleanly of the 'Armenian question' that had troubled Rome intermittently from the time of Lucullus and Pompey; and in taking from the Parthian king two highly developed countries he cut off one of his chief sources of revenue. But the price which he paid for his new provinces was excessive. In order to concentrate an overwhelming force against Armenia and Parthia the emperor had depleted the garrisons on other fronts beyond the margin of safety (p. 440). Besides, his new frontier in the East followed no natural line of defence and required a larger permanent garrison than the valley of the Euphrates. The first act of Hadrian therefore was to abandon his predecessor's conquests, so that Chosroes was allowed to resume possession of his lost provinces and Parthamaspates was transferred to Osrhoene. In 129 Hadrian restored to Chosroes his daughter, whom Trajan had captured, but not the throne of the Parthian kings. His settlement, which followed closely the lines of Nero's treaty with Vologeses I, was of similar duration. It was momentarily threatened c. 143 and again in 155, when a new Parthian king, Vologeses III, invaded Armenia in order to seize it for one of his kinsmen, but on a mere letter of remonstrance he withdrew his expedition. In 161, however, Vologeses returned to the charge and installed an Arsacid prince (another Pacorus) in Armenia after two victories over the governors of Cappadocia and Syria, who had hastened to meet him with inadequate forces. If the Parthian king had been content at this stage to make peace with M. Aurelius on the lines of Nero's previous settlement he could probably have made a permanent acquisition of Armenia on behalf of Pacorus, for the Roman emperor had no wish to draw swords against him; but by his refusal to compromise he brought upon himself the fate of Chosroes. In 163–164 a large Roman army under the nominal command of the co-emperor L. Verus, but actually under the direction of Avidius Cas-

Hadrian reverses Trajan's policy of annexation

The 'Armenian question' reopened under M. Aurelius

sius and of Statius Priscus, overran Armenia and Mesopotamia in much the same way as Trajan. In 163 Priscus captured and burnt the Armenian capital Artaxata. Cassius followed up a successful battle at Dura Europus on the Euphrates (probably 165) by joining hands with another column proceeding down the Tigris, and with the combined forces he carried the twin towns of Seleucia and Ctesiphon, both of which he destroyed (165–166). He completed the campaign with a raid into Media, the 'furthest east' of Roman arms (166). Peace was concluded. Vologeses agreed to leave Armenia in the hands of another Arsacid named Sohaemus, who had resided at Rome and held the rank of senator. At the same time he ceded the vassal-kingdom of Osrhoene in western Mesopotamia, which became a Roman dependency and was secured by a colony of veterans at Carrhae. By this arrangement M. Aurelius, while adhering in general to the line of the Euphrates, straightened his frontier by cutting off the bend in its middle reach. Soon afterwards, in order to safeguard the peace, Avidius Cassius was given supreme command over all the East, including Egypt. The wars of the second century proved once more that the Parthians might steal surprise victories over the Romans, but were no match for them in a protracted contest. But the spoil which the Romans stripped off the Parthians was a shirt of Nessus, for they brought back with them the germs of the most destructive plague in Roman history.

Extension of the Roman frontiers in Mesopo-tamia

The Roman troops bring back the plague

The Transjordanian territory annexed by Trajan was retained by his successors. Under Hadrian or Antoninus a new fortified road was constructed in advance of Trajan's *limes*. On the northern borders of the enlarged province of Cappadocia (p. 422) the forays of Alans across the Caucasian passes were beaten off without much difficulty by the Roman governors.

4. Judaea

Hadrian's decision to retire from Armenia and Mesopotamia was no doubt influenced by the rebellions which broke out in Trajan's rear in 115. These insurrections were the result of a concerted plot in which the Jews of the Dispersion co-operated with those of Palestine. This rising evidently caught Trajan by surprise, and indeed it is difficult to point to any specific grievances which the Jews could have alleged against this particular emperor: in regard to the Alexandrian Jews his attitude was so sympathetic as to provoke the indignation of the Greek residents. It is possible that the annexation of the

Renewed unrest among the Jews

38.2   Fortress at Quar al-Haar in the Syrian desert near Palmyra; second century A.D.

Widespread rishings under Trajan

Nabataean kingdom had the effect of diverting part of the Arabian trade from Palestine to Gaza or Damascus; but the main cause of the rebellion is no doubt to be sought in the Messianic hopes which had been kept alive by the surviving Rabbinical schools after the First Jewish War. The immediate occasion of the rising was the partial withdrawal of the Roman garrisons from Palestine for service against the Parthians. It may also be surmised that Chosroes, who certainly used the Jewish residents in Babylonia as agents for the uprising in the Land of the Two Rivers, likewise employed them to link up the threads of a general Jewish rebellion in Trajan's rear. The movement was so well timed that the insurgents gained the upper hand in Cyprus and Cyrene, and kept the remaining Roman troops in play in Palestine and Egypt; and wherever they obtained the ascendancy they massacred the Gentile population indiscriminately. But the termination of the Parthian War in 116 left Trajan free to round upon the Jewish insurgents. While Lusius Quietus recovered Mesopotamia and quietened Palestine, another of the emperor's chief lieutenants, Q. Marcius Turbo, crushed the rebellion in Egypt and Cyrene and abetted the usual retaliatory massacres by the Greek populations. The work of repression was achieved so thoroughly outside Palestine that the Jews of the Dispersion hence-

Severe repression of the revolts

forth ceased to give serious trouble to the Roman government.[7]

Of any fighting in Palestine itself at the end of Trajan's reign no details are known. But enough Jews survived to try their strength in another fiercely fought conflict under Hadrian, which was the result of direct provocation from the side of the Romans. In the early part of his reign this emperor had firmly upheld the rights of the Jews at Alexandria, but during his second tour through the eastern provinces he conceived the unfortunate idea of solving the Jewish problem by forcible assimilation – a policy which the Seleucid king Antiochus IV had attempted three centuries previously with disastrous results. In 131 he issued an edict against the practice of circumcision, and he founded a Roman colony, 'Aelia Capitolina', at Jerusalem, an act involving the erection of a shrine of Jupiter Capitolinus on the site of the Temple. The Jewish rising which Hadrian's measures called forth was seemingly confined to Palestine; but it was as universal within that province as the revolt against Nero. Under a leader named Bar-Cosibar (Cochbar) the rebels attempted to wear out the Romans in a war of sieges and small skirmishes (131–134). But the Roman troops, strongly reinforced by detachments from other frontiers, recovered Palestine in the same methodical manner as under Ves-

Hadrian establishes a Roman colony in Jerusalem

pasian. In 134 their commander, C. Iulius Severus, who had been summoned from Britain to take command, cut off and starved out one district after another, and in the following year he pacified the whole country. The Second Jewish War was in effect a manhunt in which the Romans exterminated a large part of the population of Palestine. The statement that they destroyed 50 fortresses, 985 villages and 580,000 men (regardless of those who perished by famine or pestilence) no doubt came nearer the truth than most bulletins of this kind.[8] The repopulation of Palestine which Hadrian had planned to begin with the colony of Aelia Capitolina was gradually carried out by the influx of Gentile settlers from the adjacent lands; the surviving Jews were forbidden to visit Jerusalem except once in a year. Judaea even lost its name and became Syria Palestina, with two legions installed. But under Antoninus the attack which Hadrian had made upon the Jewish law was called off. Though the ban upon proselytising was upheld, those born within the Jewish faith were no longer molested in the exercise of their worship, and synagogues and schools were allowed to keep alive the national traditions. At this stage a *modus vivendi* between Jews and Romans was at last established, and the Jews, though henceforth a stateless and a homeless people, were unimpeded in the exercise of their religion – a concession which enabled them to maintain themselves as a separate nation.

The Second Jewish War in Palestine

The Jews become homeless. But their religion is tolerated

5. Dacia

On the European continent the principal seat of warfare in the second century was in the Danube lands, which had again become a storm centre under Domitian. The revival of hostilities in this region was due to Trajan, who did not wait to give the treaty between Domitian and King Decebalus a full trial, but made immediate preparations for a new preventive attack upon Dacia. His wars with Decebalus are of peculiar interest, because their story is preserved in graphic form on a memorial column in Rome, on which the salient incidents of the campaigns are engraved in an ascending band of sculptures. But while this invaluable record throws a flood of light upon the equipment and organisation of the Roman armies, it does not wholly clear up the strategy of Trajan, or establish his routes of march beyond dispute.[9]

Trajan renews the preventive attacks upon Decebalus

The invasion of Dacia presented a problem of special difficulty to the Romans, both because of the mountainous and wooded nature of the country, and because its defenders could operate on inner lines, while the Roman lateral com-

munications along the Danube were of inconvenient length. Before he opened his attack Trajan improved the connexions between Pannonia and Moesia by cutting a road and towpath along the river through the defile of the Iron Gates.[10] In 101 the emperor invaded Transylvania by the Iron Gate pass in the Carpathians, while Lusius Quietus made a diversion, presumably from Moesia Inferior. Advancing by the valley of the Marisus he dislocated the Dacian defenders from a position at Tapae (the scene of Iulianus's victory in 88); but his own forces were handled so severely that he suspended operations until the next season. In 102 he advanced either by the Red Tower or the Vulcan pass, and captured a chain of fortified positions by siege warfare. After a final victory near the Dacian capital, Sarmizegethusa, Trajan obtained the surrender of Decebalus. He left the king in possession of his realm, but he dismantled some of his fortresses and placed' Roman garrisons in the remainder. On his return to Rome he received the title Dacicus.

The First Dacian War

The peace by which Trajan concluded the First Dacian War was a half-measure which effected no permanent solution to the Dacian question. In limiting his armaments and quartering Roman troops upon him, he injured Deceba-

38.3 The lower part of Trajan's Column.

38.4   Scene from Trajan's Column, showing the final Roman victory; auxiliary *alae* pursue the fleeing Decebalus and the Dacians.

38.5   Aerial view of the Saalburg fort in the Taunus mountains beyond the upper Rhine. Partial reconstruction of its third-century appearance.

The Second Dacian War

lus's pride, yet failed to reduce him to impotence. After two years' secret preparations the Dacian king destroyed or invested the Roman garrisons, and in 105 he broke into Moesia. The Second Dacian War which he thus brought on was one of the greatest in Roman history, if we measure its importance by the number of Roman troops engaged, for Trajan commanded a force of no fewer than twelve legions, which points to a total strength of not fewer than 120,000 men on the Roman side. After a hurried

campaign in defence of Moesia he recrossed the Danube in 105 by a bridge, which he had built at Drobetae at a point below the rapids of the Iron Gates, and re-entered Dacia, presumably by the Red Tower pass and the valley of the Aluta. At the end of the two hard-fought campaigns, culminating in a second battle near Sarmizegethusa, Decebalus took his own life, and his followers made their final submission.[11] Trajan's booty (estimated at more than half a million Roman pounds of gold and a million of silver, or some 700 million denarii) was the last of Rome's great war hauls.

In this war the Dacians took ruinous toll of their fighting strength, and without Decebalus to lead them they constituted no greater menace to Rome than Pontus after the death of Mithridates. But Trajan would incur no further risk from this quarter. In 107 he constituted Dacia as a Roman province, repeopling it with colonists who were forcibly transplanted from the other Danube lands and from Asia Minor. A Colonia Ulpia Traiana replaced Sarmizegethusae, and a provincial *concilium* was established at Aquae. The area annexed by Trajan did not extend beyond the Transylvanian plateau, from (perhaps) the Theiss to the Aluta and north to Porolissum. The steppe lands to east and west were but sparsely occupied with auxiliary pickets, and the Sarmatian populations were placed in a condition of merely nominal vassalage. Beyond the northern boundaries of the province (whose line has not been clearly traced) bands of Dacian refugees were allowed to settle without any form of Roman control.[12]

Annexation of Dacia

Although the new province provided a valuable bastion which separated Rome's enemies north of the Danube Trajan's protrusion of the Roman dominion across the Danube entailed the same strategic disadvantage as the annexation of Mesopotamia, in that it replaced a clearcut frontier by a more indeterminate one, and on balance it increased rather than alleviated the burden of defence. His successor therefore prepared to evacuate Dacia at the same time as the new eastern provinces, and he actually dismantled the stone bridge erected by Trajan below the Iron Gates; but on second thoughts he retained possession of the European province. To abandon Dacia would have been a desertion of the colonists whom Trajan had compelled to migrate across the Danube, and it would have deprived the fiscus of a substantial revenue from the metal deposits of the Carpathians, which imported miners from Dalmatia had already begun to work intensively. From an economic standpoint the Roman occupation of Dacia was no less beneficial to Dacia itself. In a land which had hitherto contained no town except the royal

The province of Dacia

residence, native villages and Roman garrison centres presently developed into *municipia* and *coloniae*. At the same time the penetration of Latin influence into Dacia, which had commenced as early as the days of Burebistas (p. 278), made more rapid progress, so that Transylvania soon became as much Romanised as Moesia or Pannonia and came to provide a permanent home for a Latin-speaking population in eastern Europe.

Romanisation of Dacia

Changes north of the Danube led to some alteration in the organisation of the provinces and to a redeployment of troops. To guard Dacia against the Iazyges Pannonia was divided (*c.* 103) into two provinces, Inferior (with its capital at Aquincum, Budapest, governed by a praetorian legate) and Superior (capital at Carnuntum, and a consular legate). Further east on the lower Danube the earthworks in the Dobrudja were abandoned, and the area was guarded by a legion posted at Troesmis. Both provinces of Moesia, which had been divided into a Superior and Inferior under Domitian (85–86), were extended after Trajan's Dacian campaigns, while the new province of Dacia itself was twice subdivided under Hadrian: first into Superior and Inferior (118–119) and then (*c.* 124) part of Superior was split off as Dacia Porolissensis; later (*c.* 168) the Tres Daciae were put under one governor. Stronger garrisons were needed. Three legions were posted on the lower Danube between the Black Sea and Aluta (at Troesmis, Durostorum and Novae), two in Upper Moesia (at Viminiacum and Singidunum; older legionary camps at Oescus and Ratiaria became colonies), four (five at first) in the Pannonias (at Aquincum, Brigetio, Carnuntum and Vindobona), and one in Dacia. Further south, behind the shield of these ten legions the Danubian provinces could flourish in safety. Thus Thrace was raised to the status of a praetorian province (*c.* 114) and urbanisation increased (as witness settlements named Traianopolis and Hadrianopolis), as also in Lower Moesia. But ten legions on the Danube and only four on the Rhine (contrasted with the Augustan eight) showed where the greater danger was anticipated.

Provincial changes

After Trajan's wars the Danube lands enjoyed some sixty years of almost unbroken peace. About 165 a band of marauders from Dacia or Sarmatia who went by the name of 'Costobocae' cut across the Black Sea into the Aegean, where they extended their raids as far as central Greece before the *classis Pontica* ran them down. But under M. Aurelius the districts of the middle Danube were overrun by a coalition of German tribes in a series of invasions which was the forerunner of their general migrations in subsequent centuries.

6. The Marcomannic Wars

Under the influence of contacts with the populations within the Roman Empire, which the emperors' policy of isolation could not wholly prevent, the German tribes were gradually passing out of the state of semi-nomadism into that of intensive agriculture and permanent settlements. Though the free men might leave the actual cultivation of the fields, wherever possible, to women and to prisoners of war, they were at least learning to settle down in fixed abodes. The process of settlement was relatively far advanced among the Germans in Bohemia, where King Maroboduus had deliberately introduced Roman customs, and the tribes of this region cultivated friendly relations with Rome which the brief passage of arms under Domitian did not seriously interrupt.[13]

The German tribes become more settled

But after 150 disturbances in the eastern borders of Germany drove the tribes along the Danube border to seek a more secure abode on its southern side. In 167 two of the chief peoples of southern Germany, the Marcomanni and the Quadi, together with some lesser tribes, among whom the Vandals now come into notice for the first time, broke across the Roman frontier on the middle Danube. The invaders drove under cover the Roman garrisons, which had been depleted by drafts to the Euphrates front (p. 439), and carried the entire line of the river (except at the more heavily fortified points) from Raetia to Moesia. At the same time they set in motion the Iazyges, a nomadic tribe in the valley of the Theiss, who overran Dacia and kept the garrisons beleagured in the towns. Sweeping across Pannonia and Noricum, the Marcomanni and Quadi made a descent upon Italy, where they penetrated as far as Aquileia.

German invasions across the middle Danube

This great crisis was met by M. Aurelius with the vigour of a Trajan. He raised a war fund by desperate financial devices (p. 432), recruited troops from all classes (including slaves and gladiators), and threw up new fortifications along the threatened zones. In 168 he set out in person for the Danube front, and he revisited it continuously until his death in 180 at Vindobona (modern Vienna). Of the wars of these years little is known, except that the Romans took advantage of the lack of close combination among the invaders by driving wedges between them and playing them off against each other. The literary evidence is fragmentary, and while some episodes are depicted on the Column which M. Aurelius set up in Rome after his victory, no continuous narrative is shown.[14] The wars fall into two main campaigns, one against the Marcomanni and Quadi, which Marcus fought from his base at Carnuntum, and the other against

The 'Marcomannic Wars' of M. Aurelius

the Sarmatian Iazyges. After an initial defeat (170) the Romans were successful against the Marcomanni (171–172) and Marcus took the title Germanicus, but the Quadi were not finally subdued until 174 after a battle which was celebrated in the Christian legend of the Thundering Legion: Christian soldiers in this Legio Fulminata prayed for rain to slake the thirst of the exhausted soldiers, and in the resultant storm the enemy were overcome. Directing operations from Sirmium, Marcus defeated the Iazyges in 175 and assumed the title Sarmaticus. Thus by 175 the emperor had recovered the lost ground and was preparing a counter-attack when the insubordination of Avidius Cassius in Syria (p. 428) obliged him to offer terms to the Germans, which they broke as soon as his back was turned. In 178 M. Aurelius resumed his campaigns on the Danube. Two years later he had finally cleared the trespassers out of Roman territory and was preparing to advance the *His plan* frontier to the Carpathians and the mountains *to annex* of Bohemia by the formation of two new prov- *Bohemia* inces, Sarmatia and Marcomannia. Had this plan been carried out the Roman Empire would have been provided with a continuous mountain defence in central Europe. But after the emperor's death his plans of conquest were abandoned. By the terms of peace which his successor concluded the Germans and Iazyges restored all their captives, undertook to provide *His* recruits for the Roman army, and bound them- *successor* selves not to approach within ten miles of the *reverts to* Danube. The vacant land on the farther bank *the Danube* of the river was patrolled by men stationed in *frontier* forts, linked by a chain of watch-towers.[15] At the same time several thousands of the invaders who had lost their homes were settled in the depopulated regions within the Roman borders, on condition of rendering military service as Roman auxiliaries. The efforts of M. Aurelius at least gave the Danube lands a lengthy respite from further disturbances.

The unrest which launched the Marcomanni and their associates upon the Danube lands did not communicate itself to the inhabitants of western Germany. Throughout the second century the Roman positions on the Rhine were not seriously imperilled. But the withdrawal of troops from this frontier to others which needed reinforcement obliged the Romans to strengthen its fortifications. As a prelude to his Dacian wars Trajan tightened the network of forts in the angle between the Rhine and the upper Danube and constructed new frontier-roads. Under *Fortifica-* Hadrian the earthen forts behind the frontier- *tions on* line in Upper Germany and Raetia were rebuilt *the frontier* more solidly in stone, and the chain of watch- *between* towers on the actual boundary-line of the two *Rhine and* *Danube*

provinces was connected by a continuous palisade and ditch, whose main purpose probably was to prevent a sudden break-through of mounted men. This barrier was evidently meant to serve as a permanent frontier-line; nevertheless Antoninus abandoned it in favour of a new palisade and military road which ran in long straight stretches on the summit of the ridges that overlook the Neckar valley, running from Miltenberg on the Main southward to Lorch where it met the Raetian *limes*. In this reorganisation some Britons were involved: as a result of a rising in northern Britain in 140 (p. 447) many of the insurgents from southern Scotland were drafted into *numeri* of the Roman army (new auxiliary regiments) and sent for service overseas. Thus four new *numeri Brittonum* were sent to Germany (142–145) where they were employed in building forts on the old *limes* of the Odenwald. The veterans of this earlier line were now moved forward to the new Outer line, along which they built forts. Both lines were held until *c.* 180, when the Inner line was abandoned and its troops probably moved up to reinforce the Outer line. Finally, it may be noted, at the end of the century or the beginning of the third, the whole 200-mile length of the German frontier was strengthened with an earthen rampart and trench, the so-called Pfahlgraben.[16] We may probably ascribe to Hadrian an administrative change by which Upper and Lower Germany were detached from Belgica for purposes of taxation and civil government and became two independent provinces.

7. Britain

After the decision to abandon northern Scotland and the consequent withdrawal to the Clyde–Forth isthmus as the frontier (p. 421), forts south of this line in Lowland Scotland were reconstructed (e.g. Newstead). Some disturbances followed, and the need for reinforcements for his Dacian Wars led Trajan to withdraw from the Lowlands and establish a new frontier *Trajan's* on the line of the Stanegate, Agricola's road *frontier* across the Tyne–Solway isthmus (*c.* 105). At the same time measures were taken to strengthen the province itself: the three legionary fortresses were reconstructed in stone and some new forts were built in Wales and probably at London (north-west of the inhabited area, either for an urban cohort or as an army headquarters), while two more *coloniae* had already been established, at Lindum (*c.* 90) and Glevum (96–98). Soon, however, the Selgovae and Novantae of southern Scotland and the Brigantes were on the warpath again, but the insurrection was suppressed

38.6   Hadrian's Wall. The Wall near Cuddy's Crag, Northumberland.

38.7   Hadrian's Wall. Walltown Crags, Northumberland.

38.8　Vindolanda (Chesterholm, Northumberland), by Hadrian's Wall; fort and *vicus*.

38.9　The granaries at the Roman military post at Corstopitum (near Corbridge, Northumberland), which were built by Severus and his sons, *c.* A.D. 205.

by 118. Hadrian then decided upon personal intervention. In 122 he visited Britain, bringing with him a new governor, Platorius Nepos, and probably also a new legion, the VI Victrix, to replace IX Hispana.[17]

Hadrian's Wall

Under Hadrian's instruction and Platorius's keen eye the army built a stone wall 80 miles long across Britain from the Tyne to Solway, with forts, mile-castles and turrets, and appropriate ditches. This remarkable achievement, which is reckoned to have involved moving some two million tons of rock and soil, was essentially completed by 126 after many changes of plan. These changes, which have been patiently revealed by the detective skill of modern archaeologists, resulted in a structure which comprised two main elements. In front of the wall (i.e. to the north) was a large ditch (27 feet wide and 15 deep); the wall itself was a continuous stone structure, never less than 8 feet thick and probably at least 12 feet high at its lowest; at every mile was a fortlet and between each of these were two signal-turrets (some 20 feet square); finally, at irregular intervals were sixteen forts which partly protruded from the wall. Second, behind this ran the *vallum* (or *fossatum*), a ditch 20 feet wide, 10 feet deep and with a flat bottom of 8 feet, with the upcast soil in two mounds some 100 feet apart. The system was extended for some 30 miles along the Cumbrian coast where mile-castles and signal-towers were erected but no wall was needed.[18] It required a garrison of some 9500 men in the forts, while the mile-castles were perhaps held by three or four cohorts of auxiliaries in detachments (*vexillationes*) along the wall.

Its purpose

Although the wall had a parapet sentry-walk, its function differed from that of a town-wall, since there were enemies to south as well as to north. It was designed to split the enemy, to watch and control their movements, and to enable the Romans, especially their cavalry, to sally forth from a strong base and to round up groups of the enemy against the wall itself. The purpose of the *vallum* is less clear. It probably incorporated an earlier lateral trackway, which would allow the bringing up of supplies to the wall. Since the shape of its ditch was not primarily designed for military needs (in contrast with the *vallum* in front of the wall itself), it was probably conceived as a barrier to demarcate the zone and to prevent approach to the wall from the south except by means of its causeways.

Trouble in Lowland Scotland was met partly by sending off some of the tribesmen to Germany (p. 444) and partly by a radical change of frontier. Soon after his accession Antoninus

38.10 A coin of Antoninus Pius, showing Britannia seated on a rock, holding a standard in her right hand and with her left arm resting on a shield set on a helmet.

Pius decided to abandon the garrisoning of Hadrian's Wall and advance the frontier again to the Scottish isthmus where a turf wall was to be built across the land. The task was entrusted to Lollius Urbicus, who made preparations as early as 139. On Hadrian's Wall the gates were removed from the mile-castles, and causeways made across the *vallum*. Then 30 miles of turf wall were built from the Forth to the Clyde by the legionaries (inscriptions show how the work was apportioned among the three legions). In front of the wall was a *vallum*, behind a 'Military Way'; on it were some eighteen forts, behind lay a secure base at Newstead, and in front were outlying forts. By late 142 or soon afterwards the task was completed.[19]

The Antonine Wall

In order to maintain this new commitment men were drawn from some of the forts in the Pennines and this change before long encouraged the Brigantes to revolt. They were crushed by 154 by the governor Iulius Verus, who brought reinforcements from Germany. But these were not enough and forces had to be withdrawn from Scotland: the Antonine Wall was deserted and its forts burnt by the Romans to deny their use to the enemy. Then before Antoninus's death a new policy was devised: both walls must be held. Hadrian's Wall was recommissioned and the Antonine Wall reoccupied perhaps by Verus *c.* 158. With two barriers the Scottish tribes could not communicate with their Brigantian allies, who were further checked by the rebuilding of many Pennine forts. Under M. Aurelius there were further disturbances, which Calpurnius Agricola was sent to crush (162–166), and in 175 some Sarmatian cavalry was dispatched to reinforce the garrison (p. 444). Finally, in the first year of Commodus's reign (180) disaster befell: the Antonine Wall was overrun by the tribes of central Scotland. Ulpius Marcellus, who was sent to quell the insurrection, succeeded by 184, but then withdrew the frontier to Hadrian's Wall: the

Its later history

Antonine Wall was finally abandoned. This policy was in line with Commodus's refusal to establish the new provinces of Sarmatia and Marcomannia which his father Marcus had hoped to create (p. 444). In the Lowlands beyond the new Roman frontier the tribes, now free, united in a large confederacy of the Maeatae, while further north still was a confederacy of Caledonian tribes.

The slight frontier modifications, however, carried out in Britain and elsewhere did not indicate any essential change in foreign policy. The line of fortifications which Hadrian and Antoninus drew across Europe afforded visible proof that the Roman Empire's period of growth had definitely come to an end.

8. The Roman Army

The size of the army barely adequate

The rebellions in the rear of Trajan's advance into Parthia, and the break-through of the Marcomanni during M. Aurelius's Parthian War, showed up the numerical weakness of the Roman army and the lack of an adequate reserve force to deal with emergencies. The emperors of the second century applied no radical remedy to this shortcoming. Despite new commitments entailed by the annexation of Dacia, the total number of Roman forces was but slightly augmented. The lack of a general reserve was partly met by the expedient of drafting detachments

38.11 A diploma which was given to auxiliary troops on their due discharge and granted them Roman citizenship.

(*vexillationes*) of legions from quiet to threatened fronts, and by the provision of better communications between the various sectors by means of peripheral roads.

In the second century the transformation in the personnel of the army which had begun in the days of Caesar and Augustus was all but completed. The scarcity of recruits from Italy was now such that only the praetorian cohorts were supplied from this source. The legions no less than the auxiliary units were made up almost wholly of provincials. Permanent camps encouraged local recruiting, which became normal by the time of Hadrian, including the enrolment of sons of legionaries brought up around the camps (*ex castris*). The army thus became provincialised, and the barrier between legionaries and auxiliaries was gradually weakened, but the army was not yet 'barbarised'. From Hadrian to the Severi the western provinces seem to have contributed the majority of legionaries, the Rhine–Danube area coming second, and the eastern provinces third.[20] As the Auxilia became more standardised, they were supplemented from Hadrian's time by units (*numeri*) of a new type, raised from the less Romanised provincials who fought with their own native weapons and used their native languages (e.g. *numeri* of Moors, Palmyrenes, Celts or the Britons serving in Germany, see p. 447). There were also specialist formations, as archers (*cohorts sagittariorum*), though slingers appear no longer as separate units, but the art formed part of normal auxiliary training. Some changes took place in equipment. Thus legionaries (certainly from Trajan's day and probably much earlier) wore body-armour made of metal strips (*lorica segmentata*), while on the Column of Marcus Aurelius some are shown in scale-armour (*hamata* or *squamata*). Gradually they also seem to have made use of the lance (*lancea*) and longer sword (*spatha*) used hitherto by the auxiliaries; but details of equipment may have varied slightly from province to province. Cavalry became more important, and the tactics of enemies, Parthians, Sarmatians and Celts, were studied. Regular units of mounted archers (*alae sagittariae*) were used by the Flavians, mounted but unarmoured pikemen (*contarii*) appear about this time or soon afterwards, while Hadrian created the first regular unit of auxiliary mailed cavalrymen (*alae catafractarii*; the *clibanarii*, whose horses also wore mailed armour, are a much later development of the fourth century).[21] The centurions, who trained and led the men, were mainly ex-legionaries or ex-praetorians, although some were of equestrian origin, while the higher command, chosen by the emperors, were generally

The army becomes predominantly provincial

Other changes

men of very considerable professional proficiency. Much credit for army reform has been given to Hadrian, but while not all the measures attributed to him should be set at his door, the army owed a great debt to his personal and understanding interest and to his drive for efficiency, discipline and training.

With the stabilisation of the frontiers, service in the Roman army tended more and more to resolve itself into a routine of police patrolling. Legionary base camps and the 'castella' of auxiliaries in advanced positions were alike constructed in dressed stone and arranged with a view to the comfort of the garrisons. Yet if the *The Roman army less mobile. Its training continues strict* Roman soldier of the second century was losing the mobility which distinguished him in the days of Caesar and Augustus, he was still trained with all the old-time rigour. To make up for the discipline of actual warfare Hadrian prescribed severe courses of field exercises, and at his inspections of the frontier corps he criticised their manoeuvres with an unerring eye for detail. In addition to their military drill the troops were still called upon to undertake building and digging fatigues.[22] The legionary camp at Lambaesis, the walls of Hadrian and Antoninus in Britain and the German frontier defences were the handiwork of the soldiers who occupied them. At the death of M. Aurelius the Roman army was as unconquerable and the peace of the Roman Empire was as secure as ever, provided always that the Roman army minded its business of frontier defence.

9. Conclusion

The imperial régime becomes more uniform At the death of M. Aurelius the constitution of Augustus had been in operation for two centuries; the initial difficulties that beset any new government in a transitional period had been overcome, and the merits of the system were showing through clearly. In the first century the rule of the Caesars varied considerably from emperor to emperor, in the second century it had attained a high degree of uniformity.

The comparatively unstable character of the earlier régime was partly due to the haphazard method of selecting emperors, which had the result of thrusting a quasi-absolute power into the hands of men with very diverse degrees of training and of personal ability; partly to the strain which this power placed upon its first holders. To some extent this stress arose out *Opposition to the early Caesars. The Senate and military pretenders* of the mere novelty of their position, from the lack of precedents to guide their policy. It was intensified by the misunderstandings that beset the relation of the Caesars to the Senate. Under a constitution which necessarily reduced it to

a subordinate part the Senate sullenly resented the slights, real or apparent, which the emperors placed upon it. But the principal source of anxiety for the early emperors lay, not in any collective or constitutional opposition, but in the risk of individual rebellion. Though senators might no longer govern, they could still oppose a government by the methods of M. Brutus and Cassius. An even greater danger threatened from heads of armies who might use these for their own aggrandisement — and after the 'year of the four emperors' every Roman officer was free to dream that he carried a sceptre in his kitbag.

In the second century the question of the succession had found a satisfactory solution for the *Diminished opposition in the second century* time being, and the average standard of ability of the Roman emperors was never higher. The imperial administration had learnt its business; the Senate had so far acquiesced in its new position that it was now content with mere tokens of power. Lastly, though the Caesars were never wholly free from the risk of conspiracy and rebellion, they were no longer haunted by these dangers.

The stability which the Roman government had attained in the second century gave it an opportunity for constitutional and social reforms such as the early Caesars could not have made without a risk of renewed political disorders. The times were now favourable for an attack upon two cognate social evils, slavery and the wholesale pauperising of the urban popula- *Problems now ripe for solution* tions. At best, it is true, any attempt to grapple vigorously with these problems must have offended many rooted prejudices and antagonised numerous vested interests.[23] But in the second century the physical limits of agricul- *Slavery* tural or industrial expansion were not yet within sight; the possibilities of judicious land-settlement had not yet been exhausted; and the difficulties attendant on any comprehensive social change could have been faced without the fear of general social dislocation. This problem of redistributing economic power and responsibility had its counterpart in the question of a better division of political functions, so as to counteract the tendency to excessive centralisation of power in the hands of the emperors. While a return to the government of republican times was neither practicable nor desirable, a devolution of administrative duties from the Caesars upon the provincial parliaments would at any rate have been deserving of experiment. The political utility of the *concilia* had already been proved on a small scale by the effective part which they had taken in bringing guilty governors to book, and emperors had found in *Decentralisation of government* them a serviceable link for the transmission of messages to the municipalities. Though it was imperative that the control of the army and of foreign policy should remain in the hands of the emperors, the provincial councils could fitly have been entrusted with other executive functions, such as the maintenance of internal order and the repartition of financial burdens among the constituent municipalities. A policy of decentralisation carried out on these lines would have had the double advantage of easing the burden on the shoulders of the emperors, and of giving wider scope to the administrative talents of the municipal aristocracies.[24]

These problems not touched

But no such counsels of perfection were actually offered to the emperors of the second century, for the Roman world of that age demanded nothing more than good administration on established lines. Tried by this test, the earlier Caesars gave general satisfaction, those of the second century came through with flying colours. In one respect, moreover, the Roman government of the first two centuries A.D. effected an important transformation. By its liberal policy of bestowing Roman citizenship upon the provincials it effaced the traces of former conquest and converted the Roman Empire into a commonwealth, where the way to the highest offices stood open to all educated men, regardless of race or nationality. Last but not least, the Pax Romana which Augustus had restored was upheld and consolidated under his successors. When full allowance is made for the continual unrest in some provinces and the occasional irruptions of foreign invaders on some under-garrisoned sector on the frontiers, it remains broadly true that the countries of the Roman Empire were never before and never afterwards more free from the shadow of war than in the first two centuries A.D. Of the second century it can further be said that it was an age of general goodwill, in which the inhabitants of the Empire lived together with less mutual friction than at any other time (p. 488). On these grounds the well-known words of Gibbon, that the human race was never happier than in the age of the five good Roman emperors, are not devoid of justification, and as a challenge to the modern world they have not yet lost their sting.

The Roman Empire now a commonwealth of partners

Consummation of the Pax Romana

CHAPTER 39

Roman Society from A.D. 70 to 180

1. Agriculture

The age in which the Roman Empire attained its widest extension also witnessed its highest economic development.

Agriculture becomes stabilised

In the central portions of the Empire agriculture underwent little further change. After the time of Columella no technical improvements of any consequence were made in husbandry; neither was there any notable alteration in the tenures of land or the conditions of labour. The growth of *latifundia*, which had been checked under the early emperors, was not yet resumed. In Italy the smaller peasantry derived a new lease of life from the economic policy of Nerva and his successors, for it was this class of proprietor that obtained the most benefit from the loans at easy rates which these emperors made in connexion with their 'alimentary institutions'.[1] But the most typical holding continued to be, as in the earlier part of the first century, the medium-sized plot acquired out of the profits of industry or commerce. For the cultivation of these estates servile labour was still in use, but it was giving way steadily to that of *coloni* or free tenants. On the imperial domains it now became a common practice to lease large pieces to *conductores* or tenants-in-chief who exploited a 'home farm' directly, and sub-let the remainder to *coloni* in small allotments.[2] But we may doubt whether the free tenants were appreciably better cultivators than the slaves (p. 377).

Increased recourse to free tenants

In Italy the planting of vineyards, which ranked as a safe investment in the days of Columella, was carried to a point at which wine threatened to become cheaper than water, and Domitian's scheme of restriction (p. 414) could

Over-production of wine

hardly have sufficed to bring back prosperity to this branch of husbandry. Though Italian agriculture had not yet reached the stage of decay, it did not share in the rising prosperity of the period. On the other hand the provincial land was brought under more intensive cultivation, especially in the undeveloped countries on the outskirts of the Empire. In Britain the regions best suited to tillage, and more particularly the light dry soils of the south and east, and of the Vale of York, became the chief centres of cereal production in northern Europe.[3] It may also be surmised that the wool-growing in-

Britain exports corn

39.1   Corn mill worked by an ass.

dustry which was England's main source of wealth in the Middle Ages was a legacy from Roman times: the large 'Roman villas' in Gloucestershire, and the importance which the town of Corinium (Cirencester) attained, point to the early development of the Cotswolds as a sheep-rearing centre.[4]

In the province of Belgica the proximity of the Roman camps along the Rhine gave a stimulus to corn-growing.[5] In the south of Gaul the production of wine was not arrested by Domitian's embargo; while the Narbonese province supplied the Rhineland, Aquitania opened up a new market in Britain — another anticipation of the Middle Ages. The cultivation of the olive, which Roman immigrants had successfully introduced into the steppe-lands of south-eastern Spain and southern Tunisia, now attained

Britain imports Bordeaux wine

such dimensions that these districts became the principal centres of oil-production in the Empire. The volume of the exports from these countries to Rome may be measured by the 'Monte Testaccio' on the Tiber wharf, an artificial mound of a height exceeding 100 feet and a circumference of half a mile, whose core consisted of broken jars from Spain and Africa, mostly of date A.D. 50–250.

In Egypt a fresh attack on the marginal waste land was made by Hadrian. In the Orontes valley of Syria the abundant remains of oil-presses show that this ancient home of the olive now reached its highest productivity. The lands of Transjordania, at last made safe against the secular incursion of the Bedouin by the *limes Arabicus*, were transformed into wide cornfields.

Olives in Syria; corn in Transjordania

39.2   Warehouse for storing oil or wine at Ostia, with large amphorae sunk into the ground.

2. Industry and Trade

The industrial and commercial development of the later first and of the second centuries went *pari passu* with the pacification of the Roman world and the elaboration of the road-system, which was nearing completion towards the end of the second century. The facilities for the interchange of commerce were now so manifold that the old traditions of self-contained economy broke down generally. Even in remote country districts home production of ordinary articles of necessity gave way to the purchase of goods from shops or factories. The technical processes of manufacture underwent little change, and the

Commercial exchange reaches its highest point

organisation of industry remained unaltered, but fresh sources for the supply of raw materials were laid open. An important new goldfield was vigorously developed in Dacia. In Britain the iron deposits of the Sussex Weald and of the Forest of Dean were worked intensively, and the production of lead from the mines in the Mendips and Shropshire, in Flintshire and Yorkshire, gave rise to an export trade in that metal (p. 458).[6]

The tendency of Italy to fall back in the economic race was even more marked in the domain of manufactures than in that of agriculture. About the middle of the first century the master-potters of Arretium began to lose their markets

Industrial decline of Italy

39.3 A smith at work. On the left an assistant blows up the fire with bellows. On the right, the smith's tools and a lock.

39.4 A shoemaker at work.

39.5 Relief of a vegetable stall. A greengrocer behind a trestle table with three fingers raised, perhaps indicating the price of an item. His stock includes cabbage, kale, garlic, leeks and onions.

Glass-blowing in western Europe

The Gressenich brasses

to their competitors in Gaul; in the second century the glass and bronze wares of Capua were similarly replaced by Gallic products. In the East the old-established centres of industry maintained their ascendancy, and there was a slight revival of manufacturing activity in Greece proper, where the Peloponnesian town of Patrae first attained importance by its production of fine textile fabrics.

But the most remarkable growth of industry took place in Gaul and the Rhineland, which now became the principal workshop of Europe.[7] The glass-blowing industry, which was established at Lugdunum in the first century, subsequently moved northward to Normandy and across the Channel as far as the Mersey. But later in the second century the centre of the glass-making industry was transferred to Cologne. Though the products of the Cologne kilns lacked the artistic modelling of the Campanian and Alexandrian wares, they were unsurpassed for transparency, and for the skill with which their contours were picked out with coloured threads.

The metallurgical skill of the Gauls gave rise to two new processes, tin-plating and brass-founding. An excellent brass ware with naturalistic decorations of indigenous Celtic style was produced in the second century at Gressenich near Jülich;[8] this novel product presently dis-

placed the bronze utensils of Capua in the markets of northern Europe. Above all, the ceramic industries of Gaul attained an output hitherto unknown in the ancient world. At the end of the first century the centre for the manufacture of *terra sigillata* shifted from Graufesenque (p. 380) to Lezoux in Auvergne; after 150 the headquarters of the industry moved on to Tres Tabernae (modern Rheinzabern near Speyer). Each of these districts in turn supplied western Europe with the greater part of its fine table ware.[9] Concurrently with the glossy red ware of Lezoux and Rheinzabern a black pottery which also attained a considerable vogue was manufactured near Tongres in Belgium, and a similar ware, with a grey slip and decorations that harked back to the old Celtic traditions, was produced in Britain, more particularly at Castor near Peterborough in the Nene valley and in the Colchester area. The Helvetian town of Vindonissa (Windisch) became the seat of an extensive manufacture of terracotta lamps. In the period now under review western Europe for the first time caught up with the lands of the eastern Mediterranean in regard to industrial production.

Gallic, Belgian and British pottery

The opening up of commercial relations with countries outside the Roman frontier was carried to its furthest limits in the second century. Roman coins which have been found on the east coast of Ireland may be taken as evidence of occasional visits by merchants from Britain

Trade with Scandinavia

39.6 Mosaic floor of the Piazzale delle Corporazioni, a colonnade at Ostia, with sixty-one small rooms opening off it. These were used by merchants, and the mosaics illustrate their trades. Here an *amphora* of wine is being transferred from a merchantman to a river boat.

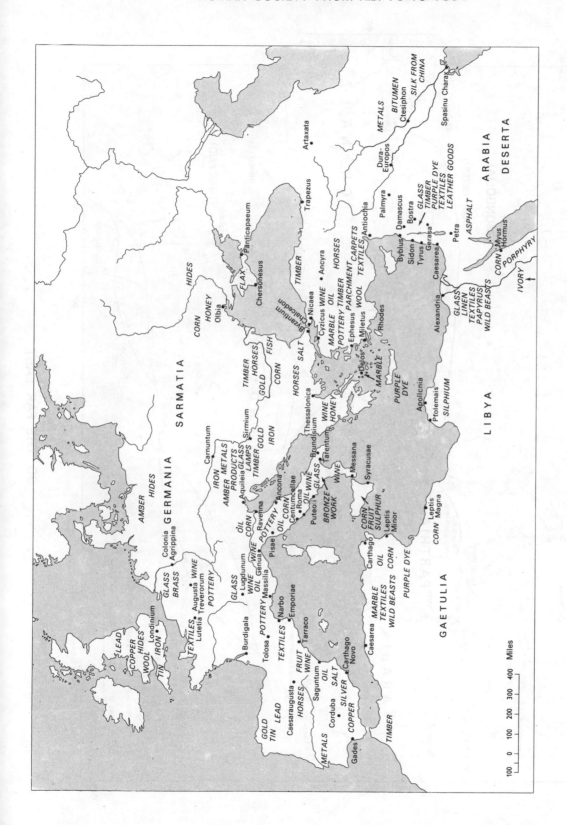

29. PRODUCTS AND TRADE OF THE EMPIRE

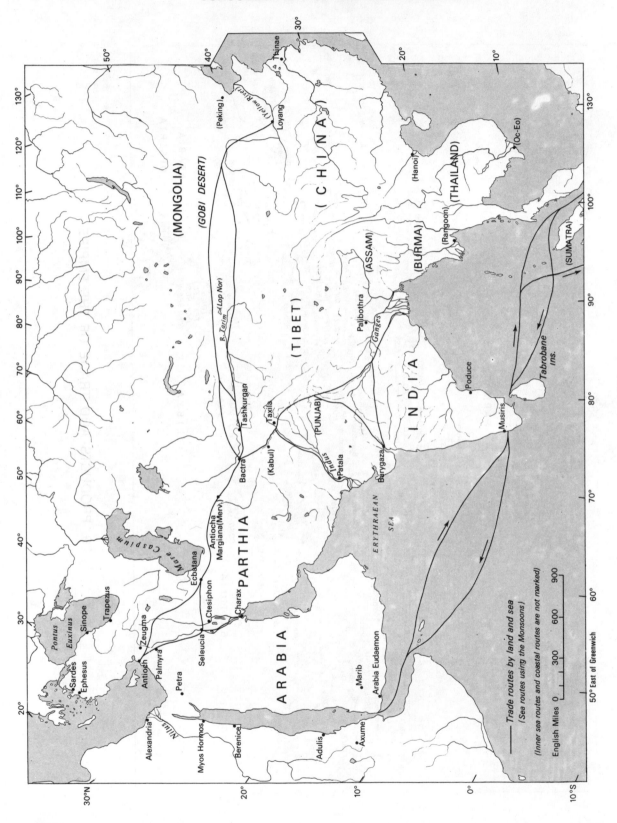

30. THE FAR EAST

rather than of regular trade.[10] Regular trade-routes connected the Roman provinces with Germany and Scandinavia. One line of traffic skirted the coast of Holland and Frisia and either turned into one of the German rivers or proceeded along the Jutish coast to Denmark. Another followed the track of the amber merchants (p. 380) from Carnuntum and the middle Danube to the Vistula, and ended by crossing the Baltic to the Swedish islands. Numerous finds of Roman coins (mostly of the second century) in Silesia and Posnania, and especially on the Swedish islands, indicate a considerable volume of commerce along the eastern road,[11] although there was little penetration of Sweden or Norway during this period. Another line went north from Carnuntum along the Oder to Pomerania and the Danish Baltic islands, especially Zealand, which were very active centres of trade.

The routes along the Russian rivers do not appear to have carried any regular current of traffic to the Baltic or to the Asian continent. On the other hand the main transcontinental road across the Parthian territory acquired a new importance at the end of the first century. The opening up of this line of traffic was mainly the work of the Han dynasty of China, whose orderly and enterprising administration formed a worthy pendant to the rule of the Caesars in the West. During the last thirty years of the first century the Chinese emperors annexed the Tarim plateau and organised two trade-routes to Bactra (modern Balkh) and Antiochia Margiana (Merv), where caravans from the Far East met the Greek or Syrian traders of Seleucia or the Mediterranean borderland. Direct commercial relations between the Roman Empire and China were hampered by the kings of Parthia, who succeeded for a time in preventing official contacts between the emperors of the East and of the West. But in 97 a Chinese envoy named Kan-Ying collected information (though perhaps not at first hand) concerning a country Ta-Tsin, in which we may probably recognise Syria. This or subsequent reports about this area especially noted the multitude of its cities, the milestones on its roads, the low price of gold, the honesty of its merchants, and the high profits with which their probity was rewarded.[12] It is possible that Trajan and Hadrian made stipulations in their treaties with the Parthian king for the freedom of transcontinental traffic. During the reign of Hadrian or Antoninus individual Greek merchants pushed their way to the halting-places on the rim of the Tarim plateau (at the Stone Tower, Tashkurgan or Darantkurgan); here agents of a 'Roman' merchant Maes Titianus met 'Chinese'.[13] To judge

Growth of the transcontinental traffic with China

Organisation of two routes by the Chinese emperors

The report of Kan-Ying on the Roman Empire

from the frescoes of Graeco-Syrian style which have been discovered in Buddhist monasteries beyond the Kuen-Lun range (north of Tibet), occasional craftsmen from the Mediterranean adventured themselves to the confines of China proper. Samples of the merchandise which passed between the Mediterranean and the Yellow seas have been recovered in the Tarim desert: bales of silk, and embroidered woollen cloths that came presumably from a Syrian loom.[14]

Greek and Roman remains in the Tarim desert

But notwithstanding the development of the overland traffic the Indian Ocean remained the chief artery of commerce with the East. By the end of the first century individual Greek venturers had penetrated from the west coast of India to the hospitable capitals of the principal rajahs in the Punjab, the Dekkan, and more particularly in the south of the peninsula. In the early or middle years of the second century Greek navigators had ventured beyond Cape Comorin, circumnavigated Ceylon (Taprobane) and explored several open-sea routes across the Bay of Bengal; one pioneer appropriately named Alexander cut across the isthmus of Malaya and skirted the Annamese coast as far as Cattigara (probably Hanoi). Finally, in 166 a deputation of Greek merchants, who styled themselves 'ambassadors' from the emperor 'An-Tun' (M. Aurelius Antoninus) but were probably private merchants, visited the court of the emperor Huan-ti at Loyang (on the Hwang-ho, Yellow River) and opened negotiations for a regular overseas trade between the Mediterranean lands and China.[15]

The eastern sea route. Extension to Malaya and Hanoi

The voyages of Greek sailors beyond Cape Comorin were not successful in establishing continuous commercial intercourse with the Far East; but the volume of Indian traffic (p. 381) attained such a scale, that in the days of Domitian special warehouses for the pepper of the Malabar coast were erected at Ostia. As the quantity of imports increased, their prices fell from the fanciful levels of the Neronian age; and payment for them, instead of being made in Roman coins, was rendered in merchandise. The spices and perfumes, the precious stones and muslins of India were exchanged for copper and tin, wine, glass and cheap woollens. Under these altered conditions the drain of precious metals from the Mediterranean, which had alarmed the elder Pliny (p. 381), came to a timely end.

Equilibrium in the eastern trade-balance

On the coast of eastern Africa Greek skippers of the late first or of the second century pushed on to Cape Delgado south of Zanzibar or struck inland towards the great lakes, bringing back true but unheeded information about the source of the Nile. Their discoveries had no appreciable

Abortive discoveries in eastern and central Africa

effect upon Mediterranean trade, except perhaps to increase the Roman supplies of ivory. Two journeys made by Roman officers, Septimius Flaccus (c. 75) and Iulius Maternus (of uncertain date), across the Sahara to the Sudan resulted in a growth of trade with the Fezzan.[16]

The expansion of foreign commerce had now attained its quickest pace, yet it could not keep up with the increase of internal trade in the Roman Empire. Of this traffic Rome still retained the lion's share. The mere magnitude of the capital city, and the presence of the court and of an ever-growing body of officials, ensured its continued supremacy among the Mediterranean markets. The preponderance of Rome among Italian cities at this period is illustrated by the diversion of traffic from the Campanian town of Puteoli to the Tiber mouth, when the great harbour works of Claudius and Trajan had made Ostia safe for large seagoing vessels.

Growth of the harbour of Ostia

In the second century the population of Ostia rose to not less than 100,000, and the remains of its spacious warehouses (usually laid out like an Oriental *fonduk*, in the form of a quadrangle, with magazines on the ground floor and showrooms above) suggest that, after Alexandria, it handled the largest volume of goods of any ancient Mediterranean harbour.[17] The attractive force of the Roman market may also be measured by the inflow of luxury wares from the Far East, and by the transport of leaden ingots from Spain and (since the second century) from Britain for the maintenance of the city's water pipes. But Rome could claim no such rapid expansion of trade as Gaul and the Rhineland, whose increased industrial activity led to a corresponding growth in the volume of their commerce. The Rhine now assumed for the first time its natural function as one of the great arteries of European traffic, and Cologne took its place beside Lyon as the chief connecting-link

Cologne and Lyon as commercial centres

between the Mediterranean lands and the regions of the Atlantic and Baltic Seas.

The growth of inter-provincial traffic was accompanied by a corresponding decline in the activity of Italian traders. The Greeks and Syrians added to their virtual monopoly of the Mediterranean carrying trade a considerable share of the commerce on outlying routes. The opening up of the Asiatic trade, so far as it did not rest with the Chinese, was the work of Greek explorers. On the European continent Syrian merchants frequented Gaul and Britain, and travellers from distant Palmyra took up their residence in Dacia. But the western traffic fell mostly to the share of the Gallic traders, who became familiar figures alike in Britain and in Italy. Even the provision of trading capital, which had formerly been the special function

Provincial intermediaries in empire trade

of the Italians, was now being left over to local bankers in the several provinces.

3. The Growth of Cities

The aggregate wealth of the Roman Empire not only was larger in the second century than at any previous period, but it was more widely distributed. The largest fortunes of which we have a record were no longer held in Rome – where the chances of making vast profits out of the public funds had now been reduced to vanishing-point – but in Asia Minor, and, strangely enough, from Greece. In the days of Trajan a Lycian grandee named Opramoas

Distribution of wealth

scattered his riches on a grandiose scale, and helped to finance the emperor's eastern campaigns in princely fashion; under Antoninus an Athenian man of letters named Herodes Atticus made himself memorable by his colossal donations to Greek cities.[18] But it is even more true of the second century than of the first that it was an age of many affluent bourgeois rather than of a few millionaires.

The second century also marks the culmination of the tendency to city-life which was characteristic of Greek and Roman civilisation. A peculiar feature of this and the previous century was the rise of civilian settlements round the permanent camps in the frontier zones.

Spontaneous growth of cities. Canabae

These *canabae* might be compared to the 'bazaars' formerly attached to military stations like Peshawar and Quetta, in that they consisted largely of native traders; but they also attracted pensioned soldiers who married and founded a home near their former place of service, and once formed, they often retained their urban character after the troops in the adjacent camp had been transferred to other quarters. In the Danube basin, where this process of town-formation was particularly common, the Roman soldier helped to create a chain of towns which were eventually constituted as *coloniae* or *municipia* by the Flavian emperors, by Trajan or Hadrian. Among these products of the camp we may enumerate Bonna (modern Bonn), Moguntiacum (Mainz), Aquae Mattiacae (Wiesbaden) and Argentorate (Strasbourg) on the Rhine, and Vindobona (Vienna), Aquincum (Budapest) and Singidunum (Belgrade) on the Danube.[19] But the chief city-forming agency was the expansion of industry and trade, and the concurrent intensification of agriculture, which

Industrial and commercial centres

enabled the rural population to cluster more closely together into small market-towns. The urbanisation of the Roman lands did not proceed at a uniform rate. In Asia Minor and the Balkan countries the population remained

39.7   Site of Calleva Atrebatum (Silchester).

sparse, except on the seaboard and in the river basins. In central Gaul and Britain the towns were fewer and smaller than might have been expected in view of the general prosperity of these regions.[20] On the other hand the valleys of the Rhine and Danube became threaded with new cities, and Dacia experienced a mushroom growth of towns. In Africa urban centres crystallised out wherever the steppe was converted into crop-land or plantation. Similarly Palestine and the wheat-belt of Transjordania grew a crop of towns,[21] and *metropoleis* or country towns began to coalesce out of the numerous hamlets of Egypt, where the larger cultivators at last abandoned their secular habit of living in the midst of their holdings and constituted themselves into bourgeoisies of the usual Graeco-Roman pattern.[22] Numidia, which could count only twelve municipalities in the first century, possessed thirty-seven at the beginning of the third;[23] in the Tunisian plains and in the Orontes valley of Syria the remains of the Roman cities form almost continuous chains. Not until the nineteenth or the present century did town life again acquire a like importance in the lands of the Roman Empire.

4. Architecture[24]

The urban character of Roman civilisation was emphasised, not only by the number of the

cities which it created, but by the brave show which these cities made. In the later first and the earlier second centuries the emperors set an example of lavish expenditure on building. At Rome although Vespasian continued to live in part of the *Domus Aurea* of Nero, which had become a public scandal, much of it was destroyed: its lake was filled in to provide a site for the Colosseum and its baths were overlaid by those of Titus (and later by Trajan's Baths). The siting of the Colosseum was a skilful move, both architecturally and politically: the basin of the old lake formed a natural arena while the diversion of part of the hated Golden House to public use and entertainment increased Vespasian's popularity. Domitian, not satisfied with Tiberius's palace on the Palatine which was associated with some of the more lurid episodes of Julio-Claudian history, built a vast new palace just to the south-east, the *Domus Augustiana*. This, the best-preserved of the imperial palaces at Rome, comprised two parts: one block, consisting of porticoed chambers in two storeys facing an inner quadrangle, formed the private residence of the imperial family; the other was the official part (sometimes called the *Domus Flavia*), consisting of a Basilica and State Rooms where the emperor gave audiences and convened his *consilium*. In fact the palace remained the official residence of the Roman emperors in Rome for centuries to come. The most extensive, and after Nero's Golden House the most

459

39.8 Wall-painting of building operations, from the tomb of Trebius Justus at Rome.

39.9 Reconstruction of Colosseum and adjacent area.

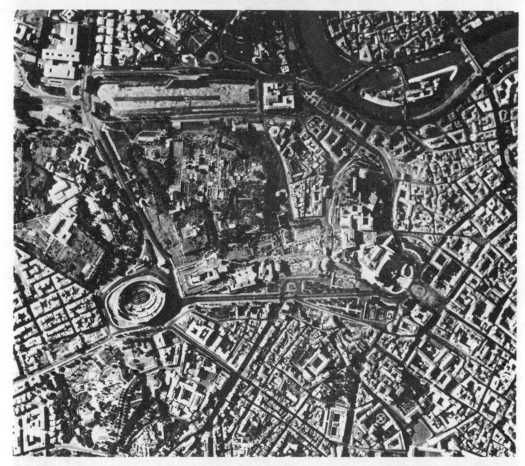

39.10 Aerial view of central Rome. At the top is the Circus Maximus, below which is the Palatine and Forum; to the right of this is the Capitol, while the Tiber Island can be seen in the top right-hand corner.

Hadrian's villa at Tibur

sumptuous, of the imperial residences was Hadrian's villa at Tibur (Tivoli), a complex of buildings scattered over 160 acres of ground: his 'villa' was, in fact, a miniature town, complete with theatre, stadium and two sets of baths. In Rome Hadrian made himself a mausoleum, a drum-shaped edifice of such massive construction that in the Middle Ages it rendered long service as a fortress and still carries the name of 'Castello Sant' Angelo'.

The Fora of Vespasian,

The most useful gift of the Flavian emperors and their successors to the general public of Rome consisted in three new Fora. To commemorate the end of the Jewish War Vespasian built the Forum that carries his name, with a Temple of Peace in the centre to house the spoils. Domitian and Nerva connected this new square with the Forum Augusti by means of a narrower piazza, the Forum Nervae or Transitorium. On the north side of Augustus's Forum Trajan cut away the shoulder of the Quirinal Hill to gain

space for the roomiest of all the public squares at Rome, the Forum Traiani. The capacious place which measured some 350 by 200 yards, contained in its centre a large covered hall, the *Basilica Ulpia*, and the 'column of Trajan' (p. 441); it was flanked at one end by the temple of Divus Traianus, while to the north on the lower slopes of the Quirinal, Trajan designed a commercial quarter, where was built Trajan's Market, a large covered hall and over 150 shops. With the completion of these Fora a commodious passage was provided between the original Forum Romanum and Campus Martius.

and of Trajan

The temple of Peace in Vespasian's Forum was reckoned among the chief show pieces of Rome. This building has now virtually disappeared; while only the Hadrianic *podium* survives of the great temple which Hadrian himself planned to *Venus et Roma* at the top of the Velia slope, a curious apsidal building with two back-to-back cells or cult-chambers (the other

Vespasian's temple of Peace

461

39.11 The Mausoleum of Hadrian, across the Tiber. It later became a fortress, the Castel S. Angelo. Originally the drum was covered by a mound of earth, planted with cypresses and crowned, probably, with a statue of Hadrian (cf. the large Etruscan *tumuli* and the Mausoleum of Augustus).

39.12 The end of Trajan's Forum, with the Basilica Ulpia and the Column.

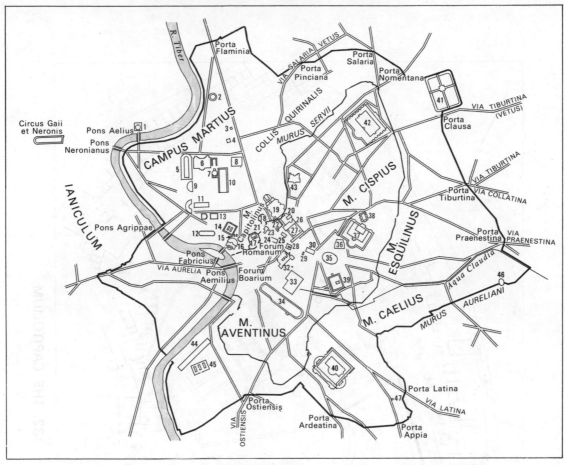

31. ROME

1. Mausoleum of Hadrian	*17. Temple of Capitoline Jupiter*	*33. Domus Augustiana*
2. Mausoleum of Augustus	*18. Temple of Juno Moneta*	*34. Circus Maximus*
3. Altar of Peace	*19. Forum of Trajan*	*35. Amphitheatrum Flavium ('Colosseum')*
4. Column of M. Aurelius	*20. Forum of Augustus*	*36. Baths of Titus*
5. Stadium of Domitian	*21. The Tabularium*	*37. Baths of Trajan*
6. Baths of Nero	*22. Forum of Caesar*	*38. Portico of Livia*
7. The Pantheon	*23. Curia (Senate-house)*	*39. Temple and Portico of Divus Claudius*
8. Temple of Divus Hadrianus	*24. Basilica Iulia*	*40. Baths of Caracalla (Thermae Antoninianae)*
9. Odeum of Domitian	*25. Basilica Aemilia*	*41. Castra Praetoria*
10. Saepta Iulia	*26. Forum of Nerva*	*42. Baths of Diocletian*
11. Theatre and Portico of Pompey	*27. Forum of Vespasian*	*43. Baths of Constantine*
12. Circus Flaminius	*28. Atrium Vestae*	*44. Porticus Aemilia*
13. Theatre of Balbus	*29. Arch of Titus*	*45. Horrea (Warehouses) Galbana*
14. Portico of Octavia	*30. Temple of Venus and Rome*	*46. Amphitheatrum Castrense*
15. Temple of Apollo	*31. Domus Tiberiana*	*47. Tomb of the Scipios*
16. Theatre of Marcellus	*32. Temple of Magna Mater*	

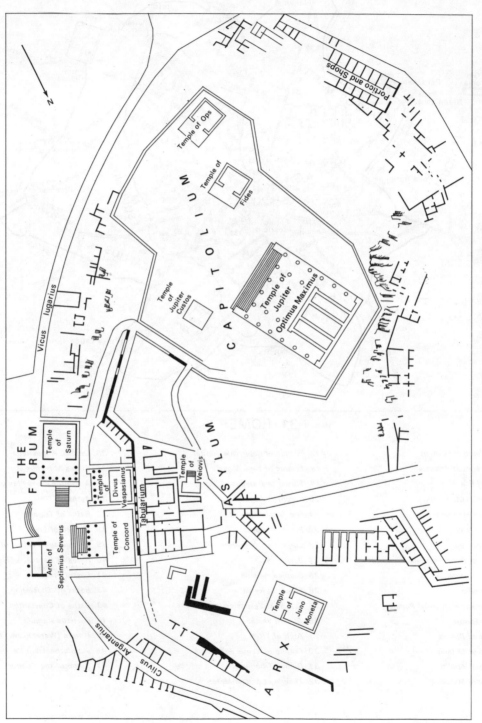

32. THE CAPITOLIUM

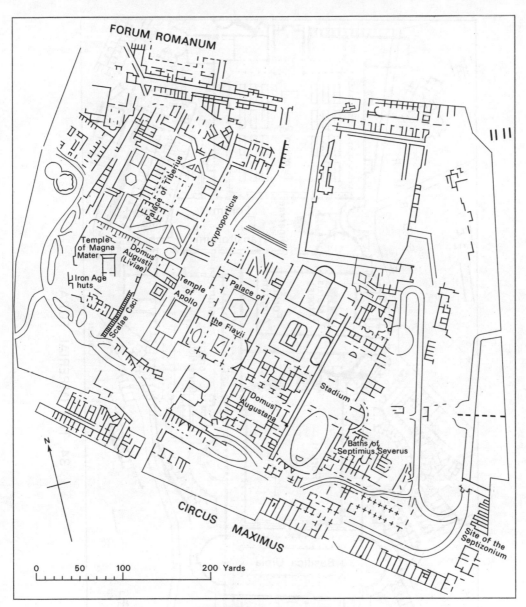

FORUM ROMANUM

Palace of Tiberius

Cryptoporticus

Temple
of Magna
Mater

Domus
Augusti
(Liviae)

Iron Age
huts

Temple
of
Apollo

Scalae Caci

Palace of

the Flavii

Domus
Augustana

Stadium

Baths of
Septimius Severus

N

CIRCUS   MAXIMUS

Site of the
Septizonium

0   50   100   200 Yards

33. THE PALATINE

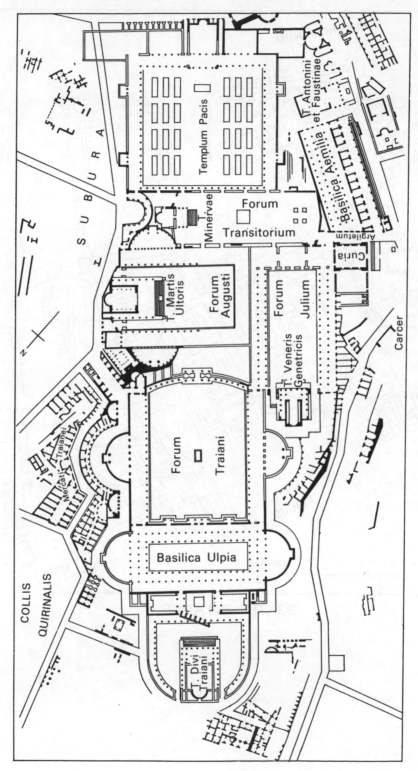

34. THE IMPERIAL FORA

39.13 Trajan's Market (Mercatus). This market complex contained 150 shops (*tabernae*) and a two-storeyed hall. Streets at the back provided access to the building at three different levels.

The Pantheon of Hadrian

remaining parts belong to a rebuilding in 307 after an earlier fire). Luckily Hadrian's other great temple in Rome has had a happier fate — the Pantheon, a sanctuary of the deities of the seven planets. The Pantheon of Hadrian replaced Agrippa's earlier and presumably rectangular temple which had already been restored by Domitian after a fire in 80. The new temple, which was provided with a huge columnar porch as a façade, was designed in the form of a spacious rotunda spanned by a concrete cupola 140 feet in diameter, with a 30-foot opening in the centre to let in the light. This dome, which was made to carry its own weight without any supporting columns, was the greatest achievement in ancient concrete construction; in 1800 years it has required only a few minor repairs, and the building which it covers served later as the burying-place for the kings of Italy. After the weighty grandeur of the porch the interior is full of light and colour and the dome seems to rest lightly above, belying its concrete mass. Another of the most impressive and best-preserved monuments of antiquity is the Arch of Titus which Domitian erected on the summit of the Velia in honour of his brother Titus and as a memorial of the Jewish War, while the stadium which he built in the Campus Martius is still partly preserved in the houses which ring the Piazza Navona. (The obelisk, which stands on Bernini's fountain

467

39.14   The Pantheon. A temple in the Campus Martius, built by Agrippa. After destruction it was rebuilt by Hadrian, whose surviving domed building is one of the architectural marvels of the ancient world. The ancient bronze doors still survive.

in the Piazza, unlike most of the obelisks which adorned ancient Rome, was not brought from Egypt but was Roman work, coming originally from the temple of Isis which Domitian rebuilt after a fire in 80.) Thus Roman architecture had triumphantly entered a new phase: Nero's Golden House (p. 387), Domitian's palace, Hadrian's villa and the Pantheon, and no less the more humble warehouses and apartment-blocks at Ostia, all owed their existence to the skill with which architects handled the use of cement. While the brick-faced exteriors of the buildings tended to maintain a functional severity, the space within was exploited with great ingenuity: light and space were no longer subordinate to the masonry but deliberately used to create illusion and to emphasise the vast soaring vaults.

The 'Colosseum'   Commenced by Vespasian, dedicated by Titus and completed by Domitian, the *Amphitheatrum Flavium* was more traditional in design if not in size and grandeur. It was well worthy of its modern name, the 'Colosseum'; it could

accommodate at least 50,000 spectators, and after serving as a quarry to successive generations of Renaissance architects it still impresses by its sheer bulk. But its mere size was less remarkable than its excellent system of concourses and stairways, and the substructure of groined vaults on which the seats were supported. Still it stands as a symbol of Roman grandeur: as Byron wrote,

'While stands the Colosseum, Rome shall stand;
When falls the Colosseum, Rome shall fall;
And when Rome falls — the World.'

Under Nerva and Trajan the last of the Roman aqueducts, the *Aqua Traiana*, was constructed; according to modern calculations the daily supply of water to Rome henceforth amounted approximately to 100 gallons a head. With the completion of two new *thermae* by Titus and Trajan the bathing facilities of the capital were enlarged to the same ultra-modern stan-   *The baths of Titus and of Trajan*

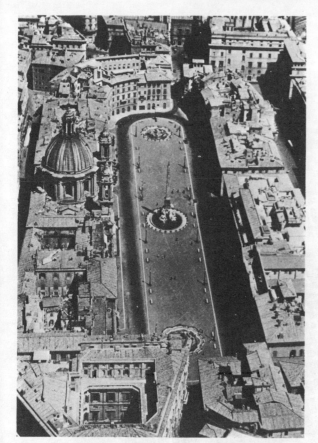

39.15 The Stadium of Domitian in the Campus Martius. The site is now occupied by the Piazza Navona, whose buildings preserve much of the original shape of the stadium.

dard. In spite of extensive rebuilding the city still contained many narrow streets and sordid quarters. Its noise and dirt and overcrowding stirred the wrath of Martial and Juvenal; we may therefore accuse Vespasian and his successors of building for ostentation rather than for the greatest welfare of the greatest number. But as a showplace Rome could now challenge comparison with the handsomest cities of the Hellenistic East.

Rome a show-town

While Rome was being reconstructed by the emperors the towns of Italy and of the provinces made successful appeals to their wealthiest residents to supply funds for new construction, or mortgaged their revenues for the satisfaction of becoming in real fact *municipia splendidissima* (p. 429). In the first and second centuries the new cities and new quarters of towns in the Roman Empire were generally made to conform to a prearranged plan. A well-preserved example of a check-board disposition of the streets may be seen in the ruins of Thamugadi (Timgad), a colony of Trajan near Mt Aures in the African

Municipal architecture

Town-planning – Timgad

province. A notable feature of town architecture at this period consisted in the long colonnaded streets which radiated outwards from the central square; at Gerasa in Transjordania the ruins of one such avenue measures half a mile; another at Palmyra extends over 1250 yards.

In the provinces the most striking examples of temple architecture were the pilgrim sanctuary of Jupiter (a Romanised form of Hadad) at Heliopolis (modern Baalbek) which was rebuilt on a colossal scale, possibly in the Augustan period, to which was added the temple of Bacchus in the reign of Antoninus, and the great temple of Zeus at Athens, which was completed at an interval of 650 years from its inception, with the help of a subsidy from Hadrian. The ruins of a large covered hall at Uriconium (Wroxeter), built under Hadrian at the expense of the surrounding canton, the *civitas Cornoviorum*, illustrate the ambitious style in which even small country towns provided for their public services.[26] But the municipalities followed the lead of Rome in bestowing special attention upon their water-supply and their places of amusement. In Britain small amphitheatres were built for instance at Isca Silurum (Caerleon: *c.* A.D. 80) and Deva where the camp arena held 7500 spectators, and also in many civilian settlements (for instance a late one at Venta Silurum, Caerwent). Theatres have been found at Verulamium, Canterbury and near Colchester. In other provinces the civilian populations built themselves stages or arenas, some with seats for 20,000 or more spectators. Among the plentiful remains of this kind of monument we may mention the amphitheatres of Arles and Nîmes and the theatre of Orange in southern France; the playhouse of Thugga in northern Africa, of Ephesus and Aspendus, of Perga and Side in Asia Minor. Even Petra and Bostra on the borders of the Arabian desert erected theatres of Roman type, and Biskra at the edge of the Sahara had its amphitheatre. The aqueducts of many cities were on a proportionately grand scale. At Cologne the water was brought from a distance of nearly 50 miles. Here and there pipe-lines were laid on the siphon principle, so as to follow the rises and falls of the ground; more often they bestrode the valleys on lofty arcades. Of the surviving monuments of Roman architecture in the European provinces, none are more impressive than the double tier of arches of the 'Puente' at Segovia in Old Castile — presumably of Flavian date — and the Pont-du-Gard near Nîmes (of uncertain date, but possibly of the reign of Augustus), whose triple arcade rises to a height of 160 feet. Lastly, two high-span bridges of Trajan's reign illus-

The town hall at Wroxeter

Provincial theatres and amphitheatres

Aqueducts

39.16   Air-view of Thamugadi (Timgad). Established by Trajan as a veteran colony, the town was laid out like a camp, with intersecting main streets and grid system. The population c. A.D. 200 is estimated at 12,000–15,000 persons.

39.17   General view of Timgad.

39.18   Part of the oval piazza at Gerasa.

39.19   Baalbek. Temple of Jupiter Heliopolitanus seen from the temple of Bacchus.

39.20   Rock-cut mausoleum at the caravan city of Petra.

39.21   The amphitheatre at El Djem in Tunisia.

39.22 The aqueduct at Segovia in Spain. It is nearly 900 yards long with 128 arches and nearly 100 feet high. It still carries the city's water supply. It is uncertain whether it dates to the early first or second century A.D.

39.23 Bridge at Alcantara over the Tagus; built by Trajan in A.D. 106.

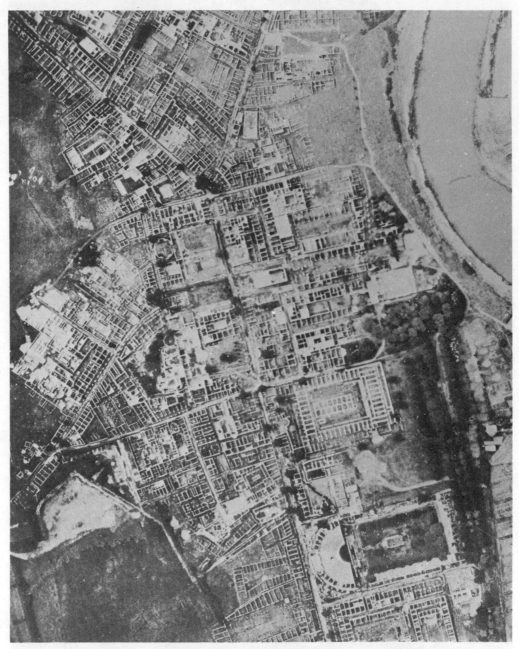

39.24   Aerial view of Ostia.

39.25 Reconstruction of houses at Ostia.

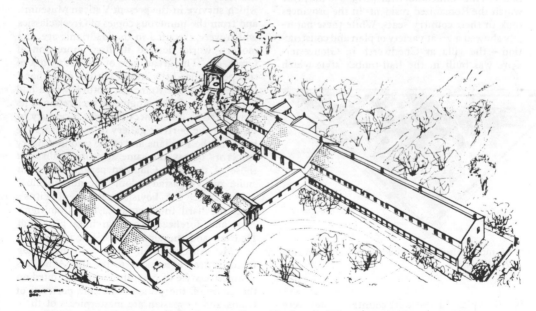

39.26 Reconstruction of the Roman villa at Chedworth (Gloucestershire), c. A.D. 300.

High-span bridges

trate the Roman architects' skill in combining practical utility with good design. One of these was built by Trajan himself near the Iron Gates of the Danube; the other, which overleaps the Tagus near Alcantara at a height of 150 feet, was erected at the cost of twelve neighbouring municipalities.[27]

The private architecture of the period cannot be adequately judged by the remains of the town houses. The relatively poor specimens at Timgad and other African cities were of the *insula* type, on the same general plan as those of Ostia.

Tenement houses at Ostia

In Ostia, which enjoyed a remarkable outburst of building activity in the first half of the second century, four-storey blocks of flats in red or yellow brick (usually but not invariably stuccoed), with large windows and occasional balconies, presented a remarkably close resemblance to the typical middle-class residences in modern continental cities. In Rome the height of tenements soared well above the legal limit of 60 feet prescribed by Augustus (p. 323), and possibly over-topped the new maximum of 70 feet which Trajan laid down. In northern Gaul and Britain the 'peristyle' house was replaced by a longitudinal dwelling with a portico to catch the sun.

Roman villas

On the other hand numerous remains of Roman villas in France and Switzerland, in Britain and the Rhineland, bear witness to the pride which the Romanised residents in the provinces took in their country seats. While these naturally showed a great variety of plan and construction – the villa at Chedworth in Gloucestershire was built in the half-timber style which

39.27 Part of mosaic from the Chedworth villa, showing the figure of 'Winter'.

is still typical of the west country – they were alike in borrowing from Italy many appliances, such as mosaic flooring, glass windows, and heating by hypocausts. The Italian summer residences of the younger Pliny, which this author has described for us with loving detail, were luxurious in their size and the number of their rooms, if not in their appointments.[28]

39.28 Part of the baths in the west wing at Chedworth villa; the mosaic floor of the warm room (*tepidarium*) with hypocaust pillars of the hot room (*caldarium*) and semi-circular hot bath.

5. Art

The brave show which the Roman world of the first and second centuries made with its architecture was matched by the profusion of its sculpture. The dilettantism of Nero was almost equalled by that of Hadrian, who converted his villa at Tibur into a veritable museum of old masters; from his collection (many pieces of which survive in the present Vatican Museum), and from the numerous copies of Greek classics which were executed in the Hadrianic age, the modern world derived its first impression of Greek art. The great mass of copyist's work of this period has little merit. On the other hand the new school of Roman sculpture, which had been formed in the Augustan age, retained its characteristic excellences for over a century to come. In the portrait gallery of the Caesars the heads of the Flavians and of the second-century emperors betray the same arresting realism as those of the Julio-Claudian period. The grim smile on Vespasian's dour but not ungenial countenance, the boyish openness of Titus's face, the hard intellectual cast of Domitian's eyes and forehead, the searching glance of Hadrian and the almost mask-like impassivity of M. Aurelius – all these distinguishing features are reproduced to the life. A no less distinctive style of portraiture was exhibited on the coins of the period. The coin-portraits of Galba and Vespasian are masterpieces of their kind.

Dilettantism of Hadrian

Roman sculpture

Portraiture

But the greatest artistic achievement of the period is to be found in its historical reliefs. The Augustan series of historical sculptures was continued on the Arch of Titus, whose inner panels were decorated with scenes from his triumph over the Jews. Though the perspective

Historical reliefs. The Arch of Titus

of these pieces is faulty, they are remarkably successful in conveying an impression of depth, and they introduce into Roman art an unwonted atmosphere of stir and bustle. On the other hand a more traditional classicising treatment, more static and idealised, appears in the two Domitianic reliefs found in 1938 near the Papal Chancellery in Rome, one depicting the arrival (*adventus*) of Vespasian in Rome in 70, the other the setting out (*profectio*) of Domitian for one of his northern campaigns.[30] However, an animation similar to that on Titus's Arch breathes through the epic in stone on Trajan's Column, which unfolds scene for scene the story of the Dacian Wars. In this monster composition the incidents of four campaigns are unrolled in a continuous spiral band of 2500 figures. In

The Column of Trajan

daring violation of the laws of perspective the more distant figures are set clear above the nearer ones, but to a spectator viewing the column from below this method of presentation would not be lacking in realism. In the somewhat bewildering mass of detail which the column presents the recurrent figure of Trajan gives unity to the whole group, and the various scenes are skilfully spaced, so as to lead up to the dramatic climax – the death of Decebalus under the walls of his capital.[31] In Hadrian's reign reliefs became once more classicised, but under the Antonines a richer pictorial style experimented again in perspective, light and shade.

Trajan's Column was followed by a similar record of the Marcomannic Wars which survives on the commemorative column of M. Aurelius in the Campus Martius. The designers of this gigantic frieze were less successful in coping with its mass of detail, which produces an effect of monotonous iteration like that of an Assyrian relief; but the execution of the single figures was as conscientious and accurate as ever.[32]

While sculpture at Rome continued to develop on its own lines, the art of the provinces tended to become largely imitative, although in Gaul, Roman Germany, Britain and northern Africa the native genius infused traditional forms and sometimes produced works of a fresh, if naïve quality. A healthy realism born of independent observation is evident in the war-scenes

Provincial art. Mosaics. Castor pottery; the 'lion of Corbridge'

carved on the tombstones of Roman soldiers in Britain and on other frontier zones; in the homely episodes from daily life on the funerary monuments of Gaul and in the scenes of rustic work and play on Gallic and African mosaics.[33] We may recognise a surviving Celtic tradition in the animation and élan of the animal friezes on the Castor pottery and the Gressenich brasses, and of the sculptured 'lion of Corbridge'. But outside of Rome the art of the

39.29 'Castor' ware, the best-known pottery of Roman Britain, named after a village near Peterborough. A hunting scene.

Roman Empire, while maintaining a tolerable standard of technical proficiency, found it difficult to emancipate itself from its classical conventions. This lack of development of art in the Roman Empire is not to be explained by any levelling action on the part of the Roman

General uniformity of art

39.30 Stone lion from Corbridge, Northumberland. Originally probably a tomb monument, it was later a fountain decoration. Made of local grit, this Romano-British work shows rugged vitality.

government, which never imposed uniformity in matters of private life upon its subjects. Classical Graeco-Roman art carried the whole field, because the peoples of the eastern Mediterranean had for the time being lost their artistic inventiveness, while the nations of Africa and of the European continent with the exception of the Celts, were largely lacking in an independent artistic tradition.

6. Social LIfe

Public amusements at Rome

At Rome the conditions of life remained unaltered for the proletariat, except that its programme of amusements became ever more prolonged; in the days of M. Aurelius the number of festival days had been extended to 130, or nearly double the total of the later age of the Republic. At the inauguration of the Colosseum Titus pandered to the coarser appetites of the

excess of them. The scrawl of a street-artist of Timgad which declared that ' 'unting [i.e. watching beast-hunts], bathing and gaming, these is life', summed up the philosophy of many a townsman of the Roman Empire.[35]

High society sobers down

On the other hand the accession of Vespasian opened a new epoch in the life of high society in the capital. The merry monarchy of Nero gave way to a century of simple or even austere living. The transition from Charles II to Dutch William at the imperial court was accompanied by a similar change of habits among the leading families at Rome, as the remaining houses of the old republican nobility died out and their place was taken by a new senatorial aristocracy, whose members held fast to the bourgeois simplicity of their Italian or provincial home. While modes of dress altered but slowly from century to century, the emperor Hadrian became a fashion-reformer *malgré lui*. To conceal a gash sustained in the hunting field (on which sport he

39.31   The Circus Maximus at Rome.

crowd by regaling them with a 100 days' run of gladiatorial games and beast-hunts.[34] A new festival in honour of the Capitoline Jupiter, but with musical, gymnastic and literary competitions of a Greek rather than a native type, was founded by Domitian, who built an *Odeum* or covered hall for the musical events. After the construction of the two new *thermae* by Titus and Trajan, the public baths absorbed so much of the townspeople's time that Hadrian found it necessary, in the interests of business, to restrict the hours of opening. The municipalities of Italy and the provinces followed the lead of the capital in providing amusements for their proletariats according to their means, or in

All-day bathing

spent many strenuous days), this emperor grew a beard, and Roman society, making a virtue of the monarch's necessity, abandoned its long tradition of clean shaving. The least pleasing feature of social life at Rome was the degeneration of the old and honourable institution of clientship, which had now outlived every practical purpose, into a mere display of wealth.[36] A more attractive trait of second-century life among the wealthier classes, in which the influence of Greek culture was evident, was the habit of travel for the purpose of sightseeing. Here again a new fashion was set by Hadrian, who took the opportunity on his tours of inspection in the Empire to visit the show-sites of Greece

Beards become fashionable

Tourist travel

and Egypt and to view a sunrise from the summit of Etna. While provincials flocked into Rome to gaze at its wonders, Italians peregrinated, guide-book in hand, to the historic sites of Greece, to Troy, or to Egypt.[37]

Social clubs

For the small masters, the retail traders and the skilled labourers (among whom a considerable servile element was included) social life was centred in the *collegia* or gilds, which reached the height of their activity in the period under review. In estimating the numbers of these we must take into account, not only the duly licensed associations, but various *collegia illicita* at which the authorities discreetly connived, so long as their activities did not take a dangerous political turn. The spread of the habit of private association is illustrated by a record from the camp at Lambaesis, relating to an officers' club whose main object was to provide travelling funds for members transferred to another command. Such mutual-aid services, it is true, were not a common function of the Roman *collegia*, though slaves and persons of slender means might join a *collegium funeraticium* and pay a low yearly premium towards their costs of burial.[38] But the dinner parties on the festival days of the club's patron deities or on the birthdays of leading members and generous donors, and the outings on public holidays, when the gild-members formed procession in their Sunday best, provided welcome diversion for the more hard-working elements in the urban populations.

7. The Spread of Latin and Greek

Literary patronage

In no century of Roman history did literature and education enjoy more ample state patronage than under the emperors from Vespasian to M. Aurelius. Vespasian, despite his obscure origin and military upbringing, knew his letters and could quote Homer fluently. Notwithstanding the financial stringency of his reign, he found means to endow chairs of Latin and Greek rhetoric at Rome. Domitian made good the ravages of a great fire in A.D. 79 among the libraries at Rome, and he gave personal encouragement to the chief Latin writers of his day. Trajan instituted the largest of Roman libraries in the *Basilica Ulpia*, and he and Hadrian rewarded the Greek man of letters Plutarch with an official post in Achaea (a procuratorship?). Of all Roman emperors Hadrian took the most catholic interest in Graeco-Roman culture. Besides being a connoisseur of art he conversed on equal terms with scholars and literary men.

Endowment of education

At Rome he founded an academy known as the *Athenaeum*, where distinguished rhetoricians and philosophers gave public recitals. Antoninus extended Trajan's lead in bestowing consulships on two distinguished men of letters, the essayist Fronto and the rhetorician Herodes Atticus. In the interests of the local treasuries he restricted the number of immunities that might be granted to teachers, but he gave subventions from the *fiscus* to the higher municipal schools. M. Aurelius endowed chairs at each of the philosophical schools at Athens.[39]

Schools and libraries

At Rome men of letters complained that private patronage was no longer being given with the ungrudging liberality of a Maecenas. In the provinces the municipalities showed greater readiness to found high schools of rhetoric — in Gaul alone eleven such university seats could be counted[40] — than to support the less showy but more solid work of the ordinary school-teacher. But discerning acts of generosity on the part of private donors were not lacking. The younger Pliny not only befriended several leading authors of his day, but endowed a secondary school and founded a library at his native town of Comum. At Timgad a public-spirited citizen provided the funds for a library of 23,000 volumes.[41] At no other period of ancient history were opportunities of acquiring some measure of school education more widespread, and the ratio of illiterates in the population was never lower. The diffusion of the art of writing in the Roman Empire is illustrated not only by the masses of surviving inscriptions carved by trained lapicides on stone or bronze — the province of Africa alone has provided more than 20,000 such texts — but by the scrawls with which idle and uncultured hands defaced the walls and pavements of cities.[42]

The book trade

By the second century Latin and Greek had virtually ousted all other written languages in the Roman Empire, and each of these tongues maintained itself in its own area with a remarkable uniformity of usage.[43] Though misspellings and solecisms were of course abundant, there was as yet little trace of local variation, or of anything resembling the 'pidgin English' of the Asiatic and African continents. The publishers' business was now so well established, and books were obtainable at such moderate prices, that even poor men could keep a few favourite texts, and private libraries were to be found even in provincial country villas. The fact that a work of the younger Pliny had a ready sale in the bookshops of Lugdunum illustrates the wide range of the reading public which a Latin author could now reach.[44]

A Greek literary renaissance

The output of literature in the period under review was enlarged by a revival of Greek letters. This Greek renaissance partly arose from the special interest which Hadrian displayed in

Greek culture – a predilection that earned him the nickname of 'Graeculus'; but its main cause no doubt lay in the renewal of security and prosperity in the eastern Mediterranean. The most typical branch of Greek literature in this age was the short essay on questions of general social interest. To this class belong the topical speeches of Dio Chrysostom (*c.* A.D. 75) and of Aelius Aristides (*c.* 117–185); the so-called *Moralia* of Plutarch (*c.* 45–120) – a collection of ethical and antiquarian miscellanies – and the satires of Lucian (*c.* 160), whose persiflage of parvenus' manners, of travellers' tales and of superstitious beliefs still remains living literature.[45]

The satires of Lucian

One aspect of this Greek revival in the second century was called the Second Sophistic movement (as opposed to the sophists who flourished in the days of Gorgias and Socrates). These sophists, whose Lives were written by Philostratus in the early third century, were not philosophers, but rather more often their rivals. They were professional rhetors whose activities were idealised in a passage of one of them (Aelius Aristides), as speaking or writing speeches, adorning festival assemblies, honouring the gods, advising cities, comforting the distressed, settling civil strife, and educating the young. They were wealthy Greeks from the cities of the East (especially Athens, Smyrna and Ephesus). They often travelled abroad, sometimes as ambassadors for their cities or provinces, but they were expected to help their own cities by holding office and by generous financial benefactions. Their local eminence naturally brought them and their families into the Roman

The Second Sophistic

upper class and they developed links with leading Romans and sometimes even with the imperial court and the emperors themselves. Though very conscious of the tradition of their Greek past, they merged easily with the new cosmopolitan world which the philhellenic Hadrian encouraged. They received favour from the Roman government and were promoted in the Equestrian and Senatorial Orders, and a few even reached the consulship. Thus these rhetors, men like Aristides and Herodes Atticus, played an important role in the economic, social and administrative life of the Empire, as well as in the world of literature. And with them may be linked men of similar interests, for instance men of letters, as Dio Prusias, Plutarch and Lucian, or even physicians as Galen, a man of immense and wide prestige.[46]

The revival of Greek national consciousness brought with it a renewed interest in the outstanding episodes of Greek history. The conquests of Alexander were recounted in an authoritative work by Flavius Arrianus, an Asiatic Greek, who entered the imperial service and became governor of his native province of Cappadocia (p. 648). The lives of the chief personages in Greek political history were narrated in a series of light yet distinctive sketches by Plutarch. At the same time a wider interest in the affairs of the Roman Empire, which Polybius had formerly endeavoured without great success to awaken among his countrymen (p. 113), was at last called forth. Plutarch matched each of his Greek biographies with a parallel life from Roman history. The civil wars that

The Lives of Plutarch

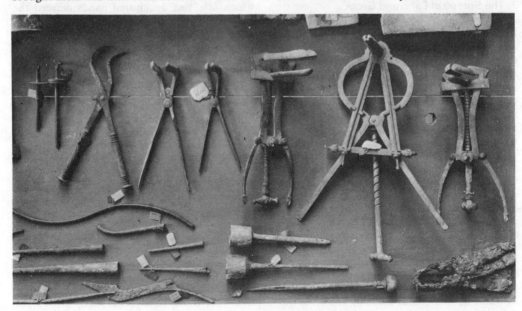

39.32   Surgical instruments from Pompeii.

led to the fall of the Republic were described in a well-planned though carelessly executed work by Appian, an Alexandrian Greek, who followed Arrian's lead in entering the Roman imperial service (*c.* 160). The detailed history of the First Jewish War by Flavius Josephus, though written by a Jewish eye-witness in Aramaic, may be included in this review, for its principal surviving text is a Greek translation, composed for the benefit of Gentile readers at the suggestion of the future emperor Titus.[47]

Josephus's history of the First Jewish War

The Greek genius for natural science manifested itself in three great resumptive works which held unchallenged sway for 1400 years, the medical encyclopaedia of the Pergamene practitioner, Claudius Galenus (*c.* 130–200), and the treatises on mathematical geography and on astronomy by the Alexandrian scholar Claudius Ptolemaeus (*c.* 150).[48]

Standard works of science: Galen and Ptolemy

8. Latin Poetry[49]

The epic poets of the Flavian age

Under the Flavian emperors Latin epic poetry experienced yet another revival, and indeed it attained its climax, as measured by quantity of output. But this resuscitation was nothing more than a literary *tour de force*. Unlike the Augustan age the Flavian period was not lifted on the crest of a wave of sentiment; it fed placidly on its own experience, and its imagination was not kindled by the consciousness of a great inheritance. The chief writers of the epic school succeeded in reproducing Virgil's smoothness of metre, but there the resemblance ended. The ablest of them, P. Papinius Statius (*c.* 45–96), went back in his *Thebais* to a subject of Greek mythology which meant little or nothing to the Romans. His personages make fine speeches, but remain mere ghosts; and the lack of dramatic unity further disperses the reader's attention. The oft-told story of the Argonauts was reiterated by C. Valerius Flaccus of the Flavian period in a poem which lacked neither unity nor skill in character-sketching; but the essential ingredient of epic tension was even more lacking in the Roman author than in his Greek prototype, Apollonius Rhodius. A third writer of hexameters, Silius Italicus (26–101), showed better discrimination in choosing for his subject the Second Punic War, but all that he could make of it was a mechanical assemblage from the stockbook of epic episodes.

The epigrams of Martial

A branch of poetry in which the Romans had not yet seriously measured themselves against the Greeks, the epigram, was attempted with unquestionable success by M. Valerius Martialis (*c.* 40–104). Though Martial could not rival his Greek masters' extreme economy of language,

he shared their gift of keen observation, and albeit a native of Spain (from Bilbilis in the Salo valley), he caught the genuine Italian note of mordant and at times riotously coarse satire, and illuminates many aspects of life in Rome where he lived from A.D. 66 to *c.* 98. But as a castigator of his own times he was thrown into the shade by a contemporary from the Volscian town of Aquinum, D. Iunius Iuvenalis (*c.* 55–130). The composition of Juvenal followed the *Satires* of Horace in form, and he, like Horace, was at his best in describing contemporary life at Rome. But far from sharing Horace's disarming *bonhomie* he was possessed by a bitter spirit of discontent, in which personal disappointment no doubt had a share, for he alone of the major poets of his age received less than his due recognition. The strokes of Juvenal's lash fell with monotonous vehemence, but they were deftly placed; and his powers of luridly vivid description compensate in some degree for his atrabilious humour.[50]

The satires of Juvenal

9. Latin Prose

The flourishing Roman school of contemporary or recent history carried on its work under the Flavian emperors, but all its productions were thrown into the shade by the work of Cornelius Tacitus (*c.* 55–120). He was probably of Gallic or northern Italian origin and started an active career in the imperial service under Vespasian. In 77 he married Agricola's daughter; absent from Rome in 93 when Agricola died, he returned in time to endure the reign of terror during Domitian's last years, an experience which shaped his whole outlook. He became suffect consul in 97 and turned to the study of history; like Sallust, he first tried his pen in two short monographs which were published in 98. His biography of his father-in-law Agricola is a *laudatio* which concentrates on the province of Agricola's main achievement, namely Britain; his *Germania*, a brief study of the German tribes, whose future importance he dimly foresaw, formed a fit preface to a new chapter of European history. In his two major works, the *Annals* and the *Histories*, Tacitus gave definite shape to the history of the emperors from Tiberius to Domitian inclusive. Among the surviving writers of Roman history Tacitus stands out for the care with which he collected and verified his facts, and by his effort to evaluate and criticise as well as to narrate. Lacking a clear political philosophy, he was carried away by his strong natural vein of satire and his rhetorical training. His portraits of the early Caesars are admittedly coloured by his own experience and

The historical writings of Tacitus

his judgments, though seldom false, are often misleading. Further, he confines his attention to certain aspects (mainly court-life and senatorial and military history to the neglect of the wider life of the Empire), and at heart he was not reconciled to the Principate, but looked back nostalgically to 'libertatem et consulatum', the free institutions of the vanished Republic which he viewed through rose-coloured spectacles, concentrating on the contemporary decline of *virtus* and of individual independence. However, he recorded the truth as he saw it, in a work of sombre magnificence and brilliant style. In the art of terse and vivid narrative Tacitus surpassed all ancient historians, and none of his Latin predecessors gives a like impression of grasp and power.[51] An instructive foil to Tacitus was provided in the *Lives of the Twelve Caesars* by C. Suetonius Tranquillus (c. 75–150). This writer followed the example of Tacitus in passing over from an administrative career, in which he rose to be secretary to Hadrian, to the profession of literature. His biographies were an avowedly uncritical collection of information raked together with the impartial zeal of a reporter in search of 'copy': his sources ranged from the letters of Augustus and the official gazette of the Senate to the gossip of the gutter. But the formal arrangement of his miscellanies of fact and fiction reveals the tidy hand of the civil servant, and the wheat in his garner considerably outweighs the chaff.

The biographies of Suetonius

Roman oratory in the period under review is represented for us by the *Panegyricus* or address of thanks which the younger Pliny delivered in the Senate on receipt of the consulship from Trajan in A.D. 100. For this type of eloquence there always remained opportunities at Rome, which were eagerly taken. But a sufficient comment on it was passed by Tacitus in a minor work (*De Oratoribus*), in which he frankly confessed that under the régime of the emperors, where eloquence had lost most of its practical efficacy, a second Cicero need not be expected. Pliny invited another damaging comparison between himself and Cicero by publishing selections of his correspondence, for his was a tame life in a settled age. Yet his letters might serve as models of a courteous but unaffected epistolary style; and in his restrained but telling description of the destruction of Pompeii he rose to a great occasion.[52] His quietly forceful Latin invites comparison with that of a more erudite letter-writer, M. Cornelius Fronto, the tutor of the future emperor Marcus Aurelius, to whom he wrote many of his letters in a spirit of mutual regard (c. 100–c. 166). In this author the quest for a pointed and distinctive style, which in the first century had called forth a riot of epigrams,

Oratory

Letter-writing

expressed itself in archaisms and phrases culled from the older Latin classics. The letters of Fronto, who was a native of Cirta, mark the entry of Africa into Latin prose. Another African writer, Apuleius of Madaura (born c. 123), made a novel experiment in his *Metamorphoses*, a work of fiction which was cast in the studiedly discursive form of a Roman *satura*, but had for its principal content a wonder-tale of Greek type – a story of a man translated into a donkey – and its Latinity was even more contorted than that of Fronto. Two of its most famous episodes are the story of Cupid and Psyche and the description of the initiation of the hero into the mysteries of Isis.[53]

The study of the Latin language and of the Latin classics of former days continued to be actively pursued. Among the several competent scholars of the period the outstanding figure was that of M. Fabius Quintilianus (c. 35–c. 100), a Spaniard (from Calagurris in Aragon), who was appointed by Vespasian to his newly endowed chair of Latin rhetoric at Rome. Quintilian's chief work, the *Institutio Oratoria*, was mainly concerned with the technique of rhetorical training. But his guiding principle was that good oratory and good literature could only be produced by a cultivated and well-informed mind. In his introductory volume he laid down an admirable code of rules for elementary education in letters; in his tenth book he passed under review the Greek and Latin classics, with a few words of sane and sincere appreciation for each.

Scholars

The study of Roman law received a stimulus from the position of influence which jurisprudents had come to occupy on the *Consilium Principis* (p. 429). In the *Institutiones* of Gaius, written c. A.D. 160, we still possess an introductory manual for Roman law students.[54]

In the middle of the second century a new branch of Greek and Latin letters, the apology for the Christian faith, came into being. This literature will require discussion later (p. 485) from a different point of view. It will suffice here to say that the chief Christian propagandists were mostly men who had received the usual rhetorical training, and in point of polemical technique they were no whit inferior to their pagan antagonists.

Christian apologetics

10. Philosophy and Religion[55]

Among the Greek philosophic sects the only ones that retained any vitality were those of the Stoics and Cynics. In the second century the Stoic school produced two of its greatest exponents, a Phrygian freedman named Epictetus, who counted the emperor Trajan among

The Meditations of M. Aurelius

his listeners, and the emperor M. Aurelius, whose *Meditations* have contributed to maintain Stoicism as a living force in the modern world. In the humbler spheres of society wandering Cynic preachers could still attract attention with their doctrine of 'living according to Nature', by which they meant disregarding conventions and limiting wants. But the teachers of the Stoic and Cynic schools, who insisted that virtue was its own reward, could not in the long run prevail against religious missionaries who were now proclaiming confidently a state of future immortality. Moreover, the tendency among the later Stoic professors to empty virtue of positive content and to attenuate it into mere impassivity put them at a disadvantage against religious reformers who were fastening on the idea of social service as the acid test of good behaviour. Though Stoicism lived on in the Christian doctrine which it influenced, it became at the most a satellite to religion after the death of M. Aurelius.

Decline of philosophical studies

Assimilation of provincial cults

Among the pagan religions of the Roman Empire there was an apparent massacre in the first and second centuries, when many of the provincial worships became merged in analogous Roman cults. The gods of the peoples on the European continent seemingly disappeared before those of the Roman pantheon; the Carthaginian Baal Hammon was swallowed by Saturn, and the Baals of Syrian towns were transmuted into Jupiters. Yet these amalgamations involved little more than a change of name and, perhaps, a modification of ritual. The tenacity of established religions was never better illustrated than in the period under review. It was no doubt a small matter that Domitian and Antoninus discharged their duties as chief pontiffs with scrupulous care, or that all the emperors from Vespasian to M. Aurelius, with the single exception of Domitian, were enrolled after death on the list of *divi*; M. Aurelius, like an orthodox Stoic, denied his personal immortality, and Vespasian could crack a joke about his impending deification. It is more significant that the traditional conceptions of the underworld were still widespread, and particularly so that even educated persons were reverting to beliefs and practices which they had tacitly abandoned or openly scoffed at in previous centuries. Oracles and omens, from being merely formal adjuncts of statecraft, were recovering much of their pristine authority. Not only the gossip-monger Suetonius, but a man of high culture like Plutarch, recorded numberless examples of divine premonition; books on the interpretation of dreams had a ready sale; the temple of Apollo at Delphi once more attracted consultants in plenty, and another Apolline

Revival of religious credulity

oracle at Claros, near Ephesus, attained a belated celebrity in the second century. While the spread of magical practices was checked by an official ban, stories of miraculous healings by pagan deities working through human agency were widely and unquestioningly accepted. Under Domitian a wandering teacher named Apollonius of Tyana (in Cappadocia) was widely credited with supernatural powers of this kind; in the days of Antoninus one Alexander of Abonutichus (in Bithynia) carried on a notorious thaumaturgical practice; and the tale went round that on his visit to Egypt Vespasian had cured the blind and the halt.[56]

Miracle-mongering

Yet the traditional religions were being eaten into by those newer worships which, by setting greater tasks and offering higher rewards, made a special appeal to the more reflective or the more adventurous. The cult of Isis (p. 400) spread in the later first and the second century, together with that of her congener Sarapis, to the northern outposts of the Roman dominions, to Cologne, London and York.[57] At the same time its somewhat indulgent moral code was made more exacting. But from the age of Antoninus it lost the primacy among the pagan missionary religions to that of another Oriental deity, the Persian Mithras.[58] Originally a god of light and truth, the agent of Ahura-Mazda, who was the power of good as opposed to Ahriman, the power of evil, Mithras was gradually transformed by unknown hands at the end of the pre-Christian period into the central figure of a Roman mystery cult. This derived partly from Persian Zoroastrianism, with Mithras being assimilated to the Sun, who was the representative of Ahura-Mazda, and partly from the worship of the Phrygian goddess Cybele from whom it borrowed an uncouth ritual of initiation by baptism with the blood of a bull. The cult of Mithras also resembled the worship of Isis in some respects: in its impressive ceremonial, conducted by highly trained priests, in its promise of future immortality, and in its possession of an ethical code. But it surpassed the worship of Isis and approximated more to Christianity in advocating active well-doing rather than mere abstinence from sin, and in giving to fraternity a prominent place among the virtues. By means of various ordeals the initiates learned of the journey of the immortal soul and sought to rid themselves of impurities by moral effort and knowledge revealed by the mysteries. The cult was exclusively for men, and on the whole appealed to the upper classes, especially army officers and substantial business men. With the connivance or active support of the emperors of the second century the cult was carried by soldiers from camp to camp from the East until

The cults of Isis

and of Mithras

39.33   The Mithraeum at Ostia. The cult of Mithras was very popular at Ostia, where at least fifteen Mithraea are known. The artificial cave was flanked by benches for worshippers to recline on at sacred banquets. At the end of the nave is a statue of Mithras, sacrificing a bull.

it reached the Rhineland and Hadrian's Wall, and spread from Dura-Europas on the Euphrates to Spain and northern Africa. But it also spread among the civilian population: it followed the Isis cult to Dacia, to Ostia, where no fewer than fifteen chapels of Mithras have been discovered, and to London.

11. The Spread of Christianity[59]

Organisation of the Christian Church

The eventual emergence of Christianity as the predominant religion in the Roman Empire was due not least to a variety of advantages which it held over rival worships. The Christians gradually provided themselves with an organisation surpassing that of all other private religions. This quickly became a necessity for the infant Church because, when the early Christian congregation broke away from the parent Jewish Church, it lost all the advantages of membership of a well-regulated society. The first Christian communities were isolated cells under a rudimentary administration of elder members. But in the first century of their existence, after a period of experimenting with apostles, prophets, teachers, bishops, presbyters, deacons and the like, they established a well-organised body of clergy possessing wide powers of discipline over the laity. Thus the letters of Ignatius (*c.* A.D. 115) show that in his own church at Antioch, as presumably in the other local churches of Asia Minor, there was a single bishop, a board of presbyters and a group of deacons. At Rome too, probably about this time, the plurality of rulers of the Church gave way to a monarchical episcopate. By the time of M. Aurelius the clerical hierarchy was complete in all essentials, and *c.* 180 the pagan writer Celsus, a detached but hostile observer, found the principal source of Christian strength in their closely knit social structure. Equally important was the creation of a unique system of intercommunication between the several Christian communities. In the first century A.D. the only means of keeping touch between the individual churches was by irregular visits or occasional epistles from authoritative leaders like Peter and Paul. In the course of the second century the churches evolved a system of regular correspondence by representatives of neighbouring congregations. Also with the increase in the number of clergy it was possible to let deacons circulate among the country congregations attached to the churches in the cities (the earliest missionaries had concentrated on the cities realising that they were the strategic points which must be captured first).

The New Testament

The spread of Christianity was also assisted by a special literature, such as was produced by no other ancient Church except that of the Jews. The teaching of Jesus, which at first was preserved by oral tradition (this long survived), was soon set down in written records (probably in Aramaic) as early as the middle of the first century, and was then expanded in Greek by the authors of the first three Gospels from their own knowledge and that of the disciples (the earliest Gospel, that of Mark, probably dates from between A.D. 65 and 70, while the genuine Pauline Epistles are earlier, c. 50–60). By c. 130 the Four Gospels and thirteen Epistles by St Paul were generally accepted as a New Testament Canon, comparable with the books of the Old Testament which had formed the first scriptures of the earliest Christians. The task of surveying the Christian creed in the light of other systems of thought, and notably of the Stoic and Platonic philosophies, was begun in the epistles of Paul and carried on in the writings of various Church Fathers, mostly of Greek nationality, among whom the Alexandrian bishops Clement and Origen (c. 200) were the pioneers. From the time of M. Aurelius the Church also kept its own historical records, among which the Acts of the Martyrs came to form a library in themselves. These vary greatly in their historical value: some embody official shorthand reports of trials and thus are both authentic and very moving, others are based on eye-witness accounts of martyrdoms, while yet others contain miraculous and legendary material.

Christian theology

Another branch of Christian literature was addressed to those outside the Church, in order to explain to them the Christian religion and to defend it against attacks from all quarters.

Apologetics

The need for this apologetic literature was all the greater, as no other ancient religion had to encounter a more sustained opposition (pp. 487, 502). These 'Apologists' belong to the period (c. 120–220) when Christian converts were first being made among the educated classes. Few were primarily theologians, but men who wanted to show both emperors and the general public what Christianity really meant, that it had been popularly defamed and misunderstood and that it was both harmless to the state and ethically superior to pagan codes. Thus a certain Quadratus addressed his apologia to Hadrian, while Justin Martyr, who set up a Christian school in Rome c. 150, addressed both Antoninus and M. Aurelius. It was under Aurelius that attacks on Christianity by two literary men, Cornelius Fronto (p. 482) and Celsus, drew several rejoinders, as from Melito, bishop of Sardes, and from Athenagoras; most famous of all were the slightly later Apologies of the African rhetorician Tertullian (c. 197) and that of Minucius Felix, the *Octavius*, written in the form of a dialogue between a Christian and a pagan (probably early third century). Though the apologists, like the fiery Tertullian, occasionally lost their patience, they maintained on the whole a tone of studious moderation and met their antagonists point by point. No other ancient religion was as fortunate as Christianity in the manner of its presentation.

One reason for the creation of an ordered organisation and a literature was the need for self-definition not only vis-à-vis clearly defined pagan cults but also against the growth of heresies within the Church. Thus among his gentile converts both at Corinth and Colossae Paul met with beliefs that are covered by the umbrella title of Gnosticism. Members of these sects, which greatly increased during the second century, claimed to possess a special 'knowledge' (*gnosis*) of a kind far more complicated than the simple faith of the Church. No attempt can be made here to summarise their complex theosophic ideas which were a weird mixture of cosmology, magic, philosophy and mythology, with only a slight infusion of basic Christian beliefs.[60]

Gnosticism

Lastly, the Christian faith was more enduringly attractive than rival worships. Its ritual was simple as yet, and made no such appeal to eyes and ears as the official pagan cults. There were of course no churches, but meetings were held in private houses. Pliny describes how the Bithynian Christians 'gathered together on a fixed day before sunrise and sang in alternate verses (antiphonally) a hymn to Christ, as to a god, and bound themselves on oath not to commit any crime but to refrain from robbery, theft and adultery, and not to break their word. . . . After this it was their custom to disperse and then re-assemble to partake of food of an ordinary and innocent kind.'[61] Further, Christianity was no respecter of persons to a degree which greatly exceeded the wide embrace of Isis: it ignored the distinction between rich and poor, man and woman, bond and free. Though it is exceedingly difficult to appraise

Christian ritual and ethics

the relative moral standards of Christians, Jews and pagans in the Roman Empire, significant testimony in favour of the Christians was given by the pagan comment, recorded by Tertullian, 'See how the Christians love one another', while much later one of their most determined opponents, the emperor Julian (361–363), exhorted the pagans to imitate their practical helpfulness in such matters as tending the sick and relieving the poor. In fact Christian charity was one of the strongest factors in promoting the success of their cause.[62] True, a persecuted minority could take no spectacular action to change the social structure in regard to the status of women and slaves, but they did emphasise the moral responsibility of the individual to treat with respect all men and women, since they were created in God's image and all were redeemed in Christ. Even more basic reasons for the growth of Christianity were, of course, the personality of its founder and the fact that the new faith seemed to many to provide a better way of life than that offered by any other contemporary religion. Also its public witness, while frightening many, attracted others; 'The blood of the martyrs is seed', said Tertullian, and it was the witness of the martyrs that won over this well-educated pagan.

Spread of Christianity

Christianity spread with remarkable speed geographically, and at a slower rate socially. The earliest adherents had been mainly humble people, although not all rich men were repelled as was the rich young ruler: as witness Joseph of Arimathaea and Nicodemus. But even if Christianity had not penetrated into the imperial family before the end of the first century (and that possibility depends on the evidence about Flavius Clemens and Domitilla, see p. 424), by the second century converts included people of all classes. The faith quickly spread from Palestine to Syria, Asia Minor and Greece, and even beyond the bounds of the Empire to Osrhoene, where there was a Christian community in the capital city Edessa during the second century.[63] In Egypt Christianity advanced up the Nile valley, though not much detail is known before the days of Clement of Alexandria (end of second century), while it flourished in northern Africa, in Numidia and Mauretania as well as in Tunisia. In Italy a considerable Church had grown up in Rome by the time that Paul wrote his Epistle to it (c. 54–59), and doubtless soon in other cities, but it made slower progress in Gaul, Britain and Spain. However, there was a flourishing Christian community in the Rhône valley in the second century. Paul's mission to Spain may never have been more than a hope, but Cyprian (who died in 258) mentions churches in four Spanish cities. Britain probably had to wait until the mid-third century before any considerable advance was made. Finally, the process of expansion may be illustrated by two quotations. Pliny describes to Trajan how Christianity spread rapidly at first in Bithynia and then was checked. 'This contagious superstition has spread not only through the cities but through the villages and country districts. It seems possible, however, to check and cure it. It is certain at any rate that the temples, which had been almost deserted [Pliny, relying on reports, may well have exaggerated the extent], begin now to be frequented, and the sacred festivals, after long disuse, are again revived; there is a general demand for sacrificial animals, which for some time past could scarcely find buyers.' Conditions in northern Africa at the end of the second century are described by Tertullian: 'We [i.e. Christians] are but of yesterday [i.e. newcomers] and we have filled all you have – cities, islands, forts, towns, assembly-halls, even military camps, tribes, town councils, the palace, senate and forum. We have left you nothing but the temples.'[64]

12. The Opposition to Christianity

The basis of the opposition to the Christians was the same as in the case of the Jews. The Christian like the Jewish religion was not content to share the world with other worships, but aimed at supplanting them altogether. This attack upon other gods, or 'atheism' as it was called, was resented by polytheists, whose maxim was to live and let live in matters of religion, as a gratuitous picking of quarrels. The dislike of Jewish and Christian aggressiveness was aggravated by the disturbance of social habits and the danger to vested interests which resulted from the refusal to 'worship idols.'[65] Neither could the Jews and Christians escape unpopularity by the self-protective device of keeping aloof from polytheistic society, for in an essentially sociable community such as a Greek or Roman city self-isolation was viewed with disfavour, and gossip-mongers were always at hand to disclose the disreputable rites which Jews and Christians were suspected of practising under cover of secrecy, or to throw out hints of political disloyalty. If a well-informed and thoughtful man like Tacitus could roundly denounce both Jews and Christians for their foul ways of life,[66] it is easy to understand that the mass of unreflecting folk would on first impression accept the most extravagant tales about them.

Opposition to monotheist cults

If the ordinary man in the Greek and Roman

world was hasty in condemning the monotheistic religions, his anger against them was seldom sustained, and he could not but admit, on a closer acquaintance with Jews and Christians, that the charges against them were unfounded. Both sects therefore lived down much of their original unpopularity. After the time of Hadrian the Jews came to a general *modus vivendi* with their neighbours. Popular indignation against the Christians declined in the third century; by the time of Constantine individual Christians and pagans had no difficulty in forming enduring friendships. But in the first two centuries of their existence the Christian communities were constantly liable to attacks by infuriated mobs, like those which have been directed against the Jews in medieval and again in recent times.

A more sustained campaign against the Jews, and more especially against the Christians, was kept up by men of letters, many of whom had been trained in philosophy or rhetoric and knew how to conduct their case. The polemics against the Jews, which were mostly carried on by Greek writers, died out in the course of the second century. The attacks upon the Christians were delivered alike in Greek and in Latin, and the war of words continued to the end of the fourth century.[67]

Lastly, the heavy arm of the Roman government came down upon both Jews and Christians. The measures taken by Roman emperors against the Jews have been discussed in previous chapters. Though they did not aim at the extermination of the Jewish religion they proved effective in arresting its diffusion among the gentile populations. It was kept alive in schools and synagogues, but it ceased to be a missionary religion. The persecutions of the Christians were an admitted failure.

The attitude of the emperors to the Christians was seemingly not defined until the reign of Trajan. The execution of Christians at Rome under

Nero was a mere afterthought (p. 359), and did not result in any general proscription of their worship. Under Vespasian the Christian community at Rome went unmolested, and the evidence of widespread martyrdoms at Rome under Domitian is of the slightest (p. 412), although the book of Revelation suggests wider persecution and disturbances in Asia Minor. During the first half-century after the crucifixion of Jesus the Roman governors in the eastern provinces took no active measures against the Christians, but in the closing years of the first century they executed a sufficient number to create a precedent for their persecution. The legal basis on which they acted has been the subject of immense discussion, since the nature of the

evidence precludes any clear-cut answer.[68] In general it may be said that provincial governors had wide discretionary powers of jurisdiction in the *cognitio* process, both in recognising *crimina* and in determining sentences *extra ordinem*. Knowledge of Nero's action might encourage local enemies of Christians to try to persuade a governor to accept their accusations and proceed against the accused on the assumption that they were in some way guilty of conduct inimical to the interests of the Roman state. This at any rate appears to be what faced Pliny, who was sent as *legatus Augusti* to reorganise the disturbed province of Bithynia-Pontus about A.D. 110.

In a letter to Trajan Pliny asked for more definite instructions in regard to the Christians, since he was ignorant of their normal punishment because he had never taken part in a trial concerning them. He reports that at the outset of his governorship he had executed those who had been accused as Christians and after a threefold inquiry still maintained that they were (apart from any Roman citizens whom he had sent to Rome for trial). He released those who denied that they were or had been Christians and who were willing to invoke the gods, sacrifice to them and to the emperor's statue and to curse Christ. He made those who admitted that they had been, but claimed they were no longer, Christians invoke the gods and worship the emperor's image, but he was puzzled whether he should release them; hence he asked for Trajan's ruling. In his reply the emperor did not lay down a universal rule; he declared that they were not to be hunted out, but if they were accused (and no anonymous accusions were to be accepted) and convicted, they must be punished. Anyone who denied that he was a Christian and sacrificed to the gods should be pardoned, even if his past was suspicious. In issuing these instructions Trajan adhered somewhat blindly to the principle of the routine administrator that a practice, once covered by precedents, must continue, and he missed the opportunity of regulating the position of the Christians on the lines of common sense laid down by Augustus, when he exempted the Jews from Caesar-worship (p. 367). True, it was a local instruction, and other governors were not bound by it, but once it was published all other governors would be likely to follow this precedent until official policy was changed (and this apparently did not occur for nearly a century and a half, under Decius). The effect of the rescript was to make every Christian into a potential traitor. But a saving lack of logic on Trajan's part protected the Christians against systematic persecution. A further instruction by Hadrian to the proconsul of Asia, Minucius Fundanus, in reply to a question by his predecessor, gave the Christians a slight additional protection by ordaining that they should not be subject to vexatious attacks by the *calumnia* (malicious or frivolous prosecution) procedure (A.D. 122–123).

Effect of the rescript

The practical effect of Trajan's rescript was that in the second century sporadic executions of Christians continued, although on the whole under Hadrian and Antoninus they enjoyed something of a lull during which the Church spread rapidly; one martyr was Ignatius of Antioch, who suffered at Rome before 117. By the mid-century, however, Christian refusal to take part in the cult of the emperor or the pagan gods led to a widespread feeling that they were enemies of the community and threatened its security by endangering the *pax deorum*; they became scapegoats for all kinds of disasters such as famine and disease. Violence broke out again under M. Aurelius,[69] Justin was condemned in Rome by the *praefectus urbi* (c. 165), and a pogrom erupted at Smyrna, where Polycarp was seized and burnt (c. 167, or possibly 155). At Lugdunum and Vienna (Vienne) outbreaks by angry mobs stimulated the governor to deal out death sentences to the victims on a liberal scale (177?), but incipient campaigns by over-zealous officials in Achaea and Macedonia were nipped in the bud by Antoninus. Christians, rather than Jews, were becoming the main targets of mob violence.

13. Conclusion

The century that began with Vespasian showed on the whole less movement than any earlier hundred years of Roman history. The wars of Trajan, the opening up of commercial intercourse with the Far East, the Pantheon and the Column of Trajan, show that it did not wholly lack the spirit of adventure; the works of Tacitus and Juvenal prove that it was still capable of deep feeling and vigorous expression. With these reserves, however, it may be admitted that it was not a heroic age. But it was, negatively, a time of freedom from strain, political and social, and, positively, an era of widespread if not very strenuous goodwill. This salient feature of the period will be found on almost every page of M. Aurelius's *Meditations*, and in a hundred letters of the younger Pliny. It recurs in Quintilian's humane precepts of education and in numerous surviving epitaphs of obscure men and women, whose chief pride was that they had lived together for half a lifetime 'without a single quarrel'. At a time when Rome was most powerful, its sense of *pietas* was also strongest.

An unheroic century

General goodwill

But in any case, the serenity of the second century must not be mistaken for the feeble contentment of a comfortable invalid. To speak of a 'decay' of the Roman Empire at this period would be premature. Economically the Empire was never sounder, politically it was never more stable, and at the death of M. Aurelius its frontiers were as secure as ever.[70]

The Empire not yet in a state of decay

CHAPTER 40

Commodus and the Severi

1. The Reign of Commodus (180–192)

M. Aurelius reintroduces hereditary succession

The wisdom with which the emperors from Nerva to Antoninus had ordered the succession was partly due to the accident that none of them had sons to survive them. But no such play of chance intervened to insure M. Aurelius against a wrong choice. Though several of his sons died prematurely, a youth (nearly eighteen years old) named L. Aurelius Commodus remained to uphold the claims of heredity, and with the same excess of family loyalty as had previously prompted him to take L. Verus into partnership, the last of the 'good emperors' accepted the risk of transmitting his power to an untried man. In promoting Commodus over the heads of several competent generals and ministers M. Aurelius no doubt speculated on his son's willingness to retain these right-hand men in his service.[1]

40.1   Commodus.

M. Aurelius's campaigns proved adequate, so far as the maintenance of frontier defence was concerned. In 180 the new emperor abandoned his father's plan to annex territory north of the Danube and made a peace with the Quadi and Marcomanni (p. 444); though the clauses in it that bound the German tribes not to draw near the Danube were not strictly enforced, it nevertheless gave the Danube front a long immunity from serious invasion. In Britain the Antonine Wall was overrun and then after the situation had been restored by Ulpius Marcellus the wall was abandoned (pp. 447 f.). Both Marcellus and his successor, P. Helvius Pertinax (185), had to face mutinies in the army, perhaps partly the result of lack of donatives.[2] On several other fronts (as Spain, Gaul and Dacia) nascent wars were stifled by officers of M. Aurelius's school. In the general administration of the empire two wise measures stood to Commodus's credit. He reaffirmed the statutory rights of the cultivating tenants on the imperial estates in Africa, where the *conductores* had introduced a system of compulsory labour not far removed from serfdom (182).[3] In 186 he instituted a regular service of ships to convey the produce of Africa to Rome, on the model of Vespasian's *classis Alexandrina* (p. 413).

Successful frontier policy of Commodus

Nevertheless, in reverting to the dynastic principle of succession, M. Aurelius saddled the Roman Empire with another Nero. From a good-natured but insignificant boy Commodus developed into a mere voluptuary; and, unlike Nero, he did not wait long before he transferred his trust from men of the stamp of Burrus and Seneca to advisers of Tigellinus's order. In the first instance he gave his confidence to a *praefectus praetorio* named Perennis, who proved himself a competent vizier. In 185, however, he executed Perennis on an unverified charge of treason, and soon transferred the command over the Guards, together with the general control of policy, to a freedman named Cleander.[4]

Commodus a second Nero

This shrewd man of business turned his office into a public market in which he made traffic of justice and state appointments: the story that he sold twenty-five consulships on one day illustrates the rate of his turn-over. He needed the money not only to line his own pocket but also to meet the drain caused by the emperor's luxurious living and extravagance in Games. In 190 Commodus sacrificed Cleander to the urban proletariat, in atonement for a famine which a jealous corn-commissioner had brought about by deliberate mismanagement. After Cleander's fall the emperor set up and removed his praetorian prefects in quick succession, according to the dictates of his mistress Marcia, who is said to have been a Christian. Under this rule of favourites the imperial finances rapidly went to rack and ruin. The payments into the chest of the alimentary institutions had been suspended in 184, benevolences were imposed upon the rich, and judicial murders were improvised, as in the worst days of Nero, in order to raise fresh funds by confiscations.[5] Commodus's own contribution to Roman statecraft was to dress up like Hercules and to shoot animals, or to lay them low with a club, at the public *venationes*. For these achievements he rewarded himself with divine honours (becoming the incarnation of Hercules, the Hercules Romanus) and by renaming Rome 'the colony of Commodus' (Colonia Commodiana).

Rule by favourites

Financial extravagance

The misrule of Commodus, which was helped by the use of secret police (*frumentarii*), allowed the Senate little chance to show more opposition than a sullen resentment, especially in view of the number of Cleander's creatures which he had managed to pack into it by *adlectio*. Though the urban proletariat cowed the emperor into dismissing this favourite, its ill humour lasted no longer than the famine which had conjured it up. Yet Commodus's reign was distracted by plots and rumours of plots. In 182 an abortive attempt by his sister Lucilla and Pompeianus Quintianus (her nephew or stepson) to assassinate him brought on a spate of denunciations and of precautionary executions. Then Paternus, the praetorian prefect, was disposed of by the intrigues of his colleague Perennis. Under these conditions of insecurity the best form of life insurance for those dwelling near the court was a real conspiracy. On the last day of 192 the praetorian prefect Aemilius Laetus and the chamberlain Eclectus, with the collusion of Marcia (who had lost the emperor's favour) stole a march upon Commodus by engaging a professional athlete to throttle him in his bath. His memory was condemned by both Senate and people.

Renewal of conspiracies

Murder of Commodus

2. The Civil Wars of 193–197

The conspiracy against Commodus recalled the conditions under which Domitian had been murdered. In this case too the assassins had made plans for the succession, and their choice had fallen on one of M. Aurelius's right-hand men, Helvius Pertinax, now aged sixty-six, who was accepted without demur by Senate and soldiery. The new emperor at once took the reins into his hands, showed respect to the Senate, and in three months' time he had begun to solve the most urgent problem of the moment, the rehabilitation of the state finances. He not only curtailed expenditure by judicious personal and public economies but he provided for future revenue by granting a title of full ownership and ten years' remission of taxes to cultivators of land left waste after the plague and the frontier wars of M. Aurelius's reign. With equal vigour he set himself to restore discipline among the household troops, for whom the reign of Commodus had been a continual Saturnalia. Though he honoured their claim to a donative by paying one-half of the promised sum as a first instalment, he reimposed stricter conditions of service. At the same time he was at pains to cultivate good relations with the Senate and to strengthen its authority, so that it might serve as a rallying-point of the orderly and responsible elements in the state against the growing licence of the soldiery. But an *entente* between emperor and Senate threatened to undermine the position of Laetus, whose object in setting up Pertinax was to acquire for himself a position such as Perennis had enjoyed under Commodus. For his attempt to restore orderly government Pertinax paid the same penalty as Galba for his endeavour to end the Neronian anarchy. After a reign of three months he was murdered by the Guards, perhaps at the instigation of Laetus (28 March 193).

The Senate appoints Pertinax

Pertinax attempts to restore discipline

He is murdered by his Guards

Having taught Pertinax their lesson the praetorian cohorts made their meaning doubly clear by their procedure in choosing his successor. When two candidates for the vacant throne offered themselves, the *praefectus urbi* Sulpicianus (Pertinax's father-in-law) and a quite incompetent but exceptionally rich senator named Didius Iulianus, the household troops put the Empire to auction between this couple and eventually knocked it down to Iulianus after he had run the bidding to the monstrous sum of 25,000 sesterces per man. The urban proletariat, to its credit, pelted Iulianus with stones, but the Senate perforce ratified the praetorians' bargain.

The Empire auctioned to Didius Iulianus

But the history of the 'Year of Four Emperors' went on repeating itself. The troops

40.2 Septimius Severus.

on the frontiers, whose opinion of the praetorians had not been enhanced by their recent performances, rediscovered the 'secret of empire' and confronted Iulianus with three rival candidates – Decimus Clodius Albinus in Britain, L. Septimius Severus in Pannonia Superior, and C. Pescennius Niger in Syria. In answer to this triple acclamation, it is true, Iulianus had the chance of playing off one pretender against another; but his opportunities of profiting by his rivals' dissensions were cut short by the prompt action of the governor of Pannonia, who was stationed nearest to Rome (at Carnuntum) and appeared first in the field.

Emperor-making in the provinces

40.3 Julia Domna, wife of Septimius.

Capture of Rome by Septimius Severus

With the support of all the Danubian and Rhenish legions Severus made a dash for Italy like Antonius Primus in 69, and captured Rome in a bloodless campaign. Iulianus, who made a vain attempt to conciliate the invader with an offer of partnership, now an emperor without any subjects, was deposed and condemned to death by the Senate; his guardsmen carried out the sentence upon him (1 June 193).

After his unopposed entry into the capital Severus stayed only long enough to consolidate his position against the other pretenders and to arrange the funeral and deification of Pertinax, whom he claimed to have avenged. But he found time to carry out an enduring reform

by cashiering the praetorian cohorts and replacing them with soldiers drawn from the legions. By this simple act of justice he broke with the tradition that the privilege of serving in the Guards' corps should be reserved for Italians, and he gave an earnest of his future levelling policy.[7]

Severus reconstitutes the Guards corps

In the game of odd-man-out Severus had already succeeded in keeping Albinus in play by conceding to him a free hand in Britain, Gaul and Spain, and by conferring upon him the title of 'Caesar', which had come by now to carry with it a claim to the succession. With his rear thus rendered secure he advanced with the full strength of the Danube armies upon Niger,

40.4 Pescennius Niger.

who, proclaimed emperor by his Syrian legions, had meanwhile secured all Asia and had thrown an advance force across the Bosporus. In a whirlwind campaign which extended through the winter of 193–194 Severus dislodged Niger's troops from the Black Sea entrance by defeating them near Cyzicus and Nicaea, stormed his second line of defence in the Cilician Gates near Issus, and cut down his rival on his final flight from Antioch to the Euphrates. The defeat of Niger involved the towns, which had supported him most steadfastly, in heavy indemnities, Antioch and Byzantium lost their municipal status and were 'attributed' to the neighbouring cities of Laodicea and Perinthus. The Byzantines at any rate gave Severus abundant excuse for severe measures, for with perverse loyalty to a cause long lost they detained his siege corps until late in 196. For reasons of security Syria was divided into two provinces, Coele and Phoenice.

Severus disposes of Pescennius Niger

In this year Severus, who had spent 195 in punitive expeditions across the Euphrates (p. 492), swung his troops back across Europe for the final round with Albinus, who had let the war in the East take its own course, but had been prescient enough to strengthen his own forces against all comers. He was raised by his army to the rank of Augustus and then crossed

40.5 Clodius Albinus.

Severus's victory over Albinus

to Gaul: the decisive action of this campaign, which was delivered near Lugdunum early in 197, involved large forces (even if Dio's estimate of 300,000 men engaged is exaggerated). The battle was Severus's hardest test, but in the event it went in his favour and left him undisputed master in the Roman Empire. Like the winner of the civil war of 68–69 Severus became the founder of a short-lived dynasty. For his soldiers the prize of victory was the city of Lugdunum, which they sacked so thoroughly that it never recovered its former ascendancy in Gaul.

3. The Military Policy of Septimius Severus

In contrast with Vespasian, Severus had won the imperial power by his own exertions, and he took personal charge of the chief foreign wars of his reign. It was a piece of good fortune for the Roman Empire that no serious invasion was attempted by the border tribes on Rhine and Danube while their garrisons were engaged in the civil wars; on these fronts the efforts of M. Aurelius had made the Roman defences secure for many years to come. In the East, however, the civil war brought a new conflict with Parthia in its train. Though the Parthian king Vologeses IV had not rendered effective aid to Niger he had made an offer of assistance to this pretender, and the native chieftain of Osroene in western Mesopotamia had taken the opportunity to renounce his recent allegiance to Rome (p. 439). After the defeat of Niger, Severus had contented himself with a punitive foray across the Euphrates and the establishment of a Roman province of Osrhoene with its capital at Nisibis; Adiabene was invaded and a formal peace made with Parthia (195). But two years later he was called back to the eastern front by an overt attack on the part of Vologeses, who made a belated attempt to recover the lost provinces in Mesopotamia while Severus lay engaged with Albinus. After a preliminary campaign in the

Severus overruns Babylonia

autumn of 197, in which he expelled the Parthians from Osroene and Adiabene, Severus repeated in the following year the victorious marches of Trajan and of Avidius Cassius upon Ctesiphon, which he reduced to ruins. With this humiliation the Roman emperor had in effect dealt the death-blow to the Parthian monarchy, and now, if ever, the moment had come to annex the entire Land of the Two Rivers. Severus went so far as to reconstruct Trajan's province of Mesopotamia and to occupy it permanently with two legions; but he withdrew his troops from Babylonia, and failed to capture Hatra.[8] Colonial status was granted to Palmyra, which entered on a period of great prosperity. Severus then visited Egypt and Syria, his wife's homeland; returning via the Danube he reached Rome in 202 where he celebrated his Decennalia and soon the Arch which still looks down on the Forum celebrated the achievements of an emperor who was now Parthicus Maximus. He then set off on a visit to his native Africa.

Caledonian forays into England

The other main seat of war in Severus's reign was Britain, whose garrison Albinus had carried off with him to Gaul. In the closing years of the second century the Caledonians and a kindred tribe named the Maeatae overran the north of England as far as York, which temporarily fell into their hands. The invaders were eventually induced by a danegeld from the governor Virius Lupus (198–202) to evacuate the land south of Hadrian's Wall. In 205 L. Alfenus Senecio started the task of repairing the Wall, which had been so badly damaged that later generations thought that it had been built in the first place by Severus; the task was finished by 207. Severus then determined to take the offensive and, despite his sixty-three years of age, arrived with his two sons, Caracalla and Geta, to conduct operations in person (208). In 209 he made a determined attempt to crush the Caledonians, advancing north of Aberdeen, perhaps nearly to the Moray Firth, while in the next year Caracalla campaigned against the Maeatae. But both father and son failed to bring the natives to battle or to make any decisive impression upon them. When Severus died at York in 211, his sons definitely evacuated Scotland and, abandoning any thought of retaining the line of the Antonine Wall, they fixed the Roman frontier on the line of the Tyne and Solway. If it is believed that sources hostile to Severus were wrong to credit him with the purpose of achieving a permanent conquest of Scotland and if his aim was in fact a punitive expedition, then he had gained a qualified success, since the northern frontier enjoyed nearly a century of peace. For reasons of security Severus

Severus's campaigns in Scotland

had already in 197 divided the province into two (Superior in the south and Inferior in the north); this division, suspended during the war, was now re-established by Caracalla.[9]

The Wall of Hadrian served as a pattern for a much longer barrier which Severus probably commenced and his son Caracalla completed for the defence of Upper Germany and Raetia. In Upper Germany the palisade was reinforced with an earth bank and ditch (*Pfahlgraben*), while in Raetia from north-west of Lorch to Heinheim it was replaced by a stone wall (*Teufelsmauer*). About A.D. 200, an earthen mound, with a wall, was thrown up east of the river Aluta, running northward from the Danube to the Carpathians. In Mauretania Caesariensis a more southerly line was occupied, but Severus's main interest probably lay in his native Tripolitania since he came from an equestrian family from Lepcis Magna. Hitherto Roman policy had aimed more at controlling tribal affairs than creating a military frontier (p. 435), but the prosperous coastal cities of Sabrata, Oea and Lepcis came to need greater protection and ultimately a Limes Tripolitanus, some 650 miles long, was created to cover the southern side of the area. Severus seems to have been the author of this development, by which the defences were pushed to the Gebel escarpment. Beyond this zone or series of zones were outlying forts, and at least from the time of Severus Alexander *limetanei* (military settlers) were established in fortified farmhouses in the more fertile wadis. The additional security which this frontier development gave made it possible not long after to replace most of the regular troops in Africa by native militias.[10] Lastly, the entire system of empire defences was improved by a thoroughgoing repair of the military roads.[11] The reign of Severus marks the last extension and the final consolidation of the Roman boundaries.

In the reign of Severus the total numbers of the Roman army were increased by the creation of three new legions, of which two were stationed in Mesopotamia, and a third in Italy at Albanum (on the west bank of the Alban Lake), where it did duty as a general reserve and as a counterpoise to the praetorian corps. This new arrangement also had the effect of diminishing the distinctions between Italy and the provinces. Another privilege which the Italians had held over provincials in the Roman military forces was removed when Severus opened the ranks of the praetorian cohorts to provincials (p. 491) and at the same time enabled them to qualify for centurions' commissions (for a term of service in the Guards continued to be the usual method of rising to the grade of centurion). Although the urban cohorts were still recruited from Italians (the Vigiles, previously freedmen, were now raised from free citizens), the army was considerably democratised. Any legionary could hope for service in the praetorians (in fact most of the new praetorians came from the Danubian legions). But, although the Guard was provincialised, the army as a whole was not 'barbarised', as sometimes suggested. The new Guard did not consist of Illyrian peasants who hardly spoke Latin, but was drawn from the towns and from sons of veterans. It is true that during the century peasants began to take the place of townsmen in the legions, but that was primarily the result of Caracalla's edict (pp. 496 f.). Nor did Severus exclude Italian officers from the army; they did in fact continue to serve in both legions and auxilia (while there had been many provincial officers before Severus's reign). Severus also lifted the ban on marriage by soldiers serving with the colours. This prohibition, which had been reasonable enough so long as the Roman army was essentially a field force and the troops changed their quarters frequently, became both unfair and impracticable, as military service more and more took the form of frontier defence in permanent camps. Indeed the formation of enduring partnerships between soldiers on garrison service and the women of the neighbourhood had the advantage of providing the army with a good supply of recruits, for the camp-children usually followed the careers of their fathers. Such unions had therefore long been connived at, and Severus did no more than recognise an accomplished fact when he gave them legal validity. The conversion of the Roman army into a frontier militia was carried one step further by Severus when he offered hereditary leases of Roman crown lands to certain auxiliary units. Finally, Severus raised the legionaries' rates of pay from 300 denarii to 500. This gift to the soldiers exposed the emperor to the charge of over-paying the troops in order to buy their favour; but the increase in their remuneration was probably intended, in part at least, to compensate them for a fall in the purchasing power of money, which seems to have occurred at this time. In any case, the concession of Severus to the army did not for the time being lead to any loss of military efficiency.

4. The Internal Reforms of Septimius Severus

Though Severus was the most active campaigner among Roman emperors since Trajan he found time to carry out extensive changes in the general administration of the Empire. A native of the African town of Lepcis Magna, he was

The northern and African frontiers

Military reforms

Troops become less mobile

nevertheless well versed in Greek and Roman letters, and he was no mere child of the camp.[12] On his accession he was at pains to legitimise his usurpation, and he made an attempt to come to a good understanding with the Senate. In the first instance he gave himself out as the avenger of the Senate's champion Pertinax; subsequently he affiliated himself to M. Aurelius by a posthumous act of adoption. At his first entry into Rome he repeated Hadrian's promise not to execute a senator except after trial in the House, and after the campaign against Niger

Severus humiliates the Senate

he killed no more than one of his partisans. But after the war against Albinus Severus reversed his attitude to the Senate, for many of its members had repaid his advances by ill-concealed expressions of sympathy with the rival pretender.[13] Though he allowed thirty-five out of sixty-four suspects whom he put on trial for treason to be acquitted, he withdrew from the senators the right of trial in their own assembly. He abandoned all pretence of partnership with the senators, and he did not disguise the fact, which Augustus had been at pains to obscure, and even Domitian had refrained from emphasising, that the authority of the emperor was based in the last resort on the support of the soldiery.

Preference given to Equites

As a soldiers' emperor Severus gave a steady preference in filling his administrative posts to persons of the Equestrian Order, whose previous training had been purely military. Though he did not directly replace the governors of the senatorial provinces by his own nominees, he prepared for their eventual extrusion from the provincial government by setting *vicarii* or deputy-governors of equestrian rank by their side, or by introducing *equites* as temporary caretakers. He did not interfere with senatorial command of the existing legions, but he did entrust his three new legions to equestrian prefects instead of to senatorial *legati*. Thus he began to drive a wedge between the civil and military administration, which ultimately in the time of Gallienus had forced them completely apart.

In excluding senators from administrative posts Severus cut away one of the chief remaining links with the Roman Republic. He abolished another surviving institution of republican times by closing down the standing jury-courts for higher crimes (the *quaestiones perpetuae*). From the time of Tiberius the competence of these courts had been partly restricted by the concurrent jurisdiction of the *praefectus urbi* (p. 361); their entire range of duties was now transferred to the *praefectus urbi*, to whom all cases originating within a hundred miles of Rome were assigned, and to the *praefectus prae-*

torio, who took cognisance of cases from the rest of Italy and from the provinces.[14] The devolution of judicial powers upon the *praefectus praetorio* is not to be explained solely by Severus's predilection for men of the camp. In the early part of his reign the emperor fell under the influence of his praetorian prefect, C. Fulvius Plautianus, to whom he conceded powers resembling those of a vizier in an eastern monarchy. In addition to his new judicial authority Plautianus was invested with an overriding control over the *praefectus annonae*, and was made vice-president of the *Consilium Principis*. After the fall of Plautianus in 205 (p. 496) Severus reverted to the practice of apportioning the duties of the prefecture between two commanders of equal rank; but he entrusted them with the same powers as Plautianus had exercised. For the discharge of the judicial duties which now attached to the prefecture the emperor appointed a distinguished jurist, Aemilius Papinianus, to one of the vacant posts.

Increased power of the prae-fectus praetorio

A notable consequence of the transfer of jurisdiction from the *quaestiones* to the imperial prefects was that higher criminal jurisdiction at Rome reverted to the condition out of which it had developed in the republican period, of being a function of administrative *coercitio*: and in the hearing of criminal cases the imperial examining magistrate exercised the same freedom of procedure as a consul of the early Republic. This change of procedure was accompanied by the increasing use of different scales of punishments according to the person of the delinquent. For purposes of criminal jurisdiction the citizen body fell into a class of *honestiores* (including members of the Senatorial and Equestrian Orders, municipal magistrates and senators, and soldiers of all ranks), and another of *humiliores*.[15] For the same crime a privileged offender might suffer simple banishment, an unprivileged one would be sentenced to penal servitude in the mines; in capital cases the *honestior* would be put to death quickly and cleanly, the *humilior* might be thrown to the beasts. A person of higher status still enjoyed the right of appeal to the emperor, and he remained exempt from torture, except in trials of treason or *maiestas*; but these privileges were withdrawn from those of the lower order. From the time of Severus the principle that the law was a respecter of persons pervaded the whole of Roman criminal jurisdiction, a rule which constituted one of Rome's most harmful legacies to the Middle Ages.

Changes in criminal jurisdiction

Honestiores and humiliores

Nevertheless in actual practice the standard of jurisdiction in the early third century probably stood as high as at any period of Roman history. The age produced several of Rome's greatest jurists (p. 500), and these eminent lawyers habitually sat as judges in the prefects' courts, or as advisory experts on the *Consilium Principis*. In other than political cases the emperor's influence was on the side of mercy, and the supplementary legislation which he introduced to protect wives' dowries or to defend the interests of minors and of slaves, followed the best tradition of the second-century emperors.

The Consilium Principis as a court of law

The process of breaking up provinces into separate administrative units, which had been begun by Augustus and continued by Trajan and Hadrian, was now carried several stages further by Severus. Numidia was detached from Africa; Syria and Britain were divided into two. The partition of Syria and Britain, where his rivals Niger and Albinus had formerly held command, suggests that Severus was taking precautions against future pretenders by preventing the concentration of military power in the hands of any one provincial governor. This measure of insurance against civil war proved effective only so long as emperors took personal command of armies engaged in major wars and maintained their control over these. In the constitution of new urban centres in the provinces Severus carried on vigorously the policy of Trajan and his successors. Thus it is probable that the British town of Eboracum (modern York) owed its elevation to the status of colony to him.[16] In Egypt, where previous emperors had inherited a policy of extreme centralisation, and had done little. or nothing to foster local autonomy, Severus introduced a larger measure of self-government by providing Alexandria and the *metropoleis* or district capitals with municipal senates.

Partition of provinces

Conferment of municipal status

In view of his African origin and his marriage with a Syrian wife it was but natural that Severus should favour the promotion of the provincials to a status of equality with the Italians. He not only placed the provincials on a level with the Italians in regard to military service (p. 493), but he admitted them in large numbers to his administrative service. A notable feature of his reign, and of the early third century in general, is the number of imperial officials from Syria and other eastern provinces. From their presence in the Roman administration it is clear that the Roman franchise had by then been extended to many towns of the eastern Mediterranean, and it may be surmised that its conferment was largely the work of Severus himself.

Grants of franchise in the eastern provinces

In the civil wars of 193–197 the districts through which the contending armies passed paid the usual heavy toll of requisitions and war-indemnities; but taken as a whole the provinces enjoyed the same good standard of adminis-

High level of provincial administration

tration as under Trajan and his successors.[17] As one who had received his own training in the school of M. Aurelius, Severus kept his officials up to a high level of efficiency. The popularity of his dynasty in the provinces is attested by many surviving monuments; though the dedications in his honour are especially frequent in his native Africa they are to be found in all parts of the empire.

Though Severus was no less lavish in his financial administration than Trajan or Hadrian he redeemed the *fiscus* from the confusion into which Commodus had thrown it and finally left it in a solvent condition. He placed a heavy additional burden on the taxpayers by raising the legionaries' rates of pay to 500 denarii. At Rome he built a new imperial palace on the Palatine and added a monumental façade, the Septizodium ('House of the Seven Planets') facing the Appian Way; he adorned the west end of the Forum with his Arch, with reliefs depicting his Parthian campaigns, including the capture of Seleucia and Ctesiphon; and he began the construction of a vast and sumptuous new suite of baths.[18] In addition to the customary distributions of grain, he indulged the populace of Rome with six *congiaria* at an estimated total of 220 million denarii, as well as with extravagant Games and free medicine for the poor. In Italy he resumed the payments on account of the alimentary institutions. In the provinces he spent large amounts on road repairs, and he took upon himself the costs of the postal service, which had hitherto rested on the shoulders of the wayside municipalities. Nevertheless he accumulated a large reserve of money in the *fiscus* and ample stocks of grain in the public magazines. The financial surplus which he realised proceeded in part from the heavy indemnities which he had imposed upon the adherents of Niger and Albinus. But these windfalls, which would have flowed under his predecessors into the *fiscus* (for the public administration) or into the *patrimonium Caesaris* (for the imperial household), were diverted by him into a new fund, the *res privata*, which he treated as heritable family property. In fact any practical distinction between public funds and those of the emperor were fast disappearing, and thus the state was closer to being identified with his own person.[19] He curtailed his expenditure by a further depreciation of the *denarius*, whose silver content he reduced to under 50 per cent – a dangerous expedient, whose ill effects, however, did not become apparent until a later time.[20] But the principal reason for Severus's success as a financier was the automatic increase of the taxation fund in a period of renewed material prosperity. During his reign the economic setback

Increased expenditure

Formation of the res privata

due to the great plague of M. Aurelius's day and the misgovernment of Commodus had been made good, and the natural buoyancy of the revenue was able to sustain an additional weight of imposts. Thus he was able to secure military support, and his advice to his sons, when dying, 'enrich the soldiers, despise all the others', indicates how this man from Africa had succeeded in gaining the Principate and establishing a dynasty.

5. Caracalla (211–217)

Caracalla murders his rivals to the succession

Severus had hardly established himself on his throne than he marked out his elder son, aged eight, for the succession by having the full imperial prerogative conferred upon him, together with the title of Augustus. The Crown Prince was hereupon officially renamed M. Aurelius Antoninus after his adoptive grandfather, but he went down to history by his popular nickname Caracallus or Caracalla (from a hooded Gallic greatcoat which he introduced into Rome).

40.6 Caracalla. ANTONINUS PIUS AUG(ustus) GERM(anicus).

Plautianus

Geta

Caracalla's chances of the succession were jeopardised for a time by the growing ascendancy of the praetorian prefect Plautianus, whose position at the court of Severus was coming to bear an ominous resemblance with that of Seianus at the side of Tiberius. Whether Plautianus actually formed a conspiracy to get rid of Caracalla is not clear; but the latter contrived to sow mistrust of the prefect in his father's mind, and once Severus lost faith in his favourite he struck him down as suddenly as Tiberius had turned upon Seianus (205). For the moment Caracalla's position was assured; but at the end of his reign Severus associated his younger son, P. Antoninus Geta, with Caracalla as co-heir to the imperial power, naming him Augustus in 209. On his death in 211 the feud, which had not failed to declare itself between the two brothers, threatened to lead to a fresh civil war;

40.7 Geta. P. SEPT(imius) GETA PIUS AUG(ustus) BRIT(annicus).

but in the following year the elder of the discordant pair cut the quarrel short by murdering Geta.[21] Having thus ended a dangerous experiment in dual monarchy Caracalla (211–217) reproduced the salient features of his father's character in an exaggerated form. Inheriting Severus's despotic humour, he showed none of his father's discrimination in striking down opposition. Though he could be generous where his personal interests were not at stake, as when he remitted the punishment inflicted by Severus upon Antioch and Byzantium, he safeguarded himself against Geta's partisans by a war of extermination, in which the jurist Papinian perished among many others. When visiting Alexandria (215) he suppressed one of the periodical ebullitions of unrest by quartering his troops on the townsmen and instigating them to a 'massacre of Glencoe'. The military character of Severus's reign was further developed by his son. In violation of the rule that only a triumphator might enter Rome in military array Caracalla habitually wore a soldier's cape in the city. Without any reason save that of currying favour with the troops he raised the pay of the legionaries from 500 to 750 denarii — an indulgence which soon converted his father's financial surplus into a deficit. Though Caracalla lived in an ostentatiously simple, not to say rough, style and spent little on public buildings at Rome, where he merely completed the great *thermae* begun by his father, he was nevertheless driven to increase taxation, and to tamper still further with the coinage by issuing in 215 a new silver piece, the *Antoninianus*, to which he gave a currency value of two denarii, although it weighed but five-thirds of a denarius; he also slightly reduced the weight of the aureus.

His despotic character

Caracalla curries favour with the troops

The financial exigencies of Caracalla are usually assigned as the reason for a remarkable edict, issued in 212, by which he practically completed the extension of the Roman citizenship to all free men within the borders of the Empire. This explanation may not be the whole

Final enfranchisement of the provinces

truth, and we shall probably do Caracalla no more than justice in attributing to him the same statesmanlike motives as had guided the franchise policy of the long line of Roman emperors since Claudius. In any case, it is unlikely that Caracalla's measure entailed any vast addition to the number of Roman citizens, for the process of enfranchisement had already been carried very far by his predecessors, though further in the western than in the eastern provinces. But if his edict did not make an epoch it certainly marked one. In 212 the long-standing distinction between Italians and provincials, between conquerors and conquered, was virtually obliterated, and the Roman Empire was definitely converted into a commonwealth of equal partners.[22]

European frontiers secured

Caracalla's military ambitions were mainly directed to the East. In Britain he surrendered all his father's gains (p. 492). On the Danube front he crossed swords with two German tribes which were to become the most persistent enemies of Rome, the Alamanni and the Goths. The Alamanni were a newly formed aggregate of displaced tribal groups in southern Germany. The Goths were an East German people who had moved from their former seats on the lower Vistula to the confines of the Black Sea, and now made acquaintance with the Romans in Lower Moesia. Caracalla beat off the attacks of these tribes (213–214), defeating the Alamanni near the Main, but he took no further measures against them except to complete his father's works along the Rhine and Upper Danube.

Caracalla's aggressive policy in the East

On the Euphrates frontier, on the other hand, Caracalla contemplated a resumption of Trajan's forward policy.[23] After his northern campaigns he did not return to Rome, which in the event was not to see him again, but went to settle a seditious disturbance in Alexandria (215) and then turned to the East. In Armenia, which his father had left undisturbed, he deposed the vassal-king Vologasus at a moment's notice and set up a Roman province (216). Following up a demand for the hand of King Artabanus V's daughter, which the Parthian ruler obligingly refused, Caracalla made a raid across Adiabene into Media (216). In the next year he resumed operations, no doubt with the intention of carrying Roman arms beyond the furthest limits of Trajan and Severus. But his anabasis was cut short at the outset by a group of officers who gratified their personal grievances or ambitions by assassinating him near Carrhae.

His death by murder

The ringleader of the conspirators, the praetorian prefect M. Opellius Macrinus, was a Mauretanian who had joined the Roman army as a common soldier. To save himself from the consequences of a stray prophecy that he was destined to become emperor, he made the oracle come true. He at once gave the title of Caesar to his young son Diadumenianus, who was later declared Augustus. But although he succeeded in the first instance in foisting himself upon the army and the Senate, which gave him recognition, he soon fell a victim to his own success. Resuming Caracalla's campaign against Artabanus with an army whose discipline he had undermined he lost two battles and was driven out of Mesopotamia. Fortunately for Macrinus, Artabanus, who was equally unsure of his followers, consented to a compromise on the lines of Nero's compact with Vologeses I. The Parthian king obtained an indemnity from Macrinus and secured Armenia for his kinsman Tiridates, who acknowledged his nominal dependence upon Rome. But the peace which he snatched on these terms gave Macrinus no more than a reprieve.

His successor Macrinus is defeated by the Parthians

40.8   Elagabulus. IMP(erator) ANTONINUS PIUS AUG(ustus).

In 218 the troops at Emesa in Syria set up as a rival emperor a grand-nephew of Julia Domna, the wife of Severus, named Bassianus, a youth who was chief priest of the local Baal; he was now passed off as a son of Caracalla and assumed the name of M. Aurelius Antoninus. Though only fourteen years of age, and quite unknown outside Syria, the new Antoninus carried all the eastern provinces by virtue of his adoptive parentage, and supplanted Macrinus after a short struggle which culminated in a battle near Antioch (218). The only importance of the brief and embarrassed reign of Macrinus was that he was the first emperor to be created out of the ranks of the Equites.

He is supplanted by Elagabalus

The second M. Aurelius surpassed all the other Caesars in good looks, but that was his only recommendation. A voluptuary of the stamp of Nero and Commodus, he allowed the administration to go to rack and ruin. His only serious purpose was to spread the worship of the sun-god of Emesa, whose name Elah-Gabal (Elagabalus) he adopted as an additional cognomen, and to introduce into Rome, which was

Elagabalus another Nero

not ripe for such a change, both the pomp and the servility of an Oriental court, and the cult of the sun-god to whom two magnificent temples were built. A slight check was placed upon his caprices by his masterful grandmother, Julia Maesa, who played the part of Agrippina to his Nero, and indeed outdid the older empress by taking open part in the debates of the Senate. In obedience to Maesa's warning Elagabalus sought to appease the rising anger of the capital by adopting his cousin M. Aurelius Severus Alexander and making him Caesar; but when he tried to go back upon this arrangement the household troops brought it to maturity by lynching him; his body was thrown into the Tiber.

6. Severus Alexander (222–235)

The substitution of Severus Alexander for Elagabalus did not seem at first sight a hopeful experiment, for Alexander, although studious and virtuous, had not attained the age of fourteen at his accession. But first his grandmother, Julia Maesa, until her death in 226, and then his mother, Iulia Mamaea, filled the part of Agrippina, and her son was a more obedient pupil than Nero had been. Indeed Alexander never attempted to throw off her tutelage, so that until 235 the Roman Empire had the unique experience of being ruled by an empress, herself Augusta and described as 'mother of Augustus and of the camp and the Senate and the fatherland'.

40.9 Severus Alexander.

Although Mamaea had taken a hand in the plot by which the praetorian troops made room for her son, she was clear-sighted enough to perceive that the most immediate danger to the Roman Empire lay in a renewal of military anarchy. Seeing that the expedient of buying off the soldiery with periodical increments of pay merely whetted their appetite, she fell back upon Pertinax's policy of enlisting the prestige

of the Senate to reinforce the imperial authority, and of relying on the civilian rather than the military element in the service of the government. Thus in order to increase the dignity of the Senate the imperial *consilium* was reorganised; details are obscure, but apparently sixteen senators now formed an important element in it and the Council itself may have comprised seventy members in all.[24] It also made clear that the praetorian prefect could hold senatorial rank and thus become *vir clarissimus*: Alexander's object was said to be to avoid any senator being judged by a non-senator. But while this measure might seem to confirm the claim of senators to be tried only by their peers, it also increased the judicial power of the prefect, since he could preside over senatorial trials. A distinguished jurist named Domitius Ulpianus was appointed as praetorian prefect and head of the entire administration. Thus although the Senators regained some dignity and in Dio's phrase remained 'the ornament of the State', the praetorian prefect and the largely equestrian imperial bureaucracy remained the chief civil authority, while not far behind the scenes the army still held ultimate control. The view expressed in the literary sources of Alexander's reign as a reversal of the reliance placed by Septimius and Caracalla upon the army and Equestrian Order, and therefore as a restoration of senatorial government, must remain unreal.

Nevertheless under the rule of Alexander and his mother Mamaea the Roman Empire enjoyed a dozen years of comparative stability, which made his reign appear to later writers as a golden interlude between two troubled periods and so gave birth to a second 'Alexander romance'.[25] The administration of Alexander was by its very nature committed to a peaceful policy, and it succeeded in avoiding any serious frontier disturbance for the first ten years of the reign. Its chief object was to win the general support of the civilian population by judicious generosities. For the benefit of the Roman populace it provided, besides the now inevitable regular doles and special *congiaria*, and an additional superfluity of public baths with the completion of Caracalla's vast *thermae*, a new scheme for the regulation of the city's supply services. It organised the special *collegia* of persons engaged in the industries and trades that provided for the needs of the capital, so that their work was carried on under official supervision. This experiment marked a new departure in the economic policy of the Roman government, which had hitherto avoided interference in commerce and manufacture except on political grounds, but found itself committed henceforth to a pervasive control (p. 501). Resuming the second-century emperors' policy of productive benevolence Alexander's government extended the alimentary institutions in Italy; it subsidised teachers and scholars; and it remitted taxes in favour of improving landlords. The revenue which it required for this liberal policy was partly raised by dint of a rigid economy at court – with a view to saving expenses it was even proposed to put the entire palace staff into uniform – and the imperial finances stood the strain of the additional outlay.

Insubordination of the Guards

But the main test of Alexander's government was whether it could put an end to military mutinies. The early years of his reign passed without serious disorder; but in 228 (if not earlier) the prefect Ulpianus was murdered by his own men, and another good disciplinarian, Dio Cassius, would not have lived to complete the history of Rome (p. 544), had the emperor not given him a peremptory if honourable dismissal. By this concession Alexander purchased a precarious armistice from his soldiers, until . the renewal of foreign war, instead of confirming their discipline, broke it down altogether.

Fall of the Arsacid monarchy

About 230 the Parthian monarchy, which had once been Rome's most formidable enemy, fell to pieces through internal weakness which had been increased by Septimius's invasion. Its Arsacid dynasty had been continually rent by internal dissensions, and it shared the fate of the late Manchu dynasty in China, of never being able to live down its foreign origin. By concessions of provincial autonomy to its outlying subjects it put off the day of dissolution, but eventually it was deposed by a rebellious vassal in southern Persia named Ardashir (Artaxerxes), who overcame Artabanus V (227) and gathered all the Parthian dominions into his hands. The new 'Sassanid' dynasty, so called from the grandfather of Ardashir, derived its strength from a temporary revival of national patriotism in Persia, and of its concomitant religion, the doctrine of Zoroaster.[26] Its founder Ardashir therefore assumed the heritage of the Achaemenid kings who had once ruled from the Indus to the Isthmus of Corinth, and claimed the reversion to their power. In 230 the Persian king began to battle for the lost Achaemenid provinces by setting siege to Nisibis. In the following year Alexander and his mother in person took charge of a Roman counter-attack. In conjunction with the Armenian king Chosroes, who had stood out successfully against Ardashir, he attempted a triple invasion of Persia through Armenia, Mesopotamia and Babylonia, in which he achieved but a half-success. Though he overawed Ardashir into a speedy cessation of hostilities he incurred heavy losses, and he failed to acquire the authority over his own troops

Aggression of its successors, the 'Sassanids'

Severus Alexander's campaign in the East

which a decisive victory would have given him; however, he held a magnificent triumph after his return to Rome in 233.

In 234 Alexander had to undertake a campaign against the Alamanni, who had resumed their incursions while the emperor was preoccupied with the Persian War, thus presenting the Roman world with the threat of war on two fronts. Alexander concentrated an army at Moguntiacum, but the growing insubordination of his troops compelled him to buy off the Germans with a danegeld. Before he could reconstitute his forces an ambitious upstart on his staff, a Thracian peasant named C. Iulius Maximinus, fomented a riot in which Alexander and his mother were killed. In committing this double murder the mutineers plunged the Roman Empire into half a century of military anarchy and all but caused its premature dissolution.

His murder on the Rhine front

7. The Severan Age

The military monarchy of the Severan period stands out clearly defined between the earlier Antonine monarchy of the 'good emperors' and the later period of military anarchy. The emperor was no longer regarded as a servant of the state, but its dominating head.[27] Thus when Macrinus and Elagabalus were accepted by the troops, they merely notified the Senate of their accession and did not allow this body any traditional share in the granting of power. More often, however, the Senate was allowed to go through the motions, and even Macrinus asked the Senate to declare Elagabalus a public enemy. But the nature of the Senate, no less than that of the emperors, was changing; its numbers increased to 900 under the Severi, and the Italian element decreased. There was much absenteeism: many senators had estates in the provinces and lived there as great landowners. The Senate lost all freedom of discussion and submitted to the monarchical initiative of the emperor. It ceased to legislate as the emperor became the sole source of new law, and it approved by acclamation decrees drafted on his orders and read to it by his quaestor (the *oratio principis*). Power had gone, but prestige remained.

The Senate

The backgrounds and personalities of the emperors made it extremely difficult for them to appreciate the constitutional traditions of Rome. Even the best of the Severi were more concerned with efficiency and the safety of the Empire: hence equestrian officials and soldiers came first. The emperor, who through his *constitutiones* was the sole source of law, was himself free from the law (*princeps legibus solutus est*, pronounced the lawyer Ulpian), although Paul

Autocratic emperors

(under Severus Alexander) did emphasise that the emperor should set an example of living in accordance with the laws. The emperor had also become the ultimate judicial authority and the final court of appeal, with the praetorian and urban prefects acting as his immediate representatives. The praetors' *quaestiones* did not survive the Severi, while the consuls were overshadowed by the imperial prefects, and the aedileship and tribunate dropped out of the *cursus honorum*. The people had of course for generations ceased to play any constitutional role; their voice was now confined to an occasional angry outburst, for instance against Plautianus in the theatre or against Macrinus in the circus. Finally mention should be made of the main policy-making body, the *Consilium*, where jurisconsults played an increasingly important part (some, as Papinian and Ulpian, doubled the role of councillor with that of praetorian prefect). Apart from their day-to-day advice to the emperor their work was of great importance: they consolidated Roman legal science and established the standard for later generations, thus bringing to an end the so-called 'classical' period of Roman law.

Role of the army

The rule of the Severi can be called a military monarchy in a sense that Augustus's rule had never been. True, Augustus's power had rested ultimately upon control of the army, but he had subordinated it to the civil authority. Under the Severi the army, which had been provincialised, overshadowed the civilians. It was the decisive force in the creation of an emperor. However, after this critical act it exercised little direct influence on constitutional development, provided that its demands were met. But this need to meet its financial requirements tended to increase the centralised control of the emperor and to give priority to the military rather than to the civilian aspects of administration: hence the beginning of the distinction between military and civil careers, with equestrians displacing senators in the army and the imperial provinces.

Italy and the provinces

The privileged position of Italy in regard to the provinces had been seriously diminished even before Caracalla took the final step of raising the provinces to its level. While consuls and praetors still had some authority in Rome, the rest of Italy was administered by agents of the emperor: procurators, curators, prefects and the like. For long the emperor had interfered in local government in Italy as well as in the provinces, but in 216 we find a *corrector* of Italy appointed (*ad corrigendum statum Italicum: ILS*, 1159); later, from the time of Aurelian, such *correctores* became regular officials. Municipal life, however, although more centrally regulated, continued to flourish both in Italy and the provinces, as witnessed by an inscription of A.D. 223 which lists the local Senate at Canusium,[28] and by Septimius's grant of local Senates in Egypt.

Towns

Although Septimius had punished some cities, as Antioch and Byzantium, with great severity, he should not be regarded as hostile to cities as such: rather, the Severi upheld Rome's traditional policy of administering the provinces through the cities, which were more privileged than the countryside. Not only were grants of colonial status numerous, but peasants were helped along the road to urbanisation through the creation of many *castella* or *stationes*, garrisoned by the agricultural population, as illustrated by documents from Sitifis in Africa and Pizus in Thrace.[29] Inscriptions in general suggest a prosperous urban life in Africa and Syria, and to a considerable extent in Asia Minor and Egypt. The rural population, however, was often oppressed and poor. This resulted partly from a fiscal policy which put increasing pressure on the towns and had repercussions in the countryside.

The country

In some parts of the Empire various forms of pressure had created very severe economic troubles, although, as the evidence comes mainly from Egypt and Asia Minor, it would be wrong to generalise too widely: the conditions in the western provinces may have been very different. One form of abuse was the exaction of too much work from the peasants on imperial estates by the *conductores*: this evil, and its correction in one instance by Commodus, has already been illustrated from the documents relating to the *saltus Burunitanus* in Africa (p. 489); there the tenants threaten even more than a strike: 'We will flee to some place where we may live as free men'. Examples of actual flight from the land (*anachoresis*) are found in Egypt, where peasants abandoned their homes and resorted to brigandage as the result of oppression from the property-owners and undue taxation and liturgies. Septimius published a proclamation granting an amnesty and summoning all peasants in Egypt to return to their homes: on this was based an edict of the Prefect of Egypt issued in connexion with the census of A.D. 201–202. A few years later, in 207, the peasants of the village of Socnopaiou Nesos, who had returned home in accordance with emperor's instructions, complained to the administrator of their district (the *strategos* of their *nome*) that they had been driven out by members of a powerful family 'who do not pay their assessments and taxes in money and kind . . . nor have they performed any liturgy, since they intimidate the successive village secretaries'. Some petitions to Septimius from Lydia reveal a similar state of affairs: 'we shall be forced to become fugitives from the imperial estate where we were born and bred and where . . . we keep our pledges to the imperial fiscus'.[30]

Despite abuses the Empire enjoyed considerable periods of peace, thanks to the army, but the army had to be paid to be controlled. Hence the emperor, who was supreme in the realm of finance as elsewhere (the senatorial Aerarium had become merely the municipal treasury of Rome), had to squeeze more money and services where he could, as well as to resort to some depreciation of the coinage. Liturgies in the municipalities were of course nothing new, but during the second century the local *decuriones* still undertook their obligations willingly in return for the honour of the office. Gradually, however, the *munera* increased to such an extent that it became difficult to find candidates for office and eligible citizens had to be forced to present themselves for office, so that by the third century magistrates were appointed by the *decuriones*, and service on the councils became compulsory for those with the requisite property qualifications. These men were now responsible for collecting the taxes due from their municipalities to the imperial government. Committees of ten (*decaprotoi* or *decem primi*) were appointed by the councils to collect the revenues with the responsibility of themselves making good any deficiencies; although they had previously made an occasional appearance, they now became a permanent feature. The municipal liturgies took three forms. *Munera patrimoniorum* taxed property and involved, for example, holding priesthoods, or providing transport or billets for the imperial army. *Munera mixta* were mainly personal but could involve payment of money, while the *munera personalia* subjected the victim to many menial jobs, as caring for public buildings, providing grain or oil, or supplying horses for the imperial service. All this resulted in a vicious circle: the townsfolk tried to exact more from the countryside, where the oppressed peasants often fled to escape the burdens, and this in turn meant that the municipalities had to put greater compulsion on their own members. And the position was still further aggravated by the great number of exemptions that were granted, nominally to people who helped the state in other ways; members of the imperial nobility, officials in the state bureaux, agents collecting taxes on the imperial estates and the *coloni* on them, serving soldiers, and members of some *collegia*, as shipowners (*navicularii*) and firemen (*centonarii*), all were exempt. Immunity from the personal *munera* was granted to people over seventy, women, fathers

of five children, veterans, doctors, schoolmasters and professors of philosophy. Hence the remainder of the population felt the burden still more heavily.[37] The increasing demand for payment in kind for troops and officials and a decrease in the importance of a fixed cash tribute was accompanied by more frequent demands for *aurum coronarium*; this payment, originally a gold crown, but later a special tax, was offered to emperors by communities on special occasions such as accessions, anniversaries or adoptions. Although partly remitted by some emperors (as Hadrian and Antoninus), it bore heavily during many reigns, as under Caracalla.

Mention has been made of the *collegia*, which played an important role in Roman life. As has been seen, some trade-gilds may go back to the regal period, while Clodius had cashed in on their political possibilities (pp. 47, 265). Thereafter Augustus had enacted that every club must be registered, and their growing importance even in the early Principate is illustrated by the central position, beside the Forum, at Pompeii which was allocated during Tiberius's reign for the building of an impressive headquarters for the gild of fullers, donated by their patroness, the priestess Eumachia. Their function was primarily social rather than designed to improve their economic status, but many were formed by men practising the same trade or craft. Burial clubs (*collegia funeratica* or *tenuiorum*) received wide sanction, but they were sometimes regarded with perhaps unnecessary suspicion: thus Trajan forbade all clubs in Bithynia. These associations, whose main activities were social (e.g. dining together), were often professional corporations and, as such, attracted the interest of the emperors; during the second century they were used for helping public services, as fire-brigades or transporting food or troops, whereas previously Rome had depended as far as possible on private initiative for securing public service, except in such vital sectors as the corn-supply which had been placed under official control. Under Septimius the state undertook the distribution of oil, and professional gilds, as shipowners (*navicularii*), bakers (*pistores*), pork merchants (*suarii*), wine merchants (*vinarii*), were officially encouraged by the grant of exemption from some municipal obligations. This encouragement had already been given under M. Aurelius, so that it was a short step when under Severus Alexander the state assumed the initiative in supervising the gilds.[32]

The age of the Severi saw not only basic changes in government and public life, but society was subjected to stronger eastern influences and became more cosmopolitan. Interest in philosophy and religion increased, while literature and the arts were not neglected. The extent of this can be seen by merely listing the names of the 'intellectuals' whom it was once supposed the empress Julia Domna gathered around herself in a literary circle: Philostratus, the biographer of sophists; the lawyers Papinian, Ulpian and Paul; the historians Dio Cassius and Marius Maximus; the doctors Serenus Sammonicus and the aged Galen; the poets Oppian and Gordian (probably the later Gordian I, rather than II); Athenaeus the Deipnosophist; and the Peripatetic philosopher Alexander of Aphrodisias. Such a catalogue reflects something of the intellectual range of the period, but not a true picture of the salon of Julia Domna, which can no longer be compared with one of the Italian princely courts of the Renaissance.[33] There was a circle around Julia, whose intellectual interests are also attested by the fact that she summoned the great Christian theologian and critic Origen, to visit her in Antioch. But while she no doubt assembled some philosophers and sophists and was visited by other men of varied interests, the only outstanding 'permanent' members of a coterie that can be established are Philostratus and a Thessalian sophist named Philiscus.

The 'circle' of Julia Domna

Sophists, doctors and lawyers made considerable contributions to the literature as well as to the life of the age. Little Latin poetry was produced, but in prose Latin was the language of the great jurists and, although the earliest

Literature

Christian 'apologies' had been in Greek, Tertullian became the father of Christian Latin literature, to be followed closely by Minucius Felix.[34] In Greek both Clement of Alexandria and Origen, who succeeded him as head of the Catechetical School in 203, made notable contributions to Christian literature, and pagan works included the history of Dio Cassius, the Lives of the Sophists and of Apollonius of Tyana by Philostratus, the Lives of the Philosophers by Diogenes Laertius, the Natural History by Aelian, the Deipnosophistai by Athenaeus (a wide-ranging discussion set at a banquet). The influential Platonic philosopher Ammonius Saccas of Alexandria wrote nothing, while poetry is represented by a work on fishing, the Halieutica by Oppian.

There was considerably more building in Rome under the Severi than under their immediate predecessors; it was mainly traditional but did not lack some glimpses of future developments. Of the new baths, those of Caracalla even in their ruins reflect something of the power and wealth of Rome, as do the massive arched substructures which supported the new palace buildings on the Palatine. Another building was the camp of the Equites Singulares, the imperial bodyguard, now beneath the Church of St John Lateran. The design of Severus's Arch in the Forum was traditional enough, but its panels look forward to later fashions, while Caracalla's temple to Sarapis with 'Asiatic'-type ornament and that of Elagabalus to Sol Invictus are reminders of the new eastern cults. In the provinces

Architecture

40.10   The Baths of Caracalla. They were dedicated in A.D. 216. This concrete architecture is, for size, one of the most impressive monuments of ancient Rome.

Tripoli in particular benefited from the birth of Septimius in Lepcis Magna: here a whole new monumental quarter was added to the city, consisting of an enclosed harbour, a bath-building, a colonnaded street, a piazza with fountain, a basilica, and a forum in which stood a large temple dedicated to the Severan family. Although built in the Romano-Hellenistic tradition, it also has a cosmopolitan air which spoke of the future.[35]

Art

Portraiture continued to maintain a high standard, both in the round and on coins and medallions; thus a bust of Caracalla, now in Berlin, shows all his ruthless cruelty in realistic mode. The tradition of historical reliefs was carried on not only on Septimius's Arch in Rome, but on the great four-way Arch at Lepcis, depicting the ceremonies enacted when the imperial family visited the city (*c.* 203). Two features of these friezes are insistence on the frontality of the chief figures, designed to rivet the onlookers' attention, and the monotonous rows of tiered frontal figures; the work was probably that of Asiatic artists. Painting of this period can be illustrated from domestic wall-paintings at Rome and Ostia, and from the well-known painting on wood of Septimius, his wife and sons, all frontal and bejewelled. Two other forms of art which flourished for a long time but not least in the Severan age are sculptured sarcophagi and mosaics; some of the most attractive of the latter come from Roman Africa and include many scenes of hunting and of agricultural life.[36]

Religion

Of the religious currents of the third century more will be said in a later chapter (Ch. 43), but brief reference must be made to the special contribution of the Severi which derived from their eastern origins. Temples were built to new gods: to the African Bacchus and Hercules, Sarapis, Dea Suria and perhaps the Carthaginian Caelestis by Septimius, and to Sarapis by Caracalla. Then Elagabalus transferred to Rome the black conical stone fetish of his sun-god of Emesa and enthroned it on the Palatine; he tried to mate it to Vesta and make it the chief deity of the Roman world. His action arose probably more from personal devotion to his local Baal than to an attempt to increase his own authority by linking it to a solar monotheism. The cult of the Sun had been popular since Septimius's reign, but its followers were not willing to identify the object of their worship with the god of Elagabalus; not until the reign of Aurelian did Sol gain a unique place in Rome.[37] However, the fanaticism of the licentious Elagabalus, abetted by his mother Julia Soaemias, was countered by the virtuous Alexander and his mother Julia Mamaea. Alexander sent the Syrian sun-god back to Emesa and showed great tolerance towards all cults, including Christianity, since he recognised each as an individual expression of a universal truth and one supreme deity. Alexander is even alleged to have had two shrines in his palace, one belonging to Orpheus, Abraham, Christ and Apollonius, the other to Virgil, Cicero and those of his own ancestors who had benefited humanity. Thus the period of the Severi ended on a note of religious syncretism in an increasingly cosmopolitan society, in which more interest was shown in intellectual, moral and spiritual matters than in politics, and one which turned naturally to a cosmopolitan pantheon.

PART VI

The Decline of the Roman Empire

CHAPTER 41

The Crisis of the Empire in the Third Century

1. Military Anarchy in Permanence

The fifty years that followed the death of Severus Alexander constitute a dark age in a double sense. They were a period of disaster and of crisis for the Roman Empire, and the record which they left of themselves is scanty and broken.[1]

Maximinus   The pretender who supplanted Alexander, C. Iulius Maximinus, resembled Macrinus, the

41.1 Maximinus.

murderer of Caracalla, in being an obscure provincial (from Thrace), who had begun his career amid the rank and file and had risen to equestrian rank.[2] Unlike Macrinus, he had pursued a purely military career and he was thoroughly competent in his own profession (and, incidentally, a man of immense physical strength). After crushing two mutinies among the northern troops, he partly justified his usurpation by restoring order on the Rhine (with a victory over the Germans in Württemberg in 235) and on

the Danube frontier (236–237). Meantime he had secured the removal of some of Alexander's counsellors and incurred the veiled antagonism of the Senate. Need for money – he had promised to double his troops' pay – led to oppression, and fiscal pressure led a group of landowners in Africa to kill the emperor's procurator; a general revolt resulted in the proclamation of M. Antonius Gordianus, the proconsul of Africa, as emperor (March 238). Said to be descended from the Gracchi and from Trajan, this 80-year-old nobleman would be acceptable to the Senate, which proceeded to appoint a committee of twenty of its members in order to help in the defence of Italy against Maximinus and possibly also in the hope of balancing the power of Gordian, who had immediately nominated his son and namesake as co-regent (Gordianus II). However, almost at once, in April, both the Gordians perished in a local war against the governor of Numidia, who sided with Maximinus. Undismayed by the death of its friend, the Senate set up two members of its commission, both elderly men, M. Clodius Pupienus Maximus and D. Caelius Balbinus, as joint emperors, possibly recalling the joint authority of the consuls of the Republic. Whereupon Maximinus, who had hitherto ignored the Senate and not visited Rome, marched on Italy from Pannonia, but he met with an unforeseen resistance. With a patriotic ardour that recalled the robust days of the Republic the Italians rallied to the defence of the Senate against the 'barbarians', and the praetorian cohorts gave momentary support to the Senate against the line troops. While the invader was making a

Maximinus is defied by the Senate

The Senate's counter-emperors: Gordian I and II;

Pupienus and Balbinus

Fiasco of Maximinus's invasion of Italy

vain attempt to reduce the frontier town of Aquileia his supply columns were cut off, and his famished army purchased its own safety by murdering him (June 238), together with his son Maximus whom he had named as Caesar three years before.

In a situation like that which followed upon the death of Caesar the Senate had snatched a sudden ascendancy out of the rivalries of different armies. But once again it was deserted in the hour of victory by its own supporters, for Maximinus had hardly been disposed of than the Guards killed Pupienus and Balbinus and forced upon the Senate a new emperor, a grandson of Gordianus I, who was a boy of some thirteen years (July 238). This sudden fancy of the household troops proved wiser than they knew, especially when in 241 Gordian III chose as praetorian prefect and adviser a very capable administrator and disciplinarian named C. Furius Timesitheus.[3] In 242 Gordian, with Timesitheus, went to the East to repel an invasion by Ardashir's son Shapur I (Sapor), who had captured Carrhae and Nisibis and was threatening Antioch. But Timesitheus's sudden death by disease in 243 delivered Gordian into the hands of the new praetorian prefect, an officer of Arab race named M. Iulius Philippus, who treacherously stirred up a mutiny and supplanted the young emperor in the now familiar brutal manner (244). The usurper was fortunate enough to negotiate a peace with Shapur, by which the frontier was secured.[4] He then turned to the northern front where he defeated German tribes (246) and the Carpi in Dacia (247). By raising his son, now aged ten, to the rank of Augustus, and other measures, he showed clearly that he hoped to establish a dynasty. He came to a good understanding with the Senate, governed well, and lived long enough to celebrate in 248 with becoming splendour the millennary of Rome's birth. But the habit of treason had now fastened like a cancer upon the Roman army. Among a whole crop of fresh pretenders a Pannonian officer, named C. Messius Decius,

The Guards set up Gordian III, who is killed by Philip the Arabian

41.3 Decius.

had his hand forced by his troops and left his command in Dacia to invade Italy.[5] Failing to come to terms with Philip he defeated him in a set battle near Verona; Philip was killed and his young son also either fell or was murdered by the praetorians in Rome (249). Decius was welcomed by the Senate and apparently even granted by it the name of Traianus: at any rate he was accepted, while his short administration was marked by a persecution of the Christians (p. 546).

Decius supplants Philip

In deserting his post on the Danube Decius handed over the Balkan peninsula to a swarm of Goths and kindred tribes, which were now being driven on by the pressure of the Alans, a nomadic people from the Asiatic steppe, to secure a permanent footing on Roman territory. The new emperor, it is true, hurried back to repel the invaders, who had meanwhile been scouring Thrace as far as Philippopolis, which fell to their siege. But after a defeat and a victory he was defeated by the Gothic king Cniva at Abrittus in the Dobrudja and perished (251). The disaster which overtook Decius was possibly due to the calculating disloyalty of the governor of the two Moesias, C. Trebonianus Gallus, who was proclaimed emperor by his own troops. Gallus, through weakness, patched up a shameful peace with the Goths, and received recognition from the Senate on a visit to Rome; his son Volusianus ruled as joint Augustus with him. But his successor in the Moesian command, a Moor named M. Aemilius Aemilianus, two years later turned the tables on him, and this with a good warrant, for instead of conniving at Cniva's raid he had driven the invader out of Moesia (253). Another civil war, whose scene was again laid in Italy, ended in the defeat and death of Gallus at Interamna (Terni). Aemilianus now endeavoured to insure himself against further mutiny by extending a hand to the Senate, but his own soldiers cut short these overtures by lynching him after a rule of three months. In the endless chain of imperial murders he that slew the slayer's slayer had the

Gothic invasion of the Balkans

New emperors: Trebonianus Gallus, Aemilianus and Valerianus

41.2 Philip.

41.4   Valerian.

shortest respite before he himself was slain. His place was taken by the last representative of the old republican nobility among the emperors, P. Licinius Valerianus, who had been appointed 'censor' in the days of Decius and had served as his vicegerent at Rome in virtue of this ghostly office (253).

2. The Empire Invaded

In proclaiming Valerian emperor the troops had blundered upon a man of integrity who won the confidence of the Senate and restored some measure of discipline in the military forces. But it was his misfortune that upon him fell with cumulative weight the stored-up effects of the chronic military anarchy of recent years. The complete disorganisation of the Roman frontier defences could no longer escape the covetous eyes of the border peoples. On the European continent the trickle of marauders which had never ceased since the days of Severus Alexander now swelled into a flood, and the history of Civilis's revolt was repeated on a larger scale and with more lasting consequences. The line of the Danube was carried at either end by Goths and Alamanni. On the lower Rhine, which had been immune from serious invasion since the days of Civilis, the Franks, an extensive new tribe that had coalesced out of fragments of Cherusci, Chatti and other old opponents of Rome, broke into European history with devastating force (256). About this time also another newly formed tribe, the Saxons of the Jutish and Frisian coasts, first ventured into the English Channel with their pirate cutters. On the Euphrates front Shapur took his opportunity in Rome's self-inflicted difficulty. Whether these attacks on different fronts were concerted or not – the lack of strict synchronism between them makes it appear improbable that there should have been any understanding between the invaders – the Roman defences were everywhere caught at a disadvantage. Nature too intervened: for nearly twenty years from the time

Loss of Danube and Rhine frontiers

of Gallus, a plague raged in different parts of the Empire. By 262 it reached Italy and Africa (where native risings also occurred). The plague is alleged to have carried off 5000 victims a day in Rome.

When Valerian, who was proclaimed in Raetia, reached Rome (autumn 253) he raised his son Gallienus to the rank of Augustus and made him partner of his Empire: with war threatening on two fronts, on the whole length of the Rhine–Danube line and against Persia, a supreme commander was needed in at least two places at once. While Valerian was preparing to meet Shapur, Gallienus successfully beat back the Alamanni on the Rhine frontier (254–256), and when his father left for the East (256 or 257) he was appointed ruler of the Western Empire. The situation, however, deteriorated. Franks obtained a firm foothold in eastern and central Gaul and in north-eastern Spain, and the Alamanni broke through into Italy itself. Gallienus hastened south and defeated the invaders near Milan (probably 258 or 259), but he had to turn back to the threatened Danube frontier to suppress a pretender named Ingenuus, the governor of Pannonia, at Mursa. No sooner was this done than a second pretender named Regillianus appeared, but he soon suffered the same fate (260). Meantime, Gallienus's general C. Latinius Postumus quarrelled with his colleague in Cologne, who was acting in the name of Gallienus's young son Saloninus, and stormed the city, killing Saloninus, who had been proclaimed Augustus. True, Postumus managed to hold the Rhine frontier, but control of the Agri Decumates (the link between Rhine and Danube) was lost. Soon Gallienus learnt that the governors of Spain and Britain were transferring their allegiance to Postumus, while from the East came the grave news that his father Valerian had been captured by the Persians and that an officer named Macrianus, who had rallied the Roman troops, had proclaimed his two sons Macrianus and Quietus emperors, feeling himself too old for the responsibility. In

Gallienus on the Rhine and Danube fronts

Pretenders

41.5   Gallienus.

The 'Thirty Tyrants'

name Gallienus was now sole emperor, but his empire was crumbling beneath his feet. Pretenders were springing up like mushrooms in this province and that. Of these 'thirty tyrants', as they were called with pardonable exaggeration (nine seem authenticated during Gallienus's reign), the majority were easily disposed of: in some instances their own troops speedily rounded upon them. But they were symptoms of the weakness of the Roman world in face of increasing and widespread barbarian attacks. Many areas, feeling themselves neglected by the central authority (as did the Danube area when Gallienus was on the Rhine), saw their safety only in the creation of an Augustus of their own, and some men must have begun to ask themselves whether the whole Empire could much longer be governed by one man alone.

In the East both Goths and Persians were on the attack, although unfortunately the chronology of their movements remains uncertain in many details. Valerian arrived in the East (probably in 256, though some would date it two or three years earlier) and found a troubled world on his northern flank.[7] In 254

Raids by Borani and Goths

Goths had raided Moesia and Thrace as far as Thessalonica, while in 256 the Borani, a Sarmatian people from southern Russia, secured ships from the Bosporan kingdom and raided the eastern Black Sea coast and captured Trapezus. Then followed a southward advance by the Goths, who captured Chalcedon and carried out extensive raids in Asia Minor. Valerian sent an officer to check them, but plague and news of the advance of Shapur diverted his attention. For several years Shapur had been pressing westward. He managed to get rid of the obstinate Armenian king Chosroes by assassination and replaced him by one of his own partisans. In an inscription in Persian and Greek which Shapur set up he claimed to have occupied Antioch, Apamea and Seleuceia, among other places, and to have defeated the Romans in a battle at Barbalissos on the middle Euphrates, while Dura-Europas on the river fell in 256.[8] Whatever the extent of his advance, contrary to the custom of the more tolerant Arsacids, he attempted to cow the population by a display of frightfulness. Valerian finally took action, although his army was decimated by plague, and he advanced into

The Sassanids overrun Syria

41.6 The surrender of the emperor Valerian to the Persian king Shapur, A.D. 260. A rock relief in the province of Fars in Iran.

Mesopotamia. He possibly suffered a reverse near Edessa, and at any rate determined to negotiate for peace. Various accounts of what happened became current. The most probable is perhaps that the negotiations, like those following upon the defeat of Crassus at the neighbouring site of Carrhae, ended in a breach of faith on the part of Shapur, who abducted Valerian and kept him in captivity until his death (260). Shapur's own version is that he defeated and personally captured Valerian. Well might the Persian show on rock-hewn reliefs, which still survive, the Roman emperor on his knees before the Great King on horseback.

Capture of Valerian

Rome's eastern provinces now lay open to Shapur, who captured Tarsus and Antioch once again, but he was checked by the forces which Macrianus (p. 509) managed to rally. After widespread raiding he withdrew, since he had to face attack from Odaenathus, a nobleman of Palmyra whom he had alienated. For Gallienus the situation was critical. Macrianus, who could expect no help from him, had proclaimed his independence in Syria and was supported by Asia Minor and Egypt, while Postumus was creating an independent empire based on Gaul. Thus Gallienus's writ ran only in Italy, Africa and in the Danubian provinces: the unity which Augustus had given to the Mediterranean world might well appear to have collapsed.

Threats to the unity of the Empire

Now sole official emperor (260), Gallienus rallied to his task. Macrianus foolishly was not content with the East, but hankered after the whole Empire. He set out for Europe, but was defeated and killed, together with his son Macrianus, by Gallienus's general Aureolus in Illyricum or Thrace. However, his other son Quietus and the praetorian prefect Ballista remained to be dealt with in Asia, so Gallienus wisely made overtures to Odaenathus, although the latter had declared himself king of Palmyra and thus independent of Rome. By granting him the title of *dux Orientis* and the command of all Roman forces in the East Gallienus secured his co-operation, which resulted in the speedy suppression of Quietus and Ballista.

Gallienus recovers the East through Odaenathus

The city of Palmyra in the next twenty years made a flight like that of a rocket across the political firmament. Situated in an extensive oasis in the desert of northern Arabia Palmyra was the principal station on the caravan route from Damascus to Seleucia, which offered the shortest cut from Antioch into the Asiatic continent. With the growth of the trans-continental trade in the second century the city attained the summit of its prosperity, and it was treated with marked favour by successive Roman emperors. In return for the protection which its well-found corps of mounted archers gave

The city-kingdom of Palmyra

to the trading parties, it was authorised to levy transit dues upon all the traffic through its territory; it was raised to the status of a Roman colony by Septimius Severus; and its leading citizens, who were of Arabian race, but tinctured with Roman culture, received the Roman franchise.[9] In a war between the Caesars and the Sassanids the economic interests of Palmyra naturally ranged it on the side of Rome against the Persians, since the Sassanids, unlike the Arsacids, interrupted the trans-continental traffic.

P. Septimius Odaenathus, now nominally the agent of Gallienus in an East in which Roman supremacy was theoretically restored, in 262 and subsequent years recovered Mesopotamia (and Armenia?) for the Romans and all but captured Ctesiphon; he was granted the title of *imperator*. But after he died in 267/8, the victim of a dynastic plot, the rising strength of Palmyra became

Odaenathus is succeeded by Zenobia

41.7 Zenobia.

a menace to Rome. While Odaenathus's prerogatives, municipal and imperial, passed into the hands of his insignificant son Vaballathus, who received none of his father's titles from Rome except recognition as king of Palmyra, the actual government was taken over by his widow Zenobia, who combined perfect Greek scholarship with a personal ambition like that of the last Cleopatra. With her advent to power Roman ascendancy in the East was once more placed in jeopardy.

Meanwhile Postumus, who defeated some Franks and Alamanni, was building up his *imperium Galliarum* to embrace western Europe which he maintained for nearly ten years. His uprising was not a national revolt; he struck coins bearing the legend 'Roma Aeterna' and followed the example of Sertorius in constituting a counterfeit Senate. He held a consulship five times, and created his own Praetorian Guard, which he stationed in Trier where he resided; here and at Cologne he established mints. In fact his position might be compared with that of a count palatine in a large medieval

Postumus's Gallic Empire

41.8 Postumus.

monarchy. But Gallienus, who naturally viewed him in the same light as Vespasian had regarded Iulius Classicus (p. 418), treated him as an open enemy, the more so when in later years Postumus used the coin-legend 'Restitutor Orbis' in place of 'Restitutor Galliarum'. In 268 Postumus defeated a rebel named Laelianus in Moguntia-cum, but succumbed to assassination; he was succeeded by a certain M. Marius and then by M. Piavonius Victorinus. Postumus's usurpation had weakened the central authority of Gallienus, but he had held the Rhine frontier against the Germans and thus saved the western provinces. Meantime the Goths had invaded the Balkans and reached Athens; though they were driven back, the presence of Gallienus himself was required (262). Then after a few years in Rome the emperor had to return to Greece to handle an invasion of the Heruli, a Germanic people who had earlier been expelled from Scandinavia by the Danes and now appeared both on the Rhine and in the Black Sea area. In 268 they captured Athens, despite the efforts of an Attic commander named Dexippus (his *Scythica* and *Chronica*, now lost, gave an excellent account of this period).[10] However, Gallienus finally met and defeated the invaders on the Nessus, but he had to hasten back to Italy where his general M'. Acilius Aureolus, whom he had left in charge of operations against Postumus, abandoned his post in order to march upon Rome. Gallienus hurried back in time to head him off and pen him up in Milan, but some Illyrian officers, including the future emperors Claudius and Aurelian, formed a conspiracy and Gallienus was murdered (268).

The literary tradition is in the main hostile to Gallienus, primarily because of his supposed enmity with the Senate, shown by his exclusion of senators from military commands, and partly because he was made a scapegoat for the troubles of his age.[11] But on these counts his conduct, if not blameless, was at least understandable. When the world was disintegrating around him, he needed officers chosen for their efficiency

Gothic invasion of Greece

Murder of Gallienus

The reign of Gallienus

rather than birth, while the problems were probably too great for any man to master quickly since resources were lacking to defeat the barbarians and regain Gaul and the East at the same time. He did in fact act with considerable vigour and success, even if the last few years after his *decennalia* showed some slackening of effort. Unlike many of the soldier-emperors of this age he was well educated and interested in literature, art and Greek culture. In fact a 'Gallienic Renaissance' has been defined in art, marked by a revival of the Antonine 'baroque' style. Gallienus followed Hadrian's example of holding the archonship at Athens and was initiated into the Eleusinian Mysteries. His concern for religion and philosophy was shown by his tolerance for Christianity, thus reversing his immediate predecessors' policy, and by his friendship for the Neoplatonist philosopher Plotinus, who hoped to persuade him to create an ideal Platonic city in Campania.

The developments during Gallienus's reign continue the trends of the age of the Severi and point forward to the reforms of Diocletian. Gallienus went further than Septimius, by transferring the command of legions from senators to equestrians: perhaps gradually rather than as the sudden result of an edict equestrian *praefecti* replaced senatorial *legati*. One effect of this was that, since *praefecti* were probably recruited from senior centurions and since common soldiers could reach the centurionate, the way to legionary command was now open to the lowest ranks. This change reacted on the position of senatorial provincial governors, who very gradually were perhaps restricted to civil administration; before long they were increasingly replaced by equestrian governors (*agentes vice praesidium*), until finally Diocletian virtually eliminated senators from provincial administration. Another office first appears under Gallienus, the *protector lateris divini*, granted to *praefecti legionum*; later junior officers received the honour and underwent special military training, thus providing skilled leadership in an army that was becoming increasingly barbarised.[12] An important reform was the development of a new cavalry corps as a highly mobile force: the existing *cataphractarii* (p. 448) were increased and supplemented by an élite body of unarmoured horsemen, the *equites Dalmatae*. Thus in many ways Gallienus prepared the way for the more radical reforms of Diocletian and Constantine.

Administrative and military reforms

3. The Frontiers Restored

In the ten years after the death of Valerianus Rome passed through its darkest hour since the

41.9   Claudius Gothicus.

battle of Cannae. But Gallienus, by not despairing of the Empire, laid the foundations of recovery, and his work was carried on by two
of his murderers, who were proclaimed
emperors in turn. His immediate successor, an
Illyrian named M. Aurelius Claudius, at once
disposed of Aureolus, and he had no difficulty
in checking another Alamannic raid, which got
no further than Lake Garda (Benacus). He then
went to Rome and was invested by the Senate.
But in 269 he was put to the test by a new.
Claudius 'Gothicus' annihilates the Gothic forces Gothic invasion, the most dangerous of all the
German inroads in the third century. Having
by now thoroughly explored the Balkan peninsula the Goths had resolved to occupy it permanently. Setting out in force, with their
families in the baggage-train, they crossed the
Danube in several relays and sailed through the
Bosporus into the Mediterranean, where they
pushed their reconnaissances as far as Cyprus.
But they received from the new emperor such
a lesson in the art of war as Scipio Africanus
or Caesar might have inflicted. Thrusting in
between their first and second wave of invaders
Claudius cut to pieces the second detachment
at Naissus (modern Nisch) in the Morava valley,
and by a resolute cross-march through the Balkan lands he intercepted the retreat of the
enemy's advance corps, while his naval squadrons made a combined drive against the sea-
raiders. Such of the invaders as did not perish
in the snows of the Balkan highlands made their
surrender and were settled as *coloni* in the vacant
spaces of the Danube provinces (269–270). This
sweeping sequence of victories removed all
serious danger from the Goths for a hundred
years to come.

In achieving this crowning mercy Claudius
'Gothicus' (as he came to be called) had to
neglect the break-away empires in West and
East. On Postumus's death Spain left the Gallo-
Roman Empire which succumbed to a fever of
military insubordination and consequent
internal unrest (p. 511), including a revolt of
Augustodunum (modern Autun) against Vic-

torinus, but the help sent by Claudius was too
weak to save the city from destruction. However,
Victorinus soon afterwards was killed and the
troops allowed the Gallic Senate to appoint a
civilian emperor named C. Pius Tetricus, who
proclaimed his peaceful disposition by transferring his capital from Augusta Trevirorum
(Trier) to Burdigala (Bordeaux). Thus Claudius
could concentrate on the Gothic danger, but
this preoccupation allowed Zenobia to extend
the Palmyrene empire by occupying Antioch
(268/9); after some setbacks her forces entered
Lower Egypt (although the Alexandrines
remained nominally subject to Rome) and then
in 270 she overran Cappadocia and Bithynia,
but failed to reach Byzantium.[13] Meanwhile
Claudius entrusted the command against the
Goths to Aurelian and was about to move to
the Danube, which was threatened by Juthungi
and Vandals, when he died of the plague (270).
The troops in Italy put forward his brother

Gaul and Palmyra

41.10   Aurelian

Quintillus to succeed him; but they removed
their own candidate by assassination on hearing
that the army in the Balkans had, with better
insight, proclaimed Claudius's compatriot and
right-hand man, L. Domitius Aurelianus. The
first act of Aurelian was to drive the Vandals
out of Pannonia and complete the reconquest
of the Danube line, the second was to recall
the remaining Roman garrisons, and such of the
civilians as preferred to retire with the Roman
forces, from the province of Dacia. Though this
country had been protected by its mountain
barriers against the full force of the German
invasions, it had not completely fulfilled its purpose as an advance outpost for the defence of
the Danube basin, and its retention merely
lengthened the line of the Roman frontier; a
new province was formed on the southern bank,
with its capital at Serdica. The new Balkan front
had hardly been secured when the Alamanni
and the Juthungi made another incursion into
Italy, in the course of which they slipped past
Ariminum (271). After a preliminary defeat
Aurelian destroyed the invaders in detail. This

Aurelian evacuates Dacia

Zenobia invades Asia Minor

victory left him free to settle accounts with Queen Zenobia, and her son Vaballathus, who in 271 took the title Augustus.[13]

While Aurelian was mounting an expedition against her, his lieutenant Probus, the future emperor, turned her flank by expelling her invading columns from Egypt (271). In the following year Aurelian swept the Palmyrenes out of Asia Minor and defeated them at Antioch. Here he arbitrated between the Christians and the heretic bishop, Paul of Samosata, whose patroness was Zenobia: Paul was expelled from the see of Antioch. The queen's forces under Zabdas rallied for another pitched battle at Emesa, but suffered a second defeat, their *clibanarii* (cavalry whose armour covered man and horse) being battered by a detachment of Palestinian 'clubmen'. Aurelian now held Syria and with the co-operation with the neighbouring Bedouin tribes he boldly transported his entire army across 80 miles of desert and put Palmyra under siege. The capture of Zenobia, who had sallied out in quest of Persian reinforcements, ended this laborious campaign, whose calculating audacity had not been seen in eastern warfare since the days of Lucullus (272). Aurelian deposed Zenobia and stationed a detachment of Roman troops in Palmyra. But he had only got back to the Danube, where he defeated the Carpi, before his garrison was massacred in a revolt fomented by the queen's kinsmen. The emperor at once retraced his steps from Thrace, where the news of the rising reached him, and pounced on the rebel city before it was ready for him. Palmyra now suffered complete destruction, and its very ruins were forgotten until the eighteenth century (273). He then had to hasten to Egypt, where a Greek merchant named Firmus was leading a revolt. This was crushed and the walls of Alexandria razed. Thus Aurelian had become the 'Restitutor Orientis': the West still had to be reduced before he could claim the title 'Restitutor Orbis'.

Aurelian's march through the desert

Capture and destruction of Palmyra

Without a pause Aurelian hurried his troops back to Europe in order to make an end of the *imperium Galliarum*, where the position of Tetricus had considerably weakened. They met at the Campi Catalaunii near Châlons-sur-Marne, where Tetricus courted defeat by deserting his troops in the heat of battle and surrendering to Aurelian (273). Tetricus and Zenobia walked in Aurelian's triumph; but with a magnanimity unparalleled in his age Aurelian gave the queen a comfortable pension and found a lucrative civil appointment for Tetricus. By his indomitable energy Aurelian had welded the Roman Empire together once more, and had earned the proud title of 'Restitutor Orbis'. In 275 he was preparing to try conclusions with the Sassanid

Aurelian recovers Gaul

'Restitutor Orbis'

monarchy when he perished at the hands of a few disaffected officers.

Aurelian, who had visited Rome in 270, spent much of the year 274 there, and introduced many reforms. The most visible was his decision to surround the city with a new wall against possible barbarian attack. This symbol of Rome's weakness at the beginning of his reign was started in 271, but was not completed until the reign of Probus. Since all available troops were needed elsewhere, the wall was built by civilian labour. It had a circumference of 12 miles, was 12 feet thick and 20 high, with eighteen gates and towers for artillery.[14] It was not designed to withstand a siege, but rather to hold back raids of barbarians who lacked siege-weapons. In 270 Aurelian had to deal with internal trouble: the mint workers, led by the mint-master Felicissimus who had 'debased the coinage', led a revolt. If there is a kernel of truth in the story that 7000 soldiers were killed fighting on the Caelian Hill, the affair appears to have been serious. Even more serious was the virtual collapse of the coinage. Gallienus had issued billon which was almost worthless, prices rocketed, trade was threatened and bankruptcy faced individuals and even the state. Aurelian called in much old money, but lacked the silver for a radical reform. He issued a new Antoninianus (of 4 per cent silver, with a silver wash) and introduced two billon coins, a single and double *sestertius*. Temporary relief may have been gained, but inflation was not stopped. However, the fall of Palmyra and restoration of the East brought some wealth, so that Aurelian cancelled arrears to the treasury and in place of the old monthly distribution of corn he provided a daily distribution of two pounds of free bread in Rome, while pork, oil and salt were distributed at regular intervals. By these measures the power of the Praefectus Annonae was increased and it is possible that the gilds of bakers and butchers were converted from voluntary to compulsory associations.

Aurelian's reforms

Aurelian, who did not suffer fools gladly (he was nicknamed 'Hand on hilt', *manu ad ferrum*), showed respect for the Senate and even asked its co-operation in building the wall and reforming the coinage, but there was no reversal of the increasing replacement of senators by equestrians in the army and civil government. His appointment of Tetricus as *corrector Lucaniae* looked back to the *iuridici* of Marcus Aurelius and forward to Diocletian's division of Italy into seven provinces. He also appointed senators as high-priests of the Sun, whose worship he officially introduced into Rome, with a temple and games (274). This cult, more sober than the excesses of Elagabalus's Sun-worship,

The Senate

Sun-worship

41.11   Aurelian's Wall at Rome, near the Porta Appia. Built of concrete, and faced with brick, the Wall
is some 12 miles long and has 381 towers.

focused the monotheistic tendencies of recent years. Aurelian sought a universal deity, of whom all local cults were individual manifestations, and at the same time hoped that the cult would act as a unifying influence through the Empire, where the imperial cult had recently been wearing a little thin. But while he showed a personal devotion to the Sun he did not try to identify himself with the god or establish a divine right to rule on that basis. In general he had served Rome so well during his short reign that his premature murder must cause regret that he lost the opportunity of carrying further his reforms in the Empire which he had reunited.[15]

The murder of Aurelian was not condoned by the troops in the usual light-hearted manner. In sudden disgust at their own wilfulness they pressed the choice of the next emperor upon a disillusioned and distrusting Senate, which reduced the army's offer *ad absurdum* by appointing against his own will a septuagenarian named M. Claudius Tacitus.[16] By a crowning paradox Tacitus took the field against

Ephemeral emperors: Tacitus and Florianus

some marauding Goths and Alans in Asia Minor and defeated them. But the spell was broken when the soldiers again smelt blood; reverting to type, they killed the senator-emperor unless in fact he died a natural death (275). The mutineers allowed the dead man's half-brother, M. Annius Florianus, to proclaim himself the next emperor (he was recognised in the western provinces), but made away with him as soon as they learnt that the other armies of the East had set up a lieutenant of Aurelian, M. Aurelius Probus, another Danubian. In this instance the soldiers chose more wisely than the Senate.

In betaking himself to Asia Minor Tacitus had overlooked a more serious inroad which was impending on the Rhine border. In his absence Alamanni and Franks descended upon Gaul on a wide front and stayed long enough to capture sixty towns; of all the Germanic invasions this onslaught struck the heaviest blow at the prosperity of Gaul. But Probus rounded upon the raiders and did not call off the pursuit until he had regained the line of the Rhine and upper Danube; he even established some forts across

Probus secures the lines of Rhine and Danube

515

the Rhine. He then campaigned against Vandals on the lower Danube (278) and in Asia Minor (279); he reached a truce with Persia, where Shapur had been succeeded by Bahram II (272). Next he returned to Gaul, where an officer named Bonosus had attoned to himself for the loss of the Rhine fleet at Cologne by proclaiming himself emperor (280); trouble may even have spread to Spain and Britain. Once this pretender had been suppressed, Probus set his hand to the

41.12   Probus.

long overdue task of economic recuperation, but in 282 when news came that the army in Raetia had proclaimed M. Aurelius Carus emperor, Probus was lynched by the Pannonian army, which he had employed, under an obsolete code of discipline, on land-reclamation. The Empire deserved well of Probus. Although he had continued the dangerous, if expedient, policy of settling barbarians within the Empire (some Scythian Bastarnae, driven from their homes by Goths, were allowed to settle in Thrace) he had crowned the work of Aurelian by continuing to restore order in the provinces and of trying to keep the army under control.

The new emperor, Carus, was a fellow Danubian of the school of Claudius and Aurelian. He had two adult sons, whom he named as Caesars. One, Carinus, he left in control of the West; the other, Numerianus, he took with him when in the following year he repeated the exploits of Trajan and Severus against the Persian king, who had reoccupied Armenia and Mesopotamia, but found his arm tied, like the former Parthian rulers, by domestic dissension. After the capture of Ctesiphon Carus intended to press on, when he was laid low by a well-aimed streak of lightning, forged no doubt in a legionary armoury. The victorious but disaffected army retired under Carus's son Numerianus, who had been nominated co-emperor by his father. On the march through Asia Minor Numerianus died as mysteriously as Carus, murdered by his father-in-law Aper, his praetorian prefect. But the troops turned to another Danubian officer named Diocles, who killed Aper with his own hand and was proclaimed emperor as C. Aurelius Valerius Diocletianus (284). Diocletian had to make good his title against Carus's elder son Carinus, who had been left in command in the West. The trial of strength between the armies of East and West ended with a hard-won victory for Diocletian on the banks of the Margus (Morava) in 285. With Diocletian's accession the Roman Empire reverted for a while to settled government. In the previous fifty years eighteen emperors on the lowest estimate had been set up and knocked down; Diocletian held power for twenty years, and when he laid down his crown he did so of his own free will.

Carus invades Mesopotamia

Numerianus: Carinus; Diocletian

CHAPTER 42

Diocletian and Constantine

1. Diocletian and the Tetrarchy

Unlike the previous soldier-emperors from the Danubian area Diocletian had no outstanding gifts as a general, although a competent soldier, but he exhibited capacity, or at any rate energy, such as was rarely found among later Roman emperors. It soon became clear that he had pondered over the problems of the Empire and had plans ready to meet them. A new start must

42.2 Maximian.

42.1 Diocletian.

be made; no longer could one emperor sit at Rome and control the whole web of interests. He must be in the field where frontiers were threatened, but his personal presence was demanded on many frontiers, since if he sent generals they might be tempted to continue the dreary process of attempted usurpation. Diocletian therefore decided to move around with his staff and court (*comitatus*) as needed (in fact throughout his reign he visited Rome only once) and at the same time to supplement his own efforts by appointing helpers of outstanding authority. In 285 therefore he named a Danubian compatriot, M. Aurelius Valerius Maxi-

mianus, as Caesar, and while himself taking the title Jovius granted that of Herculius to Maximian: the two men would act together under the shield of their patron gods, the greater god being assigned to the greater ruler, while the humble origin of the two emperors might be forgotten in the gleam of this new celestial light. In the following year Maximian was raised to the rank of Augustus as a reward for his efficient crushing of a revolt in Gaul of wandering bands of discontented peasants and others named the Bagaudae. Intermittently for the next four or five years Maximian had to contend with attacks across the upper Rhine by Alamanni and Burgundi, while further north the Franks had to be checked; in 288 a Frankish chief accepted peace in return for the title of King of the Franks. Maximian was less successful in his attempt to clear the English Channel of Saxon and Frankish pirates, since a Messapian named M. Aurelius Mausaeus Carausius, whom he had appointed as commander of a fleet based at Gesoriacum (modern Boulogne), crushed the pirates but decided to use his naval power to proclaim himself 'Augustus' and to occupy Britain, where he set up a local empire on the model

517

42.3   Carausius.

42.5   Galerius.   MAXIMIANUS   NOB(ilissimus)
Caes(ar).

*The
Tetrarchy*

of Postumus's *imperium Galliarum* (287). He was thus able to defy Maximian, who reached a working agreement with him in 290. During these years Diocletian was based at Nicomedia in Bithynia, whence he went to the Danube to defeat the Sarmatae (289 and 292), to Syria against Saracen invaders (299), and to Egypt to crush a revolt of the native Blemmyes (291). He also secured an Arsacid on the throne of Armenia without provoking Persia to war.

Although for many years Maximian had played his part well, in much the same relationship to Diocletian as Agrippa to Augustus, in 293 Diocletian carried the delegation of functions a stage further: one emperor could not be omnipresent, but four could cover more ground than two. He therefore nominated two young officers, C. Flavius Valerius Constantius (usually known as Constantius Chlorus), who was also of Illyrian–Danubian origin, and C. Galerius Valerius Maximianus to a share of the imperial power. While Diocletian and Maximian were nominally joint emperors (like M. Aurelius and L. Verus) and shared the title Augustus, Galerius and Constantius were styled Caesars and became heirs-expectant to the two senior rulers. The division of competence between Diocletian and his colleagues was made on a territorial basis. While the senior partner reserved for himself the eastern provinces he assigned Italy, Africa, Spain and the northern frontier

provinces to Maximian, whose Caesar, Constantius, received Gaul and Britain; while himself assuming responsibility for the East and Egypt, Diocletian allotted most of the Balkans to his Caesar, Galerius. The primary object of establishing this quattuorvirate was undoubtedly military, but it was also intended to provide for an orderly succession. At first sight the plan might appear as a revival of the triumvirates which had hastened rather than retarded the fall of the Republic, yet under Diocletian's supervision it worked well. By virtue of his personal authority the chief partner remained in effect sole emperor, while he secured the loyal assistance of three of the ablest military commanders. Constantius, who had been praetorian prefect, had already married Maximian's step-daughter (and put away Helena, the mother of Constantine); he was a man of statesmanlike qualities. Galerius divorced his wife in order to marry Diocletian's daughter, Valeria; he was a much rougher diamond, even if the unflattering portrait drawn by Christian writers of this persecutor of their fellow Christians is exaggerated.

Although Diocletian's reign was not free from attempted usurpations, these did not lead to any general recrudescence of civil war. In 296 an adventurer L. Domitius Domitianus with a helper named Achilleus (the two men are probably to be distinguished, not identified) assumed the imperial title in Alexandria, but was promptly crushed by Diocletian in person.[2] More serious was Carausius's claim to be a third Augustus: he must be brought to heel at last. On the whole Britain had escaped many of the troubles of the third century, except inflation, and Carausius had organised the defence of the east and south coasts against the Saxons by building some of the so-called Saxon Shore forts (e.g. at Richborough, Lympne and Portchester). However, he was murdered and supplanted by a subordinate named Allectus in 293, against whom Constantius mounted an invasion in 296. While Constantius made a demonstration in the

*Carausius
and the
British
empire
crushed*

42.4   Constantius. *Obv.* of the Arras medallion.

42.6 Aerial view of Richborough (Rutupiae) in Kent. A short stretch of the Claudian invasion ditches may be seen. The foundation (cruciform) may be the base of a triumphal monument, erected by Agricola to mark the conquest of all Britain. The main fort is that of the Saxon Shore, which can be attributed to Carausius.

Channel, his praetorian prefect, Asclepiodotus, eluded the enemy fleet in a mist and landed near Southampton Water. He then defeated Allectus's army near Silchester, while Constantius's forces sailed up the Thames just in time to save London from some of Allectus's defeated but marauding troops. Constantius's arrival (*redditor lucis aeternae*) is depicted on a famous gold medallion found near Arras.[3] Thus with the collapse of the *imperium Britanniarum* the unity of the Empire was restored.

In the absence of continuous civil wars Diocletian's colleagues were able to give a good account of themselves in frontier defence. Maximian, followed by Constantius (297–298), crushed invasions by the Alamanni in Gaul, Galerius kept order on the Danube, and Maximian in 298 subdued the Quinquegetani, a Moorish tribe in Africa (later that year Maximian appears to have visited Rome for the first time in his reign). In 296 Diocletian was called upon to defend Mesopotamia, which had been

42.7 Aerial view of Portchester in Hampshire, one of the forts of the Saxon Shore, constructed against Saxon raids. It was probably built by Carausius (A.D. 287–293). A church has been built in one corner, a castle in another.

42.8 A gold medallion found at Arras. The reverse shows the walls of London and the city of London personified in a kneeling figure, welcoming a Roman relief force. Constantius is hailed as 'the restorer of eternal light': REDDITORI LUCIS AETERNAE.

Galerius destroys a Persian army

Consolidation of gains in the East

Diocletian's retirement

ceded by the Persian king Bahram in 284. A new and vigorous king named Narses declared war. Diocletian entrusted the conduct of this Persian war to Galerius, who made good an initial defeat on open ground near Carrhae by transferring operations to Armenia, destroying Narses's army in a second battle and capturing Ctesiphon. Diocletian did not follow up his lieutenant's success, but he restored Roman suzerainty and was apparently content to let the Roman frontier lie on the line from Nisibis to Singara, with control over the whole of the upper Tigris basin. The alliance with Armenia was subsequently strengthened by the conversion of its ruler Tiridates III (261–317) to Christianity, which definitely estranged him from the Sassanids, even if it did not draw him nearer to the Caesars. With these operations the frontiers were made safe for the time being against major invasions, and an anxious period of forty years, in which crisis followed upon crisis, drew to a close. Further, the Tetrarchy had stood the strains to which it was subjected during this middle period of Diocletian's reign.

The system of Diocletian appeared to have justified itself by its results. But its success was largely due to the personal ascendancy of the emperor; for it was this, and not the system itself, that checked the ambitions of his colleagues. But he was getting old and feeling the burden of rule, while in the early years of the new century he had to face the divisive aspect of Christianity in the Empire (pp. 546 f.) and pressure from Galerius. Thus when late in 303 he went with Maximian to Rome to celebrate his twentieth anniversary as emperor he decided that both men should retire early in 305 after Maximian had celebrated his *vicennalia* in turn, and he exacted an oath from his colleague to fulfil his promise. On 1 May 305 therefore Dio-

The second Tetrarchy

cletian formally abdicated at Nicomedia and Maximian at Milan, and their Caesars, Galerius and Constantius, succeeded them as Augusti. But the appointment of two new Caesars was less easy. On a dynastic principle the two obvious candidates were Maxentius, son of Maximian, and Constantine, the bastard son of Constantius, but Diocletian did not consider the former suitable and therefore thought it wiser to pass them both by. The new Caesars were Flavius Valerius Severus, an Illyrian friend of Galerius, in the West, and C. Galerius Valerius Maximinus Daia, Galerius's nephew, in the East. By the territorial division which followed, Constantius held Britain, Gaul and Spain, and his Caesar, Severus, had Africa, Italy and Pannonia; Galerius received Asia Minor west of the Taurus Mountains, while Maximinus had the other Asiatic provinces and Egypt. Although theoretically Constantius was the senior Augustus, Galerius seemed to have got the best of the bargain, since through Severus he could

42.9 Maximinus.

control much of the West and at the same time put pressure on Constantius since he held his son Constantine at his own court. Under this arrangement the Roman Empire was virtually partitioned into separate and rival sovereignties, as in the days of the second triumvirate, and Diocletian's retirement, an act of self-denial which, in its intentions and results, recalled the abdication of Sulla, threw the constitution back into the melting pot.

2. The Rise of Constantine

While Diocletian contentedly cultivated vegetables in his great palace at Salona (modern Split) and Maximian reluctantly endured retirement in Lucania, the pattern of power changed rapidly. Constantius, who already had carried through some reconstruction in Britain, was needed there again, either to punish or anticipate attacks by the Picts (Caledonians) in the

Death of Constantius in Britain

42.10   Diocletian's Palace at Split on the Dalmatian coast, to which he retired in A.D. 305. It was a vast fortified self-contained country residence.

north of the province. He seized this chance to ask Galerius to let his son Constantine join him for the campaign; this request Galerius could scarcely refuse, unless he was prepared for civil war. Constantine, however, took no chances: he travelled by forced marches and killed the post-horses behind him, since, even if Galerius took no direct action, travelling through Severus's territory might prove hazardous. However, he safely joined his father at Boulogne early in 306 and together they carried

Gaul, where he learnt that Galerius had compromised: Severus was to be the new Augustus, but Constantine was recognised as Caesar; he acquiesced, for the moment. Civil war was averted and the tetrarchy saved.

Constantine as Caesar

Constantine's success goaded Maximian's son, Maxentius, to become the figurehead, if not the spearhead, of a revolt in Rome caused by taxation and the suppression of the Praetorian Guard (October 306). This popular movement elevated Maxentius as *Princeps* (he avoided

Maxentius's bid for power

42.11   Constantine.

42.12   Maxentius.

through a campaign which reached the north of Scotland. But after this victory Constantius died at York, and the army proclaimed Constantine as Augustus in his father's place. While awaiting Galerius's reply to a request for recognition Constantine strengthened his position by leading his main army from Britain to southern

claiming any more provocative title); he was accepted by southern Italy and Africa, but northern Italy stood by Severus. Support of the Praetorians and urban cohorts would not carry him far, so he successfully appealed to his father Maximian to come out of retirement to help him. Galerius's reaction was to order Severus to march on Rome, but Maximian resumed his title of Augustus and drove Severus back to Ravenna, where he was captured. Maxentius was proclaimed Augustus (307).

Maxentius survives Galerius's attack and Maximian's disloyalty

In order to face the expected counter-attack by Galerius, Maxentius sought the support of Constantine, whom he won over by giving him his sister Fausta in marriage and acknowledging him as Augustus in return for similar recognition. Galerius's invasion was not long delayed, and he reached as far as Interamna without opposition. However, he lacked the means for an attack on Rome itself, his troops became disaffected and he was forced to retire, while Maxentius curiously made no effort to hamper his retreat. Meantime Severus had been put to death in captivity. Maxentius next found himself double-crossed by his own father, who tried to persuade Constantine to come south in order to crush the retreating Galerius and then Maxentius. Constantine refused, although he broke off relations with Maxentius when he heard that Spain had declared for him. So the father was left to tackle his son alone: late in 307 Maximian went to Rome and, after a few months of joint rule, tried to overthrow Maxentius, tearing his purple robe from him, but he misjudged the temper of the soldiers, who rallied to the son and forced Maximian to flee to his son-in-law Constantine, leaving Maxentius in control of Rome (early 308).

Conference at Carnuntum

Galerius attempted a new settlement by appealing to the aged Diocletian to come out of his retreat and attend a conference at Carnuntum which Maximian also attended (November 308). Diocletian refused to reassume the purple and persuaded his old colleague Maximian to retire again; Galerius nominated an old companion in arms, Licinianus Licinius, to succeed Severus as junior Augustus with control of Italy, Africa and Spain (which were in fact held by Maxentius, now declared a usurper); Maximinus continued as Caesar in the East, while Constantine was demoted in rank to Caesar of Gaul and Britain. The two Caesars refused to be placated by the title of 'Sons of the Augusti',

and so in 310 Galerius had to acquiesce in their claim to be Augusti. Thus there were now four Augusti (Galerius, Licinius, Constantine and Maximinus), while Maxentius was unrecognised, although he held Italy, Africa and Spain. However, a Domitius Alexander had been proclaimed Augustus in Africa, and Spain went over to Constantine. If Galerius had reason to be satisfied with what was settled at Carnuntum, Constantine was greatly strengthened by the subsequent reshuffling.

Four Augusti

In 310 one major piece disappeared from the chess-board. Maximian, who had returned to his son-in-law Constantine in Gaul, tried to win over some troops while Constantine was busy campaigning against the Franks: the coup failed, and Constantine probably acquiesced in, if he did not order, his death. Thus a link snapped between Constantine and the 'Herculius' Augustus, who had first recognised him as Augustus, so Constantine began to look for a new basis for his authority. He propagated the idea that his father, Constantius, was descended from Claudius Gothicus, and adopted the Unconquered Sun (Sol Invictus) in place of Hercules as the patron of the dynasty. Early in 311 two claimants to power were removed. In Africa Alexander was killed by an expedition sent by Maxentius, while Galerius died after an illness which he attributed to the God of the Christians whom he had mercilessly persecuted (p. 547); a death-bed repentance resulted in an edict granting greater toleration to Christians, but not in his recovery.

Death of Maximian

and of Galerius

The four survivors played for position. Maximinus Daia overran Asia Minor before Licinius could, and then reached an agreement with him. Constantine, anticipating a struggle against Maxentius, made an agreement with Licinius (who was betrothed to his sister Constantia). This in turn drove Maximinus into the arms of Maxentius. With his immediate flank covered by Licinius, Constantine could now challenge Maxentius in Italy. Early in 312 war was declared, and Constantine advanced from Gaul.

Constantine versus Maxentius

Constantine's forces were heavily outnumbered, by at least two to one, perhaps even four to one, but he struck hard and fast. Maxentius's main forces were posted near Verona (perhaps to guard or force the Brenner Pass against Licinius). Constantine swept over the Alps by the Mont Cenis, and defeated a large force, including *clibanarii* (heavily armed cavalry) near Turin, which fell to him, while Milan surrendered. Advancing to Verona he won a decisive victory and was master of northern Italy. Maxentius prepared Rome for a siege: he got in large supplies of food and greatly strengthened the walls, but then changed his plans and

Constantine invades Italy

42.13 Licinius.

42.14 The Milvian Bridge, Rome. Here, in A.D. 312, Constantine defeated Maxentius. The Via Flaminia, built in 220 B.C., had crossed the Tiber by the Pons Mulvius, which had been rebuilt in stone in 109 B.C.; part of this can be seen in the present bridge.

Battle of the Milvian Bridge

decided to face the enemy in open battle, perhaps mistrusting the temper of the populace. He led his army northward and crossed the Tiber by the Milvian Bridge, where the Cassian and Flaminian Ways met. Following the latter along the Tiber he found his path blocked by Constantine's troops, with a strange device painted on their shields, the Chi–Rho monogram (the letter *I* with a twisted head and across it the letter *X*). Here at Red Rocks (Saxa Rubra) he was outflanked by the enemy on the Via Cassia. Hemmed in between hills and river Maxentius himself and thousands of his men perished in the river. On the next day, 29 October 312, Constantine entered Rome, while Maxentius's head was carried on a lance in order to show all that he was really dead. Soon after his victory Constantine proclaimed his allegiance to the Cross, by erecting a statue of himself, holding a cross, with an inscription which read (according to Eusebius): 'By this sign of salvation, the true mark of valour, I saved your city and freed it from the yoke of the tyrant.' And on the Arch, which still stands to commemorate the victory, can be read the words: 'because of the promptings of the Divinity and the greatness of his soul ['instinctu divinitatis, mentis magnitudine'] he with his forces avenged the commonwealth . . .'

The 'conversion' of Constantine to Christianity

In invading Italy Constantine had undertaken a great risk, which he may have faced because of a growing faith in the Christian God. Since the edicts of Diocletian in 303 Christians had been rigorously persecuted in the eastern

part of the Empire, but Constantine followed his father's example of not pressing them too hard in the West (p. 547). Then came news that Galerius, in defeat, had reversed his cruel policy with an edict of toleration (p. 547). This seeming victory of the God of the Christians apparently made a deep impression on Constantine. According to Lactantius, on the night before the battle of the Milvian Bridge Constantine was instructed in a dream to put 'the heavenly sign of God' on his soldiers' shields, and whatever may be thought of the story of the dream, the fact remains that Constantine's men did go into battle with the Chi–Rho monogram on their shields. More puzzling is the story of the heavenly vision of the Cross, which many years afterwards Constantine himself told to Eusebius. One afternoon, when marching against Maxentius, Constantine and his army saw a cross of light athwart the sun and the words 'In this conquer' written in the sky. The next night Christ appeared to him and ordered him to make a copy of what he had seen to serve as a war-standard. Constantine then had a Labarum made of precious metals: this was a banner hanging from the cross-bar of a pole which was surmounted by a wreath enclosing the Chi–Rho monogram. It was this monogram and not the Cross which he used both for the Labarum and henceforth on his own helmet. Although Constantine clearly had not spoken much about this vision (since there is no contemporary record of it before the account in Eusebius's *Life of Constantine,* which he wrote soon after 337) there is no good ground to question it. The vision itself was probably a rare but authentic 'halo phenomenon' caused by ice-crystals in the sun's rays, not unlike a rainbow. Further, it is noteworthy that the vision came from the sun, to which Constantine paid great devotion. What religious significance all this may have had for the emperor and the numerous actions which he took on behalf of the Christians is discussed later (pp. 547 f.). Here the essential point is that he believed himself borne on to victory by the favour of the God of the Christians.[4]

3. Constantine and Licinius

The battle of the Milvian Bridge gave Constantine possession of all the western portion of the Empire. In Rome the Senate transferred from Maximinus to him the title of senior Augustus. Constantine left Rome early in 313 for Milan to meet Licinius, who was to marry his sister Constantia. There, as well as arrangements for complete religious toleration for Christians (p. 547), Licinius agreed to recognise Constantine

Licinius gains supremacy in the East

as senior Augustus in return for the right to legislate in his own part of the Empire. He then had to rush to the East, which since the death of Galerius in 311 had been left as a prize to be fought for by his two former subordinates, Maximinus, who held command in Asia and Egypt, and Licinius, the ruler of the Danube provinces. Maximinus struck first: in 313 he made a spring at Licinius and drove his forces back into Thrace, capturing Byzantium on the way. But Licinius reached Adrianople with fresh troops, completely defeated his opponent and drove him across the whole length of Asia Minor to Tarsus. Too late Maximinus issued an edict of toleration; his sudden death at this stage put Licinius in possession of all the eastern provinces. The victor then murdered the family and officials of Maximinus, as well as the surviving relations of Galerius and Severus. With the death of Diocletian three years later at Salona the Jovian dynasty disappeared. Licinius and Constantine survived as joint rulers.

Joint rule of Constantine and Licinius

Constantine tried to seize the Balkans before Licinius had time to rally his troops. Although defeated in Pannonia Licinius managed to fight a second indecisive engagement in Thrace and then purchased a reprieve by ceding all the Balkans except Thrace; but with this important recruiting-area in his rival's hands the dice were loaded heavily in Constantine's favour. Ten years of uneasy peace followed, in which the Empire was officially united but in practice was divided into two parts. In 317 the emperors even agreed to create as Caesars two sons of Constantine and one son of Licinius, but their differences increased, exacerbated when Licinius reversed his policy to the Christians. In 322 Constantine had to drive Sarmatian invaders out of Pannonia and in the next year crossed into Licinius's territory to expel some Goths from Thrace. In 324 negotiations failed and war ensued. Licinius lost a battle at Adrianople (the point at which he had rallied against Maximinus in 313) and was forced out of Byzantium by Constantine's fleet. Driven out of Europe he was pursued across the Bosporus and again defeated at Chrysopolis (modern Scutari). In response to Constantia's appeal Constantine spared Licinius's life, but put him to death the next year after consulting the Senate when Licinius had been found guilty of intriguing against him.

Constantine sole ruler

After thirty-nine years the Empire now had a single ruler.

In 324 the Roman Empire was temporarily reunited under a ruler who made the last notable attempt to buttress it against further dilapidation. Constantine carried the military and administrative reforms of Diocletian several stages further (pp. 531 f.), and he provided the Roman

Empire with a new capital. From the time of the great invasions in the mid-third century the emperors had perforce spent most of their reigns on campaigns, so that their visits to Rome were short and infrequent. At the end of the century this involuntary process of desertion led on to a deliberate abandonment of the ancient capital. Diocletian set up his court at Nicomedia in Bithynia, and in 324 Constantine founded a new city on the site of Byzantium, East Rome, named after himself and formally inaugurated in 330; Constantinople was a Christian city, founded by 'the commandment of God' and as a memorial to the victory which God had granted him. This action changed the course of history, as did also the stroke of imagination, unique among Roman statesman, by which he enlisted the spiritual support of the Christian Church on behalf of the rule of the Caesars. European history started off on a new course.

Foundation of Constantinople

The reign of Constantine constitutes the sharpest break with the past in all Roman history, and it may be fitly selected as the terminal point of ancient history as a whole. It is epitomised in a scene on which N. H. Baynes focused attention in the now classic sentence with which the *Cambridge Ancient History* was brought to a close: 'Constantine sitting amongst the Christian bishops at the oecumenical council of Nicaea is in his own person the beginning of Europe's Middle Age.'

4. The Transition to Absolute Monarchy

The military cataclysms of the third century did not entail any abrupt changes in the Roman constitution. Even in this period of crisis Roman emperors felt their way in the traditional manner from precedent to precedent. But under the stress of civil wars and of foreign invasions the rate of change was accelerated, and by the cumulative effect of three centuries of patching, the Roman monarchy of Constantine had come to wear a very different aspect from that of Augustus (pp. 319 ff.). The emperors of the third and fourth centuries retained the quasi-republican titulature of the early Caesars. From time to time they assumed a consulship *pro forma,* and they nominally exercised the *tribunicia potestas*; for a full half-century after they had embraced Christianity they continued to style themselves *Pontifex Maximus*. The Senate, which remained the chief repository of ancient tradition, preserved and even added to its prestige. Its membership was now drawn from the great landowners of all parts of the Empire, who entered it by co-optation on a quasi-hereditary basis, and from the higher ranks of the emperors' civil ser-

Constitutional changes

Republican survivals

42.15 The Senate House (Curia). The earlier building had often been destroyed and rebuilt. After a fire in A.D. 283 Diocletian reconstructed it, as shown here. The prestige, if not the power, of the Senate remained high even under the Dominate.

vice, by way of *adlectio*. Under this system of recruitment the House had become fairly representative of the wealthier and more cultured classes of the whole Empire, and in the eyes of a wider public it stood for Roman civilisation in contrast with the growing barbarism of the military elements of the population. In the fourth century a Senate was still deemed an indispensable part of the constitution, so that Constantine found it necessary to create a duplicate of the Roman assembly at Constantinople.[5]

Continued prestige of the Senate

On the other hand the various republican magistracies had either died of inanition before A.D. 300 or had been reduced to merely honorary functions. The tribunate, which had been a fifth wheel on the coach since the days of Augustus, and the aediles, whose municipal duties had gradually been absorbed by imperial prefects (the *praefecti urbi, annonae*, and *vigilum*), ceased to be appointed in the reign of Severus Alexander. The consulate survived and was intermittently assumed by the emperors themselves.

Decay of the magistracies

It was even transplanted to Constantinople, where one of the pair resided after 330, while the other stayed on at Rome. But the holders of this office had been divested of all executive power; their last effective function, the presidency over the Senate, had been transferred at some unknown date to the *praefectus urbi*, and their sole duty now was to give their name to the current year. The consulship, in effect, had become a title without an office. With the closing down of the jury-courts under Septimius Severus, and the transference of the entire higher jurisdiction to the emperor and his delegates, the praetors lost their principal occupation, and the same fate befell the quaestors when the senatorial revenues from the provinces were cut off (see below). By 300 these two magistracies had been reduced to one occupant apiece, whose sole function was to organise and subsidise the circus games and theatrical performances at the Roman festivals; they were appointed by the emperor on the recommendation of the urban prefect. The praetors and quaestors of the fourth century might be compared with the sheriffs of the present day; they were men of wealth who assumed an expensive honorary office on account of the social distinction which it conferred.

Until the later part of the third century the consuls and praetors passed on to the government of a province, as in the days of the Republic. But from the reign of Septimius Severus the emperors made inroads upon this arrangement (p. 494), and in the days of the great invasions, when most of the senatorial provinces passed back into the military zone, the proconsuls were temporarily supplanted by imperial nominees. Under Gallienus imperial *praesides* of equestrian rank occasionally took over, while under Diocletian the staffing of all the provinces became an imperial prerogative (p. 512).

All provinces staffed by the emperors

The disappearance or atrophy of the executive offices, whose supervision had formerly been the principal administrative function of the Senate, robbed that body of its most important routine duty. The withdrawal of the provinces from the Senate's sphere of control entailed the loss of its chief source of income. Under Aurelian the Senate's right of issuing brass and copper coinage was withdrawn, and the mint attached to the *aerarium* was closed. By 300 the Senate had also ceased to exercise, save in rare cases, the powers of criminal jurisdiction which the early Caesars had thrust upon it. Last, but not least, the Senate's authorisation was no longer required to confer legitimacy upon the emperors. During the prolonged military anarchy of the third century the mass-production of camp-made emperors reduced the

Finance withdrawn from the Senate

The Senate ceases to invest emperors

Senate's formal right of appointment to such a self-evident farce that in 282 one of the soldiers' nominees, M. Aurelius Carus, neglected to apply to the Senate for the validation of his title. From that date the Roman emperors became autocrats ruling in their own right — subject only to the *acclamatio* of the soldiers — and the voice of the Senate, even when heard, was purely formal.[6]

The Senate a town council of Rome

The effective functions of the Senate were thus reduced to the government of Rome itself, in concurrence with its new chairman, the *praefectus urbi*. Its only other occupation was to listen to an occasional dispatch which an emperor might send down to it by way of keeping it posted up on current affairs, and to send in reply a message of effusive gratitude for the perfunctory courtesy thus offered to it. Attendance at its meetings was now confined to those few of its members (mostly imperial officials) who resided at Rome. The great majority of the senators, however highly they might value their rank, seldom left their estates to take part in the sessions of the House.

Decay of the municipal governments

In the municipalities of the Roman Empire vestiges of self-government survived here and there. In some African towns popular elections of magistrates were held as late as the reign of Constantine; and the right of appointing *curatores* (p. 500) was eventually transferred by the emperors to the local senates. But the financial embarrassments of the cities were now aggravated by the general economic regression, and by the increasing burden of imperial taxation (p. 501). The flight from office which had already set in during a more prosperous age ended by becoming a general 'every man for himself', and the emperors, who still required a skeleton of local organisation in the municipalities to assist them in the collection of their revenue, were driven to convert membership of the local senates from a voluntary office into a hereditary duty. Under such conditions the sturdy plant of municipal patriotism at last died out, and local administration fell into general neglect.[7]

5. The Emperors and their Executive

The emperors become absolute

In 282, as we have seen, the emperors ceased to be elective officials in any sense and became autocrats in law as well as in fact. This change in their legal position found expression in their titulature. From the time of Aurelian the name of *dominus*, which not even Domitian among earlier rulers had ventured to incorporate into a public document, figured regularly alongside the old republican titles, and it eventually

displaced these. At the same time the name of *princeps*, with its implication of fundamental parity between rulers and ruled, went out of use: all Romans were now equally his subjects. In official dispatches the terse and direct Latin of the early emperors made way for a turgid jargon, in which *serenitas nostra* gives directions to *devotio tua*, and not only the emperor but everything appertaining to the court is labelled 'sacred' (*sacrum*). Whatever some of his wilder predecessors may have claimed, Constantine did not wish to be worshipped as a god; nevertheless he was officially recognised as the divinely appointed vicegerent of one God. This claim was accepted in regard to secular matters even by the Church, which was generally ready to accept him as the ultimate authority even in ecclesiastical disputes. Still more obvious was the change in the emperors' outward style of life. Hitherto their court, which gradually adopted more elaborate rules of etiquette as their power became consolidated, had nevertheless retained some of the Augustan *civilitas*. But Diocletian, and more particularly Constantine, created an elaborate code of court ceremonial and imported into the Roman Empire the etiquette of a Persian court, on the assumption that their unruly soldiery might be dazzled if it could not be reasoned into obedience: at the same time it ensured them greater personal safety. Henceforth Roman emperors maintained a mysterious aloofness from their subjects; when they deigned to appear in public they wore a diadem and raiment of purple and gold and shoes sparkling with jewels and pearls, and they required those who were admitted to their presence to prostrate themselves (*adoratio*) and kiss the hem of their garments. Under Constantine probably an imperial *cubiculum* was established, controlled by a eunuch officer, *praepositus sacri cubiculi*. Other *cubicularii* included an equerry (*primicerius sacri cubiculi*) and a majordomo of the palace (*castrensis*). The majority of these eunuchs came from Persia; since they had constant contact with the emperor and could obtain for others private audiences with the emperor they clearly gained great influence and wealth. The 'Byzantinism' which modern courts have taken over from Constantinople was a legacy to the Byzantines from the later Roman emperors, who imported many of its features into Europe from Oriental monarchy.[8]

'Byzantinism' of the court

But the principal difference between the constitution of Augustus and that of Diocletian or Constantine was that in the latter all pretence of a partnership in government had been abandoned. In the fourth century the entire administration had been gathered into the hands of the emperor, and every executive official was his nominee. True he had two bodies to advise him, the Senate and the *Consilium*. But the Senate no longer advised (indeed it could scarcely have done so, since the emperor was so seldom in Rome): it merely ratified his decisions. On the other hand the council survived. Diocletian appears to have made no fundamental change in its functioning: this came with Constantine. It now became the *sacrum consistorium*, whose members no longer sat but stood in the emperor's presence. Its membership naturally depended on the emperor's choice, including his chief servants, civil and military; it was still functioning as a formal privy council in the mid-fourth century, but it represented the victory of autocracy and bureaucracy.[9]

The imperial executive underwent considerable further expansion, and it received a thoroughgoing reorganisation at the hands of Diocletian and Constantine. This proliferation was intensified as a result of the splitting up of the provinces into smaller units (see below, p. 528), as well as by the increase in court officials. The imperial court (*comitatus*) included a vast array of people. Beside the emperor's household, the eunuch *cubicularii* of the bedchamber, and the subordinate domestic staff (*castrensiani*), there was an imperial guard (*scholae palatinae*) and a corps of officer cadets (*protectores et domestici*). There were also probably (they are first mentioned under Constantius II) thirty *silentarii*, under three decurions, who served as ushers at meetings of the consistory within the palace. The minutes of the consistory were kept by secretaries called notaries (*notarii*); at first men of humble origin they became in later centuries increasingly important, while even under Constantine we hear of a notary being entrusted with an important overseas mission. The chief notary (*primicerius notariorum*), at any rate later, had the important and remunerative task of keeping the list (*Laterculum maius* or *notitia*) of all holders of high office and he probably issued their codicils of appointment. Then there was a group of four civilian and military ministers (*comites consistoriani*), with their respective offices and staffs: the quaestor (*quaestor sacri palatii*), the master of the offices (*magister officiorum*), the financial minister (*comes sacrarum largitionum*) and the minister in charge of imperial lands (*comes rei privatae*). The quaestor of the sacred palace, created by Constantine, was responsible, with the help of clerks from three ministry-departments (*scrinia*), for drafting imperial edicts and rescripts and for dealing with petitions. The *magister officiorum* was created in 320 and had a great variety of duties. He controlled the secretariats (*sacra scrinia*) which were under *magistri scriniorum*, namely

the secretarial departments of *memoria, epistolae* and *libelli*. He also controlled the corps (*schola*) of imperial couriers (*agentes in rebus*); these confidential agents replaced the *frumentarii* in the reign of Diocletian. Though ranking below the notaries, they had the important task of carrying imperial dispatches to the provinces; their senior members went out as inspectors of the post (*curiosi*), thus giving their master, the *magister*, indirect control over the *cursus publicus*. The *magister* also exercised administrative control over the bodyguard (*scholae*), had great influence on foreign affairs, and was master of ceremonies, thus regulating imperial audiences. His wide authority, extending through so many departments of state, gave him a position which might form a counterweight to that of the praetorian prefect. The *comes sacrarum largitionum* (probably still called *rationalis* under Constantine) controlled the mines and mints, while the *comes rei privatae* administered the imperial lands. Beside these high officials there were, of course, minor palatine offices and staff. To all his *palatini* Constantine granted many privileges, which included immunity from curial burdens and exemption from personal *munera*, and he gradually assimilated their status to that of the soldiers.[10]

Outside the *comitatus* the most significant office was that of the praetorian prefects who had developed from the military commanders of the guard to adjutants of the emperor with wide-ranging powers which by Diocletian's day included chief financial responsibility.[10] Constantine, however, disbanded the praetorian guard and transferred the command of the armies to *magistri militum*. The result was that the praetorian prefects became civilian officials, entrusted primarily with judicial and financial matters. They remained judges of appeal, and their sentences were made final without any further appeal to the emperor. They continued to organise levies in kind, to allocate rations for the army and civil servants, to raise recruits, and to supervise the imperial post, public buildings, state-associations (*collegia*) and provincial governors. Each member of the tetrarchy had a praetorian prefect, and the *vicarii* who controlled the twelve new dioceses which Diocletian created (see below) were officially deputies of the prefects. Thus the prefects came to be responsible for the civil administration of territorial sections of the Empire; under Constantine there were probably three prefects in the West and two collegiate prefects in the East, but ultimately there were four praetorian prefectures of the Gauls, Italy, Illyricum and the East. As the office of praetorian prefect underwent these

The city prefect

changes, so that of the *praefectus urbi* altered.[11] In line with his general levelling down of power Diocletian appointed a *vicarius* to the prefect of the city. Constantine, however, suppressed this office and transferred its function to a *vicarius in urbe* (later *vicarius urbis Romae*) who was a vicar of the praetorian prefect, not of the city prefect, whose influence was thus diminished. But the city prefect gained an important function which he had never enjoyed under the Principate: since the Senate was deprived of all its powers of ordinary jurisdiction, the court of the city prefect gained increased significance. To it all *clarissimi* brought their civil suits, and those living in Rome their criminal suits. The city prefect thus came to represent the Senatorial Order over against the praetorian prefect, the confidant of the emperor. Apart from the few surviving republican magistracies the city prefect was the only dignitary still officially to wear the toga and not the military belt (*cingulum*); he thus became the symbol of the republican traditions. One of these was revived by Constantine, who established a non-hereditary patriciate; this meant little more than a courtesy title granted to some senators, especially those who had held a consulship.

Senatorial and Equestrian Orders merged

Under Septimius Severus and his successors the imperial executive had been recruited almost exclusively from the Equestrian Order. But the economic disasters of the third century eventually made it impossible to insist on the prescribed property qualifications for aspirants to public posts, and so stultified the traditional distinction between senators and *equites*. Constantine took the final step of suppressing this distinction (before 321). Thus, although somewhat exceptionally, we find equestrian as well as senatorial *correctores*, and senatorial as well as equestrian *praesides*. Offices hitherto equestrian, as the prefectures of Annona and Vigiles, became open to both orders. Whereas during the third century men of senatorial rank had increasingly been excluded from high administrative offices, now an increasing number of posts were raised from equestrian to senatorial status, and more men entering the state service as equestrians finished up as senators: thus by the mid-fourth century the great officials, as the *magister officiorum* and the quaestor of the palace, had the permanent rank of *clarissimus*. Further, the senatorial nobility made use of the new opportunities offered to them and increasingly monopolised the best administrative posts in the West, which lent itself more readily to a feudal tendency than did the urbanised East. At the same time honorific titles increased. Under Diocletian a *clarissimus* was a member

of an exclusive Senate which comprised some 500 of the best families of the Empire; praetorian prefects held the highest equestrian title of *ementissimus,* while court ministers, vicars, *duces* and provincial governors enjoyed the next equestrian grade of *perfectissimus.* After Constantine the number of men holding such titles had vastly increased. Constantine also created an order of imperial *comites,* partly in order to blend the two classes together in loyalty to himself and partly perhaps because he appears to have liked ceremony. Men who had accompanied the emperor on his journey had always been known as *comites,* but now the title was officially granted, both to senators and commoners, with a classification into three grades (*ordinis primi, secundi* and *tertii*). Some *comites* served on the consistory, others acted in place of vicars in the provinces, while others held special commands in the field army.

Reform of provincial administration

One sphere of administration in which Diocletian introduced fundamental reform is provincial organisation. Partly in order to diminish the powers of the individual provincial governors, and partly to impose a more rigid control upon the decadent municipal governments, Diocletian carried a step further a process which had been going on since the early days of the Empire, namely a splitting up of the provinces into smaller units. A list of provinces, known as the Laterculus of Verona, shows that Diocletian roughly doubled the fifty provinces which existed at his accession: Lactantius said, critically, that the provinces were 'chopped into slices' (*in frusta concisae*).[12] In the process Italy lost its privileged position and was included in the general provincial organisation. Diocletian is often said to have made an almost universal separation of military and civil power in the provinces, but although he moved in this direction the principle was not rigidly applied. In the majority of provinces, which did not need garrisons, the governor had only civil power, being responsible for finance and jurisdiction. In some of the garrisoned provinces Diocletian did make the separation, but there are cases of governors (*praesides*) exercising military power. Military commanders (*duces*) appear to be fairly rare under Diocletian and one such might command the armies of several provinces. Senatorial governors almost disappeared; only the proconsulships of Asia and Africa survived, appointed of course by the emperor not by the Senate. *Correctores,* normally senators, were placed over the provinces into which Italy was divided and in Sicily and Achaea. The rest of the provinces were governed by equestrian *praesides.* This distinction of course disappeared after 320 when,

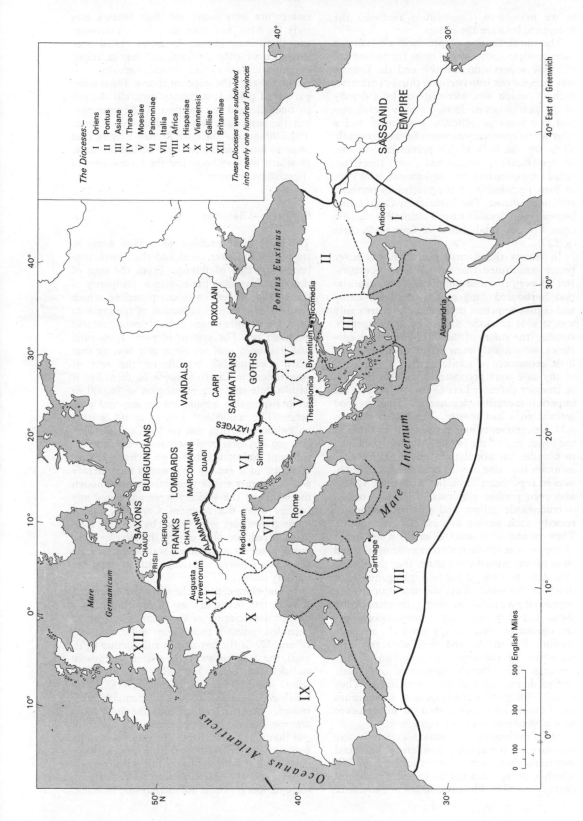

35. THE EMPIRE UNDER DIOCLETIAN

The Dioceses:—

I	Oriens
II	Pontus
III	Asiana
IV	Thrace
V	Moesiae
VI	Panonniae
VII	Italia
VIII	Africa
IX	Hispaniae
X	Viennensis
XI	Galliae
XII	Britanniae

These Dioceses were subdivided into nearly one hundred Provinces

500 English Miles

0   100   300   500

as we have seen, Constantine abolished the difference between the orders.

The multiplication of provinces necessitated their grouping into larger units for the sake of effective supervision. To this end the Empire was mapped out into twelve or thirteen dioceses, each of which was administered by a deputy of the praetorian prefects, a *vicarius*; each also had two financial officials, a *rationalis* and a *magister rei privatae*, who were of equestrian rank. Thus for the bulk of his provincial administrators (vicars, *praesides* and *duces*) Diocletian relied on equestrian *viri perfectissimi*, who were in turn responsible to the praetorian prefects, *viri eminentissimi*. The latter under Constantine became more localised until ultimately the dioceses became subdivisions of four prefectures (p. 527).

In theory the Roman executive was never better constituted than in the fourth century. But its very size and completeness of organisation harboured danger. The more self-acting and omni-competent it became, the more easily was it able to elude control by the emperors. Besides, the rulers of the third and fourth centuries were mostly men of the camp who had little experience of administrative routine, and in any case were preoccupied with the problem of frontier defence. Left to its own devices the imperial executive degenerated from a good servant to a bad master. The higher officials sold appointments and promotions to those at the lower end of the ladder. All alike combined to plunder the populations under their charge in much the same way as proconsuls and *publicani* in republican days, but with more system and even greater impunity. The emperors, it is true, made gallant and persistent efforts to remedy such abuses as came to their notice. They rained edict after edict upon the heads of the peccant officials; where remonstrance and objurgation proved unavailing, they threatened offenders, now with a public flogging, now with death at the stake. They did not wait for the oppressed peoples to lay their grievances before them, but they instituted a new inspectorate, the *agentes in rebus,* to spy upon the administration. But in the end they were regularly outwitted by the organised collusion of their servants. The officials intercepted complaints and made examples of the complainants. They quietly disregarded the emperors' admonitions and fulminations; they bribed the inspectors to turn a blind eye on their malpractices.[13]

But if the bureaucracy could successfully defy the emperors it was obliged to defer to unofficial superiors, the owners of the extensive *latifundia* which grew up after the invasions of mid-third century (p. 537). The proprietors of these large estates not only converted their tenants into serfs (p. 538), but they assumed a patronage over them which in some instances was acknowledged in a formal contract, and they exercised a domestic jurisdiction which virtually supplanted that of the imperial courts. These usurpations of political authority naturally did not go unchallenged on the part of the emperors; but the imperial executive connived at them. The *latifundia* of the later Roman Empire thus came to form miniature states within the state, in which we may recognise the forerunners of the medieval manor.[14]

6. Financial Reforms

The most acute problem of civilian administration in the later third and the fourth centuries was that of finance. From the time of the great invasions the economic prosperity of the Empire underwent a sharp decline, which resulted in a serious reduction of the taxation fund. On the other hand public expenditure still mounted up. The system of *panis et circenses* had hardened into an inexorable law, so that when Constantine transferred the seat of government to Constantinople he furnished it with a dole-receiving population of 80,000 as an indispensable adjunct to an imperial residence. The traditional duty to spend lavishly on public buildings was no less faithfully discharged. To these customary sources of expenditure was now added that of an Oriental luxury at court, of a greatly augmented bureaucracy and of a larger military establishment. Though the wages of the soldiery were not raised any further after the reign of Caracalla, and a dubious economy was realised by enlisting Germans at reduced rates of pay, the mere increase in the numbers of the army was on such a scale as to cast a heavy additional burden upon the military budget.

In mid-third century the emperors attempted to meet the increased costs of government by a drastic depreciation of the coinage and by an extended system of requisitions and compulsory labour. While the *aureus* was still further lightened, the *denarius* was progressively attenuated and debased: under Septimius Severus it contained some 50 per cent copper (p. 496), Caracalla's new *antoninianus* was substantially overvalued, while under Gallienus the diminished *denarius* became a copper piece with a wash of less than 5 per cent silver. The result was an inflationary spiral with rocketing prices, while taxes were not brought into line with the new value of money. Aurelian's reforms (p. 514) gave some temporary relief but did not stop inflation.

Excessive powers of the imperial executive

Abuse of its authority

The owners of latifundia usurp political authority

Continued rise of expenditure

Collapse of the monetary system

This continuous tampering with the coinage had less disastrous consequences than the emergency inflations of recent times, for in the Roman world there was no large class in receipt of fixed money incomes, and the typical *rentier* of ancient times, the large landowner, had no difficulty in commuting his rents into deliveries in kind. Yet the depreciation of the imperial money practically wiped out the 'alimentary institutions' and similar trusts; it drove out of the market the honest copper currencies issued by the eastern municipalities; and it caused endless confusion in the readjustment of prices and wages, which was aggravated by the government's refusal to accept its own coin from taxpayers on any terms, or only at a highly unfavourable tariff. In an attempt to restore a sound currency Diocletian raised bullion (although not sufficient) by levies on land and compulsory purchase. In 294 he issued gold *aurei* at sixty to the Roman pound, silver *denarii* (of Neronian weight) at ninety-six to the pound, and large copper (five to the new *denarius*) and small copper (at first, two to the *denarius*). This new monetary system was followed by fifteen mints, from London to Alexandria. Inflation, however, continued and in 302 Diocletian issued his famous *Edictum de pretiis*, which fixed maximum prices and wages over a very detailed range of goods, and inflicted the death penalty for infringement. This drastic measure proved a failure: goods vanished from the markets, the edict was soon disregarded, and inflation of the copper coinage increased, so that for larger transactions sealed bags (*folles*) of small coppers were used. About A.D. 309 Constantine introduced his famous gold *solidus* at seventy-two to the pound, which long retained its purity and value. Towards the end of his reign he was enabled to mint this in much greater quantity, thanks to his confiscation of temple treasures. Hardly any silver was minted between 305 and 330, when a coin of ninety-six to the pound reappeared. Though prices continued to rise, Constantine's reform can scarcely be called a failure, since his *solidus* still maintained its weight until the eleventh century.[15]

Reforms of Diocletian and Constantine

The right of requisitioning (*indictio*) victuals or transport for the Roman armies or other government service had been freely exercised under the Republic and the emperors of the first two centuries; and the burden of these demands had occasionally borne heavily upon the provincials. But the Roman governments had acknowledged a general obligation to pay for what they took, and the earlier emperors at any rate had shown some concern to keep these appropriations within reasonable bounds. But in the quasi-anarchy of the mid-third century, when

Requisitions

soldiers and officials were often left to help themselves, they made free use of their right to commandeer the goods or the services of the provincials, and the latters' right of compensation became purely illusory.[16] An effort to abolish or restrict these arbitrary practices and to revert to an equitable system of taxation was made by Diocletian. To this end he abolished the old land taxes and drastically revised the whole taxation system. He established regular and regulated *indictiones*, which were distributed evenly over the provinces, cities and individuals. From 287 the annual indictions were numbered serially in cycles of five years (from 312 in fifteen-year cycles). As a basis for the new assessment a census of the Empire was taken, province by province.[17] The tax was based on the *iugum* (unit of land) and the *caput* (a unit of human labour). This tax scheme provided, in theory, a fair balance between the various classes of taxpayers, although in fact it fell more heavily on agriculture, landlords and peasants, and its actual application gave rise to much injustice.[18] The assessment on each property was based on a rough-and-ready division of land into standard fiscal units (*iuga*), whose yield, whether of cereals, fruit or pastoral products, was reckoned as equivalent. The nature of the assessment of the *capitatio* on the rural population varied somewhat in different provinces. Under Diocletian the *capitatio* appears to have been paid in money and the land-tax (*annona*) was a requisition in kind, but before long a *iugum* was equated with a *caput*, and the *annona* was assessed on the combined total, all apparently in kind (with local variations). The tax was extended to the landowners of Italy, whose fiscal immunity had long ceased to be defensible. It was the duty of the praetorian prefects to reckon annually the quantity of food needed by the army, the civil service and the population of Rome, the number of recruits and amount of equipment for the army, and the number of animals for the post and of labourers for public works. The total was divided by the number of *iuga* and *capita*, and published in the annual indiction. Thus the taxes were adjusted in the light of the estimates of an annual budget, and the state very largely managed to do without the use of money. The payment of this tax, however, did not, in practice, confer complete immunity from the requisitions which it was intended to supersede. The old *aurum coronarium* continued, while Constantine imposed two new taxes: the *collatio lustralis*, a quinquennial tax in gold and silver on urban merchants and corporations, and the *collatio glebalis*, a graded surtax on senators, based on their land but paid in cash.

Diocletian's new taxation system

For the purpose of the very complicated assessments the prefects had a large number of financial clerks, in *scrinia* under *numerarii*, while for the actual collection of the taxes (other than the *collatio glebalis*, which was paid directly by each landowner), and for the rendering of additional services, Diocletian developed a system of corporate responsibility which had grown up in the second and third centuries. The local *decemprimi* seem to have been abolished by 310, but in any case liability was extended to the entire body of *curiales* who constituted the *ordo senatorius* of each municipality (the members who were appointed to undertake the actual collection were called *susceptores*).[19] In view of the general impoverishment of the cities, this wider distribution of liability was equitable and indeed necessary; yet it was the cause of much hardship, for the property qualification for admission to the local senates might be as low as 25 *iugera* or 15 acres of land (though clearly it will have varied in proportion to the size and wealth of each city), and many of the *curiales*, if distrained upon, would be destitute. Consequently, though the *curiales* were merciless in exacting contributions from the ultimate taxpayers, they lived perpetually under the shadow of financial ruin, and their incessant complaints necessitated a whole code of additional regulations by the emperors of the fourth and fifth centuries.

7. Compulsory Service

The grievance of the *curiales* were felt all the more acutely, in that many groups of men, all of whom had broader shoulders, were exempted from this load of responsibility, and in actual practice probably paid less than their fair share: these included senators, members of the Equestrian Order, civil servants, soldiers, doctors, official shippers, tax-farmers, and the lessees of state lands; to these Constantine later added the Christian clergy. Little wonder that many *curiales* tried to escape from these burdens by withdrawing from their order and seeking admission into one of the reserved occupations. But the government needed these landowners as agents to guarantee security for the taxes of their local communities. Thus increasing pressure was exerted on them to remain at the post of duty, and under Diocletian they had become *de facto* a hereditary class. Diocletian forbade them to enter the army, while Constantine closed the civil service to them and limited the number of clergy. The last straw came when Constantine made *curiales* legally into a heredi-

tary caste, forbidden to leave their places of residence without special permission.

Thus Diocletian's tax system, which depended upon maintaining the new grades of taxpayers and the complementary supply of labour on which the assessments were based, led to increasing state control. Voluntary service, which had flourished under the Principate, gave way to a system of compulsion which limited the individual's right of choice, and the freeer economy of earlier days was superseded by the bureaucratic controls of the state. As far as possible the *status quo* was to be upheld, with all men continuing in their current occupations and their sons following in their footsteps. Refusal might throw men out of the frying-pan into the fire: thus the hereditary principle was applied to military service, and sons of soldiers or veterans who declined their fathers' profession were drafted into the *curiae*.[20]

The new general land-tax in kind involved transporting, housing and distributing the vast quantities of natural products paid as tax, and this in turn meant the employment of more labour which must be kept available. During the third century the government had turned to the voluntary associations (*collegia*) for help in transporting food to the city and rations to the army. But this no longer could be left so uncertain, and the colleges of tradesmen, craftsmen and businessmen throughout the Empire now became corporations (*corporati*). In 314 Constantine made the *navicularii* (shipowners) into a hereditary caste, and later exempted it from all other state duties. So too other trades on which the food-supply depended were included: bakers and butchers were compelled to stay in their trades (or provide a substitute); escape into the army or other pursuits was blocked by imperial edicts. It is not certain to how many callings this kind of compulsion was extended, nor how far it was extended to gilds outside of Rome at this stage. But in view of its eventual prevalence at Constantinople it may be assumed that by the time of Constantine it had made considerable inroads upon economic freedom in the Empire. Decuriones, food-purveyors, shippers, urban craftsmen, miners, workers in state factories and in the public post, and soldiers were soon engulfed. In the circumstances agricultural workers could not expect to escape.

The status of tenants (*coloni*) on large private and imperial estates underwent a transformation. Until the third century the *coloni* on the large estates were not restricted in their personal freedom, except that they were sometimes bound to render a few days of 'boon' labour at harvest-time on the home farm of the proprietor or of

Corporate responsibility for taxes

The curiales become a hereditary caste

The spread of compulsion

Industry tied

The colonate

the *conductor* (tenant-in-chief). But henceforth the *coloni* were required, in return for the protection and patronage received, to surrender their liberty of movement and to remain permanently attached to the *latifundium*.[21] Their new status of serfdom was in some cases fastened upon them by a formal contract, and it everywhere acquired validity by the connivance of the government. In recognising the institution of tied labour for free persons the Roman government was acting against its own tradition. But – to say nothing of the fact that not a few of the higher officials themselves possessed *latifundia* and went hand in glove with the other large landowners – the emperors themselves capitulated to the plea of the landlords, that without an assured supply of labour they could not answer for the cultivation of their estates and the payment of the land-tax due from them. Since the fast-diminishing supply of slaves was now no longer adequate to the needs of the *latifundia* the Roman government had no ready answer to the arguments of the landowners. The institution of serfdom accordingly acquired a legal title through unchallenged usage. If Diocletian enacted that all the rural population had to remain at the places in which they were registered at the time of the census, this measure will not have been maintained against the freeholders but only against the tenants. By the time of Constantine the *coloni* were permanently attached to the soil, and a law of 332 allowed landlords to chain *coloni* whom they suspected of defaulting. They could not leave the estate, although they might be moved from one farm to another. In like manner their children were obliged to stay on the land. A *colonus*, however, might marry or acquire personal property with his master's agreement. The flight from the land, which had so dangerously threatened the economy of the third century, was thus largely stopped, but only at the price of individual freedom.

Reforms of the legal code

Here may be mentioned another aspect of the reforming activities of Diocletian and Constantine: the extensive alterations in the Roman criminal code, in which they exhibited a strange blend of austerity and humaneness. Diocletian prescribed the most drastic penalties for tax-evasion, and Constantine imposed the severest punishments for sexual immorality. On the other hand both emperors carried on the tradition of the second-century rulers and of Septimius Severus in making new laws to remove surviving barbarisms in the social code. Diocletian prohibited the sale of children; Constantine reduced the arbitrary disciplinary powers of the paterfamilias, made a beginning of prison reform and abolished crucifixion as well as branding on the face. In these conflicting tendencies of their legislation we may see another anticipation of the Middle Ages.

8. Defence and Army Reform

Dimensions of the Roman Empire

In the reign of Diocletian the Roman Empire had almost recovered the ground lost in the invasions of mid-third century. Its impending collapse had been averted by the remarkable series of rulers whom the blind chance of civil war cast up in the later years of the century. With the exception of Dacia no extensive piece of Roman territory had been surrendered. If the Empire had not been restored to the full dimensions of Trajan's reign, it still exceeded the limits which Augustus had marked out for it.

Fortifications

The defences of the Empire were never more complete than in A.D. 330, so far as fortifications could provide for its security. In the East Diocletian strengthened the frontier south of the Euphrates by the construction of a paved road from Damascus northward via Palmyra to Sura on the river, and by building forts on the frontier-route from Petra via Bostra and Palmyra to Circesium (also on the Euphrates); in addition he provided armouries at base cities such as Antioch and Damascus. The African *limes* was reorganised under Diocletian and Constantine, and may well have reached its final shape at this time (p. 438). New forts were established along the Rhine and Danube; a stone wall probably replaced earlier earthworks in the Dobrudja in 317, and a stone bridge was built over the Danube. In Britain Carausius had safeguarded the south-east coast by a string of forts against the depredations of the Saxon pirates (pp. 518 ff.), and in the early fourth century other defences were established along the coasts of Wales and Cumbria against inroads by Caledonians cutting across Galloway, or by Picts and Scots from Ireland. In this same period the majority of the forts of northern Britain, which needed repair either from neglect or the result of enemy action, were rebuilt. In consequence Britain enjoyed during the first half of the fourth century a period of peace and prosperity, perhaps even greater than that of the Antonine era.[22] Behind the frontiers of the Empire the towns in all the threatened areas were again making themselves secure with ring-walls. Even Rome itself was provided by Aurelian with a line of ramparts far surpassing the Wall of Servius in compass and strength (p. 514); and Constantinople was supplied with defences that defied all attacks for nearly a thousand years. In Gaul the hasty fortifications thrown up after

Britain

Rome

Gaul

the first great inroads by Alamanni and Franks were replaced in the fourth century by more substantial structures. The process started as early as Probus, and most of the town-walls which survive today belong to this period. In many of these new walls rubble from the destroyed buildings was incorporated, including statuary and funerary monuments. The walls were often massive; most were irregular in shape, being roughly circular, though a few smaller towns were rectangular in plan. The gates were protected by large towers, though not many reached the fine standard of the Porta Nigra at Trier. A good example of these rebuilt town-walls is at Le Mans, but it is symptomatic of the harshness of the days that virtually all enclosed a much smaller area than that of the earlier town.[23] In Britain London and York were refortified against Saxon raiders adventuring themselves up-river, as Danes subsequently did against Saxons. In general the network of the roads of the Empire was not only kept in repair, but was still further extended by the emperors of the third and early fourth centuries, and communications by river and sea were maintained by various detachments of the Roman navy.

Reorganisation of the army

The deficiencies in the Roman field forces which the great invasions had shown up were partly remedied in the later third century and under Constantine.[24] Gallienus, as we have seen (p. 512), had taken steps to meet two weaknesses: he had tried to improve the efficiency of the officers and to make good the long-standing lack of adequate cavalry. After the defeats inflicted by the mounted troops of the Sassanids and of the Goths (who had learnt cavalry warfare on the Russian steppes), Gallienus's new cavalry corps did good service under Claudius and Aurelian. Another weakness in the Roman defences of the mid-third century was that under the second-century emperors, and still more under the two Severi, the various units had become almost immobilised on their respective frontiers, so that they could not render each other timely support. A war in one part of the Empire often involved denuding another part of its defensive garrisons by sending detachments to act as reinforcements on the threatened front, with the resultant opportunity of attack for the barbarians on the watch beyond the frontiers. With a view to providing an adequate mobile reserve, Diocletian carried out and Constantine completed a reorganisation of the entire Roman army, which was henceforth divided into two distinct branches, the Garrison armies (*limitanei*) and the Field army (*palatini* or *comitatenses*). Both consisted of cavalry and infantry, and in both the cavalry took prece-

Frontier forces and mobile reserves

dence. The *limetanei* were commanded by *duces*, some of whom had the title of *comites*; its units were stationed in forts along the frontiers, with a detachment at headquarters under a *praefectus*. The *comitatenses* comprised both *vexillationes* (cavalry units of 500 men, under tribunes) and *legiones* (infantry units of 1000 men) and were commanded by *magistri militum*. These *magistri* had authority over the *duces* on the frontiers, while the *comitatenses* received higher pay and more privileges than the men on the frontiers, who in consequence came to be regarded as second-class troops. The units of the *comitatenses* were generally stationed away from the frontiers in towns which lay on good communication lines. In 312 Constantine disbanded the praetorian guard, but probably even before then Diocletian had created a new guard, the *scholae palatinae*, consisting of cavalry regiments, mostly barbarians, each numbering 500 strong.

Numbers

In order to correspond with his subdivision of the provinces Diocletian increased the number of the legions probably to about sixty, and assigned two (or sometimes one) to each province. At the same time he greatly increased the number of troops, perhaps at least doubling the number. John Lydus, a writer of the sixth century, says that under Diocletian the army numbered 435,266, a figure which may go back to some official record. The field army may well have numbered some 200,000 men. Thus large numbers of men had to be recruited. Under the Principate service had become largely hereditary, since most soldiers followed their fathers' calling; it was generally voluntary and conscription did not often need to be applied. Diocletian probably, rather than Constantine, introduced a rule that sons of soldiers and veterans, if fit, were obliged to serve, and he also instituted regular conscription of citizen recruits; since the latter were levied on the same assessment as the land-tax (p. 531), the burden fell on the rural population. Some voluntary enlistment no doubt continued.

Recruitment

Under these regulations the personnel of the Roman forces deteriorated considerably, as compared with the armies of the first and second centuries. From the time of the two Severi the frontiersmen included not only Roman citizens, but a considerable number of transplanted German captives; the volunteers were drawn almost exclusively from the more backward portions of the Roman Empire, or from German mercenaries, who sometimes enlisted in ready-made companies under their own chiefs. The conscripts were not picked out, as under the Republic, by the commanding officers or their agents, but were left to be supplied, according to a prearranged quota, by the owners of the large

Enrolment of Germans

estates, who naturally deputed the least efficient of their staff of tenants for military duty. The Roman soldiers of the third and fourth centuries lacked the capacity for strict discipline that had characterised the recruits from Italy and the more Romanised provinces in earlier centuries. They would not consent to wear the same weight of body-armour as the legionaries of old, nor to exercise themselves with a like thoroughness in the use of their weapons and in tactical evolutions; their insubordination is illustrated *ad nauseam* by the incessant military revolts of the third century and the frequent lynchings of their generals.

Yet if the margin of superiority which the Roman armies held over their opponents was diminishing, it remained adequate – so long as they did not desert their posts in order to wage civil wars. If the soldiers of Diocletian and Constantine were not a match for those of Scipio Africanus and Flamininus, neither were their adversaries as formidable as Hannibal and the Macedonian kings. The Sassanid monarchy, once its first flare of enthusiasm had rendered down, became as desultory in its warfare as the Arsacid dynasty which it had dispossessed. The Germans, once they had tasted the good things of the Roman Empire, came again and again; but they had no advantage in numbers,[25] they co-operated badly, and though they had abundant vigour their science of war hardly yet rose above the planning of small surprises. Though they might overrun a countryside in a sudden foray, they seldom succeeded in reducing a town, except by the process of slow starvation, for which they had no patience.

The Roman armies still hold the advantage

9. Conclusion

In the age of the civil wars and of the great invasions whatever chances the Roman Empire might have possessed of recovering a wider measure of self-government were irretrievably swept away. From the hybrid shape into which Augustus had remodelled it the Roman constitution eventually developed into a pure despotism. The active patriotism and the political resourcefulness that had once distinguished the Roman citizen had been lost beyond recovery; and the autocracy under which the old co-operative commonwealth lay submerged was more systematically oppressive than any previous Roman government.

The Roman Empire a pure autocracy

But in fairness to the later Roman emperors it should be borne in mind that they were in the position of a ship's captain labouring against time to bale out a heavily leaking vessel. Under such conditions it would be strange indeed if their work had not borne marks of hasty improvisation. But rather, if Claudius Gothicus and Aurelian are to be commended for 'not despairing of the Republic' in the face of foreign enemies, Diocletian and Constantine deserve an honourable place on the list of Rome's reforming statesmen for striving to reduce the administrative chaos which they had inherited to some degree of order. Moreover, the statesmanship of these two emperors, for all its blemishes, achieved one notable success. Though it did not prevent the process of dissolution in the western half of the Empire, it gave new stability to its eastern portion, where it provided the basis for a durable monarchy. The wonder is not that Roman history took a new course in the fourth and fifth centuries, but that it did not terminate abruptly in the third or early fourth. For this last triumph of Roman vitality the great captains of the third century perhaps deserve the chief credit, but Diocletian and Constantine may also claim the title of 'Restitutor Orbis'.

Merits of the late emperors

CHAPTER 43

Economic, Cultural and Religious Developments

1. Economic Conditions[1]

Stagnation after M. Aurelius

IN the later days of M. Aurelius the tide of prosperity which had set in under Augustus and endured through two centuries ceased to flow. The Great Plague and the Marcomannic Wars, followed by the civil wars at the end of the second century, acted as a brake on further progress. The reigns of the two Severi were an interval of partial recuperation, and the first third of the third century, taken as a whole, was a period of stability rather than of decay. But with the death of Severus Alexander an era of rapid decline and even of disintegration commenced.

The economic retrogression of the later Roman Empire was a product of the continuous civil wars and foreign invasions of the mid-third century. The effect of these disturbances was all the more disastrous, because they were no longer transient episodes, but became as it were a normal condition of Roman politics. The most harmful consequence of the political convulsions lay not so much in the immediate attendant loss, as in a pervasive sense of insecurity, which fastened on the population of the Roman Empire about A.D. 250 and was never again dispelled. The well-founded confidence in the *Pax Romana*, which had been the chief motive power in the economic development of the first two centuries A.D., had been once for all undermined; the freedom of travel which had characterised that period was rudely interrupted; and every market was dislocated in a greater or lesser degree. Abundant evidence of the prevailing nervousness in the Roman world survives in the

Insecurity after A.D. 250

numerous hoards of coins of the third and fourth centuries which have been found in the former territories of the Roman Empire; instead of capitalising their gold and silver, men stood guard over it.[2]

The havoc which political disorders played with the economic structure of the Empire was aggravated by errors of financial policy on the part of the emperors. The confusion consequent upon the depreciation of the coinage and the arbitrary incidence of taxation were added obstacles to economic activity. It is no longer held that by the fourth century payment in kind had replaced payment in money and that a natural economy of barter had superseded a money economy, but nevertheless payment in kind was used by the government to reward its officials and employees and must also have been used in many more forms of business transaction than hitherto. Further, the fiscal burdens which the emperors heaped upon the *curiales,* at the same time as they dealt tenderly with the owners of the *latifundia* took the heart out of a potentially resourceful and enterprising class, and deterred poorer men from exerting themselves in order to rise to a higher station.

Consequences of faulty finance

The improvement in the currency and the restoration of internal peace led to partial recovery, and the economic decline of the Roman Empire did not affect all its countries in an equal degree. The eastern provinces, which were less continually exposed to invasion, and in any case had a longer tradition of industry and commerce than those of the West, recaptured some of their former prosperity. On the trans-continental route to China trade lingered on into the second

Decline of Eastern trade

half of the third century, though the disintegration of the Chinese Empire towards the end of the second century, and the substitution of the Sassanid rulers for the Arsacids in Persia, disorganised communications. The overseas commerce with the Farther East crumbled away more rapidly. In the early third century the traffic with China by way of Malaya died out, and the Indian Ocean was abandoned to Hindu, Arab or Abyssinian mariners. But in the fourth and fifth centuries the exchange of Indian and Mediterranean products was resumed through these foreign intermediaries, and Roman coins again found their way as far as Ceylon.[3]

Northern Africa, which lay as yet out of the reach of the Germanic invaders and possessed a privileged and assured market for its grain and oil at Rome, remained productive to the end of the fourth century. Its decline dates from the sack of Rome by Alaric and the Vandal invasions of the fifth century (p. 551).

Relative prosperity of Britain

In Britain a period of slow decline which set in after 250 was followed by a Martinmas summer of prosperity in the days of Constantius and Constantine. Numerous hoards of fourth-century coins give evidence of waning enterprise and confidence in that period; yet as late as 350 the wheat of eastern England was still being shipped to the Roman garrisons on the Rhine. Lastly, under the shelter of the Roman camps and forts oases of highly cultivated land remained here and there between the tracks of the invaders. Among the showpieces of the Roman Empire in the fourth century was the valley of the Moselle (where viticulture had been introduced *c.* A.D. 200). Under the protection of the garrisons of Trier (the residence of emperors) and Mainz this region remained a small paradise.[4]

But the total area of cultivation in the Roman Empire underwent a serious shrinkage. Despite repeated attempts at fresh land-settlement, in which German war-captives were often given the opportunity of making good their own devastations, large zones of frontier territory relapsed into waste. After 250 Spain had little surplus of foodstuffs to export to Rome. In Italy and even in Egypt good land went out of use

Land left derelict

though after the irrigation system had been repaired Egyptian agriculture made a partial recovery. The ordinances of Aurelian and other rulers, calling upon the cities of the Empire to find cultivators for their neglected fields, show that the problem of the derelict lands was no longer confined to a few stricken areas, and could no longer be remedied by the time-honoured device of colonisation.

But the effects of the political calamities of the third century showed most clearly in the domain of industry and commerce, for once the craftsman and the trader had disappeared out of a ruined region they were more difficult to replace than the husbandman. Gaul and the Rhineland, where the seeds of western economic supremacy had been laid in the first and second centuries, lost the greater part of their manufactures and commerce. The glass industry of Cologne, which was still expanding at the beginning of the third century, suffered a decline in its middle (though it recovered somewhat in the fourth), and the flourishing ceramic industry of the western provinces fell to pieces after 250. The Danubian provinces declined both in population and prosperity.

Decay of private industry

The dearth of private enterprise obliged emperors to set up state armouries and cloth-factories to furnish their armies; and they had perforce to employ compulsion in order to keep up the supply services of Rome (p. 532). Thus the opportunities for the private trader sharply contracted. Such industry and trade as survived was mostly local rather than inter-provincial, and its objects were articles of luxury rather than of common use, although recently discovered fragments of the Edict on Prices do suggest that some trade in common objects did continue by sea.

The decline of manufactures and commerce was reflected in the dwindling acreage of the towns.[5] Rome remained a monster city; but it owed its false prosperity to the fact that even after it had ceased to be the principal seat of government it continued to be pampered by emperors and persons of wealth, and still drew its rations of free food and amusement. The shrinking of other urban sites may be particularly well observed in Gaul, where the new ring-walls of the third and fourth centuries enclosed but a quarter or less of their former area. The cities were becoming mere shelters for the administrative officials, and were ceasing to be centres of industry and trade.

Shrinkage of cities

The economic disasters of the third century greatly reduced the numbers of the bourgeois class which had thriven on industry and commerce in the first and second centuries, and of the free cultivators on the land, both proprietors and tenants. In the third and fourth centuries the concentration of landed property into fewer hands, which had hitherto been held in check, made giant strides. As in the days after the Second Punic War the favoured few who still had wealth to spare embraced the opportunity of buying or leasing on easy terms, or of simply appropriating, territory left derelict after devastation.[6] The need of protection against foreign invaders or against oppressive administrators drove many of the remaining small pro-

Growth of latifundia

43.1 Mosaic from Tunis, showing a fortified farm with look-out towers and an orchard.

prietors to surrender their holdings to their wealthier neighbours, who could provide shelter against marauders in their fortified villas, and could make a stand against tyrannous officials. Through this wholesale transference of property the *latifundium* became the prevalent type of estate in the Roman Empire, and the actual cultivation of the soil was predominantly carried on by tenants who had now become *coloni*, bound to the soil. The process was even encouraged by the government which could not afford to let deserted lands lie idle. These great landlords became immensely powerful, and their self-sufficient estates foreshadowed the later feudal manors. As the towns decayed these country villas produced for their local markets, and their owners became integrated with the countryside. As they were rich they could afford to continue to buy the luxuries which a diminished international trade still managed to handle. Thus these manor-houses, the homes of senators and other *potentiores*, not only exercised a patronage over the surrounding countryside and villages, but remained centres of that culture which had now largely forsaken the shrunken cities: here, if anywhere, something of the traditions of an older Rome survived.

2. Architecture and Art[7]

43.2 A hunting scene from northern Africa. Mosaic from Tunis.

The impoverishment of the Roman world brought with it a decline in artistic productivity which visibly foreshadowed the Dark Ages. The last Roman art, as well as the first, was architecture. There could be little building in the troubled years of the third century, and it is symbolic that Aurelian's two main constructions were his massive girdle of wall around

Renewed building activity

Rome and his temple of the Sun. With Diocletian Rome entered upon her last great period of building in antiquity, when exploitation of concrete and brick resulted in a series of vast buildings in which external beauty was sacrificed to the magnificent use of internal space; in these soaring heights the puny individual might feel as overshadowed as he did when he contemplated the all-embracing tentacles of the bureaucratic state. Diocletian built baths that surpassed in size the gigantic *thermae* of Septimius Severus and Caracalla; they are now partly converted into the church of S. Maria degli Angeli. Maxentius began and Constantine completed the construction of a basilica on an equally colossal scale. Maxentius also built a large circus (for 15,000 spectators) and a mausoleum on the Appian Way; he was also probably responsible for the so-called temple of Romulus (named after his infant son) on the Forum, where it has long since been converted into the church of SS. Cosmas and Damian. Constantine also built, in addition to his arch (see below), two imperial mausolea, one (the Tor Pignattara on the Via Praenestina) for himself but in the event used for his mother Helena, and a second for his daughter Constantina (now the church of S. Costanza). Constantius and Constantine

43.3 The baths of Diocletian, shown in the top half of the photograph. They were dedicated in A.D. 305–306. The sombre mass of the exterior was balanced by the richness of the interior of this most impressive building. The central part was converted into a church in the sixteenth century.

43.4 The so-called Porta Nigra at Trier (Augusta Treverorum) on the Moselle. Trier was the residence of Constantius, Constantine and other emperors. The gateway is probably early fourth century and was unfinished; it provided an impressive entrance to one of the major cities of the West.

Palaces and villas

embellished their residence at Trier with the most remarkable group of surviving Roman edifices in western Europe, among which, besides imperial baths, the Basilica provided one of the finest specimens of Roman work in brick, and the Porta Nigra the most elaborate of Roman city-gates. At Salona (modern Split) on the Dalmatian coast Diocletian spent his last years in a capacious palace laid out on the pattern of a legionary camp. This vast fortified villa reflected the need felt throughout the provinces for the protection of a circuit of walls; some villas indeed were abandoned, but others became isolated fortified centres. In a secluded valley in south-eastern Sicily a vast unfortified villa was built near modern Piazza Armerina for an immensely wealthy patrician, perhaps Diocletian's colleague, Maximian. There was much building at Milan, which became the leading city in the West, but little survives. When Galerius chose Thessalonica as the capital of his part of the Empire he added a palace and a mausoleum (the church of St George), between

which ran a processional way and a triumphal arch. In Constantine's new Christian capital in the East, Constantinople, many architectural traditions from both West and East united in a cosmopolitan amalgam, though little of the city built before Justinian's day survives.[8]

The builders of the later Empire possessed a technical ability scarcely inferior to that of Agrippa's or Hadrian's architects: the vaults of the *Basilica* of Maxentius and Constantine will bear comparison, in point of height and span, with the dome of the Pantheon. Yet their work achieved its effect by mere bigness or by the floridity of its decorations, rather than by its good proportions and elegance of detail. Moreover, architecture throve only in places where it enjoyed the patronage of emperors. In the cramped and reduced cities of the period there was no room for monumental display, and no municipal wealth or public spirit to provide the necessary funds. From the middle of the third century municipal building was almost restricted to the erection of new fortifications; and the country houses of the great landowners were constructed for strength rather than for beauty.

Decay of municipal architecture

Some of the best sculpture of the third and fourth centuries consisted of reliefs on the sarcophagi of some of the remaining wealthy families. Christian sarcophagi of the third century retain a similar style, with biblical subjects occasionally appearing, but from Constantine's time they are crowded with scenes from the Old and New Testaments. Romano-Christian sculpture in the round is represented by the figure of the Good Shepherd carrying a sheep (the animal-bearer was a pagan motif). Third-century portraiture, both in the round and on the coinage, is excellent, reflecting a tension between naturalism and schematisation, with a brief reversion to Antonine idealism during the days of Gallienus. But thereafter a harsher element predominates and mirrors the stern realities which faced the peasant soldier emperors. The porphyry groups of the four emperors of the first tetrarchy at Venice, with their ugly schematisation, symbolise the restored imperial unity, but the huddled figures suggest the need to stick closely together in a dangerous world. With Constantine schematisation got the upper hand: facial planes are flatter, the eye is large and often upward-gazing, so that the vicegerent of God is spiritually remote from common humanity. The tradition of historical reliefs (pp. 476 f.) was resumed after the troubles of the mid-third century: in Rome arches of Gallienus and Diocletian were erected, but little of them survives. Much more informative is the arch of Galerius at Thessalonica: its four narrow sarcophagi-like registers have

Sculpture

sculptured figures of two styles: the tetrarchs in static hieratic frontality, and other more lively scenes with the figures moving laterally. A similar combination is found on Constantine's arch in Rome in the reliefs which depict six episodes in his campaign against Maxentius. However, much of the sculptural decoration of this arch is not contemporary but taken from monuments of the time of Trajan (frieze), Hadrian (medallions, with hunting-scenes) and Marcus Aurelius (panels, showing the emperor returning to Rome or addressing his troops): the Constantinian additions are less successful.

Painting and mosaics

Mural paintings are preserved in large numbers on the walls and ceilings of tombs of varying date in Italy and many parts of the Empire. Two famous cemeteries are at Isola Sacra near Ostia, and the Vatican cemetery under St Peter's in Rome; the former served the new town of Portus during the second and third centuries, and Constantine sliced off the tops of many of the house-tombs in the Vatican to level the ground for his new Basilican church. Examples of painting in the provinces are pro-

vided by the great friezes with hunting-scenes in the 'Hunting Baths' at Lepcis Magna in Tripolitania, and by the religious murals (pagan, Jewish and Christian) from the Roman–Parthian city of Dura-Europas on the Euphrates which the Persians captured *c.* 257: here are sacrificial scenes from the temple of the Palmyrene gods, and biblical scenes on the walls of a Christian baptistery which was set up in a small private house when it was converted to a house-church. At Dura, as in many other parts of the Empire, there was a Mithraeum with painted scenes from the life of Mithras, including the bull-slaying panel. Mosaic work, no less than painting, continued to thrive, as witness, for example, the fine series at Piazza Armerina. During the first three centuries A.D. black-and-white was the favourite pavement in Italy, but the provinces preferred gayer polychrome which became commoner in Italy in the fourth century. Mosaics on walls and vaults were popular throughout the imperial period among pagans and later among Christians; a good early example of the latter is the mid-third century in the mauso-

43.5   One of the mosaics from the great villa at Piazza Armerina in Sicily. It *may* have been the country retreat of Maximian, and thus the counterpart of the residence of his colleague Diocletian at Split. Whoever in fact the owner was, he appears to have been interested in the transport of wild animals from Africa to the arenas of Italy. Part of the 'Great Hunt' mosaic, which extended the length of a 70-yard corridor, is shown here. The figure in the bottom left-hand corner is perhaps the owner.

43.6   The Arch of Constantine, erected in his honour to commemorate his victory over Maxentius in A.D. 312. Most of the sculptures and reliefs were taken from monuments of the time of Trajan, Hadrian and Marcus Aurelius.

leum of the Julii under St Peter's. Thus both in painting and mosaics a pagan art was gradually taken over by Christian usage and after a period of mixed pagan and Christian motifs art in the churches turned more exclusively to biblical and other sacred subjects. Thus in art, as in other spheres of life, the scene was set for the Middle Ages.[9]

3. Social Life

The storm and stress of the third century also left an enduring mark upon Roman social life. The only class whose habits remained immune from disturbance was the populace of Rome and of the few remaining cities that retained their former prosperity. In these favoured places the emperor or the local aristocracies maintained an unbroken round of public amusements. At Rome the number of festival days grew from

Public amusements at Rome

130 to 176 between A.D. 150 and 350. The Christian emperors of the fourth century gave no heed to the strictures of the Church upon the cruelty of gladiatorial games and beast-hunts, and upon the licence of the theatrical mimes;[10] they transplanted to Constantinople the circus games, which became the consuming passion of the new capital. But amid the general ruin of the municipal aristocracies the sources from which the public entertainments were defrayed dried up. A pampered proletariat was a luxury which the attenuated towns of the fourth century could no longer afford.

Notwithstanding the lavishness of its appointments the imperial court ceased to be a centre of social life. The rulers who now held the seat of Augustus and Hadrian had little time or taste for refined amusements; Diocletian, who purchased leisure by abdication, employed it in cultivating his palace garden. The descendants of the prosperous bourgeoisie which had

Society becomes rustic again

cultivated urbane living under the early emperors were now preoccupied with the struggle for existence; and the caste system on which industry and commerce were being reorganised formed an additional obstacle to free social intercourse. The sociableness and *humanitas* which had once distinguished Roman town life now took refuge in the villas of the great landowners.[11] Here a Pliny or even a Cicero might still have been able to make himself at home. But the country aristocracy now rarely came to town, and in its rural seclusion it gradually reverted to rustic pastimes.

4. Education and Letters

It is a paradox of later Roman history that, amid the clash of arms and the virtual bankruptcy of the state, educational institutions were not marked down for an early and heavy reduction, but enjoyed the special protection of the government. Among the later emperors Septimius Severus and Constantine had received a good literary education; Constantine took pleasure in the society of scholars, and Severus's consort Iulia Domna presided over the chief literary salon of her day (p. 502). The others, albeit mere men of the camp, held learning and letters in respect, or at any rate felt bound to follow the traditions of their predecessors in regard to educational policy. The status of teachers was confirmed by Diocletian and Constantine, who upheld the fiscal privileges previously conferred upon the profession (p. 479). At Rome and Constantinople Constantine placed educational appointments under the supervision of the Senate of either city, but he did not interfere with the curriculum.

Patronage of literature

From the third century the attitude of the Christian Church towards classical culture became a subject of persistent but indecisive discussion. The Greek Fathers, headed by Origen and Clement, remained loyal to Hellenic traditions of scholarship. The Latin Fathers were more divided in their opinions. Their earlier representatives, Tertullian and Lactantius, roundly condemned pagan *belles lettres*, though they themselves wielded their pens with some pretence to classical style; their later and greater leaders, Augustine and Jerome, could not entirely close their ears to the pagan Siren.

Attitude of the Church to literature

Thanks to the encouragement which learning and letters continued to receive at the hands of the emperors, scholarship and literature still showed some vitality. But in the third and fourth centuries Latin and Greek were no longer maintaining their ascendancy. In the eastern provinces the Greek tongue was kept by school-

Latin and Greek no longer universal tongues

masters and grammarians up to a high standard of purity and showed as yet little sign of an internal breakdown; but it was losing its virtual monopoly of literature. In Asia Minor its supremacy was so well established that the Christian Church adopted it everywhere as its liturgical language. On the other hand it lost ground in Egypt and on the Euphrates border, where the Church used the vernacular tongues for its liturgy and thus created the rudiments of the Coptic, Syriac and Armenian literatures. At the same time the teaching of Greek fell out of use in the schools of the western Mediterranean and even began to disappear from the universities. In the West the native tongues continued to lose ground before Latin, and the Church made no attempt to revive them. But after 200 the orthography and grammar of Latin began to break down, so that as a spoken language it was resolving itself into a variety of local patois. By the time of Constantine the new vernacular tongues out of which the modern Romance languages have been created were coming into existence, and Latin in its unadulterated form was being relegated to the position of a second language for the learned classes.[12]

Breakdown of spoken Latin

5. Latin and Greek Literature

Latin literature suffered an eclipse during the *années terribles* of the third century and it took some time to recover. There were no major poets. Prose-writers are best represented by the Christian authors, Arnobius, who denounced the polytheism of the pagan world *c.* 295, and Lactantius whom Diocletian summoned to Nicomedia to teach rhetoric there, and by the eulogies of rhetoricians mostly of Gallic origin: these Latin Panegyrics resembled that of Pliny the Younger in being thanksgivings to emperors for political preferment, but their style was modelled on that of Cicero, whose amplitude they reproduced without his forcefulness and wit. Later, in the fourth century and after, literature experienced a partial revival: since these writers fall outside the main scope of this book, fewer words can be spared for them than their merits demand. Claudius Claudianus, a native of Alexandria, wrote panegyrics of influential patrons, which, though overloaded with conventional rhetoric, were not unworthy successors to the similar poems of Statius in metre and style. Ausonius, a distinguished professor at Burdigala (modern Bordeaux), wrote occasional poems, of which the best is a description of a journey on the Moselle, while another Gallic poet of the early fifth century, Claudius Rutilius Namatianus, is best known for the pass-

Latin writers

age in which he grieved for the passing away of Roman world-sovereignty. The last notable historical work in Latin came from the pen of a native of Antioch named Ammianus Marcellinus (c. 330–395), who wrote a continuation of Tacitus from A.D. 96 to 378, though the surviving volumes only cover the last twenty-five years; he stood not far behind Tacitus in the accuracy of his record and in his grasp of political situations and characters. More writers followed the tradition of Suetonius than of Tacitus. The biographies known as the *Historia Augusta* are mentioned elsewhere (p. 653). The unblushing manner in which they forged documentary evidence is another sign of the approach of the Middle Ages. An older literary tradition was revived by two men of high rank of the fourth and fifth centuries, Q. Aurelius Symmachus and C. Sidonius Apollinaris, who published collections of letters in imitation of the younger Pliny, but their colourless style and commonplace thought fell woefully short of their model.[13]

The preservation and appreciation of past Latin literature was furthered by scholars of the fourth century who wrote commentaries on the classics of former ages. The surviving specimens of late Latin scholarship, such as the annotations of Aelius Donatus on Terence and of *Gram-* Marius Servius Honoratus on Virgil, are none *marians* the less of high value for the understanding of *and com-* these poets, though their learning was mostly *mentators* at second hand. Another important work of conservation was undertaken by scholars who excerpted and adapted the researches of earlier writers on the Latin language. The manual of grammar and lexicology by Nonius Marcellus, and the grammatical primer of Donatus, remained standard books through the Middle Ages and contributed to the maintenance of Latin as a language of culture. Lastly, Roman technical literature was enriched in the early years of the third century by the treatises of three leading jurisprudents who combined high erudition with a wide practical experience as legal advisers to Septimius Severus and his successors, a Syrian named Aemilius Papinianus, Domitius Ulpianus (likewise a Syrian) and Iulius *Juris-* Paulus. The voluminous treatises of these *prudence* authors on the sources of Roman law – the edicts and other communications of emperors, and the *responsa* of previous jurisconsults – provided the foundation for the *Digest* or classified commentary on Roman law, which was appended to the Code of Justinian (pp. 556 f.).

The contribution of the earlier third and the fourth centuries to Latin literature was by no means negligible. Yet in this period, despite the efforts of annotators and grammarians, many of the works of earlier Latin authors ceased to be studied or (as in the case of Livy) were only consumed in compendia and peptonised tablets. It was fortunate that in the fourth century parchment generally replaced the more fragile papyrus for literary manuscripts. To this change of materials we owe the preservation of our scanty remains of Latin literature;[14] but previous to the general use of parchment for books a considerable part of that literature had already been lost for lack of readers.

The revival of Greek letters which began under Hadrian was well maintained under the Severi; it was interrupted during the years of confusion that followed, but was resumed in the fourth century. Among the writers of the period Dio Cassius Cocceianus a praetorian prefect of *Greek* Severus Alexander, and grandson of Dio Chry- *historians* sostom (p. 480), provided a link between the long chain of classical Greek historians and the numerous and competent historical authors of the Byzantine age. His general history of Rome from Aeneas to his own day, composed in eighty books, was the most ambitious of later Greek historical works. For the period of the later Republic and the first two centuries A.D. Dio became the standard authority among Greek readers. Though he was haphazard in the selection of his sources and had obvious difficulty in understanding the politics of the republican age, he embodied much good material, and he made estimable attempts to explain as well as to narrate the course of events. A slightly later contemporary, writing perhaps after 244, was Herodian, whose *History* covered the years from A.D. 180 to 238; little is known about the man, who appears to have been from Syria and a minor official in Rome. Influenced by the Second Sophistic movement, his *History* is rhetorical and superficial, but certainly not without considerable value. It is symptomatic of the increasing vigour of Christian *vis-à-vis* pagan literature that the work of the Church historian, Eusebius of Caesarea (c. 260–340), towers above that of Herodian. He wrote a brief *Chronicle* of universal history, theological works, a *Life of Constantine*, and above all an *Ecclesiastical History*. This last work, which goes down to A.D. 324, has little claim to literary merit, but it opens a new chapter in historiography and set an example for later ecclesiastical historians. One of the great benefits of this story of Christianity from the Apostolic age until Constantine is that Eusebius quotes large numbers of authorities and documents (not faked documents, as those inserted by the authors of the *Historia Augusta*). He abandoned political history in order to describe the struggle of the Church against persecution from without and heresy from within. Although not unmindful of Jewish–Hellenistic historiography, as seen in Josephus, Eusebius was in fact breaking new ground.[15]

Greek scientific studies ran out with a treatise on arithmetic by an Alexandrian named Diophantus (of uncertain date), who made the first systematic use of algebraic notation. After the appearance of this solitary genius the Greek vein of scientific research became exhausted. The history of ancient philosophy similarly ended with one outstanding figure, an Egyptian Greek named Plotinus (205–270), who after joining Gordian's Persian expedition settled in Rome to teach philosophy. He momentarily breathed new life into the dry bones of the Platonic doctrine. The philosophy of Plotinus, set forth in six *Enneads* of nine books each, was the most methodical attempt to explain the universe since the days of Plato and Aristotle; in particular, it made a courageous study of the problem of evil which other philosophic schools tended to evade. Plotinus won distinguished converts in the emperor Gallienus and in a pupil named Porphyry, who made an able attempt to popularise his doctrine. But his system made too great a demand on the intellectual perseverance of a world which was impatient for quick and visible results. In the hands of later members of the school Neoplatonism was dissolved into a haze of impalpable half-truths which served to throw a decent mantle over all manner of popular superstitions, and Plato's doctrine of the soul's ecstasy from the body by dint of intellectual effort was transmuted into the dross of common magic. While Neoplatonism was taught or mistaught in the high school and became the fashionable creed of pagan society, popular philosophers expounded a 'Hermetic' lore (the revelations of Hermes Trismegistus and other mythical personages), in which philosophy, cosmogony and magic were compounded into a crude farrago.[16]

Plotinus

Hermetica

6. Religions

The eventual failure of Neoplatonism brings into relief the fact that the later Roman world could find no comfort in philosophy. Its only hope for the relief of mundane ills now lay in religion. The spirit of piety which had stolen over it in the second century, and the readiness to accept the most fanciful doctrines of supernatural intervention, were accentuated by the gloomy experiences of the third century. Among the old-established cults the 'religion of the

Survival of Paganism

peasant' still remained deeply rooted in the countryside. It is significant that even in the fifth century the Christian polemicists found it necessary to spend a large part of their ammunition on the pristine rural cults. The state-religion of Rome not only persisted, but in the fourth century it recovered some of its original influence among thoughtful men, whose loyalty to the ancient patron deities was quickened rather than shattered by the political misfortunes of the age. Indeed, at the end of the fourth century the Senate even reasserted itself for a moment against Christian emperors bent on abolishing the traditional state-worships. The institution of emperor-worship was somewhat damaged by the long succession of ephemeral rulers in the third century, none of whom received apotheosis after his death. Increasingly less stress was laid upon the personal divinity of the emperor himself and more upon the divine protection which he enjoyed and through which the state might secure the favour of heaven. Decius required sacrifice to the gods and offerings in honour of (not to) himself and an oath by his *genius*, as a test of loyalty. Diocletian by taking the name Iovius claimed a special relationship with the supreme god, perhaps identifying his *genius* with that of Jupiter. Thus Jupiter (and Hercules, through Maximian Herculius) were active in the world through the spirits of their earthly representatives. But whereas Aurelian by his official recognition of the worship of the Sun was moving in the direction of monotheism and syncretism as a means of securing the unity of the Empire, Diocletian's outlook was more traditional, with its emphasis on Jupiter and polytheism. His enthusiasm for the old Roman religion and practices was supported by his belief in oracles and the art of the *haruspices*. This conservatism, linked to political motives, led him to try to check the infiltration of Persian influences into the Roman Empire: from A.D. 242 a developed form of Gnosticism had been preached by a Babylonian called Mani, who had gained the favour of Shapur I. In 297 (more probably than in 302) Diocletian published an edict, which is preserved, proscribing Manichaeism throughout the Empire.[17] Soon afterwards he abandoned a tolerant policy towards Christianity and turned to persecution (pp. 546 f.).

Emperor-worship

Among the Oriental religions the Jewish worship maintained itself, but had ceased to make converts (p. 441). The cult of Isis, whose somewhat sentimental philanthropy might have been expected to find favour in an age that was losing its self-confidence, no more than held its ground after the period of the Severi. The attempt of Elagabalus to merge all other religions in that

545

of the sun-god of Emesa was merely *pour rire*; the Babylonian *Sol Invictus*, whom Aurelian permanently added to the official Roman pantheon, made no popular appeal. On the other hand the spiritualised cult of the Sun-god Mithras extended its hold on the Roman world until it became the chief rival of Christianity – at least in some areas and social classes. It was held in high favour by the Severi, and in the fourth century it became a rallying-point for those who resisted the inroads of the Galilean religion.

But in the competition between the religions of the Roman Empire the defence was in general stronger than the attack. Even such proselytising cults as those of Isis and Mithras owed much of their extension to the diffusion of their Oriental votaries over the whole Roman Empire, and conversion to them did not necessarily imply renunciation of other worships; with the decline of travel and commerce in the third and fourth centuries, the process of propagation was inevitably retarded.[18] The only religion which gained ground continuously at this period, and did so at the direct expense of other cults, was Christianity.

7. Christianity, Persecuted and Triumphant[19]

After the sporadic persecutions under Marcus Aurelius (p. 488) the Christians, whose faith

was now taking its place among the chief religions of the Graeco-Roman world, were comparatively unmolested under Commodus and in most of the Severan period. This calm was broken temporarily when Septimius, who hitherto had been favourable (he had employed a Christian nurse for his son Caracalla), suddenly in 202 banned conversion to Christianity (and to Judaism). This resulted in some martyrdoms at Carthage and the dispersion of Origen's Catechetical School at Alexandria, but under Severus Alexander, whose meticulous polytheism is said to have caused him to include Abraham and Christ among the deities of his domestic sanctuary, the Christians enjoyed a further immunity, which was only temporarily broken when Maximinus, through hatred of Alexander, took action against some Church leaders, including the bishop of Rome and his rival Hippolytus.

But in 250 the precarious safeguards of the Christians were swept away by the emperor Decius. In a wild attempt to crush the general insubordination and anarchy of his time and to create a greater unity within the Empire under its ruler, Decius expressly commanded all Christians to abjure their faith and to take part in the pagan worship of the Empire;

in order to secure the *pax deorum* the Empire's loyalty to the old gods of Rome must be demonstrated. First Decius arrested senior clergy and executed Pope Fabian; then all had to make a sacrifice or libation to the gods of Rome (among whom the emperor was not specifically included). Those Christians who refused to conform (the *confessores*) were either killed or imprisoned; those who sacrificed (the *lapsi*) were given certificates (*libelli*); others were able to flee, while some managed to buy *libelli*. The number of those who suffered for their faith cannot be estimated, although Porphyry, an anti-Christian contemporary, states that thousands were put to death. The persecution ceased with Decius's death in the summer of 251, but it was renewed in 257 by Valerian, who tried to prohibit public worship and to force all clergy to sacrifice to the gods. This was followed in 258 by a more severe edict: higher clergy who had not sacrificed were to be executed, while higher-class laymen and non-military civil servants were punished and their property confiscated. This led to numerous executions (the victims included Cyprian of Carthage), but in the next year Valerian was captured by the Persians. The persecutions, however, were too spasmodic to achieve any permanent effect. Whatever emperors might enjoin, public opinion was by now making its peace with the Christians, and provincial governors, assailed by the same doubts as the younger Pliny, salved their consciences by blowing hot and cold in turn. Gallienus, who realised that in a case of this kind a half-success was tantamount to failure, rescinded his father's orders and granted toleration and the restoration of confiscated property (260). During the next forty years the Christians were not only left unmolested, but were tacitly exempted from the obligation to worship the emperor, so that they became free to enlist in the army and enter the civil service; under Diocletian they even rose to the position of provincial governors.[20]

Yet their stiffest ordeal was still to come, for between 303 and 311 they were subjected to a more persistent persecution than ever before. This renewed attack upon the Christians was all the more strange, as Diocletian had taken a Christian to wife, was personally of a tolerant disposition and had shown no inclination to attack the Christians during the early part of his reign. Presumably he was overborne by Galerius, the most masterful of his lieutenants, whose views on conformity were those of the military martinet. After nineteen years of rule he issued his first edict against them in February 303: churches were to be destroyed, the Scriptures handed over (*traditio*) and burnt, and

43.7 A Christian catacomb, showing *loculi*, tiers of recesses for holding the bodies; they could be sealed with stone slabs or tiles.

Christians of the higher classes were to be deprived of their privileged immunities. But there was to be no bloodshed. However, two mysterious conflagrations in the emperor's palace at Nicomedia may have suggested that Nero had wrought better than he knew when he punished Christians as incendiaries. At any rate more stringent edicts followed. The clergy were imprisoned in large numbers, while a third edict ordered that they should be forced to sacrifice and then be released. Galerius next seized the opportunity occasioned by a serious illness of Diocletian to issue a fourth edict which demanded universal sacrifice on pain of death. If Diocletian had hoped to pursue a policy of reconciliation this was now wrecked. The number of victims of the persecution under Diocletian and Galerius undoubtedly exceeded all previous totals. Yet the Christians found many loop-holes of escape. After Diocletian's retirement (305) Galerius's Caesar, Maximinus Daia, issued two new edicts (in 306 and 309) which

In the East

were followed by savagely repressive measures, but even in the eastern provinces some governors were remiss in carrying out orders. Then in 311 Galerius made a death-bed repentance, stopped the persecution and granted Christians legal recognition. Apart from his personal fears Galerius perhaps recognised that his cause was lost, thanks in part to the extent to which Christianity had spread throughout the East in the countryside no less than in the towns, while the continuing brutalities were alienating much pagan sympathy. True, Maximinus, Galerius's successor as senior Augustus, made a final attempt at a pagan revival and suppression of Christianity (311–312), but he was soon ordered by Constantine to stop. Thus in the East the battle was at last won, though the cost in lives cannot be estimated: its incidence varied greatly, since we hear that 100 Christians were martyred in Egypt on one day alone, while in Palestine this number was not exceeded during many years. Meanwhile in the West the persecutions had been much lighter. Constantius seems to have gone little further than to destroy some Christian churches, and after Diocletian's abdication persecution ceased in the West.

and West

In 312 after his victory at the Milvian Bridge, which he attributed to the aid of the God of the Christians, Constantine's conversion to Christianity opened a new era for the Church. Now created senior Augustus by the Senate, he ordered Maximinus to cease persecuting, as we have seen, restored Church property and provided money for relief. Then early in 313 he met his ally Licinius at Milan and won him over to a policy of complete toleration; this policy may not have been formally expressed in a so-called 'Edict of Milan', but it was none the less real and effective: freedom of worship was granted to all the subjects of the Empire, East and West alike, and the Christian Churches were recognised as legal corporations. Thus Constantine's attitude to the Church is unambiguous but the true nature of his 'conversion' remains as enigmatic as his character.[21] He has been depicted at one extreme as religiously committed to Christ, at the other as merely using Christianity as an instrument in a policy of self-aggrandisement: the truth probably lies somewhere between. He did not accept baptism until near death or submit to the discipline of the Church and its leaders (rather, he called himself 'the bishop of those outside' and later 'the equal of the apostles'), but he showed deference to Christian advisers by his subsequent legislation on matters of private morality and by his institution of a compulsory Sunday rest from work, while in his new capital he prohibited the construction of pagan

The 'Edict of Milan'

Constantine and Christianity

43.8   The central portion of a Christian sarcophagus of *c.* A.D. 350, now in the Lateran Museum. It shows a Chi–Rho monogram within a wreath of victory, hanging from the beak of an eagle. The wreath crowns a trophy in the form of a cross, which is flanked by two soldiers who are guarding the tomb of Christ, now risen; they are in the traditional posture of barbarians who flanked imperial trophies. On the left Christ is being crowned not with a crown of thorns, but with a laurel wreath of victory. Pagan motifs are thus combined with Christian beliefs, and the age of Constantine is vividly symbolised.

temples. In rejecting paganism, he did not persecute its followers: indeed he remained conscious that he was ruler of a divided world and made every effort to heal breaches between pagans and Christians and within the Church itself. But his inmost beliefs we shall never know, though it is significant that in a letter to the bishops gathered at a conference at Arles he refers to God's blessing in showing him his past errors and guiding him into the way of truth (if the letter preserved by Optatus, a Numidian bishop, is genuine).

Imperial unity had been achieved with the defeat of Licinius (p. 524); unity within the Church must also be established. Thus Constantine became involved in Church affairs, fearing the wrath of God if he did not remove dissensions within His Holy Church. A quarrel within *The Donatists* the African Church had caused a schism between the followers of Donatus and the Catholics. When the Donatists appealed to Constantine they started a long series of events which cannot be recounted here but led to the emperor summoning an assembly of bishops at Arles to settle the issue (314), to further appeals to the emperor and ultimately to the use of force by Constantine to stamp out the Donatist churches. But then four years later he abandoned this attempt to impose unity on the African Church (321). Another schism which divided the Eastern Church arose over the nature of the divinity of Christ, the Orthodox being led by Alexander, bishop of Alexandria, the heretics by Arius. Constantine once again was concerned with the unity of the Church rather than with matters of theology, and his intervention led ultimately in 325 to the summoning of an oecumenical council of bishops at Nicaea, over which he himself presided. Here finally a creed was found *The Council of Nicaea* which was accepted by all the dissident parties: the nature of the creed was probably of far less importance to the emperor than the fact of its acceptance. But Constantine had further ecclesiastical troubles. Although Arius soon announced himself converted, Athanasius, the successor of Alexander, refused to recognise him and a bitter quarrel ensued. This ended in Constantine reluctantly banishing Athanasius, reluctantly because this one rift prevented the total success of his tireless efforts to unite the Church. Athanasius was still in exile in 337 when Constantine died. Rifts there had been also in his domestic life, which led to the execution of his eldest son Crispus and his wife Fausta, but with three other sons and many relatives he could anticipate that hereditary succession would prevail, though he could not guarantee that they would act in mutual trust. During his last illness and shortly before his death Constantine was at long last baptised.

In the days of Constantine Christianity was still a long way from being the universal religion of the Roman Empire. Except perhaps in Syria, in Asia Minor and in the city of Alexandria, its adherents nowhere included more than half the population; in Rome and the West they were as yet a small minority. Yet they had planted their propaganda-cells in every province; their clergy had constituted itself into a powerful aristocracy; above all, they had captured a high proportion of the more thoughtful inhabitants of the Empire. In the middle of the fourth century the reluctant but honest emperor Julian, the last eminent champion of the old order of things, was constrained to admit that the ultimate victory of Christianity in the Roman world was assured.

Christianity the religion of the future

CHAPTER 44

The Roman Empire. Retrospect and Prospect

1. The End of the Empire in the West

Though Diocletian and Constantine gave the Roman Empire a further lease of life, they could not eradicate the disease which had all but destroyed it. After the death of Constantine a new round of civil wars between his sons and other claimants kept the Empire in a more or less permanent state of division, and its temporary reunion under Constantius (353–361) and Julian (361–363), and again under Theodosius I (395), merely emphasised the difficulty of holding it together. In 364 the brothers Valentinian and Valens made an amicable partition of the Roman dominions, by which the former took Italy and the western districts, while Valens received the eastern provinces; and a similar compromise was made between Theodosius's two sons, Arcadius and Honorius, who became the founders of two sub-empires in the East and West respectively (395). Though in strict law Arcadius and Honorius remained joint rulers of an undivided realm, in actual practice they became independent of each other, so that the history of the eastern and western divisions henceforth ran on separate lines.

Final partition of the Empire

The East-Roman Empire remained relatively free from civil wars and enjoyed comparative immunity from foreign invasions. It passed through a critical period after 378, when the co-emperor Valens was killed in a disastrous battle against an invading army of Goths at Adrianople; but under his successor Theodosius the Goths were induced to settle down peacefully in the Balkan lands, and the Danube frontier was made fast again. A long period of

The Eastern Empire becomes stabilised

comparative tranquillity followed, during which the East-Roman emperors found leisure to continue the work of internal reorganisation. Two of the greatest monuments of Roman statecraft, the code of Theodosius II on administrative law (A.D. 438) and the general code of Justinian (528-534), had their origin at Contantinople. But the separation of the Eastern Empire from Italy inevitably caused it to lose its Roman character. The Byzantine monarchy, which grew insensibly out of the East-Roman Empire, was a Hellenistic kingdom, with a Christian Church and a Roman law-book.

but becomes Greek

The severance of Italy and the western provinces from the eastern Mediterranean resulted in their bleeding to death. In the fifth century the Western Empire had to bear the brunt of renewed German invasions at the same time as it was being distracted by internal dissensions. In 407 a rebellion by a pretender named Constantine, who deserted his post in Britain in order to cut his way through to Rome, threw open all the frontiers of western Europe. Britain, which had long been depleted of most of its effective forces, ceased to have any official connexion with the central government of Rome after 410 and had to face Saxons, Picts and Scots unaided; a final appeal, probably in 446, to Aetius, the effective Roman ruler in the West, remained unanswered. Until this latter date a British ruler, Vortigern, with the aid of Saxon federates maintained some independence in a 'sub-Roman' period during which some aspects of the older Roman framework and civilisation lingered on, but thereafter the struggle was continued less by attenuated 'Roman' elements than

Dissolution of the Western Empire

Evacuation of Britain

by the Celtic, now reinforced by the wide extension of Christianity and Christian leaders.[1] A few isolated detachments held out along the Rhine, but these could not prevent a continuous stream of German invaders from crossing the frontier. Between 406 and 419 northern Gaul was definitely conquered by the Franks, eastern Gaul by a lesser German tribe, the Burgundians, and Spain by the Suebi and Vandals. In 429 the Vandals passed over to northern Africa and converted its peaceful provinces into pirate bases, from which they cut off the sea-connexions between east and west in the Mediterranean lands. In the meantime the Visigoths (with the connivance of the East-Roman emperor Arcadius) left their new homes in the Balkans in search of better land. In the first ten years of the fifth century they repeatedly invaded Italy, while the Western emperor, Honorius, took refuge behind the marshes of Ravenna. In 408 the Visigothic chieftain Alaric broke into central Italy and extorted a danegeld from Rome; in 410 he reappeared before the 'Eternal City' and put it to sack. After his death the Visigothic marauders retired to Aquitania and founded a kingdom whose rulers came to a friendly understanding with the last Roman emperors of the West.

The Germans occupy Gaul, Spain and northern Africa

Sack of Rome by Alaric

In 451 a Roman general named Aetius won the last notable triumph of Roman armies in the West, when with the help of the Visigoths from Aquitania he beat off an alarming incursion by the Hun chieftain Attila into central France. But after the death of Aetius the West-Roman Empire hastened to its final collapse. Between 470 and 490 the Franks and Goths shared out the remaining Roman provinces in central France and Provence. In 455 the Vandal Gaiseric made a sea-raid upon Rome and plundered the city so thoroughly that it remained henceforth half derelict. In 476 a mutinous German captain of mercenaries, named Odoacer, put to death the emperor Orestes and deposed his son, Romulus Augustulus. With this act (which passed almost unnoticed at the time), the rule of Rome in the West was terminated, and the East-Roman emperor became the sole depository of the Roman *imperium*.[2]

Last Roman stand against Attila

A German chief deposes the last Western emperor

2. Decline and Fall

From the middle of the third century the Roman Empire ran a course which led to its disappearance in the West, and to its transformation into a Greek kingdom in the Byzantine East. This process, which has been summed up as the 'Decline' of the Roman Empire, has been the subject

The problem of Decline

of endless speculation, and all manner of reasons have been put forward to explain it.[3] At the same time the concept of 'Decline' has been interpreted in many different ways and this has sometimes clouded discussion. Not all elements in a culture may be declining at the same time, nor universally throughout it: thus there were elements of growth (e.g. in religious life) as well as of decline in the late Roman period, and some provinces of the Empire declined more than others. Further, full weight has to be given to the fact that, however widespread the decline, in the event only the West collapsed: East Rome survived for another thousand years. So the problem becomes one of trying to define what elements declined and for what reasons, why the result was the downfall of the Western Empire alone, and also to assess the relative part played by internal weakness against external strength.

There are those who regard the 'fall' as either natural or inevitable; others tend to deny that in any real sense there was a fall. For such the need to probe for and analyse basic causes is less. Gibbon, who in *The Decline and Fall* claimed to have 'described the triumph of Barbarism and Religion', nevertheless suggested that the fall was due to a natural internal weakness when he wrote, 'The decline of Rome was the natural and inevitable effect of immoderate greatness . . . the stupendous fabric yielded to the pressure of its own weight . . . instead of inquiring why the Roman Empire was destroyed, we should rather be surprised that it had subsisted so long.' Others attribute the fall to external circumstances: thus A. Piganiol summed up, 'Roman civilization did not die a natural death. It was murdered.' But even so, we are still faced with the problem why Rome was not strong enough to resist the murderous assaults of the barbarians. Further, the use of metaphors may lead to misunderstanding. Thus Gibbon's image of a house collapsing may obscure the fact that the Roman Empire was really a complex administrative framework which embraced a culture composed of very varied elements, or, regarded from another point of view, the beliefs held by those who lived within this framework which they had created. Further, cyclical or biological metaphors of birth, growth, decline and death as applied to civilisations, although deriving a respectable origin from Polybius or earlier, have the unfortunate effect of implying an inevitability of decline, which arises not from historical circumstances but from the use of this analogy. Thus Spengler assumed that human societies followed some natural law, like living organisms or the seasons of the year. Toynbee, though not accepting the biological analogy and Spengler's inevit-

Some views of the Decline

able end for all human societies, nevertheless sees them as subject to a common development. In particular he regards the Greek and Roman worlds as forming one 'Hellenic Society' and believes that the seeds of its fatal illness go back to the Peloponnesian War; though the hardy patient lingered on for 800 years, with intermittent periods of recovery, he was doomed from the beginning, but not doomed to annihilation in a Spenglerian sense, since when Hellenic Society ended it left as a progeny Western Christendom which was 'affiliated' to it. Finally, there are those who deny any catastrophic fall but believe that the Roman Empire was gradually changed into the medieval world without any sudden 'death' intervening: the process was one of transformation rather than decline and fall.[4]

3. Physical Causes of the Decline

However we may account for the decline of the Roman Empire we cannot simplify the process by reducing it to a single cause. Like a giant tree which has thrown out strong roots in all directions the Roman Empire could not be brought low by an attack from one quarter only. But among the variety of factors that contributed to the Decline, some require more emphasis than others; the crux of the problem *The causes* is to sort out the general and permanent from *of the* the local and transitory causes, the primary *Decline* from the derivative agencies. On this question *were* of emphasis opinions are and no doubt will *multiple* remain widely divergent. But every discussion of causes must take into account the time at which the Decline began. The later second and early third centuries may be described as a period of stagnation, but not of general retrogression. But by 250 the Roman Empire had entered on a period more critical than any since the Second Punic War, and though it emerged from its ordeal it was henceforth quite definitely on the down grade. No explanation of the Decline can be considered fully adequate unless it singles out some factor which came into play not long before 250 and acted as the *momentum rerum*.[5]

In general it may be said that the various causes of a physical order which have been invoked were, at the most, but accessory factors in the Decline. The material impoverishment of the Roman world was not in any large degree *Exhaustion* due to the exhaustion of the mines or the refusal *of land and* of the soil to yield further crops. Though care- *minerals* less cultivation no doubt ruined tracts of land here and there, evidence for a general deterioration of the land is lacking, and it cannot be inferred from the ancient methods of cultivation that these progressively robbed it of its plant food. The decrease of agricultural and industrial productivity was not so much the result of natural causes as of the political disorders and fiscal pressures of the third and following centuries.[6]

Deterioration of climate may be definitely ruled out as a serious contributory factor to the Decline. Though modifications of the weather no doubt occurred in regions subjected to excessive deforestation, climatic conditions in the Mediterranean region as a whole remained substantially unaltered through the whole course of Roman history, and they were, as at the present day, mainly favourable to the maintenance of a high civilisation.[7]

Among the causes of a medical order, to which the Decline has been ascribed, the pestilences which occasionally visited Rome, and the great plagues which swept across the Empire in 166 and 250–270, had devastating short-term results, but it is very far from certain that either the losses they inflicted were not made good or would not have been repaired but for other adverse factors.[8] Malaria, which probably had *Disease* for centuries (from the fifth century B.C. or earlier?) become endemic on the shores of Latium and Etruria and no doubt infested other low-lying shores and river-estuaries, has also been claimed as a factor of the Decline. But since the Mediterranean climate and the structure of the Mediterranean lands as a whole do not favour the formation of those stagnant backwaters which are the main breeding-grounds of the germ-carrying mosquitoes, malaria was probably, as in more recent times, *Malaria* a local disease from which the Mediterranean populations as a whole remained immune or at worst acquired a certain degree of immunity or tolerance by previous infections. And in any case we have no evidence to suggest widespread increases of the disease at periods of time which could correlate its incidence with the Decline.[9]

We may also reject the hypothesis that the Roman world was reduced to decrepitude by its profligate mode of life. The abundance of wealth *Physical* and leisure, among whom 'fast sets' developed *vice* in the usual manner, and the institution of slavery exposed all slave-owners to temptations from which the modern world is relatively free. But it would be a mistake to assess at their face value the frequent and laboured diatribes of Latin writers about Roman degeneration from the *mos maiorum*. The great majority of the population in the Roman Empire, land-workers and craftsmen, small tradesmen and professional men, had neither the means nor the cravings for dangerous self-indulgence. The general habits of the ancient as of the modern Mediterranean populations inclined towards sobriety, and evidence is not lacking that in the lands of the Roman Empire as a whole family life ran on normal healthy lines. The vices of Roman society certainly did not cut deep enough to ruin the general physical type of the Empire.[10]

Dysgenic breeding

Another theory which invokes physical causes for the Decline attributes it to dysgenic breeding. It has been contended that in the early Christian era the best strains of the Mediterranean peoples, such as those of Italy itself, broke down through excessive cross-breeding with inferior types. The mingling of races was undoubtedly facilitated under the Roman emperors by the wide diffusion of slavery and by the migrations of soldiers and traders; the population of the capital had become thoroughly mongrel even in the days of the Republic, and Italy as a whole eventually lost whatever purity of breed it may have once possessed. But racial theories find little favour today, and in any case it is difficult to single out any particular race within the Mediterranean area as specifically eugenic or dysgenic. The Oriental elements of population with which the Roman stock became saturated have often been branded as inferior; yet the eastern Mediterranean was the cradle of ancient culture, and Graeco-Roman civilisation survived in the Levant after it had become submerged in the West. Again, it cannot be assumed that unions between free persons and slaves or ex-slaves were necessarily detrimental; presumably those who inter-married with the free-born population were the soundest elements of the servile class.[11]

Excessive losses in war

An alternative theory points to the dysgenic influence of warfare, which by its very nature ensures the premature death of the fittest, and argues that the Roman wars of conquest took too heavy a toll of the best elements in the Mediterranean populations. It is perhaps not a mere accident that after the first century A.D. Italy, which had been remorselessly combed out for recruits by the Roman war-machine, supplied hardly any fighting men for the service of Rome, and produced scarcely a single important figure in the field of war or of letters. On the other hand the provinces were not systematically overburdened with conscription, and in the long era of peace under the early Caesars they were almost immune from the havoc of battle. If Italy paid too high a price for its supremacy in the Mediterranean, the Mediterranean lands as a whole were in large measure safeguarded by the *Pax Romana* against the dysgenic effects of war.

War and pestilence obviously reduced the man-power of the Empire at certain periods and a gradual decline of both free and servile popula-

Population and man-power

tion in the centuries from Augustus to Constantine may be admitted. But it may be doubted whether this led to a sufficiently critical shortage of man-power from the mid-second century as to be a major cause of the Decline, as has been recently argued.[12] True, there were vacant lands in the Empire in which barbarian troops were then settled, but much of the earlier population may have drifted to the cities rather than merely disappeared. Further, the increasing use of barbarians for defence need not imply a serious decrease in numbers but only a dislike of conditions of military service on the part of non-barbarians. Though the *pax Augusta* may have limited the number of slaves coming on to the markets as war-captives, a balance may have been established by internal breeding. In general, while the maintenance of Augustus's legislation to encourage marriage and large families suggests consciousness of a population problem, the decrease in numbers, so far as it occurred, appears to result from government demands rather than natural causes and thus falls within the category of symptoms rather than of causes of the Decline.

Another cause of physical deterioration which requires discussion is race-suicide among the governing classes of the Empire. The original patrician aristocracy of Rome suffered a rapid decline in the fifth and fourth centuries B.C. (p. 76), and in the first century A.D. it died out altogether. The nobility of the later Republic showed a similar tendency to sterility, and under the early Caesars deliberate abstention from marriage or child-bearing became so frequent among the wealthy classes of Italy that the legislation of Augustus *de maritandis ordinibus* failed to counteract it (p. 328). It is highly probable that the racial type of Italy suffered from the extinction of its most successful families. But it is quite uncertain how far the governing families in the provinces were affected by this self-effacing tendency, and in any case they in turn infused new energy into the whole body politic.[13]

Race-suicide

The incidence of physical agents in producing the Decline must remain somewhat problematic in view of the scantiness of our information on this topic. Their operation can be traced to some extent in Italy, but eludes our observation in the provinces. Taking the Roman Empire as a whole, we cannot on present evidence assign a prominent place to factors of a natural order in the history of the Decline.

4. Social and Political Causes of the Decline

Among the factors of a social and political character, Roman education has been impugned because it did not extend sufficiently far among the masses of the population.[14] Beyond doubt the masses of the people in the Roman world *One-sided* acquired no more than a smattering of Graeco-*education* Roman culture, whose roots in consequence did not strike sufficiently deep. Moreover, higher education, especially in the Latin-speaking countries, was dangerously one-sided. The almost exclusive addiction to linguistic and stylistic studies, the general neglect of natural and of social science, help to explain that perilous lack of resourcefulness and self-help which characterised Roman society after the second century. On the other hand education was more widely diffused in the first three centuries A.D. than in any other age of ancient history, and perhaps extended as far as in any subsequent period before the nineteenth century. In addition, the training in the Roman high schools was at least thorough, and so far as it went it unquestionably provided a good mental discipline.

A general failure of nerve has been seen as a cause of the Decline, but in so far as it can be detected it must be regarded as a symptom rather than a cause. Gibbon, as is well known, *Christianity* invoked Christianity: 'the introduction, or at least the abuse, of Christianity had some influence on the decline and fall of the Roman empire. The clergy successfully preached the doctrines of patience and pusillanimity; the active virtues of society were discouraged; and the last remains of the military spirit were buried in the cloister.' Such an extreme view has long been rebutted: thus J. B. Bury wrote: 'the effect of Christianity was to unite, not to sever . . . nor is there the least reason to suppose that Christian teaching had the practical effect of making men less loyal to the Empire or less ready to defend it. The Christians were as pugnacious as the pagans.'[15] Indeed few who recall how for conscience's sake numerous ordinary Christians steeled their nerves to face lions in the arena or the executioner's sword rather than cast a few grains of incense upon a pagan altar will charge them with a general failure of nerve. Equally, if early causes are sought, few would argue that Christianity had undermined society before the mid-third century, and it should be remembered that Christianity was also the religion of East Rome, which did not fall for another millennium. Nevertheless Christianity had a profound effect on society, especially from the early fourth century onwards when its power and efficiency were clearly outdistancing those of paganism, and it therefore inevitably drew to itself away from the service of the state some of the best men who otherwise would have become generals, provincial governors or im-

perial courtiers. This process was accelerated by the growth of monasticism from the second part of the fourth century. The Church also naturally tried to convert barbarians, more especially those settled within the Empire, and thus in the West it encouraged their assimilation with the state, whereas in the East the Church cooperated with the state in its fight against the barbarians. Thus, however difficult it is to analyse the impact of Christianity on later pagan society, it was clearly a major factor in a world where the basis of authority was gradually shifting.[16]

Disparity in economic efficiency forms the most striking contrast between Roman and modern civilisation. The nemesis of slave-labour was that it sterilised technical inventiveness, fostered the establishment of a stagnant rentier class, and produced permanent conditions of under-consumption. This under-consumption was fostered by the top-heavy structure of society: wealth was unduly concentrated at the top where a limited class (together with the army and to a much lesser extent markets outside the Empire) provided the main market for industry. This restricted internal market was not extended to include the masses. Consequently under ancient conditions of exchange and production rapid economic development was *Economic* scarcely possible, save where large tracts of land *failures* were being brought for the first time under intensive cultivation, where new mines were being opened or fresh trade routes explored. Further, there was a movement towards decentralisation, a drive outwards to find new markets; industry and trades tended to move from the older centres to new, while industry also gradually inclined to shift from the cities to the villages and the large manorial estates in the country, leading ultimately to a reduction of the areas open to trade. By 200, therefore, economic progress was being arrested, and in the next two centuries the economic machine could no longer repair the damage of continual wars and political disorders. Yet in the first two centuries A.D. the economic activity of the Mediterranean lands was at its highest, and there is no reason for supposing that a positive economic retrogression would have set in during the third and fourth centuries, but for the political disturbances of that period.[17]

Tension between town and country forms the basis for a famous theory of the Decline by Rostovtzeff, who superimposed on the fact of the exploitation of the peasant population by the city-dwellers a theory of class-warfare: in the *Class-* third century the army, which consisted largely *warfare* of peasants, joined hands with the rural peasants and together they opposed the bourgeoisie of the cities. But the validity of this view hardly matches the brilliance with which it was expounded, since in our surviving sources the complaints of the peasantry are not directed at the townsmen as a class, but only at individual landlords, or at officials, and the soldiers figure as oppressors of the peasants rather than as their allies or avengers.[18]

Political errors

The Decline of the Roman Empire has often, and not without reason, been attributed to faults in its political structure. From the time of the great conquests in the third and second centuries B.C. the tendency in Roman politics was towards a progressive concentration of power into the hands of a small minority. The early wars in which the Romans gained control of Italy brought about a more equable distribution of wealth and gave greater self-reliance to the common citizen; hence under the constitution of the middle Republic the sovereignty of the people was no mere empty phrase. The later wars, in which the Romans subdued the Mediterranean region, created a proletariat that lived in economic dependence on a governing class and could exercise no intelligent control over the growing complexity of politics. Under these conditions the accumulation of power in the hands of a narrow and exclusive aristocracy was an almost inevitable result. But the failure of this aristocracy to maintain order and to control the army plunged the Roman state into a chaos, for which the only remedy was a more or less unqualified dictatorship. Augustus, it is true, attempted to preserve as far as possible the republican idea of team work in the state; and the growth of new municipal aristocracies in the provinces during the first two centuries A.D. produced another governing class, to which part of the emperors' powers might fitly have been transferred by a gradual process of decentralisation (pp. 449 f.). But under the early Caesars the power of the monarchy steadily encroached on other governing bodies, and the disorders of the third century left the Roman Empire no option but to accept a dictatorship without any qualification. The problem of reconciling Empire and self-government proved too difficult for the Roman world.

Discipline and liberty not reconciled

Excessive centralisation of power

The result of this extreme concentration of political power was a general loss of those habits of self-help and resourcefulness which had been nurtured in the earlier days of the small city-state. The Roman Empire eventually found itself in the plight of an army which has engaged its last reserves and has no means left of staving off disaster if its present line does not hold. Furthermore, the Roman emperors and their officials were not more immune than other autocrats from the temptations that attend power without responsibility. In the case of the emperors, it is true, the *ultima ratio* of revolution or assassination acted as a restraint upon capricious government; on the other hand the imperial executive established itself in a virtually unassailable position. The misgovernment of the uncontrolled bureaucracy unquestionably contributed to the decline of the Empire by draining still further its attenuated resources, and by the wide and deep discontent which it caused. On the other hand it should be noted that this ever-increasing regimentation and compulsion by the state in economic and financial life was not due to an ideological policy of state enterprise, but resulted from the desperate efforts of the emperors to find a way out of certain problems of essential production and finance arising from the decline of private enterprise and of free exchange. The *laissez faire* of the earlier Empire wilted away in changing conditions of life: it was not sacrificed to any economic theory.

But the Roman Empire transcended national limits

Against these failures of Roman statecraft must be set the extension of the Roman franchise to Italy and the provinces, and the opening up of all military and political offices, not excluding that of the emperor himself, to every nationality within the Empire. In the third and fourth centuries the Roman government had at least the merit of being representative of all parts of the Roman dominions, and the sense of a common Roman citizenship was an effective safeguard against the formation of hostile nationalist groups within the Empire.[19] Furthermore, the vagaries of a Caligula and a Nero, of a Commodus and an Elagabalus, should not blind us to the fact that the Roman emperors, taken as a whole, were a vigorous and conscientious line of monarchs, and that the survival of the Empire in the third and fourth centuries was in large measure due to the personal exertions of rulers in whom the 'never-say-die' spirit of the year of Cannae was still alive.[20]

Emperors mostly capable

Disputed successions

A manifest weakness in the armour of the Roman Empire lay in its liability to disputed successions. It has been held that the lack of a rule of hereditary succession was a fatal flaw in its constitution. But — to say nothing of the fact that under a law of dynastic succession the standard of ability among the emperors would probably have been lowered — such a regulation would have been a very frail safeguard against usurpers. The existence of a dynastic law did not prevent the Ptolemaic monarchy from being seriously weakened, or the Seleucid and Arsacid monarchies from being destroyed, by wars between rival pretenders to the crown. The orgy of usurpers which momentarily imperilled and definitely weakened the Empire was predominantly due to the mutinous temper of the troops;

555

no mere alteration in the Roman constitution could have provided a remedy against this.

Of the administrative errors committed by the Roman emperors none have been more severely censured than their financial blunders. Undoubtedly the progressive depreciation of the coinage and the arbitrary incidence of taxation, for which Diocletian's reforms brought no adequate remedy, acted as a hindrance to economic recovery after the disasters of the third century; but they were the outcome, not the cause, of these disasters. Compared with the civil wars and the barbarian invasions the financial mistakes, whether of the earlier or of the later emperors, were but a minor factor in the Decline.

Arbitrary taxation

The constitutional development of the Roman Empire was dictated to a great extent by its foreign policy. Was this policy conceived on the wrong lines? It has been suggested that the Roman conquerors overreached themselves by annexing more land than they could profitably or safely hold. The extension of the Roman boundaries across the Danube to Dacia, or across the Channel to Britain, was but a matter of minor moment; the critical question is whether the Senate of the second century B.C. was well advised to make conquests in the eastern Mediterranean. It may be contended that if the Romans had left the Greeks to their own devices and had applied themselves to the consolidation of their rule in the West, they might have created a compact and homogeneous *bloc* of Latin-speaking peoples which would have been impregnable to all assailants.[21] On the other hand it cannot be said that the extension of the Roman Empire over the whole of the Mediterranean made it dangerously unwieldy, or seriously embarrassed its communications; and, if the Jews remained an alien element, the Oriental populations in the Roman dominions were none the less loyal and helpful, in spite of their differences of language and culture.

Errors of foreign policy

The most obvious of all explanations of the Decline is that the foreign enemies who broke across the frontiers in the third and following centuries were too strong for it.[22] This is a truism which may easily give a wrong impression. The Persians, Goths and Alamanni were not to be compared in point of military efficiency with the Carthaginians and Macedonians, whom the armies of the Roman Republic defeated utterly. If they nevertheless strained the Roman defences to the utmost, the reason is that these had been seriously weakened. The cause of this enfeeblement is partly to be sought in the replacement of Italian recruits to the Roman army by provincials from the less Romanised districts, who lacked the

Failure of frontier defence

versatility of the Italian soldiers and were less amenable to discipline.[23] Yet the Roman frontiers would never have been seriously imperilled but for the preoccupation of the Roman garrisons in the third century with the game of emperor-making. This beyond question was the chief proximate cause of the Decline. Of all the dangers that the Roman conquests carried with them the greatest was that the professionalised soldiery, which was the only possible instrument for holding those conquests together, should discover that as an instrument of Empire it was indispensable, and should accordingly seek to impose its own terms on Senate or emperors. Against this risk the provision of liberal pay and pensions for the troops afforded a partial insurance, but no complete guarantee. It may be suggested that a better precaution against military coups would have been to restore conscription in a modified form by supplementing the professional army with a second-line force of militiamen. To create such a force need not have imposed a severe strain upon Roman finances or undue hardships upon the conscripts. At times of foreign war a Roman militia could have rendered useful service in performing the functions which in modern armies are assigned to the older men, of securing lines of communication and of closing temporary gaps in the front. Furthermore, by its mere presence it would have spoilt the sport of emperor-making. Success in this game depended upon sudden action; delay might spell disaster, as the fate of the usurper Maximinus demonstrated (p. 507). With a second-line army between the frontiers and Rome some military coups would have failed; most of them would in all probability have never been attempted. Without such a force the professional soldiers found it fatally easy to march upon Rome, leaving the frontiers undefended. The Roman army both made and unmade the Roman Empire.

Breakdown of army discipline

5. Survivals of the Roman Empire[24]

The Decline of the Roman Empire ushered in the Middle Ages of Europe; but in the Middle Ages the Empire was not more than half dead, and even now it is mighty yet.

In the eastern Mediterranean the Byzantine monarchy was a direct continuation of the Roman Empire on a reduced scale. After the break-up of the Western Empire it preserved Roman institutions for two further centuries, and retained the use of Latin in its courts: it is to Constantinople, not to Rome, that we owe the two greatest monuments of Roman law, the Codes of Theodosius and Justinian. In the

Survivals in the East

seventh and eighth centuries the close-knit Roman administration was replaced by a more loose-jointed system analogous to the feudal governments of western Europe, and Greek ousted Latin as the official tongue. But the line of Roman emperors went on unbroken (albeit with frequent changes of dynasties) until the capture of Constantinople by Mohammed II in 1453. The Byzantine emperor Constantine XIII, who perished in the breach at the fall of his capital, might consider himself a lineal descendant of Augustus. Thus Constantinople had endured for a thousand years, thanks to the impregnability of its walls and position, the reserves of military man-power that Asia Minor provided, a generally efficient administrative machinery, and fewer economic tensions than existed in the West. To its resolute resistance to the storms of barbarism the modern world owes the preservation of much of the legacy of the ancient world since Greek literature was continuously studied there and thus survived in part; then, as the Turks finally began to close in on the capital city, numerous manuscripts were removed by fleeing scholars and teachers to Italy where they were welcomed with open arms by the humanists of the Renaissance.

In the western Mediterranean the temporary reoccupation of Rome by Justinian's generals, Belisarius and Narses, was but a brief interlude in an age of lesser German monarchies. In 489 Theodoric led his Ostrogoths into Italy to supersede Odoacer (p. 551) and established an Ostrogothic kingdom. This weakened after his death in 526 and struggled intermittently with the imperial armies of East Rome until in 568 the fierce barbarian Lombards migrated into Italy and occupied the northern part for two centuries. But on Christmas Day 800 Charlemagne, who extended to much of western Europe (though not to southern Italy) the Frankish kingdom which he had inherited from his predecessors, was crowned emperor by the Pope in St Peter's in Rome: 'Karolo piissimo Augusto a Deo coronato vita et victoria', shouted the congregation, and western Europe again had a Roman emperor. Although the Carolingian Empire later disintegrated, the heritage of the Frankish emperor. Although the Carolingian Empire later (936), who in 962 revived the title of 'Roman emperor' in western Europe, established the Holy Roman Empire and initiated a line of 'Roman' potentates which lasted intermittently until modern times. A series of vigorous German kings made determined attempts to convert the Roman Empire of the West into a reality, and the long-drawn conflict which they waged against the Popes and the revived city-republics of Italy forms one of the chief episodes in the political

The Holy Roman Empire

history of the Middle Ages.[25] After the death of Frederick II, the *stupor mundi*, in 1250, the Roman emperors' sphere of authority was definitely restricted to German soil, and after the Thirty Years War their power became quite shadowy. But it was not until 1806, when Napoleon vulgarised the style of 'emperor' by usurping it without any legal title, that Francis I of Austria renounced his Roman crown and wound up the oldest political concern in Europe by voluntary liquidation.

It is a matter of controversy whether Roman municipal institutions survived in western Europe; on the other hand there is no doubt that Roman law never went wholly out of use. Many of its elements were embodied in the 'Canon Law' which the Church administered in its particular sphere of jurisdiction. Abridgments of Theodosius's Code were made at the order of enlightened German kings in Italy *c*. A.D. 500; after 1100 Roman law became *Roman law* a leading subject of study in the universities of Europe; from the sixteenth century onward its practical application in the courts of law of the modernised European states became more and more general. At the present time the law of ancient Rome forms the basis of most of the codes in use among peoples of European race, except in some countries of English speech.[26]

The service which the Latin language rendered as an international means of communication among the clergy and other men of learning in the Middle Ages is too well known to need discussion here. Together with the Christian creed, it was the chief bond of union in a 'Balkanised' western Europe, and for several centuries it was virtually the sole vehicle of literature in the western lands. In the thirteenth century it began to be replaced by the vernacular tongues as the medium of literature, but it remained in general use in those fields of thought in which accuracy of expression was essential. English statutes were indited in Latin until the Lancastrian period, international treaties until the eighteenth century. Latin was the language *Latin* of science to the end of the seventeenth century; *literature* as an official medium of the Catholic Church it is still a living tongue.[27] The literature of ancient Rome never wholly ceased to be a subject of study in the medieval schools and monasteries. Periods of illumination shone out between years of darkness. Thus in the earlier part of the sixth century when civilisation was crumbling the works of Boëthius and Cassiodorus passed on a summary of ancient knowledge to the medieval world, and in Ireland and the Celtic fringe monks persevered in the pursuit of learning and in the transcription and preservation of books. Then followed the Carol-

The Latin language

ingian revival of learning, education and intellectual life, and it was Charlemagne's helper, Alcuin from Northumbria, whose drive led to the copying and preservation of so many manuscripts (scribes of this period were responsible for the earliest surviving copies of twelve of the major Latin writers). After a period of decadence progress was again made under the Ottos towards the end of the tenth century, as witness the growth of schools and the copying of Latin manuscripts in Saxony and elsewhere, largely by the clergy. This revival was more enduring and led on to the Schoolmen. From the twelfth century the range of Roman authors in the curriculum began to widen out again, and the so-called 'Renaissance' of scholarship in the fifteenth and sixteenth centuries merely completed a process already in operation.[28]

The Roman Church

Last but not least, the medieval Church may be regarded as a survival from ancient Rome.

Its organisation was partly based on that of the Roman Empire, and in the Dark Ages it was the principal agency for the salvaging of Roman culture.

The proud boast conveyed in the words of the Augustan poet Tibullus, 'Roma aeterna',[29] was belied by the course of events. But the prophecy which his contemporary Horace made in regard to himself, 'non omnis moriar', 'I shall not altogether die',[30] applied with no less force to the Roman Empire and to Roman civilisation. European culture is in the main a new graft upon the old Graeco-Roman stock, and Rome was the principal channel through which the modern world has entered on the heritage of the ancient. If 'all roads lead to Rome' they also lead out again from Rome. For those who have learnt to think beyond yesterday, Rome is the focusing-point of the world's history.

Rome at the centre of world history

Chronological Table

Early Italy

B.C.	
c. 5000–c. 2000	Neolithic Age.
c. 2000–1800	Chalcolithic Age.
c. 1800–c. 1000/800	Bronze Age.
c. 1800	Apennine culture begins.
c. 1500	Apennine culture fully developed.
c. 1500	Terremare culture begins.
c. 1400	Mycenaean traders in southern Italy.
c. 1250	Mycenaean pottery in Etruria (Luni).
c. 1200/1150	Late Bronze Age. Apennine and Terremare cultures draw closer.
c. 1000 (?), 900 (?), 800 (?)	Iron Age begins.
c. 750	Iron Age huts on Palatine at Rome.
c. 750	Greek colonists at Ischia and Cumae.
c. 750–700	Advanced Villanovan or early Etruscan culture?
c. 700	'Orientalising' phase in Italy begins.
c. 700	Etruscan civilisation begins to flourish.
c. 650	Etruscans begin to expand into Campania.
c. 500	Etruscan expansion into northern Italy.

Early Rome

c. 800/750	Roma Quadrata. Iron Age settlement on Palatine.
c. 750–670	Septimontium: union of settlers of Palatine, Cermalus, Velia, Fagutal, Cispius, Oppius and Caelius.
7th century	City of the Four Regions: addition of Quirinal, Viminal and part of Forum.
c. 625/600	Last Forum burials. Etruscan influences begin to appear at Rome.
6th century	'Servian' city, including Capitol and Esquiline.

Traditional Dates

753–716	Romulus.
715–673	Numa Pompilius. Cult of Vesta, etc., established.
674–642	Tullus Hostilius. Destruction of Alba Longa.
c. 655	Demaratus migrates from Corinth to Etruria.
642–617	Ancus Marcius. Extension of Rome's power to coast.

	B.C.
L. Tarquinius Priscus. Forum drained.	616–579
Servius Tullius. 'Servian' organisation begun. Treaty with Latins. Temple of Diana on Aventine.	578–535
Etruscans and Carthaginians defeat Phocaeans off Alalia.	c. 535
L. Tarquinius Superbus. Capitoline temple. Treaty with Gabii. Roman territory extended to some 350 square miles.	534–510
Etruscans defeated at Cumae, where Aristodemus gains control.	524

Roman Republic

Fall of Tarquinius and monarchy: establishment of two annual magistrates (consuls). Dedication of the Capitoline temple. Treaty between Rome and Carthage.	509
War with Porsenna (who captures Rome?).	508
Latins and Aristodemus of Cumae defeat Porsenna's son at Aricia.	506
Migration of the Claudii to Rome.	504
First dictator appointed.	501
Battle of Lake Regillus between Rome and Latin League. Cult of Liber, Libera and Ceres introduced.	496
Latin colony at Signia.	495
First secession: plebeians assert their rights. Latin colony at Velitrae.	494
Treaty of Spurius Cassius with the Latins.	493
Corn imported from Cumae. Latin colony at Norba.	492
Raid of Coriolanus.	491
Spurius Cassius proposes agrarian law. Treaty of Rome with Hernici. Wars with Aequi and Volsci: intermittently for next fifty years.	486
War with Veii.	482–474
Battle of the Cremera.	479
Etruscans defeated off Cumae by Hiero of Syracuse.	474

B.C.

471 *Lex Publilia Voleronis:* Concilium Plebis and tribunes recognised.

469? Tribunes raised to ten.

458? Minucius defeated by Aequi at Mt. Algidus; Roman army rescued by Cincinnatus.

456 *Lex Icilia de Aventino publicando.*

451–450 The decemvirates. Publication of the Twelve Tables of law.

449 Secession of the *plebs.* Valerian–Horatian laws: rights of tribunes defined.

447 Quaestors elected by the people. Comitia Tributa Populi perhaps established.

445 *Lex Canuleia.* Military tribunes with consular power replace consulship.

444 Treaty with Ardea.

443 Censorship established.

442 Latin colony at Ardea?

439 Minucius sees to corn-supply of Rome.

433 Temple of Apollo.

431 Decisive defeat of Aequi on Mt Algidus.

428–425 Rome wins Fidenae from Veii.

421 Quaestorships increased to four: opened to plebeians.

418 Latin colony at Labici.

409 Three quaestors plebeians.

406 Anxur reduced.

404 Velitrae receives garrison.

399 Lectisternium decreed.

396 Military pay introduced. Fall of Veii after long (ten years'?) siege. Peace with Volsci.

393 Latin colony at Circeii.

390? Latin colony at Sutrium.

390 Battle of Allia. Gauls sack Rome (387 according to Polybius).

388 Aequi defeated at Bola.

387 Four rustic tribes created on Ager Veiens (total now twenty-five).

386–5 Latins, Volsci and Hernici defeated.

385 Latin colony at Satricum.

383? Latin colony at Nepete.

382 Latin colony at Setia.

381 Tusculum reduced.

378 'Servian' Wall begun.

377 Latins defeated after their capture of Satricum. Licinius and Sextius begin their agitation.

367 Laws of Licinius and Sextius carried. Consulship restored. Creation of curule aedileship.

366 First plebeian consul. Creation of praetorship. Curule aedileship to alternate every year between patricians and plebeians.

361 Roman capture of Ferentinum.

359 Tarquinii revolts.

358 Hernici readmitted to alliance. Renewal of treaty with Latins. Two new tribes created on land from Antium (total twenty-seven).

357 Government tax on manumission. Maximum rate of interest fixed. Falerii revolts. Gallic raid on Latium.

356 First plebeian dictator.

354 Alliance of Rome and Samnites.

353 Caere defeated: 100 years' truce; grant of half-citizenship (or later).

352 *Quinqueviri mensarii* appointed (five men to help debtors in trouble).

B.C.

351 First plebeian censor. Tarquinii and Falerii reduced: forty years' truce.

349 (or 346) Gallic raid checked.

348 Rome's treaty with Carthage renewed.

346 Defeat of Antium and Satricum.

343 Falerii receives permanent alliance. Latin attack on Paeligni.

343–341 First Samnite War.

342 Mutiny in army and secession. *Leges Genuciae.*

340–338 Latin revolt.

339 *Leges Publiliae.*

338 Latin League dissolved. Many cities granted full or half Roman citizenship. Roman colony at Antium (and Ostia?). Land confiscated from Velitrae.

337 First plebeian praetor.

334 Latin colony at Cales.

332 Two new tribes created in Latium (total twenty-nine). Rome's treaty with Tarentum (or 303).

332–331 Rome's thirty years' truce with the Senones.

329 Privernum captured and granted half-citizenship. Roman colony at Tarracina (Anxur).

328 Latin colony at Fregellae.

328–302 Second Samnite War.

326 First use of *prorogatio imperii. Lex Poetilia* concerning debt (or 313). Roman alliance with Neapolis, Nuceria and the Apulians.

321 Roman defeat at Caudine Forks. Peace. Rome surrenders Fregellae.

318 Two tribes created in northern Campania (total thirty-one). Alliance with Teanum (Apuli) and Canusium. Roman prefects sent to Capua and Cumae.

316 Second Samnite War renewed.

315 Luceria captured. Samnite victory at Lautulae. Revolt of Capua to Samnites.

314 Roman victory at Tarracina. Capua reduced. Latin colony at Luceria.

313 (or 312) Fregellae, Sora, etc., recaptured. Latin colonies at Suessa Aurunca, Pontia, Saticula and Interamna.

312 Censorship of Appius Claudius. Via Appia and Aqua Appia started.

311 *Duoviri navales* appointed.

310 Roman advance into Etruria. Treaties with Cortona, Perusia and Arretium.

308 Alliance with Tarquinii renewed for forty years. Alliance with Camerinum.

307 Revolt of Hernici.

306 Anagnia stormed: granted half-citizenship. 'Philinus' treaty with Carthage.

304 Repeal of reform of Appius Claudius. Flavius publishes the *legis actiones.* Aequi defeated. Samnite War ended. Alliance with Marsi, Paeligni, Marrucini and Frentani.

303 Latin colonies at Alba Fucens and Sora. Half-citizenship for Arpinum. Temple of Salus at Rome.

302 Alliance with Vestini.

300 *Lex Valeria de provocatione. Lex Ogulnia,* opening Priestly Colleges to plebeians.

299 Two new tribes created, Aniensis and Terentina (total thirty-three). Latin colony at Narnia.

B.C.

298 Latin colony at Carseoli. Alliance with Picentes. Gallic raid on Roman territory.

298–290 Third Samnite War.

298 Rome captures Bovianum Vetus and Aufidena.

296 Samnite raid on Ager Falernus. Roman colonies at Minturnae and Sinuessa.

295 Roman victory over Samnites, Gauls and Umbrians at Sentinum.

294 Forty years' treaty with Volsinii, Perusia, Arretium. Samnite victory near Luceria.

293 Cult of Aesculapius introduced. *Lex Maenia* (?). Roman victory over Samnites at Aquilona.

292 Falerii reduced.

291 Venusia stormed; Latin colony there.

290 Peace with Samnites. Sabines granted half-citizenship.

289 Mint and *triumviri monetales* established at Rome. Latin colony at Hadria.

287 *Lex Hortensia*, giving *plebiscita* the force of law.

284 Revolt of Vulci, Volsinii, etc. Senones ejected from Ager Gallicus. Roman colony at Sena.

283 Boii defeated at Lake Vadimo.

282 Roman garrisons sent to Thurii, Rhegium and Locri. Roman fleet attacked by Tarentines.

281 Roman embassy to Tarentum.

280 Alliance with Vulci, Tarquinii and other Etruscan cities.

280–275 War with Pyrrhus.

280 Pyrrhus lands in Italy and defeats Romans at Heraclea. Negotiations.

279 Battle of Asculum.

278 Rome's treaty with Carthage. Pyrrhus leaves Italy.

275 Pyrrhus, on return, defeated near Malventum; he leaves Italy.

273 Latin colonies at Paestum and Cosa. Caere mulcted of some territory. Roman *amicitia* with Egypt.

272 Livius Andronicus to Rome. Anio Vetus aqueduct. Alliance with Velia, Heraclea, Thurii, Metapontum. Surrender of Tarentum.

270 Capture of Rhegium.

269 First silver coinage minted at Rome. Revolt of Picentes.

268 Picentes reduced: granted half-citizenship. Sabines receive full citizenship. Latin colonies at Beneventum and Ariminum.

267 War with Sallentini. Capture of Brundisium.

266 Apulia and Messapia reduced to alliance.

264–241 First Punic War.

264 First gladiatorial show at Rome. Latin colony at Firmum. Capture of Volsinii. Roman alliance with Mamertines. Roman army sent to Sicily.

263 Latin colony at Aesernia. Hiero becomes ally of Rome.

262 Capture of Agrigentum.

261–260 Romans build fleet.

260 Naval victory off Mylae. Duilius celebrates Rome's first naval triumph.

259 Roman occupation of Corsica.

257 Naval victory off Tyndaris.

256 Naval victory off Ecnomus. Regulus lands in Africa.

255 Defeat of Regulus's army. Naval victory off

B.C.

Cape Hermaeum, but Roman fleet wrecked off Pachynus.

Romans capture Panormus. — 254

Roman fleet wrecked off Palinurus. — 253

Victory at Panormus. Siege of Lilybaeum. — 250

Claudius's naval defeat at Drepana. Roman transport fleet wrecked. — 249

Hamilcar Barca starts Carthaginian offensive in western Sicily. — 247

Latin colony at Brundisium. — 244

Roman fleet built from voluntary loans. — 243

Institution of *praetor peregrinus*. — 242

Naval victory off Aegates Insulae. Peace. Roman occupation of Sicily. Falerii reduced. Latin colony at Spoletium. Two tribes created in Picenum (total thirty-five). 241(?) reform of the Comitia Centuriata. — 241

Revolt of the mercenaries against Carthage. — 241–238

Roman seizure of Sardinia: occupation and reduction of Sardinia and Corsica. — 238–225

Intermittent campaigns against the Ligurians. — 238–230

Hamilcar goes to Spain. — 237

First play of Naevius. Gallic raids in northern Italy. — 236

Temple of Janus closed. *c.* 235 the *quadrigatus* issued. — 235–234

Distribution of Ager Gallicus carried by Flaminius. — 232

Roman embassy to Hamilcar in Spain. — 231

Hasdrubal succeeds Hamilcar in Spain. — 230

First Illyrian War. Roman influence established on Illyrian coast. — 229–228

Roman envoys at Athens and Corinth. — 228

Praetorships raised to four. Sicily and Sardinia governed by praetors. — 227

Ebro treaty between Rome and Hasdrubal. — 226

Invading Gauls defeated at Telamon. — 225

Flaminius defeats Insubres. — 223

Battle at Clastidium; surrender of Insubres. — 222

North-eastern frontier secured to Julian Alps. — 221–220

Hannibal succeeds Hasdrubal. Saguntine appeal to Rome. — 221

Censorship of Flaminius; construction of Via Flaminia. — 220

Second Illyrian War; Demetrius defeated. Hannibal besieges and captures (November) Saguntum. — 219

Second Punic War. — 218–201

Lex Claudia. Latin colonies at Placentia and Cremona. Hannibal arrives in northern Italy. Battles of Ticinus and Trebia. — 218

Roman defeat at Lake Trasimene. Naval victory off the Ebro. — 217

Roman defeat at Cannae. Revolts in central Italy, including Capua. — 216

Tributum doubled. Hannibal in southern Italy. Alliance of Carthage with Philip and Syracuse after death of Hiero. Hasdrubal defeated at Dertosa. — 215

First Macedonian War. — 214–205

Laevinus in Illyria. — 214

Hannibal occupies Tarentum, except the citadel. Roman siege of Syracuse. — 213

Siege of Capua. Ludi Apollinares introduced. — 212

B.C.

212/211 Introduction of the *denarius*. Roman alliance with Aetolia.

211 Hannibal's march on Rome. Fall of Capua and Syracuse. Defeat of the Scipios in Spain.

210 Twelve Latin colonies refuse contingents. Fall of Agrigentum. Scipio lands in Spain.

209 Recapture of Tarentum. Capture of New Carthage.

208 Death of Marcellus. Battle of Baecula.

207 Hasdrubal defeated at Metaurus.

206 Battle of Ilipa; final reduction of Spain. Aetolians make peace with Philip.

205 Scipio in Sicily. Peace of Phoenice.

204 Ennius brought to Rome. Cult-stone of Mother Goddess brought from Asia Minor. Scipio lands in Africa.

203 Scipio defeats Syphax and wins battle of Great Plains. Armistice made and broken. Hannibal recalled to Carthage. Mago defeated in Gaul.

203–202 Pact between Philip and Antiochus.

202 Scipio's victory at Zama. Aggressions of Philip and Antiochus. Aetolian appeal to Rome rejected.

201 Peace with Carthage, which becomes a client state. Masinissa king of Greater Numidia. Appeal of Attalus and Rhodes to Rome against Philip.

200–196 Second Macedonian War.

200 War declared on Philip. Roman army sent to Greece. Insubres sack Placentia.

199 *Lex Porcia*. Death of Naevius. Aetolians join Rome.

198 Flamininus's victory at the Aous. Achaeans join Rome.

197 Praetorships raised to six. Spain organised as two provinces. Cethegus defeats the Insubres. Defeat of Philip at Cynoscephalae. Peace between Philip and Rome (winter). Revolt of Turdetani in Spain. Antiochus occupies Ephesus.

196 Final defeat of Insubres by Marcellus. Flamininus's proclamation at Corinth. Smyrna appeals to Senate. Council with Antiochus at Lysimachia. Hannibal suffete at Carthage.

195 *Lex Porcia*. Repeal of *Lex Oppia*. Hannibal exiled and joins Antiochus. Masinissa starts raids on Carthaginian territory. Cato in Spain. War against Nabis.

194 Roman colonies at Volturnum, Liternum, Puteoli, Salernum, Sipontum, Tempsa, Croton and Buxentum. Lusitani defeated: war drags on intermittently. Roman evacuation of Greece.

193 Latin colony at Thurii Copia.

192 Latin colony at Vibo Valentia. The Apuani checked. War declared on Antiochus (October), who lands in Greece.

192–189 War with Antiochus.

191 *Lex Acilia*, concerning the calendar. Boii defeated by Scipio Nasica. Antiochus defeated at Thermopylae; withdraws to Asia Minor. War in Aetolia. Antiochus's fleet defeated off Corycus. Rome rejects offer by Carthage to repay whole of indemnity.

B.C.

Placentia and Cremona resettled. The Scipios in Greece. Antiochus's fleet defeated. — 190

Antiochus defeated at Magnesia. — 190 or 189

Latin colony at Bononia. Campanians enrolled as citizens. Fall of Ambracia. Peace with Aetolia. Manlius raids Galatia. — 189

Full citizenship granted to Arpinum, Formiae and Fundi. Treaty of Apamea. Settlement of Asia. — 188

Rome liquidates war-debt. Latins sent home from Rome. Political attacks on Scipio. Via Aemilia and Via Flaminia. — 187

Senatus consultum de Bacchanalibus. Ligurians defeat Philippus. — 186

Cato censor. Basilica Porcia. Withdrawal of Scipio to Liternum. Death of Plautus. Roman colonies at Potentia and Pisaurum. Philip sends Demetrius to Rome. — 184

Death of Scipio. — 184/3

Roman colonies at Parma, Mutina and Saturnia. — 183

Death of Hannibal. — 183/2

Lex Baebia. *Lex Orchia* (sumptuary). Latin colony at Aquileia. Roman colony at Graviscae. Ingauni defeated. Revolt in Corsica and Sardinia. End of Achaeo-Spartan quarrel. — 181

First Celtiberian War. — 181–179

Lex Villia Annalis. Latin colony at Luca. Apuani defeated. Foundation of Gracchuris in Spain. Birth of Lucilius. — 180

Basilica Aemilia begun. Accession of Perseus. — 179

Expedition against the Istri. — 178

Latins sent home from Rome. Roman colony at Luna. Annexation of Istria. — 177

Sardinia reduced. — 177–176

Latins sent home. Two Epicurean philosophers expelled. Envoys sent to arbitrate between Masinissa and Carthage. — 173

Two plebeian consuls in office for first time. — 172

Third Macedonian War. — 172–167

Temporary court *de repetundis*. Latin colony at Carteia in Spain. — 171

Lex Voconia. Freedmen confined to one urban tribe. Quarrel between Senate and Equites. — 169

Defeat of Pereus at Pydna. Antiochus checked. Delos declared a free port. Foundation of Cordoba in Spain (or 151). — 168

Tributum discontinued. Perseus's library brought to Rome. Epirus plundered. Macedon divided into four republics, Illyricum into three protectorates. 1000 Achaeans deported to Rome. — 167

Production of Terence's *Comedies*. — 166–159

Final reduction of Corsica. — 163

Lex Fannia (sumptuary). Expulsion of Greek philosophers. Treaty with Jews. — 161

Law against bribery. — 159

Roman campaigns in Dalmatia and Pannonia. — 157–155

Carneades and others lecture in Rome. — 155

Oxybian Ligures defeated. — 154

Lusitanian War. — 154–138

Second Celtiberian War. — 153–151

Consuls enter office on Kalends of January. — 153

Carthage declares war on Masinissa. — 151

Lex Aelia Fufia. *Lex Aebutia*, establishing a formulary system of legal procedure. — c. 150

B.C.		B.C.
150	Return of Achaean exiles to Greece.	
149–146	Third Punic War.	
149	Permanent court *de repetundis* (*Lex Calpurnia*). Publication of Cato's *Origines*. Siege of Carthage begun. Rising of Andriscus in Macedon.	
148	Via Postumia.	
147	Viriathus successful. Scipio Aemilianus in command at Carthage. Macedonia becomes a Roman province.	
146	Destruction of Carthage. Africa becomes a province. War between Rome and Achaeans. Sack of Corinth.	
c. 145	Laelius's attempted agrarian reform.	
144	Marcian aqueduct.	
143–133	Third Celtiberian, or Numantine, War.	
142	Censorship of Scipio Aemilianus. Stone bridge over the Tiber.	
139	*Lex Gabinia:* ballot for elections. Death of Viriathus.	
137	*Lex Cassia:* ballot in law-courts. D. Brutus campaigns against the Callaici. Defeat and surrender of Mancinus in Spain.	
135–132	Slave war in Sicily.	
133	Tribunate of Tiberius Gracchus: land-law. Tribune Octavius deposed. Pergamum bequeathed to Rome by Atallus III. Gracchus killed. Scipio Aemilianus sacks Numantia and settles Spain.	
132	Quaestio to punish Gracchans. Land-commission working. Sicily reorganised by *Lex Rupilia*. Revolt of Aristonicus in Asia.	
131	*Lex Papiria:* ballot for legislation.	
130	Aristonicus defeated.	
129	Death of Scipio Aemilianus. Province of Asia organised.	
126	Law of tribune Pennus *de peregrinis*. Unrest in Sardinia.	
125	Consul Fulvius Flaccus proposes to enfranchise the Latins. Revolt of Fregellae.	
124	Colony at Fabrateria for Fregellans. War against Arverni and Allobroges in Gaul.	
123	First tribunate of Gaius Gracchus, who proposes many laws; re-elected tribune for 122. *Lex Rubria* (?122) establishes Junonia on site of Carthage. *Castellum* at Aquae Sextiae.	
122	Further legislation of C. Gracchus. Opposition of Livius Drusus. Balearic Islands subdued: colonies at Palma and Pollentia.	
121	First use of *senatus consultum ultimum*. Civil disorder: Gracchus killed; his followers executed by Opimius. *Lex agraria*. Defeat of Arverni and Allobroges. Building of Via Domitia.	
120	Trial and acquittal of Opimius.	
119	Marius, tribune, carries legislation. Abolition of Gracchan land commission. *Lex agraria*.	
118	Colony at Narbo Martius in southern Gaul. Death of Micipsa: Adherbal, Hiempsal and Jugurtha joint rulers of Numidia.	
117	Death of Hiempsal.	
116	Jugurtha strengthens his position; senatorial commission to Numidia.	
115	Aemilius Scaurus consul.	

	B.C.
Marius in Spain.	114
Cn. Carbo defeated at Noreia by Cimbri.	113
Jugurtha sacks Cirta. War declared on Jugurtha.	112
Lex agraria (*Lex Thoria?*). Temporary agreement with Jugurtha.	111
Mamilian inquiry. War in Africa: surrender of Aulus Albinus.	110
Metellus gains some successes against Jugurtha.	109
Marius, elected consul, enlists *proletarii* and succeeds Metellus: takes Capsa. Cassius defeated by Tigurini in Gaul.	107
Birth of Cicero and of Pompey. Caepio's *lex iudiciaria*. Marius penetrates western Numidia. Bocchus of Mauretania surrenders Jugurtha to Sulla.	106
Cimbri and Teutones destroy Roman armies at Arausio.	105
Judiciary law of Servilius Glaucia. Marius, consul II, reorganises Roman army. *Lex Domitia de sacerdotiis*. Second Sicilian Slave War.	104
Saturninus tribune: *lex frumentaria*, *lex de maiestate*, land-allotments for Marius's veterans. Marius, consul III, trains army in Gaul.	103
Marius, consul IV, defeats Teutones near Aquae Sextiae. M. Antonius sent to Cilicia to deal with pirates.	102
Marius, consul V, and Catulus defeat Cimbri near Vercellae.	101
Marius, consul VI. Saturninus's legislation. Marius's co-operation with Saturninus and Glaucia ends: rioting in Rome. *Senatus consultum ultimum*. Marius restores order; deaths of Saturninus and Glaucia. Birth of Julius Caesar. Colony at Eporedia. Second Sicilian Slave War ended.	100
Marius leaves Rome for Asia. *Lex Caecilia Didia*. Revolt in Lusitania.	98
Sulla (praetor 97) ordered to install Ariobarzanes on throne of Cappadocia. Ptolemy Apion dies: bequeaths Cyrene to Rome.	96
Lex Licinia Mucia: expulsion order. Mithridates ordered out of Paphlagonia and Cappadocia by Rome. Tigranes becomes king of Armenia.	95
Death of Nicomedes III of Bithynia.	94
Condemnation of Rutilius Rufus. Censors suppress Latin *rhetores*.	92
Tribunate of M. Livius Drusus; his assassination. Outbreak of Social War.	91
Roman setbacks in Social War. *Lex Iulia*.	90
Victories of Strabo and Sulla. *Lex Plautia Papiria*. *Lex Pompeia*.	89
Tribunate of Sulpicius Rufus. Proposal to transfer command in Asia from Sulla to Marius. Sulla siezes Rome, repeals Sulpicius's legislation and carries some legislation. Marius escapes. Social War confined to Samnites, who gradually yield. Mithridates overruns Asia Minor.	88
Cinna and Marius in control of Rome; massacre of Sulla's supporters. Sulla lands in Greece; siege of Athens. Cinna consul 87–84.	87
Marius, consul VII, dies. Flaccus and Fimbria	86

B.C.

organising Gaul, crosses Rubicon into Italy: beginning of civil war.

49 Pompey leaves for Greece. Caesar, dictator I for eleven days, passes emergency legislation, goes to Spain and defeats Pompeians at Ilerda. Curio defeated and killed in Africa.

48 Caesar consul II. Disturbances in Italy; Milo killed. Caesar crosses to Greece. Campaign of Dyrrhachium. Pompey defeated at Pharsalus; killed in Egypt. Alexandrine War. Cleopatra queen of Egypt.

47 Caesar dictator II (*in absentia*); Antony, his Master of Horse, attempts to maintain order in Italy. Caesar leaves Egypt, defeats Pharnaces at Zela, settles East, returns to Italy, quells a mutiny, passes legislation and sails against Pompeian forces in Africa.

46 Caesar's victory at Thapsus. Suicide of Cato. Africa Nova organised. Caesar, dictator II, consul III, returns to Rome and celebrates triumph. Legislation. Reform of calendar. Caesar leaves for Spain.

45 Caesar, dictator III, consul IV, defeats Pompeians at Munda. Returns to Rome; receives exceptional honours.

44 Caesar, dictator IV (for life), consul V. Conspiracy. Murder of Caesar. Return of Octavian from Greece. Antony receives command in Cisalpine and Transalpine Gaul. Cicero's first Philippics.

43 Antony's siege of Mutina raised; deaths of consuls Hirtius and Pansa. D. Brutus killed in Gaul. Octavian declared consul (August). Triumvirate of Antony, Octavian and Lepidus (November). Proscriptions; murder of Cicero. M. Brutus in Macedonia, Cassius in Syria.

42 Julius Caesar becomes Divus. Sextus Pompeius controls Sicily. Brutus and Cassius defeated at Philippi. Birth of emperor Tiberius.

41 Perusine War in Italy. Antony in Asia Minor, meets Cleopatra and visits Alexandria.

40 L. Antonius surrenders Perusia to Octavian. Agreement at Brundisium divides the Roman world (October). Antony marries Octavia. Parthian invasion of Syria. Herod recognised as king of Judaea by Senate. Virgil's *Fourth Eclogue*.

39 Agreement at Misenum between Antony, Octavian and Sextus Pompeius. Ventidius defeats Parthians at Mt Amanus.

38 Octavian marries Livia. Naval successes of Sex. Pompeius. Victory of Ventidius at Gindarus. Antony captures Samosata.

37 Pact of Tarentum; triumvirate probably renewed. Herod and Sosius capture Jerusalem. Antony marries Cleopatra at Antioch. Amyntas and Polemo made kings of Galatia and Pontus respectively.

36 Octavian granted tribunician sacrosanctity. Offensive against Sex. Pompeius, who is defeated off Naulochus. Lepidus ceases to be triumvir. Antony's retreat through Armenia.

35 Octavian in Illyria. Death of Sex. Pompeius.

B.C.

Octavian in Illyria. Antony invades Armenia, celebrates a triumph at Alexandria. The *Donations* of Alexandria. — 34

Octavian consul II. Antony in Armenia. — 33

Antony and Cleopatra winter at Ephesus. — 33/32

Octavia divorced by Antony. Octavian publishes Antony's will in Rome. — 32

Antony and Cleopatra in Greece. — 32/31

Octavian consul III (and successively to 23). He defeats Antony at Actium and winters in Asia. — 31

Tribunician power granted to Octavian. Suicide of Antony, Octavian enters Alexandria, suicide of Cleopatra. — 30

Crassus campaigns in Balkans. Cornelius Gallus in Egypt. — 30–28

Octavian's triple triumph. Dedication of temple of Divus Iulius. — 29

Census held by Octavian and Agrippa; *lectio senatus*. Dedication of temple of Apollo on Palatine. Mausoleum of Augustus begun. Messalla in Spain. — 28

The Principate

Constitutional settlement. Octavian, now Augustus, receives *imperium* for ten years. Triumph of Crassus. Augustus in Gaul and Spain until 25. Agrippa builds the first Pantheon. — 27

Disgrace of Cornelius Gallus. — 26

Arabian expedition of Aelius Gallus. — 26–25

Marriage of Julia and Marcellus. Varro defeats Salassi. Tarraconensis organised. Annexation of Galatia. — 25

Ethiopian War conducted by Petronius. — 25–23

Augustus ill. Conspiracy of Caepio and Murena. Constitutional resettlement. Augustus resigns consulship and receives *proconsulare imperium maius* and full tribunician power, etc. Death of Marcellus. Agrippa sent to East. Publication of the first three books of Horace's *Odes*. — 23

Augustus refuses dictatorship, and consulship for life, but accepts the *cura annonae*. Augustus in Greece and Asia for three years. — 22

Agrippa marries Julia. — 21

Roman standards returned by Parthians. Tiberius enters Armenia and crowns Tigranes. — 20

Return of Augustus. Arch of Augustus in Rome. Deaths of Virgil and Tibullus. Agrippa pacifies Spain. — 19

Augustus's *imperium* renewed for five years. Agrippa receives *imperium maius* and *tribunicia potestas*. *Leges Juliae*. *Lectio Senatus*. — 18

Augustus adopts his grandsons, Gaius and Lucius. Ludi Saeculares. Horace's *Carmen Saeculare*. — 17

Augustus in Gaul. — 16–13

Agrippa in East. Noricum incorporated. — 16

Tiberius and Drusus defeat Raeti and Vindelici, and reach Danube. — 15

Polemo receives Bosporan kingdom. — 14

Return of Augustus; renewal of his *imperium* for — 13

B.C.

five years: Tiberius consul. Return of Agrippa. Death of Lepidus. Dedication of Theatre of Marcellus. Vinicius campaigns in Pannonia.

12 Augustus becomes Pontifex Maximus. Death of Agrippa. Tiberius in Pannonia. Drusus dedicates altar near Lugdunum.

11 Tiberius divorces Agrippina and marries Julia.

9 Death of Drusus. Dedication of Ara Pacis.

8 Augustus's *imperium* renewed for ten years. Census held. Deaths of Horace and Maecenas. Tiberius in Germany.

7 Rome divided into fourteen *regiones*.

6 Tiberius received *tribunicia potestas* for five years. He withdraws to Rhodes. Paphlagonia added to Galatia.

5 Augustus's twelfth consulship. Gaius Caesar introduced to public life.

4 Death of Herod the Great.

2 Augustus, consul for thirteenth time, becomes Pater Patriae. Exile of Julia. Dedication of temple of Mars Ultor.

A.D.

1 Gaius Caesar in Syria.

2 Tiberius returns from Rhodes. Death of L. Caesar. C. Caesar settles Armenia.

3 Augustus's *imperium* renewed for ten years.

4 Death of C. Caesar in Lycia. Augustus adopts Tiberius, who receives *tribunicia potestas* for ten years. Tiberius adopts Germanicus and invades Germany. *Lex Aelia Sentia*.

5 Tiberius advances to Elbe.

6 *Aerarium militare* and office of *Praefectus vigilum* created. Revolt in Pannonia and Illyricum. Maroboduus king of the Marcomanni. Judaea made a province; assessment by Quirinius, legate of Syria.

8 Claudius becomes an augur. Pannonians give in. Ovid banished.

9 *Lex Papia Poppaea*. Revolt in Dalmatia ended. Arminius defeats Varus in Germany; loss of three legions.

12 Triumph of Tiberius.

13 Augustus's *imperium* renewed for ten years. Tiberius receives *tribunicia potestas* for ten years and proconsular *imperium*, co-ordinate with that of Augustus.

14 Lustrum. Death of Augustus. Accession of Tiberius. Sejanus made a Praetorian Prefect. Revolt of legions in Pannonia and Germany. Drusus sent to Pannonia. Germanicus crosses the Rhine against the Marsi.

15 Germanicus attacks the Chatti. Achaea and Macedonia transferred from Senate to Princeps and attached to Moesia.

16 Libo Drusus accused; suicide. Germanicus again invades Germany: recalled.

17 Triumph of Germanicus; sent to East. Cn. Piso legate of Syria. Earthquake in Asia Minor. Cappadocia and Commagene organised as imperial province. Revolt of Tacfarinas in Africa. Death of Livy.

18 Tiberius consul (III) with Germanicus. Germanicus in East. Armenia granted to Artaxias. Germanicus goes to Egypt.

A.D.

Jews banished from Rome. Arminius killed. Piso leaves Syria. Death of Germanicus at Antioch. — 19

Trial of Piso; suicide. — 20

Consulship of Tiberius (IV) with his son Drusus. Tiberius goes to Campania. Revolt of Florus and Sacrovir in Gaul. Trouble in Thrace. — 21

Castra Praetoria built in Rome. — 21–22

Drusus receives *tribunicia potestas*. — 22

Death of Drusus. — 23

Defeat of Tacfarinas. — 24

Cremutius Cordus accused; suicide. — 25

Trouble in Thrace checked. Pontius Pilate appointed prefect of Judaea. — 26

Tiberius withdraws to Capreae. — 27

Revolt of the Frisii. — 28

Death of Liva. Banishment of Agrippina. — 29

Publication of the *History* of Velleius Paterculus. — 30

Consulship (V) of Tiberius with Sejanus. Gaius receives *toga virilis*. Sejanus put to death. Macro appointed Praetorian Prefect. — 31

Death of Agrippina. Financial trouble in Rome. The Crucifixion of Jesus (probable date). — 33

Tetrarchy of Philip incorporated into Syria. — 34

Pilate sent to Rome by L. Vitellius, governor of Syria. — 36

Death of Tiberius. Accession of Gaius (Caligula); he is consul with Claudius. Commagene re-established as a client-kingdom. — 37

Death and deification of Drusilla. Jewish disturbances in Alexandria. Polemo II receives Pontus and Cotys Armenia Minor. — 38

Gaius goes to Rhine. Julia and Agrippina exiled. — 39

Gaius's expedition to the Channel; returns to Rome. Ptolemy of Mauretania murdered; revolt in Mauretania. Jewish embassy from Alexandria to Rome. Agrippa I receives kingdom of Antipas. Judaea restless. — 40

Gaius murdered (24 January). Claudius made emperor. The Chauci defeated. Claudius settles Alexandrine trouble. Agrippa I receives Judaea and Samaria. Exile of Seneca. — 41

Revolt of Scribonianus in Dalmatia; his suicide. Mauretania organised as two provinces. — 42

Expedition to Britain. Lycia made an imperial province. — 43

Claudius's triumph for Britain. Achaea and Macedonia transferred to Senate. Death of Agrippa I; Judaea again made a province. — 44

Thrace made a province. — 46

Triumph of Aulus Plautius for conquest of Britain. Censorship of Claudius and L. Vitellius. Ludi Saeculares. Corbulo campaigns against Frisii. Ostorius Scapula in Britain. — 47

Messalina put to death. Claudius marries Agrippina. — 48

Seneca recalled from Corsica and made tutor of Nero. — 49

Nero adopted by Claudius as guardian of Britannicus. Agrippa II rules in Chalcis. — 50

Burrus made Praetorian Prefect. Consulship of Vespasian. Defeat of Caratacus in Wales. 51 or 52, Vologeses king of Parthia. — 51

Gallio proconsul in Achaea. — 51–52

A.D.

53 Nero marries Octavia. Parthians occupy Armenia; Tiridates recovers his throne.

54 Death of Claudius. Accession of Nero. Claudius deified.

55 Britannicus poisoned. Pallas dismissed. Corbulo goes to East.

56 *Praefecti aerarii* replace *quaestores aerarii.*

57 Nero forces senators and knights to take part in Games.

58 Nero refuses perpetual consulship. Corbulo captures Artaxata.

59 Nero murders Agrippina and introduces Greek Games. Corbulo takes Tigranocerta.

60 *Neronia* established. Corbulo settles Armenia; governor of Syria. Festus succeeds Felix as governor of Judaea.

61 Revolt of Boudicca and the Iceni in Britain.

62 Death of Burrus. Tigellinus made a Praetorian Prefect. Seneca disgraced. Nero divorces Octavia and marries Poppaea. Octavia murdered. Paetus surrenders to the Parthians at Rhandeia.

64 Great fire in Rome. Persecution of Christians. Domus Aurea begun. Mission to Ethiopia.

64–65 Cottian Alps made a province. Pontus incorporated in Galatia.

65 Conspiracy of Piso. Suicides of Seneca and Lucan. Death of Poppaea. Musonius Rufus banished.

66 Nero crowns Tiridates in Rome and goes to Greece. Thrasea Paetus condemned. Conspiracy of Vinicius. Temple of Janus closed. Death of Petronius. Rebellion in Palestine.

67 Nero at Corinthian canal. Corbulo ordered to kill himself. Vespasian in command in Judaea. Josephus surrenders to him.

68 Nero returns to Italy; his death (June). Galba, accepted by Senate and Praetorians, enters Rome (autumn). Verginius Rufus opposes Vindex's rebellion in Gaul. Defeat and death of Vindex. Vespasian begins attack on Jerusalem.

69 Galba killed and Otho hailed as emperor by Praetorians (January). Vitellius proclaimed emperor by armies in Germany, and supported by Caecina and Valens. Otho defeated at Bedriacum; suicide (April). Rising of Civilis on the Rhine. Vespasian declared emperor in the East. His forces under Antonius sack Cremona and capture Rome; death of Vitellius (December). Vespasian emperor.

70 Vespasian arrives in Rome (summer). Classicus's attempted Imperium Galliarum. Civilis crushed. Fall of Jerusalem. Restoration of Capitoline temple started.

71 Titus returns from Judaea; receives proconsular *imperium* and shares tribunician power with Vespasian. *Astrologi* and *philosophi* expelled from Rome.

72 Armenia Minor added to Cappadocia.

73–74 Censorship of Vespasian and Titus.

75 Agrippa II and Berenice visit Rome. Alani attack Media and Armenia.

76 Birth of Hadrian.

A.D.

78 Conspiracy of Caecina Alienus and Eprius Marcellus. Agricola governor of Britain (until 85).

79 Death of Vespasian (June). Accession of Titus. Eruption of Vesuvius (24 August). Death of elder Pliny.

80 Fire at Rome. Destruction of Capitoline temple. Inauguration of Colosseum.

81 Death of Titus (September). Accession of Domitian.

82 Dedication of restored Capitoline temple.

83 Triumph of Domitian over the Chatti.

85 Domitian *censor perpetuus.* Recall of Agricola. Decebalus of Dacia defeats legate of Moesia.

86 Inauguration of Capitoline Games.

88 Ludi Saeculares. Dacians defeated at Tapae.

89 Domitian returns to Rome and triumphs. Edict against *astrologi* and *philosophi.* Saturninus hailed *imperator* at Moguntiacum.

92 Palaces on Palatine finished. Domitian's campaigns against Sarmatae and Suevi.

93 Death of Agricola.

95 Flavius Clemens and Acilius Glabrio put to death. Expulsion of philosophers from Italy.

96 Assassination of Domitian (September). Accession of Nerva. Dedication of Forum Nervae.

97 *Lex agraria* and social legislation. Rising of Praetorians.

98 Death of Nerva (January). Accession of Trajan.

99 Trajan, now emperor, returns to Rome.

100 The *Panegyricus* of Pliny.

101–102 First Dacian War.

105–106 Second Dacian War. Dacia made a province.

106 Annexation of Arabia Petraea.

109 Trajan dedicates Adam-klissi monument. Maximus appointed to Achaea.

111 Pliny sent to Bithynia.

112 Dedication of Trajan's Forum.

113 Trajan starts for Parthian War.

114 Armenia annexed.

115 Mesopotamia annexed. Jewish revolt in Cyrene.

116 Ctesiphon captured. Revolt in East. Jewish revolt spreads.

117 Trajan dies in Cilicia. Accession of Hadrian.

118 Hadrian arrives in Rome (July).

120 Consulship of Antoninus.

121 Hadrian travels in western provinces. Birth of M. Aurelius.

122 Hadrian visits Britain; orders building of Wall. Moorish revolt.

124 Hadrian in Asia Minor.

129 Hadrian at Athens.

130 Hadrian founds Antinoopolis. Aelia Capitolina founded on site of Jerusalem.

131 Jewish revolt under Bar Cocheba.

134 Alani invade Parthia.

135 Jews finally defeated. Reorganisation of Syria Palaestrina. Temple of Venus and Rome dedicated.

136 Hadrian adopts L. Aelius as Caesar. Plot of Servianus.

138 Death of L. Aelius Caesar (January). Antoninus adopted as co-regent (February). Death of Hadrian (July). Accession of Antoninus Pius.

A.D.

Gordian emperor (July). Goths and Carpi attack across the Danube.

241 Timesitheus made Praetorian Prefect. Shapur I succeeds Ardashir.

242 Timesitheus starts campaign against Persians.

244 Murder of Gordian III. Philip, the Arabian, makes peace with Persia and goes to Rome as emperor.

245–247 War on Danube frontier.

247 Philip, son of the emperor, made Augustus. Millenary of Rome's foundation.

248 Millenary Games in Rome. Decius settles Moesia and Pannonia.

249 Decius made emperor by his troops. Kills Philip and his son in battle near Verona. Goths under Cniva renew attacks.

249–251 Persecution of Christians.

251 Decius's two sons proclaimed Augusti. Defeat and death of Decius and his son Herennius Etruscus on the Danube. Trebonianus Gallus proclaimed emperor with Decius's other son, Hostilianus, who dies soon. Volusianus, son of Gallus, proclaimed Augustus.

252 Goths and barbarians attack northern frontier. Persians attack Mesopotamia.

253 Aemilianus proclaimed emperor; defeat and death of Gallus. Valerian proclaimed emperor by Rhine armies. Aemilianus murdered by his own troops. Valerian goes to Rome; his son Gallienus proclaimed second Augustus.

254 Marcomanni attack Pannonia and raid Ravenna. Goths ravage Thrace. Shapur captures Nisibis.

256 Franks attack Lower Rhine. Gothic attack by sea on Asia Minor.

257 Valerian starts new persecution of Christians. Renewed Persian invasion.

258 Martyrdom of Cyprian. 258 or 259 Gallienus defeats Alamanni.

259/260 Valerian captured by Shapur.

260 Gallienus ends Christian persecution. Macrianus and Quietus proclaimed emperors in East. Postumus in Gaul (or 259). Revolts of Ingenuus and then of Regalianus in Pannonia.

261 Macrianus killed in battle against Aureolus. Odenathus of Palmyra recognised as *dux Orientis*. Quietus executed in Emesa.

262 Plague reaches Italy and Africa. Successes of Odenathus against Persians. Dedication of Arch of Gallienus at Rome.

267 Gothic invasion of Asia Minor.

267–268 Odenathus killed; Zenobia secures power in name of infant Vaballathus.

268 Goths attack Thrace and Greece. Gallienus wins victory at Naissus, but is murdered at Milan. Claudius becomes emperor. Aureolus killed.

268/269 Postumus killed. Zenobia extends her kingdom.

269 Claudius's decisive victories over Goths.

270 Claudius dies of plague in Pannonia (January). Senate chooses Quintillus, but Aurelian is successful against him and against the Juthungi. Dacia abandoned. Zenobia's troops enter Alexandria. Death of Plotinus.

271 Aurelian's Wall started in Rome. Aurelian moves against Zenobia.

A.D.

273 Aurelian destroys Palmyra. Revolt in Egypt crushed.

274 Aurelian defeats Tetricus in Gaul; he triumphs and reforms coinage. Temple of Sun-god at Rome.

275 Aurelian murdered in Thrace. Tacitus made emperor.

276 Death of Tacitus. Murder of his brother Florian. Probus becomes emperor.

276–277 Probus clears Germans and Goths from Gaul.

278 Probus campaigns against Vandals on Danube.

279 Probus settles Asia Minor.

280 Probus suppresses Bonosus in Gaul.

282 Probus murdered. Succeeded by Carus.

283 Death of Carus near Ctesiphon. Succeeded by Carinus in West and Numerian in East. Vahram II makes peace with Rome.

284 Numerian killed. Diocles succeeds.

285 Diocles defeats Carinus, who is killed. Diocles takes name of Diocletian. Maximian named Caesar.

286 Maximian becomes Augustus after defeating the Bagaudae in Gaul.

286–287 Maximian fights against Alamanni and Burgundians. Revolt of Carausius.

289 Diocletian fights Sarmatians. Carausius defeats Maximian.

290 Diocletian reaches agreement with Vahram.

292 Diocletian fights Sarmatians.

292–293 Diocletian suppresses a revolt in Egypt.

293 Constantius and Galerius appointed Caesars in West and East respectively. Carausius killed by Allectus, who holds Britain.

296 Constantius recovers Britain from Allectus. Galerius defeats Narses, king of Persia. Rebellion of Domitius Domitianus in Egypt.

297 Diocletian's edict against the Manichaeans. Domitius crushed. Gallienus's war against Persia.

298 Maximian subdues Moors.

301 Diocletian's edict on prices.

303 Diocletian celebrates his Vicennalia in Rome. Persecution of Christians begins at Nicomedia.

305 Diocletian and Maximian abdicate. Constantius and Galerius succeeded as Augusti, Severus and Maximinus Daia as Caesars.

306 Death of Constantius at York. His troops proclaim Constantine emperor of the West. Maxentius proclaimed at Rome and supported by his father Maximian. Severus invades Italy.

307 Constantine marries Fausta, Maximian's daughter, and accepts Maxentius as Augustus. Defeat and death of Severus. Galerius goes to Italy but withdraws to Pannonia.

308 The emperors Diocletian, Galerius and Maximian confer at Carnuntum. Licinius proclaimed Augustus.

310 Death of Maximian.

311 Galerius at Nicomedia issues edict giving Christians legal recognition. Death of Galerius. Resumption of persecution (October–November). Rebellion in Africa crushed.

A.D.

312 Constantine defeats Maxentius at the Milvian Bridge. Death of Maxentius.

313 Constantine and Licinius meet at Milan and agree to partition the Roman world. Licinius defeats Maximinus, who dies at Tarsus. Licinius at Nicomedia issues a grant of freedom of worship. Donatists condemned by council in Rome.

314 Meeting of bishops at Arles.

314–315 Constantine successful in a war with Licinius.

315 Arch of Constantine erected at Rome.

316 Death of Diocletian.

317 Crispus and Constantinus, sons of Constantine, and Licinianus, son of Licinius, declared Caesars.

320 Licinius takes measures against Christians.

321 Constantine grants tolerance to Donatists.

322 Constantine drives Sarmatians from Pannonia.

323 Constantine expels Goths from Thrace.

324 War between Constantine and Licinius. Constantine victorious at Adrianople and Chrysopolis. Licinius banished. Founding of Constantinople started.

325 Licinius killed. Christian Council of Nicaea.

330 Constantinople becomes the imperial residence.

337 Death of Constantine. Division of Empire between this three sons.

A few further important dates are appended.

337–340 Constantinus II emperor in West.

337–350 Constans.

337–361 Constantius II in East.

340 Constans defeats Constantinus II and rules West.

350 Revolt of Magnentius, who kills Constans.

351–2 Constantius II defeats Magnentius at Nursa and then rules whole Empire until 361.

357 Julian defeats Alamanni near Argentorate.

359 War with Persia.

360–363 Julian emperor.

363 Julian's death on Persian Expedition; peace with Persia. End of dynasty of Constantine.

363–364 Jovian emperor.

364–375 Valentinian I emperor in West.

364–378 Valens emperor in East.

367 Gratian made a third Augustus. Britain attacked by Saxons, Picts and Scots. Situation restored by Count Theodosius.

A.D.

374–397 Ambrose bishop of Milan.

375–383 Gratian emperor in West.

375–392 Valentinian II.

376 Huns drive Visigoths across Danube.

378 Visigoths defeat and kill Valens at battle of Adrianople.

378–385 Theodosius I.

382 Altar of Victory removed from Senate House.

383 Revolt of Magnus Maximus in Britain. Death of Gratian.

383–408 Arcadius.

388 Maximus defeated and killed by Theodosius.

391 Edicts against paganism. Destruction of the Serapeum.

392 Revolt of Arbogast. Murder of Valentinian II. Eugenius proclaimed Augustus.

394 Battle of Frigidus. Deaths of Arbogast and Eugenius.

394–423 Honorius.

395 Death of Theodosius I. Division of Empire. Arcadius emperor in East (till 408) and Honorius in West (until 434). Revolt of Alaric and Visigoths.

396 Alaric defeated by Stilicho in Greece.

406 Barbarian invasion of Gaul.

408 Murder of Stilicho. Alaric invades Italy.

408–450 Theodosius II emperor in East.

409 Spain invaded by Vandals, Alans and Suevi.

410 Visigoths capture Rome (23 August). Death of Alaric. Honorius tells Britain that it must defend itself.

425–455 Valentinian III emperor in West.

429 Vandal invasion of Africa.

430 Death of Augustine of Hippo.

438 The Theodosian Code.

439 Vandals capture Carthage.

446 Britain's final appeal to Aetius.

450–457 Marcian emperor in East.

451 Battle between Aetius and Huns. Council of Chalcedon.

453 Death of Attila.

454 Murder of Aetius. Ostrogoths settle in Pannonia.

455 Maximus emperor in West. Vandals under Gaeseric sack Rome.

472 Ricimer captures Rome.

476 Deposition of Romulus Augustulus, emperor in West. Odovacer king in Italy. Zeno emperor in East and West.

The Roman Emperors, from Augustus to Constantine

Augustus	B.C. 27–A.D. 14	L. Verus	A.D. 161–169	Trebonianus	A.D. 251–253
Tiberius	A.D. 14–37	Commodus	180–192	Aemilianus	253
Caligula	37–41	Pertinax	193	Valerianus	253–260
Claudius	41–54	Didius Iulianus	193	Gallienus	253–268
Nero	54–68	Septimius Severus	193–211	Claudius Gothicus	268–270
Galba	68–69	Caracalla	211–217	Aurelian	270–275
Otho	69	Geta	211–212	Tacitus	275–276
Vitellius	69	Macrinus	217–218	Florianus	276
Vespasian	69–79	Elagabalus	218–222	Probus	276–282
Titus	79–81	Severus Alexander	222–235	Carus	282–283
Domitian	81–96	Maximinus	235–238	Carinus	283–285
Nerva	96–98	Gordian I	238	Numerianus	283–284
Trajan	98–117	Gordian II	238	Diocletian	284–305
Hadrian	117–138	Balbinus	238	Maximian	286–305
Antoninus Pius	138–161	Pupienus	238	Constantius	292–306
M. Aurelius	161–180	Gordian III	238–244	Galerius	293–311
		Philip	244–249	Licinius	311–323
		Decius	249–251	Constantine	306–337

1. Some Cornelii, Aemilii and Sempronii Gracchi

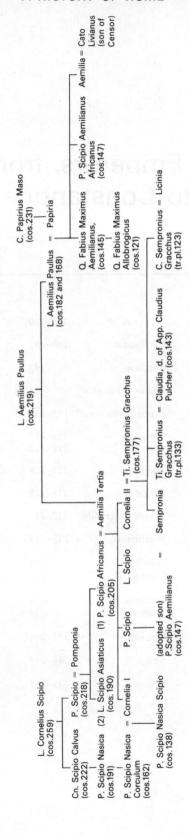

2. Some Metelli, Claudii and others

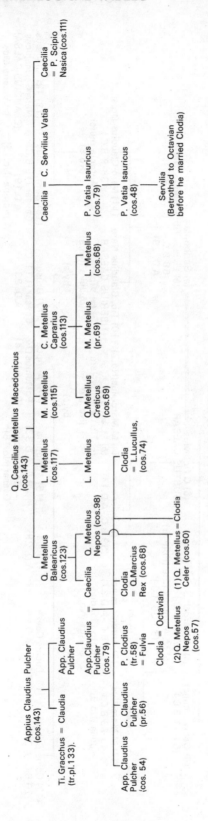

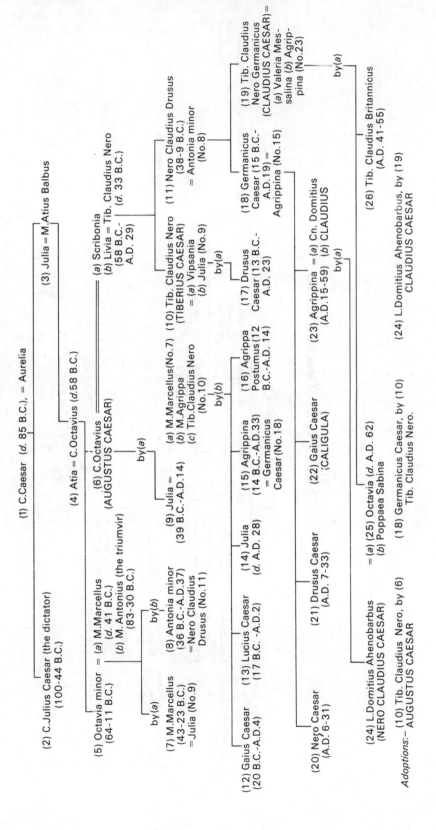

3. The Julio-Claudian Dynasty

Brief List of Books

The more important works, especially those written in English, which treat specific topics, are mentioned in the relevant notes. It may be useful to list here some of the vast number of books which deal with the whole or with long periods of Roman history.

The Cambridge Ancient History, edited by S. A. Cook, F. E. Adcock and M. P. Charlesworth: vii, *The Hellenistic Monarchies and the Rise of Rome* (1928); viii, *Rome and the Mediterranean*, 218–133 B.C. (1930); ix, The Roman Republic, 133–44 B.C. (1932); x, *The Augustan Empire, 44 B.C.–A.D. 70* (1934); xi, *The Imperial Peace, A.D. 70–192*. 1936); xii, *The Imperial Crisis and Recovery, A.D. 193–324* (1939).

Methuen's History of the Greek and Roman World, edited by M. Cary: iv, *A History of the Roman World, 753–146 B.C.* by H. H. Scullard (3rd ed. 1961); v, *146–30 B.C.* by F. B. Marsh (3rd ed. revised by H. H. Scullard, 1963); vi, *30 B.C.–A.D. 138* by E. T. Salmon (5th ed. 1966); vii, *A.D. 138–337* by H. M. D. Parker (2nd ed. revised by B. W. Warmington, 1958).

M. Rostovtzeff, *A History of the Ancient World*, ii, *Rome* (1927, revised by E. Bickerman, 1961).

A. E. R. Boak and W. G. Sinnigen, *A History of Rome to A.D. 565* (5th ed. 1965).

Th. Mommsen, *The History of Rome* (Engl. trans. 1911), i.e. of the Republic; old, but a classic.

J. Heurgon, *The Rise of Rome* (1973).

A. H. McDonald, *Republican Rome* (1966).

H. H. Scullard, *From the Gracchi to Nero* (4th ed. 1976).

M. Grant, *The World of Rome* (1960).

M. Grant, *The Climax of Rome* (1968).

J. Vogt, *The Decline of Rome* (1967).

F. Miller, *The Roman Empire and its Neighbours* (1967).

J. Wells and R. H. Barrow, *A Short History of the Roman Empire to the Death of Marcus Aurelius* (1931).

H. Mattingly, *Roman Imperial Civilisation* (1957).

G. G. Starr, *Civilisation and the Caesars* (1954).

M. Rostovtzeff, *The Social and Economic History of the Roman Empire* (2 vols, 2nd ed. 1957, by P. Fraser).

A. H. M. Jones, *The Later Roman Empire, 284–602* (3 vols, 1964).

A. H. M. Jones, *The Decline of the Ancient World* (1966), a shorter version of the above.

J. P. V. D. Balsdon, *Life and Leisure in Ancient Rome* (1969).

The Legacy of Rome, edited by C. Bailey (1924), essays on various aspects.

The Romans, edited by J. P. V. D. Balsdon (1965), also essays.

D. Dudley, *The Romans* (1970).

Aspects of Greek and Roman Life, a series edited by H. H. Scullard (some 30 volumes already published).

Aufstieg und Niedergang der römischen Welt, edited by H. Temporini, a co-operative work which aims at covering very many aspects of the Roman world, has made a beginning with the publication of vol. I, i and ii (1972).

Two useful collections of sources in translation are:

L. Lewis and M. Reinhold, *Roman Civilisation*: i, *The Republic* (1951); ii, *The Empire* (1955).

A. H. M. Jones, *A History of Rome through the Fifth Century*: i, *The Republic* (1968); ii, *The Empire* (1970).

Two works of reference are:

A Companion to Latin Studies, edited by J. E. Sandys (3rd ed. 1921).

Oxford Classical Dictionary, 2nd edition by N. G. L. Hammond and H. H. Scullard (1970).

A few useful books in French may be added:

Histoire Romaine, edited by G. Glotz, is in four volumes: i, to 133 B.C. by E. Pais and J. Bayet (2nd ed. 1940); ii, to 44 B.C. by G. Bloch and J. Carcopino (4th ed, 1950); iii, *Le Haut Empire* by L. Homo (1941); iv, *Le Bas-Empire*, i, to 325 by M. Besnier (1937) and ii, 325–395 by A. Piganiol (1947).

A. Piganiol, *Histoire de Rome* (4th ed. 1962).

A. Piganiol, *La Conquête romaine* (5th ed. 1967).

P. Petit, *La Paix Romaine* (1967); *Histoire générale de l'empire romain* (1974).

R. Remondon, *La Crise de l'empire romain* (1965).

List of Abbreviations

AJ Phil.	*American Journal of Philology*
Aufstieg NRW	*Aufstieg und Niedergang der römischen Welt*, edited by H. Temporini (1972–)
Broughton, *MRR*	T. R. S. Broughton, *The Magistrates of the Roman Republic* (1951–60)
Brunt, *Manpower*	P. A. Brunt, *Italian Manpower, 225 B.C.–A.D. 14* (1971)
CAH	*Cambridge Ancient History*
Cary, *Hist.*	M. Cary, *History of Rome*, 2nd edition (1954)
CIL	*Corpus Inscriptionum Latinarum*
Cl. Ph.	*Classical Philology*
Cl. Qu.	*Classical Quarterly*
Cl. Rev.	*Classical Review*
Crawford, *RRC*	M. Crawford, *The Roman Republican Coinage* (1975)
Degrassi, *ILLRP*	A. Degrassi, *Inscriptiones Latinae Liberae Rei Publicae* (1957–63)
De Sanctis, *Storia*	G. De Sanctis, *Storia dei Romani* (1907–66)
Dessau, *ILS*	H. Dessau, *Inscriptiones Latinae Selectae* (1892–1916)
Dittenberger, *Sylloge*	W. Dittenberger, *Sylloge Inscriptionum Graecarum*, 3rd edition (1915–24)
Entretiens Hardt, xiii	*Les Origines de la République Romaine. Entretiens sur l'antiquite classique*, Tome xiii (Fondation Hardt, Geneva, 1966)
Frank, *Econ SAR*	*An Economic Survey of Ancient Rome*, edited by T. H. Frank, 5 vols (1933–40)
JHS	*Journal of Hellenic Studies*
JRS	*Journal of Roman Studies*
Lewis–Reinhold, *R. Civ.*	N. Lewis and M. Reinhold, *Roman Civilization*, 2 vols (1951–5)
Momigliano, *Secondo, Terzo, Quarto Contrib.*	A. Momigliano, *Secondo, Terzo* and *Quarto Contributo alla storia degli studi classici* (1966, 1969)
Ogilvie, *Livy*	R. M. Ogilvie, *Commentary on Livy, Books 1–5* (1965)
OGIS	G. Dittenberger, *Orientis Graeci Inscriptiones Selectae* (1903–05)
PBSR	*Papers of the British School at Rome*
P–W	A. Pauly, G. Wissowa, *Realencyclopädie d. klassischen Altertumswissenschaft* (1893–)
Riccobono, *Fontes*	S. Riccobono, *Fontes Iuris Romani Ante-Justiniani*, i (1941)
Scullard, *Hist. Rom. World*	H. H. Scullard, *A History of the Roman World, 753–146 B.C.*, 3rd edition (1961)
Sherk, *Documents*	R. K. Sherk, *Roman Documents for the Greek East* (1969)
Sydenham, *CRR*	E. A. Sydenham, *The Coinage of the Roman Republic* (1952)
TAPA	*Transactions of the American Philological Association*
Walbank, *Polybius*	F. W. Walbank, *A Historical Commentary on Polybius*, i, ii (1957, 1967)

Notes and References

Chapter 1: Notes

[1] On Mediterranean geography in general see J. L. Myres, *The Mediterranean Lands* (1953); E. C. Semple, *The Geography of the Mediterranean Region: its Relation to Ancient History* (1931), especially chs xi–xx; M. Cary, *The Geographic Background of Greek and Roman History*; and for Italy, see *Italy*, 3 vols, Admiralty, Naval Intelligence Division, Geographical Handbooks.

[2] Evidence is forthcoming of long-term fluctuations in the volume of Mediterranean rainfall in prehistoric times: cf. C. E. P. Brooks, *Climate through the Ages* (1926). Further, it has been argued by Rhys Carpenter, *Discontinuity in Greek Civilization* (1966), 18 ff., that climatic changes through Mediterranean lands from 1200 to 850 B.C. caused drought and famine, while at points the sea-level seems to have been lower than today. This was followed by a period of abundant rainfall, so the climate may have been colder and perhaps wetter during the classical period. The effects of this change, if it is a fact, may well have been felt in the Alpine regions of Italy, where Brooks believed open communications were greatest between 1200 and 900. But thereafter changes are more likely to have been caused by local conditions: the clearing of forests and the consequent effect on the rainfall, together with the sweeping away of soil and the choking of river mouths which has continued since then (thus in Roman times difficulties of silting occurred at Ostia, Rome's port at the Tiber mouth, which today is two miles inland). J. B. Ward-Perkins (*Landscape and History in Central Italy*, Second J. L. Myres Memorial Lecture) emphasises the evil effects of deforestation upon southern Italy, including Sybaris, and points out (p. 6) that 'the great Roman ports of the northern Adriatic, Aquileia and Ravenna, are both now far inland; Spina too, the Adriatic port for northern Etruria, is high and dry'. For an attempt to discover how far the Mediterranean streams have modified their valleys during the last 2000 years see C. Vita-Finzi, *The Mediterranean Valleys* (1969) (he incidentally agrees that 'climatic conditions in Roman times were not effectively different from those of today', p. 113). This last point is also made abundantly clear from conditions described by Greek and Roman writers. Also the distribution of plants in the ancient and modern Mediterranean area shows that the isotherms remain virtually unchanged. Further, when Livy often records winter blizzards and prolonged summer rains in central Italy, this may have been because they were the reverse of normal. For further discussion see M. Cary, *The Geographic Background of Greek and Roman History* (1949), 2 ff.

On average the level of the Tyrrhenian Sea appears to have been about one metre lower c. 50 B.C.–A.D. 70 than today. See the detailed study *Il livello antico del mar Tirreno*, ed. by G. Schmiedt (1972).

[3] In Egypt the grain is ready to be harvested in April.

[4] At Rome the mean January temperature is 7° (C); the mean July temperature is 25° (C).

[5] In the lists of portents recorded by Livy there is frequent mention of automatic movement by the sacred spears of Mars. These were evidently suspended in such a manner as to oscillate, like the needle of a seismometer, in an earthquake, however slight.

Chapter 2: Notes

[1] The evidence for prehistoric Italy is naturally primarily archaeological. I have therefore included in the text the names of a certain number of small places of archaeological importance not in order to confuse the reader but to help him to orientate himself more quickly if he wishes to turn for more detail to standard archaeological works. General surveys include T. E. Peet, *The Stone and Bronze Ages in Italy and Sicily* (1909); D. Randall-MacIver, *Italy before the Romans* (1927); J. Whatmough, *The Foundations of Roman Italy* (1937); D. H. Trump, *Central and Southern Italy before Rome* (1966); L. Barfield,

Northern Italy before the Romans (1971). There is a very useful sketch and bibliography in J. Heurgon, *The Rise of Rome* (1973), while a summary is given by H. H. Scullard, *The Etruscan Cities and Rome* (1967), ch. 1.

Traces of the so-called Beaker (or Bell-Beaker) culture, which spread widely in western Europe, including Britain (originating from Spain or central Europe?), have been found in Sardinia, Sicily and northern Italy, but not hitherto in the Italian peninsula itself. Now some beakers have been discovered at Fosso Conicchio (near Viterbo) and so a new element is injected into the prehistory of central Italy. See D. Ridgway, *Antiquity* 1972, 52.

[2] See n. 1 and J. Bradford and P. R. Williams-Hunt, *Antiquity* 1946, 191 ff., and 1950, 84 ff.

[3] See Lord William Taylour, *Mycenaean Pottery in Italy* (1958).

[4] On Lipari see L. Bernabo Brea, *Sicily before the Greeks* (1957). From the seventeenth to fifteenth centuries (during the so-called Capo Graziano culture, named from a cape on the island of Filicundi), the islands imported Greek pottery (Middle Helladic, Late Helladic I, II and Mycenaean III A 1 and 2): this provides invaluable dating material. Contact with the East continued during the Middle Bronze Age cultural period (called Milazzese after a village of huts excavated on a promontory of that name on the island of Panarea). Also across the water on the opposite shore of Sicily at Milazzo (the later Greek and Roman Mylae) a cemetery has been excavated on the acropolis which contained similar material to that of Milazzese. While this Milazzese culture imported Apennine pottery, it also continued to trade further afield as witness the Mycenaean wares of *c*. 1400–1300 (LH IIIA), but a later decline in such imports implies that the culture had come to an end by 1250, while archaeology suggests that the end was abrupt.

[5] See n. 1 and D. Randall-MacIver, *The Iron Age in Italy* (1927), and *Villanovans and Early Etruscans* (1924).

[6] See J. B. Ward-Perkins, 'Veii: The Historical Topography of the Ancient City', *Papers of the British School at Rome*, 1961.

[7] On the linguistic problems see E. Pulgram, *The Tongues of Italy* (1958).

Chapter 3: Notes

[1] On the general cultural background and development of the Mediterranean world see J. Heurgon, *The Rise of Rome* (1973). On the Phoenicians see D. Harden, *The Phoenicians* (1962), and S. Moscati, *The World of the Phoenicians* (1968). Attempts have recently been made to discern Phoenician influence and traders on the site of early Rome itself. It has been argued that the sanctuary of Ara Maxima of Hercules in the Cattle Market (Forum Boarium) on the bank of the Tiber was preceded by a temple of the Phoenician god Melkart (=Hercules) and that this provides evidence for Phoenician merchants and even a Phoenician settlement, protected by a Phoenician god, at Rome. See for discussion J. Heurgon, *JRS*

1966, 2 f., and *The Rise of Rome*, 73 f. This theory should be regarded with considerable caution until confirmatory evidence appears.

[2] On the Greeks who settled in such numbers in southern Italy that the district became known as Magna Graeca, Great Greece, see T. J. Dunbabin, *The Western Greeks* (1948), A. G. Woodhead, *The Greeks in the West* (1962), and J. Boardman, *The Greeks Overseas* (1964), 175 ff.

It is noteworthy that the earliest settlements at Pithecusae and Cumae (see p. 16) were so far north: the attraction was most probably the copper and iron of Etruria and Elba, although both settlements were fertile. They were founded by Euboeans of Chalcis and Eretria. Cf. the remarks of A. J. Graham, *JHS* 1971, 143 ff. and D. Ridgway, 'The First Western Greeks', *Greeks, Celts and Romans* (ed. C. F. C. Hawkes, 1973), 5 ff. A vital sea-link with Greece was formed by the Strait of Messina: soon therefore some settlers from Cumae and Chalcis colonised Zancle-Messene (modern Messina). These in turn co-operated with Messenians from the Peloponnese in founding Rhegium across the strait in the toe of Italy. Sybaris was colonised about 720 (the traditional date) and was soon followed by Croton, Metapontum, Caulonia and others, while Taras (Tarentum) late in the eighth century occupied a territory with an ancient history. The individual names, dates and cultural contributions of these and other colonies cannot be given here, but all shared in a marvellous flowering of architecture, art, sculpture, the plastic arts, coinage, literature, science and philosophy, as seen, for instance, in the temples of Paestum, the terracottas of Locri, the bronzes of Tarentum, the philosophers of Elia and Pythagoras at Croton. It is against this brilliant background in southern Italy that Rome began to emerge in central Italy.

[3] On Demaratus see A. Blakeway, *JRS* 1935, 129 ff. Greek influence in another sphere is illustrated by a recent unexpected find: a Greek shrine, dedicated to Hera, at Graviscae, the port of the Etruscan city of Tarquinii: see M. Torelli, *Parola del Passato* 1971, 44 ff.

[4] The claim of Cumae to be the centre from which the Greek alphabet spread to the rest of Italy is strengthened by two inscriptions. One is on a cup found at Pithecusae, written in the Chalcidian alphabet, saying that anyone who drank from it would be inflamed by Aphrodite and claiming that the cup was superior to that of Nestor. It is interesting that the owner of the cup knew about Nestor's cup in the *Iliad*. Incidentally another Homeric reference *may* be contained in another locally made Geometric vase which depicts a shipwreck: it *could* refer to Odysseus or only to some other unhappy incident of Greek voyaging in the west. The other inscription which was found at Cumae is scratched on an early seventh-century vase and proclaims in the same form of letters, 'I am the vessel of Tataie; may anyone who steals me be struck blind'. It was almost certainly from here that the Etruscans borrowed their alphabet. It was soon in use at Rome and is found on the Manios *fibula* (see p. 33), but it is not certain whether it reached Rome direct from Cumae or via the Etruscans.

[5] The Greeks abandoned early 'heroic' methods of fighting, in which individual prowess was demanded, and adopted a battle-line (phalanx) of heavy-armed infantry (hoplites). The process is now shown to have been gradual; pieces of hoplite armour might be adopted by the aristocracy as they acquired them, but when the phalanx formation was adopted, social and political changes occurred in the warrior class, and a more independent middle class emerged. See A. N. Snodgrass, *Arms and Armour of the Greeks* (1967), ch. iii. This new formation was taken over by the Etruscans in the sixth century: see above, p. 53.

[6] Our knowledge of the Etruscans derives from very scattered references in the ancient writers and from archaeological discovery. Of the vast modern literature the following general surveys may be mentioned: M. Pallottino, *Etruscologia* (6th ed. 1968; English translation of this edition = *The Etruscans*, 1975); J. Heurgon, *Daily Life of the Etruscans* (1964); H. H. Scullard, *The Etruscan Cities and Rome* (1967); D. Strong, *The Early Etruscans* (1969). These works will put the reader on the track of more detailed studies and of the older literature. In H. H. Scullard *Etruscan Cities*, will be found illustrations of most of the Etruscan cities as well as of their artistic products. On architecture see A. Boëthius and J. B. Ward-Perkins, *Etruscan and Roman Architecture* (1970); on art see M. Moretti and G. Maetzke, *The Art of the Etruscans* (1970).

[7] Hesiod, *Theogony*, 1010. Herodotus, i. 94. Dionysius of Halicarnassus, i. 26–39.

[8] On Veii see J. B. Ward-Perkins, *Papers of the British School at Rome*, 1961, and on Tarquinii see H. Hencken, *Tarquinia and Etruscan Origins* (1968), which is a summary of his larger work, *Tarquinia, Villanovans and Etruscans* (1968).

[9] On the Etruscan language see, briefly, M. Pallottino, *The Etruscans* (1975), chs 10–12, and for a selection of inscriptions see his *Testimonia Linguae Etruscae²* 1968).

[10] This is the approach of M. Pallotino; see his *The Etruscans* (1955), chs 1 and 2, and for more detail his *L'origine degli Etruschi* (1947). Older views are discussed by P. Ducati, *Le Problème étrusque* (1938).

[11] An iron model of axe and *fasces* of *c.* 600 B.C. was found at Vetulonia. The twelve lictors who carried the *fasces* before kings and consuls of Rome were probably derived from the practice of the Etruscan League: when the twelve cities united for a joint enterprise the twelve axes, borne by the rulers of the individual cities, were entrusted to the supreme commander. A number of processions of magistrates is depicted on late funerary sarcophagi from southern Etruria and on alabaster urns from Volaterrae. They show the magistrate generally in a chariot, with attendants who include lictors with *fasces*; they represent both a triumphal procession when the magistrate was at the height of his glory, and also reflect his final journey to the underworld. See R. Lambrechts, *Essai sur les magistratures des républiques étrusques* (1959), with illustrations; one is reproduced in H. H. Scullard, *Etruscan Cities*, plate 102.

[12] Aristotle, *Politics* iii. 9; 1280a 35, refers to a treaty between Etruria and Carthage, without giving the date, which was probably the second half of the sixth century. The close relation between the two powers has been dramatically illustrated recently by a discovery at Pyrgi (Santa Severa), which was the port of the great Etruscan city of Caere. Between two Etruscan temples of the early fifth century were found three inscribed sheets of gold-leaf, two in Etruscan and one in Punic; although the latter is not a translation of either of the former (this would have provided the much-needed bilingual inscription which would help to a fuller interpretation of the Etruscan language), their content is similar. They record a dedication by Thefarie (Tiberius) Velianas, ruler of Caere, to Uni-Astarte, a Phoenician goddess, and the date is *c.* 500 B.C. The dedication of a shrine by an Etruscan to a Punic deity suggests very close relations and probably the existence at Pyrgi of a small settlement of Carthaginian merchants. This is the time when the Etruscans were being threatened in central Italy by Greeks and Latins and needed Carthaginian help. See J. Heurgon, *JRS* 1966, 1 ff., and J. Ferron, *Aufstieg NRW*, 1. i (1972), 189 ff.

[13] The helmet, now in the British Museum, which Hiero dedicated to Zeus at Olympia, is well known. It contained the words 'the Etruscan spoils won at Cumae'. A second inscribed helmet was found in 1959. See R. Meiggs and D. Lewis, *A Selection of Greek Historical Inscriptions* (1969), 62.

[14] The reputation for piracy which the Etruscans obtained among the Greeks was doubtless largely due to their forcible interference with Greek interlopers in the waters which they controlled.

[15] The odium in which the Etruscans were held by their subjects is illustrated by the tradition about Mezentius of Caere (the villain in the later books of Virgil's *Aeneid*), and by the solemn curses on the Etruscan race in the surviving tablets from the Umbrian town of Iguvium, for which see J. W. Poultney, *The Bronze Tables of Iguvium* (1959).

Chapter 4: Notes

[1] On the environs of Rome see T. Ashby, *The Roman Campagna in Classical Times* (1927, reprinted 1970); B. Tilly, *Vergil's Latium* (1947).

[2] T. Frank, *Economic History of Rome* (2nd ed. 1927).

[3] On Latial culture see the massive corpus by P. G. Gierow, *The Iron Age Culture of Latium*, I (1966), II. i (1964). For resemblances to and differences from southern Villanovan see I, 483 ff. Supporters of a 'long' chronology place the beginning in the tenth century, those of a 'short' chronology put it *c.* 800 B.C.

[4] Gierow, *Iron Age Culture of Latium*, i. 478, suggests they arrived in two waves, first to the Alban Hills, Rome, Ardea and perhaps Anzio and Tivoli, the second to Satricum and Palestrina.

[5] Pliny, *Nat Hist.* iii. 68–9. According to Dionysius of Halicarnassus, iv. 49, the number of Latin communities participating in the festival of Jupiter Latiaris in the sixth century was forty-seven. The Prisci Latini were those who occupied the narrow

area, between the Anio and Tiber, that separated Rome from the Sabine country: see A. N. Sherwin-White, *The Roman Citizenship* (1973), 9, and A. Bernardi, 'Dai Populi Albenses ai Prisci Latini nel Lazio arcaico', *Athenaeum* 1964, 223 ff.

[6] In the fourth century Praeneste had eight tributaries among the lesser Latin communities (Livy, vi. 29.6).

[7] The hills of ancient Rome must not be judged by those of the modern city, for the accumulation of débris from the ancient buildings in the valleys has brought about a considerable levelling of the site.

[8] For a discussion of the foundation-legends see De Sanctis, *Storia*, I, ch. vi; Ogilvie, *Livy*, 32 ff.; and, for Aeneas, G. K. Galinsky, *Aeneas, Sicily and Rome* (1969).

[9] On Romulus and Remus see C. J. Classen, *Historia* 1963, 447 ff. The origin of the second brother, Remus, is obscure. The twins may represent the Roman form of an early Indo-European myth, or they may have arisen from a misunderstanding of the Etruscan and Greek forms of the one and the same name. Or the story of Remus may have originated in the fifth or fourth century, when the plebeians formed a quasi-independent community on the Aventine, the hill with which Remus was especially associated.

[10] It need not be assumed that the suckling of Romulus by an animal was borrowed from a Greek source (such as the *Tyro* of Sophocles): similar tales recur in the folklore of Asia, Africa and America. In fact at the Etruscan city of Felsina (Bologna) a *stele* depicts a wolf suckling an infant.

[11] The twins are also depicted on the oldest silver coinage of Rome of *c.* 269 B.C. (see Sydenham, *CCR* p. 2, n. 6) and on an early bronze coin (Sydenham, n. 95), a struck semi-libral sextans. (Crawford, *RRC*, 20/1 and 39/3 respectively.)

[12] For a review of these stories see Dionysius of Halicarnassus, i. 72–4. The story of Romulus was spread abroad in Greece by the work of a certain Diocles of Peparethos, which was apparently used later by the Roman Fabius Pictor (Plutarch, *Romulus*, 3): see E. Gabba, *Entretiens Hardt*, xiii. 141 ff., who also discusses (147 ff.) the mysterious Promathion (Plut., *Romulus*, i. 3) who may draw on Etruscan traditions.

[13] See E. D. Phillips, 'Odysseus in Italy', *JHS* 1953, 53 ff.

[14] See G. K. Galinsky, *Aeneas, Sicily and Rome* (1969)

[15] See Dionys. Halic. i. 72. He adds that Aeneas named the city after Rhome, a Trojan woman who, tired of wandering, had set fire to the ships and thus forced Aeneas to settle in Latium. Alternative stories were later related about Rhome in order to attribute the foundation of Rome to the Latins rather than to Trojan Aeneas, e.g. that Rhome married Latinus, king of the Aborigines, by whom she had three sons, Romus, Romulus and Telegonus. Other stories said that Rhome was the sister of Latinus, who himself founded Rome. If Aeneas became less popular in Rome in the fifth and fourth centuries, the Greeks still linked Rome with the Trojans: thus Aristotle (fourth century) concentrates his account (Dionys. Halic.. i. 72. 3–4) on Rhome rather than on Aeneas.

[16] Lavinium, modern Pratica di Mare some sixteen miles south of Rome, is closely linked with Aeneas and the Trojan origin of Rome. It was Aeneas's first foundation in Italy according to Timaeus, who learned from local informants that among the holy objects kept at Lavinium was a Trojan earthenware jar which presumably contained the Trojan *penates*; these were originally the gods of the store cupboard (*penus*) which later were identified with the Dioscuri, Castor and Pollux. The tradition that the Trojan *penates* had come to Rome from Lavinium is strengthened by the discovery there of the archaic inscription to Castor and Pollux (CASTOREI PODLOQVEIQVE QVROIS) already mentioned (see p. 33). In addition, the fact that there was a cult of Aeneas Indiges, i.e. the divine ancestor, near Lavinium, recorded by Fabius Pictor and Naevius, has been confirmed by the discovery of a fourth-century inscription LARE AINEIA D(ONUM): see S. Weinstock, *JRS* 1960, 114 ff. There was no public cult of Aeneas at Rome itself. Beside the discovery in 1955 of the thirteen altars which suggest a federal centre at Lavinium (p. 33), an even more recent find has been made of a seventh-century tomb, surrounded by a stone circle which would have formed the base of a tumulus. In addition, in the fourth century a small shrine was erected within the circle, indicating that some famous person was venerated there. It is extremely probable that this is in fact the hero-shrine (Heroon) which tradition (Dionys. Halic. i. 64) records was erected by the Latins to Aeneas. Another indication of the importance of Lavinium is the fact that in later times after 338 B.C. high Roman magistrates (consuls, dictators, etc.) had to go there to sacrifice to the Penates and Vesta at the beginning and end of their periods of office. On Lavinium see now F. Castagnoli, *Lavinium*, i (1972), ii (in course of publication). For the Heroon see also P. Sommella, *Rend. d. pontific. accad. rom. di archeol.*, 44 (1971–2), 47 ff., G. K. Galinsky, *Vergilius* (1974), xx. 2 ff.

[17] The Roman authors no doubt reckoned a varying number of generations between the foundation of the city and the fall of Troy. On this problem see F. W. Walbank, *Polybius*, i (1957), 665 ff.

[18] The digression of Aeneas to Carthage was mentioned by Timaeus and Naevius. But neither of these writers appears to have anticipated Virgil's treatment of this episode.

[19] An excellent introduction to, and assessment of, the problems concerning early Rome is given by A. Momigliano, 'An Interim Report on the Origins of Rome', *JRS* 1963, 95 ff. (= *Terzo Contrib.* (1966), 545 ff.). Numerous papers on this topic are included in that volume (pp. 545–695) and in his *Quarto Contrib.* (1969), 273–499. The archaeological evidence is published in the monumental work of E. Gjerstad, *Early Rome*, i–vi (1953–73), vol. iv being to some extent resumptive of the earlier volumes; vol. v deals with the literary evidence and vol. vi provides an historical survey. A more popular summary is provided by R. Bloch, *The Origins of Rome* (1960), while a brief sketch is given by H. H. Scullard, *The Etruscan Cities and Rome* (1967), ch. ix. Much of great value will be found in Ogilvie, *Livy*, i–v (1965).

[20] Flint and copper implements of the Chalcolithic Age are believed to have come from the Esquiline. Apennine pottery of the Bronze Age has been found by ·E. Gjerstad in the Forum Boarium in a filling of earth which was probably put there when a temple was rebuilt in 212 B.C.; the settlement from which it originally derived was probably on one of the adjoining hills, the Aventine, Capitoline or Palatine.

[21] The date of the beginning of the Iron Age at Rome, including the huts on the Palatine, is controversial, but the early or mid-eighth century is widely accepted. H. Müller-Karpe (*Von Anfang Roms*, 1959, and *Zur Stadtwerdung Roms*, 1963), who puts it as early as the tenth century and connects it with the arrival of survivors of the Mycenaean civilisation, has been criticised by E. Gjerstad, *Opuscula Romana* (1962), 1 ff. and M. Pallottino, *Studi Etruschi* 1960, 11 ff., 1963, 3 ff., and others. H. Riemann, *Göttingische Gelehrte Anzeiger* 1960, 16 ff., argues for an intermediate date in the ninth century.

[22] On the Argei see Varro, *De Lingua Latina* v.45 54. They were puppets made of straw and were thrown into the Tiber annually on 14 May as a purificatory sacrifice. Possibly they were a substitute for human victims in earlier times.

[23] On the institutions which are attributed to Romulus in the account found in Dionysius ii. 7–29, see J. P. V. D. Balsdon, *JRS* 1971, 15 ff.

[24] Quirites may be derived from *curis* (Sabine for a spear) rather than from the Sabine town of Cures as the Romans generally asserted. Alternatively it may be from **coirion*, an assembly of people (cf. *curia*). See Ogilvie, *Livy*, 79.

[25] The tradition of Sabine influence in early Rome is rejected by J. Poncet, *Recherches sur la légende sabine, des origines de Rome* (1967) and *Aufstieg NRW*, I. i (1972), 48 ff but for a criticism of his use of the ancient sources see R. M. Ogilvie, *Cl. Rev.* 1968, 327 ff.

[26] Pompilius may be Sabine (cf. Latin Quinctilius), though it has also been claimed as Etruscan (cf. Etruscan *pumple*), while Numa is an Etruscan *praenomen*. But 'the names may have been etruscanized and then latinized in the course of history' (Ogilvie, *Livy*, 88.) For the development of the Numa legend see Ogilvie, 89 ff. As already said, this Commentary by Ogilvie is of great value for the history of these early traditions.

Chapter 5: Notes

[1] The tomb at Caere is that of the Tarchna family. The Latin equivalent is given as Tarquitius. It is not certain that this should be equated with Tarquinius and thus a possible link be established with the Tarquins of Rome. On this see M. Cristofani, *La tombe delle iscrizioni a Cerveteri* (1965), esp. appendix 1.

[2] The painting from the so-called François tomb at the Etruscan city of Vulci shows a number of warriors fighting, with their names painted on. In particular Mastarna (Macstrna) is rescuing Caelius Vibenna (Caile Vipinas), Aulus Vibenna killing his opponent, and Marcus Camitilius (Marce Camitlnas) is killing

Gnaeus Tarquinius of Rome (Cneve Tarchunies Rumach). If the last-named is to be identified with Tarquinius Priscus, this Etruscan tradition clashes with the Roman story of the latter's death. The Vibenna brothers are probably historical figures: not only were they known to the Roman tradition but a certain Aulus Vibenna dedicated a *bucchero* vase at Veii in the mid-sixth century. For the so-called Table of Claudius (a speech which he delivered at Lyons) and for a discussion of the whole problem see A. Momigliano, *Claudius²* (1961), 11 ff., 128 ff. (with bibliographies).

[3] The sixth-century date for the sanctuary stands against attempts to date it after 500 as a mere imitation of the federal sanctuary at Aricia. See A. Momigliano, *Terzo Contrib.* 641 ff., and Ogilvie, *Livy*, 182, against A. Alföldi, *Early Rome and the Latins* (1964). This book by Alföldi contains much interesting and ingenious speculation, but its main thesis cannot be sustained, namely that the picture of early Rome in relation to other Latin cities which is given by Livy was deliberately invented by Fabius Pictor in an attempt to show that sixth-century Rome was the leading Latin city, whereas in fact Rome only gained the predominance in the later fifth century. For a rejection of this thesis, which presupposes wholesale deliberate falsification by Fabius, see Momigliano, *Quarto Contrib.* 487 ff. (= *JRS* 1967, 211 ff.), and Ogilvie, *Cl. Rev.* 1966, 94 ff.; A. N. Sherwin-White, *The Roman Citizenship²* (1973), 190 ff.

[4] For the archaeological evidence see E. Gjerstad, *Early Rome*, iv (1966).

[5] For a preliminary report of the excavation of the Regia see F. E. Brown, *Entretiens Hardt*, xiii, 47 ff. The plan of the original building was respected in all later rebuildings throughout the Republic and Empire. For the *rex sacrorum* see A. Momigliano, *Quarto Contrib.*, 395 ff.

[6] On the triumph see L. B. Warren, *JRS* 1970, 49 ff. Several Etruscan tomb-paintings depict Games which resemble the traditional Roman Games, e.g. the Tomb of the Augurs (wrestlers) and Tomb of the Olympiads (runners, horse-racing) at Tarquinii and the Tomb of the Monkey (horsemen, wrestlers, athletes, boxers) at Clusium. See, for example, A. Stenico, *Roman and Etruscan Painting* (1963), plates 7, 17–19, 34–43.

[7] On the Servian Wall see G. Saflund *Le mura di Roma* (1932); Gjerstad, *Early Rome*, iii. 26 ff. On the strength of a piece of Attic pottery, Gjerstad would date the *agger* to *c.* 475, but there is evidence for an earlier phase (cf. Ogilvie, *Livy*, 179).

[8] On the vexed question as to how far private property had superseded common ownership in early Rome no final answer can be given. The later Romans, in believing that Romulus distributed conquered land to individuals (*viritim*), apparently regarded private ownership as primitive. Despite difficulties about the precise meanings and implications of the words *heredium* and *mancipatio* and the possibility that some land was still entailed within the *gentes*, private property was probably widespread if not completely unrestricted: it is presupposed in the differentiation between patricians and plebeians. (In the Twelve Tables *heredium*, hereditary estate,

meant 'orchard', not 'fields': was only the orchard private property? Does *mancipatio* imply that originally only movable objects which can be held (*manu capere*) could be sold?).

[9] The Capitoline Wolf (without the twins which were added during the Renaissance) is dated by F. Matz, *Studies presented to D. M. Robinson* (1951), i. 754 ff., to 475–450 B.C. P. J. Riis, *Introduction to Etruscan Art* (1953), 66 f., thinks its attribution to a Veientine artist of the late sixth century remains 'an open question', while G. A. Mansuelli, *Etruria and Early Rome* (1966), 122, is inclined to believe in a Veientine artist. For earlier literature see a list by Löwy, *Studi Etruschi* 1934, 77.

[10] On Greek pottery in Rome see E. Gjerstad, *Early Rome*, iv (1966), 514 ff.

[11] On Roman religion standard works are W. Warde Fowler, *The Religious Experience of the Roman People* (1911) and *The Roman Festivals* (1899); in German, G. Wissowa, *Religion und Kultus der Romer* (1912), and K. Latte, *Römische Religionsgeschichte* (1960). See also C. Bailey, *Phases in the Religion of Ancient Rome* (1932), and F. Altheim, *History of Roman Religion* (1938); the latter to be used with caution. Two excellent introductions are H. J. Rose, *Ancient Roman Religion* (1949), and R. M. Ogilvie, *The Romans and their Gods* (1969). See also H. J. Rose, *Primitive Culture in Italy* (1926); J. Bayet, *Histoire politique et psycholgique de la religion romaine*[2] (1969). For a survey of recent work on the religion of the Republic see R. Schilling *Aufstieg NRW* (1972), I. ii. 317 ff.

[12] These functional spirits (*indigamenta*) were subdivided to an almost ludicrous extent and watched over every activity from birth to death: from Cunina the spirit of the cradle to Libitina that of burial. Fabius Pictor records a list of spirits invoked by the priest of Ceres when sacrificing to Earth and Ceres: First Plougher, Second Plougher, Harrower, Sower, Top-dresser, Hoer, Raker, Harvester, Gatherer, Storer, Distributor (Vervactor, Reparator, Imporcitor, Insitor, Obarator, Ocator, Sarritor, Subruncinator, Messor, Convector, Conditor, Promitor).

[13] On the institutions of early Rome see H. Stuart Jones, *CAH*, vii, ch. xiii; the massive work in Italian by P. de Francisci, *Primordia Civitatis* (Rome, 1959); and papers by A. Momigliano, collected in *Terzo* and *Quarto Contrib*.

[14] The view that serfdom existed at Rome under the kings has now been generally abandoned, despite the advocacy of Ed. Meyer, *Kleine Schriften*, i. 351 ff.

[15] See the detailed statement in Dionys. Halic. ii. 10.

[16] On the tribal names cf. J. Heurgon, *Entretiens Hardt*, xiii, 283 f. G. Dumezil in a number of works (e.g. *Jupiter, Mars Quirinus*) has argued, on Indian and other Indo-European analogies, for a tripartite class division in early Rome, the Ramnes representing the priests, the Tities the producers and farmers, and the Luceres the warriors. This theory has not met with general approval (cf., for example, Momigliano: 'not only is his evidence weak, but his theories are unnecessary', *Terzo Contrib*. 583).

[17] On the *curiae* see A. Momigliano, *Terzo Contrib*. 571 ff. An alternative view is that the number thirty

may suggest a later creation (in the Etruscan period?) as subdivisions of the three tribes. R. E. A. Palmer, *The Archaic Community of the Romans* (1970), argues that the *curiae* were originally separate ethnic groups who gradually fused together to form the earliest community of Rome; thus they were not phratries, clans or military units, but were earlier than the three tribes which were military non-ethnic units. This view will no doubt be challenged.

[18] See Livy, i. 8.7; Dionys. Halic. ii. 12; 47; 57. The number 300 is obviously linked to the three tribes and the thirty *curiae*, but it may well be only a guess by later Romans who knew that there had originally been three tribes (though the 100 assigned to Romulus does not fit in mathematically).

[19] The origin of the phrase *patres conscripti* is obscure. Is *conscripti* a qualifying adjective or does the phrase mean *patres et conscripti* (as suggested by another phrase *qui patres qui conscripti*: Livy ii. 1.11)? If the former, then presumably at some point earlier virtual automatic membership of the Senate, which had been the privilege of certain families, had been supplemented by the inclusion of other important members of the community, and the whole body thus selected were enrolled as *patres*. Alternatively and perhaps more probably (cf. Momigliano, *Quarto Contrib*. 423 ff.), the Senate came to consist of *patres* (who did not need formal enrolment) and *non-patres* (*conscripti*) who had to be enrolled. If this view is accepted, the newcomers should not necessarily be identified either with the so-called *minores gentes* (the meaning of the distinction between *maiores* and *minores gentes* remains quite obscure) nor with plebeians (since it may be misleading to make so sharp and formal a distinction in the very early period).

[20] One much-debated problem about the early triumph is how far the king represented the god, in other words how far did the triumphal *insignia* suggest divine or only royal characteristics in the *triumphator*; it is not, however, probable that the idea of divinisation was present. On the early triumph see L. B. Warren, *JRS* 1970, 49 ff.; cf. H. S. Versnel, *Triumphus* (Leiden, 1971).

A minor and simpler form of triumph, the *ovatio*, developed in the early days of the Republic, while from the late third century we hear of generals holding unofficial triumphs on the Alban Mount during the Feriae Latinae when they were denied full triumphs by the Senate.

[21] On the calendar see A. K. Michels, *The Calendar of the Roman Republic* (1967), but her attribution of the pre-Julian calendar to the decemviral instead of the regal period should probably be rejected: cf. R. M. Ogilvie, *Cl. Rev.* 1969, 330 ff. 'Numa's' reform must surely antedate 509 since it contains no reference to the dedication of the temple of Jupiter Capitolinus in that year, while if Aprilis is an Etruscan word the reform will belong to the sixth century. It is usually believed that the introduction of the new month of January did not result in changing the beginning of the Roman year from March to January and that this change was made only in 153 B.C. However, Mrs Michels argues otherwise (97 ff.) and suggests that the change in 153 was only that the consuls entered office on 1 January instead of 1

March, i.e. the official consular year was brought into line with the older calendar year.

On the Roman calendar see also E. J. Bickerman, *Chronology of the Ancient World* (1968), 43 ff., and A. E. Samuel, *Greek and Roman Chronology* (1972), ch. v.

[22] A collection of laws was ascribed to the kings (*leges regiae*). The jurist Pomponius records (*Digest*, 1.2.2.2) that such a collection existed in his own day (second cent. A.D.) and was called *ius Papirianum* because it was compiled by a Sextus Papirius under Tarquinius Superbus, while Dionysius of Halicarnassus (iii. 36) says that C. Papirius, the first Pontifex Maximus, restored a collection, made by Ancus Marcius, of some laws of Numa which had been recorded on tablets in the Forum and become illegible. Modern scholars have collected references to the *leges regiae* preserved in the literary sources (Dionysius, Livy, etc.): e.g. Riccobono, *Fontes*, i. 1–8. The date of the collection by Papirius remains uncertain. The laws, which deal chiefly with religion or crimes regarded as infringements of religion, may represent early rules of the regal community (i.e. genuine pontifical tradition), although they will not have been published in the Forum, as were the later Twelve Tables.

[23] A. Magdalain, *Historia* 1973, 405 ff., has argued that the *duoviri perduellionis* were invented by later annalists.

[24] Cf. Momigliano, *Quarto Contrib.* 377 ff., against A. Alföldi, *Der frührömische Reiteradel und seine Ehrenbezeichnen* (1952). The controversy is continued in *Historia* 1968, 444 ff. and 385 ff.

[25] The problem of how the early army developed has, in the view of many scholars, been solved by P. Fraccaro, *Opuscula*, ii (1957, reprinting an earlier paper of 1931), but the dating of the different stages is still contested. For a brief summary see Scullard, *Hist. Rom. World*[3], 423 ff.

How varied are the interpretations that can be put upon the evidence is shown by a recent article by G. V. Sumner (*JRS* 1970, 76 ff.), who argues that Servius established a centuriate organisation of the army of 3000 based on the thirty *curiae* and the three original tribes. This lasted until the mid-fifth century when (so Sumner believes) the new territorial tribes were created, a phalanx of 3000 hoplites in thirty *centuriae*: concurrently the new model army was adapted for political purposes as a new Comitia Centuriata, no longer based on the *curiae*. This *legio* was increased to 4000 *c.* 431 B.C., and to 6000 *c.* 405 when the Comitia Centuriata assumed the classical form of five classes. After 367 it was divided into two legions and by 311 the four-legion manipular army had been created.

[26] Gellius, vi. 13.1, drawing on Cato, and Festus, p. 100L, refer to a distinction between *classici* and *infra classem*. The view has recently been revived by A. Bernardi (*Athenaeum*, 1952, 19 ff.) and Momigliano (*Terzo Contrib.* 596, *Quarto* 430 ff.) that this implies that at one time there were only these two property groups and that the Servian legion was drawn only from the *classici*: sixty centuries of infantry of the line formed the *classis*, and other lighter troops were *infra classem*. See further below, n. 29

[27] Since there is no evidence that the number of equestrian centuries was raised to eighteen during the Republic, a regal origin for the full increase is possible.

[28] The view that hoplite tactics were not introduced until the mid-fifth century (cf., for example, M. P. Nilsson, *JRS* 1929, 4 ff.) has been rejected by many: see, for example, Momigliano, *Terzo Contrib.* 593 ff., and, briefly, E. S. Staveley, *Historia* 1956, 76. The archaeological evidence also suggests a date in the mid-sixth century: see A. M. Snodgrass, *Arms and Armour of the Greeks* (1967), 74 ff. The details of the armour of the five classes, as given by Livy, i. 43, and Dionys. Halic. iv. 16–17, are not reliable and do not derive from an early source.

[29] Among the many scholars who placed the Servian reforms later than the regal period was M. Cary (see the second edition of this book, pp. 80 ff.). It is scarcely necessary to list here others who supported this view. Older views are discussed by G. W. Botsford, *The Roman Assemblies* (1909), while more recent theories are criticised by E. S. Staveley, *Historia* 1956, 74 ff. It should be noted that even Mommsen, who regarded much of the detailed account of the kings as fable, nevertheless attributed the Servian constitution to the regal period. A turning-point in modern assessments of the problem is H. Last's paper in *JRS* 1945, 30 ff. Further vindication of a more traditional position against the extreme sceptics is to be found in P. Fraccaro, *JRS* 1957, 64; P. de Francisci, *Primordia Civitatis* (1959), 672 ff.; L. R. Taylor, *Voting Districts of the Roman Republic* (1960), 3 ff.; A. Momigliano, *Terzo Contrib.* 594 ff.; Ogilvie, 166 ff. A remark by Staveley (op. cit. 76), made in regard to a specific point, may be of wider application: 'it is hardly sound historical method to prefer another date for the Servian reform to the one unanimously indicated by the ancient authorities on the strength of a theory for which those same authorities provide not the slightest support'. Thus the reforms make good historical sense in the context where tradition placed them, but nevertheless the document recording them which Livy gives (i. 43.1–9) obviously neither derives from the regal period nor quotes the authentic terms of the reforms.

[30] According to Livy (i. 43.13) Servius established the four urban tribes when he held a census of the population. Livy does not record the creation of the sixteen rural tribes, which is described by Dionys. Halic. (iv. 15: he is drawing upon Varro, but the tradition is certainly as old as Fabius Pictor and Cato), but Livy later (ii. 21.7) implies that the rural tribes antedated the beginning of the Republic.

[31] The figures for the *classes* later ranged from 100,000 *asses* for the first class to 11,000 for the fifth. They represent the attempt by later generations to turn the early ratings into terms of a bronze monetary currency which did not then exist. The proportions of the minimum qualifications for the classes may well have been 20, 15, 10, 5, $2\frac{1}{2}$/2. As mentioned above (n. 26), the phrases *infra classem* and *classici* may suggest a time when there was only one *classis* (cf. Momigliano, *Terzo Contrib.* 596, *Quarto Contrib.* 430 ff.). Indeed it could even be conjectured that Servius himself first introduced one and then later five classes: we simply do not know precisely how

and when the later system evolved. It should be noted, however, that Gellius (see n. 26) does not suggest that there was a time when there were less than five classes in the centuriate organisation. The hypothesis of a prior period of *classici/infra classem* is attractive since it avoids attributing to the regal period a complicated structure (though it is noteworthy that Solon in 590 had introduced a four-class timocratic system in early Athens), but it involves *inter alia* the need to find an appropriate date for the introduction of the five-tier system (e.g. in 445) which has escaped the notice of our surviving authorities.

[32] Unless of course the hypothesis of a one-class system at this stage is accepted: then the sixty centuries of the one *classis* would form the battle-line.

[33] The fetial procedure is described by Livy, i. 24.4–9; 32.4–13. There is no good reason to doubt the antiquity of the ritual, but many of the details given by Livy may be due to later antiquarian writers. For full discussion see Ogilvie, *Livy*, 127 ff.

[34] Although Ogilvie (*Livy*, 209 f.) thinks that the shield was a trophy for the capture of Gabii in the fourth century, the treaty it contains is widely accepted as genuine: its forgery in later times, when Gabii was an insignificant town, would be unlikely.

[35] A copy of the treaty, engraved on brass, was preserved in the Treasury at Rome and was known to Polybius, who does not claim to have seen the original document himself but said that parts of it could be understood only with considerable difficulty, i.e. the Latin was archaic (no doubt like the Manios or Lapis Niger inscriptions). He quotes two other early treaties between Rome and Carthage before the first Punic war. These raise very many questions. One main problem is whether he had antedated the first one, which he placed in the first year of the Republic. For a brief discussion and defence of the Polybian date see H. H. Scullard, *Hist. Rom. World,* appendix 7; fuller discussion in Walbank, *Polybius,* i. 337 ff.; A. J. Toynbee, *Hannibal's Legacy* (1965), i. 519 ff. Cary (*Hist.* 104) shared the opinion of those scholars who dated the first treaty to 348 (cf. Livy, vii. 17.2 and Dionys. Halic, xvi, 69.1). See also K. E. Petzold, *Aufstieg NRW,* I. i (1972), 364 ff.

[36] The two Leagues are to be distinguished. Pliny (*NH,* iii. 68) gives the names of the members of the cult of Jupiter Latiaris. On the Arician League see the fragment of Cato's *Origines* (ii. 58): 'Lucum Dianum in nemore Aricino Egerius Laevius Tusculanus dedicavit dic[t]ator Latinus, hi populi communiter, Tusculanus, Aricinus, Lanuvinus, Laurens, Coranus, Tiburtis, Pometinus, Ardeatis Rutulus.' It is almost certain that this League of Aricia is to be identified with the federation which met at *caput Ferentinae* recorded by Cincius (Festus, 276L) and Dionys. Halic. iii. 34.3. Thus when Tarquinius Superbus summoned a meeting of the Council of Ferentina, the leading part was taken by Herdonius of Aricia (Livy, i. 50–1).

[37] The killing of Cnaeus Tarquinius Romanus depicted on the François tomb at Vulci (see Chap. 5, n. 1) has been identified with the death of Sextus, on the assumption that the *praenomen* is incorrect: cf. Ogilvie, *Livy*, 230. Caere would be a natural refuge for the Tarquins if in fact the family had originated

from there, as suggested by a tomb which contains inscriptions of the fifth to third centuries of the Tarcna family. But see also n. 1 above.

[38] The name Porsenna is good Etruscan. There is a variant tradition in Pliny (*NH,* ii. 140) that he came from Volsinii, not Clusium. It has been suggested (cf. Ogilvie, *Livy*, 255; cf. 234) that the more inland Etruscan cities, such as Clusium, were pursuing a more aggressive policy than the more hellenised southern cities, such as Caere and Veii.

[39] On Horatius, Mucius and Cloelia see Ogilvie, *Livy*, 258 ff.

[40] See A. Momigliano, *Terzo Contrib.* 664 f.; E. Gabba, *Entretiens Hardt*, xiii, 144 ff.

[41] The tale of Tarquin's silent lesson in tyrant-craft to his son, the King of Gabii, when he struck off the heads of all the tallest poppies in a field (Livy, i. 54), is an obvious adaptation of a similar story about the despots of Corinth and Miletus in Herodotus, v. 92.24 ff.

[42] Cf. R. Bloch, *The Origins of Rome* (1960), 96 ff., and *Tite-Live et les premiers siècles de Rome* (1965). For a discussion of these views see M. Pallottino, *Studi Etruschi* 1963, 31 ff.

[43] So varied are the theories about the origin of the Republic and of the consulship which have been advanced in recent years that it is not feasible to try to summarise them all here. For a useful and critical discussion of them see E. S. Staveley, *Historia* 1956, 72 ff., and especially 90 ff. (with bibliography). One point which has been much discussed even more recently may be mentioned here, namely the *praetor maximus*.

According to the antiquarian Cincius (Livy, vii. 3.5) an ancient law prescribed that the *praetor maximus* every year on the Ides of September should drive a nail into the wall of the temple of Jupiter Capitolinus. The purpose presumably was to mark the passing of one year and the practice started with the dedication of the temple in the first year of the Republic. But who was the *praetor maximus*? Some scholars think that he existed under the monarchy as an officer of the king and then became head of the Republic; others would then equate him with an alleged annual dictator. But all such theories clash with Roman tradition that there was not one such head of state at the beginning of the Republic. Staveley (*op. cit.* 96 ff.) avoids the difficulty by arguing that the ancient law, or at least its wording and use of *praetor maximus*, is fourth-century (363 B.C., when Livy mentions it). The superlative *maximus* has caused trouble, but Momigliano (*Quarto Contrib.* 403 ff.) points out that in early Latin it need not mean the greatest of three or more: Terence (*Adelphoi,* 881) uses it of two brothers, and Ennius (*Ann.* 298v) of the higher of two Oscan magistrates. Thus it could mean one of two consuls, and in fact one was called *maior consul* (Festus, 154L): the two took turns in having the lictors and twelve fasces, and the one who had them at any time (for a day or month) was called *maior consul.* For this and other possible explanations of the *praetor maximus*, see Momigliano, *op. cit.*

[44] See K. Hanell, *Das altrömische eponyme Amt* (1946). A brief statement of his views is given by E. Gjerstad in *Legends and Facts of Early Roman History*

(Lund, 1962), and in ch. i of *Entretiens Hardt*, xiii, 1966; these are developed in more detail in many other of his works. For criticism see M. Pallottino, *Studi Etruschi*, 1963, 19 ff, and Momigliano, *Rivista Storia Italiana*, 1961, 802 ff.; 1963, 882 ff. (= *Terzo Contrib.* 661 ff.), and *JRS* 1963, 95 ff. (= *ibid* 545 ff.), with works cited in *JRS* 1963, 103, n. 42 for criticism of Hanell's position. For evaluation of the views of R. Werner, *Der Beginn der römschen Republik* (1963), who places the beginning in 472 and thus rejects the early consular Fasti, see Momigliano, *Terzo Contrib.* 669 ff.; R. M. Ogilvie, *Cl. Rev.* 1965, 84 ff.

Chapter 6: Notes

[1] For a text of the so-called *Lapis Niger* see Dessau, *ILS*, 4913: Degrassi, *ILLRP*, n. 3. For recent discussion see R. E. A. Palmer, *The King and the Comitium* (1969).

[2] For the text of the Twelve Tables see Riccobono, *Fontes*, i. 23 ff.; for translation with notes, A. C. Johnson, P. R. Coleman-Norton and F. C. Bourne, *Ancient Roman Statutes* (1961), 9 ff. Hypercritical attempts to lower the date of the Tables to *c.* 300 B.C. (E. Pais, *Storia critica di Roma*) or even 200 (E. Lambert, *Nouvelle Revue de droit* 1902, 149 ff.) have been rebutted (e.g. by A. H. J. Greenidge, *Eng. Hist. Rev.* 1905, 1 ff.). For general discussion see H. F. Jolowicz, *Historical Introduction to Roman Law*[3] (1972), 106 ff.

[3] See the criticisms of Cicero, *De Legibus*, iii. 46.

[4] Livy, iv. 55.13. Cf. Ogilvie, *Livy*, 503.

[5] On the credibility of the early census returns see T. Frank, *AJ Phil.* 1930, 363 ff. The received figures in our manuscripts contain some obvious copyists' errors. Those before 392 B.C. purport to include men, women and children. They are rejected by P. A. Brunt, *Italian Manpower* (1971), 27, who follows Beloch in believing that so primitive a state would not have collected statistics of this kind. However, a figure for the Servian census is given by the annalist Fabius Pictor and *may* go back to Timaeus who died in 260: see Pliny, *NH*, xxxiii. 42; Livy, i. 44.2. Cf. A. Momigliano, *Terzo Contrib.* 649 ff.

[6] The various surviving lists of consuls in the republican era, together with the Fasti Triumphales, will be found collected in *Inscriptiones Italiae*, xiii, pt i. An indispensable tool for all historians is T. R. S. Broughton, *Magistrates of the Roman Republic* (2 vols and Supplement, 1951–60), where all the known Republican magistrates are recorded, together with full references to the ancient sources for their activities. The Fasti are discussed by K. J. Beloch, *Römische Geschichte bis zum Beginn der punischen Kriege* (1926), 9 ff.

[7] On the Tabula Pontificum and the Annales Maximi see J. E. A. Crake, *Cl. Ph.* 1940, 375 ff.; P. Fraccaro, *JRS* 1957, 59 ff.; J. P. V. D. Balsdon, *Cl. Qu.* 1953, 162 ff. The view, of Mommsen and others,

that Scaevola's edition was preceded by an earlier published edition is rejected by Crake, who also argues that Scaevola did not expand his material. For the suggestion that in practice the Annales Maximi were not much used by later writers see E. Rawson, *Cl. Rev.* 1971, 158 ff.

[8] See L. G. Roberts, *Memoirs of the American Academy at Rome*, ii (1918), 55 ff. When Athens was burnt by the Persians in 480 and 479 the names of earlier eponymous magistrates survived.

[9] Ennius dates the eclipse to 5 June, whereas it was on the 21st; hardly a serious error. K. J. Beloch (*Griechische Geschichte*, IV. ii. 267) identified the eclipse with that of 13 June 288 B.C., but this involves emending the text of Cicero. (The figure for the hundreds is missing in the only surviving manuscript and a scribe has entered 'CCC'; Beloch would read 'CCCC', but that, *inter alia*, involves Cicero in a much wider margin of error in years, while the date of the month would still be wrong.) Beloch's date is rejected by J. E. A. Crake, *Cl. Ph.* 1940, 379 ff., who also deals with other arguments in favour of a third-century date for the pontifical annals (cf. Cary, *Hist.* 44), namely (*a*) in Livy the yearly list of prodigies which he transcribed from the tablets only begins under the date 296 (Obsequens's list starts only in 249). But other typical pontifical material, as the census and the founding of colonies, does appear in the fourth century, while in his later books Livy is inconsistent in the use that he makes of such material. (*b*) Our records of triumphs, which ultimately come from the same source, have been proved defective before 300 (half of the entries between 326 and 301 have been discredited). But since Livy almost certainly did not directly and personally consult the *tabulae* or the Annales Maximi, errors could easily creep in.

[10] See Ogilvie, *Livy*, 6, n. 1; 408; 581 ff.

[11] If the view of Momigliano (see p. 582) is accepted, namely that the *conscripti* were an intermediate group between patricians and plebeians (and were lesser non-patrician senators but not plebeians), then the supposed plebeian names in the Fasti will belong to the *conscripti*; thus the problem of plebeian names falls to the ground and a fatal blow is dealt to this objection to the reliability of the Fasti.

[12] The expulsion of the Tarquins, which is dated 509 in the traditional or 'Varronian' era, should be assigned to 507; the capture of Rome by the Gauls should be post-dated from 390 to 387, and the Licinian Rogations from 367 to 362.

[13] Some of these legends attached to temples and holy places, yet they were popular rather than priestly. The official Roman religion had no mythology (M. Grant, *Roman Myths* (1971).

[14] The character of these *tituli* may be illustrated from the inscriptions on the sarcophagi of the elder Scipios; Dessau, *ILS*, nos. 1 and 2.

[15] For a full discussion of the evidence for (Cicero, *Brutus*, 19.27, *Tusc. Disp.* iv. 2.3, both going back to Cato, and Varro, *de Vita Populi Romani*, ii) and the history of, the ballad theory see A. Momigliano, *Secondo Contrib.* 69 ff. (= *JRS* 1957, 104 ff.).

[16] Both Cicero (*Brutus*, 16.62) and Livy (viii. 40) commented on the mendacity of the *laudationes* or

funeral panegyrics delivered by younger members of noble families on their departed elders.

[17] On the Roman annalists see the excellent essay by E. Badian in *Latin Historians* (ed. T. A. Dorey, 1966), ch. i, with the literature there cited. Cf. also the brief accounts by A. H. McDonald, *OCD*, s.v. Historiography and the individual annalists. See also notes below dealing with the various writers. The fragments themselves are collected in H. Peter, *Historicorum Romanorum Reliquiae*, vol. i² (1914), with discussion in Latin. See also Ogilvie, *Livy*, introduction and *passim*; E. Gabba, 'Considerazioni sulla tradizione letteraria sulle origini della Republica', *Entretiens Hardt*, xiii, 135 ff.

[18] Licinius Macer claimed to have found in the temple of Juno Moneta some books written on linen (*libri lintei*), containing lists of magistrates. They purport, however, to go back earlier than 344 when this temple was founded. For a discussion of the difficulties see Ogilvie, *JRS* 1958, 40 ff. (cf. Ogilvie, *Livy*, 544 f.); he concludes that the lists went back to 509 but were not compiled before *c.* 150. They thus lacked independent value.

[19] The first book of Livy contains several such legal 'archetypes'. The story of Horatius and his appeal to the people (i. 26) is an excellent example.

[20] The brilliant analysis of the story of Spurius Cassius in Mommsen's *Römische Forschungen* (ii. 153ff.) showed the way to the discovery of such reduplications. Many more have been brought to light by Pais and Beloch, but few would care to go so far as these scholars in the pursuit of dittographies.

[21] Cf. Ogilvie, *Livy*, 10 ff., who writes about Licinius Macer, who was a *popularis*: 'all the certain Licinian throwbacks are justifications of Marius and his associates or detractions of Sulla'. By contrast Valerius Antias was an admirer of Sulla, who strengthened the Senate: hence Servius Tullius served as an excellent prototype.

[22] On the attitude of Livy and Dionysius to early Rome see D. Musti, *Tendenze nella storiografia romana e greca su Roma arcaica* (1970)

[23] *Historia Plantarum*, v. 8.2. Cf. A. Momigliano, *Interpretations* (ed. C. S. Singleton, 1969), 10 f.

[24] On Timaeus and his attitude to Rome see Momigliano, *Terzo Contrib.* 23 ff., and esp. 44 ff. On Timaeus's knowledge of early Lavinium see above, Chap. 4, n. 16.

[25] On the existence of historical works by Etruscan writers and the possible use of them by Greek and Roman writers see W. V. Harris, *Rome in Etruria and Umbria* (1971), ch. 1.

[26] The Fasti in Diodorus are printed by A. B. Drachmann, *Diodorus: Römische Annalen bis 302 a. Chr.* (1912). See also G. Perl, *Kritische Untersuchungen zu Diodors römischer Jahrzahlung* (1957), on which cf. E. S. Staveley, *Cl. Rev.* 1959, 158 ff. Bibliography by G. T. Griffith in *Fifty Years of Classical Scholarship* (ed. M. Platnauer, 1954), 190.

Chapter 7: Notes

[1] For various views about the end of the monarchy and the origin of the consulship see the end of Chap. 5 above and notes 43 and 44 to that chapter.

[2] Beloch, *Römische Geschichte*, 221.

[3] The main belief of the ancient sources is that a magistrate held a public preliminary investigation and if he condemned the accused the latter then appealed to the people (*iudicium populi*), who either confirmed or rejected the magistrate's sentence. Some scholars, however, do not believe that the right of appeal (*provocatio*) was coeval with the establishment of the Republic and suggest that the magistrate referred the question of guilt direct to the popular assembly. W. Kunkel, *Untersuchungen zue Entwicklung des römischen Kriminalverfahrens in vorsullanischer Zeit* (1962), has more recently argued that only cases concerned with political charges and offences against the State were referred to the *iudicia populi* and that the ordinary crimes were dealt with by a praetor or a triumvir capitalis. For a rejection of this view and defence of tradition see A. H. M. Jones, *The Criminal Courts of the Roman Republic and Principate* (1972), ch. 1.

[4] The change from the name praetor to consul is generally placed about the mid-fifth century. If the breastplate bearing the name of Cornelius Cossus, which the emperor Augustus saw in a temple, was genuine and correctly reported (see p. 589), then the name consul will have been in use in 428 B.C. Tradition associated no fewer than five consuls with the first year of the Republic. Three should probably be removed: L. Tarquinius Collatinus as a doublet of the king; Sp. Lucretius because of his connexion with Lucretia; and P. Valerius Poblicola as an invention of Valerius Antias. That leaves M. Horatius Pulvillus, the dedicator of the Capitoline temple and probably historical, and L. Iunius Brutus, who also may stand. Polybius mentions these two in connection with the first treaty with Carthage; this does not necessarily mean that their names were in the treaty (Polybius might have added one or both from the tradition of his own time), but his evidence certainly does not weaken their claim to historical existence.

[5] On the *fasces* see E. S. Staveley, *Historia* 1956, 103 ff.

[6] According to Livy (ii. 8.2) P. Valerius Poplicola in 509 B.C. carried a law which granted appeal (*provocatio*) from the magistrates to the people (*populus*). This is generally rejected as a doublet of later laws *de provocatione* (see p. 68).

[7] These early quaestors merely investigated crimes and determined responsibility: the consuls, with *imperium*, passed sentence.

[8] The cult of Saturn was very old (cf. the Saturnalia). The temple, which Livy (ii. 21.2) assigns to 496 B.C., may have been the replacement of an altar by a temple.

[9] On the *rex sacrorum* see Momigliano, *Quarto Contrib.* 395 ff. A *rex sacrorum* is found in other Latin cities (Tusculum, Lanuvium, Velitrae and perhaps Alba) and may have been established there at a time when these cities were losing their kings, as at Rome. In the recent excavations of the Regia a graffito with the word 'rex' was found on a *bucchero* vase. In the second century B.C. the *rex* was chosen by the Pontifex Maximus (Livy, xl. 42), though in processions he

retained his early primacy since the Pontifex Maximus had only the fifth place. Also pontifical decisions in 270 were still dated by the name of the *rex* (Pliny, *NH*, xi. 186): this incidentally, as pointed out by Momigliano, suggests that during the regal period the years were dated by the year of the king's reign (as also at Caere: the Pyrgi inscription mentions the third year of Thefarias; cf. p. 579).

[10] The disciplinary powers of the Pontifex Maximus were derived from his quasi-parental position in relation to his nominees.

[11] The tradition, preserved in Festus (305L), that the first consul Brutus added 164 plebeians to the existing 136 patrician senators, is not credible. It may reflect a late belief that at the beginning of the Republic there were 136 patrician *gentes*.

[12] Some scholars have preferred to abandon the Roman tradition and to regard the dictatorship as a relic from the regal period (e.g. a watered-down *rex* or a surviving auxiliary officer of the *rex*) rather than a creation of the Republic. For a rebuttal of such views and general discussion see E. S. Staveley, *Historia* 1956, 101 ff. The dictator had twenty-four lictors, unlike the *rex* or consuls, who had only twelve. The title dictator may have been borrowed from the Latins: in some of their cities a dictator was a permanent, often religious, officer. The first dictator was T. Larcius in 501 (Livy, ii. 18.6) or more probably in 497 (Varro: see Macrobius, i. 8.1): cf. Ogilvie, *Livy*, 281 f. This date is quite in keeping with the historical situation: there seems no good reason to follow some scholars who date the first dictatorship to a much later period merely because doubts have been expressed about the historicity of some of the early dictatorships.

[13] Livy, ii. 16.4. Much ingenuity has been expended in trying to explain away this story, but it was probably based on an authentic tradition of the Claudian *gens*, as was the date. The tradition that the migration took place under Romulus (Suet. *Tib.* 1) or under the Tarquins (Appian, *Reg.* 12), though accepted in preference to Livy by Ogilvie (*Livy*, 273), is more probably an invention of imperial times; cf. Momigliano, *Interpretations* (ed. C. S. Singleton, 1969), 26.

[14] Gjerstad, *Early Rome*, iv, 514 ff. Attic trade with Etruscan cities also decreased after 450 but not on the same scale as with Rome. *Per contra*, when trade with Rome began to revive *c.* 400, that with Etruria was reduced to a minimum.

[15] Shortage of corn is recorded in 508, 496, 492, 486, 477, 476, 456, 453, 440, 433 and 411. Although some details may be suspect, it is unnecessary to question the fact of occasional famines, since Cato (frg. 77P) expressly records that corn-shortages were one of the regular items found in the Annales, i.e. the Tabula Pontificum. It is noteworthy that a cult of Ceres, the corn-goddess, was established in Rome in the 490s and that the centres of her cult were Cumae and Sicily; Rome's treaty with Carthage will have helped trade with cities in western Sicily which were under Carthaginian influence. The account of Dionysius of Halicarnassus (vii. 1–2) of the Roman embassy sent to Sicily in 491/490 probably derives from Greek sources independent of the Roman tradition, which

is thus confirmed. In general on the corn-shortages see Ogilvie, *Livy*, 256 f., 291, 321.

[16] Thus the Senate from time to time appointed commissioners to relieve scarcity. However, the story is also told of an interested plebeian benefactor, Spurius Maelius, who in 440/439 relieved a shortage out of his own pocket for his personal ends (Livy, iv. 12–14); suspected of aiming at tyranny, he was killed. The story was told as early as Cincius (*c.* 200 B.C.) and thus is older than the time of Gaius Gracchus whose activity in the corn-supply might otherwise have been thought to have given rise to the story of Maelius. Maelius was probably a historical figure who had some connexion with a fifth-century corn-shortage. For the development of the story and the later fabrication of details see Ogilvie, *Livy*, 550 f.

Two other men are linked with the story: L. Minucius Augurinus (a consul of 458) who exposed Maelius's plot, and C. Servilius Ahala who, acting either as a private citizen or (a later tradition) as a Magister Equitum, killed Maelius (on Servilus's status and other aspects see A. W. Lintott, *Historia* 1970, 12 ff.). According to the *libri lintei* (see above, Chap. 6, n. 18) for 440 and 439 Minucius was entered as *praefectus* (*urbi*?; later interpreted as *pr. annonae*). He is said thereafter to have distributed corn and to have been rewarded with a column and statue, together with a gilded ox. This column is depicted on the later coinage of the second half of the second century (Sydenham, *CRR*, 492, 463; Crawford, *RRC*, 249/1, 242/1), but it was not set up before the fourth century (cf. Momigliano, *Quarto Contrib.* 329 ff.). Later Minucii had connexions with the corn-supply (e.g. M. Minucius Rufus, *cos*, 110, built a porticus Minucia which under the Empire was used for grain-distribution), but while L Minucius's corn-distribution need not be questioned, his alleged link with Maelius is more doubtful

[17] On Sp. Cassius see Ogilvie, *Livy*, 387 ff., and A. W. Lintott, *Historia* 1970, 18 ff., who argues that in the earliest form of the story Cassius was executed by his father by right of *patria potestas* and that a formal trial and condemnation for treason (*perduellio*) was only invented later.

[18] Since the system of *nexum* was abolished late in the fourth century B.C., knowledge of early debt procedure is obscure. For *nexum* and another method of contracting debt known as *stipulatio* (a verbal contract), see Ogilvie, *Livy*, 296 ff. Both forms were known at the time of the Twelve Tables. *Nexum* was a solemn transaction in a process of *mancipatio*, with copper and scales (*per aes et libram*), i.e. the creditor in the presence of five witnesses weighed out the copper (coined money was not yet known in Rome) which the other party wished to borrow in exchange for his services: the latter did not become a slave without civic rights but a fettered bondsman (*nexus*).

[19] A striking reconstruction has been made by A. Momigliano (*Quarto Contrib.* 419 ff. and *Interpretations*, 22 ff.), based on the supposed cleavage between *patres* and *conscripti*, between *classici* and *infra classem*, and between *populus* and *plebs*. The last is seen in sacred formulas which mention *populus plebsque*, where *populus* means citizens in their military and

political capacity (i.e. the *classici*) and the *plebs*, i.e. those who did not serve in the legion (*infra classem*). Further it is argued that the aristocracy comprised two groups, the patrician *patres* and the non-patrician (but also non-plebeian) *conscripti* (cf. Chap. 5, n. 18). But since the aristocracy was not numerous enough to fill the army (*classis*) and the *plebs* were excluded, we may assume that on the overthrow of the monarchy the patricians filled the *centuriae* with their clients. The plebeians will have been the men outside the *clientelae*, who could probably be conscripted at need but were not normally called upon to serve, men such as very small landowners, artisans and petty traders (not a few being *nexi*). During the fifth century these distinctions very gradually broke down, and the clients and *conscripti* were absorbed into the plebeian body, mainly perhaps because they found its efficient organisation attractive. In a brief note justice can scarcely be done to so radical a reconstruction: it explains many difficulties but is admittedly hypothetical in many points. It will no doubt provoke much discussion (for a beginning see *Entretiens Hardt*, xiii. 279 ff.).

[20] Livy (iii. 31.1) records that in 456 B.C. a law was passed to provide public land on the Aventine for dwellings for the plebeians. Though the bill is assigned by Dionysius of Halicarnassus to a tribune, L. Icilius, it is doubtful whether a tribune could carry a measure at this time; Dionysius adds (x. 32.4) that the text of the bill was preserved in the time of Augustus in the Aventine temple of Diana.

[21] For a defence of the historicity of the First Secession see Ogilvie, *Livy*, 309 ff.

[22] On the early tribunate see G. Niccolini, *Il tribunato della plebe* (1932). Varro, *de Lingua Latina*, v. 81, derived them from military tribunes. Ed. Meyer, *Kleine Schriften*, i. 333 ff., argued that they had been administrative officers of the tribes.

[23] Livy, ii. 56, says that the right to elect plebeian magistrates was given to the Comitia Tributa Populi. This was a different body from the Concilium Plebis; it was a meeting of patricians and plebeians alike and it was not created probably until 447 B.C. (see p. 68). On the early development of these two assemblies see E. S. Stavelely, *Athenaeum* 1955, 3 ff.

[24] For full discussion of the problems involved in the history of the decemvirs see Ogilvie, *Livy*, 451 ff. Their appointment is said to have been preceded by the sending of three commissioners to Athens to study the laws of Solon and of other Greek states. This is improbable, since Rome's purpose was to publish existing law, not to make new law. The story may have arisen from the undoubted Greek elements in the Twelve Tables, but contact with Greek states nearer home, in Magna Graecia, might explain these (the Greek word *poenē* appears as *poena*). Cf. F. Wieacker, *Entretiens Hardt*, xiii 330 ff., for the Greek elements. The names of the first ten commissioners (except one) all seem authentic, while those of the second body are suspect. It is probable that the commission lasted more than one year and that therefore a second ten were invented (in the late third century?). The romance of Appius Claudius is influenced by the history of Critias and the Thirty Tyrants at Athens. The story of Verginia, which thanks to Livy's artistry has had much influence on later writers, can scarcely be accepted; it possibly owes something to the story of Lucretia, who brought another tyranny, that of the Tarquins, to an end.

[25] The twelve bronze (perhaps originally wooden) tablets on which the laws were exhibited in the Forum have of course perished. But the code has been partly reconstructed from quotations preserved in ancient writers. These fragments are collected in Riccobono, *Fontes*, 23 ff., among other collections. They are translated in Lewis-Rheinhold, *R. Civ.* i. 102 ff. For a fuller discussion see H. F. Jolowicz, *A Historical Introduction to the Study of Roman Law*[3] (1972), chs vii–xii. See also F. Weiacker, 'Die XII. Tafeln in ihrem Jahrhundert', *Entretiens Hardt*, xiii, 293 ff., who shows (309 f.) how the funerary and sumptuary laws agree precisely with mid-fifth-century conditions.

[26] Aulus Gellius, xx. 1.48 ('partes secanto'), thinks it applies to the body, though he adds that he has never heard of anyone being dissected (cf. Quintilian, *Inst. Or.* 3. 6.84). For the view that it refers (at least in historical times) to the debtor's property see M. Radin, *AJ Phil.* 1922, 32 ff.

[27] According to Tacitus (*Ann* vi. 16) under the Twelve Tables the taking of interest on loans was limited to *unciarium foenus* ($8\frac{1}{3}$ or 12 per cent?), but this limitation may be due to a statute of 357 B.C. (p. 76).

[28] On the Valerio-Horatian laws see Scullard, *Hist. Rom. World*, appendix 6 (brief discussion); Ogilvie, *Livy*, 497 ff.; E. S. Staveley, *Athenaeum* 1955, 3 ff., *Historia* 1955, 412 ff.

[29] On the distinction between these assemblies, see E. S. Staveley, *Athenaeum* 1955, 3 ff.

[30] See E. S. Staveley, 'Tribal Legislation before the Lex Hortensia', *Athenaeum* 1955, 3 ff.

[31] *Provocatio:* in 509, Cic. *de Republica*, ii. 53, *Digest*, i. 2.2.16, Livy, ii. 8.2., Dionys. Halic. v. 19, Plutarch, *Poplicola*, ii; in the Twelve Tables, Cic. *de Republica*, ii. 54; in 449 Livy, iii. 55.5, Cic. *de Republica*, ii. 54. The issues are too complicated for detailed discussion here; see E. S. Staveley, 'Provocatio during the Fifth and Fourth Centuries B.C.', *Historia* 1955, 412 ff. It may be that the law of 509 should be rejected. That of 449 may have established a formal procedure of *provocatio* by which the magistrate was allowed but not compelled to grant appeals from his *coercitio*; if he refused he might of course be persuaded to change his mind under threat from a tribune to extend his *auxilium* to the victim. Kunkel (see n. 3 above) believes that when the Twelve Tables provided 'de capite civis nisi per maximum comitiatum . . . ne ferunto', this had nothing to do with the right of *provocatio*. On the other hand, Kunkel's view has been rejected by A. H. M. Jones (*The Criminal Courts of the Republic and Principate*, 1972, ch. 1), who defends a lex *de provocatione* of 509 and the traditional view. See further R. A. Baumann, *Historia* 1973, 34 ff., and A. W. Lintott, *Austieg NRW*, I. ii. 226 ff.

[32] Much has been written on the military tribunes, but little general agreement reached on the primary purpose of their creation. See E. S. Staveley, *JRS* 1953, 30 ff.; F. E. Adcock, *JRS* 1957, 9 ff.; A. Boddington, *Historia* 1959, 365 ff.; R. Sealey, *Latomus*, 1959, 521 ff.

[33] On the censorship see J. Suolathi, *The Roman Censors* (Helsinki, 1963). It is to this period 450–445 that many scholars (cf. Cary, *Hist.* 80 ff.) would assign the 'Servian' reform, the creation of the Comitia Centuriata, the reform of the army with the introduction of hoplite tactics, and the establishment of the dictatorship. A more traditional assessment of the evidence, however, has been made in this present book. But while the view that the basis of the reform dates from the regal period is retained, it is still possible to believe that the system of classes and centuries was extended at the time of the creation of the censorship

Chapter 8: Notes

[1] Lake Regillus is identified with Pontano Secco, 2 miles north of Frascati. It was presumably a hoplite battle, despite the story of the Dioscuri: Livy records (ii. 20.10) that the Roman cavalry rode to the battlefield, dismounted and fought on foot – that is, they were essentially hoplites who rode to the scene.

[2] On the Cassian treaty see Dionys. Halic. vi. 95 and Livy, ii. 33.4. On its reliability see A. N. Sherwin-White, *The Roman Citizenship*[2] (1973), 20 ff. It was made between Rome and the Thirty Latin cities; Dionys. Halic. v. 61 lists the Thirty, but this may be the total reached by the League some time before 338 B.C. rather than that existing at the time of the treaty. Livy (ii. 22.5) may suggest that the treaty was made in 495 by Cassius as a fetial priest rather than in 493, the year of his second consulship, where Livy (ii. 33.4) later places it; it would make better sense nearer the battle. The text of the treaty survived in the early days of Cicero (*Pro Balbo*, 53). On the machinery of the League and arrangements for military leadership (which are quite uncertain) see Ogilvie, *Livy*, 400.

[3] A record of the founding of these early federal colonies is given by the Roman annalists, who probably drew this information from the Annales Maximi. On the colonies see E. T. Salmon, *Roman Colonization* (1969), 40 ff., and, in more detail, *Phoenix* 1953, 93 ff. and 123 ff.

[4] The details of the Herdonius affair are sadly confused in Roman tradition (Livy, ii. 15–18). Although it is dismissed by some as unhistorical, the intervention of the Tusculans does not look like an invention, and thus the tradition may contain a core of truth (but see Ogilvie, *Livy*, 423 ff.).

[5] The story of Cincinnatus was embroidered by the annalists, who exalted him into a type of homespun hero (Livy, iii. 26–29). Called from the plough to assume the dictatorship, he rescued Minucius from the Aequi, whom he defeated, resigned the dictatorship and returned to his farm. Behind these embellishments we may detect a kernel of genuine folk-memory, while the defeat of the Aequi may be accepted.

[6] The story of Coriolanus, which Livy relates with dramatic brevity (ii. 39–40), is spun out interminably by Dionysius (vii. 1–59). The traditional date of his foray, 491, is of doubtful value. See Ogilvie, *Livy*, 314 ff.

[7] This incident was no doubt derived from the traditions of the Gens Fabia. The nature of the engagement might suggest (and has been adduced to suggest) that hoplite tactics had not yet been introduced. But this inference need not be drawn. During the disturbed days of the infant Republic (with incidents like those of Porsenna's activities) disciplined phalanx warfare might have given way temporarily to more 'heroic' methods of fighting, or, more probably, an irregular formation was deliberately used on a mission aimed at raiding and seizing an enemy strong point on the frontier (a mission for which the Fabii may have volunteered). Its failure is reflected in the dramatic disappearance of Fabii in the Fasti for some time to come after their dominance during the 480s.

[8] Livy records the capture of Fidenae in 435 and again, after a revolt, in 425 (iv. 21 ff.; 31.6 ff.); the former should be rejected as a reduplication of the latter. There were two traditions about Cossus; he had won the *spolia opima* either as military tribune or as consul. Augustus said that the inscription on the dedicated breastplate indicated that Cossus had been consul. But Augustus had an interest: he wished to rob M. Crassus, governor of Macedonia, of a similar honour. It is possible that he misrepresented the facts (p. 586), and that the inscription on the linen corslet had not survived, at any rate legibly, for four hundred years: see Ogilvie, *Livy*, 563 f.

[9] On the site of Veii see J. B. Ward-Perkins, *PBSR* 1961 (and for the *ager Veientanus, ibid.* 1968), and briefly H. H. Scullard, *The Etruscan Cities and Rome* (1967), 104 ff. On Livy's account (v. 1–23) of the siege see Ogilvie, *Livy*, 626 ff., etc. (he would date the fall to 392–1). Archaeological evidence shows that the natural defences were artificially strengthened at the end of the fifth century, against the Roman attack: the tufa rock was cut back and elsewhere a stone and earth wall was built. The story that the Romans captured the city by driving a long tunnel into its very centre must be rejected; it may have arisen from the fact that the neighbourhood had been honeycombed with drainage tunnels (*cuniculi*) by Etruscan engineers. It is remarkable, however, that at the Roman camp in the north-west the newly built wall was constructed over *cuniculi* which had been filled in with earth and stones. The Romans possibly could have entered the city, but not the citadel as Livy says, by clearing one of these. With this may be linked the story that an Etruscan soothsayer revealed to the Romans that they would not capture Veii until they drained the overflow of the Alban Lake. As the siege of Veii dragged on, the Romans are said to have had recourse to religious help. On the advice of the Sibylline Books (see p. 109) they held a *lectisternium* (a Greek ceremony at which the images of certain gods were exposed on couches to partake of a sacrificial feast) and also they may have consulted the oracle at Delphi. After the fall of Veii they solemnly transferred the statue and cult of Juno Regina by a ritual of *evocatio* to Rome: the statue of Veii's tutelary deity was installed by the victorious Camillus in a temple on the Aventine.

[10] On the Celts see T. G. E. Powell, *The Celts* (1958). On their invasion of northern Italy, G. A. Mansuelli and R. Scarani, *L'Emilia prima dei Romani* (1961), ch. vii; L. Barfield, *North Italy before Rome* (1971), 149 ff. Ogilvie, *Livy*, 700 ff., argues that the source for Livy's account of the Celtic migrations (v. 34–35) was Greek, either Poseidonius or Timagenes.

[11] Livy preserved a tradition that the Celtic invasions of Italy occurred *c.* 600 B.C., while modern scholars until recently have rejected this as some 200 years too early. More recent archaeological evidence, however, now suggests a possible date early in the fifth century.

[11] Cf. Ogilvie, *Livy*, 669 f., 716 f.

[13] The Allia is the Fosso della Bettina, north of Fidenae. The numbers involved are uncertain. The Romans had perhaps 15,000 men; the Gauls are variously put at 30,000–70,000. The battle was almost certainly fought on the left bank of the Tiber (despite Diodorus, xiv. 114).

[14] O. Skutsch, *JRS* 1953, 77 f., has drawn attention to traces of a tradition (which can perhaps be discerned in Ennius, *Ann.* frg. 164 and Silius Italicus, *Pun.* i. 525 f., iv. 150 f., vi. 555 f.) that the Capitol fell to the Gauls; this tradition should be rejected.

[15] For traces of devastation see L. G. Roberts, *Memoirs of the American Academy in Rome*, 1918, 55 f., and E. Gjerstad, *Early Rome*, iii (1960), index, s.v. 'Gallic invasion'.

[16] Livy tells (v. 40.9 f.) how the Vestals were helped in the evacuation by a certain Lucius Albinius. This is referred to by Aristotle (*ap.* Plutarch, *Camillus*, 22.4), who mentions a Lucius as the man who saved Rome. He thus confirms the tradition and shows that it is earlier than the later building up of Camillus as the saviour-hero of Rome.

[17] Ogilvie (*Livy*, 725 f.) is inclined to accept the story of the senators as an act of deliberate *devotio*, and that of the geese since, although geese were not sacred to Juno, birds were kept on the Capitol for purposes of divination (hens, used later, may only have been imported during the fourth century). The basic reason for the withdrawal of the Gauls may have been a report that the Veneti were attacking Cisalpine Gaul (Polybius, ii. 18.3), while Livy, v. 48.1, refers to pestilence among the Gauls. Diodorus, xiv. 117.7 says that the Gauls were defeated not by the Romans but by the Caeretans in Sabine territory and the gold thus recovered. Livy manages to turn Rome's disaster to Rome's glory: after Brennus's insolence, Camillus, the *deus ex machina*, appears and defeats the enemy soundly. The splendid oration which Livy puts into his mouth (v. 51–4), appealing for the preservation of Rome and its glory, may reflect later fears that the capital might be removed from Rome (e.g. by Julius Caesar or M. Antony), fears which Augustus finally allayed.

Chapter 9: Notes

[1] Livy places the resolution to apportion the territory in 393 B.C. (v. 30.8), the occupation of the land in 388 (vi. 4.4) and the creation of the tribes in 387 (vi. 5.8). He gives seven *iugera* as the size of each allotment, while Diodorus (xiv. 102.4) gives four *iugera*.

[2] We may compare the effect of the disaster at the Arbia in A.D. 1258 which so thinned the ranks of the Guelphs at Florence as to produce a Ghibelline revolution.

[3] P. Willems, *Le Sénat de la république romaine*, i. (1878), 103.

[4] Livy, viii. 28.1; Cicero, *de Republica*, ii. 59.

[5] Although some features of the bill (e.g. the alleged limit of 500 *iugera*) may reflect later Gracchan influences, a clause which limited tenancies of public land must be accepted. For a defence of the tradition see H. Last, *CAH*, vii. 538 ff.

[6] T. Frank, *History of Rome* (1923), 79.

[7] The *lex Genucia* of 342 is said to have declared (1) that both consuls might be plebeians (in fact two plebeian consuls were not elected until 172 B.C.) and (2) that the same office should not be held twice within ten years (if passed, this clause was certainly not observed). (1) is possible as a theoretical ruling. It is unlikely that two patricians held the consulship together after 342.

[8] On Camillus and Concord see A. Momigliano, *Cl. Qu.* 1943, 111 ff. (= *Secondo Contrib.* 89 ff.).

[9] See E. S. Staveley, *Athenaeum* 1955, 26 ff., for this solution of the problem.

[10] On the patronage which some of the premier houses of the patricians bestowed upon promising political aspirants, see F. Münzer, *Römische Adelsparteien und Adelsfamilien* (1920), esp. 8 ff., which works out the affinities and repulsions of the ruling houses in full (if at times somewhat delusive) detail. See also E. Ferenczy, 'The Rise of the Patrician–Plebeian State', *Acta antiqua Acad. Scient. Hungaricae* 1966, 113 ff.

[11] On Appius Claudius see A. Garzetti, *Athenaeum* 1947, 175 ff.; E. S. Staveley, *Historia* 1959, 410 ff.; E. Ferenczy, *Acta antiqua Acad. Scient. Hungaricae* 1967, 27 ff. (written in English). Details of his career and reforms, as given in the sources, raise very many problems which cannot be discussed here but are dealt with in the three articles quoted above. Regarding his tribal reform see also P. Fraccaro, *Athenaeum* 1935, 150 ff. (= *Opuscula*, ii (1957), 149 ff.), and L. R. Taylor, *Voting Districts of the Rom. Rep.* (1960), 11 and 133 ff. Fraccaro has disproved the earlier view that the landless had not hitherto been enrolled in any tribe. Ferenczy has argued that Appius's reform was more fundamental: he allotted all citizens to the tribes, regardless of their domicile or financial position, thus transforming the nature of the tribes (cf. Cleisthenes at Athens), and that this reform stood after 304 except that the propertyless only were relegated to the urban tribes. The purpose, apart from politics, will have been to strengthen the army. This reconstruction appears somewhat radical.

[12] Cato, *apud* Cic. *de Republica*, ii. 1.2. Polybius, vi. 10.13.

[13] See in general E. S. Staveley, *Greek and Roman Voting and Elections* (1972).

[14] At some date before 300 B.C. appeals to the Comitia Tributa had been allowed from fines exceed-

ing a certain amount, thus limiting the power of *coercitio* of a magistrate. The early history of fines is obscure. A *lex Aternia Tarpeia* of 454 allowed fines to be paid in bronze instead of cattle, while a scale was established by a lex Maenia Sestia of 452: 1 ox = 12 sheep = 100 lb. of bronze. A *lex Papiria Julia* of 430 perhaps made payment in bronze mandatory rather than optional.

[15] On alleged impeachments by tribunes before the tribal assembly see E. G. Hardy, *JRS* 1913, 25 ff.; Ogilvie, *Livy*, 323 ff. None of the tribunician state trials recorded prior to 287 should probably be accepted as historical.

In consequence of tribunes taking over the function of prosecutors in high criminal cases, the *duoviri perduellionis* disappeared and the quaestors henceforth confined themselves to their financial functions. On the other hand, soon after 300 a new board of minor magistrates, the *triumviri capitales*, was instituted to exercise a summary jurisdiction over petty offenders.

Chapter 10: Notes

[1] On the Servian Wall see p. 84 and n. 581. Pictures of the surviving portions are given in E. Nash, *A Pictorial Dictionary of Ancient Rome*, ii, 104 ff. (with bibliography).

[2] Sallust (*Cat.* 51) and the Ineditum Vaticanum date the change of armament to the Samnite Wars and believe that the Roman borrowed the *pilum* and *scutum* from the Samnites. On the other hand Livy (i. 43.1; viii. 8.3) dates the adoption of the *scutum* either to Servius Tullius or to *c.* 400 B.C. when pay for military service was first introduced. The older phalanx formation was obviously not suitable for the siege of Veii and a looser manipular system *may* have been introduced then (cf. Q. F. Maule and H. R. W. Smith, *Votive Religion at Caere* (1959), 22 ff.), but if so, it did not save the army at the Allia. More probably the reform was later (the *scutum* was in use among other Italian peoples before the Samnite Wars, and thus available for imitation: cf. P. Coussin, *Les armes romaines* (1926), 240 ff.). The 'manipular' army is described by Livy (viii. 8) under the year 340, but a rival Roman tradition preserved by Plutarch (*Camillus*, ch. 40) represented Camillus as a military reformer; thus some believe (e.g. L. Homo, *CAH*, vii, 568) that it was the Gauls whom the Romans had in mind when they remodelled their tactical formations. F. E. Adcock, however (*CAH*, vii. 596, 601), argues for a Samnite War date, while E. T. Salmon (*Samnium and the Samnites* (1967), 105 ff.) suggests the beginning of the fourth century.

[3] For details see Ed. Meyer, *Kleine Schriften*, ii, 200 ff.; Kromayer-Veith, *Heerwesen und Kriegführung der Griechen und Römer* (1928), 261 ff. See also E. Rawson, *PBSR* 1971, 13 ff.

[4] The details of these and other wars of this period are obscure and cannot be discussed here. The Gallic raids are recorded by Polybius, ii. 18 (depending on Fabius Pictor). Livy, drawing upon the later annalists, records several additional invasions, with a different

chronology. See Walbank, *Polybius*, i. 184 ff. Livy tells of two epic duels: in one T. Manlius Torquatus fought a gigantic Gaul and robbed him of his torque or collar (vii. 10; 361 B.C.), in the other the young Roman champion, M. Valerius Corvus, defeated his opponent with the help of a raven which alighted on his adversary's helmet (vii. 26; 348 B.C.). The nervousness of the Romans in the face of the Gauls was reflected in the rule that, on their coming, a state of emergency (*tumultus*) was declared and all civilian work was suspended in anticipation of a *levée en masse*.

[5] Rome's treatment of Caere is ambiguous: at some point Caere received *civitas sine suffragio* (i.e. it shared the private privileges and obligations of Roman citizenship, namely *commercium*, *conubium* and *militia*). One tradition regarded this as a benefit, granted for protecting the Vestal Virgins during the Gallic invasion of 390; another tradition saw in this treatment a punishment (for some revolt?) when *civitas sine suffragio* was considered an inferior form of citizenship. Perhaps Caere received *hospitium* in 390, a truce for a hundred years in 353, and *civitas s. suffr. c.* 274. See A. N. Sherwin-White, *Roman Citizenship*[2] (1973), 52 ff.; Toynbee, *Hannibal's Legacy*, i. 410 ff.; Brunt, *Manpower*, 515 ff.

[6] Sabelli is the Roman name for speakers of Oscan (they called themselves Sapineia); the most important group were the Samnites. They were akin to, but separate from, the Sabines. The Osci (= Opici) were originally primitive inhabitants of southern Italy, living chiefly in Campania. When they were overrun by the Sabellians in Campania, the name Oscan survived for the invaders' language, which predominated there and spread widely in southern Italy. Thus in later times it is more accurate to speak of Oscan-speaking Sabellians for a large part of the population of southern Italy, but they are often more loosely referred to as Oscans. On their occupation of Campania see T. J. Cornell, *Museum Helveticum* 1974, 193 ff.

[7] For the Samnites see E. T. Salmon, *Samnium and the Samnites* (1967); for their culture, pp. 50–186.

[8] With the Samnites we may compare the Aetolians of Hellenistic Greece and the Swiss of the later middle ages.

[9] Livy's account of the First Samnite War (vii. 29–viii. 2) is plainly impossible in its details, some of which are manifest duplicates of happenings in the second war. But neither this nor the silence of Diodorus may be sufficient reason for denying the first war altogether, as is done, for example, by F. E. Adcock, *CAH*, vii. 588. The historicity of the conflict is defended by E. T. Salmon, *Samnium and the Samnites* (1967), 195 ff., which should be consulted for all the Samnite Wars. Cf. also A. Bernardi, *Athenaeum* 1943, 21 ff. E. S. Staveley, *Historia* 1959, 419 ff., and esp. 424 ff., has argued that growing interest in industry and trade lay behind Rome's desire to extend her influence southward to Campania and that this Campanian policy was advocated by a group of men who included Q. Publilius Philo, M. Valerius Corvus, Sp. Postumius Albinus, C. Maenius and later the great Appius Claudius. E. T. Salmon, however, would attribute this southern policy to a group of patricians, though they were supported by some ple-

beian leaders (*Samnium*, 203 ff.). To what extent strategic military motives were reinforced by commercial considerations must remain doubtful, but clearly a group of senators successfully continued to urge a more active policy towards Campania.

[10] The details of this mutiny are obscure, but its historical character seems trustworthy, since Livy says that it was recorded by a consensus of ancient annalists (vii. 42.7).

[11] For the first treaty see p. 55, where the Polybian date of the first year of the Republic is accepted. Very briefly, the problem is that Polybius quotes a second (undated) treaty and a third of 279–278, while Livy records a treaty in 348 (vii. 27.2), a Punic embassy in Rome in 343 (vii. 38), a treaty *tertio renovatum* in 306 (ix. 43, 26), and a treaty in 279 (*Ep.* xiii). There is no doubt about the date of the last treaty at the time of Pyrrhus. If Polybius's first treaty is kept where he placed it, then his second treaty probably is to be equated with that mentioned by Livy in 348. Diodorus (xvi. 69.1) dates a treaty to 348/347 (though he believes it to have been the first). For further references see p. 584.

Polybius also denied a statement of a pro-Carthaginian Sicilian, named Philinus, that there was another treaty which forbade the Romans to enter Sicily and the Carthaginians Italy. If Philinus should be right (cf. A. J. Toynbee, *Hannibal's Legacy*, i (1965), 543 ff., and R. E. Mitchell, *Historia* 1971, 633 ff.), the treaty should probably be dated to 306. Cf. Chap. 12 above.

[12] Livy (viii. 5.5) represents the Latins as demanding one of the Roman consulships and half the seats in the Senate. This is clearly an anticipation of the claims for political equality which the Latins (in common with the rest of Italy) put forward in the last century of the Republic.

[13] For an elucidation of Livy's confused account of the Great Latin War (viii. 3–14) see especially F. E. Adcock, *CAH*, vii. 589 ff.

[14] The aristocracy of Capua is said to have received full citizenship, but this is improbable. On Rome's relations with Capua 343–338 see A. Bernardi, *Athenaeum* 1942, 86 ff., 1943, 21 ff. On early Capua see J. Heurgon, *Capoue préromaine* (1942).

[15] *Civitas sine suffragio* was also known as *ius Caeritum*, from the (probably erroneous) belief that Caere was the first *municipium* to receive it. This view derives from the supposed grant after 390 (see above, n. 5), whereas Caere probably received it in the third century when it was considered less honourable, in fact *ignominiosum*.

[16] On the *coloniae maritimae* see E. T. Salmon, *Roman Colonization* (1969), 70 ff., and above, Chap. 11. On early Ostia, Salmon, 71 ff. There may have been a primitive Roman settlement there during the Regal period (p. 54), but there are no traces of a formal colony until the walls of the *castrum* which belong to the second half of the fourth century; they enclose about 5 acres, just enough as the urban centre for 300 *coloni* (for photograph, Salmon, plate 43). Unlike Antium, Ostia was founded on a site where no organised town existed.

[17] Much confusion has been caused by Livy, who invented an imaginary city of 'Palaeopolis' in contrast with Neapolis (viii. 22.5). These 'old citizens' may have been refugees from Cumae. Palaeopolis was part of Neapolis, doubtless the oldest part.

[18] The site of the Caudine Forks is uncertain. E. T. Salmon, *Samnium*, 225 ff., favours the traditional site, known from medieval times as Forchia, between Santa Maria a Vico and Arpaia, in the territory of the Samnite Caudini (air-photographs, Salmon, plate 3). See further P. Sommella, *Antichi campi di battaglia in Italia* (1967), 49 ff. (fully illustrated).

Livy (ix. 5 ff.) asserts that the treaty was repudiated by the Senate and that the two consuls who negotiated it were handed over to the Samnites by way of compensation; this clearly anticipates the affair of Hostilius Mancinus in 137 (p. 149). Livy's military chronicle for the next few years is almost a blank: peace in fact was negotiated and respected.

[19] Livy (ix. 44) terminates the operations of the Second Samnite War with a disastrous Samnite defeat and the capture of Bovianum. The conditions of the peace belie such a Samnite debacle, which was probably the invention of patriotic Roman annalists, bent on providing a *revanche* for Lautulae and the Caudine Forks. The fall of Bovianum, however, is accepted by E. T. Salmon, *Samnium*, 250 f.

[20] On Rome's relations with the Etruscans from the war of 311 until the Augustan settlement see W. V. Harris, *Rome in Etruria and Umbria* (1971). It is tempting to reject Livy's account of a battle near Lake Vadimo in 310 (ix. 39) as an anticipation of the combat on that site in 283 (p. 93). But the general conditions of the campaign of 310 point to an engagement in that neighbourhood.

[21] One of these risings, which took place at Arretium in 302 (Livy, x. 3.2.), was directed against the ruling house of the Cilnii, the ancestors of Maecenas.

[22] On the inscription on his sarcophagus (Dessau, *ILS*, n. 1) Scipio Barbatus modestly claims to have 'subdued all Lucania'. For a suggestion that the Lucani conquered by Scipio were a small northern group of Lucani in the Sangro Valley in Samnium see A. La Regina, *Dialoghi di Archaeologia* 1968, 173 ff.

[23] A totally different version of the Third Samnite War and the battle of Sentinum has been given by Beloch (*Römische Geschichte*, 430 ff.), who holds that the later Roman annalists confused the Samnites ('Safinim' in their own dialect') with the Sabines; he is refuted by F. E. Adcock, *CAH*, vii. 615 f.

[24] Livy, who locates this battle near Clusium in Etruria (x. 26.7), provides the explanation of this mistake in an adjacent passage, where he mentions that Clusium had anciently been called Camars (x. 25.11).

[25] The ruins of Sentinum lie near Sassoferrato, to the north of which the battle is located by P. Sommella, *Antichi campi di battaglia in Italia* (1967). The casualties in the battle were estimated by a contemporary Greek historian, Duris, at 100,000! (see Diodorus, xxi. 6.1).

The later Roman annalists knew of three members of the family of Decius Mus, who purchased Roman victories by solemnly 'devoting' themselves to the gods of battle in three successive encounters, in the Great Latin War (340), at Sentinum (295) and at

Asculum (279). The basis for these stories is to be found in the self-sacrifice of the consul at Sentinum.

[26] Livy, x. 38–43. Pliny (*NH*, xxxiv. 43) records that the booty was so great that a bronze statue of Jupiter was made from it and set up on the Capitol where it could be seen from as far as the Alban Hills.

[27] On the treaty see Salmon, *Samnium*, 277 ff. Livy (*Epit.* xi) says that the older treaty was renewed (*renovatum*). Since Livy (*Epit.* 13) uses *renovatum* also in regard to Rome's treaties with Carthage, which are known to have differed from one another, its use here cannot be pressed to indicate that the treaty of 290 was on the same terms as that of 304.

The vast amount of bronze from booty probably enabled the Romans to start issuing coins of their own for the first time, the heavy *aes grave:* see R. Thomsen, *Early Roman Coinage*, iii (1961), 259 f., and above, p. 106. In 289 the Romans first established Triumviri Monetales.

[28] The view that the use of the word Sabines by Velleius (i. 14) in this connexion refers to less than all the Sabine people is rejected by P. A. Brunt, 'The Enfranchisement of the Sabines', *Homages à M. Renard*, ii (1969), 121 ff.

[29] Hadria: Livy, *Epit.* xi. The establishment of a maritime Roman colony at Castrum Novum in Picenum is improbable (the references belong rather to Castrum Novum in Etruria): see E. T. Salmon, *Roman Colonization* (1969), 180.

[30] On the events of 284–283 to which Polybius alludes (ii. 18–19) see Walbank, *Polybius*, i. 188 ff. cf. J. H. Corbett, *Historia* 1971, 656 ff.; M. G. Morgan, *Cl. Qu.* 1972, 309.

[31] On Tarentum see P. Wuilleumier, *Tarante* (1939). Tarentine coins of the fourth century found their way along the Po valley to France.

[32] Appian, *Samn.* vii. The date of the treaty by which the Romans were excluded from the Gulf of Tarentum is uncertain. Beloch and De Sanctis place it in 303, Mommsen in 348. For the possibility of 332, when it will have been part of the agreement with Alexander of Epirus (Livy, viii. 17.10; Justin, xii. 2.12), see M. Cary, *Journ. Phil.* 1920, 165 ff.

[33] The motives of the Romans and Tarentines are uncertain. The Roman ships were possibly on an innocent mission of showing the flag (they now had a colony in the Adriatic) or they may have intended to lend moral (or even physical) support to the pro-Roman oligarchs in Tarentum.

Roman policy to intervene in the south is sometimes attributed to the plebeian leaders whose political position had been strengthened by the lex Hortensia in 287 (e.g. by T. Frank, *CAH*, vii. 641), but E. T. Salmon (*Samnium*, 281 ff.) thinks that the 'southern lobby' in the Senate was, as earlier, a faction of the patricio-plebeian nobility, which included Ap. Claudius Caecus, P. Cornelius Rufinus, P. Valerius Corvus, L. Papirius Cursor and C. Aelius (who proposed that help should be sent to Thurii in 286/285). The possible effect on Carthage of Rome's continuing involvement in affairs of the south from 326 onwards is emphasised by R. E. Mitchell, *Historia* 1971, 633 ff.

[34] Owing to the loss of the second decade of Livy, we lack his narrative for the period 292–220. For the Epirote War our chief source is the *Life of Pyrrhus* by Plutarch, which made more use of the later Roman annalists than of the contemporary and no doubt competent history of Hieronymus of Cardia.

P. Lévêque, *Pyrrhos* (Paris, 1957), gives a detailed account of Pyrrhus's Italian campaigns. G. Nenci, *Pirro, aspirazioni egemoniche ed equilibrio mediterraneo* (1953), is more concerned with Pyrrhus's objectives (Pyrrhus was supporting the – hypothetical – anti-Carthaginian policy of the Ptolemies, i.e. Carthage, not Rome, was the primary target of his western adventure; *contra*, J. V. A. Fine, *AJ Phil.* 1957, 108 ff.).

[35] The Roman soldiers nicknamed Pyrrhus's elephants 'Lucanian oxen' (Heraclea is in Lucania). They were Indian, not African, beasts and are depicted on various objects: a painted clay dish found in southern Italy; a tiny elephant is added to an issue of Tarentine coins; and on a piece of *Aes Signatum* (p. 595). On this, and for elephants in general, see H. H. Scullard, *The Elephant in the Greek and Roman World* (1974), where the three objects are illustrated on plates vii a and xiv a and b respectively.

[36] Pyrrhus made a thank-offering dedication at Dodona: 'King Pyrrhus, the Epirotes and Tarentines [for their victory] over the Romans and their allies, to Zeus Naios' (Dittenberger, *Sylloge*, n. 392). Plutarch, *Pyrrhus*, 21.14, records the anecdote that when Pyrrhus was congratulated, he replied that another such 'victory' would be fatal to him: hence a 'Pyrrhic victor'. Victory at Heraclea had been bought at too high a price, allegedly 4000 men, in relation to his resources in man-power.

[37] The ancient authorities for the history of the negotiations are extremely confused. For analyses see G. N. Cross, *Epirus* (1932), 115 ff.; Lévêque, *Pyrrhos*, 341 ff., 404 ff.; M. R. Lefkowitz, *Harvard Studies in Cl. Phil.* 1959, 147 ff. No attempt to unravel the complicated web can be attempted here.

[38] Polybius, iii. 25. In return for Carthaginian aid Rome agreed that if either party made a treaty with Pyrrhus, it should be with the stipulation that they *might* legally render mutual aid in whichever country Pyrrhus attacked. Thus Carthage prevented Rome from making an immediate peace with Pyrrhus and perhaps alarmed him by this *rapprochement* with Rome. On the other hand the Romans got ships and money, while if Pyrrhus crossed to Sicily they were under no obligation to send help to the Carthaginians there unless they so wished. For discussion see Walbank, *Polybius*, i. 349 ff. The treaty is usually dated to 279/8. E. Will (*Histoire politique du monde hellénistique*, i (1966), 106 ff.), however, argues for 280, while G. Nenci (*Historia* 1958, 261 ff.) argued for two treaties, in 280 and 278 (but see Lefkowitz, *Harvard Studies in Cl. Phil.* 1959, 170). R. E. Mitchell, *Historia* 1971, 646 ff., argues that the essence of the negotiations in 279/8 was a reaffirmation of the Philinus treaty (see above, n. 11).

The Pyrrhic War led Rome to produce silver coins, and these possibly were minted from silver received from Carthage (see p. 595).

[39] For a novel interpretation of Rome's part in this episode at Rhegium, see F. Cassola, *I gruppi politici*

romani nel III secolo a.C. (1962), 171 ff., and A. J. Toynbee, *Hannibal's Legacy*, i (1965), 101 f.

[40] On this burst of colonisation see E. T. Salmon, *Roman Colonization* (1969), 62 ff., with many illustrations. Archaeology is revealing what some colonies, especially Cosa and Alba Fucens, looked like. For the establishment of Cosa, see Salmon, 29 ff.

[41] With this treaty we might compare the Anglo-Japanese treaty of 1902, which had the effect of introducing Japan into the circle of present-day great powers.

Chapter 11: Notes

[1] De Sanctis, *Storia*, ii. 494. Capua may have attained 70,000 inhabitants, Tarentum 60,000.

[2] The Romans provided rations for the allies on active service (whereas the Roman soldiers themselves had to pay for their own rations and equipment by stoppages of their pay), but possibly the expense in fact fell on the allied state which will have made a gross payment to Rome to cover this (see Walbank, *Polybius*, i. 722, on Polybius, vi. 39.15).

[3] Livy (x. 37.11) records a dispute among the tribunes of 293, of whom seven were upbraided by the remaining three as 'slaves of the nobles'. This is almost certainly an anticipation of the struggle between 'government' and 'opposition' tribunes in the Gracchan era.

[4] Polybius admired the Roman constitution for its accurate balance of power (vi. 11 ff.). He missed the essential point, that this equilibrium was maintained by the good sense of the Romans themselves rather than by any automatic checks in their constitutional machinery. The political sagacity of the Romans was noted *c.* 225 B.C. by the Alexandrian scholar Eratosthenes: see Strabo, i. p. 66.

[5] Prisoners awaiting execution were lodged in a well-house under the Capitol, the so-called 'Tullianum'. Women sentenced to death by a court of law were left to be executed by their father or husband.

[6] On the procedure of discussion and voting in the Comitia see G. W. Botsford, *The Roman Assemblies*, chs vi and vii (ch. vii for the *contio*), L. R. Taylor, *Roman Voting Assemblies* (1966), and E. S. Staveley, *Greek and Roman Voting and Elections* (1972). The calling of opponents to speak was due less perhaps to any desire for freedom of speech than to the opportunity to cross-question such a speaker, who might otherwise find a friendly tribune to summon another *contio* where he could express his views unchallenged.

The Comitia Centuriata was convened in the Campus Martius. The Tribal Assembly held its electoral conventions in the Campus Martius; but for other purposes it usually met in the 'Comitium', a recessed area in the Forum.

[7] See in general F. Münzer, *Röm. Adelsparteien und Adelsfamilien* (1920). (It may be doubted, however, whether all the newly ennobled *gentes* which Münzer derives from Latium and Campania were really of non-Roman origin.)

By a law of 358, which Livy (vii. 15.12) represents as an agreed measure, between patricians and plebeians, *ambitus*, or going round the country districts to solicit votes, was prohibited. In effect this law would tell most heavily against *novi homines* of the plebeian order.

[8] On the procedure of the Senate see P. Willems, *Le Sénat de la république romaine*[2] (1885), ii, 144 ff.

[9] The total number of men available for active service in 225 B.C. was according to Polybius (ii. 24) 700,000 infantry and 70,000 cavalry. These figures are in rough agreement with those given by other sources; they derive from Fabius Pictor and are basically reliable, though difficulties arise about their detailed composition. See Walbank, *Polybius*, i. 196 ff., and A. J. Toynbee, *Hannibal's Legacy*, i. 479–505. On the assumption that Polybius has counted in some items twice over and has included in his figures for Romans all adult males instead of only *iuniores* in the classes above proletarian level, Toynbee reaches the sum total of 532,800 infantry and 61,250 cavalry. Even if this reduced figure is accepted, the man-power of the Italian Confederacy was vast compared with that of any other of the contemporary Great Powers. See further Brunt, *Manpower*, ch. iv.

[10] For a detailed description of the Roman field armies of the middle of the Republic see Polybius vi. 19 ff., together with the commentary by Walbank (*Polybius*, i. 697 ff.).

The story of the dictator Postumius Tubertus, who beheaded his son for leaving his post in order to fight a gallant single action (Livy iv. 29.5), was plainly invented for edification. But it contains a core of truth.

[11] The early *coloniae Romanae* were mostly small coastguard stations, containing some 300 Roman citizens. Those of the second century, often inland, were substantial towns with wide powers of self-government. See E. T. Salmon *Roman Colonization* (1969), ch. iv, and A. J. Toynbee, *Hannibal's Legacy*, i. 178 ff.

[12] The intensive colonising activity of the Romans impressed Greek observers such as Philip V of Macedon (see his letter to the people of Larissa, where he holds up the Romans as a shining example: Dittenberger, *Sylloge*[3], 543) and Dionysius of Halicarnassus (ii. 16).

[13] Cicero, *De Republica*, iii. 33–5. Livy sharply distinguishes *iusta ac pia bella* from others (xlii. 47.8). See also M. Gelzer (*Hermes*, 1933, 129 ff. = *Kleine Schriften*, iii (1964), 51 ff.) on the conscientious regard for international right expressed by the older Roman annalists. On the *ius festiale* see above, p. 584).

[14] On the population of Italy see K. J. Beloch, *Die Bevolkerung der griechisch-römischen Welt* (1886), 388 ff. Brunt, *Manpower*, 60, reckons as maxima for 225 B.C. a free population of Italy (excluding Cisalpina) of between 3 and $3\frac{1}{2}$ millions, and a total population (including slaves) of some 4 millions (but the former will have been less than 3 millions if the census returns were more accurate than assumed in the first calculation). The Romans will have numbered some 300,000 adult males, the Latins and other allies about 640,000 (including Greeks and Bruttians). Cisalpina may have had a free population of some 1,400,000

(*Manpower*, 189). On the municipal organisation of Italy see A. N. Sherwin-White, *The Roman Citizenship*[2] (1973), ch. ii, and A. J. Toynbee, *Hannibal's Legacy*, i. 189 ff., 397 ff.

[15] The *cives sine suffragio* were incorporated primarily for service in the Roman legions. They were therefore registered in the *centuriae*, but being voteless they were excluded from the *tribus*.

The term *municipium* originally denoted all Italian communities which accepted *civitas sine suffragio*. At first this was generally regarded as an alliance which involved an exchange of social rights (though perhaps not all Rome's *municipia* were her allies as well); the *municipes* retained local autonomy except in foreign policy, and provided Rome with troops. Later, *civitas sine suffragio* came to be regarded as an inferior form of Roman citizenship. Cf. p. 591 above. On citizenship see A. N. Sherwin-White, *The Roman Citizenship*[2] (1973) and in *Aufstieg NRW*, I. ii. 23 ff.

[16] Previous to the conclusion of the treaty that regulated their future status, conquered enemies who had made a formal unconditional surrender were known as *dediticii*. By their very nature, however, the *dediticii* did not constitute a permanent category of Roman dependants. See A. Bernardi, *Nomen Latinum* (1973).

[17] The enfranchised Campanians served in separate legions until the Second Punic War, but on the same terms as the Roman legionaries.

[18] All allied troops were called up *e formula togatorum*. This formula was a schedule kept by Rome, which according to one view listed the maximum number of troops which the Romans were entitled to requisition from each of their allies: see A. J. Toynbee, *Hannibal's Legacy*, i. 424 ff. Brunt, *Manpower*, 545 ff., however, argues that it was a sliding scale, variable at Rome's wish, indicating that each ally must supply so many men for each legion that Rome put into the field any given year. On the varying proportion of allies to Romans, see Brunt, *Manpower*, 677 ff.; cf. V. Ilari, *Gli Italici nelle strutture militari romani* (1974).

[19] On the constitutions of the Italian communities see A. Rosenberg, *Der Staat der alten Italiker* (1913); E. Kornemann, *Klio*, 1914, 190 ff.; F. Sartori, *Problemi di storia costituzionale italiota* (1953). As a rule the executive was grouped in *collegia*, as at Rome. Several Latin towns were governed by a single *dictator*; but a board of three *aediles* was commoner. Campanian cities had two or three *meddices*, Umbrian towns two *marones*, Sabine cantons *octoviri*.

[20] For details see B. V. Head, *Historia Nummorum*[2] (1911). Among the towns that set up mints were eight of the Latin colonies. Most of the coinage was in bronze, but silver was not uncommon, and the Etruscan town of Volsinii was still striking gold in the third century.

[21] The Hernican town of Anagnia was thus treated in 306 (Livy ix. 43.24), and Capua suffered a like fate in 211. The Capuan *magistri* (Dessau, *ILS*, 6303) had merely religious functions. Normally, however, *praefecti* supplemented rather than entrenched upon the administration of the local magistrates in colonies and *municipia*. For the view that Rome granted such towns more self-government than is sometimes believed see Brunt, *Manpower*, 524 ff.

[22] Disputes between Italian communities were henceforth regulated by commissioners from the Senate. On Roman methods of arbitration see Dessau, *ILS*, 5944 and 5946; Coleman Philippson, *The International Law and Custom of Greece and Rome* (1911), ii. ch. xxi; L. Matthaei, *Cl. Qu.* 1908, 241 ff.; E. Badian, *Foreign Clientelae* (1957), chs 4 and 7.

[23] In 302 the Senate intervened forcibly at Arretium on behalf of the *gens* Cilnia (p. 592). In 264 it forcibly suppressed a rising against the ruling nobility of Etruscan Volsinii and settled the survivors on lower ground on Lake Bolsena. In both cases Rome supported the ruling class against the lower. From Volsinii she captured 2000 statues, while the cult of Vortumnus was transplanted to Rome, with a temple on the Aventine and a statue of the god in the Vicus Tuscus.

[24] See in general T. Frank, *An Economic Survey of Ancient Rome*, i (1933), ch. ii.

[25] The inscription reads 'Novios Plautios med Romai fecid' (Dessau, *ILS*, 8562).

[26] See R. Thomsen, *Early Roman Coinage*, 3 vols (1957–61), whose views of this complex subject are roughly followed above. Two of the Aes Signatum pieces *appear* to refer to historical events. One shows an Indian elephant/sow; this must be one of Pyrrhus's elephants, and probably refers to the battle (Asculum or Beneventum) at which according to Aelian (*NH*, i. 38) a sow grunted and frightened Pyrrhus's elephants. The second piece shows two rostra/two hens feeding. The rostra must almost certainly refer to the new Roman navy built at the beginning of the First Punic War (p. 118) and it is tempting to refer it to the battle of Drepana when Appius Claudius drowned the sacred chickens (p. 119). But would Rome have recorded her only naval defeat in the war? See further H. H. Scullard, *The Elephant in the Greek and Roman World* (1974); 113 ff.

The two other ROMANO issues mentioned showed (a) Mars/horse's head (a Carthaginian type) and (b) Apollo/horse. All this ROMANO-ROMA group are often referred to as Romano-Campanian coins.

For all these coins see also Sydenham, *CRR*, Crawford, *RRC*. On Republican coinage see also H. Zehnacker, *Moneta* (2 vols. 1973). For a general survey see C. H. V. Sutherland, *Roman Coins* (1974).

[27] On architecture in the early Republic see A. Boethius and J. B. Ward-Perkins, *Etruscan and Roman Architecture* (1970), ch. 5.; on art, J. M. C. Toynbee, *The Art of the Romans* (1965), 16 ff.

[28] For instance, Juno Lucina (375), Concordia (367), Juno Moneta (344), Salus (303) and several in the 290s. Temple C and the older temple within Temple A in the Largo Argentina in Rome were probably built before 300.

[29] For photographs of some of these towns and their walls see Boethius, Ward-Perkins, op. cit. n. 27, and E. T. Salmon, *Roman Colonization*.

[30] In view of the widespread practice of such cults, it is uncertain from which cities they reached Rome: Hercules *may* have come from Tibur, Castor and Pollux from Tusculum or Lavinium.

[31] For the Latin language see L. R. Palmer, *The Latin Language* (1954); A. Meillet, *Esquisse d'une his-*

toire de la langue Latine[4] (1930), especially ch. vi. On early Latin literature see especially J. Wight Duff, *A Literary History of Rome from the Origins to the Close of the Golden Age*[3] (1953).

[32] For example, on the sarcophagi of the elder and younger Scipio Barbatus (Dessau, *ILS*, 1 and 3). That of the younger, who was consul in 259 and censor in 258, starts, 'This one man most Romans agree was the best of all good men' ('honc oino ploirume consentiont Romane / duonoro optumo fuise viro'); his naval attack on Sardinia and Corsica, his capture of Aleria and his dedication of a temple to the Tempestates are then recorded.

[33] For specimens of Fescennine verse composed by Caesar's soldiers at his triumph in 46 B.C., see Suetonius, *Divus Iulius*, xlix and li.

[34] Livy, vii. 2.

Chapter 12: Notes

[1] Polybius originally planned to write the history of the years 220 to 168, but later (after 146?) he continued his work down to 146 in bks 30–39 in order to show how the Romans extended and used their supremacy. Of the forty books which he wrote, only bks 1–5 survive complete, but substantial parts of many others are extant. Bks. 1–2 are introductory (264–220 B.C.). In bk 6 he analysed the Roman constitution, army and early development; his analysis of the mixed constitution had a great effect on later political thinkers, including the founders of the American constitution. His main purpose was didactic: to enlighten statesmen and to show the general reader the astounding achievement of Rome's rise to world power and the resultant unity. His approach was sober and pragmatic. No historian can be completely free from all bias, but Polybius was honest, aimed at the truth and took much trouble to ascertain it, by consulting documents, travelling widely and interviewing survivors. For the First Punic War he used various written sources, especially the Roman Fabius Pictor and the pro-Carthaginian Philinus of Agrigentum in Sicily. For the Second Punic War he used Roman sources (as public archives, family records, oral tradition and writers such as Fabius) and Carthaginian material (the Greek writers Sosylus and Silenus, who lived with Hannibal). Though his narrative is lucid, his style is somewhat heavy. See above all, Walbank, *Polybius*, including the Introduction, and his Sather lectures on *Polybius* (1972). On recent work on Polybius (1950–70) see D. Must, *Aufstieg NRW*, I. ii. 1114 ff., and *Polybe* (*Entretiens Hardt*, xx, 1974).

For the history of the Punic Wars G. De Sanctis, *Storia*, vols iii and iv, pt 3, are of fundamental importance. A general account is given by T. A. Dorey and D. R. Dudley, *Rome Against Carthage* (1971). For a general account of Rome's expansion and policy during these years see R. M. Errington, *The Dawn of Empire: Rome's Rise to World Power* (1972).

[2] On Livy see p. 396. Also P. G. Walsh, *Livy: His Historical Aims and Methods* (1961), and Ogilvie, *Livy*, with Introduction. Bks 16–20, which treated

the First Punic War, are lost. For the Second Punic War Livy's account (bks 21–30) is based partly upon Polybius, partly upon less trustworthy annalists. One of the better of the latter was a Coelius Antipater who wrote a monograph on the war which was also based partly on Polybius. For the lists of magistrates and legions which he gives Livy drew on official records. His historical value at any point thus largely depends upon what source he was using then.

[3] For Carthage in general see S. Gsell, *Histoire ancienne de l'Afrique du Nord*, 8 vols (1914–28), especially vols ii and iv, and B. H. Warmington, *Carthage*[2] (1969). Cf. also G. and C. Picard, *Daily Life in Carthage* (1961), and *The Life and Death of Carthage* (1968).

[4] Archaeological evidence (proto-Corinthian pottery of *c.* 725 B.C. and some – probably slightly older – Punic pottery) found on the site suggests that the traditional foundation-date of 814 may be one or perhaps two generations too early. However, there may have been earlier tombs which so far have eluded the archaeologists.

[5] Warmington (*Carthage*, 54) argues that these were hardly commercial wars in the sense in which this term is used of wars in seventeenth-century Europe; their primary cause will have been the determination to safeguard trade-routes (especially that to the mines of Spain) rather than directly to promote the interests of producers and merchants.

[6] The statement of Strabo (xvii. 833) that Carthage at the time of its destruction contained 700,000 inhabitants is now generally discredited. Gsell (op. cit. ii. 85 ff.) points out that its area did not exceed 1 square mile. B. H. Warmington (*Carthage*[2], 133 f.) applies Strabo's figure to include the inhabitants of the Cap Bon peninsula and around the city, all of whom had a different status from the subject peoples of the interior; he reckons for the city some 200,000 in the fifth century and some 400,000 including slaves and resident aliens in the early third century.

Much early Greek pottery had been found in the cemeteries of Carthage, including Corinthian and Attic black-figure, but there is none of the later red-figure: during the fifth century Carthage suffered an economic recession (when she began to exploit the agricultural resources of North Africa), but in the following century wider trade with the Greek world was resumed.

A contributory factor to this temporary withdrawal may have been the late adoption of money by Carthage. She did not start a coinage until early in the fourth century and this at first was struck mainly for the use of her armies in Sicily, where this Siculo–Punic silver was probably minted. Soon she issued, probably at home, an impressive issue of gold on an imposing scale which far outdid any of the gold issues of Greek states in the fourth century. The gold came from West Africa, a closely guarded Carthaginian preserve. See G. K. Jenkins and R. B. Lewis, *Carthaginian Gold and Electrum Coins* (1963), 24 ff.

[7] Although at times clashes of interest may have occurred between landowners and merchants, the view that a rigid cleavage developed and affected Carthaginian policy need not be accepted. Merchants no doubt owned farms (probably of moderate size)

i.1 the country: as in England in the sixteenth century and later, merchants bought landed estates but continued in business. Cf. Warmington, *Carthage*,[2] 137 f. For the tax, Polybius, i. 72.

[8] After the conquests of Alexander the Great and the creation of the Ptolemaic empire of Egypt, Carthaginian trade became easier in the East and the presence of their merchants at Athens and Delos, two Aegean markets, is recorded by inscriptions. In the Latin play, based on Greek originals, which Plautus named *Poenulus*, 'The Little Carthaginian', we find the hero Hanno in Greece looking for his daughters who had been kidnapped and sold as slaves; he adopts the role of a trader of small goods.

[9] On Carthaginian exploration in the Atlantic see M. Cary and E. H. Warmington, *The Ancient Explorers* (1929), 31 ff., 45 ff.

[10] The extent of the liability of citizens to naval service is not known. Conditions doubtless varied at different periods of Carthage's history.

[11] When the Romans were besieging Tarentum in 272 a Carthaginian fleet suddenly appeared in the harbour and then sailed off (Livy, *Epitome*, xiv). Since Polybius, who discussed the causes of the First Punic War at some length, does not record the incident it might, on the assumption that Carthage's intention towards Rome was hostile, have been invented later by Roman annalists as an example of *Punica fides*. Or a friendly move might have been interpreted as hostile. Since in fact the Punic fleet took no direct hostile action, the episode has probably been exaggerated by Roman writers, and was not mentioned by Polybius because it did not technically infringe existing agreements between Rome and Carthage.

[12] The traditional chronology of the First Punic War has been impugned by some modern scholars, who hold that the Roman calendar at this time was seriously out of order. The traditional system is effectively defended by De Sanctis (*Storia*, III. 248 ff.). In any case, the discrepancy between the two systems amounts to a few months only.

[13] In 270 the Romans had dispossessed and severely punished a band of Campanian freebooters who had seized Rhegium (opposite Messana) (p. 96).

[14] A Greek writer of mid-third century, named Philinus, asserted that in occupying Messana the Romans had broken a previous formal treaty by which they bound themselves to keep their hands off Sicily, in return for a promise by the Carthaginians not to interfere in Italy (Polybius, iii. 26, who denied the existence of the treaty) pp. 592 and 596. This could be nothing more than misunderstanding of the pact of 279 (p. 95). But the Carthaginians had a vested interest in Sicily which the Romans could not equitably disregard, and it may be surmised that in 279 they received at very least an informal assurance of a free hand in that island (Walbank, *Polybius*, 1. 357).

[15] Presumably the Comitia Tributa to which the ratification of treaties was usually submitted. Formally the question was whether the Romans should enter into a treaty with Messana.

[16] The situation at Messana in 264 B.C. was substantially like that created at Fashoda in A.D. 1898 by the almost simultaneous arrival of a French and a British-Egyptian force. The manner in which this dispute was resolved shows what could have been done in 264 B.C. to avoid war.

[17] On the strength of this diplomatic victory Valerius assumed the somewhat inappropriate *cognomen* of 'Messalla'; this is the first instance of a 'triumphal' surname in a Roman family.

[18] Polybius (i. 20.1–2) may possibly have exaggerated the effect of the Agrigentum episode in the development of Roman imperialistic ideas (cf. Walbank, *Polybius*, i. 72 f.). If the Carthaginians would not give in and negotiate on reasonable terms, the Romans' obvious course was to try to drive them from the island.

[19] On the quinquereme see W. W. Tarn, *Hellenistic Military and Naval Developments* (1930), 129 ff. On the naval war see J. H. Thiel, *History of Roman Sea Power before the Second Punic War* (1954). On the size of the fleets, see W. W. Tarn, *JHS* 1907, 48 ff. A Punic warship has recently been found off W. Sicily.

[20] Rome's victory was due largely to the invention of the device known in their soldiers' language as the raven (*corvus*). Its precise nature, though described by Polybius (i. 22), remains obscure in detail: see H. T. Wallinga, *The Boarding-bridge of the Romans* (1956). It was either a developed grappling-iron or more probably some sort of boarding-bridge with an iron 'beak' underneath which penetrated into the enemy's deck. It was not used after 255/249 because its weight was dangerous during storms and thereafter a lighter type of quinquereme was introduced.

[21] The *columna rostrata* was decorated with the prows (*rostra*) of the captured ships. The prow on the Roman *as* (p. 107), which is that of a standard Hellenistic battleship, probably commemorates Rome's naval successes in the war; which particular victory, if any, depends on the date of the first issue, which probably falls between 260 and 235. The prow of a Carthaginian ship is shown on a slightly later coin minted in Spain, probably by Hannibal's brother Mago (see p. 132). A copy of the inscription on the Duilius column, belonging to the imperial period, survives (Dessau, *ILS*, 65).

[22] The arrangement of the Roman battle-line, and consequently of the tactics, at Ecnomus are not entirely clear. See Walbank, *Polybius*, i. 83 ff.

[23] Caecilius Metellus's tactics drove the elephants back on their own lines. After the battle he rounded up all the beasts and later displayed them at Rome. On the date see G. M. Morgan, *Cl. Qu.* 1972, 121 ff. The Caecilii Metelli adopted the elephant as a kind of family badge; it often features on coins minted by members of the family acting as mint-masters.

[24] Claudius is said to have disregarded the omens: told that the sacred chickens would not eat, he threw them overboard, saying 'Well, let them drink'. The anecdote might be true, but was more likely invented to account for his subsequent defeat (it is not related by Polybius). Despite the loss of ships many of the Roman crews managed to swim ashore.

[25] Polybius does not refer to the famous story, made familiar by Horace's well-known Ode (iii. 5), that Regulus was sent to Rome to facilitate a settlement, but patriotically broke his trust by warning his countrymen against any kind of deal with the enemy; thereafter, under oath he returned to Carthage where

he was tortured to death. The story of the peace mission is defended by T. Frank, *Cl. Ph.* 1926, 311 (and by Cary, *Hist.* 150), but is more generally rejected, as also is the story of his death on the ground that it was invented to counterbalance the story that his widow tortured some Punic prisoners in Rome. Cf. Walbank, *Polybius*, i. 92 ff. The 'legend' is, however, at least as old as the annalist Sempronius Tuditanus (*apud* Aul. Gell., *N.A.* vii. 4.1), who was quaestor in 145 and consul in 129; would such a man of affairs have repeated a completely baseless story? *Non liquet.* According to Sempronius the embassy was concerned only with an exchange of prisoners, but Livy (*Epit.* 18) adds peace.

[26] Mt Hercte (Heircte) is to be identified either with Monte Pellegrino, just north of Palermo (so De Sanctis, *Storia*, III. i. 181), or Monte Castellaccio, some 6 miles north-west (Kromayer-Veith, *Antike Schlachtfelder*, III. i. 4 ff.).

[27] On the organisation of Sicily as a province see pp. 171 ff. Rome allowed King Hiero, whose treaty had been renewed in 248, to retain his kingdom in the south-east, but undertook the direct administration of the rest of the island.

[28] Polybius regarded the war as a crucial stage in Rome's development. In bk iii. 9–10 he 'undertook to explain the grounds which led the Romans to conceive the *ambition* of a world-empire, and gave them the means to acquire it. The First Punic War, and especially Roman naval policy, provide the answer. Not by chance . . . but by deliberately schooling themselves amid dangers, the Romans conceived their ambition and accomplished it'. (Walbank, *Polybius*, i. 129).

[29] This revolt of the mercenaries, known as the Truceless War because of the relentlessness with which it was fought, threatened the very life of Carthage. It is described at length by Polybius (iii. 75 ff.), whose account forms the basis of Flaubert's well-known romance *Salammbô*. The mercenaries in effect set up a separate state and issued a wide range of coins (including gold). On their coinage see E. S. G. Robinson, *Numismatic Chronicle*, 1943, 1 ff.; 1953, 27 ff.; 1956, 9 ff.; Jenkins and Lewis, *Carthaginian Gold and Electrum Coins* (1963), 43. They first used Carthaginian types, then their own, the chief showing Head of Hercules/Lion prowling, inscribed 'of the Libyans'. The rebels in Sardinia also issued: Head of Isis/Three corn-ears. See Robinson, *Num. Chron.* 1943, 1 f.; Jenkins-Lewis, 51.

[30] Presumably the Carthaginians had in mind King Ptolemy III of Egypt, who would have been excellently qualified to act as arbitrator.

[31] For some wholesome plain speaking on the seizure of the two islands see Polybius, iii. 28 (e.g. 'contrary to all justice').

[32] Rome's relations with the Gauls are discussed by Polybius, ii. 14–35; chs 21–35 deal with 237–221 B.C. Some of the Celts, the Gaesatae, went into battle naked. A bronze figurine of this period depicts one: see T. G. E. Powell, *The Celts* (1958), plate 1. Polybius says that their swords could be used only for cutting, lacking a point for thrusting; however, 'archaeology shows that by this date Celtic swords had become

heavier and broader' (Powell, p. 107). For the site of the battle and finds in the neighbourhood see P. Sommella, *Antichi campi di battaglia in Italica* (1967), 11 ff.

[33] During the struggle with Carthage the Italian federation had remained loyal to Rome, but in 241 Falerii revolted. It was promptly stormed and the inhabitants were moved down from their strong hillsite (modern Cività Castellana) to a new city on the plain. Imposing stretches of the new city wall and a gateway survive. Half the territory of Falerii was annexed by Rome, and a Latin colony was settled at Spoletium, east of the Via Flaminia. On the Via Aurelia, whose precise dating is uncertain, see F. Castagnoli (ed.), *La Via Aurelia* (1968).

[34] On Flaminius's outstanding career see K. Jacobs, *Gaius Flaminius* (1938, written in Dutch), and Z. Yavetz, 'The Policy of Flaminius', *Athenaeum* 1962, 325 ff.

[35] The chief source for the Illyrian Wars is Polybius, ii. 2–12, iii. 16, 18–19 (on which see Walbank, *Polybius*, i). On Roman policy see M. Holleaux, *Rome, la Grèce et les monarchies hellénistiques au IIIme siècle av. J. C.* (1921); E. Badian, *PBSR* 1952, 72 ff. (= *Studies in Greek and Roman History* (1964), 1 ff.); N. G. L. Hammond, *JRS* 1968, 1 ff.; K. E. Petzold, *Historia* 1971, 199 ff. On Illyrian piracy see H. J. Dell, *Historia* 1967, 344 ff.

[36] This appears to have been Rome's first direct political dealing with Greece. The alleged Roman treaty with Rhodes in 306, her alliance with Acarnania in 266, and her intervention on behalf of Acarnania in 239 may all be dismissed as fictitious: Holleaux, op. cit. 29 ff. and in *CAH*, vii. 822 ff. Of course there had been many other contacts (not least trade) during the Etruscan period and intermittently thereafter. For some of the subsequent references to contacts see F. W. Walbank, *JRS* 1963, 2 f.

[37] On the territorial extent of the protectorate see N. G. L. Hammond, *JRS* 1968, 7 ff., with map on p. 3.

[38] Cf. Badian, op. cit. in n. 35, pp. 6 ff.

[39] Holleaux (op. cit. n. 35) showed that Rome did not pursue an expansionist eastern policy. A different view, however, is taken by Hammond (*JRS* 1968, 1 ff.) in a survey of Rome's relations with Illyris and Macedon in 229–205 B.C. He argues that both Rome and Macedon were imperialistic states 'desiring power, the power of commanding other states' and that Roman policy was anti-Macedonian. At the end of the First Illyrian War 'what Rome took was not revenge on Teuta, but command of a strategic area in Illyris' (p. 20), and this was not to stop Illyrian piracy. Rome's anti-Macedonian attitude was shown in sending embassies not to Macedon but to Macedon's enemies, the Achaean and Aetolian Leagues. In fact Rome and Macedon soon engaged in a 'cold war'. That Macedon viewed Rome's intervention in the Balkans with disfavour is plausible enough, but that Rome's policy in 228 was so far-seeing and deepseated as to envisage dominating Macedon and ultimately destroying her independence is much more doubtful.

Chapter 13: Notes

[1] Tartessus (probably = the Biblical Tarshish) lay near Gades. Its precise site has not yet been located. It was 'discovered' by the Greek mariner Colaeus of Samos *c.* 640 (Herodotus, iv. 152), but it was the Phocaeans who later developed trade-relations with its king, Arganthonius. See A. Schulten, *Tartessos* (1922); J. M. Blazquez, *Tartessos* (Salamanca, 1968). On the Iberians and their culture see P. Dixon, *The Iberians of Spain* (1940); A. Arribas, *The Iberians* (1964). On ancient Spain in general see A. Schulten, *Iberische Landeskunde* (1955).

[2] This contact with Hamilcar is recorded only in a fragment of Dio Cassius (frg. 48). Since it is not given by Polybius, some historians either reject it or regard it with some suspicion. On the part played by Massilia in these and subsequent negotiations see T. Frank, *Roman Imperialism* (1925), 121.

[3] The Ebro treaty (on which see Walbank, *Polybius*, i. 168 ff.) was a convention between Hasdrubal and the delegates of the Roman Senate (Polybius, iii. 29.3); it was probably ratified at Rome, but not at Carthage. Polybius mentions only the one clause, that the Carthaginians were not to cross the Ebro in arms. Its implications have led to much discussion and are important in the wider context of the causes and the events which led to the Second Punic War. On this question of 'war-guilt' there is a vast modern literature. Here it must suffice to refer only to Walbank, *Polybius*, i. 168 ff, 310 ff., and to three recent articles (where other literature is discussed), G. V. Sumner, *Harvard Stud. Cl. Ph.* 1967, 204 ff., *Latomus*, 1972, 469 ff., and R. M. Errington, *Latomus* 1970, 26 ff. Five other articles are reprinted in *Hannibal* (edited by K. Christ, 1974), which contains another nine articles on Hannibal.

[4] For the view that Rome had no formal *foedus* with Saguntum see E. Badian, *Foreign Clientelae* (1958), 50 f., 293. The precise date of the agreement unfortunately cannot be established: its implications for Roman policy clearly vary according to whether it fell before or after the Ebro treaty (the latter view being the more probable). The older view (e.g. J. S. Reid, *JRS* 1913, 179 ff., revived by Errington, *Latomus* 1970, 43 f.) that this agreement was made at the time when the Romans arbitrated in an internal quarrel at Saguntum (see pp. 125–6) does not seem very probable. Polybius says (iii. 30.1) that the agreement was 'several years' before the time of Hannibal, whereas the arbitration was 'a short time before' Hannibal's interview with the Roman embassy (iii. 15.7).

[5] Presumably the status of Saguntum had never been the object of an explicit understanding between Romans and Carthaginians, so that both sides could claim it, as they did Messana in 264.

[6] Polybius (iii. 8) expressly refutes the assertion of Fabius Pictor, that Hannibal forced the hand of his home government and therefore lacked its whole-hearted support (cf. Walbank, *Polybius*, i. 310).

[7] See the literature mentioned in n. 3 above.

[8] The debate continues: Sumner (see n. 3) believes that for long the Romans kept a sharp eye on Spain and that their policy was 'entirely concerned with the curbing of Carthaginian expansion' (p. 245), whereas Errington dismisses 'the wrath of the Barcids' as unknown to Fabius Pictor and thinks that 'Roman policy towards Spain was directed by nothing more potent than apathy' (p. 26). Modern views are discussed by F. Cassola, *I Gruppi politichi romani nel III sec. a. C.* (1962), 244 ff. and esp. 250 ff. On p. 251 he lists those modern writers who attribute (with various shades of emphasis) the responsibility for the war to Rome or to Carthage.

[9] Polybius (iii, vii–xv) and Livy (xxi–xxx) remain the two chief sources for the Second Punic War; other writers, as Plutarch, Appian, Dio Cassius, Florus and Eutropius (the last two follow the Livian tradition) do not add much of independent value. Of the voluminous literature on the battles of the Hannibalic War two standard works are Kromayer-Veith, *Antike Schlachtfelder*, iii (1912) and iv (1931), 609 ff. (and more briefly their *Schlachten-atlas*), and De Sanctis, *Storia*, III, ii (1917). We now have the indispensable discussion of the problems involved by Walbank, *Polybius*; throughout the present chapter continuous reference to this work will be assumed. Short discussions in Scullard, *Hist. Rom. World*[3], 436 ff.

[10] Neither Polybius (iii. 50–6) nor Livy (xxi. 31–7) gives sufficient topographical data to warrant any confident conclusions as to Hannibal's pass. The views of Sir Gavin de Beer (in *Alps and Elephants* (1955) and repeated in *Hannibal* (1969)) have been subjected to damaging criticism by F. W. Walbank, *JRS* 1956, 37 ff., and A. H. McDonald, *Alpine Journal* 1956, 93 ff. See also D. Procter, *Hannibal's March in History* (1971). If any consensus of opinion can be detected it would seem to incline to the Col du Clapier.

[11] The Trebia is a tributary of the Po, which it enters from the south just west of Placentia. Although Livy places the battle on the right bank, Polybius's site on the left bank seems the more probable.

[12] Hannibal probably used the pass of Collina between Bologna and Pistoia. Between Pistoia and Faesulae (Fiesole) he met with great difficulties in marshland. He rode on the sole surviving elephant and lost the sight of one eye through exposure.

[13] The battle-site was on the north or north-east shore of the lake, but its precise location is debated. A recent view, based on the finding of alleged ashes of the dead, by G. Susini is criticised by Walbank, *JRS* 1961, 232 ff. (cf. *Polybius*, ii. 638).

[14] The Roman forces at Cannae probably did not number as many as 80,000–90,000 men, as Polybius and Livy assert (though Livy himself knew of other assessments), but they considerably outnumbered those of Hannibal. See De Sanctis, *Storia* III. ii. 131 ff.; B. H. Hallward, *CAH*, viii. 52. Livy has preserved records of the legions in the field in the years 218–167. Their essential reliability has been maintained by De Sanctis and more recently by Brunt, *Manpower*, 416 ff., 645 ff., against the criticism of M. Gelzer, *Kleine Schriften*, iii. 220 ff.

The battle was fought either on the right or the left bank of the Aufidus (mod. Ofanto) river. The right bank, with the Roman line facing south-west, is perhaps slightly more probable.

[15] Hannibal's troops were drawn up in a single

line: (from left to right), his Spanish and Gallic cavalry, half the African infantry, the Spanish and Gallic infantry (in the centre), the rest of the Africans, the Numidian cavalry. The line was in a crescent shape (or possibly *en echelon*, though Polybius does not say this), so that its centre engaged the Romans first; as the centre fell back the Africans turned inwards against the flanks of the advancing Romans, who became too tightly packed to be able to fight properly. Cannae has always been a classic example of encirclement for military historians.

[16] Rebel Capua (and Atella and Calatia) as an act of independence issued coins (mainly bronze), inscribed not in Latin but in Oscan: one type is an elephant. At Capua Hannibal issued an electrum coinage and probably some tiny silver coins, also with elephants (cf. H. H. Scullard, *The Elephant in the Greek and Roman World* (1974), 170 ff.). For this and the rest of his coinage in Italy see the survey by E. S. G. Robinson, *Numismatic Chronicle* 1964, 37 ff. It may be appropriate to mention here Hannibal's earlier coinage, which he minted at New Carthage before leaving Spain. On it his portrait appears, at first under the guise of Hercules, then plain. Here he was following the example of his father Hamilcar, who also was depicted as Melkart–Hercules. The portraits of his brothers Hasdrubal and Mago may also appear. For a discussion of these series of fine silver coins see E. S. G. Robinson, *Essays in Roman Coinage presented to H. Mattingly* (ed. R. A. G. Carson and C. H. V. Sutherland, 1956), 34 ff., and see pp. 125, 126, 131, 132).

[17] The bearing of the Romans after Cannae fully confirms the remark of Polybius (xxvii. 8.8) that the Romans were never more intractable than after defeat.

[18] Some details regarding the numbers and distribution of the Roman legions in the Second Punic War which we read in Livy do not always tally with the data of Polybius or with each other. See M. Gelzer, *Hermes* 1935, 269 ff. (= *Kleine Schriften*, iii (1964), 220 ff.), but cf. the views of De Sanctis and Brunt cited above in n. 14.

[19] The weight of the *as* (p. 107) *may* have begun to drop before the war to a semi-libral (half-pound) standard, but it declined rapidly early in the war to a triental and then (by 214?) to a quadrantal standard. About 215 the silver *quadrigatus* was superseded by a smaller *victoriatus* (with reverse type of Victory), while a year or so earlier an emergency gold issue (Janus/Oath-scene) was produced. Another gold issue (Mars/Eagle) followed for a brief period (*c.* 212–209). But around 211 (the *precise* date is still slightly uncertain) a basic change and overhaul of all the coinage was made. With this new start a silver *denarius* (= 10 *asses*) was coined and became Rome's standard silver coin; it was linked to a sextantal bronze system. This new bimetallic system remained the basis of Rome's coinage (with of course developments in details of production) throughout the rest of the Republic and during the early Empire. In general see R. Thomsen, *Early Roman Coinage*, 3 vols (1957–63), and Crawford, *RRC* (1975): on the developments early in the Hannibalic War see Crawford, *JRS* 1964, 29 ff.

[20] Hasdrubal's force at the Metaurus probably numbered some 30,000 men, that of the Romans not less than 40,000 (Kromayer-Veith, *Antike Schlachtfelder*, iii. 490).

[21] The copious emission of Bruttian gold, silver and bronze coinage in the late third century is to be assigned to Hannibal's presence in Bruttium; he used it to finance the Punic war-effort throughout southern Italy. See E. S. G. Robinson, *Numismatic Chronicle* 1964, 54 ff.

[22] On the Roman navy from 218 to 167 B.C. see J. H. Thiel, *Studies on the History of Roman Sea-Power in Republican Times* (1946); Brunt, *Manpower*, 666 ff. Cf. also the Introduction to Admiral Mahon's classic *Influence of Sea-Power on History, 1660–1783*.

[23] The terms of the treaty are reproduced verbatim by Polybius, vii. 9, who gives a Greek translation of the Punic document which fell into Roman hands. For its interpretation see E. Bickerman, *TAPA* 1944, 87 ff., *AJ Phil.* 1952, 1 ff., who equates the oath with a Hebrew covenanted treaty (*berit*), and especially Walbank, *Polybius*, ii. 42 ff. Philip presumably swore a parallel document. The terms by which Philip promised to help Hannibal are somewhat vague, but it was arranged that with the coming of peace, which was to be the responsibility of Hannibal, the two parties should turn the compact into a defensive alliance. It is also envisaged that while Philip would deal with the Illyrian towns under Roman protection, Hannibal would deal with Italy. It is noteworthy that Hannibal's war-aims seem to be limited and do not include the annhilation of Rome.

[24] The devices which Archimedes invented for the defence of the city are described by Polybius, viii. 4 ff.; Plutarch, *Marcellus*, 14–17; Livy, xxiv. 34.1–16. See in general E. W. Marsden, *Greek and Roman Artillery* (1969), and for Archimedes at Syracuse, pp. 109 ff. For the siting of Archimedes's artillery cf. A. W. Lawrence, *JHS* 1946, 99 ff. Recent experiments by Greek sailors in setting fire to shipping by concentrating the sun's rays by means of bronze mirrors suggest that this device, attributed to Archimedes, may not be without some foundation; see *The Times*, 7 Nov. 1973.

[25] The campaigns of the Scipios in Spain are covered by Polybius (iii. 76, 95–9; x. 2–20, 34–40; xi. 20–33) and Livy (various passages in xxi–xxix). See Walbank, *Polybius*, ad loc.; H. H. Scullard, *Scipio Africanus in the Second Punic War* (1930), *Scipio Africanus: Soldier and Politician* (1970).

[26] A description of the Ebro battle is found in a fragment of the Greek historian Sosylus, who lived with Hannibal: see Jacoby, *Fr. Gr. H.* 176F.

[27] The predicament of the Scipios in 211 recalls that of Sir John Moore in 1808 and of Wellesley in 1812, when a sudden enemy concentration and difficulties of co-operation with their Spanish allies forced them to make hasty retreats.

[28] By the time of Polybius a mass of popular tradition and legend, arising from the idea that Scipio was favoured by Jupiter, had arisen. Polybius as a rationalist discounted this and believed that Scipio used this popular belief, in which he himself disbelieved, as a means to winning confidence. However, it is likely that in fact Scipio had a real trust in divine

help. On the 'legend' see R. M. Haywood, *Studies on Scipio Africanus* (1933); F. W. Walbank, *Proc. Cambr. Phil. Soc.* 1967, 54 ff.; Scullard, *Scipio Africanus: Soldier and Politician* (1970), 18 ff., 235 ff. Scipio has been called 'A Greater than Napoleon' by Sir Basil Liddell Hart in a biography of him with that title (1926).

[29] The capture of New Carthage was made easier when the northern walls were made accessible by a mysterious ebbing of the waters of the lagoon which washed them. This phenomenon (caused by a sudden wind?) confirmed the idea that Scipio received divine help (here from Neptune).

[30] Scipio's failure to pursue Hasdrubal has given rise to much discussion. Such a pursuit would have been a wild-goose chase: his inferiority in mounted troops would have prevented him from pinning Hasdrubal down, while he could not hold all the passes over the Pyrenees. It is noteworthy that the Senate did not think it necessary to recall him by the sea-route, as it had recalled Sempronius from Sicily in 218: his province was Spain, where two Punic armies still remained undefeated.

[31] On Scipio's African campaigns see Kromayer-Veith, *Antike Schlachtfelder*, iii, pt ii; Walbank, *Polybius*, ii; Scullard, *Scipio* (1930), 176 ff., (1970), 116 ff.

[32] Previously the maniples of the two rear lines had reinforced the front line, but now they were used as two independent units, ready to come up and prolong the line at each end. Further, the enemy's centre was not merely held at bay, as at Ilipa, but firmly engaged, thus minimising the possibility of a sudden retreat. Scipio is said to have experimented also with a slightly larger unit than the maniple, the cohort, of which ten later usually went to make up a legion. But the cohort was not fully developed as a separate tactical unit until the first century.

[33] The exact site of the battle cannot be determined with certainty. Polybius named the place Margaron, Livy Naraggara, and later writers (as Nepos) Zama (of which there were at least two in the area). See Scullard, *Scipio* (1970), 271 ff., and *Polis and Imperium, Studies in Honour of E. T. Salmon* (1974), 225 ff.

[34] The battle of Zama is difficult to reconstruct from the accounts of Polybius (xv. 9–14) and Livy (xxx. 32–5). Hannibal's first two lines, consisting of mercenaries and new conscripts, appear to have been thrown into temporary confusion by Scipio's first frontal attack, but whether they actually came to blows among each other is uncertain.

[35] In 204 Scipio was severely criticised in the Senate, and not without reason, for conniving at the misconduct of an officer named Q. Pleminius, who had been guilty of sacrilege and other crimes in the southern Italian town of Locri, which Scipio had managed to snatch out of Hannibal's grasp. But as a rule the discipline maintained by him was exemplary.

Chapter 14: Notes

[1] For Rome's relations with Cisalpine Gaul and the Ligurians in this period our main source consists of scattered passages in Livy (xxi–xlii). See now J. Briscoe, *A Commentary on Livy*, bks xxxi–xxxiii (1973). For the colonies see E. T. Salmon, *Roman Colonization* (1969), 96 ff. There were eight citizen colonies (Puteoli, Salernum, Volturnum, Liternum, Sipontum, Buxentum, Tempsa and Croton) and two Latin ones (Copia and Vibo Valentia). Military motives probably outweighed economic: these southern districts needed protection, not least against the menace of the fleet of Antiochus the Great (p. 163).

[2] The treaties with the Cenomani and Insubres contained the peculiar clause that no individual members of these tribes should obtain the Roman franchise (Cicero, *Pro Balbo*, 32). The practical bearing of this stipulation probably was to exclude natives from land-assignations made by the Roman government in Cisalpine Gaul.

[3] These *fora* were named after the Roman commissioners who constituted them (Forum Lepidi, Popillii, Sempronii); for purposes of jurisdiction they were 'attributed' to the nearest colony or other urban centre. Brunt, however, argues (*Manpower*, 570 ff.) that many *fora* in Cisalpina were not originally founded for the benefit of Italian immigrants, but were centres for survivors of the pacified native inhabitants; also that several should be dated later than often believed.

[4] On the early colonisation of Cisalpine Gaul see U. Ewins, *PBSR* 1952, 54 ff. On the Roman conquest see A. J. Toynbee, *Hannibal's Legacy*, ii. 252 ff., and for its population and resources see Brunt, *Manpower*, ch. xiii.

[5] On the treaty with Gades see E. Badian, *Cl. Ph.* 1954, 250 f.

[6] The main sources for the Spanish Wars are Polybius, xxxv. 1–5; Livy (various passages in xxxii, xxxv, xxxix, xl, xli); and Appian, *Iberica*, viii. 39–xvi. 98, depending in part on the lost books of Polybius, who also wrote a monograph on the Numantine War; Diodorus, xxxi. ff., with fragments from Poseidonius. The sources are collected in *Fontes Hispaniae Antiquae*, iii (1935), iv (1937), edited by A. Schulten. For modern accounts see A. Schulten, *Numantia*, ii. 261 ff., *Geschichte von Numantia* (1933); H. Simon, *Roms Kriege in Spanien, 154–133 v. Chr.* (1962); and (for 154–133) A. E. Astin, *Scipio Aemilianus* (1967), 35 ff., 137 ff. It is interesting that many Roman camps of these campaigns survive, especially in and around Numantia: see Schulten, op. cit.

[7] On the site of Numantia see Schulten, *Numantia*, ii. The town was laid out regularly with paved streets.

[8] Italica was not constituted as a colony in the strict sense. It probably ranked as a *vicus*. This was a new departure for Rome, a settlement not in Italy but hundreds of miles away. By its name it proclaimed itself an outpost of Italian civilisation; Scipio did not, like the Hellenistic rulers who founded cities, call it after himself.

[9] We may assign to this period the agricultural encyclopaedia of the Carthaginian writer Mago (Varro, *De Re Rustica*, i. 1). Presumably this work

was based on the copious Hellenistic literature on the subject.

[10] On Masinissa and his kingdom see G. Camps, *Massinissa* (= *Libyca*, viii, 1960); P. G. Walsh, *JRS* 1965, 149 ff. The latter believes that, contrary to what sometimes has been argued (e.g. by U. Kahrstedt, *Gesch. d. Karth.* iii. 615 ff.) Numidia under Masinissa cannot have given Rome any real ground for fear that it might become a rival capable of superseding Carthage, cf. A. E. Astin, *Scipio Aemilianus*, 273 ff. Numidia was permeated by Punic art, language and culture, urban life was encouraged, and Masinissa followed the pattern of Hellenistic monarchy, making many contacts with the Greek world.

[11] Masinissa was able to press into his service a clause of the peace of 201, which conceded to him 'as much land as his forefathers had possessed' within certain specified boundaries (Polybius, xv. 18.5). By reason of its indefiniteness this clause could be used as cover for successive encroachments.

[12] On the motives which led Rome to seek the destruction of Carthage there is a very large literature: see, for example, E. Badian, *Foreign Clientelae*, 125 ff., and especially 133 ff.; and A. E. Astin, *Scipio Aemilianus*, 272 ff. (with recent bibliography, p. 272, n. 1). The older view that Rome wished to remove a trade rival is not often accepted now: it is not mentioned in the sources (the silence of Polybius at xxxvi. 9 is important) and after the war the Romans made no attempt to occupy or exploit the commercial facilities of the site. 'The whole myth of economic motives in Rome's foreign policy at this time is a figment of modern anachronism, based on ancient anachronism': so wrote E. Badian, *Roman Imperialism in the Late Republic* (1968), 20. Too much has probably also been made of the role of Masinissa (see n. 10 above); Rome could have maintained the balance of power in North Africa by other means. Roman foreign policy had been hardening (thus in Greece the earlier protectorate policy was giving way to a policy which ultimately led to domination, see p. 170). This, combined with the fear, genuinely held by some, that Carthage was getting too strong, may have led to the decision to act. The opposition view, led by Scipio Nasica, is said to have been based on, first, the need for a *iusta causa* (which was supplied in religious and legal terms when the Carthaginians fought Masinissa), and then on a 'counter-weight of fear' argument, namely that an external source of fear was necessary in order to maintain Rome's military efficiency and perhaps to promote internal concord. Further, Rome was conscious of the effect on foreign opinion in going to war (Polybius, xxxvi. 2).

[13] The main sources for the Third Punic War are Polybius, xxxvi–xxxix (fragmentary), and Appian, *Libyca*, 67–135, which is based on Polybius but contaminated with less reliable annalistic material.

[14] Scipio's election to the consulship is constitutionally remarkable and significant. He was not originally standing for this office, was under the required age and had not held the praetorship. Despite these legal disabilities, and the opposition of the Senate and presiding consul, the people insisted, with tribunician backing, in suspending the relevant legislation for one year in order to exempt Scipio from the legal requirements. See A. E. Astin, *Scipio Aemilianus*, (1967), ch. vi.

[15] The only extant specimen of Punic literature is an account of an exploration of the coast of West Africa by one Hanno, part of which survives in a Greek translation (C. Müller, *Geographi Graeci Minores*, i. 1 ff.). See M. Cary and E. H. Warmington, *The Ancient Explorers* (1929), 47 ff., with translation. For a history of the wars with Rome the Carthaginians had to rely on contemporary Greek authors (Philinus and Silenus).

On Carthaginian culture in general see S. Gsell, *Histiore ancienne de l'Afrique du Nord,* iv (esp. 484 ff.), and works cited above in Chap. 12, n. 3.

Chapter 15: Notes

[1] The main literary sources for Rome's relations with the Hellenistic world from 200 to 146 B.C. are the relevant parts of Polybius, xv–xxxix, and of Livy, xxxi–xlv (which depend largely upon Polybius), and Epitome, xlvi–liii (for the years after 167 B.C.); Plutarch, *Flamininus, Cato,* and *Aemilius Paullus*; Appian, *Macedonica*, iv–xix; *Syriaca*, i–viii; Florus, ii. 23–32; Zonaras, ix. 15–31 (representing Dio Cassius, xix–xxi); Pausanias, vii. 11–116 (for the final Achaean War).

General works on the history of the Hellenistic world include *CAH*, vii–ix; W. W. Tarn and G. T. Griffith, *Hellenistic Civilization*[3] (1952); M. Cary, *A History of the Greek World from 323 to 146* B.C.[2] (1951, repr. 1963); E. Will, *Histoire politique du monde hellénistique*, i, *323–223 av. J.-C.* (1966), ii, *223–30 av. J.-C.* (1967); M. Rostovtzeff, *Social and Economic History of the Hellenistic World,* 3 vols (1941). For a good outline of Roman policy towards the Greek world see R. M. Errington, *The Dawn of Empire* (1971), pts 3–4.

On individual states see E. R. Bevan, *The House of Seleucus* (1902); E. R. Bevan, *A History of Egypt under the Ptolemaic Dynasty* (1927); E. V. Hansen, *The Attalids of Pergamum*[2] (1972); P. Fraser, *Alexandria*, 3 vols (1972); P. M. Fraser and G. L. Bean, *The Rhodian Peraea* (1952); H. H. Schmitt, *Rom und Rhodos* (1957).

[2] That Alexander ever contemplated an expedition to Italy and the West (Diodorus, xviii. 4.3) is doubted by many scholars (see W. W. Tarn, *Alexander the Great,* ii. 378 ff.), but we cannot be certain. 'What Alexander's last plans were is irrecoverable', wrote E. Badian, *Harv. Stud. Cl. Ph.* 1967, 204. But Romans of a later age believed in such a project, and Livy was at pains to prove that his compatriots (who at that juncture were being hard put to it to hold the Samnites) would have dealt with Alexander in the same manner as with Pyrrhus (ix. 17).

[3] The story that the Romans sent envoys to Alexander (e.g. Pliny, *Nat. Hist.*, iii. 57) is rightly called into doubt by Arrian (vii. 15.5–6).

[4] On Philip see F. W. Walbank, *Philip V of Macedon* (1940).

[5] Part of the text of the treaty (which is given by Livy, xxvi. 24) was found in 1949 on an inscription in Acarnania. See A. H. McDonald, *JRS* 1956, 153 ff.; E. Badian, *Latomus* 1958, 197 ff.; Walbank, *Polybius*, ii. 162, 179 f.; G. A. Lehmann, *Untersuchungen zur hist. Glaubwürdikeit des Polybios* (1967), more than half of which deals with the treaty.

[6] Livy's view (xxx. 23.5), that a Macedonian corps had fought at Zama on behalf of Hannibal, does not appear in Polybius's more detailed account and is probably the invention of a Roman annalist.

[7] Attalus and Rhodes were technically the aggressors in relation to Philip. Moreover, neither of these powers nor Athens possessed a formal treaty of alliance (*foedus*) with Rome in 200; they were official *amici*. The *ius fetiale*, however, allowed wars only in defence of Rome's oath-bound *socii*. For reasons of expediency the phrase *socius et amicus* may have been used in order to blur awkward distinctions, but the fact remains that Rome was under no *legal* obligation to intervene.

[8] A large modern literature exists on the causes of the war. Here may be mentioned M. Holleaux, *CAH*, viii. 156 ff. (whose view on the importance of the Aetolian appeal is adopted in the text, p. 153: on this appeal cf. Walbank, *Polybius*, ii. 530); A. H. McDonald and F. W. Walbank, *JRS* 1937, 180 ff.; J. P. V. D. Balsdon, *JRS* 1954, 30 ff., who rates the annalistic tradition higher than do many. B. Ferro, *Le origini della II guerra macedoniae* (1960), on which cf. McDonald, *JRS* 1963, 187 ff. F. W. Walbank, *JRS* 1963, 1 ff. who broadly supports Holleaux's position; in an examination of Polybius's attitude to Rome's eastern policy he stresses that the facts given by Polybius do not always square with his interpretation of them which will have been influenced by (*a*) Greek ideas that it was the nature of a sovereign state to expand and (*b*) by Polybius's conception of the dominating role played by Fortune (Tyche) in human affairs. He thus concludes that 'Rome did *not* become the mistress of the universe in fifty-three years as a result of imperial ambitions fostered by the directing hand of Providence. This is an oversimplification'.

Most would agree that Rome was not activated by an aggressive imperialism, territorial or commercial, since after the war she withdrew completely from Greece. However, E. Will, op. cit. n. 1 above, ii. 116 ff., has revived the old idea of personal military ambition and makes Sulpicius Galba the villain, but it may be doubted whether he and his supporters had sufficient *auctoritas* in the Senate or *clientela* in a war-weary Comitia to make both bodies change their minds so radically from a peace- to a war-policy. This is not, of course, to deny that Galba and an 'Eastern lobby' supported an aggressive policy.

Another discredited motive is phil-Hellenism. Though enthusiasm for Greek culture was gaining strength at Rome the hard-headed Romans scarcely acted from an altruistic desire to protect the Greeks because of their cultural past. If, however, self-interest coincided with the ability to appear as the champions of the Greeks, so much the better (see above, p. 153). R. M. Errington (*The Dawn of Empire* (1971), ch. x, and *Athenaeum* 1971) revives the doubtful idea that the Syro-Macedonian pact was a later invention and emphasises some alleged activity of Philip against some Illyrian territory (but these Illyrian places and their status *vis-à-vis* Rome are very uncertain). He also accepts that the Senate sent a naval squadron under Laevinius in 201 to watch the Balkan coast (Livy, xxxi. 3.3) and in general he supposes Senatorial distrust or fear of Philip was the basic cause of the war. The views of Holleaux, however, may still convince many.

[9] On the campaigns of 200–199, as far as they concern the Aoüs valley (Aoi Stena), see N. G. L. Hammond, *JRS* 1966, 39 ff.

[10] The enveloping movement of the Roman right wing at Cynoscephalae was an application of Scipionic tactics (by a veteran of Scipio's army?). Its success was largely due to Philip's weakness in cavalry. Under similar conditions Alexander or Pyrrhus would not have failed to provide a mounted flank-guard for his infantry. For a recent topographical study of the battle see W. K. Pritchett, *Studies in Ancient Greek Topography*, ii (1969), 133 ff.

[11] On the scenes of enthusiasm at the Isthmian Games at Corinth when Flamininus proclaimed the liberty of the Greeks see Plutarch, *Flamininus*, x. He was hailed as Saviour and received homage alongside the gods. He was also granted a priesthood, at which he was linked in a paean with Apollo, and gold coins were struck bearing his portrait (cf. p. 154). On Flamininus's diplomacy, which has been variously interpreted see H. H. Scullard, *Roman Politics, 220–150 B.C.*[2] (1973), index, s. v. Quinctius; J. P. V. D. Balsdon, *Phoenix*, 1967, 177 ff.; E. Badian, *Titus Quinctius Flamininus; Philhellenism and Realpolitik* (1970, University of Cincinnati), two lectures. Few would still regard Flamininus as a sentimental phil-Hellene, though his respect for Greek culture facilitated his dealing with the Greeks. To what extent he was ready to sacrifice principle to personal ambition (e.g. in his talks with Philip at Nicaea or in his interpretation of the Aetolian Treaty) is debatable. Balsdon gives a more favourable picture, Badian a more realistic assessment, reminding us that his diplomatic methods should be judged by contemporary, not modern, standards. For his family and early career see Badian, *JRS* 1971, 102 ff.

[12] On the topography of the battle see W. K. Pritchett, *Studies in Ancient Greek Topography*, i (1965), 71 ff.

[13] The Senate, and Flamininus in particular, probably used the unsuspecting Demetrius as a tool against the Macedonian royal house; if he became king, he would be pliant to Rome's wishes. Livy (lx. 23) reports that, in a letter to Philip, Flamininus charged Demetrius not only with trying to supplant Perseus but also of plotting against Philip himself. It is uncertain whether the letter was a forgery, as Livy says: see Walbank, *Philip V*, 251, Badian, *Foreign Clientelae*, 94. On Perseus see P. Meloni, *Perseo* (1953).

[14] On his journey home Eumenes was nearly killed by a falling rock at Delphi. This was more probably an accident than an attempt by Perseus to murder

him as was alleged. However, this and many other charges against Perseus figured in a letter which was sent by a Roman official to the Amphictyons at Delphi and is recorded in an inscription (Dittenberger, *Sylloge*, 643; Sherk, *Documents*, 40; translation in Lewis and Reinhold, *R. Civ.* i. 184 f.).

[15] On the sharp practice by which the Roman envoy Q. Marcius Philippus tricked Perseus until the Romans were ready to start the campaign of 171 see J. Briscoe, *JRS* 1964, 66 ff. It appears that some of the more old-fashioned senators disapproved such dishonest diplomacy.

[16] The weakness of the Macedonian cavalry was again revealed at Pydna, where the phalanx was once more left without an adequate flank-guard, as at Cynoscephalae. For recent topographical discussion see W. K. Pritchett, *Studies in Greek Topography*, ii (1969), 145 ff.

[17] On Roman action in Epirus see S. I. Oost, *Roman Policy in Epirus* (1954), 68 ff.; N. G. L. Hammond, *Epirus* (1967), 629 ff. On the part played by the Epirote traitor Charops see H. H. Scullard, *JRS*, 1945, 55 ff.

[18] On the four republics see J. A. O. Larsen, *Greek Federal States* (1968), 295 ff. E. Badian (*Foreign Clientelae*, 97) notes that the settlement involved 'for the first time the dissociation of *libertas* and *immunitas*': the states were free but paid taxes.

[19] The formal constitution of Macedonia as a Roman province is attributed by M. G. Morgan, *Historia*, 1969, 422 ff., to Mummius in 146 rather than (as is usual) to Metellus.

[20] On these campaigns see J. J. Wilkes, *Dalmatia* (1969), ch. 3, and for C. Semprinius Tuditanus see M. G. Morgan, *Philologus* 1973, 29 ff.

[21] Polybius, xxiv, 10. The Romans had little experience of arbitration, except in claims for damages between Italian communities, for the settlement of which they usually resorted to mixed commissions of *recuperatores*. On the difference between Greek and Roman methods of arbitration see L. Mathaei, *Cl. Qu.* 1908, 241 f. On Roman arbitration see E. Badian, *Foreign Clientelae* (1958), chs 4, 7.

[22] On the Roman settlement of Greece see J. A. O. Larsen in T. Frank, *Econ SAR*, iv. 306 ff.; S. Accame, *Il dominio romano in Grecia dalla guerra achaica ad Augusto* (1946). The destruction of Corinth should not be attributed to commercial jealousy on the part of Rome any more than the razing of Carthage the same year. The chief gainer by the fall of Corinth was the island of Delos. But this trading-centre did not attract any considerable number of Italian residents until later in the second century. The supposed influence of traders on Roman policy in the second century has been demolished by T. Frank, *Roman Imperialism* (1925); E. Badian, *Roman Imperialism in the Late Republic* (1968), ch. ii. Rostovtzeff, who originally accepted commercial motives, later accepted Frank's view: see *Social and Economic History of the Hellenistic World*, 787 f.

Chapter 16: Notes

[1] On the Roman negotiations with Antiochus see especially E. Badian, *Studies in Greek and Roman History* (1964), 112 ff.

[2] A surviving decree of Lampsacus in honour of its envoy to Rome (Dittenberger, n. 591) illustrates the trepidation with which the Greek city approached the Senate.

[3] Hannibal's war-policy has been defended against that of Antiochus by E. Groag (*Hannibal als Politiker* (1929), ch. vii), who holds that a general coalition of Greek states against Rome should have been formed by Antiochus. But it is most unlikely that Antiochus could have included the king of Macedon in such a coalition, and in any case an invasion of Italy by a Graeco-Punic force would have been no more feasible in the face of the superior Roman fleet than Philip's belated attempted invasion in the First Macedonian War. It is, however, possible that Antiochus encouraged Hannibal to intrigue with Rome's enemies in Carthage, and later in 192 he did allow Hannibal a limited force to operate in the West, but the project was dropped when the king decided to move into Greece.

[4] Livy relates, on the authority of a later Roman annalist, that Scipio Africanus was a member of the embassy to Ephesus and met Hannibal, with whom he exchanged compliments (xxxv. 14.5); Scipio's presence is almost certainly invented. He served on a mission of inquiry to Carthage this year, 193, and he probably went to the eastern Mediterranean; it is just conceivable that he met Hannibal and this, not a fictitious membership of the other commission, was the background to the story of the meeting. In the East Scipio made several dedications at Delos and Delphi. See Scullard, *Scipio Africanus* (1970), 285 f.

[5] The obvious man to face Antiochus and Hannibal was Africanus, but after his consulship of 194 he could not be re-elected for ten years. Hence his brother Lucius became consul, and Africanus served as his legate. For a defence of Lucius Scipio's abilities against the conventional depreciation see J. P. V. D. Balsdon, *Historia* 1972, 224 ff.

[6] At Magnesia Antiochus repeated the mistake which brought about his defeat by Ptolemy IV at the battle of Raphia in 217 (Polybius, v. 84–5).

[7] The gallant stand of Antiochus's phalanx is passed over by Livy (xxxvii. 42), but is duly mentioned by Appian (*Syriaca*, xxxv). Polybius's account of the battle has not survived.

[8] On the territorial limits imposed on Antiochus by land and sea, see A. H. McDonald, *JRS* 1967, 1 ff. (the Taurus frontier to lie along the river Calycadnus in Cilicia Tracheia), and McDonald and Walbank, *JRS* 1969, 30 ff. (naval clauses and types of ships; Antiochus's remaining ships were not to sail west of Cape Sarpedonium). E. Badian (*Foreign Clientelae*, 81 ff.), however, argues against a difference in policy between the Scipios and the Senate ('the spirit of the Scipios' armistice is the same as that of the Senate's peace treaty'), partly because Polybius's account of Scipio's terms is incomplete (xxi. 14.7 f.). We do not, however, know whether Scipio would have approved the sacrifice to Eumenes of

some of the Greek cities in the final settlement: the evidence rather suggests that he would not. We have friendly letters which he addressed to Colophon and Heraclea-by-Latmos (*SEG*, i. 440, ii. 566; Sherk, *Documents*, 36, 35). To Heraclea, which had submitted after Magnesia, and to all other cities which surrendered he promised liberty, autonomy and Rome's goodwill: 'for our part we are well disposed to all Greeks'. Unless this is interpreted as expediency disguised as phil-Hellenism, it suggests at least moderation, if not liberality, on the part of the Scipios. When the Colophonians, once tributary to Attalus, contrast their freedom with the condition of other cities which under the treaty became tributary to Eumenes, they would perhaps have been willing to give the Scipios the benefit of the doubt. If moderate to Greek cities, why should the Scipios not have shown similar moderation to Antiochus: they had no prejudice against kings as such, as shown by their letter to Prusias of Bithynia (Polybius, xxi. 11) and by the personal relations of Africanus and Philip.

[9] The Greek cities fall into three classes: free, Pergamene and Rhodian. There are difficulties, since the accounts of Polybius (xxi. 19–24 and Livy (xxxvii. 52–6) do not quite tally. See E. Bickermann, *Revue des Études grecques* 1937, 217 ff.

[10] On Asia Minor under the Romans see D. Magie, *The Roman Rule in Asia Minor*, 2 vols (1950). For an attempt to relate Rome's eastern policy during 168–146 to groups and individuals in the Senate see J. Briscoe, *Historia* 1969, 49 ff.

[11] Delos had been an independent city until 167. In that year it was placed by the Senate under Athenian administration, but on condition that no customs or harbour dues should be collected.

[12] A surviving Pergamene inscription (Dittenberger, *OGIS*, no 315, 1.52 ff.) shows that a proposed expedition by Attalus II against an unruly Galatian chieftain was abandoned on the advice of a privy councillor, who warned the king that he might offend the Romans by taking independent action.

[13] The genuineness of Attalus's will, which King Mithridates of Pontus later denounced as a forgery (Sallust, *Histories*, fr. 4.69, ed. Maurenbrecher), has been corroborated by a Pergemene inscription (Dittenberger, *OGIS*, no 338) which embodies a Pergamene decree passed before Rome had ratified the will. Another inscription (*OGIS*, no 43, Sherk, *Documents*, 11) embodies a decree of the Senate, probably in 133, about the settlement. A third (Dittenberger, *Sylloge*, 694) records the status of ally of Rome granted to a city (probably Pergamum) for help against the usurper Aristonicus. Translations of these three inscriptions are given in Lewis–Reinhold, *R. Civ.*, i. 321 ff. See also T. Drew-Bear, *Historia* 1972, 75 ff.

[14] The rising of the Pergamene slaves synchronised with the servile war in Sicily (p. 204), and with a rebellion of slaves in the silver mines of Attica. The wave of social unrest of which these movements were symptoms has no visible connexion with the Roman conquests. Aristonicus's communistic ideas will help to explain the readiness with which the neighbouring kings took the field against him. The extent of his early success is doubtful: probably south to Mysia but not Caria, and north to Cyzicus. He issued coins

(*cistophori*) bearing the title 'King', thus asserting his claim to be heir of the Attalids (see E. S. G. Robinson, *Numismatic Chronicle* 1954, 1 ff.). For the scattered sources for the war see Greenidge, Clay, Gray, *Sources for Roman History, 133–70* B.C. (1960).

[15] Demetrius's escape from Rome was abetted by the historian Polybius, who arranged to have him smuggled on board a Carthaginian ship at Ostia which was on its way to Tyre (Polybius, xxxi. 19 ff.).

[16] The treaty with Judaea, which was granted by the Senate but not ratified by the Comitia, never became operative, and its renewal in 139 was a mere matter of form. Doubts about its genuineness, however, are needless: see E. Täubler, *Imperium Romanum*, i. (1913), 240 ff. On the Jews in the Hellenistic period see, for example, E. Schürer, *The History of the Jewish People in the Age of Jesus Christ*, 5 vls, and especially the revised edition of vol. i (covering 175 B.C.–A.D. 135) edited by G. Vermes and F. Millar (1973).

[17] The will of Ptolemy VII was discovered in 1929 at Cyrene. See *SEG*, ix. 7; *JHS* 1933, 263; M. N. Tod, *Greece and Rome* (ii), 1932, 47 ff.

[18] An instruction by a high official of Ptolemy VIII to a district magistrate to 'show every consideration' to a private Roman senator L. Memmius, on tour in Egypt is preserved: Grenfell and Hunt, *Tebtunis Papyri*, i, n. 33 (112 B.C.) = Hunt and Edgar, *Select Papyri* (Loeb Cl. Lib.), ii, n. 416.

Chapter 17: Notes

[1] On alliance, *amicitia* and *clientela* see L. Mathaei, *Cl. Qu.* 1908, 182 ff.; A. Heuss, *Die volkerrechtlichen Grundlagen der römischen Aussenpolitik* (1933); and especially E. Badian, *Foreign Clientelae, 264–70* B.C. (1958), to chs. ii and iii of which the above text owes much. On client-kings see P. C. Sands, *The Client Princes of the Roman Empire* (1908).

[2] T. Frank (*Roman Imperialism*, 146 ff.) argued that the phrase *socius et amicus* was coined in order to disguise the fact that Rome had no formal treaty (*societas*) with these states. But Badian (*For. Cl.* 69, n. 1) suggests that the term is older and that these allies, because they fought by the side of Rome, were *socii* in fact, while legally *amici* because they had no treaty.

[3] On provincial administration see G. H. Stevenson, *Roman Provincial Administration* (1939); E. Badian, *Publicans and Sinners* (1972). This aspect of Roman statecraft is also discussed by T. Frank, *Roman Imperialism*; Lord Cromer, *Ancient and Modern Imperialism*; Lord Bryce, *The Ancient Roman Empire and the British Empire in India*.

[4] Thus the edict which Cicero issued as proconsul of Cilicia embodied detail from the ordinances of Scaevola in Asia (*Ad Atticum*, vi. 1.15). The influence of an eminent governor on Roman administration might be as far-reaching as that of a Lord William Bentinck or a Sir George Grey in the British Empire.

[5] In the days of the Emperor Augustus, Massilia

and its territory still remained outside the jurisdiction of the governor of Narbonese Gaul (Strabo, iv. 181).

⁶ The spheres of competence might vary considerably from province to province. For Sicily see Cicero, *In Verrem*, II. ii. 32; for Cyrene, Augustan edicts (on which see p. 629). During the Republic there is no known case of a Roman citizen being tried on a criminal charge in the provinces; after preliminary investigation the governor presumably remitted the case to Rome later.

⁷ Ordinarily propraetors were attended by one *legatus*, proconsuls by three. Governors who mistrusted their military abilities (e.g. Cicero in Cilicia) would appoint a *praefectus* to command their troops. On the *scribae* etc., see A. H. M. Jones, *JRS* 1949, 38 ff.=*Studies in Roman Government in Law* (1960), 153 ff.

⁸ Special detachments of troops (e.g. Balearic slingers) might also be engaged on a voluntary basis, like Indian Sepoys.

⁹ *In Verrem*, II. iii. 12.

¹⁰ 'II. ii. 7: *quasi* quaedam praedia populi Romani sunt vectigalia nostra atque provinciae'. The theory that Cicero's guarded hint gave rise to an established principle of Roman law has been refuted by A. H. M. Jones, *JRS* 1941, 26 ff. (= *Studies*, 141 ff.). – The doctrine of ownership of soil by right of conquest was an invention of the Hellenistic kings.

¹¹ See the speech of Petilius Cerialis to the Gauls in A.D. 70; Tacitus, *Histories*, iv. 74. I.

¹² In Spain the rate was 2 per cent, in Asia and Gaul 2½ per cent, in Sicily 5 per cent.

¹³ The *lex Hieronica* was set forth at length in the third book of Cicero's *Verrine Orations*, for a commentary on which see Carcopino, *La Loi de Hiéron et les Romains* (1919). Under this law the profits of the tax-contractors were kept within strict limits.

¹⁴ The Asiatic taxes were put up *en bloc* at Rome. Under these conditions the local contractors (who lacked the capital for operations on such a scale) were in effect debarred from competing. In Sicily the tithe of each city was adjudicated locally.

¹⁵ On Roman control of Sicilian corn see R. Scalais, *Musée Belge*, 1924, pp. 143 ff.; V. Scramuzza, in Frank, *Econ. SAR*, iii.

¹⁶ On private, as opposed to State-organised, settlement abroad, see A. J. N. Wilson, *Emigration from Italy in the Republican Age of Rome* (1966).

¹⁷ On the execution of a Roman citizen by crucifixion, a method of punishment usually reserved for slaves, see Cicero, *In Verrem*, II. v. 147–63.

¹⁸ See Badian, *Foreign Clientelae*, ch. vii, on the foreign clients of the Roman nobles.

¹⁹ In 172 the Senate allowed a former consul, named M. Popillius, who had treacherously attacked a Ligurian tribe and made a large haul of prisoners, to elude impeachment before the Tribal Assembly; but it obliged him to release all his captives (Livy, xlii. 22).

²⁰ On the incidents leading up to the constitution of the jury-court for extortion see W. S. Ferguson, *JRS* 1921, 86 ff.; E. S. Gruen, *Roman Politics and the Criminal Courts* (1968), 8 ff.

²¹ The Senate's half-measures for the protection of provincials compare unfavourably with the energetic procedure of the British Parliament in 1783 to prevent a repetition of the abuses by officials of the East India Company which had come to light under the governorship of Warren Hastings.

Chapter 18: Notes

¹ On the Tribal Assembly see L. R. Taylor, *The Voting Districts of the Roman Republic* (1960).

² The date of the reform is uncertain. It may well have been in 241 itself. An inscription from Brundisium (*L'Année Epigraphique* 1954, n. 217) refers to a magistrate who in 230 'primus senatum legit etcomiti (a ordinavit)'. This might refer to the censorship of Q. Fabius Maximus and to the reform of the Comitia. On the other hand the reference may be to a local magistrate at the Latin colony of Brundisium, and therefore irrelevant to Rome.

The reform itself is mentioned by Cicero, *De Re Publica*, ii, Livy (i. 43, 12) and Dionysius (iv. 21, 3), but none of these authors gives a clear description of it. A large modern literature exists on the topic and has been increased by the retrospective evidence provided by the discovery of the Tabula Hebana (p. 629). For general discussion see E. S. Staveley, *Historia* 1956, 112 ff. Either the centuries remained at 193 (as suggested above, p. 176) or else *all* five classes were constituted in seventy centuries (thirty-five *seniores* and thirty-five *iuniores*, correlated to the thirty-five tribes). In the latter case the Comitia would have consisted of 373 centuries (seventy in each of the five classes plus Equites and supernumeraries). But even so it is improbable that they voted in 373 groups: rather (on analogy with what the Tabula Hebana reveals about a later system) there will have been 193 voting-groups, comprising the first class and the 280 centuries of the remaining four classes which for voting purposes were amalgamated in groups of twos or threes. Cf. also Walbank, *Polybius*, i. 683 ff.

E. S. Staveley (*AJ Phil.* 1953, 1 ff.) argues that by the reform the nobles tried to restrict the influence of the wealthy traders who were enrolled in the urban tribes.

³ On the voting power of freedmen see S. Treggiari, *Roman Freedmen during the Late Republic* (1969), 37 ff.

⁴ On the fundamental importance of the decay of the Comitia see W. E. Heitland, *The Roman Fate* (1900).

⁵ In addition the Games were not infrequently prolonged beyond the regular term, on the pretext that some flaw had crept into the performance of the attendant ritual, and that therefore a repetition (*instauratio*) of the entire festival was necessary.

⁶ On the *lex Aelia* and *lex Fufia* see A. E. Astin, *Latomus* 1964, 421 ff.; A. K. Michels, *The Calendar of the Roman Republic* (1967), 94 ff.

⁷ According to P. Willems, *Le Sénat de la république romaine* (1878), i, 308 ff., the Senate of 179 B.C. contained 99 patricians and 216 plebeians.

⁸ On the new *nobilitas* see M. Gelzer's classic little book, now translated by R. Seager, *The Roman Nobility* (1969). The two most notable *novi homines*

were M. Porcius Cato, who probably owed his promotion to the good offices of the nobleman L. Valerius Flaccus, and the two protégés of Scipio Africanus, C. Laelius and M'. Acilius Glabrio.

9 For the ideas and ideals of the nobles see D. Earl, *The Moral and Political Tradition of Rome* (1967); quotation from p. 21.

10 The basis of modern study of this problem arises from the development of M. Gelzer's ideas (see n. 8 above) by F. Münzer in his *Römische Adelsparteien und Adelsfamilien* (1920). For the application of group politics to different periods see F. Cassola, *I gruppi politici romani del iii secolo a.C.* (1962); A. Lippold, *Consules . . . 264 bis 201 v.Chr.* (1963); H. H. Scullard, *Roman Politics, 220–150* B.C.² (1972); E. Badian, *Foreign Clientelae, 264–70* B.C. (1958); E. S. Gruen, *Roman Politics and the Criminal Courts, 149–78* B.C. (1968); L. R. Taylor, *Party Politics in the Age of Caesar* (1949). C. Meier, *Res Publica Amissa* (1966), minimises the existence of any durable groups in the last century B.C. See also a lecture by A. E. Astin, *Politics and Policies in the Roman Republic* (1968), and T. R. S. Broughton in *Aufstieg NRW*. I. i. 250 ff. On *factio* see R. Seager, *JRS* 1972, 55 ff.

11 The details of the 'Scipionic trials' are very obscure. See Scullard, *Roman Politics*, 290 ff., and (more briefly) *Scipio Africanus* (1970), 216 ff. On the control which a general was allowed over the disposal of booty see I. Schatzman, *Historia* 1972, 177 ff.

12 Livy (xxxviii. 56), in a speech which he attributes to the elder Gracchus, records that Scipio rebuked the people for wishing to make him perpetual consul and dictator. Any suggestion that a move was made to convert the Republic into a monarchy must be rejected. The story probably comes from a political pamphlet of the time of Sulla or Julius Caesar, both dictators.

13 In Sicily a second quaestor was appointed in 210 to administer the finances of the former kingdom of Hiero.

14 See A. E. Astin, *The Lex Annalis before Sulla* (1958).

15 In 202 one C. Servilius was nominated dictator for the formal business of holding elections. He attempted to prolong his term of office in defiance of established usage, thereby giving the finishing-stroke to a moribund institution.

16 It has generally been supposed that 153 B.C. was the date when the calendar year also was made to start in January instead of March (that it had originally started in March can be seen from the numbering of the seventh to tenth months as September to December). If true the year 153 would have had strangely world-wide consequences and have fixed Christendom's New Year Day. A. K. Michels (*The Calendar of the Roman Republic* (1967), 97 ff.), however, has suggested with good reason that only the official consular year was changed to January in 153 and that the change in the calendar year (i.e. from a lunar to a lunisolar year, in which an attempt was made to reconcile the solar and lunar years) was made much earlier. (She ascribes the change to the Decemvirate, but it was probably in the regal period.)

17 It would seem that at first the *praetor urbanus* may have retained the middle ground of cases between citizens and *peregrini* which at some time (at latest from Augustus onwards) fell to the *praetor peregrinus*. See. D. Daube, *JRS* 1951, 66 ff.

18 *Ius gentium* did not mean 'international law' (as in the seventeenth century), but it was that part of the revised Roman law which was open to citizens and non-citizens alike. This is the practical significance of the phrase, but it was also used in a wider theoretical sense which corresponded with *ius naturale*, envisaged as an ideal and universally valid set of precepts. See J. K. B. M. Nicholas, *An Introduction to Roman Law* (1962), 54 ff. The *ius gentium* was compounded of Italian rather than Greek or Carthaginian elements.

19 Details of the Leges Porciae are uncertain; see A. H. McDonald, *JRS* 1944, 19 ff., and A. H. M. Jones, *Criminal Courts of the Roman Republic and Principate* (1972), 22 ff. The first of the three laws is commemorated on a coin, a denarius of the end of the second century, issued by a namesake of the proposer of the bill: Sydenham, *CRR*, n. 571.

20 Polybius, vi. 14.7.

21 Additional praetors were made available for judicial work at Rome when the practice of staffing the provinces with ex-magistrates became general (p. 236).

22 On the procedure of the *quaestiones perpetuae* see A. H. J. Greenidge, *The Legal Procedure of Cicero's Time* (1901), 441 ff. The usual number of jurors in these courts was about thirty until 122 B.C., from fifty to seventy after that date.

23 On Roman finances from 200 to 150 see Frank, *Econ. SAR*, i. 109 ff.; *AJ Phil.* 1932, 1 ff.

24 Pliny *NH*, xxxiii, 55.

25 The general incompetence of the quaestors is illustrated by a story of Plutarch (*Cato Minor*, xvi) that Cato the Younger astonished the permanent clerks at the Treasury by his ability to check their operations.

26 Livy, xl. 43.1. Two surviving statutes from the Lucanian town of Bantia (Riccobono, *Fontes*, 82; Warmington, *Remains of Old Latin*, iv. 294) show that Oscan remained the official tongue in the second century, but had given way to Latin by 100 B.C.

27 On Roman policy to the Latins see E. T. Salmon, *JRS* 1936, 47 ff.; A. H. McDonald, *Cambr. Historical Journal* 1938, 125 ff.; *JRS* 1944, 11 ff.; A. J. Toynbee, *Hannibal's Legacy* (1965), ch. iv; A. N. Sherwin-White, *The Roman Citizenship*² (1973), 96 ff.

28 For the text of the *senatus consultum* prohibiting Bacchanalian conventicles, which records the Senate's decision and the consuls' communication of it to the allied local authorities, see Riccobono, *Fontes*, pp. 240 f. The interference of the Senate in this matter may not have been wholly unwelcome to the local governments, as Italy at that time was being agitated by spasmodic servile revolts. See also A. H. McDonald, *JRS* 1944, 26 ff.

29 On discontent and insubordination in the Roman army and the difficulty of levying troops see A. J. Toynbee, *Hannibal's Legacy*, ii. 80 ff.

30 Polybius, vi. 11 ff. On Roman probity see Polybius, vi. 56. On imperial expansion and the decline of the Roman Republic see A. W. Lintott, *Historia* 1972, 626 ff.

Chapter 19: Notes

[1] On agriculture see K. D. White, *Roman Farming* (1970), and, for technical aspects, *Agricultural Implements of the Roman World* (1967); *Farm Equipment of the Roman World* (1975).

[2] A large run of census figures is preserved in Livy and other writers, but the figures in the texts are liable to corruption, and their interpretation is extremely controversial. The numbers probably represent all adult Roman male citizens: this view is maintained in recent discussions by A. J. Toynbee, *Hannibal's Legacy*, i. 438 ff., and Brunt, *Manpower*, ch. ii. The following round figures mark the general rise and fall in the numbers:

234 B.C.	270,000
204	214,000
174	269,000
164	337,000
136	318,000

[3] The avidity with which the new rich at Rome bought up real estate may be compared with the land-hunger of the enriched traders of England in the sixteenth, seventeenth and eighteenth centuries.

[4] Those historians who reject the agrarian clause of the *lex Licinia* of 367 suppose that a law limiting the amount of public land available to each individual was passed later (*c.* 230 or *c.* 185–180), possibly by another Licinius. Livy, however, does not mention any such law. What is important is that in 167 a law existed, since in a speech Cato refers to a legal limit of 500 *iugera* (300 acres): *Oratorum Rom. Fragm.*[2], Malcovati, frg. 167. Discussion by Toynbee, *Hannibal's Legacy*, ii. 554 ff.

[5] *De Re Rustica*, ch. ii *fin.*

[6] The importation of corn from the provinces, especially Sicily and Sardinia, until about 167 and perhaps until 146 probably did not create undue hardship for the competing Italian farmer, since most of it did not reach the home market but was in fact used by the Roman armies fighting abroad. Even after this period its importation to Rome will at most have affected farmers in a very limited area around Rome and perhaps a few coastal towns, but not Italy as a whole to any extent (transport by land was too dear, though cheap by sea). See Frank, *Econ. SAR*, i, 158 ff. In the days of Polybius the price of wheat in Cisalpine Gaul was about one *as* for a *modius* (one peck), whereas the price at Rome was about one denarius, or tenfold (Polybius, ii. 15.1).

[7] Cato's manual passed over corn-growing in silence but dealt at length with the cultivation of vine and olive. The cultivation of cereals and fodder-crops is, however, essential to the system of mixed self-sufficient farming and is therefore taken for granted. On Italian oil and wine merchants at Delos see J. Hatzfeld, *Les Trafiquants italiens dans l'Orient hellénique* (1919), 212 ff. The vintage of 121 (*consule Opimio*) was long remembered for its excellence.

[8] On the meaning of *latifundia* see K. D. White, *Bulletin of the Institute of Classical Studies, London* 1967, 62 ff., where the ancient evidence is set out, and *Roman Farming*, 384 ff.

Both in southern Etruria (around Veii, Sutrium and Capena) and in Apulia (around Luceria) archaeological investigation has shown the survival of small farms during the second century. In southern Etruria, where the work has been done by members of the British School at Rome (see *Papers of BSR* 1958, 1961, 1963, 1968), small farms formed the majority of the sites investigated. Around Luceria air-photography has revealed the remains of olive-trees and trenches for vines on small individual farms, each of some 10 *iugera*, which appear to date to *c.* 120 or a little earlier. Thus they may be connected with the Gracchan settlement which started in 133 B.C. For Luceria see A. J. Toynbee, *Hannibal's Legacy* (1965), ii. 563. For a general survey of the archaeological evidence for agrarian problems of the Gracchan period see M. W. Frederiksen, *Dialoghi di Archeologia*, iv–v (1970–1), 330 ff.

[9] See K. D. White, *Roman Farming* (1970), 350 ff., and ch. xi, for personnel and personnel-management in general.

[10] Recent air-photography and excavation have dramatically revealed farming conditions in Apulia. They show a settlement of land laid out on a grid-system (*centuriatio*) and divided into small units for intensive mixed farming. They can be dated to the Gracchan period (*c.* 120 B.C.) and show that when men were settled at this time there was no question of reverting to the older type of cereal subsistence farming, but the settlers received a cash-crop plantation, each of which was, on a smaller scale, a plantation of the type described by Cato. The pattern of pits dug for olives and vines is clearly revealed and traces of farm-buildings survive. See A. J. Toynbee, *Hannibal's Legacy*, ii. 563 ff., for a summary of G. D. B. Jones's work which will be published later. For photographs see A. H. McDonald, *Republican Rome* (1966), pls 70–3.

Two rustic villas have been excavated near Capua at Villa Francolise, one dating from the end of the second century. Another farmhouse, dating from the late second century, has been excavated at Villa Sambuco near San Giovenale in southern Etruria; see McDonald, pls 67–9 and, for a plan of the Sambuco farm, p. 131.

[11] See Cato, *de Agr.* 22, Varro, 2.8.5. On harness see Lynn White, *Mediaeval Technology* (1962), 57 ff. A. Burford, *Econ. Hist. Rev.* 1960, 1 ff. On the position of craftsmen in general see A. Burford, *Craftsmen in Greek and Roman Society* (1972). Cf. P. A. Brunt, *Social Conflicts in the Roman Republic* (1971), 20 ff., on the economy. The petty scale of Roman industry in the second century is illustrated by the fact that the construction of the Aqua Marcia in 144 had to be parcelled out among 3000 contractors.

[12] According to Livy (xxi. 63.3) C. Flaminius (cf. p. 122 above) alone in the Senate supported this *lex Claudia*: this is probably an exaggeration, since at this period the interests of the senators were far more agrarian than mercantile. On the object behind the bill, which has been variously interpreted, see F. Cassola, *I gruppi politici* (1962), 215 ff.

[13] The only known instance of a 'most-favoured-nation' clause in a Roman treaty is in a compact with the Greek town of Ambracia (187 B.C.), in which it is stipulated that Italian traders shall be exempt

from custom dues (Livy, xxxviii. 44.4). At Delos Italians competed on even terms with Greeks and Orientals.

[14] On the provenance of the 'Italici' at Delos see Hatzfeld, *Bulletin de correspondance hellénique* 1912, 130 ff., and *Les Trafiquants italiens* (1919), See also Toynbee, *Hannibal's Legacy*, ii. 363 ff.

[15] On the organisation of the tax-farming companies see P–W, Supplementband xi, 1203 ff., and E. Badian, *Publicans and Sinners* (1972), esp. ch. iv.

[16] Roman money-lenders had circumvented the fourth-century legislation against usury by making their loans in the name of Italians from allied cities. But a supplementary statute of 193 brought these men-of-straw under the scope of the Roman law (Livy, xxxv. 7.2–5).

[17] On the extent of the tax contracts of the *publicani* see Polybius, vi. 17 (cf. Walbank, *Polybius*, i. 692 ff.). At 17.3 Polybius says that 'nearly everyone' had an interest in state contracts. In his later life even Cato went so far as to lend money in small amounts for shipping enterprises (Plutarch, *Cato Maior*, xxi). With this sudden craze for financial speculation we may compare the speculative fever which swept over Britain in the early eighteenth century.

[18] On the technique of ancient banking see P–W, Supplementband, s.v. Banken and Giroverkehr.

[19] On the Equites see H. Hill, *The Roman Middle Class* (1952); a lengthy work by C. Nicolet, *L'Ordre équestre à l'époque républicaine*, ii, 1966–75; a valuable paper by P. A. Brunt in *The Crisis of the Roman Republic* (ed. R. Seager, 1969), 83 ff.; and E. Badian, *Publicans and Sinners* (1972) and (briefly) *OCD²*, s.v. Equites.

[20] In 225 B.C. the number of citizens enrolled on the census-lists as available for mounted service was 23,000 according to Polybius, ii. 24.14.

[21] On the impact of Greek civilisation on Rome and the fluctuations of Roman opinion on Hellenic culture see especially G. Colin, *Rome et la Grèce de 200 à 146 av. J.-C.* (1905).

[22] On slavery in general see W. L. Westermann, *The Slave Systems of Greek and Roman Antiquity* (1955), and cf. P. A. Brunt, *JRS*, 1958 164 ff.; *Slavery in Classical Antiquity* (ed. M. I. Finley, 1960, with bibliography); and on domestic slavery at Rome (later) R. H. Barrow, *Slavery in the Roman Empire* (1928), ch. ii.

It may be assumed that Sp. Carvilius, an ex-slave who was believed to have set up the first school at Rome *c.* 250 B.C. (Plutarch, *Quaestiones Romanae*, lix), was a Greek who first introduced the Hellenic tongue into Roman schools (since these institutions were much older).

[23] On the Porticus Aemilia see Boëthius–Ward-Perkins, *Etruscan and Roman Architecture* (1970), 107: photographs, Nash, *Pict. Dict. Anc. Rome*, ii. 238 ff.

[24] On early Roman literature see especially J. W. Duff, *A Literary History of Rome from the Origins to the Close of the Golden Age³* (1950). For texts and translation of the early poets see E. H. Warmington, *Remains of Old Latin*, i–iii (1935–8). On Ennius see *Ennius, Entretiens Hardt*, xvii (1971), especially ch.

iv by E. Badian, who discusses the traditions about the poet's friends in Rome. On Lucilius see J. Christes and W. A. Krenkel, *Aufstieg NRW*, I. ii. 1182 ff. and 1240 ff.

[25] For examples of such transcripts see Riccobono, *Fontes*, 242 ff., 257 ff., etc; Sherk, *Documents*.

[26] On the early historians see literature quoted above, Chap. 6, n. 17. On Fabius Pictor see also D. Timpe, *Aufstieg NRW*, I. ii. 928 ff.

[27] Coelius was probably a chief source of Livy for the early and middle of the Second Punic War, as Polybius was for its closing campaigns.

[28] In 167 a Roman holiday-crowd gave signs of blank dismay when an imported Greek orchestra inflicted 'classical' music upon it, and of boundless delight when the players, realising their mistake, treated it to some uproarious 'pop' (Polybius, xxx. 13).

[29] On the influence of the Stoic creed upon the Romans see E. V. Arnold, *Roman Stoicism* (1900). Cf. F. H. Sandbach, *The Stoics* (1975).

[30] For books on Roman religion see above, Chap 5, n. 10, and for religion at this period see Toynbee, *Hannibal's Legacy*, ii, ch. xii.

[31] A persistent worshipper might obtain permission from the praetor in Rome who would seek the Senate's sanction that not more than five persons might celebrate the cult together; death was the penalty for infraction. On the conspiracy see A. H. McDonald, *JRS* 1944, 26 ff. For the *senatus consultum de Bacchanalibus* see Riccobono, *Fontes*, 240 ff.

[32] The skill with which the Roman aristocracy exploited religion as a means of 'keeping the lower orders in their place' is commented on by Polybius (vi. 56.7–11).

[33] For the tenacity with which the Romans retained their fundamental Italian characteristics, while they assimilated many elements of Greek culture, we may compare the attitude of modern Japan to European civilisation.

Chapter 20: Notes

[1] The main sources on the Gracchi are Plutarch's *Lives* and Appian's *Civil War,* bk i. The most important passages from these two writers and from other sources are usefully collected for the period 133–70 B.C. in A. H. J. Greenidge, A. M. Clay and E. W. Gray, *Sources for Roman History 133–70* B.C. (2nd edn, 1960).

Modern works on the Gracchi: *CAH*, ix, chs i and ii, by H. Last are still fundamental. *Autour des Gracques* (1928, 2nd edn 1967), by J. Carcopino, comprises stimulating and ingenious essays. H. C. Boren, *The Gracchi* (1968), is a general sketch. On Tiberius see D. C. Earl, *Tiberius Gracchus* (1963), A. E. Astin, *Scipio Aemilianus* (1967), esp. pp. 190–226 and E. Badian, *Aufstieg NRW*, I. i (1972), 668 ff. J. M. Riddle, *Tiberius Gracchus* (1970), is largely a collection of sources and modern interpretations, as is C. Nicolet, *Les Gracques* (1968). On recent work on the period from the Gracchi to Sulla see E. Badian, *Historia* 1962, 197 ff. (= Seager, *Crisis of Roman Republic* (1969), 3 ff.). On Cicero's views of the Gracchi see J. Béranger, *Aufstieg NRW*, I. i. 732 ff. On Tiberius

Gracchus's political supporters and opponents see J. Briscoe, *JRS* 1974, 125 ff. On the economic motives in opposition to Gracchus's agrarian law see E. Gabba in *Polis and Imperium* (ed. J. A. S. Evans, 1974), 129 ff.

² The Sicilian slave revolt is described by Diodorus (xxxix. 1–12), depending on Poseidonius: a graphic account. Cf. P. Green, *Past and Present* 1961, 10 ff. (= *The Shadow of the Parthenon* (1972), 193 ff.); W. Forrest, ibid. 1962, 87 ff.; M. I. Finley, *Ancient Sicily* (1968), 137 ff. The leader Eunus, who called himself King Antiochus and issued small coins as a Hellenistic ruler, had recourse to the tricks of the medicine-man to impose his authority. But he chose his lieutenants well, and he had the good sense to prohibit indiscriminate reprisals upon the free population. He and his fellow slaves were not seeking an ideological social revolution, but freedom and revenge on their owners.

³ Inscribed sling-bullets, bearing the name of Piso, the consul of 133 who was sent against the slaves, have been found. P. Rupilius, who finally stamped out the insurrection, issued a new definite charter for the province of Sicily. In connexion with the slave-rising, a new military road was made from the Strait of Messina to Capua, either by P. Popillius, the consul of 132, or by an Annius (praetor 131?). A headless inscription, describing this (Dessau, *ILS*, 23; Degrassi, *ILLRP*, 454), has provoked much discussion, most recently by T. P. Wiseman, *PBSR* 1969, 82 ff.

⁴ Our best tradition concerning the Gracchi is emphatic in stating that Tiberius's main concern was to repeople Italy with a healthy peasant stock, which he regarded as indispensable to Rome's military ascendancy (Appian, *Bellum Civile* i. 7–11; Plutarch, *Tib. Gracchus*, viii). Further discussion in works cited in n. 1 above; for varying views see especially Riddle's useful little book.

⁵ The additional grant was perhaps made for children rather than (as on the traditional interpretation of the evidence) for the sons: see E. Badian, *Aufstieg NRW*, I. i. 702 ff. Possibly some grazing privileges were also included. That the allotments were standardised at 30 iugera (*c*. 18 acres) each is an unwarranted inference from a mutilated paragraph in the agrarian law of 111 (see Riccobono, *Fontes*, n. 8, pp. 102 ff., and below, p. 612); they are more likely to have averaged some 10 iugera each with perhaps a legal maximum of 30. Despite some ambiguity, it is almost certain that only Roman citizens received the new allotment: Italian allies, however, who held *ager publicus* in excess of the legal limit of 500 iugera will have had to surrender the excess in the same way as Roman citizens. The fertile *ager Campanus* around Naples, which provided the Treasury with good rentals, was exempted from the scope of the bill.

⁶ On Laelius's proposal see Plutarch, *Tib. Gracchus*, 8.4. Cf. H. H. Scullard, *JRS*, 1960, 62 ff.; A. E. Astin, *Scipio Aemilianus*, 307 ff. Both date and content are uncertain.

⁷ In 167 a bellicose praetor, M'. Iuventius Thalna, summoned the Comitia Centuriata, in order to obtain a declaration of war against the Rhodians without consulting the Senate. On this occasion a veto by two tribunes (acting no doubt on the Senate's instruc-

tions) checkmated the refractory magistrate (Livy, xlv. 21). However, a tribunician veto against another tribune's proposal was unusual and thus such action by Octavius may have come as an unwelcome surprise to Tiberius. See E. Badian, *Aufstieg NRW*, I. i. 697 ff.

⁸ Plutarch (*Tib. Gracchus*, 10) says that Tiberius redrafted the bill in a more drastic form and declared a *iustitium*, a cessation of public business. Tiberius possibly proposed that the land retained by the *possessores* should not become their *ager privatus* but should remain *ager publicus* though still without rent. He may have managed by veto to check public business, but probably not by a complete *iustitium*.

⁹ In 136 the Senate deprived M. Aemilius Lepidus of his command in Spain, but Lepidus was no longer consul (as Appian, *Iberica*, 83, wrongly says; cf. Livy, *Periocha* 56), but only proconsul, which was not considered a formal magistracy.

¹⁰ The *triumviri agris iudicandis adsignandis* were probably eligible for annual re-election; in fact they changed only when vacancies were caused by death. See J. Carcopino, *Autour des Graccques* (1928, 2nd edn 1967), 149 ff.

¹¹ Whether Tiberius introduced a law (Plutarch, *Tib. Gracchus*, 14) or only threatened one (Livy, *Per.* 58), he achieved his object.

¹² The details of Tiberius's alleged programme of reform for 132, which included a judicial law, an Italian franchise law, and a measure to alleviate military service, bear a suspicious resemblance to the actual legislation of his brother Gaius ten years later, from which most items were probably borrowed. The military bill may possibly have been in Tiberius's programme. If (which is unlikely) there is any truth in the tradition (Dio Cassius, frag. 83.7 f.) that his brother Gaius was also a candidate for the tribunate and that his father-in-law Appius Claudius (already consul in 143) intended to stand again for 132, Tiberius's attempt to prolong his own office will have seemed more threatening to his opponents (from whose propaganda the story may have originated).

¹³ Nevertheless Scipio Nasica had held a second consulship within ten years in 155, as did Scipio Aemilianus in 134.

¹⁴ Nine boundary-stones (*cippi*) established by the commissioners survive (Degrassi, *ILLRP*, 269 ff.). The subject of the acephalous inscription, quoted in n. 3 above, boasted that he made the *pastores* give place to the *aratores* on the *ager publicus*. This is generally linked to the work of the Gracchan commissioners (though other interpretations are possible: see Astin, *Scipio Aemilianus*, 354). The agent may have been an Annius but perhaps was Popillius, who will then have issued an edict warning obdurate tenants not to resist the land-commissioners.

On the contribution of archaeology to the agrarian problem in the Gracchan period see M. T. Frederiksen, *Dialoghi di Archaeologia*, iv–v (1970/1), 330 ff. For the view that the effective working of the reform was brief see J. Molthagen, *Historia* 1973, 423 ff.

¹⁵ Where land originally taken by Rome from a conquered ally in the old days ran alongside land retained by the ally, cases of dispute might easily arise. It is not likely that the commissioners were concerned with *ager publicus* which had been granted

to Latin communities as corporations, with the leases guaranteed by treaty (but cf. Cary, *Hist.* 286).

[16] Scipio's precise action is not made clear by Appian (*Bell. Civ.* i. 19.2). It probably did not hamper the continuing distribution of land taken from Roman citizens. Cf. Last, *CAH*, ix. 42 ff.; F. B. Marsh, *Hist. of Rom. World, 146–31* B.C. (3rd edn 1962), 409.

[17] On the census figures see Chap. 19, n. 2. A. H. M. Jones (*Ancient Economic History*, 6 ff.), though doubtful about the reliability of some of the figures for demographic purposes, accepts the rise in 125 as the result of Tiberius's land-bill. Alternatively, the rise has been attributed to the censors of 125 having generously enrolled a number of Italians (cf. Cary, *Hist.* 289, 295 n. 15), but see P. Fraccaro, *Opuscula*, ii. 87 ff. Brunt, *Manpower*, 78 ff., connects the rise in 125/4 with the Gracchan distributions.

It was perhaps at this time (or under the impulse of Gaius Gracchus) that Roman citizenship was conferred on those men who held office in a Latin colony. This 'ius adipiscendi civitatem Romanam per magistratum' will have replaced the right 'per migrationem' (p. 184). This measure would strengthen the loyalty of the local governing class to Rome.

[18] On Scipio's death see J. Carcopino, *Autour des Gracques*[2] (1967), ch. iii.

[19] On the date of Pennus's tribunate see E. Badian, *Foreign Clientelae*, 177.

[20] The chronology of Gaius's legislation cannot be determined exactly. Probably the greater number of his measures fell into the second half of 123, but the final bill for the enfranchisement of the Italians (and perhaps the *lex Rubria* for Junonia) belongs to 122. P. A. Brunt, however, would place the majority of measures in 123 (= Seager, *Crisis of Rom. Rep.* pp. 112 f.). For the view that Gaius proceeded cautiously and that his earlier proposals were less radical than the later see H. Last, *CAH*, ix. 49 ff. See also E. Badian, *Foreign Clientelae*, 299 ff.

[21] A plague of locusts which visited Africa shortly before 123 (Livy, *Per.* lx) no doubt had its effect on prices at Rome.

[22] For the interpretation of this law suggested in the text see N. J. Miners, *Cl. Qu.* 1958, 241 ff., and U. Ewins, *JRS* 1960, 94 ff. The more usual interpretation has been to regard the law as one against judicial corruption, making bribery of jurors a criminal offence and applying only to senators and not to Equites because it was passed before the court was transferred to the Equites.

[23] A surviving judicial law, evidently of the late second century, probably preserves part of the text of Gaius's measure (Riccobono, *Fontes*, n. 7, pp. 84 ff.; translation and commentary in E. G. Hardy, *Roman Laws and Charters*, pp. 1 ff.). The resemblance between several paragraphs of this law and some details of a *lex Acilia* mentioned in the Scholia to Cicero (*Verr.* II. i, 26), renders it likely that the two are identical; if so, Gaius carried his chief judicial act in the name of another tribune. For a summary of recent views see Scullard, *From the Gracchi to Nero* (3rd edn 1970), 393 ff. See also A. N. Sherwin-White, *JRS* 1972, 83 ff., and M. T. Griffin, *Cl. Qu.* 1973, 108 ff.

On the procedure and sphere of competence of the court *de rebus repetundis* under the later Republic see A. N. Sherwin-White, *PBSR*, 1949, 5 ff., and *JRS* 1952, 43 ff., and A. H. M. Jones, *The Criminal Courts of the Roman Republic and Principate* (1972), ch. 2.

[24] The jurors were probably not drawn exclusively from the eighteen Equitum Centuriae, but from all the Equites in the wider sense; they were probably defined in the law as those possessing a fixed census of not less than 400,000 sesterces.

[25] Many passages (e.g. Velleius, ii. 6.3; Tacitus, *Ann.* xii. 60; Appian, *Bell. Civ.* 1.22) make it certain that in its final form Gaius's *lex iudiciaria* transferred the court from senators to Equites. According to Plutarch, however (*Gaius Gracchus*, 5), Gaius made up a mixed panel of 600 jurors, drawn in equal proportions from the Senate and Equites, while according to Livy (*Epit.* lx) he enrolled 600 Equites into the Senate, as an addition to the existing 300 members. These statements may represent mere misconceptions, but more probably reflect projects which Gaius never carried into law or were soon replaced by his final bill. Thus the membership of the Senate was not enlarged at this time, and the net effect of the bill was to give the equites control of the jury-court.

[26] Our sources are not clear as to the terms of the franchise act (nor whether Gaius tried to tackle the problem in two stages), but they agree that the Latins were to receive full citizenship.

[27] A large area in north-eastern Tunisia retains traces of the division of the land into units (*centuriae*) of 200 *iugera* each; part of this may represent allotments at Junonia; see J. Bradford, *Ancient Landscapes* (1957), 197 ff.; R. Chevallier, *Mélanges d'Arch.* 1958, 61 ff.

[28] The catchwords Optimates and Populares do not denote a Senatorial Party *vis-à-vis* a Democratic or Reform Party. In fact both groups were members of the same class; the difference lay primarily in themethods they adopted. But if the Populares all used similar tactics, they often varied in motive: some, as the Gracchi, were altruistic reformers, others self-seeking ambitious politicians. Before very long the situation was further complicated by the role that the army leader began to play in politics. On Cicero's use of *popularis* see R. Seager, *Cl. Qu.* 1972, 328 ff.

[29] On the Roman campaigns in the south of France, many of the details of which are uncertain, see C. Jullian, *Histoire de la Gaule*, III. 1 ff. Cf. also C. H. Benedict, 'The Romans in Southern Gaul', *AJ Phil.* 1942, 38 ff., and *A History of Narbo* (1941), ch. i.

[30] The date of the formal creation of the new province (when a Roman magistrate was regularly each year sent to administer it) is uncertain. It is generally assigned to the period of Domitius, but E. Badian (*Foreign Clientelae*, 264, n. 3, and 287 f., and more fully in *Mélanges Piganiol* (1966), 901 ff.) would date this formal organisation near the end of the century after Marius's victories over the Germans.

The earliest-known Latin inscription from Gaul is a milestone on the Via Domitia: 'Cn. Domitius Cn. f. Ahenobarbus imperator XX' (Degrassi, *ILLRP*, n. 460a: Greenidge and Clay, *Sources*[2], 49).

Velleius (i. 15.5) dates the foundation of Narbo in 118. Some coins (Sydenham, *CRR* 520, Crawford, *RRC*, 282/4) have been linked with its foundation; they depict Bituitus in a chariot and were issued by the *duoviri* appointed to found the colony, namely L. Crassus and the son of Cn. Domitius. On the assumption that they were issued at the time of the foundation and that their date is slightly later than 118 (i.e. 115/14), attempts have been made to lower the foundation date by a few years (cf. H. B. Mattingly, *Hommages à A. Grenier* (1962), iii, 1159 f.; *Num. Chron.* 1969, 95 ff.). M. Crawford (*Rom. Rep. Coin Hoards*, 5), however, prefers 118, while B. Levick (*Cl. Qu.* 1971, 170 ff.) argues for 118 as the foundation date, although allowing that the coins might be a commemorative issue of 114/13.

[31] The reduction of the Balearic Islands was doubtless undertaken to protect the sea-routes to Spain and also in connexion with the concurrent campaigns in southern Gaul. For Roman motives see M. G. Morgan, *Californian Studies in Classical Antiquity*, ii, 1969, 217 ff., who argues, on the evidence of the Livian tradition and Strabo, that there had been a recent influx of pirates (from Sardinia and Gaul) into the islands.

Chapter 21: Notes

[1] The main ancient sources for 120–100 B.C. are the same as those for the Gracchi, on which see above, Chap. 20, n. 1. Appian's narrative (*Bell. Civ.* l. 27–32) is very brief. Plutarch's *Life of Marius* and part of *Sulla* are valuable; for Marius's northern campaigns Plutarch drew on Poseidonius. For the African campaign the chief source is Sallust: see below, n. 8. Inscriptions and coins become increasingly useful sources.

The validity of Opimius's action was long debated in the later Roman rhetorical schools; the issues are given in Cicero, *de orat.* ii. 132, *part. orat.* 104. A distinction must be drawn between men still under arms against the State and those who had surrendered, in this case between the Gracchans still fighting on the Aventine and those later hauled before Opimius's assize. The former might well be dealt with summarily, but the latter, as Roman citizens, surely still had the right of appeal against any death sentence. For discussion of the *senatus consultum ultimum* see H. Last, *CAH*, ix, 85 ff.; A. W. Lintott, *Violence in Republican Rome* (1968), 149 ff. On Opimius's prosecutor, P. Decius Subulo, see E. Badian, *JRS*, 1956, 91 ff.

[2] Narbo had good agricultural land for colonists and good commercial possibilities as a focus of trade from southern Gaul and Spain as well as being at the head of a trade-route to the Atlantic and the tin of Britain. Thus it is widely believed that Equestrian interests (in line with the policy of Gaius Gracchus) stimulated the request for its foundation. Thus co-operation between the Equites and a group of senators may be suspected. Equestrian interests, however, are denied by some (e.g. P. A. Brunt, in Seager, *Crisis of Rom. Rep.* 97; E. Badian, *Rom. Imperialism*[2], 24),

who stress the *popular* interest, while some senators will have valued its strategic and protective value against Gallic aggression. The speech of Crassus, who was one of the founders, may in fact have been against a later move to dissolve the colony: cf. Badian, op. cit. 98.

[3] Three agrarian laws are described by Appian, *Bell. Civ.* i. 27, while part of the third, probably a *lex Thoria*, is preserved on a bronze tablet (which contains the *lex Acilia* on the other side: see p. 611). There are considerable difficulties in precisely identifying these laws: see a discussion by E. Badian, *Historia* 1962, 209 ff. (= Seager, *Crisis of Rom. Rep.* 15 ff.), though his conclusions are not necessarily all acceptable. For the inscription of 111 see E. G. Hardy, *Six Roman Laws*, 35 ff.; Riccobono, *Fontes*, n. 8, pp. 102 ff.; K. Johannsen, *Die lex agraria des Jahres III. v. Chr.* (Munich, 1971).

[4] On the Metelli and their political fortunes see E. S. Gruen, *Roman Politics and the Criminal Courts, 149–78 B.C.* (1968), ch. iv. On Aemilius Scaurus see G. Bloch, *Mélanges d'histoire anc.* 1909: P. Fraccaro, *Opuscula*, II (1957), 125 ff. As censor in 114 Scaurus struck no less than thirty-five senators off the roll, an exceptionally high number.

[5] On Marius see A. Passerini's articles in *Athenaeum* 1934, now reprinted as *Studi su Caio Mario* (1971); T. F. Carney, *A Biography of C. Marius* (suppl. n. 1 of *Proceedings of African Class. Assoc.* 1962); J. Van Ooteghem, *Gaius Marius* (Brussels, 1964); E. Badian, *Durham Univ. Journal* 1964, 141 ff.; Gruen, op. cit., in n. 4 above, *passim*. Marius's voting reform was to make narrower the 'bridges' (*pontes*) over which voters passed to record their votes; in this way they could be watched more carefully from the magistrate's tribunal. For the suggestion that Marius was acting in the interests of his patrons, the Metelli, see P. Bicknell, *Latomus* 1969, 327 ff. On the period of Marius and Sulla see the observations of E. Gabba, *Aufstieg NRW*, I. i. 764 ff.

[6] The transfer of Phrygian territory to Mithridates V by M'. Aquilius had never received formal confirmation from the Senate, which suspected its agent of mercenary motives in making this award; but it was not definitely repudiated until the accession of Mithridates VI.

[7] Part of the law is preserved in a Greek inscription from Delphi (text in Riccobono, *Fontes*, 121 ff.; translation of part in Lewis–Reinhold, *R. Civ.* i. 323 f.). It was probably passed in Dec. 101, and provided for a general mobilisation of Roman forces and a levy of contingents from dependent kings and city-states; all harbours of the Empire and of allied states were to be closed to pirates. See also p. 614. A second copy of what is almost certainly the same law has now been found at Cnidus: for text and discussion see M. Hassall *et al.*, *JRS* 1974, 195 ff.

King Nicomedes II of Bithynia was reported to have refused military aids to Marius in the Cimbric War on the ground that most of his subjects had been abducted by Roman money-lenders (Diodorus, xxxvi. 3.1). Presumably the *publicani* also took a hand in the Asia Minor slave-trade (cf. M. Rostovtzeff, *Social and Econ. Hist. of the Hellenistic World* (1941), ii. 828).

[8] Sallust's *Bellum Iugurthinum,* our chief source for the war, is more of a political pamphlet than a military history. Sallust, a supporter of Julius Caesar and the Populares, wanted to expose the corruption of the Optimates. Thus the virtues of Marius, a *novus homo* and Popularis, are contrasted with the corruption of the older nobility. Not all Sallust's charges of corruption against the nobles should be accepted.

On Sallust see D. C. Earl, *The Political Thought of Sallust* (1961), esp. ch. v; R. Syme, *Sallust* (1964), chs x and xi. For political repercussions cf. E. S. Gruen, *Roman Politics . . . 149–78* B.C. (1968), ch. v.

On the strategy and chronology of the war see M. Holroyd, *JRS* 1928, 1 ff.

[9] Before taking armed intervention against Jugurtha the Senate had tried a traditional policy of maintaining a balance of power by diplomatic pressure on client-kings; thus not all negotiations may have had a background of bribery as Sallust insinuates. Pressure for war gradually mounted, and it came in 111; then, after two years of inefficient fighting, pressure again mounted for an efficient general, to which Metellus was the answer. In the later phases this pressure against the Senate's handling of affairs clearly came from the Equites and people. Some historians (especially G. De Sanctis, *Problemi di storia antica* 187 ff.) have made the Equites the instigators from the beginning, but although clearly they will have been angered by the massacre of their friends at the fall of Cirta, the pressure they exerted on senatorial policy-making may have been only gradual. In any case they did not want war in order that Rome might gain more territory in Africa; what they needed was peace and order to promote their commercial interests.

[10] The fall of Cirta is not mentioned by Sallust, a bad omission in his sketchy and uneven narrative; but its capture at this stage of the war is a necessary inference from the later course of the campaigns. The identification of the Muthul is uncertain.

[11] See Brunt, *Manpower,* 402 ff. On the army in the later Republic see R. E. Smith, *Service in the Post-Marian Army* (1958), and J. Harmand, *L'Armée et le soldat à Rome de 107 à 50 avant notre ère* (1967). On some aspects of war in general see *Problèmes de la guerre à Rome,* by J. P. Briscon (1969). See also E. Gabba, *Esercito e società nella tarda repubblica romana* 1973.

[12] Sulla's perilous journey to the camp of Bocchus, and his game of diamond-cut-diamond with this wily monarch, are excellently described in the closing chapters of the *Bellum Iugurthinum* (chs cii–cxiii). Sulla, much to the annoyance of Marius, had a seal-ring which depicted Bocchus kneeling before him with the captive Jugurtha. This scene was also shown on a coin issued by Sulla's son, Faustus, when mint-master *c.* 63 B.C.: see Sydenham, *CRR,* 979; Crawford, *RRC,* 426/1; and p. 216.

[13] The Germanic origin of the Cimbri and Teutones is now generally accepted, despite the claim of Celtic affinities (some Celtic elements may of course have joined them in their wanderings).

[14] The peregrinations of the Northmen along the Rhine and Danube are marked by hoards of curiously mixed coins, which no doubt represent the leavings of their war-spoils from different countries: see R. Forrer, *Keltische Numismatik der Rhein und Donaulandes,* 316 ff.

[15] From the fact that Silanus was afterwards subjected to an unsuccessful prosecution for engaging the Cimbri *inissu populi* (Asconius, 80, Clark, 121) it does not follow that he made an unprovoked attack on them. From Florus (i. 38) it appears that the Cimbri assumed the offensive against him.

[16] The reading by F. Stahelin (*Die Schweiz in römischer Zeit²* (1931), 49) in Livy, *Epitome,* lxv, of 'in finibus Nitobrigum' for 'Allobrogum' may be accepted.

[17] Traces of the *Fossa Mariana,* which ran from Fos to Arles, have been found by underwater exploration: see P. Diole, *4000 Years under the Sea* (1954), ch. 5.

[18] A carefully planned co-ordinated three-pronged attack by the Germans is rejected as too far-sighted by E. Badian (*Historia* 1962, 217, = Seager, *Crisis of Rom. Rep.* 23). In any case the Senate had to plan to meet a triple advance.

[19] The lengthy account of the battle of Aquae Sextiae in Plutarch (*Marius,* xvii–xxi) is too incoherent to admit of systematic reconstruction. Cf. A. Donnadieu, *Revue des Études anciennes* 1954, 281 ff.

[20] Vercellae was a common Celtic place-name and the battle was probably fought near Ferrara or Rovigo: see J. Zennari, *I Vercelli dei Celti* (1956). No reliance can be put in Orosius's figure (v. 16.21) of nearly half a million German casualties (including women and children). The fact that Marius engaged the Cimbri on an open plain suggests that they did not greatly outnumber his force of 55,000 men.

[21] Marius invented a wooden rivet for the *pilum* to fasten the metal head to the wooden shaft; this rivet broke on impact and thus the enemy could not throw the *pilum* back. Cf. T. F. Carney, *Cl. Qu.* 1955, 203 ff.

[22] With this consul of 97 B.C. we may identify the 'Publius Crassus' who explored the open-sea route across the Bay of Biscay to the Cornish tin-mines (Strabo, iii. 106).

[23] The Livian tradition that the court was shared between Equites and senators is probably to be preferred to the view of Tacitus (*Ann.* xii. 60.4) that Caepio's bill restored the *quaestio* to the Senate. If other *iudicia publica,* beside the *de repetundis,* had been established at this time, they were probably included in the bill. For this measure and that of Glaucia (see especially J. P. V. D. Balsdon, *PBSR* 1938, 98 ff.=Seager, *Crisis Rom. Rep.* 132 ff.).

[24] Glaucia's law, probably of 104 (possibly 101 or even 100), also introduced some procedural improvements. It established *comperindinatio,* a system by which a trial was divided into two separate parts, and it made accessories to a crime liable to prosecution.

[25] Details are obscure. Cf. E. S. Gruen, *Roman Politics . . . 146–78* B.C., 162 ff.

[26] A fragment of Roman law, found at Bantia in southern Italy (Riccobono, *Fontes,* p. 82), has been identified with Saturninus's *lex Appuleia de maiestate* (cf. Stuart Jones, *JRS* 1926), but this is not certain. On *maiestas* see R. A. Bauman, *The Crimen Maiestatis in the Roman Republic and Augustan Principate*

(1967), who argues for an earlier possible use of the crime *maiestas* by tribunes.

[27] There is some uncertainty about the date of some of Saturninus's measures, whether they belong to his first or second tribunate (103 or 100).

On the price of the corn H. Last (*CAH*, ix. 165, n. 1) suggests that it was $5\frac{1}{3}$ *asses* (*senis et trientibus*), not the derisory sum of $\frac{5}{6}$ *as* (*semissibus et trientibus*) a peck. On the dating of a corn-law carried by a certain M. Octavius see J. G. Schovanek, *Historia* 1972, 235 ff.

[28] Details and chronology of Saturninus's laws on allotments and colonies are not always clear. The colonies also included one on Cercina, an island off the coast of north Africa, and probably one in Corsica. Inscriptions show that the African settlements were widespread. Some were apparently in Numidia (unless the Roman province of Africa was extended after the defeat of Jugurtha). This creates difficulties: thus Brunt, *Manpower* 577 ff., has revived the view of Gsell that the Marian settlers in Africa (though not those at Cercina) were not Marius's veterans but Gaetulians, to whom he is known to have granted lands (*Bellum Africum*, 56.4). A special commission of ten men was set up to supervise the land-settlements and perhaps for the colonies as well (one member was the father of Julius Caesar).

[29] For the pirate law see above, pp. 213 and 612. It has been suggested that its real purpose was to provide Marius with a new military command, and that Saturninus may have been its instigator (cf. J. Carcopino, *Mélanges Glotz*, i. 119 ff.). But there are difficulties in the way of this more sinister interpretation.

[30] This oath of obedience, *sanctio*, which is also found in the pirate law, may not, as sometimes thought, have been a distinctive feature of Saturninus's legislation. When Marius, after some demurring, took the oath (subject to the validity of the law) all the other senators followed suit, except Metellus Numidicus, who preferred exile.

[31] According to Cicero (*pro Balbo*, 48) Marius was given the right to grant Roman citizenship to three men in each colony (the reading 'ternos' has been questioned): thus the colonists were allies not Roman citizens.

[32] Saturninus's legislation of 100 was either abandoned or limited, but there is some doubt as to whether it was formally declared invalid by the Senate on the ground that it had been carried by force (*per vim*). See A. W. Lintott, *Violence in Republican Rome* (1968), 152 ff.

In 100 a colony (probably Roman) was founded at Eporedia (Ivrea) south of Aosta in the foothills of the Alps (Velleius Paterculus, l. 15.5). It is possible that the Senate authorised this settlement by way of compensation for the dropping of Saturninus's plans. Its purpose could have been military, to guard the land-route to Gallia Narbonensis or to watch over the gold-mines at Victimulae. See U. Ewins, *PBRS* 1952, 70 ff. Traces of the land-distribution (centuriation) survive: see P. Fraccaro, *Opuscula*, iii (1957), 93 ff.

[33] T. F. Carney, *Marius*, 43 f., suggests that Scaurus was behind the suppression of Saturninus

and out-manœuvred Marius in the process. Marius may have lost political support after the suppression of Saturninus less abruptly than is usually believed, according to E. Badian, *Foreign Clientelae*, 210 ff. He did not leave Rome until very late in 99 and was elected to an augurate in his absence. His choice of the East (where he met Mithridates, see above, p. 230) as his goal has been variously interpreted. His aims and political position from 100 to 88 have been discussed by T. J. Luce, *Historia* 1970, 161 ff., who argues that he went to the East to initiate steps which might lead to a war with Mithridates of which he would secure the command. At any rate, he no doubt foresaw the possibility of war some day and wanted to gain personal knowledge of the situation in the East.

Chapter 22: Notes

[1] The numismatic evidence suggests that, whatever Pliny's description (*NH*, xxxiii. 46) means (whether a debasement or the issue of one silver-plated coin to seven ordinary silver ones), nothing on these lines was in fact carried out. See M. Crawford, *Numismatic Chronicle* 1968, 57 f. Pliny's remark refers more probably to the younger Drusus than to his father, Gaius Gracchus's opponent.

[2] The ancient evidence is contradictory. Livy (*Epit.* lxxi) says Drusus carried a law to establish mixed courts; Appian (*Bell. Civ.* i. 35) that he wanted to add 300 Equites to the Senate and entrust the enlarged Senate with the courts; Velleius (ii. 13.2) that he wanted to restore them to the Senate (this is unlikely). Drusus also proposed that all jurors (i.e. including Equites) should be subject to a law against judicial corruption. For full discussion of recent views see E. J. Weinrib, *Historia* 1970, 414 ff.

[3] The ground for challenging the legality was the *lex Caecilia-Didia* of 98 B.C., which forbade the 'tacking' of disparate measures in one omnibus bill and enacted that a regular interval must elapse between the promulgation of a measure and its voting in the assembly. (The Senate had thus tried to guard against measures brought by a coalition of its opponents and at the same time against a surprise attack.) Drusus may have been guilty of some technical offence such as 'tacking' together his agrarian and colonial schemes.

[4] On Varius and his *quaestio* see E. Badian, *Historia* 1969, 447 ff.

[5] On the grievances and aims of the allies see A. N. Sherwin-White, *Roman Citizenship²*, (1973), 134 ff.; P. A. Brunt, *JRS* 1965, 90 ff.; E. T. Salmon, *Samnium and the Samnites* (1967), ch. 9.; E. Badian, *Dialoghi di Archeologia*, iv–v (1970/1) 373 ff.; D. B. Nagle, *American Journal of Archaeology* 1973, 367 ff. The struggle is sometimes called the Marsic War (because the Marsi were prominent in it) or the Social War, the 'war of the allies'. The latter title is misleading because it obscures a vital fact that the rebel allies did not include the more privileged Latin allies, all of whom (with the single exception of Venusia) remained loyal to Rome.

[6] On the constitution of the Italian confederacy see Diodorus, xxxvii. 2; Strabo, v. 241. For modern discussion of controversial details see R. Gardner, *CAH*, ix, 186 f.; Salmon, *Samnium*, 348 ff. Sherwin-White, *Roman Citizenship²* (1973), 144 ff.

[7] The war-coinage of the Marsi bore Latin inscriptions, the Samnite pieces had Oscan legends. The coinage displayed the ideals and hopes of the Italians: e.g. the new concept of Italia; groups of warriors taking oaths of allegiance; Italian bull goring the Roman wolf; the names of the commanders. See Sydenham, *CCR*; *Historia Numorum³*, i (forthcoming).

[8] An account of the war by a contemporary writer, Sisenna, is lost. Surviving information from other writers is very scrappy. On the war see E. T. Salmon, *Samnium and the Samnites* (1967), ch. 10. Some sling-bullets from the siege of Asculum survive, inscribed with such orders as 'feri Pompeium' ('hit Pompeius Strabo' – or even designating the precise target, as 'ventri').

[9] The narrower scope of the *lex Iulia* is given by Appian (*Bell. Civ.* 1.49), but Velleius (ii. 16) implies that it covered rebels who laid down their arms quickly. It also enabled generals to grant citizenship to individuals for service in battle. An inscription (Dessau, *ILS*, 8888) reveals that Strabo in his camp at Asculum thus rewarded some Spanish horsemen: for full discussion see N. Criniti, *L'Epigrafe di Asculum di Gn. Pompeo Strabone* 1970). Communities who received citizenship under the *lex Iulia* became self-governing *municipia* and their internal organisation was probably regulated by a general law (the *lex Calpurnia?*).

[10] The *lex Plautia-Papiria* (Cicero, *pro Arch.* iv. 7) was probably of much narrower range than is sometimes thought: see A. N. Sherwin-White, *Roman Citizenship²* (1973), 137. The only clause known to us dealt with *ascripti* (a kind of 'honorary freemen') who happened to be away from their town when it received citizenship under the *lex Iulia*.

[11] On the *lex Pompeia* see Asconius, *in Pisonem*, p. 3. For a slightly different interpretation of this passage, see U. Ewins, *PBSR* 1955, 73 ff., who also argues that Cisalpine Gaul was made a province in 89 and not by Sulla in 81 (even the latter date is doubted by E. Badian, *Historia* 1962, 232).

[12] Ten new tribes according to Appian (*Bell. Civ.* i. 49), eight (new or old?) according to Velleius, ii. 20, while a fragment of Sisenna refers to two new tribes. The details are less important than the agreed result, namely that the voting power of the new citizens was less than that of the old. See L. R. Taylor, *Voting Districts of the Roman Republic* (1960), ch. 8; R. G. Lewis, *Athenaeum* 1968, 273 ff.

[13] On the Asellio incident see E. Badian, *Historia* 1969, 475 ff., who links with it a *lex Plautia iudiciaria* under which jurors were chosen in a new way: each tribe elected fifteen of its own members from *any* class (not only from the Equites) and from these 525 men the jurors of the year were drawn. The nobles were perhaps attempting to win popular support against the Equites.

In 89 also the bronze coinage was reduced in weight, the *as* becoming half an ounce. It is not clear that the silver was debased at this time; in the Gracchan period the denarius had been experimentally retariffed at sixteen instead of ten *asses*; this ratio now became definite.

[14] In pronouncing sentences of outlawry upon them, the enemies of Marius and Sulpicius charged them with having called the slaves to arms (as later was also alleged against Cinna); Appian, *Bell. Civ.* i. 61, 64. These charges must remain doubtful. The military value of slaves was negligible, while their use would have alienated the Equestrian Order, on whose support both Marius and Cinna depended. In the case of Cinna it was admitted that not a single slave joined him.

On the political attitude of Sulpicius and Marius *vis-à-vis* Sulla see A. W. Lintott, *Cl. Qu.* 1971, 442 ff.

[15] Appian's account of Sulla's constitutional legislation in 88 (*Bell. Civ.* i, 59), our only source, is over-compressed and confused. His statement that Sulla at this time enrolled 300 new senators to fill gaps in its ranks is plainly an anticipation of his later reforms. On his debt-laws see T. Frank, *AJ Phil.* 1933, 54 ff.

[16] The adventures of Marius on his flight to Africa are graphically described in Plutarch (*Marius*, 35–40) and possibly over-dramatised. Cf. T. F. Carney, *Greece and Rome* 1961, 98 ff. At Minturnae, after lurking in the marshes, Marius was arrested, but with a single glance unnerved a slave sent to dispatch him; the local senate eventually took the risk of setting him free. See further E. Badian, *JRS*, 1973, 121. In Africa Marius would be nearer his veteran colonists, especially in the isle of Cercina.

[17] According to Appian (*Bell. Civ.* i. 65) Cinna complained to his troops (whether truthfully or not we cannot know) that the Senate had declared him a public enemy without the authority of the people.

[18] The artillery embrasure, still visible in the Aventine sector of the Servian Wall, was probably built into it in 87: see Saflund, *Le mura di Roma repubblicano*, 186 ff.

[19] This is the most probable explanation of the mysterious expression 'sidere afflatus' in Velleius Paterculus (ii. 21.4).

[20] If the figure of 463,000 for the census of 86/85 is accepted, it marks an increase of only 69,000 over the figures of 114. This suggests that the registration was slow in 86.

[21] On the economic reforms in general see C. M. Bulst, *Historia* 1964, 330 ff. The currency edict, issued by Marius Gratidianus, probably did not control plated coins, since the latter were never officially minted according to M. Crawford, *Numismatic Chronicle*, 1968, 57 f., *Proceedings of the Cambridge Philological Society*. 1968, 1 ff.

[22] The ancient sources which rely on Sulla's Memoirs scarcely give a true picture of Cinna's policy. He is conventionally portrayed as supported by the Equites and the new citizens, and in conflict with the oligarchy and Sulla. For a different interpretation see E. Badian, *JRS* 1962, 47 ff. Hostile sources may refer to the period as *dominatio Cinnae*, but he seems rather at first to have sought stability, moderation and unity. But Sulla, as he went from victory to vic-

tory, would not dance to Cinna's tune, nor later could Carbo hold together the government in Rome. On this period see also C. M. Bulst, *Historia* 1964, 307 ff.

[23] In the tradition which went back to Sulla's own Memoirs (Plutarch, *Sulla*, 20.1) it was asserted that the army under Flaccus was sent nominally against Mithridates, but in fact against Sulla. This 'stab in Sulla's back' version no doubt was Sulla's own and seems to be contradicted by the tradition in Memnon (Jacoby, *Fragmente der griechischen Historiker* 434, fr. 24). Cf. Badian, *JRS* 1962, 56.

Chapter 23: Notes

[1] E. Badian has shown (*Athenaeum* 1959, 379 ff. = *Studies in Gr. and Rom. Hist.* 157 ff.) that Sulla's praetorship was in 97 (not 93) and his Cilician command in 96 (not 92). This involves a considerable readjustment of subsequent events in Asia.

[2] On Mithridates and the wars see especially Appian, *Mithridatica*, and Plutarch, *Sulla*. Cf. Th. Reinach, *Mithridate Eupator* (1890); M. Rostovtzeff, *CAH*, ix, ch. v; D. Magie, *The Romans in Asia Minor* (1950), chs 8 and 9.

[3] A tolerably clear account of the battle of Chaeroneia is given by Plutarch (*Sulla*, 16–19, using the Memoirs of Sulla himself); as a native of Chaeroneia Plutarch would have interest in local detail. He numbers Sulla's forces at 16,500 strong. Archelaus's army was assessed at between 60,000 and 120,000 men (and 80,000 at Orchomenus): these figures (and the reported losses of 110,000 against some fourteen Romans) obviously do not deserve credence.

[4] Inscriptions reveal Sulla's treatment of some loyal cities, confirming (or extending) their privileges. We have his letters to Stratonicea (*OGIS*, 441; Sherk, *Documents*, 18; translation in Lewis and Reinhold, *Rom. Civ.* i. 337 f.) and to Thasos (Sherk, *Documents*, 20). Sulla, who was interested in actors (cf. S. Garton, *Phoenix* 1964, 137 ff.), in response to their appeal renewed privileges granted to the Guild of Actors of Ionia and the Hellespont, the Artists of Dionysus; a copy of the subsequent confirmation by the Senate in a Senatus Consultum, together with Sulla's covering letter, has been found in Cos (see Sherk, *Documents*, 49; translation in Lewis and Reinhold, 342).

The view that Sulla deprived the *publicani* of the right to farm the taxes of Asia should be rejected: see P. A. Brunt, *Latomus* 1956, 17 ff.

[5] According to Appian (*Bell. Civ.* i. 95) 40 senators and 1600 Equites were placed on the proscription lists. Orosius (v. 21) estimates the total number of Sulla's victims in Italy at not fewer than 9000. Both these figures appear quite credible.

[6] Sulla's colonies included Arretium, Clusium, Faesulae, Nola, Pompeii, Praeneste. The colonists apparently generally remained separate from the earlier inhabitants. See E. Gabba, *Athenaeum* 1951, 270 ff.; E. T. Salmon, *Roman Colonization* (1969), 129 ff.; Brunt, *Manpower*, 300 ff. Brunt argues for some 80,000 settlers in about 20 colonies, but this did not necessarily involve 80,000 new smallholdings

since Sulla sold many large estates to his partisans and 'to an unknown extent Sullan *latifondisti* replaced Marian, and Sullan veterans took over the homes of the "innoxia plebs" ' thus ruining many peasants (p. 311). On the relation of town and country and the problem of urbanisation in Italy in the first century B.C. see E. Galba, *Studi Classici e Orientali* 1972, 73 ff.

[7] On Sulla see E. Badian, *Historia*, 1962, 228 ff. (= Seager, *Crisis of Rom. Rep.* 34 ff.), and *Lucius Sulla; the Deadly Reformer* (Todd Memorial Lecture, Sydney, 1970).

Sulla assumed, or was granted, the name Felix: it appeared in the inscription on an equestrian statue of him erected in Rome in 82. He clearly believed in his luck: as early as 86 he had named his twin children Faustus and Fausta. In Greece his use of the name Epaphroditus suggests that he believed he enjoyed Aphrodite's favour, while *felicitas* was the required quality for a successful general. On the name Felix see J. P. V. D. Balsdon, *JRS* 1951, 1 ff.

[8] As argued by E. Badian, *Lucius Sulla*, 6 ff. (see previous note).

[9] The main thesis of J. Carcopino, *Sylla ou la monarchie manquée*[2] (1947), is that Sulla gradually lost the support of Pompey, the Metelli and the rest of the nobility, who combined against him to force his retirement when they believed he intended to maintain a *regnum* indefinitely. But this last imputed intention is not probable. On the relations of Pompey and the Metelli see B. Twyman, *Aufstieg NRW*, II. i. 816 ff.

[10] The largest recorded vote at a senatorial session was 417 in 61 B.C. (Cic. *ad Att.* 1.14.5). To this figure should be added the absentees, and the magistrates present (who did not vote). A total for the whole Senate might be either 500 or 600.

[11] On the personnel of the post-Sullan Senate, see H. Hill, *Cl. Qu.* 1932, 170 ff.; R. Syme, *PBSR* 1938, 1 ff.; E. Gabba, *Athenaeum* 1951, 267 ff.; J. R. Hawthorn, *Greece and Rome* 1962, 53 ff. See also T. P. Wiseman, *New Men in the Roman Senate 139 B.C.–A.D. 14* (1971).

[12] Of the eight praetors two were chief civil judges, holding respectively the *sors urbana* and the *sors peregrina*, six presided over the reorganised jury-courts. Additional presidents for the jury-courts were drawn from the ex-aediles, as occasion might require. Of the twenty quaestors two were attached to the aerarium (*quaestores urbani*), two to the consuls, and twelve to the provincial governors (two in Sicily). Four were distributed over Italy (*quaestores Italici*).

[13] Thus the son of the dictator, Faustus Sulla, wrote a charter for Pompeii.

[14] On Cisalpine Gaul see Chap. 22, n. 11, above. Sulla probably extended 'Italy' from the Aesis to the Rubicon for administrative purposes. It should be noted that there were now ten provinces and ten higher magistrates (two consuls and eight praetors) available for their administration.

[15] After Sulla the courts were *de repetundis, de maiestate, de ambitu, de sicariis et veneficiis, de peculatu, de iniuria, de falsis*. The first three, and probably the first five, existed before Sulla's reorganisation. Thus there were standing courts (*quaestiones perpetuae*)

dealing respectively with extortion, treason, electoral bribery, murder and poisoning, peculation, assault, and fraud. A court *de vi* (violence) was added later (in 78 by a *lex Lutatia* which was supplemented by a *lex Plautia* between 78 and 63, according to A. W. Lintott, *Violence in Republican rome* (1968), ch. viii). On the way in which these courts functioned see A. H. M. Jones, *The Criminal Courts of the Roman Republic and Principate* (1972), ch. 2.

[16] E. Badian (*Athenaeum* 1970, 3 ff.) has argued that Sulla divested himself of power by stages: he resigned the dictatorship at the end of 81, in 80 was consul without his twenty-four lictors and supreme authority, and then in 79 became a *privatus*. On the nature of Sulla's final unpleasant disease see T. F. Carney, *Acta Classica* 1960, 64 ff.

[17] Sulla did not go so far as to put his own portrait on coinage (Julius Caesar was the first to take this step at Rome), but he issued in Rome and Italy coins which bore his name, proclaimed his authority as *imperator, imperator iterum* or *felix dictator* and showed him in a triumphal chariot, his equestrian statue or two trophies (for Chaeroneia and Orchomenus?) with a *lituus* (he was one of the few Romans to add an augurate to a pontificate: see E. Badian, *Arethusa* 1968, 26 ff.). For the coins see Sydenham, *CRR*, 756 (struck for Sulla by a proquaestor), 762 (by a quaestor) and 760 and Crawford, *RRC*, 367/4, 381/1, 359/1, respectively. For discussion see M. Crawford, *Numismatic Chronicle* 1964, 148 ff.

[18] Given the road-system of ancient Italy, representative institutions or local polling were at least as practical as in Elizabethan England or in the thirteen American Colonies. Either of these systems would probably have necessitated payment for public service — another innovation left over to Augustus.

Chapter 24: Notes

[1] For the sources for 78–70 B.C. see Greenidge –Clay–Gray, *Sources*[2]: see above, Chap. 20, n. 1. The main writers are Appian (*Bell. Civ.* i. 107-21), Plutarch (*Lives of Pompey, Sertorius, Crassus, Lucullus*), Livy, *Periochae* 90–97 and *Mithridatica*. Sallust's important work, the *Histories*, covered the years 78–67, but only fragments survive. A major source which now begins to appear is Cicero's *Orations* (e.g. the *Verrines*).

For the years 69–59 see Appian, *Bell. Civ.* ii. 1–14, Dio Cassius, xxxvi–xxxviii. 12, Livy, *Periochae*, 98–103, and writers in the Livian tradition, as Velleius Paterculus, Valerius Maximus and Orosius. Cicero's *Orations* and his *Letters* form major sources, Sallust's *Bellum Catilinae* deals with one episode. Plutarch's Lives include those of *Pompey, Caesar, Crassus*, and *Cato Minor*, while Suetonius, *Divus Iulius*, begins to be relevant.

On the period 78 to 49 B.C., see now E. S. Gruen, *The Last Generation of the Roman Republic* (1974).

[2] According to Cicero (*Pro Sestio*, 109), the Tribal Assembly was sometimes so ill-attended that scarcely five members of each tribe took part.

[3] On the renewed power of the nobility in home affairs see R. Syme, *The Roman Revolution* (1939); L. R. Taylor, *Party Politics in the Age of Caesar* (1949).

[4] On this point there is remarkable unanimity of opinion between Cicero, Caesar and Sallust, all of whom were outspoken in their denunciation of the lawlessness of the preceding age.

[5] On Lepidus's revolution see T. Rice Holmes, *The Roman Republic*, i (1923) 365 ff.; N. Criniti, *Memorie dell' Istitúto Lombardo*, xxx (1969); E. Hayne, *Historia* 1972, 661 ff.

[6] Details of the *lex Terentia Cassia* are controversial. Lepidus's corn-law had probably been repealed soon after 78. Cf. T. Rice Holmes, *The Roman Republic*, i (1923), 384.

[7] The sources for the Sertorian War are collected in A. Schulten, *Fontes Hispaniae Antiquae*, iv (1937), 160 ff. The *Historiae* of Sallust (fragments) and the *Sertorius* of Plutarch are more favourable to Sertorius than are Plutarch's *Pompeius*, Appian or Livy. The best modern account is A. Schulten, *Sertorius* (1926), in German.

The sources are analysed in T. Rice Holmes, *The Roman Republic*, 3 vols (1923), to which constant reference should be made for the years 79–44 B.C.

[8] Metellus has left his name enshrined in his headquarters at Metellinum (modern Medellin), while a camp survives at Castra Caecilia (modern Caceres).

[9] In his agreement with Mithridates Sertorius conceded the king's claim to Bithynia and Cappadocia, but according to the better tradition refused to surrender the province of Asia: Appian includes Asia, thus making him a traitor rather than the loyal patriot of Plutarch.

[10] For this despatch of Pompey see Sallust, *Histories*, ii, frag. 98, Maurenbrecher; excerpted in Greenidge–Clay–Gray, *Sources*, 248; see above, n. 1.

[11] The precise date of the *lex Plautia de reditu Lepidanorum* is uncertain: it was definitely before 68, probably in 73 or 72. Cf. H. Last, *CAH*, ix. 896. Broughton, *MRR*, ii. 130, suggests 70 B.C.

[12] A *lex Gellia Cornelia* of the consuls of 72 authorised Pompey to confer Roman citizenship on the deserving: many Spaniards benefited (including Balbus of Gades), and so did Pompey's *clientela*. Instead of massacring some of the obdurate he moved them to a new settlement north of the Pyrenees, Lugdunum Convenarum.

[13] Crassus was probably praetor in 73. He was given the command against Spartacus either as proconsul or perhaps more probably as a *privatus cum imperio*: see E. Badian, *JRS* 1959, 82, n. 12 = *Stud. Gr. Rom. Hist.* (1964), 153.

Crassus inflicted the penalty of decimation, which had fallen into disuse since the days of Pyrrhus, upon two faint-hearted legions (Appian, *Bell. Civ.* i. 118). On the sources for the war see T. Rice Holmes, *The Roman Republic*, i. 385 ff.

[14] According to Ed. Meyer (*Caesars Monarchie und das Prinzipat des Pompejus*[2], 191 ff.) Pompey had political ambitions similar to those which Augustus afterwards realised. But there is nothing in Pompey's career to show that he had, or even pretended to have, any statesmanlike ability. As a political figure he is more akin to Marius than to Augustus.

On Pompey see M. Gelzer, *Pompeius* (in German,

1949); J. van Ootteghem, *Pompée le Grand* (1954); W. S. Anderson, *Pompey, his Friends and the Literature of the First Century* B.C. (1963).

[15] On Crassus see A. Garzetti, *Athenaeum* 1941, 1 ff., 1942, 13 ff., 1944–5, 1 ff.; F. E. Adcock, *Marcus Crassus, Millionaire* (1966).

Metellus's army came home separately from Spain and was not at Pompey's disposal at this time.

[16] The length of time that Pompey and Crassus retained their armies is uncertain; see Appian, *Bell. Civ.* i. 121; Plut. *Crass.* 12 and *Pomp.* 23; cf. T. Rice Holmes, *The Roman Republic*, i. 390; F. B. Marsh, *Hist. Rom. World 146–31* B.C. appendix 5. A. N. Sherwin-White (*JRS* 1956, 5 ff.) minimises Pompey's threat of force. But see D. Stockton, *Historia* 1973, 205 ff. Pompey needed land for his veterans; this may have been provided under a *lex Plotia agraria*, which included Metellus's veterans also: see R. E. Smith, *Cl. Qu.* 1957, 82 ff.

[17] Little is known about the *tribuni aerarii*. According to Varro (*De Ling. Lat.* v. 181) they had formerly been paymasters to the army. They must now have been more than a panel of officials and were probably men whose property-qualification (fixed at 300,000 sesterces) fell just below that required for membership of the Equestrian Order.

[18] This man, Chrysogonus, had murdered Sextus Roscius of Amerina and confiscated his property, and then accused Roscius's son of murdering his father. The speech which young Cicero boldly delivered (in 80 or 79) in defence of Roscius's son, *Pro Sexto Roscio Amerino*, survives and throws a vivid light on the times. On Cicero's relations (co-operative) with Pompey until 70 B.C. see A. M. Ward, *Phoenix* 1970, 58 ff., and *Latomus* 1970, 58 ff.

[19] Lentulus and Gellius carried out a census. But the arrangements which they made for registering the citizens outside Rome (presumably through the chief officials of their respective municipalities) were so defective that the total number came to no more than 910,000 (Phlegron: see Greenidge–Clay², p. 271), a figure certainly below the true total at that time.

[20] This measure stood in the joint names of Pompey and Crassus (Livy, *Epit.* xcvii), but beyond question Pompey was the real author.

[21] It is uncertain whether Manilius had instructions from Pompey or drew a bow at a venture. Unlike Gabinius he never reaped the reward of his services to Pompey. First prosecuted for *repetundae* he was soon condemned for *maiestas*.

[22] Of Cicero's speech *De Rege Alexandrino* only a few fragments survive, but these show that Crassus was the real author of the Egyptian project (so Plutarch, *Crassus*, xiii) and not Caesar (as is asserted by Suetonius, *Divus Iulius*, xi). Whether or not Egypt had much corn for export, its wealth rather than its strategic position was probably foremost in Crassus's mind. The view that Crassus and Caesar were working together at this time is sometimes questioned (see, for example, G. V. Sumner, *TAPA* 1966, 569 ff.). It is defended by A. M. Ward, *Historia* 1972, 244 ff.

[23] On the many problems arising out of the two conspiracies of Catiline see E. G. Hardy, *The Cati-*linarian Conspiracy* (1924 = *JRS* 1917, 153 ff.); T. Rice Holmes, *The Roman Republic* 455 ff. The extent to which there was any 'conspiracy' in 66/65 as suggested by Suetonius (*Div. Iul.* ix), is doubtful. Rumours told of an extensive plot, but see, for example, P. A. Brunt, *Cl. Rev.* 1957, 193 ff.; R. Seager, *Historia* 1964, 338 ff. For the modern literature on Catiline, see N. Criniti, *Bibliografia Catilinaria* (1971).

[24] The last certain case of a *novus homo* attaining the consulship before Cicero was when one C. Caelius Caldus was elected for 94.

The methods of Roman electioneering at this period are well illustrated in the pamphlet *De Petitione Consulatus* or *Commentariolum Petitionis*, which is ascribed to Cicero's brother, Quintus. This ascription is doubted by some (e.g. M. I. Henderson, *JRS* 1950; 8 ff., R. G. M. Nisbet, *JRS* 1961, 84 ff.), but accepted by others (e.g. J. P. V. D. Balsdon, *Cl. Qu.* 1963, 232 ff.; J. S. Richardson, *Historia* 1971, 436 ff.). At any rate it may contain contemporary material. On Quintus see W. C. McDermott, *Historia* 1971, 702 ff.

[25] For an analysis of Cicero's speeches *In Legem Agrariam* (in which he exaggerates the scope of Rullus's law *ad absurdum*) see Hardy, *Some Problems of Roman History* (1924), 68 ff.

[26] On the early career of Caesar, who was born in 100 B.C., see E. Badian, *JRS* 1959, 81 ff. (= *Stud. Gr. and Rom. Hist.* 140 ff.); H. Strasburger, *Caesars Eintritt in die Geschichte* (1938). After capture by the pirates (p. 25), he supported the agitation for the restoration of tribunician powers, held a military tribunate (71?), served as quaestor in Spain (69 or 68), supported the *lex Gabinia* in 67, and became aedile in 65 with Crassus's help.

[27] In 63 Caesar caused a mild sensation by initiating a suit against an aged Eques named C. Rabirius, who was reputed to have murdered Saturninus thirty-seven years previously after the passing of the Senatus Consultum Ultimum (p. 209). The curious procedure of Caesar, who revived the obsolete court of the *duoviri preduellionis* in order to strike at Rabirius, and the abrupt manner in which the trial in its final hearing before the Comitia Centuriata was broken off, suggest that the prosecution was mainly intended to keep Caesar in the limelight and that he wished to criticise possible misuse of the Senatus Consultum Ultimum. On the procedure in this case see E. G. Hardy, *Some Problems of Roman History* (1924), 99 ff.; A. H. M. Jones *Criminal Courts of the Roman Republic and Principate* (1972), 40 ff.

[28] Cicero may well have exaggerated the importance of the conspiracy and his views have been followed too literally in some modern assessments. That, however, is not to say that, as has been argued for instance by K. H. Waters (*Historia* 1970, 195 ff.), he inflated a really trivial affair into a gigantic conspiracy which allowed him to appear as saviour of the State. R. Seager (*Historia* 1973, 240 ff.) thinks that an *early* connexion of Catiline with Lepidus and Lentulus is improbable.

[29] In the first Catilinarian Oration Cicero's final request to Catiline to leave Rome for Rome's good forms a strange anticlimax to his previous vehement

denunciations of the arch-plotter. Presumably the consul had tried to rouse feeling against Catiline in the Senate, but found the House still unwilling to sanction drastic action against the conspirators.

[30] In order to guard against misrepresentation, Cicero had the proceedings of 3 and 5 December recorded by senators versed in shorthand and circulated by means of fly-sheets. It was probably this venture in journalism that suggested to Caesar his rudimentary Official Gazette (p. 249).

[31] On the legal issues involved in this debate see Hardy, *The Catilinarian Conspiracy*, 85 ff., and H. Last, *CAH*, ix, 93 ff. A citizen who was caught red-handed under arms might be regarded as having turned himself by his actions from a *civis* into a *hostis* and therefore no longer possessed of a right of appeal, but what was the position of men already captured and under guard? For a recent discussion of Cicero and the Senatus Consultum Ultimum see Th. N. Mitchell, *Historia* 1971, 47 ff.

[32] On *otium cum dignitate* see C. Wirzsubski, *JRS* 1954, 1 ff.; J. P. V. D. Balsdon, *Cl. Qu.* 1960, 45 ff. On Caesar and Vatinius see Cicero, *Vat.* 29. On the changing relations of the orders see E. Badian, *Publicans and Sinners* (1972), 101 ff., who writes:

'In the late (post-Sullan) Republic, senators shared financial interests with *equites*' (p. 99). . . . 'We can see . . . to what an extent *concordia ordinum* was an accomplished fact, except for a few recalcitrant reactionaries in high places. By the end of the Republic the principal business affairs of the *equites* must have been well on the way to being shared, if not taken over, by senators' (p. 105). . . . 'It is this solid basis (i.e. that common interests between Senate and *equites*) that helps to account for the fact that the composition of the courts never again [after 70] became a matter of controversy between the two orders. In fact the division of function between actual government and State business was breaking down' (p. 101).

[33] On the *silvae callesque* see Suetonius, *Div. Iul.* xix. 2, the only source. This tradition, though not unchallenged (see Balsdon, *JRS* 1939, 180 ff.), is generally accepted.

[34] Caesar had spoken in favour of the Gabinian and Manilian laws, and in 62 he had ostensibly supported a tribune, named Q. Metellus Nepos, who made an absurd proposal that Pompey should be invited home from the East to free the city from the tyranny of Cicero! On the other hand he abetted Crassus's intrigues against Pompey in 65–63.

[35] The order and dating of Caesar's measures are uncertain: see L. R. Taylor, *Historia* 1965, 423 ff. Caesar's first land-bill was moderate, but he brought in a very harsh supplementary bill to redistribute the fertile *ager Campanus*, which was already occupied by peasants, to some veterans and fathers of large families. The needs of these peasants and of the treasury (which was receiving rent from the land) had to give place to the needs of the military: the shadow of Marius's reforms were lengthening over the Republic. On the nature and result of this legislation see Brunt, *Manpower*, 312 ff.

[36] It is possible that Caesar also made use of fresh troops recruited by him for future service in Gaul.

Cf. F. B. Marsh, *The Founding of the Roman Empire*[2] (1927), appendix 1.

[37] Suetonius: *Div. Iul.* xx. 1. On Roman journalism see G. Bossier, *Tacitus* (1906), 197 ff.

[38] The previous status of Illyricum is uncertain. Probably it had been loosely attached to Macedonia.

[39] Crassus had supported a request from a company of tax-gatherers that the Senate should modify a bad contract they had made for the taxes of Asia. Caesar paid for Crassus's political support by getting Vatinius to carry a measure to remit one-third of the contract.

Chapter 25: Notes

[1] One of the Roman victims of the pirates was the youthful Julius Caesar, who was kidnapped on a journey to Rhodes. Caesar paid the stipulated ransom of fifty talents, but after his release he collected a punitive force on his own authority in the province of Asia and executed his captors (Velleius Paterculus, ii. 42; Plutarch, *Caesar*, ii; Suetonius, *Divus Iulius*, iv).

[2] On the campaigns of Servilius see H. A. Ormerod, *JRS* 1922, 35 ff.; D. Magie, *Roman Rule in Asia Minor* (1950), 287 ff.

[3] The fact that the Romans had left Cyrene alone ever since it had been bequeathed to them on the death of its king Ptolemy Apion in 96 shows that the Senate was avoiding any policy of expansion and that the Equites and people had acquiesced. On Cyrene from 96 to 74 B.C. see in general S. I. Oost, *Cl. Phil.* 1963, 11 ff.; E. Badian, *JRS* 1965, 119 ff.; and *Rom. Imperialism*, 29 f., 35 ff. and 99 ff. Badian argues against the formation of a formal province before the time of Pompey, since Cn. Lentulus, a legate of Pompey, acted in Cyrene in 67 in a manner which suggests there was no regular governor. A series of inscriptions referring to Cn. Lentulus has been found: see J. Reynolds, *JRS* 1962, 97 ff.

[4] On Pompey's campaign see H. A. Ormerod, *Liverpool Annals of Arch.* 1923, 46 ff. The nature of his command is uncertain; probably it was an *imperium infinitum* by sea, but by land it was equal (*aequum*) to that of any provincial governor for 50 miles inland from the coast. Cf. Velleius, ii. 31. For a revival of the view that it was *imperium maius* see Sh. Jameson, *Historia*, 1970, 539 ff. On his settlement see A. H. M. Jones, *Cities of E. Rom Prov.* 202 ff.

[5] The anxiety of Mithridates to retain free access to the Aegean Sea is shown by his preoccupation with the sieges of Chalcedon and Cyzicus in 74–73. According to Appian (*Mithridatica*, xii) he had previously denounced Nicomedes for closing the Bosporus.

[6] On the chronology of the outbreak of the war (74 or 73) see Broughton, *MRR*, ii. 106. For full discussion of the war and difficulties in the sources see D. Magie, *Roman Rule in Asia Minor*, 323 ff.

In his *elogium* (Dessau, *ILS*, 60) Lucullus later claimed to have rescued Cotta at Chalcedon. Cotta stayed on as proconsul and after a two years' siege he sacked Heraclea Pontica in 71. On his return to Rome he was accused of appropriating booty and expelled from the Senate. A fragment of a local historian of Heraclea, named Memnon, refers to these events (see Jacoby, *Fragmente der griechischen Historiker*, n. 434).

[7] For further details of the settlement see Plutarch, *Lucullus*, 20. Cf. T. R. S. Broughton in Frank, *Econ. SAR*, iv. 545.

[8] On the battle of Tigranocerta see Plutarch, *Lucullus*, xxvi–xxviii. Phlegron of Tralles, a historian of the time of Hadrian, attributes a joint force of 40,000 infantry and 30,000 cavalry to the two kings (Jacoby, *F. Gr. Hist.* n. 257, frag. 12.10). This estimate is not unlikely.

[9] Plutarch, *Lucullus*, v. Lucullus's precipitancy in attacking Tigranes without the Senate's sanction may have been due to his apprehension that Pompey (who was entitled to a proconsular province in 69) might claim Armenia for himself.

[10] With this defeat of a victorious general on his home front we may compare the frustration of Marlborough by the new Tory ministry after 1710.

[11] On Petra see M. Rostovtzeff, *Caravan Cities* (1932), ch. ii. Pompey sent his quaestor, Aemilius Scaurus, to the Nabataean king Aretas, who made a show of submission. Scaurus later issued coins showing the king kneeling beside a camel: see Sydenham, *CRR*, n. 912; Crawford, *RRC*, 422/1.

[12] On this occasion Faustus Sulla, the son of the dictator, was first over the wall. Pompey insisted on entering the Holy of Holies in the temple, but did not touch its treasures. The relations between the Jews of Palestine and the Romans under Pompey and Gabinius are described at some length by Josephus, *Antiquitates Judaicae* xiv 1–5.

[13] On Pompey's settlement of the East see Plut. *Pomp.* 38; Appian, *Mithr.* 114–15; Dio Cassius, xxxvii, 7a. Cf. A. H. M. Jones, *Cities E. Rom. Prov.* 157 ff., 202 ff., 258 ff.; D. Magie, *Roman Rule in Asia Minor*, ch. xv; A. J. Marshall, *JRS* 1968, 103 ff.; F. P. Rizzo, *Le fonti per la storia della conquista pompeiana della Siria* (1963).

[14] On Pompey's financial arrangements in the East see T. Frank, *Roman Imperialism*, 323 ff.

[15] The prospect of plundering Babylonia, which had recovered much of its old commercial importance under Greek rule, may have weighed with Crassus, though perhaps less than his desire to equal the military reputation of Pompey and Caesar.

[16] On Parthia see W. W. Tarn, *CAH*, ix, ch. xiv; N. C. Debevoise, *A Political History of Parthia* (1938); M. A. R. Colledge, *The Parthians* (1967). On the Parthian horsemen, skilled in the 'Parthian shot', fired over the crupper as they pretended to flee, see Tarn, *Hellenistic Military and Naval Developments* (1930), 73 ff.

[17] On the campaign of Carrhae see the excellent account of Plutarch, *Crassus*, xx–xxv. Tactics similar to those of Surenas at Carrhae were employed by Saladin at the battle of Hattin in 1187, in which he wore down and destroyed the more immobile Crusaders.

[18] The severed head of Crassus was brought to the Parthian court and was used for a realistic representation of the final scene in Euripides's *Bacchae*. But this bad joke originated with a Greek actor, not

with the Parthian king. Vindictiveness was not a Parthian fault.

A Chinese historian of the first century A.D. makes reference to a picture illustrating the siege of a town in Turkestan, in which were shown a palisade (as of Roman type) and a scaling party with interlocked shields over their heads (a Roman 'testudo'). The attackers may have been old soldiers of Crassus who broke loose from their captivity in Parthia and took service under the Chinese emperor. See H. H. Dubs, *AJ Phil.* 1941, 323 ff, and *Greece and Rome* 1957, 194 ff.

[19] On the implications of Carrhae see D. Timpe, *Museum Helveticum* 1962, 194 ff.

Chapter 26: Notes

[1] On ancient Gaul see C. Jullian, *Histoire de la Gaule*, esp. vols ii and iii; T. G. E. Powell, *The Celts* (1958); Stuart Piggott, *The Druids* (1968). On Caesar's military operations, see T. Rice Holmes, *Caesar's Conquest of Gaul*[2] (1911). On his war-policy, C. Hignett, *CAH*, ix. 537 ff. Other ancient sources do not add much to Caesar's own account of the Gallic campaigns given in his Commentaries *De Bello Gallico*.

[2] The bond between Ariovistus and Rome was probably *amicitia*, not a formal alliance (Plutarch, *Caesar*, xix). Caesar's motion on behalf of Ariovistus is not directly mentioned by Caesar, but is implied in *Bell. Gall.* i. 43.5.

[3] On Caesar's British expeditions see T. Rice Holmes, *Ancient Britain and the Invasions of Caesar*[2] (1935); R. G. Collingwood, *Roman Britain and the English Settlements* (1937); S. S. Frere, *Britannia* (1967), ch. 3.

[4] On the locality of Cassivellaunus's *oppidum* see R. E. M. Wheeler, *Antiquity* 1933, 21 ff.

[5] The emperor Napoleon III was the first excavator of Caesar's great siege-works round Alesia. See J. Harmand, *Une Campaigne césarienne: Alesia* (1967). For other Caesarian camps found in Gaul see O. Brogan, *Roman Gaul* (1953), 17 ff.

[6] Caesar's answer to those who look upon war as chess is contained in *Bell. Civ.* ii. 68.1.

[7] According to Plutarch (*Caesar*, xv) one million Gauls were killed and another million were captured in the Bellum Gallicum. These figures are no doubt exaggerated but the loss of life and property among the Gauls was undoubtedly immense. E. Badian (*Roman Imperialism in late Rep.*[2] 89 ff.) argues that Caesar often deliberately sought and created opportunities for such financial profits and was 'the greatest brigand of them all'. On the other hand A. N. Sherwin-White (*Greece and Rome* 1957, 36 ff.) argues that Caesar was not an imperialist, but was led on by circumstances, rather than by will, from one situation to another. For coins commemorating Caesar's Gallic victories, see Sydenham, *CRR*, n. 1010; Crawford, *RRC*, 452/4. On the contribution of Gaul to the welfare of the Roman Empire see J. Carcopino, *Points de vue sur l'impérialisme romain*, 203 ff.

[8] The main literary sources for the years 58–50 are roughly those mentioned above, Chap 24, n. 1.

[9] On the *De Re Publica* and the *De Legibus*, in which Cicero summed up his political theories, see Ed. Meyer, *Caesars Monarchie*, 177 ff.; W. W. How, *JRS* 1930, 24 ff; E. Leporé, *Il princeps ciceroniano* (1954).

[10] Before Clodius could become a tribune of the *plebs* he had to remove the disability of his patrician birth. This he accomplished (with the collaboration of Caesar as Pontifex Maximus) by his formal adoption into a plebeian family. The legal validity of his *traductio ad plebem* was not affected by the fact that his adoptive father was younger than himself. The pay for Clodius's private army may have been found by Crassus. On Clodius in general see A. W. Lintott, *Greece and Rome* 1967, 157 ff.; E. S. Gruen, *Phoenix*, 1966, 120 ff.; on his inherited family *clientelae* in the whole Greek-speaking world see E. Rawson, *Historia* 1973, 219 ff.

[11] On Clodius's legislation in regard to auspices see W. F. McDonald, *JRS* 1929, 164 ff.

[12] Cicero had incurred Clodius's undying hatred when he disproved an alibi which Clodius had put forward when he was being tried for his part in the Bona Dea scandal in 62; Clodius had dressed as a woman and attended the sacred rites which were available only to women. Despite Cicero's evidence Clodius was acquitted by gross bribery (61).

[13] On Cyprus and Cato see S. I. Oost, *Cl. Ph.* 1955, 98 ff.; E. Badian, *JRS* 1965, 110 ff.

[14] The terms of Cicero's motion are not known, but it may be taken for granted that they were framed so as to avoid offence to Pompey: see M. Cary, *Cl. Qu.* 1923, 103 ff. Shortly before he introduced this motion Cicero had restated his ideal of the *Concordia Ordinum* and delivered some unmistakable side-hits at Caesar in two forensic speeches, *Pro Sestio* and *In Vatinium*. On the political significance of these orations see L. G. Pocock, *A Commentary on Cicero, In Vatinium*. On a tribunician attempt to prosecute Caesar about this time see E. Badian in *Polis and Imperium* (ed. J. A. S. Evans, 1974), 145 ff.

[15] The conference at Luca is discussed by E. S. Gruen, *Historia* 1969, 71 ff., and C. Luibheid, *Cl. Ph.* 1970.

[16] Cicero had to accept the situation. In a letter to Pompey (*Ad Atticum*, iv. 5) he recanted and 'sang his palinode'. Then he had to make a public statement: in a speech to the Senate, *De provinciis consularibus*, he supported Caesar's request to continue in Gaul and even praised his achevements there. On this speech see the edition by H. E. Butler and M. Cary.

[17] The terminal date of Caesar's command has been placed at 1 March 50 by F. B. Marsh (*The Founding of the Roman Empire* (1927), 275 ff.); between August and early October 50 by C. E. Stevens (*AJ Phil.* 1938, 169 ff.); at 13 November 50 by F. E. Adcock (*Cl. Qu.* 1932, 14 ff.); at 1 March 49 by G. Elton (*JRS* 1946, 18 ff.) and S. Jameson (*Latomus*, 1970). According to J. P. V. D. Balsdon (*JRS* 1939, 167 ff.) the only time-limit set by the law of Pompey and Crassus was that the question of Caesar's successor should not be raised before 1 March 50. Cf. also P. J. Cuff, *Historia* 1958, 445 ff.
 The controversy turns largely on the interpretation of certain passages in the correspondence of Cicero

during 51 and 50, notably *Ad Famil.* iii. 8.4–9, 11.3; *Ad Atticum*, 7.6, 9.3. The important aspect is not the precise date but the principle behind it, namely that Caesar wished to step straight from one office to another, while his enemies were trying to create a gap in which he would be a *privatus* and so liable to prosecution (cf. n. 19 below).

[18] Cicero, who was defending Milo, for once lost his nerve in view of the troops which Pompey had ranged around the court, and failed to deliver his speech, which he later published; it survives. On Cicero's relations with Milo see A. W. Lintott, *JRS* 1974, 62 ff.

[19] In Roman law it was not admissible to prosecute the holder of a public office. From 51 onwards the practical issue therefore was whether Caesar could be reduced to the status of a private person before he took up his second consulate.
 It is not unlikely that Caesar also had in mind the alternative expedient of advancing the date of his second consulship to 49 (Adcock, *Cl. Qu.* 1932, 22, and n. 3). But he never went so far as to apply to the Senate for leave to stand for his second consulate before the legal time.

[20] On Curio see W. K. Lacey, *Historia* 1961, 318 ff.

[21] Tentative suggestions were made at Rome by those anxious to avoid civil war, that either Pompey or Caesar should be sent to Syria. This would have been almost as good a guarantee of civil peace as Curio's proposal of joint disarmament; but it would have been equally unacceptable to the extremist party in the Senate.

[22] On these eleventh-hour negotiations see H. E. Butler and M. Cary, *Suetonius, Divus Iulius*, xxii ff. On Cicero's Cilician command see A. J. Marshall, *Aufstieg NRW*, I. i. (1972), 887 ff.

[23] Caesar's hesitations on the eve of the civil war are well recounted by Plutarch (*Caesar*, xxxii). His authority was Asinius Pollio, who was then serving on Caesar's staff.

[24] On the further negotiations between Caesar and Pompey see F. B. Marsh, *Hist. of Rom. World, 146–31 B.C.*, 400 ff.; K. von Fritz, *TAPA* 1941, 125 ff.; D. R. Shackleton Bailey, *JRS* 1960, 80 ff.

[25] Suetonius, *Divus Iulius*, xxx. 4.

[26] The attitude of the average senator to the civil war is reflected in the letters of Cicero, who denied Caesar's constitutional right to the special privileges which he was demanding, but admitted that it would be better to humour him than to plunge into a civil conflict which might be fatal to the Republic, whichever party won (see esp. *Ad Attic.* vii. 5, 7 and 9).

[27] It has been suggested that Pompey was engaged in a deep-laid plot to ruin Caesar and at the same time to force himself back on the Senate as the indispensable person in a crisis: see K. von Fritz, *TAPA* 1942, 145 ff. But the simple explanation that Pompey did not know his own mind stands in good accord with his political attitude ever since his return from the East.

[28] On Caesar's *dignitas* see Caesar, *Bell. Civ.* i. 9.2. On Pompey, Tacitus, *Hist.* ii. 38.1. See also C. Wirszubski, *Libertas as a Political Idea at Rome* (1950), 77 f.

Chapter 27: Notes

[1] The main sources for 49–44 B.C. are: Cicero (a few speeches and, above all, his Letters, of which nearly 400 belong to this period). The *Corpus Caesarianum*, i.e. three books, *De Bello Civili* by Caesar himself; the *Bellum Alexandrinum*, which continues the narrative down to Zela and was perhaps written by one of his officers, named Hirtius (*cos*. 43); and the *Bellum Africum*, by a less literate soldier. Appian, *Bell. Civ.* ii. 32–117. Dio Cassius, 41–4. Livy, *Periochae* 109–16. Velleius Paterculus, ii. 49–57. Suetonius, *Div. Iul.* The relevant Lives by Plutarch. Sallust's (?) *Epistulae ad Caesarem* (see below, n. 27). Coins and inscriptions are important. Lucan's epic on the civil war, the *Pharsalia*, is interesting for his interpretations of the war and its main actors: cf. A. W. Lintott, *Cl. Qu.* 1971, 488 ff.

Suetonius's Life of Caesar has been edited by H. E. Butler and M. Cary (1927), that by Plutarch by A. Garzetti (in Italian, 1954).

On Caesar in general see M. Gelzer, *Caesar: Politician and Statesman* (1968); J. P. V. D. Balsdon, *Julius Caesar and Rome* (1967); M. Grant, *Julius Caesar* (1969). Various aspects are discussed in a special bimillenary number of *Greece and Rome*, March 1967 (iv. 1).

On the civil war in general see especially T. Rice Holmes, *The Roman Republic*, iii. On the campaign of Dyrrhachium see Veith, *Der Feldzug von Dyrrachium zwischen Caesar und Pompejus*; on Pharsalus, J. Kromayer in Kromayer–Veith, *Antike Schlachtfelder*, iv. 637 ff.; on Thapsus, Veith, op. cit. iii. 826 ff.

[2] On the campaign at Corfinium see A. Barns, *Historia* 1966, 74 ff. Domitius had been appointed governor of Transalpine Gaul in succession to Caesar; he was thus independent of Pompey, who in vain urged him not to try to hold out at Corfinium. Letters which passed between the two men are preserved in Cicero, *Ad Attic.* viii. 11.

[3] On a visit to Rome *c.* 62 B.C. Juba had suffered the indignity of having his beard pulled by Caesar in the heat of a dispute (Suetonius, *Divus Iulius*, lxxi).

[4] Caesar's success in eluding the blockade was due to no lack of vigilance on the part of the Pompeians, whose admiral-in-chief, Calpurnius Bibulus, died of the privations suffered by him on board. Ancient warships could not keep the sea for long, and were therefore ill suited for patrol work.

[5] The exact site of the battle of Pharsalus remains uncertain. For a recent discussion of earlier views see C. B. R. Pelling, *Historia* 1973, 249 ff.

According to Caesar his troops numbered 22,000 against Pompey's 47,000; at a loss of 200 men they slew 15,000 and captured 24,000 Pompeians (*Bell. Civ.* iii. 88–9, 99). According to Asinius Pollio and other sources the number of killed on Pompey's side was only 6000, as against 1200 Caesarians (Appian, *Bell. Civ.* ii. 82). If this estimate is accepted in preference to Caesar's, Pompey's effectives must be reduced to not more than 40,000.

[6] The story that the great library at Alexandria was destroyed in the 'Bellum Alexandrinum' has been proved incorrect. The 'library' that caught fire in 47

B.C. was probably a quayside dump of books for export (Rice Holmes, op. cit. iii. 487–9).

[7] On the privileges accorded by Caesar to the Jews see the documents quoted by Josephus, *Ant. Jud.* xiv. 10.

[8] For this view, according to which Caesar would have been merely consul-designate for the last months of 47, see V. Ehrenberg, *AJ Phil.* 1953, 129 ff; A. E. Raubitschek, *JRS* 1954, 70 f.

[9] Caesar addressed the mutinous troops as 'Quirites', a word of uncertain origin which had once denoted Roman citizens in general (as in the phrase *populus Romanus Quiritium*), but was eventually restricted to mean civilians only (Suetonius, *Divus Iulius*, lxx.; Dio, xlii. 53.3).

[10] At Thapsus the pursuing Caesarians probably cut off one Pompeian corps in the passage south of the lagoon.

[11] On Cato see L. R. Taylor, *Party Politics in the Age of Caesar* (1949), viii. For a portrait-bust, found at Volubilis in Africa, see *Acta Archaeologica* 1947, 117 ff.

[12] Cicero did not leave Italy until Pompey's fortunes were on the wane. His previous hesitations were not due to lack of moral courage (of which he possessed more than most Roman politicians of his day), but to simple inability to choose between two war parties, neither of which he trusted.

[13] On the population of Rome in Caesar's day see T. Rice Holmes, *The Roman Republic*, i. 360 ff. Brunt, *Manpower*, 383, reckons about three-quarters of a million inhabitants in the late Republic and under Augustus.

[14] M. W. Fredrikson (*JRS* 1966, 128 ff.) examines the problem of debt in the Ciceronian age and concludes that Caesar enacted in 49 and 48 that property should be transferred to creditors on a pre-war valuation, and in 46–45 that the hoarding of coin should be limited and investment in Italian land required. A *lex Iulia* created *cessio bonorum*, but whether it is the work of Caesar or Augustus is uncertain.

[15] Fragments of inscriptions from Ateste and Veleia in Cisalpine Gaul are relevant: the former mentions a *lex Roscia*, the latter a *lex Rubria* (see Riccobono, *Fontes*, nos 20 and 19). One may have been Caesar's enfranchising law, the other a supplement to it. See E. G. Hardy, *Six Roman Laws*, 110 ff; *Problems of Rom. Hist.* 207 ff.; U. Ewins, *PBSR* 1955, 93 ff.; M. W. Fredriksen, *JRS* 1964, 129 ff.

[16] These laws are preserved in an inscription from Heraclea in southern Italy, usually (but inaccurately) known as the *lex Iulia Municipalis*. It contains measures about the corn-dole and roads in Rome and regulations for the Italian municipalities (e.g. excluding from local magistracies and senates such undesirables as gladiators or bankrupts, but apparently allowing freedmen). This patchwork was drafted but not enacted by Caesar at the time of his death; Antony subsequently incorporated it into an omnibus bill and carried it *en bloc*. Text in Riccobono, *Fontes*, n. 13; transl. and commentary, E. G. Hardy, *Six Roman Laws*, 149 ff.; trans. Lewis–Reinhold, *R. Civ.* i. 408 ff. It is, however, possible that the content of the inscription does not consist entirely of laws of the same date: some, at least, may be earlier, i.e. the

70s or even the 80s: see M. W. Frederiksen, *JRS* 1965, 182 ff.; Brunt, *Manpower*, 519 ff. If so, it may indicate that when a census was taken in Rome, local magistrates in Italy had to register all citizens in their municipalities, i.e. local registration was practised well before Caesar's day. The statement that Caesar ordered a general survey of the Roman Empire is difficult to accept, as it rests on the sole authority of a writer of the fifth century, Iulius Honorius, and is not mentioned in Pliny's *Natural History*, where Caesar's project could hardly have failed to have received notice if Pliny had known it.

[18] On emigration see A. J. N. Wilson, *Emigration from Italy in the Republican Age of Rome* (1966); Brunt, *Manpower*, chs xiv, xv, and see below, Chap. 29, n. 2. Roman residents abroad were often organised into *conventus civium Romanorum*, but these usually had no corporate political privileges.

[19] The charter of one of these settlements, the Colonia Genetiva Iulia at Urso (modern Osuna, near Seville), has been preserved in part: see Riccobono, *Fontes*, n. 21; translation and commentary, E. G. Hardy, *Three Spanish Charters*, 23 ff; Lewis–Reinhold, *R. Civ.* i. 420 ff. It specifies the right of freedmen to hold the office of local senator (*decurio*). Like the *lex Iulia Municipalis*, this statute was formally enacted under the direction of Antony after Caesar's death.

[20] It is notoriously difficult to establish the precise date of the founding of many Caesarian, triumviral and Augustan colonies, not least because the title Iulia does not clearly distinguish the dictator from his adopted son. On colonisation in this period see P. Vittinghoff, *Römische Kolonisation unter Caesar und Augustus* (1952); E. T. Salmon, *Roman Colonization* (1969), 132 ff; and, especially Brunt, *Manpower*, ch. xv and appendices 15 and 16. Of the 80,000 colonists, whom Caesar settled according to Suetonius (*Caes.* 42.1) Brunt reckons that some 10,000 were veterans and the rest civilians.

On Caesar's grants of Latin rights in Spain, which according to M. I. Henderson (*JRS* 1942, 1 ff.) benefited some thirty southern towns, see also Brunt, 584 ff.

On the personnel of the Senate see R. Syme, *PBSR* 1938, 1 ff, *Roman Revolution*, ch. vi. The Narbonese notables were probably of Roman origin.

[21] On the kingdom of Burebistas see V. Parvan, *Dacia* (1928), ch. v.

[22] According to Appian (*Bell. Civ.* ii. 110) Caesar had in readiness a force of sixteen legions, in addition to cavalry. It may be doubted whether the whole of the infantry force (*c.* 90,000 men) would have been employed by Caesar in the actual invasion of Parthia; with a force of this size his rate of movement would have been dangerously retarded. Cf. R. Syme, *JRS* 1933, 28, n. 101.

[23] So Plutarch, *Caesar*, 58. He seems to suggest that the Parthian expedition was to come before the Dacian. Suetonius, *Divus Iulius*, xliv. 3, suggests the reverse.

[24] The interminable list of honours voted to Caesar is preserved in Suetonius (ch. 76) and Dio Cassius (xliii. 14, 44–5; xliv. 3–6). Some of these are probably fictitious (cf. F. E. Adcock, *CAH*, ix. 718 ff.) or only

planned; yet on the lowest estimate his privileges far exceeded those accorded to any other Roman of the Republican era. He did not, however, use Imperator as a permanent title: see D. McFayden, *Hist. of the title Imperator under the Roman Empire* (1920). Cf. R. Syme, *Historia* 1958, 172 ff., on the nomenclature 'Imperator Caesar'.

[25] Some far-reaching conclusions have been based on the portrait coinage of 44, but more sober views are expressed by R. A. G. Carson, *Gnomon* 1956, 181 ff., and *Greece and Rome* 1957, 46 ff.; and by C. M. Kraay, *Numismatic Chronicle*, 1954, 18 ff.

[26] On the working of the *lex Annalis* under Caesar (49–44) see G. V. Sumner, *Phoenix* 1971, 246 ff. and 357 ff.

[27] Advice to reconstruct the republican constitution on democratic, or rather on anti-plutocratic, lines was offered to Caesar in two open letters, the so-called *Suasoriae* or *Epistulae ad Caesarem senem de republica*, purporting to come from the pen of Sallust. Their authorship remains in dispute. For a sceptical view see R. Syme, *Museum Helveticum*, 1958, 177 ff. Their Sallustian authorship is upheld by L. R. Taylor, *Party Politics in the Age of Caesar*, 154 ff., etc.

[28] On Caesar's increasing autocracy during the last months of his life see J. H. Collins, *Historia* 1955, 445 ff.; J. P. V. D. Balsdon, *Historia* 1958, 80 ff. Though Caesar twice suffered from epileptic fits during his campaigns and from fainting fits near the end of his life (Suetonius, *Divus Iulius*, 45), his mental vigour seems to have been maintained to the end. On the increasing offence which his conduct gave even to some of his partisans see H. Strasburger, *Caesar im Urteil seiner Zeitgenossen* (1968).

[29] On the date (between 26 January and 15 February and probably the latter) see Ed. Meyer, *Caesars Monarchie*, 526, n. 2. For coins bearing the legend *Dictator perpetuo* see Sydenham, *CRR*, 1061 ff., Crawford, *RRC*, 480/68; C. M. Kraay, *Numismatic Chronicle*, 1954, 18 ff.

[30] The evidence for Caesar's religious policy is very confused. It is not likely that he was given the title Jupiter Julius or that a cult was established in his honour in Rome during his lifetime, though after his death a cult of Divus Iulius was created. It is uncertain whether the inscription *deo invicto*, which was on his statue in the temple of Quirinus (Dio Cassius, xliii. 45.3) was contemporary or added later. In general see F. E. Adcock, *CAH*, ix. 718 ff. In the East, where for the last 150 years Roman generals had been accustomed to receive divine honours, the position was completely different from Rome: thus at Ephesus Caesar could be described as 'god manifest and common saviour of the life of man'. The view that Caesar sought divine honours has now been powerfully reinforced by S. Weinstock, *Divus Julius* (1971), who argues that he was a daring religious reformer who stimulated the grant of extraordinary honours to himself, created new cults (e.g. Victoria Caesaris, Fortuna C., Felicitas C., Salus C., Genius C.), and claimed to be permanent Imperator; he was about to become a divine ruler when he was assassinated; thereafter his supporters took up his plan and established the new cult of Divus Iulius which inherited many of its features. Although many may

still remain sceptical about this view (believing, for example, that the author has relied too credulously on some of Dio's evidence), the book throws much light on the religious ideas of Caesar's day.

[31] In addition to Cicero Lucan took this view. Livy's verdict on Caesar likewise appears to have been unfavourable.

[32] Ed. Meyer (*Caesars Monarchie*, 508 ff.) and J. Carcopino (*Points de vue sur l'imperialisme romaine*) have emphasised Caesar's monarchical bent, but F. E. Adcock (*CAH*, ix. 718 ff.) and R. Syme (*Roman Revolution*, ch. iv) contend that Caesar never came to a final resolve to end the Republic. Support for a monarchical intention should not be sought in the fact that in September 45 Caesar adopted his grand-nephew, C. Octavius: the will was kept secret, even from Octavius himself, and there is no suggestion that Caesar was creating an heir to his power. It is impossible to foresee how Caesar would have re-shaped the constitution on his return from Parthia (he himself probably did not know in March 44), but some form of autocracy, whether the autocrat called himself *rex* or not, seems virtually unavoidable.

Chapter 28: Notes

[1] The main narrative of the years 49–31 B.C. is provided by Appian (*Bell. Civ.* iii–v, down to 35 B.C. which is based in part on the *History* of Asinius Pollio, who fought on Antony's side) and Dio Cassius (xlv–liii). For 44–43 Cicero's Letters and *Philippics* are an invaluable source. Velleius Paterculus is brief and only the *Periochae* of Livy survive, but both made use of the *Memoirs* of Augustus (now lost). The poems of Horace and Virgil begin to throw some light on the period, as do Suetonius's *Life of Augustus* and the emperor's own Res Gestae (see p. 628). Plutarch's vivid *Life of Antony* is useful. Knowledge of the latter part of the period is obscured in part by the bitter propaganda campaign waged against each other by the supporters of Octavian and Antony.

On this period see T. Rice Holmes, *The Architect of the Roman Empire*, i (1928); M. A. Levi, *Ottaviano Capoparte* (1933); R. Syme, *The Roman Revolution* (1939), chs vii–xxi; H. Frisch, *Cicero's Fight for the Republic* (1946); J. M. Carter, *The Battle of Actium* (1970. Despite its title this book covers the years 44–31).

[2] On Caesar's acta (or, more correctly, *agenda*), and the methods by which they were implemented see v. Premerstein, *Zeitschrift für die Savigny-Stiftung*, rom. Abteilung, 1922, 129 ff.

[3] 'Perpauca a se verba addidit.' So Suetonius (*Iulius*, 84.2) describes Antony's funeral oration. Appian also (*Bell. Civ.* ii. 144–5) attributes a short speech, but Dio Cassius (xliv. 36 ff.) gives a very long oration. Cicero, *Phil.* 2.91, may suggest a longer formal speech. For a defence of Suetonius's view see M. E. Deutsch, *Univ. California Publ. Class. Arch.* 1928, 127 ff. But all our sources agree in describing Antony's speech as provocative. Pre-sumably his object was to scare the conspirators out of Rome for the sake of his personal safety.

Having accomplished this he showed no further disposition to disregard the amnesty.

[4] The statement that Brutus had received Mace-donia and Cassius Syria by the dispositions of Caesar, and that Antony robbed them of these provinces for the benefit of himself and Dolabella, is repeatedly made by Appian. But it is not borne out by any other ancient writer, and is tacitly refuted by Cicero. On the distribution of provinces in 44–43 see W. Sternkopf, *Hermes* 1912, 320 ff.

[5] Ancient writers disagree as to whether there was any real plot on the part of Octavian. (See the discus-sion in T. Rice Holmes, *The Architect of the Roman Empire*, i. 27–8.) Had Antony possessed any valid evi-dence against Octavian it is hard to believe that he would have simply dropped the matter. It seems more probable that he made another ill-judged attempt to frighten Octavian.

[6] The terms are quoted by Cicero, *Philippic*, viii. 25–7. Antony's offer to the Senate suggests that at this stage he was reviving the schemes of Caesar in 58 for conquests in the Danube regions.

[7] The story that Cicero said of Octavian 'lau-dandus, ornandus, *tollendus* est' ('tollendus' with a double meaning, 'exalted' and 'destroyed'. – Velleius Paterculus, ii. 62.6; Suetonius, *Augustus*, xii) is virtu-ally admitted by himself (*Ad Fam*. xi. 21.1). His atti-tude to Octavian resembled that of the extremist sena-tors to Pompey before the Civil War. He intended to keep in with Beelzebub just so long as Satan was at large.

[8] Suetonius (*Iul* 83) records that in Caesar's will Octavian was adopted as his chief heir, and then at the end of the will (*in ima cera*) as his son, 'in familiam nomenque'. Legal difficulties have suggested that the adoption was really achieved through the *lex curiata* of 43 (see W. Schmitthenner, *Oktavian und das Testa-ment Casars* (1952)), but see the criticism by G. E. F. Chilver, *JRS* 1954, 126 ff. In any case Caesar probably intended that Octavian should be his adopted son as well as heir.

[9] All three triumvirs struck coins with their own effigy. Under their regime the mint at Rome ceased to issue money (*c.* 40), and only 'proconsular' money was put into circulation.

[10] An excellent collection of anecdotes about the proscriptions is preserved in Appian (*Bell. Civ.* iv. 11–30). During the Terror friends and kinsmen gave each other away; on the other hand, plenty of cases occurred in which wives and slaves took the utmost risks upon themselves to save the proscribed. The devotion of a wife to a proscribed husband is well illustrated in an epitaph known as the 'Laudatio Turiae'. See Dessau, *ILS*, 8393; *Éloge d'une matrone romaine* (ed. M. Durry, 1950); translation in Lewis–Reinhold, *R. Civ.* i. 584 ff.

[11] It is noteworthy that a far higher proportion of senators than of Equites was eventually pardoned by the triumvirs. Since the Equites of recent years had played little part in politics, their inclusion in the proscription lists can hardly have had a political object, as in the case of the Sullan massacres.

[12] Appian, *Bell. Civ.* iv. 32–3.

[13] Biographies of Cicero include G. Boissier, *Cicero and his Friends* (1897); J. L. Strachan-Davidson (1894);

E. G. Sihler (1914); T. Petersson (1920); H. J. Haskell, *This was Cicero* (1942); R. E. Smith (1966); M. Gelzer (in German, 1969); D. Stockton (1971); A. R. Shackleton Bailey (1971). On the impression made in Rome by the execution of Cicero see the remarkable outburst in Velleius Paterculus, ii. 66. On the influence of Cicero in forming the political thought of Augustus see E. Reitzenstein, *Nachrichten der Gesellschaft der Wissenschaften in Göttingen* (1917), pp. 399 ff., 481 ff.; E. Lepore, *Il principe Ciceroniano* 1954). See also E. Rawson, *Cicero* (1975).

[14] Brutus struck 'proconsular' coins, with the significant legend 'Idibus Martiis', and the device of a cap of liberty (such as was worn by freedmen on receiving their liberty) between two daggers. (Sydenham, *CRR*, n. 1301.). See p. 281.

[15] At the inception of the Triumvirate Antony had twenty-five legions, Octavian eleven, Lepidus seven. In the campaign of Philippi the Caesarians disposed of twenty-eight legions, Cassius commanded twelve and Brutus eight.

[16] During his governorship of Cilicia Cicero had trouble with an agent of Brutus, who was endeavouring to squeeze out of the city of Salamis the interest of a loan at compound interest of 48 per cent (*Ad Atticum*, v. 21.1).

[17] At the outset of the Perusine War L. Antonius disposed of six of his brother's legions, against four of Octavian's. Salvidienus brought six further legions to the assistance of Octavian. Against these Ventidius and Pollio could have brought eleven additional legions into action. On the war see E. Gabba, *Harvard Stud. Cl. Phil.* 1971.

[18] The identity of the child has been the subject of much speculation. For the view that he was a future son of Antony and Octavia see W. W. Tarn, *JRS* 1932, 135.

[19] On Sextus's salvage service see Appian, *Bell. Civ.* iv. 36. For the whole career of Sextus see M. Hadas, *Sextus Pompey* (1930).

[20] On the terminal date of the Second Triumvirate see T. Rice Holmes, op. cit. 231 ff. Appian asserts in one passage (*Illyrica*, ch. xxviii.) and denies in another (*Bell. Civ.* v. 95) that the prolongation of the Triumvirate was sanctioned by the Popular Assembly. The former statement appears to be derived from an apologetic source (the unfinished collection of Memoirs by Augustus), and should probably be rejected.

[21] On Agrippa's part in the war against Sextus Pompeius see M. Reinhold, *Marcus Agrippa*, (1933), 29 ff. In addition to Portus Iulius itself, Agrippa's engineer and architect constructed long underground galleries, one linking Lake Avernus with Cumae, another under the hill of Cumae itself. See R. F. Paget, *JRS* 1968, 163 ff.

[22] After the shipwreck of his fleet Octavian was reported to have declared that 'he was going to win, in spite of Neptune and all' (Suetonius, *Augustus*, xvi. 2). The craving for peace in Italy during the later years of the Triumvirate is reflected in the earlier poems of Horace, Virgil and Propertius.

[23] See Dio Cassius, xlix. 15.5 (in contrast to Appian, *Bell. Civ.*, v. 132). Cf. H. Last, *Rendiconti, Ist. Lombardo*, 1951, 95 ff.

[24] On the Illyrian Wars of Octavian see E. Swoboda, *Octavian and Illyricum* (1932); R. Syme *JRS* 1933, 66 ff. = *Dainton Papers* (1971); N. Vulic, *JRS* 1934, 163 ff.; W. Schmitthenner, *Historia* 1958, 189 ff.; J. J. Wilkes, *Dalmatia* (1969), 46 ff.

[25] Labienus commemorated his victory in a curiously hybrid coinage (no doubt intended for his ex-legionary troops), showing on one side a Parthian horse of Arab type with a quiver, on the other his own head with the legend 'Q. Labienus Parthicus Imperator'. See Sydenham, *CRR*, n. 1357 and p. 291.

[26] According to the quite credible estimate in Plutarch (*Antony*, xxxvii) 43,000 auxiliaries accompanied the 60,000 legionaries on Antony's Parthian expedition.

[27] A vivid account of the hardships of the retreat from Phraaspa (ultimately derived from an eye-witness, Q. Dellius, a lieutenant of Antony) is preserved in Plutarch, *Antony*, xli–li.

[28] That Caesarion was the son of Caesar has been widely asserted by writers ancient and modern (e.g. Plutarch, *Caesar*, xlix. 10), but Suetonius (*Iulius*, lii. 2; *Augustus*, xvii. 5) and Plutarch (*Antony*, liv) leave the matter in doubt. Some historians would also date the birth not to 47 (as Plutarch), but to 44, even just after Caesar's death. For discussion see J. P. V. D. Balsdon, *Historia* 1958, 86 ff.; *Cl. Rev.* 1960, 69 ff.

[29] On Antony see R. F. Rossi, *Marcio Antonio nelle lotta politica della tarda repubblica romana* (1959); H. Buchheim, *Die Orientpolitik des Triumvirn M. Antonius* (1961).

[30] On the date of Antony's marriage to Cleopatra see T. Rice Holmes, *Architect of the Roman Empire*, i. 227 ff. Such a marriage was not recognised in Roman law before Octavia had been divorced: in Roman law no Roman could have two wives, although other law might allow it. The marriage (under Ptolemaic law) does not prove that Antony intended to become a Hellenistic king in his own right. The commemorative coins of Cleopatra, showing her portrait on the obverse and that of Antony on the reverse, describe him by the purely Roman titulature of *imperator* and *triumvir* (in their Greek terminological equivalents. See W. Wroth, *Coins in the Br. Mus.: Cappadocia*, etc (1899), 19, n. 3).

[31] Augustus, *Res Gestae*, 7, implies that the Triumvirate terminated at the end of 33. For discussion see T. Rice Holmes, *Architect of the Roman Empire*, i. 231 ff.; G. E. F. Chilver, *Historia* 1950, 410 ff.

The publication is awaited of some very interesting documents from Aphrodisias in Caria relating to the activities in Asia of Antony and Octavian. They form part of a large archive which stretches from the Mithridatic War to Augustus, with another set of documents which run from Trajan to Gordian III. I am very grateful to Miss J. Reynolds for allowing me to see some of these.

For these triumviral documents and an assessment of the significance of the Triumvirate especially in relation to the emergence of monarchy see now F. Millar, *JRS* 1973, 50 ff.

[32] See *Res Gestae*, 25.2. On the importance of the *coniuratio* see R. Syme, *Roman Revolution*, 284 ff.;

on Octavian's followers see op. cit. 292 f., and for Antony's 266 ff. After Actium the eastern regions seem to have taken a similar oath. Its nature may be surmised from the oath of allegiance taken by resident Romans and natives at Gangra in Paphlagonia in 3 B.C. soon after its incorporation in the province of Galatia (see Ehrenberg and Jones, *Documents: Reigns of Augustus and Tiberius*, 315; also P. A. Brunt and J. M. Moore, *Res Gestae* (1967), 67 f.). The oath, which was personal, did not confer any legal power on Octavian.

[33] On the battle of Actium see W. W. Tarn, *JRS* 1931, 171 ff.; G. W. Richardson, *JRS* 1937, 153 ff.; E. Wistrand, *Horace's Ninth Epode* (1958); J. M. Carter, *The Battle of Actium* (1970). Antony's intentions are not clear. Some (e.g. Richardson, Carter) believe that his primary object was to escape, others that he sought a decisive naval action, but was let down by misunderstanding or treachery among his men (Tarn). The accounts of the battle in Plutarch (*Antony*, lxvi–lxvii) and Dio (lix. 31–5) are far from clear. After the battle Octavian founded a 'city of victory', Nicopolis, nearby.

[34] The traditional story of the deaths of Antony and Cleopatra, as given in Plutarch and Dio, is largely compounded out of untrustworthy materials, among which one may recognise a Greek romance writer and a Roman propagandist in the interest of Octavian. If we may judge by their former lives they died like a Roman nobleman and a Macedonian queen, without melodrama and without attempts at mutual betrayal. Cleopatra may have chosen to die by the bite of an asp because the Egyptians believed that it was the divine minister of the Sun-god and deified its victim. Cf. J. G. Griffiths, *Journal of Egyptian Archaeology* 1961, 181 ff.

[35] *Res Gestae*, 3.1: 'victor omnibus veniam petentibus civibus peperci'.

[36] On Cleopatra see H. Volkmann, *Cleopatra* (1958), and M. Grant, *Cleopatra* (1972); J. Lindsay, *Cleopatra* (1971), is a more popular work. On her appearance see G. M. A. Richter, *Portraits of the Greeks* (1965), 269. Her ambitions remain uncertain. According to W. W. Tarn (*CAH*, x. 76 ff.) she had a great vision of world-wide rule and believed, as a nameless Greek oracle foretold, that she would overthrow Rome, release the East, and then raise up Rome again in a partnership of East and West and inaugurate a golden age of peace and brotherhood. A more moderate assessment of her hopes is given by R. Syme, *Roman Revolution*, 274 f. Propertius (iii. 11.46) might credit her with the ambition to give judgment amid the arms and statues of Marius ('iura dare et statuas inter et arma Mari'), but at most she probably hoped to curtail rather than to destroy or dominate the Roman Empire. She wished to restore the lost glories of her inherited Ptolemaic kingdom. For the oracle, which may, but does not certainly, refer to Cleopatra, see J. Geffcken, *Oracula Sibyllina*, iii. 350 ff.

Chapter 29: Notes

[1] On the economic conditions of the Restoration period see Frank, *Econ. SAR*, 342 ff. On the land-allotment in the first century and the economic effects see Brunt, *Manpower*, ch. xix.

[2] On emigration see A. J. N. Wilson, *Emigration from Italy in the Republican Age of Rome* (1966); Brunt, *Manpower* chs xiv, xv. One key figure for estimating the number of settlers is the 80,000 Italians alleged to have been massacred by Mithridates in Asia in 88 B.C. (see p. 231). Brunt would reduce this obviously swollen total to 'a few thousand *ingenui* and freedmen'. Brunt's detailed calculations, which suggest emigration on a slightly smaller scale than the general impression given by Wilson's work, point to some 125,000 'Italians' in the transmarine provinces in 69 B.C. and some 150,000 in 49. There followed a period of considerable overseas colonisation and it may be noted here that Brunt reckons the total of adult male citizens domiciled in the provinces in 28 B.C. as some 375,000 in 8 B.C., as 575,000 and in A.D. 14 as 580,000.

[3] On the transplantation of the cherry see Pliny, *NH*, xv. 102; on the orchards of Italy, Dionys. Halic. i. 37; Varro, *De Re Rustica*, i. 2.6. According to Cicero (*De Re Publica*, iii. 16) an embargo of uncertain date, but probably in his own day, had been placed upon the plantation of vines and olives among the Transalpine peoples. If this prohibition was intended as a safeguard to Italian orchardmen, it was a seemingly superfluous measure, and indeed it was never enforced effectively.

[4] This restriction on Italian mining was probably imposed in order to prevent a dangerous concentration of servile labour in certain areas. See M. Besnier, *Revue archéologique*, 1919, 31 ff.

[5] On the Italian penetration of the Danube lands, which extended as far as Romania, see Parvan, *Dacia*, 138–40.

[6] On Italian commerce in the East in the first century see J. Hatzfeld, *Les Trafiquants italiens dans l'Orient hellénique*, 52 ff.; A. J. N. Wilson, op. cit. n. 2, 85 ff.

[7] In Cicero's estimation 'big business' i.e. financial operations on a large scale, was the only strictly respectable form of money-making, besides agriculture (*De Officiis*, i. 151).

[8] Cicero states (no doubt with some exaggeration) that in (Narbonese) Gaul the Romans financed every kind of business among the natives (*Pro Fonteio*, 11). The king of Mauretania contracted a big loan with a money-dealer named P. Sittius (Cicero, *Pro Sulla*, 56). In Egypt another adventurer, C. Rabirius Postumus, made an unsuccessful attempt to collect the money due from Ptolemy Auletes to Pompey and Caesar (Cicero, *Pro Rabirio Postumo*). On the loans of Pompey to the king of Cappadocia see Cicero, *Ad Att.* vi. 1.3; on Brutus's usury in Cyprus, *Ad Att.* v. 21.10. For examples of graceful remissions of debts by Roman lenders see *Inscriptiones Graecae*, v. i. 1146 (Gythium); XII. v. 860 (Tenos).

[9] On the sources of Crassus's fortune see Plutarch, *Crassus*, ch. ii.

[10] On social intercourse in general see Warde Fowler, *Social Life in Rome in the Days of Cicero*; W. Kroll, *Die Kultur der ciceronischen Zeit*; J. P. V. D. Balsdon, *Life and Leisure in Ancient Rome* (1969).

[11] Caesar's debts were estimated at nearly

75,000,000 denarii, those of Curio at about 50,000,000.

[12] On the conditions of the urban *plebs* see Brunt, *Manpower*, 385 ff., and in *Past and Present* 1966, 2 ff. ('The Roman Mob'), to which this paragraph owes much; on Cicero's tenements see *Ad Atticum*, xiv. 9.4. On the status of craftsmen in general see A. Burford, *Craftsmen in Greek and Roman Society* (1972).

[13] On violence in the country see Brunt, *Manpower*, 550 ff. On legislation against violence see A. W. Lintott, *Violence in Republican Rome* (1968). On the difficulty of the poor in securing their legal rights see J. M. Kelly, *Roman Litigation* (1966).

[14] On the luxurious villas of the aristocracy and their social and cultural background see J. H. D'Arms, *Romans on the Bay of Naples* (1970); J. P. V. D. Balsdon, *Life and Leisure in Ancient Rome* (1969), 193 ff.; A. G. McKay, *Houses, Villas and Palaces in the Roman World* (1975).

[15] See J. P. V. D. Balsdon, *Roman Women* (1962). On changing attitudes to life in Rome see E. S. Ramage, *Urbanitas: ancient sophistication and refinement* (1973).

[16] For wild-beast fighting (*venationes*) see G. Jennison, *Animals for Show and Pleasure in Ancient Rome* (1937). See also M. Grant, *Gladiators* (1967), and in general Balsdon, *Life and Leisure in Ancient Rome* (1969), 288 ff. On the circus races see H. A. Harris, *Sport in Greece and Rome* (1972).

[17] On Sulla's reconstruction of the Forum see E. van Deman, *JRS* 1922, 1 ff. On the buildings of Rome see Platner and Ashby, *A Topographical Dictionary of Ancient Rome* (1929); E. Nash, *A Pictorial Dictionary of Ancient Rome*, 2 vols (1961–2), illustrating the buildings described in Platner-Ashby; D. R. Dudley, *Urbs Roma* (1967); M. Grant, *The Roman Forum* (1970); and, for Italy as well as Rome, Boëthius and Ward-Perkins, *Etruscan and Roman Architecture* (1970), ch. 6.

[18] On Cossutius see Vitruvius, *Pref.* vii. 15.17; on Nicopolis, Strabo, xvii. 1.10.

[19] On Roman art see E. Strong, *Art in Ancient Rome* (1929), and *CAH*, ix. 825 ff.; G. M. A. Richter, *Ancient Italy* (1955); J. M. C. Toynbee, *The Art of the Romans* (1965); R. B. Bandinelli, *Rome, the Centre of Power: Roman Art to* A.D. *200* (1970), a sumptuous volume.

[20] On Roman schools see A. Gwynn, *Roman Education* (1926); H. I. Marrou, *A History of Education in Antiquity* (1956); M. L. Clarke, *Higher Education in the Ancient World* (1971).

[21] See L. R. Palmer, *The Latin Language* (1954).

[22] On Roman literature in the Ciceronian age see J. W. Duff, *A Literary History of Rome . . . to the Close of the Golden Age*[3] (1950), 197 ff.; T. Frank, *Life and Literature in the Roman Republic* (1930). On the mime, W. Beare, *The Roman Stage*[3] (1964), ch. xviii. On Lucretius, C. Bailey, *Lucretius*, 3 vols (1947); E. E. Sikes, *Lucretius, Poet and Philosopher* (1936); *Lucretius* (ed. D. R. Dudley, 1965). On Catullus, edition by C. J. Fordyce (1961); E. A. Havelock, *The Lyric Genius of Catullus* (1939); T. P. Wiseman, *Catullan Questions* (1969).

[23] On the annalists see literature mentioned in Chap. 6, n. 17.

[24] On Caesar's *Commentaries* see F. E. Adcock, *Caesar as a Man of Letters* (1956). Although their publication may have had a political purpose and Caesar could not help but see events through his own eyes, their essential trustworthiness has stood up well to much criticism, e.g. by M. Rambaud, *L'Art de la déformation historique dans les commentaires de César* (1953), on which work see J. P. V. D. Balsdon, *JRS* 1955, 161 ff., and cf. *Greece and Rome* 1957, 19 ff.; and by G. Walser, *Caesar und die Germanen* (1956), on which see A. N. Sherwin-White, *JRS* 1958, 188 ff. On Caesar as a political propagandist see J. H. Collins, *Aufstieg NRW*, I. i. 922 ff.

[25] The fragments of Sallust's *Historiae* are edited by B. Maurenbrecher, 2 vols (1891–3). See A. D. Leeman, *A Systematic Bibliography of Sallust, 1879–1964* (1965); M. L. W. Laistner, *The Greater Roman Historians* (1947), ch. iii; D. C. Earl, *The Political Thought of Sallust* (1961); R. Syme, *Sallust* (1964); G. M. Paul in *Latin Historians* (ed. T. A. Dorey, 1966), ch. iv.

[26] A surviving specimen is the *Invectiva in Ciceronem*, which Quintilian believed was written by Sallust, but it does not suit Sallust in 54 (its supposed date) and may be the product of an Augustan rhetorician. Its counterpart, the *Invectiva in Sallustium*, is probably a forgery.

[27] A supporter of Pompey, Varro had been pardoned by Caesar who appointed him keeper of his proposed public library. Though outlawed by Antony, Varro lived quietly after the civil war and wrote, besides his forty-one books of *Antiquitates*, two partly surviving works, a treatise on grammar and vocabulary (*De lingua Latina*, 3 books) and three books on agriculture.

[28] Of Cicero's several works on rhetoric mention may be made of his *Brutus* or *De Claris Oratoribus* (ed. by A. E. Douglas, 1966). On Cicero as a historian see B. L. Hallward, *Cambr. Hist. Journal*, iii.

[29] The surviving fragments of the Roman Orators are edited by E. Malcovati, *Oratorum Romanorum Fragmenta*[2] (1955). See M. L. Clarke, *Rhetoric at Rome* (1953); S. F. Bonner in *Fifty Years of Classical Scholarship* (ed. M. Platnauer), 335 ff.

[30] On literary patronage in the Ciceronian age see D. M. Schullian, *External Stimuli to Literary Production in Rome, 90–27* B.C., and W. S. Anderson, *Pompey, his Friends and the Literature of the First Century* B.C. (1963), who perhaps exaggerates Pompey as the centre of a literary circle.

[31] See W. Kunkel, *Herkunst und soziale Stellung der römischen Juristen* (1952). On Roman law in general see H. F. Jolowicz, *Historical Introduction to the Study of Roman Law*[3] (1972); B. Nicholas, *An Introduction to Roman Law* (1962); and especially, for law in its social setting in everyday life, J. Crook, *Law and Life of Rome* (1967). For the development of private law and its sources in the last two centuries of the Republic see A. Watson, *Law Making in the Later Roman Republic* (1974).

[32] See M. L. Clarke, *The Roman Mind* (1956); E. V. Arnold, *Roman Stoicism* (1911); A. J. Festugière, *Epicurus and his Gods* (1955); B. Farrington, *The Faith of Epicurus* (1967); F. H. Sandbach, *The Stoics* (1975).

[33] On Cicero's thought see H. A. K. Hunt, *The

Humanism of Cicero (1954); as historian and antiquarian see E. Rawson, *JRS* 1972, 33 ff.

[34] For books on Roman religion see above Chap.
5, n. 10. On many aspects of religion in Caesar's
day see S. Weinstock, *Divus Julius* (1971).

[35] See F. H. Cramer, *Astrology in Roman Law and
Politics* (1954), ch. ii.

Chapter 30: Notes

[1] The main literary sources for the principate of
Augustus are his own *Res Gestae* (ed. P. A. Brunt
and M. Moore, 1967); Suetonius, *Augustus* (ed. M.
Adams, 1939); Tacitus, *Annals*, i. 2–15; Dio Cassius,
lii–lvi; Velleius Paterculus, ii. 89–128 (on Velleius
see p. 396). A selection of documents is provided by
V. Ehrenberg and A. H. M. Jones, *Documents illustra-
ting the Reigns of Augustus and Tiberius*[2] (1955). On
Tacitus see F. R. D. Goodyear, *The Annals of Tacitus,
Annals 1, 1–54* (1972). On the coinage see H. Matting-
ly, *Brit. Museum Catalogue of the Coins of the Roman
Empire*, i: *Augustus to Vitellius* (1923); H. Mattingly
and others, *The Roman Imperial Coinage*, i (1923); M.
Grant, *From Imperium to Auctoritas* (1946); C. H. V.
Sutherland, *Coinage in Roman Imperial Policy (1951)*.

The *Res Gestae* is an official account of his reign,
composed by Augustus himself and inscribed on two
bronze pillars in front of his Mausoleum. Copies of
the document were also set up in temples throughout
the Empire. The original has perished, but an inscription on the walls of the temple of 'Roma et Augustus'
at Ancyra (modern Ankara in Turkey) preserves the
Latin text and a Greek paraphrase (hence known as
the Monumentum Ancyranum). Other fragments
have been found at Apollonia in Pisidia and at
Antioch near by. It is obviously a source of primary
importance and has been called the Queen of Latin
inscriptions.

Modern works on Augustus and his age include
T. Rice Holmes, *The Architect of the Roman Empire*,
ii (1931); R. Syme, *The Roman Revolution* (1939);
D. Earl, *The Age of Augustus* (1968); A. H. M. Jones,
Augustus (1970); G. W. Bowersock, *Augustus and the
Greek World* (1965).

[2] The importance of the mere lapse of time in
creating a new political atmosphere at Rome was aptly
emphasised by Tacitus (*Annals*, i. 3.7; *Histories* i. 1.2).
After the battle of Actium a new generation was coming into public life that knew not the Republic.

[3] The view that the 'Restoration of the Republic'
was merely intended as a screen for Augustus's personal autocracy was suggested by Tacitus and
affirmed by Dio Cassius. It has found wide modern
support but, if correct, Augustus was a most consum-
mate actor. The truth probably lies between the two
extremes; he must, in the interests of universal peace
and safety, retain autocratic control of the army, yet
he wanted to retain or restore those elements of the
republican tradition which he thought could be
revived. It is of course possible that he did dream
that at some future date, after reorganising the
whole state, he might retire into the background as
senior statesman, but it is not likely and certainly
did not happen.

[4] Octavian, though born at Rome, was brought
up in a small country town, Velitrae, some 25 miles
to the south-east. Like most country-bred people he
realised that political institutions are plants that will
not bear sudden uprooting.

[5] Since his adoption by Caesar, Octavian had been
a patrician, and as such therefore in strict law disqualified to be an actual tribune. It has been supposed
that he accepted a tribune's *ius auxilii*, which he could
exercise not only in Rome but throughout the
Empire. The view is based on a confused passage
of Dio Cassius, li. 19, and an apparent exercise of
tribunician power in Rhodes by Tiberius (Suetonius,
Tib. 11), but this is very uncertain.

[6] Augustus stated (*Res Gestae*, 8) 'senatum ter legi',
referring probably to 29, 19 and 11 (rather than 13)
B.C. See A. H. M. Jones, *Studies in Roman Government*
(1960), ch. ii. Cf. A. E. Astin, *Latomus* 1963, 226 ff.

The census figure of 28 B.C., which is 4,663,000,
contrasts with that of 70 B.C., which is 910,000 *civium
capita*. The discrepancy may arise from a great variety
of possible causes (including the unreliability of one
of the two figures). Thus Frank (*Econ. SAR*, i. 314)
rejected the earlier figure and believed that the
Augustan figure included only adult males (cf. T. P.
Wiseman, *JRS* 1959, 71 ff.). On the other hand Brunt
(*Manpower*, 100 ff., 113 ff.) champions the view that
the Augustan figure includes women and children
(excluding infants), thus making sense of the whole
series of figures; he further believes that even under
Augustus the native-born Italians were decreasing,
and that the increases in the figures of 8 B.C. and
A.D. 14 should be explained by enfranchisements of
slaves and provincials. He assumes, however, that
the enumeration may easily have been short by some
20–25 per cent, and thus would reckon the citizen
figure at about 5,000,000 in 28 B.C. (with under a
million of them living abroad) and at about 6,200,000
in A.D. 14 (with nearly 1,900,000 abroad). Brunt
would put the total population of Italy (including
Cisalpina) at no more than 7,500,000, with a high
proportion of slaves to freemen, namely some
3,000,000. This estimate of the total population,
which is higher than but of the same order as that
made by Beloch, differs strikingly from the
14,000,000 of Frank.

[7] Crassus, as proconsul of Macedonia, had defeated
the Thracian Bastarnae and killed their leader in
single combat. For this feat he claimed the *spolia
opima*, which hitherto had been granted only to
Romulus and Cornelius Cossus (p. 71). Augustus
disallowed the claim on the ground that Cossus at
the time was consul, not proconsul; however, he
granted Crassus a triumph.

[8] On the powers that Augustus received in 27 and
23 B.C. see, in addition to the books mentioned in
n. 1. above, M. Hammond, *The Augustan Principate*.
(1933); M. Grant, *From Imperium to Auctoritas*(1946);
H. Last, *JRS* 1947, 157 ff., 1950, 119 ff.; R. Syme,
JRS 1946, 149 ff.; G. E. F. Chilver, *Historia* 1950,
408 ff., (a review of work on this topic done between
1939 and 1950); A. H. M. Jones, *JRS* 1951, 112
ff. (= *Studies in Roman Government*, ch. 1); E. T.
Salmon, *Historia* 1956, 456 ff. Some of the non-
English literature will be indicated in the above works.

On Octavian's position in January 27 see W. K. Lacey, *JRS* 1974, 176 ff.

It is generally agreed that the *imperium* which Augustus exercised in the provinces from 23 was proconsular, but the nature of his provincial *imperium* from 27 to 23 is hotly debated, whether it was consular or proconsular. See the literature cited above: it is hardly possible to discuss here all the numerous controversial details of the constitutional settlement.

[9] Details and dating of the conspiracy are uncertain. Some would follow Dio Cassius and date it to 22 and identify the Murena with the cousin of the consul of 23. So K. M. T. Atkinson, *Historia* 1960, 440 ff., but see D. Stockton, ibid. 1965, 18 ff. Cf. also M. Swan, *Harvard Stud. Cl. Phil.* 1966, 235 ff., and R. A. Bauman, *Historia* 1966, 420 ff. But see S. Jameson, *Historia* 1969, 204 ff., for 23 B.C.

[10] From 12 B.C. Augustus resumed Caesar's practice of inviting the *consules ordinarii* of each year to resign after six months in favour of a supplementary pair (*consules suffecti*); after 3 B.C. he made this arrangement into a regular practice. In this way he satisfied a greater number of aspirants to the consular title, which continued to be eagerly coveted.

[11] The grant of *imperium maius*, attested by Dio Cassius (liii. 32.5), has sometimes been doubted, but is confirmed by the discovery of five edicts from Cyrene (Ehrenberg and Jones, *Documents*, n. 311; translation in Lewis–Reinhold, *R. Civ.* ii. 36 ff.). Here we have Augustus interfering in a senatorial province, but he does so when asked and with great tact; he said that the proconsuls would act 'rightly and fittingly' if they adopted his proposals for certain judicial reforms.

[12] The extent to which Augustus exercised *nominatio* or *commendatio* remains uncertain (he appears to have 'commended' four out of the twelve praetors by the end of his reign, but was sparing in direct support of consular candidates). However, B. Levick (*Historia* 1967, 207 ff.) argues that in the Julio-Claudian period *nominatio* and *commendatio* were not legally defined cut-and-dried rights.

[13] Augustus claimed (*Res Gestae*, 34.3) that from 27 'I excelled all in influence [*auctoritas*] although I possessed no more official power [*potestas*] than others who were my colleagues in the several magistracies' ('auctoritate omnibus praestiti, potestatis autem nihilo amplius habui quam ceteri qui mihi quoque in magistratu conlegae fuerant'). On whether 'quŏque' or 'quŏque' should be understood see F. E. Adcock, *JRS* 1952, 10 ff.

Much has wrongly been read into the word 'auctoritas', from a constitutional legal meaning to a semi-mystical aura. In fact it meant 'personal influence', such as the leading citizens (*principes viri*) had enjoyed; now, as leading citizen, Augustus not unnaturally claims to have more influence or moral authority than any other, resulting from his unique services to the state.

[14] Augustus lived on the Palatine in a modest house which he had acquired from the orator Q. Hortensius. This is usually identified with the surviving building known as the House of Livia. Recent excavations, however, suggest that Augustus acquired further property and built another residence just across a narrow street by the House of Livia. See C. G. Carettoni, *Rend. Pont. Accad.* xxxix (1966–7), 55 ff.; N. Degrassi, ibid. 76 ff.; A. G. McKay, *Houses, Villas and Palaces in the Roman World* (1955), 70 ff.

[15] See Dio Cassius, liv. 10.5. A. H. M. Jones (*JRS* 1951 = *Studies in Roman Government*, ch i) has argued powerfully in favour of Dio's attribution of consular *imperium* for life. But there are difficulties. See P. A. Brunt, *Cl. Rev.* 1962, 70 ff., and in his edition of the *Res Gestae*, pp. 13 ff. If Augustus did accept this power he discreetly refrained from mentioning the fact in the *Res Gestae*.

[16] It is significant that after 22 B.C. no triumphs, but only the right to wear the triumphal insignia, were granted to war-winners outside the imperial family. Similarly the 'imperatorial acclamations' (p. 134) were no longer made in the name of the actual battle-winners, but in that of Augustus, who received twenty such acclamations in all, and recorded them on public documents by assuming the cognomen of *imperator*, with an ordinal number to denote the total of acclamations received up to date. On these acclamations see T. D. Barns, *JRS* 1974, 21 ff.

[17] An early example of reference to Augustus from a senatorial province is supplied by the second edict from Cyrene. On the administration of justice during the reign see A. H. M. Jones, *Augustus* (1970), ch. xi. Augustus received so many civil appeals that he had to delegate those from Italy to the urban praetor and those from the provinces to a consular appointed in each case. We know from the Cyrene edicts that in that province there were jury-courts; they consisted of Roman citizens of standing and apparently tried both provincials and citizens. It is probable that the system, which was parallel to the *iudicia publica* in Rome, was normal throughout the provinces. It may have arisen partly to help meet the pressure of business arising from the increasing number of appeals; provincial governors may have been granted *exercitio iudicii publici*, with organised juries, to deal with crimes which at Rome would have been tried by the *iudicia publica*; for *crimina extraordinaria* they exercised *cognitio* when *provocatio* would apply in the case of Roman citizens. The juries do not appear to have survived long (not beyond the first century). See further Jones, op. cit. and *Criminal Courts of the Roman Republic and Principate* (1972), ch. 2; and P. Garnsey, 'The Lex Iulia and appeal under the Empire', *JRS* 1966, 167 ff., who argues that *provocatio* was *always* after sentence and never before trial. Cf. Garnsey, *Social Status and Legal Privilege in the Roman Empire* (1970), 75 ff.

[18] Our knowledge of the *lex Valeria Cornelia* derives from the discovery in 1947 at Magliano (ancient Heba) in Etruria of an inscription, now known as the Tabula Hebana: see Ehrenberg and Jones, *Documents²* (1955), n. 94a. It contains a *rogatio* in honour of Germanicus in A.D. 19–20, when five more voting centuries were created in his honour, and it refers back to the creation of the original ten in A.D. 5. It has provoked much discussion: see a basic work, G. Tibiletti, *Principi e magistri repubblicani* (1955).

The precise purpose of the *lex Valeria Cornelia* is not clear. It was argued by A. H. M. Jones (*JRS*

1955, 9 ff. = *Studies*, ch. iii) that since bribery was rife (anti-bribery laws were passed in 18 and 8 B.C.), elections must have been relatively free in this period; Augustus, wishing to see more men from the Italian municipalities elected, used the indirect method of introducing *destinatio* in the expectation that the predominant equestrian element in the new centuries would bring this about. However, P. A. Brunt (*JRS* 1961, 71 ff.) has shown that even after A.D. 5 the consulship still fell to men of consular lineage and that the humbler men became only *consules suffecti*. See further A. Ferrill, *Historia* 1971, 718 ff.

[19] It was an anomaly in Augustus's constitution that governors of the imperial provinces, though they might have considerable armed forces under their control, held praetorian rank, whereas the governors of even the most insignificant senatorial provinces were of proconsular status.

[20] On the lower civil servants see A. H. M. Jones, *JRS* 1949, 38 ff. (= *Studies*, ch. x). On 'Caesar's household' see P. R. C. Weaver, *Familia Caesaris* (1972).

[21] See M. Durry, *Les Cohorts pretoriennes* (1938); A. Passerini, *Le coorti pretorie* (1939). The former argues for a cohort strength of 500 (until, except under Vitellius, they were increased to 1000 by Septimius Severus).

[22] On the imperial councils see J. A. Crook, *Consilium Principis* (1955). A papyrus fragment (see E. G. Turner in *Oxyrhynchus Papyri*, xxv. 2435) describes the reception by the *Consilium Principis* of a deputation from Alexandria in A.D. 13.

[23] In his political testament according to Dio (lvi. 33) Augustus gave clear expression to the principle that a state is a partnership and should have as many active collaborators as possible.

[24] On the buildings see the works cited above in Chap. 29, n. 17. Augustus lists his new buildings in *Res Gestae*, 19–21. His boast about marble is given by Suetonius, *Aug.* 28.

[25] The duties of the 'Metropolitan Water Board' were set forth in Iulius Frontinus's surviving treatise, *De Aquis Urbis Romae*. He quotes a law and several *senatus consulta* passed in 11 B.C.

[26] The triumvir Crassus had acquired 'the greater part of Rome' by steadily buying up property ruined by fire (Plutarch, *Crassus*, ii).

[27] On the Roman fire-brigade see P. K. Baillie-Reynolds, *The Vigiles of Imperial Rome* (1926).

[28] Since 22 B.C. the distribution of corn had been controlled by *praefecti frumenti dandi ex senatus consulto*.

[29] A *praefectus urbi* was perhaps not regularly appointed until A.D. 13.

[30] Frank (*Econ. SAR*, v. 1) reckoned some 10,000,000 inhabitants, but for a much lower estimate see Brunt, quoted above, n. 6.

[31] On Augustus's colonies in Italy see Brunt, *Manpower*, 608 ff., and in general below, Chap. 31, n. 26.

[32] On the new men see T. P. Wiseman, *New Men in the Roman Senate, 139 B.C.–A.D. 14* (1971).

[33] An average daily distance covered by these couriers might be fifty miles, but 120–150 and occasionally up to 200 were reached in emergencies. See

W. Riepl, *Das Nachrichtenwesen des Altertums*, 200 ff.; A. M. Ramsay, *JRS* 1925, 60 ff.

[34] See *Res Gestae*, 8. 2–4. Cf. n. 6 above.

[35] For details of Augustus's social legislation see H. Last, *CAH*, x. 441 ff. Cf. G. Williams, *JRS*, 1962, 28 ff.; Brunt, *Manpower*, 558 ff.; A. N. Sherwin-White, *The Roman Citizenship*[2] (1973), 327 ff.

[36] On the *Severi Augustales* see A. M. Duff, *Freedmen in the Early Roman Empire* (1928), 133 ff.; L. R. Taylor, *JRS* 1924, 158 ff.

[37] On the Secular Games see J. Gagé, *Recherches sur les jeux séculaires* (1934). For the official record of the festival see Dessau, *ILS*, 5050. For commemorative coins see Mattingly and Sydenham, *Roman Imperial Coinage*, i. 75.

Chapter 31: Notes

[1] The last triumph of a man outside the imperial family was celebrated in 19 by L. Cornelius Balbus, an outstanding honour for a man of Spanish origin.

[2] The inscription is *ILS*, 8995. Gallus committed suicide in 26.

[3] For Petronius's expedition see S. Jameson, *JRS* 1968, 71 ff., who believes that Augustus's real intention was conquest. On Ethiopia see P. L. Shinnie, *Meroë* (1967).

[4] Both the Arabian and Ethiopian expeditions are recorded by Strabo, who was a personal friend of Aelius Gallus and accompanied the Arabian venture. See S. Jameson, *JRS* 1968, 71 ff. In the *Res Gestae* (26.5) Augustus says that his troops reached Mariba; though he may have hoped readers would not realise the point, this may not be identical with the Sabaean capital, Mariaba.

[5] On the destruction of Aden see M. P. Charlesworth, *Cl. Rev.* 1928, 99. On the Indian embassies (*Res Gestae*, 31.1), see E. H. Warmington, *The Commerce between the Roman Empire and India* (1928), 35 ff., who shows that more than one mission reached Rome.

[6] On Parthia see the works cited above in Chap. 26, n. 16 (p. 620). Augustus regarded the recovery of the standards lost by the troops of Crassus and Antony as one of the greatest diplomatic triumphs of his reign. Apart from placing the standards in the temple of Mars Ultor, he advertised the fact on coins with the legend *signis receptis* and the scene of surrender, which was also depicted on the centre of his breast-plate on a famous statue. Other coins showed a kneeling Armenia (*Armenia capta*). In 19 a new arch of Augustus was erected in the Forum to celebrate the victory. The event gave the poets a fertile theme.

[7] Quirinius, a *novus homo*, was consul in 12 B.C., and legate of Syria in A.D. 6. He is the 'Cyrenius' of St Luke, ii. 2. He is probably not the subject of a fragmentary inscription (*ILS*, 918) which has sometimes been applied to him. For his census in Judaea see below, p. 631. For his career see briefly, R. Syme, *OCD*[2], s.v. 'Quirinius', and literature there cited.

On the colonies see B. Levick, *Roman Colonies in Southern Asia Minor* (1967).

[8] On the Spanish Wars see R. Syme, *AJ Phil.* 1934, 293 ff.; W. Schmitthenner, *Historia* 1962, 29 ff. For the sources see A. Schulten, *Fontes Hispaniae Anti-*

quae, (1940), 183 ff. On the Augustan reorganisation see C. H. V. Sutherland, *The Romans in Spain* (1939), ch. vii.

[9] On Gaul see N. J. de Witt, *Urbanisation and the Franchise in Roman Gaul* (1940); O. Brogan, *Roman Gaul* (1953); J. J. Hatt, *Histoire de la Gaule romaine*[2] (1966); A. Grenier in T. Frank, *Econ.SRE*, iii. 379 ff. For the surviving monuments see P. MacKendrick, *Roman France* (1972). On archaeological work in Gaul carried out from 1955 to 1970 see R. Chevallier, *JRS* 1971, 243 ff.

[10] Coinage throws much light on the native British dynasties before the Claudian conquest. For the 100 years between Caesar and Claudius see S. S. Frere, *Britannia* (1967), ch. 3. On contacts and trade between Gaul and Britain see Strabo, iii. 199-201.

[11] Roman forts mark the early advances of the Romans beyond the Rhine; the invaders usually followed the valleys of the Lippe, Main or Saale. For the archaeological evidence see H. Schonberger, *JRS* 1969, 144 ff., and especially C. M. Wells, *The German Policy of Augustus* (1972). In view of the continuity of the invasions, and of the erection of an altar to Augustus on the Elbe, it is difficult to believe that the Romans were merely retaliating for German raids upon Gaul and had no intention of annexing German territory. Wells (op. cit.) argues that Augustus did not even aim specifically at an Elbe–Danube frontier and did not intend to call his conquests to a halt at any particular point.

[12] The site of the disaster has been endlessly debated: see, for example, W. John, P–W, xxiv (1963), col. 922 ff.; D. Timpe, *Arminius Studien* (1970). The dangers of introducing regular taxation in undeveloped countries were also illustrated by the Pannonian revolt and by the later British rebellion under Boudicca.

[13] D. Timpe argues (*Der Triumph des Germanicus* (1968), 31 f.), contrary to the usual view, that the Roman expeditions over the Rhine in and after A.D. 10 suggest that Augustus was still dreaming of an Elbe frontier.

[14] On the *Tropaeum Alpium*, a commemorative monument erected by Augustus near Monaco, the emperor claimed to have subdued forty-nine Alpine peoples from the Riviera to the Danube: see Ehrenberg and Jones, *Documents*, n. 40.

[15] On the Augustan conquest of this whole area see J. J. Wilkes, *Dalmatia* (1969), ch. 5. On the history of Noricum see G. Alföldy, *Noricum* (1974).

[16] The earliest mention of Moesia as a province is in connexion with the Pannonian revolt (Dio Cassius, lv. 29.3) and the earliest recorded imperial legate there is A. Caecina in A.D. 6 (P. Vinicius was possibly an earlier legate). Final organisation as a province may not have taken place until under Tiberius. Presumably it was detached from Macedonia after the rebellion in Thrace, which must have made it plain that the entire Balkan peninsula could not be controlled by a single governor. See R. Syme, *JRS* 1934, 113 ff. = *Danubian Papers* (1971), 40 ff. See also A. Mocsy, *Pannonia and Upper Moesia* (1974).

[17] On the imperial Roman army see H. M. D. Parker, *The Roman Legions*[2] (1958); G. L. Cheesman, *The Auxilia of the Imperial Roman Army* (1914); G.

Webster, *The Roman Imperial Army* (1969); on army service from the point of view of the ordinary soldier, G. R. Watson, *The Roman Soldier* (1969). See also M. Grant, *The Army of the Caesars* (1974).

[18] On the *collegia iuvenum* see L. R. Taylor, *JRS* 1924, 158 ff.

[19] On recruitment see G. Forni, *Il reclutamento delle legioni da Augusto a Diocleziano* (1953). The original garrison of Egypt was largely composed of Galatians trained in Roman fashion by King Deiotarus. But this was a temporary measure only, from which no general conclusion should be drawn.

[20] Grant of citizenship on discharge was perhaps not made automatically under Augustus, but may have depended on the extent of the soldier's Romanization, but it soon became regular. As proof of their grant of citizenship all auxiliaries were given (at least from Claudius's reign) a folded bronze tablet (*diploma*), recording the fact and copied from the official record in Rome. The *diplomata* (over 200 survive) reveal much detail about the movements of the auxiliary units. For examples see A. R. Burn, *The Romans in Britain*[2] (1969), nos. 71, 95, 100, and p. 448 above.

[21] Thus the three legions permanently stationed in Britain in the first century were named *Secunda Augusta, Nona Hispana*, and *Vicesima Valeria Victrix*.

[22] Centurions belonged to the officer class. Although the majority continued to be promoted legionaries, some were men who transferred from an equestrian career, while others might be ex-praetorians. On their promotions see B. Dobson in A. von Domaszewski, *Die Rangordnung des romischen Heeres* (2nd edition, by Dobson, 1967), xx ff.

[23] On the navy see C. G. Starr, *The Roman Imperial Navy*[2] (1960).

[24] The population of the Roman Empire under Augustus is estimated at 80–100 millions by M. Nilsson (*Imperial Rome*, 337) and at not less than 70 millions by E. Cavaignac (*La Paix romaine*, 292).

[25] On Herod and his successors see A. H. M. Jones, *The Herods of Judaea* (1938), M. Grant, *Herod the Great* (1971), and H. W. Hoehner, *Herod Antipas* (1972).

[26] On the colonies see F. Vittinghoff, *Römische Kolonization unter Caesar und Augustus* (1952); B. Levick, *Roman Colonies in Southern Asia Minor* (1967); Brunt, *Manpower*, ch. xv and appendices 15, 16; for the scale of emigration see above, Chap. 29, n. 2. The towns of Augusta Trevirorum (Trier) and Augusta Vindelicorum (Augsburg) were probably founded by Augustus, but did not attain the full status of a *Colonia* until a later date.

[27] It is improbable that Augustus ordered a simultaneous census in all the Roman provinces. A census was held in Gaul in 27 B.C., in 12 B.C. and again in A.D. 14 just after Augustus's death. He also ordered a census in Syria, through his legate Quirinius in A.D. 6. See St Luke, ii. 2, and n. 7 above. As legate of Syria Quirinius supervised the assessment of Judaea after the deposition of Archelaus and the creation of a Roman province.

[28] The theory that the emperors claimed ownership of all provincial soil has been proved untenable. See A. H. M. Jones, *JRS* 1941, 26 ff. (= *Studies*, ch. ix).

[29] The most notable scheme of road-building under Augustus was carried out in Gaul by Agrippa, who laid out a regular network with its centre at Lugdunum.

[30] On emperor-worship in general see L. Cerfaux and J. Tondriau, *Le Culte des Souverains* (1956); *Le Culte des Souverains dans l'Empire romain, Entretiens Hardt*, xix, 1973). See also L. R. Taylor, *The Divinity of the Roman Emperor* (1931). On the formula invented by Augustus for tactfully declining divine honours see M. P. Charlesworth, *PBSR* 1939, 1 ff.

[31] On the provincial *concilia* see E. G. Hardy, *Studies in Roman History* (1906), ch. 13; P. Guiraud. *Les Assemblées provinciales dans l'empire romain* (1887); D. Magie, *Roman Rule in Asia Minor* (1950); J. A. O. Larsen, *Representative Government in Greek and Roman History* (1955), 106 ff.

[32] Our knowledge of Augustus's financial system is very obscure. See. H. Last, *JRS* 1944, 51 ff.; A. H. M. Jones, *JRS* 1950, 22 ff. (= *Studies*, ch. vi); F. Millar, *JRS* 1963, 29 ff., and 1964, 33 ff.; P. A. Brunt, *JRS* 1966, 75 ff. While Millar believes that the word *fiscus* meant only the emperor's personal wealth, Jones and Brunt argue that it included public funds handled by the emperor acting on behalf of the state, and later came to include the whole financial administration controlled by the emperor.

[33] On the imperial domains in general see O. Hirschfeld, *Kleine Schriften* (1902), 545 ff. The so-called 'King's Land' of the Ptolemies (comprising most of the cultivable surface in Egypt) was renamed 'public land' under Augustus, i.e.' it became technically *ager publicus* of the Roman people. Augustus's private domains in Egypt were composed of estates previously alienated from the 'King's Land' by royal grants. See T. Frank *JRS* 1927, 159 ff. The whole administration of Egypt, with its complicated bureaucratic system inherited from the Ptolemies, differed greatly from that of other Roman provinces. See H. Idris Bell, *CAH*, x, ch. x.

[34] On Augustus's coinage see, beside the Catalogues, C. H. V. Sutherland, *Coinage in Roman Imperial Policy 31 B. C.–A.D. 68* (1951), chs 2–4.

[35] This view is perhaps preferable to that of M. Reinhold, *Marcus Agrippa* (1933), 167 ff., that Agrippa at this early stage was granted *imperium maius* over the eastern provinces (in 20 and 19 Agrippa was in Gaul and Spain not the East). Cf. R. Syme, *The Roman Revolution*, 337, n. 1. On a papyrus fragment of a Greek version of the *laudatio funebris* of Agrippa, delivered by Augustus, see I. Koenen, *Zeitschrift fur Papyrologie und Epigraphik* 1970, 217 ff. This refers, with dates (18 and 13), to the two grants of tribunician power to Agrippa, but when it appears to refer to his *imperium maius* it unfortunately gives no date. Koenen, however, argues that it refers to a grant as early as 23.

[36] Such a 'regency' had been more dimly foreshadowed by the way in which Augustus had associated Agrippa with himself. There is no need, however, to accept the view of J. Kornemann (*Doppelprinzipat und Reichtum im Imperium Romanum*, 1930) that the regencies of the Roman Empire were reduced to a regular system with a constitutional law of their own.

[37] On Augustus's physical infirmities see Suetonius, *Augustus*, lxxix–lxxxii; on his superstitions, chs xci–xcii.

[38] Beside the conspiracy of M. Aemilus Lepidus (son of the dispossessed triumvir) in 30 and that of Caepio and Murena and the activities of Egnatius Rufus, it is possible that the two lovers of the elder and younger Julia, a son of Antony and Fulvia named Iullus Antonius, and a noble named L. Aemilius Paullus, had political aims (see R. S. Rogers, *TAPA* 1931, 141 ff.).

Chapter 32: Notes

[1] The chief literary sources for Tiberius are Velleius Paterculus, ii. 123–31, a contemporary who admired Tiberius; Tacitus, *Annals*, i–vi (most of v is lost); Suetonius, *Tiberius*; Dio Cassius, lvii–lviii. Selected documents in Ehrenberg and Jones, *Documents Illustrating the Reigns of Augustus and Tiberius*[2] (1955). Coinage: see books mentioned above, Chap. 30, n. 1. These later writers drew material in part from several historians who wrote on aspects of the Julio-Claudian period but whose works are now lost. They include Aufidius Bassus (*cos.* 35), M. Servilius Nonianus (*cos. suff.* 39), Cluvius Rufus (*cos.* probably before 41), the elder Pliny (historical works), Fabius Rusticus, and Corbulo (memoirs). On these see J. Wilkes, 'The Julio-Claudian Historians', *Classical World* 1972, 177 ff. On Tacitus see F. R. D. Goodyear, *The Annals of Tacitus*, i (1972).

Modern works include F. B. Marsh, *The Reign of Tiberius* (1931); R. S. Rogers, *Criminal Trials under Tiberius* (1935); R. Syme, *Tacitus* (1958), esp. 420 ff.; R. Seager, *Tiberius* (1972). Also B. Levick, *Tiberius* (forthcoming). For the whole period to the Antonines see A. Garzetti, *From Tiberius to the Antonines* (1974), which contains a valuable assessment of the sources and discussion of relevant modern literature.

Tacitus's portrait of Tiberius is complex; it was coloured by his admiration for the Republic and by his own experiences under the reign of terror of Domitian, but he is not guilty of deliberate falsification. He aimed at the truth, even if in ambiguous cases he did not give Tiberius the benefit of the doubt. On this and on Tacitus in general see books quoted above and in Chap. 39, n. 51.

[2] For Tiberius's motto see Suetonius, *Tiberius*, lix. 2; for his diffidence, Tacitus, *Annals*, i. 80.3 ('ut callidum. eius insenium, ita anxium iudicium', shrewd in intellect, hesitant in judgment). That Tiberius was not merely shamming reluctance to office may be inferred from some of his own confessions, as in Suetonius, xxiv. 1 ('belua est imperium', rule is a monster); lxvii. 1; and Tacitus, vi. 6.1 (a letter to the Senate revealing a condition of downright mental agony).

[3] It is hardly necessary to assume that the Senate's obsequiousness to Tiberius was veiled sarcasm (as T. S. Jerome, *Aspects of the Study of Roman History*, 280), or that a solid party in the House was working in the interests of Agrippina (as F. B. Marsh, *The Reign of Tiberius*, ch. vii). Tacitus may have been influenced

by traditions unfavourable to Tiberius found in senatorial circles.

[4] On conspiracies see R. S. Rogers, *Criminal Trials under Tiberius* (1935). On Libo Drusus see D. C. A. Shotter, *Historia* 1972, 88 ff.

[5] Two edicts of Germanicus in Egypt have survived; Ehrenberg and Jones, op. cit. n. 320 a and b (translations in Lewis–Reinhold, *R. Civ.* ii. 399, 562). The first deprecates requitioning on his behalf, the second deprecates the excessive honours offered to him ('your acclamations, which are odious to me and such as are accorded to the gods, I altogether deprecate'). Another papyrus fragment, *Oxyrhynchus Papyri*, xxv (1959), n. 2453, gives Germanicus's speech on his arrival (punctuated by applause). The purpose of his visit may have been innocent (Tacitus attributes it to the desire to see the monuments), but it was tactless, as was his conduct there.

Germanicus's popularity is further shown by the extravagant honours voted to him after his death which are revealed by the Tabula Hebana (see p. 629); they include naming five voting-centuries after him.

[6] Piso, who had in Germanicus's absence cancelled some of his arrangements, was ordered by Germanicus to leave his province. After Germanicus's death Piso unwisely re-entered Syria. Recalled to Rome, he was tried before the Senate; though he cleared himself of the charge of poisoning Germanicus he was guilty of forcibly re-entering his province; he committed suicide. On Piso see D. C. A. Shotter, *Historia* 1974, 229 ff.

[7] Tiberius's formal charges against Agrippina and her sons did not mention treason but only insubordination and licentiousness. They may have connived at the schemes of C. Silius and others.

[8] It is not clear why Seianus should have plotted to hasten Tiberius's death, unless he feared that he might eventually be supplanted by Germanicus's third son Gaius. The ease with which the plot was crushed may suggest that it was not very far advanced. The seriousness of the conspiracy had been differently assessed (thus in the letter from Capreae, as recorded by Dio Cassius, Seianus is not specifically charged with treason). Attempts have been made to distinguish his political friends and enemies. See Z. Stewart, *AJ Phil.* 1953, 70 ff.; F. Adams, ibid. 1955, 70 ff.; A. Boddington, ibid. 1963, 1 ff.; R. Sealey, *Phoenix* 1961; 97 ff.; G. V. Sumner, ibid. 1965, 134 ff.; N. W. Bird, *Latomus* 1969, 61 ff.

An inscription from Alba Fucens, his home town, has revealed the true name of Q. Naevius Sutorius Macro and the fact that he had been Praefectus Vigilum: see *L'Année épigraphique* 1957, n. 250.

[9] There is no strong reason to disbelieve the story that Drusus was poisoned by his wife, who had been seduced by Seianus, though it is true that he had been ailing a long time before his death. This previous illness may well have made his death seem more natural.

[10] A typical example of Tiberius's evasiveness occurred at the very outset of his reign, when he left unexplained the sudden death of Agrippa Postumus (p. 344); his reticence gave rise to a nasty crop of rumours. The death had perhaps been ordered by a disposition of Augustus, but this is not certain.

Cf. M. P. Charlesworth, *AJ Phil.* 1923, 146 ff; R. Seager, *Tiberius* (1972), 48 ff. For the possibility that Postumus, before his disgrace, had held some official position under Augustus, see *L'Année épigraphique* 1964, n. 107, and J. Reynolds, *JRS* 1966, 119. See also B. Levick, *Historia* 1972, 674 ff.

[11] On the trials for *maiestas* see Marsh and Rogers, op. cit., n. 1 above. Suetonius and Dio Cassius clearly accepted at face value much loose gossip rejected by Tacitus. Tacitus, although careful not to admit false evidence, was so economical of truth as to be positively misleading, but it is noteworthy that he himself provides the evidence to correct his general picture of an unbridled reign of terror. Further, he himself had lived through Domitian's later terror, and could not but see Tiberius's last years in the light of his own experience. See also R. A. Bauman, *Impietas in Principem* (1974), a study of treason against the Roman emperor, especially in the first century A.D.

[12] The main sources for Caligula are Suetonius, *Gaius Caligula*; Dio Cassius, lxix; Josephus, *Ant. Iud.* xviii. 205–xix. 211; Philo, *In Flaccum* (ed. H. Box, 1939), *Legatio ad Gaium* (ed. E. M. Smallwood, 1961). The relevant books of Tacitus's *Annals* are lost. Select documents: E. M. Smallwood, *Documents Illustrating the Principates of Gaius, Claudius and Nero* (1967); on the sources see M. P. Charlesworth, *Cambr. Hist. Journal* 1933, 105 ff. See J. P. V. D. Balsdon, *The Emperor Gaius* (1934).

[13] In Suetonius Caligula is depicted as a stark lunatic of the megalomaniac type; in the account of an eye-witness, Philo (*Legatio ad Gaium*), he appears a fidgety neurotic. Though his behaviour perhaps fell short of madness, it is impossible to determine the degree of rationality he retained, especially in view of the nature of the sources. Did he, for instance, intend to make his favourite horse Incitatus consul, or is the rumour entirely baseless? Balsdon, op. cit. n. 12 above, tried to find some reason behind his military movements. When wearing the breastplate of Alexander the Great, he drove over a bridge of boats which he had built across the Bay of Naples, was he showing mere eccentricity or megalomania?

[14] The chief sources for Claudius are Tacitus, *Ann.* xi–xii (=A.D. 47–54), the earlier books being lost; Suetonius, *Divus Claudius*; Dio Cassius, lx; Seneca, *Ad Polybium, Apocolocyntosis*; Josephus, *Bell. Iud.* ii. 204, *Ant. Iud.* xix. 212 ff. Select inscriptions in Smallwood, *Documents . . . of Gaius, Claudius and Nero* (1967). Coins: see Chap. 30, n. 1, Modern books: A. Momigliano, *Claudius*[2] (1961); V. M. Scramuzza, *The Emperor Claudius* (1940).

[15] Claudius's physical ills have been variously diagnosed: see T. de C. Ruth, *The Problem of Claudius* (1924), who argues for paralytic diplegia, due to premature birth. Claudius's own mother described him as 'a monster of a man, not finished but only begun by nature' (Suetonius *Claudius*, iii. 2).

[16] Suetonius (*Claudius*, xxix. 2) estimates the number of Claudius's victims at 35 senators and over 300 *equites*. This statement, which is not borne out by Tacitus, is no doubt a great exaggeration.

[17] Tacitus (*Ann.* xii, 66–7), Suetonius (*Cl.* xliv) and Dio Cassius (lx. 34.1) agree that Claudius was poisoned; Josephus (*Ant. Iud.* xx. 8.1) is sceptical. The

alternative explanation that Claudius, who was over sixty and had always been a gross feeder, died of syncope cannot be rejected out of hand.

18 These include a speech by Claudius to the Senate on judicial matters, urging independence of judgment (Smallwood, *Documents*, n. 367); his letter to the Alexandrine Jews (n. 370); his edict regarding the grant of citizenship to the Alpine Annauni (n. 368); and his speech to the Senate about Gauls and citizenship, the so-called Lyons Tablet (n. 369).

19 On Claudius's relations with the Senate and aristocracy see D. McAlindon, *AJ Phil.* 1956, 113 ff.; 1957, 279 ff.; *JRS* 1957, 191 ff.; *Cl. Rev.* 1957, 108 ff; *Latomus* 1957, 252 ff. If Caligula himself had not already restored the elections to the Senate Claudius will have done this.

20 The chief sources for Nero are Tacitus, *Ann.* xii–xvi (to A.D. 66 only); Suetonius, *Nero*; DioCassius, lxi–lxiii. Documents in E. M. Smallwood, *Documents . . . of Gaius, Claudius and Nero* (1967). Coins: see books mentioned above Chap. 30, n. 1.

Three modern biographies are by B. W. Henderson, *Life and Principate of . . . Nero* (1903); B. H. Warmington, *Nero: Reality and Legend* (1969); and M. Grant, *Nero* (1970). Cf. also M. P. Charlesworth, *JRS* 1950, 69 ff.

21 Agrippina's eclipse is reflected in the coinage. At first her portrait dominated it, then it appeared in the remoter of two jugate busts, then it appeared only on the reverse, and finally disappeared. After 55 it had, also disappeared from some local issues, as at Antioch and Alexandria. See C. H. V. Sutherland, *Coinage in Roman Imp. Policy* (1951), 153 ff.

22 The death of Britannicus was almost certainly due to foul play. No natural cause for his collapse can be suggested, and the haste with which the body was cremated plainly points to murder. The complicity of Seneca and Burrus is uncertain. On Seneca see p. 396.; On Burrus W. C. McDermott, *Latomus* 1949, 229 ff.

23 On the place of the crime see R. Katzoff, *Historia* 1973, 72 ff. About 300 B.C. the tyrant of the Greek city of Heraclea-ad-Pontum had similarly enticed his mother on to a boat in order to drown her, see Memnon, xi. 5, *FGrH.*, n. 434 (iiiB), p. 341.

24 According to Pliny (*NB* xviii. 35) Nero made away with the six largest landowners in Africa. This statement, although not borne out by other authors, is confirmed by the existence of large imperial domains in this province in the later part of the first century.

25 The fire broke out on a mid-moon night in July, a most unlikely time for incendiaries to go to work. Clearly neither Nero nor the Christians were responsible.

The 'fiddle' of Nero is not mentioned by any ancient writer, though Dio states that the emperor dressed up in a costume of a cithara-player (lx. 18), a role in which he is depicted as Nero-Apollo, the divine musician playing a lyre, on the coinage of 64–66: see Sutherland, *Coinage in Roman Imp. Policy*, 170. There is no doubt that he took his singing very seriously and studied lyre-playing with great determination. This and his passion for horsemanship, acting and poetry were harmless enough when confined to private performance. What shocked the Roman aristocracy was his insistence on public exhibitions; they may also perhaps have looked down on his desire to introduce Greek Games (including athletics and competitions in poetry, music and oratory) in place of the bloodier Roman sports (in 57 he forbade gladiatorial fights to the death, not because he was not cruel, but because they were un-Hellenic). Thus he may well have used the fire as a fantastic background for his dramatic gifts.

26 On the Christian persecution see Tacitus *Ann.* xv 44. Its legal basis has been endlessly debated. That it was a general law passed against Christianity is not now widely held. Possibly some specific charge, as treason, arson or illegal assembly, had to be preferred, or (more probably) ordinary trial was dispensed with and magistrates exercised their powers of *coercitio* to maintain order by police action on the ground that Christianity *per se* involved *flagitium*. On this last view admission of the *nomen* would expose a man to the *coercitio* of a magistrate who would then seek to establish a *flagitium* (e.g. of arson or magic). If no general law was passed, provincial governors were not affected.

It is noteworthy that the details of the Neronian persecution were not remembered in the Church tradition. Apart from Tacitus, there is a curt allusion in Suetonius (*Nero*, xvi. 2), who does not connect the action against the Christians with the charge of arson. Tacitus's expression 'correpti [sunt] qui fatebantur' has given rise to much discussion: they confessed before arrest, but what did they confess? Surely not incendiarism, but Christianity. Tacitus, who is highly contemptuous of the Christians, and assumes them to be guilty of various kinds of foul living (*flagitia*), does not countenance the belief that they set Rome on fire; he states positively that the charges against them were a 'frame-up'. Of the immense modern literature a few items only can be mentioned: A. N. Sherwin-White, *Journal of Theological Studies*, 1952, 199 ff.; G. E. M. de Ste Croix, *Past and Present*, 1963, 6 ff. (cf. ibid. 1964, 23–33) (these articles are reprinted in *Studies in Ancient Society*, ed. M. I. Finley (1974), 210 ff.); W. H. C. Frend, *Martyrdom and Persecution in the Early Church* (1965), 161 ff.; T. D. Barnes, *JRS* 1968, 32 ff. (cf. *Tertullian* (1971), ch. xi).

27 There is no evidence for persecution outside Rome. The victims, who were thrown to the beasts in the amphitheatre or used as living torches to light the Games in the imperial gardens and the Vatican circus, may have included St Peter and Paul, as tradition asserted. Excavations under St Peter's Basilica in the Vatican City, though not revealing clear trace of Peter's burial there, have shown that a martyrshrine to him stood there as early as *c.* A.D. 160; they thus go some way to confirming the tradition that Peter was buried under this church beside the site of Nero's circus. See J. Toynbee and J. Ward-Perkins, *The Shrine of St Peter* (1956); E. Kirschbaum, *The Tombs of St Peter and St Paul* (1959); D. W. O'Connor, *Peter in Rome* (1969).

28 Nero summoned the governors of Upper and Lower Germany to him in Greece and ordered their deaths on their arrival. Corbulo soon met a similar fate. His son-in-law, Annius Vinicianus, had been involved in a conspiracy which was discovered at Beneventum in 66: hence Corbulo, as the other generals, was separated from his army and struck down, not least from the suspicion that Vinicianus had intended that Corbulo should have taken Nero's place. On Corbulo's links with persons or groups destroyed by Nero in 65 and 66, see R. Syme, *JRS* 1970, 27 ff.

[29] For a recent discussion of the implications of the phrase *quinquennium Neronis* see M. K. Thornton, *Historia* 1973, 570 ff.

[30] The stages and process by which the people (and Equites) were eliminated from the elections remain obscure. The system of *destinatio* (p. 629) survived until at least A.D. 23 when five new centuries were named after Drusus. Tacitus, however, bluntly states that under Tiberius 'tum primo e campo comitia ad patres translata sunt' (*Annals*, i 15). For discussion see works mentioned above (Chap. 30, n. 18). Whatever the technicalities the result was that the people's role was reduced to a pure formality, and the Senate was the effective electoral body.

[31] Numerous examples of these exercises in popular wit are preserved in Suetonius. Political propaganda by scribbling on walls was not unknown to the Republic: appeals of this kind had been made to Tiberius Gracchus and to M. Brutus to save Rome in their respective ways. The custom still flourished in the Rome of the Popes. See also Z. Yavetz, *Plebs and Princeps* (1969).

[32] Among the cases handled by the Senate was a severe riot at Pompeii in 59, when it sent a special commissioner to investigate and punish the ringleaders (Tacitus, *Annals*, xiv, 17).

[33] On the senatorial court, its functions and partiality or bias see P. Garnsey, *Social and Legal Privilege in the Roman Empire* (1970), chs 2 (under the Julio-Claudians) and 3 (from the Flavians to Severans). Tiberius's use of the Senate in political trials may be compared with Henry VIII's expedient of using Parliament to pass Acts of Attainder against his adversaries.

[34] The manifold activities of the imperial household may be appreciated by a glance at the funerary inscriptions of the domestic staff in vol. vi of the *Corpus Inscriptionum Latinarum*. This staff consisted mostly of freedmen and freedwomen.

[35] Tiberius became a Julius when he was adopted by Augustus; by adopting Germanicus in his turn he also admitted Caligula, as a son of Germanicus, into the Julian *gens*.

[36] According to Suetonius (*Caligula*, xxxvii. 3) this was the sum found by Caligula in the imperial chests and spent by him in less than one year. Suetonius probably exaggerated the rate of Caligula's spending.

[37] On financial problems see the works mentioned above, Chap. 31, n. 32.

[38] Traces of these works survive and are seen well in air-photography. See J. Bradford, *Ancient Landscapes* (1957), 248 ff., and pls 60 and 61; R. Meiggs, *Roman Ostia*[2] (1974). It was left to Nero to claim the credit: he showed the new harbour on his fine sesterces.

[39] Nero advertised many of these achievements on his coinage which depicts the harbour at Ostia, Ceres and Annona, and the Macellum. So too his claim to have established peace was shown by the temple of Janus with its closed doors (closed in 66, as the result of his Armenian settlement) and an Altar of Peace. Another series of coins, issued in great quantities, displays Victoria, with Augustan memories. But he also needed the loyalty of his forces; hence types showing him addressing the Praetorian Guard or taking part on horseback in their military exercises. His coinage is also noteworthy for its exceptionally fine series of portraits of Nero at various ages.

Chapter 33: Notes

[1] On the circumstances of the annexation of Mauretania see D. Fishwick, *Historia* 1971, 467 ff. On Roman rule in Mauretania see J. Carcopino, *Le Maroc antique*[2] (1947). Claudius's treatment of Volubilis in Mauretania well illustrates his generous policy. The town, which had helped Rome during the war, was given Roman citizenship, municipal status and exemption from taxation for ten years; the native tribes (*incolae*) living within the *territorium* of the *municipium*, were 'attributed' to it; that is, given some, but not all, municipal privileges as a preliminary training for the responsibilities of full citizenship. This is revealed by an inscription: see Smallwood, *Documents . . . Gaius, Claudius and Nero*, n. 407.

[2] On Tacfarinas see R. Syme, *Studies . . . in Honour of A. C. Johnson* (1951), 113 ff. Dolabella made a dedication to Victoria Augusta: see *Epigraphica*, 1938, 3 ff.

[3] On Palestine see E. Schürer, op. cit. (see Chap. 16, n. 16), and F.-M. Abel, *Histoire de la Palestine depuis la conquête d'Alexandre jusqu'à l'invasion arabe* (1952); A. H. M. Jones, *The Herods of Judaea* (1938). On the Zealots or *sicarii* see M. Hengel, *Die Zeloten* (1961); S. Applebaum, *JRS* 1971, 155 ff. On religious conditions see below, Chap. 34, n. 4b.

[4] On the Jews of the Dispersion see V. A. Tcherikover, *Hellenistic Civilization and the Jews* (1959). Jewish community in Rome: H. J. Leon, *The Jews of Ancient Rome* (1960). See also M. Grant, *The Jews in the Roman World* (1973).

[5] See H. Murillo, *The Acts of the Pagan Martyrs, Acta Alexadrinorum* (1954; with commentary).

[6] A vivid account of the Jewish embassy by Philo himself survives. See for these episodes, E. M. Smallwood, *Philo, Legatio ad Gaium* (1961); H. Box, *Philonis Alexandrini, In Flaccum* (1939). For Claudius's letter see Smallwood, *Documents of Gaius, Claudius and Nero*, n. 370 (translation in Lewis–Reinhold, *R. Civ.* ii. 366 ff.).

[7] On Corbulo's campaigns and their chronology see B. W. Henderson, *Nero*, 153 ff. and K. Gilmartin, *Historia* 1973, 583 ff. Corbulo chose the route over the plateau of Erzerum, despite its great altitude, because of its proximity to a good base of supplies at Trapezus on the Black Sea.

[8] Nero's objective may have been the Daryal Gorge

in the central Caucasus, his purpose possibly to check the Alani and bar the Caucasus to the Sarmatians.

[9] An inscription from the mausoleum of the Plautii near Tibur records Silvanus's exploits: *ILS,* 986; Smallwood, *Documents,* n. 228 (n. 384 quotes a letter of his).

[10] Germanicus's campaigns are discussed by E. Koesterman, *Historia* 1957, 429 ff., and D. Timpe, *Der Triumph des Germanicus* (1968).

[11] Another factor was probably Druidism, which helped to foster nationalistic disloyalty to Rome, and was regarded by the Romans as barbaric in some of its practices. See H. Last, *JRS* 1949, 1 ff. It was suppressed in Gaul by Tiberius (according to Pliny, *NH,* xxx. 13) or by Claudius (as Suetonius, *Div. Claud.* 25). The Aedui and Treveri presumably headed the revolt because of the withdrawal of their previous fiscal immunities. The triumphal arch at Arausio (modern Orange) in southern France probably commemorates the Roman victory over Florus and Sacrovir: on its Tiberian date see R. Amy, *L'Arc d'Orange* (1962).

[12] On the Via Claudia Augusta over the Brenner Pass see Smallwood, *Documents . . . Gaius, etc.,* n. 328.

[13] The reason why Caligula abandoned the invasion of Britain can only be surmised. Perhaps his troops were restless or he may have suddenly feared to go so far from Rome; or else he may have been guided by an emotional whim rather than by reason.

[14] On the British tribes and local dynasties, for whose history coinage provides a most valuable source, see S. S. Frere, *Britannia* (1967), chs 1–4, and the literature there cited.

[15] On Roman Britain in general see R. G. Collingwood, *Roman Britain and the English Settlements*[2] (1937); S. S. Frere, *Britannia* (1967). For the Claudian conquest, Frere, ch. 5, and G. Webster and D. R. Dudley, *The Conquest of Britain, A.D. 43–57* (1966). On the military situation from 43 to 71 see G. Webster, *Britannia,* i, 1970, 179 ff.

[16] For the inscription on Claudius's triumphal arch at Rome see A. R. Burn, *The Romans in Britain*[2] (1969), n. 1, and Smallwood, *Documents . . . Gaius, etc.,* n. 43 b. Claudius also celebrated his victory by naming his son Britannicus.

[17] Vespasian reduced Vectis (the Isle of Wight) and 'two powerful tribes' who will have been the Durotriges and Belgae in Dorset and Wiltshire. Archaeology has revealed the grim struggle the Romans had to capture the great hill-fortress of Maiden Castle and how they established a fort of their own on the captured Hod Hill (near Blandford Forum). See R. E. M. Wheeler, *Maiden Castle, Dorset* (1943); I. A. Richmond *et al., Hod Hill,* ii (1968). On the length of Vespasian's command see D. E. Eichholz, *Britannia* 1971, 149 ff. An inscribed leaden ingot found in the Mendips (Burn, n. 10) shows that the Romans had reached the Severn by 49. Meanwhile the Ninth Legion had reached Lindum (modern Lincoln) and a column had marched through the Midlands.

[18] On Gloucester see C. Green, *JRS* 1942, 39 ff., 1943, 15 ff.; I. A. Richmond, *Transact. Bristol Glos. Arch. Soc.* 1962, 14 ff., 1965, 15 ff. On Lincoln, see J. B. Whitwell, *Roman Lincolnshire* (1970).

[19] But see D. Fishwick, *Britannia* 1972, 164 ff.

[20] On the revolt see D. R. Dudley and G. Webster, *The Rebellion of Boudicca* (1962). The tombstone of Classicianus, who stood up to Suetonius, was found in London: Burn, n. 15; Smallwood, n. 268. On the coinage of the Iceni see D. F. Allen, *Britannia,* i, 1970, 1 ff.

[21] On compulsory service in Egypt see F. Ortel, *Die Liturgie* (1917), 62 ff. Under Roman rule this practice appears to have begun in the days of Tiberius. Much chicanery by local officials in Egypt is revealed in an edict by the prefect Tiberius Alexander, promising redress for accumulated grievances. See McCrum and Woodhead, *Select Documents of . . . the Flavian Emperors* (1961), n. 328. Translation in Lewis–Reinhold, *R. Civ.* ii 375 ff. For discussion see E. G. Turner, *JRS* 1954, 54 ff.; G. Chalon, *L'Édit de Tiberius Julius Alexander* (1964). He was a renegade Jew, who was governor of Judaea (*c.* 46–8), served under Corbulo in Armenia (63) and then soon became prefect of Egypt.

[22] P. A. Brunt (*Historia* 1961, 189 ff.) examines charges of provincial maladministration under the Early Empire and concludes that 'it would be wrong to assume that abuses were infrequent or redress easy to secure. The Principate often gets more credit than is due for its provincial government, and the Republic perhaps too little.' It was easier to pass laws than to enforce them.

[23] Suetonius, *Tiberius,* xxxii. 2. The general strictness of Tiberius's administration is also emphasised by Dio (lvii. 23).

[24] For the text of Claudius's speech, preserved in an inscription from Lugdunum (modern Lyons), see Smallwood, *Documents of . . . Gaius, etc.* n. 369 (translation in Lewis–Reinhold, *R. Civ.* ii. 133 ff.). We also have Tacitus's version of the speech: *Annals,* xi. 23–5. For a full discussion of Claudius's franchise policy see A. N. Sherwin-White, *The Roman Citizenship,* ch. viii. The speech was made to the Senate when some Gallic chieftains sought admission to it: this was theoretically open to anyone with Roman citizenship. The emperor emphasised republican Rome's generosity in welcoming foreign elements into the citizen body, and persuaded a reluctant Senate to state the right of all Roman citizens in Gallia Comata to stand for office in Rome; he also by-passed this stage for the Gallic nobles in question and added them to the Senate by his right of *adlectio.*

[25] The atmosphere of flattery at the imperial court has been strongly but not unduly emphasised by Tacitus. It is significant that able soldiers and administrators, like the future emperors Galba and Vespasian, thought it necessary to curry favour with empresses and freedmen (Suetonius, *Galba,* v. 2, *Vespasian,* iv. I), and that L. Vitellius, an administrator with an excellent record in the provinces, played Polonius to Claudius's Hamlet while at Rome. Of the early Caesars Tiberius alone succeeded in repelling sycophancy around him.

Chapter 34: Notes

[1] On economic conditions under the early Caesars see T. Frank, *Economic History of Rome*[2] (1927), chs xviii–xxx, *Econ. SAR*, v (Rome and Italy of the Empire), ii–iv (the provinces); M. P. Charlesworth, *Trade Routes and Commerce of the Roman Empire*[2] (1926); M. Rostovtzeff, *Social and Economic History of the Roman Empire*[2] (1957); R. D. Duncan-Jones, *The Economy of the Roman Empire: Quantitative Studies* (1974). M. I. Finley, *The Ancient Economy* (1973), discusses the concepts through which the economy of the Greeks and Romans can be analysed and the extent to which modern categories, such as capital, labour, market and credit, can be properly employed. On all aspects of farming and agriculture see K. D. White, *Roman Farming* (1970).

[2] On the labour problem of a *latifundium* see Columella, i, 7–9.

[3] The grandfather of Vespasian was said to have been a contractor who supplied hired labour from the Umbrian uplands for the larger estates on the Sabine territory (Suetonius, *Vespasian*, i. 4).

[4] On the sources of slavery in the Roman Empire see M. Bang, *Mitteilungen des deutschen archäologischen Instituts zu Rom*, (1910), pp. 223 ff.; (1912), pp. 189 ff.

[5] Dionysius of Halicarnassus states that he saw fields in Campania from which three crops (presumably of wheat or barley) were taken in a year (i. 37). Restorative courses of leguminous plants were introduced by some improving landlords, but the biennial fallow appears to have remained the prevalent system. Pliny records that recently wheeled ploughs had been invented in Raetia, but they are not likely to have been used in Italy, at any rate not south of the Po valley. See K. D. White, *Roman Farming*, 175.

[6] Some exceptional bargains made by vine-planters are recorded by Pliny (xiv. 48–51): in one case a vineyard quadrupled its capital value in ten years. On the normal profits from a vineyard see the careful calculations in Columella, iii. 3.3, on which see White, *Roman Farming*, 241 ff.

[7] On agriculture in Roman Egypt see Rostovtzeff, *Soc. Econ. Hist. of Rome. Emp*[2], 272 ff. (bibliography, 668 ff.). See further, A. C. Johnson, *Roman Egypt* (Frank, *Econ. SAR*, ii). Considerable pieces of crown land, which Augustus had appropriated in 30 B.C., were subsequently transferred in gift to members of the imperial family and to friends of the emperors.

The use of the water-wheel on Egyptian irrigation-land (in place of the swing-beam) may date back to the time of Augustus (Rostovtzeff, *Soc. Econ. Hist of Rom. Emp.*[2], 669, n. 44). On the cultivation of cotton see Pliny, xix. 14.

[8] On water-conservation in Roman Africa see Frank, *AJ Phil.* 1926, 55 ff.; J. Toutain, *Les Cités romaines de la Tunisie*, 56 ff.; and on the southern frontiers, J. Baradez, *Fossatum Africae* (1949), 164 ff. For a time-table regulating the opening and closing of sluices on an irrigation-field see Dessau, *ILS*, 5793.

[9] Pliny, xv. 102.

[10] On industry in Egypt under the Romans, see works quoted, n. 7 above.

[11] On travel in the Roman empire see L. Friedlander, *Roman LIfe and Manners under the Early Roman Empire* (Engl. transl.), i. chs vi–vii; G. H. Stevenson, in C. Bailey, *The Legacy of Rome*, 141 ff.; L. Casson, *Travel in the Ancient World* (1974).

[12] Among the imperial properties was a tile-factory, the *officina Pansiana*, whose products have been found in many parts of Italy. Pansa's brickyard at Ariminum came into imperial hands about the time of Tiberius. The making of bricks was regarded as part of agriculture rather than of industry and was therefore regarded as more or less 'respectable'.

[13] On the invention of the blow-pipe see A. Kisa, *Das Glas im Altertum* (1908), i. 296 ff.; A. B. Harden in *Hist. of Technology*, ed. C. Singer, ii (1968), 311 ff.

[14] Imports into Britain included jewellery, glass, fine pottery (Arretine ware of the early first century has been found in London), metalwork and wine. Exports included wheat, cattle, hides, slaves, hunting-dogs, gold, silver and iron.

[15] On the extent and direction of trade with Germany see O. Brogan, *JRS* 1936, 195 ff.; R. E. Mortimer Wheeler, *Rome Beyond the Imperial Frontiers* (1954), chs ii–vi. Not all the objects found beyond the Rhine reached there by trade: thus the famous silver dinner-service from Hildersheim (near Hanover) may have been loot taken from a Roman commander, while diplomatic gifts may explain the find on the Danish island of Laaland. But trade increased steadily, although much of the carrier trade probably remained in the hands of the Frisii of the Dutch coast, and not many Roman goods reached Norway or Sweden before the third century.

[16] On Greek textiles from Nion-Ula in Mongolia, see M. Rostovtzeff, *Soc. Econ. Hist. Hellen. World*, 1223, 1624. On the transcontinental road-book see W. H. Schoff, *Parthian Stations* (1914). A short cut from Syria to the lower Euphrates by way of Palmyra probably came into regular use under Augustus: see Rostovtzeff, *Caravan Cities* (1932). 103 f.

[17] See R. E. M. Wheeler, op. cit., ch. xiii.

[18] On the discovery of the open-sea routes to India see W. H. Schoff, *The Periplus of the Erythraean Sea* (1912); M. P. Charlesworth in *Studies in Roman Econ. and Soc. Hist. in Honor of A. C. Johnson* (1951), 131 ff.; M. Cary and E. H. Warmington, *The Ancient Explorers* (1929), 73 ff.; R. E. M. Wheeler, op. cit. chs ix–xii.

[19] On the Indian trade see E. H. Warmington, *The Commerce between the Roman Empire and India* (1928), esp. 272 ff.; Wheeler, op. cit. According to Pliny (vi. 101, 12.84) the annual drain of specie to India amounted to not less than 60,000,000 sesterces and not less than 100,000,000 to the East in general. Prices of Indian products at Rome were sometimes a hundredfold of prices in India.

[20] On the spice trade in general see J. I. Miller, *The Spice Trade of the Roman Empire 29 B.C.–A.D. 641* (1969). It is there argued that Pliny (*NH*, xii. 86–8) implies a cinnamon route which brought this spice to Somali from the Far East. Indonesians will have carried it by boat via Madagascar to islands off Zanzibar, whence under Arabian control it went on to the Somali ports and ultimately reached the

West. But E. Gray (*JRS* 1970, 222) believes that Pliny is referring only to cinnamon which grew in the Somali region.

[21] Seneca, *Quaestiones Naturales*, Prologus, 13.

[22] The normal rate of interest on good security fell to 4–6 per cent, the lowest level of ancient times. See G. Billeter, *Geschichte des Zinfusses im griechish-römischen Altertum* (1898), 179 ff.

[23] On the proportions of free to servile labour see H. Gummerus, in P–W, ix, cols 1500–1.

[24] On the provenance of traders see V. Parvan, *Die Nationalitat der Kaufleute im römischen Reiche* (1909). On that of slaves, M. Bang, op. cit., n. 4.; M. L. Gordon, *JRS* 1924, 93 ff., who emphasises that a Greek name is not in itself proof of Greek origin.

[25] In an essay on the economic life of the towns A. H. M. Jones (*Recueil de la Société J. Bodin*, vii. 161 ff. = *The Roman Economy* (1974), 35 ff.) argues that commerce and industry had less importance than agriculture as sources of wealth. A fine description of the life of one town is given by R. Meiggs, *Roman Ostia*[2] (1974). On Pompeii see R. C. Carrington, *Pompeii* (1936); H. H. Tanzer, *The Common People of Pompeii* (1939); M. Della Corte, *Case ed abitanti a Pompeii*[2] (1954); for its industry see T. Frank, *Econ. Hist. of Rome*[2] (1927), ch. xiv, and *Econ. SAR*, v. 252 ff. On Aquileia, which exported wine, oil, textiles, pottery, glass and sundry Oriental wares, and imported cattle, hides, slaves and amber, see A. Calderini, *Aquileia Romana* (1930). On Roman Carthage see A. Audollent, *Carthage romaine* (1900). On Lugdunum, P. Wuilleumier, *Lyon, Metropole des Gaules* (1953). On London, R. Merrifield, *The Roman City of London* (1965); W. F. Grimes, *The Excavation of Roman and Medieval London* (1968).

[26] On social life at Rome under the early emperors see Friedlander, *Roman Life and Manners under the Early Roman Empire* (Engl. trans.), i, chs i–v; J. P. V. D. Balsdon, *Life and Leisure in Ancient Rome* (1969); R. MacMullen, *Roman Social Relations, 50 B.C. to A.D. 284* (1974).

[27] A new nobility was gradually replacing the old. Members of old families, as the Scipios, Metelli and Claudii Marcelli, were disappearing from the consulship under Augustus, while some of the new families whom Augustus had ennobled failed to perpetuate their lines (as Statilius Taurus or Quirinius). And few of the republican or even Augustan noble families which did manage to survive received army commands, which went to men of less social distinction. These newer men were drawn from the whole of Italy and slowly from the more civilised regions of the West. Under Tiberius the Senate was still largely limited to *senatores Italici*, but one Narbonese man gained a consulship in 35, and then Claudius opened the doors of the Senate-House wider for Gauls. Soon Seneca from Spanish Cordoba, and Burrus from Gallic Vasio, gained great political power, and provincial senators became more common, but mainly from Italian families settled abroad; only after Nero did descendants of native provincials begin to become senators. See R. Syme, *The Roman Revolution*, ch. xxxii, and *Tacitus* (1958), 585 ff.

[28] Needless to say, young women lost their hearts

to gladiators. A 'star' at Pompeii named Celadus, was *decus* or *suspirum puellarum* (Dessau, *ILS*, 5412). On gladiators see M. Grant, *Gladiators* (1967); L. Robert *Gladiateurs dans l'Orient grec* (1940); and books quoted above, n. 26. On the Circus see H. W. Harris, *Sport in Greece and Rome* (1972).

[29] For bibliography see Chap. 29, n. 14.

[30] On this date (with a rededication to Gaius and Lucius Caesar in A.D. 1–2) see Boëthius and Ward-Perkins, *Etr. and Roman Architecture*, 371, n. 15.

[31] The podium just south of the House of Livia, which used to be attributed to Jupiter Victor, may be that of Apollo.

[32] Most of what now can be seen of Tiberius's palace is the work of later emperors. On the Domus Aurea see Boëthius–Ward-Perkins, *Roman Archit.* 214 ff. Full illustrations in Nash, *Pict. Dict. of Anc. Rome*, i. 339 ff.

[33] On the Ara Pacis, which skilfully harmonised Greek and Roman elements and embodied Augustan art at its highest, see J. M. C. Toynbee, *Proc. Brit. Acad.* xxxix (1953), and *JRS* 1961, 153 ff.

[34] On literature see H. J. Rose, *A Handbook of Latin Literature*[3] (1966); J. Wight Duff, *A Literary History of Rome . . . to the Close of the Golden Age*[3] (1953), *Lit. Hist. Rome in the Silver Age, from Tiberius to Hadrian* (1930); H. E. Butler, *Post-Augustan Poetry from Seneca to Juvenal* (1909).

[35] On Horace see L. P. Wilkinson, *Horace and his Lyric Poetry*[2] (1951); E. Fraenkel, *Horace* (1957); *Horace*, ed. C. D. N. Costa (1974).

[36] On Ovid see the essays edited by J. W. Binns in *Ovid* (1973).

[37] On Virgil see W. Y. Sellar, *Vergil*[3] (1897); Brooks Otis, *Virgil* (1963).

[38] See S. F. Bonner, *Roman Declamation in the Late Republic and Early Empire* (1949), which draws attention to the acquaintance of many declaimers with Roman law.

[39] On Livy see P. G. Walsh, (1961); *Livy* (*Greece and Rome, New Survey* 8, 1974); A. H. McDonald, *JRS* 1957, 155 ff.; Introduction of Ogilvie, *Livy*; *Livy*, essays ed. T. A. Dorey (1971).

[40] Much of the good historical material embodied in Plutarch's *Lives of Caesar* and *Antony* and in Appian's *Civil Wars* is ultimately derived from Pollio. On Pollio's relations with Augustus see A. B. Bosworth, *Historia* 1972, 441 ff.

[41] See J. P. Sullivan, *The Satyricon of Petronius* (1968). On the literary atmosphere of the Neronian period in general see A. Garzetti, *From Tiberius to the Antonines* (1974), 60 ff.

[42] Tiberius accepted the voting of a temple to himself, Livia and the Senate by the cities of Asia, which was erected at Smyrna, but he refused a similar homage from Spain, when he said that he was satisfied to be human, to perform human duties, and to occupy the first place (*principem*) among men (Tac. *Ann.* iv. 15.37–8; cf. Suetonius, *Tib.* 10). In replying to a request from Gythium in Laconia in A.D. 15 or 16, asking that the city might establish the worship of Augustus, himself and Livia, Tiberius deprecated divine honours for himself while accepting for Augustus (he adds that his mother Livia will reply for herself). See Ehrenberg and Jones, *Documents*, n.

102; partial translation in Lewis–Reinhold, *R. Civ.* ii. 560. In taking an oath of allegiance to Tiberius the Cypriotes promised to worship him and all his house (see T. B. Mitford, *JRS* 1960, 75). Claudius declined a high priest and temple in his letter to the Alexandrians: see above, p. 635.

[43] A contemporary commentary on Claudius's apotheosis was the *Apocolocyntosis* (i.e. the Pumkinification of Claudius), a brutally irreverent parody on the late emperor and the new god. It was attributed to Seneca.

[44] On astrology see above, p. 628. Roman emperors again and again expelled astrologers from Rome, yet some of them fell under its influence. Tiberius was a practitioner, under the influence of the Alexandrine scholar Thrasyllus whose son, Ti. Claudius Balbillus, shared his father's astrological lore. Balbillus won the friendship of Claudius, whom he accompanied on the British expedition; later he became Prefect of Egypt and obtained Nero's favour.

[45] See R. Witt, *Isis in the Graeco-Roman World* (1971). On the diffusion of Oriental cults in the Roman Empire see J. Toutain, *Les Cultes paiennes dans l'Empire romaine*, ii (1911); F. Cumont, *Oriental Religions in Roman Paganism* (1911); J. Ferguson, *The Religions of the Roman Empire* (1970). At this stage the cult of Mithras was still confined mainly to the eastern provinces.

[46] On the Zealots see above, Chap. 33, n. 3. On Judaism see G. F. Moore, *Judaism in the First Centuries of the Christian Era*, 2 vols (1927); *The Crucible of Christianity*, ed. A. Toynbee (1969), for various aspects (ch. iii for Judaism). On the Qumran community see M. Burrows, *The Dead Sea Scrolls* (1956); M. Black, *The Scrolls and Christian Origins* (1961); R. de Vaux, *Archaeology and the Dead Sea Scrolls*[2] (1973). On the attitude of Roman and Greek to Jew (the former being more favourable than the latter) see W. H. C. Frend, *Martyrdom and Persecution in the Early Church* (1964), ch. 5.

[47] The chronology of the life of Jesus is uncertain. This is because the disciples were more concerned with proclaiming the 'gospel' than with giving full details of the life. The keynote of the apostolic preaching (*kerugma*) was the proclamation of the crucified and risen Messiah; this had probably been recorded in some form (in Aramaic) by *c.* A.D. 50 and was then expanded by the authors of the first three Gospels from their own knowledge and that of the disciples: Luke's preface shows how he collected, sifted and arranged the written and oral tradition.

Jesus was born in the reign of Herod the Great, who died in 4 B.C.; the nativity may have been as early as 7 B.C. In the sixth century A.D. a Christian monk put the birth of Jesus too late when he established the Christian era by equating the Roman year 753 A.U.C. with 1 B.C. and 754 A.U.C. with A.D. 1. The crucifixion was probably in 29, 30 or 33. It is referred to curtly by Tacitus, *Annals*, xv, 44.4.

It is impossible here to give a bibliography of the life of Jesus. A few books may be mentioned: V. Taylor, *The Formation of the Gospel Tradition* (1933); F. C. Burkitt, *Jesus Christ* (1932); T. W. Manson, *Jesus the Messiah* (1943); C. H. Dodd, *The Founder of Christianity* (1971). On the trial, see G. D. Kilpa-

trick, *The Trial of Jesus* (1955); A. N. Sherwin-White, *Roman Society and Roman Law in the New Testament* (1963), ch. 2, and cf. his remarks in *Gnomon*, Sept. 1971, 589 ff. on the extreme views expressed by S. G. F. Brandon in *The Trial of Jesus* (1968). The story that Pilate reported the crucifixion to Tiberius (Tertullian, *Apolog.* 21.24) should be rejected: see T. D. Barnes, *JRS* 1968, 32 f.

[48] See A. D. Nock, *Essays on Religion and the Ancient World*, i. 67 (ed. Z. Stewart, 1972). The quotation comes from Nock's important study, *Early Gentile Christianity and its Hellenistic Background*, first published in 1928, which should be consulted for the influence of Hellenistic ideas upon the earliest Christians and Paul. Cf. pp. 130 ff. for a brief summary of 'why Christianity won'.

[49] On Paul see W. M. Ramsay, *St. Paul the Traveller and Roman Citizen* (1897); A Deissmann, *St Paul* (1912). His first missionary journey was made *c.* 47; he arrived in Corinth *c.* 51; he was arrested in Jerusalem *c.* 57. His epistles and the Acts throw much light on the Roman world; the Roman authorities are in general depicted favourably. See A. N. Sherwin-White, *Roman Society and Roman Law in the New Testament* (1963).

[50] Suetonius, *Claudius* 25. Suetonius himself (misunderstanding his source?) may have thought of Chrestus as an unknown Jewish agitator, but the identification with Jesus Christ (in the sense that knowledge of him led to internal dissension in the Jewish community in Rome is much more likely.

An imperial rescript from near Nazareth (Smallwood, *Documents*, n. 377) *may*, if of Claudian date, have some connexion with the Resurrection. It prescribes death for the violation of tombs. Claudius might, as the result of the disturbances in Rome, have made inquiries and tightened up penalties when hearing of the rumour that the disciples had stolen the body of Jesus (cf. St Matthew, xxviii, 12–15). See A. Momigliano, *Claudius*, 35 ff.; F. de Zulueta, *JRS* 1932, 184 ff.

Chapter 35: Notes

[1] Suetonius, *Tiberius*, 25.1.

[2] The fate of Corbulo evidently made a deep impression upon the military men. In 69 Mucianus used it to prove to Vespasian that he must insure himself against Vitellius by rebellion (Tacitus, *Histories*, ii. 75.6).

[3] The victims included the poet Lucan, who had excited Nero's literary jealousy and had been forbidden to publish his verses (Tac., *Ann.* xv. 49.3), and Seneca, whose complicity is uncertain. Later victims included Petronius and Annaeus Mela, Lucan's father and Seneca's brother. Seneca's brother Gallio was also compelled to commit suicide. The motives of the conspirators, beyond the death of Nero, are uncertain: many may have thought of Piso as the next emperor, others possibly of Seneca, while a few may have toyed with republican ideas.

[4] This watchword was taken up by Galba, on some of whose coins it appears ('Salus gen. humani'). Other

coin legends proclaimed 'concordia provinciarum', 'libertas publica', 'Roma Nascens' and 'Victoria Populi Romani'. See Mattingly and Sydenham, *Rom. Imp. Coinage*, i. 199 ff.

[5] Vindex may have wanted nothing more than a better emperor; he probably did not envisage restoring republican authority, and it is not clear how far he may have championed a Gallic nationalist movement, seeking either autonomy or greater freedom for Gaul. See G. E. F. Chilver, *JRS* 1957, 29 ff.; P. A. Brunt, *Latomus* 1959, 531 ff.; G. Townend, ibid. 1961, 337 ff.; J. C. Hainsworth, *Historia* 1962, 88 ff.; M. Raoss, *Epigrafica* 1960, 37–151. The coins which Vindex issued do not bear his name and the legends are not narrowly Gallic but words like Freedom; Mattingly–Sydenham, *Rom. Imp. Coinage*, i. 178 ff.

[6] On the campaigns of 68–69 see B. W. Henderson, *Civil War and Rebellion in the Roman Empire* (1908); P. A. L. Greenhalgh, *The Year of the Four Emperors* (1975); K. Wellesley, *The Long Year* (1975). It is estimated that Caecina's corps numbered 40,000 men, that of Valens 30,000. Otho had about 25,000 troops at hand in Italy. Of the other armies which at first declared in his favour, the Danube forces amounted to some 75,000 men.

[7] Tacitus's account of the campaign raises many topographical and other problems (cf. esp. *Histories*, ii. 40–1). See K. Wellesley, *JRS* 1971, 28 ff.

[8] Vitellius is styled 'Germanicus Imperator' on some of his coins (Mattingly–Sydenham, *Rom. Imp. Coinage*, i. 224 ff.). The military character of his rule was also set off by his neglect to assume the titles of 'Caesar' and 'Augustus'. On the attitude of the Roman *plebs* to him see R. F. Newbold, *Historia* 1972, 308 ff.

[9] The governors of Pannonia and Moesia followed Primus with their main forces. A mutiny on the way, in which the troops deposed their commanders-in-chief, had the result of giving Primus control over the whole of the expeditionary force from the Danube.

[10] The movements of Mucianus at this stage are uncertain. It may be assumed that he was the author of the terms to Vitellius. Though these were conveyed in the first instance to Vitellius by Primus, they were confirmed in a letter from Mucianus (Tacitus, *Histories*, iii. 63.3–4).

[11] This fire involved the neighbouring Tabularium (p. 304) and destroyed 3000 bronze tablets. Vespasian repaired the damage by a systematic search for duplicates (Suetonius, *Vespasian*, 8. 5).

[12] The coins of Galba, Otho and Vitellius often carry such legends as 'libertas populi', 'Roma restituta', 'Roma renascens', 'Mars Ultor', even 'pax orbis terrarum'.

Chapter 36: Notes

[1] The history of the Flavians was recorded in Tacitus's *Histories,* now lost except for the years 69–70. Surviving sources include Suetonius, *Lives of Vespasian, Titus* and *Domitian* (ed. G. W. Mooney, 1930; *Vespasian* by A. W. Braithwaite, 1927); Dio Cassius, lxv–lxvii; and, less directly, the elder Pliny, Quintilian, Frontinus, Statius, Martial, Juvenal and the early speeches of Dio Chrysostom. Select inscriptions in M. McCrum and A. G. Woodhead, *Select Documents of the Principates of the Flavian Emperors* (1961).

Modern works include B. W. Henderson, *Five Roman Emperors* (1927), chs i–vii; L. Homo, *Vespasien* (1949); S. Gsell, *Essai sur le règne de l'empereur Domitien* (1894); an essay on Domitian's character by K. H. Waters, *Phoenix* 1964, 49 ff.; A. Garzetti, *From Tiberius to the Antonines* (1974) 227 ff., with bibliographical discussions 636 ff.; R. Syme, *Tacitus* (1958), *passim*.

[2] The younger Pliny relates that when his uncle was serving as aide-de-camp to Vespasian, he had to report for duty before dawn, for the emperor worked by night as well as by day (*Epistles*, ii. 5.9). On the personal part played by individual emperors in the day-to-day administration of the Empire see F. Miller, 'Emperors at Work', *JRS* 1967, 9 ff.

[3] The act by which Vespasian was made emperor is partly preserved (*ILS*, 244; McCrum and Woodhead, *Documents*, n. 1). It was a *senatus consultum*, to which the force of law was given by a confirmatory vote of the Popular Assembly. At the end of each paragraph the words 'ita ut licuit divo Augusto', or the like, recur like a refrain. Thus Vespasian was formally granted all the miscellaneous powers which his predecessors had exercised, and, in addition, he received unlimited rights of *commendatio*. See H. Last, *CAH*, xi. 404 ff. A survey of modern interpretations is given by G. Barbieri, *Diz. Epigr.* iv (1957), 750 ff.

[4] Vespasian was ordinary (not suffect) consul every year of his reign except 73 and 78; he had Titus as colleague six times, Domitian once. Titus was consul with his father in 79 and with his brother in 80. Domitian was consul 82–88, 90, 92 and 95.

[5] On the personnel of the Senate in the Flavian period see B. Stech, *Klio*, suppl. vol., n. 10. The nominees of the Flavian emperors were usually *adlecti inter quaestorios*. Sometimes a higher grade was conferred, but there are no known cases of *adlectio inter consulares*. The first African to hold the consulship was under Vespasian in 80.

[6] Among the imperial freedmen who maintained their position by good service were Abascantus, the *praepositus ab epistulis* at Domitian's court, and Tiberius Claudius, who served every emperor from Tiberius to Domitian and was *praepositus a rationibus* under the three Flavian rulers. On these worthies see A. M. Duff, *Freedmen in the Early Roman Empire* (1928), 146, 184 f.

[7] The first known instances of such *iuridici* occur under Domitian: Dessau, *ILS*, 1011, 1015. The latter is an inscription of a famous Roman jurist, Iavolenus Priscus, who before being suffect consul in 86 had been *iuridicus provinciae Brittaniae* (he later governed Upper Germany, Syria and Africa, and was a member of Trajan's *Consilium*).

[8] Titus's second wife, who was divorced *c.* 64, bore his only child, Julia. When in Judaea (67–70), Titus had fallen in love with Berenice, sister of Agrippa II; she had a lurid marital history, and had tried to prevent the Jewish revolt. When she visited Rome

with her brother in 75, Titus openly lived with her for some time, but in face of public opinion, which recalled Cleopatra, he did not marry her. On a second visit in 79 he dismissed her, to their mutual regret: *invitus invitam*. See J. Crook, *AJ Phil.* 1951, 162 ff.

⁹ See K. Scott, *The Imperial Cult under the Flavians* (1936).

¹⁰ On the extent of the 'second persecution' of Christians see B. W. Henderson, *Five Roman Emperors* (1927), 42 ff.

¹¹ The destruction of Pompeii is vividly described in a letter by the younger Pliny (*Ep.* vi. 16), who was an eye-witness, to Tacitus. The elder Pliny, who commanded the fleet at Misenum at the time and had charge of the salvage operations, lost his life by staying too long in the danger-zone. Some 200 dead bodies (out of a total population of perhaps 30,000) have been recovered. Most of the casualties were probably due to asphyxiation by carbon monoxide or sulphur dioxide, as at the eruption of Mt Pelée in 1902. Pompeii was buried in sand, stones and mud, Stabiae in ashes, and Herculaneum in liquid tufa. See M. Grant, *Cities of Vesuvius* (1971) (a finely illustrated book).

¹² The reading *quadringenties milies* in Suetonius, *Vesp.* xvi. 3 (40,000 million sesterces), appears excessive and probably should be altered to *quadragies milies* (4000 million). Vespasian presumably was thinking of a capital sum, not annual income. Suetonius's stories of sales of office and judicial awards should be received with caution. Vespasian organised special treasuries: little is known about the *fiscus Alexandrinus* or the *fiscus Asiaticus,* but the *fiscus Iudaicus* diverted to the Capitoline temple at Rome the two drachmas which every Jew had paid annually to the temple at Jerusalem (humiliating for the conquered and profitable for the victors, since there may have been some 5,000,000 Jews in the Empire).

¹³ On the code of imperial leases see R. K. McEldery, *JRS* 1918, 95 ff. Two inscriptions contain leases of mining rights at Vipasca in Lusitania (*ILS*, 6891; Riccobono, *Fontes,* nn. 104, 105; translation in Lewis–Reinhold, *R. Civ.* ii. 188–94). The first inscription is Hadrianic and the second belongs to the same century. The middlemen, working under government contract, paid royalties of as much as 50 per cent on the ore mined.

¹⁴ On Domitian's finances see R. Syme, *JRS* 1930, 55 ff.

¹⁵ Recent excavation has revealed many vivid and grim traces of the siege and of the Roman siege-works: see Y. Yadin, *Masada* (1967). Josephus gives a detailed account: *Bell. Iud.* vii. 252–3, 275–406.

¹⁶ A court of justice at Jamnia dealt with ceremonial and civil law, and may have extended its jurisdiction under its later Patriarch. To it was probably paid any contributions made by the Jews of the Dispersion. See E. Schurer, *A History of the Jewish People* (1890), I. ii. 276 f.

¹⁷ For a detailed account of the revolt of Civilis see B. W. Henderson, *Civil War and Rebellion in the Roman Empire* (1908), ch. iii.

¹⁸ Since Durocortorum was the seat of the *legatus* of Belgica it may be assumed that he gave facilities for summoning the congress. But a delegate from

the Treveri was allowed to attend and state his case (Tacitus, *Histories,* iv. 68–9).

¹⁹ For a defence of the Roman protectorate in Gaul see the speech made by Cerialis to some of the Treveri after their surrender (Tac., *Hist.* iv. 73–4). Many Gallic chiefs would no doubt have expressed themselves in similar terms.

²⁰ For details of these campaigns see S. S. Frere, *Britannia* (1967), ch. 6.

²¹ On Wales see V. E. Nash-Williams, *The Roman Frontier in Wales* (1954).

²² The main source for Agricola's campaigns is Tacitus's monograph *De Vita Agricolae,* written in praise of his father-in-law. See the edition by R. M. Ogilvie and I. A. Richmond (1967), for a general assessment of its weaknesses and merits as history. Archaeology and especially aerial photography has done much to fill in many details.

²³ On the German and Raetian *limes* see B. W. Henderson, *Five Roman Emperors* (1927), ch. vi; O. Brogan, *Archaeological Journal,* 1935, 1 ff.; W. Schleimache, *Der römische Limes in Deutschland* (1961). For archaeological detail regarding the Flavian period see H. Schönberger, *JRS* 1969, 154 ff.

Domitian, who had longed for military glory, celebrated his victory over the Chatti by taking the title Germanicus, holding a triumph and issuing coins with the legend 'Germania capta' (Mattingly, *Coins of the Roman Empire, B.M.,* ii, pl. lxii, n. 3). On the date of the victory see B. W. Jones, *Historia* 1973, 79 ff.

²⁴ At Adamklissi an altar contained the names of over 3000 Roman casualties; these were probably the troops of Oppius Sabinus, whose defeat will have been in this area, rather than those of Cornelius Fuscus. There is also a *tropaeum* to Mars the Avenger, dedicated later by Trajan; its sculptured metopes illustrate his campaigns. See I. A. Richmond, *PBSR,* 1967, 29 ff.; L. Rossi, *Trajan's Column and the Dacian Wars* (1971), 55 ff., and *The Archaeological Journal,* 1972, 56 ff.

On the Dobrudja see H. Gajeweska, *Topographie des fortifications romains en Dobrudja* (Warsaw, 1974).

²⁵ For Syria under Vespasian see G. W. Bowersock, *JRS* 1973, 133 ff.

²⁶ For the defences of the Dariel Pass see an inscription: *ILS,* 8795; McCrum and Woodhead, *Documents,* n. 237.

²⁷ Pliny (*NH,* iii. 20) records the grant of Latin rights to all Spain, but all the surviving inscriptions relating to municipal life at this time come from Baetica. During the Flavian period some 350 Spanish towns received municipal charters. The most famous are those from Salpensa and Malaca, both Domitianic; see *ILS,* 6088, 6089; McCrum and Woodhead, *Documents,* n. 453, 454; translated in Lewis–Reinhold, *R. Civ.* ii. 32 ff. The cities received constitutions indistinguishable from those of Italian cities. They were now half-way between aliens and Roman citizens; their local office-holders received Roman citizenship and thus could take a greater share in the work of the Empire. On the gradual spread of Latin rights see A. N. Sherwin-White, *The Roman Citizenship*² (1973), 360 ff.

²⁸ On this subject see R. MacMullen, *Enemies of*

the Roman Order (1967), ch. ii; and, for the opposition under Nero, see B. H. Warmington, *Nero* (1969), ch. 12.

[29] Since Stoics and Cynics had never raised a protest against the frankly hereditary monarchies of the Hellenistic world, their objections to Vespasian's dynastic policy could not have carried much weight in genuine philosophical circles.

[30] The victims were Junius Arulenus Rusticus (suffect consul in 92) and Herennius Senecio. Domitian also arrested a wandering Greek teacher, half philosopher and half medicine-man, Apollonius of Tyana, who had criticised the emperor too freely. Apollonius, however, was acquitted (see Philostratus, *Life of Apollonius*, viii. 5). Musonius Rufus, a Stoic, had been banished by Nero and later returned to Rome. In 70 he was expressly exempted by Vespasian from the general expulsion of philosophers, but later fell into disfavour and was banished; he was recalled by Titus, whose friendship he enjoyed. He is an interesting man, in advance of his times: he denounced gladiatorial games while in Athens, advocated greater education for women, and numbered Epictetus among his pupils. See an essay on him by M. P. Charlesworth, *Five Men* (1936), ch. ii.

[31] Another cousin, Flavius Sabinus (consul with Domitian in 82 and husband of Julia, Domitian's daughter), was killed by the emperor in 84; he and his brother Clemens were probably grandsons, not sons, of Vespasian's brother Sabinus (see G. Townend, *JRS* 1961, 54). Clemens, condemned for *maiestas*, and his wife Flavia Domitilla (Domitian's niece) were alleged to have been guilty of 'atheism' or following Jewish or Christian practices. They may have been Christians, as stated by later tradition, if the early Christian Coemeterium Domitillae on the Via Ardeatina is connected with her. Domitian had intended that Clemens's two small sons should succeed him: they disappear from history after 96.

Chapter 37: Notes

[1] The main literary sources include (for Nerva and Trajan) Dio Cassius, lxvii–lxviii; Pliny, *Panygyricus* and *Epistulae* (esp. bk x); (for Hadrian) frgs of Dio Cassius, lxix; *Historia Augusta, Hadrian, L. Aelius*; (for Antoninus) frg. of Dio Cassius, lxx; *Historia Augusta, Antoninus Pius*; Aristides, *To Rome* (cf. edn by J. H. Oliver, *The Ruling Power*, 1953); Fronto, *Epistulae*; (for M. Aurelius) Dio Cassius, lxxi–lxvii; *Historia Augusta, Marcus Antoninus, L. Verus, Avidius Cassius*; Fronto, *Epistulae*. Late writers, as Aurelius Victor and Eutropius, add a little. Coins and inscriptions are, of course, invaluable. See E. M. Smallwood, *Documents Illustrating the Principates of Nerva, Trajan and Hadrian* (1966).

General modern works include M. Hammond, *The Antonine Monarchy* (1959); A. Garzetti, *From Tiberius to the Antonines* (1974), with valuable bibliographies. B. W. Henderson, *Five Roman Emperors* (1927), for Nerva and Trajan; ibid. *Life and Principate of the Emperor Hadrian* (1923); A. Birley, *Marcus Aurelius* (1966); R. Syme, *Tacitus* (1958), *passim*.

[2] Nerva had been consul in 71 and 90. His great-grandfather had been consul in 36 B.C., and through an aunt he was linked to the Julio-Claudian family. He lacked military experience as well as sons, not necessarily a disadvantage at this point, provided that the armies had come finally to accept the idea of the Principate. He was essentially a nominee of the Senate (hence well-regarded by Tacitus and Pliny).

[3] Trajan, unlike all his predecessors, was not an Italian, but came of Spanish origin. His father, adlected into the Senate by Vespasian, had been consul and proconsul of Asia. Trajan had had a senatorial career and had served in the army in different parts of the Empire. For an Italian biography see R. Paribeni, *Optimus Princeps*, 2 vols (1926–7). He did not change his gentile name after adoption. Hadrian and Antoninus followed this precedent; M. Aurelius assumed the gentile name of Antoninus. By this time the rules of Roman nomenclature, which long had lost their original significance, were falling into disregard. On the 'Spanish' emperors see the essays entitled *Les Empereurs romans d'Espagne* (1965).

[4] Hadrian was born at Italica of a senatorial family which had settled in Spain. He had gone through the regular senatorial offices (e.g. *cos. suff.* in 108) and had served in Spain, Pannonia, Moesia, Germany and, with Trajan, in Dacia. He was Trajan's legate in his eastern expedition, had been left in 117 as legate of Syria, and was at Antioch when Trajan died in Cilicia.

[5] Dio (lxix. i) says that the formal act of adoption was completed by Trajan's widow Plotina; this was perhaps the core of the truth in the tales which ascribed Hadrian's accession to Plotina's favour. We do not know why Trajan was so late in adopting a successor nor whether the death-bed adoption is true, but it is certain that he intended Hadrian to follow him: there was no other possible candidate.

[6] Antoninus Pius was born in Italy of a family which came from Nemausus (modern Nîmes). His career had not been primarily military; he had been consul (in 120), a consular judge in Italy, proconsul of Asia, and a member of the imperial council. During his reign he lived the life of a landowner in Italy, unlike the cosmopolitan Hadrian. See E. E. Bryant, *The Reign of Antoninus Pius* (1895); W. Huttl, *Antoninus Pius*, 2 vols (1933–6).

[7] M. Aurelius, who came from a consular family of Spanish origin, was born in 121 (and named M. Annius Verus). The family of his mother, Domitia Lucilla, owned large tile-factories. He was nicknamed Verissimus by Hadrian who adopted him in 138 and supervised his education. In 145 he married Pius's daughter (his own cousin), the younger Faustina. Consul in 140 and 145, he lived in friendship with Pius. His interest in rhetoric, taught by his tutor Fronto, was about 146 superseded by a greater love for Stoic philosophy, which dominated his life and was expressed in deeply felt personal terms in the twelve books of his *Meditations*. He was consul again in 161 when he succeeded Pius. See A. Birley, *Marcus Aurelius* (1966); the *Meditations* are edited by A. S. L. Farquharson (2nd ed. 1952) and discussed by P. A. Brunt, *JRS* 1974, 1 ff.

[8] On the composition of the Senate, A.D. 68–235,

see M. Hammond, *JRS* 1957, 73 ff. (with bibliography and tables), and *The Antonine Monarchy* (1959), 249 ff. He sums up (p. 252) regarding senators of known origin: 'the Italians are in a majority of over eighty per cent under Vespasian and do not sink below fifty per cent until the Severi, when they vary from forty-three to forty-nine per cent . . . the percentage of westerners sinks rapidly after Trajan and that of the easterners rises, but not so rapidly because the Africans begin to emerge in the middle of the second century and constitute about a third of the identifiable provincial senators under Marcus and Commodus, falling off slightly thereafter.' Provincial senators would naturally retain much of their wealth in their native provinces. Hence Trajan required senators to invest one-third of their property in Italian land. This appears not to have been effective, since Marcus Aurelius reduced the proportion to a quarter. It was necessary to try to link these new men closely with Italy, especially as many Italian senators were increasingly acquiring property in the provinces. In this period of social mobility the number of senators available actually to attend and the number attending remains obscure. There is evidence to suggest an attendance of 383 members in A.D. 45, and of 250 in 138 (Riccobono, *Fontes*, 289 and 292).

⁹ The four consulars may have objected to Hadrian's policy of abandoning Trajan's eastern conquests. The Senate felt that Hadrian was guilty of not keeping his promise not to execute any senator. Hadrian honoured Attianus with consular insignia: this would increase suspicion that Attianus had acted with the emperor's knowledge. In the case of Servianus it may be assumed that he was tried before the Senate, in accordance with Hadrian's oath to that body, and that the prisoner's guilt was established.

¹⁰ *Digest*, i. 2. 2.48–9; Gaius, *Instit.* 1.7. Cf. M. Hammond, *The Antonine Monarchy*, 383 ff., and (very briefly) J. Crook, *Law and Life of Rome* (1967), 25 ff.

¹¹ See J. Crook, *Consilium Principis* (1955), esp. 56 ff. There may have been a recognised membership of the *Consilium*, but perhaps different members were summoned in accordance with the nature of the business. A judicial session of the *Consilium* (before Hadrian's time) is described in Pliny, *Epist.* vi. 31. Cases referred to the emperor on appeal, but not reserved by him for the *Consilium*, were usually delegated in the second century to the *praefectus urbi*, who thus acquired a considerable general jurisdiction.

¹² See R. H. Barrow, *Slavery in the Roman Empire* (1928), *passim*.

¹³ Under Nerva the town of Glevum (Gloucester) was constituted as a colony (Dessau, *ILS*, 2365). Trajan's colonies were plentiful in Africa and Dacia. In the second century many villages which had been 'attributed' to neighbouring towns were detached from these and received municipal status. See A. N. Sherwin-White, *The Roman Citizenship*² (1973), chs ix and x.

¹⁴ On the municipalities and their internal local government see J. S. Reid, *The Municipalities of the Roman Empire* (1913); F. F. Abbott and A. C. Johnson, *Municipal Administration in the Roman Empire* (1926), with documentation; and for the eastern

cities, A. H. M. Jones, *The Greek City* (1940), esp. 174 ff., and *Cities of the Eastern Roman Provinces*² (1971).

¹⁵ On the senatorial *ordo* at Pompeii see M. L. Gordon, *JRS* 1927, 165 ff. Sons of freedmen were eligible for the municipal senates (M. L. Gordon, *JRS* 1931, 65 ff.). Property qualifications, but of a much lower amount than at Rome, were imposed in many towns.

¹⁶ For specimens of the Pompeiian 'election posters' (scrawls on any handy blank wall), see Dessau, *ILS*, 6406 ff. In Africa, and more especially in Asia Minor, the popular assemblies remained active in the second century. In Gaul they died out or became dormant.

¹⁷ Innumerable honorific inscriptions in acknowledgment of generosities are preserved. A wealthy Lydian named Opramoas had no fewer than sixty such texts engraved on his tomb (see *IGRR*, iii. 739; Smallwood, *Documents . . . Nerva, etc.*, n. 497). On the motives behind the giving and accepting of municipal honours see A. R. Hands, *Charities and Social Aid in Greece and Rome* (1968).

¹⁸ These storms in municipal tea-cups were especially frequent in Asia Minor. On the municipal police forces see O. Hirschfeld, *Kleina Schriften* (1913), 591 ff. In Asia Minor Trajan transferred the appointment of the local *irenarchs* to the provincial governors.

¹⁹ On municipal benefactions see Reid, op. cit., Hands, op. cit., (n. 14 and n. 17, above), and F. F. Abbott, *The Common People of Ancient Rome* (1912), ch. vi. At Calama in northern Africa a priest paid 600,000 sesterces into his municipal chest on his appointment. Wealthy women were appointed to priesthoods, and in Asia Minor also to magistracies (which they exercised by proxy) in consideration of a suitable fee.

²⁰ In the charter of Malaga (Chap. 51; see above, p. 64 n. 27) provision was made for the nomination of candidates by the returning-officer, should the number of voluntary entrants not be sufficient. Actual cases of compulsory enrolment into the senates occurred in Bithynia, c. 110 (Pliny, *Ep.* x. 113). In Egypt the semi-official post of *gymnasiarch* was made virtually obligatory upon the wealthier Greek residents in the second century (see F. Ortel, *Die Liturgie*, 317).

²¹ For instances of public works left unfinished see Pliny, *Ep.* x. 37.39.

²² Since Bithynia was a senatorial province the Senate ratified Pliny's appointment. But Pliny sent his reports to the emperor and received instructions from him.

²³ On the *curatores* see W. Liebenam, *Philologus*, 1897, 290 ff.; C. Lucas, *JRS* 1940, 56 ff. (*curatores* in Africa).

²⁴ On the *alimenta* see R. Duncan-Jones, *PBSR* 1964, 123 ff.; P. Garnsey, *Historia* 1968, 367 ff.; A. R. Hands, *Charities and Social Aid in Greece and Rome* (1968), 108 ff. The system arose from private philanthropy; such a benefactor is known from about Nero's time (Dessau, *ILS*, 977), while the younger Pliny had initiated such a scheme at Comum (*Ep.* vii. 18). The evidence for attributing their official establishment to Nerva is weak. Much light is thrown on the *alimenta* by two Trajanic inscriptions from

Veleia in northern Italy and from near Beneventum. Landowners gave security in land to about 12½ times the value of the sum received. At Veleia the boys (263) received 16 sesterces a month, the girls (only 35) 12 sesterces. Trajan advertised this benefaction by a relief on the arch at Beneventum and on the coinage. Antoninus Pius established a new fund, the *Puellae Faustinianae* in memory of his wife Faustina. The precise dating of the introduction of the senatorial *praefectus alimentorum* and his equestrian subordinate *procuratores ad alimenta* remains uncertain. For a discussion of the motives behind these measures, see Hands, op. cit. To what extent were they altruistic, how far did they aim at the *poorest* children, how far did they aim to improve the birth-rate all round, were they aimed at checking a decline in the population, was there such a decline (as argued by A. E. R. Boak, *Manpower Shortage and the Fall of the Roman Empire* (1955), but see M. I. Finley, *JRS* 1958, 146 ff.), or was there a belief at the time in such a supposed decline? These and similar questions scarcely admit of definite answers.

[25] *Congiaria* represented the continuation by the emperor of gifts of corn or oil made to the people by the aediles during the Republic. They increasingly took the form of cash. See *Res Gestae*, 15, for Augustus's lavish distributions. By Trajan's time a normal gift was 75 denarii per head, but he is said to have given a total of no less than 650 denarii in his three distributions (on his return to Rome in 99, and after the two Dacian Wars in 102 and 107). Most emperors (but not Domitian) celebrated these *liberalitates* by the issue of commemorative coinage.

[26] Many achievements of these emperors, even fiscal reliefs, were commemorated on their coinage. Thus we find, with appropriate pictorial types, legends such as: under Nerva, 'fisci Iudaici calumnia sublata', 'vehiculatione Italiae remissa' (as well as more constitutionally directed legends, as 'libertas publica', 'iustitia Augusti', and a hoped-for 'concordia exercitum'). Under Trajan come, e.g., 'congiarium tertium', 'alimenta Italiae', 'spes Populi Romani'. Under Hadrian, 'reliqua vetera HS novies mill. abolita' (referring to the burning of debt-bonds in the Forum). Under Antoninus, 'puellae Faustinianae'.

[27] On the *decemprimi* see Rostovtzeff, *Soc. and Econ. Hist. of Roman Empire*² (1957), 390, 706, n. 45.

[28] On the *conductores* see Rostovtzeff, ibid., index. A *lex Marciana* of uncertain date (Flavian?), dealing with imperial and private estates in north Africa, regulated relations between cultivators and the proprietors or their *conductores*. Its scope was extended by Hadrian (in the so-called *lex Hadriana*), which enabled permanent tenants to develop waste land. Text in Riccobono, *Fontes*, 484 ff.; R. M. Haywood in Frank, *Econ. SAR*, iv. 89 ff. Cf. Rostovtzeff, op. cit. 368 f.

[29] Nerva also sold off crown property, but at easy prices (Dio Cassius, lxviii. 2). His object therefore was not so much to stave off bankruptcy as to make a gesture of old-fashioned frugality.

[30] See Pliny, *Ep.* x, and notes in edition by A. N. Sherwin-White.

[31] A report (in Greek) on the conditions of navigation along the Black Sea coast, which was made at Hadrian's order by a governor of Cappadocia named Flavius Arrianus, still survives in part (C. Muller, *Geographici Graeci Minores*, i. 370 ff.).

[32] On Hadrian and Italica see R. Syme, *JRS* 1964, 142 ff. Hadrian's mother came from Gades. Although he spent little of his youth in Italica he later refurbished the city with splendid buildings and gave it colonial status (*colonia Aelia*).

[33] We may ascribe to Hadrian, who was especially liberal in his grants of the Latin status, an enlargement of the privileges which it entailed. By this Greater Latinity (*maius Latium*) full Roman franchise was conferred on all the *decuriones* of 'Latin' towns (hitherto Latin rights had conferred Roman citizenship only upon the local magistrates). In view of the numerous grants of municipal or colonial status by Hadrian to the new-grown towns in the Danube lands we may assume that it was in these regions that the half-franchise was most commonly given by him.

Chapter 38: Notes

[1] A vast series of frontier-works has been discovered through the pioneer work of Col. J. Baradez, whose publication, *Fossatum Africae* (1949), is fundamental. Air-photography, combined with selective excavation, has revealed a Numidian *limes* system, encircling the Aures frontier in the south. It is not a wall, like Hadrian's Wall, but a zone for defence in depth, with forts and some stretches of wall and of ditch where the passes through the mountains make them necessary. In its rear are extensive irrigation works, with dams and water-channels; even olive-presses and remains of trees survive. Thus the system guarded the frontier, controlled the movements of tribes, and stimulated economic growth in this wild region. The surviving remains are not all the work of one period, but the earliest work probably goes back to Hadrian, who (as shown by inscriptions of 126 and 133; see Baradez, pp. 103 ff., or Smallwood, *Documents*, n. 327) established a camp at Gemellae (near Biskra), a key point in part of the *fossatum*. Another Hadrianic inscription comes from Rapidum, far to the north-west of Gemellae. On the frontier in southern Tunisia see P. Trousset, *Recherches sur les limes Tripolitanus . . . à la frontière Tunisio-Libyenne* (1974).

[2] For the conquest, road and *limes* system see G. W. Bowersock, *JRS* 1971, 228 ff. Coins celebrated 'Arabia adquisita', not 'capta', suggesting perhaps a fairly peaceful occupation. On Trajan's road to the gulf of Aqaba see Dessau, *ILS*, 5834 (= Smallwood, n. 420). Trajan also attempted to stimulate the overseas trade to the East by cleaning out once more the old Pharaonic canal from the apex of the Nile delta to the Red Sea. But he was no more successful than his predecessors in keeping the canal free from sand-drift. A Roman fleet, designed to protect trade with India, was more likely stationed in the Persian Gulf than the Red Sea.

[3] On the Armenian and Parthian Wars, which bristle with chronological and other problems, see F. A.

Lepper, *Trajan's Parthian War* (1948); M. I. Henderson, *JRS* 1949, 121 ff.

[4] Communications between the two marching columns were kept up by means of an ancient canal from Euphrates to Tigris which Trajan opened up again for navigation. It is uncertain whether he built a *limes*, extending from the neighbourhood of Nineveh and thence down the Chaboras valley to the Euphrates, as a frontier of Roman Mesopotamia. Such a line existed later, but a Trajanic prototype is uncertain. On the Cappadocian *limes* see T. B. Mitford, *JRS* 1974, 160 ff.

[5] Trajan's conquests were marked by coin-issues with appropriate legends and types: 'Armenia et Mesopotamia in potestatem populi Romani redactae', with Armenia seated at Trajan's feet between two river-gods; 'Rex Parthis datus', Trajan placing a diadem on the head of Partamaspates; 'Parthia capta', with two Parthian captives at the foot of a trophy. Trajan adopted the title Parthicus.

[6] On the Arabian frontier see G. Macdonald, *Antiquity* 1934, 373 ff.

[7] The statement of Dio Cassius (lxviii. 32) that the Jews killed 220,000 persons in Cyrenaica, and 240,000 in Cyprus, is self-evident exaggeration. But those figures suggest that the Jews aimed at nothing less than the extermination of the Greek or hellenised population. Thereafter Jews were forbidden to set foot in Cyprus. On the revolt see A. Fuks, *JRS* 1961, 98 ff. On some letters of Hadrian concerning Cyprus after the revolt see P. M. Fraser, *JRS* 1950, 77 ff.

[8] Details of the Second Jewish War have not been preserved. According to Appian (*Syriaca*, 1) Hadrian razed Jerusalem to the ground—presumably after a siege. But the passage in which this statement occurs swarms with errors. The silence of Dio Cassius on this point rather suggests that Jerusalem remained in the hands of the Romans. On the estimated Jewish casualties see Dio, lxix. 14. Some light has been provided by discoveries in the Dead Sea caves of letters from Bar Cosiba to his commanders, one with perhaps his own signature (J. T. Milik, *Revue Biblique* 1953, 276 ff.). They show that the correct form of his name to have been Shim'on (Simon) Ben or Bar Cosiba. Documents are dated by an era, beginning 1 Tishri (October) 131, which was also used on coins struck by the Jews during the revolt. See P. Benoit *et al.*, *Discoveries in the Judaean Desert.* ii (1961), nos 24, 43–4; *Israel Explorat. Journal* 1961, 40 ff., 1962, 248 ff.; Y. Yadin, *Bar-Kokhba* (1971).

[9] The literary sources for the Dacian Wars are very defective (mainly a few pages of Dio Cassius). On the Column see L. Rossi, *Trajan's Column and the Dacian Wars* (1971). On the native Dacian hill-forts see L. Rossi, *Antiquaries Journal* 1971, 30 ff.

[10] On the Iron Gates road see Dessau, *ILS*, 5863. It has now been deliberately flooded. On Trajan's canal see J. Šašel, *JRS* 1973, 80 ff.

[11] The tombstone of Maximus, the soldier who captured Decebalus as he was dying, has been found: it depicts the scene. See M. Speidel, *JRS* 1970, 142 ff., and L. Rossi, op. cit. 229 f.

[12] A fleet on the Danube, the *classis Moesica*, had played its part in the Dacian Wars and thereafter afforded protection to Dacia and its eastern flank

on the Black Sea. (While the Moesian fleet patrolled the north-western shores of the Euxine, the rest of this vast sea was guarded by a Pontic fleet. See C. G. Starr, *The Roman Imperial Navy* (1941), 125 ff.)

[13] A comparison between the descriptions of Germany in Caesar's *Bellum Gallicum* (vi. 22) and in Tacitus's *Germania* shows that in the interval the process of settlement had advanced considerably. See E. A. Thompson, *The Early Germans* (1965), esp. chs 1 and 2. Roman ploughs have been found in central Germany: see K. Schumacher, *Siedelungs-und Kulturgeschichte der Rheinlande* (1923), ii. 246.

[14] On the problems, including chronological, of these wars see A. Birley, *Marcus Aurelius* (1966), esp. 323 ff.

[15] On Commodus's forts along the Danube see Dessau, *ILS*, 395.

[16] On the German frontier-defences see B. W. Henderson, *Five Roman Emperors* (1927), 117 ff. For a possible earlier date for the arrival of the Brittones see H. Schonberger, *JRS* 1969, 167, and, for recent archaeological evidence for the *limes* at this period, op. cit. 164 ff.

[17] The disappearance of legio IX is a mystery. The view that it was wiped out in the insurrection is not now generally held. There is some evidence to suggest that it was moved to Nijmegen *c.* 122 and then perished later, perhaps in the Jewish War of 132. See S. S. Frere, *Britannia* (1967), 137 ff. For the whole of this section Frere's book should be consulted.

[18] On the Wall see J. Collingwood Bruce, *Handbook to the Roman Wall* (11th edition by I. A. Richmond, 1957); H. M. Ordnance Survey, *Map of Hadrian's Wall* (1964); E. Birley, *Research on Hadrian's Wall* (1961); Frere, op. cit., ch. 7. The eastern part was built of stone, but its width was later changed; the western part was originally of turf and then changed to stone; the forts were also a later addition to the original plan. For details of this over-simplified statement see the works quoted. One problem that has been solved is that the Vallum was not built before the Wall, but after its construction had started: at one point it swerves to avoid a mile-castle and also the site of forts. For a recent discussion of some problems see D. J. Brege and B. Dobson, *Britannia* 1972, 182 ff.

[19] On the Antonine Wall see Sir George Macdonald, *The Roman Wall in Scotland*[2] (1934); A. S. Robertson, *The Antonine Wall* (1960); Frere, op. cit., ch. 8. Ordnance Survey map (1969). On the civilian population of the area of the two Walls see P. Salway, *The Frontier People of Roman Britain* (1965). On the fluctuations of Roman control of Scotland in the Antonine and Severan periods see B. R. Hartley, *Britannia* 1972, 1 ff.

[20] The percentage of Italians compared with provincials has been put at 65 per cent under Augustus, 48·7 per cent under Claudius and Nero, 21·4 per cent under Vespasian and Trajan, and only 0·9 per cent from Hadrian to A.D. 200. See G. Forni, *Il reclutamento delle legioni da Augusto a Diacleziano* (1953), 157 ff.

[21] See J. W. Eadie, *JRS* 1967, 161 ff.

[22] The speeches (*adlocutiones*) which Hadrian delivered to various units of the troops in Africa at

a review which he held at Lambaesis in 128 are preserved in inscriptions. See Dessau, *ILS*, 2497, 9133–5; Smallwood, *Documents*, n. 328.

[23] One of the obstacles to the abolition or restriction of slavery would have been the opposition of many small masters and cultivators of medium-sized estates, who kept a few servile workers to supplement their personal labours.

[24] For the view that the municipal aristocracies suffered from under-employment see W. E. Heitland, *The Roman Fate* (1900).

Chapter 39: Notes

[1] The rent rolls drawn up in connexion with the alimentary institutions by two local authorities in Italy, Veleia and the canton of the Ligures Baebiani (on these see above, p. 644), show that while there was a gradual decrease in the number of smallholdings the rate of decline was slow. See T. Frank, *Economic History of Rome*[2] (1927), ch. xx, and *Econ. SAR*, v. 173 f.

[2] On the management of the imperial domains much light is thrown by a series of second-century inscriptions from Africa (see above, ch. 37, n. 28). Cf. W. E. Heitland, *Agricola* (1921), 342 ff.; R. M. Haywood in Frank, *Econ. SAR*, iv. 88 ff.

[3] The only parts of the English Lowlands where large areas remained uncultivated were in the southwest, in the Sussex Weald, in the Fenlands, and in the Lancashire plain. On economic conditions in Britain see R. G. Collingwood in Frank, *Econ. SAR*, iii; S. S. Frere, *Britannia* (1967), chs 13, 14.

[4] With an area of 240 acres Corinium was second only to Londinium in size among the towns of Roman Britain. On this town see J. S. Wacher, *Antiquaries Journal* 1961–5.

[5] On Roman Belgium see F. Cumont, *Comment la Belgique fut romanisée*[2] (1918).

[6] Over a dozen ingots ('pigs') of Mendip lead are known; they all bear the name of the emperors, indicating that the mines were worked by the state, while two have the name of a *societas*. See Collingwood, in Frank, *Econ. SAR*, iii. 42 ff. The tin industry of Britain seems to have been at a standstill during the first two centuries of the Roman occupation, but woke up from the mid-third century. Presumably the Spanish mines had sufficed for the Roman market until then.

[7] On the Gallic and Rhenish industries see C. Jullian, *Histoire de la Gaule*, v; A. Grenier, in Frank, *Econ. SAR*, iii. 623 ff. (glass), 540 ff. (pottery); M. P. Charlesworth, *Trade Routes and Commerce of the Roman Empire* (1926), ch. xi. On Roman trade with free Germany see O. Brogan, *JRS* 1936, 195 ff.; M. Wheeler, *Rome Beyond the Imperial Frontiers* (1954), part I (84 ff. for glass); M. J. Eggers, *Der römische Import in freien Germanien* (1951).

[8] See H. Willers, *Neue Untersuchungen über die römische Bronzenindustrie.*

[9] On Gallic *terra sigillata* (when found in Britain it was at first misleadingly called samian ware) see C. Simpson, *Central Gaulish Potters* (1958).

[10] On Roman finds in Ireland see F. Haverfield, *English Historical Review* 1913, 1 ff.; S. P. O'Riordain, *Proc. Royal Irish Academy* 1948, 35 ff. The distribution of these finds, which are commonest on the coast of Ulster, indicates that they came from Britain (presumably from Chester), rather than from Gaul.

[11] On the island of Gothland alone more than 4000 Roman coins have been discovered.

[12] On the transcontinental route to China (from Antioch to Loyang, some 4500 miles) see F. Hirth, *China and the Roman Orient* (1885); J. I. Miller, *The Spice Trade of the Roman Empire* (1969), ch. 7.

On the expedition of Kan-Ying see W. H. Schroff, *The Periplus of the Erythraean Sea* (1912), 275 ff.; Hirth, op. cit. It was recorded in the Chinese *Annals of the Later Han Dynasty* (Hou-han-shu, 88). He was sent by the Chinese general Pan Ch'ao at a time when he was trying to keep the Silk Route open against constant attack by the Hsiung-nu (Huns).

On western objects, especially glass, found in China see C. G. Seligman, *Antiquity* 1937, 5 ff. The list of western objects exported to China, which is given in the Hou-han-shu, is discussed by J. Thorley, *Greece and Rome* 1971, 75 ff., who emphasises the profits made by the Parthian middlemen at Merv. He explains the surprising 'Coals-to-Newcastle' item in the list, the 'thin silk of various colours', as Chinese silk so skilfully woven in the eastern Roman Empire that when re-exported to the Chinese they did not recognise that they were buying back their own silk (and therefore they wrongly thought that the silkworm was cultivated in the West and so failed to recognise their own *de facto* monopoly).

[13] On Maes see Ptolemy, *Geogr.* i. 11.7. His date is generally thought to be Hadrianic: see M. Cary, *Cl. Qu.* 1956, 138 ff., who does not, however, exclude the possibility of an Augustan date. He was presumably a Syrian (Maes is Semitic; cf. Julia Maesa), who enjoyed the patronage of a member of the gens Titia.

[14] On Graeco-Roman finds on the Tarim plateau (mostly at Loulan and Miran in the Lop-Nor desert) see Sir Aurel Stein, *Serindia* (1921).

Gandhara art, which spread out from the plain of Peshawar (Gandhara), cannot be discussed here, beyond mentioning that early in the second century A.D. a new type of Buddhism, the Mahayana, emerged which allowed the depicting of the divine Buddha. This led to a new art-form in west Pakistan and Afghanistan which arose under strong western influences, helped perhaps by the actual importation of western craftsmen, coming from Syria and more especially from Alexandria. Buddhist monks and traders soon spread these new forms along the roads to Turkestan and China. For the numerous western finds at Begram (45 miles north of Kabul) see J. Hackin, *Recherches archéologiques à Begram* (1939); R. Hirshman, *Begram* (1946); R. E. M. Wheeler, *Rome beyond the Imp. Frontiers*, ch. xiii, and in *Aspects of Archaeology* (ed. Grimes, 1951).

[15] On the opening up of eastern trade by the sea-route see E. H. Warmington, *The Commerce between the Roman Empire and India* (1928); and in Cary and Warmington, *The Ancient Explorers*[2] (1963), ch. 4.; R. E. M. Wheeler, op. cit., 115 ff.

Excavation was started in 1944 at Oc-eo in the

Mekong delta near the gulf of Siam, but stopped because of war conditions. This revealed a temple and other buildings, with many objects which suggest western influence or more: two gold coins were found, one of Antoninus Pius, the other of M. Aurelius. See *Bulletin de l'École française d'extrême-Orient* 1951, 75 ff.; R. E. M. Wheeler, op. cit. 172 ff., and in *Essays in Arch.* (1951), 361.

[16] The desert south of Tripolitania was controlled by patrols or punitive expeditions until the development of a *limes* early in the third century (p. 651), but Roman goods penetrated to the Fezzan and have been found at Garama (modern Germa), the capital of the Garamantes; some date to the first century. Most remarkable is a fifteen-foot-high mausoleum, also of the latter part of the first century. The activities of Flaccus and Maternus suggest better relations with the Garamantian tribesmen, while the mausoleum is probably the tomb of a Roman agent, established at Garama by agreement. Some irrigation systems have been found which may be as early as this and suggest that Rome was trying to introduce the tribesmen to a more settled form of life. See *Monumenti Antichi* 1951; R. E. M. Wheeler, op. cit. 97 ff.

The supposed decline of Puteoli in the second century is questioned by J. H. D'Arms, *JRS* 1974, 104 ff.

[17] For all aspects of the life of this thriving town see R. Meiggs, *Roman Ostia*[2] (1974), a work which reveals the whole social and economic pattern of an Italian town. At first many of the workers in the new settlement of Portus lived in Ostia but in the third century Portus developed its own life.

[18] On Opramoas cf. above, p. 643 n. 17. On Herodes Atticus see P. Graindor, *Herode Atticus et sa famille* (1930); G. W. Bowersock, *Greek Sophists in the Roman Empire* (1969).

[19] On the *canabae* see R. MacMullen, *Soldier and Civilian in the Later Roman Empire* (1963), 119 ff.

[20] In Britain towns extending over more than a hundred acres scarcely numbered more than a dozen. See A. L. F. Rivet, *Town and Country in Roman Britain* (1958), ch. 4; J. S. Wacher, *The Towns of Roman Britain* (1975). In central Gaul Lugdunum alone attained a considerable size; Lutetia (Paris) remained comparatively undeveloped. On the growth of towns in southern Gaul to the third century see P. A. Février, *JRS* 1973, 1 ff.

[21] On the urbanisation of Palestine (which had begun under King Herod) and of other eastern provinces see A. H. M. Jones, *Cities of the eastern Roman Provinces*[2] (1971).

[22] The process was gradual: Augustus gave the Greek residents of *metropoleis* a local government, Septimius Severus added a Council (Boule), but they became official cities only in c. 297.

[23] On city life in Africa see T. R. S. Broughton, *The Romanization of Roman Africa* (1929); J. Toutain, *Les cités romaines de la Tunisie* (1895); G. C. Picard, *La Civilisation de l'Afrique romaine* (1959). On the city population and financial aspects see R. P. Duncan-Jones, *JRS* 1963, 84 ff., and *PBSR* 1962, 47 ff., respectively. For some fine illustrations see R. E. M. Wheeler, *Roman Africa in Colour* (1966).

[24] For bibliography see Chap. 29, n. 17, especially Ward-Perkins, *Roman Architecture* (1970), chs 9, 10, 11; and, for provincial architecture, chs 15–19.

[25] See C. Courtois, *Timgad, antique Thamagadi* (1951); Ward-Perkins, op. cit. 478 ff. (Timgad), 436 ff. (Gerasa), 453 ff. (Palmyra); T. Weigand, *Palmyra* (1932), and I. A. Richmond, *JRS* 1963, 43 ff.

[26] For Baalbek see Ward-Perkins, op. cit. 417 ff.; for the basilica at Wroxeter see D. Atkinson, *JRS* 1924, 226, A. R. Burn, *The Romans in Britain*, n. 42 (= *RIB* n. 288).

[27] On the Roman bridge at Alcantara see Dessau, *ILS*, 287 (= Smallwood, *Documents . . . Nerva, etc.* n. 389).

[28] See A. L. F. Rivet (ed.), *The Roman Villa in Britain* (1969); B. Thomas, *Römische Villen in Pannonien* (1964); F. Cumont, *Comment la Belgique fut romanisée* (1918). On Pliny's villa see *Ep.* ii. 17 and v. 6, and Sherwin-White, *ad loc.*, and the reconstructions in H. H. Tanzer, *The Villas of Pliny the Younger* (1924). A. G. McKay, *Houses, Villas and Palaces in the Roman World* (1975).

[29] See J. M. C. Toynbee, *The Art of the Romans* (1965), and *The Hadrianic School* (1934); D. E. Strong, *Roman Imperial Sculpture* (1961).

[30] See J. M. C. Toynbee, *The Flavian Reliefs from the Palazzo della Cancelleria in Rome* (1957).

[31] On the Column see L. Rossi, *Trajan's Column and the Dacian Wars* (1971). Another notable monument of Trajanic architecture is the Arch of Trajan at Beneventum of the end of his reign; the reliefs depict many of his achievements at home and abroad. See F. A. Lepper, *JRS* 1969, 250 ff. Such great historical reliefs are not found under Hadrian, who was content with more modest records of his pacific achievements, as on the two reliefs in the Forum, showing his *alimenta* for the children of Italy, and his burning of the debt-bonds.

[32] See C. Caprino *et al.*, *La colonna di Marco Aurelio* (1955); G. Becatti, *La colonna di M. A.* (1957); on the dating, J. Morris, *Journ. Warburg Inst.* 1952, 33 ff. Marcus is portrayed as a much more remote figure than is the emperor on Trajan's column, and the background is much less secure, with the horror and tragedy of war emphasised: cf. J. M. C. Toynbee, *The Art of the Romans* (1965), 71.

[33] See J. M. C. Toynbee, *Art in Britain under the Romans* (1964). For the art of Gaul and Africa see the illustrations in Rostovtzeff, *Social and Economic History of the Roman Empire;* M. Pobe, *The Art of Roman Gaul* (1961). For mosaics see Toynbee, *Art of Romans*, ch. ix and (for bibliography), p. 180.

[34] On the social life of the period see S. Dill, *Roman Society from Nero to M. Aurelius*[2] (1905); J. Carcopino, *Daily Life in Ancient Rome* (1940); J. P. V. D. Balsdon, *Life and Leisure in Ancient Rome* (1969). Carcopino's picture of vast crowds in Rome spending half the year in idleness (with 150,000 unemployed), kept alive by corn-doles and the excitement of public spectacles, must be modified by the more sober views of Balsdon (op. cit. 267 ff.). On festival-days all work did not stop nor all shops close; only one in twenty of the population could get into the Colosseum (if he got a ticket), though there was more room in the Circus. On the Circus games see H. A. Harris, *Sport in Greece and Rome* (1972).

[35] Dessau, *ILS*, 8826, f. 13. In Timgad, a town of hardly more than 10,000 inhabitants, there were not less than twelve bathing establishments.

[36] On the more sober tone of society see Tacitus, *Annals*, iii. 55. The sordidness of relations between patrons and clients is the subject of bitter complaints by Juvenal.

[37] For a surviving specimen of a travellers' handbook see the *Descriptio Graeciae* of Pausanias (*c.* A.D. 170). Translation and commentary by J. G. Frazer (1898), and in Loeb Classics with an extra volume of illustrations. On travel in general see L. Casson, *Travel in the Ancient World* (1974).

[38] For a full, though old, account of the Roman *collegia* see J. P. Waltzing, *Étude historique sur les corporations professionelles chez les Romains* (1895 ff.). Insurance against sickness does not appear to have been an object of these clubs.

[39] On imperial patronage of education see C. Barbagallo, *Lo stato e l'istruzione pubblica nell'impero romano* (1911), chs ii and iii; H. I. Marrou, *History of Education in Antiquity* (1956), 301 ff.

[40] On the Gallic universities see T. Haarhoff, *The Schools of Gaul* (1920).

[41] On Roman libraries see R. Cagnat, *Les Bibliothèques chez les Romains*. For Pliny's benefaction: *Ep.* i. 8. 2. Library at Timgad: H. F. Pfeiffer, *Memoirs of the American Academy at Rome*, ix. 157 ff.

[42] At Pompeii alone some 7000–8000 such scribbles (*graffiti*) have been discovered. See *Corpus Inscriptionum Latinarum*, IV. iii. 4 (1970) for inscriptions found in 1951–6. For examples from Britain see A. R. Burn, *The Romans in Britain²* (1969), nos 53 ff.

[43] On the diffusion of Latin see F. F. Abbott, *The Common People of Ancient Rome* (1912), ch. i; A Meillet, *Histoire de la langue latine*, chs ix–x. In the Balkan lands Latin conquered the inland, Greek being confined to the seaboard.

A few short texts in Celtic and in Phrygian (mostly epitaphs) survive. Among the Jews Hebrew maintained itself as a hieratic language, but the local literatures in Armenian, Coptic and Syrian did not arise until the Christian Church became firmly established in the Near East. The view that the Christian communities developed a special 'Christian Latin' (e.g. Chr. Mohrmann, *Études sur le latin des Chrétiens* i–iii (1961–5) has been questioned, since early Christian communities are likely to have used the *sermo plebeius* of their day. But beyond doubt Christianity greatly influenced the Latin language through the introduction of more Greek words and through new meanings given to old words.

[44] On the poor man's drawerful of popular classics see Juvenal, iii. 206–7; on the bookshops of Lugdunum, Pliny, *Ep.* ix. 11. 2.

[45] Both Chrysostom and Aristides throw much light on the social conditions of their day, especially in Asia Minor. Dio Cocceianus, later called Chrysostom, came from a family from Prusa in Bithynia. He was expelled from Rome, where he was practising as a rhetorician, by Domitian. He travelled in the East as an itinerant preacher of Stoic-Cynic philosophy, but although restored by Nerva he retired to Bithynia. Although an admirer of the Greek past, he was reconciled to the Roman present and ready to play his part in the local political life of his province.

Aristides, another public lecturer and writer, spent his later life in Asia Minor and is best remembered for his enthusiastic address 'To Rome' (translation and commentary by J. H. Oliver, *The Ruling Power* (1953)) and for his illnesses and hypochondria which he describes at great length. See G. W. Bowersock, *Greek Sophists in the Roman Empire* (1969).

Plutarch, although a visitor to Rome where he lectured, spent much of his time in his home town of Chaeronea, where he was influential in governing and literary circles. See R. H. Barrow, *Plutarch and his Times* (1967); C. P. Jones, *Plutarch and Rome* (1971); D. A. Russell, *Plutarch* (1973).

Lucian came from much further afield, from Samosata on the Euphrates, and his native language was probably Aramaic. He was a travelling lecturer who visited Gaul, but about 160 he settled in Athens, though it is uncertain whether he practised as a sophist. He became a minor official in Egypt, but while not an ardent admirer of Rome, like Aristides, he was probably not anti-Roman, as has been suggested.

[46] On the Second Sophistic see G. W. Bowersock, *Greek Sophists in the Roman Empire* (1969). The passage of Aristides is xlvi, p. 404 (Dindorf).

[47] Arrian of Bithynia served Rome as consul, governor of Cappadocia and victor over the Alans in 134. Beside his history of Alexander (the *Anabasis*), he wrote a history of Parthia and an account of India.

Appian who experienced the Jewish rising of A.D. 116, held office in Alexandria, moved to Rome and through the support of Fronto became *procurator Augusti*.

Josephus, the Jewish officer who tried to restrain the extremists and went over to Vespasian in 67 (see above, p. 368), wrote an account of the war which ended in 70, the *Bellum Iudaicum*, and later the *Antiquitates Iudaicae*, a history of the Jews from the Creation to A.D. 66. See H. St. J. Thackeray, *Josephus, the Man and the Historian* (1929); F. J. Foakes Jackson, *Josephus and the Jews* (1930); R. J. H. Shutt, *Studies in Josephus* (1961); and an essay by M. P. Charlesworth, *Five Men* (1936), 65 ff.

[48] On Galen, who became court-physician at Rome under Marcus Aurelius, see G. Sarton, *Galen of Pergamum* (1954); G. W. Bowersock, *Greek Sophists in the Roman Empire* (1969), ch. v; J. Scarborough, *Roman Medicine* (1970).

Ptolemy's *Geography* was the most complete of ancient times and remained a standard work until comparatively recent times.

[49] On the Latin literature of the period see especially J. W. Duff, *A Literary History of Rome in the Silver Age, from Tiberius to Hadrian* (1930); H. E. Butler, *Post-Augustan Poetry from Seneca to Juvenal* (1909).

[50] On Juvenal see G. Highet, *Juvenal the Satirist* (1954). Juvenal hated Domitian, who *may* have banished him. Like Martial, he was for long very poor and depended on the patronage of the rich, but unlike Martial he did not gain much contemporary recognition (his satire became popular only in the later fourth century). Martial was friendly with him

and indeed with most of his literary contemporaries, except Statius: Silius Italicus, Frontinus, Quintilian and the younger Pliny. Statius enjoyed the favour of Domitian, as we learn from his occasional poems entitled *Silvae* (iii. 1. 61 ff.): his extreme adulation of Domitian, a political necessity perhaps, which he shared with Martial, is one of the least pleasant features of his work (e.g. iv. 1–3).

[51] On *Agricola* see the edition by I. A. Richmond and R. M. Ogilvie (1967), on *Germania* that by J. G. C. Anderson (1938). On Tacitus see especially R. Syme, *Tacitus*, 2 vols (1958). Cf. also B. Walker, *The Annals of Tacitus, a Study in the writing of History* (1952); T. A. Dorey (ed.), *Tacitus* (1969).

[52] There is a French edition of the *Panegyricus* by M. Durry (1938). The standard edition of the Letters is A. N. Sherwin-White, *Pliny's Letters, a Social and Historical Commentary* (1966). On Vesuvius see *Epistles*, vi. 20.

[53] Apuleius travelled much, and *c.* 155 married a wealthy widow in Tripoli. He was accused before the proconsul at Sabrata on behalf of a slighted fiancé on a charge of having won the lady's affections by magic. His defence (*Apologia*) survives: he was acquitted, and later as chief priest of the province he delivered many speeches in the vein of contemporary rhetoricians.

On Fronto's letters see E. Chanplin, *JRS* 1974, 136 ff.

[54] Despite his fame, little is known about the life and personality of Gaius: see A. M. Honoré, *Gaius* (1962).

[55] On the religious life of the period see T. R. Glover, *The Conflict of Religions in the Early Roman Empire*[9] (1920); J. Beaujeu, *La religion romaine a l'apogée de l'Empire*, i (1955); E. R. Dodds, *Pagan and Christian in an Age of Anxiety* (1965); J. Ferguson, *The Religions of the Roman Empire* (1970).

[56] On Apollonius of Tyana see his life by Flavius Philostratus. On Vespasian's miracles, Suetonius *Vespasian*, ii. 2, Dio, lxvi. 8. During the second century cremation was gradually replaced by inhumation, a process which had spread to the provinces by the mid-third century. This does not seem to have been the result of any fundamental change in religious ideas. It may reflect a mere change in fashion (cf. A. D. Nock, *Harvard Theological Review* 1932, 321 ff.) or an increasing feeling of respect 'for what had been the temple and mirror of the immortal soul and enduring personality' (see J. M. C. Toynbee, *Death and Burial in the Roman World* (1971), 40 ff.).

[57] On the cult of Isis see R. E. Witt, *Isis in the Graeco-Roman World* (1971). For the cult in London, see A. R. Burn, *The Roman in Britain*[2] (1969), n. 53; on that of Serapis at York, Burn, n. 211.

[58] On Mithras see F. Cumont, *The Mysteries of Mithra* (1910); M. J. Vermaseren, *Corpus Inscriptionum et Monumentorum Religionis Mithraicae* (1956) and *Mithras, the Secret God* (1963). Two important Mithraea have been found fairly recently: that in the Walbrook in London, discovered in 1954 (cf. W. F. Grimes, *The Excavation of Roman and Medieval London* (1968)) and that under the church of Santa Prisca on the Aventine in Rome (cf. M. J. Vermaseren and C. C. van Essen, *Excavations in the Mithraeum*

of . . . *Sta Prisca* (1965)). The latter chapel has the usual statue of Mithras killing the bull, but also wall-paintings showing scenes of the ritual, metrical texts and hymns (*Mithraic Studies* (ed. J. R. Hinnalls, 1975)).

[59] See Chap. 34, n. 48. On the early Church see L. Duchesne, *Early History of the Christian Church*, i (1909); A. D. Nock, *Essays in Religion and the Ancient World*, i. 49 ff. (ed. Z. Stewart, 1972); H. Lietzman, *The Beginnings of the Christian Church*, i (1937); W. H. C. Frend, *The Early Church* (1965); H. Chadwick, *The Early Church* (1967) and *Early Christian Thought and the Classical Tradition* (1966); E. R. Dodds, *Pagan and Christian in an Age of Anxiety* (1965); R. Grant, *Augustus to Constantine: the Thrust of the Christian Movement into the Roman World* (1971). Also *The Oxford Dictionary of the Christian Church*[2] (1974). J. Stevenson, *A New Eusebius* (1957), contains a valuable collection of source-material in translation on the early Church before A.D. 337. Eusebius himself is, of course, by far the most important literary source. On the Acts of the Martyrs see H. Musurillo, *Acts of the Christian Martyrs* (1972), texts and translations. See also R. A. Markus, *Christianity in the Roman World* (1975).

[60] Gnosticism distinguished between an unknowable Divine Being and derivative 'creator god' or Demiurge, who fell through a series of aeons and created the imperfect world. Divine sparks, however, were imprisoned in certain elect men, and through *gnosis* and certain rites (thus Gnosticism was a kind of Mystery Religion), the element of spirit might be saved from the evil material body in which it lived. It was Christ who brought *gnosis*. In 1946 a large collection of Gnostic texts in Coptic was found at Nag Hammadi in Upper Egypt. See in general H. Jonas, *The Gnostic Religion* (1958); R. M. Grant, *Gnosticism and Early Christianity* (1959).

[61] See Pliny, x. 96. 7 (cf. Sherwin-White, *The Letters of Pliny*, 702 ff., and for the whole letter). Early Christians probably lived unobtrusively, but they lived in society (not in catacombs!). Churches began to acquire burial-grounds, and one of the earliest of these was on the Appian Way just south of Rome at a spot called Catacumbas: hence these cemeteries, with their underground corridors, came to be called catacombs.

[62] On Christian ethics see Herbert H. Scullard, *Early Christian Ethics in the West* (1907); C. J. Cadoux, *The Early Church and the World* (1925).

[63] When Osrhoene was incorporated in the Empire the Mesopotamian Christians used Tatian's Greek amalgam of the four Gospels in place of their earlier separate Gospels in Syriac. A fragment of this *Diatessaron* has been found in the Roman fort at Dura-Europas on the Euphrates, where also the earliest-known church-house has been discovered.

[64] Pliny, *Ep.* x. 96. 9; Tertullian, *Apol.* 37. On the spread of Christianity see K. S. Latourette, *A History of the Expansion of Christianity*, i (1938), and the interesting distribution maps in *Atlas of the Early Christian World*, ed. M. F. Hedlund and H. H. Rowley (1958).

[65] The ordinary routines of Roman life involved many incidental acts of homage to deities. Many of

these prayers or libations were quite perfunctory, yet their omission would create bad feeling. Refusal to worship the emperor, as opposed to the gods, was perhaps a less common cause of conflict than has sometimes been supposed (cf. de Ste Croix, *Past and Present* 1963, 10), though it probably accounted for the death of Christians in Asia (especially at Pergamum) under Domitian referred to in the Apocalypse.

The disturbance to trade which the spread of monotheistic religions might cause is illustrated by Pliny, *Ep.* x. 96. 10, and by the episode of Demetrius the Silversmith at Ephesus (Acts xix).

[66] For Tacitus's judgment on the Jews see *Histories*, v. 2–5; on the Christians see *Annals*, xv. 44. 4, where he refers to their hatred of the human race (*odium humani generis*) and their *exitiabilis superstitio*.

[67] On the anti-Christian propaganda of pagan men of letters see T. R. Glover, *The Conflict of Religion in the Early Roman Empire*[9] (1920).

[68] On the persecutions see the literature cited above, Chap. 22, n. 26 (p. 634). The essential point of the legal issue may be over-simplified thus: on the assumption that no general law had been passed against Christians (the so-called *institutum Neronianum*: Tertullian, *Nat.* i. 7. 9), could a magistrate, on information presented by informers and after due legal inquiry, condemn a Christian because of the name (that is, when he admitted he was a Christian) or must some crime be proved in addition? Pliny evidently at first acted on confession of the name and had such 'confessors' executed out of hand. But he then asked Trajan about 'crimes connected with the name' ('flagitia cohaerentia nomini'). His first action suggests that the name sufficed alone. But if 'flagitia' were also considered, what were they? We must of course dismiss 'Thyestian banquets', charges of cannibalism and incest, arising from a misunderstanding of celebration of the Lord's Supper; any such charge would soon be exploded, as Pliny discovered on inquiry. Although Trajan was very touchy about the risk from clubs, it is unlikely that the basis of prosecution was 'illegal association' (cf. Sherwin-White, *Letters of Pliny*, 779), despite the fact that this view has enjoyed considerable currency. Sherwin-White thinks that Pliny, after discovering that *flagitia* did not exist, punished the Christians for *contumacia*, their refusal to obey a reasonable order, but against this view see de Ste Croix, *Past and Present* 1963, 18 ff.; cf. ibid. 1964, 23 ff. (= *Studies in Ancient Society* (ed. M. I. Finley, 1974), 210 ff.).

On the attitude of Trajan and Hadrian cf. E. J. Bickerman, *Rivista di Filologia* 1968, 290 ff.

See further T. D. Barnes, *Tertullian* (1971), ch. xi, who minimises the importance of the attitude of individual Roman emperors and emphasises that of the local provincial governor, whose conduct will often have been determined by mob-pressure or his own character.

[69] Among the second-century emperors M. Aurelius has been regarded as an enemy of the Christians. He was no doubt less active than his predecessors in checking tumultuary proceedings against them, but there is no good evidence of positive hostility on his part. Possible allusions to Christians in his

Meditations (xi. 3 almost certainly refers to them, even if their name is a gloss) may suggest that he even admired their stubborn obstinacy in courting martyrdom (cf. C. R. Haines, Loeb edition of the *Meditations* (1916), 381 ff.) In general see A. Birley, *M. Aurelius* (1966), esp. app. iv, pp. 328 ff.

[70] For a fulsome but not extravagant panegyric of the Roman Empire under Antoninus see the fourteenth Oration of Aelius Aristides (ed. J. H. Oliver, *The Ruling Power* (1953)).

Chapter 40: Notes

[1] The main sources for the reign of Commodus are Herodian, i; Dio Cassius, lxxii; *Historia Augusta, Commodus*. A detailed study is that by F. Grosso, *La lotta politica al tempo di Commodo* (1964). The wild idealising of Commodus by W. Weber in *CAH*, xi, based partly upon a strained interpretation of the numismatic evidence, should be balanced by the sensible accounts given by H. Mattingly, *Brit. Mus. Catal. Coins of Rom. Emp.* (1940), pp. clxxxiii ff., and by A. Garzetti, *From Tiberius to the Antonines* (1974), 528 ff., 725 ff. Herodian wrote, in Greek, a history of the period 180–238. He himself lived through this period and published his history perhaps *c.* 248. See the Loeb edition by C. R. Whittaker, 2 vols (1969–71), with useful introduction and notes.

[2] A further source of discontent was that Perennis had appointed equestrian prefects to command legions in place of senatorial legates (a practice which became normal later in the third century). This was possibly part of a plot by Perennis aimed at the throne, aided by his son who commanded the Illyrian army: at any rate complaints are said to have been lodged by envoys from the army in Britain with Commodus in Rome.

[3] An inscription records Commodus's rescript *de saltu Burunitano*. See Riccobono, *Fontes*, n. 103; translation in Lewis–Reinhold, *R. Civ.* ii. 183 f. Tenants (*coloni*) on this imperial estate had protested to Commodus that Hadrian's law (cf. above, Chap. 37, n. 28, p. 644) was not being observed. Commodus replied: 'In view of established tradition and my order, procurators will see to it that nothing more than three periods of two days' work per man is unjustly exacted from you in violation of established practice.'

[4] In order to mislead Commodus Cleander appointed two other praetorian prefects; thus for the first time in Rome's history there were three prefects.

[5] A sharp rise in prices appears to have taken place in the Roman Empire towards the end of the second century. Y. Pekáry (*Historia* 1959, 448 ff.) discusses the finances of M. Aurelius and Commodus, but thinks that financial stringency fell far short of any threat of bankruptcy. Yet the reduced silver-content of the *denarius* suggests some measure of inflation.

[6] Lucilla, daughter of M. Aurelius, had married first L. Verus and then (169) Ti. Claudius Pompeianus, who under Commodus had withdrawn from public life. Lucilla was perhaps jealous of Commodus's wife, Augusta Crispina.

[7] On the Severi see Herodian, ii–vi; Dio Cassius,

lxviii–lxxx; *Historia Augusta*, relevant Lives. On Septimius Severus see M. Platnauer, *The Life and Reign of the Emperor L. Septimius Severus* (1918); A. Birley, *Septimius Severus* (1971). A useful and detailed bibliography of modern work published on the years A.D. 193–284 during the period 1939 to 1959 is provided by G. Walser and T. Pekary, *Die Krise der römischen Reiches* (1962).

[8] On the eastern campaigns of Septimius and Caracalla see N. C. Debevoise, *Political History of Parthia* (1938), 256 ff., and D. Magie, *Roman Rule in Asia Minor* (1950), 1540 ff., 1553 ff. On the Severan frontier see D. Oates, *Studies in the Ancient History of Northern Iraq* (1968), 73 ff.

[9] On Britain under Severus see S. S. Frere, *Britannia* (1967), ch. 9.; A. Birley, *Septimius Severus* (1971), ch. xvi. The latter argues, partly from the size of the Roman base discovered in 1961 at Carpow, not far from Perth, and numerous marching-camps stretching northward, that Septimius intended to annex a substantial portion, if not the whole, of Scotland, rather than carry out merely a punitive expedition.

[10] On the Limes Tripolitania see R. G. Goodchild and J. B. Ward-Perkins, *JRS* 1949, 81 ff., 1950, 30 ff. Cf. B. H. Warmington, *The North African Provinces* (1954), ch. iii.

[11] A curious feature of these road repairs in central Gaul and Upper Germany is the use of the Celtic measurement by leugae (*c.* 3 miles). On the military reforms see R. E. Smith, *Historia* 1972, 481 ff.

[12] For the family of Severus see A. Birley, *Septimius Severus* (1971), appendix i. It came from Lepcis, which had colonial status, and is generally believed to have Punic or Berber blood in it (T. D. Barnes, *Historia* 1967, 87 ff., argued for an immigrant family of Italian stock). Some (e.g. Kornemann and Piganiol: see G. Walser and T. Pekary, *Die Krise des römischen Reiches* (1962), 7 ff.) have concluded that his supposed Punic blood made Severus alien to the spirit of Rome and also liable to favour his native land and its outstanding citizens. Others (as M. Platnauer and A. Birley, op. cit n. 7) have played down his African tendencies, and M. Hammond (*Harvard Stud. Class. Philology*, 1940, 137 ff.) regards him as a typical Roman bureaucrat. Birley sees him and his associates as the product of the Antonine era. Gibbon took an extreme view of his achievement: he was 'the principal author of the decline of the Roman empire'. In this Gibbon was followed by J. Hasebroek, *Untersuchungen zur Geschichte des Kaisers Septimius Severus* (1921), but this point of view was dismissed by Platnauer and later scholars.

[13] With more Easterners and Africans entering the Senate the provincial element rose, *vis-à-vis* the Italian senators, to a majority of some two-thirds. The political result of this was probably much less than the social and cultural aspect.

[14] See L. L. Howe, *The Praetorian Prefect from Commodus to Diocletian* (1942); G. Vitucci, *Ricerche sulla Praefectura Urbis in età imperiale* (1956).

[15] On the *honestiores/humiliores* see P. Garnsey, *Social Status and Legal Privilege in the Roman Empire* (1970), chs 9–12.

[16] Although Londinium early became the headquarters of the financial administration (before 60?), and was the provincial capital, it was never promoted to the status of a colony, although later (in 305?) it received the official name of 'Augusta'.

[17] Beside grants of citizenship Severus also gave the highest award of *Ius Italicum* (i.e. fiscal parity with the soil of Italy) to some towns, especially in the East. He allowed the use of native languages (e.g. Punic or Celtic) in legal documents. He put alimentary institutions in the provinces in charge of the governors (he also revived those in Italy), and allowed provincials some relief from the imperial post. Thirteen decisions given by Severus during his visit to Egypt in 200 in reply to private petitions are preserved in a papyrus, see W. L. Westermann and A. A. Schiller, *Apokrimata: Decisions of Septimius Severus on Legal Matters* (1954).

[18] See E. Nash, *Pictorial Dictionary of Ancient Rome*, i. 332 ff. (Palace), ii, 302 ff. (Septizodium), i. 126 ff. (Arch). On the Arch see R. Brilliant, *The Arch of Septimius Severus in the Roman Forum = Memoirs of the American Academy at Rome*, xxix (1967).

[19] The distinction between the *res privata* and *patrimonium* and its early development are obscure. Cf. Frank, *Econ SAR*, v. 80 ff., who believes that 'Septimius Severus dealt the fatal blow to the Empire by his confiscations and his centralizing the ownership of vast estates under imperial control' (p. 85).

In Egypt the Ptolemies had instituted a 'special account' (*Idios Logos*) with a special staff to administer it, and this department survived under Roman rule. For a handbook of its departmental rules, issued under Antoninus, see H. Stuart Jones, *Fresh Light on the Roman Bureaucracy* (1920). Cf. S. L. Wallace, *Taxation in Egypt from Augustus to Diocletian* (1938). It is very uncertain whether the *Idios Logos* affected Severus's organisation of his *res privata*.

[20] From the time of Severus the level of prices appears to have remained steady (cf. F. M. Heichelheim, *Klio* 1932, 96 ff.).

[21] We may perhaps detect the influence of Severus's strong-minded wife, Julia Domna, in the ill-advised partition of the imperial power between the two brothers. But the tale that Caracalla killed Geta in the arms of his mother is of a piece with the assertion that he executed no fewer than 20,000 of Geta's adherents (Dio, lxxxvii. 2 and 4).

[22] Formerly our knowledge of Caracalla's crowning gift of franchise (the *Constitutio Antoniniana*) depended primarily on a cursory reference by Dio Cassius (lxxvi. 9), who attributed a fiscal motive to it (this appears improbable to some, because he could have increased taxation by other methods, if that had been his main purpose). A relevant fragment has now been discovered in a papyrus (*P. Giessen, 40.* The text is given in H. M. D. Parker, *Hist. Roman World, A.D. 138–337*, 333 f.; Riccobono, *Fontes*, n. 88; translation in Lewis–Reinhold, *R. Civ.* 427 ff.). Its unbusiness-like style may suggest that the fragment comes from a general proclamation of policy rather than from the *Constitutio* itself.

It adds little to our knowledge and raises problems such as the identity of the *dediticii* who are mentioned as excluded from the general grant of citizenship. One hypothesis (E. Bickermann, *Das Edikt des Kaisers Caracalla* (1926)) equates them with the barbarians who had been forcibly settled within the Empire, the so-called *laeti*, cf. A. H. M. Jones, *Studies in Roman Government and Law* (1960), ch. viii. In general see A. N. Sherwin-White, *The Roman Citizenship*[2] (1973), 279 ff. and 380 ff., who writes 'The dominant note of the papyrus is one of *maiestas*. . . . Caracalla set the *maiestas populi Romani* upon the widest possible basis.' The unity of the diverse parts of the Empire must be held together with as wide an interest in Rome as possible. For further analysis and assessment of modern views see M. Hammond, *The Antonine Monarchy* (1959), 140 ff., 161 ff. and Sherwin-White, op. cit. 388 ff. The argument of F. Millar, *J. Egyptian Archaeology* 1962, 124 ff. that the date was 214 rather than 212, has been challenged by J. F. Gillian, *Historia* 1965, 74 ff.

[23] Caracalla was fond of aping Alexander the Great, even to the extent of forming a corps of Macedonian soldiers whom he armed in the fashion of Alexander's spearmen. But we need not attribute to him, any more than to other Roman generals, plans of conquest on the scale of Alexander's.

[24] On the *Consilium* see J. Crook, *Consilium Principis* (1955), 86 ff. See also M. Hammond, *The Antonine Monarchy* (1959), 380 ff., 406 ff., who believes that the sixteen senators formed a special committee of regency, distinct from the *Consilium*.

The fifty-second book of Dio Cassius, which contains two imaginary addresses by Agrippa and Maecenas to Augustus on the outlines of an imperial constitution, is generally held to represent the political thinking of the time of Severus Alexander; Maecenas's speech is regarded as a pamphlet aimed against the 'senatorial' policy of Alexander. F. Millar, however, argues (*A Study of Cassius Dio* (1964), 102 ff.) that the speech was written under Caracalla, about 214; A. Birley, *Septimius Severus* (1971), 8 f., is less certain.

[25] This idealising tendency is unmistakeable in the Life of Alexander in the *Historia Augusta*, which has been described as a historical novel.

[26] On the Sassanid dynasty see A. Christensen, *L'Iran sous les Sassanides*[2] (1944); R. Ghirshman, *Iran, Parthians and Sassanians* (1962).

[27] See in general M. Hammond, *The Antonine Monarchy* (1959).

[28] For the decurions of Canusium see Dessau, *ILS*, 6121.

[29] For Sitifis see J. Carcopino, *Revue Africaine* 1918, and M. Rostovtzeff, *Social and Economic History of the Roman Empire*[2] (1957) 723 f.; for Pizus, Dittenberger, *Sylloge*[3], 880, and Rostovtzeff, 724 (cf. 425 ff.)

[30] The proclamation by Septimius is referred to in the appeal from Socnopaiou Nesos: see Abbott and Johnson, *Municipal Administration in the Roman Empire* (1926), n. 190. For translation, A. C. Johnson in Frank, *Econ. SAR*, ii. 119. For the Lydian documents, Abbott and Johnson, nn. 142–4.

[31] For the *munera* see the *Digest*, ll. 5 and 6. Detailed references are given by H. M. D. Parker, *Hist. of Rom. World, A.D. 138-337*, 333, with a description on pp. 123 ff.

These increased burdens should not be regarded as part of a deliberate policy to weaken the towns

as such. The famous theory of Rostovtzeff, that the Severi championed the interests of the peasants, from whom the army was drawn, against the interests of the provincial towns, has not stood up to criticism: see, for example, N. H. Baynes, *JRS* 1929, 224 ff. (= *Byzantine Studies* (1955), 307 ff.); Parker, op. cit. 27 f.

[32] On the *collegia* see J. P. Walzing, *Étude historique sue les corporations professionelles chez les Romains* (1895 ff.), and for a vivid picture of their importance in one Italian city see R. Meiggs, *Roman Ostia*[2] (1974), ch. 14. For Bithynia, Pliny, *Epist*. x. 34. For Severus Alexander, *Historia Augusta, Alex*. 33. 2.

An inscription from Beirut (*CIL*, iii. 14165a) contains a letter from the Praefectus Annonae in 201 to the five associations of shipowners at Arelate (modern Arles in southern France) who had a local office at Beirut in Syria (for helping to provision the army in Syria), as well as a central office at Ostia. In reply to their complaints the Prefect instructed the imperial procurator to attend to alleged abuses relating to money and personal safety, and to order iron fastenings and military escorts for *annona* cargoes. The inscription thus shows how the government watched over the activities of the *collegia* in order that they might not be harassed by corrupt officials. For a translation see Lewis–Reinhold, *R. Civ*. ii. 450f.

[33] On the circle of Julia Domna see G. W. Bowersock, *Greek Sophists in the Roman Empire* (1969), ch. viii.

[34] On Tertullian see T. D. Barnes, *Tertullian* (1971), a historical and literary study which sets him in his proper historical and cultural milieu.

[35] See Boëthius and Ward-Perkins, *Etruscan and Roman Architecture* (1970), 269 ff., 475 ff., and (for Severan art and architecture at Lepcis) Ward-Perkins, *JRS* 1948, 59 ff.

[36] See J. M. C. Toynbee, *The Art of the Romans* (1965) in general (pp. 73 ff. for the arch at Lepcis).

[37] Coins provide valuable evidence for these alien cults: cf. A. D. Nock in *CAH*, xii. 425 ff. Sol appears as *pacator orbis* on coins of Septimius and Caracalla. Geta appears radiant with his right hand raised in the Sun's gesture of blessing. Cybele as well as Isis appears on Julia Domna's coins, and she, while still living, was represented as Cybele.

Chapter 41: Notes

[1] For the middle of the third century we have few sources beside the scanty and unreliable biographies of the *Historia Augusta* and a few epitomes of general Roman history. The *History* of Dio Cassius runs out in the reign of Severus Alexander, that of Herodian in 238. Material to be gathered from the Church historians does not become plentiful until the end of the century. Coins and papyri help to fill some gaps. The minor writers include Aurelius Victor, *Caesares*, 25–38; *Epitome de Caesaribus*, 25–38; Eutropius, ix. 1–8; Zosimus, i. 14–40; Zonaras, xii. 16–30. Aurelius Victor, an African, was governor of Pannonia in A.D. 361 and wrote his *Caesares* from Augustus to Constantius (360). Eutropius, of the mid-fourth century,

wrote an Epitome (*Breviarium*) of Roman history from Romulus to A.D. 364. Zosimus before the end of the fifth century wrote in Greek a history from Augustus to A.D. 410. Zonaras in the twelfth century wrote a universal history.

The *Historia Augusta* is a collection of the Lives of Roman emperors from A.D. 117 to 284 (the years 244–259 are missing). They were alleged to have been written by six different authors in the time of Diocletian and Constantine. These *Scriptores Historiae Augustae* were named Spartianus, Capitolinus, Gallicanus, Lampridius, Pollio and Vopiscus. They quote a large number of documents, but these are generally regarded as either false or of dubious value. The Lives of the emperors from Hadrian to Caracalla (inclusive) go back in part to a reasonably reliable source, but many of the later Lives are little more than fiction. Vast controversy has raged over the authorship, date and purpose of this work. Various dates in the fourth and early fifth centuries have been propounded. The general tone is pro-senatorial. Of the immense literature which has been devoted to this problem only four items can be quoted here: N. H. Baynes, *The H.A., its Date and Purpose* (1926); A. Momigliano, *Secondo Contrib.* (1960), 105 ff. = *Journal of Warburg Institute* 1954, 22 ff.; R. Syme, *Ammianus and the H.A.* (1968), *Emperors and Biography* (1971) and *JRS* 1972, 123 ff., who returns to the view of Dessau, namely one author and a date in the last decade of the fourth century. On Syme's views see A. Cameron, *JRS* 1971, 253 ff.

[2] In a rehabilitation of Maximinus's reputation R. Syme (*Emperors and Biography* (1971), ch. xi) argues that Maximinus came from Moesia rather than from Thrace (and was thus a Danubian) and was a Roman citizen by birth. That the great military emperors who came from Illyricum should be called 'Danubian' rather than 'Illyrian' see R. Syme, *Historia* 1973, 310 ff.

[3] On Gordian III see P. W. Townsend, *Yale Class. Stud.* 1934, 59 ff., 1955, 49 ff. His civil administration was good. A letter of his, recently found in Aphrodisias in Caria, confirms the rights of this city and illustrates his 'senatorial' policy and his correct provincial policy: see K. T. Erim and J. Reynolds, *JRS* 1969, 56 ff.

[4] D. Oates (*Studies in the Anc. Hist. of Northern Iraq* (1968), 23 ff.) suggests that after Gordian's counter-attack Philip gave up any territory east of the line Nisibis–Singara. On Philip see J. M. York, *Historia* 1972, 320 ff.

[5] Decius was no military upstart, but a Danubian senator and consul according to R. Syme, *Emperors and Biography*, 195 ff.

[6] On the Germanic tribes see E. Demougeot, *La Formation de l'Europe et les invasions barbares* (1969), pt ii, 269 ff., and for details of the invasions of the Empire in the third century see pt iii, 391 ff.

[7] For a brief discussion of the chronological difficulties (e.g. whether Valerian arrived in the East in 254 or 256) see B. H. Warmington in Parker, *Hist. of Roman World, A.D. 138–337²*, 390 f. For a different view from that given above see T. Pekary, *Historia* 1962, 123 ff.

[8] On Shapur's inscription see E. Honnigmann and A. Maricq, *Recherches sur les Res Gestae divi Saporis* (1953). Excavation at Dura-Europas has revealed mines driven under the city-wall during the siege, together with skeletons and weapons of the defenders in a Roman counter-mine: see M. Rostovtzeff, *Dura-Europas and its Art* (1938), 28 f. Shapur's territorial advances were followed up by the missionary spread of Zoroastrianism, which was promoted by a religious leader named Kartir, known to us from four inscriptions: see K. N. Frye, *The Heritage of Persia* (1962), 218 ff., and M. L. Chaumont, *Historia* 1973, 664 ff.

[9] On Palmyra see M. Rostovtzeff, *Caravan Cities* (1932), chs iv and v; I. A. Richmond, *JRS* 1963, 43 ff. A copy of a Palmyrene customs-tariff of Hadrian's time has been preserved: Cagnat, *Inscriptiones Graecae ad Res Romanas Pertinentes*, iii. 1065; Dittenberger, *Orient. Graec. Inscr. Sel.* n. 629; partial translation in Lewis–Reinhold, *R. Civ.* ii. 330 ff.

[10] For Dexippus's work see Jacoby, *FGrH*, n. 100; it is reflected in Zosimus. On Dexippus see F. Millar, 'Dexippus: the Greek World and the Third-Century Invasions', *JRS* 1969, 12 ff.; on the Heruli at Athens see H. A. Thompson, *JRS* 1959, 61 ff.

[11] A more favourable portrait of Gallienus is given in some Greek and Christian writers than in the Latin sources such as *Historia Augusta*. His achievement has been rehabilitated in modern times by, for example, L. Homo, *Revue historique* 1913, 1 ff., 225 ff., and A. Alfoldi, *CAH*, xii. 181 ff., 223 ff. See also G. Walser and T. Pekary, *Die Krise des römischen Reiches* (1962), 28 ff.

[12] See C. W. Keyes, *The Rise of the Equites in the Third Century of the Roman Empire* (1915); H. Petersen, *JRS* 1955, 47 ff. Under Gallienus apparently senatorial *legati* and *tribuni* disappeared from the army. The process continued with Equites permanently replacing most of the senatorial governors of praetorian (but not of consular) provinces; it was completed when Diocletian left only two regular senatorial provinces, namely Africa and Asia.

[13] The Palmyrene expansion, or at any rate its beginnings, is usually dated to Claudius's reign, but A. Alfoldi, *CAH*, xii, 178 ff. would place it after his death, a view which remains very uncertain. On cultural conditions in the Fertile Crescent in this period, and in particular on the career of Paul of Samosata see F. Millar, *JRS* 1971, 1 ff.

[14] See I. A. Richmond, *The City Wall of Imperial Rome* (1930); Nash, *Pictorial Dict. of Rome*, ii. 86 ff.

[15] On Aurelian see L. Homo, *Essai sur le règne de l'empereur Aurélian* (1904).

[16] On the other hand the tradition of Tacitus as a blameless old senator may be wrong: R. Syme (*Emperors and Biography* (1971), 245 ff.) suggests that he may not have been a civilian but have stood close to the generals of Aurelian and been well known to the Danubian armies.

Chapter 42: Notes

[1] The main ancient sources for the reigns of Diocletian and Constantine are: *Panegyrici Latini*, iv–xii,

anonymous addresses to Constantius, Constantine and others; Arnobius, *Adversus nationes*, written soon after 295, and Lactantius, *De mortibus persecutorum*, written perhaps in 314 (see T. D. Barnes, *JRS* 1973, 29 ff., and for Lactantius's relationship to Constantine), both Christian polemics which contain numerous contemporary allusions; Eusebius, *Historia Ecclesiastica*, viii–ix, and *Life of Constantine*; Aurelius Victor, *Caesares*, 39–41; *Epitome de Caesaribus*, 39–40; Eutropius, ix. 20–x; Zosimus, ii; Zonaras, xii. 31 ff. Laws, coinage and papyri are all very important. On the genuineness of Eusebius's *Life* see A. H. M. Jones, *Journ. Ecclesiastical History* 1955, 196 ff.

Modern histories of the period include A. H. M. Jones, *The Later Roman Empire, 284–602*, 3 vols (1964), and a briefer account, *The Decline of the Ancient World* (1966); E. Stein, *Histoire du Bas-Empire*, i. 284–476 (1959).

On Diocletian see W. Seston, *Dioclétien et la Tetrarchie*, i (1946).

On Constantine see N. H. Baynes, *Constantine the Great and the Christian Church*[2] (1972); A. H. M. Jones, *Constantine and the Conversion of Europe* (1948); R. Macmullen, *Constantine* (1969); J. H. Smith, *Constantine the Great* (1971).

[2] On Domitius Domitianus, known from his coins, and Achilleus see W. Seston, *Dioclétien* (1946), 137 ff.

[3] On Carausius and Allectus see S. S. Frere, *Britannia* (1967), ch. 16. The coastal defences, known as the forts of the Saxon Shore, ran from the Norfolk coast to the Isle of Wight. They introduced into Britain a new type of military architecture, similar to that of the new town-walls of Gaul which can be dated to Diocletian's reign (most of the town-walls of Britain belong to a slightly earlier style). Similar forts are found on the west coast at Cardiff and Lancaster, with smaller enclosures at Caernarvon and Holyhead (Caer Gybi), but it is not known whether these are as early as Carausius. The outline of Constantius's campaign against Allectus is preserved amid the rhetoric of *Panegyricus*, viii, an address to the victorious emperor by an anonymous Gallic orator.

[4] See N. H. Baynes, *Constantine the Great and the Christian Church*[2] (1972), esp. 56 ff., and other works cited in n. 1 above.

[5] On the Senate see Ch. Lecrivain, *Le Sénat romain depuis Dioclétien* (1888); A. H. M. Jones, *Later Rom. Emp.* 523 ff.; T. W. Arnheim, *The Senatorial Aristocracy in the Later Roman Empire* (1972); A. H. M. Jones et al., *Prosopography of the Later Roman Empire*, i. (1971).

[6] In theory the Senate appears to have clung to its right. Thus as late as the mid-fifth century Majorian (457–461) could write, 'You must know, conscript fathers, that I have been made emperor by the choice of your election and by the decision of the most valiant army' (*Nov.* i. 458).

[7] The manner in which municipal authorities during the fourth century fought a losing battle (partly through their own selfishness and incompetence) against imperial governors is well illustrated in the history of Antioch: see J. H. W. F. Liebeschuetz, *Antioch* (1972).

[8] The pomp and mystery of the later Roman court owed more to the Oriental than to the Hellenistic monarchies (though Constantine's diadem was of Hellenistic origin). On the gradual elaboration of the palace ceremonial see A. Alfoldi, *Römische Mitteilungen* 1934, 1–118, 1935, 1–170, who suggests that Diocletian's role in introducing *adoratio* has been exaggerated.

[9] On the *consistorium* see A. H. M. Jones, *Later Rom. Emp.* 333 ff.

[10] On the *comitatus* see Jones, op. cit. 52 f., 104 ff., 566 ff.; E. Stein, *Histoire du Bas-empire*, i. 111 ff. The later Roman executive may be studied in the *Notitia Dignitatum*, an official handbook of the early fifth century, in which the staffs of the various government departments and military units are set out in detail. See the edition by O. Seeck (1876); A. H. M. Jones, *Later Rom. Emp.* iii, appendix ii. 347 ff.

[11] See J. R. Palanque, *Essai sur la préfecture du pretoire du Bas-empire* (1933); L. L. Howe, *The Praetorian Prefect from Commodus to Diocletian* (1942); Jones, op. cit. 587 ff. See W. Sinnigen, *The Officium of the Urban Prefecture during the Later Roman Empire* (1957); A. Chastagnol, *La Préfecture urbaine à Rome sous le bas Empire* (1960), *Les Fasti de la Préfecture de Rome* (1962).

[12] On the Verona list see A. H. M. Jones, *JRS* 1954, 21 ff., Lactantius, *Mort. Pers.* vii. 4.

[13] The struggle between the emperors and the bureaucracy is illustrated by numerous imperial ordinances in the Codex Theodosianus (p. 550). On the general character of the later Roman bureaucracy see S. Dill, *Roman Society in the Last Century of the Western Empire* (1906), bk iii; F. Lot, *The End of the Ancient World*[2] (1961), bk 1, ch. x; Jones, *Later Rom. Emp.* chs xii and xvi.

[14] On the development of the *latifundia* into miniature states – a process which can be followed out in some detail in the province of Egypt, see F. de Zulueta, *De patrociniis vicorum* – (cf. F. Lot, op. cit. pt 1, ch. vii). On the relation of the late Roman *latifundium* to the medieval manor see P. Vinogradoff, *The Growth of the Manor*, bk i, ch. ii.

[15] On the coinage see Mattingly, Sydenham *et al.*, *Roman Imperial Coinage*, vi and vii. On the reforms see also S. Bolin, *State and Currency in the Roman Empire to A.D. 300* (1958), ch. xii; A. H. M. Jones, *Later Rom. Emp.* 438 ff.; C. H. V. Sutherland, *JRS* 1955, 116 ff., 1961, 94 ff. A new inscription from Aphrodisias in Caria now reveals that Diocletian (just before his Edict of Maximum Prices of 302) issued in 301 a complementary Edict dealing with Currency Reform: see K. T. Erim, J. Reynolds and M. Crawford, *JRS* 1971, 171 ff. By this edict all new debts, etc., had to be paid in current *pecunia* with a doubled face value, i.e. the face value of the *argentarius* was doubled from fifty to a hundred *denarii* (and that of the large laureate silver-bronze from ten to twenty *denarii*).

Older versions of the *Edictum de pretiis* are given by Frank, *Econ. SAR*, v. 310 ff., and Dessau, *ILS* 642. But many further fragments have been found in recent years (cf. *JRS* 1970, 120 ff., 1973, 99 ff.), and a consolidated text is published by S. Lauffer,

Diokletian's Preisedikt (1970). The main object of the reform was to check the ravages of rapacious army contractors and currency speculators which had been giving an impetus to the spiral of inflation.

[16] Forced labour (at fair rates of pay) had been common in Ptolemaic Egypt. On its spread in the Roman Empire see M. Rostovtzeff, *Soc. Econ. Hist. Rom. Emp.*[2] index, s.v. 'Requisitions'. The burdensomeness of the requisitions is well illustrated by a petition of A.D. 238 from the people of Scaptoparene in Thrace (Abbott and Johnson, *Municipal Administration in Rom. Emp.* n. 139).

[17] On the indictions and the reformed tax-system see A. H. M. Jones, *Later Rom. Emp.* 448 ff. He believes (p. 454) that 'no systematic or regular revision of land values or population figures was made, . . . instead piecemeal reassessments were made from time to time on demand'.

[18] Under Diocletian's plan town-dwellers who had no real property were at an advantage. Galerius in 307–308 extended *capitatio* to the towns, but his measure was probably not carried out systematically even in his own part of the Empire, and in 313 the towns were again officially exempted from *capitatio*.

[19] On the *curiales* see Jones, *Later Rom. Emp.* 737 ff.

[20] On compulsory service see Jones, *Later Rom. Emp.* index, s. v. 'Hereditary Service'.

[21] On the colonate see Jones, *Later Rom. Emp.* 795 ff.

[22] See S. S. Frere, *Britannia* (1967), 248 ff., 338 ff. The dating of city-walls is notoriously difficult. It would seem that in Britain earthwork defences were widely constructed in the unsettled period between Marcus Aurelius and Severus and that masonry walls were added to the earth ramparts before (but in some cases, not long before) the time of Carausius. Their style seems to be a little earlier than that of the town-walls of Gaul, most of which are Diocletianic.

[23] See O. Brogan, *Roman Gaul* (1953), 215 ff. For an archaeological survey of the manner in which Roman methods of fortification were developed in the north-western portion of the Empire from the mid-third century onwards in order to meet the barbarian pressure see H. von Petrikovits, *JRS* 1971, 175 ff.

[24] For details of the army reforms and the individual contribution made to them by Diocletian and Constantine see D. van Berchem, *L'armée de Dioclétien et la reforme constaninienne* (1952); H. M. D. Parker, *Hist. of Rom. World, A.D. 138–337*, 269 ff.; Jones, *Later Rom. Emp.* 52 ff., 97 ff., 607 ff.

[25] The best-authenticated estimates of the numbers of invading German armies suggest that these rarely exceeded some 30,000 men, and were perhaps more often nearer 20,000. See Jones, *Later Rom. Emp.* 194 ff.

Chapter 43: Notes

[1] On economic conditions see F. Oertel, *CAH*, xii, ch. vii; F. W. Walbank, in *Cambr. Economic History of Europe*, ii. 33 ff.; C. E. Stevens, ibid. i (on land);

Jones, *Later Rom. Emp.*, esp. chs xx, xxi; F. W. Walbank, *The Awful Revolution* (1969), ch. i. For the view that the fourth century, in contrast with the third and the fifth, was not a period of economic decline: see A. Bernardi, *Studi Giuridici in memoria di E. Vanoni (Studia Ghisleriana,* ser. 1, vol. iii, 1961, 259–321). On various topics see the collected papers of A. H. M. Jones, *The Roman Economy* (1974).

[2] A notable increase of coin-hoards in Gaul during the third and fourth centuries is revealed in the inventory of A. Blanchet, *Les Trésors de monnaies romaines et les invasions germaniques en Gaule; Les Rapports entre les dépôts monétaires et les evénements militaires, polit. et économ.* (1936).

[3] Roman coins of the third century are very rare in India; those of the fourth and fifth centuries are relatively plentiful. For stray Roman coins in Iceland see H. Shetelig, *Antiquity* 1949, 161 ff.

[4] On the Moselle vineyards see Ausonius's *Mosella* (bk x). A decree of the emperor Probus, rescinding Domitian's restrictions on vine-plantation, is evidence, if such be needed, that viticulture had undergone a serious decline in the Roman provinces during the third century.

[5] The population of Rome in the third and fourth centuries is estimated to have maintained itself at about a half (or even two-thirds of) a million, but it was on the decline already when Diocletian became emperor. In the early fourth century Rome had 1800 *domus* (separate houses, occupied by one family), and about 45,000 *insulae* (tenement blocks): so the *Notitia Regionum Urbis XIV*, etc. (see Jones, *Later Rom. Emp.* iii. 212). An extreme example in Gaul is Autun, which had covered 500 acres before its capture by Tetricus and the Bagaudae, but was rebuilt by Constantius (with the help of some impressed British carpenters and masons) on a site of only 25 acres. For the walls of Arles see R. E. M. Wheeler, *JRS* 1926, 192 ff.

[6] Much of the land previously confiscated by the early Roman emperors eventually passed back by lease or sale into private hands.

[7] For bibliography see Chap. 29, n. 17. See especially Ward-Perkins, *Roman Architecture* (1970), chs 20, 21; J. M. C. Toynbee, *The Art of the Romans* (1965); R. B. Bandinclli, *Rome: the Late Empire, Roman Art A.D. 200–400* (1971); M. Grant, *The Climax of Rome* (1968), ch. 5.

[8] On Piazza Armerina see G. V. Gentili, *La villa erculia di P. Armerina* (1959). On the palace at Split see J. J. Wilkes, *Dalmatia* (1969), 287 ff. On Trier see E. M. Wightman, *Roman Trier and the Treveri* (1971).

[9] On the Isola Sacra and Vatican cemeteries see J. M. C. Toynbee, *Death and Burial in the Roman World* (1971), 82 ff., 87 ff. On Dura see M. Rostovtzeff, *Dura-Europus and its Art* (1938). On early Christian art see F. van der Meer and C. Mohrmann, *Atlas of the Early Christian World* (1958); M. Gough, *The Early Christians* (1961).

[10] Gladiatorial shows were given at Rome until *c.* 400; beast-hunts and circus games persisted until the sixth century.

[11] For a description of life on the large country estates see S. Dill, *Roman Society in the Last Century of the Roman Empire*[2] (1889), bk ii, chs iii and iv.

[18] On the methods of conversion in the Roman world see A. D. Nock, *Conversion* (1933).

On the aristocracy see M. T. W. Arnheim, *The Senatorial Aristocracy in the Later Roman Empire* (1972), and for the Senators and all men of note see A. H. M. Jones, J. R. Martindale and J. Morris, *The Prosopography of the Later Roman Empire*, vol. i, *A.D.* 260–395 (1971). Also J. Matthews, *Western Aristocracies and Imperial Court, A.D. 364–425* (1975).

[12] On the survival of Punic (*vis-à-vis* Latin) in Roman Africa see F. Millar, *JRS* 1968, 126 ff.

[13] On Claudian see A. Cameron, *Claudius, Poetry and Propaganda at the Court of Honorius* (1970). On Ammianus see E. A. Thompson, *The Historical Work of Ammianus Marcellinus* (1947); R. Syme, *Ammianus and the Historia Augusta* (1967). On the *H.A.* see further Chap. 41, n. 1 above.

[14] The use of vellum or parchment for books goes a long way back, but it became more common than papyrus in the fourth century A.D. Rolls were gradually replaced by the use of a *codex*, in notebook form, more like a modern book. This use derived partly from its employment by the Christian Church as early as the first century for the Scriptures : most biblical texts are in the form of papyrus *codex*. Its usefulness led to wider use and then the greater use of parchment in that form. Thus a more durable book was developed, and one easier to consult than the roll-form. See C. H. Roberts, *OCD²*, s.v. 'Books'.

[15] For Dio see F. Millar, *Cassius Dio* (1964). For Herodian see the Loeb edition by C. R. Whittaker, 2 vols (1969-71), with introduction and notes. For Eusebius see D. S. Wallace-Hadrill, *Eusebius of Caesarea* (1960); A. Momigliano, *The Conflict between Paganism and Christianity in the IV Century* (1963), 89 ff.

[16] See W. R. Inge, *The Philosophy of Plotinus³* (1929); T. Whittaker, *The Neoplatonists²* (1918); E. R. Dodds, *Select Passages illustrating Neoplatonism* (1924); P. Courcelle, *Les Lettres grecques en Occident* (1943). Hermes Trismegistus was a translation of the Egyptian 'Thoth the very great'. On the *Hermetica* see the edition by A. D. Nock and A. J. Festugière, i–iv (1945–54), and Festugière, *La Révélation d'Hermès Trismégistus*, i–iv (1944–54). On some of the trends of religious belief in the period for M. Aurelius to Constantine see E. R. Dodds, *Pagan and Christian in an Age of Anxiety* (1965).

[17] On Manichaeism see F. C. Burkitt, *CAH*, xii. 504 ff.; H.-C. Puech, *Le Manichéisme* (1949); G. Widergren, *Mani und der Manichaismus* (1961, Engl. trans. 1965); P. Brown, *JRS* 1969, 92 ff. Despite Diocletian's edict and attacks by Neoplatonists and Christians alike, Manichaeism later flourished in the West. When driven eastward by the advance of Islam it survived in China until the fourteenth century. Texts and paintings have been found in Chinese Turkestan and Coptic papyri in Egypt. For Diocletian's edict see Riccobono, *Fontes*, ii. 544 ff.; for translation, Lewis–Reinhold, *R. Civ.* ii. 580 f. The terms were savage: the leaders, together with their sacred books, were to be burned, and their followers executed; any highly placed Romans belonging to the sect were to be sent to the mines; the property of the victims was confiscated by the emperor. Seston (*Dioclétien*, 156 ff.) argued that Manichaeans were involved in the revolt of Achilleus in Egypt in 296.

[19] The chief sources for the persecutions are Eusebius, *Eccles. Hist.* vii and ix, and his *Martyrs of Palestine*; Lactantius, *De mortibus persecutorum*. For modern works see above p. 634, n. 26, and N. H. Baynes, *CAH*, vol. xii, ch. xix.

[20] Among the early Christians the sect of the Montanists (followers of Montanus, a prophet who started a wild and apocalyptic movement in Asia Minor in the time of Marcus Aurelius) alone opposed military service. Monasticism was a product of the fourth and fifth centuries. Apart from their refusal to participate in pagan rites, the early Christians showed no disposition to evade their civic duties. Individual Christian writers, however, might condemn military service (as Origen, Tertullian and Lactantius).

[21] On Constantine see the works quoted above, Chap. 42, n. 1 (p. 654) Documents, in translation, are collected in J. Stevenson, *The New Eusebius* (1957), in P. R. Coleman-Norton, *Roman State and Christian Church*, i (1966), and in D. Ayerst and A. S. T. Fisher, *Records of Christianity*, i, *The Roman Empire* (1971). Since with Constantine we seem to be moving into a rather changed world, less is said here about his later than his earlier years. He himself was more interested in Constantinople than in old Rome. When he had the bones of Peter and Paul transferred to new basilicas (that of St Peter on the Vatican hill lies under the later building of the seventeenth century), he did not leave the East to attend the accompanying ceremonies. On Eusebius's development of a theory of Christian sovereignty see N. H. Baynes, *Byzantine Studies* (1955), 168 ff.

Chapter 44: Notes

[1] A view based on an interpretation of the evidence in the *Notitia Dignitatum* (on this document see above, Chap. 42, n. 10, p. 654) and on the sixth-century writer Gildas, suggests that south-eastern Britain may have been reoccupied after 410 (*c.* 420?) by some Roman forces, e.g. a permanent officer and a field-army: see J. B. Bury, *JRS* 1920, 131 ff.; Collingwood-Myres, *Roman Britain*, ch. 18. But even a temporary occupation is now generally rejected. See on this and on the end of Roman Britain S. S. Frere, *Britannia* (1967), ch. 17. The latest Roman coins cease in Britain from about A.D. 402, though existing ones continued to circulate (or be hoarded) for some time, but by 430 they were no longer used as a medium of exchange.

For a retrospect on Roman Britain see M. P. Charlesworth, *The Lost Province, or the Worth of Britain* (1949).

[2] J. P. C. Kent (*Corolla memoriae E. Swoboda dedicata* (1966), 146 ff.) appears to have shown that Odoacer continued to recognise a Julius Nepos as emperor in the West until 480: thus officially the Western Empire survived four years longer than the traditional date of its end.

[3] There is of course a vast literature on the causes of the decline and fall, including discussions in the

general histories of Rome (see especially A. H. M. Jones, *Later Rom. Emp.* ch. xxv, and *The Decline of the Ancient World*, ch. xxvi). Some representative modern views are usefully collected by D. Kagan in *The Decline and Fall of the Roman Empire* (1962) and by M. Chambers in *The Fall of Rome* (1963). Two valuable surveys are N. H. Baynes, *JRS* 1943, 29 ff. (= *Byzantine Studies*, 83 ff.) and F. W. Walbank, *The Awful Revolution* (1969. This is a revised edition of his *Decline of the Rom. Emp. in the West*. The phrase 'awful revolution' is Gibbon's). See also S. Mazzarino, *The End of the Ancient World* (Engl. trans. 1966), and cf. an essay by A. R. Hands, *Greece and Rome* 1963, 153 ff.

A summary of the impressions made by the decline on thinkers of later ages will be found in W. Rehm, *Der Untergang Roms im abendlandischen Denken* (1930). A useful introductory sketch is S. Katz, *The Decline of Rome and the Rise of Mediaeval Europe* (1955).

[4] For Gibbon see J. B. Bury's edition of *The Decline and Fall of the Roman Empire*, chs 1–3, with appendix after ch. 38. How Gibbon's theme looks after 200 years is discussed in a symposium, edited by Lynn White, called *The Transformation of the Roman World* (1966). Piganiol's remark comes in his authoritative survey of the fourth century, *L'Empire chrétien (325–395)*, vol. iv, 2 in Glotz's *Histoire romaine* (1957), 422: his survey of the causes of the ruin of the Empire (pp. 411–22) ends, 'La civilisation romaine n'est pas morte de sa belle mort. Elle a été assassinée'.

O. Spengler, *The Decline of the West* (Engl. trans. 1926–8), though often misleading and 'mystical', has had great influence. A. J. Toynbee, *A Study of History*, 11 vols (1934–54. See vol. iv on problems of decline), has provoked a great literature. For a criticism of some of his views on Roman history see H. Last, *JRS* 1949, 116 ff.

A. Dopsch, *The Economic and Social Foundations of European Civilization* (Engl. trans. 1937), argued for unbroken continuity from the later Roman Empire into the Carolingian age. But even if he were right in his picture of Germans interpenetrating the Roman world and maintaining it without any real break, his view is confined too rigidly to economic aspects and too little concerned with the spirit and quality of the life which continued but which many will consider essentially different from the unified culture of the early Empire.

Regarding the use of metaphors it may be noted that the Abbé Galliani in 1744 asked, 'The fall of empires? What can that mean? Empires, being neither up nor down, do not fall' (quoted by Walbank, op. cit. 121).

[5] The general view of a decline beginning in the third century and culminating, after times of recovery, in A.D. 476 was challenged by H. Pirenne in 1927 (Engl. trans. of his book, *Economic and Social History of Mediaeval Europe*, 1936), who argued that the Empire essentially survived and the unity of the Mediterranean world was maintained until broken by the Arab conquest of Africa in the eighth century. For a criticism see N. H. Baynes, *JRS* 1929, 230 ff. (= *Byzantine Studies*, 309 ff.), who shows that it was rather Vandal sea-power in Africa in the fifth

century, based on Carthage, which cut the Mediterranean into two and shattered its unity. F. Lot (*The End of the Ancient World and the Beginning of the Middle Ages*, Engl. trans. 1932) accepts Pirenne's thesis but at the same time places the beginning of the Middle Ages in the third century with a continuous development thereafter.

[6] For the theory of soil-exhaustion see V. G. Simkhovitch, *Political Science Quarterly* 1916, 210 ff., and for criticism N. H. Baynes, *JRS* 1943, 29 ff., who finds the primary cause of agricultural decline (where it occurred) in abuses of the fiscal system, not in a hypothetical exhaustion of the soil.

[7] The most famous exponent of climatic change was Ellsworth Huntington, who tried to use the rings in the trunks of the great trees (sequoias) of California to measure this over millennia and then applied his results, arbitrarily, to Europe. For a rejection see Baynes, *JRS* 1943, 30 f.

[8] The effects of the plagues on the population of the Roman world have been assessed very differently. A. E. R. Boak, *Manpower Shortage and the Fall of the Roman Empire in the West* (1955), regards them as a major factor in an alleged decline in the population. Such a decline, however, in so far as it is accepted as a fact, can be attributed to other causes (apart from the more temporary obvious losses by plague). See below, p. 658, J. F. Gilliam, *A J Phil.* 1961, 225, however, does not consider the plague under M. Aurelius to have been a serious cause of decline.

[9] On malaria in Italy see P. A. Brunt, *Roman Manpower* (1971), 610–24, who discusses *inter alia* the views of W. H. S. Jones, *Malaria, a Neglected Factor in the History of Greece and Rome* (1907).

[10] On the normal character of Roman family life see H. Last in C. Bailey (ed.), *The Legacy of Rome* (1923), 209 ff. O. Seeck, *Geschichte des Untergangs der antiken Welt* (1901), among other views (cf. below, n. 13), called in as a factor in the Decline the nature of Roman marriage (e.g. 'arranged' marriages). But S. Mazzarino, *End of the Ancient World* (1966), 123 ff., shows that it was precisely in the later period from M. Aurelius to the Severi that a rebellion against forced marriages took place, and senatorial ladies gained great freedom, and even Seeck admitted that well-matched marriages were more likely among the lower classes; further, Christianity helped to make home life and the position of women freer.

[11] On race-deterioration in the Roman Empire see O. Seeck, op. cit.; T. Frank, *American Historical Review* 1916, 689 ff. (cf. his *Econ. Hist. of Rome* (1927), 207 ff., 211 ff.); M. Nilsson, *Imperial Rome* (1926), 361 ff.

T. Frank's view is that Italy was flooded by eastern slaves and that as these were progressively freed and became Roman citizens the whole character of the citizen body changed. But the racial origin of slaves cannot always be established (cf. M. Gordon, *JRS* 1924); further, a statistical analysis of inscriptions cannot guarantee a representative sample. For a rejection of his views see Baynes, *JRS* 1943, 32 ff. (= *Byz. Stud.* 89 ff.). Even if the number of non-Italians who entered the citizen-body was as great as Frank supposed, this is far from proving their inferiority: mongrelisation may produce good as well as bad effects, as Englishmen and Americans should know.

[12] See A. E. R. Boak, *Manpower Shortage and the Fall of the Roman Empire in the West* (1955). For trenchant criticism see M. I. Finley, *JRS* 1958, 156 ff., and (for slavery) P. A. Brunt, *JRS* 1958, 166 f. (On slavery see also S. Mazzarino, *The End of the Ancient World* (1966), 136 ff.).

[13] Beside this view of a natural decline in the stock, Seeck (op. cit. above, n. 10) argued that the third-century emperors deliberately eliminated the best among the citizens ('Ausrottung der Besten'), fearing rivalry and encouraging a slave mentality which led to the triumph of Christianity. Such a view hardly needs rebuttal. F. Lot wrote, 'if ever there were supermen in human history they are to be found in the Roman emperors of the third and fourth centuries', beside whom Baynes lined up Christian leaders as Athanasius, St Basil, Ambrose and Augustine.

[14] On the defects of Roman education see S. Dill, *Roman Society in the Last Century of the Western Empire*[2] (1906), bk v.

[15] See Gibbon, *Decline and Fall* (1901), iv. 162; Bury, *History of Later Rom. Emp.* (1923), i. 309 f. Bury's own conclusion was, 'the gradual collapse . . . was the consequence of a series of contingent events. No general cause can be assigned that made it inevitable.'

[16] On the impact of Christianity see A. Momigliano, *The Conflict between Paganism and Christianity in the Fourth Century* (1963), 1 ff., and other essays in that volume.

Even Gibbon saw some ultimate advantage in Christianity: 'the pure and genuine influence of Christianity may be traced in its beneficial, though imperfect, effects on the Barbarian proselytes of the North. If the decline of the Roman empire was hastened by the conversion of Constantine, his victorious religion broke the violence of the fall, and mollified the ferocious temper of the conquerors.'

After the sack of Rome by Alaric in 410 St Augustine in the *Civitas Dei* pondered over the decline of Rome and rejected the argument that the troubles of the Empire should be attributed to the abandonment of the pagan gods for Christianity; rather, they derived from the decline in her ancient virtues; Rome was no *urbs aeterna* and men must look instead to the City of God, which was the true goal of man's destiny.

On some aspects of the impact of Christianity upon the Graeco-Roman world see C. N. Cochrane, *Christianity and Classical Culture* (1940).

[17] On the decline of Roman economy in general see the chapters by F. W. Walbank and C. E. Stevens in *Cambr. Econ. Hist.* vols i and ii, and the former's *The Awful Revolution* (1969). On slavery M. Bloch in *Slavery in Classical Antiquity* (ed. M. I. Finley, 1960), 204 ff.; P. A. Brunt, *JRS* 1958, 164 ff.

[18] See M. Rostovtzeff, *Social and Economic History of the Roman Empire*[2] (1957). For discussion and criticism of his views see H. Last, *JRS* 1926, 120 ff.; N. H. Baynes, *JRS* 1929, 229 f.; M. Reinhold, *Science and Society*, x (1946), 301 ff. Rostovtzeff himself

had witnessed an aristocratic régime in conflict with an alliance of soldiers and workers in his own land of Russia.

[19] On the Empire's loyalty to Rome see A. N. Sherwin-White, *The Roman Citizenship*[2] (1974), ch. xix. On treason, unrest and alienation in the Empire see R. MacMullen, *Enemies of the Roman Order* (1967).

[20] On how hard emperors might have worked in the service of the Empire see F. Millar, 'Emperors at Work', *JRS* 1967, 9 ff.

[21] It is not unlikely that a Roman conquest of Germany might in the long run have proved almost as profitable to the Empire as the subjugation of Gaul. The capacity of the Germans for Romanisation was not less than that of other European peoples, and their inclusion in the Empire would probably have converted them from habitual enemies into active allies.

[22] The permanent havoc of the invasions is emphasised by N. H. Baynes (*JRS* 1948, 28 ff.). He points out that ruptured communications cause disintegration of culture.

[23] E. T. Salmon (*Transactions of the Royal Society of Canada*, 1958, 43 ff.) points out that the desire to gain Roman citizenship had during the first two centuries been a strong factor in attracting provincials into enlisting. Caracalla's extension of the citizenship in 212 robbed men who wished to improve their social status of an inducement to enlist: with men of a better type no longer volunteering to go into the army the recruits tended to be drawn from rougher and less disciplined elements of the population. Salmon compares and contrasts the Roman and British Empires in *The Nemesis of Empire* (1974).

[24] On the survival of Roman institutions in later ages see C. Bailey (ed.), *The Legacy of Rome* (1923); O. Immisch, *Das Nachleben der Antike.*

[25] On the medieval Roman Empire J. Bryce, *The Holy Roman Empire* (1905), now needs much revision. See G. Barraclough, *The Origins of Modern Germany* (1946).

A restored Roman world-empire, to match the spiritual realm of the Church Universal, was the political ideal of the two chief political theorists of the Middle Ages, St Augustine and Dante. On Augustine see P. Brown, *Augustine of Hippo* (1967), and on the *Civitas Dei*, op. cit. ch. 26.

[26] On the range of Roman law at the present day see J. Bryce, *Studies in History and Jurisprudence*, i, ch. ii.

[27] Among modern epoch-making works in Latin may be mentioned the Treaty of Utrecht (1713) and Newton's *Principia Mathematica* (1686).

[28] On the study of Latin in the Dark Ages see M. L. W. Laistner, *Thought and Letters in Western Europe, A.D. 500–900*[2] (1947); G. Haskins, *The Renaissance of the Twelfth Century.* On scholarship see J. E. Sandys, *A History of Classical Scholarship*, i[3] (1921).

[29] Tibullus, ii. 5. 24.

[30] Horace, *Odes*, iii. 30. 6.

Glossary

ACCLAMATIO Acclaim, salutation, especially on important public occasions.

ACTA . . . AGENDA Things done . . . things to be done.

ACTA DIURNA Daily doings, current events, journal.

ACTA POPULI Enactments by the people in assembly.

ACTA SENATUS Enactments of the senate.

ACTIONES IN VERREM Speeches in the prosecution of Verres.

ADLECTIO Nomination or appointment to the senate, usually granted by the emperor.

ADLECTIO INTER QUAESTORIOS Appointment to the rank of ex-quaestor.

ADVOCATI FISCI Attorneys for the treasury department.

AEDILE (plural, *aediles*) Commissioner of highways, sewers, public works, etc.

AELIA CAPITOLINA Roman colony founded by Hadrian at Jerusalem.

AERARIUM Treasury, strong-room, the main treasury of the Roman Republic.

AERARIUM MILITARE A treasury established by Augustus for the payment of the army.

AERARIUM SANCTIUS 'More sacred' treasury, set aside as reserve for extreme emergency only.

AES Bronze money.

AGENTES IN REBUS Special agents, secret-service men.

AGER Field, agricultural land, country district.

AGER FALERNUS Public domain in Falernum (northern Campania).

AGER GALLICUS Public domain in the territory of the Gauls in N. Italy.

AGER PUBLICUS Public domain.

AGNOMEN (plural, *agnomina*) Surname, nickname.

AMBITUS Canvassing, also bribery.

AMICI CAESARIS The emperor's companions or attendants.

AMICITIA Friendship, personal or political, also an inter-state agreement of friendship.

AMICUS (plural, *amici*) Friend.

AMPHITHEATRUM FLAVIUM Flavian amphitheatre (Colosseum).

ANNALES MAXIMI (also *tabulae pontificum*, priestly chronicles) Chief annals, a year-by-year chronicle of events.

ANNONA Grain supply, tax on land produce.

ANNUS CONSULARIS Consular year, term of office as consul.

AQUA TRAIANA Trajan's aqueduct.

ARA PACIS Altar of Peace.

ARBITER (plural, *arbitri*) Referee, arbiter, delegate.

ARGENTUM MULTATICIUM Money paid as fines.

AS (plural, *asses*) Unit of measure: a weight comprising 12 ounces; a bronze coin.

ATRIUM (plural, *atria*) Living-room, later vestibule or hall.

AUCTORITAS Authority, official permission or approval.

AUGURES Consulting experts, or interpreters of omens.

AUGUSTALIS *See* seviri Augustales.

AURUM CORONARIUM Gold crown, gift made to victorious generals; later a present to the emperor on accession; finally a 'voluntary gift' tax.

AUSPICIA Auspices, auguries from observation of birds.

BASILICA (plural, *basilicae*) Public hall, court-house.

BASILICA ULPIA Ulpian court-house.

BUCCHERO (*Ital.*) Black polished clay pottery.

CALUMNIA Misrepresentation, slander.

CAPITE CENSI Citizens rated or assessed only on their persons (*caput*, head), not their property.

CAPUT (plural, *capita*) Head, person; legal and political rights; citizen status.

CARMEN SAECULARE Jubilee hymn.

CELLA (plural, *cellae*) Room, vault, cult-chamber.

CENSORIUS Pertaining to the censor; ex-censor; having the rank of censor.

CENSORUM TABULAE Censors' lists.

CENSUS Census, tax assessment, national levy.

CENTURIA (plural, *centuriae*) Century, 100 men, company, a land unit.

CENTURIA PRAEROGATIVA Century allotted first vote in comitia.

CENTURIO Officer in charge of 100 men, captain.

CHARTA HIERATICA Papyrus of best quality.

CISTOPHORUS (plural, *cistophori*) Large silver coins, equivalent to four denarii.

CIVILIS Civil, pertaining to a citizen.

CIVILITAS Attribute of a citizen, courtesy, affability.

CIVIS ROMANUS SUM I am a Roman citizen.

CIVIS SINE SUFFRAGIO Citizen without voting rights.

CIVITAS OPTIMO IURE A community with full rights.

CIVITAS SINE SUFFRAGIO A community (or state) without voting rights.

CIVITATES FOEDERATAE States allied to Rome by treaty.

CIVITATES LIBERAE ET IMMUNES States free and tax-exempt.

CLADES VARIANA The disaster of Varus.

CLASSICUS Belonging to highest census class.

CLASSIS (plural, *classes*) Fleet, also class.

CLOACA MAXIMA Main sewer in the Forum.

COERCITIO Force, constraint, punishment, a right exercised by magistrates with imperium.

COGNOMEN (plural, *cognomina*) Distinguishing family name.

COHORS (plural, *cohortes*) Battalion, section of legion, staff, attendants.

COHORS PRAETORIA Battalion attached to general; guard of honour; general's staff.

COHORS URBANA Battalion assigned to city duty in Rome.

COLLATIO GLEBALIS Gift from the soil; land-tax paid in money.

COLLATIO LUSTRALIS 'Five-year gift' tax.

COLLEGIA ILLICITA Unlawful associations.

COLLEGIA IUVENUM Cadet corps.

COLLEGIUM (plural, *collegia*) Board of colleagues, society, club.

COLLEGIUM FUNERATICIUM Burial society.

COLONIA (plural, *coloniae*) Colony

COLONUS (plural, *coloni*) Colonist, farmer, tenant-farmer, serf.

COMES (plural, *comites*) Companion, member of staff, associate, 'count'.

COMES LITORIS SAXONICI Count of the Saxon shore.

COMITATENSES Mobile troops during the late Empire.

COMITIA CENTURIATA Assembly of the people voting by centuries.

COMITIA CURIATA Assembly of the people voting by wards or parishes.

COMITIATUS MAXIMUS Greatest assembly (probably same as comitia centuriata)

COMMENDATIO Recommendation, nomination, especially for magistracies.

COMMENTARII Memoranda of transactions and rules of procedure drawn up by Roman magistrates and priests. Also memoirs, diaries, journals.

COMMERCIUM Business.

CONCILIABULUM Town too small to be a municipality, 'incorporated village'.

CONCILIUM (plural, *concilia*) Council.

CONCILIUM PLEBIS Assembly of the plebeians.

CONCILIUM PLEBIS TRIBUTUM Assembly of the plebeians grouped by tribes.

CONCORDIA ORDINUM Class harmony; agreement between two highest classes – senate and equites.

CONDUCTOR (plural, *conductores*) Tenant-in-chief, chief lessor.

CONFARREATIO Form of marriage consisting of rites, celebrated under the direction of the chief priest and in the presence of ten witnesses; the oldest Roman form of marriage and confined to patricians.

CONGIARIA Gifts to the peoples, bonuses to the soldiers.

CONSILIUM (plural, *consilia*) Plan, counsel, council.

CONSILIUM FAMILIAE Family council.

CONSILIUM PRINCIPIS Emperor's privy council.

CONSUL (plural, *consules*) Colleague; one of two chief magistrates of Rome.

CONSULAR FASTI Official lists of consuls.

CONSULARES Ex-consuls; men of consular rank.

CONSULES ORDINARII The regularly elected consuls of any given year.

CONSULES SUFFECTI During the Republic they replaced consuls who had died or resigned; under the Empire they replaced the first college of consuls who resigned after a few months of holding office.

CONTIO (plural, *contiones*) Mass meeting, assembly; speech at such a meeting.

CONTROVERSIA (plural, *controversiae*) Dispute, argument, debate.

CONTUBERNIUM (plural, *contubernia*) Quasi-matrimonial union of slaves.

CONUBIUM Marriage, right of intermarriage.

CONVENTUS Circuit of judge in province.

CUNICULUS (plural, *cuniculi*) Underground passage, culvert.

CURATOR (plural, *curatores*) Curator or commissioner.

CURATOR AQUARUM Commissioner of aqueducts.

CURATORES ALVEI TIBERIS Commissioners for the Bed of the Tiber.

CURATORES OPERUM PUBLICORUM Commissioners of public works.

CURATORES VIARUM Highway commissioners.

CURIA (plural, *curiae*) Ward; one of thirty divisions of early Roman state.

CURIALES Members of the governing body of a provincial town, aldermen.

CURIO (plural, *curiones*) Presiding officer over curia.

CURSUS HONORUM Course of honours; regular succession of offices in a public career.

CURSUS PUBLICUS Government postal system, government courier service.

CURULE AEDILES Right Honourable Building Commissioners with special dignity, including use of official chair (*sella curulis*).

DAMNATIO AD METALLA Banishment to mines.

DE AMBITU Concerning bribery.

DE JURE Legally.

DE MARITANDIS ORDINIBUS Concerning classes of citizens who should marry.

DE MODO AGRORUM (Law) dealing with the status of farmland.

DE ORATORIBUS Concerning orators.

DE PROVOCATIONE (Law) on the right of appeal.

DE RE PUBLICA Concerning government.

DE RE RUSTICA Concerning agriculture.

DE REBUS REPETUNDIS (Law) regulating the recovery of money stolen by an official.

DE SICARIIS ET VENEFICIS Concerning cut-throats and poisoners.

DE VERBORUM SIGNIFICATU On the meaning of words.

DECEMPRIMI The ten senior members of the local council of a Latin or Roman municipality; under the Empire they were known in the provinces as *decaproti*.

DECEMVIR Member of an official board of ten.

DEDITICII Persons who have surrendered unconditionally; capitulants.

DEDUCTIO IN PLANA Removal of a population to flat land.

DEFENSOR Spokesman.

DEUS (plural, *dei*) God.

DICTATOR PERPETUO Permanent dictator.

DICTATOR REI PUBLICAE CONSTITUENDAE Dictator for reorganising the government.

DISCIPLINA ETRUSCA Etruscan learning or science.

DIVUS (plural, *divi*) Divine, deified.

DOMINUS Master, owner, lord.

DOMUS AUGUSTANA Augustus's palace.

DOMUS AUREA The Golden House (or palace) of Nero.

DOMUS FLAVIANA The Flavian house or dynasty.

DUOVIRI PERDUELLIONIS Board of two for the trial of traitors.

DUOVIRI SACRIS FACIUNDIS Board of two for performing the public sacrifices.

DUX ORIENTIS Leader ('Duke') or commandant of the East.

EDICTUM (plural, *edicta*) General ordinance; official pronouncement of a magistrate.

EQUESTER ORDO The class of the equites.

EQUITES 'Knights', businessmen, capitalists.

EQUITUM CENTURIAE Centuries of the 'knights'.

EX SE NATUS Born of himself; self-made man.

EXERCITUS Army.

FABULA ATELLANA (plural, *fabulae Atellanae*) A type of drama; charades imported from Atella in Campania.

FABULA TOGATA Dramatic skit on Roman manners.

FAMILIA (plural, *familiae*) Household (including slaves).

FAMILIA URBANA City establishment; slaves belonging to the town house.

FAR Species of wheat.

FASCIS (plural, *fasces*) Bundle of rods, symbol of official authority carried by lictors.

FASTI Lists of magistrates or of holy days; calendar of events.

FASTI CONSULARES List of the consuls.

FASTI MAGISTRATUUM Lists of the magistrates.

FASTI TRIUMPHALES Lists of victorious generals who celebrated triumphs.

FETIALES Commission (of priests) on procedure previous to declaration of war.

FISCUS Departmental chest; imperial treasury.

FLAMEN (plural, *flamines*) Priest; person delegated to perform religious ceremonies.

FOEDUS (plural, *foedera*) Treaty.

FORUM (plural, *fora*) Market-place, public square; settlers' communities along Roman road.

FOSSA Ditch, trench.

FRUMENTATOR Forager.

FRUMENTUM Wheat.

GENIUS AUGUSTI 'Spirit' of Augustus.

GENS (plural, *gentes*) Family groups bearing same name, 'clan'.

GENTES MINORES Families of less prestige than those of the leading aristocrats.

GRAECIA CAPTA FERUM VICTOREM CEPIT Captive Greece took prisoner its uncivilised captor.

GRAVITAS Sense of responsibility, seriousness.

HARUSPEX (plural, *haruspices*). Trained interpreter of omens (e.g. lightning, bird-flight, animal entrails).

HASTATI Spearmen, forming the front rank of the Roman legion.

HERBA MEDICA Medicinal plant.

HISTORIA NATURALIS Natural history, by Pliny the elder.

HONESTIOR (plural, *honestiores*) Men of higher birth; at first a social but, under the Empire, a legal distinction; contrasted with humiliores.

HUMANITAS Quality of being human, human sympathy; tolerance.

HUMILIORES Lower classes; humble folk; *see* honestior.

HYPOCAUST Underground system for heating rooms above.

IMPERATOR General, commander, emperor.

IMPERIUM (plural, *imperia*) Right to command, dictatorial powers of the ruler which could be enforced by the sanction of capital punishment.

IMPERIUM INFINITUM Unlimited imperium.

IMPERIUM PROCONSULARE Imperium of a proconsul (*see* proconsul).

IMPLUVIUM Skylight, opening in roof.

INDICTIO Tax-assessment, also the fifteen-year assessment period.

INFAMIS Disgraced.

INIUSSU POPULI Without orders from the people.

INSTITUTIO ORATORIA Training of an orator.

INSULA (plural, *insulae*) Large tenement house, block of buildings.

INTERCEDO Interpose or interfere. Said by the tribune of the plebs when protecting a citizen from a magistrate.

INTERREX Temporary king, viceroy.

IUDEX (plural, *iudices*) Juryman, judicial adviser, judge.

IUGERUM (plural, *iugera*) Land unit, about $\frac{3}{5}$ of an acre.

IUNIOR (plural, *iuniores*) Younger man.

IURIDICUS Legal expert.

IUS AUXILII (Tribune's) power to render assistance (to plebeians).

IUS CIVILE Civil law; the rights of citizens.

IUS COMMERCII Right of doing business under protection of law.

IUS DIVINUM General law of state ritual.

IUS FETIALE Due procedure governing declaration of war.

IUS GENTIUM Law of the 'peoples'; rights of peoples not necessarily Roman; universal law.

IUS HONORUM Right of holding office.

IUS SUFFRAGII Right of voting.

IUS TRIUM LIBERORUM Right of father of three children.

IUSTITIUM General suspension of public business.

LANCEA (plural, *lanceae*) Javelin.

LAPIS NIGER Black stone.

LAR (plural, *lares*) Household god.

LATIFUNDIUM (plural, *latifundia*) Ranch, large estate.

LAUDANDUS, ORNANDUS, TOLLEN-DUS He should be praised, honoured, promoted (i.e. removed).

LAUDATIO (plural, *laudationes*) Funeral panegyric.

LECTIO SENATUS Filling vacancies in senate, by the censors and later by the emperor.

LEGATUS (plural, *legati*) Deputy, ambassador, general.

LEGATUS AUGUSTI PRO PRAETORE Imperial deputy with rank of praetor, governor of an imperial province.

LEGES DATAE Laws imposed upon subject communities.

LEGES POPULI Laws passed by the people in its Centuriate Assembly.

LEGES ROGATAE 'Bills'; laws not yet enacted.

LEGES TABELLARIAE Laws regulating elections.

LEGIO (plural, *legiones*) Levy of soldiers; regiment.

LEGIS ACTIONES Literally, 'procedure of the law'; modes of instituting a civil action; procedure for initiating a suit.

LEX CURIATA DE IMPERIO Law passed by curiate assembly conferring imperium.

LEX DE PERMUTATIONE PROVIN-CIAE Law concerning change of a province.

LEX SACRATA Law whose violation was punished by religious curse.

LIBERTAS POPULI The people's freedom.

LIBERTI Freedmen, emancipated slaves.

LIBRI MAGISTRATUUM, PONTIFI-CUM Books of magistrates and priests, rolls on which were collected the commentarii or official records.

LICTORS Attendants to the magistrates who held imperium.

LIMES (plural, *limites*) Path, boundary, frontier.

LIMITANEI Frontier troops during the later Empire.

LUCUMO (plural, *lucumones*) Etruscan chief, aristocratic land-owner.

LUDI COMPITALICII Crossroad games, local circus performances.

LUDI PLEBEII Games in honour of the plebs; Apollinares (of Apollo); Megalenses (of the Great Mother); Ceriales (of Ceres); Florales (of Flora); Sullanae victoriae (of Sulla's victory).

LUDI SAECULARES Anniversary games.

LUDI TARENTINI Special festivals of appeasement to the Greek underworld deities, held in part of the Campus Martius called Tarentum.

LUDUS (plural, *ludi*) Game, public spectacle, festival (chiefly racing and drama).

MAGISTER (plural, *magistri*) Manager of slaves or freedmen who gathered the revenue from the individual taxpayer; master, teacher; leader.

MAGISTER BIBENDI Toast-master.

MAGISTER EQUITUM Commander-in-chief of cavalry, the subordinate of a dictator.

MAGISTER MEMORIAE Head of secretariat.

MAGISTER OFFICIORUM Head of messenger service.

MAGISTER PEDITUM Commander-in-chief of infantry.

MAGISTER UTRIUSQUE MILITIAE Commander-in-chief of both (infantry and cavalry) arms.

MAIESTAS Majesty, sovereign power; also high treason, offence against sovereign will.

MAIESTAS POPULI ROMANI IMMI-NUTA Impairment of the majesty of the Roman people, treason.

MAIUS IMPERIUM Greater (i.e. over-riding or superseding) imperium.

MANCEPS (plural, *mancipes*) Contractor, chief agent for government contracts.

MANES Spirits of the departed dead.

MANIPULUS (plural, *manipuli*) Platoon, subdivision of a century.

MANUBIAE Booty or revenue from sale of booty.

MANUS Complete disciplinary control over wife, assumed by husband at time of marriage, also possessed by paterfamilias over his household.

MARS ULTOR Mars the avenger.

MEDDIX (plural, *meddices*) Title of an Oscan magistrate.

METROPOLEIS District capitals, country towns.

MILIA PASSUUM Thousands of paces, miles.

MORALIA Ethical discussions.

MOS MAIORUM Custom of the ancestors, precedent.

MULTA (plural, *multae*) A fine, penalty.

MUNICIPIUM (plural, *municipia*) Free city, native city, municipality.

NAUMACHIA Sham sea-fights arranged as public spectacles.

NEXUM A form of contract involving rights of creditor upon the person of the debtor.

NOBILIS (plural, *nobiles*) Aristocrat; under the later Republic restricted to men whose ancestors had held a consulship.

NOBILITAS Aristocracy.

NOMEN Name.

NOMEN LATINUM Latins with a special legal status between that of a Roman citizen and that of foreign socii.

NOTAE CENSORIAE Censor's marks inserted in census lists against the names of immoral or unpatriotic persons.

NOVAE TABULAE New deal, cancellation or revaluation of debts, mortgages, etc.

NOVUS HOMO (plural, *novi homines*) New man, upstart, outsider, the first member of his family to become a consul.

NUMEN (plural, *numina*) Divinity, divine power.

NUMERUS (plural, *numeri*) A troop of auxiliary soldiers.

OCTOVIRI Board of eight men.

ODEUM Music hall.

OMEN (plural, *omina*) Signs indicating the will of the gods.

OPPIDUM (plural, *oppida*) Walled town, citadel, fortress.

OPTIMAS (plural, *optimates*) The 'best people', that is the aristocrats, especially during the later Republic.

ORDO EQUESTER, *see* equester ordo.

ORDO SENATORIUS The senatorial class.

OTIUM CUM DIGNITATE Dignified leisure.

PAGUS (plural, *pagi*) Canton, county.

PALATINUS (plural, *palatini*) Connected with palace, chamberlain, imperial guard during the later Empire.

PANIS ET CIRCENSES Bread and games.

PATER (plural, *patres*) Father; in plural, senators.

PATER PATRIAE Father of His Country.

PATERFAMILIAS Head of a family, eldest living male member.

PATRIA POTESTAS The power of a father over members of his family.

PATRICIUS (plural, *patricii*) Patrician, aristocrat, member of privileged class.

PATRIMONIUM CAESARIS Hereditary personal estate of the emperor.

PATRUM AUCTORITAS Approval of the Senate.

PAX DEORUM Covenant with the gods.

PAX ORBIS TERRARUM World peace.

PECUARIUS Grazier, cattle-breeder, farmer of public pastures.

PECULATUS Embezzlement of public money.

PECULIUM Pocket money of slaves.

PER AES ET LIBRAM In copper weighed on a balance.

PERDUELLIO Treason.

PIETAS Loyalty, devotion.

PILUM (plural, *pila*) Heavy javelin.

PLEBEIAN AEDILES Commissioners of highways, buildings. Lower social rating than curule aediles.

PLEBISCITUM (plural, *plebiscita*) Measure or ordinance passed by plebs.

PLEBS (plural, *plebes*) The common people.

PLUMBEUS AUSTER Oppressive south wind.

POMERIUM (plural, *pomeria*) Spiritual ring fence, ritual furrow around city.

PONTIFEX (plural, *pontifices*) High-priest, pontiff.

PONTIFEX MAXIMUS Chief Pontiff.

POPULARES Opponents of the senatorial nobility.

PORTORIA Tolls, transit taxes.

POSSESSOR (plural, *possessores*) Owner, possessor, also defendant in suit.

PRAEFECTURA MORUM Supervision of public morals.

PRAEFECTUS (plural, *praefecti*) Overseer, director, chief, commander, prefect, governor.

PRAEFECTUS ALIMENTORUM Supervisor of relief, poor assistance, etc.

PRAEFECTUS ANNONAE Commissioner of food supply.

PRAEFECTUS CASTRORUM Camp director, quarter-master.

PRAEFECTUS CLASSIS ET ORAE MARITIMAE Commander of the fleet and the seashore.

PRAEFECTUS FABRUM Chief engineer.

PRAEFECTUS PRAETORIO Commandant of imperial bodyguard.

PRAEFECTUS URBI Prefect in charge of the city (Rome).

PRAEFECTUS VEHICULORUM Director of conveyances for government postal system.

PRAEFECTUS VIGILUM Commander of the vigiles (q.v.).

PRAENOMEN (plural, *praenomina*) First name, personal name.

PRAEPOSITUS A LIBELLIS Examiner of petitions.

PRAEPOSITUS A RATIONIBUS Chief accountant.

PRAEPOSITUS AB EPISTULIS Chief secretary.

PRAESES (plural, *praesides*) A title of provincial governors which became increasingly common from the third century A.D. onwards.

PRAETOR (plural, *praetores*) Leader, chief magistrate, especially the magistrate whose office ranked just below the consulship in the cursus honorum.

PRAETOR FISCALIS   Magistrate in charge of imperial treasury.

PRAETOR PEREGRINUS   Judge for foreigners; magistrate charged with administration of justice for strangers. More accurately, judge of the law between citizen and non-citizen.

PRAETOR URBANUS   City judge, in charge of justice for citizens.

PRAGMATICUS   Legal expert, attorney.

PRINCEPS (plural, *principes*)   First man, prince, emperor; leading personage within the governing class.

PRINCEPS IUVENTUTIS   Leader of the (patrician) youths.

PRISCI LATINI   Original Latin communities.

PROCONSUL   Acting consul, official having consular rank.

PROCONSULARE IMPERIUM   The official rights and privileges of a proconsul.

PROCURATOR (plural, *procuratores*)   Inspector, tax-collector, financial agent; governor of a minor province.

PROCURATOR BIBLIOTHECARUM   Director of libraries.

PROCURATORES LUDORUM (or MUNERUM)   Directors of games and amusements.

PROROGATIO   Prolongation or extension of a term of office.

PROVINCIA (plural, *provinciae*)   Assignment, jurisdiction, sphere of activity, administrative district, province.

PROVOCATIO   Appeal.

PUBLICANI   Private contractors of taxes.

PULS (plural, *pultes*)   Porridge; 'oatmeal'.

QUADRIGA   Four-horse chariot.

QUAESTIO (plural, *quaestiones*)   Jury; jury-trial; judicial investigation; court.

QUAESTIO DE REBUS REPETUNDIS   Court for provincial maladministration.

QUAESTIO DE SICARIIS ET VENEFICIS   Jury court for murder.

QUAESTIO PERPETUA   Annual hearings on certain crimes (graft, treason, etc.) conducted by permanent commission presided over by praetor.

QUAESTOR PRO PRAETORE   Treasury official acting with the rank of 'judge' (normally the quaestor was subordinate to the praetor).

QUAESTOR SACRI PALATII   Financial head of imperial palace.

QUAESTORES   Financial officers, treasury officials.

QUAESTORES CONSULIS   Treasurers attached to consul's staff.

QUAESTORES ITALICI (or CLASSICI)   Four treasurers in charge of Italy.

QUAESTORES PARRICIDII   Investigators (examiners) into murder.

QUAESTORES URBANI   Four city treasurers (attached to the aerarium or treasury).

QUAESTORII   Ex-quaestors.

RATIO (plural, *rationes*)   Yearly balance sheet, reckoning, plan.

RECIPERATOR (plural, *reciperatores*)   Recoverers; board of magistrates dealing with cases of property, civil status, etc.

RECTOR   Director, ruler; tutor, master, governor.

REGIA   Official residence of Pontifex Maximus.

(LEX) REI PUBLICAE CONSTITUENDAE   Law for organising the government.

RELIGIO   Awe of the gods, religious feeling, religion.

RES DIVINA   Religious affairs.

RES GESTAE   Accomplishments, achievements.

RES HUMANA   Human affairs.

RES PRIVATA   Private affairs, private property.

RESPONSUM (plural, *responsa*)   Reply, answer.

RESTITUTOR ORBIS   Rebuilder of the World.

REX (plural, *reges*)   King, ruler.

ROGATIO (plural, *rogationes*)   Proposal, bill.

ROSTRUM (plural, *rostra*)   Prow of a ship, speaker's platform.

SACROSANCTITAS   Inviolability, under religious sanction, of certain officers of state, especially the tribune of the plebs and later the emperor.

SALTUS   Grasslands; summer pastures.

SATURA (plural, *saturae*)   Miscellany, satire.

SELLA CURULIS   Ivory chair or throne used by curule magistrate.

SENATORIUS ORDO   The senatorial class.

SENATUS   Council of elders, senate.

SENATUS CONSULTA   Resolutions of the senate.

SENATUS CONSULTUM ULTIMUM   Resolution passed by the senate which declared that the state was in danger and charged the consuls and other high magistrates 'to see to it that the republic take no harm'.

SENIOR (plural, *seniores*) Older man, veteran, senior.

SERMO (plural, *sermones*) Speech, talk, conversation.

SERVI CAESARIS Slaves of imperial household.

SEVIRI AUGUSTALES (or Augustales) A college of six men in the towns of Italy who were in charge of the imperial cult.

SICARIUS (plural, *sicarii*) Knifeman, cutthroat.

SOCII ITALICI Italian allies.

SOCIUS (plural, *socii*) Associate; community bound by treaties to Rome; partner in tax-collection, etc.

SOL INVICTUS Unconquered Sun.

SORS PEREGRINA Selection by lot of mixed juries.

SORS URBANA Selection by lot of city juries.

SPATHA (plural, *spathae*) Sword.

SUASORIA Persuasive speech.

SUI IURIS In one's own right.

SUPERSTITIO Excessive religious feeling.

TABLINUM Central room of a house at the far end of the atrium.

TABULAE PONTIFICUM Lists of religious and public events, drawn up annually by the Pontifex Maximus.

TABULARIUM (plural, *tabularia*) Record Office.

TERRA SIGILLATA Stamped clay; pottery dishes decorated with stamped designs; 'sealing-wax' ware.

THERMAE Baths, bath-houses.

TIROCINIUM FORI First experiences in the political arena.

TITULUS (plural, *tituli*) Inscription, title, label.

TOGA (plural, *togae*) Roman citizen's formal dress.

TRADUCTIO AD PLEBEM Transfer to ranks of plebeians.

TRIARII Third rank of soldiers in Roman line of battle.

TRIBUNI AERARII Literally, quartermasters; census class next to equites.

TRIBUNI CELERUM Commanders of cavalry.

TRIBUNI MILITARES CONSULARI POTESTATE Tribunes of the soldiers vested with the powers of consul.

TRIBUNI MILITUM Commanders of infantry.

TRIBUNI PLEBIS Local landowners who became champions of the plebs; tribunes.

TRIBUNICIA POTESTAS The power vested in a tribune.

TRIBUNUS (plural, *tribuni*) Tribal official; leader of ward or parish.

TRIBUS Tribe; administrative district (originally containing ten curiae or wards).

TRIBUS PRAEROGATIVA Tribe chosen by lot to vote first in the comitia.

TRIBUS RUSTICAE Tribes comprised of country dwellers.

TRIBUTUM (plural, *tributa*) Land-tax.

TRIBUTUM CAPITIS Tax on income from industries and professions.

TRIBUTUM SOLI Tax which fell upon the owners of arable and plantation land.

TRIUMVIRI CAPITALES Board of Three dealing with civil status of citizens.

TRIUMVIRI MONETALES Board of Three in charge of the Mint.

TRIUMVIRI REI PUBLICAE CONSTITUENDAE CONSULARI POTESTATE Board of Three with the power of consuls to reorganise the government.

TUMULTUS Riot.

TUNICA PRAETEXTA Bordered tunic or undergarment.

ULTRO TRIBUTA Government expenditures for public works.

URBANITAS Sophistication, urbanity.

USUS Usage; custom; use or enjoyment.

VALLUM Palisade, rampart, entrenchment, mound.

VECTIGAL Land-tax.

VELITES Light-armed soldiers.

VENATIO (plural, *venationes*) Hunt.

VENI VIDI VICI I came, saw and conquered.

VERSUS FESCENNINI Jeering dialogues of the type popular in Fescennium in Etruria.

VEXILLATIO (plural, *vexillationes*) Detachment, corps, battalion, troop, squadron.

VICARIUS Deputy, substitute, proxy, vicar.

VICESIMA HEREDITATUM 5 per cent inheritance tax.

VICOMAGISTRI Ward officers; overseers of quarters of the city, assistants to aediles.

VICUS (plural, *vici*) Open, unwalled village.

VIGILES Watchmen, guards, policemen, especially the seven cohorts of vigiles established by Augustus.

VIR CLARISSIMUS Most honourable man, title of senators.

VIR EGREGIUS Distinguished man, title of financial procurators.

VIR EMINENTISSIMUS Most eminent man, title of highest ranking equestrians.

VIR PERFECTISSIMUS Most perfect man, title of prefects, etc.

VIRITIM Individual (used of land-allotments).

Index

Roman personages, other than emperors, will usually be found under their gentile names. In cases where their family names (*cognomina*) are more familiar, cross-references are given from these to their gentile names.

The names of emperors are given as those by which they are most usually known and are printed in capitals.

Place-names are included in the form used in the text, but in some cases where ancient and modern forms differ considerably the alternative form is given in brackets.

References to material in the Notes will usually be obtained through the relevant Note-numbers in the main text. However, some direct references to the Notes are included below when this has seemed appropriate.